GENEALOGICAL, BURIAL, AND SERVICE DATA FOR REVOLUTIONARY WAR PATRIOTS BURIED IN VIRGINIA

by the

Virginia Society Sons of the American Revolution

Myron E. Lyman, Sr., Compiler and Editor

Karen Hart, Laura E. Ross and Craig M. Kilby, Assistant Editors

COLONIAL ROOTS
2016

ISBN #978-1-68034-351-9

Colonial Roots Genealogy Books and Publishing
34491 Sunset Drive
Millsboro, DE 19966

2016

Printed on acid free paper

Printed in the United States of America

Library of Congress Control Number: 2016955575

TABLE OF CONTENTS

DEDICATION

To the patriots of the Revolutionary War for their sacrifices to achieve this nation's independence and thus provide its citizens with the liberties and freedoms we all enjoy today.

To the descendants of the patriots identified within this publication and to the chapters within the Virginia Society, Sons of the American Revolution that hopefully will take the initiative to place suitable gravestones and Revolutionary War markers on these identified burial sites, for these are memorials to their struggles and sufferings in the pursuit of our liberty and visitors to these burial sites will know that they have been remembered and honored in ceremonies and have not been forgotten.

To the members of the Virginia Society, Sons of the American Revolution and to members of other SAR divisions that assisted in making this publication possible.

To all the VASSAR presidents and executive councils that for several years have enthusiastically supported this endeavor by approving annual budgets to cover expenses.

ACKNOWLEDGEMENTS

For many years the presidents and their executive councils of the Virginia Society, Sons of the American Revolution have all voted favorably to budget the funding needed to make this publication possible. I thank them dearly for doing so.

Special thanks is given to compatriot John Abbott of the Colonel Fielding Chapter, VASSAR for merging the JLARC (Joint Legislative Audit and Review Commission) of the Virginia General Assembly's Special Report: *Preservation of Revolutionary War Gravesites*, containing over 2200 veteran gravesites in Virginia into the spreadsheet of veteran and patriot graves maintained by VASSAR's Revolutionary War Graves Committee.

I thank my three assistant editors for their very important contributions to make this publication possible. The late Craig M. Kilby reviewed many marriage and pension sources that added genealogical information to the publication. Laura Ross posted the spreadsheet with all the additional information found, provided a lot of editing time, and prepared Appendix F, the Index of non-patriot names. Karen Hart converted the spreadsheet to the text format, prepared Appendix A and B and used her skills in finalizing a camera ready copy for the publisher.

Thanks goes to the VASSAR chapter graves chairmen that provided me numerous graves registry forms which furnished information on many of the patriots.

The Virginia Society, War of the War of1812 in the Commonwealth of Virginia provided a large amount of cemetery books and other burial sources that were used to identify patriot burials. This contribution saved VASSAR, and me the expense of procuring these sources.

And thanks is given to several members of VASSAR who provided me valuable details about their patriot ancestors that are used in this report.

Myron E. Lyman, Sr.
Compiler/Editor
August 2016

PREFACE

This project of identifying the burial places of Revolutionary War patriots in Virginia commenced in late 2001 when the Joint Legislative Audit and Review Committee (JLARC) of the Virginia General Assembly published its special report, *Preservation of Revolutionary War Veteran Gravesites,* House Document No. 42. It listed more than 2200 veteran graves in Virginia. The committee listed 127 sources to support its findings. The main supporting ones were reports from the National Society, Sons of the American Revolution (NSSAR), 1993 and 2000 Revolutionary Graves Registers and the National Society Daughters of the American Revolution, (NSDAR) Senate Documents 1900-1974 individual volumes and reports from NSDAR Historian General. They also received numerous reports from city/county historical societies throughout Virginia

This publication did not include patriots, defined by the NSSAR and NSDAR as those individuals that performed public service during the war period at the city, county or state level or were supporting the cause by providing material or financial support. Basically the latter was determined if they submitted a claim for the value of the goods or service provided or if it was taken from them by military units.

A project for many years by NSSAR was for state chapters and SAR members to send in graves registration forms for Revolutionary War veteran and patriot burials they found in cemeteries in cities and counties supported by their chapter. These were collected by a state chairman and after retaining a file copy were forwarded to the NSSAR chairman. Since 2001, the Virginia state chairman was William (Bill) Simpson until I, the compiler of this publication, took over the files from him in 2005.

As compiler, I merged these graves registrations which contained both veterans and patriots into the listings of those veterans identified in the JLARC report. This publication as of August 2016 contains 4164 veteran and patriot burials in Virginia and each individual is called a patriot. I felt it was necessary to provide some genealogical information in the publication, but it was also necessary to limit how much it contained as for some patriots a whole page or more could be easily written. Thus, I set the parameters that it would contain only the names and birth and death dates and places of the patriot's parents and the names of his spouses and her parent's birth and death dates and include as well a very brief summary of his major noteworthy accomplishments after the war was over. To this end, a review of some obituaries, estate records and marriage records was deemed necessary and conducted. The various sources used for this additional information are listed in Appendix E.

Soon after the project began I realized that funding was necessary to procure the necessary service and burial sources and to record the detailed information on spreadsheets. Fortunately, the War of 1812 Society in Virginia, in order to produce their book on War of 1812 burials in Virginia in which I was also the compiler, had purchased cemetery source material such as books, computer disks, etc., which contained Revolutionary War veteran service and burial data. This saved a great expense for VASSAR. To speed up the finalization of the project, a data input person was hired. It was Craig M. Kilby (now deceased), of Lancaster County, Virginia, who had assisted me with the War of 1812 publication. In addition to being a data input person, he also provided some professional genealogical services and editing. Also hired for data input, editing and preparing a by-name index was Laura E Ross. And for conversion of the spreadsheet to paragraphs, formatting the entries, and preparing the final product, Karen Hart was employed.

Like any work of this magnitude, there are no doubt some errors and omissions. With more extensive research, up-dates for content, additions, deletions and corrections will be identified. These should be saved for future revisions. In other words this is a basic start to a more complete and finalized version to be publicized by the society in the future. For example I did not have the time or resources to obtain militia records from all court records at each city/county in Virginia. The society is encouraged to obtain these and to review the sources I have used in Appendix C and D and to find additional source material. To gather more information about each patriot the Society Graves Chairman warmly welcomes any and all up-dates.

Myron E. Lyman, Sr.
Compiler/Editor

INTRODUCTION

This publication includes known burials in all Virginia Counties and Independent Cities, including the City of Alexandria which belonged to the District of Columbia during the war period. It does not include counties now in West Virginia.

EXPLANATION OF ENTRIES IN THE MAIN TEXT (pages 1-378) AND APPENDIX G:

Name, Birth, and Death

Each entry begins with surname of the patriot, followed by his first name(s), his birth date if known, place of birth if known, date of death if known, and place of death if it differs from the burial place. The many alternate spellings for some surnames are not given. Generally the spellings on the gravestones are used.

For birth years, many are derived from the age at death. Some are denoted with a "c" for "circa" before the year (e.g., b c1756). The same applies to years of death. For the most part, dates are derived from the gravestones, census records, death notices, probate records, pension and bounty land records or family records.

Rank and Service Unit ("RU" in the text)

After the name of the veteran and his birth and death information is his rank and unit. The highest rank obtained during the war period is used if known. In many instances the patriot may have obtained a higher rank after the war period which is reflected on gravestones or in other sources. This is sometimes explained further under (VI) Other Veteran Information. Some job titles like Adjutant, Aide de Camp, Quartermaster, Musician, Fifer, Drummer, Engineer and the like are used in lieu of an actual rank such as Sergeant or Lieutenant. In many cases the veteran was also a patriot by performing public service or contributing to the cause, thus his military rank is followed by the word Patriot.

Service units are a more complex matter. Only major unit assignments are generally given and the details of every assignment and when and where they served are normally not given to make the publication less voluminous. The service source code(s) (SS) in the text and the titles they refer to in Appendix C are what they are derived from. The unit assignment of the highest rank received during the war period if identified is used. In many instances the patriot may have obtained a higher rank after the war period which is reflected on gravestones or other sources

The reader should consider that many veterans served or volunteered in counties adjacent to the one in which they resided. Also, that many had service in other counties or independent cities of Virginia or in other states from which they eventually settled and were buried. Many veteran burials are not listed in this publication for this reason as further research would be needed to detect their migration to where they are buried. A sincere attempt has been made by the compiler to list the correct service. The Virginia Society, Sons of the American Revolution thus is not responsible for any errors in identifying the correct service, for listing service for those that did not have it or for not listing the burial at all. Consideration by the reader should be given to see if the service identified belongs to another person of the same name. In some instances the service selected may be for his father, son, uncle, nephew or cousin. The age of the veteran during the war period is therefore considered when making this distinction. Generally a person under the age of twenty would not attain a rank higher than a Private or Corporal or be an officer in the militia. Last, there are many cases where only the gravestone or a death notice provided the service of the veteran.

Cemetery Name, GPS, General Location, & County/Independent City ("CEM" in the text)

These are presented in the order given above. These are self-explanatory, though it should be noted that many family cemeteries and even church graveyards may go by different names from one source to another. Further searching on the internet may provide missing GPS readings. Locations and directions may vary as well. A place name and it location known by one name in the 1930s when the Works Progress Administration volunteers did its cemetery surveys may well be different than its current name. This is especially true of urban areas. With respect to family cemeteries, the names are apt to go by many names over the course of years and the person or persons who "named" it in a publication. For example, the Thornton-Forbes-Washington cemetery in Fredericksburg was known in 1963 as "Little Falls Burying Ground." The location of course had not moved, but the name is changed.

Names of burial grounds are not the only thing subject to change. For example, the modern location of a site may well have been in Princess Anne County in the 1930s, but is now part of Virginia Beach. Appendix A gives the explanation of county formations and Independent Cities status, and from what jurisdiction they were taken, and when. Last, in terms of exact location, many of our sources were vague or even silent on the matter including those in the JLARC Report. If not known at all, the veteran is not included in this publication despite the fact the veteran may have been buried in a certain county.

A list of counties and independent cities and the cemeteries and graveyards located therein is given in Appendix B. Again, these are arranged by modern day political jurisdictions.

Gravestones ("GS" in the text)

Items in this section are marked "Y", "N" and U" for "Yes," No," and "Unknown." This was one of the more vexing problems with this project. A stone that may have existed in 1890, or 1937, or even as late as 2011 when an earthquake destroyed many stones in Blandford Cemetery in Petersburg, may not exist today. Many times, stones were moved to another location while the body was not, or vice versa. St. John's, Shockoe Hill and Hollywood Cemeteries in Richmond are good examples. Not unheard of either is more than one stone for the same person in two different places (and in one case, the same cemetery.) Re-internments are listed where the gravestone is placed, however it does not mean the body is at this location. Some cemeteries have memorialized gravestones of persons buried at other locations.

For this reason, the reader is advised to consult Appendix D which gives the sources for burials, and discussed in more detail below. Further, there are many web sites available to ascertain more up-to-date research. Many of these sites were used in the research process. But like all things, even they are ephemeral and what was here today may be gone tomorrow.

Spousal Information ("SP" in the text)

The spouse information given here comes from a variety of sources as given Appendix E. In many cases, the tombstones themselves may be the only evidence of a marriage, or even multiple marriages for both spouses. This is perhaps one of the greatest contributions to genealogy this book offers. Nevertheless, other sources for marriages were also used such as marriage notices and death notices.

When known, vital statistics (birth and death, and places, date and place of marriage, and names of parents are given, as well other biographical information about the spouse. If the reader does not find the marriage in one of the published sources in Appendix E, the information came from either the gravestone(s) itself or research provided by contributors. Every effort has been made to confirm the marriage data, though there are no doubt errors in some conclusions.

Other Veteran Information ("VI" in the text)

This section provides biographical information such as names of parents, public service, occupation, cause of death, additional military service, major noteworthy accomplishments after the war was over and other anecdotal information. The reader is encouraged to search for more biographical information. A list of the children of the soldier and his decent from ancestors is generally not given otherwise each paragraph might become voluminous. In most cases, the source for this information is given in the text. Otherwise, see Appendix E.

Some men who also served in the War of 1812, are identified, though a detailed explanation of this service is not included. A thorough search for War of 1812 service was not conducted for each patriot thus many more patriots may have had this service

Information regarding pensions and bounty land warrants (BLW) are given in this portion of the text to include when received and who received it and the identifying numbers. If the individual is not listed it does not mean he did not receive one as a complete search of records at NARA and in libraries and court records was not conducted. The reader is encouraged to procure the actual pension and bounty land records from NARA as they may contain additional information about his service and family. Copies of the records may be obtained by mail using NATF form 80 and addressed to NARA References Services Branch, General Services Administration, Washington, D.C., 20408. The reader is encouraged to procure the actual records from NARA as they may contain additional information about his service and family. More information regarding bounty land may be available from the Bureau of Land Management for the state in which was awarded. Many veterans moved and took advantage of their bounty land warrants thus will not be buried in Virginia. However in many cases they simply sold their rights to them and remained in Virginia.

Pensions ("P" in the text)

Y (yes), N (no), or unk (unknown) is given. If Y, see VI (Other Veteran Information) for details.

Bounty Land Warrants ("BLW" in the text)

Y (yes), N (no), or unk (unknown) is given. If Y, see VI (Other Veteran Information) for details.

Registered with NSSAR ("RG" in the text)

An entry of Y (yes) indicates a grave registry form has been submitted though the compiler and forwarded to NSSAR. It should be noted that the NSSAR data base has been updated with the over 2200 Virginia graves in the JLARC report so if JLARC is listed as a burial code (BS) in the text it is considered previously registered with NSSAR and any further inputs on the name should be considered an up-date. Also the same applies that if an SAR ancestor number is listed as a service source (SS) in the text it has been previously registered with NSSAR. SAR members should check NSSAR's Patriot Grave Index to see if a grave has been previously registered at http://patriot.sar.org/fmi/iwp/cgi?-db=Grave%20Registry&-loadframes.

SAR/DAR grave markers ("MK" in the text)

A Y means yes. If it is a DAR marker see VI (Other Veteran Information) for details.

Photo ("PH" in the text)

This section is marked "Y" for yes and "N" for no, and indicates whether the Society or a contributor provided a photograph of the gravestone. The compiler has a file on these. The reader is encouraged to search the internet cemetery sites for photographs as they are abundant but these sources are not included in this section because of possible copyrights infringements.

Service Source ("SS" in the text)

The sources for these codes are listed in Appendix C and described in detail there.

Burial Source ("BS" in the text)

The sources for these codes are listed in Appendix D and described in detail there.

Other Sources (Appendix E), Appendix F & G: Miscellaneous Notes

Personal emails, correspondence and research notes are maintained by the compiler. At the bottom of each page of the text are some general abbreviations used. The following pages show others used in the text. The By-Name index is at Appendix F. These include names other than the veteran and unit commanders listed in the text.

A sincere effort has been made to avoid errors in this publication. Errata will be found in Appendix G for additional information that arrived after the original typeset was created. The Society greatly appreciates any corrections or additions.

Myron E. Lyman, Sr.
Compiler/Editor

LIST OF ABBREVIATIONS WITHIN THE TEXT

This list does not include standard state postal code abbreviations. Unless otherwise noted, all locales are in Virginia.

abt	about
Apr	April
acct(s)	account(s)
appl	applied or application
Att	attached or attachment
Aug	August
b	born
bef	before
bet	between
Bk	book
BLW	Bounty Land Warrant
BS	Burial Source
btw	between
bur	buried
c	circa, e.g. c1796 is circa 1796
ca	circa
Capt	Captain
Cem	Cemetery
cert	certificate
C.H. or CH	Court House
Ch	Church
cnr	corner
Co	County or Company
Cos	Counties
Col	Colonel
Cont	Continental
Ct or CT	Court
d	died
DAR	Daughters of the American Revolution Society
daug	daughter
DC	District of Columbia
Dec	December
det	detached or detachment
Doc	Document
d/o	daughter of
Dr	Doctor or Drive
E	East
Enl	Enlisted or Enlistment
Ens	Ensign
ent	entered
ES	East side
Esq	Esquire
Ext	Extension
Feb	February
fr	from

LIST OF ABBREVIATIONS WITHIN THE TEXT

(Continued)

Ft	Fort
GPS	Global position system
gr	grave
GS	Gravestone
H.R.	House Resolution (US Congress)
incl	includes
Inf	Infantry
info	information
Inv	Inventory of estate
Jan	January
jct	junction
Jr	Junior
Jul	July
Jun	June
Lib	Library
LNR	Last Known Residence
Lt	Lieutenant or Light
Lt Col	Lieutenant Colonel
LVA	Library of Virginia
Maj	Major
Mar	March
mar	married
mi	mile(s)
mo(s)	month(s)
Mt	Mount
N	No or North
NARA	National Archives and Records Administration
NE	North East
Nov	November
nr	near
NS	North side
NSDAR	National Society DAR
NSSAR	National Society SAR
NW	North West
obit	obituary
Oct	October
Pen	Pension
p	page
pg	page
PO	Post Office
Recd	Received
Reg	Regiment, Registered, or Regular
Rej	Rejected
Rep	Representative

LIST OF ABBREVIATIONS WITHIN THE TEXT

(Continued)

Rev	Reverend or Revolutionary
Rev War	Revolutionary War
Rd	Road
Rt(s)	Route(s)
RW	Revolutionary War
S	South
SAR	Sons of the American Revolution Society
SE	South East
Sep	September
Sec	Section
serv	service or served in
Soc	Society
sol	soldier
Sr	Senior
St	Street or stone
SS	South side or Service Source
sub	substituted
SW	South West
TS	Tombstone
Twp	Township
U	Unknown
Unk	Unknown
UMC	United Methodist Church
US	United States
USD	United States Daughters of 1812
VASSAR	Virginia Society SAR
V.A.	Veterans Administration
vic	vicinity
vol	volume or volunteered
VMR	Virginia Militia Regiment
W	West
WS	West side
WPA	Works Progress Administration
Y	Yes
yr(s)	year(s)

LIST OF ILLUSTRATIONS

NAME ✱ Blakemore, George

AGENCY OF PAYMENT   Richmond, Va

DATE OF ACT   1832

DATE OF PAYMENT   3rd qr 1851 (act 6 Apr.) Oct. 1849

DATE OF DEATH   July 25, 1833

**FINAL PAYMENT VOUCHER RECEIVED FROM
THE GENERAL ACCOUNTING OFFICE**

GENERAL SERVICES ADMINISTRATION   GSA DC 70-7035   GSA DEC 69 FORM 7068

Above is a sample Revolutionary War image of a Pension Final Payment Voucher that shows a death date. The image is available on the Fold3 website and at the National Archives.

Full Catalog | Books & Journals | Archives & Manuscripts | Images & Indexes

Back to Results List   Request   Save/Mail   Add to List   New Search

Full View of Record: Rev. Bounty Warrants

Choose format: Standard format   Catalog card   Name tags   MARC tags

Record 2 out of 2   PREVIOUS   NEXT

URL (Click on link) http://image.lva.virginia.gov/cgi-bin/GetRev.pl?dir=0800/B0017&card=4 Document Images

Title	**Booker, Lewis.**
Gen. note	Rank: Captain Lieutenant.
	Service: Army.
Other Format	Available on microfilm. Revolutionary War Bounty Warrants, reels 1-29.
Biog./Hist. Note	The act of the General Assembly passed on June 22, 1779, which established the Virginia Land Office, also provided for the rewarding of lands promised as bounty for specified Revolutionary War military service. The purpose of the bounty land system was to encourage longer military service. In order to qualify for bounty land, a soldier had to serve at least three (3) years continuously in the State or Continental line. Militia service did not count. Servicemen submitted various documents such as affidavits of commanding officers and fellow soldiers and discharge papers in order to substantiate their service record. When the claim was proved, the Governor's Office issued a certificate to the register of the Land Office authorizing him to issue a warrant. The first warrant was issued in 1782 and the last in 1876 as heirs of warrantees continued to seek lands for additional service. Land awarded as bounty was in the present-day states of Ohio and Kentucky.
Related Work	The papers accumulated as proof of service are now part of the records of the Executive Dept. Office of the Governor (RG#3) and are called 'Bounty Warrants' if approved and 'Rejected Claims' if disapproved. These records are housed in the Archives at the Library of Virginia.
Note	Certificate: Lieutenant Colonel Ed. Carrington.
	Certificate: Major W. Moseley.
	Voucher 1784.
	See also Papers Clement Skarrett, 1838.
	See also papers **Booker**, Lewis, 1807.
Subject - Personal	**Booker, Lewis.**
Subject - Topical	Veterans -- Virginia.
Subject -Geographic	Virginia -- History -- Revolution, 1775-1783 -- Sources.
Genre/Form	Military records -- Virginia.
Added Entry	Virginia. Governor's Office Bounty warrants, 1779-1860.
	Library of Virginia. Archives.

This above record of a BLW (Bounty Land Warrant) file is from the Library of Virginia website and is derived from microfilm images. To procure the record, open Images and Indexes in the upper margin of the Full Catalog page and scroll to Revolutionary War Bounty Warrants. Then insert a surname and select the given name. The record above shows the information for Lewis Booker. Then click the URL to see the microfilm image (see next illustration).

Booker, Lewis,- Capt. Lieut.- Army.

Cert. (1) Lt. Col. Ed. Carrington.

2 Maj. W. Moseley.

Voucher 1784.

See also papers Clement Skarrett,1838.

Booker, Lewis - 1807

I certify that Lewis Booker Sigt was appointed a Lieutenant in the Vt. Reg. of Artillery on the 18th. of Jan. 77, and remained in service until the end of the War when he was a Capt Lieutenant

Jan. 30. 1784

Eo Carrington

I certify that Capt Booker was In service In Febuary 776

Jany 31th 84

W Moseley Majr
V Line

This image of a BLW (Bounty Land Warrant) microfilm file from the Library of Virginia website obtained as shown on the previous illustration provides valuable service information of the veteran. Note that he received this in 1807 for service performed from Jan 1776 to Jan 1784.

B. | **1 Artillery.** |

Lewis Booker

Capt. Lt., { Capt. Samuel Eddens' Company in the Regiment of Artillery commanded by Col. Charles Harrison.*

(Revolutionary War.)

Appears on

Company Pay Roll

of the organization named above for the month

of .... *Sept* ...., 17 7P.

Commencement of time ...., 17 .

Commencement of pay ...., 17 .

To what time paid ...., 17 .

Pay per month .... *33⅓ doll*

Time of service ....

Whole time of service ....

Subsistence .... *10 doll*

Amount ....

Amt. of pay and subsistence ....

Pay due to sick, absent ....

Casualties ....

Remarks: ....

*This company was designated at various times as Captain William Murray's and Capt. Samuel Eddens' Company.

This regiment was organized in compliance with a Resolution of Congress of November 30, 1776. It was subsequently assigned to the State of Virginia, under Act of Congress of October 3, 1780, which provided that the Regiments of Artillery be considered as belonging to the States to which assigned, which States shall complete them to the full complement and in every respect treat them as if originally raised therein.—R. & P., 418,463.

This image of a Revolutionary War service record is available at the Fold3 website and at the National Archives.

AARON, Abraham Sr; b 1734; d 1816 **RU**: Patriot, Gave supplies and fixed guns **CEM**: Easley Family; GPS unk; Callands; Pittsylvania **GS**: Y **SP**: No info **VI**: No further data **P**: N **BLW**: N **RG**: N **MK**: N **PH**: unk **SS**: DAR Ancestor #A000005; G pg 434; AS **BS**: AS.

ABBOTT, Joseph; b 1762; d 1819 **RU**: Private, Service recorded source CZ, War, vol 4, p 83 **CEM**: Shockoe Hill; GPS 37.55190, -77.43170; 4th & Hospital Sts; Richmond City **GS**: Y **SP**: No info **VI**: No further data **P**: unk **BLW**: unk **RG**: N **MK**: N **PH**: unk **SS**: C pg 220; E pg 1; CZ pg 14 **BS**: 179 # 478.

ABENDSCHON (OBENSHAIN), Samuel; b 13 Jan 1754, PA; d Jul 1824 **RU**: Lieutenant/Patriot, Signed Oath of Allegiance, Berks Co, PA **CEM**: Abendschon Family; GPS unk; Nr Mill Creek Baptist; Botetourt **GS**: N **SP**: Phebe Daler **VI**: No further data **P**: unk **BLW**: unk **RG**: Y **MK**: unk **PH**: N **SS**: DAR Ancestor #A000227; J-NSSAR 2000 Reg; DD **BS**: JLARC 2,76.

ABERNATHY, John D Jr; b c1746; d Jun 1816 or 22 Nov 1824 **RU**: Soldier/Patriot, Military service not identified. Gave material aid to cause **CEM**: Flournoy; GPS unk; Rt 58; Brunswick **GS**: U **SP**: 1) Mar (c1768) Mary Brown 2) Mar (c1785) Mildred Harwell 3) Mar (25 Apr 1814 Brunswick) Molly King **VI**: No further data **P**: unk **BLW**: unk **RG**: Y **MK**: N **PH**: unk **SS**: D Vol 1 pg 161-2; AL Ct lists pg 5, 6; G pg 88, 90 **BS**: AS SAR regis.

ABERNATHY, John Sr; b 26 Mar 1723, Prince George Co; d 17 Feb 1812 **RU**: Patriot, Gave brandy and oats to cause **CEM**: Abernathy Family; GPS 36.50420, -77.88047; 400 yds W of Preswood Rd, Rt 646, 1.2 mi N of Linerty Rd, Rt 634; Brunswick **GS**: N **SP**: Lucy (-----) (c1728-7 Feb 1812) **VI**: Son of Robert A III & Mary (Harwell) Abernathy **P**: N **BLW**: N **RG**: unk **MK**: unk **PH**: unk **SS**: DAR Ancestor #A000241; SAR Ancestor #P-100284; D Vol 1 pg 154, 157 **BS**: 196.

ABSHIRE, Abraham; b 1755, Franklin Co; d 28 Jul 1842 **RU**: Soldier, Served in Cont Army, Specifics in Sec of War Report, 1835, Pen, Vol 2, Lib VA **CEM**: Abshire; GPS unk; Boones Mill; Franklin **GS**: U **SP**: Susannah Vinson (1767-1845) **VI**: Received VA pen 6 Apr 1842 **P**: Y **BLW**: unk **RG**: unk **MK**: unk **PH**: unk **SS**: DAR Ancestor #A000293; E pg 2; C pg 14; CA **BS**: 196.

ABYVON, George; b unk; d Bef 21 Oct 1793 **RU**: Patriot, Provided supplies of 66 rations during the war **CEM**: St Paul's Episcopal; GPS 36.84733, -76.28554; 201 St Paul's Blvd; Norfolk City **GS**: Y **SP**: Mariam (-----) Abyvon (__- bet 20 Nov 1794 & 23 Feb 1795) **VI**: Five-time Mayor of Norfolk (1754, 1767, 1771, 1776 & 1779). **P**: N **BLW**: N **RG**: Y **MK**: Y, DAR 02 Dec 2012 **PH**: Y **SS**: CB Oath as Mayor; AK **BS**: 178-8 Jan 11.

ABYVON (ABYNON), Marrim (Miriam Manim Marrim Meriam Marsam); b unk; d Bet 20 Nov 1794 to 23 Feb 1795 **RU**: Patriot, Provided supplies of 3 gallons of rum **CEM**: St Paul's Episcopal; GPS 36.84733, -76.28554; 201 St Paul's Blvd; Norfolk City **GS**: Y **SP**: George Abyvon **VI**: No further data **P**: N **BLW**: N **RG**: Y **MK**: Y **PH**: unk **SS**: CB Gave to cause **BS**: 178-8 Jan 11.

ACKISS, John; b c1740; d unk **RU**: Patriot, Was member of the Princess Anne Co Ct 28 July 1775 **CEM**: Old Baptist Meeting House; GPS 36.61001, -76.03494; Vic 664 Princess Anne Rd, Creeds; Virginia Beach City **GS**: Y **SP**: No info **VI**: No further data **P**: N **BLW**: N **RG**: unk **MK**: unk **PH**: unk **SS**: DAR Ancestor #A000321; CO pg 46 **BS**: 196.

ACKISS, John; b unk; d 1775 **RU**: Patriot, Gave provisions to Prince Anne Co Militia **CEM**: Skirmish at Kempsville Monument; GPS unk; Pleasant Hall; Virginia Beach City **GS**: U **SP**: No info **VI**: No further data **P**: N **BLW**: N **RG**: unk **MK**: unk **PH**: unk **SS**: G pg 433 **BS**: JLARC 120.

ADAM, Paul; b unk; d 1781 **RU**: Seaman, Served on "Ville de Parisa". Died from Yorktown battle **CEM**: French Memorial; GPS 36.81944, -79.39933; Yorktown; York **GS**: U **SP**: No info **VI**: No further data **P**: unk **BLW**: unk **RG**: Y **MK**: unk **PH**: unk **SS**: J-Yorktown Historian **BS**: JLARC 1,74.

ADAMS, Jacob; b unk; d 20 Oct 1807 **RU**: Soldier, Served in 7th Cont Line in Col John Gibson's Detachment, Capt Benjamin Bigg's Co, 1780 & 1781. Was in Battle of Guilford CH **CEM**: Adams-Graves-Pilson Families; GPS unk; .5 mi south of Rt 717, N side of Goblintown Creek nr Fairystone Park; Patrick **GS**: U **SP**: Mary Adams (__-1809) **VI**: BLW issued 24 Jun 1783 for 200 acres **P**: unk **BLW**: Y **RG**: unk **MK**: unk **PH**: unk **SS**: A pg 284; E pg 3; F pg 3 **BS**: JLARC 30; 196.

RU=Rank/Unit	CEM=Cemetery	GS=Gravestone	SP=Spousal Information
VI=Other Veteran Info	P=Pension	BLW=Bounty/Land Warrant	RG=Registered Grave
MK=SAR/DAR Marker	PH=Photo	SS=Service Source	BS=Burial Source

1

ADAMS, James Sr; b 1729, Goochland Co; d 15 Mar 1789 **RU:** Patriot, Gave material aid to cause **CEM:** Adams; GPS unk; Bybee; Fluvanna **GS:** U **SP:** Mar (1751) Cecily Ford, d/o William & (-----) Ford Sr. **VI:** Son of Capt Robert Sr (1689-1740) & Mourning (Lewis) (1694-1765) Adams. During the Indian Wars, James served in the VA militia under command of John Smith, taking part in Cherokee Expedition in 1760. From 1771-73, served as Justice of Peace in Albemarle Co **P:** N **BLW:** N **RG:** unk **MK:** unk **PH:** unk **SS:** DAR Ancestor #A000542; Al Ct Bk pg 29 Fluvanna Co **BS:** 196.

ADAMS, Jesse; b unk; d 7 Nov 1781 **RU:** Soldier, Served in 2d NY Line. Died from Yorktown battle **CEM:** Yorktown Victory Monument Tablet; GPS 38.28350, -78.54150; Yorktown; York **GS:** U **SP:** No info **VI:** Died in Williamsburg **P:** unk **BLW:** unk **RG:** unk **MK:** unk **PH:** unk **SS:** J-Yorktown Historian **BS:** JLARC 74.

ADAMS, Nipper (Napier); b c1732, Prince George Co; d 1820 **RU:** Patriot, Performed public duty. Also gave material aid to cause **CEM:** Adams Family; GPS unk; See county property records for location of family; Halifax **GS:** U **SP:** 1) Lucy McEndree (McKendriee) (1735-1791) 2) Obedience Atkins (c1750-bef 1795) **VI:** Son of John & (-----) Adams (1705-1769) **P:** N **BLW:** N **RG:** unk **MK:** unk **PH:** unk **SS:** DAR Ancestor #A000698; Al Ct Bk pg 12 Halifax Co; CA SAR application **BS:** 197.

ADAMS, Robert "Old Robin"; b 1727, Henrico Co; d 1785 **RU:** Patriot, 1780 was member of Vigilance Committee that helped clear the region of outlaws and Tories. Also gave material aid to cause **CEM:** Mt Zion United Methodist; GPS unk; 5662 Red House Rd, Rustburg; Campbell **GS:** N **SP:** Mar on 15 Oct 1748 to Penelope Flournoy Lynch (1734-1785) d/o Charles & Sarah (Clark) Lynch of Albemarle Co **VI:** Son of Capt Robert Adams Sr (1689-1740) & Mourning Lewis (1694-1765). One of the first Justices of Bedford Co **P:** N **BLW:** N **RG:** unk **MK:** N **PH:** N **SS:** DAR Ancestor #A000533; AL Ct Bk pg 27 **BS:** 196.

ADAMS, Robert Jr; b 1754 or 1750; d 1789 or 1790 **RU:** Captain, Appt Capt 24 Feb 1778 Bedford Militia. In Sep 1778 marched to Chiswell's Lead Mines on New River. In the Fall of 1780 led a Co to Peterburg **CEM:** Ward; GPS 37.05492, -79.43637; Hurt; Pittsylvania **GS:** Y **SP:** Mary (-----) **VI:** No further data **P:** unk **BLW:** unk **RG:** Y **MK:** unk **PH:** **SS:** DAR Ancestor #: A000553; E pg 3 **BS:** 174, JLARC 1, 4, 36, 66, 75 ,96.

ADAMS, William; b unk; d unk **RU:** Soldier, Service recorded in source CZ, War, vol 5, p 27 **CEM:** Old Burying Ground; GPS unk; Directions in Senate Doc DAR annual report 1955 vol 4 serial 11912; Arlington **GS:** N **SP:** No info **VI:** No further data **P:** unk **BLW:** unk **RG:** Y **MK:** unk **PH:** N **SS:** SAR Ancestor #P-101658; CZ pg 15 **BS:** JLARC 1, 76.

ADAMS, William; b 1746; d 1823 **RU:** Soldier, Performed personal service, specifics fr DAR not given **CEM:** Back Creek Quaker, aka Gainesboro United Methodist; GPS 39.27861, -78.25694; 166 Siler Ln, Gainesboro; Frederick **GS:** Y **SP:** No info **VI:** No further data **P:** unk **BLW:** unk **RG:** unk **MK:** Y **PH:** Y **SS:** DAR Ancestor #A000783; B **BS:** 196.

ADDISON, John; b unk; d after 1786 **RU:** Colonel, Served in a MD Flying Camp,1776 under BG Benjamin Biggs, 3rd Bn, 7th Cont Line **CEM:** Addison Family; GPS unk; Homeplace Oxen Hill on the Potomac River opposite Mt Vernon; Fairfax **GS:** U **SP:** No info **VI:** Wounded in duel with Maj Joseph Marbury 12 Oct 1786 **P:** unk **BLW:** unk **RG:** unk **MK:** N **PH:** unk **SS:** A pg 238 **BS:** JLARC 63.

ADKINS, William; b 21 Sep 1760; d 22 Oct 1748 **RU:** Private, Served in Capt Reuben Vaughan's Co, Mecklenburg Militia 1779 **CEM:** William Atkins Family; GPS unk; Rt 649 nr Cooper's Store, Callands; Pittsylvania **GS:** U **SP:** Mar (1780) Mary Hartman **VI:** No further data **P:** unk **BLW:** unk **RG:** unk **MK:** unk **PH:** unk **SS:** DB pg 11 **BS:** 196.

AGEE, Jacob; b 1756; d May 1838 **RU:** Soldier, Ent serv 1778, Buckingham Co. Served in VA Line **CEM:** Greenfield; GPS unk; On Rocky Creek nr Penlan; Buckingham **GS:** U **SP:** Elizabeth Garrett **VI:** Appl pen10 Sep 1832 Buckingham Co. Pen commenced 4 Mar 1831, $50 yr. S6470 **P:** Y **BLW:** N **RG:** unk **MK:** N **PH:** unk **SS:** DAR Ancestor #A000848; E pg 4; AG pg 758; CG pg 19 **BS:** JLARC 4, 59.

AGEE, James; b 1725; d 1820 **RU:** Patriot, Gave material aid to cause **CEM:** Agee Family; GPS unk; Nr Dillwyn; Buckingham **GS:** Y **SP:** 1) Elizabeth Ford, 2) mar (before 1747/8) Mary Ford d/o James & (-----)

RU=Rank/Unit	CEM=Cemetery	GS=Gravestone	SP=Spousal Information
VI=Other Veteran Info	P=Pension	BLW=Bounty/Land Warrant	RG=Registered Grave
MK=SAR/DAR Marker	PH=Photo	SS=Service Source	BS=Burial Source

2

Ford **VI:** No further data **P:** N **BLW:** N **RG:** N **MK:** N **PH:** unk **SS:** DAR Ancestor #A000832; AL Ct Bk pg 1, 46 Buckingham Co **BS:** AS.

AGNES, Jean; b unk; d 1781 **RU:** Seaman, Served on "Hector." Died from Yorktown battle **CEM:** French Memorial; GPS 36.81944, -79.39933; Yorktown; York **GS:** U **SP:** No info **VI:** No further data **P:** unk **BLW:** unk **RG:** Y **MK:** unk **PH:** unk **SS:** J-Yorktown Historian **BS:** JLARC 1, 74.

AIMONT, Jean; b unk; d 1781 **RU:** Soldier, Served in Regt d'Agenais,and died from Yorktown battle **CEM:** French Memorial; GPS 36.81944, -79.39933; Yorktown; York **GS:** U **SP:** No info **VI:** No further data **P:** unk **BLW:** unk **RG:** Y **MK:** unk **PH:** unk **SS:** J-Yorktown Historian **BS:** JLARC 1,74.

AKERS, William; b c1730; d 31 Mar 1810 **RU:** Patriot, Gave material aid to the cause **CEM:** First Concord Presbyterian; GPS unk; Hwy 460 E fr Lynchburg City.; Appomattox **GS:** Y **SP:** Mar (17 Mar 1798 Campbell Co) Polly Hardway, d/o Charles & (------) Hardway. Also mar to Elizabeth Martye. Order unk. **VI:** No further data **P:** N **BLW:** N **RG:** unk **MK:** unk **PH:** unk **SS:** AL Ct Bk 3 Campbell Co **BS:** 196.

ALAIN, Georges; b unk; d 1781 **RU:** Seaman, Served on "Magnanime" and died from Yorktown battle **CEM:** French Memorial; GPS 36.81944, -79.39933; Yorktown; York **GS:** U **SP:** No info **VI:** No further data **P:** unk **BLW:** unk **RG:** Y **MK:** unk **PH:** unk **SS:** J-Yorktown Historian **BS:** JLARC 1, 74.

ALARDIOT, Antoine; b unk; d 1781 **RU:** Seaman, Served on "Auguste". Died from Yorktown battle **CEM:** French Memorial; GPS 36.81944, -79.39933; Yorktown; York **GS:** U **SP:** No info **VI:** No further data **P:** unk **BLW:** unk **RG:** Y **MK:** unk **PH:** unk **SS:** J-Yorktown Historian **BS:** JLARC 1, 74.

ALBERT, Jacob Allen; b 1757; d 1856 **RU:** Private, Served in 12th Cont Line **CEM:** Doe Mountain Farm; GPS unk; Nr Pembroke; Giles **GS:** U **SP:** No info **VI:** No further data **P:** unk **BLW:** unk **RG:** unk **MK:** unk **PH:** unk **SS:** DAR Ancestor #A000947; E pg 5 **BS:** JLARC 3.

ALBRIGHT, Frederick; b Feb 1761; d 28 Aug 1824 **RU:** Private, Served in Capt Thomas Pry's Co, Col Moses Hazen's Regt 1778 **CEM:** McDowell; GPS 37.86860, -79.31080; Nr jct Rts 11 and 712, Fairfield; Rockbridge **GS:** Y **SP:** No info **VI:** No further data **P:** N **BLW:** N **RG:** N **MK:** N **PH:** unk **SS:** AP Roll **BS:** 154 Rockledge; 196.

ALDRIDGE, James; b 1760; d unk **RU:** Private, Served in Capt Thomas Catlett's Co, 2d VA Regt Cont Line for 3 yrs **CEM:** Aldridge Family; GPS unk; Off Rt 607, 2 mi E of Rt 654; Prince George **GS:** N **SP:** No info **VI:** No further data **P:** unk **BLW:** Y **RG:** unk **MK:** unk **PH:** N **SS:** DAR Ancestor #A001090; C pg 388; E pg 6; AP Payroll **BS:** 111.

ALDRIDGE, John; b 1764; d 1832 **RU:** Private, Served in 9th & 13th Cont Lines **CEM:** Goose Creek; GPS 39.11250, -77.69527; Rt 722, Lincoln; Loudoun **GS:** Y **SP:** Harriet West (1765-1857) **VI:** No further data **P:** unk **BLW:** unk **RG:** Y **MK:** N **PH:** unk **SS:** C Sec III pg 389; E pg 6 **BS:** 25 pg 54; 196.

ALESHIRE, John Conrad; b 23 Dec 1755, Shenandoah Co; d 17 Dec 1811 **RU:** Private, Served in Capts Rowsch or Denton, or Prince, Cols Bowmans & Church Regts. Was at siege of Yorktown **CEM:** Aleshire Family; GPS unk; E of Rt 616, 8 mi S of Luray, in back of canning factory; Page **GS:** Y **SP:** No info **VI:** Pen #S17816 dated 27 Aug 1832 **P:** Y **BLW:** unk **RG:** unk **MK:** unk **PH:** unk **SS:** DAR Ancestor #A001119; CI-Pension file **BS:** 120.

ALEXANDER, Andrew; b Rockbridge Co; d unk **RU:** Soldier, Served in Augusta Co Militia in Capt Long's Co 1778, Capt Kennry's Co 1779, Capt Rankin's Co 1780, and Capt Finley's Co 1782 **CEM:** Stonewall Jackson Memorial; GPS 37.78128, -79.44604; 314 S Main St; Lexington City **GS:** U **SP:** Mar (1800 Rockbridge Co) Isabelle Paxton, d/o William & Eleanor (-----) Hays **VI:** Son of William & Nancy (-----) Alexander **P:** unk **BLW:** unk **RG:** unk **MK:** unk **PH:** unk **SS:** E pg 6; N pg 1065 **BS:** JLARC 79.

ALEXANDER, Archibald; b 4 Feb 1708, Ireland; d 1 Feb 1780 **RU:** Patriot, Specific service indicated in Journal VA House of Delegates 1835-6, Doc 6, pg 75. Public service as High Sheriff & Justice, Augusta Co **CEM:** Tinkling Spring Presbyterian; GPS 38.08472, -78.98278; 30 Tinkling Spring Dr, Fishersville; Augusta **GS:** N **SP:** 1) Mar (1734 Rockbridge Co) Margaret Parks; 2) Mar (1757 Rockbridge Co) Jane McClure **VI:** Might be discrepant burial site reported for the same person **P:** unk **BLW:** unk **RG:** unk **MK:** N **PH:** N **SS:** DAR Ancestor #A001134; AD pg 242; CZ pg 16 **BS:** JLARC 63.

RU=Rank/Unit	CEM=Cemetery	GS=Gravestone	SP=Spousal Information
VI=Other Veteran Info	P=Pension	BLW=Bounty/Land Warrant	RG=Registered Grave
MK=SAR/DAR Marker	PH=Photo	SS=Service Source	BS=Burial Source

ALEXANDER, Archibald; b unk, North Ireland; d c1780 **RU:** Patriot, Performed civil service **CEM:** Muse, aka Irvine Family, aka Timber Grove, aka Timber Ridge Presbyterian; GPS unk; 9 mi N of Lexington off Rt 11, SW of jct Rts 11 & 716, 73 Sam Huston Way, Buffalo District; Rockbridge **GS:** N **SP:** No info **VI:** Might be discrepant burial site reported for the same person. GS was there but now missing **P:** unk **BLW:** unk **RG:** unk **MK:** unk **PH:** N **SS:** SAR Ancestor #P-102271 **BS:** JLARC 2 ,63;196.

ALEXANDER, Charles Sr; b 20 Jul 1737; d 1806 **RU:** Patriot, Gave wood to Minutemen in Alexandria **CEM:** Pohick Episcopal; GPS 38.42546, -77.11598; 9301 Richmond Hwy, Lorton; Fairfax **GS:** Y **SP:** Frances Brown **VI:** Son of John & Susanna (-----) Pearson **P:** N **BLW:** N **RG:** Y **MK:** N **PH:** unk **SS:** DAR Ancestor #A001140; G pg 432 **BS:** 20 pg 51.

ALEXANDER, Gabriel; b unk; d 1779 **RU:** Private, Served in Capt Baskins & Longs Cos, Augusta Co Militia **CEM:** Tinkling Spring Presbyterian; GPS 38.08472, -78.98278; 30 Tinkling Spring Dr, Fishersville; Augusta **GS:** U **SP:** No info **VI:** No further data **P:** N **BLW:** N **RG:** N **MK:** unk **PH:** unk **SS:** E pg 7 **BS:** 208 pg 458.

ALEXANDER, John; b 1763; d 1828 **RU:** Private, Served in Capt Joseph McCutchen's Co, Augusta Co Militia **CEM:** Stonewall Jackson Memorial; GPS 37.78128, -79.44604; 314 S Main St; Lexington City **GS:** U **SP:** Elizabeth Barnes, d/o Richard & (-----) Barnes **VI:** No further data **P:** unk **BLW:** unk **RG:** unk **MK:** unk **PH:** unk **SS:** E pg 7 **BS:** 245.

ALEXANDER, Robert; b Nov 1746; d 20 Nov 1820 **RU:** Captain, Oath as Capt 27 Jun 1779. Bedford Co Militia **CEM:** Alexander-Adams; GPS unk; Rt 652, Gladys; Campbell **GS:** Y **SP:** Mar (10 Mar 1774, Bedford Co) Ann Austin **VI:** No further data **P:** unk **BLW:** unk **RG:** Y **MK:** N **PH:** unk **SS:** DAR Ancestor #A001240; NSSAR Ancestor #P-102402 **BS:** JLARC 1, 2, 36; 196.

ALEXANDER, William; b 1741; d 1811 **RU:** Lieutenant Colonel, Specific Serv indicated Prince William Co, Petitions 17 Oct 1776 **CEM:** Bethel Luthern; GPS unk; 8712 Plantation Ln; Manassas City **GS:** Y **SP:** No info **VI:** No further data **P:** unk **BLW:** unk **RG:** N **MK:** N **PH:** unk **SS:** AY Muster Roll; CZ pg 16 **BS:** 190 pg 12.

ALEXANDER, William; b 3 Mar 1744, Effingham, Prince William Co; d 3 Apr 1814 **RU:** Lieutenant Colonel, Was in charge of Prince William Co Militia **CEM:** Effingham Plantation; GPS 38.38393, -77.31290; 1 mi E of Adan, 14325 Trotter's Ridge Place, Nokesville; Prince William **GS:** U **SP:** Mar (18 Apr 1765) Sigismunda Mary Massie d/o Sigismunde & Mary (Stewart) Massie **VI:** Son of Phillip M & Sarah (Hooe) Alexander. County Justice 1765-1790. SAR marker **P:** unk **BLW:** unk **RG:** Y **MK:** Y **PH:** Y **SS:** DAR Ancestor #A001271; J-NSSAR 2000 Reg; E pg 7 **BS:** JLARC 1, 2, 76; 04 CWG Chap Oct 2014.

ALEXANDER, William; b 1738, Chester Co, PA; d 1796 **RU:** Private, Served in Capt Dickey's Co, Augusta Co Militia 1782 **CEM:** Stonewall Jackson Memorial; GPS 37.78128, -79.44604; 314 S Main St; Lexington City **GS:** Y **SP:** Agnes Ann Reid (1740-11 Oct 1825) d/o Andrew & Sarah (-----) Reid **VI:** Son of Archibald (4 Feb 1818 Ireland-1780 Rockbridge Co) & (-----) Alexander **P:** unk **BLW:** unk **RG:** Y **MK:** unk **PH:** unk **SS:** DAR Ancestor #A001269; E pg 8 **BS:** JLARC 2, 63, 76; 196.

ALLARD, Andre; b unk; d 1781 **RU:** Soldier, Served in Regt d'Agenais and died from Yorktown battle **CEM:** French Memorial; GPS 36.81944, -79.39933; Yorktown; York **GS:** U **SP:** No info **VI:** No further data **P:** unk **BLW:** unk **RG:** Y **MK:** unk **PH:** unk **SS:** J-Yorktown Historian **BS:** JLARC 1, 74.

ALLEGREE, William; b 1764; d 17 Apr 1833 **RU:** Private, Served in Clarks, IL Regt, State line, Col Joseph Crockett's Regt **CEM:** St John's Episcopal; GPS 37.53183, -77.41958; 2401 E Broad St; Richmond City **GS:** Y **SP:** No info **VI:** No further data **P:** unk **BLW:** unk **RG:** unk **MK:** N **PH:** unk **SS:** C Sec III pg 324 **BS:** 28 pg 415.

ALLEN, Charles; b 1754,Cumberland Co; d 5 Feb 1814 **RU:** Lieutenant, Served in Prince Edward Co Militia in 1777. Perhaps served in 9th Cont Line **CEM:** Lakeview; GPS 37.07091, -78.01143; 8th St, Blackstone; Nottoway **GS:** U **SP:** Mar (24 Apr 1777 Prince Edward) Elizabeth Chambers **VI:** No further data **P:** unk **BLW:** unk **RG:** unk **MK:** unk **PH:** unk **SS:** DAR Ancestor #A001405; E pg 9 **BS:** 196 cem search.

RU=Rank/Unit	CEM=Cemetery	GS=Gravestone	SP=Spousal Information
VI=Other Veteran Info	P=Pension	BLW=Bounty/Land Warrant	RG=Registered Grave
MK=SAR/DAR Marker	PH=Photo	SS=Service Source	BS=Burial Source

ALLEN, Charles; b 1746, Hanover Co; d 8 Feb 1816 **RU:** Lieutenant Colonel, Served in Prince Edward's Co Militia and 9th Cont Line **CEM:** Allen-Watkins Family; GPS unk; Farmville; Prince Edward **GS:** N **SP:** Mary Venable (__-1824) **VI:** No further data **P:** unk **BLW:** unk **RG:** Y **MK:** unk **PH:** N **SS:** DAR Ancestor #A001403; E pg 9; G pg 505 **BS:** JLARC 1,76.

ALLEN, Hugh; b 4 Sep 1745, Botetourt Co; d 1816 **RU:** Second Lieutenant, Served in Capt Pryor's Co Militia. Specific serv indicated in Lib VA Auditors Accts 1779-80, pg 207 **CEM:** Allen-Carper; GPS unk; Rt 43 nr Eagle Rock; Botetourt **GS:** Y **SP:** Anna Hunter **VI:** No further data **P:** unk **BLW:** unk **RG:** Y **MK:** N **PH:** unk **SS:** DAR Ancestor #A001573; E pg 9; CZ pg 17 **BS:** 04.

ALLEN, James; b 1733; d 1810 **RU:** Private, Served in Capt Samuel McDowell's Co, Augusta Co Militia. Was in the battle at Pt Pleasant, October 1774 **CEM:** Augusta Stone Presbyterian; GPS 38.23926, -78.97356; 28 Old Stone Church Ln, Ft Defiance; Augusta **GS:** Y **SP:** Margaret Anderson **VI:** Govt stone **P:** unk **BLW:** unk **RG:** Y **MK:** unk **PH:** unk **SS:** DAR Ancestor #A001614; E pg 9; Z pg 104 **BS:** JLARC 1, 2, 8, 23, 62, 63; 196.

ALLEN, James; b 6 Dec 1762; d 26 Sep 1844 **RU:** Private, Served in Botetourt Co Militia **CEM:** Allen Family; GPS unk; 5.5 mi S of Buchanan; Botetourt **GS:** Y **SP:** Jane Steele (__-1826 **VI:** Son of Robert Allen & Mary (Walkinshaw (d 1818) **P:** unk **BLW:** unk **RG:** N **MK:** N **PH:** unk **SS:** AZ pg 103 **BS:** 115 pg 3; 196.

ALLEN, James Jr; b 7 Jul 1724, Hanover Co; d 20 Oct 1793 **RU:** Patriot, Gave material aid to cause and had patriotic public service as member of Prince Edward Co Committee of Safety, Jun & Nov 1775 **CEM:** Allen Family; GPS unk; Vic Farmville; Prince Edward **GS:** N **SP:** Elizabeth Sims **VI:** No further data **P:** N **BLW:** N **RG:** Y **MK:** N **PH:** N **SS:** DAR Ancestor #A001616; AK; AL Ct Bk pg 12 Prince Edward Co **BS:** 04.

ALLEN, John; b 1732, Ireland; d 1794 **RU:** Patriot, Gave material aid to the cause **CEM:** Opequon Presbyterian; GPS 39.13938, -78.19494; 217 Opequon Church Ln; Winchester City **GS:** N **SP:** Ann Pollock (later renamed Polk) (1743 Carlisle, Cumberland Co, PA-8 Feb 1805 Shelby Co. KY) d/o Thomas and Ann (-----) Pollock **VI:** Son of Robert (1695-1769) & Deborah (Montgomery) (1700-1740) Allen **P:** N **BLW:** N **RG:** N **MK:** N **PH:** N **SS:** DAR Ancestor #A001674; AL Ct Bk pg 4 **BS:** 59 pg 8.

ALLEN, John; b 17 Aug 1759, Botetourt Co; d 30 May 1828 **RU:** Private, Served in Capt Pryor's Co Militia **CEM:** Allen-Carper; GPS unk; Rt 43 nr Eagle Rock; Botetourt **GS:** Y **SP:** Rebecca Poague **VI:** No further data **P:** unk **BLW:** unk **RG:** Y **MK:** N **PH:** unk **SS:** DAR Ancestor #A001675; E pg 9 **BS:** 04.

ALLEN, Joseph; b unk; d 1781 **RU:** Soldier, Served fr MA, and died as result of Yorktown battle **CEM:** Yorktown Victory Monument Tablet; GPS 38.28350, -78.54150; Yorktown; York **GS:** U **SP:** No info **VI:** No further data **P:** unk **BLW:** unk **RG:** unk **MK:** unk **PH:** unk **SS:** J-Yorktown Historian **BS:** JLARC 74.

ALLEN, Malcolm; b c1710, Kilbirnie, County Ayr, Scotland; d 15 Feb 1792 **RU:** Patriot, Provided supplies/served on Petit and Grand Juries **CEM:** Allen-Carper; GPS unk; Rt 43 nr Eagle Rock; Botetourt **GS:** Y **SP:** Mary (Unreadable) **VI:** No further data **P:** N **BLW:** N **RG:** Y **MK:** N **PH:** unk **SS:** AK Mar 2007 **BS:** 04.

ALLEN, Moses; b 9 Oct 1750, Botetourt Co; d 1812 **RU:** Private, Served in Capt Pryor's Co Militia **CEM:** Allen Family; GPS unk; Off Craig Creek, nr Oriskany; Craig **GS:** Y **SP:** Lydia (-----) **VI:** No further data **P:** unk **BLW:** unk **RG:** Y **MK:** N **PH:** unk **SS:** AK Mar 2007 **BS:** 04.

ALLEN, Robert; b 1736, Ireland; d 15 Nov 1791 **RU:** Patriot, Gave material aid to cause **CEM:** Opequon Presbyterian; GPS 39.13938, -78.19494; 217 Opequon Church Ln; Winchester City **GS:** U **SP:** Martha (-----) **VI:** Son of Robert (1695-1769) & Deborah (Montgomery) (1700-1740) Allen **P:** N **BLW:** N **RG:** unk **MK:** unk **PH:** unk **SS:** DAR ancestor #A001802; D Vol 2 pg 38 **BS:** 196.

ALLEN, Robert; b 26 Nov 1748, Botetourt Co; d unk **RU:** Private, Served in Capt Pryor's Co Militia **CEM:** Allen-Carper; GPS unk; Rt 43 nr Eagle Rock; Botetourt **GS:** Y **SP:** Jane Hill **VI:** No further data **P:** unk **BLW:** unk **RG:** Y **MK:** N **PH:** unk **SS:** AK Mar 2007 **BS:** 04.

ALLEN, Robert; b 1736, Ireland; d 15 Nov 1791 **RU:** Private, Gave material aid to cause **CEM:** Opequon Presbyterian; GPS 39.13938, -78.19494; 217 Opequon Church Ln; Winchester City **GS:** U

RU=Rank/Unit	CEM=Cemetery	GS=Gravestone	SP=Spousal Information
VI=Other Veteran Info	P=Pension	BLW=Bounty/Land Warrant	RG=Registered Grave
MK=SAR/DAR Marker	PH=Photo	SS=Service Source	BS=Burial Source

SP: Martha Allen **VI**: Son of Robert (1695-1769) & Deborah (Montgomery) (1700-1740) Allen. Died in Kernstown, Frederick Co **P**: unk **BLW**: unk **RG**: Y **MK**: unk **PH**: unk **SS**: AL Bt Bk pg 22 Frederick Co **BS**: DAR Ancestor #A001802; JLARC 2, 76.

ALLEN, Robert; b 1731; d 1778 **RU**: Private/Patriot, Served in Capt Anderson's Co, Augusta Co Militia. In 1778, was exempted because of his age. Gave material aid to cause **CEM**: Allen Marker; GPS unk; E Waynesboro at Winchester Heights, lot 4, Elkin Ave; Waynesboro City **GS**: Y **SP**: No info **VI**: No further data **P**: unk **BLW**: unk **RG**: N **MK**: N **PH**: unk **SS**: E pg 10; AL Cert Augusta Co **BS**: 142 Allen Marker.

ALLEN, Thomas; b 39 Aug 1734, Ireland; d 15 Jul 1822 **RU**: Patriot, Gave material aid to cause **CEM**: Millar Family; GPS unk; W Main St, Front Royal; Warren **GS**: Y **SP**: Mar (24 Feb 1747) Abigail Millar (1747-1823) **VI**: Son of Robert (1695-1769) & (-----) Allen. Died in Shenandoah Co **P**: N **BLW**: N **RG**: N **MK**: N **PH**: unk **SS**: C pg 593; D pg 4; AL Ct Bk pg 3, 5, 7, 9 Shenandoah Co **BS**: 50, pg 36; 196.

ALLISON, Robert; b 1745; d Jun 1801 **RU**: Patriot, Signed legislative petition 25 Oct 1779 to establish a naval port in Alexandria **CEM**: Old Presbyterian Meeting House; GPS 38.48528, -77.23532; 323 S Fairfax St; Alexandria City **GS**: N **SP**: No info **VI**: Bur 11 Jun 1801, age 56. Name listed on SAR plaque in cemetery **P**: N **BLW**: N **RG**: Y **MK**: Y **PH**: N **SS**: CJ Vol 2 series 2 pg 291-3 **BS**: JLARC 1, 76; 23 pg 99; 196.

ALLMAND, Harrison; b 8 Aug 1757, Nansemond Co; d 16 Apr 1822 **RU**: Patriot, Provided supplies for the "publick service" in Nansemond Co VA "for State, a gun lost...and a horse" **CEM**: St Paul's Episcopal; GPS 36.84733, -76.28554; 201 St Paul's Blvd; Norfolk City **GS**: Y **SP**: 1) Mar (1785) Louisa Keele 2) Mar (1803) Mary Thomas Walker 3) Lucy Campbell **VI**: Original owner of "Archer-Allmand House" in Norfolk, first son of Aaron & Ann (-----) Allmand **P**: N **BLW**: N **RG**: Y **MK**: Y **PH**: unk **SS**: CB Gave to cause **BS**: 178-Jan 11.

ALSOP, Benjamin (NMI); b 17 Mar 1758, Spottsylvania Co; d 20 Dec 1832 **RU**: Major, Was Minuteman and served in Washington's army at Trenton, Princeton, Brandywine (where wounded), Germantown, Ft Mifflin, Valley Forge; returned to VA. Was in Gates army in Carolinas inRegt of Brig Gen Edward Stevens. Joined LaFayette's army and discharged Williamsburg end of Sep 1781 **CEM**: Alsop; GPS unk; Lake View Estates subdivision in small grove; Snow Hill; Spotsylvania **GS**: Y **SP**: 1) Frances Boswell (__-6 Jan 1799) 2) Mary Rogers (aunt of George Rogers Clark) (__- 6 Mar 1830) **VI**: Soldier's father d 1776 to 1778. Appl pen 7 Sep 1832 Spotsylvania Co. S9269 **P**: Y **BLW**: unk **RG**: Y **MK**: Y **PH**: unk **SS**: J-NSSAR 2000 Reg; CG pg 48 **BS**: JLARC 1, 2 ,4, 76, 91.

ALTIZER, ALTHAUSEN, Emery Emera; b 1736, Bingen, Germany; d Sep 1819 **RU**: Soldier, Served at Yorktown and in Rockbridge Militia 18 mos **CEM**: Oakley-Altizer; GPS unk; Chestnut Ridge, Riner; Montgomery **GS**: Y **SP**: 76 lists (1762) mar (Jul 1773 Hagerstown MD, but lived in Berkley Co VA) Mary Petzer (c1759-__) **VI**: Widow appl 5 Oct 1840 Montgomery Co. W4720 **P**: Y **BLW**: unk **RG**: Y **MK**: N **PH**: unk **SS**: J-NSSAR 2000 Reg; CG pg 48 **BS**: JLARC 1, 2, 4, 76.

AMBLER, Jacquelin; b 1742; d 1797 **RU**: Patriot, Served as a Commissioner of the VA Navy Board in 1779 **CEM**: Jamestown Church; GPS unk; 3827 Ironbound Rd, Williamsburg; Williamsburg City **GS**: U **SP**: No info **VI**: No further data **P**: N **BLW**: N **RG**: unk **MK**: unk **PH**: unk **SS**: CE pg 150 **BS**: 196.

AMBLER, John Esq; b 25 Sep 1762, Jamestown; d 6 Apr 1836 **RU**: Patriot, Provided provisions to cause **CEM**: Shockoe Hill; GPS 37.55190, -77.43170; 4th & Hospital Sts; Richmond City **GS**: Y **SP**: 1) Mar (31 May 1783 Henrico Co) Frances Armistead d/o Gill & (-----) Amistead 2) Mar (19 May 1791 Henrico Co) Lucy Marshall (sister of John) 3) Catherine Bush (Norton) **VI**: Son of Edward & (-----) Ambler **P**: N **BLW**: N **RG**: Y **MK**: Y **PH**: unk **SS**: D Vol 2 pg 472; AK **BS**: 04, Sep 07.

AMES, Isaac; b c1724; d 1818 **RU**: Corporal, Served in MA **CEM**: St John's Episcopal; GPS 37.53183, -77.41958; 2401 E Broad St; Richmond City **GS**: Y **SP**: No info **VI**: No further data **P**: unk **BLW**: unk **RG**: N **MK**: N **PH**: unk **SS**: AJ Vol I pg 218 **BS**: 28, pg 414.

AMIRAUD, Philippe; b unk; d 1781 **RU**: Seaman, Served on "Duc de Bourgogne" and died from Yorktown battle **CEM**: French Memorial; GPS 36.81944, -79.39933; Yorktown; York **GS**: U **SP**: No info **VI**: No further data **P**: unk **BLW**: unk **RG**: Y **MK**: unk **PH**: unk **SS**: J-Yorktown Historian **BS**: JLARC 1, 74.

RU=Rank/Unit	CEM=Cemetery	GS=Gravestone	SP=Spousal Information
VI=Other Veteran Info	P=Pension	BLW=Bounty/Land Warrant	RG=Registered Grave
MK=SAR/DAR Marker	PH=Photo	SS=Service Source	BS=Burial Source

AMISS (AMIS), Joseph; b 1710; d 1801 **RU:** Patriot, Gave material aid to cause **CEM:** Cem name unk; GPS unk; Amissville; Rappahannock **GS:** Y **SP:** Constant Jones **VI:** No further data **P:** N **BLW:** N **RG:** Y **MK:** N **PH:** unk **SS:** AL Ct bk I pg 34 **BS:** AS, SAR Rpt.

AMISS (AMIS), Levi; b 1756; d 1780 **RU:** Seaman, Served on the "Diligence" Galley **CEM:** Cem name unk; GPS unk; Amissville; Rappahannock **GS:** Y **SP:** No info **VI:** No further data **P:** unk **BLW:** unk **RG:** Y **MK:** N **PH:** unk **SS:** L pg 140 **BS:** AS, DAR Rpt.

ANDERSON, Alexander; b 1762, Augusta Co; d 25 Dec 1825 **RU:** Private/Patriot, Served in Capt John McKitrick's Co 1782 and in Capt Rankin's Co, Augusta Co Militia **CEM:** Schutterle Community; GPS 38.22030, -79.10470; Off Rt 728 SE of Rt 732, Franks Mill; Augusta **GS:** Y **SP:** 1) Esthet Kirkland (1766-1810) 2) Esther Crosby (1788 PA-18 Dec 1867) d/o George (1765-1846) & Susanna (Evans) (1767-1813) Crosby **VI:** Son of William (__-1794) & Margaret (Clendenin) (1743-1805) Anderson. Also served in War of 1812 **P:** unk **BLW:** unk **RG:** unk **MK:** unk **PH:** unk **SS:** E pg 14 **BS:** 196.

ANDERSON, Andrew; b 1750; d 1783 **RU:** Captain, Co Commander Augusta Co Militia 1783 **CEM:** Augusta Stone Presbyterian; GPS 38.23926, -78.97356; 28 Old Stone Church Ln, Ft Defiance; Augusta **GS:** N **SP:** 1) (-----) 2) Martha Crawford **VI:** No further data **P:** unk **BLW:** unk **RG:** unk **MK:** unk **PH:** N **SS:** E pg 14 **BS:** JLARC 62.

ANDERSON, Andrew; b unk; d 1835 **RU:** Private?, Served in 1st and/or 9th Cont Line **CEM:** Waterford Union of Churches; GPS 39.18557, -77.60802; Fairfax St, Waterford; Loudoun **GS:** Y **SP:** No info **VI:** No further data **P:** unk **BLW:** unk **RG:** Y **MK:** N **PH:** unk **SS:** E pg 14 **BS:** 25, pg 8.

ANDERSON, Daniel; b 1749; d 25 Jan 1813 **RU:** Sergeant, Served in 4th, 8th & 12th Cont Lines & Western Battalion VA Troops **CEM:** Blandford; GPS 37.22433, -77.38604; 319 S Crater Rd; Petersburg City **GS:** U **SP:** No info **VI:** Merchant in Petersburg. A child as his heir received pen of $8 per mo, Act of 1838, last payment 06 Nov 1840. 200 acres BLW issued 20 Jun 1783 **P:** Y **BLW:** Y **RG:** unk **MK:** unk **PH:** unk **SS:** E pg 14 **BS:** 213 pg 38.

ANDERSON, David; b 15 Jul 1756, Cumberland Co; d 18 Jun 1812 **RU:** Private, Served in Prince Edward Co Militia & Baylor's Regt **CEM:** Blandford; GPS 37.22433, -77.38604; 319 S Crater Rd; Petersburg City **GS:** U **SP:** No info **VI:** Was Chamberlain in town of Petersburg. Founder of the Corporation of Petersburg **P:** unk **BLW:** unk **RG:** unk **MK:** unk **PH:** unk **SS:** E pg 14 **BS:** 213 pg 38.

ANDERSON, David Jr; b Sep 1745, Albermarle Co VA; d 15 Mar 1795 **RU:** Captain, Vol as Minute Man Jun 1776 in Chesterfield Co; Ent serv Chesterfield Co May 1777, in Capt Cadwallader's Co of Dragoons serving 13 mos. In Mar 1781 was wagoner & collector of provisions for Army at Yorktown **CEM:** Anderson; GPS unk; Nr South Anna River, Rt 642; Louisa **GS:** U **SP:** Mar (21 Sep 1785, Prince Edward Co) Lucy Horsley (c1768-aft 10 Dec 1843 Prince Edward Co) **VI:** Chamberlain in town of Petersburg and founder of the Corporation of Petersburg. Widow pension, #SW5625 **P:** Y **BLW:** unk **RG:** Y **MK:** N **PH:** unk **SS:** DAR ancestor #A203412; E pg 14; AZ pg 53-54; DD **BS:** 04 May 07; 80 vol 1, pg 472; 13 pg 38.

ANDERSON, Edmund; b 1 Apr 1763; d 19 Apr 1810 **RU:** Private?, Service information not determined **CEM:** Locust Hill; GPS unk; Off Rt 676 N of Rt 250, Ivy; Albemarle **GS:** Y **SP:** Jane Meriwether Lewis (31 Mar 1770-15 Mar 1845) d/o William (1748-1779) & Lucy (Meriwether) (1752-1837) Lewis **VI:** No further data **P:** unk **BLW:** unk **RG:** N **MK:** N **PH:** unk **SS:** AW pg 3 **BS:** 67 vol 4 pg 105; 196.

ANDERSON, Elijah; b 1758, Culpeper Co; d Dec 1837 **RU:** Private, Served in Capt John Ball's Co, commanded by Col Elias Edmonds. Served 2 mos & 10 days 1782 in Fauquier Co Militia. **CEM:** Elijah Anderson; GPS 38.45380, -77.5833; 27 Shurgen Ln, Amissvile; Rappahannock **GS:** Y **SP:** 1) Frances Williams 2) Miriam Anderson 3) Mary Priest **VI:** Son of James & (-----) Anderson. GS replaced by family in 1999. Only stone in middle of pasture **P:** unk **BLW:** unk **RG:** Y **MK:** unk **PH:** Y **SS:** N pg 1247-1248 **BS:** 196.

ANDERSON, George; b 1745; d 1828 **RU:** Second Lieutenant, Specific service recorded source Lib VA, Archives, War, vol 4, p 79 **CEM:** Schutterle Community; GPS 38.22030, -79.10470; Off Rt 728 SE of Rt 732, Franks Mill; Augusta **GS:** N **SP:** Jane Presberry **VI:** No further data **P:** unk **BLW:** unk **RG:** Y **MK:** N **PH:** N **SS:** CZ pg 19 **BS:** JLARC 2, 76.

RU=Rank/Unit	CEM=Cemetery	GS=Gravestone	SP=Spousal Information
VI=Other Veteran Info	P=Pension	BLW=Bounty/Land Warrant	RG=Registered Grave
MK=SAR/DAR Marker	PH=Photo	SS=Service Source	BS=Burial Source

7

ANDERSON, George; b 1758; d 29 Jun 1814 **RU:** Sergeant, Served in Capt Moffett's Co Augusta Co Militia 1777 & in Capt Trimbel's Co 1781 **CEM:** Schutterle Community; GPS 38.22030, -79.10470; Off Rt 728 SE of Rt 732, Franks Mill; Augusta **GS:** Y **SP:** Mar (12 Feb 1789) Mary Breeden (__-1 Sep 1853) **VI:** Widow appl pen 26 Dec 1846 Augusta Co. Also pen to widow 12 Nov 1814 at $5.50 per mo. W5627. Govt stone says served in Moffat's Co of VA Militia **P:** Y **BLW:** unk **RG:** Y **MK:** N **PH:** unk **SS:** E pg 14; CG pg 55 **BS:** JLARC 1 ,2, 3, 62; 196; 196.

ANDERSON, Jacob; b 1756, NJ; d 1825 **RU:** Private, Specific service recorded Lib VA, Archives, Report Sec of War 1835, pen vol 2, pg 173 **CEM:** Anderson-Hash; GPS 36.66593, -81.33110; Flatridge & Old Bridle Creek Rd; Grayson **GS:** U **SP:** Mar (before 1779) Susannah Buchanan (1760-1820) **VI:** Pen list of 1820, VA **P:** Y **BLW:** unk **RG:** Y **MK:** N **PH:** unk **SS:** H; AG pg 555; CZ pg 19 **BS:** 04, e-mail 04/07.

ANDERSON, James; b 24 Jan 1740, Gloucester Co; d 8 Sep 1798 **RU:** Captain, At age 21 was Lt in Capt Robert McKenzie's Co. Was Capt in Gloucester Co Militia. Was chief armourer for colony 1776-1782. Was prisoner on parole 11 Jun 1781 **CEM:** Bruton Parish Church; GPS 37.27127, -76.70248; 331 W Duke of Gloucester St; Williamsburg City **GS:** U **SP:** No info **VI:** No further data **P:** unk **BLW:** Y **RG:** unk **MK:** unk **PH:** unk **SS:** G pg 362, 437, 433, 475, 507, 574; EE pg 4 **BS:** 196.

ANDERSON, James; b 1714, New Kent Co; d 1882 **RU:** Patriot, Gave material aid to cause **CEM:** James Anderson Family; GPS unk; Reeds; Cumberland **GS:** U **SP:** Elizabeth Baker (1737-1792) **VI:** No further data **P:** N **BLW:** N **RG:** unk **MK:** unk **PH:** unk **SS:** D pg 5; AL Ct Bk pg 1, 5, 68 Cumberland Co **BS:** 196.

ANDERSON, James; b unk; d 31 Dec 1740 **RU:** Soldier, Service information not determined **CEM:** Old Presbyterian Meeting House; GPS 38.48528, -77.23532; 323 S Fairfax St; Alexandria City **GS:** N **SP:** No info **VI:** No further data **P:** unk **BLW:** unk **RG:** Y **MK:** unk **PH:** N **SS:** J-NSSAR 1993 Reg; S NSSAR Ancestor #P-103499 **BS:** JLARC 1, 5.

ANDERSON, John; b 1707, Ireland; d 1786 **RU:** Patriot, Appraised beef and gave material aid to cause **CEM:** Augusta Stone Presbyterian; GPS 38.23925, -78.97356; 28 Old Stone Church Ln, Ft Defiance; Augusta **GS:** N **SP:** No info **VI:** No further data **P:** unk **BLW:** unk **RG:** unk **MK:** unk **PH:** unk **SS:** AL Cert Augusta Co **BS:** 196.

ANDERSON, Joseph Edward Sr; b 27 Feb 1746; d 23 Jan 1825 **RU:** Sergeant, Served in Clark's Illinois Regt or 11th VA Regt. As Patriot furnished 18 gallons of whiskey to cause **CEM:** Anderson Family; GPS 39.85160, -77.52350; "Springfield Farm," Rt 608 nr Morgan Spring Run, Webbtown; Clarke **GS:** N **SP:** Hannah D. Blue (26 Mar 1754, Wilmington, DE-28 Dec 1843, Berryville, Clarke Co) **VI:** Son of Bartholomew Anderson (1710-1754) & Phebe (-----) (1718-1799). On Pen list of 1820, VA. GS missing-- it said "Sacred to the memory of JOSEPH ANDERSON who departed this life Jan. 23 1825, aged 78 yrs, 10 mos. And 27 day" **P:** Y **BLW:** unk **RG:** N **MK:** N **PH:** N **SS:** E pg 15; AG pg 555 **BS:** 58 pg 1; 196.

ANDERSON, Matthew (Mathew); b 6 Dec 1745; d 21 Dec 1806 **RU:** Private/patriot, Served in Capt Charles Dabney's Co, Col Dabney's Legion of Calvary for 3 yrs. Also gave material aid to cause **CEM:** Ware Episcopal; GPS 37.42275, -76.50789; 7825 John Clayton Mem Hwy; Gloucester **GS:** Y **SP:** Mary (-----) (27 Aug 1749-12 Jun 1820) **VI:** Recd BLW 100 acres,14 Mar 1783. Bur at Exchange Cemetery, thus memorialized here **P:** N **BLW:** Y **RG:** N **MK:** N **PH:** unk **SS:** A pg 291; N pg 1255-6; AL Ct Bk pg ii 16 Gloucester Co **BS:** 65 Gloucester; 207; 213 pg 100-1.

ANDERSON, Nelson; b 1726, Hanover Co; d 28 Aug 1820 **RU:** Captain, Commanded a company in Bedford Co Militia **CEM:** Anderson Family; GPS 37.38970, -79.39045; 2370 Cifax Rd, Goode; Bedford **GS:** N **SP:** Frances Jackson (1741 Louisa Co-13 Mar 1818) d/o Thomas Jackson & Ann (Mills) Jackson **VI:** No further data **P:** unk **BLW:** unk **RG:** Y **MK:** N **PH:** N **SS:** AK Bedford Hist Soc **BS:** 04, Sep 07.

ANDERSON, Robert; b 1712; d 1792 **RU:** Patriot, Gave material aid to cause **CEM:** Goldmine farm; GPS unk; Rt 271, Rockville; Hanover **GS:** Y **SP:** No info **VI:** No further data **P:** N **BLW:** N **RG:** N **MK:** N **PH:** unk **SS:** AL Cert Issued **BS:** 31 pg 3.

RU=Rank/Unit   CEM=Cemetery   GS=Gravestone   SP=Spousal Information
VI=Other Veteran Info   P=Pension   BLW=Bounty/Land Warrant   RG=Registered Grave
MK=SAR/DAR Marker   PH=Photo   SS=Service Source   BS=Burial Source

8

ANDERSON, Robert; b 1739; d 1823 or 1825 **RU:** Private/Patriot, Gave material aid to the cause **CEM:** Fincastle Presbyterian; GPS 37.50017, -79.87558; 108 E Back St, Fincastle; Botetourt **GS:** N **SP:** Mary (-----) **VI:** Name is on the SAR plaque at this cemetery **P:** unk **BLW:** unk **RG:** Y **MK:** Y **PH:** N **SS:** AL Ct Bk pg 8, 9; AR pg 20; J-NSSAR 2000 Reg **BS:** 196 JLARC 1, 2 ,76; 196.

ANDERSON, Thomas; b 1754, Cumberland Co; d 14 Oct 1804 **RU:** Soldier, Served in Capt John Mountjoy's Co,10th VA Regt and Capt William Gillison's Co 6th VA Regt May 1779 **CEM:** James Anderson Family; GPS unk; Reeds; Cumberland **GS:** U **SP:** Sarah Weldon Anderson (1760-1814) Same last name. **VI:** Son of James (1714-1882) & Elizabeth (Baker) (1737-1792) Anderson **P:** unk **BLW:** unk **RG:** unk **MK:** unk **PH:** unk **SS:** E pg 16; CI: Muster Roll **BS:** 196.

ANDERSON, Thomas; b 1761; d 28 Mar 1824 **RU:** Soldier, Served in 6th and 10th Cont Line **CEM:** Stonewall Jackson Memorial; GPS 37.78128, -79.44604; 314 S Main St; Lexington City **GS:** U **SP:** No info **VI:** No further data **P:** unk **BLW:** unk **RG:** unk **MK:** unk **PH:** unk **SS:** E pg 16 **BS:** 196.

ANDERSON, William; b unk; d 1794 **RU:** Patriot, Gave material aid to cause **CEM:** Augusta Stone Presbyterian Church; GPS 38.23926, -78.97356; 28 Old Stone Church Ln, Fort Defiance; Augusta **GS:** U **SP:** Mary Margaret Reid (1720 Ireland-10 Apr 1743) **VI:** No further data **P:** N **BLW:** N **RG:** unk **MK:** unk **PH:** unk **SS:** AL Cert Augusta Co **BS:** 196.

ANDERSON, William; b 2 Jun 1764, DE; d 13 Sep 1839 **RU:** Private/Patriot, Served at 16 yrs old with Gen Green. Gave material aid to cause **CEM:** Fincastle Presbyterian; GPS 37.50017, -79.87558; 108 E Back St, Fincastle; Botetourt **GS:** Y **SP:** Anne Thomas **VI:** Served in the House of Delegates. Name is on the SAR plaque at this cemetery **P:** unk **BLW:** unk **RG:** Y **MK:** Y **PH:** unk **SS:** AL Ct Bk pg 6, 31, 32; AR pg 20; J-NSSAR 2000 Reg **BS:** JLARC 1, 2, 76; 196.

ANDES, Andrew; b 10 Feb 1749; d 21 May 1821 **RU:** Patriot, Lib of VA Public Service Claim. Gave material aid to the cause **CEM:** Mt Olivet Church of Brethern; GPS unk; 2977 Pineville Rd, McGayesville; Rockingham **GS:** Y **SP:** Barbara Bear (Baer) **VI:** No further data **P:** N **BLW:** N **RG:** Y **MK:** N **PH:** unk **SS:** AK; AL Ct bk 1 pg 12 **BS:** 4-Oct-06.

ANDRE, Jean; b unk; d 1781 **RU:** Seaman, Served on "Auguste" and died from Yorktown battle **CEM:** French Memorial; GPS 36.81944, -79.39933; Yorktown; York **GS:** U **SP:** No info **VI:** No further data **P:** unk **BLW:** unk **RG:** Y **MK:** unk **PH:** unk **SS:** J-Yorktown Historian **BS:** JLARC 1, 74.

ANDREE, John G; b unk; d 1811 **RU:** Private, Specific service recorded Lib VA, Archives, Rejected Claims for BLW **CEM:** Shockoe Hill; GPS 37.55190, -77.43170; 4th & Hospital Sts; Richmond City **GS:** Y **SP:** No info **VI:** No further data **P:** unk **BLW:** N **RG:** N **MK:** N **PH:** unk **SS:** E pg 16; CZ pg 21 **BS:** 179 # 1361.

ANDREW, Seth; b unk; d 1781 **RU:** Soldier, Served fr MA, and died as result of Yorktown battle **CEM:** Yorktown Victory Monument Tablet; GPS 38.28350, -78.54150; Yorktown; York **GS:** U **SP:** No info **VI:** No further data **P:** unk **BLW:** unk **RG:** unk **MK:** unk **PH:** unk **SS:** J-Yorktown Historian **BS:** JLARC 74.

ANDREWS, Benjamin; b 1699; d 1799 **RU:** Patriot, Gave material aid to the cause **CEM:** Andrews Family; GPS unk; Thomas Andrews Plantation, Appomattox River; Henrico **GS:** N **SP:** Ann Vodin (1722-__) **VI:** Son of Thomas (1663-1731) & Elizabeth (Thomas) (1664-__) Thomas. Died in Chesterfield Co **P:** N **BLW:** N **RG:** unk **MK:** unk **PH:** N **SS:** AL Ct Bk pg 11 Prince George Co **BS:** 196.

ANDREWS, Benjamin; b 1755; d 11 Jul 1803 **RU:** Sergeant, Served in Co Militia. Served several tours; in last tour marched prisoners fr Yorktown to Winchester, Oct 1781 **CEM:** William A. Andrews 1400 acres; GPS 36.78894, -78.13494; South Hill; Mecklenburg **GS:** U **SP:** Elizabeth (Betsy) Dodd (c1751-after 16 Mar 1843) **VI:** Son of Abraham (1725-1799) & (-----) Andrews. Widow appl pen age 92 on 16 Mar 1843 **P:** Y **BLW:** unk **RG:** unk **MK:** unk **PH:** unk **SS:** K Vol 1 pg 19 **BS:** 196.

ANDREWS, Bullard; b 20 Jul 1745, Chesterfield Co; d 7 Dec 1828 **RU:** Patriot, Paid the 1783 personal property tax in Chesterfield Co in 1783 which is considered to support the cause by partially providing funds with payment **CEM:** Thomas Andrews Plantation; GPS unk; On the Appomattox River; Henrico **GS:** Y **SP:** Sally (-----) **VI:** Son of Benjamin (1699-1799) & Ann (Vodin) (1722-__) Andrews **P:** N **BLW:** N **RG:** unk **MK:** N **PH:** N **SS:** www.southernfern.com/gjt/en-434.htm shows Personal Property tax 1783 **BS:** 196.

RU=Rank/Unit	CEM=Cemetery	GS=Gravestone	SP=Spousal Information
VI=Other Veteran Info	P=Pension	BLW=Bounty/Land Warrant	RG=Registered Grave
MK=SAR/DAR Marker	PH=Photo	SS=Service Source	BS=Burial Source

9

ANDREWS, Robert; b 24 Apr 1761; d 14 Feb 1803 **RU:** Private, Served in 6th VA Regt **CEM:** Thomas Parker Family; GPS unk; Rt 180 nr Pungoteague; Accomack **GS:** Y **SP:** No info **VI:** No further data **P:** unk **BLW:** unk **RG:** N **MK:** N **PH:** unk **SS:** AP 6th VA Regt **BS:** 178 Th. Parker.

ANDREWS, Thomas; b 12 Dec 1761, Cumberland Co; d 31 Aug 1853 **RU:** Corporal, Served in VA Line in 1st Light Dragoons **CEM:** Andrews Family; GPS unk; Evington; Bedford **GS:** U **SP:** Tabitha Lee **VI:** Appl 25 Feb 1833 Bedford Co S6506 **P:** Y **BLW:** unk **RG:** unk **MK:** N **PH:** unk **SS:** E pg 17; CG pg 64 **BS:** JLARC 4, 36, 66.

ANDREWS, Varney Sr; b 25 Jul 1760 Mecklenburg Co; d 1848 **RU:** Soldier, Vol summer 1776 or '77, in Capt Peter Rogers' Co, Col Morgans VA Regt,and marched to Gwyn's Island then Barron Point on Potomac. Served six mos as private, four mos as drummer. Served a mo, summer of 1777 or '78 in Capt Anthony Street's Co, VA Militia. Enl Feb 1781, served 2 mos as private in Capt Claybourn's Co, Col Munford's VA Regt. Was in Battle of Guilford CH. Served 3 enlistments in Rev Army, two of them under Gen Nathaniel Green **CEM:** William A. Andrews 1400 acres; GPS 36.78894, -78.13494; South Hill; Mecklenburg **GS:** Y **SP:** 1) Lucy Green (1765-__) 2) Amey Thweatt (1765-__) **VI:** Son of William A (1726-1772) & Ann Brooks (Varney) (1730-1772) Andrews. Pen claim, S 11992, based upon the service of Varney Andrews in the War of the Revolution **P:** Y **BLW:** unk **RG:** unk **MK:** unk **PH:** unk **SS:** K Vol 1 pg 20 **BS:** 196.

ANDREWS, William; b 26 Aug 1733; d 4 Apr 1777 **RU:** Seaman, Enlisted 1777 with serv in Galley "Accomack" commanded by Capt William Underhill until 1780. Served onboard ship with William Andrews. Discharged at Chincoteague **CEM:** Thomas Parker Family; GPS unk; Rt 180 nr Pungoteague; Accomack **GS:** Y **SP:** No info **VI:** Appl pen 3 Jun 1824 Accomack Co. Rejected for pension. Was 63 on 3 Jun 1834 **P:** N **BLW:** unk **RG:** N **MK:** N **PH:** unk **SS:** N pg 1267; CG pg 65 **BS:** 178 Th. Parker.

ANDREWS, William A; b 1750, Mecklenburg Co; d 1779 **RU:** Private, Served in Capt Robert Ballard's Co, 1st VA Regt, Cont Line **CEM:** Andrews Family; GPS 36.78894, -78.13494; Whittles Mill Rd, South Hill; Mecklenburg **GS:** U **SP:** No info **VI:** Son of Willam A. (1726-1772) & Ann Brooks (Varney) (1730-1772) Andrews. Died in service, had enlisted for three yrs. Service source cites Petition 05 Dec 1785. Lib of VA **P:** unk **BLW:** unk **RG:** unk **MK:** unk **PH:** unk **SS:** DB pg 15 **BS:** 196.

ANDUTEAU, Jacques; b unk; d 1781 **RU:** Seaman, Served on "Auguste" and died from Yorktown battle **CEM:** French Memorial; GPS 36.81944, -79.39933; Yorktown; York **GS:** U **SP:** No info **VI:** No further data **P:** unk **BLW:** unk **RG:** Y **MK:** unk **PH:** unk **SS:** J-Yorktown Historian **BS:** JLARC 1, 74.

ANGEVAISE, Nicolas; b unk; d 1781 **RU:** Soldier, Served in Regt d' Agenais and died from Yorktown battle **CEM:** French Memorial; GPS 36.81944, -79.39933; Yorktown; York **GS:** U **SP:** No info **VI:** No further data **P:** unk **BLW:** unk **RG:** Y **MK:** unk **PH:** unk **SS:** J-Yorktown Historian **BS:** JLARC 1, 74.

ANGIBAUD, Joseph; b unk; d 1781 **RU:** Seaman, Served on "Solitaire" and died from Yorktown battle **CEM:** French Memorial; GPS 36.81944, -79.39933; Yorktown; York **GS:** U **SP:** No info **VI:** No further data **P:** unk **BLW:** unk **RG:** Y **MK:** unk **PH:** unk **SS:** J-Yorktown Historian **BS:** JLARC 1, 74.

ANGLE (ANGELL), Peter; b 22 Apr 1754, Germany; d 25 Feb 1821 **RU:** Private, Served in Capt Baltzel's Co, Lt Col Weltner's Regt & German Regt **CEM:** Angle Family; GPS 37.06940, -79.86310; Rt 699; Franklin **GS:** Y **SP:** Elizabeth Jane Miller (4 Mar 1758 Germany-18 Apr 1827) **VI:** Died in Wirtz, Franklin Co **P:** unk **BLW:** unk **RG:** N **MK:** N **PH:** unk **SS:** DAR Ancestor #A002811; E pg 17; CI PA Archives 5th Series Vol III pg 769 **BS:** 82 pg 15; 196.

ANGLIN, Philip II or Jr; b 20 Dec 1742, Albemarle Co; d c1837 **RU:** Soldier/Patriot, Served in VA Line. Ent serv Pittsylvania Co (later Henry Co). Fought Tories in battle of Flowers Gap, NC. Supplied food to Guilford Hospital after Battle of Guilford CH **CEM:** Anglin Plantation; GPS unk; Nr Patrick Co line; Henry **GS:** U **SP:** No info **VI:** Appl 9 Apr 1834 Henry Co. R225. Will probated 13 Feb 1837 **P:** Y **BLW:** unk **RG:** Y **MK:** unk **PH:** unk **SS:** J-NSSAR 1993 Reg; CG pg 68 **BS:** JLARC 1.

ANIBEL, William; b unk; d 1781 **RU:** Soldier, Served fr MA,and died as result of Yorktown battle **CEM:** Yorktown Victory Monument Tablet; GPS 38.28350, -78.54150; Yorktown; York **GS:** U **SP:** No info **VI:** No further data **P:** unk **BLW:** unk **RG:** unk **MK:** unk **PH:** unk **SS:** J-Yorktown Historian **BS:** JLARC 74.

RU=Rank/Unit	CEM=Cemetery	GS=Gravestone	SP=Spousal Information
VI=Other Veteran Info	P=Pension	BLW=Bounty/Land Warrant	RG=Registered Grave
MK=SAR/DAR Marker	PH=Photo	SS=Service Source	BS=Burial Source

10

ANIEER, William; b unk; d unk **RU:** Soldier, Served in French unit not specified and died from Yorktown battle **CEM:** Yorktown Victory Monument Tablet; GPS 38.28350, -78.54150; Yorktown; York **GS:** U **SP:** No info **VI:** No further data **P:** unk **BLW:** unk **RG:** unk **MK:** unk **PH:** unk **SS:** http://freepages.genealogy.rootsweb.ancestry.com/~wvmystica/Yorktown_Victory_Monument_Tablet_-_American.html **BS:** Cem monument.

ANSLEY, William; b 1756; d 28 Jun 1798 **RU:** Private, Served in1st Light Dragoons **CEM:** Old Stone Methodist; GPS 39.11725, -77.56609; 168 W Cornwall St, Leesburg; Loudoun **GS:** U **SP:** Mar (1779) Nancy Ann Hereford (1766-1792) d/o John (1725-1793) & Margaret (Ammon) (1735-1809) Hereford **VI:** No further data **P:** unk **BLW:** unk **RG:** Y **MK:** unk **PH:** unk **SS:** E pg 18 **BS:** JLARC 1, 32; 196.

ANTHONY, John; b 1749; d 1822 **RU:** Private, Served in 6th Cont Line **CEM:** Walnut Hill; GPS unk; Anthony home on Otter River, Evington; Campbell **GS:** U **SP:** No info **VI:** No further data **P:** unk **BLW:** unk **RG:** Y **MK:** N **PH:** unk **SS:** DAR Ancestor #A002884; AR Vol 1 pg 23; E pg 18 **BS:** JLARC 1, 2, 66, 75.

ARBOGAST, Michael; b 1734, Baden-Wurttemberg, Germany; d 27 Aug 1812 **RU:** Private, Served in Capt Hull's Co, Augusta Co Militia **CEM:** Arbogast Family; GPS unk; Wimer Mountain Rd, Blue Grass; Highland **GS:** Y **SP:** Mar (1759 Pendleton Co, WV) Mary Elizabeth Samuels-Amanapas **VI:** Son of Michael (1694-1743) & Catherine (Konigin) (1695-aft 1736) Arbogast **P:** unk **BLW:** unk **RG:** unk **MK:** unk **PH:** unk **SS:** DAR Ancestor #A002973; J- DAR Hatcher; E pg 19; AR pg 24 **BS:** JLARC 2; 196.

ARBUCKLE, Mathew; b unk; d 22 May 1783 **RU:** Captain, Led Gen Lewis's army through the dense mountain forest to Point Pleasant and later marched a Co over same Rt to build and garrison Ft Randolf **CEM:** George Revercomb property; GPS unk; McClintic by Jackson River; Bath **GS:** U **SP:** No info **VI:** This stone probably moved (or lost) in the 1970s for the Gathright Dam project **P:** unk **BLW:** unk **RG:** Y **MK:** N **PH:** unk **SS:** DAR Ancestor #A002976; E pg 19; AK **BS:** 04, AZ, pg 33.

ARCHER, John; b 30 Sep 1746; d 3 Mar 1812 **RU:** Major, Served as Maj in Amelia Co Militia 1778 **CEM:** Archer, Red Lodge; GPS unk; Red Lodge Rd; Amelia **GS:** Y **SP:** 1) Elizabeth Bur 2) Anne Hall 3) Mar (24 Apr 1788) Elizabeth Eggleston (bond) (__-Mar 1826) **VI:** Son of William & Elizabeth (-----) Archer **P:** unk **BLW:** unk **RG:** unk **MK:** unk **PH:** Y **SS:** E pg 19; CD **BS:** 196.

ARELL, David; b unk; d 1792 **RU:** Captain, Appt Capt of Inf 7 Oct 1776. Capt of Co in 3rd VA Regt of Foot, 28 Sep 1776 fr Pittsylvania Co. Resigned 14 Feb 1778 **CEM:** Old Presbyterian Meeting House; GPS 38.48528, -77.23532; 323 S Fairfax St; Alexandria City **GS:** N **SP:** No info **VI:** Will dated 15 Aug, proved 17 Apr 1796 (WB F, pg 79). Awarded BLW of 400 acres 12 Apr 1778 **P:** unk **BLW:** Y **RG:** Y **MK:** unk **PH:** N **SS:** DAR Ancestor #A003021; J-NSSAR 1993 Reg; BX pg 18; CE pg 40; AE Virginia Genealogical Society Quarterlies: Vol 2 pg 368 **BS:** JLARC 1; 23 pg 99; 196.

ARELL, H (Henry); b 1719; d Jul 1796 **RU:** Patriot, Gave material aid to cause **CEM:** Old Presbyterian Meeting House; GPS 38.48528, -77.23532; 323 S Fairfax St; Alexandria City **GS:** N **SP:** No info **VI:** Died of consumption in Fairfax Co. Bur 13 Jul 1796, age 77 **P:** unk **BLW:** unk **RG:** N **MK:** N **PH:** N **SS:** AL Cert issued **BS:** 110, pg 118; 23 pg 99.

ARELL, Samuel; b unk; d 1795 **RU:** Lieutenant/Patriot, Served in Marines 13 Nov 1776. Recommended for Capt 13 Dec 1776. Signed a legislative petition 25 Oct 1779 to establish a naval port in Alexandria **CEM:** Old Presbyterian Meeting House; GPS 38.48528, -77.23532; 323 S Fairfax St; Alexandria City **GS:** N **SP:** No info **VI:** Died in Fairfax Co. Will dated 1 Nov 1794, proved 20 Dec 1795 (WB G, pg 130). Name is listed on SAR plaque in cemetery **P:** unk **BLW:** unk **RG:** Y **MK:** Y **PH:** N **SS:** AK; J-NSSAR 1993 Reg; CJ Vol 2 series 2 pg 291-3 **BS:** JLARC 1; 23 pg 99; 196.

ARGENBRIGHT (ARGENTINE), Augustus (Augustine); b 13 Jun 1755, Shenandoah Co; d 1833 **RU:** Soldier, Served in Capt Smith's Co, Augusta Co Militia **CEM:** Trinity Episcopal; GPS 38.14917, -79.07521; 214 Beverley St; Staunton City **GS:** U **SP:** Anna Hanger (28 Oct 1756 Woodstock, Shenandoah Co-1836) d/o Frederick (1726-1799) & Eva Margaretha (Mayer) (__-1818) Hanger **VI:** Was a blacksmith during Rev War. Recd Pension 1832 **P:** Y **BLW:** unk **RG:** Y **MK:** unk **PH:** unk **SS:** E pg 20 **BS:** JLARC 2, 62, 63, 76; 196.

RU=Rank/Unit	CEM=Cemetery	GS=Gravestone	SP=Spousal Information
VI=Other Veteran Info	P=Pension	BLW=Bounty/Land Warrant	RG=Registered Grave
MK=SAR/DAR Marker	PH=Photo	SS=Service Source	BS=Burial Source

11

ARISMENDY, Jean; b unk; d 1781 **RU:** Seaman, Served on "Ville de Paris" and died from Yorktown battle **CEM:** French Memorial; GPS 36.81944, -79.39933; Yorktown; York **GS:** U **SP:** No info **VI:** No further data **P:** unk **BLW:** unk **RG:** Y **MK:** unk **PH:** unk **SS:** J-Yorktown Historian **BS:** JLARC 1, 74.

ARMENTROUT, George; b c1760-1763, Germany; d 1805 **RU:** Private, Served in Rockingham Co Militia 24 Apr 1780 **CEM:** Old Peaked Mountain; GPS 38.37113, -78.73416; 9843 Town Hall Rd, McGaheysville; Rockingham **GS:** U **SP:** Nancy Kiser **VI:** Died in McGaheysville **P:** unk **BLW:** unk **RG:** Y **MK:** Y **PH:** unk **SS:** J-NSSAR 2000 Reg; S NSSAR Ancestor #P-104391; DAR# 1805 **BS:** JLARC 76.

ARMENTROUT, Henry; b 1755 VA or 1755; Berks Co, PA; d 16 Jun or 9 Jul 1806 **RU:** Private/Patriot, Performed public service in Rockingham Co **CEM:** Old Peaked Mountain; GPS 38.37113, -78.73416; 9843 Town Hall Rd, McGaheysville; Rockingham **GS:** U **SP:** Mar (20 Oct 1786, Rockingham Co) Elizabeth Argenbright **VI:** Son of Johan Phillip & Elizabeth (Reith) Armentrout. Died in McGaheysville or Rockingham Co **P:** unk **BLW:** unk **RG:** Y **MK:** Y **PH:** unk **SS:** DAR Ancestor #A096347; J-NSSAR 2000 Reg; DE Bk I pg 152, 209 **BS:** JLARC 76.

ARMENTROUT, John Henry; b 1722, Germany; d 1789 **RU:** Patriot, Gave material aid to cause **CEM:** Old Peaked Mountain; GPS 38.37113, -78.73416; 9843 Town Hall Rd, McGaheysville; Rockingham **GS:** U **SP:** Mary Catherine Hedrick **VI:** Died in McGaheysville **P:** N **BLW:** N **RG:** Y **MK:** Y **PH:** unk **SS:** DAR Ancestor #A00303; J-NASSR 2000 Reg; DD **BS:** JLARC 76.

ARMENTROUT, Peter; b 17 Sep 1751, Rockingham Co; d 9 Jan 1824 **RU:** Private, Served in Capt Daniel's Co, Augusta Militia **CEM:** Bethel Cemetery; GPS 38.47592, -78.75641; 3061 Armentrout Path, Keezletown; Rockingham **GS:** Y **SP:** 1) Catherine Ergebrecht 2) Margaret (Margreta) Wolf (Wolfe) **VI:** No further data **P:** unk **BLW:** unk **RG:** Y **MK:** Y **PH:** unk **SS:** DAR Ancestor #A003039; AK **BS:** 04, JLARC 2, 76.

ARMENTROUT (ERMENTRAUDT), Philip; b 26 Oct 1747, Lancaster (now Berks) Co, PA; d 1 Jul 1836 **RU:** Private, Served in Capt Daniel's Co, Augusta Militia **CEM:** Bethel Cemetery; GPS 38.47592, -78.75641; 3061 Armentrout Path, Keezletown; Rockingham **GS:** Y **SP:** Margaret Cool **VI:** No further data **P:** unk **BLW:** unk **RG:** Y **MK:** Y **PH:** unk **SS:** AK; J- DAR Hatcher **BS:** 04, JLARC 2.

ARMSTRONG, John; b 1730; d unk **RU:** Captain, Specific service recorded Lib VA, Archives, Auditors Acct 1779, pg 165 **CEM:** Armstrong Family; GPS unk; Stonewall District; Highland **GS:** Y **SP:** No info **VI:** No further data **P:** unk **BLW:** unk **RG:** N **MK:** N **PH:** unk **SS:** AS; CZ pg 23 **BS:** AS.

ARMSTRONG, John; b c1759, Augusta Co (Highland Co now); d c1821 **RU:** Private, Served in Capt Kirk's Co, Augusta Co, Militia 1783 **CEM:** Armstrong Family; GPS unk; N of McDowell; Highland **GS:** N **SP:** Agnes Ervine (Erwin) **VI:** No further data **P:** unk **BLW:** unk **RG:** Y **MK:** N **PH:** N **SS:** DAR Ancestor #A003140; E pg 21 **BS:** 04.

ARMSTRONG, William; b 12 Dec 1759; d 29 Oct 1853 **RU:** Private, Served in Capt Kinkead's Co 1778; Capt Long's Co 1779 and 1782 of Augusta Co Militia. Was at battle of Guilford CH **CEM:** Old Lebanon; GPS 38.08090, -79.37545; Off Rt 42, Craigsville; Augusta **GS:** Y **SP:** 1) Mar (26 Mar 1793) Margaret Jameson 2)Mar (Apr 1809) Margaret Kirkpatrick **VI:** Appl pen 26 Oct 1832 Augusta Co. S8032. Died in Pendleton Co (Highland now). Grave has DAR marker. Son of Archibald Armstrong who was 2nd Lt of 97th VMR. **P:** Y **BLW:** unk **RG:** Y **MK:** Y **PH:** unk **SS:** DAR Ancestor #A107191; E pg 22; BT; CG pg 78 **BS:** JLARC 2, 76; 196.

ARNOLD, William; b 1727; d Jan 1813 **RU:** Patriot, Provided a horse for cause **CEM:** Willow Hill; GPS unk; Jct Kennedy Dr and Van Buren Dr, Presidential Lake subdivision; King George **GS:** Y **SP:** Jemima Clift **VI:** Name on monument in cem **P:** N **BLW:** N **RG:** unk **MK:** unk **PH:** unk **SS:** DAR ancestor #A003335; AL Cert Caroline Co; DD **BS:** 196.

ARTEAU, Andre; b unk; d 1781 **RU:** Seaman, Served on "Auguste" and died from Yorktown battle **CEM:** French Memorial; GPS 36.81944, -79.39933; Yorktown; York **GS:** U **SP:** No info **VI:** No further data **P:** unk **BLW:** unk **RG:** Y **MK:** unk **PH:** unk **SS:** J-Yorktown Historian **BS:** JLARC 1, 74.

ARTHUR, Thomas Sr; b 1740; d Nov 1805 **RU:** Private/Patriot, Served in VA Line and Bedford Co Militia. Served over 3 yrs **CEM:** Rural; GPS unk; See property records for homeplace; Bedford **GS:** U **SP:** Mar (29 Nov 1782 Bedford Co (bond)) Sally Dixon **VI:** Widow appl pen 15 Jun 1843 Bedford Co.

RU=Rank/Unit	CEM=Cemetery	GS=Gravestone	SP=Spousal Information
VI=Other Veteran Info	P=Pension	BLW=Bounty/Land Warrant	RG=Registered Grave
MK=SAR/DAR Marker	PH=Photo	SS=Service Source	BS=Burial Source

12

Widow Sally appl for ½ pay W5636. Brother, John Arthur also served Rev War **P:** Y **BLW:** unk **RG:** N **MK**: N **PH:** unk **SS:** E pg 23; AS; CG pg 82 **BS:** AS.

ASBURY (ASHBURY), Joseph; b 1759, Paris; d 1815 **RU:** Private, Enlisted age 16, 29 May 1778. Served in Lee's Legion **CEM:** Paris Community; GPS unk; Paris; Fauquier **GS:** N **SP:** Hannah Neale Talbott **VI:** No further data **P:** unk **BLW:** unk **RG:** Y **MK:** N **PH:** N **SS:** DAR Ancestor #A003380; E pg 23; H; AK **BS:** 04; 18 pg 77.

ASH, Francis; b 1759; d 27 Apr 1828 **RU:** Second Lieutenant, Served in VA Line. Lived in Fauquier Co during service in Fauquier Co Militia. Took oath as 2nd Lt 1779 **CEM:** Ash-Blackmore; GPS unk; Delaplane; Fauquier **GS:** N **SP:**1) mar (20 Dec 1774 (bond) Fauquier Co) Ann Adams, d/o John & (-----) Adams 2) mar (12 Feb 1789) Elizabeth "Betsy" Hand (c1772-__) **VI:** Son of George & (-----) Ash. Widow appl 4 Apr 1850 Frederick Co. R274 **P:** Y **BLW:** unk **RG:** N **MK:** N **PH:** N **SS:** DAR Ancestor #A204974; E pg 24; CG pg 83; Fauquier Co Marriages pg 6 **BS:** 19 pg 235.

ASH, George; b 1732; d 1807 **RU:** Patriot, Gave material aid to cause **CEM:** Ash-Blackmore; GPS unk; Delaplane; Fauquier **GS:** Y **SP:** Mar (19 Jun 1812 (bond) Fauquier Co) Sarah Ash **VI:** No further data **P:** N **BLW:** N **RG:** N **MK:** N **PH:** unk **SS:** DAR Ancestor #A205705; D Fauquier pg 1; AL Ct Bk pg 1; Fauquier Co Marriages pg 6 **BS:** 18 pg 2.

ASHBY, John; b 1 Apr 1740, east bank Shenandoah River; d 4 Apr 1815 **RU:** Major, Served in 3rd VA Regt. Wounded at Germantown 1776. Resigned 30 Oct 1777, but later was Maj in Fauquier Co Militia 1780-81 **CEM:** Ashby Family, Belmont; GPS unk; Greenland Farm, nr Rt 724, Delaplane; Fauquier **GS:** U **SP:** Mar (22 Feb 1766 Fauquier Co) Mary Turner fr Charles Co, MD **VI:** Wounded and placed on Invalid list 1781. Inquiry made 21 Apr 1837 Norfolk. R12159, VA ½ Pay. Died at "Belmont" Greenland Farm **P:** Y **BLW:** Y **RG:** Y **MK:** unk **PH:** unk **SS:** DAR Ancestor #A003415; E pg 24; BY pg 302; CG pg 83; Fauquier Co Marriages pg 6 **BS:** JLARC 1, 4,16, 76.

ASHLEY, Warren; b 1756, New Kent Co; d 25 Feb 1829 **RU:** Midshipman, Served in VA Navy **CEM:** Cedar Grove; GPS 36.83860, -76.30810; Salter St; Portsmouth City **GS:** Y **SP:** No info **VI:** Served in Merchant service as Master **P:** unk **BLW:** unk **RG:** unk **MK:** unk **PH:** unk **SS:** L pg 67; CD **BS:** 196.

ASHLIN, John; b 1762; d 1823 **RU:** Patriot, Gave material aid to cause **CEM:** Ashlin Family; GPS unk; End Rt 606; Fluvanna **GS:** Y **SP:** No info **VI:** No further data **P:** N **BLW:** N **RG:** N **MK:** N **PH:** unk **SS:** AL Ct bk pg 1, 15 **BS:** 66 pg 4.

ASHMORE, William; b 1748; d 1834 **RU:** Patriot, Gave material aid to cause **CEM:** Lane Family; GPS unk; Cement Rd; Prince William **GS:** Y **SP:** No info **VI:** No further data **P:** N **BLW:** N **RG:** Y **MK:** N **PH:** unk **SS:** DAR Ancestor #A003508; B; I; H; AL Ct Bk pg 1 Fauquier Co **BS:** 15 pg 16.

ASHTON, Henry Alexander; b 1747; d 1806 **RU:** Patriot, Gave material aid to cause **CEM:** Mt Mariah Plantation; GPS unk; Rt 619, 10 mi NE of King George; King George **GS:** Y **SP:** Mary Dent **VI:** Son of Henry & Jane (-----) Alexander **P:** N **BLW:** N **RG:** N **MK:** N **PH:** unk **SS:** AL Ct Bk pg 2 **BS:** 163 Mt Mariah.

ASLIN, Samuel; b unk; d bef 1826 **RU:** Patriot, Gave material aid to cause **CEM:** Eastern State Hospital; GPS 37.25560, -76.71030; S Henry Street; Williamsburg City **GS:** N **SP:** No info **VI:** No further data **P:** N **BLW:** N **RG:** N **MK:** N **PH:** N **SS:** AL Lists pg 7 **BS:** 65,Williamsburg.

ASSELIN, Claude; b unk; d 1781 **RU:** Soldier, Served in Regt de Touraine and died from Yorktown battle **CEM:** French Memorial; GPS 36.81944, -79.39933; Yorktown; York **GS:** U **SP:** No info **VI:** No further data **P:** unk **BLW:** unk **RG:** Y **MK:** unk **PH:** unk **SS:** J-Yorktown Historian **BS:** JLARC 1, 74.

ATHEAN, Claude; b unk; d 1781 **RU:** Seaman, Served on "Saint-Esprit" and died from Yorktown battle **CEM:** French Memorial; GPS 36.81944, -79.39933; Yorktown; York **GS:** U **SP:** No info **VI:** No further data **P:** unk **BLW:** unk **RG:** Y **MK:** unk **PH:** unk **SS:** J-Yorktown Historian **BS:** JLARC 74,76.

ATKINSON, George; b 1755; d 1755 **RU:** Private, Served in Capt Persifor Frazer's Co, Col Anthony Wayne's PA Bn 1776 **CEM:** Blackburn-Atkinson; GPS 38.36878, -77.16685; Rippon Lodge off Rt 638, Woodbridge; Prince William **GS:** Y **SP:** No info **VI:** No further data **P:** unk **BLW:** unk **RG:** unk **MK:** unk **PH:** unk **SS:** A pg 199 **BS:** 190 name of cemetery.

RU=Rank/Unit	CEM=Cemetery	GS=Gravestone	SP=Spousal Information
VI=Other Veteran Info	P=Pension	BLW=Bounty/Land Warrant	RG=Registered Grave
MK=SAR/DAR Marker	PH=Photo	SS=Service Source	BS=Burial Source

13

AUBIN, Jean; b unk; d 1781 **RU:** Seaman, Served on "Destin" and died from Yorktown battle **CEM:** French Memorial; GPS 36.81944, -79.39933; Yorktown; York **GS:** U **SP:** No info **VI:** No further data **P:** unk **BLW:** unk **RG:** Y **MK:** unk **PH:** unk **SS:** J-Yorktown Historian **BS:** JLARC 1, 74.

AUDIGER, Henri; b unk; d 1781 **RU:** Soldier, Served in Regt de Gatinaisand died from Yorktown battle **CEM:** French Memorial; GPS 36.81944, -79.39933; Yorktown; York **GS:** U **SP:** No info **VI:** No further data **P:** unk **BLW:** unk **RG:** Y **MK:** unk **PH:** unk **SS:** J-Yorktown Historian **BS:** JLARC 1, 74.

AUDIOT, Jean; b unk; d 1781 **RU:** Seaman, Served on "Hector" and died from Yorktown battle **CEM:** French Memorial; GPS 36.81944, -79.39933; Yorktown; York **GS:** U **SP:** No info **VI:** No further data **P:** unk **BLW:** unk **RG:** Y **MK:** unk **PH:** unk **SS:** J-Yorktown Historian **BS:** JLARC 1, 74.

AUGE, Jean; b unk; d 1781 **RU:** Seaman, Served on "Caton" and died from Yorktown battle **CEM:** French Memorial; GPS 36.81944, -79.39933; Yorktown; York **GS:** U **SP:** No info **VI:** No further data **P:** unk **BLW:** unk **RG:** Y **MK:** unk **PH:** unk **SS:** J-Yorktown Historian **BS:** JLARC 1, 74.

AUGER, Etienne; b unk; d 1781 **RU:** Soldier, Served in Regt de Gatinais and died from Yorktown battle **CEM:** French Memorial; GPS 36.81944, -79.39933; Yorktown; York **GS:** U **SP:** No info **VI:** No further data **P:** unk **BLW:** unk **RG:** Y **MK:** unk **PH:** unk **SS:** J-Yorktown Historian **BS:** JLARC 1, 74.

AUGER, Pierre; b unk; d 1781 **RU:** Seaman, Served on "Languedocand" died from Yorktown battle **CEM:** French Memorial; GPS 36.81944, -79.39933; Yorktown; York **GS:** U **SP:** No info **VI:** No further data **P:** unk **BLW:** unk **RG:** Y **MK:** unk **PH:** unk **SS:** J-Yorktown Historian **BS:** JLARC 1, 74.

AULD, Hugh Sr; b 23 May 1745, Talbot Co, MD; d 7 Dec 1813 **RU:** First Lieutenant, Served in Talbot Co MD Militia in 1780 **CEM:** Arlington National; GPS 38.88377, -77.06535; Jefferson Davis Hwy Rt 110; Arlington **GS:** Y **SP:** Frances Harrison **VI:** Died and originally bur in Claiborne MD. Interred in Arlington on 11 Apr 1935. Father of Hugh, Jr also bur here and who had War of 1812 service **P:** unk **BLW:** unk **RG:** Y **MK:** Y **PH:** unk **SS:** DAR Ancestor #A003752; CF; AS **BS:** 203;196.

AUVRAY, Louis; b unk; d 1781 **RU:** Seaman, Served on "Hercule" and died from Yorktown battle **CEM:** French Memorial; GPS 36.81944, -79.39933; Yorktown; York **GS:** U **SP:** No info **VI:** No further data **P:** unk **BLW:** unk **RG:** Y **MK:** unk **PH:** unk **SS:** J-Yorktown Historian **BS:** JLARC 1, 74.

AVARY, Wiliam; b Abt 1746; d Oct 1794 **RU:** Patriot, Signed Oath of Allegience **CEM:** Avary Family; GPS unk; Avary Church Rd; Amelia **GS:** N **SP:** Hannah Clay (__-1822 Amelia Co) d/o Charles (__-1792) & (-----) Clay **VI:** Son of George & Elizabeth (-----) Avary **P:** N **BLW:** N **RG:** unk **MK:** unk **PH:** N **SS:** CQ **BS:** 32 - Kilby.

AXLINE, John; b 19 Sep 1739, Prince William Co; d 19 Feb 1833 **RU:** Patriot, Gave material aid to cause **CEM:** New Jerusalem Lutheran; GPS 39.25736, -77.63891; 12942 Lutheran Church Rd, Lovettsville; Loudoun **GS:** U **SP:** Christena Martz **VI:** No further data **P:** N **BLW:** N **RG:** Y **MK:** unk **PH:** unk **SS:** DAR Ancestor #A004044; J-NSSAR 2000 Reg; D Vol 2 pg 599 **BS:** JLARC 76.

AYLETT, William; b 1743; d 1781 **RU:** Patriot/Colonel, Was Burgess for King William Co at assemblies of 1772-1774 & 1775-1776 and member of Conventions of 1774-1775-1776. Resigned fr the Convention to accept commission as Deputy Commissary General in VA. Died in Battle of Yorktown, fr a fever he contracted (malaria?) **CEM:** Fairfield Plantation; GPS unk; Aylett; King William **GS:** U **SP:** Mar (1766) Mary Macon, d/o Col James & Elizabeth (Moore) Macon of Kennington (__-1787). Her second husband was Callohill Minnis. **VI:** Died in Yorktown, York Co. His heirs recd BLW on 6666 acres in 1809 **P:** unk **BLW:** Y **RG:** unk **MK:** unk **PH:** unk **SS:** DAR Ancestor #A004153; BX pg 24 **BS:** 196.

AYLOR, Jacob; b Feb 1749, Culpeper Co; d unk **RU:** Private, Served in VA Line. Ent serv Culpeper Co **CEM:** Aylor Family; GPS unk; .75 mi N of Novum Post Office; Madison **GS:** N **SP:** No info **VI:** Appl pen 11 Jun 1833 Madison Co. S8040 **P:** Y **BLW:** unk **RG:** N **MK:** N **PH:** N **SS:** DAR Ancestor #A204668; E pg 29; CG pg 101 **BS:** 169, Aylor.

AYRES, William; b unk; d Aug 1791 **RU:** Private, Served in Capt George Jenkin's Co, PA Militia, May & Jun 1777 **CEM:** Old Christ Church Episcopal; GPS 38.80625, -77.04718; 118 N Washington St; Alexandria City **GS:** N **SP:** No info **VI:** Burial permit issued 18 Aug 1791 **P:** unk **BLW:** unk **RG:** Y **MK:** N **PH:** N **SS:** C pg 221; E pg 29; AK; AP roll **BS:** 04; 20 pg 145.

RU=Rank/Unit	CEM=Cemetery	GS=Gravestone	SP=Spousal Information
VI=Other Veteran Info	P=Pension	BLW=Bounty/Land Warrant	RG=Registered Grave
MK=SAR/DAR Marker	PH=Photo	SS=Service Source	BS=Burial Source

BACON, Samuel; b c1734; d 22 Jul 1794 **RU:** Patriot, Submitted claim for losses suffered during burning of Norfolk **CEM:** St Paul's Episcopal; GPS 36.84733, -76.28554; 201 St Paul's Blvd; Norfolk City **GS:** Y **SP:** Mar (8 Apr 758 Norfolk Co) Mary Ann Dale **VI:** No further data **P:** N **BLW:** N **RG:** Y **MK:** Y **PH:** unk **SS:** CB Friend Amer Cause **BS:** 178-Jan 8 2011.

BAGBY, John; b 1728, Hanover Co; d 13 Jul 1789 **RU:** Patriot, Gave material aid to cause **CEM:** Mt Air/Pleasant View; GPS unk; Overton Fork, Rt 723 Bohannon Rd nr Lake Anna; Louisa **GS:** U **SP:** Theadosia Morris (1735-1792) d/o William & (-----) Morris **VI:** No further data **P:** N **BLW:** N **RG:** unk **MK:** unk **PH:** unk **SS:** DAR Ancestor #A004527; Al Ct Bk pg 30 Louisa Co **BS:** 196.

BAGGAGE, Jean; b unk; d 1781 **RU:** Soldier, Served in Agenois Bn and died from Yorktown battle **CEM:** French Memorial; GPS 36.81944, -79.39933; Yorktown; York **GS:** U **SP:** No info **VI:** No further data **P:** unk **BLW:** unk **RG:** Y **MK:** unk **PH:** unk **SS:** J-Yorktown Historian **BS:** JLARC 1, 74.

BAGOUS, Michel; b unk; d 1781 **RU:** Seaman, Served on "Saint-Esprit" and died from Yorktown battle **CEM:** French Memorial; GPS 36.81944, -79.39933; Yorktown; York **GS:** U **SP:** No info **VI:** No further data **P:** unk **BLW:** unk **RG:** Y **MK:** unk **PH:** unk **SS:** J-Yorktown Historian **BS:** JLARC 1, 74.

BAGWELL, Isaiah; b 13 Sep 1760, Accomack Co; d 8 Oct 1839 **RU:** Seaman, Served in 9th Cont Line; VA Sea Service **CEM:** Mt Holly; GPS 37.70485, -75.74185; Hill St, Onancock; Accomack **GS:** Y **SP:** Mar Accomack Co 2 Jan 1790 (bond) to Christina Newton; d 11 Jul 1819 (TS at Mt Holly) **VI:** Son of Josiah and Sarah Bagwell (tombstone.) Appl pen 4 Sep 1832 Accomack Co. S6550. Child recd final payment **P:** Y **BLW:** unk **RG:** unk **MK:** unk **PH:** unk **SS:** DAR Ancestor # A004566; E pg 30; CG pg 112 **BS:** JLARC 4, 5; 209.

BAILEY, Ansel Anselm Ansolem Anselem; b 1758; d Aft 1843 **RU:** Soldier, Served in New Kent Co Militia and 1st VA Regt, & 6th Cont Line **CEM:** Shockoe Hill; GPS 37.55190, -77.43170; 4th & Hospital Sts; Richmond City **GS:** U **SP:** Susannah (-----) (c1792-__) **VI:** Entered service in 1776 fr New Kent where also pensioned in 1820. Appl pen 9 Jul 1818 New Kent Co. S37702 **P:** Y **BLW:** unk **RG:** unk **MK:** unk **PH:** unk **SS:** E pg 30-31; CG pg 112 **BS:** JLARC 4,104.

BAILEY, Benjamin; b 1755; d 1813 **RU:** Second Lieutenant, Served in Montgomery Co Militia. Sworn in as 1st Lt at Montgomery Co on 13 May 1788 (after the war) **CEM:** Bailey Family; GPS 37.37075, -77.77635; Matoaca; Chesterfield **GS:** U **SP:** Ann Wilkins (or Watkins) **VI:** No further data **P:** unk **BLW:** unk **RG:** N **MK:** N **PH:** unk **SS:** DAR Ancestor #A004591; AS cites DAR Report **BS:** 196.

BAILEY, John; b unk; d 29 Aug 1824 **RU:** Captain, Commanded a Co in Brigadier Gen George Rogers Clark's Illinois Regt 1781 **CEM:** Presbyterian Church; GPS 37.40206, -79.13848; 2020 Grace St; Lynchburg City **GS:** Y **SP:** No info **VI:** 4000 acres BLW recd 3 Mar 1784 **P:** unk **BLW:** Y **RG:** unk **MK:** unk **PH:** unk **SS:** C pg 89; N pg1243 **BS:** 196.

BAILEY, Richard; b 1748; d 1818 **RU:** Private, Served in 15th Cont Line **CEM:** Leatherwood Farm; GPS unk; Rt 460, Bluefield; Tazewell **GS:** Y **SP:** No info **VI:** No further data **P:** unk **BLW:** unk **RG:** Y **MK:** N **PH:** unk **SS:** DAR Ancestor #A004746; E pg 31; H; AK Mar 2008 **BS:** 4.

BAILLIE, Robert; b 1744; d 1804 **RU:** Second Lieutenant, Served in Capt Joseph Warley's Co, 3rd SC Regt, Aug 1779 **CEM:** Old Presbyterian Meeting House; GPS 38.48528, -77.23532; 323 S Fairfax St; Alexandria City **GS:** N **SP:** No info **VI:** Bur 19 Aug 1804, age 60 yrs. Name is listed on SAR plaque in cemetery **P:** unk **BLW:** unk **RG:** Y **MK:** Y **PH:** N **SS:** AP roll SC Regt; J-NSSAR 1993 Reg; AK **BS:** JLARC 1; 23 pg 99; 196.

BAIN, William; b 12 Aug 1764; d 26 Nov 1815 **RU:** Private, Served in Northampton Co Militia **CEM:** Maria Robins House; GPS unk; 1 mi N of center of Eastville; Northampton **GS:** Y **SP:** 1) Mar (31 Aug 1785) Judith Stevenson 2) Mar (16 Jul 1793) Susanna (Sukey) Dunton **VI:** No further data **P:** unk **BLW:** unk **RG:** unk **MK:** N **PH:** unk **SS:** E pg 32 **BS:** 42 pg 5.

BAKER, Andrew II; b 1749, Grayson Co; d 24 Sep 1815 **RU:** Private, Served in Capt Isaac Riddle's Co **CEM:** Robert Clark Family, aka Thompson-Whitehead-Wilder; GPS 36.61376 -83.15651; Jct Rts 612 & 615, Jonesville; Lee **GS:** Y **SP:** Elizabeth Avant (12 Sep 1752 Brunswick Co-1844 Lee Co) **VI:** Son of Andrew W. (1702)-1781) & Mary Agnes (Bolling) (1702-1776) Baker. Rev. Died in Jonesville, Lee Co **P:**

RU=Rank/Unit	CEM=Cemetery	GS=Gravestone	SP=Spousal Information
VI=Other Veteran Info	P=Pension	BLW=Bounty/Land Warrant	RG=Registered Grave
MK=SAR/DAR Marker	PH=Photo	SS=Service Source	BS=Burial Source

15

unk **BLW:** unk **RG:** Y **MK**: Y **PH:** unk **SS:** DAR Ancestor #A004862; B; DD cites Hist of KY Vol I pg 13 **BS:** 04.

BAKER, Henry; b 10 Jun 1731, Rheinland-Pfatz, Germany; d 17 Mar 1809 **RU:** Private/Patriot, Served in Capt Linchfield Sharp's Co, Shenandoah Co 1781 and Col Eliza Edmondson Regt 2-5 Oct 1781. Gave 31 Oct 1775, Frederick County provisions to Dunmore Co Militia **CEM:** Mt Hebron; GPS 39.10916, -78.09497; 305 E Boscawen St; Winchester City **GS:** Y **SP:** Mary Ann Elizabeth Fink (1733-1806) **VI:** Newer GS added with "Revolutionary Patriot" at bottom, Founder of Old Lutheran Church **P:** N **BLW:** N **RG:** Y **MK**: Y **PH:** Y **SS:** DAR Ancestor #A004941; J-NSSAR Reg 2000; AL Ct Bk pg 29, 30; N pg 1265; Z pg 81 **BS:** 50 pg 43; 65, Frederick; JLARC 76.

BAKER, Henry Sr; b 1763; d 27 Dec 1837 **RU:** Patriot, Signed a legislative petition **CEM:** Baker-Ferry Family; GPS unk; East of Rt 779, Daleville; Botetourt **GS:** Y **SP:** No info **VI:** No further data **P:** N **BLW:** N **RG:** N **MK:** N **PH:** unk **SS:** DAR Ancestor #A004942; N pg 1265 **BS:** 115 pg 67.

BAKER, Hilary (Hillary) Jr; b 1746; d 1798 **RU:** Patriot, Was Clerk of Ct Henrico Co. Check DAR Senate doc 1954 serial 11831, vol 4 for military service **CEM:** Shockoe Hill; GPS 37.55190, -77.43170; 4th & Hospital Sts; Richmond City **GS:** U **SP:** No info **VI:** Clerk for militia **P:** unk **BLW:** unk **RG:** unk **MK**: unk **PH:** unk **SS:** DAR Ancestor #A004943; SAR Ancestor #P-107411; J- DAR Hatcher; S NSSAR Ancestor Nbr P-107411 **BS:** JLARC 2.

BAKER, Isaac; b 1726; d 1793 **RU:** Private, Served in Capt Joseph Bowman's Co, lower Dunmore Co (Now Shenandoah) Militia **CEM:** Baker Family, aka Spring Creek; GPS unk; N Jct with 647 Bristol-Abingdon Rd; Washington **GS:** U **SP:** No info **VI:** DAR marker **P:** unk **BLW:** unk **RG:** unk **MK**: Y **PH:** unk **SS:** J- DAR Hatcher; AR Vol 1 pg 41 **BS:** JLARC 2; 78 pg 286.

BAKER, John Sr; b 15 Sep 1754; d 15 May 1830 **RU:** Private, Served in Capt Thomas Snead's Co, Col Fleming's Regt, Cont Line Nov & Dec 1776 **CEM:** Friedens United Church of Christ; GPS 38.34848, -78.87653; 3960 Friedens Church Rd; Rockingham **GS:** Y **SP:** Anna Whitmer (4 Jun 1761-17 May 1838) **VI:** No further data **P:** unk **BLW:** unk **RG:** N **MK**: N **PH:** unk **SS:** AP roll **BS:** 191 Frieden's.

BAKER, Joseph; b 1762; d 1833 **RU:** Ensign, Served in Capt Joseph Bowman's Co Dunmore Co **CEM:** Baker Tomb; GPS unk; Albin; Frederick **GS:** Y **SP:** N o info **VI:** No further data **P:** unk **BLW:** unk **RG:** N **MK**: N **PH:** unk **SS:** C pg 601 **BS:** 59 pg 18.

BAKER, Michael; b 1747; d 6 Dec 1803 **RU:** Captain/Patriot, Served in Rockingham Co Militia. Gave material aid to cause **CEM:** Harley Good Farm; GPS unk; Brock's Gap, SW side of SR 259 in western Rockingham; Rockingham **GS:** U **SP:** Elizabeth Bok **VI:** No further data **P:** unk **BLW:** unk **RG:** unk **MK**: unk **PH:** unk **SS:** D Augusta Co **BS:** JLARC 2, 4, 64; 51.

BAKER, William Henry; b Winchester; d 1837 **RU:** Private, Served in Capt Garnell's Co 1778 **CEM:** Mt Hebron; GPS 39.10916, -78.09497; 305 E Boscawen St; Winchester City **GS:** Y **SP:** Catherine Miller fr Fredericktown, MD **VI:** Son of Henry and Ann E (-----) Baker **P:** unk **BLW:** unk **RG:** Y **MK**: unk **PH:** Y **SS:** J-NSSAR 2000 Reg; S NSSAR Ancestor Nbr P-107404; AP Payroll **BS:** JLARC 76; 196.

BALDWIN, Cornelius Dr; b 1751 or 1754; d 1826 or 1827 **RU:** Surgeon, Served in 8th Cont Line May 1777. Was prisoner Charleston 12 May 1780. Served in 1st Cont Line 1 Jan 1781 to close of war **CEM:** Mt Hebron; GPS 39.10916, -78.09497; 305 E Boscawen St; Winchester City **GS:** Y **SP:** 1) Mar (16 Oct 1783) Mary Briscoe, 2) Mar (28 Nov 1809) Nellie Conway Hite 3) Mar (31 Aug 1819) Susan Pritchard **VI:** Originally bur in a Presbyterian cemetery next to German Reformed Church cemetery in Mt Hebron. Moved 1912 with 71 other people **P:** unk **BLW:** Y **RG:** Y **MK**: Y **PH:** Y **SS:** DAR Ancestor #A005221; E pg 34; BY pg 361 **BS:** JLARC 3, 76.

BALES, Jonathan; b 22 Mar 1761, Hunting, York Co PA; d 1826 or 20 Apr 1837 **RU:** Private, Served in Capt Dobb's Co, York Co PA **CEM:** Jonathan Bales Family; GPS unk; Rt 682 vic Ewing; Lee **GS:** Y **SP:** Mar (10 Mar 1784 York Co, PA) Elizabeth McGuire Turner (20 Apr 1764-1830) **VI:** Dec 1794 made Constable, Botetourt Co. Moved to Lee Co 1814. Died in Martin's Creek, Lee Co **P:** unk **BLW:** unk **RG:** Y **MK**: N **PH:** unk **SS:** DAR Ancestor #A207527; AK Nov 06 **BS:** 04, Nov 06.

BALL, Burgess; b 28 Jul 1749, "Bewdley" Lancaster Co; d 7 Mar 1800 **RU:** Lieutenant Colonel, Served in 9th VA Regt. Was as Lt Col, Commandant in VA Line. Was Aide-de-Camp to Gen George

RU=Rank/Unit	CEM=Cemetery	GS=Gravestone	SP=Spousal Information
VI=Other Veteran Info	P=Pension	BLW=Bounty/Land Warrant	RG=Registered Grave
MK=SAR/DAR Marker	PH=Photo	SS=Service Source	BS=Burial Source

Washington. Was captured at Charleston SC May 1780 while serving in 1st VA Regt of Foot **CEM:** Ball Burial Ground; GPS 39.14404, -77.5469; Off Rt 15 nr North Spring Behavioral Healthcare; Loudoun **GS:** Y **SP:** 1) Mar (2 Jul 1770) Mary Chicheste; 2) Frances Ann (Thornton) Washington d/o Charles & Mildred Thornton **VI:** Son of Jeduthun & Elizabeth (Burgess) Ball. BLW issued 28 May 1789 #252-500-28 May 1789. R126. According to Source K was a Col and died in Leesburg **P:** Y **BLW:** Y **RG:** Y **MK:** Y **PH:** unk **SS:** DAR Ancestor #: A005389; E pg 858; K pg 42; CG pg 134; CE pg 29 **BS:** JLARC 1, 32, 76; 196.

BALL, David; b 1735, St Stephens, Northumberland Co; d 1826 **RU:** Captain/Patriot, Obtained rank of Capt by Royal Commission. Gave material aid to cause **CEM:** Ball Family; GPS 37.45912, -76.19536; Cress Field, Bay View on Balls Neck; Northumberland **GS:** Y **SP:** Hannah Haynie **VI:** Son of Capt George & Ann (Taylor) Ball **P:** unk **BLW:** unk **RG:** unk **MK:** N **PH:** Y **SS:** DAR Ancestor #A005397; AL Comm Bk IV pg 112 Northumberland; AK **BS:** 200; 04.

BALL, David; b unk; d May 1840 **RU:** Ensign, Served in Campbell's Regt **CEM:** Shockoe Hill; GPS 37.55190, -77.43170; 4th & Hospital Sts; Richmond City **GS:** Y **SP:** No info **VI:** On 1813 bur list in cem **P:** Y **BLW:** U **RG:** unk **MK:** N **PH:** N **SS:** E pg 35; BX pg 30 **BS:** 196.

BALL, George; b 2 May 1752, Glencarlyn, Arlington Co; d 24 Dec 1825 **RU:** Corporal/Patriot, Paid supply tax, Fairfax Co 1783 **CEM:** Ball Family; GPS unk; Rt 684 vic Ewing; Lee **GS:** Y **SP:** Elizabeth Tunnell (1744 Fairfax Co, VA-19 Mar 1835) **VI:** Son of Moses & Nancy Ann (Brashears) Ball **P:** unk **BLW:** unk **RG:** Y **MK:** N **PH:** unk **SS:** DAR Ancestor #A005418; AK Nov 06; DV Fairfax Co 1783 **BS:** 04, Nov 06; 196.

BALL, James; b 20 Feb 1755; d 18 Dec 1825 **RU:** Lieutenant Colonel, Was Capt VA Militia 15 Oct 1778. Promoted to Lt Col 18 Apr 1782 **CEM:** St Mary's White Chapel Episcopal; GPS 37.44782, -76.33181; 5940 White Chapel Rd, Lively; Lancaster **GS:** U **SP:** m. c1776 Fanny Downman, b. 4 May 1758 Westham, Essex Co, England, d. 23 Jan 1821; d/o Rawleigh & Frances (Ball) Downman of Morattico **VI:** Son of Col James & Lettice (Lee) Ball Lived at "Bewdley" where he d after his son William Lee Ball in 1824. Was member of Congress. Purchased "Ditchley in Northumberland Co ca1792 **P:** unk **BLW:** unk **RG:** Y **MK:** Y **PH:** unk **SS:** DAR Ancestor #A005438; J-NSSAR 1993 Reg; AK **BS:** JLARC 1; 200; 04; 47 Vol XI.

BALL, James; b 31 Dec 1718; d 24 Aug 1789 **RU:** Patriot, Elected 6 Feb 1775 as member of Lancaster Co Committee of Safety. After 1776 made Chief Justice of Ct. Also Lancaster's Commissioner of the Provision's Law that dispensed public service claims. Gave 86 # bacon to cause **CEM:** St Mary's Whitechapel Episcopal; GPS 37.44782, -76.33181; 5940 White Chapel Rd, Lively; Lancaster **GS:** U **SP:** 1) Margaret Burgess d/o Charles & Frances (Fox) Burgess; 2) Mildred Smith d/o Philip & Mary (Mathews) Smith; 3) Mar (1752) Lattice/Lettuce Lee (c1731 - 17 Nov 1811) d/o Richard & Judith (Steptoe) Lee of Ditchley **VI:** Son of Col James & Mary (Conway) Ball **P:** N **BLW:** N **RG:** Y **MK:** Y **PH:** unk **SS:** DAR Ancestor #A005436; J-NSSAR 2000 Reg; D pg 8; E pg 35; AK **BS:** JLARC 1, 2, 42, 76; 200; 04; 47 Vol XI.

BALL, John; b 1742, Stafford Co; d 1806 **RU:** Captain/Patriot, Recommended for Capt 29 Oct 1779 in Fauquier Co Militia. Provided material aid to cause **CEM:** Ball-Shumate; GPS 38.66382, -77.79851; On a knoll W & slightly S of Rts 15, 29, & 17 where it crosses Licking Run Stream; Fauquier **GS:** Y **SP:** Sarah Ellen Payne **VI:** Son of William & (-----) Ball. Father was first cousin of Washington's mother, Mary Ball **P:** unk **BLW:** unk **RG:** Y **MK:** N **PH:** unk **SS:** DAR Ancestor #A005455; AS; AV SAR applic **BS:** 83, Inv #68.

BALL, John; b 25 Jul 1746; d Dec 1814 **RU:** Ensign, Served in 6th VA Regt 26 Feb 1776 **CEM:** Old Ball Burying Ground; GPS unk; 3427 Washington Blvd, behind American Legion Bldg; Arlington **GS:** Y **SP:** Mar Mary Ann Thrift, d/o Jeremiah Thrift and Ann Trammell, b 19 Sep 1750 Fairfax Co, d 10 Oct 1804, Arlington **VI:** Son of Moses Ball (2 May 1717-3 Sep 1792) & Nancy Brashears (1729-1745). Name appears on large monument with 55 family names **P:** unk **BLW:** unk **RG:** Y **MK:** unk **PH:** unk **SS:** DAR Ancestor #A005456; E pg 79 **BS:** JLARC 1, 51; 69 pg 58, 60; 196.

RU=Rank/Unit	CEM=Cemetery	GS=Gravestone	SP=Spousal Information
VI=Other Veteran Info	P=Pension	BLW=Bounty/Land Warrant	RG=Registered Grave
MK=SAR/DAR Marker	PH=Photo	SS=Service Source	BS=Burial Source

17

BALL, John; b 1756, Augusta Co; d 28 Oct 1809 **RU:** Private?, Served in Capt Samuel Eson's Co 1782 **CEM:** Cliffton Neff Farm; GPS unk; Ewing; Lee **GS:** Y **SP:** Mary Polly Yeary **VI:** No further data **P:** unk **BLW:** unk **RG:** Y **MK:** Y **PH:** unk **SS:** DAR Ancestor #A005458; B; DF pg 122-124 **BS:** 04.

BALL, Moses; b 2 May 1717, Stafford Co; d 3 Sep 1792 **RU:** Patriot, Gave material aid to the cause **CEM:** Ball-Carlin Family; GPS unk; 300 S Kensington St; Arlington **GS:** Y **SP:** Mar (23 Jun 1745, Pr Geoge Co, MD) Ann Nancy Brashears (26 Sep 1729-30 Nov 1816) d/o Rober Cager & Charity (Dowell) Brashears **VI:** Son of John (1670-1722) & Winifred (Williams) (1690-1751) Ball **P:** N **BLW:** N **RG:** unk **MK:** unk **PH:** unk **SS:** DAR Ancestor #A210367; AL Ct Bk TBABS **BS:** 196.

BALL, Spencer; b 6 Aug 1762; d 28 Feb 1832 **RU:** Seaman, Served in VA State Navy **CEM:** Ball Family; GPS 38.80945, -77.50895; Manassas Battlefield, off Vandor Ln across fr Strayer University; Manassas City **GS:** U **SP:** Elizabeth Landon Carter (1768-1842) **VI:** Son of James (a RW soldier) & (----) Ball. Died in Prince William Co **P:** unk **BLW:** unk **RG:** unk **MK:** unk **PH:** unk **SS:** C pg 330 **BS:** JLARC 95.

BALL, William; b unk; d 2 or 7 Jul 1829 **RU:** Captain, Served in Cont & VA Line and Frederick Co Militia **CEM:** Mt Hebron; GPS 39.10916, -78.09497; 305 E Boscawen St; Winchester City **GS:** U **SP:** Mar (27 Mar 1785 Winchester) Elizabeth Riley (c1768-5 May 1855) **VI:** Served in 3rd Regt Light Dragoons which later was called 1st VA Regt. Sol appl pen 24 Jun 1828 Frederick Co, a res of Winchester. Widow appl pen 26 Jul 1838 Frederick Co. Pensioned 1828. W3376, BLW #s 356-60-55 & 356-100-22 Sep 1807 **P:** Y **BLW:** Y **RG:** unk **MK:** unk **PH:** unk **SS:** E pg 858; K pg 42; CG pg 136; EE pg 10 **BS:** JLARC 4 ,47.

BALLARD, Edward; b unk; d aft 19 Oct 1781 **RU:** Lieutenant, Was Navy pilot during the war fr enlistment in 1776 and served until after Yorktown in Oct 1781 **CEM:** Lincoln Memorial; GPS 36.80830, -76.32810; Jct Kirby St and Deep Creek Blvd; Portsmouth City **GS:** U **SP:** No info **VI:** No further data **P:** unk **BLW:** Y **RG:** unk **MK:** unk **PH:** unk **SS:** EE pg 10 **BS:** 196.

BALLARD, James; b 4 Jun 1763; d 1 Feb 1856 **RU:** Corporal, Served in VA Line. Ent serv Spotsylvania Co in Clark's Illinois Regt. Served in Capt Roberts & Maj Slaughter's Co, Col Crocket's Regt, Gen George Rogers Clarke's Brigade **CEM:** Ballard Family; GPS unk; Nr Catherine Furnace see property records for home place location; Spotsylvania **GS:** U **SP:** Isabelle Montague (1755-25 Dec 1841) d/o Clement & Ann (Bartlett) Montague **VI:** Appl pen 3 Sep 1832 Spotsylvania Co. S6584, Sol appl for BLW in 1855. BLW #36509-160-55 **P:** Y **BLW:** Y **RG:** Y **MK:** unk **PH:** unk **SS:** DAR Ancestor #A005528; E pg 36; CG pg 137 **BS:** JLARC 1, 4, 76.

BALLARD, Proctor; b 1760; d 1820 **RU:** Sergeant, Clark's Illinois Regt at Falls of Ohio River, 1781 **CEM:** Old Bardstown City; GPS unk; Bardstown; Nelson **GS:** U **SP:** No info **VI:** No further data **P:** unk **BLW:** Y **RG:** Y **MK:** unk **PH:** unk **SS:** J-NSSAR 1993 Reg; E pg 36; EE pg 10 **BS:** JLARC 1.

BALLARD, William Jr; b 8 Sep 1715, York Co; d 1794 **RU:** Patriot, Gave material aid to cause **CEM:** South River Meeting House; GPS 37.37246, -79.19194; 5810 Fort Ave; Lynchburg City **GS:** U **SP:** 1) Mary Sarah Byrum (1710-1765) 2) Mar (25 Aug 1768) Rachel (Clark) Morrman (1714-1792) **VI:** Son of William (1684-1754) & Philadelphia Ludwell (Lee) (1682-__) Ballard. Died in Bedford Co **P:** N **BLW:** N **RG:** unk **MK:** unk **PH:** unk **SS:** DAR Ancestor #A005554; D pg 11; AL Ct Bk pg 10 Bedford Co **BS:** 196.

BALSLEY (BALSEY), Christian; b 1 May 1756, Berks Co, PA; d 22 Jun 1837 **RU:** Ensign, Ent serv Reading, PA in PA Line **CEM:** Shenandoah Methodist; GPS 38.98160, -78.95773; 1919 Howardsville Turnpike, Sherando; Augusta **GS:** Y **SP:** Ann Elizabeth Koiner/Keinadt (1749-__) **VI:** Sol appl pen 3 Sep 1832 Augusta Co. Widow appl 5 Oct 1842 Augusta Co. W7231. Cenotaph monument at Sherando Methodist Church. Son of Peter Baltzly **P:** Y **BLW:** unk **RG:** unk **MK:** unk **PH:** unk **SS:** CG pg 139 **BS:** JLARC 2, 4, 62, 63.

BANISTER (BANNISTER), John Monroe; b 26 Dec 1734, Prince George Co; d 30 Sep 1788 **RU:** Lieutenant Colonel/Patriot, Served as Maj & Lt Col of VA Militia. Was in Battle of Petersburg 1781. Gave material aid to cause. Was Cont Congressman. In 1778 was signer and framer of Articles of Confederation. Was Delegate fr Virginia and member of Virginia House of Burgesses 1765-1775. Was member of conventions of 1775 & 1776. Was in VA House of delegates in 1776, 1777, & 1781-83 **CEM:** Blandford; GPS 37.22433, -77.38604; 319 S Crater Rd; Petersburg City **GS:** U **SP:** Mar (26 Feb 1779) Anne Blair (4 May 1746-23 Apr 1813) **VI:** Died in Battersea, Dinwiddie Co. Memorialized in the cemetery

RU=Rank/Unit	CEM=Cemetery	GS=Gravestone	SP=Spousal Information
VI=Other Veteran Info	P=Pension	BLW=Bounty/Land Warrant	RG=Registered Grave
MK=SAR/DAR Marker	PH=Photo	SS=Service Source	BS=Burial Source

18

as reinterred fr family cemetery at Battersea Estate. Was Col in Colonial War period **P:** N **BLW:** unk **RG:** Y **MK:** N **PH:** Y **SS:** DAR ancestor #A005765; J-NSSAR 1993 Reg, J- DAR Hatcher; AL Ct Bk pg 4, 22, 26, 32, 39 Dinwiddie Co; AR Vol I pg 94 **BS:** JLARC 1, 2; 80 vol 1 pg 47; 196.

BANKHEAD, James; b unk; d 1788 **RU:** Patriot, Gave material aid to the cause **CEM:** Dishman Fam; GPS unk; Forest Glen; Westmoreland **GS:** Y **SP:** 1) Mar (20 Aug 1738) Elinor Monroe d/o Spence & Cheistian (Tyler) Monroe 2) Mar (bet 8 Aug 1754 & 24 Sep 1764) Caty Vault d/o Dr. Robert & (-----) Vault of Washington Parish, Westmoreland Co. **VI:** Was member of Caroline Co Committee of Safety 1775-1776; 1812. Widow appl pen 21 Mar 1837 Clarke Co. Son John W Baylor appl pen 18 Feb 1802 Caroline Co. W5966, Awarded 10,000 acres BLW #114-500. Name is on family monument **P:** N **BLW:** N **RG:** N **MK:** N **PH:** unk **SS:** AL Ct Bk **BS:** 189 pg 55.

BANKS, John; b 25 Nov 1757; d 30 Aug 1850 **RU:** Sergeant, Ent serv Albemarle Co. Served in Cont Line. Disabled in service fr log falling on back **CEM:** Pine Creek Primitive Baptist; GPS 36.94622, -80.27357; Spangler Mill Rd Rt 682; Floyd **GS:** U **SP:** 1) Mary (-----) 2) Deborah (-----) **VI:** Awarded L300 gratuity 13 Nov 1780 **P:** unk **BLW:** unk **RG:** unk **MK:** unk **PH:** unk **SS:** DAR Ancestor #A005715; BX pg 31 **BS:** JLARC 4, 29, 30, 43.

BAORTON, Robert; b unk; d 1781 **RU:** Soldier, Served fr NY, and died as result of Yorktown battle **CEM:** Yorktown Victory Monument Tablet; GPS 38.28350, -78.54150; Yorktown; York **GS:** U **SP:** No info **VI:** No further data **P:** unk **BLW:** unk **RG:** unk **MK:** unk **PH:** unk **SS:** J-Yorktown Historian **BS:** JLARC 74.

BARBARAN, Francois; b unk; d 1781 **RU:** Seaman, Served on "Citoyenand" died from Yorktown battle **CEM:** French Memorial; GPS 36.81944, -79.39933; Yorktown; York **GS:** U **SP:** No info **VI:** No further data **P:** unk **BLW:** unk **RG:** Y **MK:** unk **PH:** unk **SS:** J-Yorktown Historian **BS:** JLARC 1, 74.

BARBATON, Joseph; b unk; d 1781 **RU:** Soldier, Served in Boubonnais Bn and died from Yorktown battle **CEM:** French Memorial; GPS 36.81944, -79.39933; Yorktown; York **GS:** U **SP:** No info **VI:** No further data **P:** unk **BLW:** unk **RG:** Y **MK:** unk **PH:** unk **SS:** J-Yorktown Historian **BS:** JLARC 1, 74.

BARCLAY, Hugh; b 1729; d 1806 **RU:** Patriot, Gave material aid to cause **CEM:** High Bridge Presbyterian; GPS 37.62420, -79.58610; 67 High Bridge Rd, Natural Bridge; Rockbridge **GS:** N **SP:** 1) Mary Culbertson 2) Martha Smith **VI:** No further data **P:** N **BLW:** N **RG:** unk **MK:** unk **PH:** N **SS:** DAR Ancestor #A005929; Florida SAR; AL Ct Bk Rockbridge Co pg 2, 4, 7; BY **BS:** SAR Application.

BARCY, (-----); b unk; d 1781 **RU:** Soldier, Served in Touraine Bn and died from Yorktown battle **CEM:** French Memorial; GPS 36.81944, -79.39933; Yorktown; York **GS:** U **SP:** No info **VI:** No further data **P:** unk **BLW:** unk **RG:** Y **MK:** unk **PH:** unk **SS:** J-Yorktown Historian **BS:** JLARC 1, 74.

BARDOU, Michel; b unk; d 1781 **RU:** Soldier, Served in Gatinais Bn and died from Yorktown battle **CEM:** French Memorial; GPS 36.81944, -79.39933; Yorktown; York **GS:** U **SP:** No info **VI:** Source 74 lists first name as Michel **P:** unk **BLW:** unk **RG:** Y **MK:** unk **PH:** unk **SS:** J-Yorktown Historian **BS:** JLARC 1, 74.

BARGER, Jacob; b 26 Oct 1745, Rockingham Co; d 24 Aug 1794 **RU:** Private, Served under the direct command of Washington **CEM:** Trinity Lutheran; GPS 38.17201, -78.86820; 2564 Rockfish Rd, Crimora; Augusta **GS:** Y **SP:** Mar (abt 1745) Elizabeth Hedrick **VI:** Son of Casper (1708-1715) & (-----) Barger **P:** unk **BLW:** unk **RG:** Y **MK:** unk **PH:** unk **SS:** S, NSSAR Ancestor Nbr P-108669 **BS:** JLARC 1, 4, 8, 62, 63, 76; 196.

BARGER, Philip; b 1741; d 1803 **RU:** Private, Served in Montgomery Co Militia 1779 **CEM:** Barger Family; GPS unk; Blacksburg; Montgomery **GS:** Y **SP:** 1) Eve Clements 2) Barba Eve (-----) 3) Barbara May **VI:** No further data **P:** unk **BLW:** unk **RG:** N **MK:** N **PH:** unk **SS:** AS NSSAR e-mail; DH pg 10, 45 **BS:** See SS AS.

BARKER, Edward; b 1755; d 30 May 1845 **RU:** Soldier, Served in VA Line. Ent serv King William Co & Buckingham Co **CEM:** Jackson Lewis; GPS unk; Taylors Valley; Washington **GS:** U **SP:** Mar (nr close of war, 1783?) Elizabeth (-----) (c1763-Jun 1848) **VI:** Sol appl pen 22 Aug 1833 Smyth Co. Widow appl 23 May 1848 Washington Co. R469 **P:** Y **BLW:** unk **RG:** unk **MK:** unk **PH:** unk **SS:** SAR Ancestor #P-108736; CG pg 149 **BS:** JLARC 4, 34; 196.

RU=Rank/Unit	CEM=Cemetery	GS=Gravestone	SP=Spousal Information
VI=Other Veteran Info	P=Pension	BLW=Bounty/Land Warrant	RG=Registered Grave
MK=SAR/DAR Marker	PH=Photo	SS=Service Source	BS=Burial Source

19

BARKER, Nathaniel; b 1750 or 1751, Charles Co, MD; d 13 Jul 1833 **RU:** Soldier, Served in VA Line. Ent serv Loudoun Co (later Fairfax Co) **CEM:** Frying Pan Meeting House; GPS 38.56240, -77.24480; 2615 Centreville Rd, Herndon; Fairfax **GS:** N **SP:** Mar (1 Nov 1771) Letitia or Letty or Lettiia Elsey or Elzey or Ellzey (c1756-__) **VI:** Sol appl pen 11 Dec 1832 Fairfax Co. Widow appl 21 Aug 1838. Pensioned in 1832. W5774 **P:** Y **BLW:** unk **RG:** unk **MK:** N **PH:** N **SS:** CG pg 151 **BS:** JLARC 4,14, 28.

BARKER, William; b unk; d 1820 **RU:** Private, Served in 15th VA Regt, Aug 1777 in 1st Lt Thomas Lewis's Co **CEM:** St John's Episcopal; GPS 37.53183, -77.41958; 2401 E Broad St; Richmond City **GS:** Y **SP:** Mar (27 Jul 1769, Goochland Co) Ann Evans **VI:** No further data **P:** unk **BLW:** unk **RG:** N **MK:** N **PH:** unk **SS:** AP **BS:** 28 pg 416.

BARKSDALE, Beverly; b 1756, Prince Edward Co; d Apr 1822 **RU:** Patriot, Hauled military supplies and gave material aid to cause, Pittsylvania Co **CEM:** Barksdale Family; GPS unk; End of Rt 689 at Depot, Cedar View, South Boston; Halifax **GS:** N **SP:** Mar (1 Jan 180-1) Judith Womack (1782-1830) d/o Charles (1738-1822) & Elizabeth Agnes (Williams) (1740-1800) Womack **VI:** Son of Thomas (1720-1788) & Judith (Beverly) Barksdale. Died in South Boston, Halifax Co **P:** N **BLW:** N **RG:** Y **MK:** N **PH:** N **SS:** DAR Ancestor #A006162; AL Ct Bk pg 32; AS **BS:** 196; 80 vol 1 pg 51; 215.

BARKSDALE, Peter; b 1757; d 1825 **RU:** Captain, Disabled in not identified service **CEM:** Barksdale Family; GPS unk; End of Rt 689 at Depot, Cedar View, South Boston; Halifax **GS:** U **SP:** Mar (11 Jan 1781, Halifax Co) Elizabeth Watlington, d/o Armistead & Susannah (Coleman) Watlington **VI:** Son of Nathaniel & Mourning (Dickerson) Barksdale. Awarded L90 gratuity 4 Nov 1779 **P:** unk **BLW:** unk **RG:** Y **MK:** unk **PH:** unk **SS:** DAR Ancestor #A006172; J-NSSAR 1993 Reg, J- DAR Hatcher; BX pg 34 **BS:** JLARC 1, 2; 215.

BARKSDALE, Thomas Henry; b 1710; d aft 14 Feb 1788 **RU:** Major/Patriot, Signed Oath of Allegiance **CEM:** Barksdale Family; GPS unk; Camden Parish; Henry **GS:** Y **SP:** Judith Beverly **VI:** No further data **P:** unk **BLW:** unk **RG:** N **MK:** N **PH:** unk **SS:** DAR Ancestor #A132797; AS, SAR regis; DG pg 304 **BS:** SAR regis.

BARLOW, Jesse; b 20 Sep 1740; d 1779 **RU:** Private/Patriot, Signed Oath of Allegiance Isle of Wight Co **CEM:** St Luke's Church; GPS 36.93940, -76.58670; 14477 Benns Church Blvd, Smithfield; Isle of Wight **GS:** Y **SP:** Lucy Wills **VI:** No further data **P:** unk **BLW:** unk **RG:** N **MK:** N **PH:** Y **SS:** DAR Ancestor #A006196; B; DD **BS:** Photo 2009.

BARNUM, Zeanas; b unk; d 1781 **RU:** Captain, Served fr CT and died as result of Yorktown battle **CEM:** Yorktown Victory Monument Tablet; GPS 38.28350, -78.54150; Yorktown; York **GS:** U **SP:** No info **VI:** No further data **P:** unk **BLW:** unk **RG:** unk **MK:** unk **PH:** unk **SS:** J-Yorktown Historian **BS:** JLARC 74.

BARON, Bernard; b unk; d 1781 **RU:** Seaman, Served on "Palmierand" died from Yorktown battle **CEM:** French Memorial; GPS 36.81944, -79.39933; Yorktown; York **GS:** U **SP:** No info **VI:** No further data **P:** unk **BLW:** unk **RG:** Y **MK:** unk **PH:** unk **SS:** J-Yorktown Historian **BS:** JLARC 1, 74.

BARRAT (BARRET), John; b 19 May 1748; d 9 Jun 1830 **RU:** Private, Served in Richmond Co Militia **CEM:** Hermitage; GPS unk; Cedar Hill Rd, Pendleton; Louisa **GS:** Y **SP:** Mary Strachan (1748 Scotland-19 Sep 1825) d/o Dr Peter & (-----) Strachan **VI:** Was merchant and Mayor of Richmond **P:** unk **BLW:** unk **RG:** N **MK:** N **PH:** unk **SS:** E pg 43 **BS:** 149; 196.

BARRETT, John; b unk; d 1781 **RU:** Soldier, Served fr NY, and died as result of Yorktown battle **CEM:** Yorktown Victory Monument Tablet; GPS 38.28350, -78.54150; Yorktown; York **GS:** U **SP:** No info **VI:** No further data **P:** unk **BLW:** unk **RG:** unk **MK:** unk **PH:** unk **SS:** J-Yorktown Historian **BS:** JLARC 74.

BARRON, James; b 1769; d 21 Apr 1851 **RU:** Commodore, Had VA Sea Service & USN Service. Was Aide to Com of VA Navy (father). Became Commodore & Commander in Chief of VA State Navy **CEM:** Trinity Episcopal; GPS 36.83459, -76.30105; 500 Court St; Portsmouth City **GS:** U **SP:** Mary A.B. (-----) **VI:** Killed Stephen Decator in 1820 duel. Sol appl pen 14 Jan 1834 Washington DC. Widow appl pen 27 Dec 1853 Norfolk Co. W12264 & VA 1/2 Pay **P:** Y **BLW:** unk **RG:** unk **MK:** unk **PH:** unk **SS:** CG pg 169 **BS:** JLARC 4,127.

RU=Rank/Unit	CEM=Cemetery	GS=Gravestone	SP=Spousal Information
VI=Other Veteran Info	P=Pension	BLW=Bounty/Land Warrant	RG=Registered Grave
MK=SAR/DAR Marker	PH=Photo	SS=Service Source	BS=Burial Source

20

BARTHELEMY, Louis; b unk; d 1781 **RU:** Seaman, Served on "Saint-Esprit" and died from Yorktown battle **CEM:** French Memorial; GPS 36.81944, -79.39933; Yorktown; York **GS:** U **SP:** No info **VI:** No further data **P:** unk **BLW:** unk **RG:** Y **MK:** unk **PH:** unk **SS:** J-Yorktown Historian **BS:** JLARC 1, 74.

BARTLEMAN, William; b 1767, Isle of Lewis, Ross Shire, Scotland; d 21 Dec 1742 **RU:** Soldier, Service information not determined **CEM:** Presbyterian Church; GPS 38.80015, -77.05791; Wilkes St & Hamilton Ln; Alexandria City **GS:** Y **SP:** Mar (by 1802) Margaret (-----) **VI:** Died age 77. Merchant of Alexandria **P:** unk **BLW:** unk **RG:** Y **MK:** unk **PH:** unk **SS:** J-NSSAR 1993 Reg; S NSSAR Ancestor #P-110000 **BS:** JLARC 1; 23 pg 12.

BARTON, Elisha; b 1757, Fauquier Co; d 1842 **RU:** Corporal, Ent serv Fauquier Co. Served in Bedford Co Militia, 1776 and VA Line **CEM:** McManaway Family; GPS unk; Chamblissburg; Bedford **GS:** N **SP:** Rebecca McManaway **VI:** Enlisted 1781, pensioned in Bedford 1834. Appl pen 26 Mar 1834 Bedford Co. S19198 **P:** Y **BLW:** unk **RG:** unk **MK:** N **PH:** N **SS:** DAR Ancestor #A007098; J- DAR Hatcher; E pg 45; CG pg 177 **BS:** JLARC 2.

BARTON, Richard; b 1751; d aft Jun 1837 **RU:** Private, Recd pension Chesterfield Co for militia service. Serv specifics in pension records not determined **CEM:** Hollywood; GPS 37.53560, -77.45720; 412 S Cherry St; Richmond City **GS:** U **SP:** No info **VI:** Member VA Legislature 1834-1835 **P:** Y **BLW:** unk **RG:** N **MK:** N **PH:** unk **SS:** E pg 45 **BS:** 180.

BARTON, Seth; b 29 Jul 1755, Bristol Co, RI; d 29 Dec 1813 **RU:** Lieutenant, Served in Capt Thomas Carlyle's Co, Col Robert Elliott's Regt of Artillery 1778 **CEM:** St George's Episcopal; GPS unk; 905 Princess Anne; Fredericksburg City **GS:** U **SP:** 1) Sarah Emerson Maxwell 2) Mary Chen **VI:** Shipping merchant in Fredericksburg **P:** unk **BLW:** unk **RG:** unk **MK:** unk **PH:** unk **SS:** DAR Ancestor #A007123; SAR Ancestor #P-110282; BY SAR Application **BS:** JLARC 2, 76; 196.

BASKERVILLE, William; b 12 May 1756; d 6 Nov 1814 **RU:** Captain/Patriot, Served in 2nd Lt Cont Line 1776. Commissioned capt 8 Jul 1778 in Mecklenburg Co Militia. Served as Deputy Clerk Mecklenburg Co, 9 Jul 1781 **CEM:** St James Episcopal; GPS 36.66626, -78.38683; Boydton; Mecklenburg **GS:** U **SP:** Mar (22 Jan 1786, NC) Mary Eaton (1763-1842) **VI:** Son of George (1741-1777) & Martha (Minge) (1720-1802) Baskerville **P:** unk **BLW:** unk **RG:** Y **MK:** unk **PH:** unk **SS:** DAR Ancestor #A007170; J-NSSAR 2000 Reg; CZ pg 36 Lib VA War files Vol 4 pg 28; DB pg 20 **BS:** JLARC 76.

BASKIN, Charles; b 1741; d 10 Aug 1822 **RU:** Captain, Lt in Capt Thomas Smith's Co, Augusta Co Militia, Aug 1776. As Capt commanded Co in Augusta Co Militia **CEM:** Tinkling Spring Presbyterian; GPS 38.08472, -78.98278; 30 Tinkling Spring Dr, Fishersville; Augusta **GS:** Y **SP:** Mary Craig, b 25 Sep 1746, d 13 Dec 1816 **VI:** DAR marker **P:** unk **BLW:** unk **RG:** Y **MK:** Y **PH:** Y **SS:** DAR Ancestor #A007177; E pg 7 **BS:** JLARC 62, 63; 04; 196.

BASS, William; b 10 May 1763; d 10 May 1839 **RU:** Ensign, Served in 2nd Battilion, Amelia Co, 28 Apr 1778 **CEM:** Bass Family; GPS unk; Bass St, Appomattox River at Exeter Mills; Petersburg City **GS:** N **SP:** Mar (29 Oct 1789 Chesterfield Co) Sarah Judith Shackleford (10 May 1774 Chesterfield Co-__) d/o James & Judith (-----) Shackleford **VI:** No further data **P:** unk **BLW:** N **RG:** unk **MK:** N **PH:** N **SS:** G pg 7 **BS:** 196.

BATTEZ, Pierre; b unk; d 1781 **RU:** Seaman, Served on "Languedoc" and died from Yorktown battle **CEM:** French Memorial; GPS 36.81944, -79.39933; Yorktown; York **GS:** U **SP:** No info **VI:** No further data **P:** unk **BLW:** unk **RG:** Y **MK:** unk **PH:** unk **SS:** J-Yorktown Historian **BS:** JLARC 1, 74.

BATTLES, James; b unk; d 1781 **RU:** Soldier, Served fr MA and died as result of Yorktown battle **CEM:** Yorktown Victory Monument Tablet; GPS 38.28350, -78.54150; Yorktown; York **GS:** U **SP:** No info **VI:** No further data **P:** unk **BLW:** unk **RG:** unk **MK:** unk **PH:** unk **SS:** J-Yorktown Historian **BS:** JLARC 74.

BAYLOR, George; b 1752; d 19 Nov 1784 **RU:** Brevet Brigadier General, Served in Cont Line. Served as aide to Washington as Lt Col 1775-1777; was Col of 3rd Cont Dragoons 9 Jan 1777. Was wounded and taken prisoner at Tappan 28 Sep 1778. Commanded 1st Cont Dragoons 9 Nov 1782 and was Brevet Brig Gen 30 Sep 1783 **CEM:** Baylor Family; GPS unk; Newmarket, Rt 2, 6 mi S of Bowling Green; Caroline **GS:** Y **SP:** Mar (20 May 1778, consent by Mann Page) Lucy Page (c1760-__). She Mar (2) on 24 Jan 1792, to Nathaniel Burwell of James City **VI:** Member of Caroline Co Committee of Safety

RU=Rank/Unit	CEM=Cemetery	GS=Gravestone	SP=Spousal Information
VI=Other Veteran Info	P=Pension	BLW=Bounty/Land Warrant	RG=Registered Grave
MK=SAR/DAR Marker	PH=Photo	SS=Service Source	BS=Burial Source

21

1775-1776; 1812. Widow appl 21 Mar 1837 Clarke Co. Son John W. Baylor appl pen 18 Feb 1802 Caroline Co. W5966. Awarded 10,000 acres BLW #114-500. Name is on family monument **P:** Y **BLW:** Y **RG:** unk **MK:** N **PH:** unk **SS:** DAR Ancestor #A007680; B; E pg 49; CG pg 193 **BS:** JLARC 15; 196.

BAYLOR, John; b 1750; d 1808 **RU:** Colonel, Served in 3rd Cont Dragoons **CEM:** Baylor Family; GPS unk; Newmarket, Rt 2, 6 mi S of Bowling Green; Caroline **GS:** Y **SP:** Frances Norton **VI:** Name is on family monument giving service **P:** unk **BLW:** unk **RG:** Y **MK:** N **PH:** unk **SS:** DAR Ancestor #A007685; B **BS:** JLARC 1, 15, 76; 02 pg 2; 196.

BAYLOR, Walker; b 13 Oct 1762, Caroline Co; d 14 Sp 1822 **RU:** Captain, In Jun 177? commissioned Lt in brother George Baylor's Regt. Promoted Capt 1780 **CEM:** Baylor Family; GPS unk; Newmarket, Rt 2, 6 mi S of Bowling Green; Caroline **GS:** Y **SP:** Ann Bledsoe **VI:** Resigned as Capt, thus rank of Maj obtained probably after war. His name is on a family monument here, as "progenenitor of the Baylor family of Texas." Died in Bourbon Co, KY. He is not bur here **P:** unk **BLW:** unk **RG:** unk **MK:** N **PH:** unk **SS:** DAR Ancestor #A007690; B **BS:** 196.

BAYNHAM, Richard; b 1751; d 1809 **RU:** Quartermaster, Served in Orange Co Militia **CEM:** Baynham Family; GPS unk; Rt 653, Ruther Glen; Caroline **GS:** N **SP:** No info **VI:** Son of John Baynham (1725-1768) & Johanna (-----) (1727-1807) **P:** unk **BLW:** unk **RG:** Y **MK:** N **PH:** N **SS:** E pg 49 **BS:** 02 pg 10.

BEADLES, John; b 1779; d 1824 **RU:** Second Lieutenant, Served in Capt Miller's Co, Orange Co Militia in 1780. Also gave provisions to cause **CEM:** Beadles Family; GPS unk; Btw Green Acres Rd & N side of Green Acres Lake, Greene Hills; Greene **GS:** U **SP:** 1) Elizabeth (-----) 2) Laurina or Lurenna Miller, d/o Robert Jr & Margaret (Peggy) Maupin. **VI:** Perhaps son of Robert Beadles of Orange Co **P:** unk **BLW:** unk **RG:** unk **MK:** Y **PH:** unk **SS:** DAR Ancestor #A007810; E pg 50 **BS:** JLARC 113.

BEALE, John; b 1748, Southampton Co; d 1837 **RU:** Private, Served in 5th & 9th Cont Line. Enl Southampton Co In the 5th VA Regt, served as private in Capt C. Anderson's Co, Sep & Oct 1776. Later served in consolidated 1st and 10th VA Regt 1779 **CEM:** St John's Episcopal; GPS 37.53183, -77.41958; 2401 E Broad St; Richmond City **GS:** Y **SP:** Mar (16 May 1815) Julia (-----) (c1782-__) **VI:** Sol appl pen 19 Nov 1832 Southampton Co. Widow appl 15 Aug 1853 Southampton Co. W4893, BLW #8168-160-55 **P:** Y **BLW:** Y **RG:** Y **MK:** N **PH:** unk **SS:** E pg 50; CG pg 196 **BS:** 28, pg 421.

BEALE, Reuben; b unk; d 1802 **RU:** Patriot, Gave material aid to the cause **CEM:** Repton Family; GPS unk; Vic Pratts Post Office; Madison **GS:** Y **SP:** No info **VI:** No further data **P:** N **BLW:** N **RG:** N **MK:** N **PH:** unk **SS:** AL Ct Bk pg 63 **BS:** 169 Repton.

BEALE, Robert; b 30 Jan 1759, Chestnut Hill, N Farnham Parish, Richmond Co; d 1 Sep 1843 **RU:** Major, Enlisted as ensign at age 17. Served in 13th Cont Line. Was in Battles of Trenton, Princeton, Brandywine. Captured by British in Charleston SC, when surrendered. Achieved rank of Capt by end of war **CEM:** Beale Family; GPS unk; Chestnut Hill, E of Ethel; Richmond Co **GS:** U **SP:** Martha Felicia Turberville (1786-1822). D/O George Lee & Elizabeth "Betty" Tayloe (Corbin) Turberville. **VI:** Son of Capt William (1710-1778) & Ann (Harwar) Beale. Was a twin. DAR Ancestor #A007899. Rose to rank of Maj in VA Militia. Recd 4666 acres & 555 more acres. Died in Hague, Westmoreland Co **P:** unk **BLW:** Y **RG:** unk **MK:** unk **PH:** unk **SS:** E pg 51 **BS:** 196.

BEALE, William Jr; b 31 Aug 1710; d 26 Jun 1778 **RU:** Patriot, Signer of Leedstown Resolutions **CEM:** Beale Family; GPS unk; Chestnut Hill, E of Ethel; Richmond Co **GS:** U **SP:** Ann Harwar **VI:** No further data **P:** N **BLW:** N **RG:** unk **MK:** N **PH:** N **SS:** DR **BS:** 213 pg 26; 196.

BEAN, Mordecai; b 28 Mar 1740 Chester Co, PA; d 28 Nov 1814 **RU:** Patriot, Gave material aid to cause **CEM:** St John's Lutheran; GPS 36.96500, -81.10110; 405 W Main, Wytheville; Wythe **GS:** U **SP:** Mar (18 Oct 1772) Judith Hammond (11 Apr 1753-4 Dec 1840 Frederick Co) **VI:** No further data **P:** N **BLW:** N **RG:** unk **MK:** unk **PH:** unk **SS:** DAR Ancestor #A008025; D Vol 1 pg 382; S; NSSAR Ancestor #P-111527 **BS:** JLARC 3.

BEANS, William; b 15 Jul 1752, Solebury, Bucks Co, PA; d '14 Dec 1817 **RU:** Patriot, Gave material aid to cause **CEM:** Goose Creek; GPS 39.11250, -77.69527; Rt 722, Lincoln; Loudoun **GS:** Y **SP:** Hannah Balderston (11 Mar 1751 Solebury, Bucks Co, PA-1 May 1838 Jefferson, Ashabula Co, OH) **VI:** No

RU=Rank/Unit	CEM=Cemetery	GS=Gravestone	SP=Spousal Information
VI=Other Veteran Info	P=Pension	BLW=Bounty/Land Warrant	RG=Registered Grave
MK=SAR/DAR Marker	PH=Photo	SS=Service Source	BS=Burial Source

22

further data **P:** N **BLW:** N **RG:** Y **MK:** N **PH:** unk **SS:** DAR Ancestor #A008046; E pg 51 **BS:** 25 pg 22; 196.

BEAR(BAER), Jacob Sr; b 1724; d 1783 **RU:** Patriot, Gave material aid to cause **CEM:** Bear Family; GPS unk; Bear Lithia Spring; Rockingham **GS:** U **SP:** Anna Mueller **VI:** No further data **P:** N **BLW:** N **RG:** Y **MK:** N **PH:** unk **SS:** AB; AL Ct Bk pg13 **BS:** 04.

BEARD, James; b 1761 Augusta Co; d unk **RU:** Private, Ent serv Rockingham Co in Capt Trimble's Co 1779 & Capt McCutchen's Co 1783 in the Augusta Co Militia **CEM:** Brenneman Mennonite; GPS 38.62620, -78.87588; Brenneman Church Rd; Rockingham **GS:** N **SP:** Mary Chummy, d/o John & (-----) Chummy **VI:** Appl pen 3 Nov 1845 Rockingham Co. R669 **P:** Y **BLW:** unk **RG:** Y **MK:** N **PH:** N **SS:** E pg 51; CG pg 201 **BS:** AK Sep 09.

BEATIE, David; b c1744; d 25 Apr 1814 **RU:** Captain, Capt of Militia at Kings Mountain, Oct 1780 **CEM:** Ebbing Spring; GPS unk; N side of middle fork of Holstein River, vic Glade Spring; Washington **GS:** Y **SP:** No info **VI:** No further data **P:** unk **BLW:** unk **RG:** N **MK:** N **PH:** unk **SS:** N pg 1241 **BS:** 78 pg 174.

BEATTY, Henry; b 1759, Frederick Co; MD; d 1840 **RU:** Private, Served in MD & VA Lines. Ent serv Frederick Co MD 1776, then moved to Frederick Co VA. Ent serv again 1780 and 1781. Was horseman for General John Smith **CEM:** Mt Hebron; GPS 39.10916, -78.09497; 305 E Boscawen St; Winchester City **GS:** U **SP:** Sara Hening (__-1824) **VI:** Obtained rank of Lt Col in War of 1812 and awarded a sword by US Congress..He owned a saddle shop in Winchester after the war and was an elder in the Presbyterian church. Pensioned for Rev War serv 1833, R193; appl 4 pen Mar 1834 Frederick Co. S19203 **P:** Y **BLW:** unk **RG:** unk **MK:** unk **PH:** unk **SS:** K pg 61; CG pg 204 **BS:** JLARC 2, 47, 76.

BEATTY (OR BEATTIE), William; b 4 Apr 1760 Rockbridge Co; d 4 Apr 1880 **RU:** Private, Served under Gen Campbell **CEM:** Glade Spring Presbyterian; GPS 36.76720, -81.78720; 33234 Lee Hwy, Glade Spring; Washington **GS:** U **SP:** Mary Allison **VI:** No further data **P:** unk **BLW:** unk **RG:** unk **MK:** unk **PH:** unk **SS:** DD **BS:** JLARC 2, 76.

BEAUJEARD, Francois; b unk; d 1781 **RU:** Seaman, Served on "Hector" and died from Yorktown battle **CEM:** French Memorial; GPS 36.81944, -79.39933; Yorktown; York **GS:** U **SP:** No info **VI:** No further data **P:** unk **BLW:** unk **RG:** Y **MK:** unk **PH:** unk **SS:** J-Yorktown Historian **BS:** JLARC 1, 74.

BEAUMARTIN, Jean; b unk; d 1781 **RU:** Seaman, Served on "Duc de Bourgogne" and died from Yorktown battle **CEM:** French Memorial; GPS 36.81944, -79.39933; Yorktown; York **GS:** U **SP:** No info **VI:** No further data **P:** unk **BLW:** unk **RG:** Y **MK:** unk **PH:** unk **SS:** J-Yorktown Historian **BS:** JLARC 1, 74.

BEAVER (BEAVERS), John Sr; b 1747, Prince William Co VA; d 2 Aug 1839 **RU:** Private, Served in1st Regt VA Line **CEM:** Beaver Family; GPS 38.66118, -77.47324; 13380 Bristol Rd, Nokesville; Prince William **GS:** Y **SP:** No info **VI:** No further data **P:** unk **BLW:** unk **RG:** Y **MK:** Y **PH:** Y **SS:** AK; AP roll **BS:** 04; 32, Oct 10.

BEDEL, Etienne; b unk; d 1781 **RU:** Soldier, Served in Boubonnais Bn and died from Yorktown battle **CEM:** French Memorial; GPS 36.81944, -79.39933; Yorktown; York **GS:** U **SP:** No info **VI:** No further data **P:** unk **BLW:** unk **RG:** Y **MK:** unk **PH:** unk **SS:** J-Yorktown Historian **BS:** JLARC 1, 74.

BEDEL, Jacques; b unk; d 1781 **RU:** Soldier, Served in Gatinais Bn and died from Yorktown battle **CEM:** French Memorial; GPS 36.81944, -79.39933; Yorktown; York **GS:** U **SP:** No info **VI:** No further data **P:** unk **BLW:** unk **RG:** Y **MK:** unk **PH:** unk **SS:** J-Yorktown Historian **BS:** JLARC 1, 74.

BEDEL, Jean; b unk; d 1781 **RU:** Seaman, Served on "Saint-Esprit" and died from Yorktown battle **CEM:** French Memorial; GPS 36.81944, -79.39933; Yorktown; York **GS:** U **SP:** No info **VI:** No further data **P:** unk **BLW:** unk **RG:** Y **MK:** unk **PH:** unk **SS:** J-Yorktown Historian **BS:** JLARC 1, 74.

BEDESQUE, Vincent; b unk; d 1781 **RU:** Seaman, Served on "Magnanime" and died from Yorktown battle **CEM:** French Memorial; GPS 36.81944, -79.39933; Yorktown; York **GS:** U **SP:** No info **VI:** No further data **P:** unk **BLW:** unk **RG:** Y **MK:** unk **PH:** unk **SS:** J-Yorktown Historian **BS:** JLARC 1, 74.

BEDFORD, Thomas Sr; b 16 May 1725, Gloucester Co; d Mar 1785 **RU:** Patriot, Was Justice of Charlotte Co Ct in 1779 **CEM:** Locust Grove; GPS unk; Drakes Branch; Charlotte **GS:** Y **SP:** Mary

RU=Rank/Unit	CEM=Cemetery	GS=Gravestone	SP=Spousal Information
VI=Other Veteran Info	P=Pension	BLW=Bounty/Land Warrant	RG=Registered Grave
MK=SAR/DAR Marker	PH=Photo	SS=Service Source	BS=Burial Source

23

Lignon Coleman [source?] Memorial stone says his wife was Druscilla (-----) **VI:** Memorial marker in cemetery **P:** N **BLW:** N **RG:** Y **MK:** N **PH:** unk **SS:** AL Ct bk pg 1, 3, 18, 24; AS SAR appl **BS:** 196.

BEGA, Nicolas; b unk; d 1781 **RU:** Soldier, Served in Gatinais Bn and died from Yorktown battle **CEM:** French Memorial; GPS 36.81944, -79.39933; Yorktown; York **GS:** U **SP:** No info **VI:** No further data **P:** unk **BLW:** unk **RG:** Y **MK:** unk **PH:** unk **SS:** J-Yorktown Historian **BS:** JLARC 1, 74.

BEGAIN, Francois; b unk; d 1781 **RU:** Seaman, Served on "Caton" and died from Yorktown battle **CEM:** French Memorial; GPS 36.81944, -79.39933; Yorktown; York **GS:** U **SP:** No info **VI:** No further data **P:** unk **BLW:** unk **RG:** Y **MK:** unk **PH:** unk **SS:** J-Yorktown Historian **BS:** JLARC 1, 74.

BEHER, Pierre; b unk; d 1781 **RU:** Soldier, Served in Beaujolais Bn and died from Yorktown battle **CEM:** French Memorial; GPS 36.81944, -79.39933; Yorktown; York **GS:** U **SP:** No info **VI:** No further data **P:** unk **BLW:** unk **RG:** Y **MK:** unk **PH:** unk **SS:** J-Yorktown Historian **BS:** JLARC 1, 74.

BELANGER, Vincent; b unk; d 1781 **RU:** Soldier, Served in Auxonne Bn and died from Yorktown battle **CEM:** French Memorial; GPS 36.81944, -79.39933; Yorktown; York **GS:** U **SP:** No info **VI:** No further data **P:** unk **BLW:** unk **RG:** Y **MK:** unk **PH:** unk **SS:** J-Yorktown Historian **BS:** JLARC 1, 74.

BELFIELD, John; b 23 Jun 1725; d unk **RU:** Major, Ent serv as Lt in 1st Cont Dragoons, 18 Jun 1776. Promoted to Capt 15 Mar 1777 and to Maj 3rd Cont Dragoons in 1781 **CEM:** Belfield Family; GPS 38.02316,-76.48842; 2804 County Bridge Rd, Warsaw; Richmond Co **GS:** Y **SP:** Mar (5 Apr 1744) (-----) **VI:** Son of Capt Thomas Wright & Mary Meriwether (Colson) Belfield. Member of the Society of the Cincinatti. Recd Pen & 1/2 pay as well. BLW #5397, 5333 acres for 3 yrs service & 888 more acres for 7 yrs service and 370 more acres for 5 mos longer than 7 yrs **P:** Y **BLW:** Y **RG:** unk **MK:** unk **PH:** unk **SS:** A pg 414; G pg 88,146, 313, 395, 612; K pg 65 **BS:** 32.

BELFIELD, Sydnor; b unk; d unk **RU:** Second Lieutenant, Served in Capt Beckwith's Co, Richmond Co Militia. Received rank of 2nd Lt Jun 1781 **CEM:** Belfield Family; GPS 38.02316,-76.48842; 2804 County Bridge Rd, Warsaw; Richmond Co **GS:** Y **SP:** Mar (28 Nov 1782) Ann Young, d/o Col William & Elizabeth (Smith) Young **VI:** Son of John & Ruth (Sydnor) Belfield **P:** unk **BLW:** unk **RG:** unk **MK:** unk **PH:** unk **SS:** E pg 66 **BS:** 32.

BELFIELD, Thomas Wright; b 18 Feb 1745; d 20 Oct 1803 **RU:** Captain, Commanded Co in Richmond Co Militia **CEM:** Belfield Family; GPS 38.02316,-76.48842; 2804 County Bridge Rd, Warsaw; Richmond Co **GS:** Y **SP:** Mar (25 Oct 1780) Ann Harwar Beale **VI:** Son of John & Ruth (Sydnor) Belfield **P:** unk **BLW:** unk **RG:** unk **MK:** unk **PH:** unk **SS:** G pg 314 **BS:** 32.

BELL, David; b 1722; d 1780 **RU:** Captain, Commanded a Co in the Augusta Co Militia fr 1776 to 1779. Provided a deserter fr Cont Army to Augusta Co Militia **CEM:** Augusta Stone Presbyterian; GPS 38.23926, -78.97356; 28 Old Stone Church Ln, Ft Defiance; Augusta **GS:** Y **SP:** Florence Henderson **VI:** No further data **P:** unk **BLW:** unk **RG:** Y **MK:** unk **PH:** unk **SS:** B; D pg 110, Augusta Co **BS:** JLARC 1, 2, 8, 23, 62, 63; 196.

BELL, David; b 1765; d 1 Feb 1845 **RU:** Captain, Served in Augusta Co Militia 1777-1779 **CEM:** Mossy Creek Presbyterian; GPS 38.35331, -79.04914; 372 Kyles Mill Rd, Mt Solon; Augusta **GS:** N **SP:** Mary Christian, who survived him **VI:** Son of James Bell (1740-1782) & Agnes Hogshead. Helped quell the Whiskey Rebellion **P:** unk **BLW:** unk **RG:** unk **MK:** N **PH:** N **SS:** S; NSSAR Ancestor #P-112563 **BS:** JLARC 63; 196.

BELL, George; b c1760; d 21 Apr 1834 **RU:** Corporal, Served in 9th Cont Line **CEM:** Red Bank Church; GPS unk; Jct Rts 600 & 617; Northampton **GS:** Y **SP:** Betsey (-----) (1783-24 Apr 1855) **VI:** Died age 87y 9m 16d **P:** unk **BLW:** unk **RG:** N **MK:** N **PH:** unk **SS:** E pg 55 **BS:** 42 pg 7.

BELL, George; b unk; d 1778 **RU:** Patriot, Gave material aid to the cause **CEM:** Pleasant Valley; GPS unk; Mechanicsville; Hanover **GS:** Y **SP:** No info **VI:** Body moved fr Richmond and reinterred **P:** N **BLW:** N **RG:** N **MK:** N **PH:** unk **SS:** AL Ct Bk It I pg 44 **BS:** 31 vol I pg 40.

BELL, James; b 1748; d 6 Dec 1820 **RU:** Captain, Commanded a company in Col Samuel Lewis Regt **CEM:** Fincastle Presbyterian; GPS 37.50017, -79.87558; 108 E Back St, Fincastle; Botetourt **GS:** U **SP:**

RU=Rank/Unit	CEM=Cemetery	GS=Gravestone	SP=Spousal Information
VI=Other Veteran Info	P=Pension	BLW=Bounty/Land Warrant	RG=Registered Grave
MK=SAR/DAR Marker	PH=Photo	SS=Service Source	BS=Burial Source

24

No info **VI:** No further data **P:** unk **BLW:** unk **RG:** unk **MK:** unk **PH:** unk **SS:** AZ pg 102; S; NSSAR Ancestor #P-112596 **BS:** JLARC 2, 60.

BELL, James; b unk, Ireland; d Feb 1782 **RU:** Patriot, Gave material aid to cause **CEM:** Mossy Creek Presbyterian; GPS 38.35331, -79.04914; 372 Kyles Mill Rd, Mt Solon; Augusta **GS:** N **SP:** Agnes Hogshead (Hogsett). Widow after 1782 **VI:** Died in Mt Solon, Augusta Co **P:** N **BLW:** N **RG:** unk **MK:** N **PH:** N **SS:** AL Lists III pg 7 **BS:** 196.

BELL, Joesph; b c1746; d 1833 **RU:** Private, Specific service not determined in JLARC report **CEM:** Augusta Stone Presbyterian; GPS 38.23926, -78.97356; 28 Old Stone Church Ln, Ft Defiance; Augusta **GS:** Y **SP:** No info **VI:** No further data **P:** unk **BLW:** unk **RG:** unk **MK:** unk **PH:** unk **SS:** JLARC Report; BY **BS:** JLARC 8, 23.

BELL, John; b 4 Sep 1755; d 17 Oct 1842 **RU:** Captain, Served in Augusta Co Militia. Took oath as Capt 1780 **CEM:** Mossy Creek Presbyterian; GPS 38.35331, -79.04914; 372 Kyles Mill Rd, Mt Solon; Augusta **GS:** Y **SP:** Mar (1) the widow Young; (2) Esther (-----) ; (3) Elizabeth (-----) **VI:** Son of James Bell (1740-1782) & Agnes Hogshead. Appl pen 22 Dec 1834 Augusta Co S16650. Grave has DAR marker **P:** Y **BLW:** unk **RG:** unk **MK:** Y **PH:** Y **SS:** B; E pg 55; CG pg 222; BT **BS:** JLARC 2,62,63; 196.

BELL, Joseph Jr; b Feb 1755; d 13 Sep 1833 **RU:** Captain, Drafted in 1776; served under Capt John Lyle, Col Russell's Regt in battle against Cherokees. Drafted again in 1777, and served under Capt Thomas Smith and other commanders; part of General Lafayette's Army at Yorktown. Took oath as Capt 15 Aug 1780- 18 Sep 1781, Augusta Co Militia **CEM:** Augusta Stone Presbyterian; GPS 38.23926, -78.97356; 28 Old Stone Church Ln, Ft Defiance; Augusta **GS:** Y **SP:** No info **VI:** Still lived on farm where he was b at time of pen application. Appl pen 30 Aug 1832 Augusta Co S6608; R207; Govt stone reads 1755-1833 **P:** Y **BLW:** unk **RG:** unk **MK:** unk **PH:** unk **SS:** B; E pg 56; K Vol 1 pg 66; AZ pg 104-5, 181 **BS:** JLARC 8, 23.

BELL, Joseph Sr; b c1742; d 4 Mar 1823 **RU:** Soldier, Specific service recorded Lib VA, Archives, Sec of War 1835, pen, vol 2, pg 112 **CEM:** Augusta Stone Presbyterian; GPS 38.23926, -78.97356; 28 Old Stone Church Ln, Ft Defiance; Augusta **GS:** Y **SP:** Mar Elizabeth Henderson, d/o William & Susannah (------) Henderson; b 24 Jul 1746, d 13 Sep 1833 **VI:** Died age 80 **P:** unk **BLW:** unk **RG:** unk **MK:** unk **PH:** unk **SS:** CZ pg 41 **BS:** JLARC 4, 8, 23, 62, 63, 76; 196; 197.

BELL, Nathaniel Nathan; b 11 Apr 1744, Hanover Co; d 1 Oct 1807 **RU:** Patriot, Sold 20 bushels of corn to the Cont Army 1781-1782 and furnished provisions for Ann Austin, wife of William Austin continental soldier in the 1st Regt **CEM:** Hollywood; GPS 37.53560, -77.45720; 412 S Cherry St; Richmond City **GS:** Y **SP:** 1) Sarah (-----) 2) Ann Butler Moore **VI:** Died in Pleasant Level, Hanover Co **P:** unk **BLW:** unk **RG:** Y **MK:** Y **PH:** unk **SS:** E pg 56 **BS:** 31 vol 1 pg 40.

BELL, Robert; b 25 Dec 1758; d Jul 1841 **RU:** Private, Enl Montgomery Co in Capt Aaron Skaggs, Col Preston's Regt **CEM:** Bell Family, Dunkards Bottom; GPS 37.05702, -80.62087; Claytor Lake State Park, Dublin; Pulaski **GS:** U **SP:** Keziah Farmer (1759 Montgomery Co-1836) **VI:** Pen filed 5 Aug 1833 age 74 **P:** Y **BLW:** unk **RG:** unk **MK:** unk **PH:** unk **SS:** E pg 554; G pg 222; DZ pg 64 **BS:** 196.

BELL, Robert; b 1753, Scotland; d 10 Aug 1817 **RU:** Sergeant, Probably the one this name that was Sergeant in 9th Cont Line **CEM:** Shockoe Hill; GPS 37.55190, -77.43170; 4th & Hospital Sts; Richmond City **GS:** Y **SP:** 1) Mar (4 Mar 1791, Louisa Co) Sarah Smith 2) Mar (21 Jun 1792 Louisa Co) Sarah Honson **VI:** Saddler in Richmond many yrs **P:** unk **BLW:** unk **RG:** N **MK:** N **PH:** unk **SS:** E pg 56 **BS:** 179 pg 141.

BELL, Samuel; b Feb 1759; d 15 May 1838 **RU:** Major, Ent serv Augusta Co, in VA Line. Was wounded and captured **CEM:** Hebron Presbyterian; GPS 38.14140, -79.15500; 423 Hebron Rd; Staunton City **GS:** N **SP:** Mar 1) Nancy (---) b 31 Oct 1757, d 07 Feb 1794, 2) unk 3) on 7 Dec 1815 to Rebecca Hayes, b. 6 Feb 1779, d 31 Jul 1855 **VI:** In 1834, Sol was still living on plantation where he was born. Sol appl pen 28 Jul 1834 Augusta Co. Widow appl 5 Jul 1854 Augusta Co. W12267, BLW #26094-160-55; R207 **P:** Y **BLW:** Y **RG:** unk **MK:** unk **PH:** N **SS:** E pg 56; CG pg 222; K Vol 1 pg 66 **BS:** JLARC 4, 8, 62, 63; 196.

RU=Rank/Unit	CEM=Cemetery	GS=Gravestone	SP=Spousal Information
VI=Other Veteran Info	P=Pension	BLW=Bounty/Land Warrant	RG=Registered Grave
MK=SAR/DAR Marker	PH=Photo	SS=Service Source	BS=Burial Source

25

BELL, Samuel; b 1724, Northern Ireland; d 1803 **RU:** Patriot, Gave material aid to cause **CEM:** Samuel Bell Family; GPS 38.22770, -78.89085; Nr NW jct Craigshop Rd & Rt 608 toward Middle River; Augusta **GS:** N **SP:** Mar (1) Margaret (-----) ;(2) Jane (-----) **VI:** Said to be the son of William Bell (1685-1757), immigrant fr Northern Ireland **P:** N **BLW:** N **RG:** unk **MK:** N **PH:** N **SS:** AL Cert list 1 pg 7 Augusta Co **BS:** 196.

BELL, William; b 1744; d 22 Aug 1833 **RU:** Private, Served in 1779 in Capt Simpson's and Capt Long's companies and in 1781 in Capt Given's Co, Augusta Co Militia **CEM:** Augusta Stone Presbyterian; GPS 38.23926, -78.97356; 28 Old Stone Church Ln, Ft Defiance; Augusta **GS:** U **SP:** 1) Mrs. Robert Bell (1769-1811) 2) Margaret Allen (22 Feb 1767-25 Jan 1844) **VI:** He may be the person with this name that had other service as well. He achieved the rank of major after the war period. **P:** unk **BLW:** unk **RG:** unk **MK:** unk **PH:** unk **SS:** E pg 56 **BS:** JLARC 8, 23, 62; 196.

BELL, William; b c1745; d 1804 **RU:** Surgeon, Served 11 Sep 1776 on "Caswell" Gallery, VA State Navy **CEM:** Fatherly Farm; GPS unk; Wierwood; Northampton **GS:** Y **SP:** Mar Elizabeth (-----), b c1745, d. 1802. Bur at Fatherly Farm **VI:** No further data **P:** unk **BLW:** unk **RG:** N **MK:** N **PH:** unk **SS:** C pg 4, 5 **BS:** 42 pg 8.

BELLEDENT, Pierre; b 1744; d 1781 **RU:** Soldier, Served in Soissonnais Bn and died from Yorktown battle **CEM:** French Memorial; GPS 36.81944, -79.39933; Yorktown; York **GS:** U **SP:** No info **VI:** No further data **P:** unk **BLW:** unk **RG:** Y **MK:** unk **PH:** unk **SS:** J-Yorktown Historian **BS:** JLARC 1, 74.

BENEDUM, Peter; b Bef 1755; d 1857 **RU:** Private, Served in Capt Wendell Weaver's 7th Co, 2nd Battalion, Lancaster Co PA Militia **CEM:** Benedum Family; GPS unk; Leesburg; Loudoun **GS:** Y **SP:** 1) Mary Ann Kurtz 2) Catherine Yantis **VI:** No further data **P:** unk **BLW:** unk **RG:** N **MK:** N **PH:** unk **SS:** AS SAR applic; CI PA Archives 5th Serv Vol 7 pg 182 **BS:** SAR Appl.

BENN, George; b c1762; d 24 Nov 1815 **RU:** First Lieutenant, Served in Isle of Wight Co Militia **CEM:** Benns United Methodist; GPS 36.56170, -76.35100; 1457 Benns Church Blvd, Smithfield; Isle of Wight **GS:** Y **SP:** No info **VI:** Gave the land on which Benn's Church was built. Was called Major in 1802. Originally bur in Benn family cemetery **P:** unk **BLW:** unk **RG:** Y **MK:** N **PH:** unk **SS:** G pg 192-193 **BS:** 153 Geo Benn; 196.

BENNETT, Charles; b 1720; d by 1818 **RU:** Patriot, Gave material aid to cause **CEM:** Old Christ Church Episcopal; GPS 38.80625, -77.04718; 118 N Washington St; Alexandria City **GS:** N **SP:** No info **VI:** No further data **P:** N **BLW:** N **RG:** N **MK:** N **PH:** N **SS:** AL Comm Bk III **BS:** 110 pg 95.

BENNETT, Jordan; b 1759; d 4 Oct 1822 **RU:** Private, Ent serv fr VA. Lost a leg at Battle of Builford CH **CEM:** Bennett Family; GPS unk; See county property records for location; Mecklenburg **GS:** U **SP:** Mar (17 Dec 1795 Mecklenburg Co) Ann "Nancy" Murfey/Murphey (c1776-___) **VI:** Son of Joseph Bennet, Sr. Widow appl 22 Apr 1852 Meckelburg Co. W2713, BLW #31446-160-55. R219 **P:** Y **BLW:** Y **RG:** Y **MK:** unk **PH:** unk **SS:** CG pg 238; K Vol 1 pg 67-8 **BS:** JLARC 2, 76.

BENNETT, William; b unk, Middlesex Co; d Oct 1781 **RU:** Lieutenant, Was at siege of Yorktown. Was killed in battle there **CEM:** Unidentified; GPS unk; Nr or on Battlefield; York **GS:** U **SP:** Not mar **VI:** Died in Yorktown. Gen George Washington attended his funeral. His name is not on Victory monument. Sister Catherine Williams appl for BLW **P:** unk **BLW:** Y **RG:** unk **MK:** unk **PH:** unk **SS:** EE pg 16 **BS:** Land Grant Claim.

BENNINGTON, Job; b 1758; d c1835 **RU:** Matross, Served in PA Cont Line. Enl in PA 1777 **CEM:** Bennington-Gaylor; GPS unk; Waterloo Rd; Rockbridge **GS:** N **SP:** No info **VI:** Appl 5 May 1823 Rockbridge Co. S37753. R221 **P:** Y **BLW:** unk **RG:** Y **MK:** N **PH:** N **SS:** M pg 734; CG pg 240; K Vol 1 pg 68 **BS:** 04, May 06.

BENSON, James Sr; b 3 Mar 1735; d 30 Oct 1797 **RU:** Patriot, Gave material aid to cause **CEM:** Benson Family; GPS unk; Nr Jct Cattail Rd Rt 690 & Whites Crossing Rd Rt 690; Accomack **GS:** Y **SP:** No info **VI:** No further data **P:** N **BLW:** N **RG:** N **MK:** N **PH:** unk **SS:** AL Comm Bk I-26 **BS:** 38 pg 45.

BENSON, Robert; b 1744; d 15 Jul 1799 **RU:** Patriot, Performed public service with Cont Congress 1774-1789, as witness. Was Secretary to NY Provincial Congress Feb 1776 **CEM:** Trinity Episcopal;

RU=Rank/Unit	CEM=Cemetery	GS=Gravestone	SP=Spousal Information
VI=Other Veteran Info	P=Pension	BLW=Bounty/Land Warrant	RG=Registered Grave
MK=SAR/DAR Marker	PH=Photo	SS=Service Source	BS=Burial Source

26

GPS 36.83459, -76.30105; 500 Court St; Portsmouth City **GS:** U **SP:** No info **VI:** No further data **P:** unk **BLW:** unk **RG:** unk **MK:** unk **PH:** unk **SS:** CI **BS:** 57; 196.

BENSON, William (Willis) Lee; b unk; d 1815 **RU:** Quartermaster Sergeant, Enl in Capt William Jameson's Co. Later transferred to Capt Dandridge's Co, 2d VA Regt of Calvary **CEM:** Sanford Family; GPS unk; #1 Rocky Pen area; Stafford **GS:** U **SP:** No info **VI:** No further data **P:** unk **BLW:** unk **RG:** unk **MK:** unk **PH:** unk **SS:** E pg 69; EE pg 17 **BS:** 196.

BENTON, Calab; b unk; d 26 Dec 1781 **RU:** Private, Served in CT Cont Troops and died as result of Yorktown battle **CEM:** Yorktown Victory Monument Tablet; GPS 38.28350, -78.54150; Yorktown; York **GS:** U **SP:** No info **VI:** No further data **P:** unk **BLW:** unk **RG:** unk **MK:** unk **PH:** unk **SS:** J-Yorktown Historian; DY pg 342 **BS:** JLARC 74.

BERGER, Jacob; b 21 Dec 1765, Germany; d 25 Jan 1837 **RU:** Wagoner, Was Chief Wagoner in his unit **CEM:** Bergers; GPS 36.95748, -79.48408; Nr Siloan Church nr Rt 605; Pittsylvania **GS:** Y **SP:** Mar (27 Jan 1800 Pittsylvania Co) Catey Nowlin **VI:** No further data **P:** unk **BLW:** unk **RG:** unk **MK:** unk **PH:** unk **SS:** S; NSSAR Ancestor Nbr P-113757; DAR #A017187 **BS:** 174, JLARC 76, 96.

BERGER, Jacques; b unk; d 1781 **RU:** Soldier, Served in Brie Bn and died from Yorktown battle **CEM:** French Memorial; GPS 36.81944, -79.39933; Yorktown; York **GS:** U **SP:** No info **VI:** No further data **P:** unk **BLW:** unk **RG:** Y **MK:** unk **PH:** unk **SS:** J-Yorktown Historian **BS:** JLARC 1, 74.

BERKELEY, Edmund; b 5 Dec 1730; d 1802 **RU:** Vestryman, Gave material aid to Army May 1782 **CEM:** Christ Church; GPS 37.60968, -76.54643; Rt 33 2 mi E of Saluda; Middlesex **GS:** U **SP:** 1) Mar (6 Nov 1757) Judith Randolph (1738-___) d/o William & Maria Judith (Page) Randolph 2) Mar (1768) Mary Burwell d/o Carter & (-----) Burwell of the Grove, James City Co. **VI:** No further data **P:** unk **BLW:** unk **RG:** N **MK:** N **PH:** unk **SS:** G pg 202 **BS:** 84 pg 198.

BERKELEY, Nelson; b 16 May 1733, Northumberland Co; d 24 Jan 1794 **RU:** Patriot, Member Committee of Safety **CEM:** Airwell; GPS unk; Rt 738; Hanover **GS:** Y **SP:** Elizabeth Wormley **VI:** No further data **P:** N **BLW:** N **RG:** Y **MK:** N **PH:** unk **SS:** DD **BS:** 31 vol 1 pg 2.

BERNAN, Julien; b unk; d 1781 **RU:** Seaman, Served on "Diademe" and died from Yorktown battle **CEM:** French Memorial; GPS 36.81944, -79.39933; Yorktown; York **GS:** U **SP:** No info **VI:** No further data **P:** unk **BLW:** unk **RG:** Y **MK:** unk **PH:** unk **SS:** J-Yorktown Historian **BS:** JLARC 1, 74.

BERNARD, Walter; b 1758, Frederick Co MD; d 5 Feb 1841 **RU:** Major, Served in VA Line. Ent serv Loudoun Co 1776 or 1777 for first enl. In 1778 moved to Henry Co (now Franklin Co) **CEM:** Tanyard-Bernard-Hill; GPS unk; Rocky Mount; Franklin **GS:** U **SP:** Ruth Hill **VI:** Baptized at Rock Creek Church. Appl pen 3 Sep 1832 Franklin (then Henry) Co. S6634. R225 **P:** Y **BLW:** unk **RG:** Y **MK:** unk **PH:** unk **SS:** J-NASSR 2000 Reg; CG pg 245; K Vol 1 pg 70 **BS:** JLARC 1, 2, 18, 76.

BERRY, Benjamin; b 16 Aug 1724; d Sep 1810 **RU:** Patriot, Supplied 375 lbs of beef to cause **CEM:** Grace Episcopal; GPS 39.15220, -77.98060; 110 N Church St, Berryville; Clarke **GS:** Y **SP:** No info **VI:** Son of Henry Berry of King George Co. Settled in what is now Clarke Co prior to Rev. In 1798 platted and sold the land for Berrytown **P:** N **BLW:** N **RG:** Y **MK:** Y **PH:** Y **SS:** AL Ct Bk pg 19 **BS:** 58 pg 34; 196.

BERRY, Benjamin; b 1758; near Monmouth CH, Monmouth, NJ; d 14 Dec 1834 **RU:** Private, Served in NJ & VA Lines. Drafted age 16 Shrewsbury NJ. In 1776 moved to VA & drafted Rockingham Co 1780. Served 13 mos NJ Troops in Capts Walton's and Hunn's Cos. Served in Rockingham Co Militia in Capt Harrison's VA Co and in Capt Baxter's Co, Col Halle's Virginia Regt **CEM:** Old Peaked Mountain; GPS 38.37113, -78.73416; 9843 Town Hall Rd, McGaheysville; Rockingham **GS:** U **SP:** 1) Sarah Matthews 2) Johanna (___) **VI:** Moved to VA in fall of 1778. Appl pen 2 Aug 1832 Rockingham Co age 74, S6627. R226 **P:** Y **BLW:** unk **RG:** Y **MK:** unk **PH:** unk **SS:** E pg 60; CG pg 246; K Vol 1 pg 70 **BS:** JLARC 4, 61, 76.

BERRY, Charles; b 1725; d 1789 **RU:** Patriot, Gave 350# flour in Aug 1780 to cause **CEM:** New Providence Presbyterian; GPS 37.95170, -79.30250; 1208 New Providence Rd, Raphine; Rockbridge **GS:** U **SP:** Mary Cunningham **VI:** Held rank of Col, probably obtained before RW because over military

RU=Rank/Unit CEM=Cemetery GS=Gravestone SP=Spousal Information
VI=Other Veteran Info P=Pension BLW=Bounty/Land Warrant RG=Registered Grave
MK=SAR/DAR Marker PH=Photo SS=Service Source BS=Burial Source

27

age for war service **P**: N **BLW**: N **RG**: unk **MK**: unk **PH**: unk **SS**: AL Cert 3 Augusta Co **BS**: JLARC 79; 196.

BERRY, David; b unk; d 1810 **RU**: Corporal, Served in US Army. Specific service recorded Lib VA, Archives, Bounty Land Warrants, War, vol 4,1784, pgs 96, 98 **CEM**: Leesburg Presbyterian; GPS 39.11611, -77.56722; 207 W Market St, Leesburg; Loudoun **GS**: Y **SP**: No info **VI**: No further data **P**: unk **BLW**: Y **RG**: Y **MK**: N **PH**: unk **SS**: C Sec II pg 222; CZ pg 44 **BS**: 25 pg 27.

BERRY, John; b 1743 County Antrim, Ireland; d 1786 **RU**: Lieutenant, Served in Washington Co Militia. Fought at Battle of Kings Mountain. Served in 7th VA Regt 1780-1783 **CEM**: Green Spring Presbyterian; GPS 36.63670, -81.99560; 2007 Green Spring Ch Rd, Abingdon; Washington **GS**: N **SP**: Sarah Jane Campbell (10 Apr 1743 Washington Co-27 Sep 1833) **VI**: Grave stone missing 1991 **P**: N **BLW**: N **RG**: N **MK**: unk **PH**: N **SS**: E pg 60; **CI**: Muster roll **BS**: 78, sec II pg 122; 196.

BERRY, John; b 10 Jun 1765; d 11 Nov 1831 **RU**: Private, Served in Capt Vance's Co, Augusta Co Militia **CEM**: Airy Knoll; GPS unk; E of Rt 252 abt .4 mi N of Rt 620, S of Newport; Augusta **GS**: Y **SP**: Mar (19 Oct 1797) Eleanor Jamison (21 Sep 1768-26 Aug 1959) **VI**: Son of Charles (1725-1789) & (-----) Berry **P**: N **BLW**: N **RG**: unk **MK**: N **PH**: N **SS**: E pg 60 **BS**: 196.

BERRY, John; b 1735; d 1798 **RU**: Private, Specific service recorded Lib VA, Archives, Report Sec of War, Pen, Vol 2, pg 21 **CEM**: Old Peaked Mountain; GPS 38.37113, -78.73416; 9843 Town Hall Rd, McGaheysville; Rockingham **GS**: U **SP**: Susannah Smith **VI**: No further data **P**: unk **BLW**: unk **RG**: Y **MK**: unk **PH**: unk **SS**: J-NSSAR 2000 Reg; CZ pg 44 **BS**: JLARC 76.

BERRY (BEERY), Abraham; b c1736, Lancaster Co, PA; d 25 May 1799 **RU**: Patriot, Paid supply tax 1781 in PA **CEM**: Union Church; GPS unk; Rt 679 Battlefield Rd; Rockingham **GS**: Y **SP**: 1) Elizabeth Gochenour 2) Barbara Goode **VI**: No further data **P**: unk **BLW**: unk **RG**: Y **MK**: N **PH**: unk **SS**: AK Sep 09; CI PA Archives 3d Serv Vol 21 pg 424 **BS**: AK Sep 09.

BERRYHILL, John; b 1728; d 28 Dec 1817 **RU**: Patriot, Gave material aid to cause **CEM**: Stonewall Jackson Memorial; GPS 37.78128, -79.44604; 314 S Main St; Lexington City **GS**: Y **SP**: Mar (__ Augusta Co) Rachel Moffatt (1727- 28 Sep 1812) d/o James (1700-1764) & (-----) Moffett **VI**: Son of John (1687 London, England-1751 Mecklenburg Co) & (-----) Berryhill **P**: N **BLW**: N **RG**: unk **MK**: unk **PH**: unk **SS**: AL Ct Bk pg 4 Rockbridge Co **BS**: 196.

BERTHELOT, Francois; b unk; d 1781 **RU**: Seaman, Served on "Northumberland" and died from Yorktown battle **CEM**: French Memorial; GPS 36.81944, -79.39933; Yorktown; York **GS**: U **SP**: No info **VI**: No further data **P**: unk **BLW**: unk **RG**: Y **MK**: unk **PH**: unk **SS**: J-Yorktown Historian **BS**: JLARC 1, 74."

BERTIN, Jean; b unk; d 1781 **RU**: Seaman, Served on "Hercule" and died from Yorktown battle **CEM**: French Memorial; GPS 36.81944, -79.39933; Yorktown; York **GS**: U **SP**: No info **VI**: No further data **P**: unk **BLW**: unk **RG**: Y **MK**: unk **PH**: unk **SS**: J-Yorktown Historian **BS**: JLARC 1, 74.

BESARD, Jean; b unk; d 1781 **RU**: Soldier, Served in Boubonnais Bn and died from Yorktown battle **CEM**: French Memorial; GPS 36.81944, -79.39933; Yorktown; York **GS**: U **SP**: No info **VI**: No further data **P**: unk **BLW**: unk **RG**: Y **MK**: unk **PH**: unk **SS**: J-Yorktown Historian **BS**: JLARC 1, 74.

BESCOND, Jean; b unk; d 1781 **RU**: Seaman, Served on "Saint-Esprit" and died from Yorktown battle **CEM**: French Memorial; GPS 36.81944, -79.39933; Yorktown; York **GS**: U **SP**: No info **VI**: No further data **P**: unk **BLW**: unk **RG**: Y **MK**: unk **PH**: unk **SS**: J-Yorktown Historian **BS**: JLARC 1, 74.

BESSARD, Claude; b unk; d 1781 **RU**: Seaman, Served on "Magnanime" and died from Yorktown battle **CEM**: French Memorial; GPS 36.81944, -79.39933; Yorktown; York **GS**: U **SP**: No info **VI**: No further data **P**: unk **BLW**: unk **RG**: Y **MK**: unk **PH**: unk **SS**: J-Yorktown Historian **BS**: JLARC 1, 74.

BETTS, Spencer; b 6 Apr 1759, Northumberland Co; d 2 Nov 1837 **RU**: Soldier, Service information not determined **CEM**: Betts Family at Snow Hill; GPS 36.35465, -78.57311; 2091 Snow Hill Rd, Cluster Springs; Halifax **GS**: Y **SP**: Nancy Fowlkes **VI**: Was Deacon of Baptist Church 49 yrs **P**: unk **BLW**: unk **RG**: Y **MK**: unk **PH**: unk **SS**: B **BS**: JLARC 1, 2, 4; 101; 196.

RU=Rank/Unit	CEM=Cemetery	GS=Gravestone	SP=Spousal Information
VI=Other Veteran Info	P=Pension	BLW=Bounty/Land Warrant	RG=Registered Grave
MK=SAR/DAR Marker	PH=Photo	SS=Service Source	BS=Burial Source

28

BEVEL, Abel; b unk; d 1781 **RU:** Seaman, Served on "Citoyen" and died from Yorktown battle **CEM:** French Memorial; GPS 36.81944, -79.39933; Yorktown; York **GS:** U **SP:** No info **VI:** No further data **P:** unk **BLW:** unk **RG:** Y **MK:** unk **PH:** unk **SS:** J-Yorktown Historian **BS:** JLARC 1, 74.

BEZE, Antoine; b unk; d 1781 **RU:** Soldier, Served in Gatinais Bn and died from Yorktown battle **CEM:** French Memorial; GPS 36.81944, -79.39933; Yorktown; York **GS:** U **SP:** No info **VI:** No further data **P:** unk **BLW:** unk **RG:** Y **MK:** unk **PH:** unk **SS:** J-Yorktown Historian **BS:** JLARC 1, 74.

BIBLE, Adam Jr; b c1759; d 2 Feb 1826 **RU:** Private, Served in VA 8th Cont Line. Was volunteer in Augusta Co 1775. Entered service fr Augusta Co again in 1778 **CEM:** Bible Family; GPS unk; Dull Hunt Rd at Fulks Run; Rockingham **GS:** U **SP:** Mar (Sep 1783 or Sep 1785 Rockingham Co) Magdalene or Madelean Shoemaker (c1764-__) d/o George & (-----) Shoemaker **VI:** Widow appl pen 30 May 1839 Rockingham Co. W18596. R233 **P:** unk **BLW:** unk **RG:** Y **MK:** N **PH:** unk **SS:** E pg 63; CG pg 255; K Vol 1 pg 73 **BS:** 32 Hutchens 08.

BICKLEY, Charles; b 27 Jul 1753, Amherst Co; d 1 Jun 1838 or 1839 **RU:** Private, Served in VA Line. Ent serv Russell Co 1775. Served as a guard, a driver, or a laborer in building a road over the Cumberland Mountain to KY during the Rev War period **CEM:** Bickley Family; GPS 36.88530, -82.27780; Rt 615 across rd fr Rt 640, Castlewood; Russell **GS:** U **SP:** No info **VI:** Son of John James (1713-1793) & (-----) Bickley. Sol appl pen 8 Sep 1836 Russell City age 83. Five of 7 children granted final payment 22 Apr 1840. S10091. Source 22 has picture of the gravesite. R234 **P:** unk **BLW:** unk **RG:** unk **MK:** unk **PH:** Y **SS:** K Vol 1 pg 73; N pg 1272; CG pg 256 **BS:** JLARC 2, 22; 196.

BICKLEY, John; b 1761; d 31 Aug 1834 **RU:** Soldier, Served in Russell Co Militia abt 1780 **CEM:** Bickley Family; GPS 36.88530, -82.27780; Rt 615 across fr Rt 640, Castlewood; Russell **GS:** Y **SP:** No info **VI:** Son of John James (1713-1793) & (-----) Bickley **P:** unk **BLW:** unk **RG:** N **MK:** N **PH:** unk **SS:** BK WPA Report **BS:** 158 Bickley; 196.

BICKLEY, Sebastian; b c1759; d aft 1839 **RU:** Soldier, Exact serv not determined but he & brother Charles entered service Russell Co 1775 **CEM:** Bickley Family; GPS 36.88530, -82.27780; Rt 615 across fr Rt 640, Castlewood; Russell **GS:** U **SP:** No info **VI:** Son of John James (1713-1793) & (-----) Bickley **P:** unk **BLW:** unk **RG:** N **MK:** N **PH:** unk **SS:** BK WPA Report **BS:** 158 Bickley; 196.

BIDEAU, Ange; b unk; d 1781 **RU:** Seaman, Served on "Hercule" and died from Yorktown battle **CEM:** French Memorial; GPS 36.81944, -79.39933; Yorktown; York **GS:** U **SP:** No info **VI:** No further data **P:** unk **BLW:** unk **RG:** Y **MK:** unk **PH:** unk **SS:** J-Yorktown Historian **BS:** JLARC 1, 74.

BIDOT, Jean; b unk; d 1781 **RU:** Soldier, Served in Touraine Bn and died from Yorktown battle **CEM:** French Memorial; GPS 36.81944, -79.39933; Yorktown; York **GS:** U **SP:** No info **VI:** No further data **P:** unk **BLW:** unk **RG:** Y **MK:** unk **PH:** unk **SS:** J-Yorktown Historian **BS:** JLARC 1, 74.

BILISOLY, Antonio S; b 1758; d 1845 **RU:** Seaman, Was Corsican sailing master who fought with Compte de Grasse **CEM:** Cedar Grove; GPS 36.57204, -80.02599; 301 Fort Lane Rd; Portsmouth City **GS:** U **SP:** No info **VI:** Source 2 says slab was moved to Cedar Grove Cem **P:** unk **BLW:** unk **RG:** unk **MK:** unk **PH:** unk **SS:** JLARC Appendix B-3 pg 10 **BS:** JLARC 2, 39, Appendix B-3 lot 20.

BILLEBOUX, Oliver; b unk; d 1781 **RU:** Seaman, Served on "Caton" and died from Yorktown battle **CEM:** French Memorial; GPS 36.81944, -79.39933; Yorktown; York **GS:** U **SP:** No info **VI:** No further data **P:** unk **BLW:** unk **RG:** Y **MK:** unk **PH:** unk **SS:** J-Yorktown Historian **BS:** JLARC 1, 74.

BILLUPS, Joseph; b 1723, Gloucester Co; d 1780 **RU:** Patriot, Gave material aid to cause **CEM:** Old Billups; GPS unk; Rt 643, Moon; Mathews **GS:** U **SP:** No info **VI:** Son of Joseph (1697-1790) & Margaret (Lilly) (1700-1770) Billups **P:** N **BLW:** N **RG:** unk **MK:** unk **PH:** unk **SS:** Al Ct bk pg ii, 9, Gloucester Co **BS:** 196.

BILLUPS, Joseph Jr; b 1760; d 1815 **RU:** Sergeant, Served in Capt Henry Young's Co, 7th Cont line **CEM:** Old Billups; GPS unk; Rt 643, Moon; Mathews **GS:** Y **SP:** Joice Respass **VI:** No further data **P:** unk **BLW:** Y **RG:** Y **MK:** unk **PH:** unk **SS:** E pg 64; C pg 224; CD; CZ pg 46 **BS:** JLARC 2, 76; 107.

BINNS, Charles; b 1763; d 1837 **RU:** First Lieutenant, Specific service recorded Lib VA, Archives, Auditors Acct vol XVIII, pg 558 **CEM:** Rokeby; GPS unk; Nr Leesburg; Loudoun **GS:** Y **SP:** Hannah (-----

---

RU=Rank/Unit	CEM=Cemetery	GS=Gravestone	SP=Spousal Information
VI=Other Veteran Info	P=Pension	BLW=Bounty/Land Warrant	RG=Registered Grave
MK=SAR/DAR Marker	PH=Photo	SS=Service Source	BS=Burial Source

) **VI:** Son of Charles Binns, Sr. Was clerk of Fairfax Co bef Loudoun Co was formed. His vault at home at Rokeby stored the US records during the War of 1812 **P:** unk **BLW:** unk **RG:** Y **MK:** N **PH:** unk **SS:** E pg 64; CZ pg 46 **BS:** SAR registration.

BIRD, William; b unk; d 1795 **RU:** Patriot, Signed a Legislative Petition in Alexandria **CEM:** Old Christ Church Episcopal; GPS 38.80625, -77.04718; 118 N Washington St; Alexandria City **GS:** N **SP:** No info **VI:** Burial permit issued 12 Apr 1795 **P:** N **BLW:** N **RG:** N **MK:** N **PH:** N **SS:** BB; S-Alexandria **BS:** 20 pg 145.

BIS, Georges; b unk; d 1781 **RU:** Seaman, Served on "Languedoc" and died from Yorktown battle **CEM:** French Memorial; GPS 36.81944, -79.39933; Yorktown; York **GS:** U **SP:** No info **VI:** No further data **P:** unk **BLW:** unk **RG:** Y **MK:** unk **PH:** unk **SS:** J-Yorktown Historian **BS:** JLARC 1, 74.

BISHOP, Billy; b unk; d unk **RU:** Officer's Bodyguard, Specific serv not specified in SAR registry **CEM:** Belle Air Plantation; GPS 37.20490, -77.34000; Rt 5, New Hope; Charles City Co **GS:** U **SP:** No info **VI:** No further data **P:** unk **BLW:** unk **RG:** unk **MK:** unk **PH:** unk **SS:** S, NSSAR Ancestor #P-115069 **BS:** JLARC 110.

BISHOP, Henry; b Apr 1757, Holland; d 2 Jun 1839 **RU:** Private, Served in Capt Daniel Trigg's Co, 13 Sep 1777, Montgomery Co Militia **CEM:** Wright Family; GPS 36.97658, -80.21693; Pizarro off Rt 668; Floyd **GS:** U **SP:** Mar (23 May 1785, Montgomery Co) Frances Simpkins (1768, Floyd Co-29 May 1850) **VI:** Pen # SW5823. Memorialized by DAR plaque in cem **P:** Y **BLW:** unk **RG:** unk **MK:** Y **PH:** unk **SS:** DAR Ancestor #A010438 **BS:** 196 for John Mitchell.

BISHOP, John; b 15 Nov 1764; d 25 Sep 1837 **RU:** Private, Served in Capt Daniel Triggs Co, 13 Sep 1777 **CEM:** St Clair Bottom Primitive Baptist; GPS 36.76098, -81.64556; Jct Rts 600 & 660, Chilhowie; Smyth **GS:** Y **SP:** Rhoda (-----) (17 Jun 1745-26 Sep 1817) **VI:** May be person memorialized on DAR plaque in Wright Fam cem in Floyd Co **P:** unk **BLW:** unk **RG:** unk **MK:** unk **PH:** unk **SS:** G pg 214 **BS:** 196.

BISHOP, John; b 1747; d 1822 **RU:** Soldier, Served in Capt Jason Waits Co **CEM:** Bishop Family; GPS 36.62640, -77.95580; Rt 644, Brunswick; Brunswick **GS:** N **SP:** Mar on 10 Jan 1793 (bond) to Elizabeth Jones, d/o John Jones **VI:** Son of Mathnay Bishop per his marriage bond **P:** unk **BLW:** unk **RG:** unk **MK:** U **PH:** N **SS:** A pg 147 **BS:** 196.

BISHOP, Mathew; b 1747; d 1810 **RU:** Private / Patriot, Served in Capt David Beatie's Co at battle of Kings Mountain. Also gave supplies to cause **CEM:** Bishop Family; GPS 36.62640, -77.95580; Rt 644, Brunswick; Brunswick **GS:** N **SP:** Martha (-----), b 1750, d 1828 **VI:** Pension to widow commencing 16 Jul 1814 at $48 per yr **P:** Y **BLW:** unk **RG:** unk **MK:** U **PH:** N **SS:** N pg 1241; AG pg 254 **BS:** 196.

BLACK, Benjamin; b unk; d 1789 **RU:** Private, Specific service recorded Lib VA, Archives **CEM:** Old Christ Church Episcopal; GPS 38.80625, -77.04718; 118 N Washington St; Alexandria City **GS:** N **SP:** no info **VI:** Burial permit issued 2 Jun 1789 to Andrew Wales **P:** unk **BLW:** unk **RG:** Y **MK:** N **PH:** N **SS:** A pg 191; E pg 66; CZ pg 45 **BS:** 20 pg 145.

BLACK, David; b 1762; d Jan 1831 **RU:** Captain, Gr St inscription gives rank but service not determined **CEM:** Presbyterian Church; GPS 38.80015, -77.05791; Wilkes St & Hamilton Ln; Alexandria City **GS:** Y **SP:** No info **VI:** Death notice in Alexandria Gazette, 5 Jan 1831, pg 3 **P:** unk **BLW:** unk **RG:** N **MK:** N **PH:** unk **SS:** B **BS:** 23 pg 14.

BLACK, John; b 27 Jul 1766; d 10 Jun 1839 **RU:** Private, Served in Capt Buchanan's Co, Augusta Co Militia in 1778, 1779 & 1780 **CEM:** Mossy Creek Presbyterian; GPS 38.35331, -79.04914; 372 Kyles Mill Rd, Mt Solon; Augusta **GS:** Y **SP:** Mar (1) on 20 Sep 1790 to Alice Boyd. b 4 Aug 1767, d 22 Aug 1811 Rockingham Co; (2) on 25 Mar 1756 to Mary Hogshead, b 25 Mar 1756, d 2 Apr 1850 **VI:** No further data **P:** unk **BLW:** unk **RG:** unk **MK:** N **PH:** unk **SS:** S NSSAR Ancestor #P-115465 **BS:** JLARC 62, 63; 196.

BLACK, John; b 21 Dec 1755, Albemarle Co; d 14 Jul 1849 **RU:** Private/Overseer of Roads/Patriot, Served in Capt Buchanan's Co, Augusta Co Militia. Also provided wagon with horses and other items to Col White of Lt Dragoons **CEM:** Blacksburg; GPS unk; Nr Blacksburg; Montgomery **GS:** Y **SP:** 1) Jane Alexander 2) Mary Breeden **VI:** Son of Rev Samuel & (-----) Black. Virginia Tech built on his 200 acres.

RU=Rank/Unit	CEM=Cemetery	GS=Gravestone	SP=Spousal Information
VI=Other Veteran Info	P=Pension	BLW=Bounty/Land Warrant	RG=Registered Grave
MK=SAR/DAR Marker	PH=Photo	SS=Service Source	BS=Burial Source

John Black log cabin on campus (moved for dorm) and lived in by professor. Died in Blacksburg, Montgomery Co **P:** unk **BLW:** unk **RG:** Y **MK:** unk **PH:** Y **SS:** J-NSSAR 2000 Reg; D pg 6 Augusta Co **BS:** JLARC 76.

BLACKBURN, Samuel; b 2 Jun 1759; d 2 Mar 1835 **RU:** General/Patriot, Served in VA unit that was paid at Ft Pitt. Served in Battle of Guilford CH. Gave 11 yds linen 26 Aug 1782 **CEM:** Trinity Episcopal; GPS 38.14917, -79.07521; 214 Beverley St; Staunton City **GS:** Y **SP:** Mar (Augusta Co) Ann or Anne Mathews (__-1840), d/o GA Governor George & (-----) Mathews. Later mar (-----) Blackburn. **VI:** Son of Benjamin & Mary (-----) Blackburn. Taught at Washington Academy in Wilkes Co. GA. Member of GA state legislature until 1759. Represented Bath Co in VA legislature for several terms. Died in Bath Co. In will, liberated 44 slaves,so they'd move to Liberia (42 did) **P:** unk **BLW:** unk **RG:** unk **MK:** unk **PH:** Y **SS:** CY pg 100; CZ pg 47 **BS:** JLARC 62, 63.

BLACKBURN, Thomas; b 1742; d 1807 **RU:** Lieutenant Colonel, Served as commander 2nd VA Regiment 20 Dec 1776. Wounded at Germantown Dec 1777 **CEM:** Blackburn-Atkinson; GPS 38.36878, -77.16685; Rippon Lodge off Rt 638, Woodbridge; Prince William **GS:** U **SP:** Christian Scott **VI:** Owned Rippon Lodge **P:** unk **BLW:** unk **RG:** unk **MK:** Y **PH:** unk **SS:** CZ pg 47 **BS:** JLARC 2, 76, 95.

BLACKWELL, David; b 1762 or 24 Aug 1764 (pen says 24 Aug 1765 nr New Castle in Hanover City); d 30 Dec 1837 **RU:** Private, Ent serv in 1779 in Hanover Co. Served at Yorktown, Oct 1781 **CEM:** Blackwell Family; GPS unk; Spring Grove; Hanover **GS:** Y **SP:** No info **VI:** Sol appl pen 23 Oct 1832 Hanover City age 68. S6666. R 256 **P:** Y **BLW:** unk **RG:** Y **MK:** N **PH:** unk **SS:** G pg 766; K Vol 1 pg 78; CG pg 282 **BS:** AS,SAR regis.

BLACKWELL, Joseph Jr; b 1752, Northumberland Co; d 20 Jun 1826 or Oct 1836 **RU:** Lieutenant-Quartermaster, Served in 3rd VA Regt, Cont Line. Appt quartermaster 1780 **CEM:** Blackwell Family; GPS unk; The Meadows, E of Rt 628 at the first farm past Bethel United Methodist Church; Fauquier **GS:** Y **SP:** Mar (Dec 1784) Ann Eustace Hull (1761-1840) d/o Isaac & Agatha (-----) Eustace. Her first husband was RW vet Edwin Hull (__-1780) She drew pensions for both husbands. **VI:** Son of Joseph & Lucy (Steptoe) Blackwell. Wife recd pension Fauquier Co. Govt. grave stone. R 256 **P:** Y **BLW:** Y **RG:** Y **MK:** N **PH:** unk **SS:** B; K Vol 1 pg 78; N ps 636-7 **BS:** 19 pg 8; 196.

BLACKWELL, Joseph Sr; b 9 Jul 1715, Northumberland Co; d 30 May 1787 **RU:** Patriot, Gave material aid to cause Fauquier Co **CEM:** Blackwell Family; GPS unk; The Meadows, E of Rt 628 at the first farm past Bethel United Methodist Church; Fauquier **GS:** U **SP:** Mar (Jun 1745) Lucy Steptoe (1720-26 Apr 1787) **VI:** Son of Samuel & Margery (Downing Hudnall) Blackwell **P:** N **BLW:** N **RG:** unk **MK:** unk **PH:** unk **SS:** AL Ct Bk pg 1, 21 **BS:** 196.

BLACKWELL, William; b 16 Aug 1736, Northumberland Co; d 1780 **RU:** Captain, Served in 11th VA Rgmt **CEM:** Roseland; GPS 37.51131, -76.16576; Reedville; Northumberland **GS:** U **SP:** No info **VI:** Son of Samuel & Elizabeth (Steptoe) Blackwell. Recd 4000 acres BLW. Grave relocated fr "Poplar Farm" Rt 360 near Intermediate Sch **P:** unk **BLW:** Y **RG:** unk **MK:** Y **PH:** unk **SS:** E pg 68; AK **BS:** JLARC 4; 42; 200; 04.

BLAIR, John; b 15 Oct 1759, Chester Co, PA; d 10 Jan 1823 **RU:** Private?, Served in Clark's Ill Regt **CEM:** Shockoe Hill; GPS 37.55190, -77.43170; 4th & Hospital Sts; Richmond City **GS:** Y **SP:** No info **VI:** Son of John & Elizabeth (Durbarrow) Blair **P:** unk **BLW:** unk **RG:** N **MK:** N **PH:** unk **SS:** E pg 68 **BS:** 179 pg 135; 196.

BLAIR, John Jr; b 1731; d 1800 **RU:** Patriot, Helped author VA Constitution 1776. Elected 1778 to General Ct **CEM:** Bruton Parish Church; GPS 37.27127, -76.70248; 331 W Duke of Gloucester St; Williamsburg City **GS:** N **SP:** No info **VI:** Signer, Declaration of Independence **P:** N **BLW:** N **RG:** Y **MK:** N **PH:** N **SS:** G pg 777 **BS:** 26 pg 115; 168.

BLAIR, Thomas; b 1750, Scotland; d 1805 **RU:** Private, Served in Capt O'Hara's Independent Co **CEM:** Blair; GPS unk; Cliffview; Carroll **GS:** U **SP:** No info, has child **VI:** No further data **P:** unk **BLW:** unk **RG:** unk **MK:** unk **PH:** unk **SS:** CI **BS:** 196.

BLAIR, William; b 5 Jul 1741; d Aft 1798 **RU:** Private, Served in Capt Cunningham's Co, Augusta Co Militia **CEM:** Bethel Presbyterian; GPS 38.04257, -79.17283; 563 Bethel Green Rd, Middlebrook;

RU=Rank/Unit	CEM=Cemetery	GS=Gravestone	SP=Spousal Information
VI=Other Veteran Info	P=Pension	BLW=Bounty/Land Warrant	RG=Registered Grave
MK=SAR/DAR Marker	PH=Photo	SS=Service Source	BS=Burial Source

31

Augusta **GS:** N **SP:** 1) Mary Logan 2) Elizabeth Fulton **VI:** Son of Alexander Blair & Jane Preston Scott **P:** unk **BLW:** unk **RG:** unk **MK:** unk **PH:** N **SS:** E pg 68 **BS:** 196.

BLAKEMORE, George; b 23 May 1759; d 25 Jul 1833 **RU:** Lieutenant, Served in 2nd VA Regt 19 Dec 1776. Resigned 5 Apr 1782. Served in Mid Atlantic & Southern theaters. Was at Germantown where 15 yr old brother Thomas was killed. Was sick at Valley Forge. Captured by British in SC (under Gen Green). Was on British prison ship 13 mos. Was at Yorktown at Cornwallis surrender. **CEM:** Blakemore Family; **GPS** 39.17245, -77.99008; Blakemore Ln, off Rt 7, Berryville; Clarke **GS:** Y **SP:** No info **VI:** Son of Thomas & (-----) Blakemore Sr. Brother to Thomas Blakemore Jr who was killed at Germantown and bur by George (still there). Met Gen Lafayette during Battle of Monmouth, served on his staff, & was life-long friend with him. Died in Frederick Co. Sol appl pen 26 Nov 1832 Frederick Co. S6665 BLW 1795. R 261 **P:** Y **BLW:** Y **RG:** N **MK:** N **PH:** Y **SS:** E pg 69; K Vol 1 pg 80; CG pg 289 **BS:** 58 pg 4; 196.

BLAKEMORE, Thomas Sr; b 1718; d 1808 **RU:** Patriot, Gave 144 lbs of mutton to cause **CEM:** Blakemore Family; **GPS** 39.10216, -77.59246; Byrd Farm vic Rt 7, Moreland; Clarke **GS:** Y **SP:** No info **VI:** No further data **P:** N **BLW:** N **RG:** N **MK:** N **PH:** Y **SS:** AL Ct bk pg 37 **BS:** 58 pg 4.

BLANCHET, Louis; b unk; d 1781 **RU:** Seaman, Served on "Saint-Esprit" and died from Yorktown battle **CEM:** French Memorial; **GPS** 36.81944, -79.39933; Yorktown; York **GS:** U **SP:** No info **VI:** No further data **P:** unk **BLW:** unk **RG:** Y **MK:** unk **PH:** unk **SS:** J-Yorktown Historian **BS:** JLARC 1, 74.

BLAND, Richard Jr; b 6 May 1710; d 26 Oct 1776 **RU:** Colonel, Was Paymaster, Southampton District Bn Mar 1776 and was Col of a Minuteman Bn Nov 1775 **CEM:** Bland Family; **GPS** unk; 2 mi E of Hopewell on Rt 10, 1.2 mi N on Rt 36, then 10 ft E; Prince George **GS:** U **SP:** 1) Anne Poythress 2) Martha Macon 3) Elizabeth Blank **VI:** US Continental Congressman. Member of VA House of Burgesses 1742-1775 and a member of the VA Committee of Correspondence in 1773. In 1774, elected a member of First Continental Congress, serving until 1775. Reelected to second First Continental Congress. Elected to VA House of Delegates in 1776, serving until his death **P:** unk **BLW:** unk **RG:** Y **MK:** unk **PH:** unk **SS:** J-NSSAR 2000 Reg; CE pg 22 **BS:** JLARC 1, 2, 76, 101; 196.

BLANDELET, Jean; b unk; d 1781 **RU:** Seaman, Served on "Languedoc" and died from Yorktown battle **CEM:** French Memorial; **GPS** 36.81944, -79.39933; Yorktown; York **GS:** U **SP:** No info **VI:** No further data **P:** unk **BLW:** unk **RG:** Y **MK:** unk **PH:** unk **SS:** J-Yorktown Historian **BS:** JLARC 1, 74.

BLANKENBAKER, Michael; b c1730, Orange Co; d 21 Jun 1790 **RU:** Patriot, Gave material aid to cause **CEM:** Cem name unk; **GPS** unk; Hebron Valley; Madison **GS:** N **SP:** Mar (1745 Orange Co) Elizabeth Barbara Garr (11 Feb 1730 Germany-aft 21 Jun 1790) d/o Andrew & (-----) Garr **VI:** Son of John Nicolas & (-----) Blankenbaker (immigrant). Died in Culpeper Co (now Madison) **P:** N **BLW:** N **RG:** Y **MK:** N **PH:** N **SS:** DAR Ancestor #A011152; D Vol 1 pg 274; K Vol 1 **BS:** 04.

BLANKENBECKLER (BLANKENBAKER), Zachariah Jr; b 25 Mar 1752; d 1824, Wythe Co **RU:** Private, Served in Capt Lowe's Co VA Militia **CEM:** Morgan; **GPS** unk; Rye Valley; Smyth **GS:** Y **SP:** Elizabeth (-----) **VI:** Son of Zachariah Sr. (__-1781) & Elizabeth (Weaver) Blankenbaker There is a stone to his honor & he is said to be bur there **P:** unk **BLW:** unk **RG:** unk **MK:** unk **PH:** unk **SS:** S NSSAR Ancestor #P-116251 **BS:** JLARC 114.

BLANKENSHIP, Abraham Sr; b 1759, Chesterfield Co; d 8 Mar 1845 **RU:** Private, Ent serv Chesterfield Co **CEM:** Blankenship Family; **GPS** unk; Nr Montvale; Bedford **GS:** N **SP:** Mar (1781 Chesterfield Co) Susan Wiatt **VI:** Moved to Bedford Co in 1784 where he had militia service after Rev War. Sol appl pen 7 Jan 1830 Bedford Co age 72. Pensioned in 1883 Bedford Co. Widow pensioned in Franklin Co at age 87. W10425. R266. Govt stone says he was a private in Capt Gilmore 5th Virginia Regiment **P:** Y **BLW:** unk **RG:** Y **MK:** N **PH:** unk **SS:** E pg 68; K Vol 1 pg 82; CG pg 295 **BS:** 4.

BLANKENSHIP, Hudson; b 1737, Chesterfield Co; d Bef 11 Jan 1813 **RU:** Patriot, Gave material aid to the cause **CEM:** Blankenship-Oldham; **GPS** unk; Winfall; Campbell **GS:** N **SP:** Mar Edith Wilkinson, d 1826 **VI:** Son of John Blakenship (1697-1754) & Elizabeth Hudson (1704-1789) **P:** N **BLW:** N **RG:** unk **MK:** N **PH:** N **SS:** AL Ct Bk pg 19 Campbell Co **BS:** 196.

RU=Rank/Unit	CEM=Cemetery	GS=Gravestone	SP=Spousal Information
VI=Other Veteran Info	P=Pension	BLW=Bounty/Land Warrant	RG=Registered Grave
MK=SAR/DAR Marker	PH=Photo	SS=Service Source	BS=Burial Source

32

BLANKENSHIP, James W; b unk; d 18__ **RU:** Private?, Served in 14th Cont Line **CEM:** St John's Episcopal; GPS 37.53183, -77.41958; 2401 E Broad St; Richmond City **GS:** Y **SP:** No info **VI:** No further data **P:** unk **BLW:** unk **RG:** N **MK:** N **PH:** unk **SS:** E pg 696 **BS:** 28 pg 424.

BLEUTAU, Henri; b unk; d 1781 **RU:** Seaman, Served on "Palmier" and died from Yorktown battle **CEM:** French Memorial; GPS 36.81944, -79.39933; Yorktown; York **GS:** U **SP:** No info **VI:** No further data **P:** unk **BLW:** unk **RG:** Y **MK:** unk **PH:** unk **SS:** J-Yorktown Historian **BS:** JLARC 1, 74.

BLEVEL, Guillaume; b unk; d 1781 **RU:** Seaman, Served on "Diademe" and died from Yorktown battle **CEM:** French Memorial; GPS 36.81944, -79.39933; Yorktown; York **GS:** U **SP:** No info **VI:** No further data **P:** unk **BLW:** unk **RG:** Y **MK:** unk **PH:** unk **SS:** J-Yorktown Historian **BS:** JLARC 1, 74.

BLEVENET, Paul; b unk; d 1781 **RU:** Seaman, Served on "Citoyen" and died from Yorktown battle **CEM:** French Memorial; GPS 36.81944, -79.39933; Yorktown; York **GS:** U **SP:** No info **VI:** No further data **P:** unk **BLW:** unk **RG:** Y **MK:** unk **PH:** unk **SS:** J-Yorktown Historian **BS:** JLARC 1, 74.

BLONDEL, Pierre; b unk; d 1781 **RU:** Seaman, Served on "Ville de Paris" and died from Yorktown battle **CEM:** French Memorial; GPS 36.81944, -79.39933; Yorktown; York **GS:** U **SP:** No info **VI:** No further data **P:** unk **BLW:** unk **RG:** Y **MK:** unk **PH:** unk **SS:** J-Yorktown Historian **BS:** JLARC 1, 74.

BLONDELLE, Nicolas; b unk; d 1781 **RU:** Soldier, Served in Soissonnais Bn and died from Yorktown battle **CEM:** French Memorial; GPS 36.81944, -79.39933; Yorktown; York **GS:** U **SP:** No info **VI:** No further data **P:** unk **BLW:** unk **RG:** Y **MK:** unk **PH:** unk **SS:** J-Yorktown Historian **BS:** JLARC 1, 74.

BLOW, Richard; b 1746; d 1833 **RU:** Lieutenant, Specific service recorded Lib VA, Archives, Auditors Acct vol XVIII, pg 573 **CEM:** Cedar Grove; GPS 36.57204, -80.02599; 301 Fort Lane Rd; Portsmouth City **GS:** Y **SP:** No info **VI:** No further data **P:** unk **BLW:** unk **RG:** Y **MK:** N **PH:** unk **SS:** E pg 71; CZ pg 49 **BS:** 27 pg 99.

BLUNT, Washer; b 1738; d 30 Oct 1806 **RU:** Patriot, Signed Legislative Petition in Fairfax Co **CEM:** Old Presbyterian Meeting House; GPS 38.48528, -77.23532; 323 S Fairfax St; Alexandria City **GS:** N **SP:** No info **VI:** Superintendant of Alms House, died of decay age 69 (Alexandria Gazette, 31 Oct 1806, pg 3) **P:** N **BLW:** N **RG:** N **MK:** N **PH:** N **SS:** BB **BS:** 23 pg 99.

BLY, John; b 1757; d 1821 **RU:** Lieutenant, Was received as Lt 1782 in Shenndoah Co Militia. Also was in the 8th Cont line as Sergeant **CEM:** Boehm; GPS unk; Nr Clary; Shenandoah **GS:** U **SP:** Barbara (----) (c1775-__) **VI:** Sol appl pen 25 My 1818 Shenndoah Co age 64. S37780 **P:** Y **BLW:** unk **RG:** Y **MK:** unk **PH:** unk **SS:** J-NSSAR 1993 Reg, J- DAR Hatcher; E pg 72; CG pg 307 **BS:** JLARC 1,c2.

BOATWRIGHT, Daniel; b 13 Apr 1739; d 26 Mar 1797 **RU:** Patriot, Gave material aid to cause **CEM:** Burnt Chimney; GPS unk; Cat Taile Branch; Cumberland **GS:** U **SP:** Jane Bridgewater Martin (1737-1798) d/o (-----) & Jane (Bridgewater) (1715-1778) Martin **VI:** No further data **P:** N **BLW:** N **RG:** unk **MK:** unk **PH:** unk **SS:** AL Ct Bk pg 6 **BS:** 196.

BOATWRIGHT, Reuben; b 21 Mar 1762, Cumberland Co; d unk **RU:** Private, Wounded by a bomb at Yorktown **CEM:** Boatwright Family; GPS unk; Nr Mt Zion Church, 6277 Cartersville Rd, New Canton; Buckingham **GS:** U **SP:** Mar (8 Jun 1796, Prince Edward Co) Jerusha/Lucy Penick (2 Apr 1767-__) d/o Squire William & (-----) Penick of Prince Edward Co **VI:** No further data **P:** unk **BLW:** unk **RG:** unk **MK:** N **PH:** unk **SS:** S; NSSAR Ancestor Nbr P-116936 **BS:** JLARC 59.

BOAZ, Thomas; b 27 Sep 1731; d 13 Sep 1791 **RU:** Patriot, Provided supplies for the troops **CEM:** Boaze Family; GPS 36.71055, -79.55003; 1148 Couny Rd 945, Dry Fork; Pittsylvania **GS:** Y **SP:** Mar (27 Aug 1804 Pittsylvania Co) Lucy Davis **VI:** Son of Thomas Boaz, b c1714, d 15 Aug. 1780, Buckingham Co., Virginia,and Elinor Archdeacon-Cody, b 1718, Thomastown, Co. Kilkenny, Ireland, d 25 Sep 1787, Buckingham Co. Very rough stone **P:** unk **BLW:** unk **RG:** unk **MK:** unk **PH:** unk **SS:** AL Ct Bk pg 24, 41 Pittsylvania Co **BS:** 196.

BOBBITT, John; b 1742; d 1816 **RU:** Second Lieutenant, Served in 4th VA Regt and in Pittsylvania Co Militia **CEM:** North End; GPS 36.77234, -80.73866; 101 Beaver Dam Rd, Hillsville; Carroll **GS:** Y **SP:** Sarah Gibson **VI:** Inscription illegible **P:** unk **BLW:** unk **RG:** unk **MK:** Y **PH:** unk **SS:** S; NSSAR Ancestor #P-116950 **BS:** JLARC 43.

RU=Rank/Unit   CEM=Cemetery   GS=Gravestone   SP=Spousal Information
VI=Other Veteran Info   P=Pension   BLW=Bounty/Land Warrant   RG=Registered Grave
MK=SAR/DAR Marker   PH=Photo   SS=Service Source   BS=Burial Source

33

BOBBITT, Robert; b 1744; d 1817 **RU:** Captain, Served in Montgomery Co Militia **CEM:** Bobbitt Family; GPS 36.47841, -80.40554; Rt 682 E of Rt 52, Hillsville; Carroll **GS:** N **SP:** No info **VI:** Montgomery Co Circuit Records, pg 164 is indicated also as source of service **P:** unk **BLW:** unk **RG:** Y **MK:** N **PH:** N **SS:** E pg 72 **BS:** 04 Jun 04.

BOBBITT, William Sr; b 1744, Prince George Co; d 1817 **RU:** Captain, Commanded a Co Carroll Co Militia 14 Mar 1778. Served in 6th Regt, VA Line **CEM:** Bobbitt Family; GPS 36.47841, -80.40554; Rt 682 E of Rt 52, Hillsville; Carroll **GS:** Y **SP:** Nancy Ann McKensie (__-1807) **VI:** Modern headstone identifies Bobbett's wife & children bur in family plot. R797 **P:** unk **BLW:** unk **RG:** unk **MK:** N **PH:** unk **SS:** S; NSSAR Ancestor #P-116955; DAR # A0116630 **BS:** JLARC 43; 68; 196.

BOCQ, Jean; b unk; d 1781 **RU:** Seaman, Served on "Marseillais" and died from Yorktown battle **CEM:** French Memorial; GPS 36.81944, -79.39933; Yorktown; York **GS:** U **SP:** No info **VI:** No further data **P:** unk **BLW:** unk **RG:** Y **MK:** unk **PH:** unk **SS:** J-Yorktown Historian **BS:** JLARC 1, 74.

BODEVER, Bernard; b unk; d 1781 **RU:** Seaman, Served on "Ville de Paris" and died from Yorktown battle **CEM:** French Memorial; GPS 36.81944, -79.39933; Yorktown; York **GS:** U **SP:** No info **VI:** No further data **P:** unk **BLW:** unk **RG:** Y **MK:** unk **PH:** unk **SS:** J-Yorktown Historian **BS:** JLARC 1, 74.

BOHEU, Chretian; b unk; d 1781 **RU:** Seaman, Served on "Auguste" and died from Yorktown battle **CEM:** French Memorial; GPS 36.81944, -79.39933; Yorktown; York **GS:** U **SP:** No info **VI:** No further data **P:** unk **BLW:** unk **RG:** Y **MK:** unk **PH:** unk **SS:** J-Yorktown Historian **BS:** JLARC 1, 74.

BOISSARD, Michel; b unk; d 1781 **RU:** Soldier, Served in Soissonnais Bn and died from Yorktown battle **CEM:** French Memorial; GPS 36.81944, -79.39933; Yorktown; York **GS:** U **SP:** No info **VI:** No further data **P:** unk **BLW:** unk **RG:** Y **MK:** unk **PH:** unk **SS:** J-Yorktown Historian **BS:** JLARC 1, 74.

BOISSEAU, Pierre; b unk; d 1781 **RU:** Soldier, Served in Touraine Bn and died from Yorktown battle **CEM:** French Memorial; GPS 36.81944, -79.39933; Yorktown; York **GS:** U **SP:** No info **VI:** No further data **P:** unk **BLW:** unk **RG:** Y **MK:** unk **PH:** unk **SS:** J-Yorktown Historian **BS:** JLARC 1, 74.

BOLAR, John; b 1733; d 3 Apr 1818 **RU:** Captain, Commanded a company 8 Apr 1779 Botetourt Co Militia **CEM:** Warm Springs; GPS 38.05030, -79.78110; Rt 220 Sam Snead Hwy, Warm Springs; Bath **GS:** Y **SP:** Mar (abt 1768) Margaret Thornton (c17r5-16 Jan 1815) **VI:** One of Dickenson's Rangers in French & Indian War, was at battle of Guildford CH. Justice of Bath Co 1769-1777, Sheriff in 1792. Property was "Walnut Grove." GS moved to Warm Spring in the 1970s for the Gathright Dam project **P:** unk **BLW:** unk **RG:** N **MK:** N **PH:** unk **SS:** AZ pg 191 **BS:** 159 Bolar; 196.

BOLES, William; b unk; d 1832 **RU:** Private, Served in 3rd & 4th Cont Line **CEM:** King Family; GPS unk; Rt 658 Brent Point Rd; Stafford **GS:** Y **SP:** No info **VI:** No further data **P:** unk **BLW:** unk **RG:** N **MK:** N **PH:** unk **SS:** E pg 74 **BS:** 03 pg 262.

BOLLING, Robert; b 3 Mar 1759, Petersburg, Dinwiddie Co; d 26 Jan 1839 **RU:** Captain, Volunteered 1788 in Hanover Co in Capt Thomas Nelson's Co Troop of Cavalry. In 1780 served as capt and raised a troop of cavalry in area south of James River in Col Bannister's unit of Dinwiddie Co. His Co served under Col Parker in General Muhlenberg's Brigade in Battle of Petersburg **CEM:** Blandford; GPS 37.22433, -77.38604; 319 S Crater Rd; Petersburg City **GS:** U **SP:** 1) Mary Burton (c1763- 3 Aug 1787) 2) Catharine Stith (c1776-9 Aug 1795) 3) Anna Dade, (c1778-18 Mar 1846) **VI:** Son of Robert (1730-1775) & Mary (Marshall) (1737-1814) Bolling. British General Philips d at Petersburg home of first wife, Mary and she and four daughters were made prisoners. Sol appl pen 20 Sep 1832 Petersburg age 73. S6689 Will dated 7 Sep 1789, probated 21 Feb 1791. Wardell indicates he d c1790 Dinwiddie Co. Widow had BLW in 1817 and d Aug 1832) Children appl for pen 1850. R282 **P:** Y **BLW:** Y **RG:** unk **MK:** unk **PH:** unk **SS:** J- DAR Hatcher; E pg 74; G pg 864; K Vol 1 pg 87; AZ pg 129, 130; CG pg 315 **BS:** JLARC 2, 128; 80 vol 1, pg 94; 128; 196.

BOLLING, Thomas; b 7 Jul 1735; d 7 Aug 1804 **RU:** Major/Patriot, Promoted to major rank Chesterfield Co Militia, 4 Jan 1777; as patriot gave material aid to cause **CEM:** Cobbs Family; GPS unk; Bolling Family property, Enon; Chesterfield **GS:** N **SP:** Elizabeth Gay (1738-7 Aug 1804) **VI:** Son of John (1700-1775) & Mary Elizabeth (Blair) (1708-1775) Bolling. GS destroyed during Civil War **P:** N **BLW:** N **RG:** unk **MK:** unk **PH:** unk **SS:** E pg 74; AL Ct Bk pg 10 **BS:** 196.

RU=Rank/Unit	CEM=Cemetery	GS=Gravestone	SP=Spousal Information
VI=Other Veteran Info	P=Pension	BLW=Bounty/Land Warrant	RG=Registered Grave
MK=SAR/DAR Marker	PH=Photo	SS=Service Source	BS=Burial Source

34

BONET, Guillaume; b unk; d 1781 **RU:** Seaman, Served on "Marseillais" and died from Yorktown battle **CEM:** French Memorial; GPS 36.81944, -79.39933; Yorktown; York **GS:** U **SP:** No info **VI:** No further data **P:** unk **BLW:** unk **RG:** Y **MK:** unk **PH:** unk **SS:** J-Yorktown Historian **BS:** JLARC 1, 74.

BONGAR, Francois; b unk; d 1781 **RU:** Seaman, Served on "Hector" and died from Yorktown battle **CEM:** French Memorial; GPS 36.81944, -79.39933; Yorktown; York **GS:** U **SP:** No info **VI:** No further data **P:** unk **BLW:** unk **RG:** Y **MK:** unk **PH:** unk **SS:** J-Yorktown Historian **BS:** JLARC 1, 74.

BONNET, Jean; b unk; d 1781 **RU:** Seaman, Served on "Palmier" and died from Yorktown battle **CEM:** French Memorial; GPS 36.81944, -79.39933; Yorktown; York **GS:** U **SP:** No info **VI:** No further data **P:** unk **BLW:** unk **RG:** Y **MK:** unk **PH:** unk **SS:** J-Yorktown Historian **BS:** JLARC 1, 74.

BOOKER, E Nash; b unk; d 1838 **RU:** Captain?, An Edmond Booker took oath as officer of Ameila Co Ct, 25 Jul 1776. May not be the same person **CEM:** Booker Family; GPS unk; Rt 641 outside Cumberland CH; Cumberland **GS:** Y **SP:** No info **VI:** No further data **P:** unk **BLW:** unk **RG:** N **MK:** N **PH:** unk **SS:** G pg 4 **BS:** 60, Booker; 196.

BOOKER, Edward; b 1761; d 1800 **RU:** Private, Capt Everard Meades Co, March 1777, Col Alexander Spottswoond's 2d VA Regt **CEM:** Booker Family; GPS unk; Rt 641 outside Cumberland CH; Cumberland **GS:** N **SP:** No info **VI:** No further data **P:** unk **BLW:** unk **RG:** Y **MK:** N **PH:** N **SS:** A pg 271 **BS:** 32, e-mail 07; 196.

BOOKER, George; b 1721; d Bet 13 Oct & 22 Dec 1791 **RU:** Patriot, Gave material aid to cause in Amelia Co **CEM:** Booker; GPS unk; Rt 612; Amelia **GS:** Y **SP:** Mar (12 Oct 1745, Amelia Co (bond)) Sarah Cobbs d/o Col Samuel & (-----) Cobbs **VI:** Will dated 13 Oct 1791, recorded 22 Dec 1791 **P:** N **BLW:** N **RG:** unk **MK:** unk **PH:** unk **SS:** AL Ct Bk 1 pg 53 **BS:** 196.

BOOKER, George; b c1747, Amelia Co VA; d 1816 **RU:** Patriot, Provided goods and services to Patriot forces. Was member Elizabeth City/Hampton Town Committee of Safety **CEM:** Sherwood Cemetery; GPS 37.07384, -76.34973; Langley Air Force Base; Hampton City **GS:** Y **SP:** 1) Mary Moore 2) Ann Hollier **VI:** No further data **P:** N **BLW:** N **RG:** Y **MK:** Y **PH:** Y **SS:** G pg 436-7; AK **BS:** 04; 41 pg 184; 196.

BOOKER, John; b unk; d 1842 **RU:** Private, Specific service recorded Lib VA, Archives, Council Journals 1783, pg 183 **CEM:** Sherwood Cemetery; GPS 37.07384, -76.34973; Langley Air Force Base; Hampton City **GS:** N **SP:** No info **VI:** No further data **P:** unk **BLW:** unk **RG:** Y **MK:** Y **PH:** N **SS:** N pg 1250-1; CZ pg 52 **BS:** 41 pg 184; 196.

BOOKER, Lewis; b 21 May 1754; d 23 Dec 1814 **RU:** Captain, Ent serv fr Essex Co 1777. Lt in VA Line, per pen info. Served in Lt Col Edward Carrington's Regt and in the 1st Cont Artillery. Retired 1783 **CEM:** St Paul's Episcopal; GPS 37.82921, -76.96836; 7924 Richmond-Tappahannock Hwy, Millers Tavern; Essex **GS:** Y **SP:** Mar Judith Dudley, b 1 Jan 1765, d 6 Oct 1817 **VI:** Awarded 4666 acres BLW #8-200-12 May 1803, issued to Joseph Mourse. Bur at "Laurel Cove." Memorial stone in St Paul's Episcopal Church **P:** unk **BLW:** Y **RG:** unk **MK:** N **PH:** unk **SS:** E pg 76; K Vol 1 pg 90; CG pg 322 **BS:** JLARC 2, 65; 210 pg 291; 296.

BOOKER, Richardson (Richerson); b 1754; d 27 Oct 1806 **RU:** Sergeant, Served in 5th, 11th and 15th Cont Line for 3 yrs **CEM:** Booker Family; GPS unk; Grub Hill Church Rd, check property records for location of plantation; Amelia **GS:** U **SP:** No info **VI:** Son of Richard (1720-1764) & Martha (Brunskill) Booker **P:** unk **BLW:** Y **RG:** unk **MK:** unk **PH:** unk **SS:** C pg 394; E pg 76 **BS:** 196.

BOOTH, Beverly; b 7 Jan 1753, Nottaway Parrish, Southampton Co; d 22 Nov 1833 **RU:** Private, Ent serv Southampton Co Oct 1776 in Col Benjamin Blunt's Regt, Mar 1777-May 1778, then in 1779 in Capt Joyner's Co, Col Parkers Regt until abt March 1781.Was in Battle at Petersburg in Capt Nello's Co 1781. Discharged after the Cornwallis surrender Oct 1871 at Yorktown **CEM:** Roger's Family; GPS unk; Off Rt 40, Booth Fork; Surry **GS:** Y **SP:** 1) Mar (1771) Elizabeth Cocke 2) Mar (21 Jan or 4 Feb 1819) Mary Presson Cornwall (__-2 Jul 1855) of Surry Co. Was widowed at age 73 in Surry Co. **VI:** Son of Robert & Sarah (Bailey) Booth IV. 27 Jun 1814 - Collector of the Surry Co. Levy; 15 Aug 1815 - Sheriff - Surry Co. Sol appl pen 24 Sep 1832 Surry Co age 80 in 1832 when titled "Rev". Died in Southampton Co. Widow appl pen 24 Jul 1844 Surry Co. W25267. Widow appl again 28 Mar 1855. BLW #28655-160-

RU=Rank/Unit	CEM=Cemetery	GS=Gravestone	SP=Spousal Information
VI=Other Veteran Info	P=Pension	BLW=Bounty/Land Warrant	RG=Registered Grave
MK=SAR/DAR Marker	PH=Photo	SS=Service Source	BS=Burial Source

35

55. R289 **P:** Y **BLW:** Y **RG:** Y **MK:** N **PH:** unk **SS:** E pg 77; K Vol 1 pg 91; CG pg 323 **BS:** 133 Booth Fam.

BOOTH, George; b 11 Apr 1727, England; d 28 Sep 1804 **RU:** Corporal, Served in 9th Cont Line, 3 yrs service **CEM:** Wright Family; GPS 36.97658, -80.21693; Pizarro off Rt 668; Floyd **GS:** Y **SP:** Permelia Carroll (Sep 1735 Gloucester Co-aft 1813 Montgomery Co) **VI:** Memorialized by DAR plaque in cem. BLW issued 5 May 1791 **P:** unk **BLW:** Y **RG:** unk **MK:** Y **PH:** unk **SS:** F pg 14 **BS:** 196 for John Mitchell.

BOOTH, George W; b 1768; d 1808 **RU:** Patriot, Gave material aid to cause **CEM:** Toddbury; GPS unk; On North River; Gloucester **GS:** Y **SP:** Mahala (-----) **VI:** No further data **P:** N **BLW:** N **RG:** N **MK:** N **PH:** unk **SS:** AL Ct Bk 1 **BS:** 100 pg 93.

BOOTH, John; b 1737, Amelia Co; d 17 Dec 1807 **RU:** Patriot, Gave material aid to cause **CEM:** Booth Family; GPS unk; Rt 666 nNr Smith Mountain Lake; Franklin **GS:** U **SP:** Mary Smith **VI:** No further data **P:** N **BLW:** N **RG:** Y **MK:** unk **PH:** unk **SS:** DD **BS:** JLARC 2, 76.

BOOTHE, George; b 1737; d 1813 **RU:** Corporal, Served in US Army, Specific service recorded Lib VA, Archives, Bounty Land Warrants **CEM:** Boothe Family; GPS unk; Little River, Christiansburg; Montgomery **GS:** U **SP:** No info **VI:** No further data **P:** unk **BLW:** Y **RG:** unk **MK:** unk **PH:** unk **SS:** J-DAR Hatcher; CZ pg 53; CU **BS:** JLARC 2.

BOSWELL, John Iverson; b 5 Apr 1761, Gloucester Co; d 3 Mar 1823 **RU:** Sergeant, Served in 1st VA Regt **CEM:** Boswell Family; GPS unk; Off Rt 634, SE of Rebobeth; Lunenburg **GS:** Y **SP:** 1) Mar (16 Feb 1784 Mecklenburg Co) Mary Coleman (28 Feb 1766-14 Jul 1797) 2) Mar (27 Oct 1798n Amelia Co) Barbara Walker (22 Jan 1775-13 Jun 1854). Both wives bur here **VI:** Son of Joseph Colgate & Elizabeth (Elliott) Boswell of Amelia Co **P:** unk **BLW:** unk **RG:** Y **MK:** N **PH:** unk **SS:** E pg 78 **BS:** 04; 172; 196.

BOUCAULT, Mathieu; b unk; d 1781 **RU:** Seaman, Served on "Palmier" and died from Yorktown battle **CEM:** French Memorial; GPS 36.81944, -79.39933; Yorktown; York **GS:** U **SP:** No info **VI:** No further data **P:** unk **BLW:** unk **RG:** Y **MK:** unk **PH:** unk **SS:** J-Yorktown Historian **BS:** JLARC 1, 74.

BOUILLOT, Benoist; b unk; d 1781 **RU:** Soldier, Served in Agenois Bn and died from Yorktown battle **CEM:** French Memorial; GPS 36.81944, -79.39933; Yorktown; York **GS:** U **SP:** No info **VI:** No further data **P:** unk **BLW:** unk **RG:** Y **MK:** unk **PH:** unk **SS:** J-Yorktown Historian **BS:** JLARC 1, 74.

BOULAIRE, Julien; b unk; d 1781 **RU:** Seaman, Served on "Saint-Esprit" and died from Yorktown battle **CEM:** French Memorial; GPS 36.81944, -79.39933; Yorktown; York **GS:** U **SP:** No info **VI:** No further data **P:** unk **BLW:** unk **RG:** Y **MK:** unk **PH:** unk **SS:** J-Yorktown Historian **BS:** JLARC 1, 74.

BOULANGER, Nicolas; b unk; d 1781 **RU:** Soldier, Served in Santonge Bn and died from Yorktown battle **CEM:** French Memorial; GPS 36.81944, -79.39933; Yorktown; York **GS:** U **SP:** No info **VI:** No further data **P:** unk **BLW:** unk **RG:** Y **MK:** unk **PH:** unk **SS:** J-Yorktown Historian **BS:** JLARC 1, 74.

BOULDIN, Thomas Jr; b 31 Dec 1738, Cecil Co, MD; d 1827 **RU:** Ensign, Served in Charlotte Co Militia **CEM:** Grassy Creek; GPS 36.64716, -79.91943; Nr Horsepasture, Rt 829, Drakes Branch; Henry **GS:** Y **SP:** Mar (12 Jan 1768) Martha Moseley (1742-__) d/o Edmund & Amey (Green) Moseley **VI:** Son of Thomas Sr. (1705-1783) & Anne (Clarke) (1712-__) Bouldin. Govt grave stone **P:** unk **BLW:** unk **RG:** unk **MK:** unk **PH:** unk **SS:** AR pg 98 **BS:** 196.

BOULDIN, Thomas Sr; b 15 Jan 1706, Cecil Co, MD; d 1 May 1783 **RU:** Patriot, Gave material aid to cause **CEM:** Golden Hills Estate; GPS unk; Drakes Branch; Charlotte **GS:** U **SP:** Mar (29 Jun 1783 MD) Anne Nancy Wood Clarke (1712 New Castle Del-__) d/o Richard & (-----) Clarke **VI:** No **P:** N **BLW:** N **RG:** unk **MK:** unk **PH:** unk **SS:** AL Ct Bk pg 8 **BS:** 226.

BOULDIN, Wood; b 4 Jun 1742, Cecil Co, MD; d 13 Mar 1800 **RU:** Major, Ent serv Charlotte Co 1776. Was Maj in the Cont Line and cited for gallantry at Brandywine and Germantown **CEM:** Golden Hills Estate; GPS unk; Drakes Branch; Charlotte **GS:** Y **SP:** Mar (2 or 3 Apr 1777, Charlotte Co) Joanna Tyler (1752-__) Thomas Read signed marriage bond **VI:** Son of Thomas Bouldin (1702 - 1782) & Ann Wood Clark (1715 - 1780). Fought at battles of Brandywine and Germantown. Awarded 2666 acres

---

RU=Rank/Unit   CEM=Cemetery   GS=Gravestone   SP=Spousal Information
VI=Other Veteran Info   P=Pension   BLW=Bounty/Land Warrant   RG=Registered Grave
MK=SAR/DAR Marker   PH=Photo   SS=Service Source   BS=Burial Source

36

BLW. Widow appl pen 24 Apr 1838 Charlotte Co age 86. W18637. R296 **P:** Y **BLW:** Y **RG:** Y **MK**: unk **PH:** unk **SS:** E pg 79; K Vol 1 pg 93; AL pg 79 cites 14th CL as unit; CG pg 333 **BS:** JLARC 1, 76; 186.

BOULDIN (BOUDLIN), Thomas; b 15 Jan 1702; d 2 Jun 1782 **RU:** Ensign/Patriot, Served in militia. As a patriot gave material aid to cause **CEM:** Golden Hills Estate; GPS unk; Drakes Branch; Charlotte **GS:** Y **SP:** Mar (29 Jan 1733, Cecil Co MD) Ann Wood Clark (1715 - 1780) **VI:** First sheriff of Lunenburg Co. VA. and Charlotte Co, VA. Born aboard ship in the Chesapeake Bay in move fr MD to VA. Served in French and Indian War. Widow pensioned 1838 age 86 commencing 1 Apr 1814 for $48 per yr **P:** Y **BLW:** unk **RG:** unk **MK:** unk **PH:** unk **SS:** AG pg 256; AL Ct book Charlotte pg 8 **BS:** JLARC 102; 196.

BOULWARE, Mark; b 1755; d 15 Mar 1811 **RU:** Private, Served in 2nd Cont Line **CEM:** Greenlawn; GPS 38.07030, -77.33830; Lakewood Rd, Bowling Green; Caroline **GS:** Y **SP:** Milly (-----) (__-1790) 2) Agatha Saunders (__-1836) **VI:** Govt stone gives rank as private. Memorialized on cenotaph **P:** unk **BLW:** unk **RG:** Y **MK:** N **PH:** unk **SS:** E pg 79 **BS:** JLARC 2, 76; 196.

BOUQUET, Marcel; b unk; d 1781 **RU:** Seaman, Served on "Languedoc" and died from Yorktown battle **CEM:** French Memorial; GPS 36.81944, -79.39933; Yorktown; York **GS:** U **SP:** No info **VI:** No further data **P:** unk **BLW:** unk **RG:** Y **MK:** unk **PH:** unk **SS:** J-Yorktown Historian **BS:** JLARC 1, 74.

BOURDER, Jean; b unk; d 1781 **RU:** Soldier, Served in Santonge Bn and died from Yorktown battle **CEM:** French Memorial; GPS 36.81944, -79.39933; Yorktown; York **GS:** U **SP:** No info **VI:** No further data **P:** unk **BLW:** unk **RG:** Y **MK:** unk **PH:** unk **SS:** J-Yorktown Historian **BS:** JLARC 1, 74.

BOURDIN, Nicolas; b unk; d 1781 **RU:** Soldier, Served in Agenois Bn and died from Yorktown battle **CEM:** French Memorial; GPS 36.81944, -79.39933; Yorktown; York **GS:** U **SP:** No info **VI:** No further data **P:** unk **BLW:** unk **RG:** Y **MK:** unk **PH:** unk **SS:** J-Yorktown Historian **BS:** JLARC 1, 74.

BOURGAIN, Jean; b unk; d 1781 **RU:** Seaman, Served on "Hercule" and died from Yorktown battle **CEM:** French Memorial; GPS 36.81944, -79.39933; Yorktown; York **GS:** U **SP:** No info **VI:** No further data **P:** unk **BLW:** unk **RG:** Y **MK:** unk **PH:** unk **SS:** J-Yorktown Historian **BS:** JLARC 1, 74.

BOURHIS, Francois; b unk; d 1781 **RU:** Seaman, Served on "Hector" and died from Yorktown battle **CEM:** French Memorial; GPS 36.81944, -79.39933; Yorktown; York **GS:** U **SP:** No info **VI:** No further data **P:** unk **BLW:** unk **RG:** Y **MK:** unk **PH:** unk **SS:** J-Yorktown Historian **BS:** JLARC 1, 74.

BOURHIS, Gregoire; b unk; d 1781 **RU:** Seaman, Served on "Auguste" and died from Yorktown battle **CEM:** French Memorial; GPS 36.81944, -79.39933; Yorktown; York **GS:** U **SP:** No info **VI:** No further data **P:** unk **BLW:** unk **RG:** Y **MK:** unk **PH:** unk **SS:** J-Yorktown Historian **BS:** JLARC 1, 74.

BOURIGEOT, Francois; b unk; d 1781 **RU:** Seaman, Served on "Sceptre" and died from Yorktown battle **CEM:** French Memorial; GPS 36.81944, -79.39933; Yorktown; York **GS:** U **SP:** no info **VI:** No further data **P:** unk **BLW:** unk **RG:** Y **MK:** unk **PH:** unk **SS:** J-Yorktown Historian **BS:** JLARC 1, 74.

BOUSH, William Sr; b 1739; d 1834 **RU:** Patriot, Gave material aid to cause **CEM:** Lynnhaven House; GPS unk; Shore Dr; Virginia Beach City **GS:** Y **SP:** Mary (-----) (1764-1822) **VI:** DAR plaque **P:** N **BLW:** N **RG:** Y **MK:** Y **PH:** unk **SS:** AS & AL ComBk **BS:** 80,vol1, pg 99; 212 pg 236.

BOUTWELL, John T; b unk; d unk **RU:** First Lieutenant, Appt 1st Lt in Capt Stern's Co, Caroline Co Militia Feb 1778 **CEM:** Boutwell-Smith Family; GPS unk; Rt 17, 3.1 mi S of Port Royal; Caroline **GS:** Y **SP:** No info **VI:** No further data **P:** unk **BLW:** unk **RG:** N **MK:** N **PH:** unk **SS:** E pg 80 **BS:** 98.

BOUTWELL, William; b 1734, Port Royal, Richmond Co; d 7 Jul 1803 **RU:** Patriot, Gave material aid to cause **CEM:** Boutwell-Smith Family; GPS unk; Rt 17, 3.1 mi S of Port Royal; Caroline **GS:** Y **SP:** No info **VI:** No further data **P:** N **BLW:** N **RG:** N **MK:** N **PH:** unk **SS:** Caroline Co Rec; Al Ct Bk II ps 1, 3, 4, 18, 25, Caroline Co **BS:** 98.

BOWEN, Arthur; b 17 Jan 1744, Augusta Co; d 1816 **RU:** Captain, Commanded a co in Washington Co Militia. Promoted to Capt 27 Mar 1781 **CEM:** Aspenvale; GPS 36.81420, -81.64000; Rts 641 & 642, Seven Mile Ford; Smyth **GS:** Y **SP:** Mary McMurray (1746-1816) **VI:** Son of John (1696-1761) & Lillian (McIlhaney) (1709-1780) Bowen **P:** unk **BLW:** unk **RG:** N **MK:** N **PH:** unk **SS:** E pg 80; AS, DAR Rpt **BS:** 196.

RU=Rank/Unit   CEM=Cemetery   GS=Gravestone   SP=Spousal Information
VI=Other Veteran Info   P=Pension   BLW=Bounty/Land Warrant   RG=Registered Grave
MK=SAR/DAR Marker   PH=Photo   SS=Service Source   BS=Burial Source

37

BOWEN, John Pratt; b 1754; d 1858? **RU**: Private, Served in 8th Cont Line, Was Quartermaster Dec 1778 and prisoner at Charleston 12 May 1780. Commissioned Lt 8 Feb 1781 but apparently disabled as he drew half-pay. Resigned Jan 1783 **CEM**: Pratt Family, aka Glebe; GPS 38.29934, -77.34450; 1374 White Oak; Stafford **GS**: U **SP**: Elizabeth (-----) **VI**: Plaque on cem wall indicates Rev War soldier. Pen S6761 King George Co, BLW 3222 acres **P**: Y **BLW**: Y **RG**: yes **MK**: unk **PH**: Y **SS**: A pg 414; E pg 80; CZ pg 55 **BS**: 196.

BOWEN, Micajah; b 8 Aug 1753, Meherrin, Lunenburg Co; d 24 Dec 1845 **RU**: Soldier, Ent serv Albemarle Co 1781. Albemarle Militia **CEM**: Bowen Farm; GPS unk; Red Hill; Albemarle **GS**: N **SP**: Fannie (-----) **VI**: Son of Ephraim Bowen & Anne (-----). Sol appl pen 5 Nov 1833 Albemarle Co age 80. S29643. Children recd final payment 12 Jul 1854. R300 **P**: Y **BLW**: unk **RG**: Y **MK**: unk **PH**: N **SS**: E pg 81; K Vol 1 pg 94; CG pg 338 **BS**: JLARC 2, 4, 76; 196.

BOWEN, Rees; b 1750, Augusta Co; d 7 Oct 1780 **RU**: Ensign, Served in VA Militia under Cols William Campbell, Isaac Shelby and Benjamin Cleveland. Killed in Battle at Kings Mountain **CEM**: Bowen Family; GPS unk; Cove Creek; Tazewell **GS**: Y **SP**: Mar (c1756) Louisa Smith (c1740-16 Feb 1834) **VI**: Son of John (1710 PA-19 May1761) & Lilly (McIlhaney) (1705 Ireland-20 Jun 1780) Bowen. Died in Kings Mountain, SC. Govt GS. SAR marker **P**: unk **BLW**: unk **RG**: unk **MK**: Y **PH**: unk **SS**: CD **BS**: 196.

BOWIE, William S Sr; b unk; d unk **RU**: Lieutenant, Served in MD Flying Camp in 1776 in 3rd Bn **CEM**: Fairfax City; GPS 38.84690, -77.31330; Main St & Page Ave; Fairfax City **GS**: N **SP**: No info **VI**: No further data **P**: unk **BLW**: unk **RG**: N **MK**: N **PH**: N **SS**: A pg 239 **BS**: 61 vol III pg FX-153.

BOWLES, Knight; b 8 May 1746; d 14 Feb 1820 **RU**: Private/Patriot, Served in Amherst Co Militia. Served at least 3 yrs **CEM**: Lyles Church; GPS 37.84793, -78.20337; Palmyra; Fluvanna **GS**: Y **SP**: 1) Mar (17 Feb 1767) Sarah Curd 2) Mar (24 Dec 1798) Martha Wood (26 Jun 1757-20 Nov 1846) widow of John Ellis **VI**: Son of John & Sarah (Knight) Bowles **P**: unk **BLW**: Y **RG**: N **MK**: N **PH**: unk **SS**: C pg 613; D Vol I pg 80 **BS**: 66, pg 8; 196.

BOWLES, Thomas; b 1761; d Jan 1810 or 7 Dec 1839 **RU**: Sergeant, Ent serv Hanover Co 1776. Served in VA Line **CEM**: Bowles Family; GPS unk; Waterloo, Chickahominy Point; Hanover **GS**: N **SP**: Mar (25 Nov 1793 Stafford Co) Sarah Holman or Ford. Widow moved to Indiana in 1829. **VI**: Sol appl pen 6 Aug 1832 Henrico Co. age 72. Widow appl BLW age 84 in Harrison Co, IN in 1849, which was rejected. She reappl age 93 in 1856 which was granted. Died in Spotsylvania Co. S8079. R304 **P**: Y **BLW**: Y **RG**: Y **MK**: unk **PH**: N **SS**: K Vol 1 pg 95; CG pg 343; J-NSSAR 2000 Reg **BS**: JLARC 76.

BOWLES, Thomas Philip; b 1749; d 1789 **RU**: Lieutenant, Specific service recorded Lib VA, Archives, Report of Sec of War, Vol 2, Pen, pg 148 **CEM**: Bowles Family; GPS unk; Waterloo, Chickahominy Point; Hanover **GS**: N **SP**: No info **VI**: No further data **P**: Y **BLW**: unk **RG**: unk **MK**: unk **PH**: N **SS**: J-DAR Hatcher; CZ pg 55 **BS**: JLARC 2.

BOWLES (BOLLS), William; b 1754; d 1823 **RU**: Private?, Served in 3rd, 4th, 8th, & 12th Cont Lines **CEM**: Bowles Family; GPS unk; Waterloo, Chickahominy Point; Hanover **GS**: Y **SP**: Elizabeth Napier (1758-1838) **VI**: No further data **P**: unk **BLW**: unk **RG**: Y **MK**: N **PH**: unk **SS**: E pg 82 **BS**: 31 vol 1 pg 49; 196.

BOWLING, James; b 9 Jan 1756, NC; d unk **RU**: Corporal, Served in 5th Cont Line **CEM**: Benjamin Bolling; GPS 37.07721, -82.70543; Sulpher Springs Dr, Flat Gap; Wise **GS**: U **SP**: Sarah Blevins **VI**: Son of Benjamin (1734-1832) & (-----) Bowling **P**: unk **BLW**: unk **RG**: unk **MK**: unk **PH**: unk **SS**: E pg 82 **BS**: 196.

BOWMAN, John; b 18 Jul 1750; d 7 Mar 1816 **RU**: Private, Served by running supplies in Capt Peter Hull's Co, 2nd Bn, Augusta Co Militia 1779 **CEM**: Rader Lutheran; GPS 38.65073, -78.78055; 17072 Raders Church Rd, Timberville; Rockingham **GS**: Y **SP**: Mary Magdalena Zervus (30 Oct 1755-3 Dec 1835) **VI**: No further data **P**: unk **BLW**: unk **RG**: Y **MK**: Y **PH**: Y **SS**: E pg 26 **BS**: 04.

BOWMAN, Peter; b c1762; d 22 Dec 1823 **RU**: Private, Served in Capt Jacob Holeman's Co, Dunmore Co Militia **CEM**: Bowman Family; GPS unk; War Branch, Peaked Mountain Rt 726 abt 1 mi fr jct with Rt 613 on private rd; Rockingham **GS**: Y **SP**: Mary Heatwole (18 Dec 1766 PA-Feb 1833) d/o Mathias & (--

RU=Rank/Unit   CEM=Cemetery   GS=Gravestone   SP=Spousal Information
VI=Other Veteran Info   P=Pension   BLW=Bounty/Land Warrant   RG=Registered Grave
MK=SAR/DAR Marker   PH=Photo   SS=Service Source   BS=Burial Source

38

---) Heatwole **VI:** Killed in hunting accident **P:** unk **BLW:** unk **RG:** unk **MK:** unk **PH:** unk **SS:** C pg 607 **BS:** 196.

BOWMAN, Robert; b 20 Jan 1758; d 15 Jul 1824 **RU:** Lieutenant, Serv in Cont Line in Ill Regt **CEM:** Bowman-Fariss Family; GPS 36.66541, -80.66541; Blue Ridge Pkwy MM 194, Volunteer Rd W side btw Alpine Court Rd & Boundary Rd; Carroll **GS:** Y **SP:** Mary (-----) **VI:** Modern era Govt stone **P:** unk **BLW:** unk **RG:** N **MK:** N **PH:** Y **SS:** E pg 83; B; T 63 pg 578 **BS:** 63 pg 578.

BOWYER, Henry; b 1760; d 13 Jun 1832 **RU:** Colonel, Ent serv Botetourt Co 1777. Served as Lt in Cont & VA Line **CEM:** Allen-Lauderdale; GPS unk; Fincastle; Botetourt **GS:** U **SP:** Mar (9 Aug 1792 Boutetourt Co) Agatha Madison (c1774-6 Oct 1847) **VI:** Moved to Boutetourt Co c1763 fr Augusta Co. Pensoned under Act of 1828. Widow appl pen 8 Oct 1838 Botetourt Co. W5859, BLW #283-200-31 Dec 1795. Person w/ same name, and death date is reported for Lexington. R306 **P:** Y **BLW:** Y **RG:** Y **MK:** unk **PH:** unk **SS:** K Vol 1 pg 97; CG pg 345 **BS:** JLARC 1,4,60.

BOWYER, Henry; b unk; d 1832 **RU:** Lieutenant, Specific service recorded Lib VA, Archives, Auditors Acct 1778-1783, vol VII, pg 219 **CEM:** Stonewall Jackson Memorial; GPS 37.78128, -79.44604; 314 S Main St; Lexington City **GS:** U **SP:** No info **VI:** Person w/ same name, and death date, is reported for Botetourt Co **P:** unk **BLW:** unk **RG:** unk **MK:** unk **PH:** unk **SS:** CZ pg 56 **BS:** JLARC 63.

BOWYER, John; b 1763; d 1806 **RU:** Lieutenant, Served in Capt James Gilmore's Co under command of Gen Morgan in SC, 1780 **CEM:** Stonewall Jackson Memorial; GPS 37.78128, -79.44604; 314 S Main St; Lexington City **GS:** U **SP:** 1) Madgalene Woods McDowell Borden 2) Mary (-----) **VI:** Attained rank of Col after War **P:** unk **BLW:** unk **RG:** Y **MK:** unk **PH:** unk **SS:** J-NSSAR 2000 Reg; S, NSSAR Ancestor #P-118814 **BS:** JLARC 1, 2, 63; 76.

BOXLEY, Joseph I Sr; b c1735, King William Co; d 27 Jun 1787 **RU:** Patriot, Gave material aid to cause **CEM:** Cem name unk; GPS unk; Lousia; Louisa **GS:** N **SP:** Catherine Spiller **VI:** Son of George Boxley **P:** N **BLW:** N **RG:** Y **MK:** Y **PH:** N **SS:** D Vol I pg 625, 638, 645 **BS:** 04.

BOYAR (BOYARS), John; b 1757; d 19 Nov 1802 **RU:** Sergeant, Served in Spencer's Regt, Cont Troops **CEM:** Old Christ Church Episcopal; GPS 38.80625, -77.04718; 118 N Washington St; Alexandria City **GS:** Y **SP:** No info **VI:** Cooper, died in his 46th yr **P:** unk **BLW:** unk **RG:** Y **MK:** N **PH:** unk **SS:** A pg 188; AP serv record Fold 3 **BS:** 20 pg 136; 196.

BOYD, Alexander; b 16 Aug 1743, Irvine, Scotland; d 11 Aug 1801 **RU:** Patriot, Gave 400# beef to cause 9 Apr 1782 **CEM:** Boyd Family; GPS unk; Behind Health Dept Bldg, Boyton; Mecklenburg **GS:** Y **SP:** No info **VI:** Son of Robert (1688-1786) & Elizabeth (Anderson) (1705-1786) Boyd **P:** N **BLW:** N **RG:** unk **MK:** unk **PH:** unk **SS:** DB pg 27 **BS:** 54 pg 177; 196.

BOYD, Francis; b unk; d 1850 **RU:** Private, Served in 7th VA Regt **CEM:** Boydton Presbyterian Church; GPS 36.40101, -78.23127; Boydton; Mecklenburg **GS:** Y **SP:** No info **VI:** No further data **P:** Y **BLW:** unk **RG:** Y **MK:** N **PH:** unk **SS:** C pg 395; CU **BS:** 54 pg 26.

BOYD, Robert; b unk; d 1800 **RU:** Private, Served in Capt Thomas Buford's Co, Bedford Co at Point Pleasant 10 Oct 1774 **CEM:** Boyd Family; GPS unk; Hwy 895, end of Rt 875; Mecklenburg **GS:** Y **SP:** 1) Mar(20 Apr 1789) Sarah Anderson Jones d/o of Tignal & (-----) Jones; 2) Mar (11 May 1803) Tabitha Walker **VI:** Son of Alexander & (-----) Boyd. Pen to widow commencing 30 Sep 1814 at $48 per yr. Styled Capt on GS **P:** Y **BLW:** unk **RG:** Y **MK:** N **PH:** unk **SS:** N pg 1249; Z pg 125; AG pg 256 **BS:** 54 pg 173.

BOYER, Henry; b 22 Feb 1757; d 7 Mar 1799 **RU:** Lieutenant, Served in a VA Regt in Illinois **CEM:** Old Christ Church Episcopal; GPS 38.80625, -77.04718; 118 N Washington St; Alexandria City **GS:** Y **SP:** Margaret (-----) who m (2) John Myers, RW veteran, barber, who d 17 Mar 1802 **VI:** Carpenter. GS styles him Lt, d age 43 yrs, 7 seven days; death notice in Alexandria Gazette 7 Mar 1799, pg 3 **P:** unk **BLW:** unk **RG:** Y **MK:** N **PH:** unk **SS:** J-NSSAR 1993 Reg; CZ pg 57 **BS:** JLARC 1; 20 pg 136; 196.

BOYER / BOWYER, Thomas; b unk; d 1785 **RU:** Captain, Served in 12th VA Regt of Foot as Cmdr of 10th Co 16 Dec 1776. Served in the 8th VA Regt and sent to Guilford CH Mar 1781 as temporay 3rd VA Regt. Served in Armand's Command **CEM:** Fincastle Presbyterian; GPS 37.50017, -79.87558; 108 E Back St, Fincastle; Botetourt **GS:** N **SP:** No info **VI:** Name is on the SAR plaque at this cemetery **P:** unk

RU=Rank/Unit   CEM=Cemetery   GS=Gravestone   SP=Spousal Information
VI=Other Veteran Info   P=Pension   BLW=Bounty/Land Warrant   RG=Registered Grave
MK=SAR/DAR Marker   PH=Photo   SS=Service Source   BS=Burial Source

39

BLW: unk **RG:** Y **MK:** Y **PH:** N **SS:** CE pg 58, 68; J-NSSAR 1993 Reg, J- DAR Hatcher; E pg 83 **BS:** JLARC 1, 2; 196.

BOYKIN, Simon; b unk; d 1834 **RU:** Captain, Served as Co commander in Southampton Co Militia 13 Oct 1774 extending into 1775 war period **CEM:** Boykin Family; GPS unk; Rt 460, across Blackwater River fr Zuni; Southampton **GS:** U **SP:** No info **VI:** Son of Simon (before 1731-1788) & (-----) Boykin **P:** unk **BLW:** unk **RG:** unk **MK:** unk **PH:** unk **SS:** AH pg 34 **BS:** 45 pg 18.

BOYKIN, Simon; b Before 1731; d 16 Jun 1788 **RU:** Patriot, Gave material aid to cause **CEM:** Boykin Family; GPS unk; Rt 460, across Blackwater River fr Zuni; Southampton **GS:** Y **SP:** No info **VI:** Son of William (1680-1731) & (-----) Boykin **P:** N **BLW:** N **RG:** Y **MK:** N **PH:** unk **SS:** AL Ct Bk pg 2 Southampton Co **BS:** 53 vol 7 pg 17.

BRACKETT, John I; b 1720; d 1785 **RU:** Patriot, Gave material aid to the cause **CEM:** Rural; GPS unk; See county property record for plantation; Henrico **GS:** Y **SP:** Elizabeth (-----) **VI:** Son of Thomas & Elizabeth (Ashe) Brackett **P:** N **BLW:** N **RG:** Y **MK:** N **PH:** unk **SS:** AL Ct bk pg 5 **BS:** AS, SAR registration.

BRADFORD, John; b 1717; d 1789 **RU:** Private, Served in a VA unit in Illinois **CEM:** St Paul's Episcopal; GPS 37.76570, -77.37120; 8050 St Paul's Rd, Hanover; Hanover **GS:** U **SP:** (-----) Timberlake **VI:** No further data **P:** unk **BLW:** unk **RG:** Y **MK:** unk **PH:** unk **SS:** CZ pg 59 **BS:** JLARC 2, 76.

BRADFORD, Thomas A; b 6 Mar 1764; d 8 Jul 1818 **RU:** Private, Served in Capt Levern Teakle's Co, 5th VA Regt fr 1778 to 1779 **CEM:** Bradford-Burton; GPS unk; Rt 182 and Rt 605, N fr Quinby; Accomack **GS:** Y **SP:** Mar (12 Oct 1786 (bond) Accomack Co) Alesy P. Bradford (12 Jan 1763-29 Mar 1825) **VI:** No further data **P:** unk **BLW:** unk **RG:** N **MK:** N **PH:** unk **SS:** AP 5th CL **BS:** 145 Burton.

BRADLEY, John; b 1748; d 1795 **RU:** Private, Served in Shelby's Co, Fincastle Troops. Was in battles at Long Island, Point Pleasant,and Kings Mountain **CEM:** Sinking Springs; GPS 36.71030, -81.98170; 136 E Main St, Abingdon; Washington **GS:** Y **SP:** Sarah Lillard (1745-1821) **VI:** Source 80 reports stone illegible. DAR marker **P:** unk **BLW:** unk **RG:** unk **MK:** Y **PH:** unk **SS:** J-NSSAR 2000 Reg; S, NSSAR Ancestor #P-119673 **BS:** JLARC 1, 2, 76; 80.

BRADLEY, William; b By 1758; d Aft 1774 **RU:** Sergeant, Served in Capt McKee's Co of Rockbridge Co at Point Pleasant in 1774. Later a Sgt in l5th VA Cont Line **CEM:** Cleek; GPS 38.19310, -79.73220; Rt 220 Sam Snead Hwy, Warm Springs; Bath **GS:** Y **SP:** No info **VI:** Govt stone says Sergeant, 5th VA Cont Line; R318 **P:** unk **BLW:** unk **RG:** unk **MK:** unk **PH:** unk **SS:** B; Z pg 136 **BS:** 196.

BRADLEY, William; b 1759, England; d 5 Feb 1819 **RU:** Sergeant, Served in VA Line and 3rd, 5th, 7th, and 11th Cont Lines **CEM:** Stonewall Jackson Memorial; GPS 37.78128, -79.44604; 314 S Main St; Lexington City **GS:** U **SP:** Mar (12 Mar 1791 Rockbridge Co) Mary Carlock or else wife was Elizabeth Susan (-----) (papers burned in Washington DC Fire) **VI:** Sol shown on list of invalid pensioners living in Rockbridge Co. Disability pen recd Rockbridge Co 1786. He recd pen of $60 per annum fr 13 Ju 1786 & was increased to $96 per annum under act of 24 Apr 1816. Papers destroyed in one of the Washington DC fires in War of 1812 **P:** Y **BLW:** unk **RG:** unk **MK:** unk **PH:** unk **SS:** E pg 86; CG pg 361; K Vol 1 pg 102 **BS:** JLARC 4,79.

BRAIDFOOT, John; b unk; d Aft 1781 **RU:** Chaplain, Specific service recorded Lib VA, Archives, Bounty Land Warrants shows was in US Army as Chaplain. Served with Washington throughout war period **CEM:** Trinity Episcopal; GPS 36.83459, -76.30105; 500 Court St; Portsmouth City **GS:** Y **SP:** Blondivalls or Blandinah Moseley **VI:** Believed "bur on the Glebe, and his original grave site lost". BLW 1832. DAR marker **P:** unk **BLW:** Y **RG:** Y **MK:** Y **PH:** unk **SS:** NSSAR Ancestor #P-119895; E pg 87; S; CU; CZ pg 59 **BS:** JLARC 2, 76, 105,127; 92, stone 6.

BRAME, Richens; b 2 Dec 1722; d 11 Apr 1789 **RU:** Patriot, Gave material aid to cause **CEM:** Young & Brame Family; GPS unk; 5 mi E of Boydton, 1 mi S of Antlers; Mecklenburg **GS:** N **SP:** Mar (14 Feb 1743) Susannah Chiles (13 Jun 1724 King William Co-5 Dec 1806) **VI:** Moved fr Caroline Co to Mecklenburg Co in 1760 **P:** N **BLW:** N **RG:** unk **MK:** N **PH:** N **SS:** AL Ct Bk pg 1, 17, 20 Mecklenburg Co **BS:** 196.

RU=Rank/Unit	CEM=Cemetery	GS=Gravestone	SP=Spousal Information
VI=Other Veteran Info	P=Pension	BLW=Bounty/Land Warrant	RG=Registered Grave
MK=SAR/DAR Marker	PH=Photo	SS=Service Source	BS=Burial Source

40

BRANCH, Olive; b 1758, Chesterfield Co; d 1845 **RU:** Private, Ent serv Bedford Co.Served in Buckingham Co Militia **CEM:** Branch; GPS 37.58250, -78.49000; Rt 631, Manteo; Buckingham **GS:** U **SP:** No info **VI:** Sol appl pen 10 Dec 1832 Buckingham Co age 72. S8101. R323 **P:** Y **BLW:** unk **RG:** unk **MK:** N **PH:** unk **SS:** E pg 88; K Vol 1 pg 104; CG pg 366 **BS:** JLARC 4, 44.

BRASSON, Jean; b unk; d 1781 **RU:** Seaman, Served on "Magnanime" and died from Yorktown battle **CEM:** French Memorial; GPS 36.81944, -79.39933; Yorktown; York **GS:** U **SP:** No info **VI:** No further data **P:** unk **BLW:** unk **RG:** Y **MK:** unk **PH:** unk **SS:** J-Yorktown Historian **BS:** JLARC 1, 74.

BRATTON, James; b 30 Jun 1746, Ireland; d 29 Jun 1828 **RU:** Captain, Commanded a company Augusta Co Militia, 21 Aug 1781 **CEM:** Bratton; GPS 37.99750, -79.56170; Rts 39 & 42 Mountain Valley Rd 4 mi E of Millboro Springs; Bath **GS:** Y **SP:** Mar (abt 1774) Rebecca Hogshead **VI:** Son Robert Bratton and Ann McFarland **P:** unk **BLW:** unk **RG:** N **MK:** N **PH:** unk **SS:** AZ pg 181 **BS:** 159 Bratton; 196.

BRATTON, James; b unk; d 2 Jan 1814 **RU:** Captain, Served in Augusta Co Militia. Commissioned capt 26 Aug 1781 **CEM:** Craig; GPS unk; Christiansburg; Montgomery **GS:** Y **SP:** Elizabeth M. (-----) (__-25 Jul 1806) **VI:** No further data **P:** unk **BLW:** unk **RG:** Y **MK:** N **PH:** unk **SS:** E pg 90 **BS:** 04, Jul 06; 123 pg 68; 196.

BRATTON, Robert; b 20 May 1712, Ireland; d Aft 18 Oct 1785 **RU:** Patriot, Gave material aid to cause **CEM:** Bratton Family; GPS unk; Nr Goshen; Augusta **GS:** U **SP:** Anne McFarland Dunlap **VI:** No further data **P:** N **BLW:** N **RG:** Y **MK:** unk **PH:** unk **SS:** D Vol I pg 88, 92-94, 96 **BS:** JLARC 2, 76.

BRAWNER, William Henry; b unk; d unk **RU:** Soldier, Obtain SAR application for service **CEM:** Presbyterian Church; GPS 38.80015, -77.05791; Wilkes St & Hamilton Ln; Alexandria City **GS:** U **SP:** no info **VI:** Obtain SAR application for birth and death dates **P:** unk **BLW:** unk **RG:** Y **MK:** unk **PH:** unk **SS:** SAR Ancestor #P-120258; J-NSSAR 1993 Reg **BS:** JLARC 1.

BRAXTON, Carter; b 10 Sep 1736; d 10 Oct 1797 **RU:** Patriot, Voted for independence, signed the Declaration, and then left Congress to return the next yr. In VA, supported bill to recruit slaves to fight for Rev, to be given freedom in exchange for their service (bill defeated). Gave material aid to cause. Was in Cont Congress and the Congress of the Confederation 1775-1776, 1777-1783 & 1785 **CEM:** Braxton Estate; GPS unk; Chericoke; King George **GS:** Y **SP:** 1) Judith Robinson (1736-1757) 2) Elizabeth Corbin (1745-1814) **VI:** Braxton Co in what is now WV was named for him **P:** N **BLW:** N **RG:** N **MK:** N **PH:** unk **SS:** N pg 145 **BS:** 196; 80 vol 1 pg 108.

BRECKENRIDGE, James; b 7 Mar 1763; d 13 May 1833 **RU:** Private, Served in Col Preston's Regt under Gen Green **CEM:** Breckenridge Family; GPS unk; Grove Hill Farm 1 mi NW of Fincastle on Rt 606; Botetourt **GS:** U **SP:** Mar (1 Jan 1791 Richmond) Nancy Ann Cary Selden d/o Cary & (-----) Sheldon **VI:** Son of Col Robert & (-----) Breckenridge. Resided at Grove Hill in Botetourt. US Army Brigadier General, US Congressman, member of State House of Delegates 1789-1824. In 1809 elected as a Federalist to the Eleventh Congress and to the three succeeding Congresses, serving until 1817 **P:** unk **BLW:** unk **RG:** Y **MK:** unk **PH:** unk **SS:** N pg 737 **BS:** JLARC 1,2,60,124.

BREEDEN, George; b 1764; d 1847 **RU:** Soldier, Obtain SAR application for service **CEM:** Jones-Van Lear; GPS unk; Rt 613, .3 mi S jct with Rt 742 farm of Alfred Ryder; Augusta **GS:** U **SP:** No info **VI:** No further data **P:** unk **BLW:** unk **RG:** unk **MK:** U **PH:** unk **SS:** SAR Ancestor #P-120439; JLARC 62 **BS:** JLARC 62.

BRENEMAN, Abraham; b 1744; d 1815 **RU:** Private, Served in Capt Jacob Holman's Co, Dunmore Co Militia **CEM:** Lindale Mennonite; GPS unk; Jesse Bennett Way,Linville; Rockingham **GS:** Y **SP:** Marie/Maria Reiff **VI:** No further data **P:** unk **BLW:** unk **RG:** Y **MK:** N **PH:** unk **SS:** C pg 607 **BS:** 04, 05 Oct 09.

BRENT, Richard; b 1757, Aquia Creek off Potomac, Stafford Co; d 30 Dec 1814 **RU:** Seaman, Served in US Navy **CEM:** Richland, aka Brent Family); GPS unk; Rt 637, Aquia; Stafford **GS:** U **SP:** Mar (7 Dec 1795) Rachel Moore **VI:** Was in VA House of Delegates fr Stafford Co 1788, Prince William Co 1793, 1794, 1800, 1801. US Rep to 4th & 5th Congresses 1795-99. 7th Congress 1801-03. State Senator fr

RU=Rank/Unit	CEM=Cemetery	GS=Gravestone	SP=Spousal Information
VI=Other Veteran Info	P=Pension	BLW=Bounty/Land Warrant	RG=Registered Grave
MK=SAR/DAR Marker	PH=Photo	SS=Service Source	BS=Burial Source

41

1808-09. US Senator 1809-1814. Died in Washington DC **P:** unk **BLW:** Y **RG:** unk **MK:** unk **PH:** unk **SS:** G pg 784 **BS:** 201 pg 1795.

BREWER, Lewis; b 1760; d 1839 **RU:** Private, Served in Capt Ballard's Co 20 July 1778 for 9 mos **CEM:** Rudy; GPS unk; Rt 660 near Elk Creek, Independence; Grayson **GS:** U **SP:** No info **VI:** No further data **P:** unk **BLW:** unk **RG:** Y **MK:** unk **PH:** unk **SS:** J-NSSAR 1993 Reg, J- DAR Hatcher; CH Roster of Soldiers fr NC During Rev War **BS:** JLARC 1, 2.

BRIAN, Louis; b unk; d 1781 **RU:** Soldier, Served in Gatinais Bn and died from Yorktown battle **CEM:** French Memorial; GPS 36.81944, -79.39933; Yorktown; York **GS:** U **SP:** No info **VI:** No further data **P:** unk **BLW:** unk **RG:** Y **MK:** unk **PH:** unk **SS:** J-Yorktown Historian **BS:** JLARC 1, 74.

BRICKEY, Peter; b 10 Apr 1761, Westmoreland Co; d 1836 **RU:** Private, Ent serv Botetourt Co Sep 1780 for 6 mos in Capt Saunders & Wm McClanahan's Cos. Was in Battles in NC, Reedy Fork & Guilford CH **CEM:** Brickey Family; GPS unk; See county property records for homeplace; Botetourt **GS:** U **SP:** 1) Mar (Sep 1806) Elizabeth (-----) (__- by 1820) 2) Mar (1820) Elizabeth Dunn **VI:** Pension rejected as served less than 6 mo. Source 76 has his death in 1860. BLW #44.800 (160 acres). Widow had BLW fr Carter Co TN 1855 age 56 R333 **P:** unk **BLW:** Y **RG:** Y **MK:** unk **PH:** unk **SS:** SAR Applic; K Vol 1 pg 108 **BS:** JLARC 1, 4, 60, 76.

BRIDGES, Richard; b 1752; d 1826 **RU:** Sergeant, Served in Gen Nelson's Corps in VA Light Dragoons **CEM:** Cool Spring Farm; GPS unk; 10065 Rozell Rd, Woodford; Caroline **GS:** U **SP:** Anne Johnson Norment **VI:** No further data **P:** unk **BLW:** unk **RG:** Y **MK:** N **PH:** unk **SS:** J-NSSAR 2000 Reg; E pg 93 **BS:** JLARC 76.

BRIGGS, David; b 1730; d 3 Dec 1815 **RU:** Patriot, Gave 600# fodder and 3 beeves to cause **CEM:** Stony Hill; GPS unk; Stony Hill Rd nr Curtis Lake; Stafford **GS:** Y **SP:** Jane (-----) (c1760-6 Jun 1810) **VI:** No further data **P:** N **BLW:** N **RG:** Y **MK:** N **PH:** unk **SS:** D pg 882 **BS:** 03 pg 366.

BRIGHT, John; b 8 Apr 1753, Germany; d 8 Oct 1826 **RU:** Private, Served in Capt Tate's Co in Augusta Co Militia **CEM:** Bethel Cemetery; GPS 38.47592, -78.75641; 3061 Armentrout Path, Keezletown; Rockingham **GS:** N **SP:** Ann Fawcett **VI:** No further data **P:** unk **BLW:** unk **RG:** Y **MK:** N **PH:** N **SS:** E pg 93; AK Sep 09; BD **BS:** 196.

BRIZENDINE, William Sr; b 1743, Essex Co; d 1833 **RU:** Private, Ent serv Charlotte Co 1781 **CEM:** Private; GPS unk; Nr Glade Hill; Franklin **GS:** U **SP:** Mary Dupree **VI:** Pension 1832 in Franklin Co, R (reel) 345 **P:** Y **BLW:** unk **RG:** Y **MK:** unk **PH:** unk **SS:** J-NSSAR 2000 Reg; K Vol I pg 111 **BS:** JLARC 76.

BROADWATER, Charles; b 1717; d 20 Mar 1806 **RU:** Colonel/Patriot, Served in Fairfax Co Militia, 1776-1780. Probably applies to Charles Lewis Broadwater. Gave material aid to cause **CEM:** Broadwater Family; GPS 38.88940, -77.2610; Cnr of Tapawingo Rd and Frederick St SW, Vienna; Fairfax **GS:** Y **SP:** 1) Ann Amelia Markham or Ann Pierson 2) Sarah Ann Harris **VI:** Burgess fr Fairfax in 1774. Delivered Fairfax Resolves in company of Geo. Washington to Alexandria. Helped establish VA Navy. Member Fairfax Co Committee of Safety. Rep to 1st, 2nd, 3rd, and 4th Convs. Justice of Peace, VA House of Delegates. This may apply to Charles Lewis Broadwater. Stone for Charles Broadwater simply says "Colonial Service" Obit in Alexandria Gazette 21 Mar 1806 pg 3 says he d on the 20th instant **P:** unk **BLW:** unk **RG:** Y **MK:** Y **PH:** unk **SS:** D Fairfax Co **BS:** JLARC 1, 2, 13, 27, 28; 196.

BROADWATER, Charles Lewis; b 1751; d 18 Sep 1841 **RU:** Lieutenant, Ent Serv 1776 Fairfax Co. Was Midshipman, VA State Navy 8 Mar 1776; Lt, 10th Va Regt, 18 Nov 1776. Dismissed 21 Apr 1778. Fairfax Co Militia, 1779 **CEM:** Broadwater Family; GPS 38.88940, -77.2610; Cnr of Tapawingo Rd and Frederick St SW, Vienna; Fairfax **GS:** Y **SP:** Betheland Sebastian (1750-before 1841). Died earlier than husband. **VI:** Son of Charles (1717-1806) & Ann Amelia (Markham) (1708-1796) Broadwater. Pensioned Fairfax Co 1830 age 78. Pen S.8096. R346. Small stone with engraved metal plate reads "Lieut Chas L Broadwater 10 VA Regt Rev War" **P:** Y **BLW:** unk **RG:** Y **MK:** Y **PH:** Y **SS:** K Vol 1 pg 112 **BS:** JLARC 1, 2 ,4 13, 27, 28, 45; 196.

RU=Rank/Unit	CEM=Cemetery	GS=Gravestone	SP=Spousal Information
VI=Other Veteran Info	P=Pension	BLW=Bounty/Land Warrant	RG=Registered Grave
MK=SAR/DAR Marker	PH=Photo	SS=Service Source	BS=Burial Source

42

BROCK, John P; b unk; d unk **RU:** Private, Specific service recorded Lib VA, Archives,War, vol 4, pg 28 **CEM:** Brock Spring; GPS unk; Old Telegraph Rd; Hanover **GS:** N **SP:** No info **VI:** No further data **P:** unk **BLW:** unk **RG:** Y **MK:** N **PH:** N **SS:** E pg 96; CZ pg 64 **BS:** 31 vol 1 pg 43.

BROCK, John Sr; b 28 Jun 1753; d 17 Apr 1827 **RU:** First Lieutenant, Appt 1/Lt, 2 Dec 1776. Retired 30 Sep 1778. Served in 10th VA Regt in Capt John Spotswood's Co of Foot **CEM:** Brock Family; GPS 36.71055, -79.55003; 2401 Indian Trail Rd, Keezletown 22832; Rockingham **GS:** Y **SP:** Ann Jones **VI:** No further data **P:** unk **BLW:** unk **RG:** Y **MK:** N **PH:** unk **SS:** E pg 96 **BS:** 04.

BROCKENBROUGH, John; b 1750; d 20 Nov 1801 **RU:** Private/Patriot, Served in 4th Cont Line. Gave material aid to the cause **CEM:** Doctor's Hall; GPS unk; Nr jct Rappahannock River & Creek; Richmond Co **GS:** Y **SP:** Sarah Roane (d. 1810) **VI:** Son of Col William & Margaret (Flauntleroy) Brockenbrough. Also was signer of the Westmoreland protest of 1764 against the Stamp Act. After war Judge Gen Ct of VA in 1818 **P:** unk **BLW:** unk **RG:** N **MK:** N **PH:** unk **SS:** AL Ct Bk pg 6; E pg 99 **BS:** 108 pg 556-7.

BROCKENBROUGH, William; b 5 Jun 1715; d 1778 **RU:** Colonel, Mil serv during war period not identified. Was signer of Leedstown Resolutions fr Spotsylvania Co **CEM:** Cem name unk; GPS unk; See property Records for cem loc; Richmond Co **GS:** U **SP:** Mar (25 Nov 1735) Elizabeth Fauntleroy d/o Moore & Margaret (Micou) Fautleroy **VI:** Son of Austin (1685-1717) & Mary (Metcalfe) Brockenbrough **P:** unk **BLW:** unk **RG:** Y **MK:** N **PH:** unk **SS:** E pg 97; BQ **BS:** SAR Applic.

BROCKMAN, Samuel Jr; b 1730; d 1790 **RU:** Lieutenant/Patriot, Recommended 1777 as Lt in Orange Co Militia. Gave material aid to cause **CEM:** Brockman Family; GPS unk; Greenway, Monrovia; Orange **GS:** U **SP:** 1) Rebecca Graves (4 Sep 1735, Spotsylvania Co-__) 2) Mary Woolford **VI:** Son of Samuel Sr (1685, St Marys, MD-__) & Mary Henderson (Collins) (1685, Orange Co-__) Brockman. Died in St Thomas Parish **P:** unk **BLW:** unk **RG:** unk **MK:** unk **PH:** unk **SS:** E pg 97; Al Ct Bk pg 5 **BS:** 196.

BROCKMAN, William Sr; b 1718 Newtown, King & Queen Co; d 1809 **RU:** Patriot, Donated 50 bushels of wheat and carted it 8 mi **CEM:** Brockman-Mitchell; GPS unk; Petty's Creek Annex, Stony Point; Albemarle **GS:** Y **SP:** Elizabeth "Betty" Embree (?) **VI:** Son of Samuel Brockman (1685-1766) & Mary Madison (d. 1776). In French & Indian War in 1750s, enlisted in VA militia. Lived in Orange Co **P:** N **BLW:** N **RG:** unk **MK:** unk **PH:** unk **SS:** AL Ct Book pg 2; Commissioners book: IV pg 180 Certificate 1 Lists pg 15 **BS:** 196.

BRODY, John; b unk; d 1848 **RU:** Soldier, Was black soldier who served as body guard to Capt William Campbell **CEM:** Brody Family; GPS unk; Saltville; Smyth **GS:** U **SP:** No info **VI:** Honored w/ others on monument in front of Smyth Co CH **P:** unk **BLW:** unk **RG:** unk **MK:** unk **PH:** unk **SS:** S NSSAR Ancestor #P-121619 **BS:** JLARC 114.

BRONOUGH, Thomas; b 1741; d 1794 **RU:** Patriot/Captain, Commanded a company in Fauquier Co Militia 25 May 1778. Gave material aid to the cause **CEM:** Bronough Family; GPS unk; Blue Ridge No Sub Div; Fauquier **GS:** N **SP:** Mar (19 Oct 1790 Fauquier Co) Peggy Kerr, d/o John & Sarah (-----) Kerr **VI:** Justice of Peace, 1787. County Sheriff 1790 **P:** unk **BLW:** unk **RG:** Y **MK:** N **PH:** N **SS:** AV; Fauquier Co Marriages pg 23 **BS:** 83, Inv # 61.

BROOK, Edmund (Edmond); b 1761; d 1835 **RU:** First Lieutenant, Appt Feb 1781, in 1st Regt of Artillery, Cont Line under Col Charles Harrison until Sept 1781 before Yorktown Battle **CEM:** Cem name unk; GPS unk; Snowville; Pulaski **GS:** Y **SP:** No info **VI:** Source at NARA for a claim for pay under Act of 15 May 1828 **P:** unk **BLW:** unk **RG:** Y **MK:** N **PH:** unk **SS:** A pg 388 **BS:** AS, SAR regis, Application 48, 1445, 1514.

BROOKE, Francis Taliaferro; b 27 Aug 1763; d 3 Mar 1851 **RU:** Major, Ent serv Essex Co 1781. With twin John, appointed 1st Lt in Gen Harrison's 1st Cont Regt of Artillery at age 16. Fought in VA campaign. After Battle of Green Springs joined Maj Gen Nathaniel Greene in Southern Dept, not returning to VA until Aug 1782. Was Deputy Quartermaster of Harrison's Brigade and served as Maj under General Greene **CEM:** Brooke Family; GPS unk; Rt 2, 6 mi N Fredericksburg, E side of St Julian house; Spotsylvania **GS:** Y **SP:** 1) Mar (3 Oct 1791 Nottingham) Mary Randolph Spotswood 2) Mar (14 Feb 1804, Fredericksburg Co) Mary Champe Carter, Robert S. Chew, security [Catherine L Knorr Marriages of Fredericksburg, VA 1782-1850 Pine Bluff AR 1954] pg 6 **VI:** Son of Richard & Ann May (Taliaferro) Brooke. Judge of VA Ct of Appeals 1848. Pensioned Georgetown DC, increase 1832 &

RU=Rank/Unit	CEM=Cemetery	GS=Gravestone	SP=Spousal Information
VI=Other Veteran Info	P=Pension	BLW=Bounty/Land Warrant	RG=Registered Grave
MK=SAR/DAR Marker	PH=Photo	SS=Service Source	BS=Burial Source

43

1850. Recd pen Spotsylvania Co 1832 and increase in pay under Act of 1850. R350 **P:** Y **BLW:** Y **RG:** Y **MK:** unk **PH:** unk **SS:** BY pg 14; K Vol 1 pg 113 **BS:** JLARC 1, 76; 196.

BROOKE, Robert; b 1751, Spotsylvania Co; d 25 Feb 1799 **RU:** Private, Served in Capt Larkin Smith's Calvary Co, 7th Cont Line. Was captured by British at Wesham **CEM:** Masonic Cemetery; GPS 38.30198, -77.46142; 900 Charles St; Fredericksburg City **GS:** U **SP:** Mar (1766) Mary Richie **VI:** Represented Spotsylvania Co in House of Delegates 1791-1794. Governor of VA 1794. Freemason in VA fr 1795-97. Nov 1795 succeeded John Marshall as Grand Master of Grand Lodge of Virginia **P:** unk **BLW:** unk **RG:** unk **MK:** unk **PH:** unk **SS:** E pg 98 **BS:** 196.

BROOKS, Elias; b 1759, Essex Co; d 1838 **RU:** Soldier, Ent serv in Chesterfield Co. Served in 3rd Regiment, VA State Line **CEM:** Brooks Family; GPS unk; North of Walmsley Blvd btw Angus and Shackleford roads; Chesterfield **GS:** U **SP:** No info **VI:** Son of Elias & (-----) Brooks, Sr. Pen Chestervield Co 1832, age 73 and last payment 3rd quarter 1838, R 352 **P:** Y **BLW:** unk **RG:** unk **MK:** N **PH:** unk **SS:** K Vol 1 pg 114 **BS:** JLARC 4, 35.

BROOKS, John; b 1748; d 1840 **RU:** Private, Served in Capt Wm. Bentley's Co, 3rd VA Regt in Dec 1778 **CEM:** Brooks Private; GPS unk; Rt 681 W of Halifax, Cluster Springs; Halifax **GS:** U **SP:** 1) (-----) 2) Sarah Falkner **VI:** No further data **P:** unk **BLW:** unk **RG:** Y **MK:** unk **PH:** unk **SS:** AP Payroll code; CI-Fold 3 website **BS:** JLARC 1, 76; 215.

BROOKS, John Turpin; b 1755; d 26 Jan 1821 **RU:** Private?, Specific service recorded Lib VA, Archives, Auditors Acct, vol XXXI, pg 361 **CEM:** Presbyterian Church; GPS 38.80015, -77.05791; Wilkes St & Hamilton Ln; Alexandria City **GS:** Y **SP:** No info **VI:** Died ae 66. Member Baptist Church **P:** unk **BLW:** unk **RG:** Y **MK:** N **PH:** unk **SS:** E pg 98; CZ pg 65 **BS:** 23 pg 16.

BROOKS, William; b 1752; d 24 Jan 1854 **RU:** Private, Ent serv 1777 in Culpeper Co **CEM:** Brooks; GPS unk; Rt 604, .2 mi fr grocery behind silo, Thompson Valley; Tazewell **GS:** U **SP:** Mar (5 Sep 1769) Nancy (-----) (1749-after 1843) **VI:** Pen Tazewell Co 1832, Widow pension R (reel) 355 **P:** Y **BLW:** unk **RG:** Y **MK:** unk **PH:** unk **SS:** K Vol I pg 115 **BS:** JLARC 1, 2, 89.

BROSTMAN, Jean; b unk; d 1781 **RU:** Soldier, Served in Gatinais Bn and died from Yorktown battle **CEM:** French Memorial; GPS 36.81944, -79.39933; Yorktown; York **GS:** U **SP:** No info **VI:** No further data **P:** unk **BLW:** unk **RG:** Y **MK:** unk **PH:** unk **SS:** J-Yorktown Historian **BS:** JLARC 1, 74.

BROUGH, Daniel; b 19 Jul 1762; d 26 Dec 1825 **RU:** Patriot, Paid supply tax 1783, Botetourt Co **CEM:** Old Dutch; GPS unk; W side of Rt 11 at Mill Creek, 9 mi S of Buchanan; Botetourt **GS:** U **SP:** Elizabeth (-----) **VI:** No further data **P:** N **BLW:** N **RG:** unk **MK:** N **PH:** unk **SS:** J- DAR Hatcher; DI RG 4, 61, roll #343 **BS:** JLARC 2.

BROWN, Bazael (Bazel); b unk; d unk **RU:** Captain, As Pvt serv in 1779 in Capt Abriah Springer's Co 9th VA Regt under Col Gibson; as Cpl serv in Capt James Seal's Co of 9th VA Regt **CEM:** Brown Family 1; GPS unk; Mt Fair nr Charlottesville; Charlottesville City **GS:** N **SP:** No info **VI:** Pen #S9713 **P:** Y **BLW:** unk **RG:** Y **MK:** unk **PH:** N **SS:** J-NSSAR 2000 Reg; AP record; CI fold 3 website **BS:** JLARC 76.

BROWN, Benjamin; b 1751; d 1842 **RU:** Ensign, Served in Henley's Co Cont Line **CEM:** Physics Springs; GPS unk; Buckingham; Buckingham **GS:** U **SP:** Mary Jarman **VI:** No further data **P:** unk **BLW:** unk **RG:** Y **MK:** N **PH:** unk **SS:** AP Record; CI fold 3 website **BS:** JLARC 2, 76.

BROWN, Benjamin; b 1767; d 1806 **RU:** Seaman, Served in 4th Cont Line **CEM:** St John's Episcopal; GPS unk; 100 W Queen's Way; Hampton City **GS:** Y **SP:** No info **VI:** No further data **P:** unk **BLW:** unk **RG:** N **MK:** N **PH:** unk **SS:** C pg 326; E pg 88 **BS:** 89, pg 19.

BROWN, Bernis; b 15 Aug 1752; d 30 Oct 1814 **RU:** Private? Ent serv Albemarle Co **CEM:** Brown Family 2; GPS unk; Rt 810, Brown's Cove; Albemarle **GS:** Y **SP:** Mar (14 Nov 1779, AlbeMarle Co) Henrietta Rhodes, (26 May 1761-1 Jul 1840 Brown's Cove) **VI:** Widow's pension 1842 age 81. Her pension rejected as he was not in regularly constituted military unit. R 360 **P:** Y **BLW:** unk **RG:** N **MK:** N **PH:** unk **SS:** K Vol 1 pg 117 **BS:** 80 pg 119; 176.

BROWN, Brightberry; b 13 Feb 1762; d 26 Jan 1846 **RU:** Captain, Ent serv Brown's Cove, Albemarle Co 1780 **CEM:** Brightberry Brown Family; GPS 38.20972, -78.67243; 5525 Brown's Gap Turnpike,

RU=Rank/Unit   CEM=Cemetery   GS=Gravestone   SP=Spousal Information
VI=Other Veteran Info   P=Pension   BLW=Bounty/Land Warrant   RG=Registered Grave
MK=SAR/DAR Marker   PH=Photo   SS=Service Source   BS=Burial Source

44

Brown's Cove; Albemarle **GS:** N **SP:** Mar (10 Jan 1788) Mary Susan "Suca" Madison (21 Jan 1776-14 Aug 1832) **VI:** Pension 1832 R360 **P:** Y **BLW:** unk **RG:** Y **MK:** unk **PH:** N **SS:** J-NSSAR 2000 Reg; K Vol 1 pg 117 **BS:** JLARC 76; 196.

BROWN, Christopher Sr; b 16 Jul 1751, Lancaster Co, PA; d 16 Jul 1816 **RU:** Private, Served in Capt Michael Moyer, 6th Battalion, Lancaster Co PA Militia **CEM:** St John's Lutheran; GPS 36.96500, -81.10110; 405 W Main, Wytheville; Wythe **GS:** Y **SP:** Mar (2 Jun 1772 Whytheville, Wythe Co) Anna Maria Mason (10 Oct 754 Philadelphia-10 May 1822) **VI:** Son of Johan Michael (1724-1785) & Anna Juliana (Karger) (1728-1785) Braun **P:** unk **BLW:** unk **RG:** unk **MK:** unk **PH:** unk **SS:** CI PA Archives, 5th Series Vol 7 pg 560-561 **BS:** JLARC 122, 123; 196.

BROWN, Daniel; b 1 Dec 1748, Culpeper Co (then Orange Co); d 14 Jul 1833 **RU:** Captain, Ent serv Culpeper Co 1 Dec 1748. Served as Lt in Capt Burgess Ball's Co, 5th VA Regt, appointed Capt May 1777 **CEM:** Brown; GPS unk; 1 mi NW of Reva on Rt 636, then 2 mi NW to gate; Culpeper **GS:** N **SP:** Mar (25 Dec 1779 Culpeper Co) Elizabeth Hill (she age 15 c1764-2 Jan 1852) **VI:** Pen 1832 Culpeper Co. Widow pension 1837, R362 **P:** Y **BLW:** unk **RG:** Y **MK:** unk **PH:** N **SS:** K Vol 1 pg 118 **BS:** JLARC 1, 76.

BROWN, Henry; b c1736; d 7 May 1782 **RU:** Patriot, Gave material aid to the cause **CEM:** Trinity Episcopal; GPS 36.83459, -76.30105; 500 Court St; Portsmouth City **GS:** Y **SP:** No info **VI:** Was a mariner in Norfolk Co **P:** N **BLW:** N **RG:** Y **MK:** N **PH:** unk **SS:** AL Ct Bk pg 30 **BS:** 92, stone 42.

BROWN, Henry; b 25 Oct 1759, Prince George Co; d 26 Dec 1849 **RU:** Private, ESF 1779 Bedford Co. Reenlisted 1780 as Orderly Sgt in Capt Robert Adam's Co, Col Lynch's Regt. Reenlisted 1781 in Col Parker's Regt **CEM:** Brown Family-Thompson Valley; GPS unk; New London; Campbell **GS:** U **SP:** Mar (29 Aug 1827 Buckingham Co) Elizabeth L. Jones **VI:** Recd pen 1832 Campbell Co age 72. Widow pen and drew BLW at age 76 in Campbell Co R365. Possible duplicate with Henry Brown in Bedford **P:** Y **BLW:** Y **RG:** Y **MK:** N **PH:** unk **SS:** J-NSSAR 1993 Reg; K Vol 1 pg 118 **BS:** JLARC 1.

BROWN, Henry; b 10 Aug 1760; d 13 Aug 1841 **RU:** Soldier, Wounded at Guilford CH **CEM:** Brown Family; GPS unk; Off New London Rd Rt 709, Forest; Bedford **GS:** N **SP:** Frances Thompson (6 Jun 1775-14 Aug 1822) **VI:** Opened store in New London with his brother Daniel and was Treasurer of New London Agricultural Society (New London is now in Campbell Co). Was Federal Tax Collector in Bedford 1800-1803, and serveral times Sheriff of Bedford Co **P:** unk **BLW:** unk **RG:** unk **MK:** N **PH:** N **SS:** J- DAR Hatcher; S NSSAR Ancestor #P-122498 **BS:** JLARC 2; 197.

BROWN, Isaac; b England; d 27 Aug 1785 **RU:** Sergeant, Served in Capt Wm Smith's Co, 11th Regt of Foot, commanded by Lt Col John Cropper **CEM:** Brown Family; GPS unk; New Castle; Hanover **GS:** Y **SP:** No info **VI:** No further data **P:** unk **BLW:** unk **RG:** N **MK:** N **PH:** unk **SS:** AL Lists pg 17 **BS:** 101 pg 146.

BROWN, Isaacher; b 1760; d 1840 **RU:** Private, Ent service 1780 in Upper Dublin Twp, Montgomery Co, PA **CEM:** North Fork Baptist; GPS 39.06014, -77.68509; 38130 North Folk Rd, North Fork; Loudoun **GS:** U **SP:** No info **VI:** Pensioned age 71 Loudoun Co, 1832 R366 **P:** Y **BLW:** unk **RG:** Y **MK:** unk **PH:** unk **SS:** K Vol I pg 117 **BS:** JLARC 1, 4, 32.

BROWN, James; b unk; d Sep 1801 **RU:** Private, Served in Capt Young's Co, Augusta Co Militia **CEM:** Samuel Brown Family; GPS unk; 9 mi W of Covington; Covington City **GS:** N **SP:** Agnes (-----), d Jan 1809 **VI:** No further data **P:** unk **BLW:** unk **RG:** N **MK:** N **PH:** N **SS:** E pg 100 **BS:** 160 Sam Brown.

BROWN, John; b 1749; d 2 Jun 1828 **RU:** Patriot, Gave material aid to cause **CEM:** Goose Creek; GPS 39.11250, -77.69527; Rt 722, Lincoln; Loudoun **GS:** Y **SP:** Martha Bell (1754-1784) **VI:** Son of Henry & Esther (-----) Harris **P:** N **BLW:** N **RG:** unk **MK:** unk **PH:** unk **SS:** AL Ct Bk pg 28; Comm Bk II pg 286 Loudoun Co **BS:** 196.

BROWN, John; b c1765; d 1867 **RU:** Private, Served in 3rd Regt, VA state line **CEM:** Brown-Osborne; GPS unk; 1168 White Pine Rd; Grayson **GS:** U **SP:** No info **VI:** No further data **P:** unk **BLW:** unk **RG:** Y **MK:** N **PH:** unk **SS:** AK Apr 2007 **BS:** 04, Apr 2007.

BROWN, John; b 1759; d Aft 1820 **RU:** Soldier/Patriot, Ent serv 1777, Pittsylvania Co, Served in VA Line. Gave material aid to cause **CEM:** Brown Family; GPS unk; Off Rt 705; Campbell **GS:** U **SP:** Two

RU=Rank/Unit   CEM=Cemetery   GS=Gravestone   SP=Spousal Information
VI=Other Veteran Info   P=Pension   BLW=Bounty/Land Warrant   RG=Registered Grave
MK=SAR/DAR Marker   PH=Photo   SS=Service Source   BS=Burial Source

45

marriages but do not know the order: 1) Nancy (-----); 2) Mar (19 May 1800, Campbell Co. (bond), bondsman Armistead Dudley) Phillis Dudley **VI:** No further data **P:** Y **BLW:** unk **RG:** unk **MK:** N **PH:** unk **SS:** D Campbell Co **BS:** JLARC 4, 36.

BROWN, Jonas; b unk; d 18 Oct 1781 **RU:** Sergeant, Promoted 27 Mar 1778, Capt Charles Graham's 3rd Co, Col Van Cortlandt's 2d Regt, NY Line and died as result of Yorktown battle **CEM:** Yorktown Victory Monument Tablet; GPS 38.28350, -78.54150; Yorktown; York **GS:** U **SP:** No info **VI:** No further data **P:** unk **BLW:** unk **RG:** unk **MK:** unk **PH:** unk **SS:** J-Yorktown Historian; AX pg 188 **BS:** JLARC 74.

BROWN, Low (Lowe); b 1756; d 28 Jan 1841 **RU:** Private, Ent serv Montgomery Co, 1776. Served in IL Regt under Capt George Rogers Clark on the Vincennes Expedition in 1779. Was Spy for Capt James Moore on the Bluestone, Clinch, & New Rivers. Was in Battle of Kings Mountain. **CEM:** Hezekiah Harman; GPS unk; In front of HS off Rts 460 & 19, Tazewell; Tazewell **GS:** Y **SP:** Jane Davidson, d/o John Goolman & (-----) Davidson **VI:** Son of William & Mary (Lowe) Brown, both b in Scotland. Entered service 1774, Montgomery Co for Indian Wars (Lord Dunmore's War). Pensioned Tazewell Co 1832 age 76. Govt grave stone. 1832, R373 **P:** Y **BLW:** unk **RG:** Y **MK:** unk **PH:** unk **SS:** K Vol 1 pg 121; CV pg 218 **BS:** JLARC 1, 3, 26, 89; 196.

BROWN, Richard; b 13 Nov 1735; d 27 Dec 1781 **RU:** Patriot, Gave material aid to cause **CEM:** St John's Episcopal; GPS 37.53183, -77.41958; 2401 E Broad St; Richmond City **GS:** Y **SP:** No info **VI:** No further data **P:** unk **BLW:** unk **RG:** Y **MK:** N **PH:** unk **SS:** C pg 66; Al Ct Bk pg 59 Chesterfield Co **BS:** 39 pg 99.

BROWN, William; b unk; d 1820 **RU:** Midshipman, Served on ship,"Tempest," 1779 **CEM:** St John's Episcopal; GPS 37.53183, -77.41958; 2401 E Broad St; Richmond City **GS:** Y **SP:** No info **VI:** No further data **P:** unk **BLW:** unk **RG:** N **MK:** N **PH:** unk **SS:** BE pg 71 **BS:** 28 pg 419.

BROWN, William; b 1748 or 1749, East Lothian, Scotland; d 13 Jan 1792 **RU:** Physician, Performed as Surgeon General of Hosp, 13 May 1777 and as Director General of Hosp 21 Jul 1780 **CEM:** Pohick Episcopal; GPS 38.42546, -77.11598; 9301 Richmond Hwy, Lorton; Fairfax **GS:** Y **SP:** Catherine Scott, d/o Rev James & Sarah (Brown) Scott **VI:** Son of Richard & Helen (Bailey) Brown. Graduate University of Edenburgh 1770. Originally bur at Preson in Fairfax Co. Moved to Pohick Church in 1921. BLW 6000 acres. Died in Alexandria City **P:** unk **BLW:** Y **RG:** Y **MK:** unk **PH:** Y **SS:** E pg 102 **BS:** JLARC 1, 14, 28.

BROWN, William; b 1757; d 1789 **RU:** Private, Service information not specified in SAR application **CEM:** Brown Family; GPS unk; Eagle hills; Scott **GS:** Y **SP:** No info **VI:** No further data **P:** unk **BLW:** unk **RG:** N **MK:** N **PH:** unk **SS:** AS SAR applic **BS:** 80 vol 1 pg 124.

BROWNE, William; b 17 Sep 1759; d 15 Nov 1799 **RU:** Patriot, Gave material aid to the cause **CEM:** Four Mile Tree; GPS unk; off Swan's Point Rd; Surry **GS:** Y **SP:** Elizabeth Ruffin (17 May 1771-26 Jul 1799) of Richneck Plantation, d/o William & Lucy (Cocke) Ruffin **VI:** Son of Col William (a Rev War soldier __-1786) & Sarah (Edwards) Browne. Parentage and wives are fr GS inscriptions **P:** N **BLW:** N **RG:** N **MK:** N **PH:** unk **SS:** AL Ct Bk 1 pg 3 **BS:** 147 pg 60.

BROWNE, William Burrnett; b 7 Oct 1738, Salem, Essex Co, MA; d 6 May 1784 **RU:** Private, Served in Capt Benjamin Ward Jr's Co. Enlisted 11 Jul 1775,and served 6 mo. 5 days at Salem and again 22 Jan 1776, 4 mo 7 days at Salem **CEM:** Elsing Green Plantation; GPS 37.61608, -77.04073; Off Mt Olive Cohoke Rd Rt 632; King William **GS:** Y **SP:** Judith Walker Carter **VI:** Son of William (1709-1763) & Mary (Burnett) Browne (1723-1745) **P:** unk **BLW:** unk **RG:** unk **MK:** unk **PH:** unk **SS:** AJ MA Rev War Vol 2 pg 705 **BS:** 196.

BROWNING, Francis; b 25 Nov 1753, Culpeper Co; d 18 Jul 1855 **RU:** Private, Ent serv fr Hillsborough NC. Served in NC Cont Line **CEM:** Thomas Family; GPS unk; Poor Farm Rd, Lebanon; Russell **GS:** Y **SP:** Miss Vermillion. Wife d before him. **VI:** Son of John & Elizabeth (Wimercast) Brown. Resided in Lebanon, Russell Co. Pensioned Russell Co 1832 age 79.Was 102 when he died. Govt grave stone & SAR marker. R382 **P:** unk **BLW:** unk **RG:** N **MK:** Y **PH:** unk **SS:** B Govt stone; K Vol 1 pg 125 **BS:** 32 Jul 2010.

RU=Rank/Unit CEM=Cemetery GS=Gravestone SP=Spousal Information
VI=Other Veteran Info P=Pension BLW=Bounty/Land Warrant RG=Registered Grave
MK=SAR/DAR Marker PH=Photo SS=Service Source BS=Burial Source

46

BROWNING, John; b 16 Apr 1749; d 25 Sep 1818 **RU:** Private, Served in Capt Charles Browning's Co, Culpeper Co. Was in Culpeper Co Class 56 **CEM:** Browning Family; GPS unk; Nr Salem Baptist Ch; Rappahannock **GS:** U **SP:** Elizabeth Strother **VI:** No further data **P:** unk **BLW:** unk **RG:** unk **MK:** unk **PH:** unk **SS:** DJ: Class 56 **BS:** JLARC 2, 76.

BROWNLEY, John Jr; b unk; d 1809 **RU:** Surg Mate, Served in VA Cont Line 1782 **CEM:** Castleman's Farm; GPS unk; Berryville; Frederick **GS:** Y **SP:** No info **VI:** BLW indicates he d in 1778 without issue **P:** unk **BLW:** Y **RG:** Y **MK:** N **PH:** unk **SS:** BY pg 331; E pg 103 **BS:** 50 pg 25.

BRUCE, Charles; b c1733; d 15 Dec 1791 **RU:** Captain, Commanded a Virginia Co that was paid at Ft Pitt in PA **CEM:** Soldier's Rest Plantation; GPS unk; Rt 620; Orange **GS:** Y **SP:** No info **VI:** Died in Fredericksburg **P:** unk **BLW:** unk **RG:** Y **MK:** N **PH:** unk **SS:** E pg 103; CZ pg 68 **BS:** 22 pg 89.

BRUCE, Charles; b unk, Scotland; d 1792 **RU:** Captain/Patriot, Achieved rank of Capt for gallant services. Gave 375# of beef 15 Aug 1781 **CEM:** Fredericksburg National Military Park; GPS unk; Fredericksburg; Fredericksburg City **GS:** U **SP:** 1) Diana Banks 2) Mar (1772) Frances Stubblefield (__-1833) **VI:** Served in French & Indian War under George Washington in 1754. Recd land grant **P:** unk **BLW:** Y **RG:** unk **MK:** unk **PH:** unk **SS:** AL Cert Orange Co **BS:** 196.

BRUCE, John; b 23 Apr 1759; d 10 Jan 1832 **RU:** Sergeant, Served in Capt Smith's Co of Foot,11th VA Regt Commanded by Col Charles Porterfield, Feb 1778 **CEM:** Dews Family; GPS unk; 13 mi SE of Gretna Rt 677; Pittsylvania **GS:** Y **SP:** Mar (1794 Pittsylvania Co) Lucy Doss **VI:** No further data **P:** unk **BLW:** unk **RG:** N **MK:** N **PH:** unk **SS:** E pg 103; AP record; CI Fold 3 website **BS:** 156 Dews GY.

BRUGH, Daniel Sr; b 19 Jul 1762 York Co PA; d 26 Dec 1825 **RU:** Private, Served 1782 in Capt O'Blain, 8th Co, 1st Bn, York, PA Militia **CEM:** Simmons-Brugh; GPS unk; Nr Mill Creek Baptist Church; Botetourt **GS:** Y **SP:** Mar (c1784) Elizabeth (-----) (1767-1842) **VI:** Son of Hermanus Brugh (1722-1794) & Catherine Meinhardt (1722-1801). Owned 550 acres with sawmill, grist mill, & tavern in Botetourt Co **P:** unk **BLW:** unk **RG:** N **MK:** N **PH:** unk **SS:** DD cites PA Hist & Mus Comm RG 4.61 Roll #343 **BS:** 123 pg 4; 196.

BRUGH, Hermanus; b 1722, Rheinland-Pfalz, Germany; d 13 Aug 1794 **RU:** Patriot, Overseer of the Poor 1778 **CEM:** Simmons-Brugh; GPS unk; Nr Mill Creek Baptist Church; Botetourt **GS:** Y **SP:** Mar (c1748) Catherine Meinhardt, (10 Jun 1722, Germany-1801) **VI:** Arrived in Philadelphia PA aboard the Lydia on 20 Sep 1743.Supervisor of Highways 1761. Owned sawmill & grist mill in Barwick Twp, PA, then moved to Botetourt Co 1791 **P:** N **BLW:** N **RG:** N **MK:** N **PH:** unk **SS:** H **BS:** 73 pg 2; 196.

BRULON, Francois; b unk; d 1781 **RU:** Seaman, Served on "Auguste" and died from Yorktown battle **CEM:** French Memorial; GPS 36.81944, -79.39933; Yorktown; York **GS:** U **SP:** No info **VI:** No further data **P:** unk **BLW:** unk **RG:** Y **MK:** unk **PH:** unk **SS:** J-Yorktown Historian **BS:** JLARC 1, 74.

BRUN, Jean; b unk; d 1781 **RU:** Seaman, Served on "Hercule" and died from Yorktown battle **CEM:** French Memorial; GPS 36.81944, -79.39933; Yorktown; York **GS:** U **SP:** No info **VI:** No further data **P:** unk **BLW:** unk **RG:** Y **MK:** unk **PH:** unk **SS:** J-Yorktown Historian **BS:** JLARC 1, 74.

BRUNDIGE, Timothy; b c1754; d 15 Sep 1822 **RU:** Quartermaster, Served in Westchester Co NY Militia in 2d Regt, commanded by Col Thomas Thomas, 22 May 1778 **CEM:** Dumfries Public; GPS 38.34110, -77.19964; 17821 Mine Rd, Dumfries; Prince William **GS:** Y **SP:** No info **VI:** SAR monument **P:** unk **BLW:** unk **RG:** Y **MK:** Y **PH:** unk **SS:** AX Vol 1 pg 207, 305 **BS:** 94 pg 18.

BRUNET, Jean; b unk; d 1781 **RU:** Soldier, Served in Soissonnais Bn and died from Yorktown battle **CEM:** French Memorial; GPS 36.81944, -79.39933; Yorktown; York **GS:** U **SP:** No info **VI:** No further data **P:** unk **BLW:** unk **RG:** Y **MK:** unk **PH:** unk **SS:** J-Yorktown Historian **BS:** JLARC 1, 74.

BRYAN, John Patterson; b 14 Nov 1746, NJ; d 16 Jan 1803 **RU:** Patriot, Civil service as Judge of Ct of Common Pleas, Somerset Co, NJ **CEM:** Bryan Family; GPS unk; Farmington Country Club, 10th tee; Charlottesville City **GS:** U **SP:** No info **VI:** Died in Charlottesville while collecting donations for NJ College **P:** N **BLW:** N **RG:** unk **MK:** unk **PH:** unk **SS:** CD **BS:** 196.

BRYAN, Thomas; b 1721; d 25 Feb 1793 **RU:** Patriot, Gave material aid to cause **CEM:** Spears Family; GPS unk; N of Edom Rt 42 7.3 mi; Rockingham **GS:** U **SP:** Elizabeth Palmer (1729-1793) **VI:** Son of

RU=Rank/Unit   CEM=Cemetery   GS=Gravestone   SP=Spousal Information
VI=Other Veteran Info   P=Pension   BLW=Bounty/Land Warrant   RG=Registered Grave
MK=SAR/DAR Marker   PH=Photo   SS=Service Source   BS=Burial Source

47

Cornelius & Rebecca (-----) Bryan **P:** N **BLW:** N **RG:** unk **MK**: unk **PH:** unk **SS:** D Vol III pg 830 **BS:** 196.

BRYAN, William Jr; b 1716; d 1796 **RU:** Captain, Was in Dunmore's War in Capt William Campbell's Co fr Fincastle Co 04 Aug 1776 for 3 yrs. Another this name was at Point Pleasant, perhaps father & son **CEM:** West Hill; GPS 37.29313, -80.06753; Boon St; Salem City **GS:** U **SP:** Margaret Watson (1724-1804) **VI:** Son of William Sr (1685 Ireland - 1786) & (-----) Bryan. Settled in Salem City in Roanoke Co in 1752 **P:** unk **BLW:** unk **RG:** Y **MK**: unk **PH:** unk **SS:** Z pg 163; AR pg 126 **BS:** JLARC 2, 41, 76; 196.

BRYANT, William; b 1761; d 29 Jun 1848 **RU:** Private, Served in 1st, 3rd, 4th, 6th, 10th Cont Lines **CEM:** Bryant Family; GPS unk; Charity, behind the Heidelbach School; Patrick **GS:** Y **SP:** Mar (2 Jan 1828 Patrick Co) Peggy Lewis **VI:** No further data **P:** unk **BLW:** unk **RG:** unk **MK**: unk **PH:** Y **SS:** E pg 105 **BS:** 196.

BRYARLY (BRYERLY), Thomas; b 1721, Ireland; d c1791 **RU:** Patriot, Gave material aid to cause **CEM:** Walnut Grove Plantation; GPS unk; White Post; Frederick **GS:** U **SP:** Mar (1 Feb 1752, Baltimore) Anne Tate **VI:** Son of Robert & Margaret (-----) Bryarly **P:** N **BLW:** N **RG:** unk **MK**: unk **PH:** unk **SS:** SAR Ancestor #P-329364; Al Ct Bk pg 4 **BS:** 196.

BRYSON, Robert; b unk; d 1801 **RU:** Matross, Served in Capt John Dandridge's Co of Artillery, 1st Artillery Regt, under Col John Harrison Dec 1778. Also served in Frederick Co Militia **CEM:** Dumfries Public; GPS 38.34110, -77.19964; 17821 Mine Rd, Dumfries; Prince William **GS:** N **SP:** No info **VI:** SAR monument **P:** unk **BLW:** unk **RG:** Y **MK**: Y **PH:** N **SS:** E pg 105 **BS:** 96 pg 98.

BUCHANAN, Alexander; b 28 Jan 1763; d 22 Sep 1858 **RU:** Private, Serv in Capt Buchanan's Co **CEM:** Buchanan Family; GPS 36.95610, -81.54470; New Cove, E of Saltville; Smyth **GS:** Y **SP:** No info **VI:** No further data **P:** unk **BLW:** unk **RG:** N **MK**: N **PH:** unk **SS:** G pg 212 **BS:** 97 vol 2 pg 14.

BUCHANAN, Andrew; b 1732; d 1780 **RU:** Brigadier General, Served as Maj commandant of 3rd Bn of Minutemen 1776. Later rose to rank of Brig Gen **CEM:** Buchanan Family; GPS unk; Nr Rockbridge Co line, reported on land probably owned by Ben Jacobs, btw Rts 602 & 681; Augusta **GS:** U **SP:** No info **VI:** No further data **P:** unk **BLW:** unk **RG:** Y **MK**: unk **PH:** unk **SS:** CE pg 25 **BS:** JLARC 8, 76.

BUCHANAN, John; b 1724; d 1783 **RU:** Captain, Served in VA Co that was in Illinois campaign **CEM:** Locust Grove; GPS unk; W fr Chatham Hill; Smyth **GS:** U **SP:** No info **VI:** No further data **P:** unk **BLW:** unk **RG:** Y **MK**: unk **PH:** unk **SS:** CZ pg 70 **BS:** JLARC 2, 76.

BUCHANAN, John; b 1761, Scotland; d 24 Aug 1829 **RU:** Lieutenant, Served in VA Cont Line. Appt Lt in Washington Co Militia 1778 **CEM:** Buchanan Family; GPS 36.84163, -81.75199; Rt 696, S of Saltville; Washington **GS:** Y **SP:** Anne Ryburn **VI:** BLW indicates he was killed in action, Fincastle Co, Mar 1777 and left no issue **P:** unk **BLW:** Y **RG:** N **MK**: N **PH:** unk **SS:** E pg 106; BY pg 351 **BS:** 78 pg 150; 196.

BUCHER, Philip Peter; b 6 Jun 1751, Opequon River, Frederick Co; d 1841 **RU:** Soldier, Ent serv Frederick Co **CEM:** Bucher; GPS unk; Mountain Falls; Frederick **GS:** U **SP:** Margaret (-----) **VI:** Pensioned Frederick Co 1832. R393 **P:** unk **BLW:** unk **RG:** unk **MK**: unk **PH:** unk **SS:** K Vol 1 pg 131 **BS:** JLARC 4, 47.

BUCK, Charles Jr; b 1750; d 1823 **RU:** Patriot, Gave material aid to the cause **CEM:** Buckton Family; GPS unk; 1 mi W of Buckton Station; Shenandoah **GS:** Y **SP:** Mar (17 Oct 1799) Polly Price of KY **VI:** In 1789, he erected a ferry across North Fork Shenandoah River. Was vestryman of Frederick Parish **P:** N **BLW:** N **RG:** N **MK**: N **PH:** unk **SS:** AL CT Bk pg 1 **BS:** 01, pg 32; 155.

BUCK, Thomas; b 1756 or 1757; d after 1833 **RU:** Soldier, Ent serv 1777 in Dunmore Co (later Shenandoah Co) & later again in Shenandoah Co **CEM:** Buckton Graveyard; GPS unk; Not identified; Frederick **GS:** U **SP:** No info **VI:** Drew pen 1833 in Frederick Co R395 **P:** unk **BLW:** unk **RG:** unk **MK**: unk **PH:** unk **SS:** K Vol 1 pg 131 **BS:** JLARC 4, 47.

BUCKLEY, James Jr; b Feb 1763, Loudoun Co; d 22 Nov 1835 **RU:** Sergeant/Patriot, Served in VA Militia Aug 1780 under Capt Lumpkins. Appt Sergeant of the Guard over deserters Jan 1781 in Capt John Buckley Co. Served Jul 1781 in Capt John Wynn's Co. Gave material aid to cause **CEM:** Buckley Family; GPS 36.955067, -79.141450; Mt Airy, Rt 40; Pittsylvania **GS:** Y **SP:** Mar (4 Sep 1778) Mary

RU=Rank/Unit	CEM=Cemetery	GS=Gravestone	SP=Spousal Information
VI=Other Veteran Info	P=Pension	BLW=Bounty/Land Warrant	RG=Registered Grave
MK=SAR/DAR Marker	PH=Photo	SS=Service Source	BS=Burial Source

48

Ridgeway **VI:** Pen 1832 in Weakley Co, TN. R396 **P:** Y **BLW:** unk **RG:** unk **MK:** unk **PH:** unk **SS:** D Pittsylvania Co **BS:** 174, JLARC 3101.

BUCKLEY, James Sr; b 1719 or 1722; d 6 Oct 1787 **RU:** Patriot, Provided provisions & rations & liquor for 57 militia men on march to join Gen Greene. Also provided beef, corn, & pasturage for Cont troops **CEM:** Buckley Family; GPS 36.955067, -79.141450; Mt Airy, Rt 40; Pittsylvania **GS:** Y **SP:** Mar (c1752 Prince William Co) Mary Harris (c1752-25 Apr 1817) d/o Samuel & (-----) Harris **VI:** No further data **P:** N **BLW:** N **RG:** unk **MK:** unk **PH:** unk **SS:** DAR Ancestor #A016753; SAR Ancestor #P-124183; D Vol 3 pg 767-8 **BS:** 174, JLARC 3101.

BUCKLEY, John; b c1754; d 8 Apr 1814 **RU:** Major/Patriot, Was Capt of Co Militia 17 Oct 1780. In spring 1781 led Co of PA Militia to join Gen Lafayette at Hanover Co. Marched unit through Richmond and down to "Mobbins Hill" (Malvern). Led Co to Yorktown 1781. Gave material aid to cause **CEM:** Buckley Family; GPS 36.955067, -79.141450; Mt Airy, Rt 40; Pittsylvania **GS:** Y **SP:** Mar (24 Oct 1786 Pittsylvania Co) Polley Harris **VI:** No further data **P:** unk **BLW:** unk **RG:** Y **MK:** unk **PH:** unk **SS:** D Pittsylvania Co **BS:** 174, JLARC 3, 76, 101.

BUCKNER, George; b 1760; d 1828 **RU:** Lieutenant, Specific service may be found as a Lt in the Council Journals at the Lib of VA **CEM:** Buckner-Washington-Burke; GPS unk; Off Rt 2, W on Rt 626 Woodford Rd for 4 mi to gate of "Braynefield"; Caroline **GS:** U **SP:** 1) unk; 2) Mar (c1802) Dorothea Brayne Benger (1 Mar 1765-26 Aug 1839) a widow, d/o John & Elizabeth (Johnson) Benger **VI:** Son of George & Elizabeth (Walker) Buckner. Represented Caroline Co. in House of Delegates, 1796-1800 **P:** unk **BLW:** unk **RG:** unk **MK:** N **PH:** unk **SS:** E pg 107; CZ pg 70 **BS:** JLARC 15; 02 pg 26.

BUFORD, Henry; b 19 Sep 1751, Culpeper Co; d 31 Dec 1814 **RU:** Captain, Commanded a company in Bedford Co Militia **CEM:** Locust Level; GPS 37.23180, -79.43420; Rt 460, nr Montvale; Bedford **GS:** U **SP:** 1) Mar (22 Mar 1771) Mildred Blackburn (__Norfolk-__) d/o William & Elizabeth (-----) Blackburn of Christ Church Parish, Middlesex Co 2) Jane Kent Quirk **VI:** Son of John & Judith (Early) Beauford. Built Buford's Tavern **P:** unk **BLW:** unk **RG:** Y **MK:** N **PH:** unk **SS:** J-NSSAR 1993 Reg, J- DAR Hatcher; CZ pg 71 **BS:** JLARC 1, 2; 196.

BUIS, Louis; b 1751; d 1781 **RU:** Seaman, Served on "Northumberland" and died from Yorktown battle **CEM:** French Memorial; GPS 36.81944, -79.39933; Yorktown; York **GS:** U **SP:** No info **VI:** No further data **P:** unk **BLW:** unk **RG:** Y **MK:** unk **PH:** unk **SS:** J-Yorktown Historian **BS:** JLARC 1, 74.

BULLE, Jean; b 1751; d 1781 **RU:** Soldier, Served in Gatinais Bn and died from Yorktown battle **CEM:** French Memorial; GPS 36.81944, -79.39933; Yorktown; York **GS:** U **SP:** No info **VI:** No further data **P:** unk **BLW:** unk **RG:** Y **MK:** unk **PH:** unk **SS:** J-Yorktown Historian **BS:** JLARC 1, 74.

BULLINGTON, Robert; b 1750; d Mar 1822 **RU:** Corporal, Serv in 5th Cont Line **CEM:** Bullington Family; GPS unk; Nr Sandy River; Pittsylvania **GS:** Y **SP:** Mar (1770) Elizabeth Granger Crenshaw **VI:** Son of John and Sally (Giles) Bullington **P:** unk **BLW:** unk **RG:** N **MK:** N **PH:** unk **SS:** E pg 108 **BS:** 80 vol 1, pg 131.

BULLOCK, David; b 1761, Hanover Co; d 30 Jul 1838 **RU:** Private, Ent serv Albemarle Co 1779 **CEM:** Bullock Family; GPS unk; Rt 758, Walnut Hill; Louisa **GS:** U **SP:** Mar (12 Feb 1782 Lousia Co) Jane Terry (c1756-__) **VI:** Pen Louisa Co 1832 age 71. Widow pen age 84 in 1840, rejected because she was not a widow at date of pension Act. R403 **P:** Y **BLW:** unk **RG:** Y **MK:** N **PH:** unk **SS:** E pg 108; K Vol 1 pg 133 **BS:** 4-May-07.

BUMGARDNER, Christian; b unk; d 1795 **RU:** Lieutenant, Served with Washington at Valley Forge 1778 **CEM:** St John's Reformed UCC; GPS 38.05081, -79.17761; 1515 Arbor Hill Rd, Middlebrook; Augusta **GS:** Y **SP:** Mary Gabbert **VI:** Stone reads "With Washington, Braddock's expedition 1754, Valley Forge 1778, Lieut. 1757, Mary Gabbert his wife" **P:** unk **BLW:** unk **RG:** unk **MK:** N **PH:** unk **SS:** B **BS:** JLARC 9 ,62, 63; 196.

BUMGARDNER, Jacob; b 8 Feb 1767; d 25 Aug 1857 **RU:** Soldier/Patriot, Member of Boston Tea Party 1775 and later Augusta Co Militia. **CEM:** Bethel Presbyterian; GPS 38.04257, -79.17283; 563 Bethel Green Rd, Middlebrook; Augusta **GS:** Y **SP:** Mary Waddle (25 Jul 1768-4 Dec 1849) **VI:** Son of

RU=Rank/Unit	CEM=Cemetery	GS=Gravestone	SP=Spousal Information
VI=Other Veteran Info	P=Pension	BLW=Bounty/Land Warrant	RG=Registered Grave
MK=SAR/DAR Marker	PH=Photo	SS=Service Source	BS=Burial Source

49

Christian & (-----) Bumgardner **P**: unk **BLW**: unk **RG**: unk **MK**: unk **PH**: unk **SS**: NSSAR Ancestor # 124731; DW pg 218 **BS**: JLARC 62, 63; 196.

BUMPASS, Samuel; b unk; d unk **RU**: Patriot, Signed a Legislative Petition in Hanover Co **CEM**: Still House Spring; GPS unk; Rt 669; Hanover **GS**: Y **SP**: No info **VI**: No further data **P**: N **BLW**: N **RG**: Y **MK**: N **PH**: unk **SS**: E pg 109; CZ pg 72 **BS**: 31 vol 1 pg 63.

BURCK, Justus; b unk; d 1781 **RU**: Soldier, Served fr MA, and died as result of Yorktown battle **CEM**: Yorktown Victory Monument Tablet; GPS 38.28350, -78.54150; Yorktown; York **GS**: U **SP**: No info **VI**: No further data **P**: unk **BLW**: unk **RG**: unk **MK**: unk **PH**: unk **SS**: J-Yorktown Historian **BS**: JLARC 74.

BURGESS, John; b c1744, Goochland Co; d 16 Feb 1835 **RU**: Soldier, Ent serv 1775, Fluvanna Co **CEM**: Unmarked grave; GPS unk; Overlooking Hardware River N of Rt 6.; Fluvanna **GS**: U **SP**: No info **VI**: Pen Fluvanna Co 1833, age 89 R412 **P**: Y **BLW**: unk **RG**: unk **MK**: unk **PH**: unk **SS**: K Vol 1 pg 136 **BS**: JLARC 4, 46.

BURK, John Daly; b unk; d 1808 **RU**: Private, Served in Capt Alexander Smith's Co, Col Daniel Morgan's, 11th VA Regt, 1777 **CEM**: Blandford; GPS 37.22433, -77.38604; 319 S Crater Rd; Petersburg City **GS**: Y **SP**: No info; has at least one child **VI**: Perhaps this burial is for his son who was b too late to be in Revolution. Was author of History of Virginia, portion regarding Petersburg **P**: unk **BLW**: unk **RG**: N **MK**: N **PH**: unk **SS**: AP record **BS**: 188, nbr147.

BURK (BURKE), Thomas; b 1741, Orange Co; d 1808 **RU**: Captain, Specific service will be found in the Auditors Accts, Vol XI, pg 40 Lib of VA **CEM**: Horseshoe; GPS 37.30353,-80.63395; Scenic View Dr; Giles **GS**: Y **SP**: Mar 1761, Clara Frazier (1742-1811) **VI**: DAR marker. Govt GS says "Capt Fincastle Co Militia Rev War" **P**: unk **BLW**: unk **RG**: Y **MK**: Y **PH**: unk **SS**: CZ pg 73 **BS**: JLARC 1, 2, 26.

BURKE, Richard H; b 1767; d 30 Apr 1817 **RU**: Private, Served in 5th Cont Line **CEM**: Old City; GPS 37.41472, -79.15667; 401 Taylor St; Lynchburg City **GS**: Y **SP**: No info **VI**: No further data **P**: unk **BLW**: unk **RG**: N **MK**: N **PH**: unk **SS**: E pg 111 **BS**: 162 Methodist.

BURKE, Thomas; b c1764; d 6 Feb 1807 **RU**: Private, Served in 1st & 10th Cont Lines **CEM**: Burke Family; GPS unk; 1 mile N of Burke's Bridge, on Burke's Bridge Rd Rt 654, Bowling Green; Caroline **GS**: U **SP**: Isabelle G. M. (-----) **VI**: No further data **P**: unk **BLW**: unk **RG**: Y **MK**: N **PH**: unk **SS**: D pg 225; E pg 112 **BS**: 02 pg 32; 196.

BURKE, William; b 2 Apr 1752; d 18 May 1803 **RU**: Private, Enlisted 1778 6th VA Ret, Cont Line, commanded by Col John Green, served Oct 1781 at Yorktown **CEM**: Burke-Shaw; GPS unk; Rt 688; Fauquier **GS**: Y **SP**: Susannah (-----) **VI**: Son of Thomas & Jane (-----) Burke. Recd pension in Culpeper Co **P**: Y **BLW**: unk **RG**: N **MK**: Y **PH**: unk **SS**: E pg 112 **BS**: 32, Burke 06.

BURNES (BURNS), John; b unk; d 1791 **RU**: Private, Served in 3rd and 7th VA Regts **CEM**: Old Christ Church Episcopal; GPS 38.80625, -77.04718; 118 N Washington St; Alexandria City **GS**: N **SP**: Mar (-----) Burns **VI**: Burial permit issued 1 Feb 1791 to Mrs Burns, widow **P**: unk **BLW**: unk **RG**: N **MK**: N **PH**: N **SS**: E pg 112; CI service record **BS**: 110 pg 91; 20 pg 145.

BURNETT, Williamson; b 1761, Buckingham Co; d 3 Jun 1833 **RU**: Private, Served in Capt Charles Patterson's Co, Col Fleming's Regt, & Buckingham Co Militia **CEM**: Staunton Baptist; GPS 37.06970, -79.58140; 15267 Smith Mountain Lake Pkwy, Huddleston; Bedford **GS**: Y **SP**: Mar (15 Mar 1792 Burmingham Co) Pricilla Carter (c1774-after 1843) **VI**: Widow pen age 65, Bedford Co 1840. R419. Has DAR marker on grave **P**: Y **BLW**: unk **RG**: unk **MK**: Y **PH**: unk **SS**: R 419; K Vol 1 pg 138; DD **BS**: JLARC 3; 196.

BURNLEY, Joel Terrell; b unk; d 1781 **RU**: Soldier, Service unit not determined. Died as result of Yorktown battle **CEM**: Yorktown Victory Monument Tablet; GPS 38.28350, -78.54150; Yorktown; York **GS**: U **SP**: No info **VI**: No further data **P**: unk **BLW**: unk **RG**: unk **MK**: unk **PH**: unk **SS**: J-Yorktown Historian **BS**: JLARC 74.

BURROWS, William Ward; b 16 Jan 1758, Charleston SC; d 6 Mar 1805 **RU**: Lieutenant Colonel, Aide-de-camp, 4th SC Regt (Artillery). Provided supplies to naval facilities. Gave £10,000 loan to SC and provided militia supplies **CEM**: Arlington National; GPS 38.88377, -77.06535; Jefferson Davis Hwy Rt

RU=Rank/Unit	CEM=Cemetery	GS=Gravestone	SP=Spousal Information
VI=Other Veteran Info	P=Pension	BLW=Bounty/Land Warrant	RG=Registered Grave
MK=SAR/DAR Marker	PH=Photo	SS=Service Source	BS=Burial Source

50

110; Arlington **GS:** Y **SP:** Mar (13 Sep 1783 at Kinderton Farm, North Liberties, nr Philadelphia) Mary Bond (24 Aug 1765, Philadelphia-Feb 1803, Washingoton, DC) d/o Dr. Thomas & Ann (Morga) Bond. She was originally bur at Old Presbyterian Church in Georgetown. It is not known if she was re-interred with her husband at Arlington National. **VI:** Son of William Burrows (1722-1781) & Mary Ward (1728-1775); first Commandant of the reconstituted Marine Corps (1798-1804). Died in Georgetown, DC. Originally bur by his wife at Old Presbyterian Church in Georgetown, he was reinterred at Arlington on 12 May 1892 in Sec 1, Grave 301B, Western Division **P:** unk **BLW:** unk **RG:** Y **MK:** Y **PH:** unk **SS:** AK J-NSSAR 1993 Reg **BS:** 04; JLARC 1; 196.

BURT, John; b unk; d 1781 **RU:** Soldier, Served fr MA, and died as result of Yorktown battle **CEM:** Yorktown Victory Monument Tablet; GPS 38.28350, -78.54150; Yorktown; York **GS:** U **SP:** No info **VI:** No further data **P:** unk **BLW:** unk **RG:** unk **MK:** unk **PH:** unk **SS:** J-Yorktown Historian **BS:** JLARC 74.

BURT, John M; b c1758; d 1811 **RU:** Patriot, Gave material aid to cause **CEM:** St Paul's Episcopal; GPS 36.84733, -76.28554; 201 St Paul's Blvd; Norfolk City **GS:** Y **SP:** No info **VI:** No further data **P:** N **BLW:** N **RG:** Y **MK:** N **PH:** unk **SS:** AL Com Bk IV pg 352 **BS:** 87 pg 26.

BURTON, John P; b unk; d 1848 **RU:** Patriot, Gave material aid to cause **CEM:** St John's Episcopal; GPS 37.53183, -77.41958; 2401 E Broad St; Richmond City **GS:** N **SP:** No info **VI:** No further data **P:** N **BLW:** N **RG:** N **MK:** N **PH:** N **SS:** D Vol I pg 237 **BS:** 28 pg 351.

BURTON, May Jr; b 1752; d 13 May 1829 **RU:** Captain, Entered serv 1777, Orange Co **CEM:** Burton Graveyard; GPS 38.16240, -78.20570; NE cnr of Rt 29 N and Rt 609 E; Greene **GS:** Y **SP:** Mar (29 Sep 1776 Greene Co) Sarah Head (__-Sep 1842 Greene Co) **VI:** Son of May & Hannah Medley Burton Sr. Died in "Rock Hill" Madison Co R430 **P:** Y **BLW:** unk **RG:** Y **MK:** Y **PH:** unk **SS:** AK; K Vol 1 pg 141 **BS:** 04, JLARC 113.

BURTON, Samuel; b c1755; d 16 Feb 1841 **RU:** Sergeant, Served Capt Payne's Co, Parker's Reg't, VA Line **CEM:** Burton Family; GPS 37.424557,-77.919160; 1 mi SW jct Genitoe and Brick Church Ln, property of Roger Epperson; Amherst **GS:** U **SP:** Mar (22 Dec 1800), Susannah Morris **VI:** Pen 1840 in Amelia Co age 85 **P:** Y **BLW:** Y **RG:** unk **MK:** unk **PH:** unk **SS:** C pg 223; E pg 115; G pg 752 **BS:** 32.

BURTON, Thomas; b 1741; d 1821 **RU:** Ensign, Qualified as ensign, Accomack Co Militia, 1 Oct 1777 **CEM:** Burton Private; GPS unk; Wachapreague; Accomack **GS:** N **SP:** Sinah Roberts **VI:** No further data **P:** unk **BLW:** unk **RG:** Y **MK:** unk **PH:** N **SS:** E pg 115 **BS:** JLARC 1, 76.

BURWELL, Lewis; b 26 Sep 1745; d 2 Jul 1800 **RU:** County Lieutenant, Specific service may be found as a Lt Col in the Council Journals at the Lib of VA **CEM:** Burwell Family; GPS unk; Stoneland; Mecklenburg **GS:** U **SP:** 1) Mar (24 Mar 1768) Ann Spottswood (__-14 Feb 1789) (granddaughter of Alex Spotswood, Gov of VA) 2) Mar (13 Nov 1789) Elizabeth R Harrison (__-19 Nov 1824) (Cousin of Gen Wm H. Harrison) **VI:** Son of Armistead & Christian (Blair) Burwell. For 14 yrs member of VA legislature. According to letters by researchers, he is actually bur at Stoneland Plantation, but stone was moved to church to prevent vandalism **P:** unk **BLW:** unk **RG:** Y **MK:** unk **PH:** unk **SS:** CZ pg 76 **BS:** JLARC 2, 76.

BURWELL, Nathaniel; b 15 Apr 1750, James City Co; d 1801 or 30 Mar 1802 **RU:** Captain, He commanded a Co in the King William Co Militia **CEM:** Vermont Plantation; GPS unk; W River Rd Rt 600, .5 mi E of Dorrel Rd Rt 628, River Hill; King William **GS:** N **SP:** Mar (28 Nov 1772 Middlesex Co) Susanna Grymes, Surty Phillip Grymes **VI:** Cenotaph on SAR plaque at Fincastle Presbyterian in Botetourt Co. No stones at Vermont Plantation (River Hill) graveyard for members of the Burwell family **P:** unk **BLW:** unk **RG:** unk **MK:** Y **PH:** N **SS:** J- DAR Hatcher; E pg 115 **BS:** JLARC 2; 196.

BURWELL, Nathaniel; b 1750; d 29 Mar 1814 **RU:** Colonel/Patriot, Served in 1774 James City Co Committee of Safety. Nov 1776 appt Chief Military Officer of James City Co. Procured full proportion of troops to Cont Army. Was Col James City Co Militia, and aide to Gen Robert Howe. Was prob at invasion of "Tidewater" & Yorktown serving Washington. Supplied wagons & 3972 lbs beef **CEM:** Old Chapel Episcopal; GPS 39.10677, -78.01470; Jct US 340 & Rt 255, Millwood; Clarke **GS:** Y **SP:** 1) Mar (3 Dec 1772, Middlesex Co) Susan Grymes d/o Phillip (1720-1768) & Mary (Randolph) (1729-1768) Grymes 2) Lucy (Page) Baylor (1759-11 Nov 1843) **VI:** Builder of Carter Hall. Also built Morgan Mill in Millwood with Gen Morgan. Died in Carter Hall. Rank of Col on grave stone, Recd BLW 4,666 and 300 acres **P:** unk **BLW:** Y **RG:** Y **MK:** Y **PH:** Y **SS:** E pg 115; AK **BS:** JLARC 1, 24, 76; 65 Clarke; 196.

RU=Rank/Unit	CEM=Cemetery	GS=Gravestone	SP=Spousal Information
VI=Other Veteran Info	P=Pension	BLW=Bounty/Land Warrant	RG=Registered Grave
MK=SAR/DAR Marker	PH=Photo	SS=Service Source	BS=Burial Source

BURWELL, Thomas H N; b unk; d 1841 **RU:** Major, Nominated 13 Sep 1775 for rank of Maj in Gloucester Co Militia **CEM:** Bruton Parish Church; GPS 37.27127, -76.70248; 331 W Duke of Gloucester St; Williamsburg City **GS:** Y **SP:** No info **VI:** No further data **P:** unk **BLW:** unk **RG:** Y **MK:** N **PH:** unk **SS:** N pg 562 **BS:** 26 pg 118.

BUSTER, Claudius; b unk; d unk **RU:** Private, Served in Augusta Co Militia **CEM:** Trinity Episcopal; GPS 38.14917, -79.07521; 214 Beverley St; Staunton City **GS:** N **SP:** No info **VI:** No further data **P:** unk **BLW:** unk **RG:** N **MK:** N **PH:** N **SS:** E pg 116 **BS:** 142 Trinity.

BUTCHER, John; b 1747; d 22 Nov 1811 **RU:** Patriot, Signed Legislative Petition in Alexandria **CEM:** Quaker Burial Ground; GPS 38.80749, -77.04676; 717 Queen St, Kate Walker Barrett Library; Alexandria City **GS:** Y **SP:** No info **VI:** No further data **P:** N **BLW:** N **RG:** N **MK:** N **PH:** N **SS:** S-Alexandria **BS:** 196.

BUTLER, James F; b unk; d 1847 **RU:** Patriot, Gave material aid to cause **CEM:** St John's Episcopal; GPS 37.53183, -77.41958; 2401 E Broad St; Richmond City **GS:** N **SP:** No info **VI:** No further data **P:** N **BLW:** N **RG:** N **MK:** N **PH:** N **SS:** D Vol I pg 309 **BS:** 28 pg 351.

BUTLER, Lawrence (Lance); b 1755; d 4 May 1811 **RU:** Captain, Served in 15th VA, then 11th VA. Captured at Charleston SC, in 1780 and was on parole until end of war. Discharged either 1800 (per pension) or after peace treaty with GB (per ledger) **CEM:** Butler Family; GPS 39.53680, -78.63850; Family farm in SE part of Clarke Co. Named as Dearmont Farm by one source.; Clarke **GS:** Y **SP:** No info **VI:** Grave re-found, cleaned, restored 2002. BLW 22 May 1789, R 438 **P:** unk **BLW:** Y **RG:** unk **MK:** N **PH:** Y **SS:** K Vol 1 pg 145 **BS:** JLARC 24.

BUTT, Epaphroditus; b unk; d unk **RU:** Soldier, Was in Battle of Great Bridge,1775 **CEM:** Butt Family; GPS unk; Old Brooks Farm, St Julian Creek; Chesapeake City **GS:** U **SP:** No info **VI:** No further data **P:** unk **BLW:** unk **RG:** unk **MK:** unk **PH:** unk **SS:** J- DAR Hatcher **BS:** JLARC 2.

BYBEE (BYBIE), Pleasant; b 1758; d 1835 **RU:** Soldier, Ent serv 1778 in Capt Pelham's and Ballard's Cos. VA Regt, Served in 1st, 5th, 9th Cont Lines **CEM:** Bybee Family; GPS unk; Nr Rt 633, Troy Neighborhood; Fluvanna **GS:** U **SP:** Mar (3 Sep 1789) Mildred Priddy **VI:** Widow pen Fluvanna Co 1840 age 81 and resided Sherwood, Fluvanna in 1823. He was pen there 1818 at age 60 Fluvanna Co. R443 Drew BLW of 100 acres **P:** Y **BLW:** Y **RG:** unk **MK:** unk **PH:** unk **SS:** K Vol 1 pg 147 **BS:** JLARC 4, 18.

BYRD, Thomas Taylor; b 17 Jan 1752; d 19 Aug 1821 **RU:** Sergeant, Served in 3rd and 4th Cont line **CEM:** Old Chapel Episcopal; GPS 39.106770, -78.01470; Jct US 340 & Rt 255, Millwood; Clarke **GS:** Y **SP:** No info **VI:** Obtained rank of Capt but service not identified for this rank. Recd BLW 7 Jul 1792 R444, however some sources indicate he was a Tory **P:** unk **BLW:** Y **RG:** Y **MK:** N **PH:** unk **SS:** SAR Ancestor #P-126957; E pg 119; AS; CI service record **BS:** O5.

BYRD, William; b 1752; d 31 May 1829 **RU:** Private, Entered serv 1776 in Prince Edward Co **CEM:** Samuel Byrd Family; GPS unk; Old Colonial Rd; Grayson **GS:** N **SP:** No info **VI:** Pen Grayson Co age 65 in 1818, R444 **P:** unk **BLW:** unk **RG:** Y **MK:** N **PH:** N **SS:** K pg 149 **BS:** 04, Apr 2007.

CABANNES, Jean; b unk; d 1781 **RU:** Seaman, Served on "Solitaire" and died from Yorktown battle **CEM:** French Memorial; GPS 36.81944, -79.39933; Yorktown; York **GS:** U **SP:** No info **VI:** No further data **P:** unk **BLW:** unk **RG:** Y **MK:** unk **PH:** unk **SS:** J-Yorktown Historian **BS:** JLARC 1, 74.

CABARE, Francois; b unk; d 1781 **RU:** Seaman, Served on "Marseillais" and died from Yorktown battle **CEM:** French Memorial; GPS 36.81944, -79.39933; Yorktown; York **GS:** U **SP:** No info **VI:** No further data **P:** unk **BLW:** unk **RG:** Y **MK:** unk **PH:** unk **SS:** J-Yorktown Historian **BS:** JLARC 1, 74.

CABEL, Joseph; b unk; d unk **RU:** Colonel, Specific service may be found in the Auditors Accts 1776,1779 and 1780 at the Lib of VA **CEM:** Bruton Parish Church; GPS 37.27127, -76.70248; 331 W Duke of Gloucester St; Williamsburg City **GS:** U **SP:** No info **VI:** No further data **P:** unk **BLW:** unk **RG:** unk **MK:** unk **PH:** unk **SS:** J- DAR Hatcher; CZ pg 78 **BS:** JLARC 2.

CABELL, John; b unk; d unk **RU:** Captain, Served as Lt, Buckinham Co Militia, 1780 **CEM:** Greenhill; GPS unk; James River State Park; Buckingham **GS:** U **SP:** Mar (Lynchburg City) Henrian Davies (1781-18 Mar 1843) **VI:** No further data **P:** N **BLW:** N **RG:** unk **MK:** N **PH:** unk **SS:** CZ pg 78 **BS:** JLARC 59.

RU=Rank/Unit	CEM=Cemetery	GS=Gravestone	SP=Spousal Information
VI=Other Veteran Info	P=Pension	BLW=Bounty/Land Warrant	RG=Registered Grave
MK=SAR/DAR Marker	PH=Photo	SS=Service Source	BS=Burial Source

52

CABELL, Nicholas; b 29 Oct 1750; d 18 Aug 1803 **RU:** Colonel, Raised 2 Co of Minutemen 1775. As Capt commanded a Minute Co at Amherst Co CT House Apr 1776 **CEM:** Warminster; GPS 37.68360, -78.69420; Warminster, Norwood; Nelson **GS:** Y **SP:** Mar (16 Apr 1772) Hannah Carriington (28 Mar 1751-7 Aug 1817) d/o George & Anne (Mayo) Carrington **VI:** Son of Dr. William (1699 England-12 Apr 1774) & Elizabeth (Burks) (1705-1756) Cabell. Served in VA Senate 1785-1801. R445 **P:** Y **BLW:** unk **RG:** unk **MK:** unk **PH:** unk **SS:** DC pg 154 **BS:** JLARC 4, 83; 196; 213 pg 346-7.

CABELL, Samuel Jordan; b 15 Dec 1756; d 4 Aug 1818 **RU:** Lieutenant Colonel/Patriot, Served 4 Mar 1776 as Capt of Amherst Volunteers, 6th VA Regt. Appt Maj at Saratoga 1777, Was in Gen George Washington's Cont Army until end of war. Obtained rank of Lt Col in war **CEM:** Cabell Family; GPS unk; Norwood; Nelson **GS:** U **SP:** Sarah Syme (5 Nov 1760-15 May 1814) d/o John (1729-1775) & Mildred Thurston (Meriwether) (1739-1760) Syme **VI:** Son of William (1730-1798) & Margaret Meredith (Jordan) (1742-1812) Cabell. VA State House of Delegates 1785-1792. Elected as Republican to 4th, 5th, 6th, 7th Congresses, serving until 1803. Awarded BLW 6000 acres 30 Sept 1782 and 1000 acres 25 Jun 1783 **P:** unk **BLW:** Y **RG:** unk **MK:** unk **PH:** unk **SS:** C pg 90; D pg 3 Amherst Co **BS:** 196.

CABELL, William Jr; b 1759; d 1842 **RU:** Colonel/Patriot, Served fr NC; gave material aid to cause **CEM:** Amherst; GPS 37.59640, -79.03670; Bus Rt 29, Amherst; Amherst **GS:** U **SP:** Ann "Nancy" Carrington (09 Jun 1760-30 Mar 1838) d/o Paul (1733-1818) and Margaret (Reade) (1734-1766) Carrington **VI:** No further data **P:** unk **BLW:** unk **RG:** Y **MK:** unk **PH:** unk **SS:** J-NSSAR 2000 Reg; D pg 39 **BS:** JLARC 76.

CABELL, William Sr; b unk; d 4 Aug 1818 **RU:** Patriot, Was member Committee of Safety for VA 1775 & 1776 **CEM:** Soldier's Joy; GPS unk; Wingina; Nelson **GS:** Y **SP:** Sarah Syne d/o Col John & (-----) Syne of Hanover Co. (__-15 May 1814) **VI:** Held rank of Colonel. Was member of Society of Cincinnati **P:** N **BLW:** N **RG:** N **MK:** N **PH:** unk **SS:** E pg 119 **BS:** 103 pg 349.

CABON, Yves; b unk; d 1781 **RU:** Seaman, Served on "Northumberland" and died from Yorktown battle **CEM:** French Memorial; GPS 36.81944, -79.39933; Yorktown; York **GS:** U **SP:** No info **VI:** No further data **P:** unk **BLW:** unk **RG:** Y **MK:** unk **PH:** unk **SS:** J-Yorktown Historian **BS:** JLARC 1, 74.

CADDELL, Samuel; b c1759, Ireland; d 12 Oct 1732 **RU:** Private, Vol in Rockbridge Co,1780, 2nd VA Regt Cont Line. Was in Battles of Guilford, Hobkirk's Hill, Ninety Six and Eutaw **CEM:** Caddall; GPS unk; Thornspring Farm; Pulaski **GS:** Y **SP:** Mar (1791) Nancy Ann Cecil (1769-1841) d/o Benjamin & (-----) Cecil **VI:** Emigrated fr County Down, Ireland in 1774 at abt the age of 16. Was blacksmith by trade. Pen appl 7 Aug 1832, died two mos later. DAR marker **P:** Y **BLW:** unk **RG:** Y **MK:** Y **PH:** unk **SS:** G pg 727; CZ pg 64 **BS:** 196.

CAFFEE, William; b c1764; d 1839 **RU:** Private?, Served in Capt Joseph Bowmen's Co **CEM:** Bellamy Methodist Church; GPS 37.40149, -76.58883; 4870 Chestut Fork Rd; Gloucester **GS:** Y **SP:** Martha Robins d/o Thomas & Harriet (Stubbs) Robins **VI:** No further data **P:** unk **BLW:** unk **RG:** Y **MK:** N **PH:** unk **SS:** C pg 604 **BS:** 196.

CAHOON, Charles; b Dec 1747; d Apr 1834 **RU:** Private?, Ent serv Kent Co, DE **CEM:** Cahoon Family; GPS unk; Glade Creek nr Bedford Co line; Botetourt **GS:** U **SP:** No info **VI:** Moved to VA 1795. Pen age 85, Blade Creek, Botetourt Co 1832 age 85, resided in Blade Creek R447 **P:** Y **BLW:** unk **RG:** N **MK:** N **PH:** unk **SS:** K Vol 1 pg 149-50 **BS:** AS, SAR Appl.

CAILLET, Jean; b unk; d 1781 **RU:** Soldier, Served in Soissonnais Bn and died from Yorktown battle **CEM:** French Memorial; GPS 36.81944, -79.39933; Yorktown; York **GS:** U **SP:** No info **VI:** No further data **P:** unk **BLW:** unk **RG:** unk **MK:** unk **PH:** unk **SS:** J-Yorktown Historian **BS:** JLARC 1, 74.

CAIN, Abel; b unk; d 1781 **RU:** Soldier, Served fr MA and died as result of Yorktown battle **CEM:** Yorktown Victory Monument Tablet; GPS 38.28350, -78.54150; Yorktown; York **GS:** U **SP:** No info **VI:** No further data **P:** unk **BLW:** unk **RG:** unk **MK:** unk **PH:** unk **SS:** J-Yorktown Historian **BS:** JLARC 74.

CALAGHAN, John; b unk; d 1781 **RU:** Private, Served in Col Wynkoop's NY Regt, and died as result of Yorktown battle **CEM:** Yorktown Victory Monument Tablet; GPS 38.28350, -78.54150; Yorktown; York **GS:** U **SP:** No info **VI:** No further data **P:** unk **BLW:** unk **RG:** unk **MK:** unk **PH:** unk **SS:** J-Yorktown Historian; AX pg 219 **BS:** JLARC 74.

RU=Rank/Unit	CEM=Cemetery	GS=Gravestone	SP=Spousal Information
VI=Other Veteran Info	P=Pension	BLW=Bounty/Land Warrant	RG=Registered Grave
MK=SAR/DAR Marker	PH=Photo	SS=Service Source	BS=Burial Source ·

53

CALDWELL, John F; b 20 Mar 1715, County Donegal, Ireland; d 1795 **RU:** Patriot, Gave material aid to the cause **CEM:** Cub Creek; GPS 37.03220, -78.75830; Rt 616 Cub Creek Church Rd, Brookneal; Charlotte **GS:** U **SP:** 1) Mar (11 Jun 1737, Lunenburg Co) Margaret Eleanor Ewing (1717-1745) 2) Martha Calhoun (1719-1773) 3) Mar (16 Jun 1746 Lunenburg, VA) Jane Kennedy (1727-1780) **VI:** Son of John (1682-1750) and Mary Margaret (Phillips) (1685-1748) Caldwell. Died in Halifax Co **P:** N **BLW:** N **RG:** unk **MK:** N **PH:** unk **SS:** AL Ct Bk pg 7; AL Ct Bk 16 Halifax Co **BS:** 245; 196.

CALL, Daniel; b 1765; d 1840 **RU:** Private, Service not obtained from BLW application **CEM:** Shockoe Hill; GPS 37.55190, -77.43170; 4th & Hospital Sts; Richmond City **GS:** Y **SP:** Lucy Nelson Ambler **VI:** Recd BLW of 667 acres, Was an attorney, Richmond 1808 **P:** unk **BLW:** Y **RG:** N **MK:** N **PH:** unk **SS:** C pg 614 **BS:** 179 pg 167.

CALLAND(s), Samuel; b c1750; d 8 Nov 1808 **RU:** Quartermaster/Patriot, Gave horse for state troops and corn & fodder for Conts **CEM:** Callands Family; GPS 36.85587, -79.62549; NE of Callands; Pittsylvania **GS:** Y **SP:** Elizabeth Smith **VI:** Namesake of "Callands" community in Pittsylvania Co **P:** unk **BLW:** unk **RG:** N **MK:** N **PH:** unk **SS:** E pg 121 **BS:** 174.

CALLAWAY (CALLOWAY), Charles; b 1752; d 1827 **RU:** Captain, Commanded a Co at Yorktown **CEM:** Alta Vista Plantation; GPS unk; Altavista; Pittsylvania **GS:** U **SP:** No info **VI:** No further data **P:** unk **BLW:** unk **RG:** Y **MK:** unk **PH:** unk **SS:** CZ pg 79 **BS:** JLARC 1, 2, 66, 75.

CALLAWAY (CALLOWAY), James; b 31 Dec 1736, Caroline Co; d 1 Nov 1809 **RU:** Colonel/Patriot, Served in Bedford Co Committee of Safety 1774 **CEM:** Callaway-Steptoe; GPS 37.30560, -79.29470; Rt 460, New London; Bedford **GS:** Y **SP:** 1) Mar (24 Nov 1756) Sarah P Tate (__-1773) d/o Henry & Elizabeth (Netherlannd) Tate 2) Mar (29 Sep 1777) Elizabeth Early (__-1796) d/o Col Jeremiah (1730-1779) and his 1st wife Sarah (Anderson) (1729-1770) Early 3) Mar (1799) Mary Turpin Calland Langhorne, d/o Maj Maurice & Elizabeth (Trotter) Langhorne **VI:** Son of Col William Callaway (1714-1777) & Elizabeth Tilley (1713-1750). House of Burgesses 1766-1769. Bedford Co. Committee of Safety. 1774. Treasurer New London Academy. Built 1st iron furnace south. of James River which exempted him fr military service **P:** unk **BLW:** unk **RG:** unk **MK:** Y **PH:** Y **SS:** B; CD **BS:** 196; JLARC App D.

CALLAWAY (CALLOWAY), John; b 1738; d 1820 **RU:** Colonel, Served in Bedford Co Militia and was in a VA unit at the Illinois Dept **CEM:** Otter Oaks; GPS unk; Nr Evington; Campbell **GS:** U **SP:** 1) Tabitha Tate 2) Agatha Ward **VI:** Source 90 has burial at Callaway-Hewitt Cem **P:** unk **BLW:** unk **RG:** Y **MK:** N **PH:** unk **SS:** CZ pg 79 **BS:** JLARC 1, 2, 36, 66 ,75, 90.

CALLAWAY (CALLOWAY), William; b 1714, Caroline Co; d 1777 **RU:** Lieutenant Colonel, Commanded Bedford Co Militia by 1777 **CEM:** Callaway-Steptoe; GPS 37.30560, -79.29470; Rt 460, New London; Bedford **GS:** Y **SP:** 1) Mar (8 Jan 1735) Elizabeth Tilley (1713-1750) 2) Mar (abt 1752) Elizabeth Crawford (__-22 Jan 1827) and also bur here **VI:** Son of Joseph Callaway and Catherine Ann Browning. Commander of militia during the French & Indian War as a Col. Has a Govt stone for Rev War service **P:** unk **BLW:** unk **RG:** Y **MK:** N **PH:** unk **SS:** B; E pg 122 **BS:** JLARC 1, 2, 36; 196.

CALLAWAY (CALLOWAY), William Jr; b 1748; d 22 Sep 1821 **RU:** Colonel/Patriot, Served in Bedford Co Militia. Gave material aid to cause **CEM:** Callaway-Steptoe; GPS 37.30560, -79.29470; Rt 460, New London; Bedford **GS:** Y **SP:** Anna Bowker (Mar 1751-02 Nov 1734) **VI:** Son of Col William Callaway(1714-1777) and Elizabeth Tilley (1713-1750) who also had Rev War service **P:** unk **BLW:** unk **RG:** unk **MK:** N **PH:** unk **SS:** D Bedford Co **BS:** JLARC 2, 36; 196.

CALLENDER, Eleazer; b 9 Nov 1792, MA; d 1792 **RU:** Captain/Patriot, Was Capt of ship "Dragon" built in Fredericksburg, also ship "Defiance". Petitioned for a valuable horse lost during War. Gave 68# of bacon to the cause **CEM:** Masonic Cemetery; GPS 38.30198, -77.46142; 900 Charles St; Fredericksburg City **GS:** Y **SP:** No info **VI:** Original member of Society of Cincinatti. Served as overseer of the Poor. Postmaster in Fredericksburg in 1783 **P:** unk **BLW:** unk **RG:** Y **MK:** Y **PH:** unk **SS:** L pg 57, 160 **BS:** 11 pg 23, 24.

CALLENDER, John; b unk; d 2 Oct 1797 **RU:** Major, Service information not determined **CEM:** Old Christ Church Episcopal; GPS 38.80625, -77.04718; 118 N Washington St; Alexandria City **GS:** N **SP:** No info **VI:** Teacher, "an old and respectable officer in the American War," bur with Masonic honors (The

RU=Rank/Unit	CEM=Cemetery	GS=Gravestone	SP=Spousal Information
VI=Other Veteran Info	P=Pension	BLW=Bounty/Land Warrant	RG=Registered Grave
MK=SAR/DAR Marker	PH=Photo	SS=Service Source	BS=Burial Source

54

Columbian Mirror and Alexandria Gazette, 5 Oct 1797, pg 3) **P:** unk **BLW:** unk **RG:** Y **MK:** N **PH:** N **SS:** A pg 417 ref 20 **BS:** 20 pg 136.

CALLINAN, Guillaume; b unk; d 1781 **RU:** Seaman, Served on "Diademe" and died from Yorktown battle **CEM:** French Memorial; GPS 36.81944, -79.39933; Yorktown; York **GS:** U **SP:** No info **VI:** No further data **P:** unk **BLW:** unk **RG:** Y **MK:** unk **PH:** unk **SS:** J-Yorktown Historian **BS:** JLARC 1, 74.

CALVERT, John Salvage; b c1739; d 16 Jan 1809 **RU:** Captain/Navy, Appt superintendant of the construction of a galley for James River by Committee of Safety. Was commissioned as Capt in Navy and assigned to Galley "Revenge" of Norfolk **CEM:** St Paul's Episcopal; GPS 36.84733, -76.28554; 201 St Paul's Blvd; Norfolk City **GS:** Y **SP:** Margaret "Molly" "Peggy" Walke **VI:** Son of Cornelius & Mary (Saunders) Calvert. BLW indicates he d 1809 Nansemond Co **P:** unk **BLW:** Y **RG:** Y **MK:** N **PH:** unk **SS:** L pg 160; BY pg 327; CB **BS:** 178 Jan 11.

CALVERT, Thomas; b 1725; d 2 Sep 1785 **RU:** Patriot, Took oath of Councilman 1780 **CEM:** St Paul's Episcopal; GPS 36.84733, -76.28554; 201 St Paul's Blvd; Norfolk City **GS:** Y **SP:** Mary (Thomas) Calvert **VI:** Took Oath of Office as a Common Councilman in 1780, per "The Order Book and Related Papers of the Common Hall of the Borough of Norfolk, 1736-1798" **P:** N **BLW:** N **RG:** Y **MK:** N **PH:** unk **SS:** CB Councilman 1780 **BS:** 178 Jan 11.

CAMBERNON, Antoine; b unk; d 1781 **RU:** Seaman, Served on "Citoyen" and died from Yorktown battle **CEM:** French Memorial; GPS 36.81944, -79.39933; Yorktown; York **GS:** U **SP:** No info **VI:** No further data **P:** unk **BLW:** unk **RG:** Y **MK:** unk **PH:** unk **SS:** J-Yorktown Historian **BS:** JLARC 1, 74.

CAMERON, Charles; b 22 Feb 1753; d 14 Jul 1829 **RU:** Colonel, Ent serv 1776, Augusta Co. Became as Col, Commander of Militia, Augusta Co, Aug 1781 **CEM:** Fort Dinwiddie; GPS 38.09228, -79.83140; NE of jct of Dinwiddie Trail & River Rd, Warm Springs; Bath **GS:** U **SP:** Mar on 3 May 1792 to Rachel Primrose Warwick, b 14 Mar 1772, d 6 Dec 1856 at Lexington. Stone at Warm Springs **VI:** Widow pen age 67 in Bath Co in 1839 age 67. Widow recd BLW there 1833. R453 **P:** Y **BLW:** Y **RG:** N **MK:** N **PH:** unk **SS:** E pg 399; K Vol 1 **BS:** 159 Warm Sprs; 196.

CAMERON, John; b unk; d 1815 **RU:** Sergeant, Promoted to Sgt Aug 1777 in Capt John Winston's Co, 14th VA Regt commanded by Col Charles Lewis. Was paid in a VA unit at Ft Pitt, PA. (Another person this name in the rank of corporal, was also on the payroll that listed him as a sergeant, thus he could of held the corporal rank) **CEM:** Blandford; GPS 37.22433, -77.38604; 319 S Crater Rd; Petersburg City **GS:** Y **SP:** No info **VI:** No further data **P:** Y **BLW:** unk **RG:** N **MK:** N **PH:** unk **SS:** AP Muster and Payrolls; CZ pg 80 **BS:** 188 nbr 906; CZ pg 80.

CAMPBELL, Aeneas; b 3 Oct 1757; d 15 Oct 1828 **RU:** Captain, Commanded co Washington Co, MD Jul 1776 **CEM:** Campbell-Belt Estate; GPS unk; Rock Hill, Leesburg; Loudoun **GS:** Y **SP:** 1) Sarah Hickman 2) Elizabeth Liza Ann Belt **VI:** He is reported by DAR as died in NC, so may be memorialized in this cemetery. DAR Plaque. Heirs were rejected for pension **P:** N **BLW:** unk **RG:** unk **MK:** Y **PH:** unk **SS:** J- DAR Hatcher; DK pg 48 **BS:** JLARC 2.

CAMPBELL, Alexander; b unk; d unk **RU:** Private, Served in Capt John Cropper's Co, Col Morgan's Regt **CEM:** Stonewall Jackson Memorial; GPS 37.78128, -79.44604; 314 S Main St; Lexington City **GS:** U **SP:** No info **VI:** No further data **P:** unk **BLW:** unk **RG:** unk **MK:** unk **PH:** unk **SS:** A pg 267 **BS:** JLARC 63.

CAMPBELL, Archibald; b 20 Nov 1753; d 17 Jun 1852 **RU:** Lieutenant, Became Lt 15 Jun 1781, served in 4th Cont Line **CEM:** Mt Holly; GPS 37.70485, -75.74185; Hill St, Onancock; Accomack **GS:** Y **SP:** No info **VI:** A founder of Old Friendship Church. Awarded 2666 acres BLW **P:** unk **BLW:** Y **RG:** N **MK:** N **PH:** unk **SS:** E pg 124 **BS:** 37 pg 48.

CAMPBELL, Cammuel Elias Sr; b 1730; d 1793 **RU:** Soldier/Patriot, Gave material aid to cause **CEM:** Lillard Family; GPS unk; Syria; Madison **GS:** U **SP:** Elizabeth Yowell **VI:** No further data **P:** unk **BLW:** unk **RG:** Y **MK:** unk **PH:** unk **SS:** NSSAR Ancestor #P- 128107; AL Ct bk II pg 14 Culpeper Co **BS:** JLARC 76.

CAMPBELL, Charles; b 1741; d 1826 **RU:** Captain, Promoted Capt in May 1778, Rockbridge Co Militia **CEM:** New Providence Presbyterian; GPS 37.95170, -79.30250; 1208 New Providence Rd, Raphine;

RU=Rank/Unit	CEM=Cemetery	GS=Gravestone	SP=Spousal Information
VI=Other Veteran Info	P=Pension	BLW=Bounty/Land Warrant	RG=Registered Grave
MK=SAR/DAR Marker	PH=Photo	SS=Service Source	BS=Burial Source

55

Rockbridge **GS**: Y **SP**: Mary Ann Downey **VI**: No further data **P**: unk **BLW**: unk **RG**: N **MK**: N **PH**: unk **SS**: E pg 125 **BS**: SAR Appl.

CAMPBELL, Charles; b unk; d unk **RU**: Captain., Commanded co, Rockbridge Co Militia **CEM**: New Providence Presbyterian; GPS 37.95130, -79.30250; 1208 New Providence Rd, Raphine; Rockbridge **GS**: U **SP**: No info **VI**: No further data **P**: unk **BLW**: unk **RG**: unk **MK**: unk **PH**: unk **SS**: CZ pg 81 **BS**: JLARC 63,79.

CAMPBELL, Elias; b 1730; d 1793 **RU**: Patriot, Gave material aid to the cause **CEM**: Lillard Family; GPS unk; Syria; Madison **GS**: Y **SP**: Elizabeth Yowell d/o Christopher (1720-1775) & (-----) Yowell **VI**: No further data **P**: N **BLW**: N **RG**: Y **MK**: N **PH**: unk **SS**: AL Ct Bk 2 pg 14 **BS**: SAR regis.

CAMPBELL, Francis Lee; b 1760, Scotland; d 15 Oct 1840 **RU**: Captain/Patriot, Served in Lousia Co Militia. Gave material aid to cause **CEM**: Clover Hill; GPS unk; S Anna River, Rt 647; Louisa **GS**: U **SP**: mar 01 Jan 1789, Ann Barnettb 1772, d 08 Sep 1852, daug of James Barnett, (1772-1808) & Ann (___), d 1817 **VI**: Died at "Cottage Hill" **P**: unk **BLW**: unk **RG**: Y **MK**: unk **PH**: unk **SS**: AR Vol 1 pg 149; DD **BS**: JLARC 1, 61.

CAMPBELL, Hugh; b c1750, Greenoch, Scotland; d 1791 **RU**: Private, Served in 1st VA State Regt **CEM**: Campbell Family; GPS unk; Lot 44, Tappahannock; Essex **GS**: N **SP**: Sarah Roane (1760s-early 1810) d/o Thomas of Newington & Mary Ann (Hipkins) Roane **VI**: Son of Hugh & (-----) Campbell. Land conveyance by heirs of veteran reserved permanent cemetery on this city lot for Hugh and his descendants **P**: unk **BLW**: unk **RG**: unk **MK**: unk **PH**: unk **SS**: E pg 125; CI payroll **BS**: 223 pg 125.

CAMPBELL, James; b 1745, Dumfries, Scotland; d 18 Mar 1821 **RU**: Captain - Navy, Recruited in Cont Army fr Somerset Co, MD, 30 July 1781-Dec 1781. Capt of the "Enterprise" during Rev **CEM**: Trinity United Methodist; GPS 39.13600, -77.00610; 2911 Cameron Mills Rd; Alexandria City **GS**: Y **SP**: 1) Leah (-----), (c1744-11 Oct 1803) 2) Kitty Cahale **VI**: Died age 76. Styled Capt on GS; death notice in the Alexandria Gazette 20 Mar 1821, which styles him also "Capt" **P**: unk **BLW**: unk **RG**: Y **MK**: N **PH**: Y **SS**: NSSAR Ancestor #P -127885; AR Vol 1 pg 149 **BS**: JLARC 1, 2; 23 pg 119, 196.

CAMPBELL, James; b c1753; d 5 Jan 1825 **RU**: Patriot, Gave material aid to cause **CEM**: Sinking Springs; GPS 36.71030, -81.98170; 136 E Main St, Abingdon; Washington **GS**: N **SP**: No info **VI**: DAR marker **P**: N **BLW**: N **RG**: unk **MK**: Y **PH**: N **SS**: D Montgomery Co **BS**: JLARC 80; 208 pg 73.

CAMPBELL, James; b c1745; d c1822 **RU**: Private, Served in Capt Samuel McDowell's Co fr Rockbridge Co at Point Pleasant Oct 1774 **CEM**: Campbell-Hobbs; GPS unk; Rt 682, vic Ewing; Lee **GS**: Y **SP**: No info **VI**: Son of James & Mary (Gibbs) Campbell **P**: unk **BLW**: unk **RG**: Y **MK**: N **PH**: unk **SS**: Z pg 104; AK Nov 06 **BS**: 04, Nov 06.

CAMPBELL, John; b unk; d unk **RU**: Captain, DAR Senate Documents 1836 serial # 10054, vol 5 should provide service info **CEM**: Sauger; GPS unk; Elk Creek; Grayson **GS**: U **SP**: No info **VI**: No further data **P**: unk **BLW**: unk **RG**: unk **MK**: unk **PH**: unk **SS**: AR Vol 1 pg 150; DD **BS**: JLARC 2.

CAMPBELL, John; b 1738, Augusta Co; d 1781 **RU**: Captain, Specific service may be found as a Capt in the War records, pg 23 at the Lib of VA **CEM**: Rich Valley Presbyterian; GPS 36.90248, -81.62490; 3811 Valley Rd, Saltville; Smyth **GS**: U **SP**: Mar (1767) Mary Martin (1770 or1774-__) **VI**: Died at Rich Valley **P**: unk **BLW**: unk **RG**: Y **MK**: unk **PH**: unk **SS**: J-NSSAR 1993 Reg, J- DAR Hatcher; CZ pg 81 **BS**: JLARC 1, 2.

CAMPBELL, John; b 23 Apr 1742; d 17 Dec 1825 **RU**: Captain/Patriot, Was in battles at Pt Pleasant, Long Island Flats 20 Jul 1776, Kings Mountain Oct 1780. Gave material aid to cause **CEM**: Sinking Springs; GPS 36.71030, -81.98170; 136 E Main St, Abingdon; Washington **GS**: U **SP**: Mar (10 Jun 1778 Botetourt Co) Elizabeth McDonald (29 may 1753-10 Jul 1827) d/o Edward & Elizabeth (Robinson) McDonald **VI**: Son of David (1703-1790) & Mary (Hamilton) Campbell. Was County Clerk Washington Co until 1815. Signer of Fincastle Resolutions **P**: unk **BLW**: unk **RG**: unk **MK**: unk **PH**: unk **SS**: D Augusta Co **BS**: JLARC 70, 80,101; 196; 208 pg 73.

CAMPBELL, John; b 1761; d 1793 **RU**: Private, Served in Capt John Roger's Troop of Dragoons 1 Oct 1781. Discharged 1 Jan 1782 **CEM**: Jillard & Weakley; GPS unk; Rt 600 Syria; Madison **GS**: U **SP**: No

RU=Rank/Unit	CEM=Cemetery	GS=Gravestone	SP=Spousal Information
VI=Other Veteran Info	P=Pension	BLW=Bounty/Land Warrant	RG=Registered Grave
MK=SAR/DAR Marker	PH=Photo	SS=Service Source	BS=Burial Source

56

info **VI:** Son of Elias (__-1794) & Elizabeth (Yowell) Campbell **P:** N **BLW:** N **RG:** N **MK:** unk **PH:** N **SS:** G pg 796 **BS:** 196.

CAMPBELL, Thomas; b 1749; d 1827 **RU:** Sergeant, Served in 4th Cont Line **CEM:** Campbell Family; GPS unk; Nr Irving; Bedford **GS:** Y **SP:** Mary Church **VI:** No further data **P:** unk **BLW:** unk **RG:** N **MK:** N **PH:** unk **SS:** E pg 126; SAR application **BS:** 80 vol 1 pg 150.

CAMPBELL, William; b 12 Dec 1755; d 23 Oct 1823 **RU:** Captain, Ent serv 1775, 7th Virginia Regt under Capt Gregory Smith **CEM:** Campbell Family; GPS unk; Campbellton near Barboursville; Orange **GS:** U **SP:** Mar (19 Aug 1783 King & Queen Co) Susan/Susanna Pierce (c1765-13 Mar 1852) **VI:** Nephew of Supreme Ct of Appeals Judge Edmond Pendleton. Widow pen Orange Co age 73 1838. R461. Brothers Joseph & James also served in Revolution **P:** Y **BLW:** Y **RG:** unk **MK:** unk **PH:** unk **SS:** BY pg 7; K Vol 1 pg 158 **BS:** JLARC 4.

CAMPBELL, William; b unk; d 1781 **RU:** Captain, Service unit not determined. Died as result of Yorktown battle **CEM:** Yorktown Victory Monument Tablet; GPS 38.28350, -78.54150; Yorktown; York **GS:** U **SP:** No info **VI:** No further data **P:** unk **BLW:** unk **RG:** unk **MK:** unk **PH:** unk **SS:** J-Yorktown Historian **BS:** JLARC 74.

CAMPBELL, William; b 1745, Augusta Co; d 22 Aug 1781 **RU:** Brigadier General, Was hero of Battle of Kings Mountain. Was a brigade commander **CEM:** Aspenvale; GPS 36.81420, -81.64000; Rts 641 & 642, Seven Mile Ford; Smyth **GS:** U **SP:** Elizabeth Henry (1749-1825), sister of Patrick Henry **VI:** Son of (-----) & Margaret (Buchanan) Campbell. Congratulated by U.S Congress. He d of sickness a few days before Battle of Green Springs dying in Hanover Co. Bur at Rocky Mills, Hanover Co, but in 1823, relatives moved remains to old home of Aspenville on the Holston and laid him to rest next to his mother **P:** unk **BLW:** Y **RG:** Y **MK:** unk **PH:** unk **SS:** BY pg 292; J-NSSAR 1993 Reg **BS:** JLARC 1; 196.

CANNADAY, James; b 1750 or 1755; d 1817 **RU:** Private, Served in 3rd Cont Line **CEM:** Elsie Jones; GPS unk; Nr Endicott Assembly of God Church, Rt 793; Franklin **GS:** U **SP:** Elizabeth Raikes **VI:** No further data **P:** unk **BLW:** unk **RG:** unk **MK:** unk **PH:** unk **SS:** E pg 127 **BS:** JLARC 20.

CANNELLE, Jean; b unk; d 1781 **RU:** Seaman, Served on "Citoyen" and died from Yorktown battle **CEM:** French Memorial; GPS 36.81944, -79.39933; Yorktown; York **GS:** U **SP:** No info **VI:** No further data **P:** unk **BLW:** unk **RG:** Y **MK:** unk **PH:** unk **SS:** J-Yorktown Historian **BS:** JLARC 1, 74.

CANTON, Antoine; b unk; d 1781 **RU:** Soldier, Served in Bourbonnais Bn and died from Yorktown battle **CEM:** French Memorial; GPS 36.81944, -79.39933; Yorktown; York **GS:** U **SP:** No info **VI:** No further data **P:** unk **BLW:** unk **RG:** Y **MK:** unk **PH:** unk **SS:** J-Yorktown Historian **BS:** JLARC 1, 74.

CANYS, Pierre; b unk; d 1781 **RU:** Soldier, Served in Foix Bn and died from Yorktown battle **CEM:** French Memorial; GPS 36.81944, -79.39933; Yorktown; York **GS:** U **SP:** No info **VI:** No further data **P:** unk **BLW:** unk **RG:** Y **MK:** unk **PH:** unk **SS:** J-Yorktown Historian **BS:** JLARC 1, 74.

CARBONEL, Louis; b unk; d 1781 **RU:** Soldier, Served in Auxonne Bn and died from Yorktown battle **CEM:** French Memorial; GPS 36.81944, -79.39933; Yorktown; York **GS:** U **SP:** No info **VI:** No further data **P:** unk **BLW:** unk **RG:** Y **MK:** unk **PH:** unk **SS:** J-Yorktown Historian **BS:** JLARC 1, 74.

CARDWELL, Robert; b 1746, England; d 18 Feb 1839 **RU:** Private, Served in Bedford & Amherst Co Militias. Served under Capt William Lovin in battle at Yorktown Oct 1781. Had tour guarding prisoners. Served for three yrs or more **CEM:** Dixon Family; GPS 37.18420, -79.59310; Off Rt 658, Concord quadrant, nr Rustburg; Campbell **GS:** U **SP:** 1) Elmira (-----) 2) Alice (-----) (1766-Jan 1839) **VI:** Son of Willam John (1737-1773) & Mary (Sikes/Sykes) (1738-1806) Cardwell, Recd pension in Campbell Co **P:** Y **BLW:** unk **RG:** unk **MK:** N **PH:** unk **SS:** E pg 129 **BS:** JLARC 4, 21, 36.

CARLETON, Joseph; b 1754, Beleveedre, England; d 11 May 1812 **RU:** Captain, Ent serv Bedford Co 1776 and 1781 Amherst Co. Was Paymaster, Cont Army, Pulaski Legion 1779 and Auditor of Accounts in Philadelphia May 1779 **CEM:** Arlington National; GPS 38.88377, -77.06535; Jefferson Davis Hwy Rt 110; Arlington **GS:** Y **SP:** No info **VI:** Secretary, Board of War, 1780-1783. Acting/Assistant Sec War, 1783-1785. Died in Washington DC. Orig bur in Old Presbyterian Cem in Washington DC; reinterred Arlington 13 Nov 1907. Pen age 85, Campbell Co R467 **P:** Y **BLW:** unk **RG:** Y **MK:** Y **PH:** unk **SS:** J-NSSAR 1993 Reg; E pg 130 **BS:** JLARC 1; 196.

RU=Rank/Unit	CEM=Cemetery	GS=Gravestone	SP=Spousal Information
VI=Other Veteran Info	P=Pension	BLW=Bounty/Land Warrant	RG=Registered Grave
MK=SAR/DAR Marker	PH=Photo	SS=Service Source	BS=Burial Source

57

CARLIN, William; b 1732, England; d 1820 **RU:** Patriot, Was George Washington's tailor **CEM:** Ball-Carlin; GPS unk; 300 S Kensington St; Arlington **GS:** Y **SP:** Elizabeth Ball (__-16 Jul 1869) **VI:** Died in Glencarlyn **P:** N **BLW:** N **RG:** unk **MK:** unk **PH:** unk **SS:** Sign in cemetery **BS:** 196.

CARLISLE (CARLILE)(CARLYLE), James; b 1725; d 1802 **RU:** Private, Served in a VA unit in Illinois **CEM:** Clover Creek Church; GPS unk; Clover Creek Rt 678 S of McDowell, 7.7 mi, right hand side; Highland **GS:** U **SP:** No info **VI:** No further data **P:** unk **BLW:** unk **RG:** Y **MK:** unk **PH:** unk **SS:** J-NSSAR 1993 Reg, J- DAR Hatcher; CZ pg 84 **BS:** JLARC 1, 2.

CARLOCK, Hanchrist; b 1727; d 1803 **RU:** Private, Col Willam Christian Regt in Cherokee Expedition **CEM:** Carlock Family; GPS unk; Lick Run; Botetourt **GS:** U **SP:** 1) Susan Witmer 2) Sarah Whitman **VI:** No further data **P:** unk **BLW:** unk **RG:** unk **MK:** unk **PH:** unk **SS:** J- DAR Hatcher; BC part 2 pg 1420 **BS:** JLARC 2.

CARLYLE, John; b 1720, Dumfrieshire, Scotland; d Sep 1780 **RU:** Major/Patriot, Signed Legislative Petition 25 Oct 1779 to establish Naval port in Alexandria. Gave material aid to cause **CEM:** Old Presbyterian Meeting House; GPS 38.48528, -77.23532; 323 S Fairfax St; Alexandria City **GS:** Y **SP:** 1) Leah (-----) (c1744-11 Oct 1803 2) Kitty Cahale **VI:** Son of Dr. William Carlysle & Raches Murray. Royal Customs Collector for S Potomac; merchant of Alexandria, President of the Virginia Council. One of the first trustees of Alexandria in 1748, Commissary of VA forces in 1754. Name listed on SAR plaque in cemetery **P:** unk **BLW:** unk **RG:** Y **MK:** Y **PH:** unk **SS:** D Fairfax Co **BS:** JLARC 1, 86; 23 pg 100; 196.

CARMACK, John; b 1751, Frederick Co; d 1833 **RU:** Private, Ent serv 1774 Washington Co. Served less than 6 mos **CEM:** Carmack; GPS unk; Nr Bristol; Washington **GS:** U **SP:** No info **VI:** Probably brother of William Carmack. Moved with Father to Washington Co 1773. Appl for pension 1832 there but rejected due to less than 6 mos serv. R471 Military marker. Cem #277A in source 80 **P:** unk **BLW:** unk **RG:** Y **MK:** unk **PH:** unk **SS:** K Vol 1 pg 164 **BS:** JLARC 4, 2, 34, 76, 80.

CARMACK, William; b 5 Jan 1761, Prob Frederick Co; d 24 Sep 1851 **RU:** Private, Enl Washington Co Jan 1779. Served in Capt James Shelby's Army, Montgomery's VA Regt, George Rogers Clark during the Kaskaska Campaign. Discharged 10 Jul 1780 **CEM:** Brooks; GPS unk; Ewing on Kesterson Rd Rt 690, 3 mi fr town; Lee **GS:** Y **SP:** 1) Elizabeth Walker? 2) Mary Polly (Yeary) Ball **VI:** Probably brother of John Carmack. Military marker. Pen 1832 Lee Co S9139. R471 Marker dated 2 Nov 2012 **P:** Y **BLW:** Y **RG:** Y **MK:** Y **PH:** Y **SS:** AK; K Vol 1 pg 164 **BS:** JLARC 4, 2, 34, 80.

CARPENTER, Samuel; b 15 Mar 1759; d Bef Oct 1825 **RU:** Private, Served in VA Cont Line Regt, 1st VA Brigade, commanded by BG Peter Muhlenberg, Maj Gen Nathaniel Greene **CEM:** Carpenter Family; GPS unk; on first patent land compiled 1940, VA346; Madison **GS:** N **SP:** 1) Dinah Chrisler 2) Mar (1793) Margaret Blankenbaker **VI:** Son of William (1730-1810) & Mary (Wilhoit) Carpenter. Carpenter name aka Zimmerman, GF VA Germanna Colony settler 1717 **P:** Y **BLW:** Y **RG:** unk **MK:** unk **PH:** unk **SS:** SAR Ancestor #P-129019; C pg 227; AP-pen file W6632 **BS:** 197.

CARPER, Jacob; b unk; d Aft May 1815 **RU:** Soldier/Patriot, Gave material aid to cause **CEM:** Fincastle Presbyterian; GPS 37.50017, -79.87558; 108 E Back St, Fincastle; Botetourt **GS:** N **SP:** 1) Mar (5 Jan 1795 Botetourt Co) Sally Raymer 2) Mar (3 Apr 1814 Botetourt Co) Mary Newell d/o John & (-----) Newell 3) Mar (24 May 1815) Elizabeth Nutter d/o Zadock & (-----) Nutter **VI:** Name is on the SAR plaque **P:** unk **BLW:** unk **RG:** Y **MK:** Y **PH:** N **SS:** J-NSSAR 1993 Reg; D Botetourt Co **BS:** JLARC 1.

CARPER, Nicholas; b 1749; d 1813 **RU:** Soldier, Served in Capt Uriah Springer's Co 9th VA Regt. Guarded jail Oct 1782 under Capt Robinson and served until end of war **CEM:** Fincastle Presbyterian; GPS 37.50017, -79.87558; 108 E Back St, Fincastle; Botetourt **GS:** U **SP:** Elizabeth Shrider **VI:** Was juror and constable Botetourt Co. Recd BLW #1065 **P:** unk **BLW:** unk **RG:** Y **MK:** unk **PH:** unk **SS:** DAR Ancestor #A019560; SAR Ancestor #P-129089; A pg 283 **BS:** 196, JLARC 1, 60.

CARPIER, Gilles; b unk; d 1781 **RU:** Seaman, Served on "Solitaire" and died from Yorktown battle **CEM:** French Memorial; GPS 36.81944, -79.39933; Yorktown; York **GS:** U **SP:** No info **VI:** No further data **P:** unk **BLW:** unk **RG:** Y **MK:** unk **PH:** unk **SS:** J-Yorktown Historian **BS:** JLARC 1, 74.

CARR, Dabney Jr; b 1763; d 16 May 1793 **RU:** Private?, Served in Capt William Phillips Co of volunteer rangers **CEM:** Monticello; GPS 38.00829, -78.45520; 931 Thomas Jefferson Pkwy; Charlottesville City

RU=Rank/Unit	CEM=Cemetery	GS=Gravestone	SP=Spousal Information
VI=Other Veteran Info	P=Pension	BLW=Bounty/Land Warrant	RG=Registered Grave
MK=SAR/DAR Marker	PH=Photo	SS=Service Source	BS=Burial Source

58

GS: Y **SP:** No info **VI:** Was an attorney. Recd 50 acres of bounty land. Conflicting info on burial site-- Monticello website research indicates no burial there for him. **P:** unk **BLW:** Y **RG:** N **MK**: N **PH:** unk **SS:** AH pg 295 **BS:** 80 vol 1 pg 156.

CARR, John; b 28 Aug 1738, County Down, Ireland; d 13 Nov 1807 **RU:** Ensign/Patriot, Served in1st VA Regt. Gave material aid to cause **CEM:** Union Cemetery; GPS 39.12046, -77.56239; 323 N King St, Leesburg; Loudoun **GS:** Y **SP:** No info **VI:** No further data **P:** unk **BLW:** unk **RG:** N **MK:** N **PH:** N **SS:** AL Ct bk pg 3, Loudoun Co; DD **BS:** 211 pg. 171.

CARR, John; b 1746; d 1809 **RU:** Patriot, Gave 600# meal for Albemarle Barracks **CEM:** Carr Family; GPS unk; Stoney Pt Rd Rt 20 near Charlottsville; Charlottesville City **GS:** Y **SP:** No info **VI:** DAR marker by Jack Jouett Chapter 10 Nov 1939 **P:** N **BLW:** N **RG:** N **MK:** Y **PH:** unk **SS:** AL Ct Bk pg 4, 24; Albemarle & Slatton, Arbemarle Co Public Claims pg 4 **BS:** 80 pg 156; 196

CARR, John; b 15 Jul 1764, Loudoun Co; d 15 Sep 1804 **RU:** Soldier, Served in13th VA Regt **CEM:** Fox Family; GPS unk; Waterford S on Hwy 62, Paeonian Springs; Loudoun **GS:** Y **SP:** No info **VI:** Son of Thomas (1733-1796) & Mary (Cummings) (1744-1810) Carr. Broken Gr St **P:** unk **BLW:** unk **RG:** unk **MK:** unk **PH:** unk **SS:** CI 13th VA Regt **BS:** 196.

CARR, Thomas Sr; b c1733, Ireland; d 15 Oct 1796 **RU:** Sergeant, Served in Capt William Henderson's Co, Morgan's Riflemen; also served in 9th Cont Line **CEM:** Fox Family; GPS unk; Waterford S on Hwy 62, Paeonian Springs; Loudoun **GS:** Y **SP:** Mary Cummings (1744-1810) **VI:** Son of John Carr. Inscription on stone: died age 63 yrs **P:** unk **BLW:** unk **RG:** Y **MK:** unk **PH:** unk **SS:** J-NSSAR 2000 Reg; E pg 132 **BS:** JLARC 76.

CARRE, Rene; b unk; d 1781 **RU:** Seaman, Served on "Hector" and died from Yorktown battle **CEM:** French Memorial; GPS 36.81944, -79.39933; Yorktown; York **GS:** U **SP:** No info **VI:** No further data **P:** unk **BLW:** unk **RG:** Y **MK:** unk **PH:** unk **SS:** J-Yorktown Historian **BS:** JLARC 1, 74.

CARRINGTON, Edward; b 11 Feb 1748; d 28 Oct 1810 **RU:** Lieutenant Colonel/Quartermaster General, Ent serv 1776. Was Capt of Militia Co in Cumberland Co in Dec 1775. Commissioned Lt Col of artillery in Revolutionary Army 1776 and later served as Quartermaster General on staff of Gen Nathanial Greene. Commanded artillery in Battles of Hobkirk's Hill and Yorktown 1781 **CEM:** St John's Episcopal; GPS 37.53183, -77.41958; 2401 E Broad St; Richmond City **GS:** U **SP:** Mar (8 Dec 1792 Henrico Co) Mrs. Eliza J. Brent (c1765-__), widow. Her 2nd husband. d/o (-----) and Jacquelin Amber. **VI:** A Delegate fr VA to the Continental Congress, 1789-1788. Appointed Marshal of Virginia by President Washington 1789. Served as jury foreman during Aaron Burr's trial for treason in 1807. Widow pension 1839 Richmond City 1839, age 74. R480 **P:** unk **BLW:** unk **RG:** Y **MK:** unk **PH:** unk **SS:** J-NSSAR 1993 Reg; CE pg 13; K Vol 1 pg 169. **BS:** JLARC 1; 196.

CARRINGTON, George; b 15 Mar 1711, St Philip, Barbados; d 7 Feb 1785 **RU:** Colonel, Was Col of Militia, 1778-81 **CEM:** Hollywood; GPS 37.53560, -77.45720; 412 S Cherry St; Richmond City **GS:** U **SP:** 1) Alice Adams (c1712-15 Feb 1785) 2) Anne (-----) 3) Mar (12 Dec 1792 Richmond) Eliabeth Brent **VI:** Son of Henningham, Codrington (1675-28 Jan 1744, St Philip, Barados) & (-----) (c1675-18 Jan 1744 at sea) Carrington. Died in Cumberland Co. BLW issued 21 Jan 1800. R480 **P:** unk **BLW:** Y **RG:** Y **MK:** unk **PH:** unk **SS:** J-NSSAR 1993 Reg; K Vol 1 pg 169 **BS:** JLARC 1; 196.

CARRINGTON, George; b 21 Nov 1756, Charlotte Co; d 27 May 1809 **RU:** Lieutenant, Served in Lee's Legion of Lt Dragoons, 1779-1783, and was POW 1782 **CEM:** Oak Hill; GPS unk; South Boston; Halifax **GS:** U **SP:** Sarah Coles Tucker **VI:** Son of Paul (1733-1818) & Margaret (Reade) (1734-1766) Carrington. Became a Brigadier General after war, member House of Delegates, 1802-3 and state senator. BLW 2666 acres **P:** unk **BLW:** Y **RG:** unk **MK:** unk **PH:** unk **SS:** E pg 133; F pg 17 **BS:** 196.

CARRINGTON, George Jr; b 15 Mar 1737; d 7 Nov 1784 **RU:** Major/Patriot, Served in Cumberland Co Militia 1777 to 26 Feb 1781. Performed civil service as county clerk, surveyor & member Committee of Safety **CEM:** Boston Hill Plantation; GPS unk; Cartersville; Cumberland **GS:** N **SP:** Mar (1764) Margaret Bernard **VI:** Son of George (1711-1785) & Anne (Mayo) (1711-1785) Carrington **P:** unk **BLW:** unk **RG:** unk **MK:** unk **PH:** N **SS:** E pg 133 **BS:** 196.

RU=Rank/Unit	CEM=Cemetery	GS=Gravestone	SP=Spousal Information
VI=Other Veteran Info	P=Pension	BLW=Bounty/Land Warrant	RG=Registered Grave
MK=SAR/DAR Marker	PH=Photo	SS=Service Source	BS=Burial Source

59

CARRINGTON, Paul; b 16 Mar 1733, Cumberland Co; d 23 Jan 1818 **RU:** Patriot, Gave material aid to the cause **CEM:** Mulberry Hill; GPS 36.88629, -78.70353; Staunton River Battlefield State Park, 1035 Fort Hill Trail, Randolph; Charlotte **GS:** Y **SP:** 1) Margaret Read (__-May 1766) 2) Priscilla Sims (__-1803). Both are bur here. **VI:** Son of Col George Carrington (1711-1785) & Ann Myo (1711-1785) of "Boston Hill," Cumberland Co. King's Attorney for Bedford Co in 1756. House of Delegates 1765-1776; Rev Convention 1775, 1776; VA Senate 1776-1778. Judge of High Ct of Appeals, 1779-1809. Helped form Prince Edward Academy in 1755. Died in Halifax Co. Small modern ground stone marks his grave **P:** N **BLW:** N **RG:** N **MK:** N **PH:** unk **SS:** AL Ct Bk pg 3 **BS:** DAR Rpt; 196.

CARRINGTON, Paul; b 20 Sep 1764, Charlotte Co; d 8 Jan 1816 **RU:** Soldier, Was in battles at Green Springs & Guilford CH **CEM:** Carrington Family; GPS unk; On Bruce Estate "Berry Hill" W of South Boston, off Co Rd 659, on the "River Rd" E of the house; Halifax **GS:** U **SP:** Mar (24 Aug 1786) Mildred Howell Coles (15 May 1769-14 Apr 1840) d/o Col Walter (1739-1780) and Mildred (Lightfoot) (1752-1799) Coles **VI:** No further data **P:** unk **BLW:** unk **RG:** Y **MK:** unk **PH:** unk **SS:** NSSAR Ancestor # P-129302 **BS:** JLARC 1, 2, 4, 101.

CARSON, Charles; b c1741, Ireland; d 1815 **RU:** Ensign, Served in 4th Cont Line **CEM:** Sinking Springs; GPS 36.71030, -81.98170; 136 E Main St, Abingdon; Washington **GS:** Y **SP:** Did not marry **VI:** No further data **P:** unk **BLW:** unk **RG:** N **MK:** N **PH:** unk **SS:** E pg 133 **BS:** 78 pg 73.

CARSON, James; b c1736; d 19 Jun 1814 **RU:** Patriot, Gave material aid to cause **CEM:** Second Concord Presbyterian; GPS 37.34209, -78.96585; Phoebe Pond Rd Rt 609 E of Concord; Appomattox **GS:** Y **SP:** Mar (c1765 Nelson Co) Mary Ann Helm (23 Oct 1743, Piscataway, Middlesex Co, NJ-18 Feb 1837, Henry Co, TN), d/o Moses & Sarah (Jameson) Helm. Bur at Dinwiddie Cemetery in Henry Co, TN **VI:** Died age 78 **P:** N **BLW:** N **RG:** unk **MK:** unk **PH:** unk **SS:** AL Ct Bk pg 13, Campbell Co **BS:** 196.

CARSON, Samuel; b 1744; d 20 Mar 1824 **RU:** Private, Served in Capt Tait's Co Augusta Co VA **CEM:** Old Providence; GPS 37.96151, -79.71000; 1005 Spottswood Rd, Spottswood; Augusta **GS:** Y **SP:** Sarah Gibson (1744-03 Mar 1832) **VI:** Son of Samuel & Janet (-----) Carson. New Govt stone beside original. Name also on SAR cemetery plaque **P:** unk **BLW:** unk **RG:** Y **MK:** Y **PH:** unk **SS:** E pg 134 **BS:** 44 pg 59.

CARTER, Charles; b 1 Jan 1732, Shirley Plantation; d 24 Jun 1806 **RU:** Captain, Served in Charles City Co VA Militia. Allowed Shirley to be used as supply depot towards end of war supplying Lafayette with arms and munitions to defeat Cornwallis at Yorktown **CEM:** Shirley Plantation; GPS unk; Rt 5 SE of Richmond; Charles City Co **GS:** N **SP:** 1) Mary Walker Carter; 2) Ann Butler Moore **VI:** Son of John Carter (1690-1742) & Elizabeth Hill (1703-1771). Planter and member-elect of the Council of State. SAR marker on grave **P:** unk **BLW:** unk **RG:** Y **MK:** Y **PH:** N **SS:** AK 2011 **BS:** 04; 196.

CARTER, Charles; b 1733, King George Co; d 29 Apr 1796, **RU:** Patriot, Specific serv at Lib VA Auditors Acct, 1779, pg 25 **CEM:** Willis Hill, Fredericksburg National Military Park; GPS unk; Marye Heights; Fredericksburg City **GS:** Y **SP:** No info **VI:** Son of Charles Cleve & (-----) Carter. Died at Ludlowe Plantation **P:** N **BLW:** N **RG:** Y **MK:** N **PH:** unk **SS:** D pg 871, 874; CZ pg 86 **BS:** 196.

CARTER, Edward; b 1726; d 1792 **RU:** Patriot, Specific serv at Lib VA War files vol 4, pg 140 **CEM:** Shirley Plantation; GPS unk; Rt 5, James River; Charles City Co **GS:** Y **SP:** No info **VI:** House of Delegates **P:** N **BLW:** N **RG:** N **MK:** N **PH:** unk **SS:** AS SAR applic; CZ pg 86 **BS:** 80 vol 1 pg 158.

CARTER, Edward; b 21 Apr 1736; d 13 Aug 1810 **RU:** Soldier, Served in Capt Syme's Co, 10th Cont Line **CEM:** Carter Family; GPS unk; Nr Middleburg; Loudoun **GS:** Y **SP:** No info **VI:** No further data **P:** unk **BLW:** unk **RG:** N **MK:** N **PH:** unk **SS:** E pg 134; AS **BS:** 80 vol 1 pg 158.

CARTER, James; b 16 Sep 1743, Orange Co, NC; d 14 Sep 1812 **RU:** Corporal, Served in Capt Thomas Posey's Co 7th Cont line, Sep 1777 **CEM:** South Fork Meeting House; GPS 39.02640, -77.80220; Rt 630 Unison; Loudoun **GS:** Y **SP:** Mar (31 Aug 1765 Loudoun Co) Hannah Eblin (2 Jan 1746 Chester Co, PA-16 Sep 1798 Loudoun Co) d/o John (1724-1795/7) & Mary (Warner) (__-aft 1795) Eblin **VI:** No further data **P:** unk **BLW:** unk **RG:** unk **MK:** unk **PH:** unk **SS:** E pg 134; AP Payroll **BS:** 196.

RU=Rank/Unit	CEM=Cemetery	GS=Gravestone	SP=Spousal Information
VI=Other Veteran Info	P=Pension	BLW=Bounty/Land Warrant	RG=Registered Grave
MK=SAR/DAR Marker	PH=Photo	SS=Service Source	BS=Burial Source

60

CARTER, Joseph; b 04 Sep 1736, Fauquier Co; d 16 Aug 1808 **RU:** Private, Served in 11th and 15th VA Regt **CEM:** Carter Family; GPS 36.71169,-82.69778; Rt 649, Rye Cove; Scott **GS:** Y **SP:** No info **VI:** Son of Peter (1706 Lancaster Co-1790 Amherst Co) & Judith (Norris) (1710-1765) Carter. SAR marker. Orig GS broken in half **P:** unk **BLW:** unk **RG:** Y **MK:** Y **PH:** unk **SS:** O; CZ pg 87 **BS:** 04; 196.

CARTER, Landon; b 18 Aug 1710 Christ Church, Lancaster Co; d 22 Dec 1778 **RU:** Colonel/Patriot, Was Clerk of Committee of Safety 1775 **CEM:** Lower Lunenburg Parish Church; GPS 37.96066, -76.76920; Off N Side Rt 360, Warsaw; Richmond Co **GS:** Y **SP:** 1) Mar (16 Nov 1732) Elizabeth Wormeley (1713-1740) 2) Mar (22 Sep 1742) Maria Horsmanden Byrd (1727-1744) 3) Mar (1746) Elizabeth Beale **VI:** Son of Robert King (1663-1732) and Elizabeth (Landon) (1684-1719) Carter of Corotoman Plantation in Lancaster Co **P:** unk **BLW:** unk **RG:** Y **MK:** N **PH:** unk **SS:** A part 2 pg 275; CJ 1st Series Vol 5 no 4 pg 251 **BS:** 24 pg 2184.

CARTER, Landon Jr; b Aug 1738, Richmond Co; d 1801 **RU:** Private, Served in Capt Wm Sanford's Co, Col Alexander Spotswood's 2d VA Regt, Cont Line **CEM:** Pittsylvania (Carter); GPS 38.49711, -77.31305; Manassas National Battlefield Park; Manassas City **GS:** U **SP:** Mar (1760) Judith Fauntleroy (1746-c1798) **VI:** Son of Landon Sr (7 Jun 1709-10 Aug 1778) & Elizabeth (Wormley) (1713-31 Jan 1740) Carter. His plantation house was named "Pittsylvania" **P:** unk **BLW:** unk **RG:** unk **MK:** unk **PH:** unk **SS:** DAR Ancestor #A020017; A pg 135 **BS:** 190 name of cem.

CARTER, Nicholas; b unk; d 1813 **RU:** Private, Served in 7th, 9th,13th Cont Line **CEM:** Fincastle Presbyterian; GPS 37.50017, -79.97558; 108 E Back St, Fincastle; Botetourt **GS:** U **SP:** No info **VI:** No further data **P:** unk **BLW:** unk **RG:** N **MK:** N **PH:** unk **SS:** E pg 135; BY **BS:** 197.

CARTER, Richard; b unk, Kent, England; d 1 Dec 1806 **RU:** Private, Served in Capt Springer's Co in VA Cont line. Also served in Col John Gibson's 7th Regt Cont Line; also enlisted May 1st, 1775 in Capt Jackquil Morgan's Co, at siege of Yorktown. Served also in 3rd Virginia Regt **CEM:** Richard Carter Property; GPS unk; Nr Leesburg; Loudoun **GS:** U **SP:** Mar (1780) Catherine (-----) (__-aft 1817, Loudoun) Co **VI:** No further data **P:** unk **BLW:** unk **RG:** N **MK:** N **PH:** unk **SS:** DAR Ancestor #A020050; AP roll #1022; AS SAR applic **BS:** SAR Appl.

CARTER, Robert III; b 1728; d 11 Mar 1804 **RU:** Patriot, Gave material aid to the cause **CEM:** Nomini Hall Graveyard; GPS unk; Hague; Westmoreland **GS:** N **SP:** Mar (2 Apr 1754 Anapolis MD) Francis Ann Tasker **VI:** Son of Robert & Priscilla (-----) Carter. Largest slave owner to give freedom to over 550 slaves in 1791. Died in Baltimore. He directed that no GS mark his burial place **P:** N **BLW:** N **RG:** N **MK:** N **PH:** N **SS:** AL Ct Bk pg 1, 3, 4, 5 **BS:** 121 newspaper.

CARTER, Thomas; b 27 Nov 1734; d 15 Jul 1817 **RU:** Gunner/Patriot, Enl Cumberland Co in1st Artillery Regt of Cont Army. Gave material aid to cause **CEM:** Glenrock; GPS 36.80060, -79.44548; E of Rt 824, .5 mi S of Greenbuck Branch; Pittsylvania **GS:** Y **SP:** Mar (10 Jul 1764) Winifred Hobson d/o Adcock & Joanne (Lawson) Hobson **VI:** Died in Rye Cove, Scott Co. DAR restoring grave. R 487 **P:** Y **BLW:** unk **RG:** unk **MK:** unk **PH:** unk **SS:** D Mecklenburg Co **BS:** 174, JLARC 82, 96.

CARTER, Thomas; b 24 Mar 1731, Lancaster Co; d unk **RU:** Patriot, Gave material aid to the cause **CEM:** Carter; GPS unk; Rye Cove; Scott **GS:** U **SP:** Mary Morgan **VI:** Son of Peter and Judith Norris Carter **P:** N **BLW:** N **RG:** unk **MK:** unk **PH:** unk **SS:** AL Comm Bk IV pg 268 Washington Co **BS:** 196.

CARTER, William; b unk; d 2 Jul 1828 **RU:** Lieutenant, Served in Henrico Co Militia **CEM:** Shockoe Hill; GPS 37.55190, -77.43170; 4th & Hospital Sts; Richmond City **GS:** U **SP:** No info **VI:** No further data **P:** unk **BLW:** unk **RG:** unk **MK:** unk **PH:** unk **SS:** E pg 135 **BS:** 196.

CARTER, William; b c1732; d 12 Jun 1799 **RU:** Surgeon, Served in Col Baylor's Regt of Cavalry. Recd severe cuts on both wrists at Lenew's Ferry in May 1770. Served as surgeon in Cont Hospital in Williamsburg fr Jul 1776 until end of war **CEM:** St John's Episcopal; GPS 37.53183, -77.41958; 2401 E Broad St; Richmond City **GS:** Y **SP:** No info **VI:** Resided in Caroline Co. Appl for pen. GS indicates age 67 at death **P:** Y **BLW:** unk **RG:** Y **MK:** N **PH:** unk **SS:** A pg 388; BX pg 136 **BS:** 39 pg 99.

CARTNELL (CARTMELL, CARTMILL), Nathaniel; b c1753; d Oct 1795 (will proven) **RU:** Patriot, Paid Rev War Supply Tax called Personal Property tax, Frederick Co 1782 **CEM:** St John's Lutheran; GPS 39.15310, -78.36520; 3623 Buck Mountain Rd, Hayfield; Frederick **GS:** Y **SP:** 1) Mar (23 Apr 1807)

RU=Rank/Unit	CEM=Cemetery	GS=Gravestone	SP=Spousal Information
VI=Other Veteran Info	P=Pension	BLW=Bounty/Land Warrant	RG=Registered Grave
MK=SAR/DAR Marker	PH=Photo	SS=Service Source	BS=Burial Source

61

Sarah Bean 2) Mar (7 Mar 1833) Sarah E. Lupton **VI:** No further data **P:** N **BLW:** N **RG:** Y **MK**: N **PH:** unk **SS:** E pg 135; DV **BS:** 59 pg 55.

CARWILES (CARWILE), Jacob Sr; b 1751, Goochland Co; d 1837 **RU:** Private, Served in Campbell Co Militia **CEM:** Carwile; GPS 37.08470, -78.58020; Rt 708 Seamster Rd, go to end, abt 1 mi walk, Noruna; Campbell **GS:** Y **SP:** Mar (26 Feb 1802, Campbell Co (bond)) Martha Scott **VI:** Pen awarded 16 Sep 1833 S127093. Descendents placed Govt marker there in the woods **P:** Y **BLW:** unk **RG:** unk **MK:** N **PH:** unk **SS:** NSSAR Ancestor # P -129813 **BS:** JLARC 3; 196.

CARY, George; b unk; d 1826 **RU:** Private, Was private in Hazen's Regt **CEM:** George Cary Family; GPS unk; 4.5 mi W of Courtland; Southampton **GS:** Y **SP:** No info **VI:** No further data **P:** unk **BLW:** unk **RG:** N **MK:** N **PH:** unk **SS:** AP roll **BS:** 144 Geo Cary.

CARY, John; b 1745; d 1795 **RU:** Captain, Was Co commander Elizabeth City Co Sep 1775 **CEM:** Peartree Hall; GPS unk; Nr Warwick Hall CH and Tabbs Ln; Newport News City **GS:** U **SP:** 1) Sally Slater 2) Susanna Armistead **VI:** No further data **P:** unk **BLW:** unk **RG:** Y **MK:** unk **PH:** unk **SS:** J-NSSAR 1993 Reg; CE pg 17 **BS:** JLARC 1.

CARY, Richard; b 1739; d 18 Nov 1789 **RU:** Captain/Patriot, Commanded a co in Warwick Co Militia 1775. Was member of Committee of Safety. Represented Warwick Co in VA State Convention 1776. Gave material aid to cause in Elizabeth City **CEM:** Peartree Hall; GPS unk; Nr Warwick Hall CH and Tabbs Ln; Newport News City **GS:** Y **SP:** Mary Cole **VI:** Judge of Central Ct. Died in Richmond or Newport News City **P:** unk **BLW:** unk **RG:** unk **MK:** unk **PH:** unk **SS:** J-NSSAR 1993 Reg, J- DAR Hatcher; AL Ct Bk pg 7; E pg 136 **BS:** JLARC 1, 2.

CARY, Richard Jr; b 1760; d 1800 **RU:** Captain, Commanded a Co in Warwick Co Militia **CEM:** Peartree Hall; GPS unk; Nr Warwick Hall CH and Tabbs Ln; Newport News City **GS:** N **SP:** No info **VI:** No further data **P:** unk **BLW:** unk **RG:** Y **MK**: N **PH:** N **SS:** E pg 136; CZ pg 88 **BS:** SAR Appl.

CARY, Thomas Jr; b 1720; d 1793 **RU:** Captain, Commanded a Co in Warwick Co Militia **CEM:** Windmill Point; GPS unk; N of jct Warwick River and Lucas Creek and S of Rt 173; Newport News City **GS:** U **SP:** 1) (-----) Whitaker 2) Frances Godwyn **VI:** Son of Cary Thomas Sr who d 1782 in York Co **P:** unk **BLW:** unk **RG:** Y **MK:** unk **PH:** unk **SS:** J-NSSAR 1993 Reg; CZ pg 88 **BS:** JLARC 1.

CARY, Wilson Miles; b 1734, Warwick Co; d 1817 **RU:** Colonel, Specific serv at Lib VA, Accts Committee of Safety, 1775-6, pg 40 **CEM:** Cary Family; GPS unk; Carysbrook; Fluvanna **GS:** Y **SP:** 1) Mar (25 May 1758) Sarah Blair d/o Honorable John & (-----) Blair (___-28 Feb 1799) 2) Rebecca Dawson **VI:** No further data **P:** unk **BLW:** unk **RG:** Y **MK**: N **PH:** unk **SS:** E pg 137; CZ pg 88 **BS:** SAR Appl.

CASSELL, Michael; b 1764; d 1826 **RU:** Patriot, Gave material aid to cause **CEM:** Kimberling; GPS 36.91750, -81.30440; Rt 617, Rural Retreat; Wythe **GS:** U **SP:** Catherine Tobler **VI:** No further data **P:** N **BLW:** N **RG:** unk **MK:** unk **PH:** unk **SS:** D Montgomery Co **BS:** JLARC 122, 123.

CASSIN, John; b 1758; d 1822 **RU:** Private, Served in PA military **CEM:** Arlington National; GPS 38.88377, -77.06535; Jefferson Davis Hwy Rt 110; Arlington **GS:** U **SP:** No info **VI:** No further data **P:** unk **BLW:** unk **RG:** Y **MK:** N **PH:** unk **SS:** J-NSSAR 1993 Reg **BS:** JLARC 1.

CATEL, Jean; b unk; d 1781 **RU:** Soldier, Served in Gatinais Bn and died from Yorktown battle **CEM:** French Memorial; GPS 36.81944, -79.39933; Yorktown; York **GS:** U **SP:** No info **VI:** No further data **P:** unk **BLW:** unk **RG:** Y **MK:** unk **PH:** unk **SS:** J-Yorktown Historian **BS:** JLARC 1, 74.

CATHER, Jasper; b 1740, Ulster, Trone, Ireland; d 30 Jul 1812 **RU:** Private/Patriot, Served in Frederick Co Militia, Name appears on supply tax list, Fauquier Co, PA **CEM:** Back Creek Quaker, aka Gainesboro United Methodist; GPS 39.27861, -78.25694; 166 Siler Ln, Gainesboro; Frederick **GS:** U **SP:** 1) Catherine Lawrence 2) Barbara Lawrence 3) Mar (27 Mar 1786 by Christian Streit) Sarah Moore **VI:** Son of Robert and Joanna (Thurloe) Cather **P:** unk **BLW:** unk **RG:** Y **MK:** unk **PH:** unk **SS:** AR Vol 1 pg 162; NSSAR Ancestor #P 130342 **BS:** JLARC 1, 2, 4,47; 196.

CAVALIER, Francois; b unk; d 1781 **RU:** Soldier, Served in Foix Bn and died from Yorktown battle **CEM:** French Memorial; GPS 36.81944, -79.39933; Yorktown; York **GS:** U **SP:** No info **VI:** No further data **P:** unk **BLW:** unk **RG:** Y **MK:** unk **PH:** unk **SS:** J-Yorktown Historian **BS:** JLARC 1, 74.

RU=Rank/Unit	CEM=Cemetery	GS=Gravestone	SP=Spousal Information
VI=Other Veteran Info	P=Pension	BLW=Bounty/Land Warrant	RG=Registered Grave
MK=SAR/DAR Marker	PH=Photo	SS=Service Source	BS=Burial Source

CAVE, Thomas; b 1745; d 7 Dec 1802 **RU:** Patriot, Contributed to cause by paying 1783 VA War support tax **CEM:** Dumfries Public; GPS 38.34110, -77.19964; 17821 Mine Rd, Dumfries; Prince William **GS:** Y **SP:** Mary Ann (-----) (1760-04 Feb 1818) **VI:** SAR monument **P:** N **BLW:** N **RG:** Y **MK:** Y **PH:** unk **SS:** AK CWG 2014 **BS:** 04.

CECIL, John; b 24 Jan 1750, Prince George Co, MD; d 5 Aug 1832 **RU:** Private, Served in Capt Cloyd's Co, Montgomery Co Militia Sep 1777 **CEM:** Cecil Family Farm #2; GPS unk; Neck's Creek, Belspring; Pulaski **GS:** U **SP:** Keziah Witten (19 Feb 1751 Frederick Co, MD-15 May 1837) d/o Thomas & Elizabeth (Cecil) Whitten **VI:** Son of Samuel & Rebecca (White) Cecil **P:** unk **BLW:** unk **RG:** unk **MK:** unk **PH:** unk **SS:** G pg 215 **BS:** 196.

CECIL, Samuel Witten Sr; b 23 Mar 1719 Prince George Co, MD; d 28 Mar 1786 **RU:** Patriot, Performed public service as Juror and Overseer of Roads, and took oath of allegiance, Montgomery Co **CEM:** Cecil Family; GPS unk; Nr Radford and Dublin; Pulaski **GS:** U **SP:** Rebecca White (1719-16 Mar 1815) **VI:** No further data **P:** N **BLW:** N **RG:** unk **MK:** unk **PH:** unk **SS:** DAR Ancestor #A023627; DL Part 1, pg 703, 734 **BS:** 80, vol 1, pg 162; 196.

CHABRIER, Fleury; b unk; d 1781 **RU:** Soldier, Served in Bourbonnais Bn and died from Yorktown battle **CEM:** French Memorial; GPS 36.81944, -79.39933; Yorktown; York **GS:** U **SP:** No info **VI:** No further data **P:** unk **BLW:** unk **RG:** Y **MK:** unk **PH:** unk **SS:** J-Yorktown Historian **BS:** JLARC 1,74.

CHAMBERLAIN (CHAMBERLAINE), George; b 1755, Warrwick Co; d 10 Jan 1792 **RU:** Second Lieutenant/Navy, Served in Henry & Manley Galley. Served on five vessels, two of which (the Pilot Boat "Molly" and the Light Boat "Liberty"), was commanded by him after having escaped imprisonment in England **CEM:** St Paul's Episcopal; GPS 36.84733, -76.28554; 201 St Paul's Blvd; Norfolk City **GS:** N **SP:** 1) Ann Harlow Lucas 2) Fannie Lowry Needham **VI:** No further data **P:** unk **BLW:** unk **RG:** Y **MK:** N **PH:** N **SS:** BE pg 66; CB **BS:** 28.

CHAMBERLAYNE, William; b unk; d 1838 **RU:** Brig General, Specific serv at Lib VA, Journal House of Delegates, Oct 1814, pg 114 **CEM:** St John's Episcopal; GPS 37.53183, -77.41958; 2401 E Broad St; Richmond City **GS:** N **SP:** No info **VI:** No further data **P:** unk **BLW:** unk **RG:** N **MK:** N **PH:** N **SS:** E pg 142; CZ pg 91 **BS:** 28 pg 351.

CHAMBERS, John; b 1760; d 1815 **RU:** Captain, Commanded a Co in Buckingham Co; other serv at Lib VA, Auditors Acct, XVIII, pg 177 **CEM:** Chambers Family; GPS unk; Rt 659, 2.75 mi W of Ransons; Buckingham **GS:** N **SP:** Martha Hunt Allen (1763-1805) **VI:** Stone no longer standing. Survey in 1935 noted it was very small and made of marble **P:** unk **BLW:** N **RG:** N **MK:** N **PH:** N **SS:** AP roll; CZ pg 91 **BS:** 173.

CHAMOIS, Claude; b unk; d 1781 **RU:** Soldier, Served in Gatinais Bn and died from Yorktown battle **CEM:** French Memorial; GPS 36.81944, -79.39933; Yorktown; York **GS:** U **SP:** No info **VI:** No further data **P:** unk **BLW:** unk **RG:** Y **MK:** unk **PH:** unk **SS:** J-Yorktown Historian **BS:** JLARC 1, 74.

CHANCELLOR, John; b c1726; d Aft 1815 **RU:** Patriot, Gave 3 beeves to cause **CEM:** Fairview; GPS unk; Rt 3; Spotsylvania **GS:** Y **SP:** 1) Jane Monroe (1760-1840) 2) Elizabeth Edwards **VI:** No further data **P:** N **BLW:** N **RG:** Y **MK:** N **PH:** unk **SS:** D pg 805; AL **BS:** 06 pg 81, 82; 04.

CHANDLER, Carter; b c1733; d 16 Aug 1813 **RU:** Private, Ent serv Louisa Co 1780. Sub for brother-in-law Barnett Mitchell **CEM:** Chandler Family; GPS 39.1121, -78.03; Helvestine Farm, Rt 7 vic Rt 633; Clarke **GS:** Y **SP:** No info **VI:** Resident of Spotsylvania Co after war for 4 yrs, then moved to Frederick Co. Pen. 1835 age 72. R512. BLW granted 1835. Illiterate. GSs were read in 1941, but have since been moved to side of nearby barn and are difficult to read. GPS readings is fr center of cemetery **P:** Y **BLW:** Y **RG:** N **MK:** N **PH:** unk **SS:** AP pension Rec; K Vol 1 pg 186 **BS:** 58 pg 7.

CHANPEAU, Francois; b unk; d 1781 **RU:** Seaman, Served on "Northumberland" and died from Yorktown battle **CEM:** French Memorial; GPS 36.81944, -79.39933; Yorktown; York **GS:** U **SP:** No info **VI:** No further data **P:** unk **BLW:** unk **RG:** Y **MK:** unk **PH:** unk **SS:** J-Yorktown Historian **BS:** JLARC 1,74.

CHAPIN, Benjamin; b 1736; d 1781 **RU:** Surgeon, Ent VA Navy 1777. VA State Navy on Galley "Protector" **CEM:** Old Christ Church Episcopal; GPS 38.80625, -77.04718; 118 N Washington St;

RU=Rank/Unit	CEM=Cemetery	GS=Gravestone	SP=Spousal Information
VI=Other Veteran Info	P=Pension	BLW=Bounty/Land Warrant	RG=Registered Grave
MK=SAR/DAR Marker	PH=Photo	SS=Service Source	BS=Burial Source

63

Alexandria City **GS:** N **SP:** Mar (1) Leah (-----) (c1744-11 Oct 1803); 2) Kitty Cahale **VI:** Was referred to as "Dr. Chapin." Wm R Ashton admin estate in Baltimore MD 1834. Heirs rejected for pension 1838. R516 **P:** N **BLW:** unk **RG:** Y **MK:** unk **PH:** N **SS:** J-NSSAR 1993 Reg; K Vol 1 pg 188 **BS:** JLARC 1; 196.

CHAPMAN, George; b 1749; d 1814 **RU:** Patriot, Signed petition to House of Delegates urging decrease in import duties to increase commerce, 27 May 1782 **CEM:** Pohick Episcopal; GPS 38.42546, -77.11598; 9301 Richmond Hwy, Lorton; Fairfax **GS:** Y **SP:** Amelia McCrae **VI:** No further data **P:** N **BLW:** N **RG:** Y **MK:** U **PH:** unk **SS:** I; BB **BS:** 20 pg 47; 04.

CHAPMAN, Isaac; b 1764; d 1836 **RU:** Captain, Ent serv 1776 Montgomery Co (Now Giles Co) for Indian War. Ent serv again1777. Served in 2nd Battalion, 86th Regt **CEM:** Mt Prospect; GPS unk; Rt 634, Old Strother Farm, Ripplemeade; Giles **GS:** U **SP:** Margaret Williams **VI:** Appl pen fr Giles Co 1835 age 71. Pension rejected. R520 **P:** N **BLW:** unk **RG:** unk **MK:** unk **PH:** unk **SS:** K Vol 1 pg 189 **BS:** JLARC 2, 26.

CHAPMAN, John; b 18 Jan 1740; d Aft Jun 1813 **RU:** Second Lieutenant, Served in Montgomery Co Militia **CEM:** Mt Prospect; GPS unk; Rt 634, Old Strother Farm, Ripplemeade; Giles **GS:** U **SP:** Sallie Abbott **VI:** No further data **P:** unk **BLW:** unk **RG:** unk **MK:** unk **PH:** unk **SS:** J- DAR Hatcher; E pg 144 **BS:** JLARC 2.

CHAPMAN, Nathan; b 3 May 1761; d 29 Jan 1828 or 1829 **RU:** Private, Enl Capt Beverly Stubblefield's Co, Col Richard Parker's Regt, Cont Line. Taken prisoner at Charleston, SC; exchanged at Williamsburg, Oct 1781 **CEM:** Chapman Family; GPS unk; Goodview; Bedford **GS:** U **SP:** Mar (17 Feb 1791 Franklin Co) Elizabeth "Betsy" Colema **VI:** Widow pen 1839 age 69 Bedford Co, BLW granted 1855. Perhaps he is the person by this name that BLW was issued to Nathaniel Chapman of Bedord Co for service of deceased brother Thomas, his only heir. R521 **P:** Y **BLW:** Y **RG:** unk **MK:** N **PH:** unk **SS:** AR Vol 1 pg 168; K Vol 1 pg 189 **BS:** JLARC 2.

CHAPMAN, Thomas; b unk; d unk **RU:** Patriot, Gave material aid to the cause **CEM:** Fairfax City; GPS 38.84690, -77.31330; Main St & Page Ave; Fairfax City **GS:** N **SP:** No info **VI:** No further data **P:** N **BLW:** N **RG:** N **MK:** N **PH:** N **SS:** AL Ct Bk pg 9 **BS:** 61 vol III pg FX-153.

CHAPPELL, John Sr; b unk; d 1826 **RU:** Ensign/Patriot, Served in Amelia Co Militia. Took oath 26 Oct 1780. Gave material aid to cause **CEM:** Chappell; GPS unk; Fowlkes Bridge Rd, Paineville; Amelia **GS:** N **SP:** Elizabeth (-----) **VI:** Rev War BLW issued **P:** unk **BLW:** Y **RG:** unk **MK:** unk **PH:** N **SS:** C pg 200; D pg 46; E pg 144 **BS:** 196.

CHARET, Gilbert; b unk; d 1781 **RU:** Soldier, Served in Gatinais Bn and died from Yorktown battle **CEM:** French Memorial; GPS 36.81944, -79.39933; Yorktown; York **GS:** U **SP:** No info **VI:** No further data **P:** unk **BLW:** unk **RG:** Y **MK:** unk **PH:** unk **SS:** J-Yorktown Historian **BS:** JLARC 1, 74.

CHARLES, Jean; b unk; d 1781 **RU:** Seaman, Served on "Diademe" and died from Yorktown battle **CEM:** French Memorial; GPS 36.81944, -79.39933; Yorktown; York **GS:** U **SP:** No info **VI:** No further data **P:** unk **BLW:** unk **RG:** Y **MK:** unk **PH:** unk **SS:** J-Yorktown Historian **BS:** JLARC 1, 74.

CHASE, Jonathan; b unk; d 1781 **RU:** Soldier, Served fr MA, and died as result of Yorktown battle **CEM:** Yorktown Victory Monument Tablet; GPS 38.28350, -78.54150; Yorktown; York **GS:** U **SP:** No info **VI:** No further data **P:** unk **BLW:** unk **RG:** unk **MK:** unk **PH:** unk **SS:** J-Yorktown Historian **BS:** JLARC 74.

CHATILLON, Jacques; b unk; d 1781 **RU:** Soldier, Served in Agenois Bn and died from Yorktown battle **CEM:** French Memorial; GPS 36.81944, -79.39933; Yorktown; York **GS:** U **SP:** No info **VI:** No further data **P:** unk **BLW:** unk **RG:** Y **MK:** unk **PH:** unk **SS:** J-Yorktown Historian **BS:** JLARC 1, 74.

CHATTE, Pierre; b unk; d 1781 **RU:** Seaman, Served on "Hector" and died from Yorktown battle **CEM:** French Memorial; GPS 36.81944, -79.39933; Yorktown; York **GS:** U **SP:** No info **VI:** No further data **P:** unk **BLW:** unk **RG:** Y **MK:** unk **PH:** unk **SS:** J-Yorktown Historian **BS:** JLARC 1, 74.

RU=Rank/Unit	CEM=Cemetery	GS=Gravestone	SP=Spousal Information
VI=Other Veteran Info	P=Pension	BLW=Bounty/Land Warrant	RG=Registered Grave
MK=SAR/DAR Marker	PH=Photo	SS=Service Source	BS=Burial Source

64

CHAUNIET, Guillaume; b unk; d 1781 **RU:** Seaman, Served on "Hector" and died from Yorktown battle **CEM:** French Memorial; GPS 36.81944, -79.39933; Yorktown; York **GS:** U **SP:** No info **VI:** No further data **P:** unk **BLW:** unk **RG:** Y **MK:** unk **PH:** unk **SS:** J-Yorktown Historian **BS:** JLARC 1 74.

CHAUVIN, Julien; b unk; d 1781 **RU:** Soldier, Served in Santogne Bn and died from Yorktown battle **CEM:** French Memorial; GPS 36.81944, -79.39933; Yorktown; York **GS:** U **SP:** No info **VI:** No further data **P:** unk **BLW:** unk **RG:** Y **MK:** unk **PH:** unk **SS:** J-Yorktown Historian **BS:** JLARC 1, 74.

CHAVAILLARD, Thomas; b unk; d 1781 **RU:** Soldier, Served in Gatinais Bn and died from Yorktown battle **CEM:** French Memorial; GPS 36.81944, -79.39933; Yorktown; York **GS:** U **SP:** No info **VI:** No further data **P:** unk **BLW:** unk **RG:** Y **MK:** unk **PH:** unk **SS:** J-Yorktown Historian **BS:** JLARC 1, 74.

CHEMITTE, Jean; b unk; d 1781 **RU:** Seaman, Served on "Ville de Paris" and died from Yorktown battle **CEM:** French Memorial; GPS 36.81944, -79.39933; Yorktown; York **GS:** U **SP:** No info **VI:** No further data **P:** unk **BLW:** unk **RG:** Y **MK:** unk **PH:** unk **SS:** J-Yorktown Historian **BS:** JLARC 1, 74.

CHENEY (CHANEY), Abram/Abraham; b 1760; d 25 Dec 1848 **RU:** Private, Ent serv Pittsylvania Co **CEM:** Cheney Family; GPS unk; Nr Keeling; Pittsylvania **GS:** U **SP:** 1) Mary Cheatham 2) Mar (4 Apr 1811) Nancy Donalson **VI:** Widow pen Pittsylvania Co 1853 age 77, drew BLW 1855. She resided 1855 Laurel Grove. He pen Pittsylvania Co 1832, age 72; R 575 **P:** Y **BLW:** Y **RG:** unk **MK:** unk **PH:** unk **SS:** J- DAR Hatcher **BS:** JLARC 2.

CHERET, Andre; b unk; d 1781 **RU:** Soldier, Served in Royal Deaux Ponts Bn and died from Yorktown battle **CEM:** French Memorial; GPS 36.81944, -79.39933; Yorktown; York **GS:** U **SP:** No info **VI:** No further data **P:** unk **BLW:** unk **RG:** Y **MK:** unk **PH:** unk **SS:** J-Yorktown Historian **BS:** JLARC 1, 74.

CHEROT, Jean; b unk; d 1781 **RU:** Seaman, Served on "Saint-Esprit" and died from Yorktown battle **CEM:** French Memorial; GPS 36.81944, -79.39933; Yorktown; York **GS:** U **SP:** No info **VI:** No further data **P:** unk **BLW:** unk **RG:** Y **MK:** unk **PH:** unk **SS:** J-Yorktown Historian **BS:** JLARC 1, 74.

CHEVALIER, Joseph; b unk; d 1781 **RU:** Soldier, Served in Gatinais Bn and died from Yorktown battle **CEM:** French Memorial; GPS 36.81944, -79.39933; Yorktown; York **GS:** U **SP:** No info **VI:** No further data **P:** unk **BLW:** unk **RG:** Y **MK:** unk **PH:** unk **SS:** J-Yorktown Historian **BS:** JLARC 1, 74.

CHEVALIER, Paul; b unk; d 1781 **RU:** Soldier, Served in Gatinais Bn and died from Yorktown battle **CEM:** French Memorial; GPS 36.81944, -79.39933; Yorktown; York **GS:** U **SP:** No info **VI:** No further data **P:** unk **BLW:** unk **RG:** Y **MK:** unk **PH:** unk **SS:** J-Yorktown Historian **BS:** JLARC 1, 74.

CHEW, John; b 31 Mar 1749; d 22 May 1838 **RU:** Lieutenant, Ent serv 1776. Wounded at Camden on 16 Aug 1780 **CEM:** Ketoctin Baptist; GPS 39.15746, -77.74870; Ketoctin Church Rd, Purcellville; Loudoun **GS:** U **SP:** No info **VI:** Pen for disability. Papers lost in DC fire R533 **P:** Y **BLW:** unk **RG:** Y **MK:** unk **PH:** unk **SS:** K Vol 1 pg ? **BS:** JLARC 1, 2, 32.

CHEW, John Jr; b c 1753; d 12 Feb 1806 **RU:** Lieutenant/Patriot, Appt Lt 1780. Was wounded in left arm at Battle of Camden SC 16 Aug 1780, thus arm amputated. Serv in 2nd Regt under Col George Stubblefield. Provided services, drove cattle, and gave two cattle to cause **CEM:** Masonic Cemetery; GPS 38.30198, -77.46142; 900 Charles St; Fredericksburg City **GS:** Y **SP:** 1) Elizabeth Smith 2) Ann (-----) (c1754-7 Oct 1821) **VI:** Appointed 6 August 1787 clerk of Hustings Ct of Fredericksburg. Recd gratuity and 1/2 pay pension 29 Nov 1781 **P:** Y **BLW:** unk **RG:** Y **MK:** N **PH:** unk **SS:** J-NSSAR 2000 Reg; BX pg 146 **BS:** JLARC 76.

CHEW, John Sr; b 1749; d 1838 **RU:** Cadet, Served in Capt Towles Co, Col Lees Legion of Calvary **CEM:** Ketoctin Baptist; GPS 39.15746, -77.74870; Ketoctin Church Rd, Purcellville; Loudoun **GS:** Y **SP:** No info **VI:** No further data **P:** unk **BLW:** unk **RG:** Y **MK:** N **PH:** unk **SS:** A pg 289; E pg 147 **BS:** 25 pg 53.

CHEW, Robert Beverly; b 1754; d 30 Dec 1791 **RU:** Lieutenant/patriot, Served in VA state line. Joined Marines Apr 1776 under Capt Gabriel Jones then transferred to land forces. Served as Lt of Inf in 1777. Was Ct Justice 1777 **CEM:** Masonic Cemetery; GPS 38.30198, -77.46142; 900 Charles St; Fredericksburg City **GS:** Y **SP:** No info **VI:** No further data **P:** unk **BLW:** unk **RG:** Y **MK:** N **PH:** unk **SS:** AL; D pg 869 **BS:** 04; 11 pg 30.

RU=Rank/Unit	CEM=Cemetery	GS=Gravestone	SP=Spousal Information
VI=Other Veteran Info	P=Pension	BLW=Bounty/Land Warrant	RG=Registered Grave
MK=SAR/DAR Marker	PH=Photo	SS=Service Source	BS=Burial Source

65

CHEW, Rodger; b unk; d 18 Mar 1811 **RU:** Patriot, Furnished equipment & supplies, authorized claims in Fairfax Co VA **CEM:** Old Christ Church Episcopal; GPS 38.80625, -77.04718; 118 N Washington St; Alexandria City **GS:** Y **SP:** No info **VI:** No further data **P:** N **BLW:** N **RG:** Y **MK:** N **PH:** unk **SS:** AK; AL Ct bk lt pg 13 **BS:** 04; 20 pg 136; 196.

CHEWNING, Samuel; b 21 Jan 1723, Christ Church Parish, Middlesex Co; d Bef 11 Mar 1816 **RU:** Patriot, Paid personal property taxes (considered Rev War supply Tax), 1783 Caroline Co, and gave material aid to cause **CEM:** Samuel Chewning Estate; GPS unk; See tax map for location; Caroline **GS:** U **SP:** Jennett Nancy Garrett **VI:** No further data **P:** N **BLW:** N **RG:** unk **MK:** unk **PH:** unk **SS:** DAR Ancestor #A021485; AL Ct Bk II pg 6 **BS:** 80 vol 1 pg 172.

CHICHESTER, Richard "Hard"; b 1736 Lancaster Co; d 22 Aug 1796 **RU:** Patriot, Provided beef, wheat, and pasturage **CEM:** Mt Air; GPS 38.73340, -77.17533; Newington Rd, Newington; Fairfax **GS:** Y **SP:** 1) Mar (9 Jun 1759, bond in Lancaster Co) Ann Gordon (1743-20 Apr 1766) d/o Col James (1714-1768) & Millicent (Conway) (1727-1747) Gordon; 2) Mar (c1766 Fairfax Co) Sara McCarty (1729-1826 Mt Air, Fairfax Co) d/o Daniel (__-1792) and Sinah (Ball) (1728-1798) McCarty **VI:** Son of Richard Chichester (d 1743) & Ellen Ball (d 1759) her first husband. Justice of Fairfax Co 1776-c1788; Commissioner of the Specific Tax in Fairfax Co 1780-1782. Nicknamed "Hard" by his slaves whom he apparently treated cruelly, When he d, the slaves said he ran out fr under his bed in the form of a red rabbit. In the 1920s, a severe thunderstorm hit his tombsone. When the owner when to investigate, the first three letters of first name were gone, leaving only the name "hard." No stone fragments or footprints in the soggy ground were found to explain it. Styled "Col" when he gave 272 bushels of corn to Lafayette's troops as they passed through Colston on their way to Yorktown **P:** N **BLW:** N **RG:** Y **MK:** Y **PH:** unk **SS:** D Vol II Fairfax **BS:** 04; 196.

CHILDRESS, Benjamin; b 2 Apr 1764; d 25 Mar 1852 **RU:** Private/Drummer, Ent serv 1780 age 16 in Capt John Christian and Capt James Pamplin Cos & others; and at Yorktown **CEM:** Mt Zion Methodist; GPS 37.80220, -78.59140; Rt 170 off Portress Rd Rt 627, Esmont; Albemarle **GS:** Y **SP:** Anne Key Johnson **VI:** Appl for pen 1850, R535. R1926 **P:** Y **BLW:** unk **RG:** Y **MK:** N **PH:** unk **SS:** AP pension rec; K Vol 1 pg 197 **BS:** JLARC 121; 196.

CHILTON, John; b 29 Aug 1739; d 11 Sep 1777 **RU:** Captain, Served in Culpeper Minute Men Bn, Nov 1775. Promoted to Capt 29 Apr 1776, 3rd VA Regt Cont Line. Died in Battle of Brandywine **CEM:** Rockspring; GPS unk; See property records for location; Fauquier **GS:** U **SP:** Mar (10 Apr 1768) Leticia Blackwell (3 Oct 1750-__) **VI:** No further data **P:** unk **BLW:** Y **RG:** unk **MK:** unk **PH:** unk **SS:** C pg 502; E pg 148 **BS:** 80 vol 1, pg 173.

CHILTON (CHELTON), Richard Sr; b c1740; d 15 Aug 1821 **RU:** Patriot, Gave material aid to cause **CEM:** Chilton-Moorman; GPS unk; Off Rt 221; Lynchburg City **GS:** U **SP:** Judith Arms **VI:** No further data **P:** N **BLW:** N **RG:** unk **MK:** unk **PH:** unk **SS:** AL Ct Bk I pg 21, 27, 29 Culpeper Co **BS:** JLARC 36.

CHIPLEY, William; b 1739; d 1811 **RU:** Captain/Patriot, Served in MD. Gave material aid to cause **CEM:** Opequon Presbyterian; GPS 39.13938, -78.19494; 217 Opequon Church Ln; Winchester City **GS:** U **SP:** 1) Sarah Bill 2) Ann B Ponder **VI:** No further data **P:** unk **BLW:** unk **RG:** Y **MK:** Y **PH:** unk **SS:** J-NSSAR 2000 Reg; D Frederick Co **BS:** JLARC 76, 04.

CHOWNING, William; b c1740; d unk **RU:** Captain, Appointed Lt in Lancaster Co 21 Aug 1777, and later Capt **CEM:** Chowning Ferry farm; GPS unk; Chownings Ferry Rd; Lancaster **GS:** U **SP:** Mar (28 Dec 1764 (bond) Lancaster Co) (-----) **VI:** No further data **P:** unk **BLW:** unk **RG:** N **MK:** N **PH:** unk **SS:** E pg 150 **BS:** 80 vol 1 pg 174.

CHRISMAN, George; b 1742 or 1745, Frederick Co; d 29 Aug 1816 **RU:** Captain, Commanded a co in Rockingham Co Militia after qualifying 26 Mar 1781 **CEM:** Cooks Creek Presbyterian; GPS 38.47472, -78.92997; 4222 Mt Clinton Pike, Harrisonburg; Harrisonburg City **GS:** Y **SP:** Hannah McDowell **VI:** Died in Rockingham Co **P:** unk **BLW:** unk **RG:** Y **MK:** Y **PH:** unk **SS:** E pg 150; AB; AK **BS:** AK, Sep 09, 04.

CHRISTIAN, James; b 1757; d 1825 **RU:** Corporal, Served in 6th VA Regt; also served 2d Cont line **CEM:** Soldier's Rest; GPS unk; Blanks Crossroads; Charles City Co **GS:** U **SP:** No info **VI:** No further data **P:** unk **BLW:** unk **RG:** N **MK:** N **PH:** unk **SS:** E pg 150; AP roll 6th VA R; CU **BS:** 126 Christian.

RU=Rank/Unit	CEM=Cemetery	GS=Gravestone	SP=Spousal Information
VI=Other Veteran Info	P=Pension	BLW=Bounty/Land Warrant	RG=Registered Grave
MK=SAR/DAR Marker	PH=Photo	SS=Service Source	BS=Burial Source

66

CHRISTIAN, Joseph; b 04 Sep 1757 New Kent Co; d 10 Apr 1825 **RU:** Lieutenant, Serv in Charles City Militia; and VA Cont Line **CEM:** Soldier's Rest; GPS unk; Blanks Crossroads; Charles City Co **GS:** U **SP:** Mar (1783) Elizabeth Ashfield Graves (Jul 1761-1821) **VI:** Also known as "Fightin' Joe Christian." BLW rec'd by heirs #8087SS **P:** unk **BLW:** Y **RG:** unk **MK:** unk **PH:** unk **SS:** DAR Ancestor #A021747; G pg 767; BY pg 285; CZ pg 95 **BS:** JLARC 110.

CHRISTIAN (CHRISTAIN), John; b unk; d 1822 **RU:** Soldier/Patriot, Specific serv Lib VA, War files, vol 4, pg 126. Provided wagonage for 32 days and other items to cause **CEM:** Bethel Presbyterian; GPS 38.04257, -79.17283; 563 Bethel Green Rd, Middlebrook; Augusta **GS:** N **SP:** Rachel Brownlee **VI:** No further data **P:** unk **BLW:** unk **RG:** unk **MK:** unk **PH:** N **SS:** D pg 45 Augusta Co **BS:** JLARC 62.

CHRISTOL, Jacques; b unk; d 1781 **RU:** Soldier, Served in Auxonne Bn and died from Yorktown battle **CEM:** French Memorial; GPS 36.81944, -79.39933; Yorktown; York **GS:** U **SP:** No info **VI:** No further data **P:** unk **BLW:** unk **RG:** Y **MK:** unk **PH:** unk **SS:** J-Yorktown Historian **BS:** JLARC 1, 74.

CHRYSTIE, Thomas; b 1753, Edinburgh, Scotland; d 22 Feb 1812 **RU:** Surgeon, Served in Navy and Army **CEM:** Studley; GPS 37.40100, -77.17270; Studley Farm Rd, under tree in front yard of Mr. J.A. Francieni, Jr. residence (as of 1978); Hanover **GS:** U **SP:** No info **VI:** BLW issued 19 Dec 1793, R540 & 1812 **P:** unk **BLW:** Y **RG:** unk **MK:** unk **PH:** unk **SS:** K Vol 1 pg 200; CU **BS:** JLARC 71.

CHUMARD, Thomas; b unk; d 1781 **RU:** Soldier, Served fr NJ, and died as result of Yorktown battle **CEM:** Yorktown Victory Monument Tablet; GPS 38.28350, -78.54150; Yorktown; York **GS:** U **SP:** No info **VI:** No further data **P:** unk **BLW:** unk **RG:** unk **MK:** unk **PH:** unk **SS:** J-Yorktown Historian **BS:** JLARC 74.

CHUNN, John Thomas; b 1749; d 8 Apr 1804 **RU:** Major, Commanded a Co in Fauquier Co Militia **CEM:** Chunn Family; GPS unk; Behind Mt Independence on Rt 17, north of Delaplane; Fauquier **GS:** U **SP:** Martha (-----) (22 May 1748-28 Mar 1831) **VI:** No further data **P:** unk **BLW:** unk **RG:** unk **MK:** unk **PH:** unk **SS:** CZ pg 96 **BS:** JLARC 16.

CIRCLE (CIRKLE), Peter; b 1741, Montgomery Co, PA; d Sep 1818 **RU:** Private, Served in Dunmore Co Militia, 1776 **CEM:** Locust Bottom; GPS 37.74148, -79.81456; Jct Rts 633 & 696; Pittsylvania **GS:** U **SP:** Frene Meyer (1750-1818) **VI:** No further data **P:** unk **BLW:** unk **RG:** Y **MK:** Y **PH:** unk **SS:** H source AW **BS:** 04, Jul 06.

CLAIBORNE, Augustine; b 1721, King William Co; d 3 May 1787 **RU:** Colonel/Patriot, Was Deputy Clerk of Ct and member of Committee of Safety. Gave material aid to cause **CEM:** Claiborne Family; GPS unk; See property Records for home place; Sussex **GS:** U **SP:** Mar (c1742 Petersburg) Mary Herbert (25 Aug 1728-14 Mar 1799) **VI:** No further data **P:** unk **BLW:** unk **RG:** Y **MK:** unk **PH:** unk **SS:** D Vol 3 pg 893; CZ pg 96 **BS:** JLARC 2, 76.

CLAIBORNE, Thomas; b 1 Feb 1749; d 1812 **RU:** Captain, Co Commander in Brunswick Co Militia. Served as Col & commander of same **CEM:** Claiborne Family; GPS unk; Nr jct Rts 713 & 715, Lawrenceville; Brunswick **GS:** N **SP:** No info **VI:** US Congressman 1793-1799, 1801-1805. VA House of Delegates 1783-1788. Brunswick Co Sheriff 1789-1792. State Sen 1790-1792 **P:** unk **BLW:** unk **RG:** unk **MK:** N **PH:** N **SS:** G pg 74 **BS:** 196.

CLAIBORNE, William; b 22 Jul 1748, Sweet Hall, King William Co; d 27 Sep 1809 **RU:** Patriot, Gave material aid to cause in Sussex, Hanover, New Kent Cos **CEM:** St John's Episcopal; GPS 37.53183, -77.41958; 2401 E Broad St; Richmond City **GS:** Y **SP:** No info **VI:** No further data **P:** N **BLW:** N **RG:** Y **MK:** N **PH:** Y **SS:** AM Sinks Resarch; AL Ct Bk pg 2 **BS:** 28 pg 428.

CLAIBORNE, William; b 22 Jul 1743; d 29 Sep 809 **RU:** Private, Specific Serv Lib VA, Auditors Acct, XXV, pg 35 **CEM:** Claiborne Family; GPS unk; Sweet Hall, Rocky Mount; King William **GS:** U **SP:** Mary Leigh (1750, King William Co-11 Apr 1782, Chesterfield, Co) d/o Ferdinand & Mary (Cole) Leigh **VI:** No further data **P:** unk **BLW:** unk **RG:** unk **MK:** unk **PH:** unk **SS:** AR Vol 1 pg 176; NSSAR Ancestor # P - 133142 **BS:** JLARC 2.

CLAPHAM, Josias; b unk; d 1818 **RU:** Colonel, Served 1777, Loudoun Co Militia. Was Commissary Officer, Prince William Co Battalion 1775-76 **CEM:** St James Episcopal, Old Cemetery; GPS 39.11555, -77.56250; Church St NE, Leesburg; Loudoun **GS:** Y **SP:** No info **VI:** Rev of P.G. Church. Died in

RU=Rank/Unit   CEM=Cemetery   GS=Gravestone   SP=Spousal Information
VI=Other Veteran Info   P=Pension   BLW=Bounty/Land Warrant   RG=Registered Grave
MK=SAR/DAR Marker   PH=Photo   SS=Service Source   BS=Burial Source

67

Lovettsville, Loudoun Co. Note: the service identified by DAR is likely for his father, thus more research needed **P:** unk **BLW:** unk **RG:** Y **MK:** N **PH:** unk **SS:** E pg 152; AK **BS:** 25 pg 54, 04.

CLAPP, Earl B; b 1741; d 1837 **RU:** Captain, Specific serv not given in SAR registry **CEM:** Sinking Springs; GPS 36.71030, -81.98170; 136 E Main St, Abingdon; Washington **GS:** U **SP:** No info **VI:** No further data **P:** unk **BLW:** unk **RG:** unk **MK:** unk **PH:** unk **SS:** AR Vol 1 pg 177; DD **BS:** JLARC 2; AR vol 1 pg 177.

CLARK, James; b 1700, King & Queen Co; d 1778 **RU:** Patriot, Gave material aid to cause, Gloucester Co **CEM:** First United Baptist Church; GPS 37.37133, -76.53449; 6188 George Washington Mem Hwy Rt 17; Gloucester **GS:** U **SP:** Mar (1772) Elizabeth Summers **VI:** Son of John (1665-1759) & Elizabeth Ann (Lumpkin) (1667-__) Clark. Died in Augusta Co **P:** N **BLW:** N **RG:** unk **MK:** unk **PH:** unk **SS:** AL Ct Ck ps ii, 16 **BS:** 196.

CLARK, James; b unk; d 1808 **RU:** Private, Served in Capt George Rice Co, 30 Nov 1778, Col Dan Morgan's 11th & 15th VA Regt. Also served in Capt John Wilson's Co, Augusta Co Militia **CEM:** Trinity Episcopal; GPS 38.14917, -79.07521; 214 Beverley St; Staunton City **GS:** U **SP:** No info **VI:** No further data **P:** unk **BLW:** Y **RG:** unk **MK:** unk **PH:** unk **SS:** A pg 265; CU **BS:** JLARC 2, 8; 196.

CLARK, James; b 1754, Lochgilphead, Scotland; d Dec 1818 **RU:** Sergeant, Served in VA State Regt, 6th Cont Line **CEM:** Glade Spring Presbyterian; GPS 36.76720, -81.78720; 33234 Lee Hwy, Glade Spring; Washington **GS:** U **SP:** Isabella Mary Breckenridge (1764 Scotland-09 Sep 1848) **VI:** No further data **P:** unk **BLW:** unk **RG:** unk **MK:** unk **PH:** unk **SS:** E pg 154 **BS:** 196.

CLARK, John; b 26 Dec 1745; d 2 Apr 1819 **RU:** Captain, Commanded Co in Campbell Co **CEM:** Clark Family; GPS 37.29563, -79.21086; Cnr Lawyer's Rd and Missionary Manor; Campbell **GS:** U **SP:** Mar (21 Feb 1767 Albemarle Co) Mary Moore (1 Jan 1748-5 Nov 1830) d/o (-----) & Mary Bullock (1720-1814) **VI:** Son of Micaja & Judith (Adams) Clark. Was a Justice of Campbell Co. One of the original Trustees of the City of Lynchburg City. Member of VA House of Delegates 1785-93). Sheriff of Campbell Co (1818 until death 2 Apr 1819) **P:** unk **BLW:** unk **RG:** unk **MK:** unk **PH:** unk **SS:** CD **BS:** 196.

CLARK, John; b 1761; d May 1827 **RU:** Second Lieutenant, Served in Prince Edward Co Militia **CEM:** Clark Family; GPS unk; Bannister Lodge; Halifax **GS:** U **SP:** 1) Marie Sims 2) Pricilla Sims **VI:** No further data **P:** unk **BLW:** unk **RG:** unk **MK:** unk **PH:** unk **SS:** J- DAR Hatcher; G pg 300, 301, 308, 309 **BS:** JLARC 2.

CLARK, John Shadrock (Shadrick, Shadrach); b 1759; d 1810 **RU:** Private/Patriot, Gave to cause **CEM:** Unidentified; GPS unk; See prop rec for location; Lunenburg **GS:** U **SP:** Mar (9 Jul 1789 Lunenburg) Rebecca Crymes d/o Thomas & Mary (-----) Crymes **VI:** Son of Ellison (c1695 Henrico Co-1766 Chesterfield Co) and Ann (Blanchecil) (c1762-bef 4 Jan 1771, Chesterfield Co) Clark. Son recd his pen 1841 **P:** Y **BLW:** unk **RG:** unk **MK:** unk **PH:** unk **SS:** J- DAR Hatcher; D Mecklenburg Co **BS:** JLARC 2.

CLARK, Peter; b c1761; d Sep 1821 **RU:** Private?, Served in 10th Cont Line **CEM:** Glade Spring Presbyterian; GPS 36.76720, -81.78720; 33234 Lee Hwy, Glade Spring; Washington **GS:** Y **SP:** Mary Galbreath (1758-13 Apr 1856) **VI:** No further data **P:** N **BLW:** N **RG:** N **MK:** N **PH:** unk **SS:** E pg 153; CI Serv record **BS:** 78 pg 177; 196.

CLARK, Thomas; b 1740; d 1792 **RU:** Patriot, Gave material aid to the cause **CEM:** Clark Plantation; GPS unk; Strawberry Br; Halifax **GS:** Y **SP:** No info **VI:** No further data **P:** N **BLW:** N **RG:** N **MK:** N **PH:** unk **SS:** AL Ct Bk pg 35 **BS:** 80 vol 1 pg 183.

CLARK, William; b 3 Jan 1759; d 2 Apr 1827 **RU:** Colonel, In 1781 led Co fr Halifax Co to Point of Fork on James River to a state arsenal and military stores. Commanded a reconnoitering party at Battle of Guilford CH Remained in service until discharged by Gen Lafayette **CEM:** Clark Family; GPS 36.84823, -79.32198; Pineville nr Chatham; Pittsylvania **GS:** Y **SP:** Jane Hamilton White (20 May 1762-23 Apr 1839) d/o Jeremiah & Esther (Herdon) White **VI:** No further data **P:** unk **BLW:** unk **RG:** unk **MK:** unk **PH:** unk **SS:** AR Vol 1 pg 183 **BS:** 174, JLARC 2.

CLARKE, Christopher; b 05 Apr 1753, Louisa Co; d Feb 1851 **RU:** Private/Patriot, Military service not identified. Gave material aid to cause **CEM:** Tompkins Family; GPS unk; Shipman at Burk Homestead; Nelson **GS:** U **SP:** Elizabeth Hope (22 Mar 1778-03 Apr 1873) **VI:** He is bur in Fluvanna Co where he

RU=Rank/Unit	CEM=Cemetery	GS=Gravestone	SP=Spousal Information
VI=Other Veteran Info	P=Pension	BLW=Bounty/Land Warrant	RG=Registered Grave
MK=SAR/DAR Marker	PH=Photo	SS=Service Source	BS=Burial Source

68

died, however memorial grave stone is in cemetery listed **P:** unk **BLW:** unk **RG:** unk **MK:** unk **PH:** unk **SS:** B; D Albemarle Co **BS:** 196.

CLARKE, Christopher; b unk; d unk **RU:** unk, Service not identified in SAR registry **CEM:** Clarke Family; GPS unk; Nr Woodbridge PO, Woodbridge; Prince William **GS:** U **SP:** No info **VI:** No further data **P:** unk **BLW:** unk **RG:** unk **MK:** unk **PH:** unk **SS:** AR Vol 1 pg 183; NSSAR Ancestor #P-134272 **BS:** JLARC 2.

CLARKE, James; b unk; d 13 Jan 1808 **RU:** Private, Served in Capt McCutchen's Co Augusta Co VA **CEM:** Trinity Episcopal; GPS 38.14917, -79.07521; 214 Beverley St; Staunton City **GS:** U **SP:** No info **VI:** No further data **P:** unk **BLW:** unk **RG:** Y **MK:** N **PH:** unk **SS:** E pg 154; AK **BS:** 36 pg 154.

CLARKE, William; b 28 Jan 1762; d 12 Sep 1846 **RU:** First Lieutenant, Commissioned 28 Sep 1778 Cumberland Co Militia. Also in State Line under George Roger's Clark, Illinois Regt **CEM:** Clarke Family; GPS 37.24354, -77.44655; Ravensbourne Dr, Ettrick; Chesterfield **GS:** Y **SP:** Martha Rowlett (28 Dec 1761-14 Aug 1809 **VI:** Recd BLW 2666 acres 3 Mar 1784 **P:** unk **BLW:** Y **RG:** unk **MK:** unk **PH:** unk **SS:** E pg 155; F pg 18 **BS:** 196.

CLARKSON, James; b 1764; d 5 Mar 1836 **RU:** Private, Specific service listed in BLW application **CEM:** Clarkson-Meeks, aka Clarkson #2; GPS unk; 5 mi N of Massies Mill cross Tye River Bridge; Nelson **GS:** Y **SP:** Elizabeth Jacobs (1766-13 Jan 1854) d/o John & Sarah (Crawford) Jacobs **VI:** Authorized BLW, receipt unk **P:** unk **BLW:** Y **RG:** unk **MK:** unk **PH:** unk **SS:** C pg 524 **BS:** 196.

CLAY, Eleazer; b 4 Aug 1744, Powhatan Co; d 2 May 1836 **RU:** Patriot, Gave material aid to cause **CEM:** Clay Family; GPS unk; At his homeplace, see property records for directions; Chesterfield **GS:** U **SP:** 1) Jane Apperson (1751-1787) 2) Mar (7 Jan 1789) Elizabeth Swepson Whitehead (__-1825) 3) Mar (12 Feb 1826) Phoebe Newby **VI:** Was in Colonial War Mar 1758, Became Reverend 1771 **P:** N **BLW:** N **RG:** unk **MK:** unk **PH:** unk **SS:** AL Ct Bk pg 14 Chesterfield Co **BS:** 196.

CLAY, Matthew; b 25 Mar 1754; d 27 May 1815 **RU:** Captain/Quartermaster, Served in 9th VA Regt 1776. Transferred to 1st VA Regt 1778 and to 5th VA Regt 1781 **CEM:** Clay Family; GPS unk; Danville; Danville City **GS:** U **SP:** Ann (__) **VI:** Son of Charles (1716-1789) & Martha "Patsy" (Green) (1719-1798) Clay. VA House of Delegates 1790-94. Elected to Congress as Democratic-Republican, served 8 terms fr 1797-1813 **P:** unk **BLW:** Y **RG:** unk **MK:** unk **PH:** unk **SS:** C pg 331 **BS:** 196.

CLAY, Mitchell; b 1735; d 1811 **RU:** Private, Specific Serv Lib VA, War files, 23, 1778 **CEM:** Birchlawn Burial Park; GPS 39.32610, -80.71080; Wenonah Ave Rt 460, Pearisburg; Giles **GS:** U **SP:** Phoebe Belcher **VI:** No further data **P:** unk **BLW:** unk **RG:** unk **MK:** unk **PH:** unk **SS:** CZ pg 99 **BS:** JLARC 3, 26.

CLAY, William M Sr; b 1739; d 1811 **RU:** Private, Specific Serv Lib VA, Auditors Acct, XVIII, pg 651 **CEM:** Private Grave; GPS unk; Nr Celanese, Pearisburg; Giles **GS:** U **SP:** No info **VI:** No further data **P:** unk **BLW:** unk **RG:** unk **MK:** unk **PH:** unk **SS:** J- DAR Hatcher; CZ pg 99 **BS:** JLARC 2.

CLAYTON, Phillip; b 1702, Essex Co; d 1785 **RU:** Patriot, Let the Culpeper Minutemen Bn use his property for encampment 1775 **CEM:** Catalpa Plantation; GPS unk; His homeplace on mountain nr town see property records for directions; Culpeper **GS:** Y **SP:** Anne Coleman (1703-1785) **VI:** Rank of major obtained in Colonial War in Orange Co. Member Soc of Cincinnati. Was justice in Orange Co. Was Vestryman of St Mark's Parish 1741 **P:** N **BLW:** N **RG:** unk **MK:** unk **PH:** unk **SS:** DAR ancestor #A022929; DD **BS:** 196.

CLEACH, Jean; b unk; d 1781 **RU:** Seaman, Served on "Auguste" and died from Yorktown battle **CEM:** French Memorial; GPS 36.81944, -79.39933; Yorktown; York **GS:** U **SP:** No info **VI:** No further data **P:** unk **BLW:** unk **RG:** Y **MK:** unk **PH:** unk **SS:** J-Yorktown Historian **BS:** JLARC 1, 74.

CLEMENT, Adam Sr; b 22 Apr 1738; d 11 Oct 1811 **RU:** Captain/Patriot, Served in Bedford Militia. Provided provisions to cause **CEM:** Oakdale; GPS 37.17076, -79.04768; Mollies Creek Rd, Gladys; Campbell **GS:** N **SP:** Agnes Johnson **VI:** Son of Benjamin Clement (1705-1780) & Susannah Hill (1710-1782) **P:** unk **BLW:** unk **RG:** unk **MK:** N **PH:** N **SS:** AL Ct Bk 6 **BS:** JLARC 36; 196.

RU=Rank/Unit	CEM=Cemetery	GS=Gravestone	SP=Spousal Information
VI=Other Veteran Info	P=Pension	BLW=Bounty/Land Warrant	RG=Registered Grave
MK=SAR/DAR Marker	PH=Photo	SS=Service Source	BS=Burial Source

69

CLEMENT(S), Benjamin; b unk; d Aft1781 **RU:** Patriot, Made gun powder for Army **CEM:** Clement Hill; GPS unk; Rt 29 N, btw Chatham & Hurt; Pittsylvania **GS:** Y **SP:** No info **VI:** No further data **P:** N **BLW:** N **RG:** Y **MK:** N **PH:** unk **SS:** AL Ct Bk, pg 35 **BS:** SAR report; 04.

CLOARET, Jean; b unk; d 1781 **RU:** Soldier, Served in Beaujolais Bn and died from Yorktown battle **CEM:** French Memorial; GPS 36.81944, -79.39933; Yorktown; York **GS:** U **SP:** No info **VI:** No further data **P:** unk **BLW:** unk **RG:** Y **MK:** unk **PH:** unk **SS:** J-Yorktown Historian **BS:** JLARC 1, 74.

CLOPTON, John; b 7 Feb 1756, New Kent Co; d 11 Sep 1816 **RU:** First Lieutenant, Was an artillery officer in unit not identified **CEM:** St Peter's Episcopal; GPS unk; 8400 St Peters Ln, Quinton; New Kent **GS:** U **SP:** Sarah Bacon d/o Edmund & Elizabeth (Edloe) Bacon **VI:** Son of William & Elizabeth (Ford) Cloyton. Died in "Roslin" New Kent Co **P:** unk **BLW:** unk **RG:** Y **MK:** U **PH:** unk **SS:** E pg 159; AK **BS:** 04, May 06.

CLOPTON, Robert; b 20 Feb 1755, New Kent Cod; d 22 Jan 1841 **RU:** Private, Specific Serv Lib VA, Auditors Acct, XVIII, pg 532 **CEM:** Clopton Family; GPS unk; Slatesville Rd, N of jct US Rt 360; Pittsylvania **GS:** U **SP:** Mar (5 Jan 1781 Hanover Co) Frances Anderson (1765-1837) **VI:** No further data **P:** unk **BLW:** unk **RG:** Y **MK:** N **PH:** unk **SS:** AK May 06; CZ pg 101 **BS:** 04, May 06.

CLOPTON, William; b 2 Feb 1722, New Kent Co; d 3 Aug 1796 **RU:** Captain, Commanded a co in the New Kent Co Militia **CEM:** St Peter's Episcopal; GPS unk; 8400 St Peters Ln, Quinton; New Kent **GS:** U **SP:** 1) Elizabeth Darroll Ford 20 Mar (5 Jan 1781 Hanover Co) Fanny Anderson **VI:** No further data **P:** unk **BLW:** unk **RG:** Y **MK:** unk **PH:** unk **SS:** AK; E pg 159 **BS:** 04, May 06, 197.

CLOUD, Daniel; b 8 Feb 1756; d 25 Feb 1815 **RU:** Private, Served in Capt Joseph Bowman's Co of Lower District Dunmore Co Militia **CEM:** Cloud Family; GPS unk; 1.5 mi West Front Royal; Warren **GS:** Y **SP:** Elizabeth (-----) (28 Feb 1756-17 Sep 1829) **VI:** Died in Frederick Co **P:** unk **BLW:** unk **RG:** Y **MK:** N **PH:** unk **SS:** AK; C pg 604 **BS:** 59, pg 66; 113; 197.

CLOYD, David; b 1738; d 16 Aug 1789 **RU:** Captain/Patriot, Became capt in Rockbridge Co 8 Mar 1780. Gave material aid to cause **CEM:** High Bridge Presbyterian; GPS 37.62420, -79.58610; 67 High Bridge Rd, Natural Bridge; Rockbridge **GS:** U **SP:** Elizabeth Woods (1753 Albemarle Co-Nov 1796 Rockbridge Co) **VI:** No further data **P:** unk **BLW:** unk **RG:** unk **MK:** unk **PH:** unk **SS:** D Rockbridge Co **BS:** JLARC 79; 196.

CLOYD, Joseph; b 20 Jun 1742; d 31 Aug 1833 **RU:** Major/Patriot, Served in Capt Montgomery Co Militia 1777, and as Maj in Col Preston's Regt in SC in 1781. Was member of Committee of Safety, Fincastle Co, 1775-1776 **CEM:** Cloyd; GPS 37.16166, -80.70583; Rt 100 Cleyburne Blvd N of Dublin; Pulaski **GS:** U **SP:** Mary Gordon (1750-__) **VI:** Son of David & (-----) Cloyd. Came to Back Creek around 1772 and was fr the James River area of VA **P:** unk **BLW:** unk **RG:** unk **MK:** unk **PH:** unk **SS:** A pg 207; E pg 159-160 **BS:** 196, JLARC 92; 212.

COBBS, Charles; b 1736; d Aft 13 Jan 1800 **RU:** Captain, Commanded a Co Bedford Co Militia 28 Feb 1780 **CEM:** Cobbs Hall; GPS unk; nr Rt 643, Brookneal; Campbell **GS:** U **SP:** 1) Ann Walton 2-probably) Mar (4 Dec 1783 Campbell Co (bond) Martha Bailey, d/o (-----) & Elizabeth (-----) Bailey **VI:** No further data **P:** unk **BLW:** unk **RG:** unk **MK:** N **PH:** unk **SS:** E pg 161 **BS:** JLARC 2, 36.

COBBS, Jesse; b unk; d unk **RU:** Seaman or Private, Served in VA state Navy and/or 5th Cont Line **CEM:** Cobbs Hall; GPS unk; nr Rt 643, Brookneal; Campbell **GS:** U **SP:** No info **VI:** Son of Charles Cobbs, Sr (1736-1798) & Ann Walton (1738-unk) **P:** unk **BLW:** unk **RG:** Y **MK:** N **PH:** unk **SS:** C pg 230; E pg 161 **BS:** SAR report; JLARC 36, 04; 196.

COBBS, John L; b 27 Aug 1763; d 9 Sep 1851 **RU:** Private, Served in Capt James Cobbs, Col Greene's Regt of Militia in Halifax Co. Marched to Williamsburg and placed under Command of Capt Rogers, Col Washington's Regt. Later served at Battle of Guilford CH and at Yorktown, serving 3 yrs **CEM:** St Stevens Episcopal; GPS unk; Jct Rts 663 and 221; Bedford **GS:** U **SP:** No info **VI:** Pen recd 1835 **P:** Y **BLW:** unk **RG:** unk **MK:** unk **PH:** unk **SS:** E pg 161; G pg 764; CI statement **BS:** 222, Vol 1, pg 215.

COBBS, John Sr; b 8 Oct 1759; d 6 Apr 1847 **RU:** Second Lieutenant, Ent Serv Bedford Co 1779-80 (later Campbell Co) Bedford Co Militia. Served as 2nd Lt in Capt William Craddock's Co 22 Jun 1780 **CEM:** Cobbs Hall; GPS unk; nr Rt 643, Brookneal; Campbell **GS:** U **SP:** Sarah "Sallie" McCoy, b 20 Aug

RU=Rank/Unit	CEM=Cemetery	GS=Gravestone	SP=Spousal Information
VI=Other Veteran Info	P=Pension	BLW=Bounty/Land Warrant	RG=Registered Grave
MK=SAR/DAR Marker	PH=Photo	SS=Service Source	BS=Burial Source

70

1762, d 28 Jan 1830 **VI:** Son of Charles Cobb Sr. (1736-1798) & Ann Walton (1738-unk). Member of Baptist Denomination & in his own words "A sinner saved by grace." Sr. Pen 1833, Campbell Co, R588 **P:** Y **BLW:** unk **RG:** unk **MK:** N **PH:** unk **SS:** K Vol 1 pg 216 **BS:** JLARC 2 ,36; 196.

COBBS, Robert; b 2 Mar 1754, Louisa Co; d 2 Aug 1829 **RU:** Captain, Served in Bedford Co Militia under Charles Lewis, 1779-1780 **CEM:** Cobbs Family; GPS unk; Plain Dealing, Naruna; Campbell **GS:** N **SP:** Mar (19 Nov 1783, Louisa Co) Ann Gizzage Poindexter (1762-1 Feb 1842) **VI:** Widow pen Campbell Co, age 79 in 1841 **P:** Y **BLW:** unk **RG:** unk **MK:** N **PH:** N **SS:** K Vol 1 pg 216 **BS:** JLARC 4, 36; 196.

COCHRAN, James; b 15 Feb 1756; d c1820 **RU:** Ensign, Served in Capt Moffet's Co, Augusta Co Militia **CEM:** Union Presbyterian; GPS 39.10916, -78.09497; Churchville; Augusta **GS:** N **SP:** Magdeline Moffett, d/o George Moffett; d 6 Dec 1792 **VI:** No further data **P:** unk **BLW:** unk **RG:** unk **MK:** N **PH:** N **SS:** E pg 161 **BS:** JLARC 62, 63.

COCHRAN, Samuel R; b unk; d 1847 **RU:** Sergeant, Served in 1st & 10th Cont lines **CEM:** Upperville Methodist; GPS unk; 11134 Delaplane Grade Rd, Upperville; Loudoun **GS:** Y **SP:** No info **VI:** No further data **P:** unk **BLW:** Y **RG:** Y **MK:** N **PH:** unk **SS:** A Part II pg 204 **BS:** 25 pg 57; 04.

COCHRAN, William; b 1739; d 10 Oct 1826 **RU:** Sergeant, Specific Serv Lib VA, war files, vol 4, pg 136 **CEM:** Glebe Burying Ground; GPS 38.10940, -79.22190; Glebe School Rd Rt 876, Swoopes; Augusta **GS:** Y **SP:** 1) Mary Logan, 2) Elizabeth Fulton **VI:** No further data **P:** unk **BLW:** Y **RG:** unk **MK:** N **PH:** unk **SS:** E pg 161; CU; CZ pg 103 **BS:** JLARC 8; 210 pg 395.

COCKBURN, Martin; b c1740; d unk **RU:** Patriot, Paid for collecting goods for use of the country **CEM:** Cockburn Family; GPS unk; "Springfield," Gunston Rd Rt 242, W of Gunston Hall, Mason Neck; Fairfax **GS:** N **SP:** Mar c1763 to Anne Bronaugh **VI:** GS said to have been moved to Pohick Church **P:** N **BLW:** N **RG:** N **MK:** N **PH:** N **SS:** G pg 549 **BS:** 61 vol V , pg MN-16.

COCKE, David; b c1748; d 28 Feb 1828 **RU:** Patriot, Rendered aid as a patriot in the defense of Ft Blackmore in 1777 **CEM:** Cocke Family; GPS unk; Ft Blackmore; Scott **GS:** Y **SP:** Jemima Leach **VI:** No further data **P:** unk **BLW:** unk **RG:** Y **MK:** N **PH:** unk **SS:** O **BS:** 04.

COCKE, John Hartwell; b 25 Nov 1749; d 9 Feb 1791 **RU:** Captain, Commanded co in Surry Co Militia **CEM:** Cocke Family; GPS unk; Mt Pleasant; Surry **GS:** U **SP:** Mar (28 Nov 1773) Elizabeth Kennon (13 Jul 1755-10 Jul 1791) **VI:** No further data **P:** unk **BLW:** unk **RG:** unk **PH:** unk **SS:** DAR Ancestor #A027047; G pg 456 **BS:** 224 fr Wm & Mary College Qrtly, vol 15, #2 pg 87.

COCQ, Antoine; b unk; d 1781 **RU:** Soldier, Served in Agenois Bn and died from Yorktown battle **CEM:** French Memorial; GPS 36.81944, -79.39933; Yorktown; York **GS:** U **SP:** No info **VI:** No further data **P:** unk **BLW:** unk **RG:** Y **MK:** unk **PH:** unk **SS:** J-Yorktown Historian **BS:** JLARC 1, 74.

COFER, George; b 1 Sep 1756, Culpeper Co; d 31 Aug 1837 **RU:** Corporal, Served in 1st VA State Regt **CEM:** St Stephen's Episcopal; GPS 37.37811, -79.30831; 1694 Perrowville Rd, Forest; Bedford **GS:** U **SP:** 1) Frances Dawson 2) Mary (-----) **VI:** Died in St Genevieive, MO **P:** unk **BLW:** unk **RG:** Y **MK:** N **PH:** unk **SS:** E pg 163 **BS:** SAR regis, 04; 196.

COFFER, Thomas W; b 1765; d 1784 **RU:** Patriot, Signed Legislative petition in Fairfax Co indicating public service **CEM:** Truro Parish; GPS unk; "On the middle ridge near Ox Road", the present site of Jerusalem Baptist Church off Rt 123; Fairfax **GS:** N **SP:** No info **VI:** No further data **P:** N **BLW:** N **RG:** N **MK:** N **PH:** N **SS:** BB legislative Pet **BS:** 110 pg 98.

COFFEY, Jean; b unk; d 1781 **RU:** Seaman, Served on "Saint-Esprit" and died from Yorktown battle **CEM:** French Memorial; GPS 36.81944, -79.39933; Yorktown; York **GS:** U **SP:** No info **VI:** No further data **P:** unk **BLW:** unk **RG:** Y **MK:** unk **PH:** unk **SS:** J-Yorktown Historian **BS:** JLARC 1, 74.

COFFEY (COFFEE), Edmund; b 1735; d Aft 1808 **RU:** Patriot, Obtain SAR application for service **CEM:** Coffey Family; GPS unk; Rt 789 Cub Creek Rd, Tyro; Nelson **GS:** U **SP:** Matilda (-----). Also Nancy Chena (order unk) **VI:** Will dated 1808 **P:** N **BLW:** N **RG:** unk **MK:** unk **PH:** unk **SS:** NSSAR Ancestor # P-135771 **BS:** JLARC 83.

RU=Rank/Unit   CEM=Cemetery   GS=Gravestone   SP=Spousal Information
VI=Other Veteran Info   P=Pension   BLW=Bounty/Land Warrant   RG=Registered Grave
MK=SAR/DAR Marker   PH=Photo   SS=Service Source   BS=Burial Source

71

COINER, Conrad; b unk; d 1816 **RU:** unk, Service information not shown in SAR registry **CEM:** Mt Zion Methodist; GPS 37.66596, -79.46615; Btw Buffalo & Tinkersville; Rockbridge **GS:** U **SP:** No info **VI:** No further data **P:** unk **BLW:** unk **RG:** unk **MK:** unk **PH:** unk **SS:** AR Vol 1 pg 191; NSSAR Ancestor # P-135933 **BS:** JLARC 2.

COLAR, Andre; b unk; d 1781 **RU:** Seaman, Served in Touraine Bn and died from Yorktown battle **CEM:** French Memorial; GPS 36.81944, -79.39933; Yorktown; York **GS:** U **SP:** No info **VI:** No further data **P:** unk **BLW:** unk **RG:** Y **MK:** unk **PH:** unk **SS:** J-Yorktown Historian **BS:** JLARC 1, 74.

COLE, Hugh; b 14 Mar 1744, Swansea, Bristol Co, MA; d 29 Jul 1780 **RU:** Second Lieutenant, 8th Co, Third Ulster Co Regt of Militia (western) under Capt Peleg Ramson 9 Aug 1775 **CEM:** St Clair Bottom Primitive Baptist; GPS 36.76098, -81.64556; Jct Rts 600 & 660, Chilhowie; Smyth **GS:** Y **SP:** Mar (c1771) Sarah Bishop (__-after 1780) **VI:** Son of Joseph (1716-1785) & Freelove (Mason) (1720-1785) Cole I. On 10 May 1775, signer of Articles of the Association in New-Paltz, Ulster Co, NY. Died in Washington Co. New grave marker erected 2004 - mistake on stone should say NY militia. **P:** unk **BLW:** unk **RG:** unk **MK:** unk **PH:** Y **SS:** CD **BS:** 196.

COLE, Joseph Jr; b Mar 1750, Swansea, MA; d 6 Sep 1826 **RU:** Captain, Ent serv 1777, Charlotte Co. Served in Washington Co Militia under Col William Campbell. Was in Battle of Kings Mountain **CEM:** St Clair Bottom Primitive Baptist; GPS 36.76098, -81.64556; Jct Rts 600 & 660, Chilhowie; Smyth **GS:** U **SP:** 1) Remember (-----) 2) Margaret Leuper **VI:** No further data **P:** unk **BLW:** unk **RG:** unk **MK:** N **PH:** unk **SS:** AR Vol 1 pg 193; E pg 165 **BS:** JLARC 2.

COLE, William; b 12 Dec 1752, Prince Edward Co; d 14 Oct 1838 **RU:** Buglar/Sergeant, Was Washington's bugler **CEM:** Cole Family; GPS unk; Off Rt 672, NW of Asbury Church, Asbury nr Halifax; Halifax **GS:** U **SP:** Mar (Jun 1786 Halifax Co) Mourning Hitson **VI:** Widow pen age 88 Halifax Co, 1844. He pen Halifax Co in 1835. Another W. Cole listed in sources 1+2(1745-1815) **P:** Y **BLW:** unk **RG:** Y **MK:** unk **PH:** unk **SS:** AR Vol 1 pg 194; DAR Magazine 1974-75 **BS:** JLARC 1, 2, 4.

COLEMAN, Daniel; b 7 Jun 1768; d 8 Apr 1860 **RU:** Captain, Was express rider for the militia **CEM:** Coleman Family; GPS unk; Off Yeats Store Rd, Java; Pittsylvania **GS:** Y **SP:** Anna Payne Harrison(01 Mar 1778-01 Feb 1858) **VI:** Son of Stephen Coleman (1739-1798), was Lt Col in War of 1812 **P:** unk **BLW:** unk **RG:** unk **MK:** unk **PH:** unk **SS:** AR Vol 1 pg 194 **BS:** 174; 196; JLARC 2.

COLEMAN, Hawes; b 1 Jan 1757, Spotsylvania Co; d 27 Dec 1840 **RU:** Private, Entered serv 1775 Spotsylvania Co **CEM:** Wintergreen; GPS unk; Rt 151 beyond Nellysford; Nelson **GS:** U **SP:** Nancy Anne Harris (21 Jan 1756, Albemarle Co-13 Dec 1809) **VI:** Moved 1789 to Amherst Co, now Nelson Co. Pen 1834, R 607 **P:** Y **BLW:** unk **RG:** unk **MK:** unk **PH:** unk **SS:** K Vol 1 pg 222 **BS:** JLARC 4, 83.

COLEMAN, Isaac; b unk; d Aft 1782 **RU:** Private?, SAR registration did not indicate service **CEM:** Coleman Family; GPS unk; Nr Riceville; Pittsylvania **GS:** N **SP:** No info **VI:** No further data **P:** unk **BLW:** unk **RG:** Y **MK:** N **PH:** N **SS:** AS SAR regis **BS:** SAR regis.

COLEMAN, Julius; b 1743; d 1842 **RU:** First Lieutenant/Patriot, Gave material aid to cause **CEM:** Coleman Family; GPS unk; Nr Salem Methodist Church; Buckingham **GS:** U **SP:** Elizabeth (-----) **VI:** No further data **P:** N **BLW:** N **RG:** unk **MK:** N **PH:** unk **SS:** D Caroline Co **BS:** JLARC 59.

COLEMAN, Robert; b c1766; d 1846 **RU:** Private, Entered serv 1780, Specific Serv Lib VA, Report Sec War, Pen , vol 2, pg 120 **CEM:** Coleman Family; GPS unk; Bent Creek; Buckingham **GS:** U **SP:** Elizabeth Burks **VI:** Son of Samuel Coleman. Stepmother Elizabeth Coleman. Sub for father. After RW, lived in Buckingham Co where he pen 1833, age 67. R 608 **P:** Y **BLW:** N **RG:** unk **MK:** N **PH:** unk **SS:** CZ pg 105; K Vol 1 pg 223 **BS:** JLARC 4, 59.

COLEMAN, Stephen; b 1739; d Aft 1832 **RU:** Lieutenant, Appt Lt Pittsylvania Co Militia 27 Feb 1777 **CEM:** Coleman Family; GPS unk; Nr Riceville; Pittsylvania **GS:** N **SP:** Mar (3 Sep 1799 Pittsylvania Co) Polly Williams d/o Permeneas & (-----) Williams **VI:** No further data **P:** unk **BLW:** unk **RG:** N **MK:** N **PH:** N **SS:** G pg 284 **BS:** SAR Appl.

COLERAN, Jean; b unk; d 1781 **RU:** Soldier, Served in Soissonnais Bn and died from Yorktown battle **CEM:** French Memorial; GPS 36.81944, -79.39933; Yorktown; York **GS:** U **SP:** No info **VI:** No further data **P:** unk **BLW:** unk **RG:** Y **MK:** unk **PH:** unk **SS:** J-Yorktown Historian **BS:** JLARC 1, 74.

RU=Rank/Unit	CEM=Cemetery	GS=Gravestone	SP=Spousal Information
VI=Other Veteran Info	P=Pension	BLW=Bounty/Land Warrant	RG=Registered Grave
MK=SAR/DAR Marker	PH=Photo	SS=Service Source	BS=Burial Source

72

COLES, Isaac Sr; b 2 Mar 1747, Richmond, Henrico Co; d 3 Jun 1813 **RU:** Colonel/Patriot, Served in Pittsylvania Co Militia. Gave material aid to the cause **CEM:** Coles; GPS 36.54722, -79.16470; 8 mi NE of Chatham. Source 76 has Cem as off SR 690. Source 101 has Rt 685 at Chalk Level. Java; Pittsylvania **GS:** Y **SP:** 1) Elizabeth Lightfoot (__-1781) 2) Mar (2 Jan 1790) Caterine Thompson d/o James & (-----) Coles of NYC **VI:** Son of John (1706-1747) & Mary Ann (Winston) (1721-1758) Coles. After US Constitution ratified in 1789, was among first 10 Virginians to be elected to First Congress. Served as At-Large Representative fr VA in US House of Representatives, fr 1789-1791. Later elected to VA's 6th Congressional District, serving fr 1783-1787. Died in Chatham, Pittsylvania Co **P:** unk **BLW:** unk **RG:** Y **MK:** N **PH:** unk **SS:** Al Ct Bk pg 47, 53; CD **BS:** JLARC 76, 101; 118 pg 71; 174; 196.

COLES, Walter; b 14 Nov 1739, Hanover Co; d 7 Nov 1780 **RU:** Major/Patriot, Served in Halifax Co Militia. Was Justice of Peace and elected to VA House of Delegates **CEM:** Coles-Carrington; GPS unk; Mildendo Plantation; Halifax **GS:** N **SP:** Mildred Howell Lightfoot (Feb 1752 Charles City Co-1 May 1799, Halifax Co) d/o William (1722-1764) & (-----) Lightfoot **VI:** Son of John (1706-1747) & Mary Ann (Winston) (1721-1758) Coles **P:** unk **BLW:** unk **RG:** unk **MK:** unk **PH:** N **SS:** AL Certificate & Lists, Halifax Co **BS:** 196.

COLLIER, Aaron; b 15 Jan 1750, Lee Co; d Jun 1842 **RU:** Soldier, Ent serv 1780 Montgomery Co. Served in Cont Line in William Bobbett's Co **CEM:** Collier Family; GPS 36.78160, -80.59830; Jct Rts 628 & 624, Dugspur; Carroll **GS:** Y **SP:** Elizabeth (-----), d Jul 1830 **VI:** Appl pen but not enough service time-needed 6 mos. Lived in Grayson Co 40 yrs. Appl pen 1835 Lee Co, M804 Roll 611. Newer Govt stone R2111 **P:** Y **BLW:** Y **RG:** unk **MK:** N **PH:** unk **SS:** K Vol 1 pg 225 **BS:** JLARC 4, 43; 196.

COLLINS, Benjamin; b unk; d unk **RU:** Private, Specific serv Lib VA, War files, vol 4, pg 127 **CEM:** Old Lick aka First Baptist; GPS 37.28250, -79.93690; Hart Ave bet 2nd & 4th St; Roanoke City **GS:** Y **SP:** No info **VI:** No further data **P:** unk **BLW:** unk **RG:** N **MK:** N **PH:** unk **SS:** CZ pg 106; E pg 168 **BS:** 185.

COLLINS, Thomas; b 1758; d 22 Aug 1832 **RU:** Sergeant/Patriot, Served in 1st and 10th Cont Line for 3 yrs. Gave material aid to cause **CEM:** Collins Family; GPS unk; See property records for home place; King & Queen **GS:** U **SP:** No info **VI:** No further data **P:** unk **BLW:** unk **RG:** unk **MK:** unk **PH:** unk **SS:** E pg 169; G pg 767; Al Cert King & Queen Co **BS:** 04.

COLONNA, Benjamin; b 10 Feb 1763; d 2 Jul 1851 **RU:** Soldier, Ent serv 1779, Accomack Co, Capt Americus Scarborough's Co Militia **CEM:** Waterfield Farm; GPS unk; 1.4 mi N of Rt 614, W of Rt 617, SE fr Pennyville; Accomack **GS:** N **SP:** Mar (29 Jul 1802) Elizabeth Beach (17 Oct 1784-18 Jan 1848) d/o Reuben & Mary (Wilkins) Beach **VI:** Son of Maj (22 Jul 1736-__) & Joice (Hutchinson) Colona. Appl for pension Accomack Co 1832. R616 **P:** Y **BLW:** unk **RG:** unk **MK:** unk **PH:** N **SS:** R 616; K Vol 1 pg 226 **BS:** JLARC 4, 5.

COLQUHOUN, James W; b 11 Dec 1766; d 5 Sep 1815 **RU:** Private, Served in Capt Richard Thomas's Co, 6th VA Regt, commanded by Col William Russell, Sep 1778. Served 3 yrs **CEM:** Dumfries Public; GPS 38.34110, -77.19964; 17821 Mine Rd, Dumfries; Prince William **GS:** Y **SP:** T__ (1775-Sep 1815) **VI:** SAR monument **P:** unk **BLW:** unk **RG:** Y **MK:** Y **PH:** Y **SS:** E pg 170 **BS:** 245.

COLQUITT, John; b 1775; d c18 Jun 1847 **RU:** Private?, Served US Army. Specific Serv Lib VA, War files, vol 4, pg 136 **CEM:** St John's Episcopal; GPS 37.53183, -77.41958; 2401 E Broad St; Richmond City **GS:** N **SP:** No info **VI:** His claim for BLW rejected by Gov of VA **P:** unk **BLW:** unk **RG:** N **MK:** N **PH:** N **SS:** CZ pg 107; E pg 170 **BS:** 28, pg 351.

COLSON, Thomas; b unk; d unk **RU:** Quartermaster, Served in 7th VA Cont Line **CEM:** Vauxhall Site; GPS unk; Rt 607; Spotsylvania **GS:** Y **SP:** No info **VI:** No further data **P:** unk **BLW:** unk **RG:** Y **MK:** N **PH:** unk **SS:** B; E pg 170 **BS:** 09, grid 49, 04.

COLUE, Andre; b unk; d 1781 **RU:** Soldier, Served in Gatinais Bn and died from Yorktown battle **CEM:** French Memorial; GPS 36.81944, -79.39933; Yorktown; York **GS:** U **SP:** No info **VI:** No further data **P:** unk **BLW:** unk **RG:** Y **MK:** unk **PH:** unk **SS:** J-Yorktown Historian **BS:** JLARC 1, 74.

COLVIN, Daniel; b 1737, Essex Co; d 1790 **RU:** Soldier, Served in Illinois Regt for 3 yrs. Enl 14 Nov 1779 for 3 yrs or duration of war in Capt Benjamin Roberts Co. Discharged with Slaughter's detachment and Crockett's Regt the last of 1781, pursuant to general orders. Was with George Rogers Clark at

RU=Rank/Unit	CEM=Cemetery	GS=Gravestone	SP=Spousal Information
VI=Other Veteran Info	P=Pension	BLW=Bounty/Land Warrant	RG=Registered Grave
MK=SAR/DAR Marker	PH=Photo	SS=Service Source	BS=Burial Source

73

Vincennes **CEM:** Masonic Cemetery; GPS 38.48530, -77.99470; 950 N Main, Culpeper; Culpeper **GS:** Y **SP:** Elizabeth Magdalene Hansberger **VI:** Son of Mason & Levina (Tool) Colvin. Govt stone. **P:** unk **BLW:** unk **RG:** Y **MK:** N **PH:** unk **SS:** J- DAR Hatcher; AK **BS:** JLARC 2, 04; 196.

COLVIN, Mason; b c1760 or 63, Culpeper Co; d 23 Jan 1853 **RU:** Private, Ent serv Culpeper Co 1781. Was in Illinois Regt for 3 yrs **CEM:** Slate Mills; GPS unk; Vic Woodville; Rappahannock **GS:** U **SP:** Mar (24 Apr 1788 (bond)) Elizabeth Hawkins d/o Benjamin & Judith (-----) Hawkins of Culpeper Co **VI:** Appl for pension Culpeper Co 1832, age 72. R617. Was listed as pensioner of Rappahannock Co on 1840 census, age 80 **P:** Y **BLW:** unk **RG:** Y **MK:** N **PH:** unk **SS:** M pg 830; R 617; K Vol 1 pg 227 **BS:** 04.

COMBOT, Bernard; b unk; d 1781 **RU:** Seaman, Served on "Duc De Bourgogne" and died from Yorktown battle **CEM:** French Memorial; GPS 36.81944, -79.39933; Yorktown; York **GS:** U **SP:** No info **VI:** No further data **P:** unk **BLW:** unk **RG:** Y **MK:** unk **PH:** unk **SS:** J-Yorktown Historian **BS:** JLARC 1, 74.

COMBRUN, Jean; b unk; d 1781 **RU:** Seaman, Served on "Ville de Paris" and died from Yorktown battle **CEM:** French Memorial; GPS 36.81944, -79.39933; Yorktown; York **GS:** U **SP:** No info **VI:** No further data **P:** unk **BLW:** unk **RG:** Y **MK:** unk **PH:** unk **SS:** J-Yorktown Historian **BS:** JLARC 1, 74.

COMBS, Robert; b 1753, near Berry Ferry, Shenandoah River, Frederick Co; d 7 Sep 1846 **RU:** Private, Ent Serv Loudoun Co 1775 **CEM:** Combs Family; GPS unk; Hopewell; Fauquier **GS:** N **SP:** Sarah Linton **VI:** Pensioned Fauquier Co in 1832. R618 **P:** Y **BLW:** unk **RG:** Y **MK:** N **PH:** N **SS:** K pg 228; H **BS:** 19, pg 46; 04.

COMER, John; b Jul 1753, Caroline Co; d 1836 **RU:** Soldier, Ent serv Amelia Co 1775. Was Marine on ship Hero. Ent serv again 1781 in VA Militia **CEM:** Comer; GPS unk; Rt 662, Elk Creek; Grayson **GS:** U **SP:** Amy Epps **VI:** Son of Thomas R. & Frances (Moore) Comer. Pensioned Grayson Co, 1832, where he had moved in 1782. R619 **P:** Y **BLW:** unk **RG:** unk **MK:** unk **PH:** unk **SS:** R 619; K Vol 1 pg 228 **BS:** JLARC 4.

CONDE, Pierre; b unk; d 1781 **RU:** Soldier, Served in Soissonnais Bn and died from Yorktown battle **CEM:** French Memorial; GPS 36.81944, -79.39933; Yorktown; York **GS:** U **SP:** No info **VI:** No further data **P:** unk **BLW:** unk **RG:** Y **MK:** unk **PH:** unk **SS:** J-Yorktown Historian **BS:** JLARC 1v74.

CONN, William Young; b Mar 1753, Washington DC; d 15 Apr 1837 **RU:** Navy ship pilot, Ent serv Washington DC area 1776, later ent serv Alexandria as pilot for ships evading British fleet **CEM:** Sinking Springs; GPS 36.71030, -81.98170; 136 E Main St, Abingdon; Washington **GS:** U **SP:** Jane (-----) (4 May 1746-1 Apr 1832) **VI:** Pensioned Washington DC, 1833, age 78. R627 **P:** Y **BLW:** unk **RG:** Y **MK:** unk **PH:** unk **SS:** R 627; K Vol 1 pg 230-1 **BS:** JLARC 1, 2, 4, 34 ,80.

CONNALY, Arthur Sr; b 1730; d 1805 **RU:** Patriot, Gave material aid to cause **CEM:** Augusta Stone Presbyterian; GPS 38.23926, -78.97356; 28 Old Stone Church Ln, Ft Defiance; Augusta **GS:** Y **SP:** Jean (-----) **VI:** Govt stone **P:** N **BLW:** N **RG:** Y **MK:** unk **PH:** unk **SS:** AL Ct Cert Augusta Co **BS:** JLARC 1, 2, 8, 23, 62; 196.

CONNELL, William; b unk; d 27 Mar 1795 **RU:** Private, Served in Col Francis Marion's SC Regt Nov 1779 **CEM:** Old Christ Church Episcopal; GPS 38.80625, -77.04718; 118 N Washington St; Alexandria City **GS:** N **SP:** No info **VI:** Burial permit issued 27 Mar 1795 **P:** unk **BLW:** unk **RG:** Y **MK:** N **PH:** N **SS:** A pg 290 **BS:** 20 pg 146.

CONNER, James; b unk; d 1793 **RU:** Patriot, Signed Legislative Petition **CEM:** Old Christ Church Episcopal; GPS 38.80625, -77.04718; 118 N Washington St; Alexandria City **GS:** N **SP:** No info **VI:** Burial permit issued 7 Oct 1793 **P:** N **BLW:** N **RG:** N **MK:** N **PH:** N **SS:** BB **BS:** 20 pg 146.

CONNER (CONNOR), Patrick; b unk; d 1784 **RU:** Private, Served in 3rd, 5th, & 11th Cont Line **CEM:** Truro Parish; GPS unk; "On the middle ridge near Ox Road", the present site of Jerusalem Baptist Church off Rt 123; Fairfax **GS:** N **SP:** No info **VI:** No further data **P:** unk **BLW:** unk **RG:** N **MK:** N **PH:** N **SS:** E pg 172-3 **BS:** 110, pg 103-4.

CONNOR, Daniel; b unk; d unk **RU:** Private, Served in 2nd VA Brigade & 2nd, 6th Cont Lines. Also served in Col Daniel Morgan's Riflemen Regt **CEM:** Salem Cemetery; GPS 37.05014, -80.16004; Rt

RU=Rank/Unit	CEM=Cemetery	GS=Gravestone	SP=Spousal Information
VI=Other Veteran Info	P=Pension	BLW=Bounty/Land Warrant	RG=Registered Grave
MK=SAR/DAR Marker	PH=Photo	SS=Service Source	BS=Burial Source

74

221, Head of the River Church; Floyd **GS:** U **SP:** Mary (-----) **VI:** No further data **P:** unk **BLW:** unk **RG:** unk **MK:** unk **PH:** unk **SS:** E pg 174 **BS:** JLARC 29.

CONRAD, Henry; b 1759; d 1849 **RU:** Private, WPA report indicates service but service not determined **CEM:** Elk Run; GPS 38.41042, -78.61033; North St, Elkton; Rockingham **GS:** Y **SP:** Mar (1813 Rockingham Co\) Sally Hansbarger **VI:** No further data **P:** unk **BLW:** unk **RG:** N **MK:** N **PH:** unk **SS:** AP Roll **BS:** 186.

CONRAD, John Peter; b 1745; d 1800 **RU:** Patriot, Gave material aid to the cause **CEM:** Old Peaked Mountain; GPS 38.37113, -78.73416; 9843 Town Hall Rd, McGaheysville; Rockingham **GS:** Y **SP:** Mary Nicholas, d/o Peter & (-----) Nicholas **VI:** No further data **P:** N **BLW:** N **RG:** Y **MK:** Y **PH:** unk **SS:** AL Ct Bk 1 pg 1 04 **BS:** 191 Peaked Mt 04.

CONRAD (CONROD), John Stephen Jr; b 26 Feb 1749, Tulpehocken, PA; d 28 Aug 1822 **RU:** Captain, Took oath for Lt, 7 Mar 1780 in Capt Jeremiah Beeslie's Co. Took Oath for Capt 23 Apr 1781 and commanded Co 15, Rockingham Militia until 1788 **CEM:** East Point; GPS unk; Rt 602 left fr Rt 33 E, Elkton; Rockingham **GS:** Y **SP:** Mary Margaret Moyer **VI:** No further data **P:** unk **BLW:** unk **RG:** Y **MK:** Y **PH:** unk **SS:** AS SAR Regis **BS:** SAR regis.

CONRAD (CONROD/COONROD), Jacob; b Aug 1754 or 1747, PA; d 3 Jun 1824 or 1841 **RU:** Private, Enl Redstone Settlement, Monongahola River 1 Jan 1777. Served in Capt Benjamin Harrison's Co, Cols Russell's and John Gibson's VA Regts. Was in Battle of Brandywine and Germantown. Discharged 25 Jul 1783 **CEM:** East Point; GPS unk; Rt 602 left fr Rt 33 E, Elkton; Rockingham **GS:** N **SP:** No info **VI:** Pensioned Rockingham Co 1820 S.39361 **P:** Y **BLW:** unk **RG:** Y **MK:** N **PH:** N **SS:** AH pg 146 **BS:** 142 Elk Run.

CONSTABLE, Thomas; b 1742; d 25 Apr 1805 **RU:** Ensign, Served in Baltimore MD Town Bn 23 May 1781 **CEM:** Cedar Grove; GPS 36.85860, -76.28310; 238 E Princess Anne Rd; Norfolk City **GS:** Y **SP:** no info **VI:** A person by this name was head of household in Norfolk VA in 1810. **P:** unk **BLW:** unk **RG:** N **MK:** N **PH:** unk **SS:** BF **BS:** 32 Tim Bonney.

COOK, Benjamin; b 1757; d 1830 **RU:** Private, Served in US Army, specific serv Lib VA, War files, vol 4, pg 151 **CEM:** Cook Family; GPS unk; Rt 630 nr Rt 890, nr Sago; Franklin **GS:** U **SP:** No info **VI:** No further data **P:** unk **BLW:** Y **RG:** unk **MK:** unk **PH:** unk **SS:** CU; CZ pg 110 **BS:** JLARC 2,18.

COOK, Henry; b 1761; d 13 Mar 1835 **RU:** Private, Served in 7th Cont Line **CEM:** Zion Lutheran; GPS 36.84110, -81.22310; 1417 Zion Church Rd, Crockett; Wythe **GS:** U **SP:** No info **VI:** No further data **P:** unk **BLW:** unk **RG:** unk **MK:** unk **PH:** unk **SS:** E pg 176 **BS:** 196.

COOK, Jacob; b unk; d 1789 **RU:** Patriot, Gave use of horse for six days **CEM:** Old Christ Church Episcopal; GPS 38.80625, -77.04718; 118 N Washington St; Alexandria City **GS:** N **SP:** No info **VI:** Burial permit issued 3 0 Oct 1789 **P:** N **BLW:** N **RG:** N **MK:** N **PH:** N **SS:** Z pg 61 **BS:** 20 pg 146.

COOLE, John M; b Oct 1745; d 8 Feb 1815 **RU:** Sergeant, Served in Capt Drury Ragsdale's Co, Col Chat Harrison's Regt **CEM:** Back Creek Quaker, aka Gainesboro United Methodist; GPS 39.27861, -78.25694; 166 Siler Ln, Gainesboro; Frederick **GS:** Y **SP:** Probably Nancy (-----) (__-4 May 1823), bur in cemetery listed **VI:** No further data **P:** unk **BLW:** unk **RG:** unk **MK:** unk **PH:** unk **SS:** AP-Muster Roll **BS:** 196.

COOPER, James; b 1740; d 1798 **RU:** Patriot, Gave material aid to cause **CEM:** New Hope; GPS unk; Orange; Orange **GS:** U **SP:** Mary Quisenberry (1745-1810) **VI:** No further data **P:** N **BLW:** N **RG:** unk **MK:** unk **PH:** unk **SS:** AL Ct Bk pg 6 **BS:** 196.

COOPER, John Jr; b 14 Jun 1766; d 27 Feb 1851 **RU:** Drummer, Enl Chester Co, in Capt Marshall's Co, PA Militia. Later served in VA in 1st, 3rd, 4th, 8th, 9th and 12th Cont Lines **CEM:** Cooper family; GPS unk; W side of Back Mtn Rd, 1 mi N of Mountain Falls; Frederick **GS:** U **SP:** Mar (23 Sep 1789) Catherine Secrist (1767-11 May 1849) d/o Henry & Anna Maria (-----) Secrist **VI:** Son of John Sr & (-----) Cooper. Pen filed Jun 1818 **P:** Y **BLW:** unk **RG:** unk **MK:** unk **PH:** unk **SS:** E pg 177; CZ pg 64 **BS:** 196.

COOPER, Robert; b 1738; d 20 Sep 1816 **RU:** Private, Served in Capt McCutchen's Co Augusta Co VA **CEM:** Old Providence; GPS 37.96151, -79.71000; 1005 Spottswood Rd, Spottswood; Augusta **GS:** Y

RU=Rank/Unit   CEM=Cemetery   GS=Gravestone   SP=Spousal Information
VI=Other Veteran Info   P=Pension   BLW=Bounty/Land Warrant   RG=Registered Grave
MK=SAR/DAR Marker   PH=Photo   SS=Service Source   BS=Burial Source

75

SP: Susanna H. Blair, b 1742, d 5 Nov 1817 **VI:** Son of William Cooper. Elder of Old Providence & Timber Ridge 1776 **P:** unk **BLW:** unk **RG:** Y **MK:** N **PH:** Y **SS:** E pg 571 **BS:** 44 pg 57; 196.

COOPER, Samuel; b 1756, MA; d 19 Aug 1840 **RU:** Lieutenant, Made 2nd Lt, 3rd MA CL-Artillery as of 1 Feb 1777 and Regimental Quartermaster 14 May 1778-Jun 1783, Corps Artillery 17 Jun 1783. Was Adjutant of same to 20 June 1784. Fought at Bunker Hill, Trenton, Brandywine, Germantown, Monmouth **CEM:** Christ Church Episcopal; GPS 38.80216, -77.05689; Wilkes St & Hamilton Ln; Alexandria City **GS:** Y **SP:** Sarah Maria Mason and/or Mary Horton **VI:** Member Society of Cincinnati. Rank of Maj earned after war period. Died age 84 **P:** unk **BLW:** unk **RG:** Y **MK:** Y **PH:** Y **SS:** A pg 417, 479; BT **BS:** JLARC 1, 2, 25, 86; 20 pg 92; 196.

COOPER, William Sterling; b 20 Jun 1760; d 9 Jan 1836 **RU:** Private, Served 18 mos in Capt Cunningham, 145th VA Regt at Valley Forge and Battle at Monmouth. Enl again 1780 for 3 mos under Capt Ship, and again under Capt Hayes. Was at Yorktown Battle **CEM:** Cooper Family; GPS unk; Snow Creek; Franklin **GS:** U **SP:** Mar (6 Dec 1819 Franklin Co) Lucy Willis, surety David Willis **VI:** No further data **P:** Y **BLW:** unk **RG:** unk **MK:** unk **PH:** unk **SS:** AP Pen Applic1832 **BS:** 196.

COPELAND, James (Jas); b 1 Aug 1759, Ireland; d 15 Jun 1838, Loudoun Co **RU:** Private, Ent serv Loudoun Co 1778 in11th VA Regt, Cont Line. Served in Capt William George's Co, Loudoun Co Militia 1781 **CEM:** Ketoctin Baptist; GPS 39.15746, -77.74870; Ketoctin Church Rd, Purcellville; Loudoun **GS:** Y **SP:** Mar (26 Apr 1787) Sarah Akers of Shelburne Parish (Loudoun Co). (c1762-__) **VI:** Came to VA with parents at age 4. Pensioned Loudoun Co 1832. Widow penioned age 70 Loudoun Co in 1832. Resided there in 1843, age 73. W.6730. R650 **P:** Y **BLW:** unk **RG:** Y **MK:** N **PH:** unk **SS:** R 650; AK; E pg 178; K Vol 1 pg 242 **BS:** 04, JLARC 1, 2, 32.

COPENHAVER (COPENHAVEN), Michal (Michael); b c1753; d 15 Sep 1823 **RU:** Patriot, Gave provisions to the cause **CEM:** Mt Hebron; GPS 39.10916, -78.09497; 305 E Boscawen St; Winchester City **GS:** Y **SP:** Mar (09 Mar 1786, Frederick Co by Rev Christian Streit) Margaret Price **VI:** No further data **P:** N **BLW:** N **RG:** N **MK:** N **PH:** Y **SS:** AL CT Bk 26 **BS:** 50 pg 46; 196.

COPLAND, Charles; b 1756; d 24 Nov 1836 **RU:** Private/Patriot, Signed Legislative Petition Hanover Co, 24 May 1782 **CEM:** St John's Episcopal; GPS 37.53183, -77.41958; 2401 E Broad St; Richmond City **GS:** Y **SP:** Rebecca (-----) (c1770-25 Jul 1800) **VI:** Member of the Diocese of VA and St John's Church **P:** unk **BLW:** unk **RG:** Y **MK:** N **PH:** unk **SS:** CZ pg 112; E pg 179 **BS:** 28, pg 525.

CORBIN, Gawin Tayloe; b 15 Dec 1739; d 19 Jul 1779 **RU:** Patriot, Gave material aid to Army. Was member VA Council **CEM:** Christ Church; GPS 37.60968, -76.54643; Rt 33 2 mi E of Saluda; Middlesex **GS:** U **SP:** Martha (-----) (__-11 Jun 1839, King & Queen Co) **VI:** Son of Richard)__-1790) & Betty (Tayloe) (__-1781) Corbin of Mt Airy **P:** N **BLW:** N **RG:** unk **MK:** unk **PH:** unk **SS:** G pg 202 **BS:** 196.

CORBIN, George; b 1744; d 28 Sep 1793 **RU:** Colonel, Was in charge of Accomack Co Militia. Served as County Lt, 31 Mar 1779 **CEM:** Scott Hall; GPS unk; Daugherty Rd, Onancock; Accomack **GS:** Y **SP:** Mar (17 Sep 1796 Accomack (bond)) Nancy Sterling **VI:** No further data **P:** unk **BLW:** unk **RG:** N **MK:** N **PH:** unk **SS:** E pg 179; DAR Marker **BS:** 209; 196.

CORBIN, John; b 3 Jan 1747; d 16 Jun 1813 **RU:** Private?, Served in Capt Holmes Co **CEM:** Major-Corbin; GPS unk; Amissville; Rappahannock **GS:** Y **SP:** Frances (-----) (__-1 May 1814) **VI:** Son of William (1720-1796) & Sarah (Fant) (1726-__) Corbin. **P:** unk **BLW:** unk **RG:** Y **MK:** N **PH:** unk **SS:** E pg 179 **BS:** 04.

CORBIN, Richard; b c1714; d 20 May 1790 **RU:** Patriot, Gave 3805 # of beef, 548 bushels corn & reimbursed for carting grain **CEM:** Christ Church; GPS 37.60968, -76.54643; Rt 33 2 mi E of Saluda; Middlesex **GS:** Y **SP:** Mar (1737) Elizabeth "Betty" Tayloe (1729-1784) **VI:** Son of Gawin (1659-1744) & 2nd wife Jane (Lane) Corbin. GS moved fr upper chapel **P:** N **BLW:** N **RG:** N **MK:** N **PH:** unk **SS:** AL Ct Bk pg 2; D Middlesex Co claims pg 2 May 1782 **BS:** 92 pg 6, 116.

CORBIN, William; b 1720; d 3 Dec 1796 **RU:** Patriot, Gave material aid to cause **CEM:** Major-Corbin; GPS 38.65282, -78.02353; Rt 642, Viewtown Rd nr jct with Ida Belle Ln; Rappahannock **GS:** U **SP:** Mar (1 Jan 1743) Sarah Jeenkins **VI:** Son of John (1697-1758, King George Co) & Elizabeth Jennings

RU=Rank/Unit	CEM=Cemetery	GS=Gravestone	SP=Spousal Information
VI=Other Veteran Info	P=Pension	BLW=Bounty/Land Warrant	RG=Registered Grave
MK=SAR/DAR Marker	PH=Photo	SS=Service Source	BS=Burial Source

76

(1694-1754) Corbin **P**: N **BLW**: N **RG**: unk **MK**: unk **PH**: unk **SS**: AL Ct Bk I pg 79 Culpeper Co **BS**: 196.

CORDER, John; b 1761, Fauquier Co; d 24 Jan 1849 **RU**: Private, Ent serv 1777, Fauquier Co in Col Gibson's Regt **CEM**: Corder-Pierce Family; GPS unk; Amissville; Rappahannock **GS**: Y **SP**: 1) Hannah Way (?) 2) Mar (1845) Mary (-----) Maddox, his housekeeper and widow of Samuel Maddox. **VI**: Son of William (1703-__) & Alice (-----) Corder, Fauquier Co. Recd 200 acres fr Lord Fairfax. Brother James Corder also served in Rev War. Pensioned age 71 in 1832 and states sol blind when pen. Pen fr "near Fiery Run Meeting House" Fauquier Co 1836. R654 **P**: Y **BLW**: unk **RG**: Y **MK**: N **PH**: unk **SS**: K Vol 1 pg 245 **BS**: 33.

CORLAIX, Jean; b unk; d 1781 **RU**: Seaman, Served on "Magnanime" and died from Yorktown battle **CEM**: French Memorial; GPS 36.81944, -79.39933; Yorktown; York **GS**: U **SP**: No info **VI**: No further data **P**: unk **BLW**: unk **RG**: Y **MK**: unk **PH**: unk **SS**: J-Yorktown Historian **BS**: JLARC 1, 74.

CORN, Jesse Sr; b 31 Oct 1753, Albemarle Co; d 5 May 1809 **RU**: Ensign, Ent serv Albemarle Co "early in the war". Served later in Henry Co Militia and unit was sent to support General Greene **CEM**: Patrick Henry Allied Memorial; GPS unk; Fairy Stone State Park; Patrick **GS**: Y **SP**: Mar (1780 Fluvanna Co Bond 21 Feb 1780 signed by Benjamin Hancock, Fluvanna Co) Nancy Hancock (17 Feb 1780-17 Jun 1848 in TN), d/o John & (-----) Hancock **VI**: Pen in 1841, Franklin Co. Widow pen Franklin Co TN 1841. R655 **P**: Y **BLW**: unk **RG**: N **MK**: N **PH**: unk **SS**: G pg 186; R 655; K Vol 1 pg 246 **BS**: 125 pg 420.

CORNETT (CORNET), James Jr; b 1760; d April 1824 **RU**: Private, Served in Lt John McKinney or William Walling's Co **CEM**: Cornett Family; GPS 36.72401, -81.23889; Rt 662; Grayson **GS**: U **SP**: Mary (Molly) Vaughn **VI**: No further data **P**: unk **BLW**: unk **RG**: Y **MK**: N **PH**: unk **SS**: AK Apr 2007; DD **BS**: 04, Apr 2007.

CORNISH, Daniel; b unk; d 1781 **RU**: Soldier, Served fr MA, and died as result of Yorktown battle **CEM**: Yorktown Victory Monument Tablet; GPS 38.28350, -78.54150; Yorktown; York **GS**: U **SP**: No info **VI**: No further data **P**: unk **BLW**: unk **RG**: unk **MK**: unk **PH**: unk **SS**: J-Yorktown Historian **BS**: JLARC 74.

COSBY, Overton; b c1739; d 1806 **RU**: Patriot, Gave material aid to the cause **CEM**: Landsdowne House; GPS unk; Virginia St, Urbanna; Middlesex **GS**: Y **SP**: No info **VI**: No further data **P**: N **BLW**: N **RG**: N **MK**: N **PH**: unk **SS**: AL Ct Bk pg 9 **BS**: 92, pg 58.

COSTAIL, Sidet; b unk; d 1781 **RU**: Soldier, Served in Touraine Bn and died from Yorktown battle **CEM**: French Memorial; GPS 36.81944, -79.39933; Yorktown; York **GS**: U **SP**: No info **VI**: No further data **P**: unk **BLW**: unk **RG**: Y **MK**: unk **PH**: unk **SS**: J-Yorktown Historian **BS**: JLARC 1, 74.

COSTE, Vidal; b unk; d 1781 **RU**: Soldier, Served in Touraine Bn and died from Yorktown battle **CEM**: French Memorial; GPS 36.81944, -79.39933; Yorktown; York **GS**: U **SP**: No info **VI**: No further data **P**: unk **BLW**: unk **RG**: Y **MK**: unk **PH**: unk **SS**: J-Yorktown Historian **BS**: JLARC 1, 74.

COUILLARD, Jacques; b unk; d 1781 **RU**: Seaman, Served on "Duc De Bourgogne" and died from Yorktown battle **CEM**: French Memorial; GPS 36.81944, -79.39933; Yorktown; York **GS**: U **SP**: No info **VI**: No further data **P**: unk **BLW**: unk **RG**: Y **MK**: unk **PH**: unk **SS**: J-Yorktown Historian **BS**: JLARC 1, 74.

COURBET, Antoine; b unk; d 1781 **RU**: Soldier, Served in Touraine Bn and died from Yorktown battle **CEM**: French Memorial; GPS 36.81944, -79.39933; Yorktown; York **GS**: U **SP**: No info **VI**: No further data **P**: unk **BLW**: unk **RG**: Y **MK**: unk **PH**: unk **SS**: J-Yorktown Historian **BS**: JLARC 1, 74.

COURTNEY, John; b 1741; d 1824 **RU**: Patriot, Gave material aid to cause **CEM**: Hollywood; GPS 37.53560, -77.45720; 412 S Cherry St; Richmond City **GS**: U **SP**: No info **VI**: Memorial, not indiv GS **P**: N **BLW**: N **RG**: unk **MK**: unk **PH**: unk **SS**: D Stafford Co **BS**: JLARC 99.

COURTNEY, William; b unk; d 1848 **RU**: Private, Served in Capt William Alexander's Co 1777, Col William Irvine's PA Regt **CEM**: Courtney Family; GPS unk; Nr N Bank Hamshill Creek; Page **GS**: N **SP**: No info **VI**: No further data **P**: unk **BLW**: unk **RG**: N **MK**: N **PH**: N **SS**: A pg 219 **BS**: 120.

RU=Rank/Unit   CEM=Cemetery   GS=Gravestone   SP=Spousal Information
VI=Other Veteran Info   P=Pension   BLW=Bounty/Land Warrant   RG=Registered Grave
MK=SAR/DAR Marker   PH=Photo   SS=Service Source   BS=Burial Source

77

COURTNEY (COURTNY), William; b unk; d unk **RU:** Private/Patriot, Served in 3rd, 4th, 8th Cont lines **CEM:** Courtney Family; GPS unk; Hartwood Airfield; Fauquier **GS:** N **SP:** A man by this name mar (10 Jan 1786 (bond) Fauquier Co, John Smith security) Ann Smith **VI:** Filed petition in Stafford Co. Airport removed the GSs when building the runways **P:** unk **BLW:** unk **RG:** N **MK:** N **PH:** N **SS:** CZ pg 114; E pg 183; Fauquier Co Marriages pg 42 **BS:** 19 pg 47.

COURTOIS, Etienne; b unk; d 1781 **RU:** Soldier, Served in Bourbonnais Bn and died from Yorktown battle **CEM:** French Memorial; GPS 36.81944, -79.39933; Yorktown; York **GS:** U **SP:** No info **VI:** No further data **P:** unk **BLW:** unk **RG:** Y **MK:** unk **PH:** unk **SS:** J-Yorktown Historian **BS:** JLARC 1, 74.

COUSINS, Henry; b 22 Jul 1758; d 5 Jun 1824 **RU:** Matross/Patriot, Served in Lt Shockley's Co, VA Militia. Gave material aid to cause **CEM:** Fleetwood Plantation; GPS unk; 6630 Brills Rd, McKenney; Dinwiddie **GS:** Y **SP:** Margaret Boisseau **VI:** Newer Govt stone inscribed with service as a Montross **P:** N **BLW:** unk **RG:** unk **MK:** N **PH:** unk **SS:** D Amelia Co **BS:** JLARC 116; 196.

COUTEL, Guillaume; b unk; d 1781 **RU:** Soldier, Served in Santogne Bn and died from Yorktown battle **CEM:** French Memorial; GPS 36.81944, -79.39933; Yorktown; York **GS:** U **SP:** No info **VI:** No further data **P:** unk **BLW:** unk **RG:** unk **MK:** unk **PH:** unk **SS:** J-Yorktown Historian **BS:** JLARC 1, 74.

COVINGTON, Francis L; b 1754; d 1823 **RU:** Captain, Commanded Co in Culpeper Co Militia **CEM:** Covington Family; GPS unk; Nr Washington CH. This would put it in Rappahannock Co, not Culpeper Co; Culpeper **GS:** U **SP:** No info **VI:** No further data **P:** unk **BLW:** unk **RG:** Y **MK:** N **PH:** unk **SS:** J-DAR Hatcher; CZ pg 114 **BS:** JLARC 2.

COWHERD, Francis Kirtley; b 1753; d 25 Mar 1833 **RU:** Captain, Ent serv 1779. 2nd VA Regt (Heitman). Was Lt in 2nd Regt of Foot 1778 to spring 1779. Was Capt of Milita fr Caroline Co at Guilford CH, SC 15 Mar 1781 **CEM:** Cowherd Family, "Oak Hill"; GPS unk; Gordonsville; Orange **GS:** U **SP:** Mar (Aug 1787) Lucy Scott (1763-31 Jul 1847) **VI:** Pen 1828 Orange Co. Widow pen 1838, Orange Co **P:** Y **BLW:** unk **RG:** Y **MK:** Y **PH:** unk **SS:** AK J-NSSAR 1993 Reg R 668; CE pg 37, 145 **BS:** 04, JLARC 1.

COWLING, Josiah; b 1739, Suffolk City; d Dec 1799 or 1800 **RU:** Patriot, Gave material aid to the cause **CEM:** Cedar Hill; GPS 36.73640, -76.58000; 105 Mahan St, Suffolk; Suffolk City **GS:** Y **SP:** Urania Monro (1739-1799) **VI:** Died in Chuckatuck, Suffolk City. Originally grave was located on Cowling Farm bet Reid's Ferry and Chuckatuck, VA. Markers, but not remains relocated to Cedar Hill Cemetery, Suffolk, Co in 1957 **P:** N **BLW:** N **RG:** N **MK:** N **PH:** unk **SS:** AL CT Bk pg 13, 20 **BS:** 53 pg 99; 196.

COX, Charles; b 1755; d 1832 **RU:** Patriot, Paid supply tax 1780 **CEM:** Cox Family; GPS unk; Cox, nr Turkey Pen Branch & Smith River; Henry **GS:** N **SP:** Frances Kelly (c1760-aft 1820) **VI:** No further data **P:** N **BLW:** N **RG:** unk **MK:** unk **PH:** unk **SS:** DAR Ancestor #A026979; DD cites County Deed books III, IV tax lists pg 22 **BS:** 196.

COX, Charles II; b 1721; d 1816 **RU:** Patriot, Paid supply tax, Henry Co, 1780 **CEM:** Cox Family; GPS unk; Cox, nr Turkey Pen Branch & Smith River; Henry **GS:** U **SP:** Mar (1740) Eleanor Watts (1722-1810) **VI:** Son of Charles (1690-1790) & Ida (Bennett) (1692-1786) Cox. Rec'd Land Grant 1781 for Colonial War service by Thomas Jefferson **P:** N **BLW:** Y **RG:** unk **MK:** unk **PH:** unk **SS:** EA pg 22 **BS:** 196.

COX, David; b 1737, Lancaster Co, PA; d 8 Jan 1818 **RU:** Lieutenant, Served in NC and VA. Ct order 5 April 1780 certifies military service under Preston (1755-6) on frontiers of Augusta. Served under brother Capt John Cox in battles of Point Pleasant & King's Mountain **CEM:** Cox Family Farm; GPS unk; Rt 629 W of Baywood; Grayson **GS:** Y **SP:** Mar (VA) Margaret Ann "Peggy" McGowan (1742-1811) **VI:** Son of Joshua "John" & Mary Katherine (Rankin) Cox. Owned land with brother John in "New River Settlement" with holdings across line to NC. Died in Brindle Creek, Grayson Co **P:** unk **BLW:** unk **RG:** Y **MK:** Y **PH:** unk **SS:** AK; J-NASSR 2000 Reg **BS:** 04; JLARC 1, 2, 76.

COX, Enoch Sr; b 19 Jun 1757, Orange Co, NC; d 28 Mar 1840, Grayson Co **RU:** Private, Served in VA Battalion, 14th Regt 1776. Served 1st VA Regt in battles at Brandywine and Germantown **CEM:** Old Quaker; GPS 36.64067, -80.88620; Off Old Quaker Rd Rt 727, Pipers Gap; Carroll **GS:** Y **SP:** 1) Mar (9 Jan 1781) Mary Mackey 2) Mar (5 Feb 1831 Grayson Co) Sarah Stoneman **VI:** DAR marker **P:** unk **BLW:** unk **RG:** Y **MK:** Y **PH:** Y **SS:** NSDAR Patriot Index 2003; E pg 185 **BS:** JLARC 1, 2,11, 43; 196.

RU=Rank/Unit   CEM=Cemetery   GS=Gravestone   SP=Spousal Information
VI=Other Veteran Info   P=Pension   BLW=Bounty/Land Warrant   RG=Registered Grave
MK=SAR/DAR Marker   PH=Photo   SS=Service Source   BS=Burial Source

78

COX, Peter; b 10 Jul 1744; d 6 May 1792 **RU:** Patriot, Gave material aid to cause **CEM:** Cox Homestead; GPS unk; Cherry Point; Northumberland **GS:** Y **SP:** Mar (27 Mar 1771, License in Northumberland (fee books) Jane (Harding) Garner, widow of Parish Garner (22 Sep 1746-__) d/o William & Sarah (Ball) Harding **VI:** Son of Peter & Mary (-----) Cox **P:** N **BLW:** N **RG:** N **MK:** N **PH:** unk **SS:** AL Ct Bk pg 5 **BS:** 47; 105 pg 419.

COX, Philip; b 1763 or 1764; d 1841 **RU:** Private, Specific serv Lib VA, War files, vol 4, pg 143 **CEM:** New Providence Presbyterian; GPS 37.95130, -79.30250; 1208 New Providence Rd, Raphine; Rockbridge **GS:** U **SP:** Ann Mary Wiseman **VI:** Recd BLW **P:** unk **BLW:** Y **RG:** unk **MK:** unk **PH:** unk **SS:** C sec II pg 231; CZ pg 115 **BS:** JLARC 62, 63, 79.

COX, Solomon; b 1730, New Castle, DE; d 1812 **RU:** Soldier fought at Kings Mountain 1780 **CEM:** Glenwood Methodist; GPS 36.62769, -80.88667; .1 mile E of intersection of Rt 608 Coal Creek Rd and Rt 609 Peaks Mountain Rd; Carroll **GS:** Y **SP:** No info **VI:** Fought in Battle of Alamance 1771; Died in Ross Co, Ohio. Body is probably in Ohio and only memorialized here **P:** unk **BLW:** unk **RG:** unk **MK:** N **PH:** unk **SS:** B **BS:** 199.

COX, Valentine; b c1750; d by 1812 **RU:** Patriot, Gave material aid to the cause **CEM:** Cox Family; GPS unk; Forest across fr Lake Vista; Bedford **GS:** Y **SP:** Nancy Cox (1756-1823) **VI:** Has DAR marker **P:** N **BLW:** N **RG:** Y **MK:** Y **PH:** unk **SS:** Al Ct Bk IV pg 283 **BS:** AK Sep 09.

CRABTREE, Jacob; b c1760; d 9 May 1818 **RU:** Private, Ent serv Lee Co 1766. Probably served in Capt James Crabtree's Co which was in Battle at King's Mountain **CEM:** Allison; GPS 36.91140, -81.75170; W of plaster mine on Locust Cove Rd on private property with closed gate, E of Saltville; Smyth **GS:** Y **SP:** Mar (4 Aug 1786 Russell Co) Mary Price (1768-22 Jul 1849) **VI:** Widow appl for pen which was approved after her death & distributed to heirs **P:** Y **BLW:** N **RG:** N **MK:** unk **PH:** N **SS:** K pg 255; CV pg 210 **BS:** 97 pg 1; 196.

CRADDOCK, Robert; b 1751; d 15 Oct 1842 **RU:** First Lieutenant, Ent serv in VA 11th Cont Line 1777. Was 2nd Lt 10 Aug 1777; 1st Lt 4 Jul 1779. Was prisoner at Charleston 12 May 1780 and paroled May 1783 and transferred to 4th Cont Line 1781 **CEM:** Craddock Family; GPS unk; off Darbytown Rd 5.6 mi SE of Richmond City; Henrico **GS:** Y **SP:** No info **VI:** BLW issued 15 Jul 1789. Awarded 3223 acres BLW. Pensioned at "The Hermitage" Warren Co KY, thus probably memorialized in VA cemetery. R674 **P:** Y **BLW:** Y **RG:** Y **MK:** N **PH:** unk **SS:** E pg 186; K Vol 1 pg 256 **BS:** 114, pg 2-3; 196.

CRAFFORD, Carter; b c1755; d 10 Nov 1800 **RU:** Patriot, Gave material aid to cause Surry Co **CEM:** Carter Crafford; GPS unk; Fort Eustis SW of golf course maintenance shop; York **GS:** U **SP:** Mar (25 May 1777) Sarah (-----) **VI:** No further data **P:** N **BLW:** N **RG:** unk **MK:** unk **PH:** unk **SS:** D Surry Co **BS:** 41 pg 106; 45 pg 106.

CRAFFORD, Charles; b unk; d 10 Nov 1800 VA **RU:** Patriot, Gave material aid to the cause **CEM:** Carter Crafford; GPS unk; Fort Eustis SW of golf course maintenance shop; York **GS:** Y **SP:** Martha (-----). Second husband Charlews Moore **VI:** No further data **P:** N **BLW:** N **RG:** Y **MK:** N **PH:** unk **SS:** AL Ct Bk pg 12 Surry Co; E pg 186 **BS:** 41 pg 106; 45 pg 106.

CRAGHEAD, John; b unk; d 1808 **RU:** Patriot, Gave material aid to the cause **CEM:** Graghead Family; GPS unk; Rt 1361 nr Radford; Franklin **GS:** Y **SP:** Mar (3 Apr 1789 Franklin Co) Elizabeth Hale **VI:** No further data **P:** N **BLW:** N **RG:** N **MK:** N **PH:** unk **SS:** AL O Ct Bk pg 7 **BS:** 82, pg 82.

CRAIG, Alexander; b 1757; d 30 Jun 1825 **RU:** Captain, Served in 2th PA Regt **CEM:** Old Lebanon; GPS 38.08090, -79.37545; Off Rt 42, Craigsville; Augusta **GS:** Y **SP:** Mar (c1780) Martha Crawford **VI:** SAR marker **P:** unk **BLW:** unk **RG:** Y **MK:** Y **PH:** unk **SS:** AK; CI **BS:** JLARC 62; 04; 196.

CRAIG, James; b c1762; d 8 Feb 1834 **RU:** Soldier, Served in Capt Pierce's Co 6 Apr 1781, Montgomery Co Militia **CEM:** Craig Family; GPS 37.13390, -80.39220; East Park Ln; Montgomery **GS:** Y **SP:** Anna Montgomery (__-2 Dec 1841) **VI:** No further data **P:** unk **BLW:** unk **RG:** unk **MK:** unk **PH:** Y **SS:** J- DAR Hatcher; G pg 241 **BS:** JLARC 2, 196.

CRAIG, James Jr; b 23 Jul 1745; d 22 Jun 1807 **RU:** Private, Ent serv 1777, Capt Given's Co, Augusta Co Militia **CEM:** Augusta Stone Presbyterian; GPS 38.23926, -78.97356; 28 Old Stone Church Ln, Ft Defiance; Augusta **GS:** Y **SP:** Jane Stuart **VI:** He may be the person with this name that served in a

RU=Rank/Unit	CEM=Cemetery	GS=Gravestone	SP=Spousal Information
VI=Other Veteran Info	P=Pension	BLW=Bounty/Land Warrant	RG=Registered Grave
MK=SAR/DAR Marker	PH=Photo	SS=Service Source	BS=Burial Source

79

Fincastle co commanded by Capt James Thompson at Point Pleasant in October 1774. Pensioned Augusta Co & drew BLW 5 Dec 1794. Govt stone does not show dates, but says he was in Capt Givens Co **P:** Y **BLW:** Y **RG:** Y **MK**: unk **PH**: unk **SS**: JLARC report; B; K Vol 1 pg 257; AZ pg 158 **BS:** JLARC 1, 2, 62; 196.

CRAIG, James Sr; b 1715, Ireland; d 07 Feb 1791 **RU:** Patriot, Gave material aid to the cause **CEM:** Augusta Stone Presbyterian; GPS 38.23926, -78.97356; 28 Old Stone Church Ln, Ft Defiance; Augusta **GS:** Y **SP:** Mar (1742) Mary Laird (1715-20 Feb 1785) **VI:** Stone erected by a descendant indicates he served as a private in Capt Given's Co VA Militia, Augusta Co, and was in the French & Indian War. Although he is listed on his GS as a private it was probably service before the Rev War as he would be over military age **P:** N **BLW:** N **RG:** Y **MK**: unk **PH**: unk **SS**: J-NSSAR 1993 Reg, J- DAR Hatcher; AL Ct Bk Augusta Co pg 1 **BS:** JLARC 1, 2; 196.

CRAIG, John; b 1740; d 1803 **RU:** Patriot, Gave horse to cause **CEM:** West Augusta Cemetery; GPS 38.26670, -79.33330; Rt 716 W Augusta Rd, 8 mi N of Staunton; Augusta **GS:** N **SP:** No info **VI:** No further data **P:** N **BLW:** N **RG:** N **MK**: N **PH**: N **SS**: Z pg 118 **BS:** 142.

CRAIG, John; b 1744; d 11 Jun 1811 **RU:** Private, Probably the person with this name that served in a Fincastle Co Co under Capt James Thompson at Point Pleasant, Oct 1774. Also, may be the person of this name under Capt David Beatie at King's Mountain **CEM:** Old Stone Presbyterian; GPS 38.23926, -78.97356; 28 Old Stone Church Ln, Ft Defiance; Augusta **GS:** Y **SP:** No info **VI:** Newer Govt stone **P:** unk **BLW:** unk **RG:** Y **MK**: unk **PH**: unk **SS**: B; N pg 1241; AZ pg 158 **BS:** JLARC 1, 8, 23; 196.

CRAIG, Robert; b 1746; d 1834 or 4 Feb 1851 **RU:** Captain, Ent serv first in Lancaster PA. Was Capt in Washington Co Militia. Was at Battle of Kings Mountain 1780 **CEM:** Sinking Springs; GPS 36.71030, -81.98170; 136 E Main St, Abingdon; Washington **GS:** U **SP:** Jean Denny **VI:** Widow appl for pension age 89, Washington Co. Not approved as service short of 6 mos. R677 **P:** N **BLW:** unk **RG:** Y **MK**: Y **PH**: unk **SS**: E pg 187; K Vol 1 pg 257 **BS:** JLARC 1,80; 196.

CRAIG, Samuel; b 1762; d Jan 1808 **RU:** Captain, Served in Clark's Illinois Regt. He is not person this name as Sgt at Battle of Point Pleasant as he would be too young **CEM:** Old Presbyterian Meeting House; GPS 38.48528, -77.23532; 323 S Fairfax St; Alexandria City **GS:** N **SP:** Joanna (-----) (c1756-21 Oct 1806) **VI:** Alexandria merchant. Bur 24 Jan 1808, age 45. Listed on an SAR plaque in cemetery **P:** unk **BLW:** unk **RG:** Y **MK**: Y **PH**: N **SS**: A part II pg 416; AK **BS:** 23 pg 101; 196.

CRAIG, Samuel; b unk; d unk **RU:** Sergeant, Served in Capt Alexander McClanahan's Co of Augusta Co Militia in Battle at Point Pleasant **CEM:** John Sterrett Family; GPS unk; 1 mi W of Craigsville; Augusta **GS:** Y **SP:** No info **VI:** No further data **P:** unk **BLW:** unk **RG:** N **MK**: N **PH**: unk **SS**: Z pg 116 **BS:** 142 WPA.

CRAIG, William; b 18 Jan 1750; d 8 Sep 1829 **RU:** Private, Served in Capt Given's Co, Augusta Co Militia; perhaps is the person of this name that served in the VA 7th Cont Line in Capt Springer's Co and served over three yrs **CEM:** Augusta Stone Presbyterian; GPS 38.23926, -78.97356; 28 Old Stone Church Ln, Ft Defiance; Augusta **GS:** Y **SP:** Jean/Jane Anderson (1744-1811) **VI:** Died age 79 **P:** unk **BLW:** unk **RG:** Y **MK**: unk **PH**: unk **SS**: E pg 187; N pg 442 **BS:** JLARC 1, 2, 8, 62, 63; 196.

CRAIK, James Dr; b 1727, Dumfries, Scotland; d 4 Feb 1814 **RU:** Surgeon, Physician, chief surgeon of Cont Army. Personal physician of George Washington **CEM:** Old Presbyterian Meeting House; GPS 38.48528, -77.23532; 323 S Fairfax St; Alexandria City **GS:** Y **SP:** Marianne Ewell (__VA-20 Apr 1815) **VI:** After war was Washington's personal physician and was present by Washington's side when Washington d at Mt Vernon. Modern monument. Original table stone disappeared during the Civil War. Listed on an SAR plaque in cemetery **P:** unk **BLW:** Y **RG:** Y **MK**: Y **PH**: unk **SS**: AK; BY pg 378 **BS:** JLARC 1, 86; 23 pg 101; 196.

CRAWFORD, Alexander; b 1751, Augusta Co; d 19 Jun 1830 **RU:** Private, Served in Capt Young's Co, Augusta Co Militia **CEM:** New Providence Presbyterian; GPS 37.95130, -79.30250; 1208 New Providence Rd, Raphine; Rockbridge **GS:** U **SP:** 1) (-----) 2) (-----) McClure **VI:** No further data **P:** unk **BLW:** unk **RG:** unk **MK**: unk **PH**: unk **SS**: E pg 189 **BS:** JLARC 63, 79.

RU=Rank/Unit	CEM=Cemetery	GS=Gravestone	SP=Spousal Information
VI=Other Veteran Info	P=Pension	BLW=Bounty/Land Warrant	RG=Registered Grave
MK=SAR/DAR Marker	PH=Photo	SS=Service Source	BS=Burial Source

CRAWFORD, Ann (Anderson); b 1708; d 1803 **RU:** Patriot, Gave material aid to cause in Amherst Co VA **CEM:** David Crawford Plantation; GPS unk; See property records for plantation location; Amherst **GS:** Y **SP:** David Crawford **VI:** Maiden name, Anderson **P:** N **BLW:** N **RG:** Y **MK:** N **PH:** unk **SS:** AL Ct Bk pg 11 **BS:** SAR regis.

CRAWFORD, George Jr; b 1748; d 1790 **RU:** Private, Served in Capt Rankin's Co Augusta Co **CEM:** Augusta Stone Presbyterian; GPS 38.23926, -78.97356; 28 Old Stone Church Ln, Ft Defiance; Augusta **GS:** Y **SP:** Florence Henderson d/o of Samuel & Jane (Henderson) Thompson. She mar (2) Christian Surface in 1799 **VI:** His Govt stone indicates he d in 1791, but his will was probated 21 Sep 1790 **P:** unk **BLW:** unk **RG:** unk **MK:** unk **PH:** unk **SS:** E pg 189 **BS:** JLARC 2, 62, 63; 196.

CRAWFORD, John; b 1741; d 13 Jan 1832 **RU:** Captain/Patriot, Served 2d VA Regt. Provided horse and flour to cause   **CEM:** Hebron Presbyterian; GPS 38.14140, -79.15500; 423 Hebron Rd; Staunton City **GS:** Y **SP:** 1) Margaret Crawford 2) Mary Craig 3) Sarah Newman **VI:** No further data **P:** N **BLW:** N **RG:** unk **MK:** unk **PH:** unk **SS:** D pg 67 Augusta Co; BS pg 32, 37, 56 **BS:** JLARC 2 ,8, 62, 63; 196.

CRAWFORD, John; b 1765; d 6 Apr 1845 **RU:** Private, Served in Capt Given's Co, Augusta Co Militia **CEM:** Bethel Presbyterian; GPS 38.04257, -79.17283; 563 Bethel Green Rd, Middlebrook; Augusta **GS:** N **SP:** No info **VI:** No further data **P:** unk **BLW:** unk **RG:** N **MK:** N **PH:** N **SS:** E pg 189 **BS:** 142 Bethel.

CRAWFORD, John; b 29 Mar 1761; d 17 Dec 1846 **RU:** Private/Ensign?, Served in Capt Given's Co, Augusta Co Militia; perhaps became an ensign in this militia before Oct 1783 in Capt Simpson's Co **CEM:** Augusta Stone Presbyterian; GPS 38.23926, -78.97356; 28 Old Stone Church Ln, Ft Defiance; Augusta **GS:** Y **SP:** Rebecca Allen (22 Feb 1769-6 Jun 1851) **VI:** Son of Patrick (1723-1787) and Sally (Willson) (1726-1787) Crawford. Although the title "Maj" is styled on his GS, because of his age he would have probably obtained that rank after the war period ending Oct 1783 **P:** unk **BLW:** unk **RG:** unk **MK:** unk **PH:** unk **SS:** E pg 189 **BS:** JLARC 2, 8, 23, 63; 196.

CRAWFORD, Nathan; b 1750, Antrim, Ireland; d 1822 **RU:** Patriot, Furnished a substitute to serve **CEM:** Cleek; GPS 38.19310, -79.73220; Rt 220 Sam Snead Hwy, Warm Springs; Bath **GS:** Y **SP:** Jane/Jean Sitlington (___-1829) **VI:** Son of James & Mary (Gilbert) Crawford. Govt marker on grave **P:** N **BLW:** N **RG:** Y **MK:** N **PH:** Y **SS:** J-NSSAR 1993 Reg; B; DD **BS:** JLARC 1, 196.

CRAWFORD, Patrick; b 1723, Northern Ireland; d 18 Dec 1787 **RU:** Patriot, Gave material aid to cause **CEM:** Augusta Stone Presbyterian; GPS 38.23926, -78.97356; 28 Old Stone Church Ln, Ft Defiance; Augusta **GS:** Y **SP:** Mar (c1747) Sally Willson (1726 Northern Ireland-1787) **VI:** Son of William & Mary Ann (Douglas) Crawford of Scotland. Although the title "Maj" is styled on his GS, because of his age he would have probably obtained that rank other than in the war period ending in October 1783 **P:** N **BLW:** N **RG:** unk **MK:** unk **PH:** unk **SS:** B; AL Certificate Augusta Co **BS:** JLARC 62; 196.

CRAWFORD, Thomas; b unk; d 1794 **RU:** Private, Served in Cont Line for three yrs **CEM:** Old Christ Church Episcopal; GPS 38.80625, -77.04718; 118 N Washington St; Alexandria City **GS:** N **SP:** No info **VI:** Drew pension in Frederick Co **P:** Y **BLW:** unk **RG:** N **MK:** N **PH:** N **SS:** E pg 189 **BS:** 110 pg 92.

CRAWFORD, William; b 1764; d 22 Feb 1832 **RU:** Lieutenant, Served in Monongalia Co Militia and is listed on payrolls of VA soldiers paid at Romney, IL **CEM:** Crawford Family #2; GPS unk; Rt 726, .6 mi fr jct with Rt 613 on Sam Brown property, Peaked Mountain; Rockingham **GS:** Y **SP:** Mar (1803) Nancy Smith (1783-25 Aug 1853) **VI:** Son of Patrick (1723 Ireland-1 Dec 1787) & Sally (Wilson) (1732-__) Crawford **P:** unk **BLW:** unk **RG:** unk **MK:** unk **PH:** unk **SS:** E pg 189; CZ pg 117 fr MS at LVA **BS:** 51.

CREANCE, Guillaume; b unk; d 1781 **RU:** Seaman, Served on "Saint-Esprit" and died from Yorktown battle **CEM:** French Memorial; GPS 36.81944, -79.39933; Yorktown; York **GS:** U **SP:** No info **VI:** No further data **P:** unk **BLW:** unk **RG:** Y **MK:** unk **PH:** unk **SS:** J-Yorktown Historian **BS:** JLARC 1, 74.

CREASY, William; b unk; d 1828 **RU:** Patriot, Gave material aid to cause **CEM:** Creasy Family; GPS unk; nr jct Rts 615 and 648; Campbell **GS:** U **SP:** No info **VI:** No further data **P:** N **BLW:** N **RG:** unk **MK:** N **PH:** unk **SS:** D Campbell Co **BS:** JLARC 36.

CREGER, George; b 1763; d 1838 **RU:** Private, Served in Montgomery Co Militia **CEM:** Browning's Mill; GPS unk; Old Stage Rd; Wythe **GS:** U **SP:** Elizabeth Catron **VI:** No further data **P:** unk **BLW:** unk **RG:** unk **MK:** unk **PH:** unk **SS:** G pg 232 **BS:** JLARC 123.

RU=Rank/Unit	CEM=Cemetery	GS=Gravestone	SP=Spousal Information
VI=Other Veteran Info	P=Pension	BLW=Bounty/Land Warrant	RG=Registered Grave
MK=SAR/DAR Marker	PH=Photo	SS=Service Source	BS=Burial Source

81

CREIGHTON, Robert Dr; b c1735, Scotland; d 18 Nov 1801 **RU:** Physician, Served in Braddock's Army **CEM:** Old Presbyterian Meeting House; GPS 38.48528, -77.23532; 323 S Fairfax St; Alexandria City **GS:** Y **SP:** Left a widow, not named **VI:** Moved to Jamaica after Braddock's defeat for 40 yrs, returned to Alexandria for medical attention, and d of consumption age 66 (GS inscription) **P:** unk **BLW:** unk **RG:** Y **MK:** N **PH:** unk **SS:** AK; AL Ct Bk lt pg 5, 6, 7; B **BS:** 04; 23 pg 101.

CREPEL, Pierre; b unk; d 1781 **RU:** Seaman, Served on "Languedoc" and died from Yorktown battle **CEM:** French Memorial; GPS 36.81944, -79.39933; Yorktown; York **GS:** U **SP:** No info **VI:** No further data **P:** unk **BLW:** unk **RG:** Y **MK:** unk **PH:** unk **SS:** J-Yorktown Historian **BS:** JLARC 1,74.

CRESPOT, Francois; b unk; d 1781 **RU:** Seaman, Served on "Duc De Bourgogne" and died from Yorktown battle **CEM:** French Memorial; GPS 36.81944, -79.39933; Yorktown; York **GS:** U **SP:** No info **VI:** No further data **P:** unk **BLW:** unk **RG:** Y **MK:** unk **PH:** unk **SS:** J-Yorktown Historian **BS:** JLARC 1,74.

CREWS, Joseph; b c1757; d 26 May 1843 **RU:** Private, Ent serv Amherst Co during war period **CEM:** Crews Family; GPS unk; Nr Big Island; Bedford **GS:** Y **SP:** Mar (4 Jan 1822 Bedord Co (bond)) Nancy Eubank/Newbank (c1790-__) She also drew pension as blind person, that was cut off during Civil War until she signed oath of allegiance to US Govt. Then granddaughter granted another BLW. **VI:** Pensioned age 75 in Bedford Co in 1832. Widow granded BLW 1855 age 65. R690 **P:** Y **BLW:** Y **RG:** N **MK:** N **PH:** unk **SS:** K Vol 1 pg 263 **BS:** 80 vol pg 217.

CRIM (KRIM/GRIM), Johann Peter; b 23 May 1749, Germany; d 6 Sept 1825 **RU:** Soldier, Served in Capt Exekiel Harrison's Co, East District **CEM:** Rader Lutheran; GPS 38.65073, -78.78055; 17072 Raders Church Rd, Timberville; Rockingham **GS:** Y **SP:** Anna Maria Sophia Mueller **VI:** No further data **P:** unk **BLW:** unk **RG:** Y **MK:** N **PH:** unk **SS:** E; I **BS:** Church records JLARC 2.

CRITTENDEN, William; b c1729; d 27 Mar 1817 **RU:** Private, Served in VA State Line **CEM:** Schuler Place; GPS unk; Rt 705; Orange **GS:** Y **SP:** No info **VI:** No further data **P:** unk **BLW:** unk **RG:** Y **MK:** N **PH:** unk **SS:** AK; Al app l pg 89 **BS:** 04; 22 pg 86.

CRITZ, Hamon Jr (Herman); b 1760; d 5 Aug 1828 **RU:** Captain, Ent serv Henry Co Militia 1777 **CEM:** Critz Baptist Church; GPS unk; 3294 Dogwood Rd, Critz; Patrick **GS:** U **SP:** Mar (1786) Nancy Dalton c1766-__). Resided as widow near Stokes Co NC line. **VI:** Widow pen 1841 Patrick Co. R692 **P:** Y **BLW:** unk **RG:** unk **MK:** unk **PH:** unk **SS:** K Vol 1 pg 265 **BS:** JLARC 2, 4, 30.

CROCKETT, Hugh; b 1730 Lancaster, PA; d 1816 **RU:** Colonel, Specific serv Lib VA, War files, Auditors Acct XV, pg 401 **CEM:** White; GPS 37.15829,-80.25423; Rt 637, S of Shawsville; Montgomery **GS:** U **SP:** Mar (1773) Rebecca Larton (1749, Montgomery Co-1836 Crockett Springs) **VI:** No further data **P:** unk **BLW:** unk **RG:** Y **MK:** unk **PH:** unk **SS:** J-NSSAR 1993 Reg, J- DAR Hatcher; CZ pg 119 **BS:** JLARC 1, 2; 196.

CROCKETT, John; b 1737, Orange Co; d Aft 14 Feb 1798 **RU:** First Lieutenant, Served in Montgomery Co Militia. Promoted 3 Feb 1777 **CEM:** Crockett Family; GPS 37.01560, -81.05500; Off Rt 600, Crockett's Cove; Wythe **GS:** U **SP:** Elizabeth Betsey Montgomery **VI:** Son of Samuel (1694-1749) & Esther Thomson (Sayers) (1710-1770) Crockett. Was a juryman and a surveyor. DAR marker **P:** unk **BLW:** unk **RG:** unk **MK:** Y **PH:** unk **SS:** E pg 193 **BS:** JLARC 2, 101; 196.

CROCKETT, Joseph; b 1767; d 1853 **RU:** Captain/Patriot, Gave material aid to cause **CEM:** Crockett; GPS unk; SR 649, turn left to cross RR tracks, to Suthers home; Wythe **GS:** U **SP:** Mar (1800) Catherine Montgomery (20 Jan 1772-18 Jan 1833) **VI:** No further data **P:** unk **BLW:** unk **RG:** unk **MK:** unk **PH:** unk **SS:** D Cumberland Co **BS:** JLARC 76, 123.

CROPPER, John; b 23 Dec 1755; d 15 Jan 1821 **RU:** Colonel, Ent serv Accomac Co 1778. Served in 7th, 9th,11th Cont Line. Resigned 16 Aug 1779, then was appointed Col of the militia to close of war **CEM:** Bowman's Folly; GPS unk; End of Rt 652, private lane, 2.4 mi NE of Accomac, Joynes Neck; Accomack **GS:** Y **SP:** 1) Mar (15 Aug 1776 Northampton Co) Margaret Pettit (__-Jun 1784, Occahannock, Northhampton Co) d/o William & Mary (-----) Pettit; 2) Mar (18 Sep 1790 Hill's Farm, Accomack Co) Catharine Bayley (24 Jan 1772- 24 Jan 1855) d/o Thomas & Ann (-----) Bayly. **VI:** Son of Sebastian & Sabra (-----) Cropper. Father was also a RW soldier. Member of General Assembly 1784.

RU=Rank/Unit	CEM=Cemetery	GS=Gravestone	SP=Spousal Information
VI=Other Veteran Info	P=Pension	BLW=Bounty/Land Warrant	RG=Registered Grave
MK=SAR/DAR Marker	PH=Photo	SS=Service Source	BS=Burial Source

Styled "General" on his GS. Widow pensioned 1838 Accomack Co. Awarded BLW of 8,888 acres. R696 **P:** Y **BLW:** Y **RG:** Y **MK**: unk **PH:** unk **SS:** J-NSSAR 1993 Reg; K Vol 1 pg 267 **BS:** JLARC 1.

CROPPER, Sebastian; b 1731; d 20 Mar 1776 **RU:** Captain, Served in Accomac Co Militia **CEM:** Bowman's Folly; GPS unk; End of Rt 652, private lane, 2.4 mi NE of Accomac, Joynes Neck; Accomack **GS:** Y **SP:** Sabra Corbin (__-2 Nov 1791) d/o Gen John & Sarah (-----) Corbin **VI:** Died age 45. Son of Boman & Tabitha (-----) Cropper **P:** unk **BLW:** unk **RG:** Y **MK:** N **PH:** unk **SS:** AK; E pg 194 **BS:** 04; 37 pg 60.

CROSS, William; b 1748; d 1836 **RU:** Lieutenant, Was Lt under command of Maj James Crew, Monongalia Co Militia. Stationed at Ft Pitt in Oct 1777 **CEM:** High Bridge Presbyterian; GPS 37.62420, -79.58610; 67 High Bridge Rd, Natural Bridge; Rockbridge **GS:** Y **SP:** No info **VI:** No further data **P:** unk **BLW:** unk **RG:** Y **MK:** N **PH:** unk **SS:** E pg 680 **BS:** 154.

CROSS, William; b 1733, England; d 1798 **RU:** Patriot, Gave material aid to cause **CEM:** Cross Family Farm; GPS unk; Nr Roanoke; Botetourt **GS:** N **SP:** Elizabeth (-----) **VI:** No further data **P:** N **BLW:** N **RG:** unk **MK:** unk **PH:** N **SS:** AL Ct Bk pg 6, 9, 13 **BS:** 196 Crumley.

CROUCHER, Thomas; b 1768, Dumfries, Scotland; d 22 May 1792 **RU:** Captain, In charge of taking prisoners fr Battle of Yorktown to Noland's Ferry on Potomac. Served in 10th Cont Line **CEM:** Old Christ Church Episcopal; GPS 38.80625, -77.04718; 118 N Washington St; Alexandria City **GS:** Y **SP:** No info **VI:** Died in his 25th yr (age 24). Place of birth on stone **P:** unk **BLW:** unk **RG:** Y **MK:** N **PH:** unk **SS:** AZ pg 169 **BS:** 110 pg 96; 20 pg 136; 196.

CROW, James; b unk, Spotsylvania Co; d 1798 **RU:** Patriot, Specific serv at Lib VA, War files, vol 4, pg 131 **CEM:** Nicholson Family; GPS unk; Syria; Madison **GS:** N **SP:** Elizabeth (-----) **VI:** No further data **P:** N **BLW:** N **RG:** Y **MK:** N **PH:** N **SS:** D pg 346; CZ pg 120 **BS:** 04.

CROWE, Edward; b 1751; d 1830 **RU:** Soldier, Served 41 days in Capt William Campbell's Co **CEM:** Royal Oak; GPS 36.84315, -81.49660; Behind Marion Baptist Church, Marion; Smyth **GS:** U **SP:** June Mackey **VI:** No further data **P:** unk **BLW:** unk **RG:** unk **MK:** Y **PH:** unk **SS:** NSSAR Ancestor #P-141774 **BS:** JLARC 114.

CRUMLEY, William; b 1735, Chester Co, PA; d 30 Sep 1792 **RU:** Patriot, Gave material aid to cause **CEM:** Back Creek Quaker, aka Gainesboro United Methodist; GPS 39.27861, -78.25694; 166 Siler Ln, Gainesboro; Frederick **GS:** U **SP:** Mar (1763) Hannah Mercer (__-1774) **VI:** Son of James (1712-1764 & (-----) Crumley. **P:** N **BLW:** N **RG:** unk **MK:** unk **PH:** unk **SS:** AL three cert, Berkeley Co **BS:** 196.

CRUTCHFIELD, John; b 1756; d Aft 1820 **RU:** Private, Specific serv Lib VA, Report Sec of War re pensions, vol 2, pg 50 **CEM:** Belle Air Plantation; GPS 37.20490, -77.34000; Rt 5, New Hope; Charles City Co **GS:** U **SP:** No info **VI:** Grave near gate **P:** unk **BLW:** unk **RG:** N **MK:** N **PH:** unk **SS:** K Vol 1 Crutchfield; CZ pg 122 **BS:** 127 Crutchfield.

CRUTCHFIELD, Lewis; b unk; d unk **RU:** Soldier, Served in Charles City Co Militia **CEM:** Belle Air Plantation; GPS 37.20490, -77.34000; Rt 5, New Hope; Charles City Co **GS:** U **SP:** Mar (29 Oct 1779 Charles City Co) Mildred Jamison, spinster **VI:** Cem betw Belair house and gate, thereafter called "Soldiers' Burying Ground" **P:** unk **BLW:** unk **RG:** unk **MK:** unk **PH:** unk **SS:** CZ pg 122 **BS:** JLARC 110.

CULLEN (CULLINS), John; b 11 Mar 1748, Scotland; d 7 Aug 1827 **RU:** Sergeant, Served in 3rd VA Regt commanded by Col Thomas Marshall in Nov 1777 **CEM:** Bethleham Lutheran; GPS 38.05454, -78.95222; 1148 Ladd Rd; Waynesboro City **GS:** Y **SP:** Nancy Foster (23-6 Feb 1758, England-24 Mar 1831) **VI:** Son of Dr William & (-----) Cullen **P:** unk **BLW:** unk **RG:** N **MK:** N **PH:** unk **SS:** AP roll VA 3d Div **BS:** 142.

CUMMINGS, Charles Rev; b 1731; d 1812 **RU:** Patriot, Was a member of Fincastles Resolutions Committee of Safety 1775 **CEM:** Sinking Springs; GPS 36.71030, -81.98170; 136 E Main St, Abingdon; Washington **GS:** U **SP:** Mildred Carter (__-__Abingdon Washington Co) d/o John & (-----) Carter of Lancaster Co **VI:** No further data **P:** N **BLW:** N **RG:** Y **MK:** unk **PH:** unk **SS:** J-NSSAR 1993 Reg, J-DAR Hatcher; plaque in cemetery **BS:** JLARC 1, 2; 212 pg 73.

RU=Rank/Unit	CEM=Cemetery	GS=Gravestone	SP=Spousal Information
VI=Other Veteran Info	P=Pension	BLW=Bounty/Land Warrant	RG=Registered Grave
MK=SAR/DAR Marker	PH=Photo	SS=Service Source	BS=Burial Source

83

CURDINET, Francois; b unk; d 1781 **RU:** Soldier, Served in Gatinais Bn and died fr battle at Yorktown **CEM:** French Memorial; GPS 36.81944, -79.39933; Yorktown; York **GS:** U **SP:** No info **VI:** No further data **P:** unk **BLW:** unk **RG:** unk **MK:** unk **PH:** unk **SS:** J-Yorktown Historian **BS:** JLARC 74.

CURDON, Louis; b unk; d 1781 **RU:** Soldier, Served in Gatinais Bn and died fr battle at Yorktown **CEM:** French Memorial; GPS 36.81944, -79.39933; Yorktown; York **GS:** U **SP:** No info **VI:** No further data **P:** unk **BLW:** unk **RG:** unk **MK:** unk **PH:** unk **SS:** J-Yorktown Historian **BS:** JLARC 74.

CURRIE, James; b 1744, Annandale, Scotland; d 23 Apr 1807 **RU:** Captain, Served in Cont Line. Specific serv Lib VA, MS Involved with arrangement of Cont Line pgs 10,16 **CEM:** St John's Episcopal; GPS 37.53183, -77.41958; 2401 E Broad St; Richmond City **GS:** Y **SP:** No info **VI:** Was a doctor in Richmond for 40 yrs **P:** unk **BLW:** unk **RG:** Y **MK:** N **PH:** unk **SS:** CZ pg 124; E pg 201 **BS:** 28 pg 426.

CURRY, Robert; b 10 Nov 1717 Ulster, Ireland; d 5 Jan 1800 **RU:** Captain, Served as Capt of Homeguards during the Rev War **CEM:** Augusta Stone Presbyterian; GPS 38.23926, -78.97356; 28 Old Stone Church Ln, Ft Defiance; Augusta **GS:** Y **SP:** Anne (-----) (25 Sep 1727, Ulster, Ireland-15 May 1819) **VI:** Commanded a Co in the Augusta Co Militia before the war on 16 August 1774. Elder of Augusta Church and was styled "Doctor" **P:** unk **BLW:** unk **RG:** unk **MK:** Y **PH:** Y **SS:** B; AH pg 7 **BS:** JLARC 2, 8, 63; 196.

CURTIS, James; b 1763; d 6 Jan 1810 **RU:** Lieutenant/Patriot, Served in US Navy on ship "Lancaster." Gave material aid to the cause **CEM:** Old Stone Methodist; GPS 39.11725, -77.56609; 168 W Cornwall St, Leesburg; Loudoun **GS:** Y **SP:** Unmarried **VI:** No further data **P:** unk **BLW:** unk **RG:** N **MK:** N **PH:** unk **SS:** L pg 177; AL Ct Booklet **BS:** 25 pg 73.

CURTIS, John; b 1763; d 6 Jan 1810 **RU:** Corporal, Served in Capt Bullen's Co, Stafford Co Militia **CEM:** Jett Family #2; GPS unk; End Broad Oak Ln. See property records for homestead location; Stafford **GS:** Y **SP:** No info **VI:** No further data **P:** unk **BLW:** unk **RG:** N **MK:** N **PH:** unk **SS:** AP NARA fdr364 **BS:** 03 Addenump, 26.

CURTIS, John Parke; b unk; d 1781 **RU:** Soldier, Served fr VA. Was Aide to Washington. Died at battle at Yorktown **CEM:** Yorktown Victory Monument Tablet; GPS 38.28350, -78.54150; Yorktown; York **GS:** U **SP:** No info **VI:** No further data **P:** unk **BLW:** unk **RG:** unk **MK:** unk **PH:** unk **SS:** J-Yorktown Historian **BS:** JLARC 74.

CURTIS, William; b c1759; d 22 Apr 1808 **RU:** Ensign, Served in Middlesex Co Militia. Recommended as officer 28 Jul 1777; oath as Ens 24 Nov 1777 **CEM:** Highgate; GPS unk; Cash Post Office; Gloucester **GS:** Y **SP:** Ariana M Grymes (second husband was Peter Kemp Jr.) **VI:** No further data **P:** unk **BLW:** unk **RG:** Y **MK:** Y **PH:** unk **SS:** AK; E pg 02 **BS:** 04; 48 pg 38.

CUSTER (CUSTARD), Richard Sr; b 1 Jun 1757, PA; d 14 Feb 1837 **RU:** Private, Ent serv Rockingham Co 1781. Early in 1781, served 3 mos in Capt George Huston's Co, Col Nall's Regt. Was in skirmishes at Wiliamsburg & Hot Water Creek. In 1781, served 3 mos in Capt Anthony Rader's Co **CEM:** Custer Family; GPS unk; Dry River S of Rt 259, Fulks Run; Rockingham **GS:** Y **SP:** Mar (18 Mar 1790) Jane Humble (c1771-__) d/o Conrad & (-----) Humble. **VI:** Pensioned Rockingham Co 1832. Widow pen Rockingham Co 1841 age 70. R725. W6749 **P:** Y **BLW:** unk **RG:** Y **MK:** Y **PH:** unk **SS:** K Vol 1 pg 278-9; O; AK **BS:** 04, JLARC 4, 64.

CUSTIS, Henry; b 27 Jul 1743; d 28 Jul 1793 **RU:** Lieutenant Colonel, Oath as Maj 30 Jul 1777, and rec as Lt Col 30 Apr 1782 Accomack Co VA Militia **CEM:** Mt Custis; GPS unk; Off Rt 622 2.5 mi of Rt 13, Bayley's Neck; Accomack **GS:** Y **SP:** Mar (c1765) Matilda Hack **VI:** Son of Robinson Custis & Mary Parramore. Stone styles him Lt Col. DAR marker on gravesite **P:** unk **BLW:** unk **RG:** Y **MK:** Y **PH:** unk **SS:** E pg 202; BT **BS:** AS SAR reg; 196.

CUSTIS, Thomas; b 1721; d 21 Dec 1810 **RU:** Patriot, Gave material aid to the cause **CEM:** Deep Creek Plantation; GPS unk; Onancock; Accomack **GS:** N **SP:** No info **VI:** In 1792 Deep Creek House (at end of Mink Farm Rd) was built for him **P:** N **BLW:** N **RG:** unk **MK:** unk **PH:** N **SS:** AI Cert Accomack Co **BS:** 196.

CUTLER, William; b c1762; d 17 May 1836 **RU:** Private, Specific serv Lib VA, Journal House of Delegates 1833-4, Doc 33 pg 11 **CEM:** Mt Pleasant; GPS unk; Rt 609; Dinwiddie **GS:** Y **SP:** 1) Mar (20

RU=Rank/Unit	CEM=Cemetery	GS=Gravestone	SP=Spousal Information
VI=Other Veteran Info	P=Pension	BLW=Bounty/Land Warrant	RG=Registered Grave
MK=SAR/DAR Marker	PH=Photo	SS=Service Source	BS=Burial Source

84

Jul 1790 Boston MA) Sally Henderson 2) Susan (-----) widow of Windfield Mason **VI:** Was called Dr fr Weston at time of marriage. After war owned a celebrated racing stable **P:** unk **BLW:** unk **RG:** N **MK**: N **PH:** unk **SS:** AJ Middlesex Co; CZ pg 125 **BS:** 70 pg 121.

DABNEY, Charles; b 1745, Montpelier, Hanover Co; d 15 Dec 1829 **RU:** Colonel, Marched fr Hanover Co with Patrick Henry to exhort public powder taken fr Williamsburg by Lord Dunmore, 1775. Organized Hanover District minutemen. Was Maj 3rd VA State Regt at Germantown & Princeton 1777. Was Col of state Militia 1778-1781. Was Commander at York & Portsmouth Nov 1781. Served 1778 with Gen "Mad Anthony" Wayne at Stony Point in Lt Col of "Dabney's Legion." Joined Cont Line with 2nd VA State Line Regt at Valley Forge. Served under Lafayette during 1781 at Yorktown and held confidence of the Marquis **CEM:** Aldingham; GPS unk; On Plantation this name. See property records for directions.; Hanover **GS:** N **SP:** No info **VI:** Son of William (1707-1773) & Anne (Barret) (1715-1779) Dabney. On 19 Oct 1781, Articles of Capitulation of Cornwallis given at dinner with Geo. Washington. Jan 1782 state line units consolidated to Charles Dabney's Virginia State Legion. Stopped mutiny Sep 1782. Legion disbanded Apr 1783. Charter member of The Society of the Cincinnati. Died in Montpelier, Hanover Co. Probably bur in cnr of garden of "Aldinham." BLW 6667 acres **P:** unk **BLW:** Y **RG:** unk **MK:** unk **PH:** N **SS:** E pg 203 **BS:** 196.

DABNEY, Samuel; b 14 Apr 1752; d 1793 **RU:** Ensign, Promoted to Ens 9 Jun 1777, Louisa Co Militia **CEM:** Dabney Family; GPS unk; 4.3 mi NE of Orchid; Louisa **GS:** Y **SP:** Jane Meriwether (8 Apr 1757-1833) **VI:** No further data **P:** unk **BLW:** unk **RG:** N **MK:** N **PH:** unk **SS:** AZ pg 214 **BS:** 149 Dabney.

DADE, Francis L; b 1760; d 1791 **RU:** Captain, Served in 3rd Cont Dragoons. Was taken prisoner at Tappan 18 Sep 1778. Was promoted to Capt 1781. Retired 9 Nov 1782 **CEM:** Dade Family; GPS unk; Rose Hill; Orange **GS:** U **SP:** Mar (13 Mar 1782 Orange Co) Sarah Taliaferro d/o Lawrence & (-----) Taliaferro **VI:** BLW issued 7 Jul 1799. 4000 acres to minor children. R728 **P:** unk **BLW:** Y **RG:** unk **MK:** unk **PH:** unk **SS:** J- DAR Hatcher; E pg 203-4; F-S21153; K Vol II pg 1 **BS:** JLARC 2.

DAGGETT, Ebenezer; b unk; d 20 Nov 1781 **RU:** Ensign, Served in Capt Chapman's Co, CT Cont Troops; died on return fr siege at Yorktown **CEM:** Yorktown Victory Monument Tablet; GPS 38.28350, -78.54150; Yorktown; York **GS:** U **SP:** No info **VI:** Died in Head of Elk, MD **P:** unk **BLW:** unk **RG:** unk **MK:** unk **PH:** unk **SS:** J-Yorktown Historian; DY pg 328 **BS:** JLARC 74.

DAGONARD, Claude; b unk; d 1781 **RU:** Seaman, Served on "Caton" and died from Yorktown battle **CEM:** French Memorial; GPS 36.81944, -79.39933; Yorktown; York **GS:** U **SP:** No info **VI:** No further data **P:** unk **BLW:** unk **RG:** Y **MK:** unk **PH:** unk **SS:** J-Yorktown Historian **BS:** JLARC 1, 74.

DALTON, William; b 27 Apr 1740, Pittsylvania Co; d 14 Jan 1811 **RU:** Private, Served in Col William Nelson's Regt and 2 yrs in VA Line **CEM:** William Dalton Cem; GPS 36.79595, -80.64369; off Rt 221, Dugspur; Carroll **GS:** N **SP:** Elizabeth Sturman, probably also bur here **VI:** S 8295. NC 12202 **P:** Y **BLW:** unk **RG:** unk **MK:** N **PH:** N **SS:** VA Pen appl V26 **BS:** JLARC 43; 68; 196.

DAME, George; b 1752 King & Queen Co; d Aft 16 Oct 1805 **RU:** Private/Patriot, GS indicates soldier but serv not identified, Gave material aid to cause **CEM:** Christ Church; GPS 37.60968, -76.54643; Rt 33 2 mi E of Saluda; Middlesex **GS:** U **SP:** Mary Green (1752 Culpeper Co-29 Jun 1832 Jones Co) d/o Nicholas & Elizabeth (Price) Green **VI:** Son of Solomon (1722-1780) & Martha (Brookings) (1712-1845) Dame **P:** unk **BLW:** unk **RG:** unk **MK:** unk **PH:** unk **SS:** J- DAR Hatcher; D Vol 2 pg 396 **BS:** JLARC 2; 196.

DAMERON, John; b unk; d unk **RU:** Private, Specific service information not determined **CEM:** Dameron Family; GPS unk; 20 mi W of Covington; Covington City **GS:** U **SP:** No info **VI:** No further data **P:** unk **BLW:** unk **RG:** N **MK:** N **PH:** unk **SS:** E pg 205 **BS:** 160 Dameron.

DANDRIDGE, William; b 1734, King William Co; d May 1784 **RU:** Patriot, Gave material aid to cause **CEM:** Huntington, aka Old Fox; GPS unk; On Mattaponi River in King William Co adj New Kent Co; King William **GS:** U **SP:** Agnes West (1734-1759) d/o Francis & Susan (Littlepage) West **VI:** Son of William (1689-1744) & Unity (West) (1700-1753) Dandridge. Died in New Kent Co **P:** N **BLW:** N **RG:** unk **MK:** unk **PH:** unk **SS:** Al Comm Bk III pg 56 Henrico Co **BS:** 196.

RU=Rank/Unit   CEM=Cemetery   GS=Gravestone   SP=Spousal Information
VI=Other Veteran Info   P=Pension   BLW=Bounty/Land Warrant   RG=Registered Grave
MK=SAR/DAR Marker   PH=Photo   SS=Service Source   BS=Burial Source

85

DANIEL, Frances (Moncure); b c1745; d 1800 **RU:** Patriot, Gave 6 beeves, 65# bacon, and 172# more beef to cause **CEM:** Crows Nest; GPS unk; Crows Nest area; Stafford **GS:** Y **SP:** Travers Daniel **VI:** Daughter of Rev John & Frances (Brown) Moncure **P:** N **BLW:** N **RG:** Y **MK:** N **PH:** unk **SS:** AK; D pg 871, 874 **BS:** 04; 03 pg 186.

DANIEL, Marie; b unk; d 1781 **RU:** Seaman, Served on "Auguste" and died from Yorktown battle **CEM:** French Memorial; GPS 36.81944, -79.39933; Yorktown; York **GS:** U **SP:** No info **VI:** No further data **P:** unk **BLW:** unk **RG:** Y **MK:** unk **PH:** unk **SS:** J-Yorktown Historian **BS:** JLARC 1, 74.

DANIEL, Travers D Sr; b 16 Mar 1741, Mount Pleasant, Stafford Co; d 28 Jun 1824 **RU:** Soldier/Patriot, Served on Stafford Resolutions Committee 1774. Gave musket, bayonet & beeves to cause **CEM:** Crows Nest; GPS unk; Crows Nest area; Stafford **GS:** Y **SP:** Mar (7 Oct 1762) Frances Moncure (1745-1800) Daughter of Rev John & Frances (Brown) Moncure. He also had service as he received pension. **VI:** Son of Peter (1706-1789 & Sarah (Travers) (__-1788) Daniel. County Surveyor fr 1777 **P:** N **BLW:** N **RG:** Y **MK:** N **PH:** unk **SS:** AK; D pg 877 **BS:** 04; 03 pg 186.

DANIEL, William Sr; b 18 Jan 1762; d 15 May 1845 **RU:** First Lieutenant, Took oath as 1st Lt Cumberland Co Militia 23 Apr 1781 **CEM:** Old City; GPS 37.41472, -79.15667; 401 Taylor St; Lynchburg City **GS:** N **SP:** Ann Goode d/o Samuel & (-----) Goode **VI:** Pen 24 Jun 1833, Campbell Co R736 **P:** Y **BLW:** unk **RG:** N **MK:** N **PH:** N **SS:** E pg 206; F-S3263; K Vol 2 pg 6-7 **BS:** 62 pg 103.

DANIK, Pierre; b unk; d 1781 **RU:** Seaman, Served on "Saint-Esprit" and died from Yorktown battle **CEM:** French Memorial; GPS 36.81944, -79.39933; Yorktown; York **GS:** U **SP:** No info **VI:** No further data **P:** unk **BLW:** unk **RG:** Y **MK:** unk **PH:** unk **SS:** J-Yorktown Historian **BS:** JLARC 1, 74.

DANNER (TANNER), Jacob; b 4 Dec 1763; d 17 Jun 1850 **RU:** Private, Entered serv 1775-76. Served in PA Line **CEM:** Mt Carmel; GPS 39.03170, -78.28720; 3rd & Commerce St, Middletown; Frederick **GS:** Y **SP:** Mar (25 Oct 1795 Frederick Co by Rev Simon Haar) Hannah Senseney (14 Aug 1775-12 Sep 1823) d/o Dr Peter & (-----) Sensensey **VI:** His company manufactured compasses in Middleton. Also a clockmaker and jeweler. Pensioned 1818 Botetourt Co. Resident Botetourt Co in 1820 age 65 when wife as age 56 or 7. R739 **P:** Y **BLW:** unk **RG:** N **MK:** N **PH:** unk **SS:** E pg 757 (for Tanner); F-S39411; K Vol 2 pg 7 **BS:** 59 pg 82.

DARAY, Bertrand; b unk; d 1781 **RU:** Soldier, Served in Gatinais Bn and died fr battle at Yorktown **CEM:** French Memorial; GPS 36.81944, -79.39933; Yorktown; York **GS:** U **SP:** No info **VI:** No further data **P:** unk **BLW:** unk **RG:** unk **MK:** unk **PH:** unk **SS:** J-Yorktown Historian **BS:** JLARC 1, 74.

DARBY, John; b 1751; d 21 Sep 1789 **RU:** Lieutenant Colonel, Promoted in Co Militia to Lt Col 14 May 1782. Became the county Lt 14 Oct 1783 **CEM:** Darby's Wharf Farm; GPS unk; Nr Shields' Bridge, Belle Haven; Northampton **GS:** N **SP:** Mar (31 Dec 1777) Esther Harmanson (1 Oct 1762-12 Mar 1834) d/o John Sr. & (-----) Harmanson **VI:** Died age 38. Styled "Col" on his wife's stone **P:** unk **BLW:** unk **RG:** unk **MK:** unk **PH:** N **SS:** E pg 207 **BS:** JLARC 4, 69; 42 pg 21.

DARBY, Nathaniel; b 15 Jun 1754; d 13 Nov 1811 **RU:** Lieutenant, Ent serv VA 9th Cont Line 1776. Promoted to 2nd Lt, 7 Mar 1777. Prisoner of war Germantown 4 Oct 1777. After release serv in 5th Cont Line until end of war **CEM:** Darby's Wharf Farm; GPS unk; Nr Shields Bridge, Belle Haven; Northampton **GS:** Y **SP:** No info **VI:** "As an officer he served his country with unsullied reputation, during her glorious contest with Greath Britain" (epitaph). BLW of 3480 acres issued 26 Jun 1789. R740 **P:** unk **BLW:** Y **RG:** unk **MK:** unk **PH:** unk **SS:** E pg 207, 220; K Vol II pg 8; F-BLW605. **BS:** JLARC 4, 69; 42 pg 21.

DARLINGTON, Gabriel; b 16 Aug 1767; d 30 Jul 1841 **RU:** Private, Service information not determined fr BLW **CEM:** Back Creek Quaker, aka Gainesboro United Methodist; GPS 39.27861, -78.25694; 166 Siler Ln, Gainesboro; Frederick **GS:** N **SP:** 1) Mar (19 Apr 1792 Frederick Co by Rev Christian Streit) Margaret Edwards (1777-c1841) 2) Mar (8 May 1798 Frederick Co (return) by Rev Alexander Balmain) Margaret Edwards 3) Mar (8 May 1798 Frederick Co) Martha Edwards **VI:** GS indicates he d in 1844. Recd BLW **P:** unk **BLW:** Y **RG:** Y **MK:** N **PH:** N **SS:** C pg 615; BY **BS:** 59 pg 82.

DARNALL, Jeremiah; b 1720; d 1795 **RU:** Patriot, Sold hay and mutton to militia **CEM:** Germantown Glebe; GPS unk; Rt 643 nr Licking Run, Midland; Fauquier **GS:** Y **SP:** 1) Catherine Holzclaw 2)

RU=Rank/Unit	CEM=Cemetery	GS=Gravestone	SP=Spousal Information
VI=Other Veteran Info	P=Pension	BLW=Bounty/Land Warrant	RG=Registered Grave
MK=SAR/DAR Marker	PH=Photo	SS=Service Source	BS=Burial Source

Catherine (-----) **VI:** Died in Germantown **P:** N **BLW:** N **RG:** Y **MK:** N **PH:** unk **SS:** AK; D Fauquier pg 30 **BS:** 04;19 pg 66.

DARTER (TARTER), Nicholas; b 12 Mar 1746, Philadelphia; d 28 Apr 1821 **RU:** Soldier, Procure SAR application for service unit **CEM:** St John's Lutheran; **GPS** 36.96500, -81.10110; 405 W Main, Wytheville; Wythe **GS:** Y **SP:** Maria Parcell and Firwell Newbry Henderson **VI:** Son of Johann & Maria Elizabeth Kurtz (Darter) Anthon **P:** unk **BLW:** unk **RG:** unk **MK:** unk **PH:** unk **SS:** SAR applic; NSSAR Ancestor #P-143940 **BS:** JLARC 11, 23.

DAUCAN, Guillaume; b unk; d 1781 **RU:** Soldier, Served in Touraine Bn and died fr battle at Yorktown **CEM:** French Memorial; **GPS** 36.81944, -79.39933; Yorktown; York **GS:** U **SP:** No info **VI:** No further data **P:** unk **BLW:** unk **RG:** Y **MK:** unk **PH:** unk **SS:** J-Yorktown Historian **BS:** JLARC 1, 74.

DAULIN, Jean; b unk; d 1781 **RU:** Seaman, Served on "Citoyen" and died from Yorktown battle **CEM:** French Memorial; **GPS** 36.81944, -79.39933; Yorktown; York **GS:** U **SP:** No info **VI:** No further data **P:** unk **BLW:** unk **RG:** Y **MK:** unk **PH:** unk **SS:** J-Yorktown Historian **BS:** JLARC 1, 74.

DAUSSENT, Pierre; b unk; d 1781 **RU:** Soldier, Served in Gatinais Bn and died fr battle at Yorktown **CEM:** French Memorial; **GPS** 36.81944, -79.39933; Yorktown; York **GS:** U **SP:** No info **VI:** No further data **P:** unk **BLW:** unk **RG:** Y **MK:** unk **PH:** unk **SS:** J-Yorktown Historian **BS:** JLARC 1, 74.

DAUVERGNE, Jacques; b unk; d 1781 **RU:** Soldier, Served in Soissonnais Bn and died fr battle at Yorktown **CEM:** French Memorial; **GPS** 36.81944, -79.39933; Yorktown; York **GS:** U **SP:** No info **VI:** No further data **P:** unk **BLW:** unk **RG:** Y **MK:** unk **PH:** unk **SS:** J-Yorktown Historian **BS:** JLARC 1, 74.

DAVENPORT, Bedford; b 21 Nov 1748, Halifax Co; d 16 Aug 1852 **RU:** Second Lieutenant, Served in Capt Danile Parker's Co, Col John Crane's Regt 1778, 3rd & 4th Cont Line **CEM:** Davenport Family; **GPS** unk; Nr jct Rts 360 & 344, Scottsburg; Halifax **GS:** N **SP:** Annie Comer **VI:** No further data **P:** unk **BLW:** unk **RG:** Y **MK:** N **PH:** N **SS:** J-NASSR 2000 Reg; NSSAR Ancestor #P-144022 **BS:** JLARC 76.

DAVENPORT, Catrin (Catherine?); b 1727; d Aft 29 Nov 1782 **RU:** Patriot, Gave material aid to cause **CEM:** Davenport Family; **GPS** unk; Nr jct Rts 360 & 344, Scottsburg; Halifax **GS:** N **SP:** James Davenport **VI:** No further data **P:** N **BLW:** N **RG:** Y **MK:** N **PH:** N **SS:** D Vol II pg 430 **BS:** 04.

DAVENPORT, David; b unk; d unk **RU:** Patriot, Gave material aid to cause **CEM:** Cherrydale; **GPS** unk; Rt 667; Hanover **GS:** N **SP:** No info **VI:** No further data **P:** N **BLW:** N **RG:** N **MK:** N **PH:** N **SS:** AL Ct Bk pg 8 **BS:** 31 vol 2 pg 80.

DAVID, Francois; b unk; d 1781 **RU:** Seaman, Served on "Victorie" and died from Yorktown battle **CEM:** French Memorial; **GPS** 36.81944, -79.39933; Yorktown; York **GS:** U **SP:** No info **VI:** No further data **P:** unk **BLW:** unk **RG:** Y **MK:** unk **PH:** unk **SS:** J-Yorktown Historian **BS:** JLARC 1, 74.

DAVID, Yves; b unk; d 1781 **RU:** Soldier, Served in Agenois Bn and died fr battle at Yorktown **CEM:** French Memorial; **GPS** 36.81944, -79.39933; Yorktown; York **GS:** U **SP:** No info **VI:** No further data **P:** unk **BLW:** unk **RG:** Y **MK:** unk **PH:** unk **SS:** J-Yorktown Historian **BS:** JLARC 1, 74.

DAVIES, James II; b 1741; d unk **RU:** Sergeant, Served in 7th Cont Line. Served in VA unit in Illinois **CEM:** Davies Farm; **GPS** unk; See property records nr Abingdon; Washington **GS:** U **SP:** No info **VI:** No further data **P:** unk **BLW:** unk **RG:** Y **MK:** unk **PH:** unk **SS:** SAR Ancestor #P-144290; J-NSSAR 1993 Reg; E pg 209; CZ pg 129 **BS:** JLARC 1; 197.

DAVIES, Joseph Sr; b 1740; d 1781 **RU:** Soldier/Patriot, Gave material aid to cause **CEM:** Rural; **GPS** unk; Reed Creek; Montgomery **GS:** U **SP:** No info **VI:** No further data **P:** unk **BLW:** unk **RG:** Y **MK:** unk **PH:** unk **SS:** J-NSSAR 1993 Reg; D Montgomery Co **BS:** JLARC 1; 197.

DAVIS, Abraham; b 1750; d 1830 or 30 May 1839 **RU:** Private, Ent Serv 1775. 3rd VA Regt in Capt Thomas Cutleet's Co under Col Buford. Wounded at Buford's defeat near Hanging Rock, SC. Recd two wounds in left arm and suffered fr rupture lifting artillery pieces **CEM:** Tolersville Tavern burial ground; **GPS** 38.01321, -77.90345; Rt 677 nr Mineral Baptist Church, Mineral; Louisa **GS:** N **SP:** Mar (19 Feb 1818 Louisa Co) Mary or Polly Talley (c1790-__) **VI:** Given gratuity of £500 on 29 Nov 1780. Recd pen of £12 on 4 Mar 1789. Also on 1813 pen list. Pen in Louisa Co 1818. Widow pen Louisa Co 1853.

RU=Rank/Unit   CEM=Cemetery   GS=Gravestone   SP=Spousal Information
VI=Other Veteran Info   P=Pension   BLW=Bounty/Land Warrant   RG=Registered Grave
MK=SAR/DAR Marker   PH=Photo   SS=Service Source   BS=Burial Source

87

Birth/death dates taken fr marker **P:** Y **BLW:** unk **RG:** N **MK**: Y **PH:** N **SS:** E pg 210; BX pg 201; K Vol II pg 13 **BS:** 196.

DAVIS, Augustine; b 1752,Yorktown; d 2 Nov 1825 **RU:** Patriot, Gave material aid to the cause **CEM:** Shockoe Hill; GPS 37.55190, -77.43170; 4th & Hospital Sts; Richmond City **GS:** Y **SP:** No info **VI:** After war in Jun 1788 was appointed printer to the convention that considered the formation of the Federal Gov't. Later in 1786, started newspaper Virginia Independent Chronicle but later was publisher of The Virginia Gazette & Richmond Advertiser **P:** N **BLW:** N **RG:** N **MK:** N **PH:** unk **SS:** AL Ct Bk pg 3 **BS:** 57 pg 3.

DAVIS, Benjamin; b 1762; d 1836 **RU:** Private, Served in 4th, 8th, 12th Cont Line. Was in Battle of Gilford CH, NC **CEM:** Davis Family; GPS unk; Cherrystone Plantation; Pittsylvania **GS:** U **SP:** Lydia Meadows (__-1848) **VI:** Son of William and (-----) Davis **P:** Y **BLW:** unk **RG:** unk **MK:** unk **PH:** unk **SS:** E pg 210 **BS:** 196.

DAVIS, David; b 1749; d 1799 **RU:** Soldier/Patriot, Gave material aid to cause **CEM:** Pughtown; GPS unk; Gainesboro; Frederick **GS:** U **SP:** No info **VI:** No further data **P:** unk **BLW:** unk **RG:** unk **MK:** unk **PH:** unk **SS:** J- DAR Hatcher; D Frederick Co **BS:** JLARC 2.

DAVIS, Hugh; b Nov 1758; d 26 Feb 1843 **RU:** Sergeant, Ent serv Prince William Co in 9th & 13th Cont Lines. Crippled for life fr bullet through knee at Battle of Paulus Hook near Trenton, NJ **CEM:** Davis Family; GPS unk; Wolf Run Shoals Rd; Prince William **GS:** Y **SP:** Mar (1788) Jane (-----) (__-20 Sep 1796) **VI:** Pen 1819, Prince William Co. Resided near Dumfries, VA 1829. S10136 **P:** Y **BLW:** unk **RG:** N **MK:** N **PH:** unk **SS:** K Vol 2 pg 15 **BS:** 94 pg 199.

DAVIS, Isaac; b 9 Jun 1754, Albemarle Co; d 8 Aug 1835 **RU:** Captain, Ent serv Albemarle Co. Served in 6th, 10th, 11th Cont Lines. Became Capt 1781 **CEM:** Locust Grove; GPS unk; From Rt 623 take 641 .4 mi to Locust Grove farm road, .35 mi; Greene **GS:** U **SP:** Elizabeth Kirtley (1 Apr 1766-1 Mar 1821) **VI:** After war moved to Orange Co in 1786 where he was pen 1833. Was bur in Greene Co, which was formed fr Orange Co in 1838. S17916 **P:** Y **BLW:** unk **RG:** unk **MK:** unk **PH:** unk **SS:** K Vol II pg 15 **BS:** JLARC 113.

DAVIS, James; b 1745; d 1819 **RU:** Captain, Served in VA line **CEM:** Davis Family; GPS unk; Morefield; Russell **GS:** U **SP:** No info **VI:** Heirs recd BLW for 300 acres **P:** unk **BLW:** Y **RG:** N **MK:** N **PH:** unk **SS:** AS SAR applic; Gen Publ Co Baltimore MD 1975 **BS:** SAR Appl.

DAVIS, James; b c1761; d 1849 **RU:** Fifer, Ent serv Loudoun Co 1777 **CEM:** Sharon; GPS unk; Middleburg; Loudoun **GS:** Y **SP:** No info **VI:** Pen Loudoun Co 1832 S8288 **P:** unk **BLW:** unk **RG:** Y **MK:** N **PH:** unk **SS:** E pg 211; K Vol II pg 15 **BS:** 25 pg 76.

DAVIS, Jesse; b 3 Feb 1756; d unk **RU:** unk, SAR registry did not specify service **CEM:** Davis Family; GPS unk; Edgehill; King George **GS:** U **SP:** m. 14 Dec 1789 (bond), Richmond Co, to Priscilla Downman, b. 3 Mar 1763, North Farnham Parish, Richmond Co, daughter of James Downman & Lucy Sydnor, d. bef 4 May 1801 when her brother Traverse Downman wrote his will. Groom was of Northumberland Co at the time. **VI:** Resident of Northumberland Co when mar in 1789. Pen 1830. Baptist minister **P:** Y **BLW:** unk **RG:** unk **MK:** unk **PH:** unk **SS:** NSSAR Ancestor # P-144627; AR Vol 1 pg 238 **BS:** JLARC 2.

DAVIS, John A; b unk; d unk **RU:** Lieutenant, Served in Navy **CEM:** Arlington National; GPS 38.88377, -77.06535; Jefferson Davis Hwy Rt 110; Arlington **GS:** U **SP:** No info **VI:** No further data **P:** unk **BLW:** unk **RG:** Y **MK:** unk **PH:** unk **SS:** J-NASSR 2000 Reg **BS:** JLARC 76.

DAVIS, Joseph; b unk, Pittsylvania Co; d unk **RU:** Second Lieutenant, Served in Bedford Co Militia **CEM:** Davis Family; GPS unk; Cherrystone Plantation; Pittsylvania **GS:** U **SP:** Lucy McGehee Hodnett **VI:** Son of William (1729-1791) & (-----) (__-1789) Davis **P:** unk **BLW:** unk **RG:** unk **MK:** unk **PH:** unk **SS:** E pg 212 **BS:** 196.

DAVIS, Samuel; b unk; d 1819 **RU:** Patriot, Gave material aid to the cause **CEM:** Cedar Grove; GPS 36.57204, -80.02599; 301 Fort Lane Rd; Portsmouth City **GS:** Y **SP:** No info **VI:** No further data **P:** N **BLW:** N **RG:** N **MK:** N **PH:** unk **SS:** AL Ct Bk pg 2 **BS:** 27 pg 108.

RU=Rank/Unit	CEM=Cemetery	GS=Gravestone	SP=Spousal Information
VI=Other Veteran Info	P=Pension	BLW=Bounty/Land Warrant	RG=Registered Grave
MK=SAR/DAR Marker	PH=Photo	SS=Service Source	BS=Burial Source

88

DAVIS, Thomas; b 1760, Orange Co; d 1811 **RU**: Patriot, Provided beef 300# 2 Nov 1781 **CEM**: Mount Valley; GPS unk; Vic jct Rts 663 & 522; Orange **GS**: N **SP**: 1) Mar (24 Apr 1783) Elizabeth Early, d/o (-----) & Theodosia Early 2) Elizabeth EarlyMar (10 Jan 1789 Orange Co) Elizabeth Pannill, d/o William & (-----) Pannill, Sr. **VI**: No further data **P**: N **BLW**: N **RG**: Y **MK**: N **PH**: N **SS**: AK Jun 2007 **BS**: 04, Jun 2007.

DAVIS, Thomas; b 1760; d 1781 **RU**: Soldier, Served fr PA, and died fr the battle at Yorktown **CEM**: Yorktown Victory Monument Tablet; GPS 38.28350, -78.54150; Yorktown; York **GS**: U **SP**: No info **VI**: No further data **P**: unk **BLW**: unk **RG**: unk **MK**: unk **PH**: unk **SS**: J-Yorktown Historian **BS**: JLARC 74.

DAVIS, Walter; b c1733, Ireland; d 20 Mar 1803 **RU**: Private, Serv in 6th & 10th Cont Line **CEM**: Tinkling Spring Presbyterian; GPS 38.08472, -78.98278; 30 Tinkling Spring Dr, Fishersville; Augusta **GS**: U **SP**: Martha Cunningham (1731 PA-12 Jan 1806) **VI**: No further data **P**: unk **BLW**: unk **RG**: unk **MK**: unk **PH**: unk **SS**: C pg 165 **BS**: 196.

DAVIS, William; b 9 Aug 1729; d 4 Jun 1791 **RU**: Patriot, Gave material aid to cause **CEM**: Davis Family; GPS unk; Cherrystone Plantation; Pittsylvania **GS**: U **SP**: No info **VI**: No further data **P**: N **BLW**: N **RG**: unk **MK**: unk **PH**: unk **SS**: AL Ct Bk pg 2, 12, 31 **BS**: 196.

DAVIS, William; b 13 Aut 1755, Louisa Co; d 1 Sep 1829 **RU**: Private, Served in 15th VA Regt **CEM**: South River Meeting House; GPS 37.37246, -79.19194; 5810 Fort Ave; Lynchburg City **GS**: Y **SP**: Judith (-----) (__-after 1787) **VI**: Widow recd pen in Louisa Co 1787 **P**: Y **BLW**: unk **RG**: N **MK**: N **PH**: N **SS**: G pg 718 **BS**: 196.

DAVIS, William D; b 12 Dec 1765; d 3 Feb 1852 **RU**: Private, Served in Capt Finley's Co, Augusta Co Militia **CEM**: Tinkling Spring Presbyterian; GPS 38.08472, -78.98278; 30 Tinkling Spring Dr, Fishersville; Augusta **GS**: Y **SP**: Mar (24 Jul 1789) Mary Howard **VI**: Was of Brunswick Co **P**: unk **BLW**: unk **RG**: N **MK**: N **PH**: unk **SS**: E pg 213 **BS**: 142 Tinkling Spr.

DAVIS (DAVIES), Jesse; b 1756; d 7 May or March 1837 **RU**: Private, Ent serv 1776 Westmoreland Co. Served in 5th Cont line **CEM**: Private; GPS unk; Edgehill; King George **GS**: U **SP**: No info **VI**: Pen age 74 recd King George Co 1830 when he was Baptist minister. S8282 **P**: Y **BLW**: unk **RG**: unk **MK**: unk **PH**: unk **SS**: J- DAR Hatcher; E pg 209; K Vol II pg 13; CZ pg 130 **BS**: JLARC 2.

DAVIS (DAVIES), William; b 1745; d 1805 **RU**: Colonel, Served in Cont Line **CEM**: Whittle and Davis Family; GPS unk; Left of old Whittle House off Hwy 636; Mecklenburg **GS**: U **SP**: No info **VI**: No further data **P**: unk **BLW**: unk **RG**: unk **MK**: unk **PH**: unk **SS**: CZ pg 129 **BS**: JLARC 2, 72.

DAWSON, Benjamin; b 1758 or 1760; d 4 Nov 1825 **RU**: Private, Ent Serv Fauquier Co **CEM**: Dawson Family; GPS unk; Culpeper; Culpeper **GS**: U **SP**: 1) (-----) 2) Ann Pope LeRoy **VI**: Pen Prince William Co 1818 age 60. S39405 **P**: Y **BLW**: unk **RG**: N **MK**: N **PH**: unk **SS**: AS, DAR Report; K Vol II pg 24 **BS**: DAR Rpt.

DAWSON, Martin; b 1722; d 16 Mar 1812 **RU**: Patriot, Gave material aid to cause **CEM**: Valentine Cox; GPS unk; Forest; Bedford **GS**: Y **SP**: Mar (__ Amherst Co) Priscilla Sowell (c1719 James City Co-c1770 Amherst Co) **VI**: No further data **P**: N **BLW**: N **RG**: unk **MK**: unk **PH**: unk **SS**: DAR ancestor #A030822; AL CT Bk Amherst Co pg 8, 12, 13, 31 **BS**: 196.

DAY, Benjamin; b 24 Sep 1752, London, England; d 16 Feb 1821 **RU**: Major, Was Adjutant, 2nd VA Regt and Aide de Camp to Gen Woodford **CEM**: Masonic Cemetery; GPS 38.30198, -77.46142; 900 Charles St; Fredericksburg City **GS**: Y **SP**: Mar (3 Nov 1804) (-----) d/o Ebenezer & (-----) (-----) **VI**: Twice Mayor of Fredericksburg; Grand Master, Grand Lodge of VA **P**: unk **BLW**: unk **RG**: Y **MK**: N **PH**: unk **SS**: J-NSSAR 1993 Reg,; NSSAR Ancestor #P-145303; AR Vol 1 pg 242 **BS**: JLARC 1, 2.

DE BERTHELOT, Augustin; b unk; d 1781 **RU**: Soldier, Served in Gatinais Bn and died fr battle at Yorktown **CEM**: French Memorial; GPS 36.81944, -79.39933; Yorktown; York **GS**: U **SP**: No info **VI**: No further data **P**: unk **BLW**: unk **RG**: Y **MK**: unk **PH**: unk **SS**: J-Yorktown Historian **BS**: JLARC 1, 74.

DEAN, Joseph; b 1763; d 21 Apr 1818 **RU**: Private, Served 3 yrs in Cont line, ending 20 Jun 1783 **CEM**: Presbyterian Church; GPS 38.80015, -77.05791; Wilkes St & Hamilton Ln; Alexandria City **GS**: Y **SP**: Hannah (----), b c1767, d 6 Feb 1843 **VI**: Received 100 acres bounty land. Death notice in the

RU=Rank/Unit   CEM=Cemetery   GS=Gravestone   SP=Spousal Information
VI=Other Veteran Info   P=Pension   BLW=Bounty/Land Warrant   RG=Registered Grave
MK=SAR/DAR Marker   PH=Photo   SS=Service Source   BS=Burial Source

89

Alexandria Gazette 23 Apr 1818 pg 3 **P:** unk **BLW: Y RG: Y MK:** N **PH:** unk **SS:** F pg 21; AK **BS:** 04; 23 pg 25.

DEARING, John; b 1745; d 9 Sep 1822 **RU:** Captain, Served in Louisa Co as Lt and later promoted to capt **CEM:** Dearing Family; GPS unk; Caledonia Farm, 47 Dearing Rd, Flint Hill; Rappahannock **GS:** Y **SP:** Anna (Nancy) Jett (c1751-30 Jun 1823), d/o Francis & (-----) Jett **VI:** He built the farm house called Fountain Hill in 1812 **P:** unk **BLW:** unk **RG: Y MK:** N **PH:** unk **SS:** AK; E pg 216 **BS:** 04; 33.

DEARING / DEERING, James; b 1755; d 1811 **RU:** Captain/Patriot, Served in 2nd VA Regt. Gave material aid to cause **CEM:** Deering Family; GPS unk; At Otterburne, Old Deering Place on Otter River, Altavista/nr Evington; Campbell **GS:** U **SP:** Mar (3 Apr 1783 Campbell Co (bond) James Adams, bondsman) Elizabeth Adams **VI:** No further data **P:** unk **BLW:** unk **RG: Y MK:** N **PH:** unk **SS:** D Lousia Co **BS:** JLARC 1, 2, 4, 36, 66, 75.

DEBAPTIST (deBAPTIST, D. BAPTIST), John; b c1740, St Kitts, West Indies; d 3 Sep 1804 **RU:** Seaman, Served as crewman on the "Dragon" fr Fredericksburg, Fall 1776 to end of war **CEM:** Union Church; GPS 38.32268, -77.46615; Carter St, Falmouth; Stafford **GS: Y SP:** Frances (-----) **VI:** Because of dark skin was considered a free black. Owned land in Fredericksburg area to include the wharf and ferry betw Fredericksburg and Falmouth. Died in Falmouth or Fredericksburg. SAR marker **P:** unk **BLW:** unk **RG: Y MK: Y PH: Y SS:** AK **BS:** 04, JLARC 48; CMM Chap 1998; GW Chap 2015.

DEBASE, Pierre; b unk; d 1781 **RU:** Seaman, Served on "Sceptre" and died from Yorktown battle **CEM:** French Memorial; GPS 36.81944, -79.39933; Yorktown; York **GS:** U **SP:** No info **VI:** No further data **P:** unk **BLW:** unk **RG: Y MK:** unk **PH:** unk **SS:** J-Yorktown Historian **BS:** JLARC 1 ,74.

DECOUNE, Louis; b unk; d 1781 **RU:** Soldier, Served in Gatinais Bn and died fr battle at Yorktown **CEM:** French Memorial; GPS 36.81944, -79.39933; Yorktown; York **GS:** U **SP:** No info **VI:** No further data **P:** unk **BLW:** unk **RG: Y MK:** unk **PH:** unk **SS:** J-Yorktown Historian **BS:** JLARC 1, 74.

DEDERICK, Jacob; b 1752; d 28 Nov 1830 **RU:** Private, Served in PA Militia 14 Sep 1777 **CEM:** Neriah Baptist; GPS 37.78778, -79.36482; Jct Rts 631 & 706, South River; Rockbridge **GS: Y SP:** No info **VI:** No further data **P:** unk **BLW:** unk **RG: N MK:** N **PH:** unk **SS:** CI PA Archives **BS:** 154 Neriah.

DEGRAFENREIDT, Tscharner; b 9 Feb 1752; d 1811 **RU:** Sergeant/Patriot, Wounded in Battle at Guilford CH. Gave material aid to cause **CEM:** DeGrafenreidt Family; GPS unk; See county property records; Lunenburg **GS:** U **SP:** Not mar **VI:** Son of Anthony & Mary (Baker) Degrafenreid. BLW recd 1810 of 400 acres **P:** N **BLW: Y RG:** unk **MK:** unk **PH:** unk **SS:** J- DAR Hatcher; AL Ct Bk pg 17 Lunenburg Co **BS:** JLARC 2.

DEGRES, Michel; b unk; d 1781 **RU:** Soldier, Served in Santogne Bn and died fr battle at Yorktown **CEM:** French Memorial; GPS 36.81944, -79.39933; Yorktown; York **GS:** U **SP:** No info **VI:** No further data **P:** unk **BLW:** unk **RG: Y MK:** unk **PH:** unk **SS:** J-Yorktown Historian **BS:** JLARC 1, 74.

DEHAVEN, Isaac; b 18 Feb 1750; d Bef 23 Dec 1835 **RU:** Private, Entered serv in Loudoun Co. Previously was private in 4th Bn, PA Militia **CEM:** Back Creek Quaker, aka Gainesboro United Methodist; GPS 39.27861, -78.25694; 166 Siler Ln, Gainesboro; Frederick **GS: Y SP:** Mar (Frederick Co) Abigail Phillips **VI:** Pen 1832 Franklin Co. S8313 **P: Y BLW:** unk **RG: Y MK:** N **PH:** unk **SS:** K Vol 2 pg 29; AK **BS:** 59 pg 87; 04.

DEHAVEN, Peter; b 31 Jan 1741, Philadelphia, PA; d 4 Jan 1822 **RU:** Private, Served in 4th Battalion PA Militia **CEM:** Back Creek Quaker, aka Gainesboro United Methodist; GPS 39.27861, -78.25694; 166 Siler Ln, Gainesboro; Frederick **GS: Y SP:** Mar (1 Jan 1763) Abigail West (__-Jan 1818) **VI:** Govt GS **P:** unk **BLW:** unk **RG:** unk **MK:** unk **PH:** unk **SS:** B **BS:** 196.

DEJARNETTE, Joseph Jr; b 9 Oct 1747; d Sep 1824 **RU:** First Lieutenant, Served May 1781 under Capt James Sutton, McAllister's Militia **CEM:** DeJarnette Family; GPS unk; Rt 2, 5.5 mi fr Bowling Green; Caroline **GS:** U **SP:** Mary Hampton **VI:** No further data **P:** unk **BLW:** unk **RG:** unk **MK:** N **PH:** unk **SS:** AZ pg 194 **BS:** JLARC 15.

DELAGNEL, Julius Adolphus; b 31 Oct 1744; d 21 May 1840 **RU:** Captain, Was a Capt of Ordinance in the US Army **CEM:** St Paul's Episcopal; GPS 38.79959, -77.05860; 228 S Pitt St; Alexandria City **GS:** Y

RU=Rank/Unit	CEM=Cemetery	GS=Gravestone	SP=Spousal Information
VI=Other Veteran Info	P=Pension	BLW=Bounty/Land Warrant	RG=Registered Grave
MK=SAR/DAR Marker	PH=Photo	SS=Service Source	BS=Burial Source

90

SP: Harriet Sandford (1801-28 May 1891). After his death, she moved to Alexandria with his children and lived with her sister and Rev James T. Johnson **VI:** His stone here may be a cenotaph as he died in New York and his widow then moved to Alexandria **P:** unk **BLW:** unk **RG:** Y **MK:** unk **PH:** unk **SS:** J-NSSAR 1993 Reg; NSSAR Ancestor #P-146494 **BS:** JLARC 1; 174 pg 392; 196.

DELAHAYE, Pierre; b unk; d 1781 **RU:** Seaman, Served on "Ville de Paris" and died from Yorktown battle **CEM:** French Memorial; GPS 36.81944, -79.39933; Yorktown; York **GS:** U **SP:** No info **VI:** No further data **P:** unk **BLW:** unk **RG:** Y **MK:** unk **PH:** unk **SS:** J-Yorktown Historian **BS:** JLARC 1,74.

DELANY, John; b 11 Jun 1740; d 5 Jan 1831 **RU:** Private, Ent serv 1776 in MD **CEM:** Old Stone Methodist; GPS 39.11725, -77.56609; 168 W Cornwall St, Leesburg; Loudoun **GS:** Y **SP:** No info **VI:** Pensioned age 88 in Fairfax Co in 1828. FS46Y38 recd 1780. S46438 **P:** Y **BLW:** unk **RG:** Y **MK:** N **PH:** unk **SS:** K Vol 2 pg 29; AK **BS:** 04, 25 pg 78.

DELAPORT, Ubal; b unk; d 1781 **RU:** Seaman, Served on "Auguste" and died from Yorktown battle **CEM:** French Memorial; GPS 36.81944, -79.39933; Yorktown; York **GS:** U **SP:** No info **VI:** No further data **P:** unk **BLW:** unk **RG:** unk **MK:** unk **PH:** unk **SS:** J-Yorktown Historian **BS:** JLARC 1, 74.

DELLINGER, Christian Jr; b 13 Feb 1764, Swover Creek, Shenandoah Co; d 22 Sep 1856 **RU:** Private, Ent serv 1781 Shenandoah Co. Was in Battle of Yorktown. After surrender of Cornwallis, detailed as guard & marched prisoners to Fredericksburg **CEM:** Dellinger Family; GPS 38.5037, -78.4054; Madison District Conicville; Shenandoah **GS:** Y **SP:** Eva Mary Foltz **VI:** Appl for pension age 71 1836 and again in 1850 age 86. Both rejected. R2857. Died in Conicville, Shenandoah Co **P:** N **BLW:** unk **RG:** Y **MK:** N **PH:** unk **SS:** J- DAR Hatcher; BY; K Vol II pg 29 **BS:** 197; JLARC 2.

DELONG, John Nicholas; b 19 Jul 1756, Berks Co, PA; d 21 Feb 1823 **RU:** Private, Served in 13th Cont Line **CEM:** Trinity Evangelical Lutheran; GPS 39.08280, -78.21679; Mulberry St, Stephens City; Frederick **GS:** Y **SP:** Mar (20 May 1794 by Rev Christian Streit) Mary Toomy **VI:** Son of Johannes (1730-1813) & Maria Katherina (Dussinger) (1725-1782) DeLang **P:** unk **BLW:** unk **RG:** Y **MK:** N **PH:** unk **SS:** E pg 218 **BS:** 59 pg 91; 196.

DELTRIEUX, Pierre; b unk; d 1781 **RU:** Seaman, Served on "Solitaire" and died from Yorktown battle **CEM:** French Memorial; GPS 36.81944, -79.39933; Yorktown; York **GS:** U **SP:** No info **VI:** No further data **P:** unk **BLW:** unk **RG:** Y **MK:** unk **PH:** unk **SS:** J-Yorktown Historian **BS:** JLARC 1, 74.

DEMARET, Nicolas; b unk; d 1781 **RU:** Soldier, Served in Gatinais Bn and died fr battle at Yorktown **CEM:** French Memorial; GPS 36.81944, -79.39933; Yorktown; York **GS:** U **SP:** No info **VI:** No further data **P:** unk **BLW:** unk **RG:** Y **MK:** unk **PH:** unk **SS:** J-Yorktown Historian **BS:** JLARC 1, 74.

DEMBRE, Pierre; b unk; d 1781 **RU:** Seaman, Served on "Diademe" and died from Yorktown battle **CEM:** French Memorial; GPS 36.81944, -79.39933; Yorktown; York **GS:** U **SP:** No info **VI:** No further data **P:** unk **BLW:** unk **RG:** Y **MK:** unk **PH:** unk **SS:** J-Yorktown Historian **BS:** JLARC 1, 74.

DENNETT, John; b unk; d 15 Jul 1787 **RU:** Patriot, Gave material support in Richmond Co **CEM:** St Peter's Episcopal; GPS unk; 8400 St Peters Ln, Quinton; New Kent **GS:** N **SP:** No info **VI:** No further data **P:** N **BLW:** N **RG:** N **MK:** N **PH:** N **SS:** G pg 317 **BS:** 85 pg 58.

DENSON, Jordan; b unk; d 1806 **RU:** Patriot, Gave material aid to the cause **CEM:** Jerico; GPS unk; Courtland; Southampton **GS:** Y **SP:** Ann Copeland **VI:** No further data **P:** N **BLW:** N **RG:** N **MK:** N **PH:** unk **SS:** AL Ct Bk pg 4 **BS:** 53 vol 5.

DEREUT, Pierre; b unk; d 1781 **RU:** Seaman, Served on "Citoyen" and died from Yorktown battle **CEM:** French Memorial; GPS 36.81944, -79.39933; Yorktown; York **GS:** U **SP:** No info **VI:** No further data **P:** unk **BLW:** unk **RG:** Y **MK:** unk **PH:** unk **SS:** J-Yorktown Historian **BS:** JLARC 1, 74.

DERINIER, Louis; b unk; d 1781 **RU:** Seaman, Served on "Palmier" and died from Yorktown battle **CEM:** French Memorial; GPS 36.81944, -79.39933; Yorktown; York **GS:** U **SP:** No info **VI:** No further data **P:** unk **BLW:** unk **RG:** Y **MK:** unk **PH:** unk **SS:** J-Yorktown Historian **BS:** JLARC 1, 74.

DESCHAMPS, Joseph; b unk; d 1781 **RU:** Soldier, Served in Gatinais Bn and died fr battle at Yorktown **CEM:** French Memorial; GPS 36.81944, -79.39933; Yorktown; York **GS:** U **SP:** No info **VI:** No further data **P:** unk **BLW:** unk **RG:** Y **MK:** unk **PH:** unk **SS:** J-Yorktown Historian **BS:** JLARC 1, 74.

RU=Rank/Unit CEM=Cemetery GS=Gravestone SP=Spousal Information
VI=Other Veteran Info P=Pension BLW=Bounty/Land Warrant RG=Registered Grave
MK=SAR/DAR Marker PH=Photo SS=Service Source BS=Burial Source

91

DESHAY, Francois; b unk; d 1781 **RU:** Soldier, Served in Gatinais Bn and died fr battle at Yorktown **CEM:** French Memorial; GPS 36.81944, -79.39933; Yorktown; York **GS:** U **SP:** No info **VI:** No further data **P:** unk **BLW:** unk **RG:** Y **MK:** unk **PH:** unk **SS:** J-Yorktown Historian **BS:** JLARC 1, 74.

DESHAZO, William; b unk; d 24 or 27 Apr 1839 **RU:** Soldier, Enl Winter 1777 in Capt Henry Dudley's Co for 3 yrs. Served in 2nd VA State Regt, under Col Gregory Smith and marched to Valley Forge and after to Brigade of Gen Muhlenburg. Was in Battle of Monmouth on 28 Jun 1778. Was in attack on Stoney Point on Paulus's Hook. Left service Spring 1780 at Williamsburg **CEM:** DeShazo; GPS unk; Leatherwood; Henry **GS:** U **SP:** Mar (Nov 1794, bond dated 5 Nov 1794) Person Co NC, Jane Cincy King (1770-__) **VI:** Recd pension 1832 age 73 Henry Co. Pension says he d 27 Apr. 1839. Widow pen Henry Co age 74 and was resident there 1855 age 85. W1832 & R801 **P:** Y **BLW:** Y **RG:** unk **MK:** unk **PH:** unk **SS:** K Vol II pg 34; R Vol 2 pg 34 **BS:** 196.

DESMONT, Antoine; b unk; d 1781 **RU:** Soldier, Served in Bourbonnais Bn and died fr battle at Yorktown **CEM:** French Memorial; GPS 36.81944, -79.39933; Yorktown; York **GS:** U **SP:** No info **VI:** No further data **P:** unk **BLW:** unk **RG:** Y **MK:** unk **PH:** unk **SS:** J-Yorktown Historian **BS:** JLARC 1 ,74.

DESRIEU, Louis Sr; b unk; d 1781 **RU:** Seaman, Served on "Auguste" and died from Yorktown battle **CEM:** French Memorial; GPS 36.81944, -79.39933; Yorktown; York **GS:** U **SP:** No info **VI:** No further data **P:** unk **BLW:** unk **RG:** Y **MK:** unk **PH:** unk **SS:** J-Yorktown Historian **BS:** JLARC 1, 74.

DETERMINE, Nicolas; b unk; d 1781 **RU:** Soldier, Served in Santogne Bn and died fr battle at Yorktown **CEM:** French Memorial; GPS 36.81944, -79.39933; Yorktown; York **GS:** U **SP:** No info **VI:** No further data **P:** unk **BLW:** unk **RG:** Y **MK:** unk **PH:** unk **SS:** J-Yorktown Historian **BS:** JLARC 1, 74.

DEVAISE, Joseph; b unk; d 1781 **RU:** Soldier, Served in Touraine Bn and died fr battle at Yorktown **CEM:** French Memorial; GPS 36.81944, -79.39933; Yorktown; York **GS:** U **SP:** No info **VI:** No further data **P:** unk **BLW:** unk **RG:** Y **MK:** unk **PH:** unk **SS:** J-Yorktown Historian **BS:** JLARC 1, 74.

DEVERLE (DEYERLE), Peter; b c1734, Germany; d Jan 1813 **RU:** Patriot, Surveyor of Road, 1780 **CEM:** Deyerle Family; GPS unk; West part; Roanoke Co **GS:** U **SP:** Mar (c1763) Regina Ann Bowman (13 Jan 1743, Orange Co-May 1828, Montgomery Co) **VI:** Died in Montgomery Co **P:** N **BLW:** N **RG:** N **MK:** N **PH:** unk **SS:** DAR Ancestor # A033362; AR Vol 1 pg 254; AS DAR Report; DL pg 307 **BS:** DAR Rpt.

DEVILLIERS, Gabriel; b unk; d 1781 **RU:** Soldier, Served in Bourbonnais Bn and died fr battle at Yorktown **CEM:** French Memorial; GPS 36.81944, -79.39933; Yorktown; York **GS:** U **SP:** No info **VI:** No further data **P:** unk **BLW:** unk **RG:** Y **MK:** unk **PH:** unk **SS:** J-Yorktown Historian **BS:** JLARC 1, 74.

DEW, Thomas; b 28 May 1763, MD; d 23 Apr 1849 **RU:** Private, Ent serv Caroline Co 1780. Serv from fr King and Queen Co in Gen Steven's Bde, and was in Battle of Camden, SC and at Battle at Guilford CH. Served again Apr 1781 under Weeden's Bde & Marquis de Lafayette **CEM:** Dewsville plantation; GPS unk; Newtown; King & Queen **GS:** Y **SP:** Mar (07 Jan 1793) Lucy Gatewood (24 Mar 1776-17 Nov 1832) **VI:** Was later a Capt in War of 1812. Marker placed Nov 2012. Was President of William & Mary College 1836 to death. Appl for pension fr King & Queen Co 1842 age 78. Pension rejected due to less than six mos serv. R2909 & R803 **P:** No **BLW:** unk **RG:** Y **MK:** Y **PH:** Y **SS:** K Vol II pg 34; AK **BS:** JLARC 1, 4, 37.

DEZE, Andre; b unk; d 1781 **RU:** Soldier, Served in Gatinais Bn and died fr battle at Yorktown **CEM:** French Memorial; GPS 36.81944, -79.39933; Yorktown; York **GS:** U **SP:** No info **VI:** No further data **P:** unk **BLW:** unk **RG:** Y **MK:** unk **PH:** unk **SS:** J-Yorktown Historian **BS:** JLARC 1, 74.

DIALE, Jean; b unk; d 1781 **RU:** Seaman, Served on "Sceptre" and died from Yorktown battle **CEM:** French Memorial; GPS 36.81944, -79.39933; Yorktown; York **GS:** U **SP:** No info **VI:** No further data **P:** unk **BLW:** unk **RG:** Y **MK:** unk **PH:** unk **SS:** J-Yorktown Historian **BS:** JLARC 1, 74.

DIAMOND, Moses; b unk; d 1781 **RU:** Private, Served in Col Lewis Duboys 5th NY Regt. Killed in the battle at Yorktown **CEM:** Yorktown Victory Monument Tablet; GPS 38.28350, -78.54150; Yorktown; York **GS:** U **SP:** No info **VI:** No further data **P:** unk **BLW:** unk **RG:** unk **MK:** unk **PH:** unk **SS:** J-Yorktown Historian. AX pg 56 **BS:** JLARC 74.

RU=Rank/Unit	CEM=Cemetery	GS=Gravestone	SP=Spousal Information
VI=Other Veteran Info	P=Pension	BLW=Bounty/Land Warrant	RG=Registered Grave
MK=SAR/DAR Marker	PH=Photo	SS=Service Source	BS=Burial Source

92

DICK, Archibald; b 1725; d 1811 **RU:** Patriot, Gave material aid to cause in Caroline Co **CEM:** Dick-Smith Family; GPS unk; Bullock's Rd; Caroline **GS:** Y **SP:** No info **VI:** Minister of St Margaret's Parish **P:** N **BLW:** N **RG:** Y **MK:** N **PH:** unk **SS:** AL Ct Bk lt II pg 24 **BS:** 02 pg 54.

DICK, Elisha Cullen Dr; b 15 Mar 1762, Chester Co, PA; d 22 Sep 1825 **RU:** Private, Private 5th class, 5th Co. (Capt Jacob Martin, 4th Bn (Lt Col Paul Coxe) Philadelphia City, PA 1780 or 81 as Elisha Dick. Private 7th Class, 8th Co (Capt Joh Cornish) 4th Battalion (Lt Col Paule Coxe, Philadelphia City Militia 1780 or 81. Listed as Doctor Dick **CEM:** Quaker Burial Ground; GPS 38.80749, -77.04676; 717 Queen St, Kate Walker Barrett Library; Alexandria City **GS:** N **SP:** Mar (Oct 1793 Chester Co, PA) to Hannah Harmon, (__-1843 Roanake, VA) **VI:** Recd medical degree fr Univ. PA in 1782. Studied w/ Dr. Benjamin Rush and Dr. William Shippen. Transcript of letter fr J.A. Pearce written 20 Aug 1885 shows he was b 15 Mar 1762, contrary to 1750 on 1937 plaque. Died in Cottage Farm, Fairfax Co. In 1937 Kate Waller Barrett Library was constructed on the burying ground. No GS found & marker moved **P:** unk **BLW:** unk **RG:** Y **MK:** Y **PH:** N **SS:** www.digitalarchives.state.pa.us/archive.asp?view=ArchiveItems&ArchiveID=13&FL=D&FID=457214&LID=457313 card 41&42. PA Mil records; AK Sep 2009 **BS:** 34 pg 63.

DICKENSON, Griffith; b 8 Aug 1757 Hanover Co; d 16 Oct 1843 **RU:** Corporal, Enl Oct 1776 under Capt Thomas Scott as musician. Discharged Nov 1779 after 3 mos as fifer and 33 mos as corporal **CEM:** Berger burial ground; GPS 36.92909, -79.25041; Rt 685, or Rt 927 E of Chalk Level, E fr Gretna 6 mi; Pittsylvania **GS:** Y **SP:** Susanna Shelton (1752 Christchurch, Middlesex Co-20 Oct 1747 Chalk Level, Pittsylvania Co) **VI:** Source 90 has second graveyard,also says a Baptist minister **P:** unk **BLW:** unk **RG:** unk **MK:** unk **PH:** unk **SS:** E pg 223 **BS:** 174; JLARC 2, 90, 96.

DICKERSON, Elijah; b 1755, Halifax Co; d Aft 4 Sep 1834 **RU:** Private, Served in Montgomery Co Militia, commanded by Col Christie **CEM:** Wright Family; GPS 36.97658, -80.21693; Pizarro off Rt 668; Floyd **GS:** U **SP:** Mar (23 May 1785, Montgomery Co) (-----) **VI:** Memorialized by DAR plaque in cem. Pen in 1835 list at age 79 **P:** Y **BLW:** unk **RG:** unk **MK:** Y **PH:** unk **SS:** DAR member #A034128; E pg 223 **BS:** 196 for John Mitchell.

DICKERSON, Joseph; b 11 Apr 1742; d 16 Sep 1818 **RU:** Patriot, Gave material aid to the cause **CEM:** Dickerson Family; GPS unk; Nr Moneta; Bedford **GS:** Y **SP:** Mar (5 Mar 1769) Elizabeth Wooldridge (11 Jan 1744, Buckingham Co-7 Nov 1818) **VI:** No further data **P:** N **BLW:** N **RG:** N **MK:** N **PH:** unk **SS:** AL Ct Bk pg 11 **BS:** 80 vol 1 pg 255.

DICKERSON, Moses; b 1756; d 23 Mar 1834 **RU:** Patriot, Took oath of allegiance in Henry Co 1776 **CEM:** Pine Creek Primitive Baptist; GPS 36.94622, -80.27357; Spangler Mill Rd Rt 682; Floyd **GS:** Y **SP:** Jemima (Jemina) Sullivan (1756-26 May 1846) **VI:** No further data **P:** N **BLW:** N **RG:** unk **MK:** unk **PH:** unk **SS:** DAR vol 1 pg 192 **BS:** JLARC 29.

DICKINSON, James; b 1742; d 1828 **RU:** Private, Specific service may be found at the Lib of VA in Auditor's Acct Bk XVIII, pg 474 **CEM:** Belle Isle; GPS unk; Nr Frederick Hall; Louisa **GS:** U **SP:** Mary (Cole) Barclay **VI:** No further data **P:** unk **BLW:** unk **RG:** Y **MK:** unk **PH:** unk **SS:** J-NASSR 2000 Reg; CZ pg 137 **BS:** JLARC 76.

DICKINSON, John; b 1731; d 1799 **RU:** Captain, Served in battle of Point Pleasant in Capt Charles Lewis's Co, Oct 1774 **CEM:** Augusta; GPS unk; See DAR Senate Doc year 1959; Bath **GS:** U **SP:** Mar (21 May 1767) Martha Usher (1745 Philadelphia-__) **VI:** SAR applic indicates cem name is Augusta **P:** unk **BLW:** unk **RG:** unk **MK:** unk **PH:** unk **SS:** NSSAR Ancestor #P-147922; SAR applic; AR Vol 1 pg 254 **BS:** JLARC 2.

DICKINSON, Thomas Bowers; b c1751; d 25 Apr 1785 **RU:** Captain, Specific service may be found at the Lib of VA in War files vol 4 pg 167 **CEM:** Trinity Episcopal; GPS 36.83459, -76.30105; 500 Court St; Portsmouth City **GS:** Y **SP:** No info **VI:** No further data **P:** unk **BLW:** unk **RG:** N **MK:** N **PH:** unk **SS:** B shows rank; CZ pg 137 **BS:** 92 stone 63.

DICKINSON (DICKSON), Henry; b 28 Oct 1747; d 6 Jul 1825 **RU:** Colonel, Served in 6th SC Regt Cont Line **CEM:** Dickinson Family; GPS unk; Nr Old Courthouse; Russell **GS:** U **SP:** Mar (3 Apr 1842) Mary Powell (1 Dec 1750-23 Apr 1842) **VI:** No further data **P:** Y **BLW:** unk **RG:** unk **MK:** unk **PH:** unk **SS:** J-DAR Hatcher; E pg 224; CI pen records of several soldiers; CZ pg 137; DD **BS:** JLARC 2.

RU=Rank/Unit	CEM=Cemetery	GS=Gravestone	SP=Spousal Information
VI=Other Veteran Info	P=Pension	BLW=Bounty/Land Warrant	RG=Registered Grave
MK=SAR/DAR Marker	PH=Photo	SS=Service Source	BS=Burial Source

93

DICKSON, Henry; b 1743 Hull, York, England; d 10 Dec 1810 **RU:** Captain, Probably had naval service, specifics not found **CEM:** Trinity Episcopal; GPS 36.83459, -76.30105; 500 Court St; Portsmouth City **GS:** Y **SP:** Janet Brown **VI:** Trustee Portsmouth 1796 & 1800 **P:** unk **BLW:** unk **RG:** N **MK:** N **PH:** unk **SS:** B; H NC Service **BS:** 75 Portsmouth.

DIDIERRE, Nicolas; b unk; d 1781 **RU:** Soldier, Served in Touraine Bn and died fr battle at Yorktown **CEM:** French Memorial; GPS 36.81944, -79.39933; Yorktown; York **GS:** U **SP:** No info **VI:** No further data **P:** unk **BLW:** unk **RG:** Y **MK:** unk **PH:** unk **SS:** J Yorktown Historian **BS:** JLARC 1, 74.

DIGGES, Dudley Power; b 1728, Bellfield Plantation, York Co; d 3 May 1790, Yorktown **RU:** Patriot, Was member Rev Conventions & Committee of Correspondence, and Committee of Safety, 1775 and member of VA Assembly. Was captured by British during Charlottesville raid 4 Jun 1781. Was former Lt Gov **CEM:** Abingdon Episcopal; GPS 37.33355, -76.51364; 4645 George Washington Mem Hwy Rt 17; Gloucester **GS:** U **SP:** 1) Mar (1745 Yorktown) Martha Burwell Armistead 2) Mar (1760 Yorktown) Elizabeth Wormeley, d/o Ralph & (-----) Wormeley of "Rosegill" **VI:** Son of Col Cole (1692-1744) & Elizabeth (Follott Power) (1697-__) Digges, Esq. Burgess fr York Co 1752-1776. Cenotaph. Orig bur Bluefield Cem, James City Co (source SAR) **P:** N **BLW:** N **RG:** N **MK:** N **PH:** unk **SS:** AS DAR Report, CD; NSSAR Ancestor #P-148151 **BS:** DAR Rpt; 196.

DIGGES, Edward; b 22 Jan 1746; d 29 Oct 1818 **RU:** Captain, Commanded an Artillery Co in VA State Line, 2nd Bn, Fauquier Co Militia Nov 1777. Served in State Line for 3 yrs **CEM:** Diggs Family; GPS unk; Cliff Mill; Fauquier **GS:** N **SP:** 1) Mar (11 Jun 1775) Elizabeth Ann Gaskins (1756-__) 2) Mar (29 Mar 1798 Fauquier Co, Charles Marshal, security) Ann E. Gaskins, no stone **VI:** Son of Col Edward (1715-1769) & Anne (Harrison) (1720-1775) Digges. Justice of Peace Fauquier Co 1787. Received BLW. Fieldstone only **P:** unk **BLW:** Y **RG:** Y **MK:** N **PH:** N **SS:** E pg 225; N; H; AK; CD; Fauquier Co Marriages pg 50 **BS:** 04;19 pg 212.

DIGGES (DIGGS), Dudley Jr; b 6 Apr 1766; d 4 Apr 1839 **RU:** Lieutenant, Served in Calvary, VA line 1779 to 1783. Joined Southern Army 1780. Probably disabled in serv as authorized half pay **CEM:** Fork Episcopal Church; GPS 37.85340, -77.53100; 12566 Old Ridge Rd, Doswell; Hanover **GS:** Y **SP:** Alicy Grymes Page (__-1846) **VI:** Son of Dudley Power (1728-1790) & Elizabeth (Wormeley) Digges. Pensioned 8 Jan 1820, Louisa Co, $90 per annum and $100 immediate relief in lieu of half pay **P:** Y **BLW:** unk **RG:** N **MK:** N **PH:** unk **SS:** AH pg 219; M Vol 3 pg 514 **BS:** 109 pg 570.

DIGGS, Edward; b 1721; d 1810 **RU:** Colonel, Was Maj in 2d Bn Fauquier Co Militia 1777. Obtained rank of Colonel **CEM:** Denbigh United Presbyterian; GPS unk; 302 Denbigh Blvd; Newport News City **GS:** U **SP:** No info **VI:** No further data **P:** unk **BLW:** unk **RG:** unk **MK:** unk **PH:** unk **SS:** NSSAR Ancestor #P-148155; E pg 225; AR Vol 1 pg 256 **BS:** JLARC 2.

DILLARD, George; b 1720, Williamsburg; d 3 Feb 1790 **RU:** Patriot, Gave material aid to cause **CEM:** St Mark's, aka Little Fork Church; GPS unk; See DAR Senate Doc 1956, serial #11999, vol 8; Culpeper **GS:** U **SP:** Priscilla Major (1716 New Kent Co-2 Mar 1790) **VI:** Son of Edward & (-----) Dillard. DAR indicates he d 20 Sep 1790 **P:** N **BLW:** N **RG:** unk **MK:** unk **PH:** unk **SS:** J- DAR Hatcher; D Vol 1 pg 263 **BS:** JLARC 2; AR vol 1 pg 257.

DILLARD, James B; b 15 Oct 1727, James City Co; d 24 Aug 1794 **RU:** Patriot, Gave material aid to cause **CEM:** Mansion House; GPS unk; Buffalo Island; Amherst **GS:** U **SP:** Mar (8 Jul 1748) Mary Ann Hunt (28 Apr 1734-26 Aug 1787) **VI:** No further data **P:** N **BLW:** N **RG:** unk **MK:** unk **PH:** unk **SS:** AL Ct Bk pg 13 Amherst Co **BS:** JLARC 115.

DILLARD, John; b 1751, Amherst Co; d 1 Dec 1822 **RU:** Captain/Patriot, Commanded a co, Henry Co Militia, 1780. Was wounded in Battle at Princeton **CEM:** Font Hill; GPS unk; Leatherwood Creek, Irisburg; Henry **GS:** U **SP:** Mar (23 Dec 1771) Sarah Stoval (c1758 Pittsylvania Co-aft 1800) **VI:** Son of James (1727-1794) & Mary (Hunt) (1748-1784) Dillard of Essex Co **P:** unk **BLW:** unk **RG:** unk **MK:** unk **PH:** unk **SS:** DAR #A036086; D Vol II pg 507, 510, 516; E pg 225; CZ **BS:** 196.

DILLARD, John; b unk; d 10 Jun 1808 **RU:** Patriot, Gave material aid to the cause **CEM:** Coons Family; GPS unk; vic Rixeyville Rt 640; Culpeper **GS:** Y **SP:** Ann Robertson, (1750-15 May 1815) also bur here **VI:** No further data **P:** N **BLW:** N **RG:** N **MK:** N **PH:** unk **SS:** ALCt bk I pg 47 **BS:** 75 Culpeper; 196.

RU=Rank/Unit	CEM=Cemetery	GS=Gravestone	SP=Spousal Information
VI=Other Veteran Info	P=Pension	BLW=Bounty/Land Warrant	RG=Registered Grave
MK=SAR/DAR Marker	PH=Photo	SS=Service Source	BS=Burial Source

94

DILLON, Jesse; b unk; d 1833 **RU:** Bombardier, Served in Capt Thomas Baytop's Co, 1st Artillery at Valley Forge, Jun 1778 **CEM:** Dillon Family; GPS unk; Rt 900; Franklin **GS:** Y **SP:** Mar (18 Jan 1808 Franklin Co) Rebecca Plybon **VI:** No further data **P:** unk **BLW:** unk **RG:** N **MK:** N **PH:** unk **SS:** A pg 251 **BS:** 82 pg 95.

DILTZER, Jean; b unk; d 1781 **RU:** Soldier, Served in Royal Deaux Ponts Bn and died fr battle at Yorktown **CEM:** French Memorial; GPS 36.81944, -79.39933; Yorktown; York **GS:** U **SP:** No info **VI:** No further data **P:** unk **BLW:** unk **RG:** Y **MK:** unk **PH:** unk **SS:** J-Yorktown Historian **BS:** JLARC 1, 74.

DIQUE-DOUNIER, Francois; b unk; d 1781 **RU:** Soldier, Served in Soissonnais Bn and died fr battle at Yorktown **CEM:** French Memorial; GPS 36.81944, -79.39933; Yorktown; York **GS:** U **SP:** No info **VI:** No further data **P:** unk **BLW:** unk **RG:** Y **MK:** unk **PH:** unk **SS:** J-Yorktown Historian **BS:** JLARC 1, 74.

DIRONDELLES, Francois; b unk; d 1781 **RU:** Seaman, Served on "Citoyen" and died from Yorktown battle **CEM:** French Memorial; GPS 36.81944, -79.39933; Yorktown; York **GS:** U **SP:** No info **VI:** No further data **P:** unk **BLW:** unk **RG:** Y **MK:** unk **PH:** unk **SS:** J-Yorktown Historian **BS:** JLARC 1, 74.

DISHMAN, Samuel; b 26 Apr 1756, Westmoreland Co; d 14 May 1817 **RU:** Patriot, Gave material aid to the cause **CEM:** Dishman Family at Pine Hill; GPS unk; Off Rt 621, Shiloh; King George **GS:** Y **SP:** Mar (1830) Susanna Baker (1750 Tudex, King George Co) **VI:** No further data **P:** N **BLW:** N **RG:** N **MK:** N **PH:** unk **SS:** ALCom Bk pg 334 **BS:** 60 King George; 196.

DISHMAN, Sarah; b 1712; d 1782 **RU:** Patriot, Gave material aid to the cause **CEM:** Dishman Family; GPS unk; Pine Hill Hunt Club; Essex **GS:** Y **SP:** No info **VI:** No further data **P:** N **BLW:** N **RG:** Y **MK:** N **PH:** unk **SS:** AL Ct Bk pg 7 Essex Co; AS; SAR applic **BS:** SAR Appl.

DIUGUID, George; b Oct 1762, Buckingham Co; d Aft 10 Sep 1832 **RU:** Private, Served in Capts Robert Hews', William Poor's, & David Patterson's Cos **CEM:** Diuguid; GPS unk; On Barry Jones Farm near Rt 460, on Co Rd 757, btw Concord & Lynchburg City; Campbell **GS:** U **SP:** Nancy Simpson **VI:** No further data **P:** unk **BLW:** unk **RG:** Y **MK:** Y **PH:** unk **SS:** DD **BS:** JLARC 1, 3, 4, 36.

DIVERS, George; b 1747; d 2 May 1830 **RU:** Paymaster/Patriot, Served in the 14th VA Regt, and resigned 28 Apr 1777. Paid Personal Property Tax Albemarle Co yrs 1782 and 1783 (considered as supply tax for Rev War expenses) **CEM:** Castle Hill; GPS 38.05683,-78.31828; 1625 Country Club Dr, can be seen 150 yds E of Wood Ln, Farmington; Albemarle **GS:** Y **SP:** Mar (1780) Martha Walker (2 May 1760, Albemarle Co-1829) d/o Thomas & Mildred (Thornton) Walker **VI:** No further data **P:** N **BLW:** N **RG:** unk **MK:** unk **PH:** unk **SS:** E pg 227 **BS:** 196.

DIVET, Henri; b unk; d 1781 **RU:** Seaman, Served on "Hector" and died from Yorktown battle **CEM:** French Memorial; GPS 36.81944, -79.39933; Yorktown; York **GS:** U **SP:** No info **VI:** No further data **P:** unk **BLW:** unk **RG:** Y **MK:** unk **PH:** unk **SS:** J-Yorktown Historian **BS:** JLARC 1, 74.

DIXON, James; b 1748 or 14 Feb 1749, Carlisle, Cumberland Co, PA; d 1786 **RU:** Captain, Served in Bedford Co Militia **CEM:** Dixon Family; GPS 37.18420, -79.59310; Off Rt 658, Concord quadrant, nr Rustburg; Campbell **GS:** U **SP:** 1) Elizabeth (-----) 2) Mar (18 Aug 1776 Bedford Co) Susanna Helm **VI:** Son of Thomas Dixon & Mary Ann Dinwiddie Bell **P:** unk **BLW:** unk **RG:** unk **MK:** N **PH:** unk **SS:** E pg 227 **BS:** JLARC 36.

DIXON, John; b unk; d 1777 **RU:** Patriot, Gave material aid to the cause **CEM:** Trinity Episcopal; GPS 37.41069, -76.33578; Off Rt 614 nr jct Khyber Pass Trail; Mathews **GS:** U **SP:** No info **VI:** Son of John (of Bristol) & Lucy (Reade) (of Gloucester) Dixon **P:** N **BLW:** N **RG:** N **MK:** N **PH:** unk **SS:** AL Ct Bk pg ii **BS:** 124 pg 117; 196.

DOAK, David D; b 1752; d 16 Jan 1829 **RU:** Patriot, Provided use of horses for 23 days. Was collector of public tax 1782,1783 **CEM:** Black Lick Rural Retreat; GPS 36.94435, -81.24377; 2390 Black Lick Rd; Wythe **GS:** U **SP:** Mary Hanna (Polly) (1753-19 Aug 1829) **VI:** No further data **P:** N **BLW:** N **RG:** unk **MK:** unk **PH:** unk **SS:** CL pg 125; Public Service Claims Augusta Co pg 12 **BS:** 196.

DOAK, David Sr; b 1710; d 2 Oct 1787 **RU:** Patriot, Gave material aid to the cause in Augusta Co **CEM:** Black Lick Rural Retreat; GPS 36.94435, -81.24377; 2390 Black Lick Rd; Wythe **GS:** U **SP:** Mar (1745) Mary Breckinridge (1736-__) **VI:** DAR indicates he was also a soldier in the Montgomery Co Militia

RU=Rank/Unit   CEM=Cemetery   GS=Gravestone   SP=Spousal Information
VI=Other Veteran Info   P=Pension   BLW=Bounty/Land Warrant   RG=Registered Grave
MK=SAR/DAR Marker   PH=Photo   SS=Service Source   BS=Burial Source

95

under Capt John Ward, however doubtful because would be too old **P:** N **BLW:** N **RG:** unk **MK:** unk **PH:** unk **SS:** AL Ct Bk pg 15 Augusta Co **BS:** 196.

DOAK, Joseph; b unk; d unk **RU:** Second Lieutenant, Served in Montgomery Co Militia 6 Nov 1781 **CEM:** Black Lick Rural Retreat; GPS 36.94435, -81.24377; 2390 Black Lick Rd; Wythe **GS:** U **SP:** No info **VI:** No further data **P:** unk **BLW:** unk **RG:** unk **MK:** unk **PH:** unk **SS:** E pg 203 **BS:** JLARC 122.

DOAK, Robert; b 1751, Greenville, Augusta Co; d 12 Mar 1832 **RU:** Colonel, Capt of a Tazewell Co Co which fought at Battle of Point Pleasant Oct 1774 **CEM:** Bethel Presbyterian; GPS 38.04257, -79.17283; 563 Bethel Green Rd, Middlebrook; Augusta **GS:** Y **SP:** 1) Mar (28 Mar 1774 Augusta Co) Elizabeth Mitchell, (__-25 Dec 1824 Greenville, Augusta Co) 2) Mar (24 Aug 1826) Ann Tempelton McGuffin (c1780-1866 elsewhere) **VI:** Son of Samuel and Jane (Mitchell) Doak Sr. of Ireland. Source indicates served in Capt James Tate's Co of VA Militia 12 Mar 1832 on date of death, but doubtful. Bethel Presbyterian Church sign says was built by Elder Doak in 1779. Member VA House of Delegates 1812, raised troops 1813, high sheriff of Co. Died in Greenville, Augusta Co **P:** no **BLW:** no **RG:** Y **MK:** Y **PH:** Y **SS:** B; CD; Z pg 169 **BS:** JLARC 2, 8, 62, 63; 196.

DOAK, Samuel; b 1746; d 1826 **RU:** Ensign, Served in Montgomery Co Militia 8 Sep 1779. **CEM:** Bethel Presbyterian; GPS 38.04257, -79.17283; 563 Bethel Green Rd, Middlebrook; Augusta **GS:** N **SP:** No info **VI:** No further data **P:** unk **BLW:** unk **RG:** unk **MK:** unk **PH:** N **SS:** E pg 227 **BS:** JLARC 62.

DOAK, William; b unk; d unk **RU:** Captain, Served in Montgomery Co Militia. Resigned 6 Nov 1781 **CEM:** Black Lick Rural Retreat; GPS 36.94435, -81.24377; 2390 Black Lick Rd; Wythe **GS:** U **SP:** No info **VI:** No further data **P:** unk **BLW:** unk **RG:** unk **MK:** unk **PH:** unk **SS:** E pg 227 **BS:** JLARC 122.

DOAK (DOACK), David; b 9 Dec 1740; d aft 1784 **RU:** Patriot, Gave use of horse 23 days and 6 days public hire **CEM:** North Mountain; GPS unk; 7 mi S of Staunton on N side Rt 252; Augusta **GS:** U **SP:** Jenet Davis **VI:** Son of Samuel & Jane (Mitchell) Doak. Name on monument in cemetery **P:** N **BLW:** N **RG:** unk **MK:** unk **PH:** unk **SS:** Al Ct Bk pg 15 and certificates **BS:** 73; 196.

DOBLER, Jacob; b 20 May 1764; d 7 Feb 1820 **RU:** Private, Served in Capt Robert Doad's Co of Militia, Jun 1774 **CEM:** Dobler Family; GPS unk; nr Kimbersville; Wythe **GS:** Y **SP:** No info **VI:** No further data **P:** unk **BLW:** unk **RG:** N **MK:** N **PH:** unk **SS:** Z pg 79-80 **BS:** 140 Doblerhome.

DOGAN, Henry; b 23 Nov 1759; d 20 Dec 1823 **RU:** Soldier, Served in Capt George Rice Co, Nov 1778. Served in 7th, 11th & 15th Cont Lines **CEM:** Stonewall Memory Gardens; GPS 38.81530, -77.55170; 12004 Lee Hwy; Manassas City **GS:** U **SP:** Mar (11 Nov 1782) Mary Wheeler (4 Jul 1765-9 Jan 1832 Groveton, Prince William Co) d/o Drummond & (-----) Wheeler **VI:** SAR and DAR marker **P:** unk **BLW:** unk **RG:** unk **MK:** Y **PH:** Y **SS:** E pg 228 **BS:** JLARC 2, 3, 95; 196.

DOMINO, Jean; b unk; d 1781 **RU:** Soldier, Served in Gatinais Bn and died fr battle at Yorktown **CEM:** French Memorial; GPS 36.81944, -79.39933; Yorktown; York **GS:** U **SP:** No info **VI:** No further data **P:** unk **BLW:** unk **RG:** Y **MK:** unk **PH:** unk **SS:** J-Yorktown Historian **BS:** JLARC 1, 74.

DONALDSON, Robert; b 4 Mar 1764, Fayetteville Co, NC; d 1 Jul 1808 **RU:** Private, Served in Capt Charles Polk's Co of Foot in NC **CEM:** Blandford; GPS 37.22433, -77.38604; 319 S Crater Rd; Petersburg City **GS:** Y **SP:** No info **VI:** Was a merchant in Petersburg **P:** unk **BLW:** unk **RG:** N **MK:** N **PH:** unk **SS:** AP roll NC Militia **BS:** 128 Donaldson; 213 pg 33.

DONOHOE, John V; b 16 May 1761; d 4 Dec 1821 **RU:** Corporal, Served in 8th Cont Line **CEM:** Mountain Chapel; GPS unk; Jct Rts 734 & 630; Loudoun **GS:** Y **SP:** No info **VI:** No further data **P:** unk **BLW:** unk **RG:** Y **MK:** N **PH:** unk **SS:** E pg 231 **BS:** 25 pg 83.

DORTON, William Jr; b 1750; d 1826 **RU:** Captain, Served in Washington Co Militia **CEM:** Dorton; GPS unk; Rt 71 near Dickensonville; Russell **GS:** U **SP:** Mary (-----) **VI:** No further data **P:** unk **BLW:** unk **RG:** unk **MK:** unk **PH:** unk **SS:** NSSAR Ancestor #P-149447 **BS:** JLARC 81.

DOUGHERTY (DOUGHTY), Edward; b c1750; d 6 Feb 1801 **RU:** Private, Served in Capt Robert Burns's Co, Col Moses Hazens's Regt, Jan 1779 **CEM:** Sanderson Home; GPS unk; Near NC line; Norfolk City **GS:** Y **SP:** No info **VI:** No further data **P:** N **BLW:** N **RG:** N **MK:** unk **PH:** unk **SS:** AP payroll Fold 3 **BS:** 75 pg 92.

RU=Rank/Unit   CEM=Cemetery   GS=Gravestone   SP=Spousal Information
VI=Other Veteran Info   P=Pension   BLW=Bounty/Land Warrant   RG=Registered Grave
MK=SAR/DAR Marker   PH=Photo   SS=Service Source   BS=Burial Source

96

DOUGLAS, William; b c1752; d 1803 **RU:** Seaman, Served on the "Dragon" 22 Oct 1777-16 Dec 1777 **CEM:** St Paul's Episcopal; **GPS** 36.84733, -76.28554; 201 St Paul's Blvd; Norfolk City **GS:** Y **SP:** No info **VI:** No further data **P:** unk **BLW:** unk **RG:** N **MK:** N **PH:** unk **SS:** L pg 182 **BS:** 87 pg 26.

DOUGLAS (DOUGLASS), Hugh; b 1760; d 1815 **RU:** Captain, Served in Loudoun Co Militia May 1781 **CEM:** St James Episcopal, Old Cemetery; **GPS** 39.11555, -77.56250; Church St NE, Leesburg; Loudoun **GS:** U **SP:** No info **VI:** No further data **P:** unk **BLW:** unk **RG:** unk **MK:** unk **PH:** unk **SS:** E pg 233 **BS:** JLARC 1, 32.

DOUGLASS, Achilles; b 22 Feb 1752; d 5 Nov 1810 **RU:** Patriot, Gave material aid to cause **CEM:** South River Meeting House; **GPS** 37.37246, -79.19194; 5810 Fort Ave; Lynchburg City **GS:** U **SP:** No info **VI:** No further data **P:** N **BLW:** N **RG:** unk **MK:** unk **PH:** unk **SS:** AL Ct Bk pg 18 Albemarle Co **BS:** 196.

DOUGLASS, Daniel; b unk; d Sep 1803 **RU:** Private, Served in Harford Co, MD, Oct 1780 **CEM:** Old Presbyterian Meeting House; **GPS** 38.48528, -77.23532; 323 S Fairfax St; Alexandria City **GS:** N **SP:** No info **VI:** Died of bilious fever age 35, bur 7 Sep 1803 **P:** unk **BLW:** unk **RG:** N **MK:** N **PH:** N **SS:** AP roll **BS:** 23 pg 102.

DOUGLASS, John; b unk; d 1776 **RU:** Scout, Killed by Indians on way back fr Black's fort to warn settlement at Castle Woods of impending attack **CEM:** John Douglass; **GPS** unk; 100 yds N of John B Douglass Wayside Rt 19, 9 mi N of Abingdon; Washington **GS:** Y **SP:** No info **VI:** DAR monument erected 1929 **P:** unk **BLW:** unk **RG:** N **MK:** Y **PH:** unk **SS:** AR Vol 1 pg 264 **BS:** 78 pg 142.

DOVE, William; b 27 Nov 1758, Charles Co, MD; d 20 Sep 1847 **RU:** Sergeant, Served in Capt Thomas Co, Col Rumley Regt, Alexandria. Marched to Gen Washington's headquarters, 1777. Enl Sep 1778-Jun 1779 as Marine on ship "Gen'l Washington" to France, Spain; enl again Mar 1780 same vessel to Holland; again Jul 1781-Oct 1781 under Capt Powell **CEM:** George Family; **GPS** 36.58210,-79.19222; Gretna; Pittsylvania **GS:** Y **SP:** Mary Baker (1745 Culpeper Co-__) **VI:** Son of Joseph & Mary (-----) Dove. Moved to Fairfax Co as child. Moved to Pittsylvania Co after 1781 tour. Pen recd S-8336 **P:** Y **BLW:** unk **RG:** unk **MK:** unk **PH:** unk **SS:** E pg 234; G pg 263-5 **BS:** 196.

DOWNER, Ezra; b unk; d 1781 **RU:** Private, Served in CT Cont Line. Died fr battle at Yorktown **CEM:** Yorktown Victory Monument Tablet; **GPS** 38.28350, -78.54150; Yorktown; York **GS:** U **SP:** No info **VI:** No further data **P:** unk **BLW:** unk **RG:** unk **MK:** unk **PH:** unk **SS:** J-Yorktown Historian; DY pg 353 **BS:** JLARC 74.

DOWNMAN, Rawleigh; b c1719; d 18 Mar 1781 **RU:** Patriot, Gave matreial to cause for military certificates as will and inventory mentions several thousand dollars of Cont Certificates, left to his daughter Fanny Ball **CEM:** Morrattico House; **GPS** unk; Morattico House, Morattico; Lancaster **GS:** N **SP:** Fanny Ball d/o Joseph (1690-1760) & Frances (Ravenscroft) (1679-1762) Ball **VI:** Son of Rawleigh Downman (-- 1719) & Margaret Ball (1690-1758). His will bequeathed Continental certificates to be valued at £1000 specie to daughter Fanny Ball. His inventory listed £3894 in 17 Continental Certifcates. He and his wife Frances are bur in the orchard per the Downman family bible. Exact location is not known, but is vic Morattico House **P:** N **BLW:** N **RG:** unk **MK:** N **PH:** N **SS:** DT **BS:** 214.

DRAKE, James Sr; b 1725; d 1791 **RU:** Patriot, Gave material aid to cause **CEM:** St John's Episcopal; **GPS** 37.53183, -77.41958; 2401 E Broad St; Richmond City **GS:** N **SP:** No info **VI:** No further data **P:** N **BLW:** N **RG:** N **MK:** N **PH:** N **SS:** AL Ct Bk pg 25 Powhatan Co **BS:** 80 vol 1 pg 266.

DRAKE, Thomas; b 13 Jul 1728, Piscataway, Middlesex Co, NJ; d 25 Jun 1811 **RU:** Soldier/Patriot, Served in Loudoun Co Militia. Gave material aid to the cause **CEM:** Unidentified; **GPS** unk; See DAR Senate report 1961, serial #12449, vol 6 for loc; Loudoun **GS:** U **SP:** Mar (4 Mar 1760) Eurah Humphrey **VI:** Son of Jonathan (1689-1754) & Mary (Clawson) (c1696,-1762) Drake. DAR report & AR vol 1, pg 267 show cem name as Loudoun **P:** N **BLW:** N **RG:** N **MK:** N **PH:** unk **SS:** DAR Ancestor #A033498; AL Ct Bk pg 44 **BS:** 80 vol1 pg 267; 196.

DREUILHET, Dominique; b unk; d 1781 **RU:** Soldier, Served in Touraine Bn and died fr battle at Yorktown **CEM:** French Memorial; **GPS** 36.81944, -79.39933; Yorktown; York **GS:** U **SP:** No info **VI:** No further data **P:** unk **BLW:** unk **RG:** Y **MK:** unk **PH:** unk **SS:** J-Yorktown Historian **BS:** JLARC 1, 74.

RU=Rank/Unit	CEM=Cemetery	GS=Gravestone	SP=Spousal Information
VI=Other Veteran Info	P=Pension	BLW=Bounty/Land Warrant	RG=Registered Grave
MK=SAR/DAR Marker	PH=Photo	SS=Service Source	BS=Burial Source

97

DRISKILL, Daniel; b unk; d 1813 **RU:** Soldier, Served in KY Milita **CEM:** Driskill; GPS unk; SE of Rt 40, Dog Creek; Campbell **GS:** U **SP:** Anne (-----) **VI:** No further data **P:** unk **BLW:** unk **RG:** unk **MK**: N **PH:** unk **SS:** E pg 237 **BS:** JLARC 36.

DRUMMOND, William; b c1765; d 1804 or 14 Oct 1809 **RU:** Patriot, Was town Alderman during war period **CEM:** Masonic Cemetery; GPS 38.30198, -77.46142; 900 Charles St; Fredericksburg City **GS:** Y **SP:** No info **VI:** Wine merchant and trustee of Fredericksburg Charity school **P:** N **BLW:** N **RG:** Y **MK**: N **PH:** unk **SS:** 08 Vol 3 pg 421 **BS:** 08 vol 3 pg 421.

DRYDEN, James Jr; b 1730; d 1792 **RU:** Soldier/Patriot, Was in Battle at Kings Mountain 1780 in Col Campbell's Regt. Gave material aid to cause **CEM:** Dryden Family; GPS unk; See DAR Senate Doc 1958 serial 12259, vol 4; Rockbridge **GS:** U **SP:** No info **VI:** DAR source AR vol 1 pg 268 and SAR gives name of cem as Rockbridge **P:** unk **BLW:** unk **RG:** unk **MK**: unk **PH:** unk **SS:** DAR Ancestor #A033893; J- DAR Hatcher; AL Ct Bk pg 4 Rockbridge Co **BS:** JLARC 2.

DUBEAU, Pierre; b unk; d 1781 **RU:** Seaman, Served on "Auguste" and died from Yorktown battle **CEM:** French Memorial; GPS 36.81944, -79.39933; Yorktown; York **GS:** U **SP:** No info **VI:** No further data **P:** unk **BLW:** unk **RG:** Y **MK**: unk **PH:** unk **SS:** J-Yorktown Historian **BS:** JLARC 1, 74.

DUBOURG, Nicolas; b unk; d 1781 **RU:** Soldier, Served in Soissonnais Bn and died fr battle at Yorktown **CEM:** French Memorial; GPS 36.81944, -79.39933; Yorktown; York **GS:** U **SP:** No info **VI:** No further data **P:** unk **BLW:** unk **RG:** Y **MK**: unk **PH:** unk **SS:** J-Yorktown Historian **BS:** JLARC 1, 74.

DUCROS, Lue; b unk; d 1781 **RU:** Soldier, Served in Santogne Bn and died fr battle at Yorktown **CEM:** French Memorial; GPS 36.81944, -79.39933; Yorktown; York **GS:** U **SP:** No info **VI:** No further data **P:** unk **BLW:** unk **RG:** Y **MK**: unk **PH:** unk **SS:** J-Yorktown Historian **BS:** JLARC 1, 74.

DUFF, Robert; b 23 Jun 1759, County Antrim, Northern Ireland; d 20 Jun 1820 **RU:** Private, Served in Capt David Clarks Co 138th PA Militia Regt **CEM:** Duff family; GPS unk; 3.2 mi E on Rt 612, fr jct Rts 58E and 421 E, Stickleyville; Lee **GS:** Y **SP:** Mary Powell Dickenson (15 Mar 1770-20 Dec 1859) **VI:** No further data **P:** unk **BLW:** unk **RG:** unk **MK**: unk **PH:** unk **SS:** CI PA Archives Vol X pg 109 **BS:** 196.

DUFF, Samuel; b 1745; d 1824 **RU:** Private, Was in Kings Mountain Battle in Capt David Beatie's Co **CEM:** Green Spring Presbyterian; GPS 36.63670, -81.99560; 2007 Green Spring Ch Rd, Abingdon; Washington **GS:** U **SP:** No info **VI:** No further data **P:** unk **BLW:** unk **RG:** unk **MK**: unk **PH:** unk **SS:** J-DAR Hatcher; N pg 1241 **BS:** JLARC 2.

DUFFEL, Edward; b 1754; d 1835 **RU:** Private, Was POW of British during RW **CEM:** Old City; GPS 37.41472, -79.15667; 401 Taylor St; Lynchburg City **GS:** U **SP:** No info **VI:** No further data **P:** unk **BLW:** unk **RG:** unk **MK**: unk **PH:** unk **SS:** BT Blud Ridge Chapter NS DAR **BS:** JLARC 4; 196.

DUFFEL, James C; b 1761; d 1835 **RU:** Corporal, Served in 5th & 11th Cont Lines **CEM:** Old City; GPS 37.41472, -79.15667; 401 Taylor St; Lynchburg City **GS:** U **SP:** No info **VI:** No further data **P:** unk **BLW:** unk **RG:** unk **MK**: unk **PH:** unk **SS:** AR Vol 1 pg 270 **BS:** JLARC 2.

DUFOUR, Charles; b unk; d 1781 **RU:** Soldier, Served in Gatinais Bn and died fr battle at Yorktown **CEM:** French Memorial; GPS 36.81944, -79.39933; Yorktown; York **GS:** U **SP:** No info **VI:** No further data **P:** unk **BLW:** unk **RG:** Y **MK**: unk **PH:** unk **SS:** J-Yorktown Historian **BS:** JLARC 1, 74.

DUFUT, Michel; b unk; d 1781 **RU:** Soldier, Served in Gatinais Bn and died fr battle at Yorktown **CEM:** French Memorial; GPS 36.81944, -79.39933; Yorktown; York **GS:** U **SP:** No info **VI:** No further data **P:** unk **BLW:** unk **RG:** Y **MK**: unk **PH:** unk **SS:** J-Yorktown Historian **BS:** JLARC 1, 74.

DUGUE, Joseph; b unk; d 1781 **RU:** Seaman, Served on "Ville de Paris" and died from Yorktown battle **CEM:** French Memorial; GPS 36.81944, -79.39933; Yorktown; York **GS:** U **SP:** No info **VI:** No further data **P:** unk **BLW:** unk **RG:** Y **MK**: unk **PH:** unk **SS:** J-Yorktown Historian **BS:** JLARC 1, 74.

DULAC, Jean; b unk; d 1781 **RU:** Seaman, Served on "Auguste" and died from Yorktown battle **CEM:** French Memorial; GPS 36.81944, -79.39933; Yorktown; York **GS:** U **SP:** No info **VI:** No further data **P:** unk **BLW:** unk **RG:** Y **MK**: unk **PH:** unk **SS:** J-Yorktown Historian **BS:** JLARC 1, 74.

RU=Rank/Unit	CEM=Cemetery	GS=Gravestone	SP=Spousal Information
VI=Other Veteran Info	P=Pension	BLW=Bounty/Land Warrant	RG=Registered Grave
MK=SAR/DAR Marker	PH=Photo	SS=Service Source	BS=Burial Source

DULANEY, John; b 27 Jun 1747; d 1817 **RU:** Patriot, Gave material aid to cause **CEM:** Dulaney Family; GPS unk; See DAR Senate Doc1956, serial # 11999; vol 8; Fairfax **GS:** U **SP:** Mar (5 Mar 1773) Susannah Watts **VI:** Died in Culpeper Co **P:** N **BLW:** N **RG:** unk **MK:** N **PH:** unk **SS:** J- DAR Hatcher; AL Ct Bk I pg 45 Culpeper Co; AR pg 270 **BS:** JLARC 2.

DUMONT, Denis; b unk; d 1781 **RU:** Soldier, Served in Gatinais Bn and died fr battle at Yorktown **CEM:** French Memorial; GPS 36.81944, -79.39933; Yorktown; York **GS:** U **SP:** No info **VI:** No further data **P:** unk **BLW:** unk **RG:** Y **MK:** unk **PH:** unk **SS:** J-Yorktown Historian **BS:** JLARC 1, 74.

DUNCAN, Andrew; b 1761; d 1826 **RU:** Private, Served in Capt Edward's Co, Montgomery Co Militia **CEM:** Shockoe Hill; GPS 37.55190, -77.43170; 4th & Hospital Sts; Richmond City **GS:** U **SP:** No info **VI:** Bur on 13 Nov 1826. Age at death: 85 **P:** N **BLW:** N **RG:** N **MK:** N **PH:** N **SS:** G pg 224 **BS:** 196.

DUNCAN, Charles; b 1738, Strathblane Parish, Scotland; d 29 Jan 1808 **RU:** Patriot, Gave material aid to the cause **CEM:** Duncan Family; GPS unk; Roslyn Ave, 2 mi E of Town Hall, Chester; Chesterfield **GS:** Y **SP:** Elizabeth Peachy(---, 09 Jun 1806) **VI:** Died in his 70th yr while visiting a daughter in London, England. Bur at church at Hampstead in Middlesex. Memorial stone **P:** N **BLW:** N **RG:** unk **MK:** N **PH:** unk **SS:** Al CT Bk Chesterfield Co pg 16, 55 **BS:** 196.

DUNCAN, Charles; b 1712, Perth and Kinross, Scotland; d 1780 **RU:** Patriot, Gave material aid to the cause **CEM:** Duncan; GPS 38.59068, -77.96277; Nr Oakshade; Culpeper **GS:** N **SP:** No info **VI:** Son of Henry (1664-1725) and Rebekkah Grace (Elson) (1684-1744) Duncan **P:** N **BLW:** N **RG:** unk **MK:** unk **PH:** N **SS:** AL Ct Bk 1 Culpeper Co pg 13, 46, 47 **BS:** 196.

DUNCAN, George; b 1730, Scotland; d 1783 **RU:** Captain, Promoted to Capt, Fluvanna Co Militia in Sep 1777 **CEM:** Duncan Family; GPS unk; Nr Hardware River; Fluvanna **GS:** Y **SP:** Mar (1754) Ann Hall (1732-1783) **VI:** No further data **P:** unk **BLW:** unk **RG:** N **MK:** N **PH:** unk **SS:** E pg 240 **BS:** 80 vol 1 pg 270.

DUNCAN, John; b 1741; d 1833 **RU:** Soldier, Specific service may be found at the Lib of VA in Auditor's Acct 1778-83 pg 106 **CEM:** Sumpter; GPS unk; Rt 619, Floyd; Floyd **GS:** U **SP:** Elizabeth (-----) **VI:** No further data **P:** unk **BLW:** unk **RG:** unk **MK:** unk **PH:** unk **SS:** CZ pg 146 **BS:** JLARC 4, 29.

DUNCANSON, James; b 11 Feb 1735, Scotland; d 1 Mar 1791 **RU:** Colonel/Patriot, Served in 2d VA Regt. Gave material aid to cause **CEM:** St George's Episcopal; GPS unk; 905 Princess Anne; Fredericksburg City **GS:** U **SP:** Mar (12 Jan 1766) Mary McCauley(3 Feb 1718-10 Oct 1790) **VI:** Arr in VA Jul 1752 **P:** unk **BLW:** unk **RG:** unk **MK:** unk **PH:** unk **SS:** J- DAR Hatcher; AL Ct Bk 1 pg 24, 47, 50 Culpeper Co; DD **BS:** JLARC 2; 213 pg 577.

DUNGAN (DUNCAN), Elisha; b 1735, Bucks Co, PA; d 1 Dec 1808 **RU:** Patriot, Was member of Road Committee and Juror, Washington Co **CEM:** St Clair Bottom Primitive Baptist; GPS 36.76098, -81.64556; Jct Rts 600 & 660, Chilhowie; Smyth **GS:** U **SP:** Mar (1760) Hannah Rogers (__-1800 Clair's Bottom) **VI:** Died in Washington Co **P:** N **BLW:** N **RG:** unk **MK:** N **PH:** unk **SS:** DL Part 2 pg 1053, 1058 **BS:** JLARC 114.

DUNKIN, John Jr; b 25 Feb 1765; d 8 Apr 1832 **RU:** Sergeant, Served in 3rd & 4th Cont Lines **CEM:** Green Spring Presbyterian; GPS 36.63670, -81.99560; 2007 Green Spring Ch Rd, Abingdon; Washington **GS:** U **SP:** Mary Laughlin (20 Jul 1767 KY_22 Feb 1846, Lineville, VA) **VI:** Son of John Sr (1735-27 Oct 1740 Abingdon) & (-----) Dunkin. Died in Kentucky **P:** unk **BLW:** unk **RG:** unk **MK:** unk **PH:** unk **SS:** J- DAR Hatcher; E pg 241 **BS:** JLARC 2; 80 vol 1 pg 272.

DUNKIN, John Thomas; b 1743, Lancaster Co, PA; d 6 Aug 1818 **RU:** Captain, Promoted to Capt 1777 in Washington Co Militia. Was Sgt in 3rd & 4th Cont Lines **CEM:** Green Spring Presbyterian; GPS 36.63670, -81.99560; 2007 Green Spring Ch Rd, Abingdon; Washington **GS:** U **SP:** Eleanor Sharp **VI:** Son of (-----) & Elizabeth (Alexander) (1710-1814) Dunkin. POW in Quebec **P:** unk **BLW:** unk **RG:** unk **MK:** Y **PH:** Y **SS:** E pg 241; BT USDAR Gr Mkr **BS:** 80 vol 1 pg 272.

DUNLOP, John; b 1756; d 1806 **RU:** Private, Served in Capt Durval Harrison Co, in 2nd VA Regt **CEM:** Old Presbyterian Meeting House; GPS 38.48528, -77.23532; 323 S Fairfax St; Alexandria City **GS:** N **SP:** No info **VI:** Died after a lingering illness age 50, bur 2 Nov 1806. Listed on an SAR plaque in

RU=Rank/Unit   CEM=Cemetery   GS=Gravestone   SP=Spousal Information
VI=Other Veteran Info   P=Pension   BLW=Bounty/Land Warrant   RG=Registered Grave
MK=SAR/DAR Marker   PH=Photo   SS=Service Source   BS=Burial Source

99

cemetery **P:** unk **BLW:** unk **RG:** Y **MK**: Y **PH:** N **SS:** J-NSSAR 1993 Reg; AP roll; AK **BS:** JLARC 1; 23 pg 102; 196.

DUNN, John; b 1750; d 11 Apr 1827 **RU:** Private, Served 3 yrs **CEM:** St James Episcopal, Old Cemetery; GPS 39.11555, -77.56250; Church St NE, Leesburg; Loudoun **GS:** Y **SP:** No info **VI:** Rector of St James Episcopal Church nearly 25 yrs. Was a Mason **P:** unk **BLW:** unk **RG:** Y **MK:** N **PH:** unk **SS:** C Sec III pg 420 **BS:** 25 pg 87.

DUNN, William; b 1748; d 25 Dec 1787 **RU:** Corporal, Served in 9th & 13th Cont Line **CEM:** Old Christ Church Episcopal; GPS 38.80625, -77.04718; 118 N Washington St; Alexandria City **GS:** Y **SP:** No info **VI:** Died age 39 **P:** unk **BLW:** unk **RG:** Y **MK:** unk **PH:** unk **SS:** J-NSSAR 1993 Reg; E pg 242 **BS:** JLARC 1; 20 pg 137; 196.

DUPLAT, Michel; b unk; d 1781 **RU:** Seaman, Served on "Diademe" and died from Yorktown battle **CEM:** French Memorial; GPS 36.81944, -79.39933; Yorktown; York **GS:** U **SP:** No info **VI:** No further data **P:** unk **BLW:** unk **RG:** Y **MK:** unk **PH:** unk **SS:** J-Yorktown Historian **BS:** JLARC 1, 74.

DUPREX, Joseph; b unk; d 1781 **RU:** Seaman, Served on "Hector" and died from Yorktown battle **CEM:** French Memorial; GPS 36.81944, -79.39933; Yorktown; York **GS:** U **SP:** No info **VI:** No further data **P:** unk **BLW:** unk **RG:** Y **MK:** unk **PH:** unk **SS:** J-Yorktown Historian **BS:** JLARC 1, 74.

DUPUIS, Jean; b unk; d 1781 **RU:** Seaman, Served on "Diademe" and died from Yorktown battle **CEM:** French Memorial; GPS 36.81944, -79.39933; Yorktown; York **GS:** U **SP:** No info **VI:** No further data **P:** unk **BLW:** unk **RG:** Y **MK:** unk **PH:** unk **SS:** J-Yorktown Historian **BS:** JLARC 1, 74.

DUPUY, James; b 1758; d 1823 **RU:** Patriot, Signed Legislative petition **CEM:** Dupuy; GPS unk; Jennings Ordinary, NW 647 for 1 mi to Carrington home; Nottoway **GS:** U **SP:** Mary Purnall **VI:** No further data **P:** N **BLW:** N **RG:** unk **MK:** unk **PH:** unk **SS:** E pg 243 **BS:** JLARC 85.

DURAND, Pierre; b unk; d 1781 **RU:** Seaman, Served on "Saint-Esprit" and died from Yorktown battle **CEM:** French Memorial; GPS 36.81944, -79.39933; Yorktown; York **GS:** U **SP:** No info **VI:** No further data **P:** unk **BLW:** unk **RG:** Y **MK:** unk **PH:** unk **SS:** J-Yorktown Historian **BS:** JLARC 1, 74.

DUVAL, Pilip Jr; b 1758; d 1817 **RU:** Patriot, Gave material aid to the cause **CEM:** Shockoe Hill; GPS 37.55190, -77.43170; 4th & Hospital Sts; Richmond City **GS:** Y **SP:** No info **VI:** No further data **P:** N **BLW:** N **RG:** N **MK:** N **PH:** unk **SS:** AL Ct Bk pg 26 **BS:** 179 pg 131.

DYER, George; b 1753, Prince Georges Co, MD; d 1827 **RU:** Lieutenant, Served in Capt Daniel Hankins Co in the MD Cont Line. Also in Capt Charles Williamson's Co, Prince George's Co, MD **CEM:** Dyer Family; GPS 36.45261, -79.48125; Foxpipe Rd, Leatherwood; Henry **GS:** N **SP:** Rachel Dalton 1759-1862) **VI:** Son of James & Eleanoer (Brown) Dyer. Will dated 15 Mar 1823 age 70 **P:** unk **BLW:** unk **RG:** Y **MK:** N **PH:** N **SS:** Archives of MD Vol 18 pg 328; AK **BS:** 04.

EALEY, John; b unk; d by 1826 **RU:** Private?, Served in 5th, 11th, 15th Cont lines **CEM:** Eastern State Hospital; GPS 37.25560 -76.71030; S Henry Street; Williamsburg City **GS:** N **SP:** No info **VI:** His name is on a plaque in the cemetery **P:** unk **BLW:** unk **RG:** N **MK:** N **PH:** unk **SS:** E pg 245-246 **BS:** 65 Williamsburg.

EARLY, James; b 1750; d 1822 **RU:** Ensign, Served in Capt Shackleford's Co, 27 Sep 1781, Orange Co Militia **CEM:** Wakefield Cemetery; GPS unk; Wakefield Farm Rd, Earlysville; Albemarle **GS:** U **SP:** Mar (1772) Elizabeth Thompson **VI:** No further data **P:** unk **BLW:** unk **RG:** unk **MK:** unk **PH:** unk **SS:** J- DAR Hatcher; E pg 246 **BS:** JLARC 2.

EARLY, James Matten; b 1752; d 1807 **RU:** Soldier, Served in 3rd, 4th & 9th Cont Line **CEM:** Fincastle Presbyterian; GPS 37.50017, -79.87558; 108 E Back St, Fincastle; Botetourt **GS:** N **SP:** Mar (c1780 in Albemarle Co) Jane Gatewood (1758-9 Mar 1832, Benton, Franklin Co., IL) d/o William & Ann (Ronsom) Gatewood of Albemarle Co **VI:** Name is on the SAR plaque at this cemetery. His cabin built ca 1796 serves today as loc of the Fincastle Museum **P:** unk **BLW:** unk **RG:** unk **MK:** Y **PH:** N **SS:** AR Vol 2 pg 2; E pg 246, J-NSSAR 1993 Reg, J- DAR Hatcher **BS:** 196; JLARC 1, 2.

EARLY, Jeremiah; b 1730; d 1779 **RU:** Colonel/Patriot, Served in Bedford Co Militia. Gave material aid to cause **CEM:** Wyndholm, aka Early Family; GPS unk; Flat Creek nr Evington; Campbell **GS:** U **SP:** 1)

RU=Rank/Unit VI=Other Veteran Info MK=SAR/DAR Marker CEM=Cemetery P=Pension PH=Photo GS=Gravestone BLW=Bounty/Land Warrant SS=Service Source SP=Spousal Information RG=Registered Grave BS=Burial Source

100

Sarah (-----); 2) Mary (-----) **VI:** No further data **P:** unk **BLW:** unk **RG:** unk **MK:** N **PH:** unk **SS:** D Campbell Co **BS:** JLARC 2, 36.

EASLEY, Robert; b 2 May 1754, Cumberland Co; d 5 Dec 1814 **RU:** Soldier/Patriot, Served in 5th, 11th, 15th Cont Lines. Gave material aid to cause **CEM:** Oak Ridge; GPS 36.71912, -78.90321; Main St & Hamiliton St, South Boston; Halifax **GS:** Y **SP:** 1) Mar (1779) (-----) Jennings 2) Mar (1799) Ann Stephens **VI:** No further data **P:** unk **BLW:** unk **RG:** Y **MK:** unk **PH:** unk **SS:** D Halifax Co; DD **BS:** JLARC 1, 2, 4.

EAST, Thomas; b 1740, Henrico Co; d Aft 17 Jul 1797 **RU:** Patriot, Took oath of Allegiance, Pittsylvania Co **CEM:** Alta Vista Plantation; GPS unk; Altavista; Pittsylvania **GS:** Y **SP:** Mar (1761) Obedience (-----) (__-19 Oct 1807) **VI:** No further data **P:** N **BLW:** N **RG:** N **MK:** N **PH:** unk **SS:** AR DAR report; BV Thomas Dillard's list **BS:** 80 vol 2 pg 2.

EASTHAM, George; b unk; d 1 Jan 1841 **RU:** Patriot, Served as wagoner for Militia **CEM:** Eastman Family; GPS unk; Jct Rts 17 & 660; Fauquier **GS:** Y **SP:** No info **VI:** No further data **P:** N **BLW:** N **RG:** Y **MK:** N **PH:** unk **SS:** D Fauquier pg 5 **BS:** 19 pg 50.

EASTON, William; b unk; d unk **RU:** Sergeant, Served in Capt William Motte Co in Col Francis Marion's SC Regt, 1 Nov 1779. Later promoted to Sgt in Hazen's Corps **CEM:** Eastin Family; GPS unk; Rt 601; Fluvanna **GS:** Y **SP:** No info **VI:** Recd BLW **P:** unk **BLW:** Y **RG:** N **MK:** N **PH:** unk **SS:** A pg 114 **BS:** 66 pg 26.

EDMON, Maurice; b unk; d 1781 **RU:** Soldier, Served in Touraine Bn and died fr battle at Yorktown **CEM:** French Memorial; GPS 36.81944, -79.39933; Yorktown; York **GS:** U **SP:** No info **VI:** No further data **P:** unk **BLW:** unk **RG:** Y **MK:** unk **PH:** unk **SS:** J-Yorktown Historian **BS:** JLARC 1, 74.

EDMONDS, Elias Jr; b 1756; d Aft 1828 **RU:** Captain, Served in Fauquier Co Militia 1776-1777 **CEM:** Oak Springs; GPS unk; 770 Fletcher Dr; Fauquier **GS:** N **SP:** A man of this name mar (11 Jan 1786 Fauquier Co, Simon Morgan security) Frances Edmonds **VI:** No further data **P:** unk **BLW:** unk **RG:** Y **MK:** N **PH:** N **SS:** AV; Fauquier Co Marriages pg 56 **BS:** 83, Inv # NF-20.

EDMONDS, John; b 1737, Lancaster Co; d 1798 **RU:** Lieutenant/Captain, Served in 9th Cont Line **CEM:** Oak Springs; GPS unk; 770 Fletcher Dr; Fauquier **GS:** N **SP:** 1) Francis Jane Wildly (Wilder) 2) Helen Hack (nee Shepard, noted English actress) widow of Hack of Hacks Neck, VA. A John Edmonds Jr. mar (5 Jun 1793 (bond) Fauquier Co) Naomi Hicks d/o Kimble & (-----) Hicks **VI:** No further data **P:** unk **BLW:** unk **RG:** Y **MK:** N **PH:** N **SS:** E pg 248; AK; AV; Fauquier Co Marriages pg 56 **BS:** 04; 83, Inv # NF-20.

EDMONDS, William; b 1734 or 1736, Lancaster Co; d 19 Feb 1816 **RU:** Colonel, Served in 1st Bn of Fauquier Co Militia. Was in 1st battle of Revolution fought on VA soil at Great Bridge, VA Dec 1775. Recd 24 Mar 1778 as Maj and as Lt Col Aug 1781. Served in 1st Bn Fauquier Co Militia. Resigned May 1783 **CEM:** Edmonds Family; GPS unk; Warrenton; Fauquier **GS:** Y **SP:** Mar (16 mar 1764 Fauquier Co, William Blackwell security) Elizabeth Blackwell (1742-28 Feb 1817) **VI:** Also has a stone placed at Warrenton Cem by his daughter **P:** unk **BLW:** unk **RG:** unk **MK:** unk **PH:** unk **SS:** AK; Fauquier Co Marriages pg 56 **BS:** 04; JLARC 16.

EDWARDS, Ambrose; b 17 Feb 1747, Albemarle Co; d 1812 **RU:** Patriot, Gave material aid to the cause **CEM:** Leatherwood Plantation; GPS 36.44534, -79.4558; Nr Martinsville; Henry **GS:** U **SP:** Mar (15 Mar 1774) Olive Martin (1754-1826) **VI:** No further data **P:** N **BLW:** N **RG:** unk **MK:** unk **PH:** unk **SS:** NSSAR Ancestor #P-153293; AR Vol 2 pg 7 **BS:** JLARC 2.

EDWARDS, Ambrose; b c1726, England; d Dec 1810 **RU:** Patriot, Gave material aid to the cause **CEM:** Edwards Family; GPS unk; Cherry Grove; King William **GS:** U **SP:** 1) Mar (1750) Wealthean Butler (__-22 Dec 1800) 2) Barbara Finch **VI:** No further data **P:** N **BLW:** N **RG:** N **MK:** N **PH:** unk **SS:** AL Ct Bk pg 20 **BS:** 86 pg 43.

EDWARDS, Benjamin; b c1758; d Aft 1835 **RU:** Private, Served in VA State Line for 3 yrs **CEM:** Wright Family; GPS 36.97658, -80.21693; Pizarro off Rt 668; Floyd **GS:** U **SP:** No info **VI:** Memorialized by DAR plaque in cem. Pensioned per 1835 list at age 77. BLW of 299 acres issued 1 May 1783 **P:** Y **BLW:** Y **RG:** unk **MK:** Y **PH:** unk **SS:** E pg 250; F pg 25 **BS:** 196 for John Mitchell.

RU=Rank/Unit   CEM=Cemetery   GS=Gravestone   SP=Spousal Information
VI=Other Veteran Info   P=Pension   BLW=Bounty/Land Warrant   RG=Registered Grave
MK=SAR/DAR Marker   PH=Photo   SS=Service Source   BS=Burial Source

101

EDWARDS, Elias; b 1753; d 1830 **RU:** Lieutenant Colonel, Commanded 3rd VA Regt **CEM:** North End; GPS 36.77234, -80.73866; 101 Beaver Dam Rd, Hillsville; Carroll **GS:** U **SP:** No info **VI:** No further data **P:** unk **BLW:** unk **RG:** N **MK:** N **PH:** unk **SS:** E pg 255; CI pensions of soldiers **BS:** 123 pg 67.

EDWARDS, Isaac; b 25 Dec 1747; d 29 Jul 1825 **RU:** Private, Specific service may be found at the Lib of VA in Auditor's Acct Bk XXII, pg 19. **CEM:** North End; GPS 36.77234, -80.73866; 101 Beaver Dam Rd, Hillsville; Carroll **GS:** Y **SP:** Mar (27 Jan 1769, Rowan Co, NC) Catherine Rosanna Boone (1 Feb 1755 Guilford Co, NC-Feb 1835 Grayson Co) **VI:** Son of Thomas Hanuel (1706-1768) & Eleanor (Scaif) Edwards. Died in Grayson Co. Illegible stone has DAR marker mounted on it **P:** unk **BLW:** unk **RG:** unk **MK:** Y **PH:** unk **SS:** E pg 250; CZ pg 137 **BS:** JLARC 43; 196.

EFFINGER, John Ignatius; b 4 Dec 1756, Mannheim, Germany; d 1 Sep 1839 **RU:** Sergeant, Served in Capt Bartholomew Von Heers Co of Dragoons, PA Line **CEM:** St Paul's Reformed Church; GPS 38.87780, -78.50663; Cnr S Church St & E South St, Woodstock; Shenandoah **GS:** U **SP:** 1) Ann Catherine Spatz 2) Barbara Cook **VI:** Pensioned in 1828. Died in Woodstock **P:** Y **BLW:** unk **RG:** Y **MK:** unk **PH:** unk **SS:** J-NSSAR 1993 Reg; DD **BS:** JLARC 1; 196.

EGE, Jacob; b 13 Mar 1754; d 6 Oct 1795 **RU:** Patriot, Gave material aid to cause **CEM:** St John's Episcopal; GPS 37.53183, -77.41958; 2401 E Broad St; Richmond City **GS:** Y **SP:** Elizah W(-----) (14 Feb 1746-8 Jan 1829) **VI:** No further data **P:** N **BLW:** N **RG:** N **MK:** N **PH:** unk **SS:** D Vol II pg 499; AL Ct Bk pg 7 Henrico Co **BS:** 28 pg 439; 196.

EGE, Samuel; b 22 Jan 1742, Germany; d 11 Feb 1801 **RU:** Quartermaster, Served in Richmond E Co **CEM:** St John's Episcopal; GPS 37.53183, -77.41958; 2401 E Broad St; Richmond City **GS:** Y **SP:** Mar (1777) Elizabeth Walker (14 Jan 1746-8 Jan 1829) **VI:** No further data **P:** unk **BLW:** unk **RG:** Y **MK:** Y **PH:** unk **SS:** AK; E pg 251; D vol 2 pg 500 **BS:** 04; 28 pg 439.

EGGERS, Elijah; b unk; d 17 Dec 1781 **RU:** Private, Served in Capt Samuel Pell's 4th Co, Col Courtland's 2d NY Line Regt and died fr battle at Yorktown **CEM:** Yorktown Victory Monument Tablet; GPS 38.28350, -78.54150; Yorktown; York **GS:** U **SP:** No info **VI:** No further data **P:** unk **BLW:** unk **RG:** unk **MK:** unk **PH:** unk **SS:** J-Yorktown Historian; AX pg 190 **BS:** JLARC 74.

EGGLESTON, Joseph; b 24 Nov 1754; d 13 Feb 1811 **RU:** Major, Ent serv Amelia Co 1778 while student at W&M. Served as Cavalry major in Army. Prisoner at Elizabethtown, 25 Jan 1780 **CEM:** Grub Hill; GPS 37.39940, -77.97030; Grub Hill Church Rd Rt 609; Amelia **GS:** Y **SP:** 1) Mar (17 Oct 1776 (bond)) Judith Bentley, a widow; 2) Mar (7 May 1796 (bond) Amelia Co) Judith Cary (c1766-19 Feb 1859) **VI:** BLW #675 issued 10 Aug 1789 for 5,333 acres. Widow pen Amelia Co 1848 age 82. W8687. Maj in Lee's Legion during the War; member Virginia House of Delegates, 1785 to 1788 ;member Virginia Privy Council in 1787. In 1798, he was elected to Congress to fill the vacancy caused by the resignation of William B. Giles and reelected to the Sixth Congress, serving until 1801 **P:** Y **BLW:** Y **RG:** unk **MK:** unk **PH:** unk **SS:** E pg 251; K Vol II pg 74 **BS:** JLARC 4, 55; 196.

EGRE, Paul; b unk; d 1781 **RU:** Soldier, Served in Royal Deaux Ponts Bn and died fr battle at Yorktown **CEM:** French Memorial; GPS 36.81944, -79.39933; Yorktown; York **GS:** U **SP:** Mar (25 Feb 1788) Sally Meade **VI:** No further data **P:** unk **BLW:** unk **RG:** Y **MK:** unk **PH:** unk **SS:** J-Yorktown Historian **BS:** JLARC 1, 74.

ELDRIDGE, Rolfe; b 29 Dec 1745, Prince George Co; d 1831 **RU:** Patriot, Gave material aid to the cause **CEM:** Eldridge Family; GPS unk; Fork of North & Slate Rivers; Buckingham **GS:** U **SP:** Mar (26 Nov 1773) Susanna Everard (c1760-1808 Elizabeth City Co) **VI:** County Clerk of Buckingham Co **P:** N **BLW:** N **RG:** N **MK:** N **PH:** unk **SS:** AL Ct Bk pg 7 **BS:** 173 Eldridge.

ELGIN, Francis Jr; b 1758, St Mary's Co, MD; d 6 Dec 1813 **RU:** Ensign, Took oath 9 Aug 1779 Loudoun Co Militia **CEM:** Elgin Family; GPS unk; Kingdom Farm on Evergreen Mill Rd, Sycolin, S of Leesburg; Loudoun **GS:** N **SP:** Jane Adams (1 Jul 1759 d/0 Andrew & Catherine (-----) Adams **VI:** Son of Francis Sr. & Rebecca (Cartwright) Elgin **P:** unk **BLW:** unk **RG:** unk **MK:** unk **PH:** N **SS:** E pg 252 **BS:** 196.

ELGIN, Gustavus; b 17 Sep 1754, St Mary's Co, MD; d 24 Jan 1834 **RU:** Captain, Served in Loudoun Co Militia 1780 **CEM:** Elgin Family; GPS unk; Kingdom Farm on Evergreen Mill Rd, Sycolin, S of

RU=Rank/Unit	CEM=Cemetery	GS=Gravestone	SP=Spousal Information
VI=Other Veteran Info	P=Pension	BLW=Bounty/Land Warrant	RG=Registered Grave
MK=SAR/DAR Marker	PH=Photo	SS=Service Source	BS=Burial Source

102

Leesburg; Loudoun **GS:** N **SP:** Rebecca Thrift (24 Dec 1767 Fairfax Co-9 Oct 1822) d/o Charles & Rebekah (Hamilton) Thrift **VI:** No further data **P:** unk **BLW:** unk **RG:** unk **MK:** unk **PH:** N **SS:** E pg 252 **BS:** 196.

ELGIN, Walter; b 12 Apr 1756, St Mary's Co, MD; d 9 Aug 1836 **RU:** Sergeant, Served in Loudoun Co Militia 1778 **CEM:** Elgin Family; GPS unk; Kingdom Farm on Evergreen Mill Rd, Sycolin, S of Leesburg; Loudoun **GS:** N **SP:** Diadama Pancoast (3 Apr 1768-29 Sep 1826) d/o Adin & Abigail (Boone) Pancoast **VI:** Son of Francis Sr. & Rebecca (Cartwright) Elgin **P:** Y **BLW:** N **RG:** unk **MK:** unk **PH:** N **SS:** E pg 252 **BS:** 196.

ELIE, Claude; b unk; d 1781 **RU:** Soldier, Served in Touraine Bn and died fr battle at Yorktown **CEM:** French Memorial; GPS 36.81944, -79.39933; Yorktown; York **GS:** U **SP:** No info **VI:** No further data **P:** unk **BLW:** unk **RG:** Y **MK:** unk **PH:** unk **SS:** J-Yorktown Historian **BS:** JLARC 1, 74.

ELLIOTT, William; b 20 Oct 1754; d 23 Sep 1836 **RU:** Soldier, Ent serv age 16 1771, Accomack Co. Served again Capt William Polk's Co, Col Southey Simpson's Co at Melompkin Creek **CEM:** Bradford-Burton; GPS unk; Rt 182 and Rt 605, N fr Quinby; Accomack **GS:** Y **SP:** Mar (10 Dec 1781) Anzele A. Wallace (16 Sep 1757-aft 1851) **VI:** Pen recd 1832. Widow recd pen 1851 **P:** Y **BLW:** unk **RG:** unk **MK:** unk **PH:** unk **SS:** JLARC app B; K Vol II pg 82 **BS:** JLARC 4, 5; 196.

ELLIOTT (ELLIOT), Thomas; b 14 Feb 1744; d 19 Jul 1811 **RU:** Colonel, Served in 4th Cont Line. Commanded forces at Hampton fr 23 Dec 1775-Jan 1776. Commanded 4th VA Regt of Foot 3 Sep 1776-28 Sep 1777, then resigned. Served in 4th Cont Line to 3 Sep 1776 to 28 Sep 1777 **CEM:** Shockoe Hill; GPS 37.55190, -77.43170; 4th & Hospital Sts; Richmond City **GS:** Y **SP:** Mary (-----) (c1751-12 Mar 1796) **VI:** Awarded 6666 acres BLW **P:** unk **BLW:** Y **RG:** Y **MK:** N **PH:** unk **SS:** E pg 253; CE pg 41 **BS:** 21 pg iv.

ELLIS, Jacob; b unk; d 19 Dec 1781 **RU:** Private, Served in Capt Philip DeBevier's 4th Co, Col Lewis Dubois's 5th NY Line Regt. Died fr Yorktown battle **CEM:** Yorktown Victory Monument Tablet; GPS 38.28350, -78.54150; Yorktown; York **GS:** U **SP:** No info **VI:** No further data **P:** unk **BLW:** unk **RG:** unk **MK:** unk **PH:** unk **SS:** J-Yorktown Historian; AX pg 226 **BS:** JLARC 74.

ELLIS, Josiah B; b 1745; d 1810 **RU:** Patriot, Gave material aid to cause **CEM:** Shelton-Ellis-Watts; GPS unk; Winesap Rd; Amherst **GS:** U **SP:** Jane Shelton Ellis **VI:** No further data **P:** N **BLW:** N **RG:** unk **MK:** unk **PH:** unk **SS:** AL Ct Bk pg 9, 39 Amherst Co **BS:** JLARC 115.

ELLIS, Richard; b unk; d Aft 1774 **RU:** Private, Serv in Capt John Lynch's Co, 5th MD Regt of Foot, commanded by Col William Richardson **CEM:** Fairfax City; GPS 38.84690, -77.31330; Main St & Page Ave; Fairfax City **GS:** N **SP:** No info **VI:** No further data **P:** unk **BLW:** unk **RG:** N **MK:** N **PH:** N **SS:** AP roll MD 5th R **BS:** 61 vol III pg FX-153.

ELLZEY, William; b unk, Loudoun Co; d 30 Nov 1835 **RU:** Captain, Gave material aid to the cause **CEM:** Ellzey Family; GPS unk; Rt 621, Middleton; Loudoun **GS:** Y **SP:** Mar (4 Mar 1799) Frances Hill Westwood, (26 Jun 1780 Elizabeth City Co-16 Apr 1820) d/o William (1738 Elizabeth City Co-24 Jan 1782) & Anne (Stith) (1742-1780) Westwood **VI:** No further data **P:** unk **BLW:** unk **RG:** N **MK:** N **PH:** unk **SS:** AL Cert Issued **BS:** 25 pg 90.

ELY, William; b 25 Mar 1748, PA or 1753; d 1850 **RU:** Private, Ent serv Bedford Co 1779. Served in Capt Thomas Helm's Co 15 Feb 1779. Served 18 mos Capt Hughes Woodson's & Capt Lawson's cos of Col Abraham Buford's command. Was in Battle of Hanging Rock, NC **CEM:** Russell Family; GPS unk; Rt 58 Rose Hill; Lee **GS:** Y **SP:** Rebecca Rawlings **VI:** Pensioned Lee Co 1820 age abt 80. S39493 **P:** Y **BLW:** unk **RG:** Y **MK:** Y **PH:** unk **SS:** K Vol II pg 82; AK; AP **BS:** 04, Nov 06.

ENAUD, Antoine; b unk; d 1781 **RU:** Seaman, Served on "Languedoc" and died from Yorktown battle **CEM:** French Memorial; GPS 36.81944, -79.39933; Yorktown; York **GS:** U **SP:** No info **VI:** No further data **P:** unk **BLW:** unk **RG:** Y **MK:** unk **PH:** unk **SS:** J-Yorktown Historian **BS:** JLARC 1, 74.

ENGLAND, John; b c1757 or 1 Apr 1767, Goochland Co; d 18 Mar 1840 **RU:** Private, Served in Goochland Co in Cont Line **CEM:** England; GPS 36.60323, -82.94029; Looneys Gap #14; Scott **GS:** Y **SP:** Mar (22 Feb 1786 Amherst Co) Mary Parsons (c1765-after 1846) d/o John & (-----) Parsons **VI:** Son of William and (-----) England. Pen 1833 Scott Co age 76. Died in England Valley, Scott Co. Widow pen

---

RU=Rank/Unit	CEM=Cemetery	GS=Gravestone	SP=Spousal Information
VI=Other Veteran Info	P=Pension	BLW=Bounty/Land Warrant	RG=Registered Grave
MK=SAR/DAR Marker	PH=Photo	SS=Service Source	BS=Burial Source

103

Hawkins Co, TN 1843 and was living there in 1846 age 81. Bronze marker ordered fr War Dept, placed 1983. W5270 **P:** Y **BLW:** unk **RG:** unk **MK:** Y **PH:** unk **SS:** K Vol II pg 84 **BS:** JLARC 4, 22.

ENGLISH, William; b Bef 1765, Bedford Co; d 4 July 1816 **RU:** Private, Ent serv Bedford Co in Capt Jno Triga? 1780-1781; Capt Peter Weller 1781; Capt Coleman or Clements at Siege of '96 **CEM:** English Family; GPS unk; Kemps Mill; Franklin **GS:** N **SP:** Mar (Oct or Nov 1793 - bond dated 4 Nov 1793 - while living on Blackwater River) Adria or Addria or Addry Kemp (Dudley) (1768 or 1771-__) of Franklin Co. - "former widow". **VI:** Widow pen Franklin Co age 74 in 1845 and pension increased there 1850 age 82. Grave now underwater beneath Smith Mountain Lake. W7970 **P:** Y **BLW:** unk **RG:** Y **MK:** N **PH:** N **SS:** K Vol II pg 85; AK; E pg 256 **BS:** 04.

ENSORIEL, Espirit; b unk; d 1781 **RU:** Seaman, Served on "Diademe" and died from Yorktown battle **CEM:** French Memorial; GPS 36.81944, -79.39933; Yorktown; York **GS:** U **SP:** No info **VI:** No further data **P:** unk **BLW:** unk **RG:** Y **MK:** unk **PH:** unk **SS:** J-Yorktown Historian **BS:** JLARC 1, 74.

EPES (EPPES), Francis; b 1730, Amelia Co; d 1789 **RU:** Lieutenant Colonel, Was Capt of Guard, Charles City Co. Promoted to Lt Col 18 Mar 1776. Was wounded at Long Isand in 1st VA Regt of Foot 27 Aug 1776 **CEM:** The Old Place; GPS unk; 5 mi NW of Blackstone; Nottoway **GS:** N **SP:** Mar (c1754) Mary Williams (unk, Amelia Co-Mar 1795) **VI:** BLW of 6000 acres recd while residing in Dinwidde Co **P:** unk **BLW:** unk **RG:** N **MK:** N **PH:** N **SS:** E pg 256; G pg 115; CE pg 29 **BS:** 151.

EPPERSON, David; b 22 Jun 1734, New Kent Co; d Btw 1776 & 1780; or Dec 1799 **RU:** Private, Served in14th Cont Line. Records indicate he died in service bet 1776 and 1780 **CEM:** Blue Ridge Farm; GPS unk; Rt 261, 2.1 mi off Rt 250 W, Greenwood; Albemarle **GS:** Y **SP:** Hannah Judith Thompson (1735-1814.) She moved to Estill Co, KY with her son after her husband d **VI:** Son of John Epperson, Sr. (1703-1737) & Elizabeth Michaux. Widow recd gratuity of 164 acres in Albemarle Co on 14 Dec 1780. His will is dated 2 Feb 1799 and probated Oct 1799. DAR marker **P:** unk **BLW:** Y **RG:** N **MK:** Y **PH:** Y **SS:** J- DAR Hatcher; E pg 256; BT **BS:** JLARC 2; 67 vol 2 pg 291; 196.

EPPES, Francis; b unk; d 1844 **RU:** Patriot, Gave material aid to cause **CEM:** Eppes Family; GPS unk; Off Rt 616, 3.9 mi SE of jct with Rt 37; Prince George **GS:** U **SP:** Mildred (-----) **VI:** No further data **P:** N **BLW:** N **RG:** unk **MK:** unk **PH:** unk **SS:** AL Ct Bk pg 17 Chesterfield Co **BS:** 51.

EPPES, Peter; b 1759, Charles City Co; d 9 Dec 1828 **RU:** Sergeant, Served in 6th Regt. Ent serv Apr 1777. Discharged Mar 26 1778 **CEM:** Shockoe Hill; GPS 37.55190, -77.43170; 4th & Hospital Sts; Richmond City **GS:** Y **SP:** Mar (1796) Lucy Ballard (1764 Charles City Co-11 Dec 1844) **VI:** Pen 1832 Dinwiddie Co S8424 **P:** unk **BLW:** unk **RG:** Y **MK:** Y **PH:** unk **SS:** E pg 257; K Vol II pg 86 **BS:** 57 pg 6.

ERVIN, William; b 1760; d Mar 1817 **RU:** Sergeant, Served in 1st, 8th,10th Cont Lines **CEM:** Mossy Creek Presbyterian; GPS 38.35331, -79.04914; 372 Kyles Mill Rd, Mt Solon; Augusta **GS:** Y **SP:** Margaret Robertson (1778-15 Mar 1797) d/o Col James & Margaret (Poage) Robertson **VI:** Son of Francis & Jane (Curry) Ervin **P:** unk **BLW:** unk **RG:** N **MK:** N **PH:** unk **SS:** E pg 257 **BS:** 142; 196.

ESKRIDGE, Margaret (Mrs Kenner); b c1715; d 8 Oct 1801 **RU:** Patriot, Service in helping soldiers **CEM:** Kenner Family; GPS unk; 2452 Kenner Ln; Fauquier **GS:** Y **SP:** Mar (June 1732 Sandy Point) Howson Francis Kenner **VI:** Daug of Col George & Rebecca (Bonum) Eskridge **P:** N **BLW:** N **RG:** Y **MK:** N **PH:** unk **SS:** AL Ct Bk pg 2, 19 **BS:** AV Inv # 69.

ESOM (ESCOM), Hannah; b 1752; d 1843 **RU:** Patriot, Gave material aid to cause **CEM:** Esom Family; GPS unk; Nr Cave Spring; Roanoke Co **GS:** Y **SP:** No info **VI:** No further data **P:** N **BLW:** N **RG:** N **MK:** N **PH:** unk **SS:** AR DAR report **BS:** 80 vol 2 pg 16.

ESTES, Elisha; b 1749, Albemarle Co; d 1 Feb 1821 **RU:** Sergeant, Served in 1st & 10th Cont Line, Maj Nocholas Co #5 **CEM:** Estes Family; GPS unk; Check property records for location, also in DAR 1959 Senate Doc serial # 12260, vol 5; Nelson **GS:** U **SP:** Catherine Tompkins (1 Oct 1759-25 Apr 1804) **VI:** Son of Abraham Jr and Elizabeth (-----) Eases **P:** unk **BLW:** unk **RG:** unk **MK:** unk **PH:** unk **SS:** DAR Ancestor #A037271; A pg 273; E pg 246 **BS:** JLARC 2.

ESTES, George; b 3 Feb 1763 Amelia Co; d Jul 1859 **RU:** Private, Ent serv Halifax Co as substitute for father. Ent serv fr TN 1782.Served in 2nd, 6th, 10th Cont Lines **CEM:** Oak Ridge; GPS 36.71912, -78.90321; Main St & Hamilton St, South Boston; Halifax **GS:** U **SP:** Mary Younger (1772-__) **VI:** Son of

RU=Rank/Unit	CEM=Cemetery	GS=Gravestone	SP=Spousal Information
VI=Other Veteran Info	P=Pension	BLW=Bounty/Land Warrant	RG=Registered Grave
MK=SAR/DAR Marker	PH=Photo	SS=Service Source	BS=Burial Source

104

Moses & (-----) Estates. Moved "a family of people" in 1781 to NC and later TN by 1782. Recd pension 1833 Halifax Co. Granted BLW #26130 S18394 **P:** Y **BLW:** Y **RG:** unk **MK:** unk **PH:** unk **SS:** E pg 258; K Vol II pg 87 **BS:** 196.

ESTES, Richard; b 1758; d 5 Aug 1832 **RU:** Private, Served in Capt Cloyd's Co, Cont Line, 12 Sep 1777 **CEM:** Greenfield; GPS unk; Fawn Lake Pwy; Spotsylvania **GS:** Y **SP:** No info **VI:** Son of Abraham & Annie (Clark) Estes **P:** unk **BLW:** unk **RG:** Y **MK:** N **PH:** unk **SS:** E pg 258 **BS:** 07 pg 2, 3.

ESTES, William; b 1745; d 1827 **RU:** Corporal/Patriot, Served in Bedford Co Militia. Served in 2nd & 6th Cont Line. Gave material aid to cause **CEM:** Unidentified; GPS unk; South/left side of Rt 648 after crossing Buffalo River fr Rt 604; Greene **GS:** U **SP:** Frances Cox **VI:** Field stone "W.E. Dec ? 1827". RW service noted Greene Co Magazine **P:** unk **BLW:** unk **RG:** unk **MK:** unk **PH:** unk **SS:** D Orange Co **BS:** JLARC 113.

ETTER, Daniel; b 28 Apr 1750, Lebanon Co, PA; d 5 Sep 1803 **RU:** Fife & Drummer, Served in PA **CEM:** St John's Lutheran; GPS 36.96500, -81.10110; 405 W Main, Wytheville; Wythe **GS:** U **SP:** 1) Elizabeth McMahon (1759-1781) 2) Mar (25 Apr 1781 in PA) Mary Magdalena Reihn (1749-1821) **VI:** Son of Gerhand (27 Jan 1718 Bern, Switzerland-26 Apr 1783) & Caterine (Banga) (26 Oct 1717 Bern, Switzerland-20 Apr 1788) Etter **P:** unk **BLW:** unk **RG:** unk **MK:** unk **PH:** unk **SS:** CD **BS:** JLARC 123; 196.

EUBANK (EUBANKS), Richard; b 1758 Glouchester Co; d 1855 **RU:** Sergeant, Served in 1st, 10th, 14th Cont Lines. Served in Capt John Marks Co, Col Charles Lewis,14th Regt **CEM:** Forkquarter; GPS unk; Calno Rd Rt 601, Norment Ferry; King William **GS:** U **SP:** Mar (1797) Susan Gary (__-1857) **VI:** No further data **P:** unk **BLW:** unk **RG:** unk **MK:** unk **PH:** unk **SS:** J- DAR Hatcher; E pg 259 **BS:** JLARC 2.

EVANS, Daniel; b 22 Mar 1750, Wales; d 1 Jan 1829 **RU:** Soldier, Served in Chesterfield Co Militia and a VA unit in Illinois campaign **CEM:** Dixon Family; GPS 37.18420, -79.59310; Off Rt 658, Concord quadrant, nr Rustburg; Campbell **GS:** U **SP:** Mar (1781) Jane Davis (6 Aug 1751 PA-23 Sep 1819) **VI:** No further data **P:** unk **BLW:** unk **RG:** unk **MK:** N **PH:** unk **SS:** E pg 260 **BS:** JLARC 36.

EVANS, John; b unk; d Feb 1790 **RU:** Seaman, Specific service may be found at the Lib of VA in Auditor's Acct Bk XXII, pg 441 and in War Files vol 5 pg 65 **CEM:** Old Christ Church Episcopal; GPS 38.80625, -77.04718; 118 N Washington St; Alexandria City **GS:** N **SP:** No info **VI:** Burial permit issued 23 Feb 1790 **P:** unk **BLW:** unk **RG:** N **MK:** N **PH:** N **SS:** L pg 186; CZ pg 156 **BS:** 20 pg 147.

EVANS, Reese; b unk; d unk **RU:** Ensign, Served in PA troops **CEM:** Dixon Family; GPS 37.18420, -79.59310; Off Rt 658, Concord quadrant, nr Rustburg; Campbell **GS:** U **SP:** Bridgett (-----) **VI:** No further data **P:** unk **BLW:** unk **RG:** unk **MK:** N **PH:** unk **SS:** NSSAR Ancestor #P-155599 **BS:** JLARC 36.

EVANS, William; b 1756; d 1840 **RU:** Lieutenant, Served in Buckingham Miltia **CEM:** Merionette; GPS unk; Nr Willis Mountain; Buckingham **GS:** U **SP:** Mary (-----) **VI:** Drew pen in Buckingham Co **P:** Y **BLW:** N **RG:** unk **MK:** N **PH:** unk **SS:** E pg 261 **BS:** JLARC 4, 59.

EVERLET, Gaspard; b unk; d 1781 **RU:** Soldier, Served in Dillon Bn and died fr battle at Yorktown **CEM:** French Memorial; GPS 36.81944, -79.39933; Yorktown; York **GS:** U **SP:** No info **VI:** No further data **P:** unk **BLW:** unk **RG:** Y **MK:** unk **PH:** unk **SS:** J-Yorktown Historian **BS:** JLARC 1, 74.

EVINS, William; b unk; d 1780 **RU:** Corporal, Served in 8th & 12th Cont Line **CEM:** Sinking Springs; GPS 36.71030, -81.98170; 136 E Main St, Abingdon; Washington **GS:** U **SP:** Ann Covill (1733-1790) **VI:** No further data **P:** N **BLW:** N **RG:** N **MK:** unk **PH:** N **SS:** E pg 262 **BS:** 212 pg 74.

EWELL, Jesse; b 24 Sep 1743; d 30 Sep 1805 **RU:** Colonel/Patriot, Was a member of Prince William Co Committee of Safety,1775. Gave material aid to cause **CEM:** Ewell-Weems; GPS unk; Rt 640; Prince William **GS:** N **SP:** Mar (10 Oct 1767) Charlotte Ewell (14 Feb 1750-13 Apr 1823) d/o Bertrand & Frances (Kenner) Ewell **VI:** Son of Charles (1713-__) & Sarah (Ball) (1712-__) Ewell **P:** unk **BLW:** unk **RG:** Y **MK:** N **PH:** N **SS:** E pg 262; AL Ct Bk pg 5 Prince William Co **BS:** 16 pg 180.

EWER (EWERS), John; b 27 Dec 1735, Bucks Co, PA; d 9 May 1815 **RU:** Private, Served in Capt David Marpole Co, Philadelphia Co PA Militia **CEM:** Unison; GPS unk; Unison; Loudoun **GS:** U **SP:**

RU=Rank/Unit	CEM=Cemetery	GS=Gravestone	SP=Spousal Information
VI=Other Veteran Info	P=Pension	BLW=Bounty/Land Warrant	RG=Registered Grave
MK=SAR/DAR Marker	PH=Photo	SS=Service Source	BS=Burial Source

Sarah Gladny **VI:** No further data **P:** unk **BLW:** unk **RG:** Y **MK:** unk **PH:** unk **SS:** J-NSSAR 1993 Reg, J-DAR Hatcher; AP PA Archives 2nd series vol 13 pg 721 & 6th series Vol 1 pg 637, 649 **BS:** JLARC 1, 2.

EWING, James; b unk; d 16 Feb 1796 **RU:** Captain, Commanded a co in Augusta Co Militia, Mar 1776-17 Apr 1777 **CEM:** Glebe Burying Ground; GPS 38.10940, -79.22190; Glebe School Rd Rt 876, Swoopes; Augusta **GS:** Y **SP:** Martha (-----), named in his will **VI:** DAR marker (plaque) which styles him Capt. GS only gives date of death **P:** unk **BLW:** unk **RG:** unk **MK:** Y **PH:** unk **SS:** E pg 262; BT; CZ pg 157 **BS:** JLARC 8, 62, 63; 196.

EWING, James; b 1740; d 14 Apr 1809 **RU:** Patriot, Gave material aid to the cause **CEM:** North Mountain; GPS unk; 7 mi S of Staunton on N side Rt 252; Augusta **GS:** Y **SP:** Jean Finley **VI:** No further data **P:** N **BLW:** N **RG:** N **MK:** N **PH:** unk **SS:** AL Com BK II pg 362 **BS:** 142; 196.

EWING, James; b 4 Mar 1762; d 26 Sep 1794 **RU:** Captain/Patriot, Served in Capt McCutchen's Co, Augusta Co Militia. Gave material aid to cause **CEM:** Glebe Burying Ground; GPS 38.10940, -79.22190; Glebe School Rd Rt 876, Swoopes; Augusta **GS:** Y **SP:** Martha (-----) (15 Feb 1741-2 Jul 1828) **VI:** Called Capt James Ewing on DAR plaque in cemetery **P:** unk **BLW:** unk **RG:** unk **MK:** Y **PH:** unk **SS:** D pg 94; E pg 262 **BS:** 210 pg 394; 196.

EWING, Robert Sr; b 1718, County Londonderry, Ireland; d 1787 **RU:** Private/Patriot, Was in Battle of Point Pleasant, Oct 1774. Had civil service as Justice of the Peace, Bedford Co and gave material aid to the cause **CEM:** Ewing-Patterson Cem; GPS unk; Penick's Mill; Bedford **GS:** N **SP:** Mar (c1746) Mary Baker (1728 Prince Edward Co-__) **VI:** No further data **P:** unk **BLW:** unk **RG:** Y **MK:** N **PH:** N **SS:** J-NSSAR 1993 Reg, J- DAR Hatcher; AL Ct Bk pg 11, 12, 30 and cert listed as Capt military officer **BS:** JLARC 1, 2.

EWING, Samuel; b unk, Fahan, Donegal, Ireland; d 24 Aug 1798 **RU:** unk, Specific service is at the Lib of VA, Auditors Acct vol XVIII pg 515 **CEM:** Ewing Family; GPS unk; Off Stickley Dr to Hayvenhurst Ct; Winchester City **GS:** U **SP:** Margaret McMichael (1773-__) **VI:** Son of John (1648-1745) & Jennet (Wilson) (1633-__) Ewing. Died in Stephen City, Frederick Co **P:** unk **BLW:** unk **RG:** unk **MK:** N **PH:** unk **SS:** J- DAR Hatcher; CZ pg 158 **BS:** JLARC 2; 196.

EWING, William; b 9 May 1721; d 17 Jun 1794 **RU:** Patriot, Gave material aid to the cause **CEM:** Glebe Burying Ground; GPS 38.10940, -79.22190; Glebe School Rd Rt 876, Swoopes; Augusta **GS:** Y **SP:** No info **VI:** No further data **P:** N **BLW:** N **RG:** N **MK:** N **PH:** unk **SS:** AL Ct Bk pg 6 **BS:** 142; 196.

EWING, William; b 1764; d 1852 **RU:** Sergeant, Served in VA Cont Line **CEM:** Ewing-McClure (aka Friendship Church); GPS unk; Jonesville; Lee **GS:** Y **SP:** 1) Elizabeth Saunders 2) Sarah Wynn (Hix) **VI:** No further data **P:** unk **BLW:** unk **RG:** Y **MK:** Y **PH:** unk **SS:** AK Dec 06 **BS:** 04, Dec 06.

FABRE, Paul; b unk; d 1781 **RU:** Soldier, Served in Touraine Bn and died fr battle at Yorktown **CEM:** French Memorial; GPS 36.81944, -79.39933; Yorktown; York **GS:** U **SP:** No info **VI:** No further data **P:** unk **BLW:** unk **RG:** Y **MK:** unk **PH:** unk **SS:** J-Yorktown Historian **BS:** JLARC 1, 74.

FAIRFAX, Thomas; b 22 Oct 1693 Leeds Castle, Scotland; d 9 Dec 1781 **RU:** Patriot, Publically denounced British policies and urged neighbors to defend privileges. Helped stabilize currency by directing it be accepted for quit-rents. Helped with exchange of prisoners **CEM:** Christ Episcopal, Courtyard; GPS unk; 114 W Boscawen St; Winchester City **GS:** Y **SP:** No info **VI:** 6th Baron of Cameron. Gave provisions. Died in Frederick Co **P:** N **BLW:** N **RG:** Y **MK:** N **PH:** unk **SS:** AK; J-NSSAR 1993 Reg; 156201 **BS:** 04 JLARC 1.

FAIRFAX, William; b 1720, Charles Co, MD; d 1793 **RU:** Patriot, Gave Oath of Allegiance 1778, MD. Also gave wheat to military Jul 1782 **CEM:** Bacon Race; GPS 38.69145, -77.46439; Davis Ford Rd & Bacon Race Rd; Prince William **GS:** Y **SP:** 1) Benedicta Blancett 2) Elizabeth Buckner **VI:** No further data **P:** N **BLW:** N **RG:** Y **MK:** Y **PH:** Y **SS:** AK **BS:** 4.

FAISSANS, Maurice; b unk; d 1781 **RU:** Seaman, Served on "Saint-Esprit" and died from Yorktown battle **CEM:** French Memorial; GPS 36.81944, -79.39933; Yorktown; York **GS:** U **SP:** No info **VI:** No further data **P:** unk **BLW:** unk **RG:** unk **MK:** unk **PH:** unk **SS:** J-Yorktown Historian **BS:** JLARC 1, 74.

RU=Rank/Unit	CEM=Cemetery	GS=Gravestone	SP=Spousal Information
VI=Other Veteran Info	P=Pension	BLW=Bounty/Land Warrant	RG=Registered Grave
MK=SAR/DAR Marker	PH=Photo	SS=Service Source	BS=Burial Source

106

FALL, George; b 1743, PA; d 1818 **RU:** Private, Served in 6th Bn, Berk's Co PA Militia. Served in Capt George Baxter's Co, Rockingham Co Militia as guard of prisoners going to Winchester Feb & Mar 1782 **CEM:** St James Methodist; GPS unk; 3777 Churchville Ave, Churchville; Augusta **GS:** Y **SP:** Catharine (-----) **VI:** Newer stone with engraved plaque of Pennsylvania **P:** unk **BLW:** unk **RG:** Y **MK:** N **PH:** unk **SS:** N pg 123 **BS:** JLARC 1 ,2, 62; 196.

FARLEY, Thomas Jr; b 1760; d 11 Jun 1839 **RU:** Private, Ent serv 1776 Walker's Creek, Montgomery Co (Later Giles Co). Served in VA Line **CEM:** Sugar Run, Farmer Family; GPS unk; Staffordsville; Giles **GS:** U **SP:** Mar (8 May 1793 Montgomery Co) Patty/Patsey Lester/Lister (c1772-18 Nov 1853). QLF states he mar Martha V. Peck. **VI:** Sol appl pen 30 Jun 1834 Giles Co age 73 or 74. Widow appl 25 Sep 1848 Giles Co, age 76. W7244 **P:** Y **BLW:** unk **RG:** unk **MK:** unk **PH:** unk **SS:** J- DAR Hatcher. CG Vol 2 pg 1152; K Vol II pg 101 **BS:** JLARC 2.

FARMER, James; b 1758; d 12 Aug 1838 **RU:** Private, Specific service is at the Lib of VA, Auditors Acct vol XVIII pg 531 **CEM:** North End; GPS 36.77234, -80.73866; 101 Beaver Dam Rd, Hillsville; Carroll **GS:** Y **SP:** Susannah (----- (1765-20 Sep 1850) **VI:** Son of Michael Farmer & Martha Latham **P:** unk **BLW:** unk **RG:** N **MK:** N **PH:** unk **SS:** E pg 264; CA pg 158 **BS:** 123 pg 67; 196.

FARRIS, Gideon; b 1748; d 1818 **RU:** Private/Patriot, Served in Washington Co Militia 1776, commanded by Col William Christian. Performed public service as Juror 19 Nov 1778 **CEM:** Rock Spring; GPS 37.78126, -79.44585; Jct Rt 803 & Liberty Hall Rd, Lodi; Washington **GS:** U **SP:** Sarah McSpadden (1745 Augusta Co-1820) d/o Thomas (1720-1765) & (-----) Spaden **VI:** Son of (------) & Deborah Faries **P:** unk **BLW:** unk **RG:** unk **MK:** unk **PH:** unk **SS:** DD **BS:** 196.

FAULEY (FAWLEY), John; b Jan 1720, Loudoun Co; d 11 Jun 1803 **RU:** Private, Unit not identified but available at Lib of VA **CEM:** New Jerusalem Lutheran; GPS 39.25736, -77.63891; 12942 Lutheran Church Rd, Lovettsville; Loudoun **GS:** Y **SP:** Anna Maria Ault (1737-1803) **VI:** No further data **P:** unk **BLW:** unk **RG:** unk **MK:** unk **PH:** Y **SS:** E pg 266 cites Eckenrode, Dr. H J Index to Rev War Records in VA State Archives **BS:** 196.

FAULKNER, Jacob; b 1744; d 24 Mar 1823 **RU:** Ensign, Served in Halifax Co Militia 1774-1777 **CEM:** Faulkner Family; GPS unk; Nr Cherry Hill, 1 mi W of Hyco, nr Omega; Halifax **GS:** U **SP:** Mar (1770) Catherine Howerton (1750-__) **VI:** No further data **P:** unk **BLW:** unk **RG:** unk **MK:** unk **PH:** unk **SS:** J- NSSAR 1993 Reg, J- DAR Hatcher; G pg 184 **BS:** JLARC 1, 2.

FAUNTLEROY, Moore; b unk; d 1791 **RU:** Major/Patriot, Served in 4th Regt of Dragoons Gave material aid to cause **CEM:** Farnham Episcopal; GPS unk; 231 N Farnham Church Rd, Farnham; Richmond Co **GS:** N **SP:** No info **VI:** BLW issued 21 Mar 1795. Records lost in Pension Office fire. F959 **P:** unk **BLW:** Y **RG:** N **MK:** N **PH:** N **SS:** AL Ct Bk pg 9 Richmond Co; K Vol II pg 105 **BS:** See SS BQ pg 7162.

FAUNTLEROY, Samuel Griffin; b 7 May 1759; d 8 Dec 1826 **RU:** Captain, Served in Richmond Co Militia 1781 **CEM:** Fauntleroy Family at Farmers Mt Plantation; GPS unk; Whitehall; King & Queen **GS:** Y **SP:** Sarah Lowry (25 Mar 1776-24 Nov 1840) **VI:** No further data **P:** unk **BLW:** unk **RG:** N **MK:** N **PH:** unk **SS:** G pg 316 **BS:** 129 pg 479.

FAW, Abraham; b 14 May 1747, (Bapt) Basel, Switzerland; d 26 Jun 1828 **RU:** Patriot, Member of Committee of Obervation; cared for prisoners in the "Poorhouse." Also loans Treasury of state of MD $1000 20 Jun 1780 **CEM:** Trinity United Methodist; GPS 39.13600, -77.00610; 2911 Cameron Mills Rd; Alexandria City **GS:** Y **SP:** 1) Mar (16 Oct 1770) Juliana boyer Lowe 2) Mar (28 Mar 1790) Mary Ann Steiner (20 Nov 1760-19 Jan 1805) 3) Mar (20 Apr 1806) Sarah Moody (28 Mar 1764-28 Aug 1818) **VI:** Son of Jacob & Cathrine (Dyssly/Disslin) Pfau **P:** N **BLW:** N **RG:** Y **MK:** Y **PH:** Y **SS:** AK GW Chapter 2015 **BS:** 04.

FELIX, (-----); b unk; d 1781 **RU:** Seaman, Served on "Solitaire" and died from Yorktown battle **CEM:** French Memorial; GPS 36.81944, -79.39933; Yorktown; York **GS:** U **SP:** No info **VI:** No further data **P:** unk **BLW:** unk **RG:** unk **MK:** unk **PH:** unk **SS:** J-Yorktown Historian **BS:** JLARC 1, 74.

FENDALL, Philip Richard; b 24 Nov 1734; d Mar 1805 **RU:** Patriot, Public service claim **CEM:** Fendall Family; GPS unk; 614 N Washington St; Alexandria City **GS:** N **SP:** Mary Lee (__ 10 Nov 1827,

---

RU=Rank/Unit	CEM=Cemetery	GS=Gravestone	SP=Spousal Information
VI=Other Veteran Info	P=Pension	BLW=Bounty/Land Warrant	RG=Registered Grave
MK=SAR/DAR Marker	PH=Photo	SS=Service Source	BS=Burial Source

Washington DC) sister of Henry "Lighthorse Harry" Lee **VI:** His 1799 will directed he be bur in the burying ground on his farm **P:** N **BLW:** N **RG:** N **MK:** N **PH:** N **SS:** AL Cert Issued **BS:** 20 pg 28.

FERET, Dominique; b unk; d 1781 **RU:** Soldier, Served in Gatinais Bn and died fr battle at Yorktown **CEM:** French Memorial; GPS 36.81944, -79.39933; Yorktown; York **GS:** U **SP:** No info **VI:** No further data **P:** unk **BLW:** unk **RG:** unk **MK:** unk **PH:** unk **SS:** J-Yorktown Historian **BS:** JLARC 1, 74.

FERGUSON, Daniel; b 1752; d 3 Sep 1785 **RU:** Private, Served in Capt Francis Muir's 7th Co, Col Nathaniel Gist's VA Regt 1777 **CEM:** St Paul's Episcopal; GPS 36.84733, -76.28554; 201 St Paul's Blvd; Norfolk City **GS:** Y **SP:** No info **VI:** No further data **P:** unk **BLW:** unk **RG:** Y **MK:** N **PH:** unk **SS:** A pg 287; G pg 253 **BS:** 87 pg 27; 196.

FERGUSON, Robert; b 30 Mar 1733; d 17 Sep 1796 **RU:** Soldier, Served in1st Lt Dragoons **CEM:** Ferguson Family; GPS unk; 31356 Rochelle Swamp Rd, Vic Newsoms; Southampton **GS:** U **SP:** Sarah (-----) (1733-1800) **VI:** No further data **P:** unk **BLW:** unk **RG:** unk **MK:** unk **PH:** unk **SS:** E pg 269 **BS:** 40 vol II pg 48; 196.

FERGUSSON (FARGUSSON FURGUSSON FURGUSON), Moses; b 1760; d 1851 **RU:** Captain, Served in Col Proctor's VA State 4th Regt of Artillery **CEM:** Farguson Family; GPS unk; 12951 Blue Stack Ct.; Chesterfield **GS:** U **SP:** No info **VI:** BLW 4 Jun 1789. Grave marked only by fieldstone **P:** unk **BLW:** Y **RG:** unk **MK:** N **PH:** unk **SS:** CG pg 1294 **BS:** JLARC 4, 35.

FERRAND, Antoine; b unk; d 1781 **RU:** Seaman, Served on "Citoyen" and died from Yorktown battle **CEM:** French Memorial; GPS 36.81944, -79.39933; Yorktown; York **GS:** U **SP:** No info **VI:** No further data **P:** unk **BLW:** unk **RG:** Y **MK:** unk **PH:** unk **SS:** J-Yorktown Historian **BS:** JLARC 1,74.

FERRELL (FERRILL), William H; b 1752, Halifax Co; d 26 Nov 1826 **RU:** Private, Ent serv 1778 Halifax Co. Served in SC & VA Lines **CEM:** Ferrell Family; GPS unk; Cherry Hill, W of Halifax; Halifax **GS:** U **SP:** Mar (16 Aug 1787) Frances Martin (unk Halifax Co-__) **VI:** Sol appl pen 28 Aug 1833 Halifax Co age 81. S13015 **P:** Y **BLW:** unk **RG:** Y **MK:** unk **PH:** unk **SS:** J-NSSAR 1993 Reg, J- DAR Hatcher; CG Vol 2 pg 1179; K Vol II pg 109 **BS:** JLARC 1, 2.

FERREY, Claude; b unk; d 1781 **RU:** Soldier, Served in Auxonne Bn and died fr battle at Yorktown **CEM:** French Memorial; GPS 36.81944, -79.39933; Yorktown; York **GS:** U **SP:** No info **VI:** No further data **P:** unk **BLW:** unk **RG:** Y **MK:** unk **PH:** unk **SS:** J-Yorktown Historian **BS:** JLARC 1, 74.

FIELDS, Andrew; b c1751; d 1794 **RU:** Ensign, Served in Bedford Co or Campbell Co Militia in Capt Thomas Helm's Co. Was in Battle of Guilford CH **CEM:** Falling River Baptist; GPS 37.07531, -78.91543; 2874 Wickliffe Ave, Brookneal; Campbell **GS:** U **SP:** Margaret Galbraith (c1754 Northampton Co, PA-1835 Campbell Co) d/o Alexander & (-----) Galbreath **VI:** Son of John & Sarah (Milbert) Fields. JLARC indicates location of cem is in Spring Mills which may not be location of the church by that name **P:** unk **BLW:** unk **RG:** unk **MK:** N **PH:** unk **SS:** NSSAR Ancestor #P-157994 **BS:** JLARC 36.

FINCOMB, Amos; b unk; d 25 Nov 1781 **RU:** Private, Served in Capt Dunscomb Co, Lewis Dubois's 5th NY Line Regt. Died fr the battle at Yorktown **CEM:** Yorktown Victory Monument Tablet; GPS 38.28350, -78.54150; Yorktown; York **GS:** U **SP:** No info **VI:** No further data **P:** unk **BLW:** unk **RG:** Y **MK:** unk **PH:** unk **SS:** J-Yorktown Historian; AX pg 220 **BS:** JLARC 74.

FINLEY, John; b 1706; d 1791 **RU:** Patriot, Gave material aid to cause **CEM:** Tinkling Spring Presbyterian; GPS 38.08472, -78.98278; 30 Tinkling Spring Dr, Fishersville; Augusta **GS:** U **SP:** Thankful Doak (__-after 1791) **VI:** No further data **P:** N **BLW:** N **RG:** unk **MK:** unk **PH:** unk **SS:** AL Commissioners Bk II pg 358 Augusta Co **BS:** 196.

FISHBACK, John Frederick; b 1716, Germanna Colony, Orange Co; d 20 Sep 1782 **RU:** Patriot, Gave material aid to cause **CEM:** Fleetwood; GPS unk; Fleetwood Ln off Rt 621, Jeffersonton; Culpeper **GS:** U **SP:** 1) Mar (abt 1740) Ann Elizabeth Holtzclaw 2) Mar (abt. 1757) Eve Mertain (Martin) **VI:** Son of Johannes & Agnes (Hager) Fishback **P:** N **BLW:** N **RG:** unk **MK:** unk **PH:** unk **SS:** AL Cert Fauquier Co **BS:** 196.

FISHBACK, Martin; b 12 Oct 1763; d 24 Jan 1842 **RU:** Private, Was in the battle of Yorktown **CEM:** Fleetwood; GPS unk; Fleetwood Ln off Rt 621, Jeffersonton; Culpeper **GS:** Y **SP:** Lucy Amiss (8 July

RU=Rank/Unit	CEM=Cemetery	GS=Gravestone	SP=Spousal Information
VI=Other Veteran Info	P=Pension	BLW=Bounty/Land Warrant	RG=Registered Grave
MK=SAR/DAR Marker	PH=Photo	SS=Service Source	BS=Burial Source

108

176_-12 Sep 1843) **VI:** Son of Johann Freidrich Fishback & Eve Martin. Born and d in the same room of "Fleetwood" the family home. SAR marker on Gr **P:** unk **BLW:** unk **RG:** Y **MK:** Y **PH:** unk **SS:** N pg 1109 **BS:** 04; 196.

FISHBURNE, Dietrick (Detrich); b 29 Jan 1760, PA; d Oct 1822 **RU:** Private, Served in Laird's Co of PA Militia **CEM:** Fishburne; GPS unk; At the end of Rt 847, behind Verona Methodist Church, Verona; Augusta **GS:** U **SP:** Mar (2 Mar 1784 Frederick, MD) Catharine/Catherine Burckardt **VI:** No further data **P:** unk **BLW:** unk **RG:** unk **MK:** unk **PH:** unk **SS:** CI PA Archives 5th Series Vol 7 pg 942, 944 **BS:** JLARC 8, 52, 62.

FISHER, John; b unk; d 1815 **RU:** Patriot, Gave material aid to the cause **CEM:** Back Creek Quaker, aka Gainesboro United Methodist; GPS 39.27861, -78.25694; 166 Siler Ln, Gainesboro; Frederick **GS:** N **SP:** No info **VI:** No further data **P:** N **BLW:** N **RG:** N **MK:** N **PH:** N **SS:** AL Cert Issued **BS:** 59 pg 110.

FISSY, Antoine; b unk; d 1781 **RU:** Soldier, Served in Gatinais Bn and died fr battle at Yorktown **CEM:** French Memorial; GPS 36.81944, -79.39933; Yorktown; York **GS:** U **SP:** No info **VI:** No further data **P:** unk **BLW:** unk **RG:** Y **MK:** unk **PH:** unk **SS:** J-Yorktown Historian **BS:** JLARC 1,74.

FITZ (FITTS), Robert Walker; b 1755 or 1756, Dinwiddie Co; d Sep 1840 **RU:** Soldier, Ent Serv Mecklenburg Co 1776 in Capt James Anderson Co. In 1779 was in Capt Reuben Vaughan's Co, at Battle of Stono. In 1781 was in Halifax Co, Capt Marmaduke Standfield's Co, and transferred at Cabin Point to Col Wm Dix, Jesse Conway's Co. In Apr or May 1781 was in Capt Edward King's Co, in Battle of Ninety-Six. Guarded prisoners to Halifax Old Town, Pittsylvania Co Aug 1781. Was in Capt Fleming Bates Co to Little York, and at surrender of Cornwallis **CEM:** Fitts; GPS 36.58428, -79.69962; Rt 621 off Rt 610, Aiken Summit; Pittsylvania **GS:** Y **SP:** Mar (16 May 1782) Susannah Pass (1762-21 Dec 1849 in TN) **VI:** Pen Mecklenburg Co 1832. Was residing in Pittsylvania Co in 1840. S8475 **P:** Y **BLW:** unk **RG:** unk **MK:** unk **PH:** unk **SS:** K Vol II pg 119 **BS:** 174, JLARC 4, 76, 96.

FITZGERALD, Edmund (Edmond); b 18 Mar 1745; d 6 Jun 1848 **RU:** First Lieutenant, Pittsylvania Co Militia 25 Nov 1778. 1st Lt 18 Apr 1781 **CEM:** Fitzgerald Family; GPS 36.80353, -79.24233; 1 mi E of Shockoe on Rt 832; Pittsylvania **GS:** Y **SP:** Mar (1774 Campbell Co) Mildred Payne (1752-12 Mar 1837) d/o Reuben & Agnes (Wade) Payne **VI:** Son of James & Mary (O'Brian) Fitzgerald of Ireland **P:** unk **BLW:** unk **RG:** unk **MK:** unk **PH:** unk **SS:** NSSAR Ancestor #P-158999; AR Vol 2 pg 37 **BS:** 174, JLARC 2, 90.

FITZGERALD, John; b unk, County Wiclow, Ireland; d 3 Dec 1799 **RU:** Lieutenant Colonel, Aide de Camp Gen Washington 1778. Wounded at Monmouth **CEM:** St Marys Catholic; GPS 38.79390, -77.04750; 310 S Royal St; Alexandria City **GS:** Y **SP:** Jane Digges (1754-__) d/o Charles & (-----) Digges **VI:** Awarded BLW of 4,666 acres **P:** unk **BLW:** Y **RG:** unk **MK:** unk **PH:** unk **SS:** NSSAR Ancestor # P-159007; E pg 275; SAR application **BS:** JLARC ;196.

FITZHUGH, Thomas; b 15 Jun 1753, Bel Air, Stafford Co; d Oct 1829 **RU:** Patriot, Contributed Mar 1782 Prince William Co two beeves weighing 600 lbs & two cattle weighing 550 lbs **CEM:** Fitzhugh Plantation; GPS unk; Check property records for location of home; Prince William **GS:** U **SP:** Mar (1775) Lucinda Helm **VI:** Son of John & Alice Catlett (Thornton) Fitzhugh **P:** N **BLW:** N **RG:** unk **MK:** unk **PH:** unk **SS:** CC Pr Wm Co Court Order Book 1778-1784 **BS:** 196.

FITZHUGH, William; b 24 Aug 1741, Eagles Nest, King George Co; d 8 Jun 1809 **RU:** Patriot, Was Delegate 1st, 2nd, 3rd, 4th, 5th VA Conv; VA House of Delegates 1776-7 & 1780-1; Cont Congress 1779; VA State Senate 1782-3; signed Articles Non-importation 1775; Caroline [Military] District Comm 1776; Commissioner arms factory at Fredericksburg & Falmouth **CEM:** Pohick Episcopal; GPS 38.42546, -77.11598; 9301 Richmond Hwy, Lorton; Fairfax **GS:** Y **SP:** Ann Randolph **VI:** Died in Ravensworth, Fairfax Co **P:** N **BLW:** N **RG:** Y **MK:** Y **PH:** unk **SS:** I; D **BS:** 01; 201.

FITZPATRICK (FITTZPATRICK), John; b 1740, Ireland; d 28 May 1801 **RU:** Patriot, Gave material aid to cause; also performed public service as member of Comm of Safety, Sheriff, and Justice of Peace **CEM:** Fitzpatrick Family; GPS unk; Nathalie; Halifax **GS:** U **SP:** Mar (9 Oct 1762) Behetherand Brent (c1740-27 Sep 1813) **VI:** Died in Pittsylvania Co **P:** unk **BLW:** unk **RG:** Y **MK:** unk **PH:** unk **SS:** J-NASSR 2000 Reg; AL Ct Bk pg 4, 10 Campbell Co **BS:** JLARC 76.

RU=Rank/Unit	CEM=Cemetery	GS=Gravestone	SP=Spousal Information
VI=Other Veteran Info	P=Pension	BLW=Bounty/Land Warrant	RG=Registered Grave
MK=SAR/DAR Marker	PH=Photo	SS=Service Source	BS=Burial Source

109

FIX, Phillip; b 2 Jun 1754 or 1759, Schuykill river below Reading, Berks Co, PA; d 2 Dec 1834 **RU:** Private, Ent serv Loudoun Co and later Augusta Co **CEM:** Old Monmouth Presbyterian; GPS 37.80810, -79.47280; Jct Rts 60 & 669; Lexington City **GS:** Y **SP:** Mar (15 Mar 1780 Augusta Co) Margaret Swink (c1762-__) **VI:** Sol appl 8 Aug 1833 Rockbridge Co age 79. Died in Rockbridge Co. Widow appl pen 26 Jan 1846 Rockbridge Co age 84. W7264 **P:** Y **BLW:** unk **RG:** Y **MK:** N **PH:** unk **SS:** E pg 226; K Vol II pg 121-2; CG Vol 2 pg 1207 **BS:** 04.

FLAGLY (FLAGLEY), John; b unk; d 1781 **RU:** Private, Col John Lamb's 2d NY Artillery Regt. Killed in the battle at Yorktown **CEM:** Yorktown Victory Monument Tablet; GPS 38.28350, -78.54150; Yorktown; York **GS:** U **SP:** No info **VI:** No further data **P:** unk **BLW:** unk **RG:** unk **MK:** unk **PH:** unk **SS:** J-Yorktown Historian; AX pg 64 **BS:** JLARC 74.

FLEENOR, Michael; b c1757, Berks Co, PA; d 3 Aug 1837 **RU:** Soldier, Served in VA Line. Ent serv Washington Co 1777 as sub for brother (Jacob) **CEM:** Fleenor; GPS unk; North Fork, Holston; Washington **GS:** U **SP:** Mar (10 Dec 1781 Washington Co) Sally Lyndor (c1765-aft 1848) **VI:** Sol appl pen 26 Mar 1833 Washington Co age 76. Widow appl 21 Aug 1844 Washington Co age 79. W7288. Pensioned in 1833 **P:** Y **BLW:** unk **RG:** unk **MK:** unk **PH:** unk **SS:** CG Vol 2 pg 1210; K Vol II pg 123 **BS:** JLARC 4, 34.

FLEET, William; b 1757; d 1833 **RU:** Lieutenant, Specific service is at the Lib of VA, Collection of Loose Manuscripts re pensions, vol 2 **CEM:** Private graveyard nr St Stephens Church; GPS unk; Goshen; Rockbridge **GS:** U **SP:** No info **VI:** No further data **P:** Y **BLW:** unk **RG:** unk **MK:** unk **PH:** unk **SS:** J-DAR Hatcher; CZ pg 165 **BS:** JLARC 2.

FLEET, William; b 18 Dec 1757, King & Queen Co; d 11 Apr 1833 **RU:** Lieutenant/Patriot, Served in King & Queen Co Militia and had other unidentified service to qualify him for a pension. Gave material aid to cause **CEM:** Goshen; GPS unk; Check property records for Fleet Family at "Goshen" also see Senate Document 1952,serial 11670, vol 3; King & Queen **GS:** Y **SP:** Mar (1 Oct 1795) Sarah Tomlin or Browne (1 Apr 1776 Essex Co-27Jan 1818) **VI:** This may or may not be the same person with same birth and death yrs that is buried in Rockbridge Co **P:** Y **BLW:** unk **RG:** N **MK:** N **PH:** unk **SS:** D King & Queen Co; E pg 277; AR Vol 2 pg 38 **BS:** 129 pg 485.

FLEMING, Andrew; b 1759; d 6 Jan 1820 **RU:** Soldier, Specific service is at the Lib of VA, Journals House of Delegates, Dec 1824 pg 18 **CEM:** Presbyterian Church; GPS 38.80015, -77.05791; Wilkes St & Hamilton Ln; Alexandria City **GS:** Y **SP:** Prob mar Catherine (-----) (c1773-26 Mar 1846) also bur here **VI:** Died age 61 **P:** unk **BLW:** unk **RG:** Y **MK:** unk **PH:** unk **SS:** J-NSSAR 1993 Reg; CZ pg 165 **BS:** JLARC 1; 23 pg 32.

FLEMING, William; b 6 Jul 1736, Cumberland Co; d 15 Feb 1824 **RU:** Patriot, Delegate to 1775 & 1776 colonial conventions. Served in VA State House of Delegates fr 1776-1778. Cont Congress 1778-1779 **CEM:** Fleming Family; GPS unk; Midlothian; Chesterfield **GS:** U **SP:** No info **VI:** Judge of the General Ct. In 1789 was elected to Virginia's first Supreme Ct of Appeals to 1809 when he became presiding judge **P:** N **BLW:** N **RG:** unk **MK:** unk **PH:** unk **SS:** CD **BS:** 196.

FLEMING, William; b 18 Feb 1729, Jedburgh, Scotland; d 24 Aug 1795 **RU:** Surgeon/Colonel, Gave orders as Co Lt to send troops to Fincastle Co who were being invaded by enemy. Wounded as Col at Battle of Point Pleasant in Oct 1774 **CEM:** Belmont; GPS unk; Frank Rd, Roanoke; Roanoke City **GS:** U **SP:** Mar (1763) Anne Christian (1744-1811) **VI:** Acting governor for 10 days in 1781 **P:** unk **BLW:** unk **RG:** unk **MK:** Y **PH:** unk **SS:** C pg 589; Z pg 198 **BS:** JLARC 2,41, 109.

FLINT, John; b 1763, Amherst Co; d 1818 **RU:** Private, Served in 4th Troop, 1st Battalion Light Dragoons, Jan 1783 **CEM:** Stonewall Jackson Memorial; GPS 37.78128, -79.44604; 314 S Main St; Lexington City **GS:** U **SP:** Mar (21 Oct 1784) Elizabeth Williams (1754 Rockbridge Co-1 Mar 1839) **VI:** Son of Richard (1739-1790) & Hannah (-----) (1742-1839) Flynt **P:** unk **BLW:** unk **RG:** unk **MK:** unk **PH:** unk **SS:** E pg 278; AP-Payroll **BS:** 196.

FLOOD, Henry; b 1755; d 1827 **RU:** Soldier, Served in 2nd Regt Cont Line 1777-1780 **CEM:** Flood Family; GPS unk; Vera; Appomattox **GS:** Y **SP:** Mary Walker (1754- 24 Jul 1828) **VI:** No further data **P:** unk **BLW:** unk **RG:** unk **MK:** unk **PH:** unk **SS:** AP Muster roll **BS:** 196.

RU=Rank/Unit	CEM=Cemetery	GS=Gravestone	SP=Spousal Information
VI=Other Veteran Info	P=Pension	BLW=Bounty/Land Warrant	RG=Registered Grave
MK=SAR/DAR Marker	PH=Photo	SS=Service Source	BS=Burial Source

FLOOD, Nicholas Dr; b Abt 1710; d 1776 **RU:** Patriot, His estate gave material aid to the cause **CEM:** North Farnham Episcopal; GPS unk; Farnham; Richmond Co **GS:** N **SP:** Eliabeth Peachey (18 Nov 1721, d. 1792 Richmond Co) d/o Samuel & Catherine (McCarty) Peachey **VI:** His will directed that he be bur next to his only daughter Catherine (Flood) McCall at North Farnham Church. His estate gave material aid to the cause. Only a fragment of the stone remains **P:** N **BLW:** N **RG:** unk **MK:** N **PH:** N **SS:** AL Ct Bk pg 1, 7; DU pg 111 **BS:** 196.

FLOOD, Noah; b unk; d 2 Oct 1818 **RU:** Soldier, Served in VA Line **CEM:** Flood Family, "Toga"; GPS unk; Rt 24; Buckingham **GS:** U **SP:** Mar (29 or 30 Nov 1785 in Buckingham Co) Sarah Fuqua (1763-aft 1841) **VI:** Widow appl pen 16 Oct 1841 Buckingham Co age 78- rejected. R3615 **P:** Y **BLW:** N **RG:** unk **MK:** N **PH:** unk **SS:** CG Vol 2 pg 1218; K Vol II pg 126 **BS:** JLARC 4, 10, 44, 59.

FLOOK (FLUCK), Henry (John Henry); b 2 Nov 1759, Middleton, MD; d 26 Sep 1841 **RU:** Private, Served in 33rd Bn MA Militia **CEM:** Bethel Cemetery; GPS 38.47592, -78.75641; 3061 Armentrout Path, Keezletown; Rockingham **GS:** Y **SP:** Elizabeth Rossel **VI:** No further data **P:** unk **BLW:** unk **RG:** unk **MK:** Y **PH:** unk **SS:** NSSAR Ancestor #P-159577 **BS:** JLARC 3.

FLORI, Pierre; b unk; d 1781 **RU:** Seaman, Served on "Diademe" and died from Yorktown battle **CEM:** French Memorial; GPS 36.81944, -79.39933; Yorktown; York **GS:** U **SP:** No info **VI:** No further data **P:** unk **BLW:** unk **RG:** Y **MK:** unk **PH:** unk **SS:** J-Yorktown Historian **BS:** JLARC 1, 74.

FLOURANCE, George Jr; b c1753, Prince William Co; d c1822 **RU:** Private, Served in 3rd VA Cont Line **CEM:** Flourance Family; GPS 38.71577, -77.46386; Lake Jackson; Prince William **GS:** Y **SP:** Eve (-----) (1778-__) **VI:** Son of George & (-----) Flourance Sr **P:** unk **BLW:** unk **RG:** Y **MK:** Y **PH:** Y **SS:** 04 **BS:** 04.

FLOURANCE (FLORENCE, FLORANCE), William; b 7 Jan 1736, Prince William Co; d 14 Sep 1821 or 22 Oct 1822 **RU:** Lieutenant, Ent serv Col Buford's Brigade, Fauquier Co Militia **CEM:** Camp Glen Kirk; GPS 38.77367, -77.62360; Gainesville, Rt 29 N, Linter Hall Rd; Prince William **GS:** Y **SP:** 1) Mary Nash 2) Mar (21 Apr 1784 Prince William Co, bond dated 13 Apr 1784) Sarah Hutchison (c1759-__) **VI:** Widow pensioned Prince William Co 1838 age 79. F-W7291 R992, 7291 **P:** Y **BLW:** unk **RG:** Y **MK:** Y **PH:** Y **SS:** K Vol II pg 127 **BS:** 04.

FLOYD, Matthew; b 7 Mar 1763; d 20 Aug 1844 **RU:** Soldier, VA Line. Enl St George Parrish, Accomack Co **CEM:** Morrison Hill; GPS unk; .8 mi S of Rt 622, W of Rt 600, Frogstool; Accomack **GS:** Y **SP:** 1) Elizabeth Custis 2) Lizzie Glenn (3 Feb 1789-1 Mar 1807) TS shared with husband Matthew Floyd. **VI:** Sol appl 1 Aug 1832 in St George Parish in Accomack Co. S184402. Was minister of gospel. Recd pen 1832. S2553. DAR marker on Gr **P:** Y **BLW:** unk **RG:** unk **MK:** unk **PH:** unk **SS:** CG Vol 2 pg 1219; K Vol II pg 129; BT **BS:** JLARC 4, 5; 196.

FOLE, Nicolas; b unk; d 1781 **RU:** Soldier, Served in Auxonne Bn and died fr battle at Yorktown **CEM:** French Memorial; GPS 36.81944, -79.39933; Yorktown; York **GS:** U **SP:** No info **VI:** No further data **P:** unk **BLW:** unk **RG:** unk **MK:** unk **PH:** unk **SS:** J-Yorktown Historian **BS:** JLARC 1, 74.

FOLLIN, Catherine (Sandford); b 1765; d 1813 **RU:** Patriot, Service information not determined fr DAR **CEM:** Arlington National; GPS 38.88377, -77.06535; Jefferson Davis Hwy Rt 110; Arlington **GS:** Y **SP:** John Fallin, also bur here, shared stone **VI:** No further data **P:** N **BLW:** N **RG:** Y **MK:** N **PH:** unk **SS:** AR DAR report **BS:** 80 vol 2 pg 41; 196.

FOLLIN, John; b 5 Sept 1761, Fairfax Co; d 17 Apr 1841 **RU:** Seaman, US Navy, Ent serv Fairfax Co, age 17. Captured aboard the vessel "Neptune". Imprisoned for 3 yrs. Exchanged near close of the Revolution. Was Paymaster **CEM:** Arlington National; GPS 38.88377, -77.06535; Jefferson Davis Hwy Rt 110; Arlington **GS:** Y **SP:** 1) Catherine Follin (1767-1813) 2) Mary Barker (1787-1863) **VI:** Died & bur Fairfax Co; reinterred at Arlington 23 May 1911. Shared stone with both wives **P:** unk **BLW:** unk **RG:** Y **MK:** Y **PH:** unk **SS:** B **BS:** JLARC 1, 27; 196.

FONTAINE, William; b 1754; d 6 Oct 1810 **RU:** Lieutenant Colonel, Ent serv Amherst Co. Served in VA Line. At Yorktown, commanded 5th Co, 21 Oct 1775 of 2nd VA Regt of Foot. As Maj was in the Conventional Army Guard Regt 24 Dec 1779-15 June 1781 which transferred prisoners fr MA to VA. Was promoted to Lt Col Mar 1781 **CEM:** Beaver Dam; GPS unk; Rt 738; Hanover **GS:** U **SP:** Mar (27

RU=Rank/Unit   CEM=Cemetery   GS=Gravestone   SP=Spousal Information
VI=Other Veteran Info   P=Pension   BLW=Bounty/Land Warrant   RG=Registered Grave
MK=SAR/DAR Marker   PH=Photo   SS=Service Source   BS=Burial Source

111

Dec 1787 Hanover Co) Ann Morris (c1766-aft 1843) **VI:** Teacher in Amherst Co, 1773. Widow appl pen 20 Aug 1838 Hanover Co age 72. W7319, BLW #1949-450 issued to heirs 28 Jun 1833, also VA 1/2 pay **P:** Y **BLW:** Y **RG:** unk **MK:** unk **PH:** N **SS:** CE pg 36, 117, 118; CG Vol 2 pg 1224; K Vol II pg 130 **BS:** JLARC 4, 71.

FONTENAY, Guillaume; b unk; d 1781 **RU:** Seaman, Served on "Diademe" and died from Yorktown battle **CEM:** French Memorial; GPS 36.81944, -79.39933; Yorktown; York **GS:** U **SP:** No info **VI:** No further data **P:** unk **BLW:** unk **RG:** Y **MK:** unk **PH:** N **SS:** J-Yorktown Historian **BS:** JLARC 1, 74.

FORBES, Alexander; b 1763, Stafford Co; d 22 Feb 1838 **RU:** Soldier, Ent serv Buckingham Co 1780. Served in VA Line **CEM:** Loch Lomond; GPS unk; Check property records; Buckingham **GS:** U **SP:** 1) Mar (28 Jan 1787 Buckingham Co) Lucy Scruggs 2) Mar (27 Mar 1815 Buckingham Co) Judith Ammonette (c1778-aft 1855) **VI:** Sol appl pen 13 Aug 1832 Buckingham Co. Widow appl 20 Dec 1854 Buckingham Co age 76 and also 24 Mar 1855. W10998, BLW #26642-160-55 **P:** Y **BLW:** Y **RG:** unk **MK:** N **PH:** N **SS:** CG Vol 2 pg 1226; K Vol II pg 130 **BS:** 80; JLARC 2.

FORD, John; b 17 Jun 1755, Stafford Co; d Apr 1825 **RU:** Private, Served in 5th, 6th Cont Lines **CEM:** Ford Family; GPS unk; Nr Leon; Madison **GS:** Y **SP:** 1) Myrtle (-----) 2) Mar (4 Apr 1788) Rosanna Newmann **VI:** Son of John & Elizabeth (Thornton) Ford **P:** unk **BLW:** unk **RG:** N **MK:** N **PH:** unk **SS:** E pg 281 **BS:** 80 vol 2 pg 43.

FORD, John Thomas; b 17 Jun 1725, King George Co; d 19 Dec 1791 (WP 1792) **RU:** Lieutenant/Patriot, Served in 5th and 6th Cont line and Clark's Illinois Regt. Was entitled to 1/2 pay **CEM:** Ford Family; GPS unk; Merrimac; Culpeper **GS:** U **SP:** Elizabeth Myrtle Thornton (1733-1788) **VI:** No further data **P:** N **BLW:** N **RG:** unk **MK:** unk **PH:** N **SS:** A pg 419; AL Ct Bk I pg 19; EF pg 37 **BS:** 196.

FORD, William; b unk; d 1794 **RU:** Private, Served in Capt Ephraim Rucker's Co of Col Field's Regt at the Battle of Point Pleasant Oct 1784 **CEM:** Dumfries Public; GPS 38.34110, -77.19964; 17821 Mine Rd, Dumfries; Prince William **GS:** N **SP:** No info **VI:** SAR monument **P:** unk **BLW:** unk **RG:** Y **MK:** Y **PH:** N **SS:** Z pg 87 **BS:** 04; 96 pg 83.

FOREHAND, John Sr; b 29 Mar 1755, PA; d 27 Feb 1838 **RU:** Private, Served in Capts McGuire and Bell's Cos, 6th VA Regt **CEM:** Hattan Family; GPS unk; Rt 629, behind house on Frances Hostetter's property, Kerr's District; Rockbridge **GS:** Y **SP:** Rebecca Campbell (17 Mar 1754-29 Jan 1846) **VI:** Govt GS **P:** unk **BLW:** unk **RG:** unk **MK:** unk **PH:** unk **SS:** DAR Ancestor #A041018; B **BS:** 204.

FOREMAN, Robert; b 1740; d 4 Mar 1790 **RU:** Paymaster, 9th Cont Line in Apr 1777. Resigned 16 June 1778 **CEM:** Foreman Plot; GPS unk; NW of jct Rts 709 & 708, nr Miona; Accomack **GS:** Y **SP:** No info **VI:** Died age 50 **P:** unk **BLW:** unk **RG:** N **MK:** N **PH:** unk **SS:** E pg 281 **BS:** 38 pg 119.

FORREST, George; b c1747; d aft 1818 **RU:** Soldier, Ent serv 1776 **CEM:** St James Church; GPS unk; Mathews CH; Mathews **GS:** U **SP:** No info **VI:** Pen in Mathews Co in 1818. Resident there in 1820 when he was 73 **P:** Y **BLW:** unk **RG:** unk **MK:** unk **PH:** N **SS:** J- DAR Hatcher; K Vol II pg 114 **BS:** JLARC 2.

FORT, Lewis; b unk; d 1826 **RU:** Private, Probably served in Southampton Co Militia **CEM:** Mason Family; GPS unk; Rt 612 Fortsville Rd, 4 mi NW of Adam Grove; Southampton **GS:** Y **SP:** Elizabeth Harris Coleman (__-1823) **VI:** No further data **P:** unk **BLW:** unk **RG:** N **MK:** N **PH:** unk **SS:** AP roll **BS:** 144 Mason.

FORTUNE, Benjamin; b 1742; d 1784 **RU:** Private, Served in 10th Cont Line **CEM:** Fortune; GPS unk; Lovingston; Nelson **GS:** U **SP:** Sarah Eubank (1747-1824) d/o John & Hannah (-----) Eubank **VI:** Son of John & Lucey (-----) Fortune **P:** unk **BLW:** unk **RG:** unk **MK:** unk **PH:** unk **SS:** E pg 283 **BS:** 196.

FORTUNE, Thomas; b 1740; d 1804 **RU:** Private, Served in Caroline Co Militia, 1781 **CEM:** Fortune; GPS unk; Lovingston; Nelson **GS:** U **SP:** Elizabeth Eubank (1745-1821) d/o John (1715-1789) & Hannah (-----) Eubank **VI:** Son of John (1711-1790) & Lucry (Fletcher) Fortune **P:** unk **BLW:** unk **RG:** unk **MK:** unk **PH:** unk **SS:** CQ **BS:** 196.

FOSTER, Isaac; b c1750 Gloucester Co; d c1804 **RU:** Captain, Served in a VA unit in Illinois **CEM:** Foster; GPS unk; See property records for him and his wife in Mathews Co; Mathews **GS:** U **SP:** Mar (1776) Elizabeth Cayles Hodges (__Gloucester Co-aft 1810, Mathews Co) **VI:** DAR applic indicates he

RU=Rank/Unit   CEM=Cemetery   GS=Gravestone   SP=Spousal Information
VI=Other Veteran Info   P=Pension   BLW=Bounty/Land Warrant   RG=Registered Grave
MK=SAR/DAR Marker   PH=Photo   SS=Service Source   BS=Burial Source

112

died in Gloucester County and his wife died in Mathews Co **P:** unk **BLW:** unk **RG:** unk **MK:** unk **PH:** unk **SS:** DAR Ancestor #A041568; NSSAR Ancestor #P-160760; CZ pg 168 **BS:** JLARC 68.

FOSTER, James; b Jun 1750, Prince William Co; d 10 Sep 1800 **RU:** Patriot, Gave material aid to the cause. Paid Supply Tax, Prince William Co in 1783 **CEM:** Whitewood; GPS unk; 2 mi N of The Plains; Fauquier **GS:** Y **SP:** Mar (15 May 1772) Elizabeth Grigsby (12 Jan 1755-20 May 1837) **VI:** Son of Robert & Sarah (Haley) Foster. Remains reinterred here fr Prince William Co where he died **P:** N **BLW:** N **RG:** N **MK:** N **PH:** unk **SS:** AL Ct Bk pg 5; DD **BS:** 95 Whitewood; 196.

FOSTER, Joseph; b c1757; d 1837 **RU:** Corporal, Served in 4th & 7th Cont lines **CEM:** Shockoe Hill; GPS 37.55190, -77.43170; 4th & Hospital Sts; Richmond City **GS:** Y **SP:** No info **VI:** No further data **P:** unk **BLW:** unk **RG:** N **MK:** N **PH:** unk **SS:** E pg 283 **BS:** 57 pg 14.

FOSTER, Peter G; b Mar 1756; d 31 Dec 1819 **RU:** Sergeant, Served 3 yrs in 1st VA Regt **CEM:** Richard Foster; GPS unk; Rt 650, Hicks Wharf Rd, Rose Hill Plantation; Mathews **GS:** Y **SP:** Nancy Ann Hall (Sep 1756, Gloucester Co-Jan 1820) d/o Robert & Nancy (Johnston) Hall **VI:** Son of Richard (1723-1795) & (-----) Foster. BLW 200 acres, recd 28 Jul 1783 **P:** unk **BLW:** Y **RG:** unk **MK:** unk **PH:** unk **SS:** E pg 284; F pg 27 **BS:** 196.

FOURNIER, Charles; b unk; d 1781 **RU:** Seaman, Served on "Sceptre" and died from Yorktown battle **CEM:** French Memorial; GPS 36.81944, -79.39933; Yorktown; York **GS:** U **SP:** No info **VI:** No further data **P:** unk **BLW:** unk **RG:** Y **MK:** unk **PH:** unk **SS:** J-Yorktown Historian **BS:** JLARC 1, 74.

FOUSHEE, William; b 26 Oct 1749; d 21 Aug 1824 **RU:** Surgeon, Ent serv as army surgeon. Was Medical Director for VA **CEM:** Shockoe Hill; GPS 37.55190, -77.43170; 4th & Hospital Sts; Richmond City **GS:** Y **SP:** Elizabeth Harmondson **VI:** Recd pen R14223. Also VA 1/2 Pay (See N.A. Acc #874 #050068 1/2 Pay). Heirs recd BLW 28 Mar 1832. Was first mayor of Richmond **P:** Y **BLW:** Y **RG:** unk **MK:** N **PH:** Y **SS:** AK; BY pg 277; CG Vol 2 pg 1246; K Vol II pg 139 **BS:** 04, JLARC 4, 77, 104.

FOWLER, Samuel; b c1764, Salisbury, MA; d 31 Jul 1814 **RU:** Captain, Serv in Salisbury, MA fr 2 Dec 1780 to 24 Apr 1781. Was made capt by end of war **CEM:** Trinity Episcopal; GPS 36.83459, -76.30105; 500 Court St; Portsmouth City **GS:** Y **SP:** No info **VI:** No further data **P:** unk **BLW:** unk **RG:** N **MK:** N **PH:** unk **SS:** AJ MA Service **BS:** 57; 75 Portsmouth.

FOWLES, James; b unk; d 1781 **RU:** Private, Served in Col James Clinton's 3rd NY Line Regt. Killed in the battle at Yorktown **CEM:** Yorktown Victory Monument Tablet; GPS 38.28350, -78.54150; Yorktown; York **GS:** U **SP:** No info **VI:** No further data **P:** unk **BLW:** unk **RG:** unk **MK:** unk **PH:** unk **SS:** J-Yorktown Historian; AX pg 42 **BS:** JLARC 74.

FOX, John; b 29 Jun 1760, King William Co; d 29 Dec 1814 **RU:** Captain, Commanded a co in Louisa Co Militia Apr 178? **CEM:** Retreat; GPS unk; Aylett; King William **GS:** U **SP:** 1) Judith Turner (___-1780) 2) Frances Wyatt Woolfork (1762-1823) **VI:** No further data **P:** unk **BLW:** unk **RG:** unk **MK:** N **PH:** unk **SS:** E pg 285 **BS:** 196.

FOX, Samuel; b c1732, Bitton, Gloucestershire, England; d 13 Mar 1801 **RU:** Patriot, Gave material aid to cause **CEM:** St George's Episcopal; GPS unk; 905 Princess Anne; Fredericksburg City **GS:** Y **SP:** Elizabeth (-----) **VI:** No further data **P:** N **BLW:** N **RG:** Y **MK:** N **PH:** unk **SS:** D pg 346 **BS:** 12 pg 105.

FRANCISCO, Peter; b 9 Jul 1760 1759; d 16 Jan 1831 **RU:** Private, Ent serv Prince Edward Co 1776. Served in 10th VA Regt, part of Cont Army in Dec '76. Was at Brandywine, Germantown, Ft Mifflin (at Valley Forge), Monmouth, Stony Pt; Camden, SC and saved Col Mayo's life. Was at Cowpens, and Guilford CH NC where severely wounded. Killed 3 Tarelton's Raiders near Ward's Tavern in Amelia Co **CEM:** Shockoe Hill; GPS 37.55190, -77.43170; 4th & Hospital Sts; Richmond City **GS:** Y **SP:** One or more?) (-----) 2) Mar (3 Jun 1823 Buckingham Co, later Appomattox Co) Mrs. Mary B West (soldier's last wife) **VI:** Was 6'6" 260-pound hero. Lifelong friend of Lafayette. Sergeant-at-Arms of house of Delegates. Bur with full military & Masonic honors. Also in War of 1812. Sol recd pen 1 Jan 1819 age 60. Widow appl pen 27 Feb 1854 Botetourt Co & for BLW 24 Mar 1855. W11021. BLW #8002-160-55 **P:** Y **BLW:** Y **RG:** Y **MK:** Y **PH:** unk **SS:** CG Vol 2 pg 1256 **BS:** JLARC 1, 2, 4, 77.

FRANKLIN, James; b 1750; d 1813 **RU:** Corporal/Patriot, Served in 3rd, 4th, 5th Cont Line. Gave material aid to cause **CEM:** Franklin; GPS unk; Amherst; Amherst **GS:** U **SP:** Mar (15 Dec 1796

RU=Rank/Unit   CEM=Cemetery   GS=Gravestone   SP=Spousal Information
VI=Other Veteran Info   P=Pension   BLW=Bounty/Land Warrant   RG=Registered Grave
MK=SAR/DAR Marker   PH=Photo   SS=Service Source   BS=Burial Source

113

Amherst Co) Nancy Crews **VI:** No further data **P:** unk **BLW:** unk **RG:** unk **MK:** unk **PH:** unk **SS:** E pg 287; AL Ct Bk pg 9 Amherst Co **BS:** JLARC 4.

FRANKLIN, John Sr; b 1763; d 1845 **RU:** Soldier/Patriot, Gave material aid to cause **CEM:** Franklin Family; GPS unk; Twp 50; Chesterfield **GS:** U **SP:** No info **VI:** Son of John (c1735-aft 1783 Chesterfield Co) & Ann (Hatcher(Franklin (c1738-1801 Chesterfield Co) **P:** unk **BLW:** unk **RG:** Y **MK:** N **PH:** unk **SS:** J-NSSAR 2000 Reg; NSSAR Ancestor #P-161654; Al Ct Bk pg 22 **BS:** JLARC 76.

FRANKLIN, Lewis; b 1758, prob Orange Co; d 11 Apr 1842 **RU:** Private, Served in NC & VA Line. Ent serv Surry Co NC. Also Ent serv Orange Co 1779. Ent serv Henry Co 1780. Served in Orange Co Militia & guarded POWs at the Albemarle Barracks. While in Henry Co Militia, served against Tories in Western VA & served with Gen Greene during the "Race to the Dan" in 1781. Was wagon driver (QM dept) for 5 mos, 1781 **CEM:** Franklin Family; GPS 36.71597,-79.94299; Off US 57, btw Shadyview Rd SR 1404 and US 220 Bypass, behind "Old Franklin Home Place," nr community of Fieldale; Henry **GS:** Y **SP:** Milly Stone, d 1841 **VI:** Sol appl pen 13 Nov 1832 Henry Co age 74. S8519 Family records - cemetery still owned by extended family member **P:** Y **BLW:** unk **RG:** Y **MK:** Y **PH:** unk **SS:** Pension affidavit; CG Vol 2 pg 1259; K Vol II pg 144 **BS:** 196.

FRANKLIN, Thomas; b 8 Sep 1758, Bedford Co; d 23 Mar 1841 **RU:** Private, Ent serv Bedford Co. Served in VA Line and Campbell Co Militia **CEM:** Franklin Family; GPS 37.07200, -79.05100; SW Rt 646 3.2 mi N of Rt 615, Gladys quadrant; Campbell **GS:** N **SP:** Mar (29 Mar 1796) Letitia Evans (c1759-28-Jul 1862 Campbell Co) **VI:** Sol appl 2 Oct 1832 Campbell Co age 69. S8517. Widow pen Campbell Co 1850 age 81. BLW #26969 granted fr Campbell Co 1856. Her pen cut off during Civil War, then pen appl rejected. W1590. Survey at site of family in 1936 found one Gr (his). DAR marker on Gr **P:** Y **BLW:** Y **RG:** unk **MK:** Y **PH:** N **SS:** E pg 287; CG Vol 2 pg 1259; K Vol II pg 144 **BS:** JLARC 4, 36; 196.

FRANTZ, Christian; b 1740; d Feb 1824 **RU:** Private, Served in Capt John Anapach Co, Berks Co, PA **CEM:** Frantz Family; GPS unk; Check property records for location; Bedford **GS:** U **SP:** Mar (1763) Anna (-----) (__-1821) **VI:** Died in Botetourt Co. SAR database has correct burial county (Bedford), but wrong location of Fincastle which is in Botetourt Co. **P:** unk **BLW:** unk **RG:** Y **MK:** N **PH:** unk **SS:** J-NASSR 2000 Reg; CI, PA Archives Series 5 Vol 5 pg 185 **BS:** JLARC 76.

FRAY, Ephraim; b 1762; d 3 Feb 1846 **RU:** Private, Was placed on a draft list in Culpeper Co **CEM:** Hebron Lutheran; GPS 38.40676, -78.24808; 899 Blankenbaker Rd, Madison; Madison **GS:** Y **SP:** 1) Maria Huffman 2) Nancy Snyder (1781-22 Dec 1849) **VI:** No further data **P:** unk **BLW:** unk **RG:** Y **MK:** N **PH:** unk **SS:** O; DJ Jan 1781 pg 25 **BS:** 04.

FRAYSER (FRAZIER), Jesse; b 27 Jul 1754 or 1764; d 28 Mar 1827 **RU:** Private, Served at Yorktown **CEM:** Glendale/Frayser Farm Family; GPS unk; 11 mi SE of Richmond City on Rt 5; Henrico **GS:** Y **SP:** Kesiah Hobson (12 May 1761-5 Dec 1854) **VI:** No further data **P:** unk **BLW:** unk **RG:** Y **MK:** unk **PH:** unk **SS:** J-NASSR 2000 Reg; B; DD **BS:** 114, JLARC 76.

FRAZIER, James; b unk; d 1818 **RU:** Private, Served in Booker's Co, 11th VA Inf Regt **CEM:** Bethel Presbyterian; GPS 38.04257, -79.17283; 563 Bethel Green Rd, Middlebrook; Augusta **GS:** Y **SP:** No info **VI:** Govt stone. Was a Capt of militia in 1794 **P:** unk **BLW:** unk **RG:** unk **MK:** Y **PH:** unk **SS:** B **BS:** JLARC 2, 8, 62, 63; 196.

FRAZIER, John; b 1750; d 1832 **RU:** Soldier, Served in 8th Cont Line **CEM:** New Providence Presbyterian; GPS 37.95130, -79.30250; 1208 New Providence Rd, Raphine; Rockbridge **GS:** U **SP:** No info **VI:** No further data **P:** unk **BLW:** unk **RG:** unk **MK:** unk **PH:** unk **SS:** E pg 287 **BS:** JLARC 63, 79.

FREEMAN, William; b 1754; d 2 Aug 1829 **RU:** Private, Ent serv 1775. Served in Cont & VA Lines. Served under many Capts in Col Henry Henderson's Regt **CEM:** Freeman Family; GPS unk; Rt778, Weber City; Scott **GS:** Y **SP:** Mar (1778) Hannah Epperson (1756-25 Nov 1836) **VI:** Sol appl pen 2 Jun 1818 Scott Co age 64. S39547 **P:** Y **BLW:** unk **RG:** Y **MK:** N **PH:** unk **SS:** O; CG Vol 2 pg 1269; K Vol II pg 147 **BS:** 04.

FRENCH, Matthew; b unk; d unk **RU:** Private, Served in Capt Cloyd's Co, Cont Line 12 Sep 1777 **CEM:** French (possibly same as Boyd); GPS unk; Wolf Creek near Curve; Giles **GS:** U **SP:** Sarah Paine **VI:**

RU=Rank/Unit	CEM=Cemetery	GS=Gravestone	SP=Spousal Information
VI=Other Veteran Info	P=Pension	BLW=Bounty/Land Warrant	RG=Registered Grave
MK=SAR/DAR Marker	PH=Photo	SS=Service Source	BS=Burial Source

114

No further data **P:** unk **BLW:** unk **RG:** Y **MK:** unk **PH:** unk **SS:** G pg 215 Montgomery Co **BS:** JLARC 1, 2, 26, 63.

FRIEZ (FREIS, FREISE, FREIZE), Martin; b 1748; d 1830 **RU:** Patriot, Gave material aid to cause **CEM:** Old Stone Church; GPS 39.30110, -78.16750; nr 461 Green Spring Rd, Green Spring; Frederick **GS:** Y **SP:** No record of marriage **VI:** No further data **P:** N **BLW:** N **RG:** N **MK:** N **PH:** unk **SS:** AL Cert Issued **BS:** 59 pg 116.

FRIMIER, John; b unk; d 1781 **RU:** Private, Served in Col Van Cortlandt's 2d Regt, NY Line. Killed in the battle at Yorktown **CEM:** Yorktown Victory Monument Tablet; GPS 38.28350, -78.54150; Yorktown; York **GS:** U **SP:** No info **VI:** No further data **P:** unk **BLW:** unk **RG:** unk **MK:** unk **PH:** unk **SS:** J-Yorktown Historian; AX pg 33 **BS:** JLARC 74.

FRITTS, John; b c1762, Shenandoah Co; d c1847 **RU:** Private, Served in NC & VA Militias 1781-1782, in Capt John Lopp & then Capt Peter Faust Cos. Enl Rowan Co NC **CEM:** Fritts Family; GPS unk; Rumored to be next to federal prison, check property records of family; Lee **GS:** U **SP:** Mary Beaver **VI:** Son of Hans Ulrich & (-----) Fritts, also a Rev War veteran. Sol appl pen 27 May 1834 Hawkins Co TN age 72 S10701. Came back to Lee Co before death **P:** Y **BLW:** unk **RG:** Y **MK:** N **PH:** N **SS:** K pg 14; CG Vol 2 pg 1277 **BS:** 4.

FROLEAUX, Julien; b unk; d 1781 **RU:** Seaman, Served on "Victorie" and died from Yorktown battle **CEM:** French Memorial; GPS 36.81944, -79.39933; Yorktown; York **GS:** U **SP:** No info **VI:** No further data **P:** unk **BLW:** unk **RG:** Y **MK:** unk **PH:** unk **SS:** J-Yorktown Historian **BS:** JLARC 1, 74.

FROMENT, Pierre; b unk; d 1781 **RU:** Soldier, Served in Touraine Bn and died fr battle at Yorktown **CEM:** French Memorial; GPS 36.81944, -79.39933; Yorktown; York **GS:** U **SP:** No info **VI:** No further data **P:** unk **BLW:** unk **RG:** Y **MK:** unk **PH:** unk **SS:** J-Yorktown Historian **BS:** JLARC 1, 74.

FROST, John; b 1756, Morristown, NJ; d 13 Jul 1834 **RU:** Corporal, Ent serv Morris Co, NJ, served in 4th NJ Regt. Ent serv Bedford Co Militia **CEM:** John Frost; GPS 36.71845, -80.89540; Roseberry Ln nr Hillsville; Carroll **GS:** N **SP:** Mar (8 Jul 1834 Rockingham Co, NC) Mary (-----) **VI:** Son of Ezekial Frost (1716-1762) & Alice Hopkins. Moved to NC after Rev War for 18 mos, then to Montgomery Co (later Grayson Co) 1784. Widow recd pen Grayson Co 1840 age 76. W7324 **P:** Y **BLW:** unk **RG:** unk **MK:** unk **PH:** N **SS:** K Vol II pg 149 **BS:** JLARC 4, 43; 196.

FROST, William; b unk; d unk **RU:** Captain/Patriot, Served in Frederick Co Militia 4 Aug 1779. Supplied hay, bushels of corn, 880# beef **CEM:** Frost; GPS unk; Vic Hopewell; Clarke **GS:** N **SP:** No info **VI:** "Middle Farm" owned by Mrs. Lorenzo Lewis in 1941; marked by a few trees. **P:** unk **BLW:** unk **RG:** unk **MK:** N **PH:** N **SS:** E pg 291 **BS:** JLARC 24.

FRY, Christopher; b c1728; d 10 May 1801 **RU:** Patriot, Provided waggonage to militia 1775 **CEM:** Mt Hebron; GPS 39.10916, -78.09497; 305 E Boscawen St; Winchester City **GS:** Y **SP:** No info **VI:** He served in the Colonial War in the Old VA Regt as an NCO in 1754 and on 08 Mar 1780 received bounty land of 200 acres for this service **P:** N **BLW:** N **RG:** N **MK:** N **PH:** N **SS:** Z pg 77; AH pg 311 **BS:** 196.

FRY, Henry; b ,; d 6 Sep 1823 **RU:** Patriot, Was member of House of Burgess, and the VA Legislature **CEM:** Fry Family; GPS unk; Meander Plantation; Madison **GS:** Y **SP:** Susan Thorton Walker (1746-1808) **VI:** Son of Joshua (1700-1754) & Mary Hill (Micou) Fry (1716-1772). After overcoming severe alcoholism, became a Methodist minister and served 40 yrs. Was clerk of Albemarle Co for 8 yrs **P:** N **BLW:** N **RG:** N **MK:** N **PH:** Y **SS:** AK; AL Commissioner of Provisioners Law for Culpeper Co 1780/civil service **BS:** 196; 32 Oct 08.

FRYE, Benjamin; b 1754; d 8 Apr 1823 **RU:** Captain, Commissioned Capt 1779. Served in Christopher Lippett's Regt **CEM:** Frye Family; GPS unk; Wheatfield; Shenandoah **GS:** U **SP:** Mary Magdalena Secrist (__-__ Morgantown, WV) **VI:** No further data **P:** unk **BLW:** unk **RG:** unk **MK:** unk **PH:** unk **SS:** C pg 155 **BS:** 196.

FUGENOT, Noel; b unk; d 1781 **RU:** Soldier, Served in Agenois Bn and died fr battle at Yorktown **CEM:** French Memorial; GPS 36.81944, -79.39933; Yorktown; York **GS:** U **SP:** No info **VI:** No further data **P:** unk **BLW:** unk **RG:** Y **MK:** unk **PH:** unk **SS:** J-Yorktown Historian **BS:** JLARC 1, 74.

RU=Rank/Unit	CEM=Cemetery	GS=Gravestone	SP=Spousal Information
VI=Other Veteran Info	P=Pension	BLW=Bounty/Land Warrant	RG=Registered Grave
MK=SAR/DAR Marker	PH=Photo	SS=Service Source	BS=Burial Source

115

FULCHER, William; b c1762; d 30 May 1844 **RU:** Private?, Refer to pension or BLW records for service **CEM:** Longrow; GPS unk; Rt 658; Hanover **GS:** Y **SP:** No info **VI:** No further data **P:** Y **BLW:** Y **RG:** Y **MK:** N **PH:** unk **SS:** E pg 291 **BS:** 31 vol 1 pg 8.

FULFERSON, Frederick; b 1739; d 1796 **RU:** Private, Served in Pittsylvania Co Militia **CEM:** Mayo Baptist Church; GPS unk; 85 Penn Store Rd, Spencer; Henry **GS:** Y **SP:** No info **VI:** Actual burial place on land owned by Frederick Fulkerson. SAR marker **P:** unk **BLW:** unk **RG:** N **MK:** Y **PH:** unk **SS:** AK correspondence **BS:** 32 Jun 2010; 196.

FULKERSON, James (Jacobus); b 22 Jun 1737, NJ; d 22 Sep 1799 **RU:** Lieutenant, Served in Washington Co Militia **CEM:** Burson Family, originally Fulkerson; GPS 36.66440, -82.17500; Nr Jct of Rt 633 & Spur Strap Rd, Burson's Cnr; Washington **GS:** N **SP:** Mary (-----) (19 Sep 1747-12 Jul 1830) **VI:** DAR marker **P:** unk **BLW:** unk **RG:** Y **MK:** Y **PH:** N **SS:** E pg 291 **BS:** JLARC 1, 80; 78 pg 388; 196.

FULTON, James; b 10 Aug 1755; d 14 Feb 1834 **RU:** Private/Patriot, Served in Capt John Tates Co, Augusta Co Militia. Gave material aid to cause **CEM:** Bethel Presbyterian; GPS 38.04256, -79.17283; 563 Bethel Green Rd, Middlebrook; Augusta **GS:** U **SP:** Mar (Sep 1809 or 1810) Elizabeth "Betsey" Mitchell (1 Mar 1776-11 Sep 1850) d/o Thomas & Elizabeth (McClahan) Mitchell **VI:** Son of John & Mary (Steele) Fulton **P:** unk **BLW:** unk **RG:** unk **MK:** unk **PH:** unk **SS:** JLARC 63; E pg 292; AL Cert Augusta Co 79 **BS:** 196.

FULWEIDER, Johannes; b 19 Apr 1756; d 30 Sep 1831 **RU:** Soldier, SAR registration did not specify service **CEM:** Hanger Family; GPS unk; Rt 670, near Greenville; Augusta **GS:** U **SP:** Catharinea Elizabeth (-----) (17 Dec 1757-8 Feb 1827) **VI:** No further data **P:** unk **BLW:** unk **RG:** unk **MK:** unk **PH:** unk **SS:** NSSAR Ancestor # P-163188 **BS:** JLARC 8.

FUNK, Jacob; b 16 Feb 1767; d 7 Jun 1847 **RU:** Private, Served in Capt Joseph Bowman's Co in the lower district of Dunmore Co (now Shenandoah Co) **CEM:** Funk Family; GPS unk; behind Travel Trailer Park, vic Strasburg; Shenandoah **GS:** N **SP:** No info **VI:** No further data **P:** unk **BLW:** unk **RG:** N **MK:** N **PH:** N **SS:** C pg 606 **BS:** 79 pg 120.

FUNKHOUSER, Abraham; b 1742; d 1796 **RU:** Private, Served in Capt Alexander Machir's Co, Strasburg District Militia **CEM:** Funkhouser Family; GPS unk; Vic Fishers Hill; Shenandoah **GS:** Y **SP:** Mary Magdalena Campbell **VI:** No further data **P:** unk **BLW:** unk **RG:** N **MK:** N **PH:** unk **SS:** C pg 606 **BS:** 79 pg 121; 196.

FUNKHOUSER, Jacob Jr; b 1766; d 1846 **RU:** Private, Served in Capt Alexander Machir's Co, Strasburg District Militia **CEM:** Funkhouser Family; GPS 38.801981, -78.78390; Resort Dr Rt 835, Basye; Shenandoah **GS:** Y **SP:** No info **VI:** No further data **P:** unk **BLW:** unk **RG:** N **MK:** N **PH:** unk **SS:** C pg 606 **BS:** 155 Funkhouser.

FUNKHOUSER, Jacob Sr; b 1750, Shenandoah Co; d 27 Nov 1801 **RU:** Private/Patriot, Served in Capt Alexander Machir's Co. Gave to cause in Shenandoah Co **CEM:** Funkhouser Family; GPS unk; Mt Jackson; Shenandoah **GS:** Y **SP:** Mar (c1775) Dorothy Hottel (1755, Mt Olive-6 Oct 1802) **VI:** No further data **P:** unk **BLW:** unk **RG:** Y **MK:** Y **PH:** unk **SS:** T **BS:** 04.

FUNKHOUSER, John III; b unk; d 11 Jun 1826 **RU:** Private, Served in Capt Alexander Machir's Co, Strasburg District Militia **CEM:** Funkhouser Family; GPS unk; Waxwing Ln on Shipe farm; Shenandoah **GS:** Y **SP:** No info **VI:** No further data **P:** unk **BLW:** unk **RG:** N **MK:** N **PH:** unk **SS:** C pg 606 **BS:** 79 pg 129; 196.

FUQUA, Joseph; b 4 May 1756; d 4 May 1829 **RU:** Private, Ent serv 1776 in 4th or 5th VA Regt. Fought at Cowpens and Brandywine **CEM:** Fuqua Family; GPS 37.33344, -79.48352; Orange Street; Bedford City **GS:** Y **SP:** Mar (13 Nov 1782 Bedford Co (bond)) Celia Bondurant (23 Dec 1762-28 Mar 1847) **VI:** Son of Ralph Fuqua (1693-1770) & Priscilla Owen (1702-1779). Donated 100 acres for the town of Liberty. First Deacon of Meeting House (now Timber Ridge Baptist). Widow appl pen 27 Jan 1840 Bedford Co age 77. W734. Small Govt marker on grave **P:** Y **BLW:** unk **RG:** Y **MK:** N **PH:** unk **SS:** CG Vol 2 pg 1293; K Vol II pg 153 **BS:** JLARC 1, 56; 196.

FUQUA, Ralph Jr; b 1737, Lunenburg Co; d Feb 1777 **RU:** Soldier, Served in 5th VA Regt 1777 **CEM:** Fuqua Family; GPS 37.33344, -79.48352; Orange Street; Bedford **GS:** Y **SP:** Mar (17 May 1804) Fanny

RU=Rank/Unit	CEM=Cemetery	GS=Gravestone	SP=Spousal Information
VI=Other Veteran Info	P=Pension	BLW=Bounty/Land Warrant	RG=Registered Grave
MK=SAR/DAR Marker	PH=Photo	SS=Service Source	BS=Burial Source

116

Minor, d/o William & (-----) Minor **VI:** Son of Ralph Fuqua (1693-1770) & Pricilia Owen (1702-1779). Small Govt marker denoting unit and death date (Feb 1777) **P:** unk **BLW:** unk **RG:** Y **MK:** N **PH:** unk **SS:** B; J-NSSAR 1993 Reg **BS:** JLARC 1; 196.

FURR, Enoch; b 1756, Fauquier Co; d 3 Apr 1845 **RU:** Soldier, Served in VA Line. Ent serv Loudoun Co **CEM:** Ebenezer Baptist; GPS 39.05824, -77.84142; 20421 Airmont Rd, Bluemont; Loudoun **GS:** U **SP:** Mar (Mar 1786) Sarah "Sally" Clawson (c1768-__) **VI:** Sol appl pen 9 May 1836 Loudoun Co, age 80. Widow appl pen 4 Feb 1846 Loudoun Co age 78. W11030 **P:** Y **BLW:** unk **RG:** unk **MK:** unk **PH:** unk **SS:** CG Vol 2 pg 1294 **BS:** JLARC 4, 32.

GAAR, Andrew; b 1750; d 1811 **RU:** Patriot, Gave material aid to the cause **CEM:** Gaar Mountain; GPS 38.43374, -78.29048; Mulatto Run nr Beamer Hd Rd; Madison **GS:** Y **SP:** Christina Wilhoite d/o John & (-----) Wilhoit) **VI:** Brother of John, mar sister of John's wife **P:** N **BLW:** N **RG:** Y **MK:** Y **PH:** unk **SS:** AK AL Ct bk pg 3 **BS:** 04; 32 Apr 09.

GAAR, Johann (John) Adam aka Adam; b 1711, Illenschwang, Barvaria (Kingdom); d 11 Jan 1790 **RU:** Patriot, Performed public Service **CEM:** Mt Pisgah Church; GPS 38.39265, -78.30396; Rt 652 nr intersection of Ruth Rd; Madison **GS:** N **SP:** Elizabeth Kaffer (Kaffier) **VI:** Died at Gaar Mtn, Madison Co at his farm **P:** N **BLW:** N **RG:** Y **MK:** N **PH:** N **SS:** AK **BS:** 04.

GAAR, John (Johannes); b 1744, Lorenz Gaar home at Gaar Mtn and Mulatto (Pass) Run, Madison Co; d 1898 or 1809 **RU:** Militiaman, Served in a Culpeper Co, VA State Militia. Gave material aid to the cause **CEM:** Lorenz Gaar Family; GPS unk; Mulatto Run nr Beamer Hd Rd; Madison **GS:** Y **SP:** Margaritha Wilhoite (Margaretha Willheit) d/o John & (-----) Wilhoit) **VI:** Brother of Andrew, mar sister of Andrew's wife. Died at Gaar Mountain, Madison **P:** unk **BLW:** unk **RG:** Y **MK:** Y **PH:** unk **SS:** AK; AL Ct Bk 1 pg 44-6 **BS:** 04; 32 Apr 09.

GABIANT, Benoit; b unk; d 1781 **RU:** Seaman, Served on "Hercule" and died from Yorktown battle **CEM:** French Memorial; GPS 36.81944, -79.39933; Yorktown; York **GS:** U **SP:** No info **VI:** No further data **P:** unk **BLW:** unk **RG:** Y **MK:** unk **PH:** unk **SS:** J-Yorktown Historian **BS:** JLARC 1, 74.

GAGUEBEY, Bernard; b unk; d 1781 **RU:** Soldier, Served in Foix Bn and died fr battle at Yorktown **CEM:** French Memorial; GPS 36.81944, -79.39933; Yorktown; York **GS:** U **SP:** No info **VI:** No further data **P:** unk **BLW:** unk **RG:** Y **MK:** unk **PH:** unk **SS:** J-Yorktown Historian **BS:** JLARC 1, 74.

GAINES, James; b 1710, King & Queen Co; d 1786 **RU:** Private/Patriot, Served in Capt Josiah Parker's VA Regt. Gave material aid to cause **CEM:** Gaines Family; GPS unk; See tax map for location; Madison **GS:** N **SP:** Mary Pendleton, b 1717, d 1803; d/o Henry Pendleton (1683-1721) & Mary Taylor (1688-1770) **VI:** Son of Richard (1686-1755) & (-----) Gaines. Died in Culpeper Co. VA. Widow pensioned commencing 08 May 1813 at $48 per yr **P:** Y **BLW:** N **RG:** unk **MK:** unk **PH:** N **SS:** AG pg 264; AK Ct Bk #1 pg 19, 25 **BS:** 65 cites Notable Southern Families, Vol 1; 196.

GAINES, Richard; b 1726, King William Co; d 1801 **RU:** Sergeant, Enl 13 Feb 1778. Promoted to Sgt May 1778. Transferred fr Capt Reuben Lipscomb's Co, 7th VA Regt Nov 1778. Served in Lt Col Hold Richeson's 5th VA Regt. Discharged 16 Feb 1779 **CEM:** Cub Creek; GPS 37.03220, -78.75830; Rt 616 Cub Creek Church Rd, Brookneal; Charlotte **GS:** U **SP:** Mar (1747) Mildred Hollinger. She was mentioned in will. **VI:** BLW as Sgt **P:** unk **BLW:** Y **RG:** unk **MK:** unk **PH:** unk **SS:** C pg 239; E pg 294 **BS:** 196.

GAINES, Thomas; b 1738; d 1811 **RU:** Corporal, Served in 7th, 11th, 15th Cont line **CEM:** Fairview; GPS 38.48080,-78.00470; Sperryville Pike Rt 522, Culpeper; Culpeper **GS:** U **SP:** No info **VI:** No further data **P:** unk **BLW:** unk **RG:** unk **MK:** unk **PH:** unk **SS:** J- DAR Hatcher; E pg 294 **BS:** JLARC 2.

GALBURE, Jean; b unk; d 1781 **RU:** Seaman, Served on "Magnanime" and died from Yorktown battle **CEM:** French Memorial; GPS 36.81944, -79.39933; Yorktown; York **GS:** U **SP:** No info **VI:** No further data **P:** unk **BLW:** unk **RG:** Y **MK:** unk **PH:** unk **SS:** J-Yorktown Historian **BS:** JLARC 1, 74.

GALI (GALLIN) (GALING), Samuel; b 1763; d 1796 **RU:** Private, Capt Thomas Massie's Co, 6th VA Regt commanded by Col Simms, Oct 1777 **CEM:** Thomas Parker Family; GPS unk; Rt 180 nr Pungoteague; Accomack **GS:** Y **SP:** No info **VI:** No further data **P:** unk **BLW:** unk **RG:** N **MK:** N **PH:** unk **SS:** P 6th VA Regt **BS:** 178 Th. Parker.

RU=Rank/Unit	CEM=Cemetery	GS=Gravestone	SP=Spousal Information
VI=Other Veteran Info	P=Pension	BLW=Bounty/Land Warrant	RG=Registered Grave
MK=SAR/DAR Marker	PH=Photo	SS=Service Source	BS=Burial Source

117

GALLAGHER, Bernard; b c1749, Ireland; d 16 Oct 1821 **RU:** Seaman/Midshipman/Ships Master, Served first as a seaman, then as Acting Midshipman under John Paul Jones on sloop "Providence"; Mate on PA brigatine "Minerva"; Master of "St Patrick," "Bachelor" and others **CEM:** Dumfries Public; GPS 38.34110, -77.19964; 17821 Mine Rd, Dumfries; Prince William **GS:** Y **SP:** Mar (1785) Margaret Strother (1773-2 Feb 1834) **VI:** SAR monument **P:** unk **BLW:** unk **RG:** Y **MK:** Y **PH:** unk **SS:** H; I; AK **BS:** 16 pg 21.

GALOTET, Jean; b unk; d 1781 **RU:** Soldier, Served in Bourbonnais Bn and died fr battle at Yorktown **CEM:** French Memorial; GPS 36.81944, -79.39933; Yorktown; York **GS:** U **SP:** No info **VI:** No further data **P:** unk **BLW:** unk **RG:** Y **MK:** unk **PH:** unk **SS:** J-Yorktown Historian **BS:** JLARC 1, 74.

GALT, John Minson; b 17 Oct 1744, Williamsburg; d 12 Jun 1808 **RU:** Surgeon, Served in 15th Cont Line, 1777. Taken prisoner at Germantown 4 Oct 1777. Was disabled due to service **CEM:** Bruton Parish Church; GPS 37.27127, -76.70248; 331 W Duke of Gloucester St; Williamsburg City **GS:** U **SP:** Mar (6 Apr 1769) Judith Craig (30 Aug 1749, Williamsburg-12 Jun 1808, Williamsburg) **VI:** Recd pen 1/2 pay 28 Mar 1849 indicating disabled during service. Recd BLW 6000 acres. Pension paid to James Lyon, Attorney for John M. Galt, administrator of soldier's estate R14353 **P:** Y **BLW:** Y **RG:** Y **MK:** unk **PH:** unk **SS:** J-NSSAR 1993 Reg; E pg 258; K pg 158; CG pg 1302 **BS:** JLARC 1.

GALTIER, Jean; b unk; d 1781 **RU:** Soldier, Served in Bourbonnais Bn and died fr battle at Yorktown **CEM:** French Memorial; GPS 36.81944, -79.39933; Yorktown; York **GS:** U **SP:** No info **VI:** No further data **P:** unk **BLW:** unk **RG:** Y **MK:** unk **PH:** unk **SS:** J-Yorktown Historian **BS:** JLARC 1,74.

GAMBLE, George; b 1755, Ireland; d 1836 **RU:** Soldier, Served in PA & VA Lines. Ent serv Lancaster Co PA. Also Ent serv Washington Co VA. Was in Battle of King's Mountain **CEM:** Glade Spring Presbyterian; GPS 36.76720, -81.78720; 33234 Lee Hwy, Glade Spring; Washington **GS:** U **SP:** Margaret (-----) (__-1847) **VI:** Sol appl pen 31 Mar 1834 Washington Co Age 79. S10720 **P:** Y **BLW:** unk **RG:** unk **MK:** unk **PH:** unk **SS:** CG Vol 2 pg 1303 **BS:** JLARC 4,34; 196.

GAMBLE, John; b 1760; d 14 Jan 1831 **RU:** Captain, Commanded cavalry troop in Augusta Co Militia 19 Nov 1782 **CEM:** Augusta Stone Presbyterian; GPS 38.23926, -78.97356; 28 Old Stone Church Ln, Ft Defiance; Augusta **GS:** Y **SP:** Rebecca McPheeters (27 Nov 1767-18 May 1832) d/o F Reverend William (1729-1807) & Rebecca Moore (__-1826) McPheeters **VI:** Govt stone, indicates Capt of VA Co of Troop **P:** unk **BLW:** unk **RG:** Y **MK:** unk **PH:** unk **SS:** B; E pg 296 **BS:** JLARC 1,2,8, 23 ,63; 196.

GAMBLE, Robert; b 3 Sep 1754, Augusta Co; d 12 Apr 1810 **RU:** Captain, Served in VA Line and Augusta Co Militia. Fought at Yorktown **CEM:** St John's Episcopal; GPS 37.53183, -77.41958; 2401 E Broad St; Richmond City **GS:** Y **SP:** Catherine Grattan **VI:** Sol appl 3 Jun 1805 Richmond for BLW that was issued 18 Sep 1789 but not rec'd until soldier requested at Richmond in 1805 a survey of the bounty land. John G Gamble witness to the request BLW869 **P:** unk **BLW:** Y **RG:** Y **MK:** N **PH:** unk **SS:** K pg 158; J-NSSAR 1993 Reg; CG Vol 2 pg 1303 **BS:** JLARC 1.

GARDINER, Francis; b 1762; d 26 Jul 1842 **RU:** Private, Served in Capt Joseph Patterson's Co. Marched to Jamestown in Jan 1781 and was in skirmishes there **CEM:** Hebron Presbyterian; GPS 38.14140, -79.15500; 423 Hebron Rd; Staunton City **GS:** Y **SP:** Ann Bell **VI:** Died age 80 (stone) **P:** unk **BLW:** unk **RG:** N **MK:** N **PH:** unk **SS:** AZ pg 103 **BS:** JLARC 62, 63; 142 Hebron; 196.

GARDNER, James; b 26 Apr 1755, NY; d 21 April 1849 **RU:** Private, Ent serv 1777 Essex Co, NJ **CEM:** Gardner Family; GPS 36.76610, -80.72080; End of Lynhaven Rd, Hillsville; Carroll **GS:** Y **SP:** 1) ?Rachael Wilson? 2) Tabitha Martin (16 Dec 1780-7 Sep 1862) d/o William Martin & Delphia Walden **VI:** Son of Isaac Martin (1700-1774, Halifax C) & Phylis (-----) **P:** unk **BLW:** unk **RG:** unk **MK:** Y **PH:** unk **SS:** Winchester Account Book 37; NSDAR **BS:** JLARC 2, 4, 11, 43; 68; 196.

GARDNER, John; b 3 Jun 1760, Montgomery Co; d 15 Nov 1833 **RU:** Private, Served in Capt McCreevy's Co, Augusta Co Militia **CEM:** Sunset; GPS 37.12390, -80.40420; South Franklin near I-81, Christiansburg; Montgomery **GS:** U **SP:** Mar (20 Jan 1813 Montgomery Co) Betsy Page d/o John & (----) Page **VI:** No further data **P:** unk **BLW:** unk **RG:** unk **MK:** unk **PH:** Y **SS:** E pg 297 **BS:** 196.

GARDNER, John; b 1750 Chester Co, PA; d 1807 **RU:** Sergeant, Served in 5th & 11th Cont Line **CEM:** Leesburg Presbyterian; GPS 39.11611, -77.56722; 207 W Market St, Leesburg; Loudoun **GS:** U **SP:**

RU=Rank/Unit CEM=Cemetery GS=Gravestone SP=Spousal Information
VI=Other Veteran Info P=Pension BLW=Bounty/Land Warrant RG=Registered Grave
MK=SAR/DAR Marker PH=Photo SS=Service Source BS=Burial Source

118

Mar (1782) Mary Douglas (__-10 Jul 1818) **VI:** DAR indicates he was a Colonel but perhaps too young to obtain this rank during the war period having been born in 1750. Recd BLW **P:** unk **BLW: Y RG:** unk **MK:** unk **PH:** unk **SS:** J- DAR Hatcher; E pg 296 **BS:** JLARC 2.

GARDNER, Nathanial; b 1760; d 12 Dec 1832 **RU:** Private, Serv at Massey's Ferry in SC, then at Battle of Guilford CH **CEM:** Mill Meeting House; GPS unk; Nr Chatham; Pittsylvania **GS:** Y **SP:** No info **VI:** Perhaps son of Nathaniel (1739/40-Feb 1833) & Margaret (Heath) Gardner **P:** unk **BLW:** unk **RG:** N **MK:** N **PH:** unk **SS:** G, pg 287 **BS:** AW pg 2; 196.

GAREL, Julien; b unk; d 1781 **RU:** Seaman, Served on "Diademe" and died from Yorktown battle **CEM:** French Memorial; GPS 36.81944, -79.39933; Yorktown; York **GS:** U **SP:** No info **VI:** No further data **P:** unk **BLW:** unk **RG:** Y **MK:** unk **PH:** unk **SS:** J-Yorktown Historian **BS:** JLARC 1, 74.

GARIQUE, Jacques; b unk; d 1781 **RU:** Seaman, Served on "Diademe" and died from Yorktown battle **CEM:** French Memorial; GPS 36.81944, -79.39933; Yorktown; York **GS:** U **SP:** No info **VI:** No further data **P:** unk **BLW:** unk **RG:** Y **MK:** unk **PH:** unk **SS:** J-Yorktown Historian **BS:** JLARC 1, 74.

GARLAND, Nathaniel; b 1750; d 1793 **RU:** Lieutenant, Served in Albemarle Co Militia **CEM:** Garland Family; GPS unk; Refer to county property records for location; Albemarle **GS:** N **SP:** Mar (7 Dec 1772) Jane Rodes (c1754-1830) **VI:** Son of Rev War patriot James (c1722 Hanover Co-1812) & Mary (Rice) (c1732 Hanover Co-1812) Garland **P:** unk **BLW:** unk **RG:** unk **MK:** unk **PH:** N **SS:** J- DAR Hatcher; E pg 297; G pg 445 **BS:** JLARC 2.

GARNETT, James Rev; b Nov 1743; d 16 Apr 1830 **RU:** Patriot, Gave material aid to cause **CEM:** Crooked Run Baptist Church; GPS unk; 7351 James Madison Hwy, Rapidan; Culpeper **GS:** N **SP:** (-----) Rowe **VI:** Baptist minister, was pastor of Crooked Run Church 55 yrs serving fr 1774-1830 **P:** N **BLW:** N **RG:** unk **MK:** N **PH:** N **SS:** AL CT BK 1 pg 12, 44, 54 **BS:** 196.

GARNETT, Muscoe; b 17 Aug 1736; d Jan 1803 **RU:** Patriot, Gave material aid to cause **CEM:** Garnett Family; GPS unk; Elmwood, Loretto; Essex **GS:** U **SP:** Grace Fenton Mercer (20 Feb 1751 Stafford Co-14 Jun 1814) d/o John (1704 Dublin, Ireland-__) & Ann (Roy) Mercer **VI:** Son of James (1691-1765) & Elizabeth (Muscoe) (1699-__) Garnett **P:** N **BLW:** N **RG:** unk **MK:** unk **PH:** unk **SS:** AL Ct Bk pg 9, 10 Essex Co **BS:** 196.

GARNETT, Reuben; b 27 Jul 1753; d 16 Jun 1839 **RU:** Second Lieutenant, Served in Essex Co Militia in Capt Hancock Lee's Co 21 Jul 1777, took oath as 2nd Lt 20 Apr 1779. **CEM:** Garnett Family; GPS unk; Rt 648, 10 mi off Rt 15; Culpeper **GS:** Y **SP:** Mary Twyman (7 Jul 1757-1841) **VI:** No further data **P:** unk **BLW:** unk **RG:** N **MK:** N **PH:** Y **SS:** E pg 298 **BS:** 167 Garnett; 196.

GARRETT, William; b 24 Dec 1752; d 11 Jul 1825 **RU:** Private, Served in Capt Everard Meade's Co & Capt William Taylor's Co; Col Alexander Spotswood & Col Christian Febiger's Regts **CEM:** Pitts Farm; GPS unk; Nr Slaydo; Essex **GS:** U **SP:** 1) Elizabeth (-----); 2) Mar (1803) Clara Favor (__-aft 15 Aug 1825) **VI:** No further data **P:** unk **BLW:** unk **RG:** unk **MK:** N **PH:** unk **SS:** AP roll #941 **BS:** JLARC 2, 76.

GARST, Frederick; b 24 Dec 1752; d 1842 **RU:** Private, Served fr PA **CEM:** Garst Family; GPS unk; Kesler Mill Rd up hill behind a business near RR tracks; Salem City **GS:** Y **SP:** Magdalena Rauch (1752-1845) **VI:** No further data **P:** unk **BLW:** unk **RG:** Y **MK:** N **PH:** unk **SS:** J-NASSR 2000 Reg **BS:** JLARC 76; 196.

GARY(GERY), James; b 1764; d 23 Apr 1831 **RU:** Private, Enl age 16, served in 1st VA State Regt **CEM:** Gary Family; GPS unk; Centreville; Fairfax **GS:** U **SP:** No info **VI:** Was a Private in the War of 1812, as member of Petersburg Volunteers **P:** unk **BLW:** unk **RG:** Y **MK:** N **PH:** unk **SS:** E pg 299; AS, SAR regis G pg 139 **BS:** SAR regis.

GASKINS, John; b 13 July 1754; d 12 Mar 1838 **RU:** Private, Served in Capt Thomas Gaskin's Co, 5th VA Regt in 1777 **CEM:** Union Church; GPS 38.32268, -77.46615; Carter St, Falmouth; Stafford **GS:** Y **SP:** No info **VI:** No further data **P:** unk **BLW:** unk **RG:** N **MK:** N **PH:** unk **SS:** E pg 299; AP roll **BS:** 03 addendum.

GATES, Elijah; b 22 Jun 1744, Preston, New London, CT; d 11 Apr 1802 **RU:** Captain, Served in Vt in Col Olcott and Col Wait's Regts **CEM:** Wood; GPS unk; Wood; Scott **GS:** Y **SP:** Mar (23 Nov 1769,

RU=Rank/Unit	CEM=Cemetery	GS=Gravestone	SP=Spousal Information
VI=Other Veteran Info	P=Pension	BLW=Bounty/Land Warrant	RG=Registered Grave
MK=SAR/DAR Marker	PH=Photo	SS=Service Source	BS=Burial Source

119

Norwich, VT) Eunice Hatch (16 Jun 1741 Preston, CT-__) **VI:** No further data **P:** unk **BLW:** unk **RG:** Y **MK:** N **PH:** unk **SS:** AS SAR applic; DD **BS:** SAR Appl.

GATES, William; b 1760; d 9 Mar 1816 **RU:** Soldier, Served in VA Line **CEM:** Gates Family; GPS unk; Rt 614, .4 mi west on private road next to "Fairfield" Farm; Chesterfield **GS:** Y **SP:** Mar (May 1784) Lydia "Liddy" Granger **VI:** Widow appl pen 25 Feb 1840 Chesterfield Co age 80. W19485. Newer Govt stone **P:** Y **BLW:** unk **RG:** unk **MK:** N **PH:** unk **SS:** K pg 165; CG Vol 2 pg 1324 **BS:** JLARC 4, 35; 196.

GAUDARD, Jean; b unk; d 1781 **RU:** Soldier, Served in Gatinais Bn and died fr battle at Yorktown **CEM:** French Memorial; GPS 36.81944, -79.39933; Yorktown; York **GS:** U **SP:** No info **VI:** No further data **P:** unk **BLW:** unk **RG:** Y **MK:** unk **PH:** unk **SS:** J-Yorktown Historian **BS:** JLARC 1, 74.

GAUSSE, Philippe; b unk; d 1781 **RU:** Soldier, Served in Soissonnais Bn and died fr battle at Yorktown **CEM:** French Memorial; GPS 36.81944, -79.39933; Yorktown; York **GS:** U **SP:** No info **VI:** No further data **P:** unk **BLW:** unk **RG:** Y **MK:** unk **PH:** unk **SS:** J-Yorktown Historian **BS:** JLARC 1, 74.

GAUTIER, Jean; b unk; d 1781 **RU:** Seaman, Served on "Caton" and died from Yorktown battle **CEM:** French Memorial; GPS 36.81944, -79.39933; Yorktown; York **GS:** U **SP:** No info **VI:** No further data **P:** unk **BLW:** unk **RG:** Y **MK:** unk **PH:** unk **SS:** J-Yorktown Historian **BS:** JLARC 1, 74.

GAVAUDANT, Michel; b unk; d 1781 **RU:** Soldier, Served in Soissonnais Bn and died fr battle at Yorktown **CEM:** French Memorial; GPS 36.81944, -79.39933; Yorktown; York **GS:** U **SP:** No info **VI:** No further data **P:** unk **BLW:** unk **RG:** Y **MK:** unk **PH:** unk **SS:** J-Yorktown Historian **BS:** JLARC 1, 74.

GAY, William; b c1755; d 2 May 1815 **RU:** Captain, Commanded a co in Powhatan Co Militia until resignation 21 Aug 1777 **CEM:** Fairfield; GPS unk; 5.5 mi W of Goochland Rt 6, then S Rt 614 .4 mi; Goochland **GS:** Y **SP:** No info **VI:** No further data **P:** unk **BLW:** unk **RG:** N **MK:** unk **PH:** unk **SS:** G pg 288 G-VA Mil records pg 288; E pg 301 **BS:** 196; 46, pg 140.

GEDDES, Winston; b c1721; d 9 Jun 1781 **RU:** Patriot, Provided two beeves to cause **CEM:** St John's Episcopal; GPS 37.53183, -77.41958; 2401 E Broad St; Richmond City **GS:** Y **SP:** No info **VI:** No further data **P:** N **BLW:** N **RG:** Y **MK:** N **PH:** unk **SS:** D Vol 2 pg 497 **BS:** AK Dec 2006.

GELLY, Jacques; b unk; d 1781 **RU:** Seaman, Served on "Citoyen" and died from Yorktown battle **CEM:** French Memorial; GPS 36.81944, -79.39933; Yorktown; York **GS:** U **SP:** No info **VI:** No further data **P:** unk **BLW:** unk **RG:** Y **MK:** unk **PH:** unk **SS:** J-Yorktown Historian **BS:** JLARC 1, 74.

GENIES, Joseph; b unk; d 1781 **RU:** Soldier, Served in Foix Bn and died fr battle at Yorktown **CEM:** French Memorial; GPS 36.81944, -79.39933; Yorktown; York **GS:** U **SP:** no info **VI:** No further data **P:** unk **BLW:** unk **RG:** Y **MK:** unk **PH:** unk **SS:** J-Yorktown Historian **BS:** JLARC 1, 74.

GENTIL, Joseph; b unk; d 1781 **RU:** Seaman, Served on "Marseillais" and died from Yorktown battle **CEM:** French Memorial; GPS 36.81944, -79.39933; Yorktown; York **GS:** U **SP:** No info **VI:** No further data **P:** unk **BLW:** unk **RG:** Y **MK:** unk **PH:** unk **SS:** J-Yorktown Historian **BS:** JLARC 1, 74.

GENTRY, James; b 1754 or 1757, Hanover Co; d 22 Jun 1851 **RU:** Captain, Served in VA Cont Line. Ent serv Hanover Co **CEM:** Rockgate; GPS 38.06170, -78.70170; 981 Crozet Ave, Crozet; Albemarle **GS:** N **SP:** Mar (c1779) Mary Hicks (9 May 1763 Goochland Co-1835) d/o Stephen & Agnes (Hancock) Hicks **VI:** Son of George (c1732 Hanover Co-5 Nov 1810) & Elizabeth (___) (__-5 Nov 1810) Gentry. Sol appl pen 2 Oct 1832 Albemarle Co. S8555 **P:** Y **BLW:** unk **RG:** unk **MK:** unk **PH:** N **SS:** J- DAR Hatcher; K pg 168; CG Vol 2 pg 1332 **BS:** JLARC 2; 196.

GEOFFROY, Jean; b unk; d 1781 **RU:** Soldier, Served in Soissonnais Bn and died fr battle at Yorktown **CEM:** French Memorial; GPS 36.81944, -79.39933; Yorktown; York **GS:** U **SP:** No info **VI:** No further data **P:** unk **BLW:** unk **RG:** Y **MK:** unk **PH:** unk **SS:** J-Yorktown Historian **BS:** JLARC 1, 74.

GEORGE, Benjamin; b c1740; d 5 Aug 1811 **RU:** Private, Served in 6th Cont Line **CEM:** George Family; GPS unk; Catlett; Fauquier **GS:** N **SP:** Mar (1768) Hannah (-----) (1749-1833) **VI:** Died in Prince William Co. GS destroyed by cattle **P:** unk **BLW:** unk **RG:** Y **MK:** N **PH:** N **SS:** E pg 302 **BS:** 19, pg 64.

GEORGE, Byrd; b 17 May 1758; d 7 Dec 1836 **RU:** Private, Served in Capt Newell's Co, Montgomery Co Militia **CEM:** George Family; GPS unk; 9.7 mi E of Richmond City, on Rt 60, Briel's Farm Rd;

RU=Rank/Unit	CEM=Cemetery	GS=Gravestone	SP=Spousal Information
VI=Other Veteran Info	P=Pension	BLW=Bounty/Land Warrant	RG=Registered Grave
MK=SAR/DAR Marker	PH=Photo	SS=Service Source	BS=Burial Source

120

Henrico **GS:** Y **SP:** Mary Crutchfield (20 May 1777-27 Sep 1807) **VI:** Also Maj in War of 1812, Henrico Co **P:** unk **BLW:** unk **RG:** unk **MK:** unk **PH:** unk **SS:** G pg 238 **BS:** 114, Byrd Fam.

GEORGE, Reuben; b unk; d 1834 **RU:** Private, Served 3 yrs in Cont Line **CEM:** Old City; GPS 37.41472, -79.15667; 401 Taylor St; Lynchburg City **GS:** Y **SP:** No info **VI:** Recd BLW 100 acres 14 Dec 1831 **P:** unk **BLW:** Y **RG:** N **MK:** N **PH:** unk **SS:** N pg 112 **BS:** 62 pg 112.

GEORGE, Reuben; b 25 Nov 1749; d 16 Jan 1832 **RU:** Sergeant, Ent serv Culpeper Co. Served in Capt John Gillison's Co, Col Edward Stephen's 10th VA Regt; also in Capt Peter Ward's Co. Was in Battles of Brandywine, Germantown & White Marsh **CEM:** Fairford; GPS unk; Nr Penola; Caroline **GS:** U **SP:** Mar (27 Dec 1780, NJ) Elsey Frazy **VI:** Appl for pen 04 Dec 1818 **P:** Y **BLW:** unk **RG:** unk **MK:** unk **PH:** unk **SS:** CG pg 1334 **BS:** 196.

GEORGE, William; b unk; d 11 Sep 27 **RU:** Captain, Served in VA Line **CEM:** Friendship Rest; GPS unk; Rt 623; Goochland **GS:** Y **SP:** Mar (21 Sep 1784) Miss Nancy Garthright, d/o William & (-----) Garthright of Henrico Co (__-21 Jun 1838) **VI:** R3977 **P:** Y **BLW:** unk **RG:** N **MK:** N **PH:** unk **SS:** E pg 303; K pg 169; CG Vol 2 pg 1334 **BS:** 46 pg 150.

GERAUD, Guillaume; b unk; d 1781 **RU:** Seaman, Served on "Languedoc" and died from Yorktown battle **CEM:** French Memorial; GPS 36.81944, -79.39933; Yorktown; York **GS:** U **SP:** No info **VI:** No further data **P:** unk **BLW:** unk **RG:** Y **MK:** unk **PH:** unk **SS:** J-Yorktown Historian **BS:** JLARC 1, 74.

GERRY, Philippe; b unk; d 1781 **RU:** Seaman, Served on "Ville de Paris" and died from Yorktown battle **CEM:** French Memorial; GPS 36.81944, -79.39933; Yorktown; York **GS:** U **SP:** No info **VI:** No further data **P:** unk **BLW:** unk **RG:** Y **MK:** unk **PH:** unk **SS:** J-Yorktown Historian **BS:** JLARC 1, 74.

GERTHIER, Francois; b unk; d 1781 **RU:** Soldier, Served in Auxonne Bn and died fr battle at Yorktown **CEM:** French Memorial; GPS 36.81944, -79.39933; Yorktown; York **GS:** U **SP:** No info **VI:** No further data **P:** unk **BLW:** unk **RG:** Y **MK:** unk **PH:** unk **SS:** J-Yorktown Historian **BS:** JLARC 1, 74.

GIBBON, James; b 1759, PA; d 1 July 1835 **RU:** Major, PA Line. "Hero of Stony Point." Aide de Camp to Brig Gen Irwin **CEM:** Shockoe Hill; GPS 37.55190, -77.43170; 4th & Hospital Sts; Richmond City **GS:** U **SP:** Mar (17 Mar 1782) Ann Elizabeth Phyle (4 Jan 1762, Philadelphia, PA-25 Nov 1853) **VI:** Sol appl pen 8 Sep 1828 Richmond VA. S13138. BLW #1538-300. Was collector at Richmond port for 30 yrs **P:** Y **BLW:** Y **RG:** Y **MK:** unk **PH:** unk **SS:** K pg 170; CG Vol 2 pg 1336 **BS:** JLARC 1, 77.

GIBBONS, Isaac; b 13 Mar 1757, Bethlehem, PA; d 22 Dec 1826 **RU:** Private, Served in PA Cont Line. Enl Easton PA and served in Capt John Craig's Co. 4th PA Dragoons **CEM:** Old Peaked Mountain; GPS 38.37113, -78.73416; 9843 Town Hall Rd, McGaheysville; Rockingham **GS:** U **SP:** Mar (28 Dec 1782 Allentown PA) Mary Gongwer (14 Nov 1760-__) **VI:** Sol appl pen 25 May 1818 Shenandoah Co age 61. He d in Shenandoah Co. Widow appl pen 22 Oct 1839 Rockingham Co. Son appl BLW on 16 Mar 1840. W4204. BLW 22282-100 **P:** Y **BLW:** Y **RG:** unk **MK:** unk **PH:** unk **SS:** K pg 171; CG Vol 2 pg 1337 **BS:** JLARC 4, 76.

GIBBONS, John; b 1740; d 1812 **RU:** Private, Served in General Nelson's Corps **CEM:** Augusta Stone Presbyterian; GPS 38.23926, -78.97356; 28 Old Stone Church Ln, Ft Defiance; Augusta **GS:** U **SP:** No info **VI:** No further data **P:** unk **BLW:** unk **RG:** unk **MK:** unk **PH:** unk **SS:** E pg 304; BY **BS:** JLARC 63.

GIBSON, George; b 1732 Cork Co, Ireland; d 3 Apr 1819 **RU:** Lt Colonel, Was at Point Pleasant 10 Oct 1774 as Lt in Capt James Ewing's Co fr Augusta Co. Was at Valley Forge during winter 1777-8 as Maj. Served 22 Mar 1777-5 Jun 1777. Later was Col of 1st VA Regt at Yorktown **CEM:** Gibson Family; GPS unk; Gibson Station; Lee **GS:** Y **SP:** Elizabeth Smith **VI:** No further data **P:** unk **BLW:** unk **RG:** Y **MK:** Y **PH:** unk **SS:** AK Nov 06; CF pg 42, 110, 184 **BS:** 04, Nov 06.

GIBSON, Joseph; b unk; d 1796 **RU:** Patroit, Gave material aid to the cause **CEM:** South Fork Meeting House; GPS 39.02640, -77.80220; Rt 630, Unison; Loudoun **GS:** Y **SP:** No info **VI:** No further data **P:** unk **BLW:** unk **RG:** N **MK:** N **PH:** unk **SS:** AL Ct Booklet pg 4 **BS:** 25 pg 111.

GIBSON, William; b 1740, Louisa Co; d After 1832 **RU:** Corporal, Enl 12 Jan 1776 Louisa Co in 9th, 10th, 13th Cont Lines **CEM:** Gibson Farm; GPS unk; Louisa; Louisa **GS:** U **SP:** Mary Nappter (1770-

RU=Rank/Unit	CEM=Cemetery	GS=Gravestone	SP=Spousal Information
VI=Other Veteran Info	P=Pension	BLW=Bounty/Land Warrant	RG=Registered Grave
MK=SAR/DAR Marker	PH=Photo	SS=Service Source	BS=Burial Source

121

1821) **VI:** Appl for pen 14 Aug 1832 age 72 **P:** Y **BLW:** unk **RG:** unk **MK:** unk **PH:** unk **SS:** A pg 201; E pg 305; CG pg 1342 **BS:** 196.

GIDEON, Peter; b 22 Mar 1752, near Philadelphia PA; d 5 Feb 1844 **RU:** Soldier, Served in MD Line. Ent serv Taneytown MD **CEM:** Potts Family; GPS unk; Rts 716 & 714, Hillsboro; Loudoun **GS:** U **SP:** (------) was living in 1833 **VI:** Sol appl pen 22 Mar 1752 Loudoun Co. S6887 **P:** Y **BLW:** unk **RG:** unk **MK:** unk **PH:** unk **SS:** CG Vol 2 pg 1342-3 **BS:** JLARC 4, 32.

GILBERT, Samuel; b 1761; d 1845 **RU:** Private?, Served in VA Line. Ent serv Washington Co (later Russell Co), Capt James Crabree's Co under Col Aurthur Campbell. Served in militia commanded by Capt James Montgomery **CEM:** Tritt-Gilbert; GPS unk; Rt 642, Woodway; Lee **GS:** Y **SP:** Mary (-----) **VI:** Sol appl pen 18 Feb 1833 Lee Co age 72. S8569. He died in Lee Co at Thomas Gilbert's **P:** Y **BLW:** unk **RG:** Y **MK:** N **PH:** unk **SS:** 32 Pension list; CG Vol 2 pg 1347 **BS:** 04, Dec 06.

GILCHRIST, Robert; b c1721, Scotland; d 16 July 1790 **RU:** Patriot, Performed public service as Commissioner for specific taxes **CEM:** Townsfield Farm; GPS unk; Port Royal; Caroline **GS:** Y **SP:** Catherine (-----) (c1720-5 May 1789?) **VI:** No further data **P:** N **BLW:** N **RG:** N **MK:** N **PH:** unk **SS:** AL, CT Bk It II pg 8 **BS:** 02 pg 75; 196.

GILES, Thomas; b 30 Nov 1763, Hartford Co, MD; d 21 Mar 1842 **RU:** Private, Served in VA troops, Northumberland Co **CEM:** Westview; GPS 37.23390, -80.40830; Blacksburg; Montgomery **GS:** U **SP:** Mar (10 May 1762) Anne Wheeler **VI:** No further data **P:** unk **BLW:** unk **RG:** Y **MK:** unk **PH:** unk **SS:** J-NSSAR 1993 Reg, NSSAR Ancestor #P-166148; AR Vol 2 pg 73 **BS:** JLARC 1, 2.

GILES, William; b 1727; d unk **RU:** Colonel, Commissionary officer Amelia Co Militia, 22 Jan 1780 **CEM:** Jeter-Cadwell; GPS unk; Giles Rd Rt 636; Amelia **GS:** N **SP:** Ann Branch **VI:** Father of Governor William Branch Giles **P:** unk **BLW:** unk **RG:** unk **MK:** unk **PH:** N **SS:** G pg 14 **BS:** 196.

GILES, William Branch; b 21 Aug 1762; d 4 Dec 1830 **RU:** Ensign, Served in Henrico Co Militia 1 Oct 1781 **CEM:** Wigwam Estate; GPS unk; Amelia CH; Amelia **GS:** Y **SP:** No info **VI:** US Rep 1790-98. US Senator 1804 & 1805-15. Governor 1827-30. Sponsored admission of TN as 18th state of Union 1809. Giles Co in TN named for him **P:** unk **BLW:** unk **RG:** unk **MK:** unk **PH:** unk **SS:** E pg 306 **BS:** 196.

GILKESON, Hugh; b 1744; d Feb 1806 **RU:** Private, Served in Capt Long's Co, Augusta Militia **CEM:** Tinkling Spring Presbyterian; GPS 38.08472, -78.98278; 30 Tinkling Spring Dr, Fishersville; Augusta **GS:** N **SP:** Elizabeth (-----) (1744-May 1830) **VI:** No further data **P:** unk **BLW:** unk **RG:** unk **MK:** N **PH:** N **SS:** E pg 307 **BS:** 208 pg 468.

GILKESON, John; b c1749, PA; d 1 Jun 1793 **RU:** Major, Served as Capt 3rd Co 2nd VA Regt. Promoted to Maj **CEM:** Opequon Presbyterian; GPS 39.13938, -78.19494; 217 Opequon Church Ln; Winchester City **GS:** Y **SP:** Sarah Vance **VI:** No further data **P:** unk **BLW:** unk **RG:** Y **MK:** Y **PH:** unk **SS:** J-NASSR 2000 Reg; CE pg 33 **BS:** JLARC 76.

GILKESON, Samuel; b unk; d unk **RU:** Major, Promoted to Capt in Frederick Co Militia 4 Aug 1779. Promoted to Maj 2 May 1780 **CEM:** Opequon Presbyterian; GPS 39.13938, -78.19494; 217 Opequon Church Ln; Winchester City **GS:** U **SP:** Mar (3 Jul 1777 Frederick Co (bond) John Peyton, security) Susannah Hayn **VI:** No further data **P:** unk **BLW:** unk **RG:** Y **MK:** Y **PH:** unk **SS:** J-NASSR 2000 Reg; E pg 307 **BS:** JLARC 76.

GILKESON, William; b 29 Aug 1750; d 3 Jul 1828 **RU:** Private, Served in Capt Robert McClannahan's Co, Dunmore's War of 1774 at Point Pleasant **CEM:** Bethel Presbyterian; GPS 38.04257, -79.17283; 563 Bethel Green Rd, Middlebrook; Augusta **GS:** Y **SP:** Sarah Love (29 Aug 1752-27 Jun 1826) **VI:** No further data **P:** unk **BLW:** unk **RG:** unk **MK:** unk **PH:** unk **SS:** CP Dunmore's War **BS:** JLARC 62; 196.

GILL, Erasmus; b 15 Jul 1752; d 16 Mar 1807 **RU:** Captain, Served in 4th Cont Dragoons, Feb 1779 and taken prisoner at siege of Savannah 3 Oct 1779, and exchanged 22 Oct 1780, and served to close of war **CEM:** Blandford; GPS 37.22433, -77.38604; 319 S Crater Rd; Petersburg City **GS:** Y **SP:** Mar (8 Jun 1786, Dinnwiddie Co) Sarah Newsum (17 Aug 1765-16 Apr 1826) d/o Benjamin & Lucy (Jones) Newsum **VI:** Rank of Major perhaps made before Oct 1783. Recd BLW # 839-300-27, 27 Aug 1795 5,333 acres **P:** unk **BLW:** Y **RG:** unk **MK:** unk **PH:** unk **SS:** DAR ancestor #A044666; E pg 307; CG pg 1350 **BS:** 196; 217.

RU=Rank/Unit	CEM=Cemetery	GS=Gravestone	SP=Spousal Information
VI=Other Veteran Info	P=Pension	BLW=Bounty/Land Warrant	RG=Registered Grave
MK=SAR/DAR Marker	PH=Photo	SS=Service Source	BS=Burial Source

122

GILLES, Pierre; b unk; d 1781 **RU:** Soldier, Served in Gatinais Bn and died fr battle at Yorktown **CEM:** French Memorial; GPS 36.81944, -79.39933; Yorktown; York **GS:** U **SP:** No info **VI:** No further data **P:** unk **BLW:** unk **RG:** unk **MK:** unk **PH:** unk **SS:** J-Yorktown Historian **BS:** JLARC 1, 74.

GILLESPIE (GILLASPY), Thomas II; b 1760; d 1842 **RU:** Private, Served in Capt Alexander Breckenridge Co, Col Nathaniel Gist's Regt 1777 **CEM:** Sayer's Farm; GPS unk; Mouth of Thompson Valley, Foot of Clinch Mountain, Dry Fork; Tazewell **GS:** U **SP:** Mar (c1781 Washington Co) Margaret Bowen (c1760 Augusta Co-d1799) d/o Rees (c1737 Augusta Co-7 Oct 1780 Kings Mountain, SC) & Louisa (Smith c1740-16 Feb 1834) Bowen **VI:** No further data **P:** unk **BLW:** unk **RG:** unk **MK:** unk **PH:** unk **SS:** J- DAR Hatcher; A pg 285 **BS:** JLARC 2.

GILLET, Guillaume; b unk; d 1781 **RU:** Seaman, Served on "Diademe" and died from Yorktown battle **CEM:** French Memorial; GPS 36.81944, -79.39933; Yorktown; York **GS:** U **SP:** No info **VI:** No further data **P:** unk **BLW:** unk **RG:** Y **MK:** unk **PH:** unk **SS:** J-Yorktown Historian **BS:** JLARC 1, 74.

GILLIES (GILLES), James Dr; b 1758; d 24 Aug 1807 **RU:** Soldier/Patriot, Mil serv info not determined. Paid the supply tax in Fairfax Co 1782 **CEM:** Old Presbyterian Meeting House; GPS 38.48528, -77.23532; 323 S Fairfax St; Alexandria City **GS:** N **SP:** No info **VI:** Died of decline age 49, bur 25 Aug 1807. Was Vice President of St Andrew's Society (Alexandria Gazette 7 Aug 1807). Listed on SAR plaque in cemetery **P:** unk **BLW:** unk **RG:** Y **MK:** Y **PH:** N **SS:** J-NSSAR 1993 Reg; AK; DV **BS:** JLARC 1; 23 pg 102; 196.

GILMER, George Dr; b 27 Nov 1742, Williamsburg; d 29 Nov 1795 **RU:** Lieutenant, Was Surgeon for 11th VA. Was Lt in Albemarle Co 1775. Was 1st Lt in an independent Co of Albemarle Co Apr to Jul 1775 **CEM:** Gilner Family; GPS 38.04851, -78.44964; Pen Park off Rio Rd; Charlottesville City **GS:** U **SP:** Mar (27 Aug 176_) first cousin Lucy Walker, d/o Dr. Thomas Walker **VI:** Son of George Gilmer (1700-1757) & Mary Peachey (1710-1745). Died in Pen Park, Charlottesvillle **P:** unk **BLW:** unk **RG:** unk **MK:** unk **PH:** unk **SS:** E pg 308; CE pg 10 **BS:** JLARC 2,3,58; 67 Vol 1 pg 234; 196.

GILMORE, James; b 1710; d 1782 **RU:** Captain, Commanded co Rockbridge Co Militia,1780 **CEM:** High Bridge Presbyterian; GPS 37.62420, -79.58610; 67 High Bridge Rd, Natural Bridge; Rockbridge **GS:** U **SP:** Martha Dennison (1738-17850 **VI:** Son of John (1692-1759) & Agnes (Anderson) (1702-1759) Gilmore **P:** unk **BLW:** unk **RG:** unk **MK:** unk **PH:** unk **SS:** J- DAR Hatcher; AL Ct Bk pg 3a Rockbridge Co **BS:** JLARC 2; 196.

GILMORE (GILMOR, GILMER), Samuel; b 24 Mar 1760, Bucks Co, PA; d 25 Jan 1848 **RU:** Private, Severely wounded at Battle of Waxhaw, 1780 **CEM:** Gilmore Family; GPS unk; In woods in back of Briscoe's Grocery Store. (Rt 84). Mill Gap.; Highland **GS:** Y **SP:** Mar (Feb 1799) Eleanor Bailey McQuillen **VI:** Died in Back Creek, Highland Co. Stone found lying on ground, broken into three pieces **P:** unk **BLW:** unk **RG:** unk **MK:** N **PH:** unk **SS:** NSSAR Ancestor #P-166615; AR Vol 2 pg 76 **BS:** JLARC 2, 4,103.

GILPIN, George; b 4 Mar 1740; d Dec 1813 **RU:** Major, Served in Fairfax Militia 1777-78. Was 1/Lt in independent Co of Fairfax 1775. Gave material aid to cause **CEM:** Old Christ Church Episcopal; GPS 38.80625, -77.04718; 118 N Washington St; Alexandria City **GS:** N **SP:** 1) Catherine Peters 2) Jane Peters **VI:** Records of Ct Martial of Fairfax Co Militia of 29 Oct 1776 contain charges against 11 men in Capt George Gilpin's Co. At tiime of his death, at age 72, he was Postmaster and Magistrate for Fairfax Co and Alexandria, bur with Masonic orders (Alexandria Gazette, 28 Dec 1813) **P:** unk **BLW:** unk **RG:** Y **MK:** N **PH:** N **SS:** E pg 309; R pg 7, 12, 14; CE pg 10 **BS:** 20 pg 97-8.

GINBERT, Julien; b unk; d 1781 **RU:** Seaman, Served on "Citoyen" and died from Yorktown battle **CEM:** French Memorial; GPS 36.81944, -79.39933; Yorktown; York **GS:** U **SP:** No info **VI:** No further data **P:** unk **BLW:** unk **RG:** Y **MK:** unk **PH:** unk **SS:** J-Yorktown Historian **BS:** JLARC 1, 74.

GIRARD, Joseph; b unk; d 1781 **RU:** Seaman, Served on "Citoyen" and died from Yorktown battle **CEM:** French Memorial; GPS 36.81944, -79.39933; Yorktown; York **GS:** U **SP:** No info **VI:** No further data **P:** unk **BLW:** unk **RG:** unk **MK:** unk **PH:** unk **SS:** J-Yorktown Historian **BS:** JLARC 74.

RU=Rank/Unit	CEM=Cemetery	GS=Gravestone	SP=Spousal Information
VI=Other Veteran Info	P=Pension	BLW=Bounty/Land Warrant	RG=Registered Grave
MK=SAR/DAR Marker	PH=Photo	SS=Service Source	BS=Burial Source

123

GIRAUD, Joseph; b unk; d 1781 **RU:** Soldier, Served in Gatinais Bn and died fr battle at Yorktown **CEM:** French Memorial; GPS 36.81944, -79.39933; Yorktown; York **GS:** U **SP:** No info **VI:** No further data **P:** unk **BLW:** unk **RG:** Y **MK:** unk **PH:** unk **SS:** J-Yorktown Historian **BS:** JLARC 1, 74.

GISH, Jacob; b 5 Feb 1761; d 2 Aug 1836 **RU:** Private, Served in Lancaster Co, PA Militia **CEM:** Daleville; GPS 37.39869, -79.91069; Roanoke Rd Rt 220 nr Kroger store, Daleville; Botetourt **GS:** Y **SP:** Mar (PA) Ann Vineyard (2 Feb 1761 Botetourt Co-Dec 1830) **VI:** Son of Christain Sr & Sophia (Hook) Gish **P:** unk **BLW:** unk **RG:** unk **MK:** unk **PH:** unk **SS:** CI PA Archives 5th series Vol 14 pg 323 **BS:** 123 pg 67; 196.

GIVEN, William; b 21 Mar 1746; d 29 Sep 1793 **RU:** Private/Patriot, Served in PA Militia. Signed petition to separate Bath Co fr Augusta Co in 1779 **CEM:** Cleek; GPS 38.19310, -79.73220; Rt 220 Sam Snead Hwy, Warm Springs; Bath **GS:** N **SP:** Perhaps mar (21 Mar 1764 Augusta Co) Agnes Bratton (17Apr 1747-22 Jul 1827) d/o Robert & Ann (McFarland) Bratton **VI:** Perhaps son of John & Margaret (Sitlington) Givens (This info fr Findagrave.com. It is expected that war service, spouse, & parents are incorrect on this site with that of a William Givens, not William Given. His children have surname of Given, not Givens) **P:** unk **BLW:** unk **RG:** N **MK:** N **PH:** N **SS:** BM Gleek; CD **BS:** 159 Cleek.

GIVENS, John; b May 1740; d 13 Apr 1812 **RU:** Captain, Commanded a company Augusta Co Militia 17 Feb 1778-October 1783 Marched his unit to near Jamestown in 1781 **CEM:** Augusta Stone Presbyterian; GPS 38.23926, -78.97356; 28 Old Stone Church Ln, Ft Defiance; Augusta **GS:** Y **SP:** Mary Margaret Sitlington **VI:** No further data **P:** unk **BLW:** unk **RG:** unk **MK:** unk **PH:** unk **SS:** E pg 310; G pg 470; AZ pg 122, 182 **BS:** JLARC 1, 8, 23, 62, 63; 196.

GLANET, Louis; b unk; d 1781 **RU:** Soldier, Served in Santogne Bn and died fr battle at Yorktown **CEM:** French Memorial; GPS 36.81944, -79.39933; Yorktown; York **GS:** U **SP:** No info **VI:** No further data **P:** unk **BLW:** unk **RG:** Y **MK:** unk **PH:** unk **SS:** J-Yorktown Historian **BS:** JLARC 1, 74.

GLASCOCK, Hezekiah; b 21 Jun 1746; d 1 Aug 1818 **RU:** Patriot, Gave material aid to cause **CEM:** Clascock "Glenmore"; GPS unk; Rectortown; Fauquier **GS:** U **SP:** Sarah (-----) (__-13 Oct 1815) **VI:** No further data **P:** N **BLW:** N **RG:** unk **MK:** unk **PH:** unk **SS:** AL Cert & List pg 1 Fauquier Co **BS:** 196.

GLASGOW, Arthur; b 1750, Rockbridge Co; d May 1822 **RU:** Soldier, DAR application does not specify service other than soldier **CEM:** Falling Springs Presbyterian; GPS 37.68494, -79.45105; 410 Falling Springs Rd, Glasgow; Rockbridge **GS:** Y **SP:** Mar (1782) Rebeckah McCorkle (1755-Jan 1818) **VI:** No further data **P:** N **BLW:** N **RG:** unk **MK:** unk **PH:** unk **SS:** DAR Ancestor #A045298 **BS:** 204.

GLASSBURN, David; b 1730, Germany; d 1830 **RU:** Private, Served in Capt Arbuckle's Co, Botetourt Co Militia **CEM:** Mallow Tract; GPS unk; nr Hot Springs; Bath **GS:** U **SP:** Mar (18 Mar 1778) Elizabeth Carpenter (1758-1837) **VI:** Died in Covington, Botetourt Co **P:** unk **BLW:** unk **RG:** unk **MK:** unk **PH:** unk **SS:** J- DAR Hatcher; DD **BS:** JLARC 2.

GLASSCOCK, John; b 14 Jan 1699, Richmond; d 28 Jun 1784 **RU:** Patriot, Gave material aid to cause **CEM:** Rockburn (Rachburn); GPS unk; Nr Warrenton; Fauquier **GS:** Y **SP:** Margaret (-----) **VI:** No further data **P:** N **BLW:** N **RG:** Y **MK:** N **PH:** unk **SS:** AL lists pg 6 Fauquier Co **BS:** SAR regis.

GLASSCOCK (GLASCOCK), George; b 1741; d 4 Mar 1826 **RU:** Patriot, Gave material aid to cause, Richmond Co **CEM:** Rockburn; GPS unk; Rockburn Farm, 224 Crenshaw Rd, Rectortown; Fauquier **GS:** Y **SP:** Hannah Rector (1750-Sep 1816) **VI:** No further data **P:** N **BLW:** N **RG:** Y **MK:** N **PH:** unk **SS:** J-NSSAR 1993 Reg; NSSAR Ancestor # P-166878 **BS:** JLARC 1; 196.

GLASSCOCK (GLASCOCK), Thomas; b 1731; d 1793 **RU:** Lieutenant/Patriot, Gave material aid to cause **CEM:** Glasscock Family Farm; GPS unk; Nr Marshall; Fauquier **GS:** U **SP:** 1) Catherine Rector and 2) Agatha Rector **VI:** No further data **P:** unk **BLW:** unk **RG:** unk **MK:** unk **PH:** unk **SS:** NSSAR Ancestor #P-166832; AR Vol 2 pg 77; AL Ct Bk pg 25 Fauquier Co **BS:** JLARC 2.

GLEAVES, Michael; b unk; d unk **RU:** Private, Capt James Newell's Co, Montgomery Co Militia, 5 Apr 1781 **CEM:** Gleaves Farm; GPS unk; Dunkley farm, Cripple Creek; Wythe **GS:** U **SP:** No info **VI:** No further data **P:** unk **BLW:** unk **RG:** Y **MK:** unk **PH:** unk **SS:** J-NASSR 2000 Reg; G pg 226 **BS:** JLARC 76.

RU=Rank/Unit	CEM=Cemetery	GS=Gravestone	SP=Spousal Information
VI=Other Veteran Info	P=Pension	BLW=Bounty/Land Warrant	RG=Registered Grave
MK=SAR/DAR Marker	PH=Photo	SS=Service Source	BS=Burial Source

124

GLEAVES, William Benjamin; b 1750; d 1820 **RU:** First Lieutenant, Capt James Newell's Co, Montgomery Co Militia, 5 Apr 1781 **CEM:** Gleaves Farm; GPS unk; Dunkley farm, Cripple Creek; Wythe **GS:** U **SP:** Mar (3 May 1770) Elizabeth Turk (c1752-1840) **VI:** Son of Matthew & Esther (-----) Gleaves **P:** unk **BLW:** unk **RG:** unk **MK:** unk **PH:** unk **SS:** G pg 226 **BS:** JLARC 40; 196.

GLENN, George; b 1720, Londonderry, Ireland; d Feb 1815 **RU:** Private, Served in Capt Reuben Harrison's & Capt Anderson's companies, Augusta Co Militia **CEM:** Augusta Stone Presbyterian; GPS 38.23925, -78.97356; 28 Old Stone Church Ln, Ft Defiance; Augusta **GS:** U **SP:** Mary Young **VI:** Came to VA fr PA **P:** unk **BLW:** unk **RG:** unk **MK:** Y **PH:** Y **SS:** AK **BS:** 04; 196.

GLOVER, Anthony; b 15 Apr 1755; d 1838 **RU:** Patriot, Gave material aid to the cause **CEM:** Anthony Glover Cem; GPS unk; Dirt lane 1 mi S of Alcoma; Buckingham **GS:** N **SP:** Ann Tyndall (1770-27 May 1838) d/o Benjamin & Anne (Lewis) Tyndall **VI:** Son of Samuel & Judith (Benning) Glover **P:** N **BLW:** N **RG:** N **MK:** N **PH:** N **SS:** AL Ct bk pg 2, 49 **BS:** 52 pg 272.

GLOVER, Joseph; b c1767; d 1792 **RU:** Private, Served in Capt Williamson's Co, VA line. Was at siege of Yorktown Oct 1781 **CEM:** Tooker Family, Brandon Home; GPS unk; 5 mi NE of Burrowsville; Prince George **GS:** Y **SP:** No info **VI:** No further data **P:** Y **BLW:** unk **RG:** N **MK:** N **PH:** unk **SS:** AJ MA Service; CI applic for pension **BS:** 111 Part 2 pg 43.

GLOVER, Samuel Jr; b 2 Jun 1759; d 7 Jun 1820 **RU:** Soldier, Served in VA Line **CEM:** Samuel Glover; GPS unk; Rt 742; Buckingham **GS:** N **SP:** Mar (16 Oct 1782 Buckingham) Mary Tindale, (__-11 Apr 1839) **VI:** Son of Samuel & Judith (Benning) Glover. R4074 **P:** Y **BLW:** N **RG:** unk **MK:** N **PH:** N **SS:** K pg 189; CG Vol 2 pg 1368 **BS:** JLARC 4, 10, 59; 196.

GODARD, Jean; b unk; d 1781 **RU:** Soldier, Served in Beaujolais Bn and died fr battle at Yorktown **CEM:** French Memorial; GPS 36.81944, -79.39933; Yorktown; York **GS:** U **SP:** No info **VI:** No further data **P:** unk **BLW:** unk **RG:** Y **MK:** unk **PH:** unk **SS:** J-Yorktown Historian **BS:** JLARC 1, 74.

GODEAU, Nicolas; b unk; d 1781 **RU:** Seaman, Served on "Sceptre" and died from Yorktown battle **CEM:** French Memorial; GPS 36.81944, -79.39933; Yorktown; York **GS:** U **SP:** No info **VI:** No further data **P:** unk **BLW:** unk **RG:** Y **MK:** unk **PH:** unk **SS:** J-Yorktown Historian **BS:** JLARC 1, 74.

GODSEY, Austin; b c1752, Chester, Chesterfield Co; d c1818 **RU:** Private, Served in VA Line. Enl serv Granville Co, NC **CEM:** Godsey Family; GPS unk; Rt 613, Nickelsville; Scott **GS:** Y **SP:** Mar (30 Dec 1782 Granville Co NC) Frances "Frankey" or "Franky" Hicks (__-18 Nov 1855) **VI:** Died in Russell Co (later Scott Co). Widow appl pen 30 July 1855 Lincoln Co GA age 90. R21991. Memorialized in Scott Co on widow's GS **P:** Y **BLW:** unk **RG:** Y **MK:** Y **PH:** unk **SS:** K pg 191; AK Amherst Rec; CG Vol 2 pg 1371 **BS:** 04, Nov 06.

GOGGIN, Stephen Jr; b unk; d 1802 **RU:** First Lieutenant, Served in Bedford Co Militia. Served in 1779 as 1st Lt, marched to Charlotte, NC & served under Gen Greene **CEM:** Quaker Baptist; GPS 37.20619, -79.51623; 4665 Chestnut Fork Rd, Chestnut Fork; Bedford **GS:** Y **SP:** Rachel Moorman (1754 Hanover Co-1835 Bedford Co) d/o Thomas (1705-1767) & Rachel (Clark) (1714-1792) Moorman. No stone **VI:** Govt marker inscribed "1st Lieut Bedford Cty Mil Rev War" **P:** unk **BLW:** unk **RG:** Y **MK:** N **PH:** unk **SS:** B; AZ pg 135 **BS:** 196.

GOLLADAY, David; b 15 Sep 1759, Gaithersburg, Montgomery Co, MD; d 23 Sep 1823 **RU:** Major, Served as staff officer in Shenandoah Co Militia **CEM:** Leland Brown Farm; GPS unk; Nr Weyers Cave; Augusta **GS:** Y **SP:** One son by Abigail Combs out of wedlock, who was Jacob Gallady (Aug 1785-__). Mar (24 Jun 1785) Rebecca Hockman (1764-1 Oct 1840 Montgomery Co) **VI:** Son of Jacob & Elinor (----) Galladay. Govt stone. There is an image of a fine oil portrait of him on his memorial page at findagrave.com **P:** unk **BLW:** unk **RG:** unk **MK:** unk **PH:** unk **SS:** NSSAR Ancestor #P-167485; B lists serv **BS:** JLARC 62.

GOLLADAY (GOLLIDAY), Jacob; b 1735, Lancaster Co, PA; d 28 Feb 1795 **RU:** Lieutenant, Served in Shenandoah Co Militia **CEM:** Dry Run Church; GPS 38.85929, -78.40075; Rt 678, Fort Valley Rd nr jct with Dry Run Rd, Seven Fountains; Shenandoah **GS:** Y **SP:** Elinor (-----)(__ Lancaster Co, PA-1774) **VI:** Son of Joseph (1703-1758) & Sybilla (Kneisley) (1709-1758) Golladay **P:** unk **BLW:** unk **RG:** N **MK:** N **PH:** unk **SS:** B Govt; E pg 314 **BS:** 32 May 11; 196.

RU=Rank/Unit   CEM=Cemetery   GS=Gravestone   SP=Spousal Information
VI=Other Veteran Info   P=Pension   BLW=Bounty/Land Warrant   RG=Registered Grave
MK=SAR/DAR Marker   PH=Photo   SS=Service Source   BS=Burial Source

125

GOLLADAY (GOLLODAY), Joseph; b 1758; d Sep 1826 **RU**: Private, Served in VA Line. Enl Woodstock, VA **CEM**: Dry Run Church; GPS 38.85929, -78.40075; Rt 678, Fort Valley Rd nr jct with Dry Run Rd, Seven Fountains; Shenandoah **GS**: Y **SP**: Mar (1784 NY State) Mary Huslander or Hulslander (22 Jan 1753-__) **VI**: Sol appl pen 27 Oct 1819 Shenandoah Co age 61. Widow appl pen 16 Mar 1839 Shenandoah Co. W7555 **P**: Y **BLW**: unk **RG**: N **MK**: N **PH**: unk **SS**: E pg 314; CG Vol 2 pg 1375 **BS**: 32 May 11.

GOODALL, Parke; b 1742; d 1816 **RU**: Ensign, Served in an Independent Co in Hanover Co, May-Jun 1775 **CEM**: Goodall's Tavern Property; GPS unk; .75 mi W of jct Rts 623 & 33; Hanover **GS**: N **SP**: Mary (-----) **VI**: No further data **P**: unk **BLW**: unk **RG**: unk **MK**: unk **PH**: N **SS**: CE pg 11 **BS**: JLARC 71.

GOODE, Francis; b 1744; d 1795 **RU**: Colonel, Capt of Militia, Chesterfield Co, Nov 1775, later obtained rank of Col **CEM**: Skinquarter Baptist; GPS 37.40916, -77.792655; 6900 Moseley Rd, Moseley; Chesterfield **GS**: Y **SP**: No info **VI**: Marker. Bur at sea **P**: unk **BLW**: unk **RG**: unk **MK**: Y **PH**: N **SS**: CF pg 13 **BS**: JLARC 4, 35.

GOODE, John; b 1738; d 1790 **RU**: Private/Patriot, Served in Buckingham Co Militia. Gave material aid to cause **CEM**: Skinquarter Baptist; GPS 37.40916, -77.792655; 6900 Moseley Rd, Moseley; Chesterfield **GS**: N **SP**: Sarah Brown (1745-1812), d/o George & (-----) Brown **VI**: Rev Son of Benjamin Goode (c1700-aft 1764) & Susanna (-----) of Henrico Co, VA Colony. Widow pensioned commencing 27 Aug 1814 at $48 per yr **P**: Y **BLW**: N **RG**: Y **MK**: N **PH**: N **SS**: J-NASSR 2000 Reg; E pg 315; G pg 559; AG pg 264; AL Ct Bk pg 24 **BS**: JLARC 76; 196.

GOODE, Samuel; b 1756; d 14 Nov 1822 **RU**: Lieutenant, Served in VA Dragoons 1776-1779 **CEM**: Invernay Family Center; GPS unk; Rt 138 at Invernay PO; Mecklenburg **GS**: U **SP**: Mar (28 Sep 1786) Mary Armistead Burwell d/o of Lewis Burwell **VI**: No further data **P**: unk **BLW**: unk **RG**: Y **MK**: unk **PH**: unk **SS**: J-NASSR 2000 Reg; E pg 315 **BS**: JLARC 76.

GOODRICH, David; b unk; d 1781 **RU**: Private, Served in Capt Chapman's Co, CT Cont line. Died fr battle at Yorktown **CEM**: Yorktown Victory Monument Tablet; GPS 38.28350, -78.54150; Yorktown; York **GS**: U **SP**: No info **VI**: No further data **P**: unk **BLW**: unk **RG**: unk **MK**: unk **PH**: unk **SS**: J-Yorktown Historian; DY pg 352 **BS**: JLARC 74.

GOODSON, Thomas H II; b 18 Aug 1755, Frederick Co, MD; d 3 Sep 1837 **RU**: Lieutenant, Served in VA Line. Ent serv Botetourt Co. Promoted to 1st Lt in Isle of Wight Co Militia; served in 7th Cont Line **CEM**: Goodson Family; GPS unk; Pine Creek, near Turtle Rock; Floyd **GS**: U **SP**: Elizabeth Pogue or Poague (__-5 Feb 1837) **VI**: Son of Thomas Sr (1735-14 Mar 1815 Montgomery Co) & (-----) Goodson. Moved to New River, Augusta Co with his father when he was five yrs old. Sol appl pen 17 Dec 1832 Floyd Co. S6901 **P**: Y **BLW**: unk **RG**: unk **MK**: N **PH**: unk **SS**: G pg 192-4; K pg 196; CG Vol 2 pg 1382 **BS**: JLARC 2, 4, 29.

GOODSON, Thomas Washington I; b Aug 1735, Frederick Co MD; d 11 Mar 1815 **RU**: Major/Patriot, Gave material aid to cause. Also Juror 1780 **CEM**: Pine Creek Primitive Baptist; GPS 36.94622, -80.27357; Spangler Mill Rd Rt 682; Floyd **GS**: Y **SP**: Sarah Riddle Goodson (1740-1816). Mar also Keziah Harris. **VI**: Son of Thomas and 1) (-----) Goodson. Died in Montgomery Co (now Floyd Co) **P**: unk **BLW**: unk **RG**: unk **MK**: unk **PH**: Y **SS**: AN; AL Ct Bk pg 10 Isle of Wight Co; BC Part 1 pg 329-331 **BS**: 196.

GOODWYN, Joseph; b unk; d Aft 1781 **RU**: Soldier/Patriot, Served in VA andGA. Gave material aid to cause **CEM**: Sweden Plantation; GPS 37.15854, -77.54751; Nr jct Claiborne & White Oak rds, Sutherland; Dinwiddie **GS**: N **SP**: No info **VI**: Twin brother of Peterson Goodwyn **P**: N **BLW**: unk **RG**: unk **MK**: N **PH**: N **SS**: AL Cert Dinwiddie Co **BS**: JLARC 116.

GOODWYN, Peterson; b 1745; d 21 Feb 1818 **RU**: Colonel, Served in Goodwyn's Co. Commanded co at Great Bridge. Promoted fr Capt to Col for gallantry at Battle of Great Bridge **CEM**: Sweden Plantation; GPS 37.15854, -77.54751; Nr jct Claiborne & White Oak rds, Sutherland; Dinwiddie **GS**: Y **SP**: Elizabeth Peterson (1757-1818). Her inscription is on the back of her husband's V.A. marker. Daughter of Peter Peterson & Lucy Osborn **VI**: Was an attorney, House of Delegates 1789-1802; US Congress 1803-1818. Grave has a Vet Admin marker erected in the 1990s. Listed on cenotaph at Congressional

RU=Rank/Unit	CEM=Cemetery	GS=Gravestone	SP=Spousal Information
VI=Other Veteran Info	P=Pension	BLW=Bounty/Land Warrant	RG=Registered Grave
MK=SAR/DAR Marker	PH=Photo	SS=Service Source	BS=Burial Source

126

Cemetery in Washington, DC **P:** N **BLW:** unk **RG:** unk **MK:** Y **PH:** unk **SS:** CD **BS:** JLARC 2, 4, 57,116; 196.

GOODWYN (GOODWIN), Robert; b 1739, York Co; d 12 May 1789 **RU:** Patriot, Gave material aid to cause **CEM:** Goodwyn house cem; GPS unk; Rt 16, 3.4 mi fr Louisa; Louisa **GS:** U **SP:** Jane Tulloch **VI:** No further data **P:** N **BLW:** N **RG:** unk **MK:** unk **PH:** unk **SS:** D Vol II pg 625, 633; BY **BS:** JLARC 61.

GORDON, James (Col); b 2 Aug 1750; d 29 Sep 1794 **RU:** Patriot, Had public service as Sheriff of Lancaster Co 17 Oct 1782 **CEM:** Old St John's Cemetery; GPS 37.68920, -76.38530; Off Rt 1066 (Harris Rd), abt .5 mi S of DMV Dr; Lancaster **GS:** N **SP:** Ann Payne, d/o John & (-----) Payne of Goochland Co **VI:** Son of Col James Gordon (1714 Newry Ireland-2 Jun 1768 Lancaster Co) & Mary (Harrison) ((1731-May 1771). **P:** N **BLW:** N **RG:** unk **MK:** unk **PH:** N **SS:** DS pg 249 **BS:** 40 pg 128; 196.

GORDON, Nathaniel; b 28 Aug 1763, Lancaster Co; d -29160 **RU:** Patriot, Gave material aid to cause **CEM:** Maplewood; GPS 38.14640, -78.20060; Rt 33 W Gordonsville; Orange **GS:** U **SP:** Mar (20 Oct 1785) Mary Gordon, d/o John & Lucy (Churchill) Gordon **VI:** Son of James & Mary (Harrison) Gordon. Founder of Gordonsville 1787 **P:** N **BLW:** N **RG:** unk **MK:** unk **PH:** unk **SS:** AL Ct Bk pg 3; Commissioner's Book III pg 273 **BS:** 196.

GORDON, Thomas; b 1752, Muddy Creek, Rockingham Co; d 2 Apr 1814 **RU:** Second Lieutenant/Patriot, Served in 6th Cont Line. Gave material aid to cause **CEM:** Salem Presbyterian; GPS unk; Cooks Creek; Rockingham **GS:** U **SP:** Catherine Davis **VI:** No further data **P:** unk **BLW:** unk **RG:** Y **MK:** unk **PH:** unk **SS:** J-NASSR 2000 Reg; D Rockbridge Co **BS:** JLARC 76.

GORE, Joshua Sr; b 1752; d 1830 **RU:** Patriot, Gave material aid to cause **CEM:** Goose Creek; GPS 39.11250, -77.69527; Rt 722, Lincoln; Loudoun **GS:** Y **SP:** No info **VI:** No further data **P:** N **BLW:** N **RG:** unk **MK:** unk **PH:** unk **SS:** AL Ct Bk pg 19, 37; Comm Bk III pg 298 **BS:** 196.

GORRELIER, Pierre; b 1752; d 1781 **RU:** Soldier, Served in Beaujolais Bn and died fr battle at Yorktown **CEM:** French Memorial; GPS 36.81944, -79.39933; Yorktown; York **GS:** U **SP:** No info **VI:** No further data **P:** unk **BLW:** unk **RG:** Y **MK:** unk **PH:** unk **SS:** J-Yorktown Historian **BS:** JLARC 1, 74.

GOSSAN, Jean; b 1752; d 1781 **RU:** Seaman, Served on "Sceptre" and died from Yorktown battle **CEM:** French Memorial; GPS 36.81944, -79.39933; Yorktown; York **GS:** U **SP:** No info **VI:** No further data **P:** unk **BLW:** unk **RG:** Y **MK:** unk **PH:** unk **SS:** J-Yorktown Historian **BS:** JLARC 1, 74.

GOULD, William; b 1752; d 1781 **RU:** Soldier, Served fr MA and died as result of Yorktown battle **CEM:** Yorktown Victory Monument Tablet; GPS 38.28350, -78.54150; Yorktown; York **GS:** U **SP:** No info **VI:** No further data **P:** unk **BLW:** unk **RG:** unk **MK:** unk **PH:** unk **SS:** J-Yorktown Historian **BS:** JLARC 74.

GOUYA, Antoine; b 1752; d 1781 **RU:** Soldier, Served in Gatinais Bn and died fr battle at Yorktown **CEM:** French Memorial; GPS 36.81944, -79.39933; Yorktown; York **GS:** U **SP:** No info **VI:** No further data **P:** unk **BLW:** unk **RG:** Y **MK:** unk **PH:** unk **SS:** J-Yorktown Historian **BS:** JLARC 1, 74.

GOUZER, Albin; b 1752; d 1781 **RU:** Seaman, Served on "Citoyen" and died from Yorktown battle **CEM:** French Memorial; GPS 36.81944, -79.39933; Yorktown; York **GS:** U **SP:** No info **VI:** No further data **P:** unk **BLW:** unk **RG:** Y **MK:** unk **PH:** unk **SS:** J-Yorktown Historian **BS:** JLARC 1, 4.

GRADY, James Sr; b 1747; d 9 Jan 1815 **RU:** Private?, Served in 6th & 10th Va Cont Lines. Signed for clothing in 1779, perhaps for unit **CEM:** Ebenezer Baptist; GPS 39.05824, -77.84142; 20421 Airmont Rd, Bluemont; Loudoun **GS:** Y **SP:** Susanna Butcher (1754-26 Feb 1818) **VI:** Died in Bloomfield, Loudoun Co **P:** unk **BLW:** unk **RG:** Y **MK:** N **PH:** unk **SS:** E pg 319 **BS:** 25 pg 116; 196.

GRAHAM, Andrew; b 1757; d 1823 **RU:** Private?, Served in 2d VA Regt Jan 1777 **CEM:** Old Lebanon; GPS 38.08090, -79.37545; Off Rt 42, Craigsville; Augusta **GS:** Y **SP:** Elizabeth (Warren) Cooper, widow of John Cooper **VI:** No further data **P:** unk **BLW:** unk **RG:** Y **MK:** Y **PH:** unk **SS:** CI Numbered Record Book **BS:** 04; 196.

GRAHAM, David; b 1758; d Oct 1803 **RU:** Soldier, Service information not determined **CEM:** Old Presbyterian Meeting House; GPS 38.48528, -77.23532; 323 S Fairfax St; Alexandria City **GS:** N **SP:**

RU=Rank/Unit	CEM=Cemetery	GS=Gravestone	SP=Spousal Information
VI=Other Veteran Info	P=Pension	BLW=Bounty/Land Warrant	RG=Registered Grave
MK=SAR/DAR Marker	PH=Photo	SS=Service Source	BS=Burial Source

127

No info **VI:** Died of fever, bur 8 Oct 1803, age 45. Listed on SAR plaque in cemetery **P:** unk **BLW:** unk **RG:** Y **MK:** Y **PH:** N **SS:** J-NSSAR 1993 Reg; AK **BS:** JLARC 1; 23 pg 102; 196.

GRAHAM, Michael; b 6 Apr 1758, Lancaster Co, PA; d 18 May 1834 **RU:** Private, Served in PA & VA Line. Lived Paxton Twp, Lancaster Co, PA at enl. Moved to Rockbridge Co VA 1777 and Ent serv there again **CEM:** Longwood; GPS 37.34170, -79.51190; Nr jct Oakwood & Longwood Ave Rt 122; Bedford City **GS:** Y **SP:** Mar (Feb 1786 Rockbridge Co) Elizabeth Lyle **VI:** Sol appl pen 24 Dec 1832 Bedford Co. S8621. Was Bedford Co Magistrate 17 or 18 yrs,and High Sheriff of county. In1832, was Escheator & Commissioner of Revenue **P:** unk **BLW:** unk **RG:** unk **MK:** N **PH:** unk **SS:** J- DAR Hatcher; K pg 202; CG Vol 2 pg 1400 **BS:** JLARC 2.

GRAHAM, Robert; b 1750, Ireland; d 9 May 1811 **RU:** Private, Served in Capt Baskin's Co, Augusta Co Militia **CEM:** Horseshoe Bend, Graham Family; GPS 36.94917, -80.90010; N side of Reed Creek on Formato Dr nr jct with E Lee Hwy; Wythe **GS:** U **SP:** 1) Mary Craig (1750 Ireland-26 Oct 1786) 2) Mary Cowen (17 Jun 1768-28 Dec 1819, Locust Hill, Wythe Co) **VI:** DAR marker **P:** unk **BLW:** unk **RG:** unk **MK:** Y **PH:** unk **SS:** E pg 320 **BS:** JLARC 123; 196.

GRAHAM, William; b 19 Dec 1746, PA; d 17 Jun 1799 **RU:** Captain, Led troops to Rockfish Gap in search of Tarleton. Later joined LaFayette **CEM:** Washington & Lee Univ Campus; GPS 36.60863, -81.01593; Nr Jefferson St; Lexington City **GS:** Y **SP:** No info **VI:** Was rector of Washington Academy in Rockbridge Co for 24 yrs. Rev Graham was 1st Rector of Liberty Hall, later to become Washington & Lee University. Died in Richmond. First bur at St John's Church, Richmond, but later reburied on campus of Washington & Lee Univ **P:** unk **BLW:** unk **RG:** Y **MK:** Y **PH:** unk **SS:** AD **BS:** JLARC 1, 79.

GRAHAM, William; b 1746; d 1799 **RU:** Private, Served in Capt Benjamin Bartholaman's Co of Foot, 5th VA Regt, commanded by Col Thomas Johnson, July 1777 **CEM:** St John's Episcopal; GPS 37.53183, -77.41958; 2401 E Broad St; Richmond City **GS:** Y **SP:** No info **VI:** No further data **P:** unk **BLW:** unk **RG:** N **MK:** N **PH:** unk **SS:** AP **BS:** 28 pg 448.

GRANBON, Claude; b unk; d 1781 **RU:** Soldier, Served in Soissonnais Bn and died fr battle at Yorktown **CEM:** French Memorial; GPS 36.81944, -79.39933; Yorktown; York **GS:** U **SP:** No info **VI:** No further data **P:** unk **BLW:** unk **RG:** Y **MK:** unk **PH:** unk **SS:** J-Yorktown Historian **BS:** JLARC 1, 74.

GRANDSTAFF (GRINSTAFF), George; b 8 Aug 1741, Lancaster Co, PA; d 7 Jun 1823 **RU:** Private/Patriot, Gave material aid to cause **CEM:** Grandstaff Family; GPS unk; Narrow Pass Creek; Shenandoah **GS:** Y **SP:** Madeline Hough **VI:** No further data **P:** unk **BLW:** unk **RG:** Y **MK:** Y **PH:** unk **SS:** E pg 330; AL Ct Bk pg 7, 12 **BS:** 04.

GRANDY, James; b unk; d 1781 **RU:** Soldier, Served fr MA and died as result of Yorktown battle **CEM:** Yorktown Victory Monument Tablet; GPS 38.28350, -78.54150; Yorktown; York **GS:** U **SP:** No info **VI:** No further data **P:** unk **BLW:** unk **RG:** unk **MK:** unk **PH:** unk **SS:** J-Yorktown Historian **BS:** JLARC 74.

GRAVELY, Joseph; b 10 Jan 1744, Hartfordshire, England; d 1834 or 3 Oct 1844 **RU:** Private, Served in Capt James Tarrant's Co Henry Co Militia. Fought at Guilford CH **CEM:** Leatherwood Plantation; GPS 36.44534, -79.4558; Nr Martinsville; Henry **GS:** N **SP:** Eleanor Cox **VI:** Died in Leatherwood **P:** unk **BLW:** unk **RG:** unk **MK:** Y **PH:** N **SS:** G pg 181; J- DAR Hatcher **BS:** JLARC 2.

GRAVES, John; b 1760, Culpeper Co; d 1828 **RU:** Private, Served fr Orange Co. Was at Yorktown. Guarded prisoners that were taken **CEM:** Graves Family; GPS unk; Property records may reveal location within County; Madison **GS:** U **SP:** Mar (25 Nov 1788) Elizabeth Eddins (c1770, Culpeper Co-1828) d/o Joseph (c1745 Culpeper Co-Jun 1825 Orange Co) & Sarah (Blakey) (c1749 Middlesex Co-1790 Orange Co 1790) Eddins **VI:** No further data **P:** unk **BLW:** unk **RG:** unk **MK:** unk **PH:** unk **SS:** J-DAR Hatcher; DA pg 49 & 89 **BS:** JLARC 2.

GRAY, Francis; b 1759; d 24 or 27 Apr 1827 **RU:** Lieutenant, Served in Cont & VA Lines. Enl serv Culpeper Co. Lost hearing fr sword wound at Battle of Lanneau's Ferry, SC **CEM:** Old City; GPS 37.41472, -79.15667; 401 Taylor St; Lynchburg City **GS:** U **SP:** Mar (23 Jun 1785 Culpeper Co) Eleanor Hening or Henning, d/o David & Mary (-----) Hening or Henning (1764-31 Aug 1839) **VI:** Widow appl pen 15 Aug 1838 Lynchburg City age 74. W7575. Recd BLW #873-200-24 Jun 1793. VA 1/2 Pay. In 1820

RU=Rank/Unit	CEM=Cemetery	GS=Gravestone	SP=Spousal Information
VI=Other Veteran Info	P=Pension	BLW=Bounty/Land Warrant	RG=Registered Grave
MK=SAR/DAR Marker	PH=Photo	SS=Service Source	BS=Burial Source

sol stated he was age 62 **P:** Y **BLW:** Y **RG:** Y **MK:** unk **PH:** unk **SS:** J-NSSAR 1993 Reg, J- DAR Hatcher; K pg 205; CG Vol 2 pg 1411 **BS:** JLARC 1, 2.

GRAY, James; b unk; d Dec 83 **RU:** Captain, Had sea serv as 2nd Lt on ship "Liberty" 27 Mar 1776. In 2nd overseas voyage in "Liberty" it was commanded by Capt J. Gray. Later he was Commander of "Cormorant" **CEM:** St John's Episcopal; GPS 37.53183, -77.41958; 2401 E Broad St; Richmond City **GS:** N **SP:** No info **VI:** R56 also VA 1/2 Pay (see Acc #837 VA State Navy, YS File VA 1/2 Pay). BLW #8026 for 4677 acres issued to heirs 16 Sep 1834. George W. Mallicote was estate admin and granted BLW 2026 for sailor's heirs 1846, who were granted 1/2 pay pension 1847 **P:** Y **BLW:** Y **RG:** Y **MK:** Y **PH:** N **SS:** AK; N pg 193; K pg 206; CG Vol 2 pg 1412 **BS:** 04; 28 pg 448.

GRAY(GREY), Daniel; b 1765; d Jan 1844 **RU:** Private, Served in VA Line. Ent serv Leesburg VA. Served in Lee's Legion & 3rd Lt Dragoons. Served three yrs in Cont Line **CEM:** Union Church; GPS 38.44480, -78.38350; Mt Jackson nr jct Main St & Bridge St; Shenandoah **GS:** Y **SP:** Polly (-----) (c1766-__) **VI:** Sol appl 28 May 1818 Shenandoah Co age 56.S39621. Source 1 has burial at Mt Calvary Baptist Church Cem. Heirs recd bounty land in 1840. DAR Plaque by headstone **P:** Y **BLW:** Y **RG:** Y **MK:** Y **PH:** unk **SS:** J-NSSAR 1993 Reg; J- DAR Hatcher; E pg 322; CG Vol 2 pg 1411 **BS:** JLARC 1, 2.

GRAYSON, Spencer; b 1734; d Dec 1792 **RU:** Chaplain, Served as Chaplain in Grayson's Regt May 1777 **CEM:** Grayson; GPS 38.64775, -77.27648; West Longview Dr, Woodbridge; Prince William **GS:** Y **SP:** No info **VI:** Son of Benjamin (1684-1757) & Susannah Monroe Tyler (Linton) (1695-1752) Grayson. SAR marker **P:** unk **BLW:** unk **RG:** Y **MK:** Y **PH:** Y **SS:** E pg 323 **BS:** JLARC 4.

GRAYSON, William; b 1736; d 12 Mar 1790 **RU:** Lieutenant Colonel, Was Capt of Independent Co of Cadets 1774-75 and Col of Prince William District Bn. Resigned 21 Mar 1776 **CEM:** Grayson; GPS 38.64775, -77.27648; West Longview Dr, Woodbridge; Prince William **GS:** Y **SP:** Eleanor Smallwood **VI:** Son of Benjamin (1684-1757) & Susannah (Monroe) Tyler Linton (1695-1752) Grayson. Assistant Secretary to Gen George Washington 21 Jun 1776. DAR plaque; He was one of the first two US senators fr VA **P:** unk **BLW:** Y **RG:** Y **MK:** Y **PH:** Y **SS:** CE pg 9, 22 **BS:** JLARC 3.

GRAYSON, William; b 25 Nov 1732, Spotsylvania Co; d 17 May 1829 **RU:** Captain, Served in Cont Army & VA Militia. Was Capt in Albemarle Co Militia and Signer of Leedstown Resolutions fr Spotsylvania Co **CEM:** Carver; GPS 38.52735, -77.56054; Rt 610 vic jct with Rt 612; Prince William **GS:** Y **SP:** Elizabeth Smith **VI:** Son of Ambrose & Alice (Sharpe) Grayson. He died in Albemarle Co **P:** unk **BLW:** unk **RG:** unk **MK:** unk **PH:** unk **SS:** E pg 323; BQ **BS:** 196.

GREEN, Fortunatus; b 6 Apr 1754; d unk **RU:** Sergeant, Served in VA Line. Ent serv Hanover Co **CEM:** Green; GPS unk; Greenlands Farm, abt 4 mi N Ashland; Hanover **GS:** N **SP:** Sarah White (16 Jul 1760-27 Jan 1825) **VI:** Sol appl pen 7 Jun 1833 Hanover Co age 79. S15155 **P:** Y **BLW:** unk **RG:** unk **MK:** unk **PH:** N **SS:** CG Vol 2 pg 1419 **BS:** JLARC 4, 71; 196.

GREEN, John; b 1730, Liberty Hall; d 1793 **RU:** Colonel, Capt 1st VA Regt 16 Sep 1775. Promoted to Maj 13 Aug 1776. Wounded at Mamaroneck 21 Oct 1776. Was Lt Col 1st VA, 22 Mar 1777 and Col 10th VA Regt 26 Jan 1778. Fought at Brandywine, Monmouth, Guilford CH. Retired 1783 **CEM:** Arlington National; GPS 38.88377, -77.06535; Jefferson Davis Hwy Rt 110; Arlington **GS:** Y **SP:** Susannah Blackwell (1739-1791) **VI:** BLW #866-500-20 Sep 1800. Died in Liberty Hall, Culpeper Co. Reinterred to Arlington National cem on 23 Apr 1931 in Sec 1, lot 503. He is one of eleven Rev War veterans bur there **P:** unk **BLW:** Y **RG:** Y **MK:** Y **PH:** unk **SS:** J-NSSAR 1993 Reg, J- DAR Hatcher; CG Vol 2 pg 1422 **BS:** JLARC 1, 2.

GREEN, John; b 1747, Amelia Co; d 22 Jan 1798 **RU:** Patriot, Gave material aid to cause **CEM:** Green Family; GPS unk; Rt 622; Amelia **GS:** N **SP:** Mar 5 Dec 1772 (bond) in Brunswick Co to Dolly Jones, b. c1754, d 14 Jun 1847 Lunenburg Co **VI:** Son of William (1705-1747) & Amey (Clay) (1708-1774) Green. Died in Brunswick Co **P:** N **BLW:** N **RG:** unk **MK:** unk **PH:** N **SS:** AL Ct Bk 1 pg 25, 59, II pg 34 **BS:** 196.

GREEN, John; b unk; d 1827 **RU:** Patriot, Gave material aid to the cause **CEM:** Goose Creek; GPS 39.11250, -77.69527; Rt 722, Lincoln; Loudoun **GS:** Y **SP:** No info **VI:** No further data **P:** N **BLW:** N **RG:** N **MK:** N **PH:** unk **SS:** AL Ct bk lt 46 **BS:** 25 pg 120.

RU=Rank/Unit	CEM=Cemetery	GS=Gravestone	SP=Spousal Information
VI=Other Veteran Info	P=Pension	BLW=Bounty/Land Warrant	RG=Registered Grave
MK=SAR/DAR Marker	PH=Photo	SS=Service Source	BS=Burial Source

129

GREEN, Joseph; b unk; d 1782 **RU:** Private, Served in 6th Cont Line **CEM:** Spears Family; GPS unk; N of Edom Rt 42 7.3 mi; Rockingham **GS:** Y **SP:** 1) Mar (1794 Rockingham Co) Amelia Matthews d/o Solloman & (-----) Matthews 2) Mar (1809 Rockingham Co) Mary Blain d/o Joseph & (-----) Blain **VI:** No further data **P:** unk **BLW:** unk **RG:** Y **MK:** N **PH:** unk **SS:** AK; E pg 324 **BS:** 04; 191 Spears fam.

GREEN, Samuel; b unk; d 1822 **RU:** 2d Lt, Appointed 2nd Lt Amelia Co Militia 23 Apr 1778 **CEM:** Fairfax Meeting House; GPS 39.18557, -77.60589; Water St & Waterford Rd, Waterford; Loudoun **GS:** Y **SP:** No info **VI:** No further data **P:** unk **BLW:** unk **RG:** N **MK:** N **PH:** unk **SS:** AZ pg 178; E pg 324 **BS:** 25 pg 121.

GREEN, Thomas; b unk; d 30 Apr 1791 **RU:** Patriot, Gave material aid to cause **CEM:** Green Family; GPS unk; Rt 622; Amelia **GS:** N **SP:** No info **VI:** Son of William (1705-1747) & Amey (Clay) (1708-1774) Green **P:** N **BLW:** N **RG:** unk **MK:** unk **PH:** N **SS:** AL Ct Bi II pg 10 **BS:** 196.

GREEN, William; b unk; d 1790 **RU:** Private/Patriot, Served in 1st, 4th, 5th, 11th, 14th & 15th Cont Lines. Gave material aid to cause **CEM:** Green Family; GPS unk; Rt 622; Amelia **GS:** N **SP:** Obedience Green (first cousin). She mar Richard Foster in 1793 after William Green's death. **VI:** Son of William Green (1705-1747) & Amey (Clay) (1708-1774) Green. Died in "Greenland." Widow recd pen commencing 8 Dec 1813 at $48 per yr **P:** Y **BLW:** N **RG:** unk **MK:** unk **PH:** N **SS:** E pg 325; AG pg 264; AL Ct Bk 1, pg 6, 43, 48 Amelia Co **BS:** 196.

GREEN (GREENE), Berryman; b 26 Jan 1754, Westmoreland Co; d 13 Sep 1825 **RU:** Captain, As 1st Lt was Paymaster, 1st Cont Dragoons, 31 Mar 1777 Westmoreland Co. Appt Capt 31 Mar 1777; resigned 1779; Asst. Deputy QM 1781. Aide to Washington 1776. Deputy Sheriff Charlotte Co 1780 **CEM:** Terry Family; GPS unk; 1154 N Terry Rd, Halifax; Halifax **GS:** U **SP:** Mar (6 Jan 1789) Nancy Terry (__ Halifax Co-20 Feb 1836, Green's Folly, Halifax Co) **VI:** Recd BLW 4000 acres **P:** N **BLW:** Y **RG:** Y **MK:** unk **PH:** N **SS:** J-NSSAR 1993 Reg; J- DAR Hatcher; E pg 323; BY **BS:** JLARC 1, 2; 196.

GREENHOW, John; b 12 Nov 1724, England; d 1787 **RU:** Patriot, Gave material aid to the cause **CEM:** Bruton Parish Church; GPS 37.27127, -76.70248; 331 W Duke of Gloucester St; Williamsburg City **GS:** Y **SP:** 1) Mar (29 Nov 1759, Williamsburg) Judith Davenport (1738-1765) 2) Elizabeth Tyler (1744-1781) **VI:** No further data **P:** unk **BLW:** unk **RG:** N **MK:** N **PH:** unk **SS:** AL Ct Bk pg 4, 8 **BS:** 26 pg 105.

GREENHOW, Robert; b 11 May 1761 Williamsburg; d Jun 1840 **RU:** Private?, In 1775 was in volunteer unit with other youth in Williamsburg under Capt Henry Nicholson to retrieve powder fr magazine that Dunmore was abt to take **CEM:** Shockoe Hill; GPS 37.55190, -77.43170; 4th & Hospital Sts; Richmond City **GS:** Y **SP:** Mar (1 Jul 1786, St John's Episcopal Church) Mary Ann Wills (4 May 1768, Fluvanna Co-26 Dec 1811, in the Richmond Theatre fire) d/o Elias & (-----) Wills of Richmond **VI:** No further data **P:** unk **BLW:** unk **RG:** N **MK:** N **PH:** unk **SS:** C pg 558 **BS:** 57 pg 20.

GREENWAY, James; b 1720, Cumbria, England; d 1797 **RU:** Patriot, Gave material aid to cause **CEM:** The Grove; GPS unk; Rt 662, 12 mi S of Dinwiddie; Dinwiddie **GS:** Y **SP:** Martha Dixon **VI:** Botanist, physician, surveyor, miller & planter. Came to Virginia c1758 where he is first found in Sussex Co records. Justice of Dinwiddie Co **P:** N **BLW:** N **RG:** N **MK:** N **PH:** unk **SS:** AL Ct Justice; Ct Bk pg 32 Dinwiddie Co **BS:** 70 pg 147; 166; 196.

GREER, Moses Sr; b 2 Jun 1744, MD; d 10 May 1834 **RU:** Officer, Served in VA Line. Ent serv Bedford Co (now Franklin Co) **CEM:** Greer Family; GPS unk; .5 mi W of Rts 812 & 919; Franklin **GS:** U **SP:** Mar (4 Nov 1794 Franklin Co) Susannah Wood **VI:** After Rev War, elected to State Legislature from Franklin Co. Was presiding Judge of Franklin County Ct. Sol appl pen 12 Sep 1832, Bedford Co (the part that became Franklin) S8609 **P:** Y **BLW:** unk **RG:** unk **MK:** unk **PH:** unk **SS:** K pg 213; CG Vol 2 pg 1431 **BS:** JLARC 4,20.

GREEVER (GREWER), Phillip Sr; b 2 Oct 1745 Holland; d 26 Mar 1830 **RU:** Soldier/Patriot, Served in VA Militia under Col Campbell. Fired 1st shot at Battle of Kings Mtn, 7 Oct 1780. Was Overseer of Roads Washington Co 1743 **CEM:** Old Grewer (Greever) Burial Ground; GPS 36.79250, -81.69860; W end of Skyview Dr, Chilhowie; Smyth **GS:** U **SP:** Mar (1773) Margaret Bosang (1758, Augusta Co-6 Mar 1831) **VI:** See entry, same name, Washington Co (memorial placed by descendants) **P:** unk **BLW:** unk **RG:** unk **MK:** unk **PH:** unk **SS:** B-Memorial stone; CV pg 204 **BS:** JLARC 2114; 78 pg 173; 196.

RU=Rank/Unit	CEM=Cemetery	GS=Gravestone	SP=Spousal Information
VI=Other Veteran Info	P=Pension	BLW=Bounty/Land Warrant	RG=Registered Grave
MK=SAR/DAR Marker	PH=Photo	SS=Service Source	BS=Burial Source

130

GREGG, John; b 16 Jan 1733, Chester Co, PA; d 9 Sep 1804 **RU:** Ensign, Served in Col McGaw's 6th Regt, PA Cont Line **CEM:** Goose Creek; **GPS** 39.11250, -77.69527; Rt 722, Lincoln; Loudoun **GS:** Y **SP:** Ruth Smith (6 Jun 1734 New Garden, PA-9 Sep 1804) **VI:** Son of Thomas (1703-1748) & Dinah (Harlan) (1707-1763) Gregg **P:** unk **BLW:** unk **RG:** unk **MK:** unk **PH:** unk **SS:** Fold 3 Muster Roll **BS:** 196.

GREGG, John C; b 1756; d 1 Oct 1825 **RU:** Private, Served in Capt Francis Willis's Co, Col William Grayson's Regt, Jan 1777-Mar 1778 **CEM:** Goose Creek; **GPS** 39.11250, -77.69527; Rt 722, Lincoln; Loudoun **GS:** Y **SP:** No info **VI:** Son of John (1733-1804) & Ruth (Smith) (1734-1763) Gregg **P:** unk **BLW:** unk **RG:** unk **MK:** unk **PH:** unk **SS:** Fold 3 Muster Roll **BS:** 196.

GREGORY, Roger; b 1 May 1729 King William Co; d 2 Oct 1803 **RU:** Patriot, Gave 550# beef for Cont use **CEM:** Gregory Family; **GPS** unk; Jct Rts 655 & 657; Mecklenburg **GS:** Y **SP:** Mar (31 Mar 1776) Fanny Garland Lory (__-30 Jun 1816) **VI:** No further data **P:** N **BLW:** N **RG:** N **MK:** N **PH:** unk **SS:** AL Ct Bk pg 6; DB pg 20 **BS:** 54 pg 255.

GRENON, Andre; b unk; d 1781 **RU:** Seaman, Served on "Duc De Bourgogne" and died from Yorktown battle **CEM:** French Memorial; **GPS** 36.81944, -79.39933; Yorktown; York **GS:** U **SP:** No info **VI:** No further data **P:** unk **BLW:** unk **RG:** Y **MK:** unk **PH:** unk **SS:** J-Yorktown Historian **BS:** JLARC 1, 74.

GREROUA, Jean; b unk; d 1781 **RU:** Seaman, Served on "Diademe" and died from Yorktown battle **CEM:** French Memorial; **GPS** 36.81944, -79.39933; Yorktown; York **GS:** U **SP:** No info **VI:** No further data **P:** unk **BLW:** unk **RG:** Y **MK:** unk **PH:** unk **SS:** J-Yorktown Historian **BS:** JLARC 1, 74.

GRICE, Joseph; b 1759; d 20 Aug 1820 **RU:** Private, Served in 5th VA Regt, Sep 1782 **CEM:** Trinity Episcopal; **GPS** 36.83459, -76.30105; 500 Court St; Portsmouth City **GS:** U **SP:** Mary (-----) (1757-2 Dec 1838) **VI:** No further data **P:** unk **BLW:** unk **RG:** unk **MK:** unk **PH:** unk **SS:** AP-roll **BS:** 57.

GRIFFIN, Cyrus; b 16 Jul 1748, Farnham, Richmond Co; d 14 Dec 1810 **RU:** Patriot, Gave material aid to cause. Was member VA House of Delegates 1777-78,1786-87. Was member of Cont Congress 1787-88 and president Cont Congress 1788 **CEM:** Bruton Parish Church; **GPS** 37.27127, -76.70248; 331 W Duke of Gloucester St; Williamsburg City **GS:** U **SP:** Mar (c1779, Scotland) Lady Christina Stuart (1752, Scotland-8 Oct 1807, Williamsburg) **VI:** President of Ct of Admiralty. Commissioner to Creek nation. Judge of US District Ct of VA fr Dec 1789 until death. Died in Yorktown **P:** N **BLW:** N **RG:** unk **MK:** unk **PH:** unk **SS:** DD **BS:** 201 pg 7389, 7390.

GRIFFIN, Henry; b unk; d 1812 **RU:** Captain, Service information not given in WPA report and not found **CEM:** Tapp & Griffin Families; **GPS** unk; Vic Amissville; Rappahannock **GS:** Y **SP:** No info **VI:** No further data **P:** unk **BLW:** unk **RG:** N **MK:** N **PH:** unk **SS:** BO WPA report **BS:** 163 Tapp.

GRIFFIN, Thomas; b unk; d 25 Oct 1843 **RU:** Private, Served in Capt Nicolas Cabell's Co, Albemarle Co Militia, Apr 1776 **CEM:** Shockoe Hill; **GPS** 37.55190, -77.43170; 4th & Hospital Sts; Richmond City **GS:** U **SP:** no info **VI:** GS indicates death date **P:** unk **BLW:** unk **RG:** unk **MK:** unk **PH:** unk **SS:** DC pg 154 **BS:** 196.

GRIFFITH, Benjamin; b c1775, Bedford Co; d 26 Nov 1830 **RU:** Ensign/Patriot, Appt 23 Nov 1778, Franklin Co Militia. Paid supply tax in Franklin Co 1783 **CEM:** Overfelt; **GPS** 37.07377, -79.94785; Grassy Hill Rd, Helm; Franklin **GS:** U **SP:** Mar (c1774) Catherine (__) (1756-1829) **VI:** No further data **P:** unk **BLW:** unk **RG:** unk **MK:** unk **PH:** unk **SS:** E pg 348 **BS:** 32, 196.

GRIGG, Abner; b 1720, Londonderry, Ireland; d 1795 **RU:** Private, Was an Artificer in an artillery unit of VA State Line **CEM:** Goshen Family; **GPS** unk; 8 mi S of Petersburg and W of Old Stage Rd on the "Goshen" site; Dinwiddie **GS:** U **SP:** Mar (1744) Mary Stokes (c1726-1782) **VI:** Recd BLW of 100 acres **P:** N **BLW:** Y **RG:** unk **MK:** N **PH:** unk **SS:** AR Vol 2 pg 96; C pg 203, 342; F pg 31 **BS:** JLARC 2.

GRIGG, Burwell; b 1741; d 1805 **RU:** First Lieutenant, Recommended 1st Lt Brunswick Co Militia 25 Oct 1779 **CEM:** Grigg Family; **GPS** unk; Jarratt; Greensville **GS:** Y **SP:** Mary Carroll **VI:** No further data **P:** unk **BLW:** unk **RG:** unk **MK:** unk **PH:** Y **SS:** G pg 78 **BS:** 196.

GRIGG, William Sr; b 3 Dec 1746, Dinwiddie Co; d unk **RU:** unk, Specific service may be found at the Lib of VA, Auditors Acct XVIII pg 444 **CEM:** Goshen Family; **GPS** unk; 8 mi S of Petersburg and W of

RU=Rank/Unit   CEM=Cemetery   GS=Gravestone   SP=Spousal Information
VI=Other Veteran Info   P=Pension   BLW=Bounty/Land Warrant   RG=Registered Grave
MK=SAR/DAR Marker   PH=Photo   SS=Service Source   BS=Burial Source

131

Old Stage Rd on the "Goshen" site; Dinwiddie **GS:** U **SP:** Mar (31 Jan 1767 Dinwiddie Co) Charlotte Williamson (1749-1800) **VI:** Son of Abner & Mary (Stokes) Grigg. Died in Bedford Co **P:** N **BLW:** unk **RG:** unk **MK:** N **PH:** unk **SS:** J- DAR Hatcher; CZ pg 192 **BS:** JLARC 2.

GRIGNON, Thomas; b unk; d 1781 **RU:** Seaman, Served on "Palmier" and died from Yorktown battle **CEM:** French Memorial; GPS 36.81944, -79.39933; Yorktown; York **GS:** U **SP:** No info **VI:** No further data **P:** unk **BLW:** unk **RG:** Y **MK:** unk **PH:** unk **SS:** J-Yorktown Historian **BS:** JLARC 1, 74.

GRIGSBY, John; b 1720, Stafford Co; d 7 April 1794 **RU:** Private, Served in Capt William Nalle's Co of Rangers. Served in Rockingham Co Militia. Was in Battle of Point Pleasant Oct 1774. Served in 13th Regt of VA Line **CEM:** Falling Springs Presbyterian; GPS 37.68526, -79.44972; 410 Falling Springs Rd, Glasgow; Rockbridge **GS:** Y **SP:** 1) Mar (1745) Rosanna Etchison 2) Mar (1764) Elizabeth Porter (1734-1807) **VI:** First person bur in this cem **P:** unk **BLW:** unk **RG:** Y **MK:** Y **PH:** Y **SS:** Z pg 113 **BS:** JLARC 1, 2, 63, 79; 196.

GRIM, Charles; b c1755; d 13 Dec1815 **RU:** Private, Marched under Morgan to Boston and was taken prisoner in the battle at Quebec in 1775 **CEM:** Mt Hebron; GPS 39.10916, -78.09497; 305 E Boscawen St; Winchester City **GS:** Y **SP:** No info **VI:** Stayed with militia after the war and earned rank of Capt. Bur in Centenary Reformed UCC portion of Mt Hebron Cemetery. Govt GS. SAR marker **P:** N **BLW:** N **RG:** N **MK:** Y **PH:** Y **SS:** J-NSSAR reg; NSSAR Ancestor # P-170906 **BS:** 196.

GRIM, John; b 15 Oct 1753, York, PA; d 19 Apr 1840 **RU:** Private, Served in Virginia militia. Ent serv in Winchester **CEM:** Mt Hebron; GPS 39.10916, -78.09497; 305 E Boscawen St; Winchester City **GS:** N **SP:** Mar (21 Mar 1821) Julianna Mainzer (__-21 May 1821) **VI:** Sol appl 5 Feb 1833 Winchester. S8628 **P:** Y **BLW:** unk **RG:** Y **MK:** Y **PH:** N **SS:** J-NSSAR 1993 Reg; CG Vol 2 pg 1443 **BS:** JLARC 1; 196.

GRIMES, James S; b 25 Feb 1745; d 18 Jan 1804 **RU:** Private/Patriot, Served in Capt Powell's Co, 2nd Co, 3rd VA Regt 1778-1779. Also gave material to cause **CEM:** Dick Warren Farm; GPS unk; Lake Drummond; Norfolk City **GS:** Y **SP:** No info **VI:** No further data **P:** unk **BLW:** unk **RG:** N **MK:** N **PH:** unk **SS:** AL Ct Bk pg 11; AP payroll fr Fold 3 **BS:** 63 pg 169.

GRIMES, John; b unk; d May 1795 **RU:** Private, Served in Clarks III Regt at Ft Nelson, Portsmouth **CEM:** Old Christ Church Episcopal; GPS 38.80625, -77.04718; 118 N Washington St; Alexandria City **GS:** N **SP:** No info **VI:** Burial permit issued 3 May 1795 **P:** unk **BLW:** unk **RG:** Y **MK:** N **PH:** N **SS:** E pg 329, 332 **BS:** 20 pg 148.

GRIMES, Thomas; b 1738, Norfolk; d 8 May 1797 **RU:** Patriot, Gave material aid to cause in Norfolk **CEM:** Trinity Episcopal; GPS 36.83459, -76.30105; 500 Court St; Portsmouth City **GS:** Y **SP:** Chloe Grimes **VI:** Son of James & Mary (-----) Grimes. D in Edgecombe Co, NC. Memorialized on monument (stone # 117) in cemetery as one of the first vestrymen **P:** N **BLW:** N **RG:** unk **MK:** unk **PH:** unk **SS:** D pg 105 **BS:** 00:00.0.

GRINNAN, Daniel Sr; b 1739, Accomack Co; d 25 Mar 1830 **RU:** Private, Served in Gen Edward Stevens unit. Was captured at Battle of Guilford CH but escaped on British officer's horse **CEM:** Masonic Cemetery; GPS 38.30198, -77.46142; 900 Charles St; Fredericksburg City **GS:** Y **SP:** Mar (31 Jul 1804) Eliza Richards Green (12 Jan 1787-7 Jul 1813) d/o Timothy & (-----) Green **VI:** Elder in 1st Presbyterian Church in Fredreickburg. Originally fr Madison Co **P:** unk **BLW:** unk **RG:** Y **MK:** N **PH:** unk **SS:** D pg 267, 273 **BS:** 08 vol 1 pg 99.

GROOM, Jonathan; b 5 Feb 1756, London, England; d 1834 **RU:** Soldier, Ent serv Bedford Co in VA Line **CEM:** Groom Family; GPS unk; Nr Shady Grove Church; Bedford **GS:** N **SP:** Elizabeth Moon (1765-1835) **VI:** Sol appl pen 28 Jan 1833 Bedford Co. S19305 **P:** Y **BLW:** unk **RG:** unk **MK:** N **PH:** N **SS:** J- DAR Hatcher; CG Vol 2 pg 1448 **BS:** JLARC 2; 196.

GROSECLOSE, Peter Jr; b 20 May 1757, Lancaster Co, PA; d Dec 1805 **RU:** Private, Served in Capt Thomas Ingles Co of Militia 7 Apr 1781 **CEM:** Sharon Lutheran; GPS 37.05800, -81.20590; Rt 42 W of Ceres; Bland **GS:** Y **SP:** Mar (May 1782) Elizabeth Sluss (18 Mar 1766-12 Jul 1855, Smyth Co). Most of the Sluss family were massacred by Indians on 2 Aug 1774 during Lord Dunmore's War. She is bur at Kimberling Cemetery in Smyth Co. **VI:** Son of Peter Gloseclose Sr (1730-1803) & Mary Magdalena Ott

RU=Rank/Unit	CEM=Cemetery	GS=Gravestone	SP=Spousal Information
VI=Other Veteran Info	P=Pension	BLW=Bounty/Land Warrant	RG=Registered Grave
MK=SAR/DAR Marker	PH=Photo	SS=Service Source	BS=Burial Source

132

(1732-1805). Widow appl pen fr Smyth Co 1853, age 87, rejected. R4354. Small Govt marker **P:** N **BLW:** unk **RG:** N **MK:** Y **PH:** unk **SS:** B; G pg 227; K pg 221 **BS:** 60 Bland Co; 196.

GROSECLOSE, Peter Sr; b 23 Feb 1730, Miesau, Rheinland-Pfalz; d 6 Dec 1803 **RU:** Private/Patriot, Serv not identified. Gave gun to cause Oct 1781 & two beeves Dec 1781 **CEM:** Sharon Lutheran; GPS 37.05800, -81.20590; Rt 42 W of Ceres; Bland **GS:** Y **SP:** Mar (abt 1755 PA) Mary Magdalena Ott (17 Aug 1732, Wila, Zurich, Switzerland-27 Oct 1805) **VI:** No further data **P:** unk **BLW:** unk **RG:** Y **MK:** N **PH:** unk **SS:** G pg 227; J-NASSR 2000 Reg **BS:** JLARC 76; 196.

GROSNIER, Jacques; b unk; d 1781 **RU:** unk, Served on "Northumberland". Died fr battle at Yorktown **CEM:** French Memorial; GPS 36.81944, -79.39933; Yorktown; York **GS:** U **SP:** No info **VI:** No further data **P:** unk **BLW:** unk **RG:** Y **MK:** unk **PH:** unk **SS:** J-Yorktown Historian **BS:** JLARC 1, 74.

GROSSETETE, Antoine; b unk; d 1781 **RU:** unk, Served in Auxonne Bn. Died fr battle at Yorktown **CEM:** French Memorial; GPS 36.81944, -79.39933; Yorktown; York **GS:** U **SP:** No info **VI:** No further data **P:** unk **BLW:** unk **RG:** Y **MK:** unk **PH:** unk **SS:** J-Yorktown Historian **BS:** JLARC 1, 74.

GROULT, Jean; b unk; d 1781 **RU:** unk, Served on "Northumberland." Died fr battle at Yorktown **CEM:** French Memorial; GPS 36.81944, -79.39933; Yorktown; York **GS:** U **SP:** No info **VI:** No further data **P:** unk **BLW:** unk **RG:** Y **MK:** unk **PH:** unk **SS:** J-Yorktown Historian **BS:** JLARC 1, 74.

GROVE, Marcus; b 1739, East Earl, Lancaster Co, PA; d 19 Sep 1808 **RU:** Private/Patriot, Served in Reader's VA Inf Co, Shenandoah Co Militia. Gave material aid to cause in Shenandoah Co **CEM:** Grove Family; GPS unk; Slade Farm on Rt 615 near Luray, Bixler's Ferry; Page **GS:** U **SP:** 1) Susan/Susannah Elizabeth Roades/Rhodes (massacred by Indians) 2) Mary Maria Strickler **VI:** Son of Rev Martin & (-----) Graff **P:** unk **BLW:** unk **RG:** unk **MK:** Y **PH:** unk **SS:** C pg 602; D pg 106 **BS:** JLARC 67; 196.

GROVE (GROFF), Christian Sr (or Christley); b c1735, Lancaster PA; d 9 Jun 1786 **RU:** Private, Served in Michael Reader's Co **CEM:** Grove Family; GPS unk; Meadow Mills, off Rt 340, S fr Luray; Page **GS:** U **SP:** 1) Anna (-----) 2) Esther (-----) **VI:** Died in Shenandoah Co **P:** unk **BLW:** unk **RG:** Y **MK:** unk **PH:** unk **SS:** 171388 **BS:** JLARC 1, 2, 67.

GRUBBS, Hensley (Henry); b 1754; d 1842 **RU:** Lieutenant, Served in VA Line Cont Army and wintered at Valley Forge **CEM:** Grubbs Family, aka called Spring Grove; GPS 37.43510, -77.36520; Spring Grove #2 Farm, nr Calvary Christian jct Rts 623 & 624; Hanover **GS:** U **SP:** (-----) in 1820 had wife age 54 **VI:** Sol appl pen 24 Jun 1818 Hanover Co. S37962, DAR marker 1997 **P:** Y **BLW:** unk **RG:** unk **MK:** unk **PH:** unk **SS:** CG Vol 2 pg 1453; B **BS:** JLARC 4, 71.

GRUBBS (b VAN KRUPPS), William; b unk, New York City; d aft 1782 **RU:** unk, SAR registration did not specify service **CEM:** Grubbs Family, aka Spring Grove; GPS 37.43510, 77.36520; Spring Grove #2 Farm, nr Calvary Christian jct Rts 623 & 624; Hanover **GS:** Y **SP:** No info **VI:** Was a resident of Hanover Co in 1782 census **P:** unk **BLW:** unk **RG:** unk **MK:** unk **PH:** unk **SS:** NSSAR Ancestor # P-171485 **BS:** JLARC 71.

GRYMES, Benjamin Jr; b 2 Jan 1756; d 13 Feb 1804 **RU:** Captain, Served in Clark's Ill Regt. Was at Ft Nelson 1782. Served in 1st Lt Dragoons, Col W Grayson Cont Line Regt **CEM:** Eagle's Nest; GPS unk; Rt 218 E to Rt 242 N to to Rt 682. Take immediate rt into cemetery.; King George **GS:** Y **SP:** Ann Nicolas **VI:** Awarded 4000 acres BLW **P:** unk **BLW:** Y **RG:** Y **MK:** N **PH:** unk **SS:** E pg 331; BY **BS:** 17 pg 37.

GRYMES, Philip Ludwell; b unk; d 1805 **RU:** Patriot, Gave material aid to cause **CEM:** Christ Church; GPS 37.60968, -76.54643; Rt 33 2 mi E of Saluda; Middlesex **GS:** U **SP:** Judith (-----) **VI:** No further data **P:** N **BLW:** N **RG:** N **MK:** N **PH:** unk **SS:** G pg 202; CT Bk pg iv, 6 Gloucester Co **BS:** 84 pg 198.

GUBIAUD, Benoist; b unk; d 1781 **RU:** Soldier, Served in Foix Bn and died fr battle at Yorktown **CEM:** French Memorial; GPS 36.81944, -79.39933; Yorktown; York **GS:** U **SP:** No info **VI:** No further data **P:** unk **BLW:** unk **RG:** Y **MK:** unk **PH:** unk **SS:** J-Yorktown Historian **BS:** JLARC 1, 74.

RU=Rank/Unit	CEM=Cemetery	GS=Gravestone	SP=Spousal Information
VI=Other Veteran Info	P=Pension	BLW=Bounty/Land Warrant	RG=Registered Grave
MK=SAR/DAR Marker	PH=Photo	SS=Service Source	BS=Burial Source

GUEGUEN, Joachim; b unk; d 1781 **RU:** Seaman, Served on "Magnanime" and died from Yorktown battle **CEM:** French Memorial; GPS 36.81944, -79.39933; Yorktown; York **GS:** U **SP:** No info **VI:** No further data **P:** unk **BLW:** unk **RG:** Y **MK:** unk **PH:** unk **SS:** J-Yorktown Historian **BS:** JLARC 1, 74.

GUELIN, Nicolas; b unk; d 1781 **RU:** Soldier, Served in Gatinais Bn and died fr battle at Yorktown **CEM:** French Memorial; GPS 36.81944, -79.39933; Yorktown; York **GS:** U **SP:** No info **VI:** No further data **P:** unk **BLW:** unk **RG:** Y **MK:** unk **PH:** unk **SS:** J-Yorktown Historian **BS:** JLARC 1, 74.

GUENARD, Pierre; b unk; d 1781 **RU:** Soldier, Served in Gatinais Bn and died fr battle at Yorktown **CEM:** French Memorial; GPS 36.81944, -79.39933; Yorktown; York **GS:** U **SP:** No info **VI:** No further data **P:** unk **BLW:** unk **RG:** Y **MK:** unk **PH:** unk **SS:** J-Yorktown Historian **BS:** JLARC 1, 74.

GUIBOISEAU, Francois; b unk; d 1781 **RU:** Soldier, Served in Agenois Bn and died fr battle at Yorktown **CEM:** French Memorial; GPS 36.81944, -79.39933; Yorktown; York **GS:** U **SP:** No info **VI:** No further data **P:** unk **BLW:** unk **RG:** Y **MK:** unk **PH:** unk **SS:** J-Yorktown Historian **BS:** JLARC 1, 74.

GUILIFORD, Allen; b unk; d 1815 **RU:** Patriot, Gave a horse to the army **CEM:** Fincastle Presbyterian; GPS 37.50017, -79.87558; 108 E Back St, Fincastle; Botetourt **GS:** N **SP:** No info **VI:** Name is on the SAR plaque at this cemetery **P:** N **BLW:** N **RG:** N **MK:** Y **PH:** N **SS:** AR Vol 2 pg 100; Z pg 172; J-NSSAR 1993 Reg; J- DAR Hatcher **BS:** 196; JLARC 1, 2.

GUILLAUME, Joseph; b unk; d 1781 **RU:** Soldier, Served in Bourbonnais Bn and died fr battle at Yorktown **CEM:** French Memorial; GPS 36.81944, -79.39933; Yorktown; York **GS:** U **SP:** No info **VI:** No further data **P:** unk **BLW:** unk **RG:** Y **MK:** unk **PH:** unk **SS:** J-Yorktown Historian **BS:** JLARC 1, 74.

GUILLERAUX, Joseph; b unk; d 1781 **RU:** Soldier, Served in Gatinais Bn and died fr battle at Yorktown **CEM:** French Memorial; GPS 36.81944, -79.39933; Yorktown; York **GS:** U **SP:** no info **VI:** No further data **P:** unk **BLW:** unk **RG:** Y **MK:** unk **PH:** unk **SS:** J-Yorktown Historian **BS:** JLARC 1, 74.

GUILLON, Francois; b unk; d 1781 **RU:** Soldier, Served in Soissonnais Bn and died fr battle at Yorktown **CEM:** French Memorial; GPS 36.81944, -79.39933; Yorktown; York **GS:** U **SP:** No info **VI:** No further data **P:** unk **BLW:** unk **RG:** Y **MK:** unk **PH:** unk **SS:** J-Yorktown Historian **BS:** JLARC 1, 74.

GUILLOT, Mathieu; b unk; d 1781 **RU:** Seaman, Served on "Languedoc" and died from Yorktown battle **CEM:** French Memorial; GPS 36.81944, -79.39933; Yorktown; York **GS:** U **SP:** No info **VI:** No further data **P:** unk **BLW:** unk **RG:** Y **MK:** unk **PH:** unk **SS:** J-Yorktown Historian **BS:** JLARC 1, 74.

GUINELS, Francois; b unk; d 1781 **RU:** Seaman, Served on "Citoyen" and died from Yorktown battle **CEM:** French Memorial; GPS 36.81944, -79.39933; Yorktown; York **GS:** U **SP:** No info **VI:** No further data **P:** unk **BLW:** unk **RG:** Y **MK:** unk **PH:** unk **SS:** J-Yorktown Historian **BS:** JLARC 1, 74.

GULLAMEBOURG, Antoine; b unk; d 1781 **RU:** Soldier, Served in Gatinais Bn and died fr battle at Yorktown **CEM:** French Memorial; GPS 36.81944, -79.39933; Yorktown; York **GS:** U **SP:** No info **VI:** No further data **P:** unk **BLW:** unk **RG:** Y **MK:** unk **PH:** unk **SS:** J-Yorktown Historian **BS:** JLARC 1, 74.

GUM, Isaac; b 1746; d Bef 7 Apr 1830 **RU:** Private, Served in Capt Peter Hull's Co, Augusta Co Militia **CEM:** Gum Family, aka Walker Wilfong Family; GPS unk; Hightown; Highland **GS:** Y **SP:** 1) Martha Jane McBride 2) Jane Erwin (__-12 May 1833) **VI:** No further data **P:** unk **BLW:** unk **RG:** Y **MK:** unk **PH:** unk **SS:** J-NSSAR 1993 Reg; E pg 333 **BS:** JLARC 1; 196.

GUNNELL, Henry M; b 1705; d 20 Feb 1792 **RU:** Patriot, Gave material aid to cause **CEM:** Gunnell Family; GPS unk; 600 Innsbrook Ave, Great Falls; Fairfax **GS:** U **SP:** Catherine O'Daniel (1706-__) **VI:** No further data **P:** N **BLW:** N **RG:** unk **MK:** N **PH:** unk **SS:** AL Certificate Fairfax **BS:** 196.

GUNNELL, John II; b 1763; d 1836 **RU:** Private/Patriot, Gave material aid to cause **CEM:** Gunnell Family; GPS unk; Buckner; Louisa **GS:** U **SP:** Mar (21 Aug 1807) Lucy Fleming (1790, Louisa Co-Aug 1856) **VI:** Son of John (1730, Hanover Co-13 Oct 1803) 7 Sarah Pons (Mountcastle) (1735-1735) Gunnell **P:** unk **BLW:** unk **RG:** unk **MK:** unk **PH:** unk **SS:** AL Ct Bk pg 2 Fairfax Co **BS:** JLARC 2, 61.

GUNNELL, William; b 30 Jan 1750; d 1820 **RU:** Private, Served in 1st Light Dragoons **CEM:** Gunnell Family; GPS unk; 600 Innsbrook Ave, Great Falls; Fairfax **GS:** Y **SP:** Sarah Coleman (1781-1812) **VI:**

RU=Rank/Unit	CEM=Cemetery	GS=Gravestone	SP=Spousal Information
VI=Other Veteran Info	P=Pension	BLW=Bounty/Land Warrant	RG=Registered Grave
MK=SAR/DAR Marker	PH=Photo	SS=Service Source	BS=Burial Source

134

Son of Henry & Catherine (Daniel) Gunnell. Death yr is not part of stone, but was entered by findagrave contributor **P:** unk **BLW:** unk **RG:** N **MK:** N **PH:** unk **SS:** E pg 333 **BS:** 61 vol VI, pg MN-72; 196.

GUNNELL (GUNNILL), John Sr; b 1730, Louisa Co; d 13 Oct 1803 **RU:** Patriot, Gave material aid to the cause **CEM:** Gunnell Family; GPS unk; Buckner; Louisa **GS:** Y **SP:** Sarah Pons Mountcastle (__-6 Sep 1811) **VI:** BLW #12150 issued Mar 1794 **P:** N **BLW:** Y **RG:** N **MK:** N **PH:** unk **SS:** K pg 255; AL Ct Bk pg 17 **BS:** 80 vol 2 pg 101.

GUTHRIE, John; b c1762; d 27 Jan 1845 **RU:** Private, Ent serv 1777, Capt Given's Co, Augusta Co Militia **CEM:** Tinkling Spring Presbyterian; GPS 38.08472, -78.98278; 30 Tinkling Spring Dr, Fishersville; Augusta **GS:** Y **SP:** 1) Ann (-----) (1772-27 Apr 1832) 2) Margaret Guthrie (c1762-7 Dec 1815) **VI:** No further data **P:** unk **BLW:** unk **RG:** unk **MK:** unk **PH:** Y **SS:** E pg 333 **BS:** 196; 208.

GUY, Rene; b unk; d 1781 **RU:** Seaman, Served on "Ville de Paris" and died from Yorktown battle **CEM:** French Memorial; GPS 36.81944, -79.39933; Yorktown; York **GS:** U **SP:** No info **VI:** No further data **P:** unk **BLW:** unk **RG:** Y **MK:** unk **PH:** unk **SS:** J-Yorktown Historian **BS:** JLARC 1, 74.

GWINN (GWIN), David; b c1742, Orange, Wales, UK; d Jan 1822 **RU:** Captain/Patriot, Was in Battle of Guilford CH. Gave material aid to cause **CEM:** Clover Creek Church; GPS unk; Clover Creek Rt 678 S of McDowell, 7.7 mi, right hand side; Highland **GS:** U **SP:** 1) Viola Jane Crawford 2) Jane Carlisle/Carlile **VI:** Also served in Colonial Wars in 1756 in Capt William Preston's Co of Rangers **P:** unk **BLW:** unk **RG:** Y **MK:** Y **PH:** unk **SS:** D Augusta Co **BS:** JLARC 2, 103.

HADEN, Anthony; b 1748; d 28 Apr 1828 **RU:** Captain, Served in VA Line and Albemarle Co Militia **CEM:** Haden family; GPS unk; Phillips Farm, Evington; Campbell **GS:** U **SP:** Mar on 21 Dec 1787 Albemarle Co to Anna Dabney d 24 Dec 1824 **VI:** Recd pen R4418 **P:** Y **BLW:** unk **RG:** unk **MK:** N **PH:** unk **SS:** CG Vol 2 pg 1466-67 **BS:** JLARC 36.

HADEN, Benjamin; b 1762, Goochland Co; d 14 Aug 1837 **RU:** Soldier, Served in Albemarle Co Militia **CEM:** Haden family; GPS unk; Phillips Farm, Evington; Campbell **GS:** U **SP:** Mar (2 Dec 1780) Martha Moorman (__Bedford Co-__) **VI:** Son of John (1723-1817) & Jean (Moseley) (1 Oct 1723, Middlesex Co-1796) Haden **P:** unk **BLW:** unk **RG:** unk **MK:** N **PH:** unk **SS:** NSSAR Ancestor #P-172118 **BS:** JLARC 36.

HADEN, John Sr; b 1723; d 1817 **RU:** Patriot, Gave material aid to cause **CEM:** Haden family; GPS unk; Phillips Farm, Evington; Campbell **GS:** U **SP:** Jean Moseley (1 Oct 1723, Middlesex Co-1796) **VI:** No further data **P:** N **BLW:** N **RG:** unk **MK:** N **PH:** unk **SS:** AL CT Bk pg 2 Fluvanna Co **BS:** JLARC 36.

HAGAN, Francis Ignatius; b c1754, Fairfax Co; d 15 Dec 1830 **RU:** Corporal, Served in 3rd VA Cont line. Ent serv Hampton1775. Private under Capt David Arell 1777. Enl 7 Jan 1777 in Hagan's Corps **CEM:** St Mary's Catholic; GPS 38.79390, -77.04750; 310 S Royal St; Alexandria City **GS:** Y **SP:** Never mar **VI:** Sol appl 1 Apr 1818 Dist of Columbia. S36007. Died age 76 per death notice, funeral held fr home of Mrs. Sherfield's, upper end of King Street. He had entered service at the commencement of the war and served until its end (Alexandria Gazette, 17 Dec 1830) **P:** Y **BLW:** unk **RG:** Y **MK:** N **PH:** Y **SS:** SAR Ancestor #P-334430; E pg 336; K pg 231; AK Feb 2006; CG Vol 2 pg 1469 **BS:** 196.

HAGAN, Michael; b unk; d unk **RU:** Drummer, Served in 2d PA Regt **CEM:** Shockoe Hill; GPS 37.55190, -77.43170; 4th & Hospital Sts; Richmond City **GS:** Y **SP:** No info **VI:** No further data **P:** unk **BLW:** unk **RG:** N **MK:** N **PH:** unk **SS:** AP 2d PA Regt **BS:** 179 #939.

HAGERTY, Patrick; b unk; d Jul 1791 **RU:** Sergeant, Served in Capt Buller Clarborney Co, Col Alex Spotwood's 2nd VA Regt, 1777 **CEM:** Old Christ Church Episcopal; GPS 38.80625, -77.04718; 118 N Washington St; Alexandria City **GS:** N **SP:** No info **VI:** Burial permit issued 22 Jul 1791 **P:** unk **BLW:** unk **RG:** Y **MK:** N **PH:** N **SS:** A pg 270 **BS:** 20 pg 148.

HAGUENEAU, Jerome; b unk; d 1781 **RU:** Soldier, Served in Beaujolais Bn and died fr battle at Yorktown **CEM:** French Memorial; GPS 36.81944, -79.39933; Yorktown; York **GS:** U **SP:** No info **VI:** No further data **P:** unk **BLW:** unk **RG:** Y **MK:** unk **PH:** unk **SS:** J-Yorktown Historian **BS:** JLARC 1, 74.

HAINES, Casper; b unk; d unk **RU:** Lieutenant, Served in VA Militia in Capt Stephen Conrad's Co **CEM:** Old Peaked Mountain; GPS 38.37113, -78.73416; 9843 Town Hall Rd, McGaheysville; Rockingham **GS:**

RU=Rank/Unit   CEM=Cemetery   GS=Gravestone   SP=Spousal Information
VI=Other Veteran Info   P=Pension   BLW=Bounty/Land Warrant   RG=Registered Grave
MK=SAR/DAR Marker   PH=Photo   SS=Service Source   BS=Burial Source

135

Y **SP:** No info **VI:** Name is on a plaque in cemetery of those that served in the Rev War **P:** unk **BLW:** unk **RG:** Y **MK:** Y **PH:** unk **SS:** J-NSSAR 2000 Reg; NSSAR Ancestor #P-172386 **BS:** JLARC 76.

HAINES, George; b unk; d unk **RU:** Private, Served in 6th Cont Line **CEM:** Old Peaked Mountain; GPS 38.37113, -78.73416; 9843 Town Hall Rd, McGaheysville; Rockingham **GS:** Y **SP:** No info **VI:** Name is on a plaque in cemetery of those that served in the Rev War. Recd BLW 4000 acres 27 Jun 1783 **P:** unk **BLW:** Y **RG:** Y **MK:** Y **PH:** unk **SS:** J-NASSR 2000 Reg; BY **BS:** JLARC 76.

HAINES, John; b unk; d unk **RU:** Corporal, Enl 14 Mar 1777 and served in 4th & 11h Cont lines under Col Daniel Morgan 31 May 1777-30 Nov 1778 **CEM:** Old Peaked Mountain; GPS 38.37113, -78.73416; 9843 Town Hall Rd, McGaheysville; Rockingham **GS:** Y **SP:** Person this name mar (8 Dec 1791 Lunenburg Co) Martha Walker. Mar (1797 Rockingham Co) Dorothy Cash d/o Mathias & (-----) Cash **VI:** Name is on a plaque in cemetery of those that served in the Rev War **P:** unk **BLW:** unk **RG:** Y **MK:** Y **PH:** unk **SS:** E pg 337 **BS:** 04.

HAINES, Jonas; b unk; d unk **RU:** Patriot, Gave material aid to cause **CEM:** Old Peaked Mountain; GPS 38.37113, -78.73416; 9843 Town Hall Rd, McGaheysville; Rockingham **GS:** Y **SP:** No info **VI:** Name is on a plaque in cemetery of those that served in the Rev War **P:** N **BLW:** N **RG:** Y **MK:** Y **PH:** unk **SS:** O pg 242 **BS:** 04.

HAINES, Joseph; b unk; d unk **RU:** Patriot, Gave material aid to cause **CEM:** Old Peaked Mountain; GPS 38.37113, -78.73416; 9843 Town Hall Rd, McGaheysville; Rockingham **GS:** Y **SP:** No info **VI:** Name is on a plaque in cemetery of those that served in the Rev War **P:** N **BLW:** N **RG:** Y **MK:** Y **PH:** unk **SS:** P pg 85 **BS:** 04.

HAINES (HAINS), Peter M; b c1754; d unk **RU:** Private, Served in VA Cont Line for 3 yrs **CEM:** Old Peaked Mountain; GPS 38.37113, -78.73416; 9843 Town Hall Rd, McGaheysville; Rockingham **GS:** Y **SP:** Mar (1775) Margaret Willis (1757-1831) **VI:** Sol appl 21 Apr 1818 Jefferson Co. Name is on a plaque in cemetery of those that served in the Rev War. S38008. Recd. BLW 100 acres 23 Jun 1787 **P:** Y **BLW:** Y **RG:** Y **MK:** Y **PH:** unk **SS:** E pg 337; CG Vol 2 pg 1472 **BS:** 04.

HAINES (HAYNES), Frederick; b unk; d unk **RU:** Patriot, Gave 500# beef 2 Nov 1780 to Frederick Co Militia **CEM:** Old Peaked Mountain; GPS 38.37113, -78.73416; 9843 Town Hall Rd, McGaheysville; Rockingham **GS:** Y **SP:** Mar (1804 Rockingham Co) Barbara Pence **VI:** Name is on a plaque in cemetery of those that served in the Rev War **P:** N **BLW:** N **RG:** Y **MK:** Y **PH:** unk **SS:** O pg 242 **BS:** 04.

HAIRSTON, George; b 1750; d 1827 **RU:** Captain, Commanded Co in the Henry Co Militia **CEM:** Hairston Family; GPS unk; SR 108, Beaver Creek, N of Martinsville; Henry **GS:** U **SP:** Mar (1781) Elizabeth Letcher (1759-1819) **VI:** Mar William Letcher's widow. Became General in War of 1812 **P:** unk **BLW:** unk **RG:** unk **MK:** unk **PH:** unk **SS:** E pg 337 **BS:** JLARC 2, 30.

HALE, Edward; b 1750, Franklin Co; d 1820 **RU:** Captain, Served in 13th Cont Line, Capt John Lucas Co of Militia, Montgomery Co **CEM:** Hale Farm; GPS unk; Wolf Creek nr Narrows; Giles **GS:** Y **SP:** Mar (1785) Patsy Perdue (c1760-c1820) **VI:** Settled in Giles Co 1779 **P:** unk **BLW:** unk **RG:** Y **MK:** unk **PH:** unk **SS:** G pg 234; E pg 234; J-NSSAR 1993 Reg; J- DAR Hatcher **BS:** 196; JLARC 1,2.

HALE, Lewis; b 2 Nov 1742; d 12 Mar 1802 **RU:** Private/Patriot, Served at Kings Mountain. Took oath of allegiance in Grayson Co **CEM:** Hale Family; GPS unk; Nr Elk Creek; Grayson **GS:** Y **SP:** Mary Burwell **VI:** No further data **P:** unk **BLW:** unk **RG:** N **MK:** N **PH:** unk **SS:** AS SAR applic; CE Vol 9 pg 139 **BS:** 80 vol 2 pg 106.

HALEY, James; b 4 May 1732; d 25 Aug 1827 **RU:** Sergeant, Served in 1st VA Regt **CEM:** Haley/Halley Family; GPS unk; 4422 San Carlos Rd, Fairfax; Fairfax **GS:** U **SP:** Mar (1767) Frances (-----) (19 May 1737 Fairfax-7 Oct 1824) **VI:** No further data **P:** unk **BLW:** Y **RG:** unk **MK:** unk **PH:** unk **SS:** C pg 242; E pg 338 **BS:** JLARC 27, 14.

HALL, Asa Sr; b 13 Feb 1841, RI; d 6 Mar 1841 or 1849 **RU:** Private, Ent serv Dutchess Co NY 1776. Served in Capt Vail's Co, Graham's Regt, NY State Troops **CEM:** Mack Creek Village; GPS unk; W fr Snowville on Lead Mine Rd abt 5 mi to Little River Dam Rd, then N .7 mi, on left just past Burleigh Ln; Montgomery **GS:** Y **SP:** 1)) Mar (c1779) Sarah Adams (1760-1802) 2) Mar (31 Jul 1803, Montgomery

RU=Rank/Unit   CEM=Cemetery   GS=Gravestone   SP=Spousal Information
VI=Other Veteran Info   P=Pension   BLW=Bounty/Land Warrant   RG=Registered Grave
MK=SAR/DAR Marker   PH=Photo   SS=Service Source   BS=Burial Source

136

Co) Mary Vanover d/o Henry & (-----) Vanover **VI:** Was pensioned 1833 in Montgomery Co. Moved to Montgomery Co in 1808. S6945. SAR Gr marker **P:** Y **BLW:** unk **RG:** unk **MK:** Y **PH:** Y **SS:** DAR Ancestor #A049416; K pg 234 & BS pg 386; J- DAR Hatcher **BS:** 196, JLARC 2.

HALL, James; b Bef1752; d Oct 1816 **RU:** Captain/Patriot, Served in Botetourt Co. Was Capt in Rockbridge Militia. Gave material aid to cause **CEM:** Oxford Presbyterian; GPS 37.75302, -79.56023; 18 Churchview Ln, Lexington; Lexington City **GS:** Y **SP:** Martha Gilmore **VI:** Died in Rockbridge Co **P:** unk **BLW:** unk **RG:** unk **MK:** N **PH:** unk **SS:** NSDAR #490826; D Rockbridge Co **BS:** JLARC 11, 26.

HALL, Jesse; b 22 Mar 1760, Charleston, Washington Co, RI; d 2 Oct 1848 **RU:** Private, Served in NY Line. Moved fr RI to Dutchess Co NY where he entered service in 1776. Was in Battle at White Plains, NY **CEM:** Barnett Family; GPS 36.80751, -80.15219; Alleghany Spring Rd, left side of Sisson Farm; Montgomery Co **GS:** Y **SP:** Mar (c1778 Dudley, MA) Phoebe Wilbur (13 Jul 1761, RI-aft 1830. Montgomery Co) d/o Christopher & Sarah (Vaughn) Wilbur **VI:** Son of Benajah & Sarah (Crandall) Hall. Sol appl pen 7 Jan 1833 Montgomery Co. S8666. Pen 1837. Moved to Montgomery Co. 1789. SAR gr marker **P:** Y **BLW:** unk **RG:** Y **MK:** Y **PH:** Y **SS:** A part 2 pg 266; CG Vol 3 pg 1481 **BS:** 04; 196.

HALL, Patrick; b 1751, Ireland; d 23 Nov 1814 **RU:** Private, Served in Capt McCutchen's Co, Augusta Co Militia **CEM:** Old Providence; GPS 37.96151, -79.71000; 1005 Spottswood Rd, Spottswood; Augusta **GS:** Y **SP:** Mar (1773) Susanna McChesney (1749-19 Nov 1814). Both she and her husband d of yellow fever contracted by nursing their son William who had brought it back fr Norfolk during War of 1812 **VI:** Weaver by occupation, deeded land for Old Stone Church in 1794. Name also on SAR plaque at cemetery **P:** unk **BLW:** unk **RG:** unk **MK:** Y **PH:** unk **SS:** E pg 339; BT **BS:** JLARC 2, 8, 62, 63; 196.

HALL, Thomas Sr; b 1746; d 26 Jul 1804 **RU:** Private, Was in Battle at Point Pleasant in Capt Thomas Buford's Co of independents **CEM:** Hall Family; GPS unk; Rt 658 vic Winston; Culpeper **GS:** Y **SP:** No info **VI:** No further data **P:** unk **BLW:** unk **RG:** N **MK:** N **PH:** unk **SS:** Z pg 125 **BS:** 167 Hall.

HALL, William; b 1749; d 1814 **RU:** Captain, Commanded a co in Augusta Co Militia **CEM:** Old Providence; GPS 37.96151, -79.71000; 1005 Spottswood Rd, Spottswood; Augusta **GS:** Y **SP:** No info **VI:** Newer Govt stone. Name also on SAR cemetery plaque **P:** unk **BLW:** unk **RG:** unk **MK:** Y **PH:** unk **SS:** B; G pg 632; BT **BS:** JLARC 2, 8, 62, 63; 196.

HALL, William Sr; b 1766; d 17 Oct 1844 **RU:** Private, Served in Capt William Campbell's Co against the Indians in 1782 in Montgomery Co **CEM:** North Mountain; GPS unk; 7 mi S of Staunton on N side Rt 252; Augusta **GS:** Y **SP:** No info **VI:** Died age 78 **P:** unk **BLW:** unk **RG:** N **MK:** N **PH:** unk **SS:** G pg 239 **BS:** 142; 196.

HALLEY, Henry Simpson; b 10 May 1762; d 28 Nov 1838 **RU:** Soldier, Served in VA Line. Ent serv Fairfax Co. Served in Capt Little's Co, Gen Weadon's Regt and under Marquis De Lafayette **CEM:** Haley/Halley Family; GPS unk; 4422 San Carlos Rd, Fairfax; Fairfax **GS:** U **SP:** Mar (8 Jun 1786) Elizabeth Hampton (21 Sep 1762, Fairfax Co-24 Sep 1824) **VI:** Pension applic rejected. Died with six children but no wife. R4493 **P:** Y **BLW:** unk **RG:** unk **MK:** unk **PH:** unk **SS:** K pg 239; CG Vol 2 pg 1489 **BS:** JLARC 4, 28.

HALLEY, James Jr; b 4 Apr 1737; d 1795 **RU:** Sergeant/Patriot, Served in VA Inf unit. Gave material aid to cause **CEM:** Pleasant Green Farm-Popes Head Run; GPS unk; Nr Occoquan; Fairfax **GS:** U **SP:** Mar (1767) Frances Hampton (19 May 1737-25 Aug 1827) **VI:** No further data **P:** unk **BLW:** unk **RG:** unk **MK:** unk **PH:** unk **SS:** J- DAR Hatcher; AL Ct Bk pg 16 Fairfax Co **BS:** JLARC 2.

HALSTEAD (HOLSTEAD), Matt; b 26 Sep 1760; d 30 Mar 1829 **RU:** Private, Served in Capt William Crane's Troop of Horse, 20 Apr-20 May 1780 in NJ **CEM:** Halstead Family; GPS unk; Pond Lake; Chesapeake City **GS:** Y **SP:** Mary (-----) (29 Mar 1771-10 Jan 1832) **VI:** Listed with wife on monument **P:** N **BLW:** N **RG:** N **MK:** unk **PH:** unk **SS:** AP Payroll on Fold 3 **BS:** 63 pg 175.

HAMILTON, Alexander; b unk; d unk **RU:** Captain, Commanded a company Botetourt Co Militia 1777 **CEM:** Fincastle Presbyterian; GPS 37.50017, -79.87558; 108 E Back St, Fincastle; Botetourt **GS:** N **SP:** No info **VI:** Name is on VASSAR plaque at cemetery **P:** unk **BLW:** unk **RG:** Y **MK:** Y **PH:** N **SS:** E pg 341; J-NASSR 2000 Reg **BS:** 196; JLARC 76.

RU=Rank/Unit	CEM=Cemetery	GS=Gravestone	SP=Spousal Information
VI=Other Veteran Info	P=Pension	BLW=Bounty/Land Warrant	RG=Registered Grave
MK=SAR/DAR Marker	PH=Photo	SS=Service Source	BS=Burial Source

137

HAMILTON, Alexander; b Sep 1759, Augusta Co; d 1845 **RU:** Soldier, Ent Serv Augusta Co 1778. Served in VA Line. Brother James served with him and was severely wounded in Battle of Hot Water. Another brother John took his place **CEM:** Bethel Presbyterian; GPS 38.04257, -79.17283; 563 Bethel Green Rd, Middlebrook; Augusta **GS:** N **SP:** No info **VI:** Sol appl 29 Aug 1833 Augusta Co. S9556. No stone **P:** Y **BLW:** unk **RG:** unk **MK:** unk **PH:** N **SS:** K pg 240; CG Vol 2 pg 1493 **BS:** JLARC 2, 62, 63.

HAMILTON, Andrew; b unk; d 1823 **RU:** Captain, Served in Capt McClanahan's Co at Point Pleasant in 1774. Co Cmdr Botetourt Militia in 1777 **CEM:** Fincastle Presbyterian; GPS 37.50017, -79.87558; 108 E Back St, Fincastle; Botetourt **GS:** N **SP:** Mar (8 Nov 1800 Botetourt Co) Sarah C. Seldon **VI:** Name is on the SAR plaque at this cemetery **P:** unk **BLW:** unk **RG:** Y **MK:** Y **PH:** N **SS:** AR Vol 2 pg 100; Z pg 128; AZ pg 191; J-NSSAR 1993 Reg, J- DAR Hatcher **BS:** 196; JLARC 1,2.

HAMILTON, David; b 1762; d 15 Mar 1828 **RU:** Soldier, Capt Cunningham's Co Augusta Co Militia **CEM:** Bethel Presbyterian; GPS 38.04257, -79.17283; 563 Bethel Green Rd, Middlebrook; Augusta **GS:** Y **SP:** No info **VI:** Died age 66 **P:** N **BLW:** N **RG:** unk **MK:** unk **PH:** unk **SS:** NSSAR Ancestor # P-173732; E pg 341 **BS:** JLARC 62, 63; 196.

HAMILTON, James; b 1739; d 1807 **RU:** Private, Served in Capt John Lewis's Co, Augusta Co Militia for 112 days **CEM:** Tinkling Spring Presbyterian; GPS 38.08472, -78.98278; 30 Tinkling Spring Dr, Fishersville; Augusta **GS:** N **SP:** No info **VI:** No further data **P:** unk **BLW:** unk **RG:** N **MK:** N **PH:** N **SS:** Z pg 116 **BS:** 142 Tinkling Spr.

HAMILTON, James; b c1714, Glen Carland, County Tyrone, Ireland; d c1798 **RU:** Private, VA Line. Enl Berkeley Co **CEM:** Old Opequon Church; GPS 39.82237, -78.11412; 217 Opequon Church Ln, Kernstown; Frederick **GS:** Y **SP:** Mar (26 Dec 1793 near Bucks Co PA line) Rebecca (-----) **VI:** Sol appl pen 15 May 1818 Frederick Co age 60. Pen info says soldier d Apr 1830. Widow appl pen 14 May 1839 Loudoun Co age 68. W24403 **P:** Y **BLW:** unk **RG:** Y **MK:** N **PH:** unk **SS:** E pg 341; CG Vol 2 pg 1494 **BS:** 112 Old Opeeq.

HAMILTON, James; b 2 Sep 1748, Tyrone Co, Ireland; d 19 Jan 1812 **RU:** Private, Served in Morgan's riflemen unit **CEM:** Opequon Presbyterian; GPS 39.13938, -78.19494; 217 Opequon Church Ln; Winchester City **GS:** Y **SP:** Jane Gilbreath **VI:** Recd pension in Frederick Co. Died in Botetourt Co **P:** unk **BLW:** unk **RG:** Y **MK:** N **PH:** Y **SS:** E pg 341; DAR Index Patriot pg 1287; J-NSSAR 2000 Reg **BS:** JLARC 76.

HAMILTON, James; b 1755; d 29 Mar 1831 or 1834 **RU:** Soldier, Served in Capt Patrick Buchanan's Co, Col Thomas Hugart's Regt in battle of Hot Water 1781 and was severely wounded **CEM:** Bethel Presbyterian; GPS 38.04257, -79.17283; 563 Bethel Green Rd, Middlebrook; Augusta **GS:** Y **SP:** Mar (26 Mar 1794) Belenah (-----) **VI:** Appl for disability pen 13 Nov 1786 Augusta Co VA age 30. Recd 18 Nov 1786. S25128. Increased under Act of 24 Apr 1816. Was still living 14 Sep 1822 Augusta Co. Papers burned in fire of 1800. Only dates on stone are death on March 29th (year not readable) **P:** Y **BLW:** unk **RG:** unk **MK:** unk **PH:** unk **SS:** AZ pg 111; CG Vol 2 pg 1494 **BS:** JLARC 62, 63; 196.

HAMILTON, John; b 1750; d Mar 1829 **RU:** Soldier, Nurse in 1781; was in Battle at Hot Water & replaced brother Alexander **CEM:** Bethel Presbyterian; GPS 38.04257, -79.17283; 563 Bethel Green Rd, Middlebrook; Augusta **GS:** Y **SP:** No info **VI:** Died age 79 **P:** unk **BLW:** unk **RG:** unk **MK:** unk **PH:** unk **SS:** AZ pg 112 **BS:** JLARC 62, 63; 196.

HAMILTON, William; b 1748; d 1795 **RU:** Private, Served in Capt Johnston's Co, Augusta Co Militia and in 1st Light Dragoons **CEM:** Tinkling Spring Presbyterian; GPS 38.08472, -78.98278; 30 Tinkling Spring Dr, Fishersville; Augusta **GS:** N **SP:** No info **VI:** No further data **P:** unk **BLW:** unk **RG:** unk **MK:** unk **PH:** N **SS:** E pg 342 **BS:** 208 pg 469; 196.

HAMILTON, William T; b unk; d 7 Jun 1810 **RU:** Patriot, Gave material aid to the cause **CEM:** Mt Zion Methodist; GPS 37.66596, -79.46615; Btw Buffalo & Tinkersville; Rockbridge **GS:** Y **SP:** No info **VI:** No further data **P:** N **BLW:** N **RG:** N **MK:** N **PH:** unk **SS:** AL Ct bk 3 **BS:** 154 Rockbridge.

HAMMER, Henry; b 26 Nov 1759, Winchester; d 5 Feb 1841 **RU:** Private, Served in VA Line. Ent serv Rockingham Co, May 1778. Served 3 mos/10 days in Capt Robert Craven's VA Co. Enl early 1781 and served 3 mos/8 days Capt Michael Coger's Co in Col Hall's VA Regt **CEM:** Elk Run; GPS 38.41042, -

RU=Rank/Unit	CEM=Cemetery	GS=Gravestone	SP=Spousal Information
VI=Other Veteran Info	P=Pension	BLW=Bounty/Land Warrant	RG=Registered Grave
MK=SAR/DAR Marker	PH=Photo	SS=Service Source	BS=Burial Source

138

78.61033; North St, Elkton; Rockingham **GS:** Y **SP:** Mar (21 Jun 1786 Rockingham Co) Mary Davis d/o Joseph & (-----) Davis of Rockingham Co **VI:** Moved as infant with father to Shenandoah Co for six yrs, then to Rockingham Co. Source 76 has Old Peaked Mountain Church Cem. Mem. Stone at Elk Run Cem. He was bur at Old Peake Mountain Church Cem in McGaheysville. At Old Peake Mountain, his name listed with other Rev soldiers bur there. SAR marker at that site. Death listed on pen 5 Feb 1841-- on stone is listed as 1842. Sol appl pen 29 Aug 1835 Rockingham Co. Widow appl pen 12 May 1843 Rockingham Co age 76. W7652 **P:** Y **BLW:** unk **RG:** unk **MK:** N **PH:** unk **SS:** K pg 243; CG Vol 2 pg 1498-99 **BS:** JLARC 4, 64, 76.

HAMMON, Edward; b 1764; d 1801 **RU:** Matross, Enlisted in Capt William Waters Co Jan 1777. Served in VA 1st Artillery and as Private in 14th VA Regt **CEM:** Blandford; GPS 37.22433, -77.38604; 319 S Crater Rd; Petersburg City **GS:** Y **SP:** No info **VI:** No further data **P:** unk **BLW:** unk **RG:** N **MK:** N **PH:** unk **SS:** E pg 342 **BS:** 188.

HAMMOND, Stephen; b unk; d 1781 **RU:** Soldier, Served fr MA, killed in the battle at Yorktown **CEM:** Yorktown Victory Monument Tablet; GPS 38.28350, -78.54150; Yorktown; York **GS:** U **SP:** No info **VI:** No further data **P:** unk **BLW:** unk **RG:** unk **MK:** unk **PH:** unk **SS:** J-Yorktown Historian **BS:** JLARC 74.

HAMNER, Nicholas; b 1743; d 1793 **RU:** Captain, Commanded Co Albemarle Co Militia 14 Apr 1781. **VI:** Source cites unindexed lot of Executive Papers at the VA State library containing recommendations for militia officers **CEM:** Hamner Family; GPS unk; Carter's Bridge, Keene; Albemarle **GS:** N **SP:** Mar (1768) Agnes Tomkins 9 (1751 Spotsylvania Co.-1825) d/o Giles (1719-1795) & Virginia (Chiles) Tomkins **VI:** No further data **P:** unk **BLW:** unk **RG:** Y **MK:** unk **PH:** N **SS:** J-NSSAR 1993 Reg; E pg 343 **BS:** JLARC 1.

HAMON, Guenole; b unk; d 1781 **RU:** Seaman, Served on "Saint-Esprit" and died from Yorktown battle **CEM:** French Memorial; GPS 36.81944, -79.39933; Yorktown; York **GS:** U **SP:** No info **VI:** No further data **P:** unk **BLW:** unk **RG:** Y **MK:** unk **PH:** unk **SS:** J-Yorktown Historian **BS:** JLARC 1, 74.

HAMON, Yves; b unk; d 1781 **RU:** Seaman, Served on "Auguste" and died from Yorktown battle **CEM:** French Memorial; GPS 36.81944, -79.39933; Yorktown; York **GS:** U **SP:** No info **VI:** No further data **P:** unk **BLW:** unk **RG:** Y **MK:** unk **PH:** unk **SS:** J-Yorktown Historian **BS:** JLARC 1, 74.

HAMPTON, Thomas; b 17 Oct 1728, Fairfax Co; d 17 Dec 1796 **RU:** Sergeant/Patriot, Gave material aid to cause **CEM:** Hampton Family; GPS unk; Cascade; Pittsylvania **GS:** U **SP:** Sarah Pattison Conyers (1728-1765) **VI:** Son of John II & Margaret (Wade) Hampton **P:** unk **BLW:** unk **RG:** unk **MK:** unk **PH:** unk **SS:** J- DAR Hatcher; AL Ct Bk pg 8 Pittsylvania Co **BS:** JLARC 2.

HANBY, Jonathan; b 9 Dec 1741, Patrick Co; d 26 Mar 1817 **RU:** Captain, Ent serv Henry Co Militia 1777 **CEM:** Creasey's Chapel; GPS unk; Stuart; Patrick **GS:** U **SP:** Mar (6 Apr 1769 on home of father on Mayo River, Guilford Co NC) Sarah Dalton **VI:** Justice of the Peace in Patrick Co. W4687 **P:** unk **BLW:** unk **RG:** Y **MK:** unk **PH:** unk **SS:** K pg 248 **BS:** JLARC 1, 4, 30.

HANCOCK, Austin; b 5 Oct 1760, Hanover Co; d 12 Nov 1849 **RU:** Sergeant, Lived in Hanover Co at enl. Served in Capt John White's Co, VA Line **CEM:** Little River Baptist; GPS unk; Bumpass; Louisa **GS:** Y **SP:** Mar (1781 Louisa Co) Anna Nuckolls (1762-__) d/o Charles N. & Sarah Keziah (Yancey) Nuckolls **VI:** Son of Benjamin & Mary (Beadles) Hancock. Govt Gr stone. Sol appl pen 14 Jan 1833 Louisa Co. S5499 **P:** Y **BLW:** unk **RG:** Y **MK:** unk **PH:** unk **SS:** J-NSSAR 1993 Reg, J- DAR Hatcher; CG Vol 2 pg 1503 **BS:** JLARC 1, 2.

HANCOCK, George; b 13 Jun 1754; d 18 Jul 1820 **RU:** Colonel, Served in VA Line. Was aide-de-camp to Gen Pulaski **CEM:** Fortheringay; GPS 37.19101, -80.23193; Nr Graham St, Shawsville; Montgomery **GS:** U **SP:** Mar (24 Aug 1781) Margaret Strother (16 Sep 1763-22 Oct 1834) d/o (-----) & Mary Kennerly (1746-1834) **VI:** US Congressman 1793 to 1797 **P:** unk **BLW:** unk **RG:** Y **MK:** unk **PH:** unk **SS:** J-NSSAR 1993 Reg, J- DAR Hatcher **BS:** JLARC 1, 2; 196.

HANCOCK, John (D?); b 1733, James Northern Parish, Goochland Co; d 10 Nov 1802 **RU:** Patriot, Gave material aid to the cause **CEM:** Liberty Primitive Baptist; GPS 36.69494, -80.16269; Patrick Springs; Patrick **GS:** N **SP:** Mar (16 Oct 1755 Goochland Co) Elizabeth Maddox (1732-__) d/o John & Elizabeth (-----) Maddox of Goochland and Powhatan Cos. **VI:** Son of Benjamin & (-----) Hancock. Bur

RU=Rank/Unit   CEM=Cemetery   GS=Gravestone   SP=Spousal Information
VI=Other Veteran Info   P=Pension   BLW=Bounty/Land Warrant   RG=Registered Grave
MK=SAR/DAR Marker   PH=Photo   SS=Service Source   BS=Burial Source

139

on the "NE slope of Bull Mountain." This cemetery seems to fit that description **P:** N **BLW:** N **RG:** unk **MK:** unk **PH:** N **SS:** AL Ct Bk pg 2 Fluvanna Co **BS:** 196.

HANDLEY, John; b c1760; d 1804 **RU:** Private?, Served in Clark's III Regt in 1781 **CEM:** North Fork Baptist; GPS 39.06014, -77.68509; 38130 North Folk Rd, North Fork; Loudoun **GS:** Y **SP:** No info **VI:** No further data **P:** unk **BLW:** unk **RG:** N **MK:** N **PH:** unk **SS:** E pg 344 **BS:** 75 Loudoun; 196.

HANGER, Frederick Jr; b 1755; d 1812 **RU:** Ensign, Served in Capt Buchanan's Co, Augusta Co Militia fr 30 Mar 1780 to end of war **CEM:** St John's Reformed UCC; GPS 38.05081, -79.17761; 1515 Arbor Hill Rd, Middlebrook; Augusta **GS:** N **SP:** 1) Elizabeth Rush 2) Maria Hull Rush **VI:** Son of Frederick Sr. (17 Nov 1726 Germany-Jul 1799 VA) & Eva Margaretha (Mayer) Hanger **P:** unk **BLW:** unk **RG:** unk **MK:** N **PH:** N **SS:** E pg 345 **BS:** JLARC 9, 62; 196.

HANGER, Peter; b 15 Feb 1729, Germany; d 1802 **RU:** Private/Patriot, Served in Capt Thomas Smith's Co, Augusta Co Militia. Also gave 17 bushels of rye to cause 25 Apr 1782 & 26 Aug 1782 **CEM:** Trinity Episcopal; GPS 38.14917, -79.07521; 214 Beverley St; Staunton City **GS:** U **SP:** Anna Sabina Hannah Gabbert (1724-1801) **VI:** Died in Staunton, Augusta Co **P:** unk **BLW:** unk **RG:** unk **MK:** unk **PH:** unk **SS:** E pg 345; CY pg 46, 92 **BS:** 196.

HANGER, Peter; b 29 Jan 1761; d 23 Dec 1828 **RU:** Soldier, Served in Capt Thomas Smith's Co Augusta Co Militia **CEM:** Old Link; GPS unk; .5 mi W of Ft Defiance; Augusta **GS:** Y **SP:** Catherine Line/Link (1767-1837) d/o Matthias (1737-1815) & Anna Maria (Schmidt) (1746-1817) Link. **VI:** Son of Peter Sr (1729-1802) & (-----) Hangar **P:** unk **BLW:** unk **RG:** unk **MK:** unk **PH:** unk **SS:** E pg 345 **BS:** JLARC 8, 62; 196.

HANKS, Abraham; b 1745, Northern Neck of VA; d In 1790s **RU:** Private, Served in Lt Col Richard Taylor's 2nd VA Regt of Foot 1779-1781 **CEM:** Hat Creek Presbyterian; GPS 37.06570, -78.54240; 6442 Hat Creek Rd, Brookneal; Campbell **GS:** N **SP:** Sarah Harper Hanks (__ Prince William Co)-1790 Campbell Co), daughter of George & Elizabeth (Shipley) Harper **VI:** Farrier for the William Clark party which were going to meet Daniel Boone in KY. Met on the Rapidan River 14 Mar 1775 according to Clark's journal. Grandfather of Abraham Lincoln **P:** unk **BLW:** unk **RG:** unk **MK:** N **PH:** N **SS:** E pg 345 **BS:** 196.

HANKS, Abraham; b 2 Apr 1759, Amelia Co; d 10 July 1833 **RU:** Soldier, Served in VA Line. Ent serv Bedford Co **CEM:** Harper Family; GPS unk; Nr Hat Creek Church, Brookneal; Campbell **GS:** N **SP:** 1) Sarah Harper; 2) mar (5 Apr 1788 Campbell Co) Lucy Jennings **VI:** Appl 16 Oct 1832 Lincoln TN. Widow appl 21 Dec 1840 Lincoln Co TN age 70. R4569. Died in Lincoln Co TN. Some say he was the grandfather of Abraham Lincoln **P:** Y **BLW:** unk **RG:** unk **MK:** N **PH:** N **SS:** CG Vol 2 pg 1508 **BS:** 196.

HANKS, Joshua; b c1760, Amelia Co; d Feb 1854 **RU:** Private, Served in Capt Flower Swift's Co, Montgomery Co Militia **CEM:** Old Quaker; GPS 36.64067, -80.88620; Off Old Quaker Rd Rt 727, Pipers Gap; Carroll **GS:** Y **SP:** Ruth Bryant, b 1764 in NC, d 1840 Grayson Co **VI:** Recd land grant 15 Oct 178? Supposed to be bur next to wife **P:** unk **BLW:** Y **RG:** Y **MK:** N **PH:** unk **SS:** AK May 07; BW pg 41, 43; BY **BS:** 04; 196.

HANNA, Joseph; b 1722; d 27 Jul 1789 **RU:** Patriot, Operated a gunpowder mill and provided gunpowder for militia **CEM:** Hanna Family; GPS unk; Nr Grottoes; Augusta **GS:** Y **SP:** Anna (-----) **VI:** No further data **P:** N **BLW:** N **RG:** Y **MK:** N **PH:** unk **SS:** DAR Ancestor #A051192; SAR Ancestor #P-174586; D, Vol 3 pg 833; AS; SAR applic **BS:** SAR Appl.

HANNA, Robert; b 1750; d 1825 **RU:** Private, Served in Capt Brent's Co, 4th VA Brigade **CEM:** Bethel Presbyterian; GPS 38.04257, -79.17283; 563 Bethel Green Rd, Middlebrook; Augusta **GS:** Y **SP:** Mary Ann Kilpatrick **VI:** Govt stone (cenotaph) **P:** unk **BLW:** unk **RG:** unk **MK:** unk **PH:** unk **SS:** NSSAR Ancestor # P-174593 **BS:** JLARC 4, 62, 63; 196.

HANNAH, Alexander; b 1728; d Nov 1803 **RU:** Patriot, Gave material aid to cause **CEM:** Old Presbyterian Meeting House; GPS 38.48528, -77.23532; 323 S Fairfax St; Alexandria City **GS:** N **SP:** No info **VI:** Died of old age, bur 22 Nov 1803 age 74 **P:** N **BLW:** N **RG:** N **MK:** N **PH:** N **SS:** AL Cert Issued **BS:** 23 pg 103.

RU=Rank/Unit	CEM=Cemetery	GS=Gravestone	SP=Spousal Information
VI=Other Veteran Info	P=Pension	BLW=Bounty/Land Warrant	RG=Registered Grave
MK=SAR/DAR Marker	PH=Photo	SS=Service Source	BS=Burial Source

140

HANNAN, Esom; b 1752; d 20 Mar 1843 **RU:** Private, Served in Cont & VA Lines. Ent Botetourt Co **CEM:** Greenwood Family; GPS unk; Cave Springs; Roanoke Co **GS:** U **SP:** Mar (15 Sep 1783) Mary Greenlee d/o William & (-----) Greenlee of Botetourt Co **VI:** Sol appl pen 12 Nov 1833. Widow appl pen 11 Oct 1843 Roanoke Co. W7644 **P:** Y **BLW:** unk **RG:** unk **MK:** unk **PH:** unk **SS:** J- DAR Hatcher; CG Vol 2 pg 1510 **BS:** JLARC 2.

HANSBROUGH (HANSBOROUGH), William; b 1755, Amherst Co; d 18 Jan 1816 **RU:** Private, Served in Capt William Fontaine's Co, VA Line **CEM:** Stevensburg Baptist; GPS unk; Stevensburg; Culpeper **GS:** Y **SP:** Mar (5 Nov 1786) Sarah/ Sally Vaughn (c1767-23 Mar 1857) daughter of William & (-----) Vaughn (father signed bond w/ sol 2 Nov 1786 in Culpeper Co) **VI:** Pen rec Jan 1816. Widow appl pen 18 Sep 1845 Culpeper Co age 77. W3808. Recd BLW #28518-160-55.Source 4 has esf 1775 and d in Stevensburg. Stone reads he d in 1815. Has SAR marker **P:** Y **BLW:** Y **RG:** Y **MK:** Y **PH:** unk **SS:** J-NSSAR 1993 Reg, J- DAR Hatcher; K pg 254; CG Vol 2 pg 1511 **BS:** JLARC 1, 2; 196.

HANSFORD, Cary H; b unk; d 29 Oct 1801 **RU:** Surg Mate/Patriot, Served in VA Line and Navy. Served 3 yrs on galley, "Dragon".Was at siege of Yorktown. Took oath as a Common Councilman in 1782 **CEM:** St Paul's Episcopal; GPS 36.84733, -76.28554; 201 St Paul's Blvd; Norfolk City **GS:** Y **SP:** Maria T__ **VI:** Alderman and eminent physician, Mayor of Norfok in 1785, 1791-2. Half pay pen paid to wife and son. R14850 **P:** Y **BLW:** unk **RG:** Y **MK:** N **PH:** unk **SS:** CB K,Vol 2 pg 254; K pg 254; CG Vol 2 pg 1512 **BS:** 87 pg 27.

HARDING, Aesop; b unk; d 1781 **RU:** Soldier, Served fr MA, killed in the battle at Yorktown **CEM:** Yorktown Victory Monument Tablet; GPS 38.28350, -78.54150; Yorktown; York **GS:** U **SP:** No info **VI:** No further data **P:** unk **BLW:** unk **RG:** unk **MK:** unk **PH:** unk **SS:** J-Yorktown Historian **BS:** JLARC 74.

HARDING, Isaac; b 1736; d 1820 **RU:** Patriot, Gave 139 # of beef for guard of prisoners **CEM:** Old Hardin (Shirley) Property; GPS unk; Nr Greenwood; Albemarle **GS:** Y **SP:** No info **VI:** No further data **P:** N **BLW:** N **RG:** N **MK:** N **PH:** unk **SS:** AL Ct Bk pg 22, 23; D Albemarle Co pg 25 **BS:** 80 vol 2 pg 117.

HARDY, Joseph Austin; b 1756, Lunenburg Co; d 22 May 1831 **RU:** Soldier, Served in Harrison's Co, 2nd VA Regt, Cont Line **CEM:** Hardy Family; GPS 37.23460, -79.30230; State Rts 122 & 640, Forbes Mill; Bedford **GS:** U **SP:** Mar (31 Aug 1788) Margaret Mackinzie (1768 Scotland-__) **VI:** Son of Thomas (4 May 1705-1791 KY) & Elizabeth (Austin) Hardy **P:** unk **BLW:** unk **RG:** unk **MK:** N **PH:** unk **SS:** J-DAR Hatcher; E pg 348 Govt marker shows service **BS:** JLARC 2; App D;196.

HARDY, Joshua; b unk; d unk **RU:** Soldier, Served in Harrison's Co 2nd VA Regt, Cont Line **CEM:** Hardy Family; GPS unk; State Rts 122 & 640, Forbes Mill; Bedford **GS:** Y **SP:** No info **VI:** No further data **P:** unk **BLW:** unk **RG:** Y **MK:** N **PH:** unk **SS:** J-NSSAR 1993 Reg **BS:** JLARC 1.

HARE, Joseph; b 1749, SC; d Sep 1853 **RU:** Scout, Served in militia **CEM:** Boyd, Wolf Creek; GPS unk; Wolf Creek Rd nr Narrows; Giles **GS:** U **SP:** 1) Nannie Clay 2) Phoebe Perdue **VI:** No further data **P:** unk **BLW:** unk **RG:** unk **MK:** unk **PH:** unk **SS:** J- DAR Hatcher; DD **BS:** JLARC 2.

HARKRADER (HARKRIDER), John; b 1 Oct 1750, Maxatawny Twp, Berks Co, PA; d 24 Nov 1837 **RU:** Captain, Served in PA Line. Ent serv Lancaster Co PA **CEM:** St John's Lutheran; GPS 36.96500, -81.10110; 405 W Main, Wytheville; Wythe **GS:** U **SP:** Barbara Sophia (-----) (7 Feb 1753-6 May 1802) **VI:** Son of Johannes (1714, Germany-19 Dec 1773, Middletown, Frederick Co, MD) & Anna Dorthea (Manuschmidt) (1719-1753) Herrgereder. Sol appl pen 12 Nov 1832 Wythe Co. S13323 **P:** Y **BLW:** unk **RG:** unk **MK:** unk **PH:** unk **SS:** K pg 259; CG Vol 2 pg 1520 **BS:** JLARC 3, 4, 40; 196.

HARLESS, David Anthony; b 5 Jan 1745, Lancaster, Lancaster Co, PA; d 1817 **RU:** Private, Served in Capt John Taylor's Co, Montgomery Co Militia **CEM:** Harless Family; GPS 37.21331, -80.54910; Vic jct Rt 744 & Long Shop Rd, Blacksburg; Montgomery **GS:** U **SP:** Mar (20 Jan 1813 Montgomery Co) Polly Hill, surty - John Hill (This marriage could be for another same name) **VI:** Son of John Phillip (1716-1772) & Anna Margaretha (Price) (1713-1784) Harless. Born on what is now Rockbridge Co on Cow Pasture River 4 mi fr Natural Bridge **P:** unk **BLW:** unk **RG:** unk **MK:** unk **PH:** unk **SS:** G pg 234-5 **BS:** 196.

HARLESS (HORLESS), Philip; b 1748 (pen rec 1760 or 1761, Botetourt Co); d 1822 **RU:** Private, Served in VA Line. Ent serv Botetourt Co (now Montgomery) **CEM:** Harless Family; GPS 37.21331, -

RU=Rank/Unit   CEM=Cemetery   GS=Gravestone   SP=Spousal Information
VI=Other Veteran Info   P=Pension   BLW=Bounty/Land Warrant   RG=Registered Grave
MK=SAR/DAR Marker   PH=Photo   SS=Service Source   BS=Burial Source

141

80.54910; Vic jct Rt 744 & Long Shop Rd, Blacksburg; Montgomery **GS:** U **SP:** Mar (7 Jun 1790 Montgomery Co) Milly Stanley **VI:** Sol appl pen 22 Mar 1834 Giles Co age 73. R4613 **P:** Y **BLW:** unk **RG:** unk **MK:** unk **PH:** unk **SS:** J- DAR Hatcher; CG Vol 2 pg 1520 **BS:** JLARC 2.

HARMAN, Daniel Conrad; b 26 Jan 1760 Rowan Co, NC; d 10 Jul 1791 **RU:** Patriot, Gave material aid to cause **CEM:** Henry Harmon; GPS unk; Fourway; Tazewell **GS:** Y **SP:** Phebey (Pheby) Davidson (1762 Rowan Co NC-1791 Tazewell Co) **VI:** Son of Henry Sr. (1726-1822) & Nancy Ann (Welburn/Wilburn) (1730-1808) Harman and brother of Daniel Harman. Was killed and scalped by an Indian a mile or two east of Five Oaks, in Tazewell Co. 1791 **P:** N **BLW:** N **RG:** N **MK:** N **PH:** N **SS:** AL Ct Bk pg 43 Montgomery Co **BS:** 196.

HARMAN, Henry Sr; b 30 Oct 1726, Isles of Man, Ireland; d 23 May or Jun 1822 **RU:** Patriot, Member of the Committee of Safety, Rowan Co, NC **CEM:** Holly Brook; GPS unk; Rt 606 off Hwy 42 adj Holly Brook Community Center; Bland **GS:** Y **SP:** Nancy Ann Wilburn (1734-1808) **VI:** Govt marker and another monument celebrating his and his two sons' victory over seven Black Hawk Indians in 1788. DAR Marker **P:** N **BLW:** N **RG:** Y **MK:** Y **PH:** unk **SS:** J-NSSAR 1993 Reg; DD cites book by Saunders Colonial Records of NC Vol 9 pg 1073 **BS:** JLARC 1; 196.

HARMAN, Mathias (Matthias); b c1736; d 2 Apr 1832 **RU:** Captain, Served in Cont Line **CEM:** Dry Fork, Sayer's Farm, or Harman; GPS unk; Rt 637, Dry Fork State marker nearby; Tazewell **GS:** U **SP:** Lydia Skaggs (1755-2 Oct 1814) d/o James & Rachel (Moredock) Skaggs **VI:** Son of Heinrich Adam (1700-1767) & Louisa Katrina (Martias) (1704-1749) Harman. He with others in a hunting party built a lodge in E KY in 1787 or 1789 which became a stockade called Harman Station which was later burned by Indians **P:** unk **BLW:** unk **RG:** Y **MK:** unk **PH:** unk **SS:** B Military Marker; NSSAR Ancestor #P-175290; DAR #A050869 **BS:** JLARC 1, 2, 89; 196.

HARMAN, Michael; b 4 Nov 1766, Frederick Co, MD; d 11 Aug 1808 **RU:** Private, Served in German Bn Cont Troops. Also served in 4th PA Regt **CEM:** Trinity Episcopal; GPS 38.14917, -79.07521; 214 Beverley St; Staunton City **GS:** U **SP:** No info **VI:** No further data **P:** unk **BLW:** unk **RG:** unk **MK:** unk **PH:** unk **SS:** CI **BS:** 196.

HARMAN (HARMON), Daniel; b 26 Jun 1760, Tazewell Co; d 10 Jul 1791 **RU:** Private, Served in Capt James Maxwell's Co Montgomery Co **CEM:** Wynn-Peery; GPS 37.12620, -81.4988; Campbell Ln, Tazewell; Tazewell **GS:** Y **SP:** No info **VI:** No further data **P:** unk **BLW:** unk **RG:** Y **MK:** N **PH:** unk **SS:** G pg 237 **BS:** 135 vol 3 pg 52.

HARMON, Henry; b 1726, Isle of Mann, Scotland; d Aft 23 Jul 1822 **RU:** Private?, Served in the battle at Point Pleasant **CEM:** Old Peaked Mountain; GPS 38.37113, -78.73416; 9843 Town Hall Rd, McGaheysville; Rockingham **GS:** Y **SP:** Nancy Wilburn **VI:** A person this name is buried in Tazewell Co, who had civil service in Rowan Co, NC who married Anna Wilburn **P:** unk **BLW:** Y **RG:** Y **MK:** Y **PH:** unk **SS:** Q pg 70; CU Vol 9 pg 1073; SAR Ancestor #P-175326 **BS:** 04.

HARMON, Jacob Jr; b 2 Feb 1754; d 1792 **RU:** Private/Patriot, Served in Capt James Maxwell's Co, Montgomery Co. Signed Oath of Alligiance Sep 1777 Montgomery Co **CEM:** Old Peaked Mountain; GPS 38.37113, -78.73416; 9843 Town Hall Rd, McGaheysville; Rockingham **GS:** N **SP:** No info **VI:** No further data **P:** unk **BLW:** unk **RG:** N **MK:** N **PH:** N **SS:** G pg 209, 237 **BS:** 116.

HARMON, Mathias; b Feb 1769; d 20 Dec 1802 **RU:** Soldier, Served in Capt James Maxwell's Co, Montgomery Co Militia **CEM:** Harmon Family; GPS 36.95470, -81.40080; Rt 610 Old Valley Rd, S of Hamon Creek nr Bland Co line; Smyth **GS:** Y **SP:** Mar (25 Jan 1791) Mary (-----) **VI:** SWS **P:** unk **BLW:** unk **RG:** unk **MK:** unk **PH:** unk **SS:** G pg 237 **BS:** 97 pg 30.

HARNSBERGER, Adam; b 1751; d 1816 **RU:** Private/Patriot, Gave material aid to cause **CEM:** Elk Run; GPS 38.41042, -78.61033; North St, Elkton; Rockingham **GS:** U **SP:** Catherine Null **VI:** No further data **P:** unk **BLW:** unk **RG:** unk **MK:** unk **PH:** unk **SS:** J- DAR Hatcher; D Vol 3 pg 828, 832 **BS:** JLARC 2.

HARNSBERGER, Robert; b 1760; d 7 Feb 1840 **RU:** Private, Served in Capt William Hall's Co **CEM:** Augusta Stone Presbyterian; GPS 38.23926, -78.97356; 28 Old Stone Church Ln, Ft Defiance; Augusta

RU=Rank/Unit	CEM=Cemetery	GS=Gravestone	SP=Spousal Information
VI=Other Veteran Info	P=Pension	BLW=Bounty/Land Warrant	RG=Registered Grave
MK=SAR/DAR Marker	PH=Photo	SS=Service Source	BS=Burial Source

142

GS: N **SP:** Christena Miller **VI:** No further data **P:** unk **BLW:** unk **RG:** unk **MK**: unk **PH:** N **SS:** AP NARA Service Record, Pension rec Thomas Lewis & John Pence; AR Vol 2 pg 119 **BS:** JLARC 2, 62.

HARPER, Edward; b 1763; d 4 Dec 1803 **RU:** Soldier, SAR registration did not specify service **CEM:** Old Presbyterian Meeting House; GPS 38.48528, -77.23532; 323 S Fairfax St; Alexandria City **GS:** N **SP:** No info **VI:** No further data **P:** unk **BLW:** unk **RG:** Y **MK:** unk **PH:** N **SS:** J-NSSAR 1993 Reg; NSSAR Ancestor #P-175440 **BS:** JLARC 1; 5.

HARPER, John; b 3 Oct 1728, Philadelphia, PA; d 7 May 1804 **RU:** Captain/Patriot, Served in Navy. Was Councilman in Alexandria and took Oath of Allegiance 1780 **CEM:** Old Presbyterian Meeting House; GPS 38.48528, -77.23532; 323 S Fairfax St; Alexandria City **GS:** Y **SP:** 1) Sarah Wells 2) Mary Reynolds Cunningham **VI:** Died age 76. Bur 7 May 1704. Styled Capt on stone, which is mostly obscured by the church wall. Listed on SAR plaque in cemetery **P:** unk **BLW:** unk **RG:** Y **MK:** unk **PH:** unk **SS:** J-NSSAR 1993 Reg, J- DAR Hatcher; AK; CT Order Bk Vol 6 pg 2, 3 Alexandria **BS:** JLARC 1 ,2; 23 pg 103; 196.

HARPER, Joseph; b 1751; d 31 Nov 1809 **RU:** Patriot, Signed a legislative petition **CEM:** Old Presbyterian Meeting House; GPS 38.48528, -77.23532; 323 S Fairfax St; Alexandria City **GS:** N **SP:** No info **VI:** Was rope maker. Died of palsey age 58 (Alexandria Gazette, 1 Dec 1809), bur 1 Dec 1809 **P:** N **BLW:** N **RG:** N **MK:** N **PH:** N **SS:** BB **BS:** 23 pg 111.

HARPER, William; b 1760; d 18 Apr 1829 **RU:** Captain, Served under Gen Washington at Princeton, Monmouth, Brandywine, & Valley Forge **CEM:** Presbyterian Church; GPS 38.80015, -77.05791; Wilkes St & Hamilton Ln; Alexandria City **GS:** Y **SP:** Mar (May 1763) Mary Scull, d/o William & (-----) Scull **VI:** Recd pen R4629 Died age 69. Death notice in Alexandria Gazette 22 Apr 1829 **P:** unk **BLW:** unk **RG:** Y **MK:** N **PH:** unk **SS:** K pg 263; AK GW 2015 **BS:** 23 pg 39.

HARRIS, Benjamin; b 3 Jan 1754; d 25 Mar 1834 **RU:** Captain, Served in VA Line. Ent serv Albemarle Co **CEM:** Harris Family; GPS 37.81867, -78.66393; Irish Rd, Esmont; Albemarle **GS:** Y **SP:** Mar (27 Oct 1785 Albemarle Co) Mary Woods (c1767-15 Aug 1844) **VI:** Sol appl pen 8 Jan 1834 Albemarle Co. Widow appl pen 2 Oct 1841 Albemarle Co age 74. W7664 **P:** Y **BLW:** unk **RG:** unk **MK:** unk **PH:** unk **SS:** CG Vol 2 pg 1530 **BS:** JLARC 4; 196.

HARRIS, David; b c1761; d 1841 **RU:** Private, Served in 1st, 2nd, 7th, 11th, 15th Cont Lines **CEM:** Shockoe Hill; GPS 37.55190, -77.43170; 4th & Hospital Sts; Richmond City **GS:** Y **SP:** No info **VI:** Pensioned in Hanover Co. Recd BLW of 100 acres for 3 yrs service Jun 1786 **P:** Y **BLW:** Y **RG:** N **MK**: N **PH:** unk **SS:** E pg 352; F pg 39 **BS:** 57 pg 22.

HARRIS, Francis E; b unk; d 20 Oct 1820 **RU:** Patriot, Gave material aid to cause **CEM:** Patrick Harris Homesite; GPS unk; dirt rd off Rt 614 abt 3 mi; Powhatan **GS:** Y **SP:** Col Thomas Harris **VI:** No further data **P:** N **BLW:** N **RG:** unk **MK**: unk **PH:** unk **SS:** AL Ct Bk pg 9 **BS:** 187.

HARRIS, James; b 22 May 1722 Hanover Co; d 14 Apr 1792 **RU:** Patriot, Gave material aid to cause **CEM:** Stonewall Jackson Memorial; GPS 37.78128, -79.44604; 314 S Main St; Lexington City **GS:** Y **SP:** Mary (-----) Harris (10 Feb 1730 Hanover Co-4 Jan 1819 Albemarle Co) **VI:** Died in Albemarle Co **P:** N **BLW:** N **RG:** N **MK:** N **PH:** N **SS:** AL Ct Bk V pg 72 Rockbridge Co **BS:** 196.

HARRIS, John; b unk; d bef 1826 **RU:** Patriot, Gave material aid to cause **CEM:** Eastern State Hospital; GPS 37.25560, -76.71030; S Henry Street; Williamsburg City **GS:** N **SP:** No info **VI:** No further data **P:** N **BLW:** N **RG:** N **MK:** N **PH:** N **SS:** AL Ct bk pg 1 **BS:** 65 Williamsburg.

HARRIS, John C; b 24 Dec 1754 or 1755, New Kent Co; d 1824 **RU:** Soldier, Ent Serv Lousia Co. Served in Lt Wm Harris Co **CEM:** Liberty Baptist; GPS 37.35181, -78.82862; 1709 Church St, Appomatox; Appomattox **GS:** N **SP:** Mary (-----) **VI:** Sol appl pen 26 Nov 1832 Nelson Co. S6953 **P:** Y **BLW:** unk **RG:** unk **MK:** unk **PH:** N **SS:** CG Vol 2 pg 1534 **BS:** JLARC 4, 59.

HARRIS, Jordan; b 20 May 1763, Goochland Co; d 7 Oct 1826 **RU:** Line Lieutenant, Served in Cont Army in VA Line **CEM:** Grubbs Family, aka Spring Grove; GPS 37.43510, 77.36520; Spring Grove #2 Farm, nr Calvary Christian jct Rts 623 & 624; Hanover **GS:** U **SP:** Mar (1789) Elizabeth Mosby Cannon (1771-1801) **VI:** BLW #1083-150-2 Apr 1796 to Joseph Fenwick. Record lost in 1814 fire **P:** unk **BLW:** Y **RG:** unk **MK:** unk **PH:** unk **SS:** K pg 267; CG Vol 2 pg 1534 **BS:** JLARC 71.

RU=Rank/Unit	CEM=Cemetery	GS=Gravestone	SP=Spousal Information
VI=Other Veteran Info	P=Pension	BLW=Bounty/Land Warrant	RG=Registered Grave
MK=SAR/DAR Marker	PH=Photo	SS=Service Source	BS=Burial Source

143

HARRIS, Robert; b unk; d 1805 **RU:** Second Lieutenant, Took oath 17 Sep 1777 as 2nd Lt in Capt Samuel McCutchen's Co, Augusta Co Militia **CEM:** New Providence Presbyterian; GPS 37.95170, -79.30250; 1208 New Providence Rd, Raphine; Rockbridge **GS:** U **SP:** No info **VI:** No further data **P:** unk **BLW:** unk **RG:** unk **MK:** unk **PH:** unk **SS:** E pg 353 **BS:** 196.

HARRIS, Samuel; b 1724; d 1799 **RU:** Colonel/Patriot, Gave material aid to cause **CEM:** Harris Family; GPS unk; Rt 816 or Rt 703, 10 mi fr Chatham nr Chatham HS; Pittsylvania **GS:** U **SP:** Lucy Camp **VI:** Organizer of Baptists **P:** unk **BLW:** unk **RG:** unk **MK:** unk **PH:** unk **SS:** AL Ct Bk pg 30, 47, 53, 59 Pittsylvania Co **BS:** JLARC 76,96.

HARRIS, William; b 13 Jul 1748, Goochland Co (pen rec) or 1749; d 1815 **RU:** Major, Served in VA Line. Ent serv Amherst Co **CEM:** Rockfish Presbyterian; GPS unk; 5016 Rockfish Valley Hwy, Nellysford; Nelson **GS:** U **SP:** Elizabeth Wagstaff **VI:** Sol appl pen 22 Oct 1832 Nelson Co (formerly Amherst Co). S6956 **P:** Y **BLW:** unk **RG:** unk **MK:** unk **PH:** unk **SS:** CG Vol 2 pg 1537 **BS:** JLARC 83.

HARRIS, William; b 1712; d 1788 **RU:** Patriot, Gave material aid to cause in Albemarle Co **CEM:** Harris Family; GPS 37.81867, -78.66393; Irish Rd, Esmont; Albemarle **GS:** Y **SP:** Mary Netherland (1719-1789) **VI:** No further data **P:** unk **BLW:** unk **RG:** unk **MK:** unk **PH:** Y **SS:** AL Ct Bk pg 7, 15 **BS:** 196.

HARRIS, William E; b 1752; d 1826 **RU:** Patriot, Gave material aid to the cause **CEM:** Spring Grove; GPS 39.10916, -78.09970; Rockville; Hanover **GS:** Y **SP:** Mar (20 Dec 1780 Hanover Co) Diana Goodwin **VI:** No further data **P:** N **BLW:** N **RG:** N **MK:** N **PH:** unk **SS:** AL Ct Bk lt I pg 24 **BS:** 31 vol I pg 104.

HARRISON, Benjamin; b 1755 or 1757, Charles City Co; d 1799 **RU:** Captain, Commanded a co in Charles Co Militia, Dec 1776 **CEM:** Berkeley Plantation; GPS 37.31450, -77.17840; Rt 5, Harrison Landing Rd; Charles City Co **GS:** U **SP:** Mar (15 Nov 1785) Anne Mercer (9 Sep 1760, Stafford Co-29 Jun 1822, Cabin Point, Surry Co) **VI:** Son of Benjamin (13 Dec 1730, Charles City Co-24 Apr 1791) & Elizabeth (Bassett) (13 Dec 1730, Eltham, VA-1792, Berkeley) Harrison. Rec'd BLW of 266.66 acres **P:** unk **BLW:** Y **RG:** unk **MK:** unk **PH:** unk **SS:** A pg 534; G pg 116; N pg 1093; CZ **BS:** 196.

HARRISON, Benjamin; b 1741, Dayton, Rockingham Co; d 1819 **RU:** Colonel/Patriot, Was Capt in Battle of Point Pleasant 1774. Held rank of Col in VA Militia. Served under General LaFayette & General Andrew Lewis. Gave material aid to cause **CEM:** Dayton; GPS 38.42000, -78.94303; Bowman Rd, Dayton; Rockingham **GS:** Y **SP:** Mary McClure **VI:** NSSAR Graves database shows Benjamin's wife as Margaret Cravens. Benjamin is the son of Daniel Harrison and Margaret Cravens **P:** unk **BLW:** unk **RG:** Y **MK:** Y **PH:** unk **SS:** J-NSSAR 1993 Reg; D Rockingham Co **BS:** JLARC 1.

HARRISON, Benjamin; b 1743; d 1797 **RU:** Lieutenant/Patriot, Gave material aid to cause **CEM:** Harrison Family; GPS unk; 5.5 mi NE of Burrowsville; Prince George **GS:** Y **SP:** No info **VI:** No further data **P:** unk **BLW:** unk **RG:** Y **MK:** N **PH:** unk **SS:** E pg 354; AL Ct Bk pg 4 Prince George Co **BS:** 111 Part 5 pg 113.

HARRISON, Benjamin; b unk; d Aft 1781 **RU:** Lt Colonel/Patriot, Served in Rockingham Co Militia. Took oath as Lt Col 25 May 1778, and oath as Co Lt 1782.Gave material aid to cause in Rockingham Co adjacent to Shenandoah Co **CEM:** St Mathew's; GPS 36.65131, -78.67121; Breckenridge Ln, New Market; Shenandoah **GS:** U **SP:** No info **VI:** No further data **P:** unk **BLW:** unk **RG:** unk **MK:** unk **PH:** unk **SS:** J- DAR Hatcher; AL Ct Bk II pg 36 **BS:** JLARC 2.

HARRISON, Benjamin; b 13 Dec 1730; d 24 Apr 1791 **RU:** Patriot, Signer Declaration of Independence, member Cont Congress **CEM:** Berkeley Plantation; GPS 37.31450, -77.17840; Rt 5, Harrison Landing Rd; Charles City Co **GS:** U **SP:** Mar (1748) Elizabeth Bassett (13 Dec 1730, Eltham, VA-1792 Berkeley) **VI:** Governor of VA. Member of General Assembly **P:** N **BLW:** N **RG:** unk **MK:** unk **PH:** unk **SS:** DD cites Dictionary of American Biography Vol 4 pg 330, 331 **BS:** 196.

HARRISON, Carter Henry; b 22 Aug 1736, Fairfax Co; d 8 Oct 1793 **RU:** Captain/Patriot, Served at Ft Cumberland on 17 Sep 1775 in a VA Regt. Was on a committee of safety **CEM:** Clifton Cemetery; GPS 37.40752, -78.07579; Off Rt 690 N of Hamilton; Cumberland **GS:** Y **SP:** Mar (9 Nov 1760 Goochland Co) Susannah Randolph (25 Sep 1738, Goochland Co-__) d/o Isham Randolph (1685-1742) & Jane Lilburne Rogers (1692-1760) **VI:** Son of Benjamin Harrison (1694-1745) & Anne Carter (1704-1745).

RU=Rank/Unit	CEM=Cemetery	GS=Gravestone	SP=Spousal Information
VI=Other Veteran Info	P=Pension	BLW=Bounty/Land Warrant	RG=Registered Grave
MK=SAR/DAR Marker	PH=Photo	SS=Service Source	BS=Burial Source

144

Was in Cumberland Co Committee of Safety,and author of Resolutions of Independence 22 Apr 1776; member House of Delegates 1782-1787 **P:** unk **BLW:** unk **RG:** N **MK:** Y **PH:** unk **SS:** G pg 357 **BS:** 32 e-mail 01/07; 196.

HARRISON, John Peyton; b 9 Mar 1748 Augusta Co; d Nov 1789 **RU:** Captain, Served in 2nd Cont Line May 1777 **CEM:** Lacey Springs; GPS 38.54475, -78.77072; Lacey Springs; Rockingham **GS:** U **SP:** Mar (c1772) Hannah Lincoln (9 Mar 1748, PA-Dec 1803) **VI:** Son of Zebulon (1718, Long Island, NY-Rockingham Co 1792) & Margaret (Cravens) (23 Jul 1724,Morristown, NJ-1800) Harrison. Recd BLW 4000 acres 4 May 1777 **P:** unk **BLW:** Y **RG:** unk **MK:** unk **PH:** unk **SS:** E pg 355 **BS:** 196.

HARRISON, John Sr; b 1760; d 28 May 1808 **RU:** Private, Served in VA Line. Lived w/ father in King George Co at enl. Was age 15 at enl in 1776 **CEM:** Harrison Family; GPS 38.43373, -78.29048; Shelby; Madison **GS:** U **SP:** Jane Campbell **VI:** Sol appl pen 23 Aug 1832 Madison Co, age 72 where he lived for 42 yrs. S5471 **P:** Y **BLW:** unk **RG:** Y **MK:** unk **PH:** unk **SS:** J-NSSAR 2000 Reg; K pg 271; CG Vol 2 pg 1540 **BS:** JLARC 76.

HARRISON, Nathaniel; b 1703; d 1 Oct 1781 **RU:** Patriot, Gave material aid to cause. Was member of Prince George Co Committee of Safety & member of the State Senate, Oct 1779 **CEM:** Brandon Plantation; GPS 37.15271, -76.59362; Burrowsville; Prince George **GS:** Y **SP:** 1) Mary Digges d/o Cole & (-----) Digges of "Belfield" York Co 2) mar (bef 15 Feb 1748) Lucy Carter, d/o Robert & (-----) Carter of "Corotoman" **VI:** No further data **P:** unk **BLW:** unk **RG:** N **MK:** N **PH:** unk **SS:** AS, DAR Report; AL Ct Bk I pg 5, 7 Prince George Co **BS:** 80 vol 2 pg 123; 213 pg 425.

HARRISON, Reuben; b 1731; d 1807 **RU:** Captain/Patriot, Took oath as Capt, 25 May 1778 and commanded a co in Rockingham Co Militia. Gave material aid to cause **CEM:** Harrison Family, Smith's Creek; GPS 38.4200, -78.94303; Nr Lacy Springs; Rockingham **GS:** U **SP:** 1) Lydia Harrison 2) Mary McDonald **VI:** Recd pen # W7689 **P:** Y **BLW:** unk **RG:** unk **MK:** unk **PH:** unk **SS:** J- DAR Hatcher; AL Ct Bk I pg 5, 7 Rockingham Co **BS:** JLARC 2.

HARRISON, Reuben; b c1754 or 1757, Augusta Co, (later Rockingham Co); d 15 Aug 1840 **RU:** Private/Wagoneer, Served in VA Line. Ent serv Augusta Co (later became Rockingham). Served in Capt Robert Cravens Co Rockingham Militia at Tygarts Valley, Col Hamilton's, VA Regt. Also served under Gen Wayne at Jamestown **CEM:** Woodbine; GPS unk; Cnr of E Market St and Ott St, Harrisonburg; Rockingham **GS:** Y **SP:** Mar (27 Apr 1791) Mary Matthews or Mathews (3 Jul 1772-__) **VI:** Sol appl pen 22 May 1833 Augusta Co (later Rockingham) age abt 76. Widow appl pen 14 Jun 1843 Rockingham Co. She was there in 1848. W7689 **P:** Y **BLW:** unk **RG:** Y **MK:** N **PH:** unk **SS:** K pg 272; CG Vol 2 pg 1541 **BS:** JLARC 4.

HARRISON, Robert; b 11 Feb 1755; d 17 Aug 1836 **RU:** Private, Served in Cont Line for 3 yrs **CEM:** Bicars; GPS unk; 75 yards behind house site on private road off Rt 641, Huntington; Prince George **GS:** N **SP:** Henrietta Maria Hardeman of Flower de Hundred **VI:** Recd 100 acres BLW **P:** N **BLW:** Y **RG:** unk **MK:** unk **PH:** N **SS:** J- DAR Hatcher; A pg 192; G pg 426 **BS:** JLARC 2; 111.

HARRISON, Thomas; b 1704, Smithtown, Suffolk Co, NY; d 1785 **RU:** Patriot, Gave material aid to cause **CEM:** Woodbine; GPS 38.44803, -78.86244; Jct Rt 33 & Reservoir St, Harrisonburg; Harrisonburg City **GS:** U **SP:** No info **VI:** Son of Isaiah (1666-1738) & Abigail (Herring) (1710-1780) Harrison. 23 names including his are listed on crypt moved to Woodbine fr another location **P:** N **BLW:** N **RG:** unk **MK:** unk **PH:** unk **SS:** AL Ct Bk I pg 2, 8, 11, 12 **BS:** 196.

HARRISON, Thomas; b 1750; d 1811 **RU:** Sergeant, Served in Col Gist's Regt **CEM:** Fairview; GPS unk; Chopawamic Creek; Stafford **GS:** Y **SP:** No info **VI:** Son of Thomas & Ann (Peyton) Harrioson. Was a reverend **P:** unk **BLW:** unk **RG:** N **MK:** N **PH:** unk **SS:** E pg 356 **BS:** 03 pg 198.

HARRISON, William; b c1730; d 20 Nov 1814 **RU:** Captain/Patriot, Commanded a Co in the Amelia Co Militia. Gave material aid to cause **CEM:** Blandford; GPS 37.22433, -77.38604; 319 S Crater Rd; Petersburg City **GS:** Y **SP:** Mar (1793) Anne Vaughn (1769-2 Jul 1829) **VI:** Was a reverend after the war **P:** unk **BLW:** unk **RG:** N **MK:** N **PH:** Y **SS:** AL Ct Bk pg 30, 57 Brunswick Co; G pg 116; AZ pg 178; CD **BS:** 47 vol 8 pg 179.

RU=Rank/Unit	CEM=Cemetery	GS=Gravestone	SP=Spousal Information
VI=Other Veteran Info	P=Pension	BLW=Bounty/Land Warrant	RG=Registered Grave
MK=SAR/DAR Marker	PH=Photo	SS=Service Source	BS=Burial Source

145

HARRISON, William H; b 1761; d 1817 **RU:** Sergeant, Served in Charles City Co Militia under Capt Benjamin Harrison fr 21 Nov 1776-11 Dec 1776. Was Sgt in Pulaski's Legion **CEM:** Harrison-Pinkards; GPS unk; 4.5 mi E Prince George, then N; Prince George **GS:** Y **SP:** No info **VI:** No further data **P:** unk **BLW:** unk **RG:** N **MK:** N **PH:** unk **SS:** E pg 356; G pg 116 **BS:** 111 pg 15.

HARRISON, William; b 1762; d 22 Jan 1849 **RU:** Drummer boy, Ent Serv Mecklenburg Co. Served in VA Line **CEM:** Grace Church; GPS unk; Manteo; Buckingham **GS:** U **SP:** Sina or Lina Wootton or Wooton (c1800-after 1868) **VI:** Sol appl pen 15 Aug 1832 Buckingham Co. W4481. Widow appl pen 9 May 1853 Buckingham Co age 53 & was still there 1868. Recd BLW #3977-160-55 **P:** Y **BLW:** Y **RG:** unk **MK:** N **PH:** unk **SS:** CG Vol 2 pg 1542 **BS:** JLARC 4 , 44, 59.

HARSHBARGER, Christian Sr; b 20 Aug 1756, Lancaster Co, PA; d 29 Jun 1827 **RU:** Private/Patriot, Served in Lancaster Co PA in Capt Bradley's Co. Gave material aid to cause **CEM:** Old German; GPS unk; Roanoke; Roanoke City **GS:** U **SP:** Mar (Jun 1779) Barbara Ammen (19 Feb 1760, Lincoln Co, PA-9 Jan 1803) **VI:** Died in Mill Creek, Fincastle Co **P:** unk **BLW:** unk **RG:** unk **MK:** unk **PH:** unk **SS:** J-NSSAR 1993 Reg, J- DAR Hatcher; D Shenandoah Co; CI **BS:** JLARC 1, 2.

HARTSHORNE, William; b Jun 1742, Burlington Co, NJ; d 13 Dec 1816 **RU:** Patriot, Signed legislative petition in Alexandria during RW period. Member of Fairfax Co Committee of Safety **CEM:** Quaker Burial Ground; GPS 38.80749, -77.04676; 717 Queen St, Kate Walker Barrett Library; Alexandria City **GS:** U **SP:** Mar (8 Oct 1767) Susannah Saunders (13 Jun 1745-1801) **VI:** Son of Hugh & Hannah (Pattison) Hartshorne. Alexandria Gazette says age75 yrs at death **P:** N **BLW:** N **RG:** unk **MK:** unk **PH:** unk **SS:** S - Alexandria; DD cites DAR Mag (1916) Vol 49 pg 239 **BS:** 196.

HARVEY, John; b 1742; d 1807 **RU:** Captain, Served in 1776 or 1777 in US Navy. Taken prisoner for 12 to 18 mos. Served three yrs **CEM:** Harvey Family; GPS unk; Specific location not identified; Norfolk City **GS:** U **SP:** No info **VI:** Son of John (__-by 1749 (will proved) Northumberland Co) & Mary (-----) (__-aft 1749) Harvey. Fr Northumberland Co. Rank of Col on GS **P:** unk **BLW:** Y **RG:** unk **MK:** unk **PH:** unk **SS:** B; E pg 357; L pg 199 **BS:** 196.

HARVEY, Matthew; b 1760, Elkton, Cecil Co, MD; d 19 Sep 1825 **RU:** Private, Served in Cont Line (MD). Ent serv Head of the Elk in MD at age 16. Was in the Battle at Guilford CH **CEM:** Fincastle Presbyterian; GPS 37.50017, -79.87558; 108 E Back St, Fincastle; Botetourt **GS:** Y **SP:** Mar (18 Aug 1788 at Catawba Creek, two mi fr Fincastle, at home of his brother Robert Harvey) Magdalene Hawkins (24 Jul 1775, Rockbridge Co-20 Apr 1845). Pensioned at age 67 in 1841. **VI:** Soldier at 16, with all three brothers, Robert, William, James, all of head of Elk River MD. William killed in Battle of Guilford CH (4). Widow appl pen 3 Apr 1841 Botetourt Co age 67. W19681. Recd BLW on 09 Apr 1796. No BLW number. Name is on the SAR plaque at this cemetery **P:** Y **BLW:** Y **RG:** unk **MK:** Y **PH:** unk **SS:** K pg 276; AR Vol 2 pg 126; BY; CG Vol 2 pg 1550 **BS:** 196, JLARC 1,2,4.

HARVEY, Mungo; b unk; d 21 Mar 1794 **RU:** Patriot, Gave material aid to the cause **CEM:** St Paul's Episcopal; GPS 38.33200, -77.12500; 5486 St Paul's Rd off Rt 206; King George **GS:** N **SP:** Mar (18 Aug 1769 Lancaster Co (bond) Priscilla Glascock (18 Aug 1769-__), d/o William & Ester (Ball) Glascock of Richmond Co. Widow of Williamson Ball (__-1764 Westmoreland Co, bur King George Co)—she mar Ball 24 Mar 1763 Richmond Co bond. **VI:** No further data **P:** N **BLW:** N **RG:** N **MK:** N **PH:** N **SS:** D Lancaster Co; AL Ct Bk **BS:** 189 pg 59.

HARVEY, Robert; b 1756; d 1831 **RU:** Soldier, Served in Lee's Legion **CEM:** Fincastle Presbyterian; GPS 37.50017, -79.87558; 108 E Back St, Fincastle; Botetourt **GS:** N **SP:** Martha Woods Borden **VI:** Name is on the SAR plaque at this cemetery, and the monument to Rev War soldiers **P:** unk **BLW:** unk **RG:** Y **MK:** Y **PH:** N **SS:** J-NSSAR 1993 Reg; J- DAR Hatcher; E pg 358 **BS:** JLARC 1, 2; 196.

HARVIE, John; b 1742, Albemarle Co; d 1807 **RU:** Colonel/Patriot, Commanded Albermarle Co Militia 1776-1781. Was Delegate fr VA to Cont Congress 1777-78 **CEM:** Hollywood; GPS 37.53560, -77.45720; 412 S Cherry St; Richmond City **GS:** Y **SP:** No info **VI:** Signer of the Articles of Confederation. Secretary of Commonwealth 1788. His estate became the location of the Hollywood Cemetery **P:** unk **BLW:** unk **RG:** N **MK:** N **PH:** unk **SS:** E pg 358 **BS:** 130; 196.

HASH, John Sr; b 1724; d 13 Apr 1784 **RU:** Private, Served in Capt Enoch Osburn's Co and Draper's Co, Montgomery Co Militia **CEM:** Silas Ward Family; GPS unk; Bridle Creek; Grayson **GS:** Y **SP:**

RU=Rank/Unit	CEM=Cemetery	GS=Gravestone	SP=Spousal Information
VI=Other Veteran Info	P=Pension	BLW=Bounty/Land Warrant	RG=Registered Grave
MK=SAR/DAR Marker	PH=Photo	SS=Service Source	BS=Burial Source

Elizabeth Stodgill (1734, Orange Co-1785) d/o James (1700-1753) & (-----) Sturgill **VI:** Govt Gr St **P:** unk **BLW:** unk **RG:** unk **MK:** unk **PH:** unk **SS:** G pg 212 **BS:** 196.

HASH, William; b 1750; d 1818 **RU:** Private, Served in Capt Enoch Osburn Co, Montgomery Co Militia **CEM:** Silas Ward Family; GPS unk; Bridle Creek; Grayson **GS:** Y **SP:** Mar (1774) Eleanor Osborne, (__, Rowan Co, NC-1820) **VI:** Son of John (__-1784) & Elizabeth (Stodgill) (1734-1785) Hash. Govt Gr St **P:** unk **BLW:** unk **RG:** Y **MK:** unk **PH:** unk **SS:** J-NSSAR 1993 Reg, J- DAR Hatcher; G pg 224 **BS:** JLARC 1, 2.

HATCHER, Elijah Sr; b c1762, Bedford Co; d 10 Dec 1829 **RU:** Patriot, Gave material aid to cause **CEM:** Hatcher Family; GPS unk; Scruggs; Franklin **GS:** Y **SP:** Mar (c1782) Sarah Hale (c1764-1829) d/o Richard (1740-28 Jun 1784) & Elizabeth (-----) (__- c1797) Hale **VI:** SAR Gr marker **P:** N **BLW:** N **RG:** Y **MK:** Y **PH:** unk **SS:** AE Vol 2 pg 84-6 **BS:** 04.

HATCHER, James Sr; b 1732; d 1816 **RU:** Sergeant, Served in Capt Charles Thomas Co, 7th VA Regt 1777 **CEM:** Goose Creek; GPS 39.11250, -77.69527; Rt 722, Lincoln; Loudoun **GS:** N **SP:** No info **VI:** Son of William (1704-1780) & (-----) Hatcher **P:** unk **BLW:** unk **RG:** unk **MK:** unk **PH:** N **SS:** CI NARA Muster Role **BS:** 196.

HATHAWAY, John; b 11 May 1733, Lancaster Co; d 19 Apr 1786 **RU:** Major/Patriot, Commanded a Co in Fauquier Co Militia Mar 1780. Promoted to Maj, resigned May 1783. Gave material aid to cause **CEM:** The Hatherage; GPS unk; Warrenton; Fauquier **GS:** U **SP:** Mar (26 Dec 1754) Sarah Timberlake (21 Apr 1739, Northumberland Co-1809) **VI:** No further data **P:** unk **BLW:** unk **RG:** unk **MK:** unk **PH:** unk **SS:** J- DAR Hatcher; E pg 359; AL Cert list pg 14 Fauquier Co **BS:** JLARC 2.

HAUTVILLE, Joseph; b unk; d 1781 **RU:** Soldier, Served in Agenois Bn and died fr battle at Yorktown **CEM:** French Memorial; GPS 36.81944, -79.39933; Yorktown; York **GS:** U **SP:** No info **VI:** No further data **P:** unk **BLW:** unk **RG:** Y **MK:** unk **PH:** unk **SS:** J-Yorktown Historian **BS:** JLARC 1, 74.

HAWKINS, Issac; b unk; d 1781 **RU:** Private, Served in Capt Benjamin Hick's 4th Co, 1st Regt NY Line. Died fr the battle at Yorktown **CEM:** Yorktown Victory Monument Tablet; GPS 38.28350, -78.54150; Yorktown; York **GS:** U **SP:** No info **VI:** No further data **P:** unk **BLW:** unk **RG:** unk **MK:** unk **PH:** unk **SS:** J-Yorktown Historian; AX pg 179 **BS:** JLARC 74.

HAWKINS, John; b 1750,Charles Co, MD; d 1802 or 1805 **RU:** Captain, Served 3 yrs in 3rd VA Regt Cont Line 1776 and was 3rd Regt Adjutant 28 Dec 1776. On rolls to Feb 1781 **CEM:** Hawkins Family; GPS 38.77367, -77.62359; Buckland Farm, 6342 Pleasant Colony Ln, Warrenton; Fauquier **GS:** U **SP:** Alice Corbin Thompson, daughter of Dr. Adam & Lettice (Lee) Thompson **VI:** Possibly d in Alexandria. Recd BLW of 1333 acres 28 Apr 1785 **P:** unk **BLW:** Y **RG:** N **MK:** Y **PH:** Y **SS:** BX, pg 351, G, pg 405 & 626; E pg 361; BY; CE pg 41 **BS:** 196; SAR Appl.

HAY, William; b 10 Nov 1825, Kilsyth, Scotland; d unk **RU:** Soldier, Served in Capt Burgess Balls Co, Col Parker's VA Regt of Foot, Oct & Nov 1778 **CEM:** Old Chapel Episcopal; GPS 39.10677, -78.01470; Jct US 340 & Rt 255, Millwood; Clarke **GS:** U **SP:** (1) (-----) Cory; (2) (-----) Both mar in Richmond.) **VI:** Resided in Richmond. Died at home called "Farnley", Clarke Co **P:** unk **BLW:** unk **RG:** unk **MK:** N **PH:** unk **SS:** E pg 362; AP Roll **BS:** 206.

HAYLEY, James; b unk; d Aug 1789 **RU:** Sergeant, Served in 1st VA State Regt **CEM:** Old Christ Church Episcopal; GPS 38.80625, -77.04718; 118 N Washington St; Alexandria City **GS:** N **SP:** No info **VI:** Burial permit issued 15 Aug 1789 to Mr Carville **P:** unk **BLW:** unk **RG:** Y **MK:** N **PH:** N **SS:** E pg 363 **BS:** 20 pg 149.

HAYNES, Benjamin; b 1738; d 1808 **RU:** Private, Served in Capt Joseph Hayne's Co, Rockingham Co that was in the Point Pleasant Battle **CEM:** Mountain View; GPS 37.81360, -79.81390; Clifton Forge; Alleghany **GS:** U **SP:** No info **VI:** No further data **P:** unk **BLW:** unk **RG:** unk **MK:** N **PH:** unk **SS:** J- DAR Hatcher; Z pg 107 **BS:** JLARC 2.

HAYNES, Joseph; b 3 Aug 1742, England; d 9 Aug 1815 **RU:** Captain, Served in Co in Rockingham Co that was in the Point Pleasant Battle **CEM:** Mountain View; GPS 37.81360, -79.81390; Clifton Forge; Alleghany **GS:** U **SP:** Jeanette/Janette T. Young (16 Sep 1756, Ireland-Jun 1827) **VI:** No further data **P:** unk **BLW:** unk **RG:** unk **MK:** N **PH:** unk **SS:** J- DAR Hatcher; Z pg 107 **BS:** JLARC 2; 196.

RU=Rank/Unit	CEM=Cemetery	GS=Gravestone	SP=Spousal Information
VI=Other Veteran Info	P=Pension	BLW=Bounty/Land Warrant	RG=Registered Grave
MK=SAR/DAR Marker	PH=Photo	SS=Service Source	BS=Burial Source

147

HAYNIE, Bridgar II; b 1745; d 1791 **RU:** Lieutenant/Patriot, Gave material aid to cause **CEM:** Haynie Family; GPS unk; Heathsville; Northumberland **GS:** U **SP:** Mar (16 Jun 1766 (bond) Lancaster Co) Sarah Shearman d/o Martin & Ann (Chinn) Shearman. Her brother owned "Pop Castle" in War of 1812. **VI:** No further data **P:** unk **BLW:** unk **RG:** Y **MK:** unk **PH:** unk **SS:** J-NASSR 2000 Reg; AL Ct Bk pg 12 Northumberland Co **BS:** JLARC 76.

HAYS, John; b unk; d 1808 **RU:** Captain, Commanded a Co in Montgomery Co in Nov 1781 (Giles Co formed fr Montgomery Co in 1806) **CEM:** Indian Bottom Farm; GPS unk; Walkers Creek District Twp; Giles **GS:** U **SP:** No info **VI:** No further data **P:** unk **BLW:** unk **RG:** Y **MK:** unk **PH:** unk **SS:** J-NSSAR 1993 Reg; E pg 364; AL Cert lists pg 2, 7, 11 Botetourt Co **BS:** JLARC 1.

HAYS, John; b 1739; d 1808 **RU:** Major, Served in 3rd VA Regt of Foot as Maj fr 23 Apr 1778-12 Feb 1781. Taken prisoner at Germantown Oct 1777 and remained captive until retirement **CEM:** Stone House Plantation; GPS unk; Hill behind Hays Creek, nr Staunton; Staunton City **GS:** U **SP:** No info **VI:** No further data **P:** unk **BLW:** unk **RG:** Y **MK:** unk **PH:** unk **SS:** J-NSSAR 1993 Reg, J- DAR Hatcher; CE pg 39 **BS:** JLARC 1, 2.

HAYTER, Israel; b 2 Oct 1754, Frederick Co, MD; d 11 Feb 1829 **RU:** Private, Served in Capt James Dysart's Co, Col William Campbell's VA Militia. Was wounded in thigh at Kings Mountain **CEM:** Hayter-Litton; GPS 36.84443, -81.92628; Nr the Litton Home, 7261 Hayter's Gap Rd; Washington **GS:** U **SP:** Mar (20 Apr 1781) Anne Crawford (19 Feb 1754-25 Apr 1843) **VI:** DAR plaque **P:** N **BLW:** N **RG:** no reg **MK:** Y **PH:** N **SS:** AR pg 135 **BS:** JLARC 2,80; 196; 208 pg 49.

HAYWARD, James; b unk; d 1781 **RU:** Soldier, Served fr MA and died as result of Yorktown battle **CEM:** Yorktown Victory Monument Tablet; GPS 38.28350, -78.54150; Yorktown; York **GS:** U **SP:** No info **VI:** No further data **P:** unk **BLW:** unk **RG:** unk **MK:** unk **PH:** unk **SS:** J-Yorktown Historian **BS:** JLARC 74.

HEAD, Benjamin Sr; b 1731, Spotsylvania Co; d 19 Aug 1803 **RU:** Captain, Commanded a co of militia in Orange Co 1778-9 **CEM:** Westover United Methodist; GPS 38.28130, -78.38607; 2801 Fredericksburg Rd; Orange **GS:** Y **SP:** Mar (1754) Martha Sharman (c1734,-1803) d/o Robert & Lucy (-----) Sharman **VI:** Son of Henry (1695-1765) of Spotsylvania Co & Frances (Spence) Head. Cenotaph abt him in cem. SAR marker **P:** unk **BLW:** unk **RG:** unk **MK:** Y **PH:** Y **SS:** AR Vol 2 pg 137; NSSAR Ancestor #P-178532; Orange Co Order Bk 2 pg 86-7 **BS:** JLARC 2.

HEADRICK, Charles; b unk; d unk **RU:** Patriot, Gave material aid to cause **CEM:** Old Peaked Mountain; GPS 38.37113, -78.73416; 9843 Town Hall Rd, McGaheysville; Rockingham **GS:** Y **SP:** No info **VI:** Listed on a plaque in the cemetery with others that had Rev War service **P:** unk **BLW:** unk **RG:** Y **MK:** Y **PH:** unk **SS:** O pg 143; AL Ct Bk pg 6 Rockingham Co **BS:** 04.

HEALY, James; b 1756; d 1820 **RU:** Sergeant, Served in VA battalion, 1st VA Regt **CEM:** Clark's Neck; GPS unk; See property records for Clark's Neck & Healy family residence; Middlesex **GS:** U **SP:** Ruth Bristow **VI:** No further data **P:** unk **BLW:** unk **RG:** Y **MK:** unk **PH:** unk **SS:** SAR Ancestor #P-178802; J-NSSAR 2000 Reg; E pg 365 **BS:** JLARC 76.

HEARD, John; b c1761, Albemarle Co; d Aft 1835 **RU:** Private, Served first under Capt Hairston. Served six tours of six weeks each **CEM:** Wright Family; GPS 36.97658, -80.21693; Pizarro off Rt 668; Floyd **GS:** U **SP:** No info **VI:** #S8709 pen commenced 26 Aug 1833 age 74, annual amount of $23.33 **P:** Y **BLW:** unk **RG:** unk **MK:** unk **PH:** unk **SS:** E pg 366; CG pg 1588 **BS:** 196 for John Mitchell.

HEATH, Henry; b 25 Oct 1753, Sussex Co; d 3 Apr 1797 **RU:** Captain, Served with Capt Bland's Co of Horse with his brother Howell, who was killed in battle **CEM:** Heath Family; GPS unk; See US Senate Doc 1938, serial 10448, vol 2; Prince George **GS:** U **SP:** (1779) Susanna Williams (c1753-1 Sep 1811) **VI:** Perhaps another person this name in rank of sergeant drew a pension and received a BLW. BLW indicates he d 1790, Prince George Co **P:** unk **BLW:** Y **RG:** unk **MK:** unk **PH:** unk **SS:** DAR Ancestor #A053934; BY pg 394, J- DAR Hatcher **BS:** JLARC 2.

HEATH, Jesse; b 1765; d 1850 **RU:** Private, Enl 25 Apr 1777 for 3 yrs in Capt Amos Emerson's Co, Prince George Co Militia **CEM:** Blandford; GPS 37.22433, -77.38604; 319 S Crater Rd; Petersburg City **GS:** Y **SP:** Agnes Peebles **VI:** Son of William (1731-1771) of Surry Co and Margaret (Bonner) Heath.

RU=Rank/Unit	CEM=Cemetery	GS=Gravestone	SP=Spousal Information
VI=Other Veteran Info	P=Pension	BLW=Bounty/Land Warrant	RG=Registered Grave
MK=SAR/DAR Marker	PH=Photo	SS=Service Source	BS=Burial Source

148

Plaque with his name is att to GS of Heartwell Peeples Heath; memorialized in the cemetery as bur elsewhere **P:** unk **BLW:** unk **RG:** N **MK:** N **PH:** unk **SS:** A pg 149; G pg 116 **BS:** 128 Heath; 196.

HEATH / HAYTH, Thomas; b 1750, Bedford Co; d 1821 **RU:** First Lieutenant, Served in 6th VA Regt, Cont Line **CEM:** Jones Family; GPS unk; Gladys Twp; Campbell **GS:** U **SP:** Mar (25 Dec 1772) Martha Gilbert **VI:** No further data **P:** unk **BLW:** unk **RG:** Y **MK:** N **PH:** unk **SS:** J-NSSAR 1993 Reg; E pg 366 **BS:** JLARC 1.

HEATON, James; b 12 Jan 1759, Sussex Co NJ; d 14 Jul 1824 **RU:** Lieutenant Surgeon, Served in Frederick Co Militia 4 Aug 1779 **CEM:** Ketoctin Baptist; GPS 39.15746, -77.74870; Ketoctin Church Rd, Purcellville; Loudoun **GS:** Y **SP:** 1) Hannah Rachel Smith (1762-1784) 2) Lydia Osburn (1778-1839) **VI:** No further data **P:** unk **BLW:** unk **RG:** Y **MK:** N **PH:** unk **SS:** E pg 366 **BS:** JLARC 1, 32; 25 pg 137; 196.

HEDGES, John; b 1755; d 4 Jun 1804 **RU:** Captain/Patriot, Served in Prince William Co Militia. Gave material aid to cause **CEM:** Hedges Family; GPS unk; Quantico Marine Base; Stafford **GS:** U **SP:** Elizabeth Worsham **VI:** No further data **P:** unk **BLW:** unk **RG:** unk **MK:** unk **PH:** unk **SS:** DAR Ancestor #A054114; SAR Ancestor #P-179107; AL Ct Bk pg 7 Prince William Co **BS:** JLARC 48; 03 pg 243.

HEISKELL (HISKILL), Peter; b 1760; d 4 Nov 1841 **RU:** Ensign, Served in Frederick Co Militia 4 Aug 1779 **CEM:** Trinity Episcopal; GPS 38.14917, -79.07521; 214 Beverley St; Staunton City **GS:** Y **SP:** 1) Susan Wetzel 2) Caroline Heiskell (__-1833) Later mar (-----) Brikenridge **VI:** No further data **P:** unk **BLW:** unk **RG:** unk **MK:** unk **PH:** Y **SS:** E pg 380 **BS:** JLARC 62; 196.

HELEH, Jean; b unk; d 1781 **RU:** Seaman, Served on "Ville de Paris" and died from Yorktown battle **CEM:** French Memorial; GPS 36.81944, -79.39933; Yorktown; York **GS:** U **SP:** No info **VI:** No further data **P:** unk **BLW:** unk **RG:** Y **MK:** unk **PH:** unk **SS:** J-Yorktown Historian **BS:** JLARC 1, 74.

HELM, Meridith Jr; b 19 Nov 1753, Frederick Co; d 12 Oct 1804 **RU:** Captain, Daniels Morgan's Riflemen. Also furnished supplies to cause. Frederick Co Militia 1 Apr 1783 **CEM:** Milburn Chapel; GPS 39.22360, -78.11360; Milburn Rd Rt 622, Stephenson; Frederick **GS:** Y **SP:** Frances Sanford Fowler **VI:** Son of Major Meridith & Margaret Ann (Neill) Helm. Styled Col after the War. Lived and d at "Belleville Farm", 4 mi fr Winchester, Frederick Co. Granted land in Ohio. Memorial for him at Rest United Methodist Church Cemetery, Frederick Co. Original stone was at Milburn Chapel Cemetery in Frederick Co. Repaired, moved to another cem at Milburn **P:** unk **BLW:** unk **RG:** N **MK:** N **PH:** unk **SS:** E pg 367 **BS:** 59 pg 145; 196.

HELM, Meridith Sr; b c1724; d 12 Jun 1804 **RU:** Patriot, Gave material aid to the cause **CEM:** Goose Creek; GPS 39.11250, -77.69527; Rt 722, Lincoln; Loudoun **GS:** U **SP:** Mar (1745) Calmes (-----) **VI:** No further data **P:** N **BLW:** N **RG:** unk **MK:** unk **PH:** unk **SS:** AL Ct Bk 8 **BS:** 196.

HELPHENSTINE (HELVESTON, HELPHENSTIEN), Peter; b 17 Jun 1724, Koln, Germany; d 11 May 1779 **RU:** Major, Was Capt in General Mulenburg's 8th Cont Line. Appt Maj Dec 1775 in 8th VA Regt **CEM:** Mt Hebron; GPS 39.10916, -78.09497; 305 E Boscawen St; Winchester City **GS:** U **SP:** Mar (3 Jul 1750, Germany) Catherine Berger **VI:** Son of Pieter & Mary (Biedermann) Helfenstien. Took ill in SC, furlough, d at home (Source 112). Name listed on NSDAR plaque in cemetery **P:** unk **BLW:** Y **RG:** Y **MK:** unk **PH:** unk **SS:** BY pg 350; J-NSSAR 1993 Reg **BS:** JLARC 1; 112; 196.

HEMPENSTALL, Abraham; b 1740, NJ; d 1783 **RU:** Ensign, Served in Augusta Co Militia **CEM:** Doe Hill; GPS 38.25976, -79.26629; Across St fr Doe Hill Methodist Ch Rt 654; Highland **GS:** U **SP:** Mar (soon after Mar 1775) Mary Peter d/o of Capt (------) & Mary (Lewis) Peter (__-1789 Greenbriar Co) **VI:** No further data **P:** unk **BLW:** unk **RG:** unk **MK:** unk **PH:** unk **SS:** CM Vol 1 pg 197 **BS:** JLARC 103.

HENDERSON, Alexander; b 2 Mar 1737, Glasglow, Scotland; d 22 Nov 1815 **RU:** Patriot, Was member of House of Burgesses & General Assembly of VA **CEM:** Henderson; GPS unk; Mountclair; Prince William **GS:** Y **SP:** Mar (19 Jan 1773, Fairfax Co) Sarah Moore (1752-Dec 1816) **VI:** Died in Dumfries. A plaque in cemetery with his story erected by the Montclair Bicentennial Commission 1976 **P:** N **BLW:** N **RG:** Y **MK:** Y **PH:** unk **SS:** H; I **BS:** 16 pg 17-8.

HENDERSON, David; b 1 Jan 1754; d 28 Jan 1838 **RU:** Midshipman Sailor Patriot, Had VA Sea Serv. Ent serv 1777. Served on Warship "Dragon". Provided bolt of canvas to cause **CEM:** Masonic

RU=Rank/Unit	CEM=Cemetery	GS=Gravestone	SP=Spousal Information
VI=Other Veteran Info	P=Pension	BLW=Bounty/Land Warrant	RG=Registered Grave
MK=SAR/DAR Marker	PH=Photo	SS=Service Source	BS=Burial Source

149

Cemetery; GPS 38.30198, -77.46142; 900 Charles St; Fredericksburg City **GS:** Y **SP:** No info **VI:** Sailor appl pen 12 Sep 1832 Spotsylvania Co age 78. Pen rec 28 Feb 1838. S5506 **P:** Y **BLW:** unk **RG:** Y **MK:** N **PH:** unk **SS:** C Vol 1 pg 11; K Vol 3 pg 292; CG Vol 2 pg 1600 **BS:** 11 pg 57-8.

HENDERSON, James; b c1739, Scotland; d 8 Nov 1819 **RU:** Patriot, Carried arms fr Richmond for 24th Regt **CEM:** Blendon; GPS 37.14110, -78.08030; Rt F656 & Rt 460 Nottoway CH Rd; Nottaway **GS:** Y **SP:** No info **VI:** GS indicates member of county for 60 yrs, thus arrived c1759 Amelia Co of which portion became Nottoway 1789 **P:** N **BLW:** N **RG:** unk **MK:** N **PH:** Y **SS:** G pg 96 **BS:** 196.

HENDERSON, James; b 1764; d 1818 **RU:** Private, Served in 9th & 15th Cont lines **CEM:** Bruton Parish Church; GPS 37.27127, -76.70248; 331 W Duke of Gloucester St; Williamsburg City **GS:** Y **SP:** Elizabeth (-----) **VI:** Was Reverend **P:** unk **BLW:** unk **RG:** unk **MK:** unk **PH:** Y **SS:** E pg 368; CD **BS:** 196.

HENDERSON, John; b 1740, Montgomery Co; d Dec 1812 **RU:** Captain, Commanded a co in Montgomery Co Militia. Commissioned Capt 4 Mar 1778 **CEM:** Henderson; GPS unk; Catawba Rd Rt 785 Blacksburg; Montgomery **GS:** U **SP:** Mary O'Brian Downard 1750-1834) **VI:** Son of George & Elizabeth (Moore) Henderson **P:** unk **BLW:** unk **RG:** unk **MK:** unk **PH:** unk **SS:** J- DAR Hatcher; E pg 368 **BS:** JLARC 2, 196.

HENINGER (HENEGAR) (HENNINGAR), Jacob; b c1763; d 26 Mar 1830 **RU:** Soldier, Was in Battle at Kings Mountain **CEM:** Greever; GPS 36.79250, -81.69860; Rt 1019 off Rt 11, Chilhwie; Smyth **GS:** Y **SP:** No info **VI:** No further data **P:** unk **BLW:** unk **RG:** N **MK:** N **PH:** unk **SS:** CV pg 121 **BS:** 97 pg 29.

HENKEL, Paul Rev; b 15 Dec 1754, Rowan Co, NC; d 17 Nov 1825 **RU:** Soldier, Served in Capt John Skidmore's Co, Greenbrier Co at Ft Hinkle **CEM:** St Martin's Lutheran; GPS 38.64480, -78.67124; 2235 River Rd, New Market; Shenandoah **GS:** Y **SP:** Elizabeth Nagley (1757-1843) **VI:** Son of Jacob (1732-1779) & Mary Barbara (Teter) (1734-1814) Henkle, a traveling Baptist reverend **P:** unk **BLW:** unk **RG:** unk **MK:** unk **PH:** unk **SS:** J- DAR Hatcher; G pg 514; DD **BS:** JLARC 2; 196.

HENLEY, James; b 19 Sep 1764; d 23 Jul 1832 **RU:** Private, Served in 1st Cont Line **CEM:** Cedar Grove; GPS 36.85860, -76.28310; 238 E Princess Anne Rd; Norfolk City **GS:** Y **SP:** Elizabeth (-----) (1781-1829) **VI:** Is listed as Capt on GS. Was not old enough to be capt in Rev War, therefore perhaps War of 1812 **P:** unk **BLW:** unk **RG:** unk **MK:** unk **PH:** unk **SS:** E pg 370 **BS:** 245.

HENLEY, Leonard; b 1748/49, James City Co; d 19 Nov 1798 **RU:** Sergeant/ Patriot, Was Quarter Master Sergeant, Capt John Belfield's Co, Col Theodoric Bland's 6th Troop, Light Dragoons. As patriot furnished two wagonloads wood and a gun to Kent Co Militia **CEM:** Cedar Grove; GPS 37.26140, -76.70720; Jct Rt 132 and Hunting Cove; Williamsburg City **GS:** U **SP:** Mar (31 Jan 1779) Elizabeth Dandridge (25 May 1749, New Kent Co-__) **VI:** No further data **P:** N **BLW:** N **RG:** unk **MK:** unk **PH:** unk **SS:** DAR Ancestor #A055043; G pg 472, 580 **BS:** AR pg 142.

HENNONE, Jean; b unk; d 1781 **RU:** Soldier, Served in Soissonnais Bn and died fr battle at Yorktown **CEM:** French Memorial; GPS 36.81944, -79.39933; Yorktown; York **GS:** U **SP:** No info **VI:** No further data **P:** unk **BLW:** unk **RG:** Y **MK:** unk **PH:** unk **SS:** J-Yorktown Historian **BS:** JLARC 1, 74.

HENRY, Didier; b unk; d 1781 **RU:** Seaman, Served on "Duc De Bourgogne" and died from Yorktown battle **CEM:** French Memorial; GPS 36.81944, -79.39933; Yorktown; York **GS:** U **SP:** No info **VI:** No further data **P:** unk **BLW:** unk **RG:** Y **MK:** unk **PH:** unk **SS:** J-Yorktown Historian **BS:** JLARC 1, 74.

HENRY, Isaac; b 1738; d 1829 **RU:** Private, Served in VA unit in Illinois **CEM:** Pittsylvania (Carter); GPS 38.49711, -77.31305; Manassas National Battlefield Park; Manassas City **GS:** U **SP:** Judith Carter d/o Landon Jr. & (-----) Carter **VI:** He was a doctor. Some historians indicate he was a Navy officer **P:** unk **BLW:** unk **RG:** unk **MK:** unk **PH:** unk **SS:** E pg 370 **BS:** 190 under cem name.

HENRY, James Jr; b 1762, Augusta Co; d 21 Mar 1828 **RU:** Private, Served in Capt Tate's Co, Augusta Co Militia **CEM:** New Providence Presbyterian; GPS 37.95130, -79.30250; 1208 New Providence Rd, Raphine; Rockbridge **GS:** U **SP:** Mar (13 Dec 1787 Augusta Co) Mary Berry (1862-1828) **VI:** Son of James & Mary (-----) Henry **P:** unk **BLW:** unk **RG:** unk **MK:** unk **PH:** unk **SS:** E pg 370 **BS:** JLARC 62; 196.

RU=Rank/Unit	CEM=Cemetery	GS=Gravestone	SP=Spousal Information
VI=Other Veteran Info	P=Pension	BLW=Bounty/Land Warrant	RG=Registered Grave
MK=SAR/DAR Marker	PH=Photo	SS=Service Source	BS=Burial Source

HENRY, Patrick; b 29 May 1739, Hanover Co; d 6 Jun 1799 **RU:** Colonel/Patriot, Col in command of 1st VA Regt of Foot Jul 1775-13 Feb 1776. Commander in chief of VA forces. Resigned 28 Feb 1776 **CEM:** Henry Family; GPS unk; Red Hill Plantation, 1250 Red Hill Rd, Brookneal; Charlotte **GS:** Y **SP:** Mar (1) in 1754 at wife's family's house Rural Plains to Sarah Shelton, b 1738, d 1775; (2) on 25 Oct 1777 to Dorothea Spotswood Dandridge, b 175, d 1831 **VI:** Son of John Henry & Sarah Windson. Best known for his "Give me liberty or give me death" speech. Attorney. House of Burgesses 1764-1765, 1st & 2nd Continental Congress. First Governor of Virginia. Died in Campbell Co. Daug, Ms. Dorothea Spotswood Winsto, age 76 of Linestone AL appl 13 Dec 1853 Limestone Co AL age 76. Rej due to no record according to War Office. R4898 **P:** Y **BLW:** unk **RG:** Y **MK:** unk **PH:** unk **SS:** J-NSSAR 1993 Reg, J-DAR Hatcher; K Vol I pg 296; CG Vol 2 pg 1607 **BS:** JLARC 1, 2; 196.

HENRY, William; b 1734, Hanover Co; d 1784 **RU:** Captain, Commanded a Co of minutemen. Wounded at Battle of Brandywine **CEM:** Winton Plantation; GPS unk; adj Winton Country Club, Clifford; Amherst **GS:** Y **SP:** 1) Lucy Taylor 2) Peggy McNair **VI:** Died in Fluvanna Co. Has a Vet Admin stone engraved "Lieutenant, Virginia Militia, Revolutionary War" **P:** unk **BLW:** unk **RG:** Y **MK:** unk **PH:** unk **SS:** B; Wm & Mary Qrtly, Vol 6 pg 189 **BS:** JLARC 1 ,4, 7, 46; 196.

HENSLEY, Samuel; b 1754, d 1841 **RU:** Soldier, Ent serv 1774 against Shawnee Indians. Ent serv again 1776 "on frontiers of VA" **CEM:** Hensley; GPS 36.64426, -82.71960; Sleepy Hollow Ln; Scott **GS:** U **SP:** 1) Eleanor Elliott 2) Margaret Crawford **VI:** Sol appl pen 20 Aug 1834 Washington Co. Formerly lived in Sullivan Co TN. S21278 **P:** Y **BLW:** unk **RG:** unk **MK:** unk **PH:** unk **SS:** J-NSSAR 2000; K Vol 3 pg 296; Reg CG Vol 2 pg 1608 **BS:** JLARC 76.

HERBERT, Pascow (Pasco); b 1741; d 21 May 1801 **RU:** Lieutenant, Served in VA State Navy. Had sea service on ship "Liberty" **CEM:** Herbert; GPS 39.01475, -76.35013; Off Armstrong Ln; Hampton City **GS:** U **SP:** Mary Jones **VI:** R43, also VA 1/2 pay (see N.A. Acc #837 VA State Navy, file for Pascow Herbert). Died in Elizabeth City Co **P:** Y **BLW:** unk **RG:** unk **MK:** unk **PH:** unk **SS:** BY pg 202; J- DAR Hatcher; K Vol 3 pg 298; L pg 200; CG Vol 2 pg 1610 **BS:** JLARC 2, 196.

HERBERT, William; b 1746 Ireland; d 24 Feb 1819 **RU:** Private, Served in Capt William Rummey's Co, Fairfax Co. Militia, c1776-1779 **CEM:** Christ Church Episcopal; GPS 38.80216, -77.05689; Wilkes St & Hamilton Ln; Alexandria City **GS:** Y **SP:** Mar (c1776 Alexandria) Sarah Fairfax Carlyle (4 Jan 1757-Jul 1827) d/o John & (-----) Carlyle **VI:** Merchant. Moved to VA in 1773. Provided horse to unit under Gen Lafayette's command & 700 lbs beef. First of two Commissioners of Taxes for Alexandria 1780. Justice of Hustings Ct. Alexandria 1781-2. Mayor Alexandria 1781-2. City Council member 1783-8. Secretary, Masonic Lodge No. 39. President, Bank of Alexandria. Death notice in the Alexandria Gazette 27 Feb 1819, pg 3 **P:** unk **BLW:** unk **RG:** Y **MK:** Y **PH:** unk **SS:** I; R pg 2, 9 **BS:** 2 pg 99; 20 pg 99; 196.

HEREFORD, John E; b 1725; d 8 Apr 1793 **RU:** Sergeant/Patriot, Gave material aid to cause **CEM:** Old Stone Methodist; GPS 39.11725, -77.56609; 168 W Cornwall St, Leesburg; Loudoun **GS:** Y **SP:** Margaret Ammon (1735 Loudoun Co-23 Oct 1809 Fauquier Co) **VI:** No further data **P:** unk **BLW:** unk **RG:** Y **MK:** N **PH:** unk **SS:** E pg 372; AL Ct Bk pg 30, 86 Loudoun Co **BS:** 25 pg 138.

HERMAIN, Jean; b unk; d 1781 **RU:** Soldier, Served in Touraine Bn and died fr battle at Yorktown **CEM:** French Memorial; GPS 36.81944, -79.39933; Yorktown; York **GS:** U **SP:** No info **VI:** No further data **P:** unk **BLW:** unk **RG:** Y **MK:** unk **PH:** unk **SS:** J-Yorktown Historian **BS:** JLARC 1, 74.

HERNDON, Edward Jr; b 1761; d 10 or 12 Nov 1837 **RU:** Private, Ent service 1781, and served as Assistant Quartermaster of VA Troops **CEM:** Laurel Hill, Nywood Farm; GPS unk; Rt 210 3.3 mi east of courthouse; Spotsylvania **GS:** U **SP:** No info **VI:** Probably son of Edward (1730-1799) and Mary (Duerson) Herndon. Was wounded in service and drew half-pay for it. Wife not named as predeceased him. S30478 **P:** Y **BLW:** unk **RG:** unk **MK:** unk **PH:** unk **SS:** K Vol 3 pg 299; CG pg 1611 **BS:** JLARC 2, 91.

HERNDON, Edward Sr; b 5 Mar 1730, Spotsylvania Co; d 3 Sep 1799 **RU:** Patriot, Was member of County Committee of Safety **CEM:** Gordon Herndon; GPS 38.15467, -77.65341; Rt 656 S off Rt 208, Post Oak; Spotsylvania **GS:** Y **SP:** Mar (c1754/55) Mary Duerson **VI:** No further data **P:** N **BLW:** N **RG:** unk **MK:** unk **PH:** unk **SS:** DD cites Force American Archives 4th series Vol 3 pg 1570 **BS:** 196.

RU=Rank/Unit	CEM=Cemetery	GS=Gravestone	SP=Spousal Information
VI=Other Veteran Info	P=Pension	BLW=Bounty/Land Warrant	RG=Registered Grave
MK=SAR/DAR Marker	PH=Photo	SS=Service Source	BS=Burial Source

151

HERNDON, William; b 1751; d 1823 **RU:** Private/Patriot, Served in VA 1st State Regt **CEM:** Belvoir House; GPS unk; Jct 608 E & 635; Spotsylvania **GS:** N **SP:** No info **VI:** No further data **P:** unk **BLW:** unk **RG:** Y **MK:** N **PH:** N **SS:** D pg 260; E pg 372 **BS:** 08 vol 1 pg 90-5.

HERON, James; b 1749; d 29 Sep 1801 **RU:** Captain, Served in Hazen's Regt in 1777 **CEM:** St John's Episcopal; GPS 37.53183, -77.41958; 2401 E Broad St; Richmond City **GS:** Y **SP:** Mar (11 Sep 1790) Sarah Taylor (25 Dec 1771-26 Dec 1811 in Richmond theatre fire). She also has headstone at St John's Church, Richmond. **VI:** No further data **P:** unk **BLW:** unk **RG:** N **MK:** N **PH:** unk **SS:** AP **BS:** 28 pg 454.

HERRING, Bethual (Bethuel Bethuard); b 1751, Sussex Co; d c1815 **RU:** Private/Patriot, Served in Capt William Herring's Co, Rockingham Co Militia. Gave material aid to cause **CEM:** Old Peaked Mountain; GPS 38.37113, -78.73416; 9843 Town Hall Rd, McGaheysville; Rockingham **GS:** U **SP:** Mar (16 Aug 1782) Mary Miller (__-c1800) **VI:** Son of Alexander (1708-1778) & Abigail (Harrison) (1710-1780) Herring. Name is on plaque in cemetery **P:** unk **BLW:** unk **RG:** Y **MK:** Y **PH:** unk **SS:** J-NSSAR 2000 Reg; AL Ct Bk II, pg 26, 37 Rockingham Co; DAR Chapter publication on Rev War soldiers in Rockingham Co pg 12 **BS:** JLARC 76.

HERRING, Leonard; b 1735; d 1805 **RU:** Patriot, Gave material aid to cause **CEM:** Old Peaked Mountain; GPS 38.37113, -78.73416; 9843 Town Hall Rd, McGaheysville; Rockingham **GS:** Y **SP:** Mar (1805 Rockingham Co) Anne Ervin d/o Benjamin & (-----) Ervin **VI:** Son of Alexander (1708-1778) & Abigail (Harrison) (1710-1780) Herring **P:** N **BLW:** N **RG:** Y **MK:** Y **PH:** unk **SS:** O pg 128; AL Ct Bk I pg 1, 7, 8 Rockbridge Co **BS:** 04; 196.

HERRING, William; b c1760; d 8 Oct 1812 **RU:** Captain, Served under Capt Cravens. Took oath as Capt in Militia. Served under Col Benjamin Harrison **CEM:** Old Peaked Mountain; GPS 38.37113, -78.73416; 9843 Town Hall Rd, McGaheysville; Rockingham **GS:** U **SP:** 1) Susannah Parham 2) Betsy T__) **VI:** No further data **P:** unk **BLW:** unk **RG:** Y **MK:** Y **PH:** unk **SS:** Court minutes 23 Oct. 1780; J-NSSAR 2000 Reg **BS:** JLARC 76.

HERRINGTON, William; b unk; d 1781 **RU:** Soldier, Served fr MA, killed in the battle at Yorktown **CEM:** Yorktown Victory Monument Tablet; GPS 38.28350, -78.54150; Yorktown; York **GS:** U **SP:** No info **VI:** No further data **P:** unk **BLW:** unk **RG:** unk **MK:** unk **PH:** unk **SS:** J-Yorktown Historian **BS:** JLARC 74.

HERVE, Guillaume; b unk; d 1781 **RU:** Seaman, Served on "Saint-Esprit" and died from Yorktown battle **CEM:** French Memorial; GPS 36.81944, -79.39933; Yorktown; York **GS:** U **SP:** No info **VI:** No further data **P:** unk **BLW:** unk **RG:** Y **MK:** unk **PH:** unk **SS:** J-Yorktown Historian **BS:** JLARC 1, 74.

HERVE, Jean; b unk; d 1781 **RU:** Seaman, Served on "Citoyen" and died from Yorktown battle **CEM:** French Memorial; GPS 36.81944, -79.39933; Yorktown; York **GS:** U **SP:** No info **VI:** No further data **P:** unk **BLW:** unk **RG:** Y **MK:** unk **PH:** unk **SS:** J-Yorktown Historian **BS:** JLARC 1, 74.

HERVE, Michel; b unk; d 1781 **RU:** Soldier, Served in Gatinais Bn and died fr battle at Yorktown **CEM:** French Memorial; GPS 36.81944, -79.39933; Yorktown; York **GS:** U **SP:** No info **VI:** No further data **P:** unk **BLW:** unk **RG:** Y **MK:** unk **PH:** unk **SS:** J-Yorktown Historian **BS:** JLARC 1, 74.

HESS, Jacob; b unk; d Mar 1788 **RU:** Private, Served in Capt Driesback's Co, Col Armand's Command, 26 Feb 1777 **CEM:** Old Christ Church Episcopal; GPS 38.80625, -77.04718; 118 N Washington St; Alexandria City **GS:** N **SP:** No info **VI:** Burial permit issued 6 Mar 1788 to his estate **P:** unk **BLW:** unk **RG:** N **MK:** N **PH:** unk **SS:** A pg 219 **BS:** 20 pg 149.

HEYDE (HIDY), Johann Henrich (John); b 1751, Germany; d Aft 21 Mar 1823 **RU:** Asst Drill Master, Served in PA. Enl Philadelphia 25 Jan 1776, 3rd VA Regt. Was at Valley Forge and was Assistant Drill Master there. **CEM:** Heyde; GPS unk; Rt 644, Blue Grass; Highland **GS:** U **SP:** Mar (27 Feb 1781) Christian Ann Trexler (1763 Northumberland Co PA-1836) d/o Peter (1727-1764) & Maria (Albrecht) Trexler **VI:** Arrived in USA a Johann Heinrich Heyde. Changed name to John Hidy **P:** unk **BLW:** unk **RG:** Y **MK:** Y **PH:** unk **SS:** J-NSSAR 1993 Reg; CD; CI, PA Archives, 5th series, 19 Feb Vol 2, pg 109, 947 **BS:** JLARC 1; 196.

HICKLE, Lewis; b 1751; d 1808 **RU:** Soldier, Served in VA Line. Also Capt Robinson's Co, Frederick Co Militia **CEM:** Fincastle Presbyterian; GPS 37.50017, -79.87558; 108 E Back St, Fincastle; Botetourt **GS:** N **SP:** Elizabeth Huber **VI:** Son appl 30 Apr 1855 Grainger Co TN. R4947. Will dated of 21 Mar 1823.

RU=Rank/Unit	CEM=Cemetery	GS=Gravestone	SP=Spousal Information
VI=Other Veteran Info	P=Pension	BLW=Bounty/Land Warrant	RG=Registered Grave
MK=SAR/DAR Marker	PH=Photo	SS=Service Source	BS=Burial Source

152

Name is on the SAR plaque at this cemetery and the monument to Rev War soldiers **P:** Y **BLW:** unk **RG:** Y **MK**: Y **PH:** N **SS:** J-NSSAR 1993 Reg, J- DAR Hatcher; AR Vol 2 pg 147; BW pg 479; CG Vol 2 pg 1622 **BS:** 196; JLARC 1, 2.

HICKMAN, Jacob; b 1765; d 24 Nov 1848 **RU:** Patriot, Gave material aid to the cause **CEM:** Mt Zion Methodist; GPS 37.66596, -79.46615; Btw Buffalo & Tinkersville; Rockbridge **GS:** Y **SP:** No info **VI:** No further data **P:** N **BLW:** N **RG:** N **MK:** N **PH:** unk **SS:** AL Certificate **BS:** 154 Rockbridge.

HICKOK, Ebenezer; b 02 Feb 1759, Stamford, CT; d Feb 1843 **RU:** Private, Served in CT Line. Ent ser 1775 in Fairfield, CT **CEM:** Fincastle Presbyterian; GPS 37.50017, -79.87558; 108 E Back St, Fincastle; Botetourt **GS:** N **SP:** Mar (Amherst Co) widow Jane Linn **VI:** He moved to Amherst Co in 1782. Appl 17 Oct 1832 Amherst Co. S5541. Name is on VASSAR plaque at cemetery **P:** Y **BLW:** unk **RG:** N **MK**: Y **PH:** N **SS:** K Vol 2 pg 303; CG Vol 2 pg 1623 **BS:** 196.

HICKS, Kimble; b 1746; d 2 Feb 1837 **RU:** Patriot, Gave material aid to the cause **CEM:** Sherman-Hicks Family, aka Liberty Farm; GPS unk; Paris; Fauquier **GS:** Y **SP:** Matilda (-----) Hicks **VI:** Son of Charles & Mary (Kimble) Hicks of Bucks Co, PA **P:** N **BLW:** N **RG:** N **MK:** N **PH:** unk **SS:** AL Ct Bk II pg 239 **BS:** 95 Liberty farm.

HIELDEN, (------); b unk; d 1781 **RU:** Soldier, Served in Royal Deaux Ponts Bn and died fr battle at Yorktown **CEM:** French Memorial; GPS 36.81944, -79.39933; Yorktown; York **GS:** U **SP:** No info **VI:** No further data **P:** unk **BLW:** unk **RG:** Y **MK:** unk **PH:** unk **SS:** J-Yorktown Historian **BS:** JLARC 1, 74.

HIGGINBOTHAM, James; b 25 Dec 1729; d 14 Mar 1813 **RU:** Colonel/Patriot, Was Maj in Amherst Co Militia. In 1778 promoted to Col in 9th VA Regt 1777-1780. Furnished part of clothing & beef for 16th Division **CEM:** Higginbotham Family; GPS 37.69140, -79.14280; Rt 617 N of jct with 761, Amherst; Amherst **GS:** N **SP:** Mar (30 May 1779) Rachel Campbell (1755-17 Apr 1805) **VI:** Son of Joseph Higginbotham. Widower at death. Surviving children appl pen which was rejected **P:** N **BLW:** unk **RG:** unk **MK:** unk **PH:** N **SS:** E pg 376; G pg 72; K Vol 3 pg 306; Order bk pg 498 **BS:** 196.

HIGGINS, Thomas; b unk; d 1781 **RU:** Soldier, Served fr NY, killed in the battle at Yorktown **CEM:** Yorktown Victory Monument Tablet; GPS 38.28350, -78.54150; Yorktown; York **GS:** U **SP:** No info **VI:** No further data **P:** unk **BLW:** unk **RG:** unk **MK:** unk **PH:** unk **SS:** J-Yorktown Historian **BS:** JLARC 74.

HIGHT, George; b 3 Jul 1755, King & Queen Co; d 21 Aug 1837 **RU:** Private, Ent serv Botetourt Co, Jan 1776. Volunteered serv against Cherokees under Capt Bilmore Aug 1777. Served in Col George Baylors Regt of Light Dragoons and Cont VA Line **CEM:** Mt Zion Methodist; GPS 37.66596, -79.46615; Btw Buffalo & Tinkersville; Rockbridge **GS:** Y **SP:** Mar (24 May 1782) Lovia Lunsford (24 Jun 1760-3 Jun 1843) (Find A Grave says d. 1840) **VI:** Moved age 8 (1763) Albemarle Co, then Amherst (1767), then 1776 Botetourt. Sol appl pen 3 Dec 1832. W19769 Rockbridge Co. Died in Nelson Co. Widow appl pen 3 Jun 1843. Source 101 has Haines Chapel, South Mountain Cem **P:** Y **BLW:** unk **RG:** unk **MK:** unk **PH:** Y **SS:** K Vol 3 pg 307; CD; CG Vol 2 pg 1630 **BS:** JLARC 2, 79,101.

HIGIE, Richard; b unk; d 1781 **RU:** Seaman, Served on "Auguste" and died from Yorktown battle **CEM:** French Memorial; GPS 36.81944, -79.39933; Yorktown; York **GS:** U **SP:** No info **VI:** No further data **P:** unk **BLW:** unk **RG:** Y **MK:** unk **PH:** unk **SS:** J-Yorktown Historian **BS:** JLARC 1, 74.

HILL, Amos; b unk; d 1781 **RU:** Soldier, Service unit not determined. Died fr battle at Yorktown **CEM:** Yorktown Victory Monument Tablet; GPS 38.28350, -78.54150; Yorktown; York **GS:** U **SP:** No info **VI:** No further data **P:** unk **BLW:** unk **RG:** unk **MK:** unk **PH:** unk **SS:** J-Yorktown Historian **BS:** JLARC 74.

HILL, Humphrey; b 2 Apr 1756; d 27 Jun 1841 **RU:** Soldier, Ent serv Middlesex Co. Served in VA Line **CEM:** Hill Family; GPS 37.93764, -77.55152; 5498 Mt Airy Dr, Mt Airy, Ruther Glen; Caroline **GS:** Y **SP:** 1) Mary Garlick (1771-1819) 2) Elizabeth Minor (1776-1833) **VI:** Sol appl pen 16 Jul 1832 Culpeper Co. S5530 **P:** Y **BLW:** N **RG:** unk **MK:** N **PH:** Y **SS:** K pg 308; CG pg 1635; CI Serv Record; served VA Line **BS:** 196.

HILL, James; b unk; d 1802 **RU:** Patriot, Gave material aid to cause **CEM:** Springfield; GPS unk; Abt 2 mi south of King William CH, on right side of Rt 621, leading fr Skyron to Palls; King William **GS:** N **SP:** Mildred Clopton **VI:** Formerly of "Porto Bello", located on Queens Creek, York Co VA. Moved to Springfield abt 1771 **P:** N **BLW:** N **RG:** Y **MK:** N **PH:** N **SS:** AL Ct Bk II pg 3, 9 York Co **BS:** 196.

RU=Rank/Unit	CEM=Cemetery	GS=Gravestone	SP=Spousal Information
VI=Other Veteran Info	P=Pension	BLW=Bounty/Land Warrant	RG=Registered Grave
MK=SAR/DAR Marker	PH=Photo	SS=Service Source	BS=Burial Source

HILL, James; b unk; d 1817 **RU:** Private, Served in Capt Thomas Hill's Co, Col Holt Richison's 7th VA Regt, Jun 1778 **CEM:** North End; **GPS** 36.77234, -80.73866; 101 Beaver Dam Rd, Hillsville; Carroll **GS:** N **SP:** Keziah (-----) (1761-3 Apr 1815) **VI:** No further data **P:** unk **BLW:** unk **RG:** N **MK:** N **PH:** N **SS:** E pg 377; CI Rev War Rolls **BS:** 123 pg 67; 196.

HILL, John Berry; b 1727; d 28 Dec 1817 **RU:** Patriot, Gave material aid to cause **CEM:** Stonewall Jackson Memorial; **GPS** 37.78128, -79.44604; 314 S Main St; Lexington City **GS:** U **SP:** Rachel Berry (___-28 Sep 1812) **VI:** No further data **P:** N **BLW:** N **RG:** unk **MK:** unk **PH:** N **SS:** CI record book Officers & Men **BS:** 196.

HILL, Nathaniel; b 1740; d 1808 **RU:** Soldier, Served in VA unit in Illinois **CEM:** Hill Family; **GPS** unk; Cub Creek Rd Rt 789, Tyro; Nelson **GS:** U **SP:** Mar (3 Sep 1767) Nanny Parrish (c1745, Goochland Co-1808) **VI:** No further data **P:** unk **BLW:** unk **RG:** unk **MK:** unk **PH:** unk **SS:** E pg 377 **BS:** JLARC 83.

HILL, Robert; b 10 Sep 1713, Dublin, Ireland; d 17 Aug 1778 **RU:** Soldier, Served in Capt Thomas Buford's Co, Bedford Co, at the Battle of Point Pleasant 1774 **CEM:** Tanyard-Barnard-Hill; **GPS** unk; Rocky Mount; Franklin **GS:** U **SP:** mar (12 Sep 1741 Chester Co, PA) Violett Linnes (1725-1808) **VI:** Son of Sinfield & Mary (Wilson) Hill. Name on a DAR plaque in cemetery that shows his service **P:** unk **BLW:** unk **RG:** unk **MK:** unk **PH:** unk **SS:** Z pg 125; BT **BS:** JLARC 20; 196.

HILL, Thomas; b 1745; d 5 Feb 1827 **RU:** Ensign, Ent serv 1779. Serv in 5th VA Regt 1778-9 **CEM:** Tanyard-Bernard-Hill; **GPS** unk; Rocky Mount; Franklin **GS:** U **SP:** Alianna Stranifer (c1756-15 Jun 1827) **VI:** Son of Robert (1713-1778) & Violet (Linus) (1725-1808) Hill. DAR plaque in cem. BLW issued 24 Aug 1789 #1429. Another BLW issued to brother James residing in Bedford Co on 6 Dec 1828 **P:** unk **BLW:** Y **RG:** Y **MK:** Y **PH:** unk **SS:** K pg 310; CG pg 1640; CI Rev War roll **BS:** JLARC 1, 2,18; 196.

HILL, Thomas M or H; b 1758; d 29 Mar 1815 **RU:** Patriot, Was member of the trustees of the town of Portsmouth 1783 **CEM:** Trinity Episcopal; **GPS** 36.83459, -76.30105; 500 Court St; Portsmouth City **GS:** Y **SP:** No info **VI:** No further data **P:** N **BLW:** N **RG:** N **MK:** N **PH:** unk **SS:** B gives service **BS:** 92 stone 64.

HILL, Violet (Linus); b 1725; d 1808 **RU:** Patriot, Gave material aid to the cause **CEM:** Tanyard-Bernard-Hill; **GPS** unk; Rocky Mount; Franklin **GS:** Y **SP:** Thomas Hill (1745-1827) **VI:** No further data **P:** N **BLW:** N **RG:** Y **MK:** N **PH:** unk **SS:** AL Ct Bk pg 33 **BS:** 80 vol 2 pg 151.

HILL, William; b unk; d 1800? **RU:** Private, Served in Capt Tate's Co, Augusta Co **CEM:** Hill Family; **GPS** unk; Cub Creek Rd Rt 789, Tyro; Nelson **GS:** U **SP:** Susanne Jacobs **VI:** No further data **P:** unk **BLW:** unk **RG:** unk **MK:** unk **PH:** unk **SS:** NSSAR Ancestor # P-181635; E pg 378 **BS:** JLARC 83.

HILLENBERG (HILLENBURG), Daniel; b 10 Sep 1752, Rohenfurth, Hesse-Kassel, Germany; d 19 Jun 1819 **RU:** unk, Serv listed in Wythe Co Historical Review, #18, Jul 1980, pub by Wythe Co Hist Soc **CEM:** Hillenberg; **GPS** unk; SW of Crockett?; Wythe **GS:** U **SP:** Mar (25 Mar 1787, Montgomery Co) Mary Barbara Shrader d/o John & Johannas (Christian) Shrader **VI:** Son of Christian & Anna Catherina (Sinninger) Hillenburg. Arrived Staten Island 24 Aug 1776. Was in British Army at Savannah; deserted with weapons and full pack. Family tradition is that he fought for American forces **P:** unk **BLW:** unk **RG:** unk **MK:** unk **PH:** unk **SS:** JLARC Rpt App B-2 pg 71 **BS:** JLARC 122.

HILTON, Samuel; b 1759; d 1852 **RU:** Private, Served in 3rd MD Regt **CEM:** Trinity United Methodist; **GPS** 39.13600, -77.00610; 2911 Cameron Mills Rd; Alexandria City **GS:** N **SP:** No info **VI:** No further data **P:** unk **BLW:** unk **RG:** N **MK:** N **PH:** N **SS:** AP MD roll **BS:** 126 vol 2 pg 157.

HILTZENBERGER, Francois; b unk; d 1781 **RU:** Soldier, Served in Royal Deaux Ponts Bn and died fr battle at Yorktown **CEM:** French Memorial; **GPS** 36.81944, -79.39933; Yorktown; York **GS:** U **SP:** No info **VI:** No further data **P:** unk **BLW:** unk **RG:** Y **MK:** unk **PH:** unk **SS:** J-Yorktown Historian **BS:** JLARC 1, 74.

HINKLE, Isaac; b 5 Dec 1754 Mocksville, Davie County, NC; d 1 Nov 1824 **RU:** Captain, Was corporal in WVA. Commanded a Co in Rockingham Co Militia 24 Sep 1781 **CEM:** Old Peaked Mountain; **GPS** 38.37113, -78.73416; 9843 Town Hall Rd, McGaheysville; Rockingham **GS:** U **SP:** Mar (13 Dec 1781) Mary Cunningham (1758, Chillicothe, Ross Co, Ohio-2 Mar 1819, Pendleton Co, WV) **VI:** Son of John

RU=Rank/Unit	CEM=Cemetery	GS=Gravestone	SP=Spousal Information
VI=Other Veteran Info	P=Pension	BLW=Bounty/Land Warrant	RG=Registered Grave
MK=SAR/DAR Marker	PH=Photo	SS=Service Source	BS=Burial Source

154

Justus (1706-1778) & Maria Magdelena (Eschmann) (1710-1798) Hinkel. Died in Riverton, Pendleton Co, WV. Though bur in WV, memorialized on DAR plaque in cemetery **P:** unk **BLW:** unk **RG:** Y **MK:** Y **PH:** unk **SS:** J-NSSAR 2000 Reg; AZ pg 230 **BS:** JLARC 76; 196.

HINKLE, Yost; b unk; d unk **RU:** Ensign, Served in Capt Isacc Hinkle's Co **CEM:** Old Peaked Mountain; GPS 38.37113, -78.73416; 9843 Town Hall Rd, McGaheysville; Rockingham **GS:** U **SP:** No info **VI:** Memorialized on DAR plaque in cemetery **P:** unk **BLW:** unk **RG:** Y **MK:** Y **PH:** unk **SS:** J-NSSAR 2000 Reg; NSSAR Ancestor # P-182116 **BS:** JLARC 76.

HIPKINS, John; b unk; d 1804 **RU:** Partiot, Gave material aid to the cause **CEM:** Emmanuel Episcopal; GPS unk; US 301, Port Conway; King George **GS:** N **SP:** Elizabeth Pratt (1754-1829) **VI:** His name is on a memorial plaque at the Port Royal Church at the Emmanuel Cemetery **P:** unk **BLW:** unk **RG:** Y **MK:** N **PH:** N **SS:** AL Ct Bk I pg 5 **BS:** 64 pg 15.

HITE, Isaac; b 1758; d 24 Nov 1836 **RU:** Ensign, Served in VA Line. Ent Serv Frederick Co 1780 **CEM:** Old Hite Farm; GPS unk; Long Meadows, Middletown; Frederick **GS:** U **SP:** Ann T__) Still living in 1844 **VI:** Sol appl pen 23 Jun 1828 Frederick Co. S8714. Recd BLW #189-200 **P:** Y **BLW:** Y **RG:** Y **MK:** unk **PH:** unk **SS:** J-NSSAR 1993 Reg; BY; CG Vol 2 pg 1656 **BS:** JLARC 1.

HITE, Isaac; b 12 May 1723, Perkiomen Creek, PA; d 18 Sep 1795 **RU:** Patriot, Approved 25 Oct 1775 in Frederick Co for reimbursement for provisions he provided. Performed public service as Justice of Frederick Co **CEM:** Hite Family; GPS unk; Middletown; Frederick **GS:** Y **SP:** Mar (12 Apr 1745) Eleanor Eltinge (29 Apr 1724, Kingston, NY-10 Nov 1792; Middletown, Frederick Co) **VI:** Son of Joseph (__-1761) & (-----) Hite **P:** N **BLW:** N **RG:** Y **MK:** N **PH:** unk **SS:** Z pg 78; DD cites Norris History of the Lower Shenandoah Valley pg 136 **BS:** 113 (see Cem); 196.

HITE, Julius; b 10 Oct 1756, Sussex Co; d 2 Dec 1851 **RU:** Corporal, Served in Cont & VA Line. Lived in Sussex Co at enl. Served in Col Henry Lee's Legion in 1783 **CEM:** Hite Family; GPS unk; Forksville; Lunenburg **GS:** Y **SP:** Agnes Land of Sussex Co. **VI:** Wrote to Washington DC abt war penson. Walked all the way to Washington to collect pension in silver, then walked all the way back. Sol appl pen 4 Jul 1832 Lunenburg Co age 73, a res of Oak Grove. S18024. BLW #12223-130-8 May 1794 **P:** Y **BLW:** Y **RG:** unk **MK:** unk **PH:** unk **SS:** G pg 649-650; J- DAR Hatcher; CG Vol 2 pg 1656 **BS:** 196; JLARC 2.

HITT, Nimrod (Nimrods); b 21 Jul 1765, Germantown, Fauquier Co; d 17 Sep 1825 **RU:** Soldier, Served in VA unit in Illinois **CEM:** Miller; GPS unk; Rt 248 in Harris Hollow, Washington; Rappahannock **GS:** Y **SP:** Never mar **VI:** Died in Culpeper Co **P:** unk **BLW:** unk **RG:** Y **MK:** N **PH:** unk **SS:** E pg 381 **BS:** 33.

HITT, Peter; b 1755; d 31 Aug 1802 **RU:** Private?, Served in VA Line. Ent serv Fauquier Co 1777 **CEM:** Hitt family; GPS unk; Rt 645; Fauquier **GS:** Y **SP:** Mar (Apr 1783 Fauquier Co) Hannah (-----) (__-1846 Fauquier Co) **VI:** Son of John & Sarah (Pace) Hitt. Widow appl pen 7 Sep 1841 Fauquier Co age 78. F-W7732 R1291 **P:** Y **BLW:** unk **RG:** Y **MK:** N **PH:** Y **SS:** K pg 313; CG Vol 2 pg 1656; Germanna Record No 1 **BS:** 19 pg 88.

HIX, James; b unk; d 1781 **RU:** Soldier, Served fr MA, killed in the battle at Yorktown **CEM:** Yorktown Victory Monument Tablet; GPS 38.28350, -78.54150; Yorktown; York **GS:** U **SP:** No info **VI:** No further data **P:** unk **BLW:** unk **RG:** unk **MK:** unk **PH:** unk **SS:** J-Yorktown Historian **BS:** JLARC 74.

HIXON, Timothy; b 1730, Hunterdon Co, NJ; d Sep 1822 **RU:** Captain, Took oath as Capt in Loudoun Co 13 Oct 1782. Rec to command a Co in 1st Battalion of Militia 10 Feb 1783 **CEM:** Hixon Family; GPS unk; Check property records for home place as burial site; Loudoun **GS:** Y **SP:** Mar (c1762) Rachel Lacey (1735 Essex, NJ- 1786 Leesburg) **VI:** Son of William (1647-1736) & Mary (Patterson) Hixon **P:** unk **BLW:** unk **RG:** N **MK:** N **PH:** unk **SS:** E pg 381; DD; BY **BS:** SAR Appl.

HOAGON, Cyprien; b unk; d 1781 **RU:** Seaman, Served on "Saint-Esprit" and died from Yorktown battle **CEM:** French Memorial; GPS 36.81944, -79.39933; Yorktown; York **GS:** U **SP:** No info **VI:** No further data **P:** unk **BLW:** unk **RG:** Y **MK:** unk **PH:** unk **SS:** J-Yorktown Historian **BS:** JLARC 1, 74.

HOBBS, Ezekiel; b 1762; d 13 Jun 1835 **RU:** Soldier, Served in VA Line. Ent serv Washington Co **CEM:** Hobbs; GPS unk; North Fork, Holston River; Washington **GS:** U **SP:** Elizabeth Lilley (a Hardy Lilley signed mar bond with sol 27 Jul 1803 Washington Co) (c1785-__) **VI:** Was Reverend. Sol appl pen 6 Oct 1834 Washington Co age 70. Widow appl pen 28 Jun 1853 & 24 Mar 1855 age 70. W8940. Recd

RU=Rank/Unit	CEM=Cemetery	GS=Gravestone	SP=Spousal Information
VI=Other Veteran Info	P=Pension	BLW=Bounty/Land Warrant	RG=Registered Grave
MK=SAR/DAR Marker	PH=Photo	SS=Service Source	BS=Burial Source

155

BLW #26632-160-55. **P:** Y **BLW:** Y **RG:** unk **MK:** unk **PH:** unk **SS:** K Vol 3 pg 314; CG Vol 2 pg 1659 **BS:** JLARC 4,34,80; 80 cem #6

HOBBS, Vincent; b 1720, Dorchester, Dorest, England; d unk **RU:** Private, Served in Dunsmore's War of 1774 at Point Pleasant fr Fincastle Co under Capt Joseph Cloyd **CEM:** Hobbs family, also called Debusk Family; GPS unk; Dryden; Lee **GS:** Y **SP:** No info **VI:** Plaque on GS, DAR marker **P:** unk **BLW:** unk **RG:** N **MK:** Y **PH:** unk **SS:** G pg 216; CP Dunmore's War **BS:** 196; Email Sep 09.

HOBSON (HOPSON), Joseph Calip/Caleb; b unk; d 1814 **RU:** First Lieutenant, Served in Capt Thomas Posey's Co, Col Morgan's picked riflemen. Promoted to 1st Lt 28 Nov 1776. Resigned 20 May 1778 **CEM:** Old Hobson; GPS unk; Blenheim, nr Balleville; Powhatan **GS:** Y **SP:** Pheobe Brackett **VI:** No further data **P:** unk **BLW:** unk **RG:** N **MK:** N **PH:** unk **SS:** E pg 381 **BS:** 187.

HOFF, Lewis; b c1738; d 29 May 1803 **RU:** Patriot, Filed claim 25 Oct 1775, Frederick Co, for gun carriage he gave to Dunmore Co Militia **CEM:** Mt Hebron; GPS 39.10916, -78.09497; 305 E Boscawen St; Winchester City **GS:** Y **SP:** Susanna Catherine Fortney **VI:** No further data **P:** N **BLW:** N **RG:** N **MK:** N **PH:** Y **SS:** Z pg 78 **BS:** 50 pg 53; 196.

HOFFMAN, Andre; b unk; d 1781 **RU:** Soldier, Served in Royal Deaux Ponts Bn and died fr battle at Yorktown **CEM:** French Memorial; GPS 36.81944, -79.39933; Yorktown; York **GS:** U **SP:** No info **VI:** No further data **P:** unk **BLW:** unk **RG:** Y **MK:** unk **PH:** unk **SS:** J-Yorktown Historian **BS:** JLARC 1, 74.

HOGE, Edward; b unk; d 1782 **RU:** Patriot, Gave material aid to the cause **CEM:** Old Opequon Church; GPS 39.82237, -78.11412; 217 Opequon Church Ln, Kernstown; Frederick **GS:** Y **SP:** Elizabeth Brown (__ Ireland 1754-14 Apr 1844) **VI:** Son of James & Agnes (Crawford) Hoge **P:** N **BLW:** N **RG:** Y **MK:** N **PH:** unk **SS:** AL Ct Bk, pg 8 **BS:** 59 pg 153; 196.

HOGE, James; b 4 Jul 1706, PA; d 2 Jun 1795 **RU:** Patriot, Gave material aid to cause **CEM:** Old Opequon Church; GPS 39.82237, -78.11412; 217 Opequon Church Ln, Kernstown; Frederick **GS:** Y **SP:** 1) Agnes Crawford (14 Apr 1700-1743) 2) Nancy Griffith **VI:** Son of William (1660 Scotland-Aug 1749, Kernstown) & Barbara (Hume,) (1670 Scotland-1745) Hoge **P:** N **BLW:** N **RG:** unk **MK:** unk **PH:** unk **SS:** Al Ct Bk pg 5, 16, 22 **BS:** 196.

HOGE, James; b 22 Jan 1742; d 8 Apr 1812 **RU:** Private, Served in Capt Mayes Co, Montgomery Co Militia **CEM:** Sunnyside; GPS unk; Btw Radford and Dublin at Old Joseph Howe place, Back Creek; Pulaski **GS:** Y **SP:** Mar (21 Jan 1768) Elizabeth Howe (10 May 1750-1804) **VI:** No further data **P:** unk **BLW:** unk **RG:** unk **MK:** unk **PH:** unk **SS:** DAR #A056515; G pg 238 **BS:** 196.

HOGE, William; b unk; d 1842 **RU:** Corporal, Served in 7th,11th & 15th Cont Lines **CEM:** Goose Creek; GPS 39.11250, -77.69527; Rt 722, Lincoln; Loudoun **GS:** Y **SP:** No info **VI:** No further data **P:** unk **BLW:** unk **RG:** Y **MK:** N **PH:** unk **SS:** C pg 243; E pg 38 **BS:** 25 pg 144.

HOGE, William; b c1727; d 1815 **RU:** Corporal/Patriot, Gave material aid to cause **CEM:** Back Creek Quaker, aka Gainesboro United Methodist; GPS 39.27861, -78.25694; 166 Siler Ln, Gainesboro; Frederick **GS:** Y **SP:** mar (16 Jun 1795 Frederick Co by Rev Alexander Balmain) Rachel Steel **VI:** No further data **P:** unk **BLW:** unk **RG:** Y **MK:** N **PH:** unk **SS:** E pg 383; AL Ct Bk pg 10 Frederick Co **BS:** 59 pg 153.

HOGE (HOGG), James Sr; b 4 Jul 1706, PA; d 2 Jun 1795 **RU:** Patriot, Gave material aid to the cause **CEM:** Old Opequon Church; GPS 39.82237, -78.11412; 217 Opequon Church Ln, Kernstown; Frederick **GS:** Y **SP:** 1) Agnes Crawford (14 Apr 1700, Minnigaff, Kirkcudbright, Scotland-1743 VA) 2) Nancy Griffith **VI:** Son of William (1660-1749) & Barbara (Hume) (1670-1745) Hoge. Died in Winchester **P:** N **BLW:** N **RG:** N **MK:** N **PH:** unk **SS:** AL Ct bk pg 5, 16 **BS:** AS DAR report; 196.

HOGG (HOGE), James Jr; b 27 Jan 1742; d 8 Apr 1812 **RU:** Private, Served in Capt Maye's Co, Montgomery Co Militia **CEM:** Sunnyside; GPS unk; Btw Radford and Dublin at Old Joseph Howe place, Back Creek; Pulaski **GS:** U **SP:** Elizabeth Howe (11 May 1751-11 Jul 1835) d/o Samuel Joseph (1720-1794) & Eleanor (Dunbar) (1730-1790) Howe **VI:** No further data **P:** unk **BLW:** unk **RG:** unk **MK:** unk **PH:** unk **SS:** J- DAR Hatcher; G pg 237 **BS:** JLARC 2; 196.

RU=Rank/Unit	CEM=Cemetery	GS=Gravestone	SP=Spousal Information
VI=Other Veteran Info	P=Pension	BLW=Bounty/Land Warrant	RG=Registered Grave
MK=SAR/DAR Marker	PH=Photo	SS=Service Source	BS=Burial Source

HOGSHEAD, David Jr; b c1761; d 1814 **RU:** Private/Patriot, Gave material aid to cause **CEM:** Hogshead Family; GPS unk; Off Rt 736 btw Rts 42 & 250, N of Jennings Gap; Augusta **GS:** Y **SP:** No info **VI:** No further data **P:** unk **BLW:** unk **RG:** N **MK:** N **PH:** unk **SS:** E pg 384; AL Cert Aubusta Co **BS:** 36 pg 73; 196.

HOGSHEAD, Michael; b unk; d 1818 **RU:** Patriot, Gave material aid to cause **CEM:** Hogshead Family; GPS unk; Off Rt 736 btw Rts 42 & 250, N of Jennings Gap; Augusta **GS:** Y **SP:** No info **VI:** No further data **P:** N **BLW:** N **RG:** N **MK:** N **PH:** unk **SS:** E pg 384; AL Cert Augusta Co **BS:** 36 pg 72-3; 196.

HOLKER, John; b 1743, England; d Jun 1820 **RU:** Patriot, Sent to USA during the Rev War c1778 by Govt of Louis XVI, or rather by Beaumarchais, to inquire into probability of the success of our armies against England. Favorable report and treaty made bet Louis and USA **CEM:** Stone Chapel Presbyterian; GPS 39.22610, -78.01060; Old Charles Town Rd, Berryville; Clarke **GS:** U **SP:** 1) (-----) 2) (-----) 3) Mrs. Nancy Davis (Stackpole) Stillman of Boston MA **VI:** Son of Jean and (-----) Holker of France. John Holker became Consul General of France & agent of Royal Marine. Brought letters fr Benjamin Franklin to Robert Morris and Congress. Died in Springsberry, Clarke Co. Originally bur in holy ground in Winchester, but reinterred in Autumn 1904 to "Old Chapel" Clarke Co **P:** N **BLW:** N **RG:** unk **MK:** N **PH:** unk **SS:** CD **BS:** 196.

HOLLADAY, Joseph; b c1726, Spotsylvania Co; d 24 Jul or 23 Sep 1785 **RU:** Patriot, Was inspector of tobacco and also gave material aid to cause in 1781 **CEM:** Elmwood; GPS unk; Rt 614; Spotsylvania **GS:** N **SP:** Elizabeth Lewis d/o Harry & (-----) Lewis **VI:** Son of John (__-Nov 1742) & Elizabeth (-----) Holladay of Spotsylvania Co. Will proved 4 Apr 1787 **P:** N **BLW:** N **RG:** Y **MK:** N **PH:** N **SS:** D pg 857 **BS:** 09 Part 2.

HOLLADAY, Lewis; b 1761; d 1842 **RU:** Lieutenant, Served through Rev War. Commissioned Lt of Spotsylvania Co Militia by the VA Committee of Safety, 5 Oct 1775. In 1785 & 1787 appointed Capt by Govrs Henry & Randolph, & Maj in 1793 by Governor Lee **CEM:** Holladay Family; GPS unk; Bellefont House; Fredericksburg City **GS:** Y **SP:** No info **VI:** Appointed Coroner in 1793, having previously been a Justice of Spotsylvania Co in 1790. Was Sheriff of the county, Justice and Overseer of the Poor, Farmer and planter **P:** unk **BLW:** unk **RG:** Y **MK:** unk **PH:** unk **SS:** AR vol 2 pg 161; J-NSSAR 2000 Reg **BS:** 08 JLARC 76.

HOLLADAY, Lewis; b 22 May 1751, Spotsylvania Co; d 20 Oct 1820 **RU:** Major, Served in VA troops through Rev War. Appointed Maj 1793 by VA Gov Light Horse Harry Lee **CEM:** Bellefonte; GPS unk; Leiston; Spotsylvania **GS:** Y **SP:** Mar (15 Mar 1774) Elizabeth Lewis Littlepage (9 Oct 1732 Spotsylvania-1809) **VI:** Son of Capt Joseph & Ann Elizabeth (Lewis) Holladay. Sheriff of Spotsylvania Co **P:** unk **BLW:** unk **RG:** unk **MK:** Y **PH:** unk **SS:** BZ **BS:** 196.

HOLLAND, Nathaniel; b c1760; d 4 Jan 1838 **RU:** Private, Served in Northampton Co Militia **CEM:** Poplar Hill; GPS unk; Rt 631, Cherrystone; Northampton **GS:** Y **SP:** mar (20 Dec 1788) Susan Bryan (c1771-24 Dec 1843) d/o Henry & (-----) Bryan (__-1788) **VI:** Died age 78 **P:** unk **BLW:** unk **RG:** Y **MK:** N **PH:** unk **SS:** J-NSSAR 1993 Reg; E pg 385 **BS:** JLARC 1; 42 pg 40.

HOLLAND, Richard; b 1755, Prince Edward Co; d 1820 **RU:** Captain, Served in Capt Walker's Regt in battle of Guilford CH, NC 1779. Was Capt in Prince Edward Co Militia, Aug 1779, serving until end of war **CEM:** Old Walker Home; GPS unk; 5 mi N of Pamplin on Rt 600, then .4 mi W on Rt 627, then .4 mi NW on Rt 628; Appomattox **GS:** U **SP:** mar Capt Walker's widow at the end of the war after 2 yrs of courtship **VI:** No further data **P:** unk **BLW:** unk **RG:** Y **MK:** Y **PH:** unk **SS:** G pg 298 **BS:** JLARC 33; 196.

HOLLAND, Thomas; b 2 Feb 1764, Bedford Co; d 1 Jan 1816 or 1842 **RU:** Corporal, Served in 3rd, 4th, 5th Cont Line **CEM:** Holland Family; GPS unk; Rt 616 nr HancockCem; Franklin **GS:** Y **SP:** 1) Lydia Meador 2) Sally Gilbert **VI:** No further data **P:** unk **BLW:** unk **RG:** Y **MK:** N **PH:** unk **SS:** E pg 385 **BS:** 82 pg 174.

HOLLANDSWORTH, Thomas; b 1740; d 1842 **RU:** Private/Patriot, Served in Capt John Cunningham's Co, Lt Col Abraham Penn's Regt. Took oath of allegiance Henry Co 1777 **CEM:** Blackberry Creek Private; GPS unk; Bassett; Henry **GS:** U **SP:** Susannah Mayze **VI:** No further data **P:** unk **BLW:** unk **RG:** Y **MK:** unk **PH:** unk **SS:** J-NSSAR 1993 Reg; DM pg 72-73 **BS:** JLARC 1.

RU=Rank/Unit	CEM=Cemetery	GS=Gravestone	SP=Spousal Information
VI=Other Veteran Info	P=Pension	BLW=Bounty/Land Warrant	RG=Registered Grave
MK=SAR/DAR Marker	PH=Photo	SS=Service Source	BS=Burial Source

157

HOLLENBACH (HOLLENBECK), Daniel; b unk; d 11 Oct 1808 **RU:** Ensign/Patriot, Was acting wagonmaster for militia 27 Oct 1775 in Frederick Co. Served in 12th Cont Line in Dec 1776. Resigned as Ens Aug 1777. **CEM:** Mt Hebron; GPS 39.10916, -78.09497; 305 E Boscawen St; Winchester City **GS:** Y **SP:** No info **VI:** He was fr Harpers Ferry when he d in Winchester **P:** N **BLW:** N **RG:** Y **MK:** N **PH:** N **SS:** E pg 386; Z pg 79 **BS:** 196.

HOLLIDAY, Israel Ellsworth; b 1750 or 1751, Simsbury Twp, Hartford Co, CT; d Aft 1832 **RU:** Soldier, Served in Cont & VT Line, also Green Mountain Boys. Ent serv Rutland Co, VT **CEM:** Dranesville United Methodist Church; GPS 39.00240, -77.35082; 11720 Sugarland Rd, Dranesville; Fairfax **GS:** U **SP:** Mar (1790) Ann Bennett (1768 Fairfax Co-__) **VI:** Sol appl pen 15 Oct 1832, Fairfax Co. S10856 **P:** Y **BLW:** unk **RG:** unk **MK:** N **PH:** unk **SS:** K Vol 3 pg 320; CG Vol 2 pg 1681 **BS:** JLARC 4,14, 28.

HOLLOWAY, Daniel; b c1761; d 1824 **RU:** Patriot, On 25 Feb 1782 recd reimbursement for property impressed or taken for public use during war period **CEM:** Shockoe Hill; GPS 37.55190, -77.43170; 4th & Hospital Sts; Richmond City **GS:** Y **SP:** No info **VI:** No further data **P:** N **BLW:** N **RG:** N **MK:** N **PH:** unk **SS:** G pg 85; Brunswick Co Ct order Bk #13 **BS:** 57 pg 20.

HOLLOWAY, George; b 1760, England; d 1810 **RU:** Private, Served in Capt Steven's Co, 6th and 10th Regt Cont Lines for duration of War **CEM:** Holloway Family; GPS unk; Orange; Orange **GS:** U **SP:** 1) Mar (c1770) Martha Hall 2) Mar (1785) Frances Tiller (1762, Culpeper-1820, Clark Co, KY) **VI:** Elizabeth Holloway, heir in law recd BLW #3357 of 200 acres **P:** unk **BLW:** Y **RG:** N **MK:** N **PH:** unk **SS:** N pg 1259; NSSAR Ancestor # P-183776 **BS:** AS DAR report.

HOLMAN, John; b 21 Apr 1757; d 13 Jan 1852 **RU:** Private, Served in VA Line. Ent serv Cumberland Co **CEM:** Cotton Town; GPS unk; Holman Square; Cumberland **GS:** U **SP:** Mar (1784) Anne Wright (1766-18 Feb 1833) **VI:** JP for Cumberland Co for several yrs. Sol appl 23 Feb 1850 Cumberland Co. S8738 **P:** Y **BLW:** unk **RG:** unk **MK:** N **PH:** unk **SS:** J- DAR Hatcher; CG Vol 2 pg 1686 **BS:** JLARC 2.

HOLMAN, William Jr; b 1753; d 1776 **RU:** Ensign, Served in 9th Cont Line, 13 Mar 1776 **CEM:** Holman Family; GPS unk; Rt 645; Goochland **GS:** Y **SP:** No info **VI:** No further data **P:** unk **BLW:** unk **RG:** N **MK:** N **PH:** unk **SS:** E pg 387 **BS:** 46 pg 167.

HOLMAN, William Sr; b 1725; d 1796 **RU:** Patriot, Gave material aid to the cause **CEM:** Holman Family; GPS unk; Rt 645; Goochland **GS:** Y **SP:** 1) mar (by 30 Nov 1763) Jean Martin 2) 31 Aug 1766) Susannah Thompson 3) (1766) Becky Woodward. **VI:** No further data **P:** N **BLW:** N **RG:** N **MK:** N **PH:** unk **SS:** AL Ct Bk lt pg 2, 6 **BS:** 46 pg 167.

HOLMES, Hugh; b unk; d 1825 **RU:** Patriot, Performed public service as Judge **CEM:** Mt Hebron; GPS 39.10916, -78.09497; 305 E Boscawen St; Winchester City **GS:** Y **SP:** Mar (1797) Elizabeth Thomas **VI:** On chart of RW soldiers at Mt Hebron Cem **P:** N **BLW:** N **RG:** N **MK:** N **PH:** unk **SS:** BT: DAR Rev War chart I listing patriot burials in cemetery files **BS:** 119 chart.

HOLSINGER, Micheal; b 1740, Germany; d Aug 1819 **RU:** Private, Served in Augusta Co 1776-78 under Capt Reuben Harrison. In 1778 served fr Rockingham Co under Capt Joseph (Josiah) Harrison. Was listed as "Vocher" **CEM:** Holsinger Family; GPS 38.61139, -78.76164; 2805 Holsinger Rd, Broadway; Rockingham **GS:** Y **SP:** Barbara (-----) **VI:** No further data **P:** unk **BLW:** unk **RG:** Y **MK:** N **PH:** unk **SS:** BC pg 46; AK Sep 09; BY **BS:** 4.

HONAKER, Henry S Sr; b 10 Feb 1756, Philadelphia, PA; d 16 Sep 1830 **RU:** Private, Served in Capt Buck's Co, Dunmore Co Militia **CEM:** Honaker; GPS unk; Draper; Pulaski **GS:** U **SP:** 1) Mar (18 Jul 1785) Anna Baker 2) (Wythe Co) Edith Smith **VI:** Son of Hans Jacob & Maria (Goetz) Honaker. Died in Wythe Co **P:** unk **BLW:** unk **RG:** unk **MK:** unk **PH:** unk **SS:** E pg 389; J- DAR Hatcher **BS:** 196; JLARC 2.

HONAKER, John; b 1755, Philadelphia, PA; d 1786 **RU:** Private, Served in Capt John Bright's Co, Col Nichols City Guard of Philadelphia, Feb 1777 **CEM:** Richardson Family; GPS 38.95750, -78.29610; 1.5 mi fr entrance to GW National Forest, Rt 678 nr Fortsmouth Vol Fire Dept; Warren **GS:** U **SP:** No info **VI:** Son of Hans Jacob (1718-1796) & Maria (Goetz/Gotz) Honaker **P:** unk **BLW:** unk **RG:** unk **MK:** unk **PH:** unk **SS:** AP Muster Roll PA Archives **BS:** 196.

RU=Rank/Unit   CEM=Cemetery   GS=Gravestone   SP=Spousal Information
VI=Other Veteran Info   P=Pension   BLW=Bounty/Land Warrant   RG=Registered Grave
MK=SAR/DAR Marker   PH=Photo   SS=Service Source   BS=Burial Source

158

HONAKER, HONEGGER, Hans Jacob; b 24 Jul 1718, Hinwil, outside Zurich, Switzerland; d 10 May 1796 **RU:** Patriot, Gave material aid to cause **CEM:** Honaker; GPS unk; Draper; Pulaski **GS:** U **SP:** 1) Maria Goetz 2) Anna Bleyer (1726-1749) **VI:** Son of Hans Jacob & Elsbeth (Bosshart) Honegger. Carpenter. Indentured servant. Arrived HMS Crown in Phila. 30 Aug 1749. Freedom dues were horse and suit. Died in Wythe Co **P:** N **BLW:** N **RG:** unk **MK:** unk **PH:** unk **SS:** AL Ct bk pg 2,17 Shenandoah Co **BS:** 196.

HONORE, Jean; b unk; d 1781 **RU:** Soldier, Served in Bourbonnais Bn and died fr battle at Yorktown **CEM:** French Memorial; GPS 36.81944, -79.39933; Yorktown; York **GS:** U **SP:** No info **VI:** No further data **P:** unk **BLW:** unk **RG:** Y **MK:** unk **PH:** unk **SS:** J Yorktown Historian **BS:** JLARC 1, 74.

HOOE, Bernard; b 1740; d 1825 **RU:** Captain, Commanded a co in Prince William Co Militia 1777-1778 **CEM:** Hooe Family; GPS 38.80555, -77.53451; Chinn Ridge, Manassas National Battlefield Park; Manassas City **GS:** Y **SP:** Eleanor Buchanan Briscoe **VI:** Died in Prince William Co **P:** unk **BLW:** unk **RG:** Y **MK:** Y **PH:** Y **SS:** E pg 369; G pg 473 **BS:** 16 pg 184.

HOOE, Gerard (Garrard); b 14 Sep 1733; d 29 Sep 1785 **RU:** Patriot, Gave 1300 #, then 1000 # of beef to cause **CEM:** St Paul's Episcopal; GPS 38.33200, -77.12500; 5486 St Paul's Rd off Rt 206; King George **GS:** Y **SP:** 1) Sarah (-----) (20 Jul 1742-__) 2) mar (1 Jan 1761) (-----) 3) (-----) (__-8 May 1805) **VI:** Son of Capt Jonathan & Ann (-----) Hooe **P:** N **BLW:** N **RG:** unk **MK:** N **PH:** unk **SS:** D pg 563; E pg 242 **BS:** JLARC 48; 17 pg 632.

HOOE, Robert Howson; b 1748; d 1833 **RU:** Captain, Served in Cont Line & Prince William Co Militia **CEM:** Mayfield Plantation; GPS 38.75290, -77.35571; Mayfield Park; Manassas City **GS:** Y **SP:** Mary Waugh **VI:** No further data **P:** unk **BLW:** unk **RG:** Y **MK:** Y **PH:** Y **SS:** J-NSSAR 2000 Reg; NSSAR Ancestor # P-184359 **BS:** JLARC 76.

HOOF, Lawrence; b 1756; d 26 May 1834 **RU:** Patriot, Signed petition of Alexandria citizens to House of Delegates 27 May 1782 for ferry across Potomac & representation in House of Delegates (Petition 1614-P). Signed petition to House of Delegates fr Fairfax Co on 27 May 1782 to reduce duties on commerce (Petition 1612-P) **CEM:** St Paul's Episcopal; GPS 38.79959, -77.05860; 228 S Pitt St; Alexandria City **GS:** Y **SP:** Ann Gretter (1760-8 Jun 1846_ **VI:** Signed 3 petitions: 3 Dec 1778 Incorp Alexandria as town; 27 May 1782 Reduce VA import fees to that of MD; 21 Nov 1783 Parish elections. First Senior Warden of St Paul's Episcopal **P:** N **BLW:** N **RG:** Y **MK:** unk **PH:** unk **SS:** S #1612 **BS:** 04; 196.

HOOK, John; b 1745; d 1808 **RU:** Private, Served in Capt Charles Cameron's Co in 1781. Gave material aid, a rug to Capt Irvine for Cherokee Expedition **CEM:** Hook Family; GPS unk; Rt 122 nr US Cellular; Franklin **GS:** Y **SP:** No info **VI:** No further data **P:** unk **BLW:** unk **RG:** N **MK:** N **PH:** unk **SS:** E pg 389 **BS:** 82 pg 176.

HOOK, William; b 1750; d 1826 **RU:** Private/Patriot, Gave material aid to cause. Service as private not identified **CEM:** Augusta Stone Presbyterian; GPS 38.23926, -78.97356; 28 Old Stone Church Ln, Ft Defiance; Augusta **GS:** N **SP:** No info **VI:** No further data **P:** unk **BLW:** unk **RG:** unk **MK:** unk **PH:** N **SS:** AL Ct Bk 1 pg 2, 23, 46 Buckingham Co **BS:** JLARC 62; 71 pg ??.

HOOKE (HOOK), Robert Sr; b 1712; d 1802 **RU:** Private/Patriot, A person with this name served in Capt Hewett's Co Augusta Co Militia, however would be above military age to have had this service. Served in Dunmore's War of 1774 at Point Pleasant fr Augusta Co under Sgt Joseph Dictorn. Gave material aid to cause **CEM:** Augusta Stone Presbyterian; GPS 38.23926, -78.97356; 28 Old Stone Church Ln, Ft Defiance; Augusta **GS:** Y **SP:** No info **VI:** Status verification: Source 76 has "furnished supplies." Memorial stone erected in 1958 states he was elected Capt of the Augusta militia on 13 Sep 1756 and had Rev War service **P:** unk **BLW:** unk **RG:** Y **MK:** unk **PH:** unk **SS:** CP Dunmore's War; J-NSSAR 2000 Reg; B; AL Comm Bk V pg 122 **BS:** JLARC 1, 2, 62, 76; 196.

HOOKE (HOOK), William Sr; b 1738, Ireland; d 25 Sep 1817 **RU:** Private, Served in Capt Hewett's Co, Augusta Co Militia **CEM:** Augusta Stone Presbyterian; GPS 38.23926, -78.97356; 28 Old Stone Church Ln, Ft Defiance; Augusta **GS:** Y **SP:** Mar (1772) Sarah (-----) (__-15 Apr 1790, Cross Keys, VA) **VI:** Memorial stone erected in 1958 says he had Rev War service, and that he was a private in the Augusta

RU=Rank/Unit   CEM=Cemetery   GS=Gravestone   SP=Spousal Information
VI=Other Veteran Info   P=Pension   BLW=Bounty/Land Warrant   RG=Registered Grave
MK=SAR/DAR Marker   PH=Photo   SS=Service Source   BS=Burial Source

159

Co militia during the French and Indian War **P:** unk **BLW:** unk **RG:** Y **MK:** unk **PH:** unk **SS:** J-NSSAR 1993 Reg, J- DAR Hatcher; E pg 390 **BS:** JLARC 1, 2; 196.

HOOMES, John; b unk; d 14 Mar 1824 **RU:** Ensign, Appt ensign 10 Oct 1776 in Capt P. Johnson's Co of Caroline Co **CEM:** Old Mansion; GPS unk; S end of Main St, Bowling Green; Caroline **GS:** N **SP:** No info **VI:** Son of John Hoomes (1749-1805) & Judith Church Allen (1748-1822) **P:** unk **BLW:** unk **RG:** Y **MK:** N **PH:** N **SS:** E pg 390 **BS:** 02 pg 87; 196.

HOOMES, John; b 1749; d Dec 1805 **RU:** Patriot, Gave material aid to cause **CEM:** Old Mansion; GPS unk; S end of Main St, Bowling Green; Caroline **GS:** N **SP:** Judith Churchill Allen b c1748, d 11 Aug 1822 **VI:** Richmond Enquirer gives death notice rank as Col. Was Ct Justice 1777 Caroline Co **P:** N **BLW:** N **RG:** Y **MK:** N **PH:** N **SS:** G pg 105, 559; AL Ct Bk 1 pg 2 Caroline Co **BS:** 02 pg 87; 196.

HOOPER, George; b 1736; d 1800 **RU:** Colonel/Patriot, Served in Buckingham Co Militia. Resigned 11 Jun 1781. Gave material aid to cause **CEM:** Hooper Family; GPS unk; Hooper's Mount, Arcanum; Buckingham **GS:** U **SP:** Mar (c1758 Cumberland Co) Elizabeth Cooke (174?-1817) **VI:** No further data **P:** N **BLW:** N **RG:** N **MK:** N **PH:** unk **SS:** E pg 369, 390; AL Ct Bk pg 2, 23, 46 Buckingham Co; CD **BS:** 32 e-mail 07; 196.

HOOVER, John; b c1764; d 1815 **RU:** Second Lieutenant, Appointed 2nd Lt 28 Feb 1782, Shenandoah Co **CEM:** Mt Hebron; GPS 39.10916, -78.09497; 305 E Boscawen St; Winchester City **GS:** Y **SP:** 1) Mar (20 Jun 1787 Frederick Co by John Montgomery) Elizabeth Erehart 2) Mar (28 Mar 1799 Frederick Co by Christian Streit) Mary Martin 3) mar (5 Feb 1800 Frederick Co by Alexander Balmain) Nancy McKeever d/o Paul & Rachel (Cheshire) McKeever **VI:** Died in Frederick Co **P:** no **BLW:** no **RG:** Y **MK:** N **PH:** Y **SS:** E pg 390 **BS:** 50 pg 48.

HOOVER, John Henry; b 05 Dec 1732; d 28 Mar 1815 **RU:** Private, Served in Capt Thomas Buck's Co of Volunteers, Dunmore Co, 1777 **CEM:** Mt Hebron; GPS 39.10916, -78.09497; 305 E Boscawen St; Winchester City **GS:** Y **SP:** Mar (5 Feb 1800 Frederick Co) Mary McKeever **VI:** No further data **P:** no **BLW:** no **RG:** no **MK:** N **PH:** Y **SS:** E pg 106, 390 **BS:** 50 pg 49; 196.

HOOVER, Michael; b 1761; d 12 Jun 1829 **RU:** Soldier, Served in Capt Hull's Co, Augusta Co Militia **CEM:** Hebron Presbyterian; GPS 38.14140, -79.15500; 423 Hebron Rd; Staunton City **GS:** Y **SP:** No info **VI:** Died age 68 (stone) **P:** unk **BLW:** unk **RG:** unk **MK:** unk **PH:** unk **SS:** E pg 390 **BS:** JLARC 62, 63; 196.

HOPE, Adam; b 1729; d 3 Aug 1802 **RU:** Patriot, Performed public service as Overseer of Roads, also gave material aid to cause **CEM:** Green Springs Presbyterian; GPS 36.63670, -81,99560; 2007 Gr Spr Ch Rd, Abingdon; Washington **GS:** U **SP:** Agnes Kincaid (1722-1804) **VI:** No further data **P:** N **BLW:** N **RG:** unk **MK:** unk **PH:** unk **SS:** DAR Ancestor #A135161; DD **BS:** 200 pg 139.

HOPE, James; b 1754 PA; d 15 Oct 1811 **RU:** Private, Served in McFarland's Co **CEM:** Green Spring Presbyterian; GPS 36.63670, -81.99560; 2007 Green Spring Ch Rd, Abingdon; Washington **GS:** Y **SP:** Mar (21 Feb 1753 Washington Co) Margaret Dryden (25 Feb 1776 Augusta Co-5 May 1854) d/o Nathaniel & Mary (-----) Dryden **VI:** Son of Adam (1729-1802) & Agnes (Kincaid) (1722-1804) Hope **P:** unk **BLW:** unk **RG:** unk **MK:** unk **PH:** unk **SS:** J- DAR Hatcher; DL pg 1394 **BS:** JLARC 2.

HOPKIN, HOPKINS, Archibald; b Bef 1737, Northern Ireland; d 8 May 1799 **RU:** Patriot, Personal service (specifics not given in SAR registry) **CEM:** Old Peaked Mountain; GPS 38.37113, -78.73416; 9843 Town Hall Rd, McGaheysville; Rockingham **GS:** Y **SP:** Jannet Love **VI:** No further data **P:** N **BLW:** N **RG:** Y **MK:** Y **PH:** unk **SS:** SAR Ancestor #P-184606 **BS:** 04.

HOPKIN, HOPKINS, John; b 1732, Goochland; d 25 Feb 1788 **RU:** Captain/Patriot, Was Private in David Stephens Co, Col Abraham Bowman's 8th Regt. Enl 21 Feb 1778 and served 3 yrs in Capt Croghan's Co 4th, 8th, 12th VA Regt commanded by Col James Wood 1778. Date promoted to Capt not determined. Gave material aid to cause **CEM:** Old Peaked Mountain; GPS 38.37113, -78.73416; 9843 Town Hall Rd, McGaheysville; Rockingham **GS:** U **SP:** Mar (12 Oct 1759, Augusta Co) Jean Jordon **VI:** No further data **P:** unk **BLW:** unk **RG:** Y **MK:** Y **PH:** unk **SS:** J-NSSAR 2000 Reg; D Rockingham Co; SAR Ancestor #P-184607 **BS:** JLARC 76.

RU=Rank/Unit	CEM=Cemetery	GS=Gravestone	SP=Spousal Information
VI=Other Veteran Info	P=Pension	BLW=Bounty/Land Warrant	RG=Registered Grave
MK=SAR/DAR Marker	PH=Photo	SS=Service Source	BS=Burial Source

160

HOPKINS, James; b 22 Feb 1765; d 20 Jul 1844 **RU:** Private, Enl Amherst Co in Capt Azh Martin's Eighth Co of the 4th Regt of Line, 15 Jun-7 Sep 1780. Unit was at battle of Camden and Hillborough **CEM:** Hopkins; GPS unk; Behind Thomas Muse house near Franklin Co Line, Sago; Pittsylvania **GS:** Y **SP:** 1) (-----) 2) mar (15 Nov 1797 at home of her uncle Thomas Carter in Pittsylvania Co) Mary (-----) (c1761-31 May 1853) **VI:** Sol appl pen 17 Sep 1832 Pittsylvnia Co. Widow appl pen 2 Mar 1853 age 92. W3553. Sub for father (James, Sr). Cemetery moved when Quantico Marine Base took over a portion of Stafford Co **P:** Y **BLW:** unk **RG:** unk **MK:** unk **PH:** no **SS:** G pg 17; K Vol 3 pg 328; CG Vol 2 pg 1703 **BS:** JLARC 4, 90.

HOPKINS, Walter; b 1757; d 1800 **RU:** Captain, As Lt was Paymaster in Capt Ander's Co. Later was Capt in New Kent Co Militia 1775-6 **CEM:** Shockoe Hill; GPS 37.55190, -77.43170; 4th & Hospital Sts; Richmond City **GS:** U **SP:** Abigail Herbert Osborne (1762-1840) d/o Henry (1710-1778) & (-----) Herbert of Herbertsville, Norfolk Co. She later remarried. **VI:** No further data **P:** unk **BLW:** unk **RG:** unk **MK:** unk **PH:** unk **SS:** E pg 391; G pg 624 **BS:** 196.

HOPPESS, John; b 1745; d 1836 **RU:** Soldier, Served in PA **CEM:** St Paul's Lutheran; GPS 36.91173, -81.23484; 330 St Pauls Church Rd, Rural Retreat; Wythe **GS:** U **SP:** No info **VI:** No further data **P:** unk **BLW:** unk **RG:** unk **MK:** unk **PH:** unk **SS:** JLARC pg 72 **BS:** JLARC 40, 123.

HORE, Elias; b 1747; d 10 Jul 1832 **RU:** Patriot, Gave material aid to the cause **CEM:** Cedar Run; GPS 38.36299, -77.33694; Quantico Marine Base; Stafford **GS:** U **SP:** No info **VI:** Remains moved there when base established. Burial source 95 says bur in Prince William Co **P:** N **BLW:** N **RG:** Y **MK:** N **PH:** Y **SS:** Al Ct Bk I pg 9, Bk II pg 6 **BS:** JLARC 48, 95; 3 pg 170; 95.

HORNER, Gustavus Brown; b 28 Feb 1761, Newport, Charles Co, MD; d 24 Jan 1815 **RU:** Surgeon's Mate, Served in Cont Army in MD commencing age 15, served 5 yrs **CEM:** Clermont; GPS 38.71262,-77.8003; Warrenton; Fauquier **GS:** Y **SP:** Mar (14 Apr 1786 Clermont) Frances Harrison Scott (1764-27 Nov 1837 Washington DC) d/o Capt James & Eliza (Harrison) Scott **VI:** Studied medicine in Alexandria VA. Finished training Philadelphia. Surgeon in War of 1812. Settled in Warrenton. Served VA Legislature & was presidential elector. Wife recd pen of 1/2 pay starting 4 Mar 1834 in MD **P:** Y **BLW:** unk **RG:** unk **MK:** unk **PH:** unk **SS:** BX pg 384 **BS:** 196.

HOSKINS, Robert; b c1755; d 1815 **RU:** Lieutenant, Promoted to Lt in Cont Army at Williamsburg. Served at Valley Forge, Monmouth, Middlebrook, Stony Point, and King's Ferry **CEM:** Bird-Boyd-Todd Family; GPS unk; Popular Grove Plantation, Stevensville; King & Queen **GS:** U **SP:** No info **VI:** No further data **P:** unk **BLW:** unk **RG:** unk **MK:** unk **PH:** unk **SS:** SAR Ancestor #P-185240; J-NSSAR 1993 Reg; CZ **BS:** JLARC 1.

HOSKINS, Thomas Coleman; b 1752, Halifax Co; d 11 Feb 1833 **RU:** Corporal, Ent serv Lunenburg Co, 6th VA Regt **CEM:** Brightwood; GPS unk; Marilla Ln, Chatham; Pittsylvania **GS:** Y **SP:** Mar (19 Jul 1790 Campbell Co) Betsy Ellington **VI:** Son of William & Dorothy (-----) Hoskins. Appl pen 17 Sep 1827 age 75. S38044 **P:** Y **BLW:** N **RG:** N **MK:** N **PH:** Y **SS:** E pg 393 **BS:** 196 modified fr pension rec.

HOSTETTER, Ulrich; b 1749 York, PA; d 26 Feb 1840 **RU:** Ensign, Served in PA Militia. Ent serv York Co PA 1776 **CEM:** Hostetter Family; GPS unk; Lexington; Lexington City **GS:** U **SP:** Elizabeth (-----) **VI:** Son of Ulrich Sr (1720 Switzerland-1785 York Co, PA) & Anna Marie (-----) Hostetter. Sol appl 7 Aug 1832 Rockbridge Co VA. S5563 **P:** Y **BLW:** unk **RG:** Y **MK:** N **PH:** unk **SS:** K Vol 3 pg 333; AG, pg 514; CG Vol 2 pg 1714 **BS:** SAR report.

HOTT, George; b c1700; d 1797 **RU:** Patriot, Paid Personal Property Tax 1782, Frederick Co. Considered tax to support Rev war cause **CEM:** George Hott, Sr; GPS unk; Rt 654 fr Nain 7 mi to Pleasant Valley Church, on right on top of hill; Frederick **GS:** U **SP:** Magdalena Shantz (__-1801) d/o Jacob & (----) Shantz **VI:** No further data **P:** N **BLW:** N **RG:** unk **MK:** unk **PH:** N **SS:** DV **BS:** 228.

HOTTEL, Johann; b 12 Apr 1722, Germany; d 28 Mar 1782 **RU:** Patriot, Gave material aid to cause **CEM:** Keller; GPS 38.56480, -78.46220; Tom's Brook nr Mt Olive; Shenandoah **GS:** U **SP:** No info **VI:** Died in Woodstock, Shenandoah Co **P:** N **BLW:** N **RG:** unk **MK:** unk **PH:** unk **SS:** AL Cert Shenandoah Co **BS:** 196.

RU=Rank/Unit CEM=Cemetery GS=Gravestone SP=Spousal Information
VI=Other Veteran Info P=Pension BLW=Bounty/Land Warrant RG=Registered Grave
MK=SAR/DAR Marker PH=Photo SS=Service Source BS=Burial Source

161

HOTTEL, John Jacob; b 20 Jan 1752, Frederick Co; d Aug 1820 **RU:** Private, Served in Capt Michael Reader and Capt Alexander Machir's Cos, Shenandoah Militia **CEM:** Keller; GPS 38.56480, -78.46220; Tom's Brook nr Mt Olive; Shenandoah **GS:** U **SP:** Mar (21 Jun 1774) Mary Dorothea Rinker (20 Jan 1755 York Co, PA-c1820) **VI:** No further data **P:** unk **BLW:** unk **RG:** unk **MK:** unk **PH:** unk **SS:** DAR Ancestor #A058954; J- DAR Hatcher; C pg 602-607; BY **BS:** JLARC 2.

HOTTEL, Joseph; b 1761, Frederick Co; d 1814 **RU:** Private, Served in VA line **CEM:** Keller; GPS 38.56480, -78.46220; Tom's Brook nr Mt Olive; Shenandoah **GS:** U **SP:** Barbara Dull **VI:** No further data **P:** unk **BLW:** unk **RG:** unk **MK:** unk **PH:** unk **SS:** J- DAR Hatcher; AP serv rec Muster roll **BS:** JLARC 2.

HOTTENSTEIN, Jacob; b 1735, Barvaria; d After 7 Jun 1803 **RU:** Soldier, Cont Line **CEM:** Lutheran; GPS unk; Washington; Rappahannock **GS:** U **SP:** Catherine Widener **VI:** No further data **P:** unk **BLW:** unk **RG:** unk **MK:** unk **PH:** unk **SS:** J- DAR Hatcher; BC part 2 pg 1394 **BS:** JLARC 2.

HOUBA, Remy; b unk; d 1781 **RU:** Soldier, Served in Gatinais Bn and died fr battle at Yorktown **CEM:** French Memorial; GPS 36.81944, -79.39933; Yorktown; York **GS:** U **SP:** No info **VI:** No further data **P:** unk **BLW:** unk **RG:** Y **MK:** unk **PH:** unk **SS:** J-Yorktown Historian **BS:** JLARC 1, 74.

HOUCHOIS, Charles; b unk; d 1781 **RU:** Seaman, Served on "Duc De Bourgogne" and died from Yorktown battle **CEM:** French Memorial; GPS 36.81944, -79.39933; Yorktown; York **GS:** U **SP:** No info **VI:** No further data **P:** unk **BLW:** unk **RG:** Y **MK:** unk **PH:** unk **SS:** J-Yorktown Historian **BS:** JLARC 1, 74.

HOUCK, George Michael; b 1757; d 13 Jan 1845 **RU:** Private, Served in Montgomery Co Militia **CEM:** St Paul's Lutheran; GPS 38.99140, -78.36250; 156 W Washington, Strasburg; Shenandoah **GS:** U **SP:** Margaretta Funk (Dec 1757-28 Jan 1841) **VI:** No further data **P:** unk **BLW:** unk **RG:** unk **MK:** unk **PH:** unk **SS:** G pg 232 **BS:** 196.

HOUGH, Benjamin; b unk; d 22 Sep 1816 **RU:** Private?, See Bounty Land Warrant application for service units **CEM:** Fairfax Meeting House; GPS 39.18557, -77.60589; Water St & Waterford Rd, Waterford; Loudoun **GS:** Y **SP:** No info **VI:** Recd bounty land 1060 acres **P:** unk **BLW:** unk **RG:** Y **MK:** N **PH:** unk **SS:** C pg 610 **BS:** 25 pg 147.

HOUGH (HUFF), John; b 1763; d 1840 **RU:** Sergeant, Served in 2nd Cont Line **CEM:** Pigg River Primitive Baptist; GPS 36.96913, -80.07368; Rt 750 nr Callaway; Franklin **GS:** U **SP:** 1) (-----) 2) (-----) 3) Elizabeth **VI:** No further data **P:** unk **BLW:** unk **RG:** Y **MK:** unk **PH:** unk **SS:** E pg 393 **BS:** JLARC 1,2,4,19.

HOUGH (HUFF), William; b 24 Nov 1744, Fairfax Co; d 18 Feb 1815 **RU:** Private, Served in VA Cont Line. Gave for cause 325# beef; 42 days wagon team and driver **CEM:** Fairfax Meeting House; GPS 39.18557, -77.60589; Water St & Waterford Rd, Waterford; Loudoun **GS:** Y **SP:** Eleanor Hite **VI:** US VA-style marker is intact and legible **P:** unk **BLW:** unk **RG:** unk **MK:** N **PH:** unk **SS:** J- DAR Hatcher; AK; D pg 6, 7; E pg 393 **BS:** JLARC 2; 04.

HOUNSHELL, John; b 5 Oct 1756; d 11 Aug 1827 **RU:** Private, Served in Capt Daniel Trigg's Co, Montgomery Co Militia Sep 1777 **CEM:** St Paul's Lutheran; GPS 36.91173, -81.23484; 330 St Pauls Church Rd, Rural Retreat; Wythe **GS:** Y **SP:** Susannah (-----) (1766-1828) **VI:** Obtained rank of major probably after war period. DAR marker fr KY society **P:** unk **BLW:** unk **RG:** Y **MK:** Y **PH:** unk **SS:** J-NSSAR 1993 Reg, J- DAR Hatcher; G pg 214 **BS:** JLARC 1, 2; 196.

HOUPILLARD, Jacques; b unk; d 1781 **RU:** Soldier, Served in Santogne Bn and died fr battle at Yorktown **CEM:** French Memorial; GPS 36.81944, -79.39933; Yorktown; York **GS:** U **SP:** No info **VI:** No further data **P:** unk **BLW:** unk **RG:** Y **MK:** unk **PH:** unk **SS:** J-Yorktown Historian **BS:** JLARC 1, 74.

HOUSE, James; b 1761 CT; d 17 Nov 1834 **RU:** Matross, Served in Capt Ragsdale's Co, 1st Battalion Artillery, Cont Line **CEM:** Arlington National; GPS 38.88377, -77.06535; Jefferson Davis Hwy Rt 110; Arlington **GS:** Y **SP:** No info **VI:** Died in DC. Originally bur at Old Presbyterian Church in Georgetown, reinterred 12 May 1892. One of 11 Rev War soldiers bur at Arlington **P:** unk **BLW:** unk **RG:** Y **MK:** Y **PH:** unk **SS:** J-NSSAR 2000 Reg; NSSAR Ancestor #P-185624 **BS:** JLARC 76; 196.

RU=Rank/Unit	CEM=Cemetery	GS=Gravestone	SP=Spousal Information
VI=Other Veteran Info	P=Pension	BLW=Bounty/Land Warrant	RG=Registered Grave
MK=SAR/DAR Marker	PH=Photo	SS=Service Source	BS=Burial Source

162

HOUSE, Matthias; b 8 Aug 1739; d 20 Oct 1829 **RU:** Patriot, Listed on the Culpeper Co Classes (recruiting list 1781) number 87 covering a portion of Madison Co **CEM:** House Hollow Farm; GPS unk; Slate Mills; Madison **GS:** N **SP:** Maria Margaretha Jaeckler (1743-1812) **VI:** No further data **P:** N **BLW:** N **RG:** unk **MK:** unk **PH:** unk **SS:** unk **BS:** 229 Madison Co.

HOUSTON, George; b unk; d 1819 **RU:** Captain, Served in Rockbridge Co Militia & 9th Cont line **CEM:** New Providence Presbyterian; GPS 37.95130, -79.30250; 1208 New Providence Rd, Raphine; Rockbridge **GS:** U **SP:** No info **VI:** No further data **P:** unk **BLW:** unk **RG:** unk **MK:** unk **PH:** unk **SS:** E pg 394 **BS:** JLARC 63, 79.

HOUSTON, James; b 1745; d 1803 **RU:** Ensign, Was in Battle of Point Pleasant Oct 1774, in Capt Samuel McDowell's Co of Rockbridge Co. Was Ens Rockbridge Co Militia 2 Nov 1779 **CEM:** New Providence Presbyterian; GPS 37.95130, -79.30250; 1208 New Providence Rd, Raphine; Rockbridge **GS:** Y **SP:** No info **VI:** No further data **P:** unk **BLW:** unk **RG:** unk **MK:** unk **PH:** unk **SS:** Z pg 103 **BS:** JLARC 63, 79; 196.

HOUSTON, John Sr; b 1726, Ireland; d 1798 **RU:** Soldier/Patriot, Mil serv not identified. Gave material aid to cause **CEM:** Old Stone Presbyterian; GPS unk; 73 Sam Huston Way; Rockbridge **GS:** U **SP:** Sarah Todd **VI:** Son of John & Margaret (Cunningham) Houston **P:** unk **BLW:** unk **RG:** unk **MK:** unk **PH:** unk **SS:** SAR Ancestor #P-185776; AL Ct Bk pg 2, 5 Rockbridge Co **BS:** JLARC 63.

HOUSTON, Samuel; b 1745; d 1807 **RU:** Captain/Patriot, Served in Morgan's Rifle Brigade. Gave material aid to cause **CEM:** High Bridge Presbyterian; GPS 37.62420, -79.58610; 67 High Bridge Rd, Natural Bridge; Rockbridge **GS:** U **SP:** Elizabeth Blair Paxton (1757-8 Sep 1831 Blount Co, TN) d/o John & Mary (Blair) Paxton **VI:** Son of Robert H. (1720-1760) & Margaret Dunlap (Davidson) (1720-___) Houston. Obtained rank of Maj after war period. Was VA Militia inspector. Died in Bath Co, KY in military duty after war. Body returned to VA **P:** unk **BLW:** unk **RG:** unk **MK:** unk **PH:** unk **SS:** J- DAR Hatcher; D Vol 3, pg 825, Bath Co; CD **BS:** JLARC 2.

HOUSTON, Samuel; b 1737; d 18 Apr 1813 **RU:** Patriot, Gave material aid to cause **CEM:** North Mountain; GPS unk; 7 mi S of Staunton on N side Rt 252; Augusta **GS:** Y **SP:** No info **VI:** No further data **P:** N **BLW:** N **RG:** N **MK:** N **PH:** unk **SS:** AL Ct bk p5,8 **BS:** 75; 196.

HOUSTON, Samuel; b 1 Jan 1758, Hays Creek, now Rockbridge Co; d 20 Jan 1839 **RU:** Private, Served in Gen Stevens Brigade in Battle of Guildford CH, NC **CEM:** High Bridge Presbyterian; GPS 37.62420, -79.58610; 67 High Bridge Rd, Natural Bridge; Rockbridge **GS:** Y **SP:** Margaret (-----) **VI:** Cousin of General Sam Houston. Pastor of High Bridge Church for 43 yrs. Addition to church building is said to have been built over his grave **P:** unk **BLW:** unk **RG:** Y **MK:** Y **PH:** Y **SS:** AR Vol 2 pg 171; NSSAR Ancestor #P-185752 **BS:** JLARC 1, 2, 79.

HOWARD, James; b 1763, Goochland Co; d c1841 **RU:** Private, Ent serv Bedford Co. Served in VA Line **CEM:** Howard Family; GPS unk; Nr Campbell Co CH, Rustburg; Campbell **GS:** Y **SP:** Mary (-----) **VI:** Appl for pension in Campbell Co 09 Sep 1833, #S9563 **P:** Y **BLW:** unk **RG:** N **MK:** N **PH:** unk **SS:** SAR Ancestor #P-185998; AS DAR Report; CG pg 1727 **BS:** 80 vol 2 pg 173.

HOWARD, James; b 1752; d aft 1820 **RU:** Private, Served in VA battalion & 4th, 8th, 9th, & 12th Cont Lines. Served in Taylor's Regt. Was wounded at Guilford CH **CEM:** Union Baptist; GPS 37.94660, -77.65160; 16230 Union Church Rd, Beaverdam; Hanover **GS:** Y **SP:** No info **VI:** No family after 1820. Recd pen 1813 & appl again 27 May 18181 Hanover Co. S38045 **P:** Y **BLW:** unk **RG:** unk **MK:** N **PH:** N **SS:** E pg 394-5; BX pg 388; CG pg 1721 **BS:** 196.

HOWARD, Peter Rev; b 4 Apr 1762, York County, England; d 9 May 1827 **RU:** Private, Served in 5th and 7th Regts in Co 10, Col Daniel's 11th & 15th Regts. Listed in Regt 10 Nov 1778 **CEM:** Pine Creek Primitive Baptist; GPS 36.94622, -80.27357; Spangler Mill Rd Rt 682; Floyd **GS:** Y **SP:** Sarah Jane Strickland (12 Mar 1761-23 Nov 1846) **VI:** X893 **P:** Y **BLW:** unk **RG:** unk **MK:** N **PH:** unk **SS:** NSSAR Ancestor #P-186150; DAR #A058102; Pen Appl **BS:** JLARC 2, 29.

HOWARD, Robert; b c1757; d 1821 **RU:** Sergeant, Served in Regular Army Inf unit **CEM:** Pine Creek Primitive Baptist; GPS 36.94622, -80.27357; Spangler Mill Rd Rt 682; Floyd **GS:** Y **SP:** No info **VI:** BLW issued 1783 **P:** unk **BLW:** Y **RG:** N **MK:** N **PH:** unk **SS:** E pg 395; CU- VA BLW **BS:** 64 pg 122; 196.

RU=Rank/Unit   CEM=Cemetery   GS=Gravestone   SP=Spousal Information
VI=Other Veteran Info   P=Pension   BLW=Bounty/Land Warrant   RG=Registered Grave
MK=SAR/DAR Marker   PH=Photo   SS=Service Source   BS=Burial Source

163

HOWARD, William; b 1727; d 1815 **RU:** Patriot, Gave material aid to cause **CEM:** Howard-Palmer; **GPS** 37.05575, -80.50448; 4165 Piney Woods Rd, behind House, Childress; Montgomery **GS:** Y **SP:** Hannah Psalter (1738-1810) **VI:** No further data **P:** N **BLW:** N **RG:** N **MK:** N **PH:** unk **SS:** AS DAR Report **BS:** 80 vol 2 pg 174; 196.

HOWARD, William Lawrence; b unk; d 1797 **RU:** Private?, Served in 13th Cont Line **CEM:** Pine Creek Primitive Baptist; **GPS** 36.94622, -80.27357; Spangler Mill Rd Rt 682; Floyd **GS:** Y **SP:** No info **VI:** No further data **P:** unk **BLW:** unk **RG:** N **MK:** N **PH:** unk **SS:** E pg 395 **BS:** 64 pg 122.

HOWE, Daniel; b c1758; d 1 Jan 1838 **RU:** Major, Enl Montgomery Co 1776 and served until 1781. Was at surrender of Cornwallis **CEM:** Sunnyside; **GPS** unk; Btw Radford and Dublin at Old Joseph Howe place, Back Creek; Pulaski **GS:** U **SP:** Nancy Haven (3 Jan 1771-1 Mar 1830) **VI:** Appl pen 2 Oct 1832 Montgomery Co age 74. S5565. Died in Newbern, Montgomery Co **P:** Y **BLW:** unk **RG:** unk **MK:** unk **PH:** unk **SS:** J- DAR Hatcher; K Vol 3 pg 337; CG Vol 2 pg 1730 **BS:** JLARC 2; 196.

HOWELL, Daniel Sr; b 1759, Philadelphia Co, PA; d 5 Mar 1836 **RU:** Private, Served in Capt Josuha Wilson's Co 1778. Served three tours. Was in Col Martin's and Crockett's Regts in the Cherokee Exposition **CEM:** Wright Family; **GPS** 36.97658, -80.21693; Pizarro off Rt 668; Floyd **GS:** U **SP:** Mar (c1784) Frances (-----) **VI:** Son of Benjamin & Maria Elizabeth (Beest) Howell. Memorialized by DAR plaque in cem. Pensioned 1835 age 75 making death date in 1840; #S 13413 **P:** Y **BLW:** unk **RG:** unk **MK:** Y **PH:** unk **SS:** DAR Ancestor #A058496; E pg 395 **BS:** 196 for John Mitchell.

HOWELL, John F; b unk; d 1821 **RU:** Lieutenant/Patriot, Gave material aid to cause **CEM:** St Paul's Episcopal; **GPS** 36.84733, -76.28554; 201 St Paul's Blvd; Norfolk City **GS:** Y **SP:** No info **VI:** No further data **P:** unk **BLW:** unk **RG:** Y **MK:** N **PH:** unk **SS:** E pg 395; AL Ct Bk 1 pg 11 Nansemond Co **BS:** 87 pg 28.

HOWISON, Stephen; b 31 Jan 1736, St Mary's or Charles Co, MD; d 1 Feb 1815 **RU:** Second Lieutenant, Served in Prince William Co Militia **CEM:** Howison Family; **GPS** 38.63313, -77.38399; Minniville Rd; Prince William **GS:** Y **SP:** Mary Brooke (1752-14 Apr 1808) **VI:** No further data **P:** unk **BLW:** unk **RG:** Y **MK:** Y **PH:** Y **SS:** AK; AL Ct Bk pg 7 **BS:** 04; 80 vol 2 pg 176.

HUBARD, William; b unk; d 1802 **RU:** Sergeant, Served in 1st & 10th Cont Lines **CEM:** St Luke's Church; **GPS** 36.93940, -76.58670; 14477 Benns Church Blvd, Smithfield; Isle of Wight **GS:** Y **SP:** No info **VI:** No further data **P:** N **BLW:** N **RG:** N **MK:** N **PH:** unk **SS:** E pg 396 **BS:** 117 pg 26.

HUBERT, Jean; b unk; d 1781 **RU:** Seaman, Served on "Saint-Esprit"and died from Yorktown battle **CEM:** French Memorial; **GPS** 36.81944, -79.39933; Yorktown; York **GS:** U **SP:** No info **VI:** No further data **P:** unk **BLW:** unk **RG:** Y **MK:** unk **PH:** unk **SS:** J-Yorktown Historian **BS:** JLARC 1, 74.

HUDSON, Christopher; b 20 Jul 1758, Hanover Co; d 1 May 1825 **RU:** Captain, Goochland Co Militia 1779. Was also serving as Capt in Louisa Co 1781-3 period **CEM:** Mt Air; **GPS** unk; Hardware River, Keene, NW of Scottsville; Albemarle **GS:** Y **SP:** Mar (19 Mar 1783 Hanover Co) Sarah Anderson (20 Jul 1758 Hanover Co-2 Apr 1807) d/o David Overton & Elizabeth (Mills) Anderson **VI:** Resided Louisa Co 1782. Moved to Albemarle Co in 1786 **P:** unk **BLW:** unk **RG:** unk **MK:** unk **PH:** unk **SS:** J- DAR Hatcher; E pg 398; AL Cert Louisa Co **BS:** JLARC 2; 196.

HUDSON, James; b c1754; d 1820 **RU:** Private, Served in 5th Cont Line **CEM:** Hudson Family; **GPS** unk; Rt 721; Culpeper **GS:** Y **SP:** Sarah (-----) **VI:** Son of David Hudson (1727-14 Jan 1811) & Keziah Plunkett (1728-1807). Will proved 1820. Weathered chiseled limestone or fieldstone **P:** unk **BLW:** unk **RG:** Y **MK:** N **PH:** unk **SS:** E pg 398; H pg 481; Research by CMK **BS:** 04.

HUDSON, John; b 1750; d 1801 **RU:** Captain/Patriot, Served in Albemarle Co Militia. Also gave material aid to cause **CEM:** Mt Air; **GPS** unk; Hardware River, Keene, NW of Scottsville; Albemarle **GS:** N **SP:** no info **VI:** No further data **P:** unk **BLW:** unk **RG:** Y **MK:** unk **PH:** N **SS:** AL Ct Bk pg 28; E pg 398 **BS:** JLARC 2, 76.

HUDSON, Thomas; b 1763; d 11 Mar 1843 **RU:** Soldier, Ent serv Augusta Co in 2nd VA State Regt & 14th Cont Line **CEM:** Rinker; **GPS** unk; Conicville; Shenandoah **GS:** U **SP:** Mar (31 Aug 1784) Dorothy (-----) (c1756-__) **VI:** Sol appl pen 10 Sep 1832 Shenandoah Co. In 18 Aug 1837 Warren Co, sol made

RU=Rank/Unit   CEM=Cemetery   GS=Gravestone   SP=Spousal Information
VI=Other Veteran Info P=Pension   BLW=Bounty/Land Warrant RG=Registered Grave
MK=SAR/DAR Marker PH=Photo   SS=Service Source   BS=Burial Source

164

inquiry concerning BLW for services. Widow appl pen 30 Aug 1834 Shenandoah Co. W7832 **P:** Y **BLW:** unk **RG:** unk **MK:** unk **PH:** unk **SS:** E pg 398; CG Vol 2 pg 1749 **BS:** JLARC 3.

HUDSON, Vincent; b c1763, Essex Co; d 27 Sep 1819 **RU:** Fifer, Joined 7th VA Regt Feb 1776. Discharged Valley Forge Feb 1778. Reenlisted 21st Gloucester Co Militia 1779. Was Fife Maj until 1781 **CEM:** Union Baptist; **GPS** 37.27882, -76.44331; 9524 Guinea Rd, Achilles; Gloucester **GS:** N **SP:** Mar (1794 at her father's, Gloucester Co) Mildred Shackelford (c1774-after 1851) **VI:** Also soldier in War of 1812. Sol appl pen 22 May 1818 Gloucester Co. He died in Saddler's Neck, Gloucester Co. Widow appl pen 27 Mar 1746 age 74. 6876. Widow's pension W7833 **P:** Y **BLW:** unk **RG:** Y **MK:** N **PH:** N **SS:** S #1274; K Vol 3 pg 343 **BS:** 04.

HUFF, Francis Jr; b 1758, Augusta Co; d 27 Aug 1832 **RU:** Private, Served in Capt John McKittrick's Co, Augusta Co Militia **CEM:** Trinity Episcopal; **GPS** 38.14917, -79.07521; 214 Beverley St; Staunton City **GS:** N **SP:** Sarah Salley (4 Mar 1764-13 Apr 1810) **VI:** Died in Augusta Co **P:** unk **BLW:** unk **RG:** unk **MK:** unk **PH:** N **SS:** E pg 399 **BS:** 196.

HUFF, John; b Nov 1743; d 10 Feb 1804 **RU:** Patriot, Gave provisions to the cause **CEM:** Mt Hebron; **GPS** 39.10916, -78.09497; 305 E Boscawen St; Winchester City **GS:** Y **SP:** Mar Elizabeth (-----) (c1757-14 Jun 1838) **VI:** No further data **P:** N **BLW:** N **RG:** Y **MK:** N **PH:** unk **SS:** AL Comm Bk II-211 **BS:** 01 pg 47; 09.

HUFF, John; b 1763, Pittsylvania Co; d 10 May 1840 **RU:** Private, Served in VA Line. Ent serv Henry Co **CEM:** Pigg River Primitive Baptist; **GPS** 36.96913, -80.07368; Rt 750 nr Callaway; Franklin **GS:** Y **SP:** 1) Mar (21 Nov 1784 Frederick Co by Alexander Balmain) Catherine Lemly 2) Mar (14 Jul 1786 Franklin Co) Mary (Polly) Gearhart 3) Mar (c 9 Feb 1837) Elizabeth Gulliams of Floyd Co. (Mar bond signed by James Ferguson 1 Feb 1837). Widow mar next Stephen A. Payne & moved to Athens Co, OH. **VI:** Sol appl pen 1 Jul 1833 Franklin Co. S5590, Recd BLW #87034-160-55 **P:** Y **BLW:** Y **RG:** N **MK:** N **PH:** unk **SS:** E pg 399; CG Vol 2 pg 1750 **BS:** 82 pg 181.

HUFFER(HUFFORD)(HUFFERT), Jacob; b 6 Nov 1755, Lancaster Co, PA; d 1848 **RU:** Private, Served in PA Companies **CEM:** Emmanuel; **GPS** unk; Mt Solon; Augusta **GS:** N **SP:** Anna Schoenauer (1760 Berks Co, PA-__) **VI:** No further data **P:** unk **BLW:** unk **RG:** unk **MK:** unk **PH:** N **SS:** JLARC Rpt App B-2 pg 9 **BS:** JLARC 125; 196.

HUFFMAN, Barnard; b unk; d 1826 **RU:** Private, Served at Ft Pitt (Pittsburgh PA) 1775 **CEM:** North End; **GPS** 36.77234, -80.73866; 101 Beaver Dam Rd, Hillsville; Carroll **GS:** N **SP:** No info **VI:** No further data **P:** unk **BLW:** unk **RG:** N **MK:** N **PH:** N **SS:** E pg 399 **BS:** 123 pg 67.

HUFFMAN (HOOFMAN), Valentine (Valentin); b c1720-1730, Germany; d c1803 **RU:** Captain, Served in Chaplin, Berks Co PA Militia **CEM:** Friedens United Church of Christ; **GPS** 38.34848, -78.87653; 3960 Friedens Church Rd; Rockingham **GS:** Y **SP:** Ann Maria Franck **VI:** Son of John Jacob & (-----) Hoofman **P:** unk **BLW:** unk **RG:** Y **MK:** Y **PH:** Y **SS:** J-NSSAR 2000 Reg **BS:** JLARC 76; 196.

HUGHART, Thomas; b 1725; d 23 May 1810 **RU:** Colonel/Patriot, Performed public and military service **CEM:** Rocky Spring Presbyterian; **GPS** 38.11470, -79.24250; 1 mi S of Deerfield; Augusta **GS:** Y **SP:** Rebecca Estill **VI:** Stone reads "A soldier of the Revolution in command of Augusta troops at the seige of Yorktown." Col rank fr Colonial war period **P:** unk **BLW:** unk **RG:** unk **MK:** N **PH:** unk **SS:** B; AL signature approval given Augusta Co 1781-3 period for public Claim **BS:** JLARC 2, 62, 63; 196.

HUGHART, Thomas; b unk; d Aft 1781 **RU:** Patriot, Gave material aid to cause **CEM:** Trinity Episcopal; **GPS** 38.14917, -79.07521; 214 Beverley St; Staunton City **GS:** U **SP:** No info **VI:** May be duplicate of Thomas Hughart reported bur at Rock Spring Cem **P:** N **BLW:** N **RG:** unk **MK:** unk **PH:** unk **SS:** J- DAR Hatcher; AL Cert Augusta Co **BS:** JLARC 2.

HUGHES, Archelaus; b 1747; d 1796 **RU:** Colonel/Patriot, Was Appointed Apr 1780 as Henry Co Lt. Gave material aid to cause **CEM:** Hughesville; **GPS** unk; Hwy 631 nr Stuart; Patrick **GS:** U **SP:** Mary Dalton **VI:** No further data **P:** unk **BLW:** unk **RG:** Y **MK:** unk **PH:** unk **SS:** AL Ct Bk pg 7a, 26, 30 **BS:** JLARC 1,30, 102.

HUGHES, Isaac; b 15 Jun 1740, Bucks Co, PA; d 23 Mar 1803 **RU:** Private, Served in Col John Alexander's Regt **CEM:** Leesburg Presbyterian; **GPS** 39.11611, -77.56722; 207 W Market St, Leesburg;

RU=Rank/Unit	CEM=Cemetery	GS=Gravestone	SP=Spousal Information
VI=Other Veteran Info	P=Pension	BLW=Bounty/Land Warrant	RG=Registered Grave
MK=SAR/DAR Marker	PH=Photo	SS=Service Source	BS=Burial Source

165

Loudoun **GS:** U **SP:** Mar (13 Mar 1764 Hunterdon Co NY) Mary Warne (25 Jul 1743 Cranbury, Middlesex Co NJ-1803) d/o George & Abigail (Warford) Warne **VI:** Son of Mathew & Elizabeth (Stevenson) Hughes **P:** unk **BLW:** unk **RG:** Y **MK:** unk **PH:** unk **SS:** J-NSSAR 1993 Reg, J- DAR Hatcher; CD **BS:** JLARC 1, 2; 196.

HUGHES, James; b 1750; d 1801 **RU:** Soldier, Served in Capt Tate's Co, Augusta Co Militia **CEM:** Trinity Episcopal; GPS 38.14917, -79.07521; 214 Beverley St; Staunton City **GS:** U **SP:** Mar (1772) Cassandra Dunn (__ Jefferson Co-__) **VI:** Son of Felix (1723 Ireland-__) & Cynthia (Kaigan) (1723-1805) Hughes. Died in Waynesboro **P:** unk **BLW:** unk **RG:** unk **MK:** unk **PH:** unk **SS:** J- DAR Hatcher; E pg 400; NSSAR Ancestor #P-187416 **BS:** JLARC 2.

HUGHES, John W; b 4 Oct 1750, Wales; d 9 Feb 1851 **RU:** Private, Served in Capt Barton Lucas's 3rd Co, Smallwood's 1st MD Regt. Fought at Long Island & White Plains. Wounded and discharged at White Plains **CEM:** Neriah Baptist; GPS 37.78778, -79.36482; Jct Rts 631 & 706, South River; Rockbridge **GS:** Y **SP:** mar (c1778) Rebecca Taylor (1753 Orange Co-26 Apr 1850 Fairfield, Rockbridge Co) **VI:** Appl pen 3 Sep 1832 Rockbridge Co. Died in Fairfield, Rockbridge Co. Widow recd pen #5594 **P:** Y **BLW:** unk **RG:** Y **MK:** Y **PH:** Y **SS:** CG Vol 2 pg 1753 **BS:** JLARC 1, 2, 79; 196.

HUGHES, Thomas A; b 10 Jan 1752, Bucks Co, PA; d 18 Jul 1822 **RU:** Soldier, Served in 3rd Cont Line **CEM:** Goose Creek; GPS 39.11250, -77.69527; Rt 722, Lincoln; Loudoun **GS:** U **SP:** mar (13 Jan 1779 at Fairfax Monthly Meeting, Loudoun Co) Sarah Schooley (31 Jan 1760 Waterford, Loudoun Co-5 Dec 1845 Franklin Co, IN) d/o John (1727-1814) & Mary (Wright) Schooley. Moved to Franklin Co IN as widow. **VI:** Son of Matthew & Elizabeth (Stephenson) Hughes of Bucks Co, PA **P:** N **BLW:** N **RG:** unk **MK:** unk **PH:** unk **SS:** E pg 400 **BS:** 196.

HUGUETT, Louis; b unk; d 1781 **RU:** Seaman, Served on "Auguste" and died from Yorktown battle **CEM:** French Memorial; GPS 36.81944, -79.39933; Yorktown; York **GS:** U **SP:** No info **VI:** No further data **P:** unk **BLW:** unk **RG:** Y **MK:** unk **PH:** unk **SS:** J-Yorktown Historian **BS:** JLARC 1, 74.

HULL, George; b 15 Oct 1757, Rockingham Co; d 4 Sep 1849 **RU:** Private, Served in Capt Fraizer's Co Augusta Co, then VA Line **CEM:** Hull Family; GPS unk; Rt 640 to Rt 637, .9 mi to Elmer Ruckman farm; Highland **GS:** Y **SP:** Hannah Keister (1757 Brandywine, Pendleton Co WV-1837) d/o Frederick (1730-1815) & Hannah (Dyer) (1735-1811) Keister **VI:** Son of Peter Thomas (1706-1776) & Susanna Margetetha (Dieffenbach) (1725-1790) Hull. Resided in Augusta Co (part that became Pendleton Co), later moved to Bath Co. GS not readable, but there. Appl for pen 27 Aug 1832 age 74. S13317 **P:** Y **BLW:** N **RG:** unk **MK:** N **PH:** N **SS:** E pg 411; CG pg 1759 **BS:** 196.

HULL, Henry; b 27 Mar 1762, Lancaster Co, PA; d 16 Sep 1835 **RU:** Soldier, Served in Augusta Co Militia 1780-82 **CEM:** Peterstown; GPS 37.39470, -80.80140; Off Rt 219 btw Peterstown & Midway, on WV state line; Giles **GS:** N **SP:** 1) Elizabeth (-----) 2) mar (11 Sep 1821 Monroe Co VA/WVA) Elizabeth Hawkins **VI:** Son of Franz "Francis" Philip (1733-1808) and Maria "Mary" Agnes (Klingel) (1732-__) Hull. Recd pen for war service 1802. DAR plaque. Grave stone has been removed and probably stolen. Widow recd pen and BLW **P:** Y **BLW:** Y **RG:** unk **MK:** unk **PH:** N **SS:** B; CG pg 1759 **BS:** 196.

HULL, Johiel; b unk; d 1781 **RU:** Soldier, Served fr NJ; killed in the battle at Yorktown **CEM:** Yorktown Victory Monument Tablet; GPS 38.28350, -78.54150; Yorktown; York **GS:** U **SP:** No info **VI:** No further data **P:** unk **BLW:** unk **RG:** unk **MK:** unk **PH:** unk **SS:** J-Yorktown Historian **BS:** JLARC 74.

HULL, Peter; b c1742-1755; d Jan 1818 **RU:** Captain, Served in Capt Hull's Co, 2nd Augusta Co Militia. Also commanded a troop of Calvary, Col John McCreey's Regt at Yorktown in Oct 1781 **CEM:** Hull Family; GPS unk; Rt 640 to Rt 637, .9 mi to Elmer Ruckman farm; Highland **GS:** U **SP:** Barbara Penniger **VI:** Son of Peter Thomas (1706-1776) & Susanna Margetetha (Dieffenbach) (1725-1790) Hull **P:** unk **BLW:** unk **RG:** unk **MK:** unk **PH:** unk **SS:** E pg 402 **BS:** JLARC 103; 196.

HUME, Francis; b 1730, Tridelphia, Spotsylvania Co; d 1813 **RU:** Captain/Patriot, Served in VA state troops and Culpeper Minutemen Bn. Served w/ Morgan and later Washington at Yorktown Oct 1781. Gave material aid to cause **CEM:** Hume; GPS unk; Nr Remington on James Madison St; Culpeper **GS:** Y **SP:** Mar (30 Aug 1763) Elizabeth Duncan (1728, Fauquier Co-__, Columbia, Boome Co, MO) **VI:** Original member Society of Cincinnati. Died in Walnut Plantation, Culpeper Co. SAR Marker **P:** unk **BLW:** unk **RG:** Y **MK:** Y **PH:** Y **SS:** J-NSSAR 2000 Reg; D Vol 1 pg 264 Culpeper Co **BS:** JLARC 76.

RU=Rank/Unit	CEM=Cemetery	GS=Gravestone	SP=Spousal Information
VI=Other Veteran Info	P=Pension	BLW=Bounty/Land Warrant	RG=Registered Grave
MK=SAR/DAR Marker	PH=Photo	SS=Service Source	BS=Burial Source

166

HUMES (HUME), William; b 1758; d 3 May 1808 **RU:** Private, Served in Fauquier Co Militia. Wounded near Williamsburg 1781 **CEM:** Mt Union; GPS 37.45133, -79.97055; 4614 Catawba Rd, Mt Union; Botetourt **GS:** Y **SP:** No info **VI:** Pen recd 19 Dec 1783. Was on 1785 pen list. Died age 50 **P:** Y **BLW:** unk **RG:** N **MK:** N **PH:** unk **SS:** A pg 402; BX pg 397 **BS:** 115 pg 41; 196.

HUMPHREY, Jesse; b 29 Sep 1766; d 1 Jan 1815 **RU:** Private, Ent serv Caroline Co **CEM:** Ebenezer Baptist; GPS 39.05824, -77.84142; 20421 Airmont Rd, Bluemont; Loudoun **GS:** Y **SP:** Winey (-----) **VI:** Died in Bloomfield, Loudoun Co **P:** unk **BLW:** unk **RG:** Y **MK:** N **PH:** unk **SS:** E pg 402 **BS:** 25 pg 154.

HUMPHREY, William; b 1748; d 1827 **RU:** Private, Served in Capt Tates Co, Augusta Co Militia **CEM:** Humphries Lone Graves; GPS unk; 11 mi SW of Covington; Alleghany **GS:** N **SP:** Ruth (-----) **VI:** No further data **P:** unk **BLW:** unk **RG:** N **MK:** N **PH:** N **SS:** E pg 403 **BS:** 160 Humphrey.

HUMPHREY (HUMPHREYS), Abner; b 27 Oct 1763; d 17 Dec 1824 **RU:** Private, Specific service info is at the Lib VA in Auditors Accts XV pg 513 **CEM:** Ebenezer Baptist; GPS 39.05824, -77.84142; 20421 Airmont Rd, Bluemont; Loudoun **GS:** Y **SP:** Mary Van Hook Purcell (11 Sep 1758-11 Mar 1824) d/o Thomas (1720-1779) & Mary (Van Hook) (1723-1771) Purcell **VI:** No further data **P:** unk **BLW:** unk **RG:** Y **MK:** unk **PH:** unk **SS:** CZ pg 232 **BS:** JLARC 1, 2, 32; 196.

HUMPHREY (HUMPHREYS), Thomas; b 2 Jun 1742, PA; d 7 Jun 1822 **RU:** Captain, Served in 2nd VA Regt & Loudoun Co Militia, 1777-1783 **CEM:** Ketoctin Baptist; GPS 39.15746, -77.74870; Ketoctin Church Rd, Purcellville; Loudoun **GS:** Y **SP:** Mary Marks **VI:** No further data **P:** unk **BLW:** unk **RG:** Y **MK:** N **PH:** unk **SS:** AK; E pg 403; AZ pg 211 **BS:** 04 JLARC 1, 2, 32.

HUMPHREYS (HUMPHRIES), David; b 1743, County Armagh, Ireland; d 15 Aug 1826 **RU:** Soldier/Patriot, Served in Capt Cunningham's Co, Augusta Co Regt, VA Militia. Also gave 365# beef to cause **CEM:** Bethel Presbyterian; GPS 38.04257, -79.17283; 563 Bethel Green Rd, Middlebrook; Augusta **GS:** Y **SP:** Margaret Finley (__-22 Sep 1849) **VI:** Died age 83 nr Greenville, Augusta Co **P:** unk **BLW:** unk **RG:** Y **MK:** Y **PH:** unk **SS:** D pg 51 Augusta Co; DD **BS:** JLARC 1, 62, 63; 196.

HUNDLEY, Josiah; b 1756; d 11 Aug 1827 **RU:** Private, Ent serv Amelia Co. Served in VA Line under Patrick Henry **CEM:** Bethel Baptist; GPS 37.50986, -77.71166; 1100 Huguenot Springs Rd, Midlothian; Chesterfield **GS:** Y **SP:** Mar (1758) Ann Holmes (13 May 1768-19 Jan 1852). **VI:** Newer stone says he was b in England, but this is doubtful as there were several Josias Hundleys long established in nearby Amelia Co. Sol appl pen age 62 on 27 Aug 1818 Mecklenburg Co without receipt. DAR plaque. Widow appl pen 8 July 1840 Mecklenburg Co. W7844 **P:** Y **BLW:** unk **RG:** Y **MK:** Y **PH:** unk **SS:** CG pg 1766 **BS:** JLARC 1, 2, 4,12, 35; 196.

HUNGATE, William; b unk; d Aft Jan 1833 **RU:** Lieutenant, Served in Montgomery Co Militia Aug 1775 **CEM:** Hungate Family; GPS unk; Rt 615 nr Little River; Floyd **GS:** U **SP:** No info **VI:** Will dated Jan 1833. Memorialized by DAR plaque in cem **P:** unk **BLW:** unk **RG:** unk **MK:** unk **PH:** unk **SS:** SAR Ancestor #P-188027; E pg 404; AZ pg 139 **BS:** JLARC 2, 29; 196 for John Mitchell.

HUNGERFORD, John Pratt; b 2 Jan 1761, Westmoreland Co; d 21 Dec 1833 **RU:** Captain, Served in VA State Regt in 1779 & 1780 **CEM:** Hungerford-Griffin; GPS unk; 373 Resolutions Rd, Leedstown; Westmoreland **GS:** Y **SP:** no info **VI:** Rev War. VA House Delegates 1797-1801. VA Senate 1801-09. 12th Congress Member-elect 4 Mar-29 Nov 1811 but succeeded by John Taliaferro. US Rep 13th 14th Congress 1813-17. Brigadier Gen of militia in War of 1812. Sol appl pen Westmoreland Co. S5586. Died inTwiford, Westmoreland Co **P:** Y **BLW:** unk **RG:** N **MK:** N **PH:** unk **SS:** E pg 404; CG Vol 2 pg 1766 **BS:** 75 pg 1; 201 pg 7397.

HUNGERFORD, Thomas; b 1740; d 1803 **RU:** First Lieutenant, Served in 3rd VA Regt VA Line **CEM:** Hungerford-Griffin; GPS unk; 373 Resolutions Rd, Leedstown; Westmoreland **GS:** U **SP:** No info **VI:** Govt GS indicates service. Recd BLW #934-200-26 May 1789 (also recorded at #2476) **P:** unk **BLW:** Y **RG:** Y **MK:** unk **PH:** unk **SS:** J-NSSAR 1993 Reg; CG Vol 2 pg 1767 **BS:** JLARC 1.

HUNSICKER, Peter; b 1761, Lancaster Co, PA; d 1816 **RU:** Patriot, Provided provisions to Cont Army, including 261# flour **CEM:** Stone Chapel Presbyterian; GPS 39.22610, -78.01060; Old Charles Town Rd, Berryville; Clarke **GS:** Y **SP:** Ann Eve Schmidt (c1761-30 Apr 1850) **VI:** Son of Daniel & Christina

RU=Rank/Unit   CEM=Cemetery   GS=Gravestone   SP=Spousal Information
VI=Other Veteran Info   P=Pension   BLW=Bounty/Land Warrant   RG=Registered Grave
MK=SAR/DAR Marker   PH=Photo   SS=Service Source   BS=Burial Source

167

Hunsicke, natives of Wolfersheim, Germany. Had public service claims **P:** N **BLW:** N **RG:** Y **MK**: N **PH:** Y **SS:** AL Cert Issued **BS:** 58 pg 90; 196.

HUNT, David; b 1745; d 1826 **RU:** Colonel/Patriot, In Aug 1781 marched fr Pittsylvania in Capt William Dix Co to Little York until surrender of Cornwallis. Marched with Capt Charles Williams to guard British prisoners at Noland's Ferry on Potomac. Gave material aid to cause **CEM:** Hunt; GPS 37.007097, -79.224135; Mt Airy Rt 640 near Renan; Pittsylvania **GS:** Y **SP:** No info **VI:** No further data **P:** unk **BLW:** unk **RG:** Y **MK**: unk **PH:** unk **SS:** D Pittsylvania Co **BS:** 174; JLARC 76, 90, 96.

HUNT, James; b 1750; d 7 Nov 1820 **RU:** Private, Served in VA Line; entered serv 1776 **CEM:** Walnut Tree Farm; GPS unk; Btw Vienna & Oakton; Fairfax **GS:** Y **SP:** Mar (12 Jan 1792 in MD) Una Lovelace **VI:** Moved to Fairfax Co in 1814. Appl pen 29 May 1818 Prince William Co age 57. (however 24 May 1820 gave age as 70, living in Fairfax Co) S38062 **P:** Y **BLW:** unk **RG:** N **MK:** N **PH:** unk **SS:** KI Vol 2 pg 355; CG Vol 2 pg 1770 **BS:** 80 vol 2 pg 184.

HUNTER, Alexander; b 1706; d Jun 1798 **RU:** Patriot, Public service claim **CEM:** Old Presbyterian Meeting House; GPS 38.48528, -77.23532; 323 S Fairfax St; Alexandria City **GS:** N **SP:** No info **VI:** Bur 27 Jun 1798, age 82 **P:** N **BLW:** N **RG:** N **MK**: N **PH:** N **SS:** AL Comm Bk V **BS:** 110 pg 131.

HUNTER, Elizabeth (nee Chapman); b 13 Jun 1733; d 1783 **RU:** Patriot, Provided driver and horses for 40 days (claim filed 1782 under Act of 1780) **CEM:** Pohick Episcopal; GPS 38.42546, -77.11598; 9301 Richmond Hwy, Lorton; Fairfax **GS:** Y **SP:** John Hunter MD **VI:** Originally interred at family cem at Summer Hill in Fairfax Co. 28 Mar 1940, Grs at Summer Hill were removed & reinterred at Pohick Church **P:** N **BLW:** N **RG:** Y **MK**: N **PH:** Y **SS:** R pg 2 **BS:** 04.

HUNTER, George; b 1742; d Feb 1798 **RU:** Patriot, Signed Legislative Petition at First Presbyterian Church, Alexandria **CEM:** Old Presbyterian Meeting House; GPS 38.48528, -77.23532; 323 S Fairfax St; Alexandria City **GS:** N **SP:** No info **VI:** Died of intemperance age 56, bur 15 Feb 1798 **P:** N **BLW:** N **RG:** unk **MK:** unk **PH:** N **SS:** BB **BS:** 196; 23 pg 103.

HUNTER, George Dr; b 1753; d 1776 **RU:** Surgeon, Served in Revolutionary Navy, aboard the sloop "Congress" **CEM:** Pohick Episcopal; GPS 38.42546, -77.11598; 9301 Richmond Hwy, Lorton; Fairfax **GS:** Y **SP:** No info **VI:** Son of (-----) and Elizabeth (-----) Hunter. Died at sea. Grave moved fr Summer Hill Plantation. DAR plaque placed by Mount Vernon chapter **P:** unk **BLW:** Y **RG:** Y **MK:** Y **PH:** Y **SS:** E pg 405 **BS:** JLARC 1, 14, 28, 51; 69 pg 83.

HUNTER, James; b 23 Oct 1721, Legenwood, Berwickshire Scotland; d c1785 **RU:** Patriot, Was owner of Hunter Ironworks, Falmouth. Made camp utensils, weapons, equipment for continental forces. Was not fully compensated-lost entire estate in debt **CEM:** Union Church; GPS 38.32268, -77.46615; Carter St, Falmouth; Stafford **GS:** Y **SP:** No info **VI:** Son of James & Helen (Simson) Hunter of Duns Scotland. Gravesite has iron fence with his name. Iron Works in operation by 1761; by 1775 largest iron works in colonies. Sample musket was made standard. Will dated 18 Nov 1784 **P:** N **BLW:** N **RG:** Y **MK**: Y **PH:** Y **SS:** D pg 883 **BS:** 30 pg 308-313; 04 1998.

HUNTER, John; b 1762; d 1849 **RU:** Patriot, Gave material aid to the cause **CEM:** Old Presbyterian Meeting House; GPS 38.48528, -77.23532; 323 S Fairfax St; Alexandria City **GS:** N **SP:** No info **VI:** Died age 66. Death notice in Alexandria Gazette, 6 Sep 1826, pg 3. Listed on SAR plaque in cemetery **P:** N **BLW:** N **RG:** N **MK:** N **PH:** N **SS:** AL Ct BK pg 1; J-NSSAR 1993 Reg; AK **BS:** JLARCK 1; 23 pg 103; 196.

HUNTER, John Chapman; b c1762; d 14 Feb 1849 **RU:** Private?/Patriot, Specific service not identified. Styled "General" in his obit. Paid the supply tax in Fairfax Co 1782 **CEM:** Flint Hill; GPS 38.88190, -77.29390; Chain Bridge Rd, Oakton; Fairfax **GS:** Y **SP:** Sarah Dade (c1775-3 Oct 1845) **VI:** GS has been removed fr Hunter Family graveyard (now on Glengyle Dr) to Flint Hill Cemetery. Was presiding justice of Fairfax Co at his death. Styled "General" in his obit in the Alexandria Gazette on 22 Feb 1849, pg 3 **P:** unk **BLW:** unk **RG:** Y **MK:** N **PH:** unk **SS:** E pg 405-406; DV **BS:** 32 e-mail; 196.

HUNTER, John Jr; b 10 Jul 1760, Bedford Co, later Campbell Co; d unk **RU:** Soldier, Ent Serv Campbell Co. Served in VA Line **CEM:** Concord Presbyterian #2; GPS unk; .5 mi S of Hunter's Tavern; Campbell

RU=Rank/Unit   CEM=Cemetery   GS=Gravestone   SP=Spousal Information
VI=Other Veteran Info   P=Pension   BLW=Bounty/Land Warrant   RG=Registered Grave
MK=SAR/DAR Marker   PH=Photo   SS=Service Source   BS=Burial Source

168

GS: U SP: Rachel (-----) VI: Son of John Hunter Sr. Lived in NC, TN, KY. Appl 14 Oct 1833 Campbell Co. S15897 P: Y BLW: unk RG: unk MK: N PH: unk SS: CG Vol 2 pg 1775 BS: JLARC 36.

HUNTER, Nathaniel Chapman; b 1764, Alexandria; d 28 Apr 1812 RU: Private, Serv in VA Line for duration of war; recd wounds during serv CEM: Pohick Episcopal; GPS 38.42546, -77.11598; 9301 Richmond Hwy, Lorton; Fairfax GS: Y SP: Ann Tyler, d/o Charles & (-----) Tyler, Esq VI: Son of Dr. John & (__ Chapman) Hunter. Was a merchant in Dumfries, Prince William Co. In 1806 moved to Alexandria and was officer in a bank. Bur first in Summer Hill cem in Arlington moved to Pohick Church cem on 6 Apr 1940 P: unk BLW: unk RG: N MK: N PH: unk SS: AO Vol I pg 198 BS: 69 pg 83, 83A.

HUNTER, Robert; b unk; d Aft 1781 RU: Patriot, Gave material aid to cause in Bedford Co CEM: Concord Presbyterian #3; GPS unk; 4909 Reedy Spring Rd, Sprout Springs; Campbell GS: U SP: Nancy (-----) VI: No further data P: N BLW: N RG: unk MK: N PH: unk SS: AL resided and gave in Bedford Co; NSSAR Ancestor #P-188460 BS: JLARC 36.

HUNTER, Samuel; b 1737; d 18 Apr 1813 RU: Patriot, Gave material aid to cause CEM: North Mountain; GPS unk; 7 mi S of Staunton on N side Rt 252; Augusta GS: Y SP: Susannah Alexander VI: Name also on cenotaph monument here P: N BLW: N RG: Y MK: N PH: unk SS: AL cert issued; BY BS: 80 vol 2 pg 186;196.

HUNTER, William; b 1749; d Oct 1803 RU: Soldier/Patriot, Gave material aid to cause CEM: Old Presbyterian Meeting House; GPS 38.48528, -77.23532; 323 S Fairfax St; Alexandria City GS: N SP: No info VI: Bur 18 Oct 1803, age 54 P: unk BLW: unk RG: Y MK: unk PH: N SS: J-NSSAR 1993 Reg; AL Ct Bk pg 4 Fairfax Co BS: JLARC 1; 23 pg 104.

HUNTER, William Jr; b 20 Jan 1731, Galston, Scotland; d 19 Nov 1792 RU: Patriot, Gave material aid to cause. Signed a Legislative Petition in Alexandria CEM: Old Presbyterian Meeting House; GPS 38.48528, -77.23532; 323 S Fairfax St; Alexandria City GS: Y SP: No info VI: Mayor of Alexandria, and founder of St Andrew's Society in Alexandria. A slab in cemetery lists his RW service. Death notice in Alexandria Gazette, 22 Nov 1792 P: N BLW: N RG: N MK: N PH: unk SS: AL Ct bk lt pg 4; AK; S-Alexandria BS: 23 pg 103; 196.

HURDLE, Lawrence; b 1750, MD; d 1 Dec 1848 RU: Private, Served in MD Line 1776-1782. Was in battles at Harlan Height, NY & Camden, SC CEM: St Mary's Catholic; GPS 38.79390, -77.04750; 310 S Royal St; Alexandria City GS: Y SP: Mar (20 Oct 1792 Georgetown, MD) Nancy Wheeler, (__-13 Dec 1863) VI: Sol appl pen 21 Aug 1818 Montgomery Co MD. Widow appl pen 30 Aug 1849 Alexandria Co. Widow appl for BLW 15 Mar 1855 Alexandria Co. W2157. BLW #1-60-55. Death notice in the Alexandria Gazette 2 Dec 1848, pg 3 says he died 1 Dec 1848 age 98 yrs. No dates on stone P: Y BLW: Y RG: Y MK: Y PH: Y SS: SAR Ancestor #P-188773; M Vol 3 pg 514; CG pg 1781 BS: 174 pg 164; 196.

HURSIN, Francois; b unk; d 1781 RU: Soldier, Served in Agenois Bn and died fr battle at Yorktown CEM: French Memorial; GPS 36.81944, -79.39933; Yorktown; York GS: U SP: No info VI: No further data P: unk BLW: unk RG: unk MK: unk PH: unk SS: J-Yorktown Historian BS: JLARC 74.

HURST, John; b 1713, Stafford Co; d 26 Apr 1789 RU: Patriot, Gave material aid to cause CEM: Summers; GPS 38.82121, -77.14098; Jct Rt 613 & Beaugard St, Lincolnia; Fairfax GS: U SP: Elizabeth Summers (1724-1781) d/o John (__-6 Dec 1747) & (-----) Hurst of Stafford Co VI: No further data P: N BLW: N RG: unk MK: unk PH: unk SS: AL Ct Bk pg 10, 22 BS: 196.

HURT, Moses; b 1730; d 1806 RU: Lieutenant/Patriot, Gave material aid to cause CEM: Hurt Family; GPS unk; Nr Mobley's Creek; Bedford GS: N SP: Ruth Turner, d/o James Turner VI: No further data P: unk BLW: unk RG: unk MK: N PH: N SS: J- DAR Hatcher; AL Cert Bedford Co BS: JLARC 2; 196.

HUTCHESON, Benjamin; b 3 Apr 1756; d 7 Sep 1823 RU: Patriot, Gave material aid to cause CEM: Hutchinson-Whaley; GPS unk; next to 4319 General Kearney Ct, Chantilly; Fairfax GS: Y SP: Elizabeth (----) (10 May 1756-30 Oct 1833) also bur here, "wife of B. Hutchinson" VI: No further data P: N BLW: N RG: N MK: N PH: unk SS: AL CT Bk pg 54 BS: 61 vol 4 pg CH-21.

HUTCHESON, William; b unk; d 1779 RU: Private, Served in Capt Robert McClanahan's Co at Point Pleasant, Oct 1774 CEM: Old Hoges Chapel; GPS unk; Mount Lake Rd; Giles GS: U SP: No info VI: No further data P: unk BLW: unk RG: unk MK: unk PH: unk SS: E pg 407; Z pg 128-9 BS: 196.

RU=Rank/Unit   CEM=Cemetery   GS=Gravestone   SP=Spousal Information
VI=Other Veteran Info   P=Pension   BLW=Bounty/Land Warrant   RG=Registered Grave
MK=SAR/DAR Marker   PH=Photo   SS=Service Source   BS=Burial Source

169

HUTCHINGS, Moses; b 1 Mar 1754, Culpeper Co; d 2 Apr 1836 **RU:** Lieutenant, Ent serv Pittsylvania Co Mar 1777 in Capt John Conelson's Co. Marched to Long Island under Col Shelby against Cherokee & Chickamauga. Was Indian spy under Capt Thomas Dillard 1778. 1779, and Lt under Capt Armistead Shelton.In Feb 1781 harrassed British pickets with 9 others.Was in Capt Thomas Smith's Co Campbell's Regt at Battle of Guilford CH **CEM:** Hutchings, Jack Crane Farm; **GPS** 36.74674, -79.42226; Dry Fork Rt 718; Pittsylvania **GS:** Y **SP:** No info **VI:** Son of Christopher and Elizabeth (-----) Hutchings. Pensioned in Pittsylvania 1832. S8742 **P:** Y **BLW:** unk **RG:** Y **MK:** Y **PH:** unk **SS:** K Vol 3 pg 360 **BS:** 174; JLARC 1, 2, 96.

HUTCHINS (HUTCHINGS), Christopher; b 1722, England; d 20 May 1807 **RU:** Patriot, Gave material aid to cause **CEM:** Rock Wall; **GPS** unk; Dry Fork; Pittsylvania **GS:** Y **SP:** Elizabeth Parks (1724-1807) d/o Thomas & Sarah (Miller) Parks **VI:** No further data **P:** N **BLW:** N **RG:** Y **MK:** N **PH:** unk **SS:** D Vol 3 pg 762, 769; AS SAR regis **BS:** SAR regis.

INSKEEP, James; b 1734, Burlington, NJ; d 1802 **RU:** Patriot, Gave material aid to cause **CEM:** Fairview; **GPS** 38.48080,-78.00470; Sperryville Pike Rt 522, Culpeper; Culpeper **GS:** Y **SP:** Mar (1760) Hope Collins (1745 Burlington, NJ-1806) **VI:** No further data **P:** N **BLW:** N **RG:** N **MK:** N **PH:** unk **SS:** AL Ct Bk pg 24 **BS:** 29 pg 27.

IRELAND, James; b 3 Dec 1745, Edinburgh, Scotland; d 5 May 1806 **RU:** Patriot, DAR marker calls him a patriot. He was a Baptist minister imprisoned for proselytizing in early 1770s in Culpeper Co **CEM:** Berryville Baptist; **GPS** 39.94700, -77.53700; 114 Academy St, Berryville; Clarke **GS:** Y **SP:** Mar (22 Apr 1771) Jane Burgess (c1750-Apr 1790, Page Co) **VI:** Imprisoned for proselytizing in early 1770s, Culpeper Co. Died in Crooked Run, Frederick Co. Buck Marsh Baptist Church location not known. Memorial stone at Berryville Baptist which says he was bur at Buck Marsh Baptist Church "near here." Served as pastor at Buck Mark Baptist 1778-1806 **P:** N **BLW:** N **RG:** Y **MK:** Y **PH:** N **SS:** AR Vol 2 pg 195; BT **BS:** JLARC 1, 2; 196.

IRONS, John; b 16 Dec 1825; d 1821 **RU:** Private, Served in Capt Lawson Smith's MD Rifle Co, Lt Col Moses Rawlings' Regt **CEM:** Royal Oak; **GPS** 36.84315, -81.49660; Behind Marion Baptist Church, Marion; Smyth **GS:** Y **SP:** No info **VI:** No further data **P:** unk **BLW:** unk **RG:** N **MK:** N **PH:** unk **SS:** A pg 240 **BS:** 97 vol I pg 139.

IRVINE, John Jr; b 1735, PA; d 1814 **RU:** Patriot, Gave material aid to cause **CEM:** Hat Creek Presbyterian; **GPS** 37.06570, -78.54240; 6442 Hat Creek Rd, Brookneal; Campbell **GS:** Y **SP:** Mar (4 Aug 1772, Amherst Co) Mary Anne Tucker (1752-1817) **VI:** Son of John (1700-1788) & Mary Margaret (Boyd) (1707-__) Irvine. Died in Hat Creek, Campbell Co. Newer monument shared with his parents styles him "Maj"—achieved rank of Maj after RW **P:** N **BLW:** N **RG:** unk **MK:** N **PH:** Y **SS:** AL Ct Bk 3 **BS:** JLARC 36; 196.

IRVINE, John Sr; b 1700; d 1788 **RU:** Patriot, Gave to cause in Bedford Co **CEM:** Hat Creek Presbyterian; **GPS** 37.06570, -78.54240; 6442 Hat Creek Rd, Brookneal; Campbell **GS:** Y **SP:** Mary Margaret Boyd **VI:** Newer monument, shared with his son John Irvine Jr **P:** N **BLW:** N **RG:** unk **MK:** N **PH:** unk **SS:** AL Certificate J- DAR Hatcher **BS:** JLARC 2; 196.

IRVINE, William; b unk; d unk **RU:** Soldier, Served in 1st, 10th, & 14th Cont Lines **CEM:** Stonewall Jackson Memorial; **GPS** 37.78128, -79.44604; 314 S Main St; Lexington City **GS:** U **SP:** No info **VI:** No further data **P:** unk **BLW:** unk **RG:** unk **MK:** unk **PH:** unk **SS:** NSSAR Ancestor p-189903; E pg 410 **BS:** JLARC 63.

IRVINE (ERWIN, IRWIN), Edward; b 1740; d 1814 **RU:** Soldier/Patriot, Gave material aid to cause **CEM:** Mossy Creek Presbyterian; **GPS** 38.35331 -79.04914; 372 Kyles Mill Rd, Mt Solon; Augusta **GS:** Y **SP:** 1) Mary Curry; 2) Sarah Percy **VI:** Son of John and Jean (-----) Erwin **P:** unk **BLW:** unk **RG:** unk **MK:** N **PH:** unk **SS:** AL List 1 pg 10 Augusta Co **BS:** JLARC 62, 63; 196.

IRWIN, James; b 1757, Belfast, Ireland; d 5 Sep 1822 **RU:** Private?, Served in 1st, 10th, 14th Cont Line **CEM:** Presbyterian Church; **GPS** 38.80015, -77.05791; Wilkes St & Hamilton Ln; Alexandria City **GS:** Y **SP:** No info **VI:** Guardian of John Adams, church elder. Died of fever age 64 **P:** unk **BLW:** unk **RG:** Y **MK:** N **PH:** unk **SS:** E pg 410 **BS:** 23 pg 44.

RU=Rank/Unit · VI=Other Veteran Info · MK=SAR/DAR Marker · CEM=Cemetery · P=Pension · PH=Photo · GS=Gravestone · BLW=Bounty/Land Warrant · SS=Service Source · SP=Spousal Information · RG=Registered Grave · BS=Burial Source

170

ISBELL, Joseph; b 1747, Caroline Co; d 20 Jul 1823 **RU:** Patriot, Gave material aid to cause **CEM:** Isbell Family; GPS unk; Rt 619; Goochland **GS:** U **SP:** No info **VI:** Son of William (1720-1807) & Ann (Dillard) (1724-1829) Isbell **P:** N **BLW:** N **RG:** unk **MK:** unk **PH:** unk **SS:** AL Ct Bk pg 33 Louisa Co **BS:** 196.

ISBELL, William; b c1716-1726; d 1807 **RU:** Patriot, Gave 11 pounds, 20 shillings to cause **CEM:** Isbell Family; GPS unk; Rt 619; Goochland **GS:** U **SP:** Mar (before 5 Mar 1757) Ann Dillard (1724-1829) **VI:** Lived in Lickinghold Twp, St James Parish, Goochland. No marker has been found **P:** N **BLW:** N **RG:** unk **MK:** unk **PH:** unk **SS:** AL Ct Bk pg 1, 13, 22 **BS:** 196.

IVEY, John; b unk; d unk **RU:** Patriot, Gave material aid to the cause **CEM:** Ivey Family; GPS unk; Rt 611 5.5 mi W of Emporia; Greensville **GS:** Y **SP:** No info **VI:** No further data **P:** N **BLW:** N **RG:** N **MK:** N **PH:** unk **SS:** AL Ct bk pg 7 **BS:** 141 Ivey house.

JACKSON, Francis; b 1725, Henrico Co; d 1792 **RU:** Patriot, Gave material aid to cause and paid personal Property Tax Amelia Co 1782 (considered supply tax to support war) **CEM:** Jackson Family; GPS unk; 6101 Buckskin Rd, Rt 640, Jetersville; Amelia **GS:** U **SP:** Mar (1783) Mary Franklin (c1745-1790) **VI:** No further data **P:** N **BLW:** N **RG:** unk **MK:** unk **PH:** unk **SS:** DAR Ancestor #A061251; Al Ct Bk II pg 15, 21, 75; DV **BS:** 196.

JACKSON, George; b 1764; d 18 Mar 1847 **RU:** Captain, Was in charge of Monongalia Co Militia; served in VA Line as volunteer. Was wounded in service **CEM:** Burnt Factory United Methodist Church; GPS 38,18490, -78.07550; 1943 Jordan Springs Rd Rt 664, Burnt Factory; Frederick **GS:** Y **SP:** Mar (18 May 1809 Jefferson Co, VA, now WV) Susan Goldsborough (__-14 Feb 1840) **VI:** Son of John (1715-1801 Clarksburg WVA) & (-----) Jackson. Recd pen R15396. Also recd 1/2 pay under Act of 5 Jul 1832 (disabled due to RW service) **P:** Y **BLW:** U **RG:** N **MK:** unk **PH:** Y **SS:** E pg 411; N pg 1228; CG pg 1810 **BS:** 196.

JACKSON, John; b unk; d 1795 **RU:** Patriot, Performed public service as Assistant Commissary officer, 24 Jun 1782 in Middlesex Co **CEM:** Christ Church; GPS 37.60968, -76.54643; Rt 33 2 mi E of Saluda; Middlesex **GS:** U **SP:** No info **VI:** No further data **P:** N **BLW:** N **RG:** N **MK:** N **PH:** unk **SS:** G pg 202-3 **BS:** 84, pg 198.

JACKSON, Josiah; b 5 Mar 1732, Chester Co, PA; d Apr 1794 **RU:** Patriot, Gave material aid to the cause **CEM:** Back Creek Quaker, aka Gainesboro United Methodist; GPS 39.27861, -78.25694; 166 Siler Ln, Gainesboro; Frederick **GS:** U **SP:** Mar (Lampeter M.M., Chester Co, PA) Ruth Steer (1747-1825) **VI:** No further data **P:** N **BLW:** N **RG:** unk **MK:** unk **PH:** unk **SS:** AL Ct bk pg 7 **BS:** 196.

JACKSON, Thomas; b c1755; d Bef 15 Jul 1807 **RU:** Private, Served in Lousia Co Militia **CEM:** Jackson Family; GPS unk; Catalpa Hall, Rt 522; Louisa **GS:** U **SP:** No info **VI:** No further data **P:** unk **BLW:** unk **RG:** Y **MK:** N **PH:** unk **SS:** AK May 2006 **BS:** 04, May 06.

JACKSON, Thomas; b 1740; d 14 Aug 1843 **RU:** Soldier, Served in Benjamin Brigg's and Uriah Springer's companies under Col Gibson **CEM:** Green Hill; GPS 39.15810, -77.97690; Berryville; Clarke **GS:** Y **SP:** No info **VI:** Originally bur on "Cherry Hill" farm GS, but not body, moved to Green Hill Cemetery sometime after 1842, BLW 200 acres awarded 24 Jun 1783 **P:** unk **BLW:** Y **RG:** unk **MK:** N **PH:** Y **SS:** F pg 40 **BS:** JLARC 24.

JACKSON, William; b 1742 Louisa Co; d 13 Sep 1781 **RU:** Lieutenant, Sworn in 11 Aug 1777. Retired 1 Jun 1778 **CEM:** Jackson Family; GPS unk; Catalpa Hall, Rt 522; Louisa **GS:** U **SP:** Susannah Goodwin **VI:** No further data **P:** unk **BLW:** unk **RG:** Y **MK:** unk **PH:** unk **SS:** E pg 412 **BS:** 04, May 06.

JACKSON, William Sullivan; b 1759, Dorset Co, MD; d 22 Aug 1849 **RU:** Soldier, Served in MD Line. Ent serv 1777 **CEM:** Jackson Family; GPS unk; Rt 658, along Bear Creek; Grayson **GS:** U **SP:** Mar (8 Aug 1814) Jemima Burnet (c1787-__) **VI:** Sol appl pen 12 Nov 1834 Grayson Co. Widow appl pen 3 Oct 1853 Carroll Co age 66. W7883 **P:** Y **BLW:** unk **RG:** unk **MK:** unk **PH:** unk **SS:** K Vol 3 pg 10; CG pg 1815 **BS:** JLARC 4.

JACOBS, George; b 1755; d 1840 **RU:** Private, Was paid at Romney in 1775 **CEM:** Cub Creek; GPS unk; Off Rt 789 Cub Creek Rd at Beech Grove Community; Nelson **GS:** U **SP:** No info **VI:** No further data **P:** unk **BLW:** unk **RG:** unk **MK:** unk **PH:** unk **SS:** E pg 412 **BS:** JLARC 83.

RU=Rank/Unit	CEM=Cemetery	GS=Gravestone	SP=Spousal Information
VI=Other Veteran Info	P=Pension	BLW=Bounty/Land Warrant	RG=Registered Grave
MK=SAR/DAR Marker	PH=Photo	SS=Service Source	BS=Burial Source

171

JACOBS, John; b 1740, Germany; d 24 Feb 1812 **RU**: Captain/Patriot, Gave material aid to cause **CEM**: Cub Creek; GPS unk; Off Rt 789 Cub Creek Rd at Beech Grove Community; Nelson **GS**: U **SP**: Mar (21 May 1740, Amherst Co) Sarah (Sally) Crawford (26 Sep 1740-1832, Nelson Co) d/o David & Ann (Anderson) Crawford **VI**: No further data **P**: unk **BLW**: unk **RG**: unk **MK**: unk **PH**: unk **SS**: AL Cert Amherst Co **BS**: JLARC 83.

JACOBS, John; b unk; d 1781 **RU**: Corporal, Capt Van Rensselears 4th Co, Col James Livingston's Battalion, NY line Regt. Killed in the battle at Yorktown **CEM**: Yorktown Victory Monument Tablet; GPS 38.28350, -78.54150; Yorktown; York **GS**: U **SP**: No info **VI**: No further data **P**: unk **BLW**: unk **RG**: unk **MK**: unk **PH**: unk **SS**: J-Yorktown Historian; AX pg 237 **BS**: JLARC 74.

JACOBS, William H; b unk; d unk **RU**: Private, Served in Frederick Co Militia **CEM**: Trenary Farm; GPS unk; Bayard Post Office; Warren **GS**: Y **SP**: No info **VI**: No further data **P**: unk **BLW**: unk **RG**: N **MK**: N **PH**: unk **SS**: E pg 412 **BS**: 50 pg 24.

JACOBY, Nicolas; b unk; d 1781 **RU**: Soldier, Served in Soissonnais Bn and died fr battle at Yorktown **CEM**: French Memorial; GPS 36.81944, -79.39933; Yorktown; York **GS**: U **SP**: No info **VI**: No further data **P**: unk **BLW**: unk **RG**: Y **MK**: unk **PH**: unk **SS**: J-Yorktown Historian **BS**: JLARC 1, 74.

JAGOUS, Francois; b unk; d 1781 **RU**: Seaman, Served on "Saint-Esprit" and died from Yorktown battle **CEM**: French Memorial; GPS 36.81944, -79.39933; Yorktown; York **GS**: U **SP**: No info **VI**: No further data **P**: unk **BLW**: unk **RG**: Y **MK**: unk **PH**: unk **SS**: J-Yorktown Historian **BS**: JLARC 1, 74.

JAMAIS, Sebastian; b unk; d 1781 **RU**: Soldier, Served in Touraine Bn and died fr battle at Yorktown **CEM**: French Memorial; GPS 36.81944, -79.39933; Yorktown; York **GS**: U **SP**: No info **VI**: No further data **P**: unk **BLW**: unk **RG**: Y **MK**: unk **PH**: unk **SS**: J-Yorktown Historian **BS**: JLARC 1, 74.

JAMES, Edward; b unk; d Aft 1814 **RU**: USN Lieutenant, Was Lt on sloop "Scorpion" under Capt Westcott 20 Sep 1776 **CEM**: Red Mill Farm; GPS unk; Hedgelawn Rd; Virginia Beach City **GS**: Y **SP**: No info **VI**: No further data **P**: unk **BLW**: unk **RG**: N **MK**: N **PH**: unk **SS**: L pg 206 **BS**: 93 Red Mill Fm.

JAMES, John; b 16 Mar 1709, Stafford Co; d 2 Jan 1778 **RU**: Patriot, He or son John James Jr gave use of wagon & beef to cause **CEM**: James Family; GPS unk; Midland; Fauquier **GS**: Y **SP**: Mar (before 16 Aug 1738 Stafford Co) Dinah Allen (1716 Stafford Co-16 May 1800), dau of Willam & (-----) Allen **VI**: Son of William & (-----) James **P**: N **BLW**: N **RG**: Y **MK**: N **PH**: unk **SS**: H; D Vol III pg 873, 879, 880 **BS**: 19 pg 131.

JAMES, Thomas; b 1759; d 1828 **RU**: Patriot, Performed civil service as clerk of Kingston Parish **CEM**: James Family; GPS 37.35835, -76.33166; End of Bar Neck Rd, Susan; Mathews **GS**: U **SP**: Betsy Davis, (1763-1830) **VI**: No further data **P**: N **BLW**: N **RG**: unk **MK**: unk **PH**: unk **SS**: B **BS**: 196.

JAMES, Thomas; b unk; d 1833 **RU**: Private?, Served in 9th & 15th Cont Lines of VA **CEM**: Goose Creek; GPS 39.11250, -77.69527; Rt 722, Lincoln; Loudoun **GS**: Y **SP**: No info **VI**: No further data **P**: unk **BLW**: unk **RG**: Y **MK**: N **PH**: unk **SS**: E pg 413 **BS**: 25 pg 160.

JAMESON, David; b 19 Aug 1752, Orange Co; d 2 Oct 1839 **RU**: Lieutenant/Patriot, Served in VA Line. Lived in Culpeper Co at enl. Served as JP and Col of Militia. Served under Capt John Jameson **CEM**: Masonic Cemetery; GPS 38.48530, -77.99470; 950 N Main, Culpeper; Culpeper **GS**: Y **SP**: Mary Mennis **VI**: Source 4 has pensioned in 1832. Served 2 sessions in VA Assembly. Sol appl pen 16 Aug 1832 Culpeper Co. S5607. DAR plaque placed 14 May 1883 to him and Col John Jameson, both members of the Culpeper Minute Men Battalion in 1775 **P**: Y **BLW**: unk **RG**: unk **MK**: Y **PH**: unk **SS**: CG pg 1821 **BS**: JLARC 3; 196.

JAMESON, John; b 1751; d 20 Nov 1810 **RU**: Lieutenant Colonel, Served as Lt Col in Cont & VA Line and First Cont Dragoons. Wounded at Valley Forge **CEM**: Masonic Cemetery; GPS 38.48530, -77.99470; 950 N Main, Culpeper; Culpeper **GS**: Y **SP**: No info **VI**: Recd pen R15404, also VA 1/2 pay. Recd BLW #1164-450-10 Aug 1789. Settlement made 20 Mar 1783 (See Hening's Statutes at Large, Vol 10 pg 462) Inquiry made 17 May 1751 Norfolk VA. DAR plaque placed 14 May 1883 to him and David Jameson, both members of the Culpeper Minute Men in 1775, that states under Col John's orders he became the captor and executioner of one "Andre" for being a spy on 2 Oct 1780. Member Society of Cincinnati **P**: Y **BLW**: Y **RG**: unk **MK**: Y **PH**: unk **SS**: CG pg 1821 **BS**: JLARC 3; 196.

RU=Rank/Unit	CEM=Cemetery	GS=Gravestone	SP=Spousal Information
VI=Other Veteran Info	P=Pension	BLW=Bounty/Land Warrant	RG=Registered Grave
MK=SAR/DAR Marker	PH=Photo	SS=Service Source	BS=Burial Source

172

JANNEY, Abel; b unk; d 13 Apr 1812 **RU:** Patriot, Signed Legislative Petition in Alexandria **CEM:** Quaker Burial Ground; GPS 38.80749, -77.04676; 717 Queen St, Kate Walker Barrett Library; Alexandria City **GS:** N **SP:** No info **VI:** Death notice in Alexandria Gazette 14 Apr 1812 **P:** N **BLW:** N **RG:** unk **MK:** N **PH:** N **SS:** BB **BS:** 196.

JARRETT (JARRATT), Devereux; b 6 Jan 1733, New Kent Co; d 29 Jan 1801 **RU:** Patriot, Gave material aid to cause **CEM:** Old Saponey Church; GPS 36.97110, -77.63610; E of Rt 709 on Rt 692; Dinwiddie **GS:** U **SP:** Martha Claiborne (1744-9 Mar 1826) d/o Durnell & Hannah (Ravenscrott) Claiborne **VI:** Son of Robert II & Sarah (Bradley) Jarratt. A plate on wall of church is to him and his wife. They were first bur in Diamond Hill in Amelia Co and remains moved to under the church **P:** N **BLW:** N **RG:** unk **MK:** unk **PH:** unk **SS:** AL Ct Bk pg 21 Dinwiddie Co **BS:** 213 pg 49, 196.

JARVIS, John Sr; b 1754; d 1822 **RU:** Patriot, Was approved for claim of loss by British troops in York Co in 1781 **CEM:** Cedar Grove; GPS 36.57204, -80.02599; 301 Fort Lane Rd; Portsmouth City **GS:** Y **SP:** No info **VI:** No further data **P:** N **BLW:** N **RG:** N **MK:** N **PH:** unk **SS:** G pg 330 **BS:** 27 pg 121.

JAUBERT, Jean; b unk; d 1781 **RU:** Soldier, Served in Beaujolais Bn and died fr battle at Yorktown **CEM:** French Memorial; GPS 36.81944, -79.39933; Yorktown; York **GS:** U **SP:** No info **VI:** No further data **P:** unk **BLW:** unk **RG:** Y **MK:** unk **PH:** unk **SS:** J-Yorktown Historian **BS:** JLARC 1, 74.

JAUBERT, Joseph; b unk; d 1781 **RU:** Soldier, Served in Beaujolais Bn and died fr battle at Yorktown **CEM:** French Memorial; GPS 36.81944, -79.39933; Yorktown; York **GS:** U **SP:** No info **VI:** No further data **P:** unk **BLW:** unk **RG:** Y **MK:** unk **PH:** unk **SS:** J-Yorktown Historian **BS:** JLARC 1, 74.

JAUNEAU, Julien; b unk; d 1781 **RU:** Seaman, Served on "Palmier" and died from Yorktown battle **CEM:** French Memorial; GPS 36.81944, -79.39933; Yorktown; York **GS:** U **SP:** No info **VI:** No further data **P:** unk **BLW:** unk **RG:** Y **MK:** unk **PH:** unk **SS:** J-Yorktown Historian **BS:** JLARC 1,74.

JAYNE, Henry; b 14 Mar 1754, Florida, Orange Co, NY; d 23 Jan 1828 **RU:** Private/Patriot, Served in NY Troops. Also on 8 Jun 1775 signed the revolutionary pledge at Goshen, NY **CEM:** St Clair Bottom Primitive Baptist; GPS 36.76098, -81.64556; Jct Rts 600 & 660, Chilhowie; Smyth **GS:** U **SP:** Abigail Wheeler (31 Jan 1751 Orang Co, NY-12 July 1824) d/o James & (-----) Wheeler **VI:** Son of Isaac (1715-1781) & Mary (Jones) (1718-1818) Jayne. Died in Washington Co **P:** unk **BLW:** unk **RG:** unk **MK:** unk **PH:** unk **SS:** B; CD **BS:** 196.

JEAN, Jean; b unk; d 1781 **RU:** Seaman, Served on "Languedoc" and died from Yorktown battle **CEM:** French Memorial; GPS 36.81944, -79.39933; Yorktown; York **GS:** U **SP:** No info **VI:** No further data **P:** unk **BLW:** unk **RG:** Y **MK:** unk **PH:** unk **SS:** J-Yorktown Historian **BS:** JLARC 1, 74.

JEAN, Pierre; b unk; d 1781 **RU:** Soldier, Served in Gatinais Bn and died fr battle at Yorktown **CEM:** French Memorial; GPS 36.81944, -79.39933; Yorktown; York **GS:** U **SP:** No info **VI:** No further data **P:** unk **BLW:** unk **RG:** Y **MK:** unk **PH:** unk **SS:** J-Yorktown Historian **BS:** JLARC 1, 74.

JEFF, Henry; b May 1704; d 8 Jun 1784 **RU:** Patriot, Gave material aid to cause **CEM:** Neff-Kagey; GPS 38.69443, -78.65895; Rt 827, Old Bridge Rd, New Market; Shenandoah **GS:** U **SP:** No info **VI:** No further data **P:** unk **BLW:** unk **RG:** unk **MK:** unk **PH:** unk **SS:** AL Certificate, Hampshire Co (now WV) **BS:** 196.

JEFFERS (JEFFRIES), John; b 1761; d 14 Nov 1795 **RU:** Private/Patriot, Served in Capt Jeffries Co, Pittsylvania Co Militia. Gave material aid to cause in Mecklenburg Co **CEM:** Blandford; GPS 37.22433, -77.38604; 319 S Crater Rd; Petersburg City **GS:** Y **SP:** Deliah (-----) **VI:** Soldier drew BLW. Widow drew pen W26158; BLW 26840-160-55 was received by spouse. After war Capt in the Pershing Troop of Horse. Was a Magistrate **P:** Y **BLW:** Y **RG:** Y **MK:** N **PH:** unk **SS:** E pg 415; AL Ct Bk pg 4, 9, 10 Mecklenburg Co; AP service rec, pension rec & BLW rec; CG pg 1826 **BS:** 99 pg 44; 196.

JEFFERSON, Thomas; b 13 Apr 1743, Shadwell, Albemarle Co; d 4 Jul 1826 **RU:** Private/Patriot, Served in Albemarle Co, Independent Co 1775 **CEM:** Monticello; GPS 38.00829, -78.45520; 931 Thomas Jefferson Pkwy; Charlottesville City **GS:** Y **SP:** Mar (1722) Martha Wayles (30 Oct 1748 Charles City Co-6 Sep 1782) d/o John (1715-1773) & Martha (Epps) (1721-1748) Wayles **VI:** Son of Peter (1707-1757) & Jane (Randolph) (1720-1776) Jefferson. First Secretary of State under

RU=Rank/Unit   CEM=Cemetery   GS=Gravestone   SP=Spousal Information
VI=Other Veteran Info   P=Pension   BLW=Bounty/Land Warrant   RG=Registered Grave
MK=SAR/DAR Marker   PH=Photo   SS=Service Source   BS=Burial Source

173

Washington, 1789-1793; third U.S. President 1881-1809 **P:** unk **BLW:** unk **RG:** N **MK:** Y **PH:** unk **SS:** E pg 415; AS SAR applic **BS:** 80 vol 2 pg 201.

JENKINS, William; b unk; d 28 Dec 1794 **RU:** Patriot, Gave material aid to cause **CEM:** Masonic Cemetery; GPS 38.30198, -77.46142; 900 Charles St; Fredericksburg City **GS:** U **SP:** No info **VI:** Bur with Masonic honors **P:** N **BLW:** N **RG:** unk **MK:** unk **PH:** unk **SS:** AL Ct Bk 1 pg 51 **BS:** 196.

JENNINGS, Charles; b 1749; d 1 Jan 1816 **RU:** unk, Specific service is in the Lib of VA, Auditor's Acct 1780-1781, pg 164 **CEM:** St John's Episcopal; GPS unk; 100 W Queen's Way; Hampton City **GS:** U **SP:** Jane (-----) (1759-15 Oct 1781) **VI:** No further data **P:** unk **BLW:** unk **RG:** unk **MK:** unk **PH:** unk **SS:** CZ pg 240 **BS:** 213 pg 588.

JENNINGS, Lewis; b 1765; d Apr 1831 **RU:** First Lieutenant, Was Ens Fauquier Militia 1781, 1st Lt for 6 mos Jun 1780 under John Marshall **CEM:** Jennings-Foster Family; GPS unk; 11446 FreemansFord; Fauquier **GS:** N **SP:** 1) Mar (4 Oct 1786 Fauquier Co, William Churchhlll security) Lucinda Bradfird (c1770-before 1820) 2) Mar (23 Oct 1820 Fauquier Co, Alex L. Kelley security) Mrs. Margaret Franklin, a widow (1786-Dec 1842) **VI:** No further data **P:** unk **BLW:** unk **RG:** Y **MK:** N **PH:** N **SS:** AV; Fauquier Co Marriages pg 108 **BS:** 83, Inv# 13.

JENNINGS, William; b 1750; d 10 Oct 1791 **RU:** Captain, Served in VA Line. Commissioned as an officer in 1777, rec pay as Lt and Capt **CEM:** St John's Episcopal; GPS unk; 100 W Queen's Way; Hampton City **GS:** U **SP:** No info **VI:** Appl pen 23 Aug 1832 Elizabeth City Co. S5615 **P:** Y **BLW:** unk **RG:** unk **MK:** unk **PH:** unk **SS:** CG pg 1834 **BS:** JLARC 4, 117.

JENNINGS, William; b 1758; d 21 Aug 1838 **RU:** Seaman, Had VA Sea Service. Ent serv 1777 on ship "Patriot" **CEM:** St John's Episcopal; GPS unk; 100 W Queen's Way; Hampton City **GS:** U **SP:** No info **VI:** Recd Pen 1838. R15422. Also VA 1/2 pay (See N.A. Acc #874 #050092 1/2 Pay also papers in N.A. Acc #837, VA State Navy, YS File) **P:** Y **BLW:** unk **RG:** unk **MK:** unk **PH:** unk **SS:** K Vol 3 pg 20; CG pg 1834 **BS:** JLARC 4, 117.

JERDONE, Francis; b 1756; d 1841 **RU:** Patriot, Gave material aid to cause **CEM:** Jerdone Castle; GPS unk; 4.4 mi NW of Buckner; Louisa **GS:** Y **SP:** No info **VI:** No further data **P:** N **BLW:** N **RG:** N **MK:** N **PH:** unk **SS:** AL Cert Issued **BS:** 102 pg 291.

JERIFAFIN, Jean; b unk; d 1781 **RU:** Soldier, Served in Bourbonnais Bn and died fr battle at Yorktown **CEM:** French Memorial; GPS 36.81944, -79.39933; Yorktown; York **GS:** U **SP:** No info **VI:** No further data **P:** unk **BLW:** unk **RG:** Y **MK:** unk **PH:** unk **SS:** J-Yorktown Historian **BS:** JLARC 1 ,74.

JETER, Henry; b 1744, Caroline Co; d 1821 **RU:** First Lieutenant, Served in Bedford Co Militia 28 May 1780 **CEM:** Jeter Family; GPS unk; Btw Centerville & Otterville; Bedford **GS:** N **SP:** Elizabeth Bel (1747-1833) **VI:** Moved with his parents at an early age to Amelia Co, and upon their death moved to Bedford Co. Govt Gr stone **P:** unk **BLW:** unk **RG:** unk **MK:** N **PH:** N **SS:** J- DAR Hatcher; E pg 418 **BS:** JLARC 2.

JOBART, Joseph; b unk; d 1781 **RU:** Seaman, Served on "Citoyen" and died from Yorktown battle **CEM:** French Memorial; GPS 36.81944, -79.39933; Yorktown; York **GS:** U **SP:** No info **VI:** No further data **P:** unk **BLW:** unk **RG:** Y **MK:** unk **PH:** unk **SS:** J-Yorktown Historian **BS:** JLARC 1, 74.

JOHNS, William; b 1765; d 1856 **RU:** Captain, Served in Buckingham Co Militia 1777 **CEM:** Indian Graveyard; GPS unk; Bear Mtn, Rt 643; Amherst **GS:** N **SP:** No info **VI:** No further data **P:** unk **BLW:** unk **RG:** N **MK:** N **PH:** N **SS:** E pg 419 **BS:** 01 pg 70.

JOHNSON, Andrew; b unk; d 1785 **RU:** Private/Patriot, Served in Clark's Illinois Regt, VA State Troops. Gave material aid to cause in Prince Edward Co **CEM:** Blandford; GPS 37.22433, -77.38604; 319 S Crater Rd; Petersburg City **GS:** Y **SP:** No info **VI:** No further data **P:** unk **BLW:** unk **RG:** N **MK:** N **PH:** unk **SS:** G ps 479, 480; AL Ct Bk ps 34, 37; AP record **BS:** JLARC 1; 188 #1359; 196.

JOHNSON, Dennis; b c1765; d 19 Jul 1811 **RU:** Soldier, Possibly the soldier fr ME that was in the Battle of Saratoga in 1777 **CEM:** Old Presbyterian Meeting House; GPS 38.48528, -77.23532; 323 S Fairfax St; Alexandria City **GS:** N **SP:** No info **VI:** No further data **P:** Y **BLW:** unk **RG:** Y **MK:** unk **PH:** N **SS:** J-NSSAR 1993 Reg; NSSAR Ancestor # P-225025; CI pension files **BS:** JLARC 1; 5.

RU=Rank/Unit	CEM=Cemetery	GS=Gravestone	SP=Spousal Information
VI=Other Veteran Info	P=Pension	BLW=Bounty/Land Warrant	RG=Registered Grave
MK=SAR/DAR Marker	PH=Photo	SS=Service Source	BS=Burial Source

JOHNSON, Thomas Jr; b 6 Mar 1736, King William Co; d 12 Aug 1803 **RU:** Captain, Served as commander of 10th Co, 3rd VA Regt of Foot 21 Mar 1776-Jan 1777 fr Louisa Co **CEM:** Roundabout Castle; GPS unk; 3998 Yanceyville Rd; Louisa **GS:** U **SP:** Elizabeth Meriwether (3 Mar 1745-14 Sep 1812) d/o Thomas (1713-1757) and Elizabeth (Thornton) (1713-1774) Meriwether **VI:** No further data **P:** unk **BLW:** unk **RG:** unk **MK:** unk **PH:** unk **SS:** AR Vol 2 pg 208; CE pg 39 **BS:** JLARC 2; 196.

JOHNSTON, David; b 1726; d 1786 **RU:** Private, Served in Capt James Maxwell's Co, Montgomery Co Militia **CEM:** Phlegar Farm; GPS unk; Rt 626, Ripplemead; Giles **GS:** U **SP:** Nannie Abbott (__-1813) **VI:** No further data **P:** unk **BLW:** unk **RG:** unk **MK:** unk **PH:** unk **SS:** J- DAR Hatcher; G pg 237 **BS:** JLARC 2; 196.

JOHNSTON, John; b 15 Nov 1761; d 8 Apr 1845 **RU:** Private, Served in Capt Rankins Co Augusta Co Militia **CEM:** West Hill; GPS 37.29313, -80.06753; Boon St; Salem City **GS:** Y **SP:** Mar (16 Sep 1794) Elizabeth Bell **VI:** Son of Zachariah (1742-1800) & Ann (Robertson) (1742-1818) Johnston. Died in Augusta Co **P:** unk **BLW:** unk **RG:** Y **MK:** N **PH:** unk **SS:** E pg 424 **BS:** 122, pg 242.

JOHNSTON, William; b 1752, Fairfax Co; d 13 Apr 1815 **RU:** Captain, Served in VA Line. Served in 7th VA Cont Regt Nov 1779-May 1780. Commander of co in 3rd VA Regt. Was captured 1781 and POW to end of war **CEM:** Belle Vale; GPS unk; Belle Vale Manor, Doeg's Run; Fairfax **GS:** U **SP:** Mar (1785) Ann Simpson (1763, Fairfax Co-4 Mar 1815) **VI:** Recd BLW #1166-300-5 Jul 1799 **P:** unk **BLW:** Y **RG:** unk **MK:** N **PH:** unk **SS:** J- DAR Hatcher; CG pg 1865; CE pg 32, 41 **BS:** JLARC 2.

JOHNSTON, William Z; b 1742; d unk **RU:** Captain/Patriot, Gave material aid to cause **CEM:** Tinkling Spring Presbyterian; GPS 38.08472, -78.98278; 30 Tinkling Spring Dr, Fishersville; Augusta **GS:** N **SP:** No info **VI:** No further data **P:** unk **BLW:** unk **RG:** unk **MK:** N **PH:** N **SS:** J- DAR Hatcher; AL Lists 1 pg 10 Augusta Co **BS:** JLARC 2.

JOHNSTON (JOHNSON), Peter; b unk; d 18 Dec 1831 **RU:** Officer, Served in Lee's Legion **CEM:** Johnston; GPS unk; 1 mi on ext of Valley St, Abingdon; Washington **GS:** U **SP:** 1) Mary (-----) 2) Mar (13 Dec 1831 home of Charles Copland Esq. Richmond VA) Ann or Anne Bernard (c1774-29 Jun 1865), d/o John & Henningham (Carrington) Bernard Esq. According to nephew who appl for pen, mentally incompetent when she wrote will. **VI:** Speaker of VA House of Delegates. Member Society of the Cincinatti. Was judge when he mar 2nd time. Grave at #130 in Source 80. Sol had recd pen under act of 15 May 1828. Widow appl BLW 4 May 1855 Richmond City. W27629. BLW #1171-200-9 Sep 1789 **P:** Y **BLW:** Y **RG:** unk **MK:** unk **PH:** unk **SS:** K Vol 3 pg 34; CG pg 1864 **BS:** JLARC 4, 34, 80.

JOHNSTON (JOHNSON), Zachariah; b 1742, near Staunton, Augusta Co; d 7 Jan 1800 **RU:** Captain/Patriot, Served in VA Militia, Was in campaigns against Indians in west and Battle of Jamestown VA 1781. Was member of House of Delegates fr Augusta & Rockbridge. Was leader in passage of religious freedom. Was member of delegation to ratify constitution **CEM:** Stonewall Jackson Memorial; GPS 37.78128, -79.44604; 314 S Main St; Lexington City **GS:** Y **SP:** Ann Robertson **VI:** Source 79 says he moved fr Augusta to Rockbridge in 1790. Died in Rockbridge Co **P:** unk **BLW:** unk **RG:** Y **MK:** N **PH:** unk **SS:** AD **BS:** JLARC 1, 2, 63, 79.

JOLIVET, Francois; b unk; d 1781 **RU:** Soldier, Served in Bourbonnais Bn and died fr battle at Yorktown **CEM:** French Memorial; GPS 36.81944, -79.39933; Yorktown; York **GS:** U **SP:** No info **VI:** No further data **P:** unk **BLW:** unk **RG:** Y **MK:** unk **PH:** unk **SS:** J-Yorktown Historian **BS:** JLARC 1, 74.

JOLY (JOLLEY), (-----); b unk; d 1781 **RU:** Soldier, Service unit not determined. Died fr battle at Yorktown **CEM:** French Memorial; GPS 36.81944, -79.39933; Yorktown; York **GS:** U **SP:** No info **VI:** No further data **P:** unk **BLW:** unk **RG:** Y **MK:** unk **PH:** unk **SS:** J-NSSAR 1993 Reg **BS:** JLARC 1.

JONES, Benjamin Dr; b 5 Feb 1752, Culpeper Co; d 22 Aug 1843 **RU:** Surgeon, Was Surgeon 3rd VA Regt. **CEM:** Oakwood; GPS 36.38690, -79.88000; 199 Cemetery St; Martinsville City **GS:** Y **SP:** Mar (7 Sep 1776 Prince William Co) Elizabeth de Remi (Reamey) (5 Feb 1756-22 Apr 1856) **VI:** Politician. Several times represented Henry Co in state legislature. Died in Henry Co. Govt Gr stone **P:** N **BLW:** N **RG:** Y **MK:** N **PH:** N **SS:** DD **BS:** JLARC 1, 2,102.

JONES, Charles; b unk; d 1810 **RU:** Seaman, Served in Navy. Had sea service until 1781 **CEM:** Cub Creek; GPS unk; Off Rt 789 Cub Creek Rd at Beech Grove Community; Nelson **GS:** U **SP:** Elizabeth (--

RU=Rank/Unit	CEM=Cemetery	GS=Gravestone	SP=Spousal Information
VI=Other Veteran Info	P=Pension	BLW=Bounty/Land Warrant	RG=Registered Grave
MK=SAR/DAR Marker	PH=Photo	SS=Service Source	BS=Burial Source

175

---) **VI:** Administration granted to William Woodward of Norfolk for 1/2 pay pen. R50 **P:** Y **BLW:** unk **RG:** unk **MK:** unk **PH:** unk **SS:** K Vol 3 pg 37 **BS:** JLARC 83.

JONES, Charles G; b unk; d 1818 **RU:** Patriot, Gave material aid to cause **CEM:** St John's Episcopal; GPS 37.53183, -77.41958; 2401 E Broad St; Richmond City **GS:** Y **SP:** No info **VI:** No further data **P:** N **BLW:** N **RG:** N **MK:** N **PH:** unk **SS:** AL Lists I pg 2 **BS:** 28 pg 462.

JONES, Churchill; b 1748, Middlesex Co; d Sep 1822 **RU:** Major/Patriot, Provided 1655# beef to Lafayette Jun 1781 **CEM:** Ellwood Burial Ground; GPS unk; Wilderness Battlefield; Orange **GS:** N **SP:** 1) Judith Churchill 2) Mary Thornton Champe 3) Martha Selden Douglas **VI:** Lived at "Chatham" in Stafford Co. Appl pen 1806 fr "Chatham." BLW 304 issued 3 Jan 1807. Died at Woodville Plantation, Orange Co. QLF says he d in 1828 **P:** Y **BLW:** unk **RG:** Y **MK:** Y **PH:** N **SS:** D Vol 2 pg 741; K Vol 3 pg 37 **BS:** 04.

JONES, Daniel; b 1748; d 16 Dec 1822 **RU:** Patriot, Furnished supplies to VA troops **CEM:** Jones-Nunn Family; GPS 37.21246, -76.47290; Farmville Ln, Norge; James City Co **GS:** Y **SP:** Mary Morris **VI:** No further data **P:** N **BLW:** N **RG:** N **MK:** N **PH:** unk **SS:** AL Ct Bk pg 10 **BS:** 32 Boelt; 04.

JONES, Edward; b 15 Dec 1754, New York; d 17 Sep 1829 **RU:** Private/Patriot, Treasury official under George Washington. Served in Capt Ackerson Co, Col Hays Regt, NY State **CEM:** Arlington National; GPS 38.88377, -77.06535; Jefferson Davis Hwy Rt 110; Arlington **GS:** Y **SP:** No info **VI:** Died age 78 yr 9 mos (Richmond Enquirer, 22 Sep 1829) **P:** unk **BLW:** N **RG:** unk **MK:** unk **PH:** unk **SS:** H; BS pg 405; SAR applic **BS:** JLARC 76; 196.

JONES, Gabriel Jr; b 1748; d 1777 **RU:** Captain, Served in VA State Line under Col George Gibson, joined the State Marines and died in service in 1777 **CEM:** Slaughter-Jones Family; GPS 38.45500, -77.84131; Stone's Mill Rd Rt 676, LaGrange; Culpeper **GS:** U **SP:** 1) Mary Waller 2) Martha Slaughter **VI:** Son of Gabriel Jones and Mary (Johnson) Edmondson. Created first Marine unit in Fredericksburg in 1775, which was abandoned and he joined the 1st VA Regiment. Govt stone styles him Capt, Virginia State Navy **P:** unk **BLW:** Y **RG:** N **MK:** N **PH:** unk **SS:** 49710.289537 **BS:** 29 pg 61; 196.

JONES, George; b 1763, MD; d 12 May 1843 **RU:** Private, with service in MD **CEM:** Old Jones Place; GPS unk; Rt 600 nr Troy; Fluvanna **GS:** Y **SP:** No info **VI:** No further data **P:** unk **BLW:** unk **RG:** N **MK:** N **PH:** unk **SS:** BJ pg 95 **BS:** 164 Old Jones.

JONES, Henry; b 1748; d 1807 **RU:** Private, Served in 9th VA Regt, Cont Line **CEM:** Jones Family; GPS unk; Left fr US 250 on Rt 614 traveling fr McDowell. Farm of Clay Botkins; Highland **GS:** U **SP:** 1) (-----) 2) Emily Jane Carlile **VI:** No further data **P:** unk **BLW:** unk **RG:** unk **MK:** unk **PH:** unk **SS:** NSSAR Ancestor #P-226145 **BS:** JLARC 62, 103.

JONES, Holmes; b 15 Jun 1758, Sussex Co; d 4 Oct 1810 **RU:** Sergeant, Served in Capt Edmunds Co, Lt Col Innes Regt, 15th Cont Line **CEM:** Jones Family; GPS unk; See US Senate Doc 1937 vol 1, serial 10173 DAR Report; Sussex **GS:** U **SP:** Mar (17 Oct 1783) Susanna Moss (4 Oct 1760, Sussex Co-aft 21 Jun 1816) **VI:** No further data **P:** unk **BLW:** unk **RG:** unk **MK:** unk **PH:** unk **SS:** DAR Ancestor #A062199; J- DAR Hatcher; E pg 426; DD **BS:** JLARC 2.

JONES, Jacob; b unk; d 1781 **RU:** Soldier, Served fr MA, and died fr the battle at Yorktown **CEM:** Yorktown Victory Monument Tablet; GPS 38.28350, -78.54150; Yorktown; York **GS:** U **SP:** No info **VI:** No further data **P:** unk **BLW:** unk **RG:** unk **MK:** unk **PH:** unk **SS:** J-Yorktown Historian **BS:** JLARC 74.

JONES, John; b 1752; d 1797 **RU:** Patriot, Gave material aid to the cause **CEM:** St John's Episcopal; GPS unk; 100 W Queen's Way; Hampton City **GS:** Y **SP:** No info **VI:** No further data **P:** N **BLW:** N **RG:** N **MK:** N **PH:** unk **SS:** AL Ct Bk pg 4,6 **BS:** 89 pg 81.

JONES, John; b 1738; d 1784 **RU:** Patriot, Gave material aid to the cause **CEM:** Jones Family; GPS unk; Rt 742 Nicholas St; Hanover **GS:** N **SP:** No info **VI:** No further data **P:** N **BLW:** N **RG:** N **MK:** N **PH:** N **SS:** AL Ct Bk lt I pg 34 **BS:** 31 vol 2 pg 75.

JONES, Joseph; b 1749; d 1824 **RU:** Captain/Patriot, Commanded a Co in Dinwiddie Co Militia. As patriot had public service as a member of the Committee of Public Safety, 1775 **CEM:** Blandford; GPS 37.22433, -77.38604; 319 S Crater Rd; Petersburg City **GS:** Y **SP:** No info **VI:** Postmaster of Petersburg

RU=Rank/Unit	CEM=Cemetery	GS=Gravestone	SP=Spousal Information
VI=Other Veteran Info	P=Pension	BLW=Bounty/Land Warrant	RG=Registered Grave
MK=SAR/DAR Marker	PH=Photo	SS=Service Source	BS=Burial Source

176

and Collector of Port 1821-24 **P:** unk **BLW:** unk **RG:** Y **MK:** unk **PH:** Y **SS:** J-NSSAR 1993 Reg; NSSAR Ancestor #P-226322; G pg 479, 480; AL Ct Bk pg 34, 37 **BS:** JLARC 1; 196.

JONES, Joseph; b 172, King George Co; d 28 Oct 1805 **RU:** Commissary Officer/Patriot, Was commissary officer at Fredericksburg factory 1775-6. Gave material aid to cause. Elected 5th VA Convention 1775 **CEM:** Not identified; GPS unk; Check newspapers & other sources; Fredericksburg City **GS:** U **SP:** Mary Taliaferro d.of John & (-----) Taliaferro of Spotsylvania Co **VI:** Son of James & Hester (-----) Jones. Member of state convention in 1788 which ratified US Constitution **P:** unk **BLW:** unk **RG:** unk **MK:** unk **PH:** unk **SS:** D Fredericksburg; E pg 427; CZ **BS:** 138 Joseph Jones, VA.

JONES, Michael; b unk; d 1821 **RU:** Private, Served in Mitchel's Co, 12th VA **CEM:** Jones; GPS unk; Rt 24, S of Togson, abt 2.5 mi then 1.5 mi on private road; Buckingham **GS:** U **SP:** No info **VI:** Has Govt GS **P:** N **BLW:** N **RG:** unk **MK:** N **PH:** unk **SS:** E pg 428 **BS:** JLARC 59.

JONES, Nicholas; b 3 Jul 1760; d 7 Apr 1831 or 1834 **RU:** Private, Ent serv Amherst Co in VA Line **CEM:** Neriah Baptist; GPS 37.78778, -79.36482; Jct Rts 631 & 706, South River; Rockbridge **GS:** U **SP:** Mar (3 Jul 1783 Rockbridge Co) Amarella (-----) (1765-aft 3 Apr 1838) **VI:** Stone Broken. Widow appl pen 3 Apr 1738 Rockbridge Co age 73. W7907 **P:** Y **BLW:** unk **RG:** unk **MK:** unk **PH:** unk **SS:** CG pg 1878 **BS:** 196.

JONES, Peter; b unk; d 7 Apr 1815 **RU:** Patriot, Gave material aid to the cause **CEM:** Locust Grove; GPS unk; Rt 66 abt 5 mi S of Victoria; Amelia **GS:** N **SP:** Mar (Lunenburg Co) Jane Stokes, d/o David & (-----) Stokes **VI:** No further data **P:** N **BLW:** N **RG:** N **MK:** N **PH:** N **SS:** AL Ct Bk pg 64, 69 **BS:** 171 Locust Gr; 172.

JONES, Richard; b unk; d 1781 **RU:** Private, Was killed in the Battle of Green Spring near Williamsburg in 1781 **CEM:** Williamsburg Land Conservancy; GPS unk; 5000 New Point Rd; Williamsburg City **GS:** N **SP:** No info **VI:** No further data **P:** unk **BLW:** unk **RG:** N **MK:** N **PH:** N **SS:** AU, SAR study **BS:** 32.

JONES, Robert; b unk; d unk **RU:** Patriot, Gave material aid to cause **CEM:** Wade-Cox; GPS unk; Check property records, Floyd and Montgomery Co for loc of residence; Floyd **GS:** U **SP:** No info **VI:** Cem not listed with this name in Floyd Co Hist Soc listings **P:** N **BLW:** N **RG:** unk **MK:** unk **PH:** unk **SS:** SAR Ancestor #P-226466; J- DAR Hatcher; AL Ct Bk pg 19 Henry Co **BS:** JLARC 2; 80 vol 2 pg 212.

JONES, Robert Jr; b 1736; d 1820 **RU:** Patriot, Gave material aid to cause **CEM:** Ward Feazell; GPS unk; Ferrum; Franklin **GS:** U **SP:** Martha Riley (1736-__) **VI:** Son of Robert (1696-1775) & Margaret (Van Metre) (1706-1775) Jones **P:** unk **BLW:** unk **RG:** unk **MK:** unk **PH:** unk **SS:** Al Ct Bk pg 19 Henry Co **BS:** 196.

JONES, Strother; b 1758; d 1790 **RU:** Captain, Served in VA Cont Line **CEM:** Jones Family; GPS unk; Vanchese; Frederick **GS:** U **SP:** No info **VI:** Daughter Nancy Ann Jones appl pen 7 Nov 1855 Columbia Co, GA. BLW #2442-300 **P:** unk **BLW:** Y **RG:** unk **MK:** unk **PH:** unk **SS:** J- DAR Hatcher; CG pg 1882 **BS:** JLARC 2.

JONES, Thomas; b 6 Nov 1754, Bedford Co; d 1826 **RU:** Ensign/Patriot, Was Ensign 24 Apr 1781, Bedford Co Militia. Gave material aid to cause **CEM:** Blenheim; GPS 37.13150, -78.5700; Rt 648, Gladys; Campbell **GS:** N **SP:** Mar (1775) Betty Jones (09 Nov 1757, Bedford Co-13 Nov 1837) **VI:** No further data **P:** unk **BLW:** unk **RG:** unk **MK:** N **PH:** N **SS:** AL Ct Bk pg 3, 10 Campbell Co; AZ pg 187 **BS:** JLARC 36.

JONES, Thomas; b 21 May 1748, Frederick Co, MD; d 22 Mar 1830 **RU:** First Lieutenant, Served in Henry Co Militia 1780 **CEM:** Pigg River Primitive Baptist; GPS 36.96913, -80.07368; Rt 750 nr Callaway; Franklin **GS:** N **SP:** Mar (1770 Pittsylvania Co) Joanna Hill (24 Jan 1752 Lunenburg Co-2 Mar 1833 Callaway, Franklin Co). d/o Robert (1713-1778) & Violett (Linus) (1725-1808) Hill **VI:** Son of Robert (1696-1796) & Mary Marie Jansen (VanMeter) (1709-1796) Jones. Was a minister **P:** unk **BLW:** unk **RG:** Y **MK:** N **PH:** N **SS:** E pg 429; AK cites DAR app **BS:** 04 cites DAR appl.

JONES, Thomas; b unk; d unk **RU:** Patriot, Gave material aid to cause **CEM:** Jones Family; GPS unk; Crooked Run; Culpeper **GS:** U **SP:** No info **VI:** No further data **P:** N **BLW:** N **RG:** Y **MK:** unk **PH:** unk **SS:** J-NSSAR 1993 Reg; AL Cert Culpeper Co **BS:** JLARC 1.

RU=Rank/Unit   CEM=Cemetery   GS=Gravestone   SP=Spousal Information
VI=Other Veteran Info   P=Pension   BLW=Bounty/Land Warrant RG=Registered Grave
MK=SAR/DAR Marker   PH=Photo   SS=Service Source   BS=Burial Source

177

JONES, Thomas; b 1758; d 8 Jul 1835 **RU:** Sergeant, Served in VA Line. Ent serv Amherst Co that became Nelson. Enlisted US Army 1776, 10th Regt, VA Line later 6th Regt. Was in Battle of Brandywine and Germantown. Was wounded but served 3 yrs **CEM:** Jones-Clarkson; GPS 37.79438, -78.98530; Persimmon Hill Rd, Roseland; Nelson **GS:** N **SP:** Mar (17 Oct 1780) Catharine Clarkson (1 or 11 Jun 1760-1847) **VI:** Sol appl pen 8 Jul 1835 at Jonesboro in Nelson Co. Died in Jonesboro, Nelson Co. Widow appl pen 19 Oct 1838 Nelson Co. Recd BLW of 200 acres. W7905 **P:** Y **BLW:** Y **RG:** unk **MK:** unk **PH:** N **SS:** CG pg 1883 **BS:** JLARC 4, 83; 196.

JONES, Thomas C Sr; b 1736; d 15 Oct 1818 **RU:** Patriot, Gave material aid to cause **CEM:** South River Meeting House; GPS 37.37246, -79.19194; 5810 Fort Ave; Lynchburg City **GS:** U **SP:** Mar (abt 1765) Hannal Erwin (Irwin) (1747 Augusta Co-1826) **VI:** Cem records indicate b 1735, d 1815 with perhaps spouse Patsey, b 1743, d 1825 **P:** N **BLW:** N **RG:** unk **MK:** unk **PH:** unk **SS:** AL Cert 1 Bedford Co **BS:** 196; 221.

JONES, Thomas Sr; b c1746; d 1786 **RU:** First Lieutenant, Served in Pittsylvania Co Militia 27 Sep 1775 **CEM:** Jones Family; GPS 36.84300, -79.26227; Nr Mtn Top, 7 mi E Chatham; Pittsylvania **GS:** Y **SP:** Mar (12 May 1763) Mary (-----) (__-1798 Pittsylvania Co) **VI:** No further data **P:** unk **BLW:** unk **RG:** N **MK:** N **PH:** unk **SS:** G pg 284; DD **BS:** 174, 91.

JONES, Walter; b 18 Dec 1745; d 31 Dec 1815 **RU:** Physician General, Served in Hospital Middle Department 11 Apr-1 Jul 1777. **CEM:** Hayfield; GPS unk; Nr Callao; Northumberland **GS:** U **SP:** Mar (c1773) Alice Flood **VI:** Rep in 5th Congress 1797-1799. VA House of Delegates 1802-03. US Congress 1803-1811 **P:** unk **BLW:** unk **RG:** unk **MK:** unk **PH:** unk **SS:** E pg 429 **BS:** 201 pg 7397.

JONES, William; b 25 Oct 1734, Caroline Co; d Aft 1788 **RU:** Patriot, Gave material aid to cause **CEM:** Marlfield Plantation; GPS 37.44928, -76.62239; Rt 610 at 3780 Pebble Ln, Marlfield; Gloucester **GS:** U **SP:** Mar (1766) Lucy (Taliaferro) Carter, the widow of Charles Carter (1707-1764). D/o William & Anne (Walker) Talioferro. **VI:** Purchased Marlfield 1782 fr John Buckner, who built it 1732. Among first VA planters to use marl in agriculture **P:** N **BLW:** N **RG:** unk **MK:** unk **PH:** unk **SS:** AL Ct Bk IV pg 184 Caroline Co **BS:** 196.

JONES, William; b 1730, Mecklenburg Co; d 15 Apr 1818 **RU:** Patriot, Gave material aid to the cause **CEM:** Dishman Family at Pine Hill; GPS unk; Off Rt 621, Shiloh; King George **GS:** U **SP:** Elizabeth Buckner **VI:** No further data **P:** N **BLW:** N **RG:** unk **MK:** unk **PH:** unk **SS:** AL Ct Bk pg 3; Commissioner's Bk II pg 336 **BS:** 196.

JONES, William; b 1750, Middlesex Co; d 1845 **RU:** Patriot, Provided 700 lbs beef to Lafayette June 1781 **CEM:** Ellwood Burial Ground; GPS unk; Wilderness Battlefield; Orange **GS:** N **SP:** 1) Betty Churchill 2) Lucinda Gordon Jones Green **VI:** Died in Ellwood, Orange Co **P:** N **BLW:** N **RG:** Y **MK:** N **PH:** N **SS:** D Vol 2 pg 741 **BS:** 04.

JONES, William; b unk; d 12 Nov 1828 **RU:** Private, Served in VA Line **CEM:** Cross Road Baptist; GPS 36.62690, -79.04780; 1098 Flint Rock Rd, South Boston; Halifax **GS:** N **SP:** Mar (9 Oct 1776) Martha (-----) (1756-18 Aug 1843 Carroll Co TN) **VI:** Widow appl pen 25 Aug 1843 Carroll Co, TN R5724 **P:** Y **BLW:** N **RG:** unk **MK:** unk **PH:** N **SS:** CG pg 1886 **BS:** 196.

JONES, William; b unk; d 1781 **RU:** Private, Was killed in the Battle of Green Springs near Williamsburg in 1781 **CEM:** Williamsburg Land Conservancy; GPS unk; 5000 New Point Rd; Williamsburg City **GS:** N **SP:** Mar (Dec 1776 James City Co) Elizabeth Roberts **VI:** No further data **P:** unk **BLW:** unk **RG:** N **MK:** N **PH:** N **SS:** AU SAR study **BS:** 32 Willbg chap.

JONES, William (John) Paul; b 6 Jul 1747; d 18 Jul 1792 **RU:** Commodore, Cont Navy as 1st Lt 22 Dec 1775 on "Alfred." Capt on ship "Ranger" 14 Feb 1777. Capt on "Bonhomme Richard" 1779; later served as Commodore **CEM:** St George's Episcopal; GPS unk; 905 Princess Anne; Fredericksburg City **GS:** U **SP:** No info **VI:** Honorary GS in St Georges Cem in Fredericksburg erected by his brother. Died in Paris, France. Remains fr burial in Paris moved Apr 1906 to US Navy Academy Chapel, Annapolis MD **P:** unk **BLW:** unk **RG:** Y **MK:** unk **PH:** unk **SS:** J-NSSAR 2000 Reg; L pg 210 **BS:** JLARC 76.

JORDAN, John; b 10 Apr 1757; d 1835 **RU:** Captain, Taken prisoner in Charleston SC in 2nd Cont Line 12 May 1780. Exchanged Apr 1781. Commanded a co 8 Sep 1781. Wounded in battle of Edge Hill

RU=Rank/Unit	CEM=Cemetery	GS=Gravestone	SP=Spousal Information
VI=Other Veteran Info	P=Pension	BLW=Bounty/Land Warrant	RG=Registered Grave
MK=SAR/DAR Marker	PH=Photo	SS=Service Source	BS=Burial Source

178

CEM: Locust Bottom Church; GPS 37.74170, -79.8150; Eagle Rock; Botetourt **GS:** U **SP:** Catharine/Catherine Beale **VI:** Source 4 has Member of Society of Cincinnati. Pensioned 1811. Recd BLW 4666 acres **P:** Y **BLW:** Y **RG:** unk **MK:** N **PH:** unk **SS:** J- DAR Hatcher; E pg 430; CZ pg 248; BX pg 428; NSSAR Ancestor # P-226775 **BS:** JLARC 2.

JORDAN, John; b unk; d Feb 1795 **RU:** Private, Service information not determined **CEM:** Old Christ Church Episcopal; GPS 38.80625, -77.04718; 118 N Washington St; Alexandria City **GS:** N **SP:** No info **VI:** Burial permit issued 17 Feb 1795 **P:** unk **BLW:** unk **RG:** N **MK:** N **PH:** N **SS:** Z pg 36 **BS:** 20 pg 149.

JOSEPH, Jean; b unk; d 1781 **RU:** Seaman, Served on "Duc De Bourgogne" and died from Yorktown battle **CEM:** French Memorial; GPS 36.81944, -79.39933; Yorktown; York **GS:** U **SP:** No info **VI:** No further data **P:** unk **BLW:** unk **RG:** Y **MK:** unk **PH:** unk **SS:** J-Yorktown Historian **BS:** JLARC 1, 74.

JOSSARD, Jean; b unk; d 1781 **RU:** Soldier, Served in Soissonnais Bn and died fr battle at Yorktown **CEM:** French Memorial; GPS 36.81944, -79.39933; Yorktown; York **GS:** U **SP:** No info **VI:** No further data **P:** unk **BLW:** unk **RG:** Y **MK:** unk **PH:** unk **SS:** J-Yorktown Historian **BS:** JLARC 1, 74.

JOSSE, Jean; b unk; d 1781 **RU:** Seaman, Served on "Hercule" and died from Yorktown battle **CEM:** French Memorial; GPS 36.81944, -79.39933; Yorktown; York **GS:** U **SP:** No info **VI:** No further data **P:** unk **BLW:** unk **RG:** unk **MK:** unk **PH:** unk **SS:** J-Yorktown Historian **BS:** JLARC 74.

JOSSE, Oliver; b unk; d 1781 **RU:** Seaman, Served on "Citoyen" and died from Yorktown battle **CEM:** French Memorial; GPS 36.81944, -79.39933; Yorktown; York **GS:** U **SP:** No info **VI:** No further data **P:** unk **BLW:** unk **RG:** Y **MK:** unk **PH:** unk **SS:** J-Yorktown Historian **BS:** JLARC 1, 74.

JOUE, Jean; b unk; d 1781 **RU:** Seaman, Served on "Ville de Paris" and died from Yorktown battle **CEM:** French Memorial; GPS 36.81944, -79.39933; Yorktown; York **GS:** U **SP:** No info **VI:** No further data **P:** unk **BLW:** unk **RG:** Y **MK:** unk **PH:** unk **SS:** J-Yorktown Historian **BS:** JLARC 1, 74.

JOULIN, Jean; b unk; d 1781 **RU:** Soldier, Served in Auxonne Bn and died fr battle at Yorktown **CEM:** French Memorial; GPS 36.81944, -79.39933; Yorktown; York **GS:** U **SP:** No info **VI:** No further data **P:** unk **BLW:** unk **RG:** Y **MK:** unk **PH:** unk **SS:** J-Yorktown Historian **BS:** JLARC 1, 74.

JOYNES, Levin S; b 6 Jan 1753; d 16 Oct 1794 **RU:** Lieutenant Colonel, Served 7 yrs, 10 mos in VA Line of Cont Establishment. Comm Lt Col 11 Dec 1777. Wounded & taken prisoner at Germantown in Oct 1777 **CEM:** Joynes-Bayne; GPS unk; W end of Meadville Dr, Onancock; Accomack **GS:** Y **SP:** Anne (-----) (10 Jun 1756-16 Aug 1815) **VI:** Aft war member VA Senate.Recd BLW #63-500-24 Nov 1792 **P:** unk **BLW:** Y **RG:** N **MK:** N **PH:** unk **SS:** CG pg 1892 **BS:** 37 pg 133; 196.

JULIAN, John; b 1748 or 1749; d 1785 or 1788 **RU:** Surgeon, Served in VA Cont Line **CEM:** Masonic Cemetery; GPS 38.30198, -77.46142; 900 Charles St; Fredericksburg City **GS:** Y **SP:** Mar (c1762) Margaret Isabella Lounds **VI:** Son of Charles & Phebe (Wilson) Julian. Was in practice with Hugh Mercer MD c1772. Was Vestryman at St George's Church. BLW file indicates he d before 1787 in Fredericksburg **P:** unk **BLW:** Y **RG:** unk **MK:** Y **PH:** unk **SS:** BY pg 285; J- DAR Hatcher **BS:** JLARC 2; 196.

JULIEN, Claude; b unk; d 1781 **RU:** Soldier, Served in Gatinais Bn and died fr battle at Yorktown **CEM:** French Memorial; GPS 36.81944, -79.39933; Yorktown; York **GS:** U **SP:** No info **VI:** No further data **P:** unk **BLW:** unk **RG:** Y **MK:** unk **PH:** unk **SS:** J-Yorktown Historian **BS:** JLARC 1, 74.

JUND, Francois; b unk; d 1781 **RU:** Soldier, Served in Auxonne Bn and died fr battle at Yorktown **CEM:** French Memorial; GPS 36.81944, -79.39933; Yorktown; York **GS:** U **SP:** No info **VI:** No further data **P:** unk **BLW:** unk **RG:** Y **MK:** unk **PH:** unk **SS:** J-Yorktown Historian **BS:** JLARC 1, 74.

JUPIN, Laurent; b unk; d 1781 **RU:** Seaman, Served on "Diademe" and died from Yorktown battle **CEM:** French Memorial; GPS 36.81944, -79.39933; Yorktown; York **GS:** U **SP:** No info **VI:** No further data **P:** unk **BLW:** unk **RG:** Y **MK:** unk **PH:** unk **SS:** J-Yorktown Historian **BS:** JLARC 1, 74.

JUVET, Barthelemy; b unk; d 1781 **RU:** Seaman, Served on "Hector" and died from Yorktown battle **CEM:** French Memorial; GPS 36.81944, -79.39933; Yorktown; York **GS:** U **SP:** No info **VI:** No further data **P:** unk **BLW:** unk **RG:** Y **MK:** unk **PH:** unk **SS:** J-Yorktown Historian **BS:** JLARC 1, 74.

RU=Rank/Unit	CEM=Cemetery	GS=Gravestone	SP=Spousal Information
VI=Other Veteran Info	P=Pension	BLW=Bounty/Land Warrant	RG=Registered Grave
MK=SAR/DAR Marker	PH=Photo	SS=Service Source	BS=Burial Source

179

KABLER, Frederick; b 1695, Baden-Wurttemberg, Germany; d 1779 **RU:** Patriot, Gave material aid to cause **CEM:** Kabler Family; GPS unk; See property records for home place location; Chesterfield **GS:** U **SP:** Martha Miles (__-aft 7 Dec 1793) **VI:** Died in Culpeper Co **P:** N **BLW:** N **RG:** unk **MK:** unk **PH:** N **SS:** DAR ancestor #A208552; Al Ct bk pg 30 **BS:** 196.

KAYLOR, Micheal; b 1771; d Apr 1807 **RU:** Private, Ent serv 1788 age abt 16, enrolled in Capt Conrad's Co. At 21 yrs 1792, enrolled in Capt Haines Co **CEM:** Old Peaked Mountain; GPS 38.37113, -78.73416; 9843 Town Hall Rd, McGaheysville; Rockingham **GS:** Y **SP:** No info **VI:** No further data **P:** unk **BLW:** unk **RG:** Y **MK:** Y **PH:** unk **SS:** U **BS:** 04. (See Appendix G -deleted for being too young)

KAYSER / KEYSER, John J; b c1762; d 12 Sep 1823 **RU:** Private, Served in 8th Cont Line **CEM:** Locust Bottom; GPS unk; Jct Rts 622 & 696; Botetourt **GS:** N **SP:** No info **VI:** No further data **P:** unk **BLW:** unk **RG:** N **MK:** N **PH:** N **SS:** E pg 444 **BS:** 115 pg 12.

KEARFOOT (KERFOOT), William; b May 1749, Frederick Co; d 4 Feb 1811 **RU:** Sergeant/Patriot, Served full 8 yrs of war. Was 1st Sergeant in Capt Stith's Co 4th VA Regt of Cont Line. He or father supplied mutton. Gave material aid to cause **CEM:** White Post aka Wheeler Family; GPS 39.71170, -78.5419; Nr White Post, nr Clarke-Frederick co line, Dearfield Farm; Frederick **GS:** U **SP:** 1) Mary Bryarly 2) Mar (27 Jan 1785 Frederick Co by Rev Alexander Balmain) Ann Peters **VI:** Son of William Sr (1724 Spotsylvania Co-7 Dec 1779) & Mary Margaret (Carter) Kerfoot **P:** unk **BLW:** unk **RG:** unk **MK:** N **PH:** Y **SS:** J- DAR Hatcher; AL Ct Bk pg 5; DD **BS:** JLARC 2.

KEARNES, John; b 1753; d 1799 **RU:** Corporal, Served in 7th & 11th Cont Lines **CEM:** Trinity Episcopal; GPS 36.83459, -76.30105; 500 Court St; Portsmouth City **GS:** Y **SP:** No info **VI:** No further data **P:** unk **BLW:** unk **RG:** N **MK:** N **PH:** unk **SS:** E pg 434 **BS:** 92 stone 85.

KEATTS, William Sr; b unk, Lunenburg Co; d 22 Aug 1829 **RU:** Colonel/Patriot, Was in battle at Guilford Ct House. Had all the baggage fr the battle delivered to Halifax Co **CEM:** Keatts Family; GPS unk; Nr Mulberry Baptist Church, nr Pittsylvania; Halifax **GS:** U **SP:** Mary Lewis of Amelia Co **VI:** Son of Curtis & Tabitha (Dennis?) Keatts **P:** unk **BLW:** unk **RG:** Y **MK:** unk **PH:** unk **SS:** J-NSSAR 1993 Reg, J- DAR Hatcher; AL Ct Bk pg 13 Pittsylvania Co **BS:** JLARC 1, 2; 196.

KEELING, Jacob; b 1750; d 20 Feb 1815 **RU:** Patriot, Gave material aid to the cause **CEM:** Keeling Family; GPS unk; Back of Laurel Manor; Virginia Beach City **GS:** Y **SP:** Mary (-----) (1749-7 Oct 1821) **VI:** No further data **P:** N **BLW:** N **RG:** unk **MK:** unk **PH:** unk **SS:** AL CT BK pg S 4, 8 Princess Anne Co; AL Ct Bk pg 1 Norfolk Co **BS:** 212.

KEEN, Abraham (Abram); b c1762; d Aft 1847 **RU:** Private?, Served in VA Line. Ent serv Halifax Co 1777. Moved to Amelia in 1777 where ent serv 1781 **CEM:** Keen Family; GPS unk; Rt 92; Mecklenburg **GS:** Y **SP:** Mar (29 Dec 1790) Margaret Tabb **VI:** Moved to Mecklenburg 1785. Appl pen 31 May 1839 age 77. Mecklenburg Co. S11710; Edward L. Tabb, Security, pg 30 **P:** Y **BLW:** unk **RG:** N **MK:** N **PH:** unk **SS:** K Vol 3 pg 55; CG pg 1904 **BS:** 54, pg 235.

KEESEE (KEEZEE), Jeremiah; b 12 Oct 1751; d 2 Jan 1825 **RU:** Private, Served in Capt Abston's Co VA Militia **CEM:** Keesee Family; GPS 36.87683, -79.52109; Nr Green Pond; Pittsylvania **GS:** Y **SP:** 1) Mar (4 Sep 1793 Pittsylvania Co) Dorcas Perkins 2) Sarah Burch Else (4 Oct 1757-3 Dec 1813) **VI:** No further data **P:** unk **BLW:** unk **RG:** N **MK:** N **PH:** unk **SS:** BU **BS:** 174, 194.

KEESLING, Conrad; b 1744, Berks Co, PA; d Dec 1818 **RU:** Private, Served in Capt Jacob Baldy's Co. Served fr Berks Co PA **CEM:** Old Keesling; GPS unk; unk; Wythe **GS:** U **SP:** Mar (1794) Rebecca Ann Kegley (__-__Delaware Co, IN) **VI:** No further data **P:** unk **BLW:** unk **RG:** unk **MK:** unk **PH:** unk **SS:** NSSAR Ancestor # P-258078; CI PA Archives 5th series Vol 5 pg 235 **BS:** JLARC 2, 40,123.

KEITH, Alexander; b unk; d Dec 1788 **RU:** Patriot, Gave material aid to cause **CEM:** Old Christ Church Episcopal; GPS 38.80625, -77.04718; 118 N Washington St; Alexandria City **GS:** N **SP:** No info **VI:** Burial permit issued 3 Dec 1788 to the widow **P:** N **BLW:** N **RG:** Y **MK:** N **PH:** N **SS:** E pg 435; AL Ct Bk pg 8 Prince William Co **BS:** 20 pg 149.

KEITH, Thomas Randolph; b 14 Mar 1736, Fauquier Co; d 1805 **RU:** Captain, Served in Fauquier Co Militia as 2nd Lt 24 Mar 1778. Listed as Capt in BLW records. Pen rec indicates was in VA Line **CEM:** Blackwell Family; GPS unk; The Meadows, E of Rt 628 at first farm past Bethel Methodist Ch, Bethel;

RU=Rank/Unit	CEM=Cemetery	GS=Gravestone	SP=Spousal Information
VI=Other Veteran Info	P=Pension	BLW=Bounty/Land Warrant	RG=Registered Grave
MK=SAR/DAR Marker	PH=Photo	SS=Service Source	BS=Burial Source

180

Fauquier **GS:** N **SP:** Mar (25 May 1775) Judth Blackwell (1758-17 Apr 1837) **VI:** Son of James (1696-1758) & Mary Isham (Randolph) (1758-17 Apr 1837) Keith. Died on trip to GA in 1805 with son, but not known if body brought back. In some records, Thomas & Judith are bur in Blackwell Fam Cem in Fauquier Co. Wife appl pen 27 Dec 1836 Fauquier Co **P:** Y **BLW:** Y **RG:** unk **MK:** unk **PH:** N **SS:** E pg 436; CG pg 1907 **BS:** 196.

KELL, Michel; b unk; d 1781 **RU:** Soldier, Served in Bourbonnais Bn and died fr battle at Yorktown **CEM:** French Memorial; GPS 36.81944, -79.39933; Yorktown; York **GS:** U **SP:** No info **VI:** No further data **P:** unk **BLW:** unk **RG:** Y **MK:** unk **PH:** unk **SS:** J-Yorktown Historian **BS:** JLARC 1, 74.

KELLER, Frederick Sr; b 1767; d 1839 **RU:** Patriot, Gave material aid to cause **CEM:** Keller Family; GPS unk; On Dr. Knopp's Farm, Churchville; Augusta **GS:** N **SP:** Barbara Baylor **VI:** No further data **P:** N **BLW:** N **RG:** unk **MK:** unk **PH:** N **SS:** AL Ct Bk pg 5 Augusta Co **BS:** JLARC 62.

KELLER, George; b 19 Apr 1758, nr Stovertown, Shenandoah Co; d 27 Jan 1844 **RU:** Ensign, Served in Augusta Co Militia & VA line **CEM:** Keller Family; GPS unk; On Dr. Knopp's Farm, Churchville; Augusta **GS:** U **SP:** Sophie Mowry (1776 PA-18 Oct 1759 West View, Augusta Co) **VI:** Son of George (1735-1818) & Anna Barbara (Hanger) (1766-1859) Keller. Appl pen in Monongolia Co 22 Aug 1832, S5649. Died in West View, Augusta Co **P:** Y **BLW:** N **RG:** unk **MK:** unk **PH:** unk **SS:** E pg 436; G pg 446; CG pg 1908 **BS:** 196.

KELLER, George; b 1735, PA; d 1818 **RU:** Patriot, Gave material aid to cause **CEM:** Keller Family; GPS unk; On Dr Knopp's Farm, Churchville; Augusta **GS:** N **SP:** Anna Barbara Hanger (7 Nov 1736 Germany-__) **VI:** Son of George (1711-1782) & Barbara (Hottel) (1713-1798) Keller **P:** unk **BLW:** unk **RG:** unk **MK:** unk **PH:** N **SS:** AL Ct Bk pg 5 Augusta Co **BS:** 196.

KELLER, George; b 17 May 1711; d 1782 **RU:** Patriot, Gave material aid to cause and was a member of the Committee of Safety, Dunmore Co, which Shanandoah became a part **CEM:** Keller Family; GPS 38.96580, -78.46220; Sand Ridge Rd, Mt Olive; Shenandoah **GS:** N **SP:** Barbara Hottel (1713-1798) **VI:** Son of Bastian & Elizabeth (Hildebrant) Keller, both German immigrants **P:** N **BLW:** N **RG:** unk **MK:** unk **PH:** N **SS:** AL Ct Bk pg 11 Shenandoah Co **BS:** 196.

KELLER, George Jr; b 4 Mar 1731, Rotherfluh, Switzerland; d Jan 1788 **RU:** Patriot, Performed public service & gave material aid to cause **CEM:** Keller Family; GPS 38.49457, -78.25335; Burner Ln off Fort Valley Rd; Shenandoah **GS:** U **SP:** Mar (1760) Barbara Zimmerman **VI:** Was a doctor. Died in Ft Valley, Shenandoah Co. DAR marker **P:** N **BLW:** N **RG:** unk **MK:** Y **PH:** unk **SS:** CA **BS:** 04.

KELLEY, James; b 1735; d 1795 **RU:** Patriot, Gave material aid to the cause **CEM:** Christ Church; GPS 37.61019, -76.54606; 420 Christ Church Rd, Weems; Lancaster **GS:** Y **SP:** No info **VI:** No further data **P:** N **BLW:** N **RG:** N **MK:** N **PH:** unk **SS:** AL Ct bk pg 20 **BS:** 40 pg 68.

KELLY, Edward; b c1752; d 17 Aug 1834 Russell Co **RU:** Private, Served in Capt Thomas Young in Western Bn commanded by Col Joseph Crockett in VA State service and Capt Edwin Hull in 15th VA Regt commanded by Lt Col Innes **CEM:** Kelly; GPS 36.95690, -82.09360; Just off Rt 621 on Sandy Ridge, nr home of Rev & Mrs Gonan Kelly; Russell **GS:** U **SP:** Mar (9 Apr 1774 Shenandoah Co) Bridget "Biddy" Nugent (c1752 Ireland-__ Russell Co) **VI:** Said to have preached sermon for Gen George Washington at Valley Forge. Moderator of Washington Baptist Assoc. (Regular Baptist) 1815, 1816, 1818, and a delegate fr Reed's Valley Church 1814-1822, 1826, 1827 **P:** unk **BLW:** unk **RG:** unk **MK:** unk **PH:** unk **SS:** E pg 437 indicates record at War Department at Nat Archives **BS:** 196.

KELLY, John; b 1747, County Donegal, Ireland; d 4 Dec 1822 **RU:** Soldier, Served 1780 in Cont Army at Battle of Kings Mountain. Served in 1st, 4th, 8th, 9th, 12th Cont Lines **CEM:** Ebbing Spring; GPS unk; N side of middle fork of Holstein River, vic Glade Spring; Washington **GS:** U **SP:** Jean Kirkham (__-bef 1822) Will specified husband to be bur next to her. **VI:** Honored 4 Jul 2001 when Black's Ft chapter of DAR put monument in Sinking Spring Cemetery in Abingdon to honor soldiers bur in Washington Co **P:** unk **BLW:** unk **RG:** unk **MK:** Y **PH:** unk **SS:** E pg 436 **BS:** 196.

KELSO, Robert; b 10 Apr 1761; d 21 Jul 1842 **RU:** Private, Served in Capt Edward Mumford's Co, Dec 1779 commanded by Col Willis & Col Mays Duval. Was in skirmish with British at Bland's Ordinary in Southampton Co. In 1780 or 1781 served in Capt Richard Crump's Co in Powhatan Co. **CEM:** Kelso

RU=Rank/Unit CEM=Cemetery GS=Gravestone SP=Spousal Information
VI=Other Veteran Info P=Pension BLW=Bounty/Land Warrant RG=Registered Grave
MK=SAR/DAR Marker PH=Photo SS=Service Source BS=Burial Source

181

Family; GPS unk; 1 mi N of Pamplin on Rt 600; Appomattox **GS:** Y **SP:** Susan Pollard (3 Aug 1773 Hanover Co-21 Nov 1848) d/o William & Mary (-----) Pollard **VI:** No further data **P:** unk **BLW:** unk **RG:** unk **MK:** unk **PH:** unk **SS:** AP pension rec **BS:** 196; 201.

KEMPER (KAMPER), Charles Sr; b 27 Jun 1756; d 1 Dec 1841 **RU:** Private, Served in VA Line. Ent serv Fauquier Co 1777 **CEM:** Kemper Family; GPS unk; Rt 802 Nr Warrenton; Fauquier **GS:** Y **SP:** Mar (29 Nov 1774 or 1786 Fauquier Co) Susanna Mawzey by John Pickett, Baptist minister (c1766-__) **VI:** Sol appl pen 25 Jun 1833 Fauquier Co. Widow appl pen 4 May 1843 Fauquier Co. W20292 **P:** Y **BLW:** unk **RG:** N **MK:** N **PH:** unk **SS:** K Vol 3 pg 61; N pg 1258; CG pg 1919; Fauquier Co Marriages pg 112 **BS:** JLARC 4,16; 19 pg 132.

KENDALL, George; b 1759; d 24 Nov 1784 **RU:** Patriot, Gave material aid to cause **CEM:** Kendall Grove; GPS unk; Rt 674; Northampton **GS:** Y **SP:** No info **VI:** Died age 25. Stone erected by his friend George Parker **P:** N **BLW:** N **RG:** N **MK:** N **PH:** unk **SS:** G pg 483 **BS:** 42 pg 48.

KENDALL, William; b 1763; d 1807 **RU:** Private, Served in VA Battalion and was in Clark's Illinois Regt **CEM:** Hungerford-Griffin; GPS unk; 373 Resolutions Rd, Leedstown; Westmoreland **GS:** Y **SP:** No info **VI:** Received BLW **P:** unk **BLW:** Y **RG:** N **MK:** N **PH:** unk **SS:** E pg 439; AP rec **BS:** 189.

KENNAHORN, William Jr; b 20 Nov 1747; d 30 Nov 1840 **RU:** Soldier, Served in VA Line. Ent serv Accomack Co, 1776. Served in Capt Levin Jones Co for two yrs, discharged at Valley Forge, PA **CEM:** Kennahorn Family; GPS unk; N side of Rt 638, .4 mi E of 637, W fr Cashville; Accomack **GS:** Y **SP:** 1) unk 2) Mar (14 Jan 1824 Accomack) Delaney Butler (c1779-__) **VI:** Occupation cooper in 1829 age 82 & wife Delaney age 50. Sol appl pen 9 Jul 1818 Williamsburg. Pensioned Accomack Co 1818 age 70. Widow appl pen 28 Sep 1853 age 78 Accomack Co. Widow appl for BLW 3 Apr 1855. W26642, BLW #8175-160-55. DAR marker placed on the Gr of William Kennahorn, Sr **P:** Y **BLW:** Y **RG:** unk **MK:** Y **PH:** unk **SS:** K Vol 3 pg 64; CG pg 1923; BT **BS:** JLARC 4, 5; 209.

KENNAHORN, William Sr; b 20 Mar 1717; d 20 Nov 1810 **RU:** Soldier, Specific service not identified **CEM:** Kennahorn Family; GPS unk; N side of Rt 638, .4 mi E of 637, W fr Cashville; Accomack **GS:** Y **SP:** No info **VI:** GS reads "Soldier in the War of 1776", however over military age **P:** unk **BLW:** unk **RG:** unk **MK:** unk **PH:** unk **SS:** BT **BS:** 209.

KENNEDY, James Dr; b c1753, Dumfrieshire, Scotland; d 6 Jan 1816 **RU:** Sergeant, Served 13th Cont Line as pvt; served 3rd, 5th, 7th, 11th Cont Line **CEM:** Presbyterian Church; GPS 38.80015, -77.05791; Wilkes St & Hamilton Ln; Alexandria City **GS:** Y **SP:** Mar (12 May 1780) Susannah (-----) (25 Jul 1766-30 May 1845) **VI:** Death notice in the Alexandria Gazette, 8 Jan 1816 **P:** unk **BLW:** unk **RG:** Y **MK:** N **PH:** unk **SS:** E pg 439 **BS:** 23 pg 49.

KENNER, Howson Francis; b 10 Mar 1712, Northumberland Co; d 24 May 1778 **RU:** Midshipman, Navy service particulars not identified **CEM:** Kenner; GPS unk; Rt 616, Somerville; Fauquier **GS:** Y **SP:** Margaret Eskridge (19 May 1712 Westmoreland Co-8 Oct 1801 Warrenton, Fauquier Co) **VI:** Son of Francis (1675-1728) & Hannah (Howson) (1677-1712) Kenner. Recd BLW **P:** unk **BLW:** Y **RG:** unk **MK:** unk **PH:** unk **SS:** E pg 441; CZ pg 252; CU **BS:** JLARC 16; 196.

KENNEY (KENNY, KINNEY), Robert; b 1743; d 28 Nov 1806 **RU:** Captain, Commanded a Co in Augusta Co Militia after being commissioned as Capt 18 August 1778 **CEM:** Augusta Stone Presbyterian; GPS 38.23926, -78.97356; 28 Old Stone Church Ln, Ft Defiance; Augusta **GS:** Y **SP:** Pheobe Huston (11 May 1788-23 Apr 1806) d/o James (1726 Baltimore-1818 Fayette Co, KY) & (-----) Huston **VI:** Gov't GS shows rank **P:** unk **BLW:** unk **RG:** unk **MK:** unk **PH:** unk **SS:** E pg 441 **BS:** 196.

KENNEY (KENNY, KINNEY), Robert; b 1748; d unk **RU:** Private, Served in Dunmore's War 1774 at Point Pleasant fr Augusta Co under Capt George Matthews and later Capt Rankin's Co, Augusta Militia **CEM:** Augusta Stone Presbyterian; GPS 38.23926, -78.97356; 28 Old Stone Church Ln, Ft Defiance; Augusta **GS:** Y **SP:** No info **VI:** Stone erected in 1953 styles him a Capt of the Rev War **P:** unk **BLW:** unk **RG:** Y **MK:** unk **PH:** unk **SS:** B; E pg 441; Z pg 105-6; CP Dunmore's War; J-NSSAR 2000 Reg **BS:** JLARC 1, 2, 8, 23 ,62, 76; 196.

KENNON, Richard; b 1759, Mecklenburg Co; d 4 Feb 1805 **RU:** Captain, Served in VA Line. Ent serv Mecklenburg Co **CEM:** Wimmer King; GPS unk; Copper Hill; Floyd **GS:** Y **SP:** Mar (16 May 1780)

RU=Rank/Unit CEM=Cemetery GS=Gravestone   SP=Spousal Information
VI=Other Veteran Info P=Pension   BLW=Bounty/Land Warrant RG=Registered Grave
MK=SAR/DAR Marker PH=Photo   SS=Service Source   BS=Burial Source

182

Elizabeth Beverley Munford (28 Mar 1762 Mecklenburg Co-1825) **VI:** Gov't gr st shows rank and service. BLW #2298-300 issued 22 Nov 1842 to heirs **P:** unk **BLW:** Y **RG:** unk **MK:** unk **PH:** unk **SS:** E pg 441; CG pg 1926; DD **BS:** JLARC 2, 72; 196.

KENNY, William; b c1764; d 1851 **RU:** Private?, Served in 3rd Cont Line **CEM:** Kenny Family; GPS unk; Vic jct Rts 802 & 709; Carroll **GS:** U **SP:** No info **VI:** No further data **P:** unk **BLW:** unk **RG:** N **MK:** N **PH:** unk **SS:** E pg 442 **BS:** 63 pg 384.

KENT, Luke; b c1762; d 28 Apr 1789 **RU:** Patriot, Supplied the militia with material aid **CEM:** Kent Family; GPS unk; Poplar Creek; Halifax **GS:** N **SP:** Mar (8Jan 1782 Bedford Co) Sarah Cocke (1767-Dec 1801) d/o George Sr (1725 Hanover Co-___) & Agnes (-----) (___-1785) Cocke **VI:** Died in Cumberland Co **P:** N **BLW:** N **RG:** Y **MK:** N **PH:** N **SS:** V bk 2 pg 279-280 **BS:** 04.

KENT, Robert; b c1710-1715, Goochland Co; d 17 Jul 1783 **RU:** Patriot, Supplied the militia with material aid **CEM:** Kent Family; GPS unk; Poplar Creek; Halifax **GS:** N **SP:** Mary Easley (___-13 Oct 1782) **VI:** No further data **P:** N **BLW:** N **RG:** Y **MK:** N **PH:** N **SS:** DAR Ancestor #A065044; V bk 2 pg 279-280 **BS:** 04.

KER, Edward; b unk; d 1790 **RU:** Patriot, Gave material aid to cause **CEM:** Melrose & Ker Family; GPS unk; Abt 2 mi SW Pungoteague; Accomack **GS:** N **SP:** No info **VI:** No further data **P:** N **BLW:** N **RG:** N **MK:** N **PH:** N **SS:** G pg 483 **BS:** 145 Melrose Ker.

KER, John Shepard; b 1762; d Sep 1800 **RU:** Private, Served in Capt Stephenson's Co, 9th VA Regt, May 1776 **CEM:** Scott Hall, aka Edward Snead; GPS 37.71115; -75.75250; Nr River btw Mt Prospect Ave and South St, Onancock; Accomack **GS:** Y **SP:** Perhaps Agnes Drummond Corbin (Jan 1775-Feb 1814) as she has adjacent stone in cem **VI:** Son of Edward Jr & Margaret (Shepard) Ker **P:** N **BLW:** N **RG:** N **MK:** N **PH:** unk **SS:** AP Payroll 9th VA Regt **BS:** 145 Snead; 196.

KERFOOT (KEARFOOT), William; b c 1719 or 1724, Castle Blaney, Monaghan, Ireland; d 1779 **RU:** Sergeant, Served in Capt John Stiths's Co 4th VA Regt. Served 3 yrs **CEM:** White Post aka Wheeler Family; GPS 39.71170, -78.5419; Nr White Post, nr Clarke-Frederick co line, Dearfield Farm; Frederick **GS:** U **SP:** Mar (1745) Mary Margaret Carter (1727 Frederick Co-1777) **VI:** Deed for 192 acres on Opequon Creek in 1763. Recd BLW **P:** unk **BLW:** Y **RG:** unk **MK:** unk **PH:** unk **SS:** C pg 459; E pg 443; BY **BS:** 80 vol 2 pg 217.

KERR, James; b 1726, Lancaster Co, PA; d 5 Jan 1812 **RU:** Private, Served in Capt Rankin's Co, Augusta Co Militia. Augusta Co record of 16 Oct 1776 indicates "exempted fr military duty until he comes the use of his arm." He may be the person of this name that served in the 3rd, 5th, 7th, and 11th Cont Line and was at Valley Forge **CEM:** Augusta Stone Presbyterian; GPS 38.23926, -78.97356; 28 Old Stone Church Ln, Ft Defiance; Augusta **GS:** Y **SP:** Mar (c1755) Jane Robertson (1739-11 Feb 1824) **VI:** Stone reads b 1724 but other sources indicate 1734 and 1737. Also was at Valley Forge **P:** unk **BLW:** unk **RG:** unk **MK:** unk **PH:** unk **SS:** B; E pg 443 **BS:** JLARC 63; 196.

KERR, John Jr; b unk; d 1794 **RU:** Soldier, Served in Capt Rankin's or Capt Kenny's Co, Augusta Co Militia, also in 1st VA Regt & Cont Line **CEM:** Augusta Stone Presbyterian; GPS 38.23926, -78.97356; 28 Old Stone Church Ln, Ft Defiance; Augusta **GS:** Y **SP:** Christine Niswonger **VI:** Family stone erected in 1930, does not mention Rev War service, and gives no date of birth. A person this name recd BLW **P:** unk **BLW:** Y **RG:** unk **MK:** unk **PH:** unk **SS:** C pg 249; E pg 443 **BS:** JLARC 63; 196.

KERR, John Sr; b unk; d 8 Jul 1830 **RU:** Private, Served in Capt Kenny's Co, Augusta Militia. He may be the person of this name that served in the 1st VA State Regt and the 4th, 7th, 8th, and 12th Cont Line **CEM:** Augusta Stone Presbyterian; GPS 38.23926, -78.97356; 28 Old Stone Church Ln, Ft Defiance; Augusta **GS:** Y **SP:** Elizabeth Hogsettker (___-1842) **VI:** Family stone erected in 1930, does not mention Rev War service, and gives no date of birth **P:** unk **BLW:** unk **RG:** Y **MK:** unk **PH:** unk **SS:** E pg 443 **BS:** JLARC 1, 8, 23, 62; 196.

KERR, Joseph; b unk; d 1839 **RU:** Private?, Served in Capt Teater's Co, Augusta Co Militia **CEM:** Old Stone Presbyterian; GPS 38.23926, -78.97356; 28 Old Stone Church Ln, Ft Defiance; Augusta **GS:** Y **SP:** No info **VI:** No further data **P:** unk **BLW:** unk **RG:** Y **MK:** N **PH:** unk **SS:** E pg 443 **BS:** 71 pg 16.

RU=Rank/Unit	CEM=Cemetery	GS=Gravestone	SP=Spousal Information
VI=Other Veteran Info	P=Pension	BLW=Bounty/Land Warrant	RG=Registered Grave
MK=SAR/DAR Marker	PH=Photo	SS=Service Source	BS=Burial Source

183

KERR, William; b 1760, Fifeshare, Scotland; d 16 Jul 1828 **RU:** Private/Patriot, Served in VA & PA. Served in 3rd Co Rifleman, 5th Battalion, Washington Co, PA. Gave one bag of beef to cause **CEM:** Bethel Presbyterian; GPS 38.04257, -79.17283; 563 Bethel Green Rd, Middlebrook; Augusta **GS:** N **SP:** Mar (22 Dec 1796) Mary Ann Grove **VI:** No further data **P:** unk **BLW:** unk **RG:** unk **MK:** unk **PH:** N **SS:** D pg 45 Augusta Co; N **BS:** JLARC 63.

KESSLER, John; b 8 Feb 1761; d 2 Jan 1847 **RU:** Private, Enl 28 Jan 1776 in 9th Co of Light Artillery **CEM:** Kessler Family; GPS unk; Nr Brick Union Ch; Botetourt **GS:** Y **SP:** Elizabeth (-----) (30 Sep 1822-c1883) **VI:** No further data **P:** unk **BLW:** unk **RG:** N **MK:** N **PH:** unk **SS:** AP pension **BS:** 165.

KEY, John; b unk; d unk **RU:** Ensign, Served in 8th Cont Line. Was Ens 3 Feb 1777. Resigned 24 Apr 1778 **CEM:** Trinity Episcopal; GPS 36.83459, -76.30105; 500 Court St; Portsmouth City **GS:** Y **SP:** No info **VI:** Stone 86 B in W.B. Butt inventory. Govt marker **P:** unk **BLW:** unk **RG:** unk **MK:** unk **PH:** unk **SS:** E pg 444 **BS:** JLARC 105, 127; 196; 57.

KEYSER, Andrew Sr; b 16 Dec 1758, Shenandoah Co; d 23 Nov 1833 **RU:** Private/Major, Ent serv Shenandoah Co 1780 for 18 mos in Capt Conway Oldham's Co, Col Richard Campbell's VA Regt. Was in battles of Guilford, Camden, Ninety-Six, and Eutaw Springs **CEM:** Keyser Family; GPS unk; Rt 684, NW fr Luray 8 mi; Page **GS:** N **SP:** 1) Sarah Margaret "Sally" Rinehart 2) Elizabeth Grove Strickler **VI:** Other writings show him as Maj in the VA Troop which may have been for service after the Revolution. Sol appl pen 23 Jul 1832 Page Co. Died in Shenandoah Co, now Page Co. S5651 **P:** Y **BLW:** unk **RG:** unk **MK:** N **PH:** N **SS:** Pen Appl; CG pg 1937 **BS:** JLARC 2, 4, 49; 120.

KEYSER, Charles Jr; b 1750; d Aft 12 Sep 1796 **RU:** Private, Served in Capt Michael Reader's Co, Shenandoah Militia **CEM:** Keyser Family; GPS unk; Rt 684, NW fr Luray 8 mi; Page **GS:** U **SP:** Elizabeth Baker **VI:** No further data **P:** unk **BLW:** unk **RG:** unk **MK:** unk **PH:** unk **SS:** J- DAR Hatcher; C pg 602 **BS:** JLARC 2.

KEYSER (KEYSOR), William; b 1755; d 4 Dec 1837 **RU:** Private, Ent serv Gloucester Co in Capt Thomas Baytop's Co, 2d VA State Regt. Was at Valley Forge with Washington's Army, later Col Charles Dabney's Regt at Monmouth Battle & Battles at Sawmill River Bridge & Stoney Point **CEM:** Keyser Family; GPS 37.96885,-79.83694; nr Jct Rts 612 & 618, Warm Springs; Bath **GS:** N **SP:** Keziah Snead (1761 Hanover Co-1849 Alleghany Co) **VI:** Memorial GS placed at Healing Springs Baptist Church. Pen recd 9 Oct 1832; widow pen Bath Co W3427 **P:** Y **BLW:** unk **RG:** unk **MK:** unk **PH:** unk **SS:** G pg 723; CG pg 1937 **BS:** 196.

KIBLER, Henry; b c1746, Germany; d 9 Sep 1796 **RU:** Patriot, Gave material aid to cause **CEM:** Robert T Kemp Farm; GPS unk; Luray; Page **GS:** U **SP:** Mary Amelia (__-1796) **VI:** No further data **P:** N **BLW:** N **RG:** Y **MK:** unk **PH:** unk **SS:** J-NSSAR 2000 Reg; AL Ct Bk pg 12 Shenandoah Co **BS:** JLARC 76.

KIDD, James; b unk; d Nov 1795 **RU:** Private, Served in Capt Thomas Tebbe Co #4, 30 Apr 1777, 2nd Cont Line **CEM:** Old Christ Church Episcopal; GPS 38.80625, -77.04718; 118 N Washington St; Alexandria City **GS:** N **SP:** No info **VI:** Burial permit issued 4 Nov 1795 **P:** unk **BLW:** unk **RG:** Y **MK:** N **PH:** N **SS:** A pg 273; E pg 444 **BS:** 20 pg 149.

KILLINGER, George; b c1756, PA; d Bet 19 Aug 1841 - 23 Mar 1842 **RU:** Private, Served in PA Line. Ent serv Lancaster Co PA. Was in 4th class in 2nd Co of 9th Battalion of Lancaster Co PA Militia under Col John Rogers **CEM:** Royal Oak; GPS 36.84315, -81.49660; Behind Marion Baptist Church, Marion; Smyth **GS:** Y **SP:** No info **VI:** Appl pen 20 Mar 1841 Smyth Co. R5919. Rejected **P:** N **BLW:** unk **RG:** Y **MK:** N **PH:** unk **SS:** J-NSSAR 1993 Reg; CG pg 1942 **BS:** JLARC 1; 196.

KILPATRICK, Ann; b 1739; d 2 Aug 1815 **RU:** Patriot, Gave material aid to cause **CEM:** Hogshead Family; GPS unk; Off Rt 736 btw Rts 42 & 250, N of Jennings Gap; Augusta **GS:** U **SP:** Prob widow of David Hogshead, Sr; maiden name Kilpatrick **VI:** No further data **P:** N **BLW:** N **RG:** unk **MK:** unk **PH:** unk **SS:** Al Cert, Augusta Co as Mrs Ann Hogstead **BS:** 36 pg 72-3; 196.

KIMBALL, Benjamin; b unk; d 1781 **RU:** Soldier, Served fr MA, and died fr the Battle at Yorktown **CEM:** Yorktown Victory Monument Tablet; GPS 38.28350, -78.54150; Yorktown; York **GS:** U **SP:** No info **VI:** No further data **P:** unk **BLW:** unk **RG:** unk **MK:** unk **PH:** unk **SS:** J-Yorktown Historian **BS:** JLARC 74.

RU=Rank/Unit	CEM=Cemetery	GS=Gravestone	SP=Spousal Information
VI=Other Veteran Info	P=Pension	BLW=Bounty/Land Warrant	RG=Registered Grave
MK=SAR/DAR Marker	PH=Photo	SS=Service Source	BS=Burial Source

184

KINCAID, John; b 1754, Ireland; d 30 Jan 1811 **RU:** Soldier, Served in VA unit in Illinois **CEM:** Presbyterian Church; GPS 38.80015, -77.05791; Wilkes St & Hamilton Ln; Alexandria City **GS:** Y **SP:** Lucy (-----), (1759-18 Apr 1842) **VI:** Died age 57 **P:** unk **BLW:** unk **RG:** Y **MK**: unk **PH:** unk **SS:** J-NSSAR 1993 Reg; E pg 446 **BS:** JLARC 1; 23 pg 49-50.

KINCAID, John; b 11 Jan 1758, Augusta Co; d 5 Aug 1835 **RU:** Private, Served in VA Line. Ent serv Botetourt Co in Hanley's Co of militia **CEM:** Falling Springs Presbyterian; GPS 37.68526, -79.44972; 410 Falling Springs Rd, Glasgow; Rockbridge **GS:** Y **SP:** Mar (25 Jul 1787) Alice "Alley" Dean (her marriage record says Alcy Elliott), (1767-25 Feb 1861) **VI:** Sol appl pen 19 Nov 1833 Alleghany Co. Widow appl pen 6 Jun 1842 Alleghany Co. W3428.Recd BLW #38513-160-55 **P:** Y **BLW:** Y **RG:** unk **MK**: unk **PH:** unk **SS:** CG pg 1947 **BS:** JLARC 2, 4, 53; 196.

KING, Elisha; b 10 Apr 1756; d 13 May 1821 **RU:** Major, Served in VA Line and as 1st Lt 10th Cont Line. Later Maj in Dragoons **CEM:** Sweden Plantation; GPS 37.15854, -77.54751; nr jct Claiborne & White Oak rds, Sutherland; Dinwiddie **GS:** N **SP:** Mar (1789) Judith Brent (__-4 May 1807) **VI:** Recd BLW #324-200-14 Feb 1807. **P:** unk **BLW:** Y **RG:** unk **MK**: N **PH:** N **SS:** DAR #A066428; E pg 447; K Vol 3 pg 76; CG pg 1951 **BS:** JLARC 116.

KING, George; b 1730, Brunswick Co; d 6 May 1806 **RU:** Private, Served in Gen George Rogers Ill Regt and Joseph Crocketts Regt **CEM:** King; GPS unk; Leatherwood; Henry **GS:** U **SP:** Mar (1766) Mary Niblet (c1740-1848) **VI:** No further data **P:** unk **BLW:** unk **RG:** unk **MK**: unk **PH:** unk **SS:** DAR #A066468; G pg 701 **BS:** 196.

KING, John; b 1746; d 11 Sep 1810 **RU:** Ensign, Served in Capt William Doak's Co, Montgomery Co Militia **CEM:** King; GPS unk; W side of SR 625, S of jct with SR 667, Crockett; Wythe **GS:** U **SP:** Mar (1775) Savannah Sabine (c1757-12 Oct 1844) **VI:** Reported burial said to be on Claude Copernhaver farm. **P:** unk **BLW:** unk **RG:** unk **MK**: unk **PH:** unk **SS:** DAR Ancestor #A012224; G pg 220; BW pg 1, 12, 13 **BS:** JLARC 40, 123.

KING, John; b 1760; d 1840 **RU:** Private, Probably the man by this name who served in Capt Campbell's Co, Augusta Co Militia **CEM:** Stull Family; GPS unk; 10 mi S of Lowmoor; Alleghany **GS:** Y **SP:** No info **VI:** No further data **P:** unk **BLW:** unk **RG:** N **MK**: N **PH:** unk **SS:** E pg 447 **BS:** 160 Stull.

KING, John; b 1759, MD; d Mar 1843 **RU:** Private, Served in Capt Daniel Stull's Co, Col John Gunby, 7th MD Regt, MD Militia **CEM:** King; GPS unk; Nr MM 141 on Blue Ridge Pkwy; Floyd **GS:** U **SP:** Mar (4 Nov or Dec 1799) Sarah Addair (c1781-Mar 1843) **VI:** Recd VA pension in Floyd Co #S5553 **P:** Y **BLW:** unk **RG:** unk **MK**: unk **PH:** unk **SS:** DAR Ancestor #A066603; E pg 447; DD **BS:** JLARC 4, 29; 196.

KING, John; b 1744; d 1802 **RU:** Private, Served in Capt Campbell's Co, Augusta Co Militia. Also in Capt George Moffat's Co at Point Pleasant Battle Oct 1774 **CEM:** Kring Salvage; GPS unk; Off John Deere Dr, behind Harman Machinery, Broadway; Rockingham **GS:** Y **SP:** No info **VI:** No further data **P:** unk **BLW:** unk **RG:** N **MK**: N **PH:** unk **SS:** E pg 447; Z pg 117-8 **BS:** 191 Salvage.

KING, John Sr; b 1758, Brunswick Co; d 1821 **RU:** Soldier, Served in Brunswick Co Militia Oct 1782 **CEM:** King; GPS unk; Leatherwood; Henry **GS:** U **SP:** 1) Mar (c1779) Mary Elizabeth Seward (1750-1760 Brunswick Co-Feb 1829) 2) Mary Love (1774-1847) **VI:** Son of George (1734-__) & Mary (Niblett) King. Pastor at Beaver Creek and Leatherwood Churches **P:** unk **BLW:** unk **RG:** unk **MK**: unk **PH:** unk **SS:** DAR Ancestor #A066681; G pg 90 **BS:** 196.

KING, Miles Sr; b 2 Nov 1746, Elizabeth City Co; d 9 Jun 1814 **RU:** Surg Mate Captain, Ent Serv Hampton in Elizabeth City Co. Commanded a co of Minutemen. Served when French arrived at Chesapeake and during siege of York **CEM:** St Paul's Episcopal; GPS 36.84733, -76.28554; 201 St Paul's Blvd; Norfolk City **GS:** Y **SP:** 1) Barbara Jones 2) Mar (27 Apr 1782 Elizabeth City Co) Martha Kirby (Nov 1765-29 Jan 1849 Norfolk) **VI:** One of first elected to VA legislature after Rev. Had 40+ yrs service to country, Burgoise representing Elizabeth City Co to Colonial assembly. Delegate & Justice of Peace Elizabeth City Co. In 1800 moved to Norfolk, as Alderman. Pen says he d in August. Widow appl pen Jan 1838 Norfolk. DAR marker 02 Dec 2012. W20342 **P:** unk **BLW:** Y **RG:** Y **MK**: Y **PH:** Y **SS:** CB; K Vol 3 pg 78; BY, pg 290; AK; CG pg 1955 **BS:** 04.

RU=Rank/Unit	CEM=Cemetery	GS=Gravestone	SP=Spousal Information
VI=Other Veteran Info	P=Pension	BLW=Bounty/Land Warrant	RG=Registered Grave
MK=SAR/DAR Marker	PH=Photo	SS=Service Source	BS=Burial Source

185

KING, Robert; b 1765; d 1814 **RU:** Private, Served in 7th Cont Line **CEM:** King Family; GPS unk; Rt 658 Brent Point Rd; Stafford **GS:** Y **SP:** No info **VI:** No further data **P:** unk **BLW:** unk **RG:** N **MK:** N **PH:** unk **SS:** E pg 447 **BS:** 03 pg 262.

KING, Robert; b 1752; d 1821 **RU:** Soldier, Served in Capt John Smith's Co, Augusta Co **CEM:** West End; GPS 36.94140, -81.11670; off Rt 11, Wytheville; Wythe **GS:** U **SP:** No info **VI:** Remains moved fr Old West End Cemetery in 1959. Name listed on plaque in the cemetery **P:** unk **BLW:** unk **RG:** unk **MK:** unk **PH:** unk **SS:** G pg 24 **BS:** 196.

KING, Stephen; b 2 Apr 1752; d 2 Apr 1836 **RU:** Soldier, Ent serv Henry Co 1780.Served in Capt James Shelton & Daniel Richardson's Co **CEM:** Ramsey-Stanley; GPS unk; Rt 764 nr Rt 606; Franklin **GS:** U **SP:** Mar (16 Dec 1785) Laurana Maupine (1750-1840) **VI:** Pen 1832 Franklin Co age 81. S5551 **P:** unk **BLW:** unk **RG:** unk **MK:** unk **PH:** unk **SS:** DAR #A064788; K Vol 3 pg 79; DD **BS:** JLARC 4,19.

KING, William; b 1752; d 1810 **RU:** Private, Served in Christy's NC Regt **CEM:** Green Spring Presbyterian; GPS 36.63670, -81.99560; 2007 Green Spring Ch Rd, Abingdon; Washington **GS:** U **SP:** No info **VI:** Source 80 has d at age 88 **P:** unk **BLW:** unk **RG:** unk **MK:** unk **PH:** unk **SS:** NSSAR Ancestor #P-260583 **BS:** JLARC 2, 70, 80,101.

KING, William; b 1752; d 1817 **RU:** Soldier, Served in VA militia. Ent serv Bedford Co 1778. Assigned as guard at lead mines, Wythe Co in Capt Robert Adams Co **CEM:** King; GPS unk; W side of SR 625, S of jct with SR 667, Crockett; Wythe **GS:** U **SP:** Catherine Creger (9 Jun 1754-8 Feb 1841) d/o Michael & Catherine (-----) Creger **VI:** Cem reported in good condition in Oct 1998 **P:** unk **BLW:** unk **RG:** unk **MK:** unk **PH:** unk **SS:** AZ pg 134 **BS:** JLARC 40, 123.

KING, William Sr; b unk; d unk **RU:** Private/Patriot, Ent serv Bedford Co 1778, then 2d VA State Regt and 3rd, 4th, 7th and 14th Cont Lines. Gave material aid to cause **CEM:** Trinity Episcopal; GPS 38.14917, -79.07521; 214 Beverley St; Staunton City **GS:** N **SP:** (-----) - she did receive a pension. **VI:** Son of Avra & (-----) King. Pen to widow commencing 2 Feb 1814 at $48 per yr **P:** Y **BLW:** N **RG:** N **MK:** N **PH:** N **SS:** E pg 448; AG pg 268; AL Ct Bk pg 43 Montgomery Co; AZ pg 134 **BS:** 142 Trinity.

KINHEAD (KINKEAD), Thomas; b unk; d 20 Nov 1841 **RU:** Private, Served in Capt Lockridge's Co, Augusta Co Militia **CEM:** Shinaberry; GPS unk; 3 mi N Hightown, Crabbottom; Highland **GS:** Y **SP:** Susan Hull (__-2 oct 1816) d/o Peter & Barbara (Penninger) Hull **VI:** Recd pension in Pendleton Co, WV **P:** unk **BLW:** unk **RG:** N **MK:** N **PH:** unk **SS:** E pg 448 **BS:** 181; 196.

KINSER (KENSOR), Michael; b 25 Feb 1762; d Dec 1822 **RU:** Private, Ent serv Wythe Co, 1st VA Regt. Wounded at Battle at Camden **CEM:** Broce-Kenser; GPS 37.23061, -80.45373; Boxwood Dr, Blacksburg; Montgomery **GS:** Y **SP:** Mar (4 Sep 1783 or 1784) Elizabeth (-----) **VI:** Pen disability commencing 1 Jan 1786. Widow appl pen 10 Jun 1844 in Wythe Co at 78 yrs, 11 mos, 21 days. Died (WP), Wythe Co. Pen records indicate death in Nov 1823. Will probated 10 Dec 1822, Wythe Co. W8001 **P:** Y **BLW:** unk **RG:** N **MK:** N **PH:** N **SS:** E pg 719; K Vol 3 pg 81; CG pg 962 **BS:** 196.

KIPPS (KEPPS) (KIPS), Jacob; b 11 Nov 1760; d 20 Apr 1849 **RU:** Private, Served in VA Line **CEM:** Zirkle Family; GPS 38.65900, -78.69580; River Rd, New Market; Shenandoah **GS:** Y **SP:** Elizabeth Zirkle (19 May 1766-21 Jun 1857) d/o George Adam (1740-1800) & Elizabeth (Ridenour) (1752-1829) Zirkle **VI:** Son of George Michael & (-----) Kipps. Widow appl pen 1851.W7993. Also granted BLW 1855. BLW #35835 **P:** Y **BLW:** Y **RG:** unk **MK:** unk **PH:** unk **SS:** E pg 153; K Vol 3 pg 67; CG pg 1964 **BS:** 196.

KIRK, John II; b 10 Oct 1754, Fauquier Co; d 10 Dec 1850 **RU:** Soldier, Ent serv Fauquier Co 1776. Was at Valley Forge under command of Gen Washington **CEM:** Kirk Burial Grounds; GPS unk; Chapman-Straley Farm Rt 730, nr Eggleston Springs; Giles **GS:** Y **SP:** Elizabeth O'Bryant or O'Brien (1760-1829) **VI:** Appl for pension 27 Aug 1832 Giles Co S5558 **P:** Y **BLW:** unk **RG:** Y **MK:** unk **PH:** unk **SS:** E pg 449; K Vol 3 pg 82; CG pg 1965 **BS:** JLARC 1, 26; 196.

KIRKPATRICK, Robert; b 31 Dec 1764; d 12 Mar 1832 **RU:** Soldier, Served in 5th Cont line **CEM:** Alone Community, aka Bethany Lutheran; GPS unk; Rts 602 & 525, Kerrs Dist part 6; Rockbridge **GS:** U **SP:** Mar (5 Feb 1799) Anna Davidson (15 Dec 1780-18 Mar 1826) d/o Samuel (c1753-1799) &

RU=Rank/Unit	CEM=Cemetery	GS=Gravestone	SP=Spousal Information
VI=Other Veteran Info	P=Pension	BLW=Bounty/Land Warrant	RG=Registered Grave
MK=SAR/DAR Marker	PH=Photo	SS=Service Source	BS=Burial Source

186

Elizabeth (Gilmore) Davidson **VI**: No further data **P**: N **BLW**: N **RG**: unk **MK**: unk **PH**: unk **SS**: E pg 445 **BS**: 204.

KISLING, George; b 1759, Berks Co, PA; d 19 Mar 1840 **RU**: Lieutenant, Served in Berks Co PA 1777-1780 **CEM**: Keesling; GPS unk; Rural Retreat; Wythe **GS**: Y **SP**: Catherine Gose (1766-1808) **VI**: Died in Speedwell, Wythe Co **P**: unk **BLW**: unk **RG**: unk **MK**: unk **PH**: Y **SS**: CI PA Archives Series 3 Vol VI Stat of Accts pg Jacob Morgan **BS**: 196.

KISLING (KISSLING), Jacob; b 18 Jan 1760, Rockingham Co; d 1835 **RU**: Private, Ent serv Rockingham Co. Served in Capt Huston's Co, Maj Hamilton command at Wiliamsburg and at Yorktown 1781 in Capt Cowger's Co under Gen Muhlenburg & Washington **CEM**: Old Peaked Mountain; GPS 38.37113, -78.73416; 9843 Town Hall Rd, McGaheysville; Rockingham **GS**: Y **SP**: Mar (1782) Barbara Lingell (12 Mar 1742-14 Apr 1827) **VI**: Sol appl pen 15 Oct 1832 Rockingham Co S5554 **P**: Y **BLW**: unk **RG**: unk **MK**: Y **PH**: unk **SS**: J- DAR Hatcher, DAR #A065206; O pg 355; CG pg 1967 **BS**: JLARC 2.

KISSLING, Ditrick; b 12 Jan 1760; d 23 May 1785 **RU**: Private, Served 3 mos in Capt Knawl's VA Co. Enl fall 1780 for 3 mos in Capt John Rush's Co, Col Smith's VA Regt **CEM**: Old Peaked Mountain; GPS 38.37113, -78.73416; 9843 Town Hall Rd, McGaheysville; Rockingham **GS**: Y **SP**: No info **VI**: Common monument. Recd pen S16178 **P**: Y **BLW**: unk **RG**: Y **MK**: Y **PH**: unk **SS**: J-NSSAR 2000 Reg, B, C pg 38; P pg 383 **BS**: JLARC 76.

KISSLING, John; b unk; d unk **RU**: Patriot, Gave material aid to cause **CEM**: Old Peaked Mountain; GPS 38.37113, -78.73416; 9843 Town Hall Rd, McGaheysville; Rockingham **GS**: Y **SP**: No info **VI**: No further data **P**: N **BLW**: N **RG**: Y **MK**: Y **PH**: unk **SS**: P pg 353 **BS**: 04.

KISSLING (KISLING, KESLING), Hugh Conrad; b 1762, Berks Co, PA; d 12 May 1818 **RU**: Private, Served in PA Line. Enlisted Co Heisters Battalion. Served in Capt Baldys Co of Berks Co, PA Militia fr Aug-7 Sep 1780 **CEM**: Keesling; GPS unk; Grahams Forge; Wythe **GS**: Y **SP**: No info, has children **VI**: Son of Johann Georg (17 Feb 1734 Truchtelfinger, Baden-Wuerttemberg, Germany-3 Jun 1788 Wythe Co) & (-----) Kissling. Died in Max Meadows, Wythe Co **P**: unk **BLW**: unk **RG**: Y **MK**: Y **PH**: Y **SS**: J-NSSAR 2000 Reg; P pg 353 **BS**: JLARC 76; 47; 196.

KLEIN, George Jr; b 19 Dec 1740, Amwell, NJ; d 19 Aug 1798 **RU**: Private, Served in Armand's Legion, Capt Jacob Bauer's Co, in PA **CEM**: Kline Family; GPS 38.58118, -78.82895; Rt 1415 nr Broadway; Rockingham **GS**: Y **SP**: Elizabeth "Lizzie" Altaffer (1739-1825) **VI**: Son of Johannes George (1715-1783) & Dorothy (Rebman) (1714-1777) Klein **P**: unk **BLW**: unk **RG**: Y **MK**: N **PH**: unk **SS**: AK; A pg 221 **BS**: 04; 191 Kline; 196.

KLINE, Jacob; b 23 Aug 1736; d 27 Aug 1816 **RU**: Private, Served in German Regt Cont Forces 1778, 1779 **CEM**: Trinity Evangelical Lutheran; GPS 39.08280, -78.21679; Mulberry St, Stephens City; Frederick **GS**: Y **SP**: Eva Dusong (6 Oct 1739 Germany-3 May 1815) **VI**: No further data **P**: unk **BLW**: unk **RG**: Y **MK**: N **PH**: unk **SS**: AP Service Roll; CI payroll **BS**: 112 pg 2.

KOINER, George Adam; b 7 Aug 1753, New Holland, Lancaster Co, PA; d 9 Dec 1830 **RU**: Private, Served in 2nd Bn, Col Samuel Lyon's Co **CEM**: Trinity Lutheran; GPS 38.17201, -78.86820; 2564 Rockfish Rd, Crimora; Augusta **GS**: Y **SP**: Barbara Smith **VI**: Son of Michael Keinadt (1720-1796) and Margaret Diller (1734-1813). DAR marker **P**: unk **BLW**: unk **RG**: Y **MK**: Y **PH**: unk **SS**: BT; CD Cumberland Co, PA militia **BS**: JLARC 1,3,8,62; 196.

KOINER, George Michael; b 1758, Lancaster Co, PA; d 10 Jun 1840 **RU**: Private, Served in PA Militia **CEM**: Trinity Lutheran; GPS 38.17201, -78.86820; 2564 Rockfish Rd, Crimora; Augusta **GS**: Y **SP**: Susanna Hawpe (1773-18 Dec 1848) d/o Rudolph (___-1802) & Catherine (Heilman) Hawpe **VI**: Son of Michael (1720-1796) & Margaret (Diller) (1734-1813) Keinadt. DAR marker **P**: unk **BLW**: unk **RG**: unk **MK**: Y **PH**: unk **SS**: AS SAR regis; AK cites DAR; BT **BS**: JLARC 62, 63; 196.

KOINER, Kasper; b 25 Sep 1764 Millersville, Lancaster Co, PA; d 31 Oct 1856 **RU**: Private, Served in Capt John Stone Co, PA Militia 1781 **CEM**: Trinity Lutheran; GPS 38.17201, -78.86820; 2564 Rockfish Rd, Crimora; Augusta **GS**: Y **SP**: Anna Margaret Barger, d/o Jacob & (-----) Barger. "Eloped to Staunton" **VI**: Son of Michael Keinadt (1720-1796) and Margaret Diller (1734-1813). DAR marker **P**: unk

---

RU=Rank/Unit	CEM=Cemetery	GS=Gravestone	SP=Spousal Information
VI=Other Veteran Info	P=Pension	BLW=Bounty/Land Warrant	RG=Registered Grave
MK=SAR/DAR Marker	PH=Photo	SS=Service Source	BS=Burial Source

187

BLW: unk **RG:** Y **MK:** Y **PH:** unk **SS:** AS; AK cites DAR; BT; CI PA Archives 5th Serv Vol 7 pg 137, 138 **BS:** 04 Aug 08; 80 vol 2 pg 240; JLARC 2, 8, 62; 196.

KREMER, KRAMER), Conrad; b 1748, Germany; d 29 May 1837 **RU:** Private, Served in PA Cont Line **CEM:** Mt Hebron; GPS 39.10916, -78.09497; 305 E Boscawen St; Winchester City **GS:** Y **SP:** Mar (before 1819) Catharine Helphenstine, (04 Jun 1761 Frederick Co-3 Jun 1825) d/o Major Peter & (-----) Helphenstine. **VI:** He appl pen 2 Jun 1825 in Winchester, Frederick Co, age 77. S19372 **P:** Y **BLW:** N **RG:** N **MK:** N **PH:** N **SS:** K Vol 3 pg 87; CG pg 1985 **BS:** 196; JLARC 4, 47.

KRIM (GRIM, CRIM), John; b Oct 1755/1756; d 19 Apr 1840 Frederick Co **RU:** Private, Ent serv Lancaster Co PA. Served in PA & NJ Lines. Fought at Trenton, Statton Island, Ft Washington **CEM:** Trinity Evangelical Lutheran; GPS 39.08280, -78.21679; Mulberry St, Stephens City; Frederick **GS:** Y **SP:** 1) Juliana Mainger 2) mar (2 Nov 1821) Phoebe (Coleman) Drake (c1776-__) **VI:** Sol appl pen 7 Nov 1832 Frederick Co. S26182. Widow appl pen 23 Nov 1853 Belmont Co OH; Widow appl BLW 3 Sep 1855, BLW 338508-160-55 **P:** Y **BLW:** Y **RG:** Y **MK:** Y **PH:** Y **SS:** B; CG pg 1986 **BS:** 04.

KRING, John; b 2 Sep 1744, Haiger, Germany; d 16 Dec 1802 **RU:** Sergeant, Served in 3rd, 5th, 7th, & 11th Cont Lines **CEM:** Kring Salvage; GPS unk; Off John Deere Dr, behind Harman Machinery, Broadway; Rockingham **GS:** N **SP:** Catherine Arnold (1746-1820) **VI:** Son of Johannes & Catherine (Arnold) (Kring) Jost of Lancaster, PA. Died at Linville Creek, Rockingham Co **P:** unk **BLW:** unk **RG:** Y **MK:** N **PH:** N **SS:** AK; E pg 447 **BS:** 04; 191 Salvage.

KULLERS (CULLERS), Jacob; b 1725; d 1805 **RU:** Private?, For service, check DAR who installed grave marker **CEM:** Dry Run Church; GPS 38.85929, -78.40075; Rt 678, Fort Valley Rd nr jct with Dry Run Rd, Seven Fountains; Shenandoah **GS:** Y **SP:** Mar (1742 Germany) Mary Magdalena (-----) (1723-__) **VI:** No further data **P:** unk **BLW:** unk **RG:** N **MK:** N **PH:** unk **SS:** BT **BS:** 04; 196.

KULLERS (KULLER, CULLERS), John; b 1747, Germany; d 1796 **RU:** Private?, Served in PA troops 5 Mar 1780 **CEM:** Dry Run Church; GPS 38.85929, -78.40075; Rt 678, Fort Valley Rd nr jct with Dry Run Rd, Seven Fountains; Shenandoah **GS:** Y **SP:** Mar (4 Apr 1775 Frederick Co MD) Anna Marie Muller (1750-1832) **VI:** Son of Jacob (1725-1805) & (-----) Cullers/Kullers **P:** unk **BLW:** unk **RG:** N **MK:** N **PH:** unk **SS:** BT; CI PA archives series 3 Vol XXIII pg 394 **BS:** 04; 196.

KURTZ, Adam; b 1747, Germany; d 1815 **RU:** Private, Served in Gen Daniel Morgan's Riflemen fr Frederick Co. Was in Battle of Quebec, captured and was POW for 6 mos. Was member of Morgan's Dutch Mess **CEM:** Mt Hebron; GPS 39.10916, -78.09497; 305 E Boscawen St; Winchester City **GS:** Y **SP:** Mar (30 Dec 1813, Frederick Co) Elizabeth Bennett (Return) **VI:** Owned a boot and shoemakers shop in Winchester. Bur in the Centenary Reformed UCC portion of the Mt Hebron Cemetery. Marriage to Elizabeth may be for another member of his family **P:** unk **BLW:** unk **RG:** Y **MK:** N **PH:** Y **SS:** E pg 452 **BS:** J-NSSAR 1993 Reg.

KYGER, Christian; b 27 Nov 1748, Lancaster Co, PA; d Bef Jan 1830 **RU:** Lieutenant, Took oath 27 Aug 1781 **CEM:** Old Peaked Mountain; GPS 38.37113, -78.73416; 9843 Town Hall Rd, McGaheysville; Rockingham **GS:** U **SP:** Mar (c1762) Margaret Armentrout . 2) Caty Dundore **VI:** Son of Wilhelm & Eva Barbara (Stober) Geiger **P:** unk **BLW:** unk **RG:** Y **MK:** unk **PH:** unk **SS:** J-NSSAR 2000 Reg; NSSAR Ancestor #P-262438 **BS:** JLARC 76.

KYLE, David Sr; b 1757; d 25 Oct 1844 **RU:** Patriot, Gave material aid to cause **CEM:** Massanutten Cross Keys; GPS 38.35817, -78.84124; Rt 679 at Cross Keys, vic jct Rts 276 & 679; Rockingham **GS:** Y **SP:** Mar (period 1 Dec 1775-78 Buckingham Co) Elizabeth Chambers (__-1846) **VI:** No further data **P:** N **BLW:** N **RG:** N **MK:** N **PH:** Y **SS:** AL Ct Bk pg 33 **BS:** 191 Massan; 196.

KYLE, William; b 1736, Tyrone Co, Ireland; d 25 Jun 1832 **RU:** Private, Served in Botetourt Co Militia **CEM:** Fincastle Presbyterian; GPS 37.50017, -79.87558; 108 E Back St, Fincastle; Botetourt **GS:** Y **SP:** Mar (1750, Ireland) Sara Ann Stevens **VI:** Son of Robert Kyle & Betty Ann Campbell. Came to VA with his parents in 1759 first settling in Richmond Co. Pensioner. Name is on the SAR plaque at this cemetery **P:** Y **BLW:** unk **RG:** N **MK:** Y **PH:** unk **SS:** E pg 452 **BS:** 196.

RU=Rank/Unit CEM=Cemetery GS=Gravestone SP=Spousal Information
VI=Other Veteran Info P=Pension BLW=Bounty/Land Warrant RG=Registered Grave
MK=SAR/DAR Marker PH=Photo SS=Service Source BS=Burial Source

188

KYNION, William; b unk; d 1781 **RU:** Soldier, Served fr NY, killed in the battle at Yorktown **CEM:** Yorktown Victory Monument Tablet; GPS 38.28350, -78.54150; Yorktown; York **GS:** U **SP:** No info **VI:** No further data **P:** unk **BLW:** unk **RG:** unk **MK:** unk **PH:** unk **SS:** J-Yorktown Historian **BS:** JLARC 74.

LABBE, Jean; b unk; d 1781 **RU:** Seaman, Served on "Caton" and died from Yorktown battle **CEM:** French Memorial; GPS 36.81944, -79.39933; Yorktown; York **GS:** U **SP:** No info **VI:** No further data **P:** unk **BLW:** unk **RG:** Y **MK:** unk **PH:** unk **SS:** J-Yorktown Historian **BS:** JLARC 1, 74.

LACOSTE, Jean; b unk; d 1781 **RU:** Soldier, Served in Gatinais Bn and died fr battle at Yorktown **CEM:** French Memorial; GPS 36.81944, -79.39933; Yorktown; York **GS:** U **SP:** no info **VI:** No further data **P:** unk **BLW:** unk **RG:** Y **MK:** unk **PH:** unk **SS:** J-Yorktown Historian **BS:** JLARC 1, 74.

LACROIX, Guillaume; b unk; d 1781 **RU:** Soldier, Served in Gatinais Bn and died fr battle at Yorktown **CEM:** French Memorial; GPS 36.81944, -79.39933; Yorktown; York **GS:** U **SP:** No info **VI:** No further data **P:** unk **BLW:** unk **RG:** Y **MK:** unk **PH:** unk **SS:** J-Yorktown Historian **BS:** JLARC 1, 74.

LACROIX, Jean; b unk; d 1781 **RU:** Soldier, Served in Soissonnais Bn and died fr battle at Yorktown **CEM:** French Memorial; GPS 36.81944, -79.39933; Yorktown; York **GS:** U **SP:** No info **VI:** No further data **P:** unk **BLW:** unk **RG:** Y **MK:** unk **PH:** unk **SS:** J-Yorktown Historian **BS:** JLARC 1, 74.

LACROIX, Pierre; b c1743; d 22 Sep 1830 **RU:** Private?, Check Geo Washington Chapter files for service **CEM:** St Mary's Catholic; GPS 38.79390, -77.04750; 310 S Royal St; Alexandria City **GS:** Y **SP:** No info **VI:** Served as drummer boy in the French & Indian War (for the French) and his death notice says he later served in the Revolution. Died at the home of Mr. Edward Smyth (Alexandria Gazette, 27 Sep 1831, pg 3) **P:** unk **BLW:** unk **RG:** N **MK:** Y **PH:** Y **SS:** SAR Ancestor #P-334431; BP Obit **BS:** 174 pg 304;196.

LACY, Mathew; b unk; d 7 Mar 23 **RU:** Ensign Second Lieutenant/ Patriot, Ent serv Goochland Co 1779. Served in Capt Humphrey Parrish's Co, Taylors Regt, VA Troops **CEM:** Lacy Family; GPS 37.80571, -77.99405; Rt 615; Goochland **GS:** Y **SP:** Mar (8 Apr 1772) Susanna Rutherford (6 Apr 1750 Goochland Co-26 Jun 1839 Goochland Co) **VI:** Brother Charles Lacy also served fr Hanover Co. Widow appl pen 7 Mar 1838 age 88 Goochland Co. W8077 **P:** Y **BLW:** unk **RG:** N **MK:** N **PH:** Y **SS:** D pg 143; E pg 453; K Vol 3 pg 88; CG pg 1990 **BS:** 46 pg 176; 196.

LADD, William; b 30 Dec 1736, Little Compton, RI; d 3 Dec 1800 **RU:** Captain, Served in Rhode Island **CEM:** Old Presbyterian Meeting House; GPS 38.48528, -77.23532; 323 S Fairfax St; Alexandria City **GS:** Y **SP:** Sarah Gardner (1725-30 Oct 1807) d/o Benoni & (-----) Gardner, Esq. of Newport, RI, "consort of William Ladd" **VI:** State legislator fr Rhode Island that ratified the US Constitution. Died visiting his children. Death notice in the Alexandria Gazette, 6 Dec 1800. Listed on SAR plaque in cemetery **P:** unk **BLW:** unk **RG:** Y **MK:** Y **PH:** unk **SS:** B; AK **BS:** JLARC 1, 86; 23 pg 104; 196.

LAFAYETTE, James; b unk; d 9 Aug 1830 **RU:** Soldier, Served as a double agent and spy **CEM:** Afro-American aka East End; GPS 37.53640, -77.38640; Bulheller Rd; Henrico **GS:** U **SP:** No info **VI:** Black Soldier. Petitioned for pension in New Kent Co **P:** Y **BLW:** unk **RG:** Y **MK:** unk **PH:** unk **SS:** J-NSSAR 1993 Reg **BS:** JLARC 1.

LAFOSSE, Antoine; b unk; d 1781 **RU:** Soldier, Served in Bourbonnais Bn and died fr battle at Yorktown **CEM:** French Memorial; GPS 36.81944, -79.39933; Yorktown; York **GS:** U **SP:** No info **VI:** No further data **P:** unk **BLW:** unk **RG:** Y **MK:** unk **PH:** unk **SS:** J-Yorktown Historian **BS:** JLARC 1, 74.

LAFOSSE, Charles; b unk; d 1781 **RU:** Seaman, Served on "Duc De Bourgogne" and died from Yorktown battle **CEM:** French Memorial; GPS 36.81944, -79.39933; Yorktown; York **GS:** U **SP:** No info **VI:** No further data **P:** unk **BLW:** unk **RG:** Y **MK:** unk **PH:** unk **SS:** J-Yorktown Historian **BS:** JLARC 1, 74.

LAFRANCE, Nicolas; b unk; d 1781 **RU:** Seaman, Served on "Diademe" and died from Yorktown battle **CEM:** French Memorial; GPS 36.81944, -79.39933; Yorktown; York **GS:** U **SP:** No info **VI:** No further data **P:** unk **BLW:** unk **RG:** Y **MK:** unk **PH:** unk **SS:** J-Yorktown Historian **BS:** JLARC 1, 74.

RU=Rank/Unit CEM=Cemetery GS=Gravestone SP=Spousal Information
VI=Other Veteran Info P=Pension BLW=Bounty/Land Warrant RG=Registered Grave
MK=SAR/DAR Marker PH=Photo SS=Service Source BS=Burial Source

189

LAGADENE, Jean; b unk; d 1781 **RU:** Seaman, Served on "Languedoc" and died from Yorktown battle **CEM:** French Memorial; GPS 36.81944, -79.39933; Yorktown; York **GS:** U **SP:** No info **VI:** No further data **P:** unk **BLW:** unk **RG:** Y **MK:** unk **PH:** unk **SS:** J-Yorktown Historian **BS:** JLARC 1, 74.

LAGNEL, Louis; b unk; d 1781 **RU:** Seaman, Served on "Diademe" and died from Yorktown battle **CEM:** French Memorial; GPS 36.81944, -79.39933; Yorktown; York **GS:** U **SP:** No info **VI:** No further data **P:** unk **BLW:** unk **RG:** Y **MK:** unk **PH:** unk **SS:** J-Yorktown Historian **BS:** JLARC 1, 74.

LAINE, Philippe; b unk; d 1781 **RU:** Solider, Served in Gatinais Bn and died fr battle at Yorktown **CEM:** French Memorial; GPS 36.81944, -79.39933; Yorktown; York **GS:** U **SP:** No info **VI:** No further data **P:** unk **BLW:** unk **RG:** Y **MK:** unk **PH:** unk **SS:** J-Yorktown Historian **BS:** JLARC 1, 74.

LAINE, William; b 1760; d 1807 **RU:** Private, Served in 1st & 10th Cont Lines **CEM:** Laine Family; GPS unk; Amherst; Amherst **GS:** U **SP:** 1) (-----) 2) Mar (5 May 1794 Amherst Co) Rebeccah Berry, spinster **VI:** No further data **P:** unk **BLW:** unk **RG:** N **MK:** N **PH:** unk **SS:** E pg 454 **BS:** SAR report.

LAIRD, James; b 1740; d 18 Nov 1827 **RU:** Private, Served in Capt Peachy Gilmore's Co, Augusta Co Militia **CEM:** Falling Springs Presbyterian; GPS 37.68494, -79.45105; 410 Falling Springs Rd, Glasgow; Rockbridge **GS:** Y **SP:** No info **VI:** No further data **P:** unk **BLW:** unk **RG:** unk **MK:** unk **PH:** unk **SS:** E pg 454 **BS:** 204.

LALOGE, Pierre de; b unk; d 1781 **RU:** Soldier, Served in Auxonne Bn and died fr battle at Yorktown **CEM:** French Memorial; GPS 36.81944, -79.39933; Yorktown; York **GS:** U **SP:** No info **VI:** No further data **P:** unk **BLW:** unk **RG:** Y **MK:** unk **PH:** unk **SS:** J-Yorktown Historian **BS:** JLARC 1, 74.

LAMBERT, Blaise; b unk; d 1781 **RU:** Soldier, Served in Touraine Bn and died fr battle at Yorktown **CEM:** French Memorial; GPS 36.81944, -79.39933; Yorktown; York **GS:** U **SP:** No info **VI:** No further data **P:** unk **BLW:** unk **RG:** Y **MK:** unk **PH:** unk **SS:** J-Yorktown Historian **BS:** JLARC 1, 74.

LAMESSE, Etienne; b unk; d 1781 **RU:** Seaman, Served on "Marseillais" and died from Yorktown battle **CEM:** French Memorial; GPS 36.81944, -79.39933; Yorktown; York **GS:** U **SP:** No info **VI:** No further data **P:** unk **BLW:** unk **RG:** Y **MK:** unk **PH:** unk **SS:** J-Yorktown Historian **BS:** JLARC 1, 74.

LAMM (LAMIE), John; b 1763; d 6 Mar 1830 **RU:** Private, Served in10th Cont Line **CEM:** Lamie Family; GPS unk; 2 mi E of Saltville; Smyth **GS:** N **SP:** Eleanor (-----) (__-1846) **VI:** Cemetery may have been destroyed by cattle. **P:** unk **BLW:** unk **RG:** Y **MK:** N **PH:** unk **SS:** E pg 455 **BS:** 97 vol 1 pg 44.

LAMME, James; b 1732; d 3 Apr 1819 **RU:** Sergeant, Served in 8th Cont Line **CEM:** Lamie Family; GPS unk; 2 mi E of Saltville; Smyth **GS:** Y **SP:** No info **VI:** No further data **P:** unk **BLW:** unk **RG:** Y **MK:** N **PH:** unk **SS:** E pg 455 **BS:** 97 vol 1 pg 44.

LAMY, Pierre; b unk; d 1781 **RU:** Seaman, Served on "Languedoc" and died from Yorktown battle **CEM:** French Memorial; GPS 36.81944, -79.39933; Yorktown; York **GS:** U **SP:** No info **VI:** No further data **P:** unk **BLW:** unk **RG:** Y **MK:** unk **PH:** unk **SS:** J-Yorktown Historian **BS:** JLARC 1,74.

LANCASTER, John; b 3 Mar 1763, Goochland Co; d 28 Jan 1826 **RU:** Private, For service check special report by Department of Archives and History, Lib of VA **CEM:** Clover Forest; GPS unk; 3 mi W of Farmville nr Sandy Fork Bridge; Prince Edward **GS:** U **SP:** Drusilla Legrand (13 Apr 1769-14 Dec 1825) d/o Alexander (1728-1825) & Lucy (Walker) (1735-1825) Legrand **VI:** No further data **P:** unk **BLW:** unk **RG:** unk **MK:** unk **PH:** unk **SS:** E pg 455; CZ **BS:** 196.

LANDES, John; b 1752, Windsor, York Co, PA; d Oct 1819 **RU:** Private, Served in Kaufflet's Co, PA Troops **CEM:** Landes Family; GPS 38.30110, -78.97170; W fr Burketown 2 mi, near Weyers Cave; Augusta **GS:** Y **SP:** Catherine Miller (1749-May 1834) **VI:** Son of Christian Landes (1728-1782). Govt stone **P:** unk **BLW:** unk **RG:** unk **MK:** unk **PH:** unk **SS:** B; CI PA Archives 5th serv Vol 2 pg 443 **BS:** JLARC 2, 8, 62; 196.

LANE, Anna Maria; b unk, prob NH; d 1810 **RU:** Soldier, Served when husband was wounded in 1776-1777 at Battle of Germantown by using his clothes. Was also wounded. Later served in Light Horse Harry Lee's Regt, in 2d siege of Augusta, GA, 22 May to 5 Jan 1781 **CEM:** Cem name unk; GPS 37.32337, -77.26132; Nr State Capitol; Richmond City **GS:** U **SP:** John Lane (1723-14 Jul 1823) **VI:** Only documented woman veteran of the Rev War to reside in Virginia. After war served in public guard

RU=Rank/Unit CEM=Cemetery GS=Gravestone SP=Spousal Information
VI=Other Veteran Info P=Pension BLW=Bounty/Land Warrant RG=Registered Grave
MK=SAR/DAR Marker PH=Photo SS=Service Source BS=Burial Source

190

in city and at military hospital. Rec'd $100 a yr effective 1808. Memorialized on Va Historical Road sign **P:** Y **BLW:** N **RG:** unk **MK:** Y **PH:** N **SS:** BX pg 460 **BS:** 196.

LANE, Corbin; b 1750, Baltimore MD; d 2 Sept 1816 or 8 Dec 1817 **RU:** Patriot, Served in NC Cont Line **CEM:** Pendleton; GPS 36.67145, -82.66248; Rt 664, Manville; Scott **GS:** Y **SP:** Frances "Fanny" Preck (possibly Brock, Prock, or Proctor) **VI:** Son of Samuel (1700-1799) & Mary Jane (Corbin) Lane (1708-1773) **P:** N **BLW:** N **RG:** Y **MK:** N **PH:** Y **SS:** O; H **BS:** 04.

LANE, John; b 1723; d 14 July 1823 **RU:** Private, Ent serv NH 1778. Was taken POW & released. Served in Capt Ambrose Madison's Co, Francis Taylor's VA Regt, & 3rd & 5th Cont Line **CEM:** Shockoe Hill; GPS 37.55190, -77.43170; 4th & Hospital Sts; Richmond City **GS:** Y **SP:** Ann Maria (-----) (1733-__). Wife also fought as man at Germantown and was seriously wounded and drew a pension in 1807, she being the only woman pensioned in VA for RW service. **VI:** Sol appl pen in Chesterfield Co 4 Dec 1819. S38129, R1520 **P:** Y **BLW:** unk **RG:** N **MK:** N **PH:** unk **SS:** E pg 456; G pg 1, 2; K Vol 3 pg 95; CG pg 2007 **BS:** 196.

LANE, Joseph; b 1750; d 12 Mar 1803 **RU:** Lieutenant Colonel/Patriot, Served in Westmoreland Co Militia. Was Commissioner of Provisional Law in 1780 **CEM:** Lane Family; GPS unk; Leithtown; Loudoun **GS:** Y **SP:** Mar (c1763) Katherine Newton (c1745-__) **VI:** No further data **P:** unk **BLW:** unk **RG:** Y **MK:** N **PH:** unk **SS:** E pg 456; J-Yorktown Historian **BS:** 25 pg 174.

LANE, William; b 30 Aug 1740; d 16 Mar 1808 **RU:** Captain, Served in Loudoun Co Militia. Promoted 9 Sep 1777 **CEM:** Lane Family; GPS 38.90658, -77.38822; 12700 Franklin Farm Rd, Centreville; Fairfax **GS:** U **SP:** 1) Katherine Eskridge 2) Sarah (Sally) Rowles Higgs (1760-1826) **VI:** Son of James L & Lydia (Hardage) Lane. Pen records indicate birthdate of 10 Mar 1754. Appl for pen 2 Mar 1824 Charlotte Co, VA **P:** Y **BLW:** unk **RG:** unk **MK:** unk **PH:** unk **SS:** E pg 456; CG pg 2010 **BS:** 196.

LANGBORNE, William; b 1750; d 1814 **RU:** Major/Patriot, Was Ens 6th Cont Line 27 Apr 1777. Later was promoted to Maj. Recd Brevet Commission fr US Congress of Lt Col 6 Oct 1783. Also gave 2250# beef to cause **CEM:** Langborne Family; GPS unk; At Langborne on bank of Pamunkey River; King William **GS:** U **SP:** Elizabeth (-----) **VI:** Awarded 6224 acres BLW in 1824 as a major. Tomb reported in 1897 source: "A hero and patriot of the Revolution" **P:** unk **BLW:** Y **RG:** unk **MK:** unk **PH:** unk **SS:** D pg 17 King William Co; G pg 402 **BS:** JLARC 106.

LANGLOIS, Jacques; b 1750; d 1781 **RU:** Soldier, Served in Soissonnais Bn and died fr battle at Yorktown **CEM:** French Memorial; GPS 36.81944, -79.39933; Yorktown; York **GS:** U **SP:** No info **VI:** No further data **P:** unk **BLW:** unk **RG:** Y **MK:** unk **PH:** unk **SS:** J-Yorktown Historian **BS:** JLARC 1, 74.

LANIER, Benjamin Bird; b 1711, Surry Co; d 12 Dec 1796 **RU:** Patriot, Signed Oath of Allegiance 10 Oct 1778. Gave money & supplies to aid the Revolution **CEM:** Lanier Family; GPS unk; Nr Smoky Ordinary & Poarch Store; Brunswick **GS:** N **SP:** 1) Mar (c1737 Surry Co) Elizabeth Warren (?) (1719-1775) 2) Mar (26 Nov 1776) Lucy (-----) Pennington (__-Dec 1781 or Jan 1782), a widow 3) Mar (28 Apr 1783 Brunswick Co) Ann (-----) Wilkinson, a widow **VI:** Son of John Lanier (1680-1727) DAR marker on Gr **P:** N **BLW:** N **RG:** unk **MK:** Y **PH:** N **SS:** AI Ct Bk 1 pg 121 **BS:** 196.

LANNOY, Jean de; b 1750; d 1781 **RU:** Soldier, Served in Gatinais Bn and died fr battle at Yorktown **CEM:** French Memorial; GPS 36.81944, -79.39933; Yorktown; York **GS:** U **SP:** No info **VI:** No further data **P:** unk **BLW:** unk **RG:** Y **MK:** unk **PH:** unk **SS:** J-Yorktown Historian **BS:** JLARC 1, 74.

LAROCHE, Etienne; b 1750; d 1781 **RU:** Soldier, Served in Soissonnais Bn and died fr battle at Yorktown **CEM:** French Memorial; GPS 36.81944, -79.39933; Yorktown; York **GS:** U **SP:** No info **VI:** No further data **P:** unk **BLW:** unk **RG:** Y **MK:** unk **PH:** unk **SS:** J-Yorktown Historian **BS:** JLARC 1, 74.

LAROSE, Jean; b 1750; d 1781 **RU:** Seaman, Served on "Saint-Esprit" and died from Yorktown battle **CEM:** French Memorial; GPS 36.81944, -79.39933; Yorktown; York **GS:** U **SP:** No info **VI:** No further data **P:** unk **BLW:** unk **RG:** Y **MK:** unk **PH:** unk **SS:** J-Yorktown Historian **BS:** JLARC 1, 74.

LARRICK, Casper; b c1730, France; d 1801 **RU:** Soldier/Patriot, Served in Ohio 1775-76. Gave material aid to cause **CEM:** Mt Olive; GPS 39.22610, -78.72000; 327 Mt Olive Rd, Hayfield; Frederick **GS:** Y **SP:** 1) (-----) 2) Mar (1772, Frederick Co) Elizabeth Sundown (c1750-23 Aug 1847) **VI:** Came to

RU=Rank/Unit   CEM=Cemetery   GS=Gravestone   SP=Spousal Information
VI=Other Veteran Info   P=Pension   BLW=Bounty/Land Warrant   RG=Registered Grave
MK=SAR/DAR Marker   PH=Photo   SS=Service Source   BS=Burial Source

191

America abt 1755 with surname of La Roque, next revision was Laruck. DAR marker. **P:** unk **BLW:** unk **RG:** N **MK:** Y **PH:** unk **SS:** DAR #A066852; AL cert issued **BS:** 59 pg 185; 196.

LARUE, Isaac; b 11 Jan 1713, Hunterdon Co, NJ; d 20 Mar 1795 **RU:** Patriot, Gave 2419# beef, 1756# flour, over 150# bacon, pasturage for livestock **CEM:** Old Buck Marsh Meeting House; GPS 39.94730, -77.58370; nr Barryville Meeting House; Clarke **GS:** Y **SP:** Mar (1743) Phebe Carmen (4 Mar 1725, Cranbury, Middlesex Co, NJ-25 Jan 1804, Berryville, Clark Co) d/o James (1677-1756) & (-----) Carman **VI:** GS lost. Actually bur in field outside Berryville **P:** N **BLW:** N **RG:** N **MK:** N **PH:** unk **SS:** DAR #A066874; AL Ct Bk pg 22, 23, 36 Frederick Co; AS DAR Report; AR Vol 3 pg 1 **BS:** Serv Source AR vol 3 pg 1; DAR report; 196.

LATAUPE, Gilbert; b unk; d 1781 **RU:** Soldier, Served in Soissonnais Bn and died fr battle at Yorktown **CEM:** French Memorial; GPS 36.81944, -79.39933; Yorktown; York **GS:** U **SP:** No info **VI:** No further data **P:** unk **BLW:** unk **RG:** Y **MK:** unk **PH:** unk **SS:** J-Yorktown Historian **BS:** JLARC 1, 74.

LAUCK, Simon; b 1760; d 1815 **RU:** Private, Participated in march to Boston under Morgan's riflemen **CEM:** Mt Hebron; GPS 39.10916, -78.09497; 305 E Boscawen St; Winchester City **GS:** Y **SP:** 1) Catherine Starr 2) Mar (26 Oct 1803 Frederick Co) Mary Sensency (Return) **VI:** He owned a gunsmith shop in Winchester and manufactured a rifle with his name. Bur in the Centenary Reformed UCC portion of the Mt Hebron Cemetery. DAR marker. **P:** N **BLW:** N **RG:** Y **MK:** Y **PH:** N **SS:** CG pg 2024; J-NSSAR 1993 Reg **BS:** 196; JLARC 1.

LAUCK (LAUK), Peter; b 31 Dec 1753; d 2 Oct 1839 **RU:** Private, Served in Gen Daniel Morgan's Riflemen in Frederick Co. Ent serv 1775 in Winchester. Marched to Boston and was in the Battle at Quebec. Lost his hearing in the battle **CEM:** Mt Hebron; GPS 39.10916, -78.09497; 305 E Boscawen St; Winchester City **GS:** Y **SP:** Mar (27 Oct 1779) Emily (QLF says Amelia) Heiskell. (c1766-1840) **VI:** Built and ran the Red Lion Tavern in Winchester. Bur in the Centenary Reformed UCC portion of the Mt Hebron Cemetery. DAR marker. Sol appl pen 9 Aug 1832 Frederick Co. Widow appl pen 2 Apr 1840 Winchester VA. F-R6183, R1530 1832 Frederick Co. Her application rejected. **P:** Y **BLW:** unk **RG:** Y **MK:** Y **PH:** N **SS:** J-NSSAR 1993 Reg; K Vol 3 pg 102; CG pg 2024 **BS:** 196; JLARC 1.

LAUGHLIN, Alexander; b c1746; d 25 Nov 1806 **RU:** Patriot, Gave to cause in Montgomery Co **CEM:** Walnut Grove; GPS unk; Lee Hwy, Bristol; Washington **GS:** Y **SP:** Mar (9 Nov 1769 Hanover, York Co, PA) Ann Sharp (9 Nov 1751 Lancaster PA-18 Feb 1834) **VI:** No further data **P:** N **BLW:** N **RG:** N **MK:** N **PH:** unk **SS:** G pg 217-218 **BS:** 78 pg 375; 196.

LAURENCEAU, Jean; b unk; d 1781 **RU:** Soldier, Served in Gatinais Bn and died fr battle at Yorktown **CEM:** French Memorial; GPS 36.81944, -79.39933; Yorktown; York **GS:** U **SP:** No info **VI:** No further data **P:** unk **BLW:** unk **RG:** Y **MK:** unk **PH:** unk **SS:** J-Yorktown Historian **BS:** JLARC 1, 74.

LAURENS, Jean; b unk; d 1781 **RU:** Soldier, Served on "Caton" and died from Yorktown battle **CEM:** French Memorial; GPS 36.81944, -79.39933; Yorktown; York **GS:** U **SP:** No info **VI:** No further data **P:** unk **BLW:** unk **RG:** Y **MK:** unk **PH:** unk **SS:** J-Yorktown Historian **BS:** JLARC 1, 74.

LAURENT, Daniel; b unk; d 1781 **RU:** Soldier, Served in Touraine Bn and died fr battle at Yorktown **CEM:** French Memorial; GPS 36.81944, -79.39933; Yorktown; York **GS:** U **SP:** No info **VI:** No further data **P:** unk **BLW:** unk **RG:** Y **MK:** unk **PH:** unk **SS:** J-Yorktown Historian **BS:** JLARC 1, 74.

LAURENT, Jacques; b unk; d 1781 **RU:** Soldier, Served in Gatinais Bn and died fr battle at Yorktown **CEM:** French Memorial; GPS 36.81944, -79.39933; Yorktown; York **GS:** U **SP:** No info **VI:** No further data **P:** unk **BLW:** unk **RG:** Y **MK:** unk **PH:** unk **SS:** J-Yorktown Historian **BS:** JLARC 1, 74.

LAVERTY, Ralph; b 1715, Ireland; d Aft Jun 1792 **RU:** Patriot, Gave material aid to cause **CEM:** Laverty Farm; GPS unk; Cow pasture; Bath **GS:** U **SP:** 1) Elizabeth Stuart; 2) Jane Hicklin **VI:** No further data **P:** N **BLW:** N **RG:** Y **MK:** unk **PH:** unk **SS:** J-NSSAR 2000 Reg; CM Vol 1 pg 248 **BS:** JLARC 76.

LAWRASON, James; b 2 Dec 1753, Sussex Co, NJ; d 18 Apr 1824 **RU:** Lieutenant/Patriot, Steward, Cont Army Hospital, Alexandria, 1777. Receiver for specific tax, Fairfax Co. Legislative petitions & civil positions in Alexandria. Was president of Bank of Alexandria **CEM:** Christ Church Episcopal; GPS 38.80216, -77.05689; Wilkes St & Hamilton Ln; Alexandria City **GS:** Y **SP:** Mar (23 Jun 1779 Loudoun

RU=Rank/Unit   CEM=Cemetery   GS=Gravestone   SP=Spousal Information
VI=Other Veteran Info   P=Pension   BLW=Bounty/Land Warrant   RG=Registered Grave
MK=SAR/DAR Marker   PH=Photo   SS=Service Source   BS=Burial Source

192

Co) Alice Levering **VI:** GS records yr of death as 1823, but obit (20 Apr 1824) is taken to be more reliable. **P:** unk **BLW:** unk **RG:** Y **MK:** Y **PH:** Y **SS:** J-NSSAR 1993 Reg **BS:** JLARC 1; 20 pg 102; 196.

LAWRENCE, John; b c1734, Great Britain; d 25 Dec 1814 **RU:** Patriot, Served on Committee of Observation for the Borough of Norfolk in 1775. On 22 Aug 1774, was member of committee that recommended tea be sent back (refuse delivery fr Brigantine "Mary and Jane"). Gave material aid to the cause **CEM:** St Paul's Episcopal; GPS 36.84733, -76.28554; 201 St Paul's Blvd; Norfolk City **GS:** Y **SP:** No info **VI:** Served on the Committee of Observation for the Borough of Norfolk in 1775. Died Christmas day, 1814 at age of 80. **P:** N **BLW:** N **RG:** Y **MK:** Y **PH:** unk **SS:** CB AL Ct Bk I pg 7, 17 **BS:** 87 pg 28.

LAWRENCE, John; b unk; d 4 Feb 1821 **RU:** Patriot, Gave material aid to cause **CEM:** St John's Episcopal; GPS 37.53183, -77.41958; 2401 E Broad St; Richmond City **GS:** Y **SP:** No info **VI:** Was delegate fr Isle of Wight Co to General Assembly after war in 1821. **P:** N **BLW:** N **RG:** N **MK:** N **PH:** unk **SS:** D Vol 2 pg 470; AL Ct Bk 1 pg 28 Hanover Co **BS:** 28 pg 469; 196.

LAWS, John; b 1764; d 1 Dec 1839 **RU:** Private, Served for 3 yrs **CEM:** Laws Family; GPS unk; Rt 13 nr Nelsonia; Accomack **GS:** Y **SP:** no info **VI:** Son of Robert W & Mary (Williams) Laws. Received 100 acres bounty land, 22 Nov 1784. **P:** unk **BLW:** Y **RG:** N **MK:** N **PH:** unk **SS:** F pg 46 **BS:** 178 Laws.

LAWSON, Robert; b 23 Jan 1748, Yorkshire, England; d Apr 1805 **RU:** General, Served in 4th Regt Dec 1775-13 Feb 1776. As Col, was commander of 4th VA Regt of Foot 1 Apr 1777-17 Dec 1777. Later was Brigadier Gen of VA Militia **CEM:** St John's Episcopal; GPS 37.53183, -77.41958; 2401 E Broad St; Richmond City **GS:** Y **SP:** Mar (30 Nov 1769) Sarah Meriwether Pierce (1747, England-1809) **VI:** No further data **P:** unk **BLW:** unk **RG:** Y **MK:** N **PH:** unk **SS:** DAR #A067381; E pg 462; N pg 1240; CE pg 41 **BS:** SAR regis.

LAWSON, William; b 1731; d Bef 1826 **RU:** Patriot, Gave material aid to the cause **CEM:** Eastern State Hospital; GPS 37.25560 -76.71030; S Henry Street; Williamsburg City **GS:** N **SP:** No info **VI:** No further data **P:** N **BLW:** N **RG:** N **MK:** N **PH:** N **SS:** E pg 462; AL Ct Bk pg 23 **BS:** 65 Williamsburg.

LAWSON, William II; b Bef 1763, NC; d 30 Jan 1852 **RU:** Private, Ent serv Franklin Co, NC. Served in Capt Levary's Co. NC Militia **CEM:** Lawson Confederate Memorial; GPS 36.68728, -82.50114; Rt 71, Snowflake; Scott **GS:** Y **SP:** Nancy Baker **VI:** S10969, 12 Dec 1832 Scott Co **P:** Y **BLW:** unk **RG:** Y **MK:** Y **PH:** Y **SS:** O; CG pg 2031 **BS:** 04.

LAWSON, William Sr; b 26 Jun 1731, Montrose, Scotland; d 18 Apr 1826 **RU:** Sergeant, Served in Montgomery Co Militia 13 Sept 1777 and was in Battle of Kings Mountain, SC 7 Oct 1780 **CEM:** Lawson Confederate Memorial; GPS 36.68728, -82.50114; Rt 71, Snowflake; Scott **GS:** Y **SP:** Rebecca (-----) (__-16 Jan 1827) **VI:** Son (also William) served too, and is believed bur in Wabash, Illinois **P:** unk **BLW:** unk **RG:** unk **MK:** Y **PH:** unk **SS:** DAR #A067400; NSSAR Ancestor #P-234046 **BS:** JLARC 22, 81.

LAYMAN, Benjamin; b 1723, PA; d 1787 **RU:** Patriot, Gave material aid to cause **CEM:** Clover Hill; GPS unk; Saumsville; Shenandoah **GS:** Y **SP:** Barbara Baughman (__PA-__) d/o John & (-----) Baughman of Lancaster Co, PA **VI:** No further data **P:** N **BLW:** N **RG:** unk **MK:** unk **PH:** unk **SS:** AL Ct Bk pg 8 Shenandoah Co **BS:** 196.

LAYMAN, George; b 1760, Frderick Co MD; d 1854 **RU:** Private, Served in VA Line. Final pay received 11 April 1787 **CEM:** Laymantown; GPS 37.36278, -79.84909; Laymantown Rd, Laymantown; Botetourt **GS:** Y **SP:** Barbara Baumgartner **VI:** New monument placed by Willliam Preston Chapter DAR **P:** unk **BLW:** unk **RG:** Y **MK:** Y **PH:** unk **SS:** B **BS:** JLARC 1, 2, 124; 196.

LAYMAN, John; b 13 Mar 1763, Frederick Co, MD; d 25 Apr 1836 **RU:** Private?, Service used to support SAR grave marker not identified **CEM:** Bethel Cemetery; GPS 38.47592, -78.75641; 3061 Armentrout Path, Keezletown; Rockingham **GS:** U **SP:** Mar (23 Jan 1787 Frederick Co, MD) Maria Elizabeth Enhald (3 Feb 1762-21 Jul 1834) **VI:** SAR Gr Marker **P:** unk **BLW:** unk **RG:** unk **MK:** Y **PH:** unk **SS:** CS **BS:** 196.

LEACH, John; b 1739, Ireland; d 1820 **RU:** Private, Cont Line **CEM:** Oxford Presbyterian; GPS 37.75302, -79.56023; 18 Churchview Ln, Lexington; Lexington City **GS:** U **SP:** Martha McComb **VI:** Recd Cont Line warrant. Reported as unmarked grave **P:** unk **BLW:** Y **RG:** unk **MK:** unk **PH:** unk **SS:** C pg 465 **BS:** JLARC 126.

RU=Rank/Unit	CEM=Cemetery	GS=Gravestone	SP=Spousal Information
VI=Other Veteran Info	P=Pension	BLW=Bounty/Land Warrant	RG=Registered Grave
MK=SAR/DAR Marker	PH=Photo	SS=Service Source	BS=Burial Source

LEAKE, Josiah; b 1730; d Prob 1795 **RU:** Captain, Commanded a co Goochland Co Militia. Resigned 16 May 1780 **CEM:** Rocky Spring Leake; GPS unk; Jct Rts 6 & 600; Goochland **GS:** Y **SP:** Mar (1 Jan 1759 Henrico Co) Ann Fenton by Rev William Douglas. **VI:** Probably the Josiah Leake who died 1795. Will recorded in Goochland Co in WB 16 pg 475 **P:** unk **BLW:** unk **RG:** N **MK:** N **PH:** unk **SS:** E pg 463 **BS:** 46 pg 224.

LEAKE (LEAK), Elisha; b 1739, Goochland Co; d 19 Oct 1806 **RU:** Captain, Commanded a co Goochland Co Militia, 1779-80 **CEM:** Woodlawn; GPS unk; Jct Rts 250 & 612; Goochland **GS:** Y **SP:** 1) (-----) 2) Mar (23 Mar 1791) Frances Curd (__-aft 1806) **VI:** No further data **P:** unk **BLW:** unk **RG:** N **MK:** N **PH:** unk **SS:** DAR #A067940; E pg 463; CZ Vol 1 pg 264 **BS:** 46 pg 251.

LEBAIL, Guillaume; b unk; d 1781 **RU:** Seaman, Served on "Hector" and died from Yorktown battle **CEM:** French Memorial; GPS 36.81944, -79.39933; Yorktown; York **GS:** U **SP:** No info **VI:** No further data **P:** unk **BLW:** unk **RG:** Y **MK:** unk **PH:** unk **SS:** J-Yorktown Historian **BS:** JLARC 1, 74.

LEBARS, Louis; b unk; d 1781 **RU:** Seaman, Served on "Languedoc" and died from Yorktown battle **CEM:** French Memorial; GPS 36.81944, -79.39933; Yorktown; York **GS:** U **SP:** No info **VI:** No further data **P:** unk **BLW:** unk **RG:** Y **MK:** unk **PH:** unk **SS:** J-Yorktown Historian **BS:** JLARC 1, 74.

LEBERRE, Yves; b unk; d 1781 **RU:** Seaman, Served on "Ville de Paris" and died from Yorktown battle **CEM:** French Memorial; GPS 36.81944, -79.39933; Yorktown; York **GS:** U **SP:** No info **VI:** No further data **P:** unk **BLW:** unk **RG:** Y **MK:** unk **PH:** unk **SS:** J-Yorktown Historian **BS:** JLARC 1, 74.

LEBIHAN, Isaac; b unk; d 1781 **RU:** Seaman, Served on "Palmier" and died from Yorktown battle **CEM:** French Memorial; GPS 36.81944, -79.39933; Yorktown; York **GS:** U **SP:** No info **VI:** No further data **P:** unk **BLW:** unk **RG:** Y **MK:** unk **PH:** unk **SS:** J-Yorktown Historian **BS:** JLARC 1, 74.

LEBOURG, Jacques; b unk; d 1781 **RU:** Seaman, Served on "Languedoc" and died from Yorktown battle **CEM:** French Memorial; GPS 36.81944, -79.39933; Yorktown; York **GS:** U **SP:** No info **VI:** No further data **P:** unk **BLW:** unk **RG:** Y **MK:** unk **PH:** unk **SS:** J-Yorktown Historian **BS:** JLARC 1, 74.

LEBREHEL, Pierre; b unk; d 1781 **RU:** Seaman, Served on "Victorie" and died from Yorktown battle **CEM:** French Memorial; GPS 36.81944, -79.39933; Yorktown; York **GS:** U **SP:** No info **VI:** No further data **P:** unk **BLW:** unk **RG:** Y **MK:** unk **PH:** unk **SS:** J-Yorktown Historian **BS:** JLARC 1, 74.

LEBRUN, Edme; b unk; d 1781 **RU:** Soldier, Served in Touraine Bn and died fr battle at Yorktown **CEM:** French Memorial; GPS 36.81944, -79.39933; Yorktown; York **GS:** U **SP:** No info **VI:** No further data **P:** unk **BLW:** unk **RG:** Y **MK:** unk **PH:** unk **SS:** J-Yorktown Historian **BS:** JLARC 1, 74.

LECAMUS, Francois; b unk; d 1781 **RU:** Seaman, Served on "Northumberland" and died from Yorktown battle **CEM:** French Memorial; GPS 36.81944, -79.39933; Yorktown; York **GS:** U **SP:** No info **VI:** No further data **P:** unk **BLW:** unk **RG:** Y **MK:** unk **PH:** unk **SS:** J-Yorktown Historian **BS:** JLARC 1, 74.

LECLAIR, Francois; b unk; d 1781 **RU:** Seaman, Served on "Victorie" and died from Yorktown battle **CEM:** French Memorial; GPS 36.81944, -79.39933; Yorktown; York **GS:** U **SP:** No info **VI:** No further data **P:** unk **BLW:** unk **RG:** Y **MK:** unk **PH:** unk **SS:** J-Yorktown Historian **BS:** JLARC 1, 74.

LECOEUR, Jean; b unk; d 1781 **RU:** Seaman, Served on "Hector" and died from Yorktown battle **CEM:** French Memorial; GPS 36.81944, -79.39933; Yorktown; York **GS:** U **SP:** No info **VI:** No further data **P:** unk **BLW:** unk **RG:** Y **MK:** unk **PH:** unk **SS:** J-Yorktown Historian **BS:** JLARC 1, 74.

LECOMTE, Pierre; b unk; d 1781 **RU:** Soldier, Served in Soissonnais Bn and died fr battle at Yorktown **CEM:** French Memorial; GPS 36.81944, -79.39933; Yorktown; York **GS:** U **SP:** No info **VI:** No further data **P:** unk **BLW:** unk **RG:** Y **MK:** unk **PH:** unk **SS:** J-Yorktown Historian **BS:** JLARC 1, 74.

LECOURTOIS, Philippe; b unk; d 1781 **RU:** Seaman, Served on "Languedoc" and died from Yorktown battle **CEM:** French Memorial; GPS 36.81944, -79.39933; Yorktown; York **GS:** U **SP:** No info **VI:** No further data **P:** unk **BLW:** unk **RG:** Y **MK:** unk **PH:** unk **SS:** J-Yorktown Historian **BS:** JLARC 1, 74.

LECUNFF, Joseph; b unk; d 1781 **RU:** Seaman, Served on "Hector: and died from Yorktown battle **CEM:** French Memorial; GPS 36.81944, -79.39933; Yorktown; York **GS:** U **SP:** No info **VI:** No further data **P:** unk **BLW:** unk **RG:** Y **MK:** unk **PH:** unk **SS:** J-Yorktown Historian **BS:** JLARC 1, 74.

RU=Rank/Unit	CEM=Cemetery	GS=Gravestone	SP=Spousal Information
VI=Other Veteran Info	P=Pension	BLW=Bounty/Land Warrant	RG=Registered Grave
MK=SAR/DAR Marker	PH=Photo	SS=Service Source	BS=Burial Source

194

LEDUC, Jean; b unk; d 1781 **RU:** Seaman, Served on "Auguste" and died from Yorktown battle **CEM:** French Memorial; GPS 36.81944, -79.39933; Yorktown; York **GS:** U **SP:** No info **VI:** No further data **P:** unk **BLW:** unk **RG:** Y **MK:** unk **PH:** unk **SS:** J-Yorktown Historian **BS:** JLARC 1, 74.

LEDUC, Jean; b unk; d 1781 **RU:** Seaman, Served on "Northumberland" and died from Yorktown battle **CEM:** French Memorial; GPS 36.81944, -79.39933; Yorktown; York **GS:** U **SP:** No info **VI:** No further data **P:** unk **BLW:** unk **RG:** Y **MK:** unk **PH:** unk **SS:** J-Yorktown Historian **BS:** JLARC 1, 74.

LEE, Arthur; b 20 Dec 1740, Westmoreland Co; d 12 Dec 1792 **RU:** Patriot, Was Commissioner to France 1776, Spain 1777. Was in VA House of Delegates & Cont Congress 1782-84. Also served on Treasury Board **CEM:** Landsdowne House; GPS unk; Virginia St, Urbanna; Middlesex **GS:** Y **SP:** Mary Ball **VI:** Son of Thomas (1690-1750 Stradford) & Hannah Harrison (Ludwell) (1701-1749 Green Spring) Lee. Diplomat with Franklin and Adams to France. Graduated fr Edenburgh University in medicine **P:** N **BLW:** N **RG:** Y **MK:** N **PH:** unk **SS:** AS SAR regis **BS:** 92 pg 58; 201 pg 73, 90.

LEE, Charles; b 1758; d 24 Jun 1815 **RU:** Patriot, Was Delegate to Cont Congress **CEM:** Warrenton; GPS unk; Chestnut St, Warrenton; Fauquier **GS:** Y **SP:** 1) Mar (11 Feb 1789) Anne Lee (1 Dec 1770-9 Sep 1804), d/o Richard Henry & Anne (Gaskins-Pinckard) Lee. 2) Mar (18 Jul 1809 Fauquier Co. Chandler Peyton, security) Margaret C. Peyton, widow of Yelverton Peyton, d/o Rev John & Elizabeth (Gordon) Scott **VI:** Brother of Light-Horse Harry Lee. Studied law with Jared Ingersoll in Philadelphia. Served in VA Assembly. Naval officer of Potomac District until 1795. Collector of customs at Alexandria. Appointed US Attorney General 10 Dec 1795-1801. Was offered Chief Justice of Supreme Ct by Jefferson, but declined **P:** N **BLW:** N **RG:** N **MK:** N **PH:** unk **SS:** AT pg 541 **BS:** 18 pg 145.

LEE, David; b unk; d 1781 **RU:** Sergeant/Patriot, Was Sergeant in Capt Giles Meads co, 1st NJ Regt in 1780, and died fr the battle at Yorktown **CEM:** Yorktown Victory Monument Tablet; GPS 38.28350, -78.54150; Yorktown; York **GS:** U **SP:** No info **VI:** No further data **P:** unk **BLW:** unk **RG:** unk **MK:** unk **PH:** unk **SS:** J-Yorktown Historian; AL Ct Bk pg 8 Prince William Co **BS:** JLARC 74.

LEE, Edward; b 25 Dec 1760; d 16 Apr 1822 **RU:** Private, Served in Capt Hawkins Boone's Co of Riflemen, Col Daniel Morgan's Regt, Mar 1778 **CEM:** Blandford; GPS 37.22433, -77.38604; 319 S Crater Rd; Petersburg City **GS:** Y **SP:** 1) Nancy Price 2) Mary (-----) (__-Mar 1745) **VI:** Rec'd 26 Apr 1783, BLW 200 acres **P:** N **BLW:** Y **RG:** unk **MK:** unk **PH:** unk **SS:** F pg 44; AP service record; DAR Newsletter Sep/Oct 2015 Vol 15 No 5 pg 417 **BS:** 196.

LEE, Francis Lightfoot; b 14 Oct 1734, Stratford Hall, Westmoreland Co; d 11 Jan 1797 **RU:** Patriot, Served in Cont Congress 1775-79. Signed Leedstown Resolutions in 1766 in protest of Stamp Act. Signed Declaration of Independence with brother Richard Henry Lee. Was member VA House of Delegates, and VA Senate **CEM:** Tayloe Family; GPS 37.58200, -76.47290; Mt Airy, Rt 360, Warsaw; Richmond Co **GS:** Y **SP:** 1) Rebecca Tayloe (1752-1797) 2) Reecca Plater Tayloe (1751-1797) **VI:** Son of Thomas (1690-1750) & Hannah (Ludwell) (1701-1750) Lee. Died in Menokin, Richmond Co **P:** N **BLW:** N **RG:** N **MK:** N **PH:** unk **SS:** E pg 464 **BS:** Serv Source AS vol 3 pg 14; 201 pg 73, 90, 91.

LEE, George Fairfax; b 1754; d 1804 **RU:** Ensign, Served in Lee's Regt Cont troops. Was Ens in Capt John Rice's Westmoreland Co Militia **CEM:** Unidentified; GPS unk; Rt 675, nr Lee Creek, Hague; Westmoreland **GS:** N **SP:** No info **VI:** Son of George Lee (18 Aug 1714-19 Nov 1761) and Anne Fairfax (1728-14 Mar 1761) **P:** unk **BLW:** unk **RG:** N **MK:** N **PH:** N **SS:** AP rec; CN pg 85 **BS:** 189 pg 88.

LEE, Henry II; b 1729, Stratford Hall, Westmoreland Co; d 1787 **RU:** Lieutenant Colonel/Patriot, Was member of Convention 1774,75,76 and State Senator 1780. Also gave use of wagons, horses, hay shoes and other items to militia **CEM:** Leesylvania Plantation; GPS 38.35240, -77.15200; On a ridge overlooking Occoquan Bay, Woodbridge; Prince William **GS:** U **SP:** Lucy Grymes, d/o Charles & Frances (Jennings) Grymes **VI:** Resided at "Leesylvania" Prince William Co. Justice of Peace, Burgess before war. Will probated Oct 1787. Cem stone missing; replaced with bronze plaque. **P:** unk **BLW:** unk **RG:** Y **MK:** unk **PH:** unk **SS:** J-NSSAR 1993 Reg; D pg Prince William Co **BS:** JLARC 1

LEE, Henry III; b 29 Jan 1756, Prince William Co; d 25 Mar 1818 **RU:** Lieutenant Colonel, Was Lt Col in Lee's Legion. Served in Rev War. As "Lighthorse Harry". Served in VA House Delegate fr Westmoreland Co **CEM:** Washington & Lee Univ Campus; GPS 36.60863, -81.01593; Nr Jefferson St; Lexington City **GS:** U **SP:** Mar (1782) (-----) **VI:** Cont Congress 1787-88. Gov of VA 1791-94. US Rep 6th Congress

RU=Rank/Unit	CEM=Cemetery	GS=Gravestone	SP=Spousal Information
VI=Other Veteran Info	P=Pension	BLW=Bounty/Land Warrant	RG=Registered Grave
MK=SAR/DAR Marker	PH=Photo	SS=Service Source	BS=Burial Source

195

1799-1801. After Rev War became General. July 1812 severely hurt at Baltimore riots. Federalist. Support editor of Baltimore Federalist that editorialized against War of 1812. Gave George Washington eulogy: "first in war, first in peace, and first in the hearts of his countrymen." Father of Robert E. Lee. Died in Camden Co, GA. Reinterred to Lee Chapel Cem 1913. Recd BLW #1299-500-3 Jul 1789 **P:** unk **BLW: Y RG: Y MK:** unk **PH:** unk **SS:** J-NSSAR 1993 Reg; CG pg 2043 **BS:** JLARC 1; 201 pg 7392.

LEE, John; b c1736-1740; d c1819-1822 **RU:** Captain, Served in the Marines **CEM:** Lee Family; GPS unk; Leesville; Campbell **GS: Y SP:** No info **VI:** Founder of Leesville, Campbell Co **P:** unk **BLW:** unk **RG: Y MK: N PH:** unk **SS:** J-NSSAR 1993 Reg; J- DAR Hatcher; G pg 783 **BS:** JLARC 1, 2; 196.

LEE, John; b 1750; d 1821 **RU:** Major, Served under Col Charles Dabney, Supernumerary Feb-Apr 1782 in rank of Maj **CEM:** Old Kiskiak; GPS unk; Nr Yorktown; York **GS: U SP:** No info **VI:** No further data **P:** unk **BLW:** unk **RG:** unk **MK:** unk **PH:** unk **SS:** J- DAR Hatcher; G pg 852 **BS:** JLARC 2.

LEE, John; b 1757; d 19 Apr 1797 **RU:** Patriot, Submitted claim for losses suffered during burning of Norfolk **CEM:** St Paul's Episcopal; GPS 36.84733, -76.28554; 201 St Paul's Blvd; Norfolk City **GS: Y SP:** Mar (4 Dec 1769) Jane Brazill **VI:** No further data **P: N BLW: N RG: Y MK: Y PH:** unk **SS:** CB Friend Amer cause **BS:** 178 Jan 11.

LEE, Ludwell; b 13 Oct 1760, Westmoreland Co; d 25 Mar 1835 **RU:** Soldier? Served in VA Line. Lived in Westmoreland Co at enl. Was Aide-de-camp to General Lafayette, with unetermined rank **CEM:** St James Episcopal, Old Cemetery; GPS 39.11555, -77.56250; Church St NE, Leesburg; Loudoun **GS: U SP:** Flora Lee (Jun 1771, Stratford Hall, Westmoreland Co-1795, Fairfax Co) d/o Phillip Ludwell (1727-1775) & Elizabeth (Steptoe) (1743-1789) Lee **VI:** Son of Richard Henry (1732-1794) & (-----) Lee. Achieved rank of colonel after war. Appl pen 14 Jan 1833 Loudoun Co. S8829 **P: Y BLW:** unk **RG: Y MK:** unk **PH:** unk **SS:** CG pg 2045 **BS:** JLARC 1, 4, 32.

LEE, Nathaniel; b 1730; d 1820 **RU:** Patriot, Gave material aid to cause **CEM:** Nathaniel Lee Home; GPS unk; NE of Carson; Prince George **GS: N SP:** No info **VI:** No further data **P: N BLW: N RG: N MK: N PH: N SS:** E pg 465; AL Com Bk IV pg 363 Prince George Co **BS:** 148 Lee.

LEE, Philip Ludwell; b 1726; d 1775 **RU:** Patriot, Gave material aid to cause in Westmoreland Co **CEM:** Lee Family; GPS unk; Stratford Hall; Westmoreland **GS: N SP:** Elizabeth Steptoe **VI:** Son of Thomas Lee (1690-1750) and Hannah Ludwell **P: N BLW: N RG: N MK: N PH: N SS:** AL Ct Bk **BS:** 189 pg 88.

LEE, Richard Bland; b 20 Jan 1761, Leesylvania, Prince William Co; d 12 Mar 1827 **RU:** Matross/Patriot, Served in 1st Artillery. 1st congressman fr N. VA. State House of Delegates (1784-88) 1st, 2nd, 3rd Congresses (1789-95). Convinced Congress to locate nation's capital in Washington DC. Gave 223 pounds of beef to cause **CEM:** Sully Plantation; GPS unk; Sully Rd Rt 28, adj Dulles National Airport, Chantilly; Fairfax **GS: Y SP:** Elizabeth Collins (1770-1858) **VI:** Son of Henry Lee & Lucy Ludwell Grymes. Appointed by Madison as commissioner in 1816 to adjust claims of loss fr War of 1812. Judge in Orphans Ct in DC until death there. Originally interred at Congressional Cem, Washington DC. Monument erected by Lee Family Association **P:** unk **BLW:** unk **RG: Y MK: Y PH: Y SS:** E pg 466; AL Ct Bk pg 43 **BS:** 61 vol IV pg CH 24; JLARC 14; 196.

LEE, Richard Henry; b 18 or 20 Jan 1732, Stratford Hall, Westmoreland Co; d 19 Jun 1794 **RU:** Patriot, Was member VA House of Burgesses 1758 -76. Believed in VA's resistance to Stamp & Townshend Acts. Was member 1774 of 1st Cont Congress. **CEM:** Burnt House Field; GPS unk; Hague; Westmoreland **GS: Y SP:** 1) Anne Aylette 2) Anne Pinckard **VI:** Son of Thomas & Hannah (Ludwell) Lee. Signer of the Declar. Independence fr VA; brother of Francis Lightfoot Lee who also signed. Brother of Gen "Lighthorse Harry" Lee, uncle of Civil War Conf Gen Robert E Lee. President of Congress (1784-1785) under Articles of Confederation, unofficially President of USA. Died in Chantilly **P: N BLW: N RG: Y MK: N PH:** unk **SS:** W pg 22-23 **BS:** 189 pg 85; 201 pg 7392-93.

LEE, Thomas Ludwell; b 13 Dec 1730, Stratford Hall, Westmoreland Co; d 13 Apr 1778 **RU:** Patriot, Was active in VA Convention, Committee of Safety for Colony of VA. Served in House of Burgesses. Was judge of General Ct of VA **CEM:** Belleview Plantation; GPS unk; Rt 604; Stafford **GS: N SP:** Mary Aylett, daughter of William & (-----) Aylett **VI:** Known to have d at his plantation "Bellevue" and is thought to have been bur nearby. **P: N BLW: N RG: Y MK: N PH: N SS:** E pg 466 **BS:** 04; 30 pg 230.

RU=Rank/Unit   CEM=Cemetery   GS=Gravestone   SP=Spousal Information
VI=Other Veteran Info   P=Pension   BLW=Bounty/Land Warrant   RG=Registered Grave
MK=SAR/DAR Marker   PH=Photo   SS=Service Source   BS=Burial Source

196

LEE, William; b c1750; d Sep 1803 **RU:** Private/Patriot, Served in Capt Cobbs Co, Bedford Co Militia. Gave material aid to cause **CEM:** Lee Family; GPS unk; New London; Bedford **GS:** U **SP:** Ava Noel (1745-1820) **VI:** Son of Charles (c1720, Goochland Co-15 Mar 1799, Cumberland Co) & Ann (Dabbs) (c1722-1795) Lee. Source 2 has burial near Evington in Campbell Co. Source 66 has burial at Old Lee graveyard at the home of Mr. Edward Leftwick, bet Evington and New London **P:** unk **BLW:** unk **RG:** Y **MK:** N **PH:** unk **SS:** E pg 466; AL Ct Bk pg 13 Amherst Co; CZ **BS:** JLARC 1, 2, 4, 66, 75; 196.

LEE, William "Billy"; b 1750; d 1828 **RU:** Valet, Served as Washington's valet servant man **CEM:** Mt Vernon; GPS 38.42280, -77.05090; Mt Vernon Estate; Fairfax **GS:** N **SP:** Margaret Thomas Lee, a free black fr Philadelphia. It is not known if she ever moved to Mt Vernon **VI:** Emancipated in Washington's will for his service to him during the Rev War. Bur in the negro cemetery which only has a generic memorial stone for all the slaves as a group **P:** unk **BLW:** unk **RG:** Y **MK:** N **PH:** N **SS:** J-NSSAR 1993 Reg; NSSAR Ancestor #P-234885 **BS:** JLARC 1.

LEE, Zachariah Jr; b 1765; d 1854 **RU:** Soldier, Served in VA line **CEM:** Brickey-Lee; GPS unk; Rt 779, McAfees Knob; Botetourt **GS:** U **SP:** Mar (23 Dec 1813 Botetourt Co) Agnes Brickey d/o Peter & (-----) Brickey **VI:** Appl pen 12 May 1834 Botetourt Co. R6260 **P:** Y **BLW:** unk **RG:** unk **MK:** unk **PH:** unk **SS:** CG pg 2048 **BS:** JLARC 4, 60.

LEE, Zephaniah; b 1755; d unk **RU:** Private, Served in Capt Fraizer's Co, Augusta Co Militia **CEM:** Greenwood; GPS 38.38470, -78.97610; Vic Green St & North Grove St, Bridgewater; Rockingham **GS:** N **SP:** Mar (1781 Rockingham Co) Jean Bright **VI:** No further data **P:** unk **BLW:** unk **RG:** unk **MK:** unk **PH:** N **SS:** E pg 466 **BS:** 196.

LEECH, John Sr; b 1739; d 1820 **RU:** Private, Served in 2nd PA Regt Jan 1781 to Jan 1782 **CEM:** Oxford Presbyterian; GPS 37.75302, -79.56023; 18 Churchview Ln, Lexington; Rockbridge **GS:** N **SP:** Mar (1761) Martha McComb **VI:** Moved to Rockbridge Co 1778 **P:** unk **BLW:** unk **RG:** N **MK:** N **PH:** N **SS:** AP **BS:** 32 Jan 2011.

LEFERME, Pierre; b unk; d 1781 **RU:** Soldier, Served in Gatinais Bn and died fr battle at Yorktown **CEM:** French Memorial; GPS 36.81944, -79.39933; Yorktown; York **GS:** U **SP:** No info **VI:** No further data **P:** unk **BLW:** unk **RG:** Y **MK:** unk **PH:** unk **SS:** J-Yorktown Historian **BS:** JLARC 1, 74.

LEFEVRE, Jean; b unk; d 1781 **RU:** Seaman, Served on "Citoyen" and died from Yorktown battle **CEM:** French Memorial; GPS 36.81944, -79.39933; Yorktown; York **GS:** U **SP:** No info **VI:** No further data **P:** unk **BLW:** unk **RG:** Y **MK:** unk **PH:** unk **SS:** J-Yorktown Historian **BS:** JLARC 1, 74.

LEFEVRE, Joseph; b unk; d 1781 **RU:** Soldier, Served in Touraine Bn and died fr battle at Yorktown **CEM:** French Memorial; GPS 36.81944, -79.39933; Yorktown; York **GS:** U **SP:** No info **VI:** No further data **P:** unk **BLW:** unk **RG:** Y **MK:** unk **PH:** unk **SS:** J-Yorktown Historian **BS:** JLARC 1, 74.

LEFLOCH, Francois; b unk; d 1781 **RU:** Seaman, Served on "Northumberland" and died from Yorktown battle **CEM:** French Memorial; GPS 36.81944, -79.39933; Yorktown; York **GS:** U **SP:** No info **VI:** No further data **P:** unk **BLW:** unk **RG:** Y **MK:** unk **PH:** unk **SS:** J-Yorktown Historian **BS:** JLARC 1, 74.

LEFTWICH, Augustine Jr; b 10 Sep 1744, Caroline Co; d unk **RU:** Lieutenant, Ent serv Bedford Co in VA Line **CEM:** Leftwich Family; GPS unk; Mt Airy, nr Leesville; Bedford **GS:** N **SP:** Mary (-----) **VI:** Sol appl pen 26 Oct 1833 Bedford Co. S11364 **P:** Y **BLW:** unk **RG:** Y **MK:** N **PH:** N **SS:** K Vol 3 pg 114; CG pg 2050 **BS:** JLARC 1, 4, 36.

LEFTWICH, Augustine Sr; b 1712, New Kent Co; d 1795 **RU:** Soldier/Patriot, Served in Co F, 10th VA Militia, Gave material aid to cause **CEM:** Goose Creek; GPS unk; Lynch Station; Campbell **GS:** Y **SP:** 1) Mar (c1736) Mary Mosley (1720 Bedford Co-__) 2) Mar (c1777) Elizabeth (Fuqua) Stovall (1736 Bedford Co-24 Jun 1795), widow of John Stovall, d/o of Ralph & Priscilla (Owen) Fuqua **VI:** Also fought in French & Indian War. Died in Bedford Co. Govt stone says "Rev War Co. F, 10th VA Militia" **P:** unk **BLW:** unk **RG:** unk **MK:** N **PH:** unk **SS:** B; AL Lists pg 16, 18 **BS:** 196.

LEFTWICH, Joel; b 17 Nov 1760, Caroline Co; d 20 Oct 1846 **RU:** Sergeant, Ent serv Bedford Co in VA Line. Ent serv again as Orderly Sergeant in Thomas Leftwich Co (no kinship given) **CEM:** Leftwich Family; GPS unk; Mt Airy, nr Leesville; Bedford **GS:** N **SP:** Mar (24 Dec 1781 Bedford Co) Nancy Turner **VI:** Son of Augustine Leftwich (1712-1795). Lived in Bedford Co after RW, then moved 1827 to

RU=Rank/Unit	CEM=Cemetery	GS=Gravestone	SP=Spousal Information
VI=Other Veteran Info	P=Pension	BLW=Bounty/Land Warrant	RG=Registered Grave
MK=SAR/DAR Marker	PH=Photo	SS=Service Source	BS=Burial Source

197

Campbell Co where pen. Legislator & Justice of Peace after War. Commanded brigade as Brig Gen that marched to relieve Gen Harrison in Ohio, in 1812. Helped build Ft Meigs. Led brigade in Battle of Baltimore 1813. Sol appl pen 8 Oct 1832 Campbell Co. S8830. **P:** Y **BLW:** unk **RG:** unk **MK:** N **PH:** N **SS:** J- DAR Hatcher; K Vol 3 pg 114; CG pg 2050 **BS:** JLARC 2; 196.

LEFTWICH, Thomas; b 1740, Caroline Co; d 3 May 1816 **RU:** Colonel/Patriot, Served in Lunenburg & Bedford Co Militias 1758. Became Lt in Bedford Co Militia early part of Rev War, promoted to Capt & reassigned to Gen Edward Stevens Regt. At Battle of Camden, commanded rear-guard of Gen Gates' Division. Gave material aid to cause **CEM:** Leftwich Family; GPS unk; Mt Airy, nr Leesville; Bedford **GS:** N **SP:** 1) Mar (10 Dec 1764) Mary Challis (__-1777); 2) Mar (2 Apr 1771, prob Amherst Co) Bethunia Ellis (__-1780); 3) Mar (27 Oct 1783) Jane Gincey Stratton (1762-1806) **VI:** Son of Augustine (1712-1795). Soon after Rev War, served as Maj, Lt Col and Col, respectively, of 10th Regt of VA Militia **P:** unk **BLW:** unk **RG:** Y **MK:** N **PH:** N **SS:** D Bedford Co **BS:** JLARC 1, 2, 36; 196.

LEFTWICH, Uriah; b 1748, Caroline Co; d 1838 **RU:** Second Lieutenant/Patriot, Served in Bedford Co Militia. Gave material aid to cause **CEM:** Leftwich Family; GPS unk; Mt Airy, nr Leesville; Bedford **GS:** N **SP:** Mar (c1769) Nancy Keith **VI:** Son of Augustine (1712-1795) & (-----) Leftwich. Appointed Ens 1779, Capt 1789 (Bedford Co). Pen recd by widow commencing 16 Sep 1812 at $12.50 per mo **P:** Y **BLW:** N **RG:** Y **MK:** N **PH:** N **SS:** E pg 467; AG pg 269; AK Sep 2007; AL Ct Bk pg 8, 18 Bedford Co **BS:** 04 Sep 07; 196.

LEFTWICH, William; b 1737; d 31 May 1820 **RU:** Lieutenant Colonel/Patriot, Gave material aid to cause **CEM:** Leftwich Family; GPS unk; Mt Airy, nr Leesville; Bedford **GS:** N **SP:** Elizabeth Haynes (1732-1780) **VI:** Capt of Militia 1772, Committee of Safety 1775, Justice 1777, Maj 1778, Lt Col 1780, Sheriff in 1796, Virginia Legislature 1786-87 **P:** unk **BLW:** unk **RG:** unk **MK:** N **PH:** N **SS:** AL Ct Bk pg 8, 9, 12, 32 Bedford Co **BS:** JLARC 2, 36.

LEGG, John; b unk; d April 1799 **RU:** Private/Patriot, Served in VA Cont Line for 3 yrs. Also as patriot gave 26 gal rum to cause on Jul 1780 **CEM:** Masonic Cemetery; GPS 38.30198, -77.46142; 900 Charles St; Fredericksburg City **GS:** N **SP:** Lucy Lee (c1763 - 11 May 1787) **VI:** The Virginia Herald in April 1799 indicates he was a capt, but BLW indicates private thus rank obtained after war **P:** unk **BLW:** Y **RG:** Y **MK:** N **PH:** N **SS:** AK; F pg 44 **BS:** 04; 11 pg 68.

LEGOFF, Jean; b unk; d 1781 **RU:** Seaman, Served on "Saint-Esprit" and died from Yorktown battle **CEM:** French Memorial; GPS 36.81944, -79.39933; Yorktown; York **GS:** U **SP:** No info **VI:** No further data **P:** unk **BLW:** unk **RG:** Y **MK:** unk **PH:** unk **SS:** J-Yorktown Historian **BS:** JLARC 1, 74.

LEGROSS, Pierre; b unk; d 1781 **RU:** Seaman, Served on "Duc De Bourgogne" and died from Yorktown battle **CEM:** French Memorial; GPS 36.81944, -79.39933; Yorktown; York **GS:** U **SP:** No info **VI:** No further data **P:** unk **BLW:** unk **RG:** Y **MK:** unk **PH:** unk **SS:** J-Yorktown Historian **BS:** JLARC 1, 74.

LEGUEN, Louis; b unk; d 1781 **RU:** Seaman, Served on "Ville De Paris" and died from Yorktown battle **CEM:** French Memorial; GPS 36.81944, -79.39933; Yorktown; York **GS:** U **SP:** No info **VI:** No further data **P:** unk **BLW:** unk **RG:** Y **MK:** unk **PH:** unk **SS:** J-Yorktown Historian **BS:** JLARC 1, 74.

LEGUERN, Guillaume; b unk; d 1781 **RU:** Seaman, Served on "Hercule" and died from Yorktown battle **CEM:** French Memorial; GPS 36.81944, -79.39933; Yorktown; York **GS:** U **SP:** No info **VI:** No further data **P:** unk **BLW:** unk **RG:** Y **MK:** unk **PH:** unk **SS:** J-Yorktown Historian **BS:** JLARC 1, 74.

LEGUILLOUX, Rene; b unk; d 1781 **RU:** Seaman, Served on "Marseillais" and died from Yorktown battle **CEM:** French Memorial; GPS 36.81944, -79.39933; Yorktown; York **GS:** U **SP:** No info **VI:** No further data **P:** unk **BLW:** unk **RG:** Y **MK:** unk **PH:** unk **SS:** J-Yorktown Historian **BS:** JLARC 1, 74.

LEHMAN, Ludwick; b 1740, Philadelphia Co, PA; d 16 Mar 1820 **RU:** Private, Listed in 8th Class, 2nd Battalion, Lancaster Co PA Militia **CEM:** Bethel Cemetery; GPS 38.47592, -78.75641; 3061 Armentrout Path, Keezletown; Rockingham **GS:** Y **SP:** No info **VI:** Son of Christain K (__-1748) & Ann Margaret (-----) Lehman **P:** unk **BLW:** unk **RG:** unk **MK:** unk **PH:** unk **SS:** AP PA Archives Series 5 Vol VII pg 172 **BS:** 196.

RU=Rank/Unit	CEM=Cemetery	GS=Gravestone	SP=Spousal Information
VI=Other Veteran Info	P=Pension	BLW=Bounty/Land Warrant	RG=Registered Grave
MK=SAR/DAR Marker	PH=Photo	SS=Service Source	BS=Burial Source

198

LEHUP, Pierre; b unk; d 1781 **RU:** Soldier, Served in Soissonnais Bn and died fr battle at Yorktown **CEM:** French Memorial; GPS 36.81944, -79.39933; Yorktown; York **GS:** U **SP:** No info **VI:** No further data **P:** unk **BLW:** unk **RG:** Y **MK:** unk **PH:** unk **SS:** J-Yorktown Historian **BS:** JLARC 1, 74.

LEIGH, John; b 1737, King William Co; d 14 Aug 1785 **RU:** Lieutenant, Served in 5th and 7th VA Regts. Was sick at end of service but received a certificate for full pay 14 Feb 1783 **CEM:** Leigh Family; GPS unk; Base of Leigh Mountain, Farmville; Prince Edward **GS:** U **SP:** Mar (21 Nov 1757) Virginia Greenhill (c1741 Amelia Co-9 Jul 1820 Madison Co) d/o David & Catherine (Clairborne) Greenhill **VI:** Son of Zacheriah (1704-1770) & Ellen (Jones) (1705-1745) Leigh. Recd BLW of 200 acres and another for 2487 acres, 5 Jan 1824 **P:** unk **BLW:** Y **RG:** unk **MK:** unk **PH:** unk **SS:** DAR ancestor #A069201; C pg 463; AP Ser Rec **BS:** 196.

LEJORE, Jean; b unk; d 1781 **RU:** Soldier, Served in Gatinais Bn and died fr battle at Yorktown **CEM:** French Memorial; GPS 36.81944, -79.39933; Yorktown; York **GS:** U **SP:** No info **VI:** No further data **P:** unk **BLW:** unk **RG:** Y **MK:** unk **PH:** unk **SS:** J-Yorktown Historian **BS:** JLARC 1, 74.

LELAYER, Yves; b unk; d 1781 **RU:** Seaman, Served on "Ville de Paris" and died from Yorktown battle **CEM:** French Memorial; GPS 36.81944, -79.39933; Yorktown; York **GS:** U **SP:** No info **VI:** No further data **P:** unk **BLW:** unk **RG:** Y **MK:** unk **PH:** unk **SS:** J-Yorktown Historian **BS:** JLARC 1, 74.

LEMAY, Jacques; b unk; d 1781 **RU:** Soldier, Served in Gatinais Bn and died fr battle at Yorktown **CEM:** French Memorial; GPS 36.81944, -79.39933; Yorktown; York **GS:** U **SP:** No info **VI:** No further data **P:** unk **BLW:** unk **RG:** Y **MK:** unk **PH:** unk **SS:** J-Yorktown Historian **BS:** JLARC 1, 74.

LEMAY, Julien; b unk; d 1781 **RU:** Seaman, Served on "Diademe" and died from Yorktown battle **CEM:** French Memorial; GPS 36.81944, -79.39933; Yorktown; York **GS:** U **SP:** No info **VI:** No further data **P:** unk **BLW:** unk **RG:** Y **MK:** unk **PH:** unk **SS:** J-Yorktown Historian **BS:** JLARC 1, 74.

LEMINGNON, Jean; b unk; d 1781 **RU:** Seaman, Served on "Magnanime" and died from Yorktown battle) **CEM:** French Memorial; GPS 36.81944, -79.39933; Yorktown; York **GS:** U **SP:** No info **VI:** No further data **P:** unk **BLW:** unk **RG:** Y **MK:** unk **PH:** unk **SS:** J-Yorktown Historian **BS:** JLARC 1, 74.

LEMOING, Jean; b unk; d 1781 **RU:** Seaman, Served on "Hercule" and died from Yorktown battle **CEM:** French Memorial; GPS 36.81944, -79.39933; Yorktown; York **GS:** U **SP:** No info **VI:** No further data **P:** unk **BLW:** unk **RG:** Y **MK:** unk **PH:** unk **SS:** J-Yorktown Historian **BS:** JLARC 1, 74.

LEMON, Jacob; b 7 May 1763, Frederick Co, MD; d 6 Nov 1848 **RU:** Soldier, Served in MD & VA Lines. Lived in Augusta Co VA at enl 1780. Nov 1781 visited relatives in Frederick Co MD, reenlisted for relative Andrew Hull. Returned to Augusta Co VA and reenlisted **CEM:** Lemon Family; GPS 37.77126, -79.78160; Nr jct Rts 220 & 698 Lick Run Rd, Lick Run; Botetourt **GS:** Y **SP:** Mar (3 Jan 1797 Botetourt "at her father's house on James River) Jane Gilliland (3 Jan 1773, Rockingham Co-30 Nov 1858) d/o James & Susan (Young) Gilliland **VI:** Son of George Lemon (1738-1807) & Marie Elizabeth Young. Moved to Augusta Co when 10 yrs old (1773). Fought at battle of Cowpens. Ent service again 1782 fr Augusta Co against Indians. Moved abt 1790 to Botetourt Co. Sol appl pen13 Aug 1832 Botetourt Co. Widow appl pen 15 Sep 1850 age 80 Botetourt Co & appl BLW 1855 same. W3698. BLW #26990-160-55. Widow recd pension. **P:** Y **BLW:** Y **RG:** unk **MK:** N **PH:** unk **SS:** K Vol 3 pg 115; CG pg 2054 **BS:** JLARC 4, 60; 196.

L'ENFANT, Pierre Charles; b 2 Aug 1754, France; d 14 Jun 1825 **RU:** Major of Engineers, One of the first French volunteers to enlist in the Cont Army in 1776. Under Gen Washington at Valley Forge, PA during winter 1777-78. Wounded 1779 Savannah GA. Taken prisoner Charleston, SC. Awarded rank of Maj in Corps of Engineers 1783 **CEM:** Arlington National; GPS 38.88377, -77.06535; Jefferson Davis Hwy Rt 110; Arlington **GS:** Y **SP:** No info **VI:** Known for pencil portraits of officers, including Washington. Developed city plan for Washington DC where he died. Reinterred fr Digges Farm (aka Green Hill), Princes George Co, Maryland 28 Apr 1909 **P:** unk **BLW:** unk **RG:** N **MK:** N **PH:** unk **SS:** AS DAR mag **BS:** JLARC 1, 2, 111; 80 vol 1 pg 169; 196.

LENOIR, Rene; b unk; d 1781 **RU:** Seaman, Served on "Auguste" and died from Yorktown battle **CEM:** French Memorial; GPS 36.81944, -79.39933; Yorktown; York **GS:** U **SP:** No info **VI:** No further data **P:** unk **BLW:** unk **RG:** Y **MK:** unk **PH:** unk **SS:** J-Yorktown Historian **BS:** JLARC 1, 74.

RU=Rank/Unit CEM=Cemetery GS=Gravestone SP=Spousal Information
VI=Other Veteran Info P=Pension BLW=Bounty/Land Warrant RG=Registered Grave
MK=SAR/DAR Marker PH=Photo SS=Service Source BS=Burial Source

199

LEONARD, Frederick; b 1761, Lancaster, Lancaster Co, PA; d 1845 **RU:** Private, Enl in Col Stuart's Regt, PA Line **CEM:** Malone Family; GPS unk; Three Springs; Washington **GS:** Y **SP:** Anna Maria Braun or Brown (1762-1855) **VI:** Pen appl for 18 May 1829. Died in Three Springs, Washington Co. BLW given to son Henry. Error on Govt issued stone says VA Line, but is actually PA Line. **P:** Y **BLW:** Y **RG:** Y **MK:** N **PH:** Y **SS:** E pg 469; CG pg 2057; AS SAR regis **BS:** SAR regis.

LEPAGE, Pierre; b unk; d 1781 **RU:** Soldier, Served in Gatinais Bn and died fr battle at Yorktown **CEM:** French Memorial; GPS 36.81944, -79.39933; Yorktown; York **GS:** U **SP:** No info **VI:** No further data **P:** unk **BLW:** unk **RG:** Y **MK:** unk **PH:** unk **SS:** J-Yorktown Historian **BS:** JLARC 1, 74.

LEPARC, Jean; b unk; d 1781 **RU:** Seaman, Served on "Citoyen" and died from Yorktown battle **CEM:** French Memorial; GPS 36.81944, -79.39933; Yorktown; York **GS:** U **SP:** No info **VI:** No further data **P:** unk **BLW:** unk **RG:** Y **MK:** unk **PH:** unk **SS:** J-Yorktown Historian **BS:** JLARC 1, 74.

LEPELLE, Julien; b unk; d 1781 **RU:** Seaman, Served on "Auguste" and died from Yorktown battle **CEM:** French Memorial; GPS 36.81944, -79.39933; Yorktown; York **GS:** U **SP:** No info **VI:** No further data **P:** unk **BLW:** unk **RG:** Y **MK:** unk **PH:** unk **SS:** J-Yorktown Historian **BS:** JLARC 1, 74.

LERICHE, Jacques; b unk; d 1781 **RU:** Soldier, Served in Auxonne Bn and died fr battle at Yorktown **CEM:** French Memorial; GPS 36.81944, -79.39933; Yorktown; York **GS:** U **SP:** No info **VI:** No further data **P:** unk **BLW:** unk **RG:** Y **MK:** unk **PH:** unk **SS:** J-Yorktown Historian **BS:** JLARC 1, 74.

LEROUX, Etienne; b unk; d 1781 **RU:** Seaman, Served on "Magnanime" and died from Yorktown battle **CEM:** French Memorial; GPS 36.81944, -79.39933; Yorktown; York **GS:** U **SP:** No info **VI:** No further data **P:** unk **BLW:** unk **RG:** Y **MK:** unk **PH:** unk **SS:** J-Yorktown Historian **BS:** JLARC 1, 74.

LEROUX, Jean; b unk; d 1781 **RU:** Soldier, Served in Touraine Bn and died fr battle at Yorktown **CEM:** French Memorial; GPS 36.81944, -79.39933; Yorktown; York **GS:** U **SP:** No info **VI:** No further data **P:** unk **BLW:** unk **RG:** Y **MK:** unk **PH:** unk **SS:** J-Yorktown Historian **BS:** JLARC 1, 74.

LERSNE, Augustin; b unk; d 1781 **RU:** Soldier, Served in Touraine Bn and died fr battle at Yorktown **CEM:** French Memorial; GPS 36.81944, -79.39933; Yorktown; York **GS:** U **SP:** no info **VI:** No further data **P:** unk **BLW:** unk **RG:** Y **MK:** unk **PH:** unk **SS:** J-Yorktown Historian **BS:** JLARC 1, 74.

LESAGNE, Pierre; b unk; d 1781 **RU:** Seaman, Served on "Magnanime" and died from Yorktown battle **CEM:** French Memorial; GPS 36.81944, -79.39933; Yorktown; York **GS:** U **SP:** No info **VI:** No further data **P:** unk **BLW:** unk **RG:** Y **MK:** unk **PH:** unk **SS:** J-Yorktown Historian **BS:** JLARC 1, 74.

LESOURD, Sebastien; b unk; d 1781 **RU:** Seaman, Served on "Saint-Esprit" and died from Yorktown battle **CEM:** French Memorial; GPS 36.81944, -79.39933; Yorktown; York **GS:** U **SP:** No info **VI:** No further data **P:** unk **BLW:** unk **RG:** Y **MK:** unk **PH:** unk **SS:** J-Yorktown Historian **BS:** JLARC 1, 74.

LESTER, John; b 1 Jan 1752, Bucks Co, PA; d 29 Jan 1825 **RU:** Private, Served in Capt David Trigg Co Montgomery Co Militia. Also in Capt Helvan's Co, 1st VA Regt, commanded by Col Green **CEM:** Lester; GPS 37.11698, -80.25156; S fr Riner; Montgomery **GS:** Y **SP:** Catherine Plick or Plickenstalver (1759 Bedford Co-15 Sep 1833 Montgomery Co) **VI:** No further data **P:** unk **BLW:** unk **RG:** Y **MK:** unk **PH:** unk **SS:** J-NSSAR 1993 Reg; J- DAR Hatcher; AP roll **BS:** JLARC 1, 2.

LESTER, John; b 1748, Sul, Suffolk Co, Great Britain; d 19 Dec 1804 **RU:** Sergeant, Served in1st Cont Line **CEM:** St John's Episcopal; GPS 37.53183, -77.41958; 2401 E Broad St; Richmond City **GS:** Y **SP:** No info **VI:** Merchant of the city of Richmond. White marble slab on pedestals. **P:** unk **BLW:** unk **RG:** N **MK:** N **PH:** unk **SS:** E pg 469; AP **BS:** 28 pg 465; 196.

LESUEUR, Martel; b 6 Mar 1758, Manakin, Cumberland Co; d 10 Aug 1843 **RU:** Private, Ent serv Cumberland Co. Served in militia **CEM:** Prillman-Turner; GPS unk; Btw Ferrun & Philpott Res; Franklin **GS:** U **SP:** Mar (10 Jun 1781 Chesterfield Co) Elizabeth Bacon **VI:** Moved to Charlotte Co, then Henry Co, then Patrick Co, then Grayson Co, then Franklin Co where pen in 1832. Widow recd pension 1844 at age 79. F-W8035, R1552 **P:** Y **BLW:** unk **RG:** Y **MK:** N **PH:** Y **SS:** K Vol 3 pg 118 **BS:** 04, Jul 07.

LETCHER, William; b 1741, Petersburg; d 7 Aug 1780 **RU:** Colonel/Patriot, Serv not identified. Was killed by a Tory, thus DAR considers him a patriot. **CEM:** Delionback Home; GPS 36.34040, -80.33240; End of Rt 749 on Ararat River; Patrick **GS:** U **SP:** Mar (20 Nov 1778) Elizabeth Perkins (May 1759-__)

RU=Rank/Unit   CEM=Cemetery   GS=Gravestone   SP=Spousal Information
VI=Other Veteran Info   P=Pension   BLW=Bounty/Land Warrant   RG=Registered Grave
MK=SAR/DAR Marker   PH=Photo   SS=Service Source   BS=Burial Source

200

VI: Great-grandfather of J.E.B. Stuart. Was assasinated by a Tory. DAR marker **P:** unk **BLW:** unk **RG:** unk **MK:** Y **PH:** unk **SS:** BT; DD DAR #A069559 **BS:** JLARC 30, 108; 196.

LETCHER, William; b unk; d 1781 **RU:** Private, Was killed at Battle of Green Springs, Williamsburg. Listed in the Lib of VA "Rev War Dead" Database as "Killed in Action" **CEM:** Williamsburg Land Conservancy; GPS unk; 5000 New Point Rd; Williamsburg City **GS:** N **SP:** No info **VI:** No further data **P:** unk **BLW:** unk **RG:** N **MK:** N **PH:** N **SS:** AU SAR study **BS:** 32.

LETOUX, Clement; b unk; d 1781 **RU:** Seaman, Served on "Saint-Esprit" and died from Yorktown battle **CEM:** French Memorial; GPS 36.81944, -79.39933; Yorktown; York **GS:** U **SP:** No info **VI:** No further data **P:** unk **BLW:** unk **RG:** Y **MK:** unk **PH:** unk **SS:** J-Yorktown Historian **BS:** JLARC 1, 74.

LEVENT, Jean; b unk; d 1781 **RU:** Seaman, Served on "Northumberland" and died from Yorktown battle **CEM:** French Memorial; GPS 36.81944, -79.39933; Yorktown; York **GS:** U **SP:** No info **VI:** No further data **P:** unk **BLW:** unk **RG:** Y **MK:** unk **PH:** unk **SS:** J-Yorktown Historian **BS:** JLARC 1, 74.

LEWIS, Andrew; b 9 Oct 1716 County Donegal, Ulster Ireland; d 26 Sep 1781 **RU:** General/Patriot, Served as Brig General in VA Line. Was in Battle of Point Pleasant. Promoted to Gen 1776. Resigned commission 1777. Performed patriotic service securing troops supporting Battle of Point Pleasant 1774 **CEM:** King; GPS unk; Bent Mountain, S fr Roanoke; Roanoke Co **GS:** U **SP:** Mar (1749) Elizabeth Givens **VI:** Monument to him at Point Pleasant. Died in Bedford Co. Was Brig Gen after war. Great-great-granddaughter Margaret W. Juny appl pen 17 Jun 1858 Christian Co, KY. Pen says d 1782. R6308. DAR Monument **P:** Y **BLW:** unk **RG:** Y **MK:** Y **PH:** unk **SS:** J-NSSAR 1993 Reg; K Vol 3 pg 120; AZ various pages; CG pg 2066; DD DAR Ancestor #A069714 **BS:** JLARC 1, 4, 41.

LEWIS, Andrew Jr; b Oct 1758; d 25 Sep 1844 **RU:** Private, Served in VA Line. Ent serv Botetourt Co **CEM:** King; GPS unk; Bent Mountain, S fr Roanoke; Roanoke Co **GS:** U **SP:** Mar (10 Jun 1788) Margaret Briant (c1766 Botetourt Co.-__) **VI:** Sol appl pen 29 Apr 1833 Montgomery Co. Widow appl pen 22 Jan 1845 Montgomery Co. W3431 **P:** Y **BLW:** unk **RG:** unk **MK:** unk **PH:** unk **SS:** K Vol 3 pg 120; CG pg 2065 **BS:** JLARC 2, 4,109.

LEWIS, Benjamin; b Nov 1763; d 25 Sep 1824 **RU:** Sergeant, Served in Illinois & Western Army under Gen George Rogers Clark 1778-1783 **CEM:** Lewis Family; GPS 38.80276, -77.96242; Woodstock Plantation, Meredithville; Brunswick **GS:** Y **SP:** Mar (8 Sep 1787 Brunswick Co (bond) by Rev Thomas Lundie) Elizabeth Edmunds, d/o John Flood & (-----) Edwards **VI:** Son of Zebulon and Sandal (Jackson) Lewis **P:** unk **BLW:** unk **RG:** unk **MK:** N **PH:** unk **SS:** G pg 697 **BS:** 196.

LEWIS, Benjamin; b unk; d 1781 **RU:** Soldier, Served fr NJ, and died fr the battle at Yorktown **CEM:** Yorktown Victory Monument Tablet; GPS 38.28350, -78.54150; Yorktown; York **GS:** U **SP:** No info **VI:** No further data **P:** unk **BLW:** unk **RG:** unk **MK:** unk **PH:** unk **SS:** J-Yorktown Historian **BS:** JLARC 74.

LEWIS, Betty (Washington); b 20 Jun 1773, Westmoreland Co; d 31 Mar 1797 **RU:** Patriot, With husband's death as only heir she gave the use of a warehouse in Fredericksburg for militia use **CEM:** Western View; GPS unk; 17434 Boldaker Ln; Culpeper **GS:** Y **SP:** Mar (7 May 1750 Fredericksburg) Fielding Lewis (7 Jul 1725 Warner Hall, Gloucester Co-7 Dec 1781 Fredericksburg) s/o John & Frances (Fielding) Lewis **VI:** Daughter of Augustine Washington (1694-1743) & Mary Ball (c1708-1789). DAR. Sister of President George Washington. Died at home of her daughter at "Western View" Culpeper Co **P:** N **BLW:** N **RG:** N **MK:** N **PH:** unk **SS:** D Vol 3 pg 866 **BS:** 32 Lyman; 196.

LEWIS, Charles; b 1730 or c1744; d 1779 **RU:** Colonel, Served in VA Cont Line. As Capt commanded an Infantry Co fr Albemarle Co Apr-Jun 1775. Commissioned Col of 2d Bn of Minutemen,10 May 1776. Serv as Col 14th Cont Line 12 Nov 1776. Killed by Shawnee Indians **CEM:** Berry Hill; GPS unk; 1.5 mi N of Sweet Briar College; Albemarle **GS:** Y **SP:** Mary Randolph **VI:** Awarded BLW of 6666 acres. Died in Canada **P:** unk **BLW:** Y **RG:** N **MK:** N **PH:** unk **SS:** BY pg 225; E pg 471; CE pg 10, 14 **BS:** 161 Berry Hill.

LEWIS, Edward; b 1747; d 6 Jan 1800 **RU:** Private, VA service, specifics not identified **CEM:** Old Christ Church Episcopal; GPS 38.80625, -77.04718; 118 N Washington St; Alexandria City **GS:** Y **SP:** No info **VI:** Died age 53. Perhaps son of Patrick Lewis. Recd pen 1787 **P:** unk **BLW:** unk **RG:** Y **MK:** N **PH:** unk **SS:** G pg 720, plus **BS:** 20 pg 138.

RU=Rank/Unit   CEM=Cemetery   GS=Gravestone   SP=Spousal Information
VI=Other Veteran Info   P=Pension   BLW=Bounty/Land Warrant   RG=Registered Grave
MK=SAR/DAR Marker   PH=Photo   SS=Service Source   BS=Burial Source

201

LEWIS, Edward; b Dec 1760; d 13 Oct 1828 **RU:** Soldier, Was incapacitated by his war service **CEM:** Lewis Family; GPS unk; 712 Heidleback School Rd, Dodson; Patrick **GS:** Y **SP:** Nancy Price (1759 Orange Co.-30 Dec 1835) d/o William (1726-1807) & Mary (Moore) Price **VI:** Son of Charles & Elizabeth (Parham) Lewis. Pen. Patrick Co, 27 Feb 1801 **P:** Y **BLW:** unk **RG:** unk **MK:** unk **PH:** unk **SS:** G pg 712 **BS:** JLARC 30; 196.

LEWIS, Fielding; b 7 Jul 1725, Warner Hall, Gloucester Co; d Dec 1781 **RU:** Patriot, Was church leader, judge, County Lt, Chairman Committees of Correspondence and Safety, Director of Defense of the Rappahannock, Commissioner of Gun Manufactory **CEM:** St George's Episcopal; GPS unk; 905 Princess Anne; Fredericksburg City **GS:** N **SP:** 1) Mar (18 Oct 1748) Catharine Washington (11 Feb 1723/4-19 Feb 1749/50) d/o John & Catharine (Whiting) Washingto; 2) Mar (7 May 1750, Stafford Co) Elizabeth "Betty" Washington (20 Jun 1733 Wakefield, Westmoreland Co-31 Mar 1797 Western View, Culpeper Co) d/o Augustine & Mary (Ball) Washington. Bur in Culpeper Co. **VI:** Cenotaph. Son of John (1694-1754) & Frances (Fielding) (1701-1731) Lewis. Washington's brother-in-law. Not bur at St Georges Church in Fredericksburg. Bur in Clarke Co but memorialized at St Georges Cemetery in Fredericksburg. **P:** unk **BLW:** unk **RG:** Y **MK:** N **PH:** N **SS:** D Spotsylvania Co & Fredericksburg **BS:** JLARC 1, 2, 91; 196.

LEWIS, George Washington; b 13 Mar 1757, Fredericksburg; d 13 Nov 1821 **RU:** Captain/Lieutenant, Served in 3rd Regt, Light Dragoons. On 12 Mar 1776, Gen Washington created the "Commander-in-Chief Guard" and appt Capt Caleb Gibbs as Commandant & George Lewis as 1st Lt as Second in Command. (George Lewis was 19). Was in 2nd & 3rd Cont Dragoons. Resigned as Capt 1779 **CEM:** Willis Hill, Fredericksburg National Military Park; GPS unk; Marye Heights; Fredericksburg City **GS:** Y **SP:** Mar (15 Oct 1779) Catherine Daingerfield (1764-1820), d/o Col William & (-----) Daingerfield, Commander of 7th VA Regt of Cont Line. **VI:** Son of Col Fielding (1725-1781) & Betty (Washington) (1733-1797) Lewis. George Washington's nephew. Attended Princeton College. When Pres. Washington died, he gave George Lewis first choice of swords. Died at Kenmore Plantation, Fredericksburg. DAR marker **P:** unk **BLW:** unk **RG:** Y **MK:** Y **PH:** unk **SS:** D Fredericksburg **BS:** JLARC 76, 91.

LEWIS, Jesse Pitman; b 13 May 1763. Albemarle Co; d 1849 **RU:** Soldier, Served in VA Line. Ent serv Albemarle Co **CEM:** Lewis Family, University Heights; GPS 38.02390, -78.31000; Jct 250 W and Colonnade Dr, nr Old Ivy Rd; Charlottesville City **GS:** U **SP:** Nancy (-----) **VI:** Sol appl pen 13 Oct 1832 Albemarle Co. S5680, DAR marker **P:** Y **BLW:** unk **RG:** unk **MK:** unk **PH:** unk **SS:** CG pg 2069 **BS:** JLARC 2, 4.

LEWIS, John; b 1749; d 1797 **RU:** Captain, Appt Capt 1 Nov 1777. Resigned 1780 **CEM:** Lewis Family; GPS unk; Nr Staunton; Augusta **GS:** N **SP:** No info **VI:** Awarded 5000 acres bounty land **P:** unk **BLW:** Y **RG:** N **MK:** N **PH:** N **SS:** E pg 471-2 **BS:** 80 vol 3 pg 21.

LEWIS, John T; b 1757 (per pen info, b 1761); d 1835 **RU:** Private?, Served in VA Line. Ent serv Mecklenberg Co **CEM:** Lewis Family; GPS unk; Rt 727; Mecklenburg **GS:** Y **SP:** No info **VI:** Sol appl pen 19 Aug 1835 Halifax Co, age 74. S10249 **P:** Y **BLW:** unk **RG:** N **MK:** N **PH:** unk **SS:** K Vol 3 pg 122; CG pg 2070 **BS:** 54 pg 366.

LEWIS, Mary; b 24 Jul 1742, Albemarle Co; d 9 Feb 1824 **RU:** Patriot, Gave material aid to the cause **CEM:** Riverview; GPS 38.02610, -78.45810; 1701 Chesapeake St; Charlottesville City **GS:** Y **SP:** Mar (2 Nov 1808, Charlottesville) Nicholas Lewis (19 Jan 1734, Henrico Co-8 Dec 1808 Charlottesville) **VI:** Daug of Dr Thomas & Mildred (Thornton) Walker **P:** unk **BLW:** unk **RG:** unk **MK:** unk **PH:** unk **SS:** Al Ct Bk pg 28 Albemarle Co **BS:** 196.

LEWIS, Nicholas; b 19 Jan 1734; d 8 Dec 1808 **RU:** Colonel, Commanded a co of Militiamen in Albemarle Co 1776-7. Later became Col of Co Militia there in 1781 **CEM:** Lewis-Clarkson; GPS 38.04407, -78.51706; Collonade Dr; Charlottesville City **GS:** N **SP:** Mary Walker (24 Jul 1742-9 Feb 1824) d/o Dr Thomas (1715-1794) & Mildred (Thornton) (1734 1808) Walker **VI:** Son of Robert (1704-1765) & Jane Meriwether (1705-1757) Lewis. Stone is no longer visible **P:** unk **BLW:** unk **RG:** unk **MK:** unk **PH:** N **SS:** E pg 472 **BS:** 200 William & Mary Quarterly; JLARC 2; 196.

RU=Rank/Unit	CEM=Cemetery	GS=Gravestone	SP=Spousal Information
VI=Other Veteran Info	P=Pension	BLW=Bounty/Land Warrant	RG=Registered Grave
MK=SAR/DAR Marker	PH=Photo	SS=Service Source	BS=Burial Source

202

LEWIS, Taliaferro; b 4 Feb 1754; d 12 Jul 1810 **RU:** Corporal, Served in 9 VA Cav. Was at battle at Germantown, taken prisoner **CEM:** Lewis Family, University Heights; GPS 38.02390,-78.31000; Jct 250 W and Colonnade Dr, nr Old Ivy Rd; Charlottesville City **GS:** Y **SP:** No info **VI:** Son of John Terrell (1728-1784) & Sarah (Taliaferro) (1728-1789) Lewis. Govt issue marker and old stone. **P:** unk **BLW:** unk **RG:** N **MK:** N **PH:** unk **SS:** E pg 472 **BS:** JLARC 2; 67 vol 1 pg 153.

LEWIS, Thomas; b 27 Apr 1718, County Donegal, Ulster, Ireland; d 31 Jan 1790 **RU:** Patriot, Was Delegate to 3rd, 4th, 5th VA Conventions 1775-1776 and voted for independence. Was Delegate to VA Contitutional Convention June 1778 and voted for US Constitution **CEM:** Lewis Family; GPS unk; Rt 708 & 340; Rockingham **GS:** Y **SP:** Mar (26 Jan 1749) Jane Strother (1732, Stafford Co-19 Sep 1820) **VI:** Died at Lynnwood, Rt 1, Port Republic **P:** N **BLW:** N **RG:** Y **MK:** Y **PH:** Y **SS:** DAR #A070144; X **BS:** 04.

LEWIS, Thomas; b 26 Jan 1760; d Aft 1832 **RU:** Private, Ent serv Augusta Co, that part that is now Rockingham. Served in VA Line **CEM:** Western State Hospital; GPS 38.14299, -79.06571; Village Dr; Staunton City **GS:** N **SP:** No info **VI:** Sol appl pen 20 Aug 1832. S7138 **P:** Y **BLW:** unk **RG:** N **MK:** N **PH:** N **SS:** E pg 472; CG pg 2073 **BS:** 80 pg 22; 196.

LEWIS, Thomas Walker; b 24 Jun 1763; d 7 Jun 1807 **RU:** Private, SAR registration did not provide service **CEM:** Lewis-Clarkson; GPS 38.04407, -78.51706; Collonade Dr; Charlottesville City **GS:** Y **SP:** Elizabeth Meriwether (24 Feb 1771 Albemarle Co-17 Apr 1855 Lincoln Co, Missouri) d/o Nicholas & Margaret (Douglas) Meriwether **VI:** Son of Nicolas (1734-1808) & Mary (Walker) (1742-1824) Lewis. Stone is no longer visible **P:** unk **BLW:** unk **RG:** unk **MK:** unk **PH:** unk **SS:** AR Vol 3 pg 22; NSSAR Ancestor #P-236185 **BS:** JLARC 2; 196.

LEWIS, Warner II; b c1747; d 1791 **RU:** Captain/Patriot, Served as County Lt of Gloucester 1775 and was officer in Gloucester Co Militia **CEM:** Warner Hall; GPS 37.20403, -76.28539; 4750 Warner Hall Rd; Gloucester **GS:** Y **SP:** 1) Mary Criswell 2) Mary Fleming **VI:** No further data **P:** unk **BLW:** unk **RG:** Y **MK:** N **PH:** Y **SS:** E pg 473 **BS:** 32.

LEWIS, William; b 1748; d 14 Nov 1779 **RU:** Lieutenant, Served in 1st Regt. Was Sgt in an independent Co of Albemarle Co 1775. Member of Lee's Legion **CEM:** Clover Fields; GPS unk; Rt 22 NE off I-64, W of Charlottesville; Charlottesville City **GS:** Y **SP:** Lucy Meriweather, d/o Thomas Merweather & Elizabeth Thornton, b, 4 Feb 1752, d 8 Sep 1837. She m(2) ----- Marks; bur at Locust Hill, Ivy, Albemarle Co **VI:** Son of Robert Lewis & Jane Meriweather. Stone indicates "1740-1780" which was erected by the DAR. BLW states he d 14 Nov 1779 at battle of Yorktown (Battle was in Oct 1781).Is Meriwether Lewis' father. BLW 12308 issued 12 Nov 1791 **P:** unk **BLW:** Y **RG:** unk **MK:** Y **PH:** unk **SS:** K Vol 3 pg 125; BY pg 317; CF pg 10 **BS:** JLARC 2, 4, 58; 196.

LEWIS, William; b 1750; d 1824 or 1830 **RU:** Private, Probably served in Clark's Illinois Regt fr VA; possibly at Ft Nelson **CEM:** Lewis Family; GPS unk; Little Georgetown; Fauquier **GS:** Y **SP:** Ann Montgomery (3 Sep 1759 - __), daughter of Capt Wm & Catherine (Morris) Montgomery of Prince William Co **VI:** A Maj by this name served in 3rd VA Regt of Foot 12 Feb 1781-1 Jan 1783 as POW taken at Charleston, SC **P:** unk **BLW:** unk **RG:** Y **MK:** unk **PH:** unk **SS:** J-NSSAR 1993 Reg; AK; CE pg 39 **BS:** JLARC 1; 04; 18 pg 137.

LEWIS, William J; b 4 Jul 1766, Augusta Co; d 1 Nov 1828 **RU:** Private, Serv at Ft Nelson in Portsmouth in 1782 **CEM:** Mt Athos; GPS unk; Rt 460, Kelly; Campbell **GS:** N **SP:** Elizabeth Cabel (1773-1855) **VI:** Son of William (1724-1811) & Ann (Montgomery) (1737-1808) Lewis. US Congressman 1817-1819. VA House of Delegates. 1800 built "Mount Athos" above James River in Campbell Co **P:** unk **BLW:** unk **RG:** unk **MK:** N **PH:** N **SS:** E pg 473 **BS:** 196.

LIEBERT, Jean; b unk; d 1781 **RU:** Soldier, Served in Santogne Bn and died fr battle at Yorktown **CEM:** French Memorial; GPS 36.81944, -79.39933; Yorktown; York **GS:** U **SP:** No info **VI:** No further data **P:** unk **BLW:** unk **RG:** Y **MK:** unk **PH:** unk **SS:** J-Yorktown Historian **BS:** JLARC 1, 74.

LIGHT, Peter; b unk; d 30 Nov 1813 **RU:** Patriot, Gave material aid to cause **CEM:** Back Creek Quaker, aka Gainesboro United Methodist; GPS 39.27861, -78.25694; 166 Siler Ln, Gainesboro; Frederick **GS:** Y **SP:** Catherine (-----) **VI:** No further data **P:** N **BLW:** N **RG:** unk **MK:** unk **PH:** unk **SS:** AL Ct Bk 1 pg 25, 28 Berkeley Co, VA (now WVA) **BS:** 196.

RU=Rank/Unit	CEM=Cemetery	GS=Gravestone	SP=Spousal Information
VI=Other Veteran Info	P=Pension	BLW=Bounty/Land Warrant	RG=Registered Grave
MK=SAR/DAR Marker	PH=Photo	SS=Service Source	BS=Burial Source

203

LIGHTFOOT, Mildred Howell; b Feb 1752, Charles City Co; d 01 May 1799 **RU:** Patriot, Gave material aid to cause **CEM:** Coles-Carrington; GPS unk; Mildendo Plantation; Halifax **GS:** U **SP:** Walter Coles (14 Nov 1739-07 Nov 1780) **VI:** No further data **P:** N **BLW:** N **RG:** unk **MK:** unk **PH:** unk **SS:** AL Ct Bk pg 58 Halifax Co **BS:** 196.

LIGHTFOOT, William; b 1758, James City Co; d 1809 **RU:** Lieutenant/Patriot, Gave material aid to cause **CEM:** Lightfoot Family; GPS unk; Teddington, Sandy Point; Charles City Co **GS:** Y **SP:** Mar (c1795) Lucy Armistead Digges (c1773, James City Co-__) d/o Cole (31 Dec 1748-__) Martha (Walker) Digges of Hampton **VI:** No further data **P:** unk **BLW:** unk **RG:** Y **MK:** unk **PH:** unk **SS:** J-NSSAR 1993 Reg; AL Ct Bk pg 13, 14, 18 Charles City Co **BS:** JLARC 1; 196.

LIGNOT, Pierre; b unk; d 1781 **RU:** Soldier, Served in Agenois Bn and died fr battle at Yorktown **CEM:** French Memorial; GPS 36.81944, -79.39933; Yorktown; York **GS:** U **SP:** No info **VI:** No further data **P:** unk **BLW:** unk **RG:** Y **MK:** unk **PH:** unk **SS:** J-Yorktown Historian **BS:** JLARC 1, 74.

LILLARD, Benjamin; b c1740, Orange Co; d 26 Mar 1829 **RU:** Captain/Patriot, Commanded a co in Culpeper Co Militia. Furnished supplies to the Cont Army **CEM:** Hot Mountain; GPS unk; Nethers; Rappahannock **GS:** U **SP:** Mar (c1772) Frances Crow (__-26 Apr 1832, Madison Co) **VI:** Died in Madison Co **P:** unk **BLW:** unk **RG:** Y **MK:** unk **PH:** unk **SS:** J-NSSAR 2000 Reg; DD; DAR #A070354 **BS:** JLARC 76.

LILLARD, James; b c1725 or c1735, Spotsylvania Co; d 1804 **RU:** Patriot, Gave material aid to cause **CEM:** Lillard Family; GPS unk; Nethers; Madison **GS:** N **SP:** Keziah Bradley **VI:** No further data **P:** N **BLW:** N **RG:** Y **MK:** Y **PH:** N **SS:** AL Ct Bk 1 pg 14, 29 Culpeper Co **BS:** 04.

LINCOLN, Jacob; b 18 Nov 1751, Carnavon, PA; d 20 Feb 1822 **RU:** Lieutenant, Ent serv 1781. Served in Capt Abraham Lincoln's Co, Rockingham Co Militia, 26 Mar 1781 **CEM:** Lincoln Family; GPS 36.68726, -82.56917; 7884 Harpine Rd Rt 42, Linville, 3 mi S of Broadway on SR 42, N of Edom exit.; Rockingham **GS:** Y **SP:** Mar (Aug 1870) Dorcas Robertson (15 Mar 1822-25 Jan 1840) **VI:** SAR marker Widow R6347 **P:** Y **BLW:** unk **RG:** unk **MK:** Y **PH:** Y **SS:** E pg 475; K Vol 3 pg 128 **BS:** JLARC 4, 64.

LINDSAY, Reuben; b 15 Jan 1747, Caroline Co; d 7 Nov 1831 **RU:** Colonel/Patriot, Was commander of Caroline Co Militia. Gave material aid to cause **CEM:** Lidsay Family, Springfield Farm; GPS unk; W fr Gordonsville; Orange **GS:** U **SP:** Mar (1778) Sarah Walker (__Castle Hill, Albemarle Co- __) **VI:** No further data **P:** unk **BLW:** unk **RG:** Y **MK:** unk **PH:** unk **SS:** J-NSSAR 1993 Reg, J- DAR Hatcher; DAR #A070619; AL Ct Bk 1 pg 11 Albemarle Co **BS:** JLARC 1,2.

LINDSAY, Thomas; b 13 Nov 1750, "The Mount"; d 14 Sep 1830 **RU:** Patriot, Gave material aid to the cause **CEM:** The Mount; GPS unk; 2312 Col Lindsey Ct, Falls Church; Fairfax **GS:** Y **SP:** No info **VI:** No further data **P:** N **BLW:** N **RG:** N **MK:** N **PH:** unk **SS:** AL Ct Bk pg 4, 13 **BS:** 61 vol III pg FC-40.

LINDSAY, William; b Mar 1742; d 15 Sep 1792 **RU:** Major, Served in 1st Cont Lt Dragoons Regt. Wounded 31 Mar 1777 near Valley Forge 20 Jan 1778, then assigned Lee's Corps of Partisan Lt Dragoons. Appt Maj Mar 1781 in 1st VA State Legion. Wounded again at Bulford Ct House May 1781. **CEM:** Laurel Hill; GPS 38.70961, -77.23464; Ground of former Lorton Reformatory, Lorton; Fairfax **GS:** Y **SP:** No info **VI:** Recd BLW 4000 acres 26 Jun 1783. DAR & SAR markers **P:** unk **BLW:** unk **RG:** unk **MK:** Y **PH:** Y **SS:** E pg 225; F pg 45; AK-GW Chap 2014 **BS:** 04.

LINDSAY, William; b 1742; d 15 Sep 1792 **RU:** Major, Recd as Maj 9 Nov 1780, Fairfax Co Militia. severely wounded at Guilford CH; Served in Taylor's Legion **CEM:** Lindsay Family; GPS 38.70958, -77.23767; Off Lorton Rd nr Laurel Golf Club, Lorton; Fairfax **GS:** Y **SP:** Mar (c1766) Ann Calvert (1751-1822) **VI:** Older Govt stone, does not give birth yr **P:** unk **BLW:** unk **RG:** Y **MK:** Y **PH:** Y **SS:** E pg 476 **BS:** JLARC 1 ,2, 14, 27, 28; 196.

LINGAN, James McCubbin; b 13 May 1751, MD; d 28 Jul 1812 **RU:** Bridgadier General, Capt MD Line. 2nd Lt of Stephenson's MD & VA Rifle Regt. Fought at Long Island, York Island, Ft Washington. Wounded & taken prisoner at Ft Washington Nov 1776 aboard British ship Jersey, exchanged Oct 1780; retired Jan 1781 **CEM:** Arlington National; GPS 38.88377, -77.06535; Jefferson Davis Hwy Rt 110; Arlington **GS:** Y **SP:** Janet Henderson (2 Sep 1765-5 Jul 1832) **VI:** Collector of port of Georgetown. Free speech advocate who defended Alexander Hanson, publisher of the Federal Republican & Commercial

RU=Rank/Unit   CEM=Cemetery   GS=Gravestone   SP=Spousal Information
VI=Other Veteran Info   P=Pension   BLW=Bounty/Land Warrant   RG=Registered Grave
MK=SAR/DAR Marker   PH=Photo   SS=Service Source   BS=Burial Source

204

Gazette, who criticized US for participation in War of 1812 and was killed by angry mob who stormed the publisher's offices. Died in Baltimore, MD. Originally bur Washington DC, reinterred 5 Nov 1908. BLW #1294-300-19 Mar 1792 **P:** unk **BLW:** Y **RG:** Y **MK:** Y **PH:** unk **SS:** J-NSSAR 1993 Reg; CG pg 2087 **BS:** JLARC 1; 196.

LINK, Matthias; b 11 Feb 1737, PA; d 8 Feb 1815 **RU:** Patriot, Gave material aid to cause **CEM:** Old Link; GPS unk; .5 mi W of Ft Defiance; Augusta **GS:** U **SP:** Mary Christiana Schmidt (c1746 MD-12 Jun 1817) **VI:** No further data **P:** N **BLW:** N **RG:** unk **MK:** unk **PH:** unk **SS:** DAR Ancestor #132196; DD cites Augusta Co Ct Bk pg ? **BS:** 225.

LINN, William Sr; b unk; d 1808 **RU:** Patriot, Gave material aid to cause **CEM:** Linn Family Farm; GPS unk; Morgantown; Fauquier **GS:** U **SP:** No info **VI:** No further data **P:** N **BLW:** N **RG:** unk **MK:** unk **PH:** unk **SS:** J- DAR Hatcher; AL Lists pg 9 Fauquier Co **BS:** JLARC 2.

LINSEY, Stephen; b unk; d 1781 **RU:** Soldier, Served fr MA, and died fr the battle at Yorktown **CEM:** Yorktown Victory Monument Tablet; GPS 38.28350, -78.54150; Yorktown; York **GS:** U **SP:** No info **VI:** No further data **P:** unk **BLW:** unk **RG:** unk **MK:** unk **PH:** unk **SS:** J-Yorktown Historian **BS:** JLARC 74.

LIPSCOMB, John; b 1756; d 28 Sep 1824 **RU:** Private, Served in VA Cont Line. Ent serv King William Co 1778 **CEM:** Meadow Hill Estate; GPS unk; Off Rt 613, 1.8 mi N of Luck's Store; Spotsylvania **GS:** Y **SP:** Mar (24 Dec 1783 King William Co) Elizabeth Lipscomb (c1761-__) d/o Ambrose & (-----) Lipscomb **VI:** Sol appl pen 27 May 1819 King William Co. age 67. Widow appl pen 25 Feb 1839 King William Co. W5323 **P:** Y **BLW:** unk **RG:** N **MK:** N **PH:** unk **SS:** B; K Vol 3 pg 132; CG pg 2091 **BS:** 09 grid 71.

LIPSCOMB, Thomas; b 1730, Albemarle Co; d 1799 **RU:** Captain, Served in 7th Cont Line as Ens 28 Oct 1776. Resigned 20 May 1778 **CEM:** Meadow Hill Estate; GPS unk; Off Rt 613, 1.8 mi N of Luck's Store; Spotsylvania **GS:** Y **SP:** Dorothy (-----) (__-aft 1799) as widow mar Thomas's brother Archibald Lipscomb. Another soldier same name (__-12 Jun 1825 Spotsylvania Co) mar Mary Smith (14 Dec 1733-__) relation not determined. **VI:** Son of Anderson & (-----) Lipscomb. Anderson was a delegate in the VA Assembly. Pen spouse Dorothy. BLW 2,666 acres **P:** Y **BLW:** Y **RG:** Y **MK:** N **PH:** unk **SS:** E pg 478; BG pg 2091 **BS:** 09 part 2.

LITTLEPAGE, Lewis; b 19 Dec 1762, Hanover Co; d 19 Jul 1802 **RU:** Soldier/Statesman, Was in VA & US Govt. Was one of William and Mary College students at Williamsburg that fought British raids spring 1779. Member Jay Commission to Spain. American volunteer in Monorcan Campaign 1781-82 which captured Minorca fr GB **CEM:** Masonic Cemetery; GPS 38.30198, -77.46142; 900 Charles St; Fredericksburg City **GS:** Y **SP:** No info **VI:** Son of Col James & Elizabeth (Lewis) (09 Oct 1732-1809) Littlepage **P:** unk **BLW:** unk **RG:** Y **MK:** N **PH:** Y **SS:** O **BS:** 13 Gr 183; 196.

LITTON, Martha (Duncan); b 22 Sep 1756, Lancaster Co, PA; d 21 Mar 1821 **RU:** Patriot, Was POW in Canada in 1780-1783 during Rev War **CEM:** Soloman Litton Hollow; GPS unk; nr Pinnacle Preserve; Russell **GS:** Y **SP:** Solomon Caleb Litton (1751-1814) **VI:** Daughter of Thomas & Elizabeth (Alexander) (1710-1814) Duncan. Died in Whitley Co, KY **P:** N **BLW:** N **RG:** Y **MK:** N **PH:** unk **SS:** AS, SAR regis; BT - DAR marker **BS:** SAR regis; 196.

LITTON (LINTON), Burton Caleb (Caleb Burton) Sr; b 5 Aug 1763, Botetourt Co; d 5 May 1778 **RU:** Private, Served in Capt William Russell's Co, Russell Co Militia **CEM:** Soloman Litton Hollow; GPS unk; nr Pinnacle Preserve; Russell **GS:** U **SP:** No info **VI:** Son of John Richard (1726-1804) & Sarah Ann (Wilcoxen) (1728-1808) Litton. Killed at Glade Hollow Ft, Washington Co by Indians. SAR Gr marker. Govt Gr stone lists service **P:** unk **BLW:** unk **RG:** Y **MK:** Y **PH:** unk **SS:** J-NSSAR 2000 Reg; B; Z pg 152 **BS:** JLARC 76; 196.

LITTON (LINTON), Solomon Caleb Sr; b 1730; d 1843 **RU:** Ensign, Served in Washington Co Militia. Also in Dunmore's War 1774 **CEM:** Soloman Litton Hollow; GPS unk; nr Pinnacle Preserve; Russell **GS:** U **SP:** Marta Duncan **VI:** No further data **P:** unk **BLW:** unk **RG:** Y **MK:** unk **PH:** unk **SS:** J-NSSAR 2000 Reg; E pg 479; Z pg 160 **BS:** JLARC 76.

LITTON (LITION), Thomas W; b 13 May 1754, Botetourt Co; d 11 June 1840 **RU:** Private, Served in Cont Line **CEM:** Soloman Litton Hollow; GPS unk; nr Pinnacle Preserve; Russell **GS:** Y **SP:** Carleen Dempsey (20 Feb 1760-16 Nov 1840) **VI:** Son of John Richard (1726-1804) & Sarah Ann (Wilcoxen)

RU=Rank/Unit   CEM=Cemetery   GS=Gravestone   SP=Spousal Information
VI=Other Veteran Info   P=Pension   BLW=Bounty/Land Warrant   RG=Registered Grave
MK=SAR/DAR Marker   PH=Photo   SS=Service Source   BS=Burial Source

205

(1726-1808) Litton. Govt. Gr stone shows last name as "Lition" but suspect it is in error. SAR marker **P:** unk **BLW:** unk **RG:** N **MK:** Y **PH:** N **SS:** J-NSSAR 2000 Reg; B govt Gr stone **BS:** JLARC 76; 196.

LIVERNOIS, Jacques; b unk; d 1781 **RU:** Soldier, Served in Gatinais Bn and died fr battle at Yorktown **CEM:** French Memorial; GPS 36.81944, -79.39933; Yorktown; York **GS:** U **SP:** No info **VI:** No further data **P:** unk **BLW:** unk **RG:** Y **MK:** unk **PH:** unk **SS:** J-Yorktown Historian **BS:** JLARC 1, 74.

LIVINGSTON, Peter; b 1755, Russell Co; d 1815 **RU:** Captain, Served in VA Militia **CEM:** Livingston Family; GPS 36.67987, -82.35273; Rt 689, Mendota; Scott **GS:** Y **SP:** Elizabeth Head **VI:** Died in Mendota, Scott Co **P:** unk **BLW:** unk **RG:** Y **MK:** Y **PH:** unk **SS:** O **BS:** 04.

LOCKETT, Edmund Sr; b 1755 (pen info says 3 Jun 1761); d 24 Jun 1834 **RU:** Captain, Served in VA Line. Ent serv 1780 Chesterfield Co **CEM:** Lockett Family; GPS unk; Brandermill, cnr of Long Gate & Huntgate; Chesterfield **GS:** U **SP:** Mar (8 Dec 1785 Powhatan Co) Sally Bryant (5 Nov 1762-__), d/o James & Jane (-----) Bryant **VI:** Son of Richard & Mary (-----) Lockett. JP and High Sheriff of Chesterfield Co. Sol appl pen 14 Aug 1832. Widow appl pen 27 Oct 1840 Chesterfield Co. W8064 **P:** Y **BLW:** unk **RG:** unk **MK:** N **PH:** unk **SS:** K Vol 3 pg 136; CG pg 2102 **BS:** JLARC 4, 12, 35.

LOCKHART, Patrick; b 1749; d 1810 **RU:** Major, Promoted to Maj 12 Jul 1781 **CEM:** Fincastle Presbyterian; GPS 37.50017, -79.87558; 108 E Back St, Fincastle; Botetourt **GS:** N **SP:** No info **VI:** Name is on the SAR plaque at this cemetery **P:** unk **BLW:** unk **RG:** Y **MK:** Y **PH:** N **SS:** AZ pg 192, J-NSSAR 1993 Reg; J- DAR Hatcher **BS:** 196; JLARC 1, 2.

LOCKRIDGE, Andrew; b 1755; d 1791 **RU:** Major, Served in 2nd Battalion, Rockbridge Co Militia 15 Sep 1788-Oct 1779 **CEM:** Rocky Spring Presbyterian; GPS 38.11470, -79.24250; 1 mi S of Deerfield; Augusta **GS:** N **SP:** Mar (6 Apr 1762) Jane Graham (1742 Augusta Co-1796) **VI:** No further data **P:** unk **BLW:** unk **RG:** unk **MK:** N **PH:** N **SS:** DAR #A071780; E pg 480; AZ pg 82, 93; 183 **BS:** JLARC 62, 103.

LOGAN, James; b 1733 Lurgan, Ireland; d 19 Jun 1825 **RU:** Patriot, Gave material aid to cause **CEM:** New Monmouth Presbyterian; GPS 37.83960, -79.48586; 2343 West Midland Rd; Lexington City **GS:** U **SP:** Mar (c1765) Hannah Erwin (Irwin) **VI:** Died in Rockbridge Co **P:** N **BLW:** N **RG:** unk **MK:** unk **PH:** unk **SS:** NSSAR Ancestor #P-237841 **BS:** JLARC 2.

LOGAN, James; b 1755; d 1825 **RU:** Private, Served in 4th, 8th, & 12th Cont Lines **CEM:** New Monmouth Presbyterian; GPS 37.83960, -79.48586; 2343 West Midland Rd; Lexington City **GS:** U **SP:** No info **VI:** No further data **P:** unk **BLW:** unk **RG:** unk **MK:** unk **PH:** unk **SS:** J- DAR Hatcher; E pg 481 **BS:** JLARC 2.

LOGAN, John; b 26 Dec 1767; d 9 Jan 1837 **RU:** Private, Served in Capt McCutchen's Co, Augusta Co Militia **CEM:** Bethel Presbyterian; GPS 38.04257, -79.17283; 563 Bethel Green Rd, Middlebrook; Augusta **GS:** Y **SP:** Mar (30 Aug 179_ Augusta Co) Rachel McPheeters (28 Dec 1774-16 Dec 1849) d/o Rev William (1729-1807) and Rachel (Moore) (__-1826) McPheeters **VI:** Son of James (1733-1825) & Hannah (Irvine) (1747-1826) Logan **P:** unk **BLW:** unk **RG:** unk **MK:** unk **PH:** unk **SS:** E pg 481 **BS:** JLARC 62, 63; 196.

LOGAN, Robert; b 1755; d 9 Oct 1828 **RU:** Drummer, Served in Capt Thomas Moultrie's 6th Co, Col Francis Marion's Regt Cont Line, Nov 1779 **CEM:** Fincastle Presbyterian; GPS 37.50017, -79.87558; 108 E Back St, Fincastle; Botetourt **GS:** Y **SP:** Margaret (-----) (c1781-10 May 1830) **VI:** Minister of church 30 yrs. Name is on the SAR plaque at this cemetery **P:** unk **BLW:** unk **RG:** N **MK:** Y **PH:** unk **SS:** A pg 292 **BS:** 196.

LOGAN, William; b 1740; d 26 May 1812 **RU:** Private, Served in 8th and 12th Cont Line **CEM:** Logan Family; GPS unk; Off Rt 672, NE jct with Rt 666, .4 mi on private Rd; Halifax **GS:** Y **SP:** Nancy Sydnor (25 Sep 1764-2 Dec 1826) **VI:** Will indicated burial in cem at residence. BLW # 7761, 100 acres **P:** unk **BLW:** Y **RG:** unk **MK:** unk **PH:** unk **SS:** C pg 318, 467; E pg 481 **BS:** 198.

LOGWOOD, Thomas; b 1740, Henrico Co; d 10 Sep 1821 **RU:** Major/Patriot, Commanded a company in Bedford Co Militia. Gave material aid to cause **CEM:** Logwood Family; GPS unk; Locust Hill; Bedford **GS:** U **SP:** Mar (c1775) Ann Aiken (__Chesterfield Co-1815 Bedford Co) **VI:** No further data **P:** unk

RU=Rank/Unit	CEM=Cemetery	GS=Gravestone	SP=Spousal Information
VI=Other Veteran Info	P=Pension	BLW=Bounty/Land Warrant	RG=Registered Grave
MK=SAR/DAR Marker	PH=Photo	SS=Service Source	BS=Burial Source

206

BLW: unk **RG:** Y **MK:** N **PH:** unk **SS:** J-NSSAR 1993 Reg, J- DAR Hatcher; DAR #A071176; D Vol 1, pg 100, 102, 103, 112, 115; E pg 481 **BS:** JLARC 1, 2.

LOHR, Johan Peter; b 25 Jan 1756, Codorus Furnace, York Co, PA; d 21 Sep 1841 **RU:** Soldier, Served in MD Line. Ent serv Hagerstown MD 1776. Was buried with military honors **CEM:** Trinity Episcopal; GPS 38.14917, -79.07521; 214 Beverley St; Staunton City **GS:** U **SP:** 1) Catherine Eyler 2) Elizabeth Satzer **VI:** Son of Johan George & Maria Margaretta (-----) Lohr. Moved to Maryland as a small child. Moved to Augusta Co VA c1790. Appl pen 24 Sep 1832. S5699 **P:** Y **BLW:** unk **RG:** unk **MK:** unk **PH:** unk **SS:** K Vol 3 pg 138; CG pg 2107 **BS:** JLARC 2, 4 ,62.

LOMAX, Thomas; b 1746 or 1755; d 1811 **RU:** Major, Served in Caroline Co, VA Militia **CEM:** Lomax-White; GPS unk; Rt 758, Port Tobago; Caroline **GS:** N **SP:** Ann Corbin Taylor (__-1835) **VI:** Son of Lunsford & Judith (-----) Lomax **P:** unk **BLW:** unk **RG:** Y **MK:** N **PH:** N **SS:** E pg 481; H **BS:** 02 pg 101.

LONG, John; b 1742; d 14 Feb 1807 **RU:** Private, Served in Capt James McDaniel's Co, Montgomery Co Militia **CEM:** Thornrose; GPS 38,15120, -79.08460; 1041 W Beverly St; Staunton City **GS:** Y **SP:** No info **VI:** Son of James & Johanna (H-----) Long. **P:** N **BLW:** N **RG:** N **MK:** N **PH:** N **SS:** G pg 236 **BS:** 196.

LONG, Joseph Sr; b 8 Sep 1744 (bapt 16 Sep 1774); d 15 Jun 1829 **RU:** Captain, Commanded a company in Augusta Co Militia, Oct 1782. Served in Battle of Point Pleasant 1794 **CEM:** Tinkling Spring Presbyterian; GPS 38.08472, -78.98278; 30 Tinkling Spring Dr, Fishersville; Augusta **GS:** Y **SP:** Catherine Long (16 Feb 1762-Nov 1836) **VI:** Son of William Long (1715-1781), DAR plaque **P:** unk **BLW:** unk **RG:** Y **MK:** Y **PH:** unk **SS:** E pg 482 **BS:** JLARC 1, 4, 62; Wilson, HM, The Tinkling Spring Headwater of Freedom, the Church & Her People, pub 1954 pg 185, 464; 196.

LONG, Mary; b c1755; d 10 Apr 1797 **RU:** Patriot, Gave material aid to cause **CEM:** Friedens United Church of Christ; GPS 38.34848, -78.87653; 3960 Friedens Church Rd; Rockingham **GS:** U **SP:** John Long **VI:** No further data **P:** N **BLW:** N **RG:** unk **MK:** unk **PH:** unk **SS:** DAR Newsletter, Sep/Oct 2015 Vol 15 No 5 pg 417 **BS:** 196.

LONG, Philip; b 18 Dec 1742 or 1755; d 5 Feb 1826 **RU:** Private, Served in Capt Michael Reader's Co, Shenandoah Co, and in Clark's Regt in Illinois **CEM:** Long Family Price Farm; GPS unk; Rt 616, Alma; Page **GS:** Y **SP:** 1) Katherine (-----) 2) Elizabeth Arey 3) Mary Hay **VI:** Son of Paul & Mary (Miller) Long. Died in Ft Long, Shenandoah, Rockingham Co. Common monument. **P:** unk **BLW:** unk **RG:** Y **MK:** Y **PH:** unk **SS:** C pg 207, 602; E pg 482 **BS:** JLARC 76, 94; 196.

LONGDEN, John; b c1754 or 1755; d 31 Mar 1830 **RU:** Corporal, Served in Cont & VA Line. Lived in Alexandria at enl. Served in the First Light Dragoons, Lee's Legion **CEM:** Trinity United Methodist; GPS 39.13600, -77.00610; 2911 Cameron Mills Rd; Alexandria City **GS:** Y **SP:** No info **VI:** Son of Ralph Longden. Died age 76. F-S 18033 R 15-81 BLW #423-100-28 19 Apr 1808. Death notice in the Alexandria Gazette 1 Apr 1830 **P:** Y **BLW:** Y **RG:** Y **MK:** N **PH:** unk **SS:** AK; E pg 483; K Vol 3 pg 142; CG pg 2112 **BS:** 04; 23 pg 130.

LORIVAT, Jean; b unk; d 1781 **RU:** Seaman, Served on "Solitaire" and died from Yorktown battle **CEM:** French Memorial; GPS 36.81944, -79.39933; Yorktown; York **GS:** U **SP:** No info **VI:** No further data **P:** unk **BLW:** unk **RG:** Y **MK:** unk **PH:** unk **SS:** J-Yorktown Historian **BS:** JLARC 1, 74.

LORMIER, Augustin; b unk; d 1781 **RU:** Soldier, Served in Touraine Bn and died fr battle at Yorktown **CEM:** French Memorial; GPS 36.81944, -79.39933; Yorktown; York **GS:** U **SP:** No info **VI:** No further data **P:** unk **BLW:** unk **RG:** Y **MK:** unk **PH:** unk **SS:** J-Yorktown Historian **BS:** JLARC 1, 74.

LORRAIN, Georges; b unk; d 1781 **RU:** Soldier, Served in Santogne Bn and died fr battle at Yorktown **CEM:** French Memorial; GPS 36.81944, -79.39933; Yorktown; York **GS:** U **SP:** No info **VI:** No further data **P:** unk **BLW:** unk **RG:** Y **MK:** unk **PH:** unk **SS:** J-Yorktown Historian **BS:** JLARC 1, 74.

LOUIS, Jean; b unk; d 1781 **RU:** Seaman, Served on "Citoyen: and died from Yorktown battle **CEM:** French Memorial; GPS 36.81944, -79.39933; Yorktown; York **GS:** U **SP:** No info **VI:** No further data **P:** unk **BLW:** unk **RG:** Y **MK:** unk **PH:** unk **SS:** J-Yorktown Historian **BS:** JLARC 1, 74.

RU=Rank/Unit CEM=Cemetery GS=Gravestone SP=Spousal Information
VI=Other Veteran Info P=Pension BLW=Bounty/Land Warrant RG=Registered Grave
MK=SAR/DAR Marker PH=Photo SS=Service Source BS=Burial Source

207

LOVE, Charles; b 1748, Charles Co, MD; d 1792 **RU:** Private/Patriot, Served in MD Line. Enlisted 17 Apr 1782. Gave material aid to cause **CEM:** Love Family; GPS 38.43950, -77.40266; Buckland Farm, 6342 Pleasant Colony Ln, Warrenton; Fauquier **GS:** Y **SP:** Mar (c1734) Mary Harris (c1772 Charles City, MD-22 Jul 1757) **VI:** Died in Buckland, Prince William Co ("Buckland" is now in Fauquier Co). GS without data **P:** unk **BLW:** unk **RG:** unk **MK:** Y **PH:** Y **SS:** DAR #A071808; D Vol 3 pg 806; BK MD Settlers & Soldiers 1700-1800 **BS:** Buckland Farm rcds.

LOVE, James; b c1766; d 1846 **RU:** Private, Served in Cumberland Co PA Militia **CEM:** Goose Creek; GPS 39.11250, -77.69527; Rt 772, Lincoln; Loudoun **GS:** Y **SP:** Susanna (-----))1766-25 Jan 1847) **VI:** Stone illegible **P:** unk **BLW:** unk **RG:** unk **MK:** unk **PH:** unk **SS:** Fold 3 Series 5 Vol VI pg 159 **BS:** 196.

LOVE, Samuel; b 1720, Charles Co, MD; d 24 Apr 1787 **RU:** Sergeant/Patriot, Served as Sgt in 3rd Cont Line. Gave beef, a very large amount of flour, meal, milk, cider and a 10-yr-old horse **CEM:** Love Family; GPS 38.43950, -77.40266; Buckland Farm, 6342 Pleasant Colony Ln, Warrenton; Fauquier **GS:** Y **SP:** Rebecca (-----) (__-1821) **VI:** Died in Buckland, Prince William Co ("Buckland" is now in Fauquier Co). Stone broken & nearly illegible. Foot marker initials legible **P:** unk **BLW:** unk **RG:** N **MK:** Y **PH:** Y **SS:** E pg 484 public claims bk **BS:** 94 Buckland Hall.

LOVELACE, Thomas; b 8 Feb 1739, Richmond Co; d 1792 **RU:** Patriot, Gave material aid to cause **CEM:** Lovelace Family; GPS unk; Off Rt 676, W of Asbury Church; Halifax **GS:** U **SP:** Tabitha Oldham d/o James & Tabitha (Haydon) Oldham **VI:** Son of Charles & Bridget (McLaughlin) Lovelace of North Farnham Parish **P:** N **BLW:** N **RG:** unk **MK:** unk **PH:** unk **SS:** AL Ct Bk pg 27,57 **BS:** 215.

LOVELL, Joseph; b c1765, Boston, MA; d 9 Oct 1784 **RU:** Private, Served in MA **CEM:** St John's Episcopal; GPS 37.53183, -77.41958; 2401 E Broad St; Richmond City **GS:** Y **SP:** No info **VI:** No further data **P:** unk **BLW:** unk **RG:** N **MK:** N **PH:** unk **SS:** AJ Vol 9 pg 1008 **BS:** 28 pg 467; 196.

LOVING, William; b 14 Feb 1740, Culpeper Co; d 30 Jan 1792 **RU:** Captain/Patriot, Co Commander in Amherst Co Militia. Gave material aid to cause **CEM:** Old Keys Church; GPS unk; Jct Rt 647 & 722; Amherst **GS:** N **SP:** Mar (21 Sep 1763) Elizabeth Hargrave (1750-1808) **VI:** No further data **P:** unk **BLW:** unk **RG:** N **MK:** N **PH:** N **SS:** DAR #A071988; D Vol 1 pg 80, 81; AH pg 3 **BS:** 01 pg 3.

LOVINGS (LOVING), John Jr; b 4 Oct 1739, Culpeper Co; d 10 May 1804 **RU:** Captain, Commanded a co in Amherst Co Militia 1780-1781. Was at Yorktown Oct 1781 **CEM:** Lovings Gap; GPS unk; Lovington; Nelson **GS:** U **SP:** Naomi "Amy" Seay (1741-1819) **VI:** Was sheriff of Amherst Co **P:** unk **BLW:** unk **RG:** N **MK:** unk **PH:** N **SS:** E pg 485 **BS:** JLARC 115; 196.

LOYD, Henry; b 1756; d 4 May 1817 **RU:** Ensign, Served in Cont Navy **CEM:** Stiff Family; GPS unk; Union Church Rd 1 mi past Union Methodist, Thaxton; Bedford **GS:** Y **SP:** No info **VI:** Govt stone with SAR marker att **P:** unk **BLW:** unk **RG:** Y **MK:** Y **PH:** unk **SS:** AK Bedford Museum **BS:** 196.

LUCAS, Basil; b 20 Aug 1757, MD; d 6 Jul 1841 **RU:** Sergeant, Served in MD Line. Ent serv MD 1776 **CEM:** Mt Hebron; GPS 39.10916, -78.09497; 305 E Boscawen St; Winchester City **GS:** U **SP:** Mar (26 Feb 1786) Elizabeth (-----) **VI:** Sol appl pen 11 May 1833 Berkeley Co. In 1831 stated name was on MD pen roll. S18097. Die in Berkeley Co **P:** Y **BLW:** unk **RG:** Y **MK:** unk **PH:** unk **SS:** E pg 486; K Vol 3 pg 148; CG pg 2136; J-NSSAR 2000 Reg **BS:** JLARC 76.

LUCAS, Parker; b 1756; d 27 Mar 1835 **RU:** Soldier, Ent serv Montgomery Co. Served in Capt John Lucas's Co, VA Line **CEM:** Cloverhollow; GPS 37.33470, -80.47580; Rt 715 Deerfield Ln before first sharp turn; Giles **GS:** U **SP:** Margaret (-----) **VI:** Sol appl pen 23 Sep 1832 Giles Co age 76. S8868 **P:** Y **BLW:** unk **RG:** unk **MK:** unk **PH:** unk **SS:** CG pg 2137 **BS:** JLARC 4, 26.

LUCAS (LUCASS), John; b 15 Jul 1749, Augusta Co; d 19 Apr 1836 **RU:** Captain, VA Line. Ent serv Montgomery Co 1778. Served under Col Preston to end of war **CEM:** Lucas Family (source 1), Old Cooper (source 2); GPS unk; S or E fr Riner; Montgomery **GS:** N **SP:** Mar (15 Feb 1777 Montgomery Co) Mary Polly Wilson (1 Jan 1758-17 May 1843) **VI:** Lucas family research & patriot ancestor war service produced DAR marker in Lucas fam cem indicates Capt John Lucas is bur in Old Cooper cem, 2-3 mi E of Calfees Mountain. Sol appl pen 8 Aug 1832 Montgomery Co. Widow appl pen 6 May 1839 Montgomery Co. W5468 **P:** Y **BLW:** unk **RG:** Y **MK:** Y **PH:** N **SS:** J-NSSAR 1993 Reg, J- DAR Hatcher; K Vol 3 pg 149; CG pg 2137 **BS:** JLARC 1, 2.

RU=Rank/Unit	CEM=Cemetery	GS=Gravestone	SP=Spousal Information
VI=Other Veteran Info	P=Pension	BLW=Bounty/Land Warrant	RG=Registered Grave
MK=SAR/DAR Marker	PH=Photo	SS=Service Source	BS=Burial Source

208

LUCKETT, John B; b 1747; d 10 Mar 1794 **RU:** Captain, Served in Loudoun Co Militia. Took oath as Capt 8 Jun 1778 **CEM:** Luckett; GPS unk; Nr Quantico Marine Base; Prince William **GS:** Y **SP:** No info **VI:** No further data **P:** unk **BLW:** unk **RG:** Y **MK:** N **PH:** unk **SS:** E pg 487 **BS:** 15 pg 195.

LUKE, Issac Sr; b 26 Nov 1729; d 31 Oct 1784 **RU:** Patriot, Gave 48 bushels of lime to the cause **CEM:** Trinity Episcopal; GPS 36.83459, -76.30105; 500 Court St; Portsmouth City **GS:** Y **SP:** Rachel Dale (11 Feb 1737-27 Jan 1775) **VI:** No further data **P:** N **BLW:** N **RG:** Y **MK:** N **PH:** unk **SS:** G pg 485 **BS:** 75 Portsmouth.

LUMSDEN, John; b 1738, Bedford Co; d 1788 **RU:** Corporal/Patriot, Served in 1st, 5th and 9th Cont Lines. Gave material aid to cause **CEM:** John Fisher Farm; GPS 37.03640, -79.72470; Rt 669; Franklin **GS:** U **SP:** Mar (1752) Wilmouth Steele (1732-1788) **VI:** Rec'd BLW 1 Sep 1783, 409 acres in Franklin Co and on 31 March 1786, 440 acres **P:** unk **BLW:** Y **RG:** unk **MK:** unk **PH:** unk **SS:** E pg 488; AL Ct Bk pg 47 Henry Co; CD **BS:** JLARC 2,18; 196.

LUNDY, John; b 19 Nov 1751, Sussex Co, NJ; d 5 May 1831 **RU:** Private, Served in 6th PA Regt **CEM:** Nuckolls Family; GPS 36.63551, -80.95944; Beyond the end of Wild Turkey Ln, jct US-58 & Rt 94; Grayson **GS:** U **SP:** Mar (11 Dec 1777 NJ) Rebecca Silverthorn (8 May 1754 Morris Co, NJ-24 Dec 1839 Oldtown, Grayson Co) d/o Thomas & Johanna (Newman) Silverthorn **VI:** No further data **P:** unk **BLW:** unk **RG:** unk **MK:** unk **PH:** unk **SS:** AP Service Rec **BS:** 196.

LYBROOK, John; b 20 Nov 1763, PA; d 18 Dec 1837 **RU:** Private, Ent serv Botetourt Co (now Giles). Served 6 mo under Capt Floyd in 1778, 1779 to 1782 and in Capt Lucas Co, VA Line **CEM:** Lybrook Family; GPS 37.33385, -80.61087; End Rt 65, Pembroke; Giles **GS:** Y **SP:** Anne L Chapman (1761, Culpeper Co-1831) d/o John C (1740-1813) & (-----) Chapman **VI:** Son of Balzar Palzer (1729-1804) & Catherine (Reihm) (1761-1831) Lybrook. Sol appl pen 19 Mar 1834 Giles Co. R6540 **P:** Y **BLW:** unk **RG:** unk **MK:** unk **PH:** unk **SS:** J- DAR Hatcher; K Vol 3 pg 153; CD; CG pg 2149 **BS:** JLARC 2; 196.

LYNCH, Anselm; b 8 Jun 1764; d 18 Feb 1826 **RU:** First Lieutenant, Served in Bedford Co Militia. Appointed 1st Lt 24 Sep 1781 **CEM:** Lynch Family; GPS 37.12946, -79.26853; Avoca Museum, 1514 Main St, Altavista; Campbell **GS:** Y **SP:** Susan Miller (___-1808) **VI:** Son of Charles Lynch (1736-1796) & Anne Terrell (d 1804) **P:** unk **BLW:** unk **RG:** unk **MK:** N **PH:** unk **SS:** E pg 489 **BS:** JLARC 36; 196.

LYNCH, Charles Sr; b 1736; d 29 Oct 1796 **RU:** Colonel, Bedford Militia. Appointed Col Bedford Co Militia 24 Feb 1778 **CEM:** Lynch Family; GPS 37.12946, -79.26853; Avoca Museum, 1514 Main St, Altavista; Campbell **GS:** Y **SP:** Anne Terrell (___-1804) **VI:** Connected with lead mines in county. Justice of Bedford Co and was disowned by the Quakers for taking the oath of office. House of Burgesses 1769-1778. At battle of Guilford CH. VA Senate 1784-1789 **P:** unk **BLW:** unk **RG:** unk **MK:** N **PH:** unk **SS:** E pg 489 **BS:** JLARC 36, 66, 75; 196.

LYNCH, John; b 1740; d 13 Oct 1820 **RU:** PrivatePatriot, Served in 1st Cont Line, 2nd VA Regt. Served as ferry operator **CEM:** South River Meeting House; GPS 37.37246, -79.19194; 5810 Fort Ave; Lynchburg City **GS:** U **SP:** Mar (1 Aug 1769, Bedford Co) Mary Bowles (1752-5 Aug 1829) **VI:** Founder of Petersburg; petitioned VA Legislature 1784 to found city on land he possessed. City Council dedicated a plaque to him which is in cemetery **P:** unk **BLW:** unk **RG:** unk **MK:** Y **PH:** unk **SS:** DAR #072647; E pg 489 **BS:** 196; 221.

LYNE, William; b 30 Jan 1734, Belfast Ireland; d 10 Sep 1808 **RU:** Colonel, Served as Ranger on frontier under Ens James Lynch, Westmoreland Co, PA. Was commander of King and Queen Co Militia. Was the County Lt in 1782 and was President of a Cts Marshall **CEM:** Lyne Family; GPS unk; See property records for location; King & Queen **GS:** U **SP:** Mar (1778) Lucy Foster Lyne (__ Granville Co, NC-aft 1799) d/o Henry & (-----) Lyne **VI:** Son of Willam of Bristol Co, NC & (-----) Lyne. DAR indicates burial in Richmond City **P:** unk **BLW:** unk **RG:** N **MK:** N **PH:** unk **SS:** DAR #A072676; E pg 490; CI: PA Archives 5th Series Vol 2 pg 675, 727, Vol 4, pg 597, 734, 747 **BS:** DAR report; 80.

LYONNOIS, Jean; b unk; d 1781 **RU:** Soldier, Served in Foix Bn and died fr battle at Yorktown **CEM:** French Memorial; GPS 36.81944, -79.39933; Yorktown; York **GS:** U **SP:** No info **VI:** No further data **P:** unk **BLW:** unk **RG:** Y **MK:** unk **PH:** unk **SS:** J-Yorktown Historian **BS:** JLARC 1, 74.

RU=Rank/Unit	CEM=Cemetery	GS=Gravestone	SP=Spousal Information
VI=Other Veteran Info	P=Pension	BLW=Bounty/Land Warrant	RG=Registered Grave
MK=SAR/DAR Marker	PH=Photo	SS=Service Source	BS=Burial Source

209

LYONNOIS, Pierre; b unk; d 1781 **RU:** Seaman, Served in Soissonnais Bn and died fr battle at Yorktown **CEM:** French Memorial; GPS 36.81944, -79.39933; Yorktown; York **GS:** U **SP:** No info **VI:** No further data **P:** unk **BLW:** unk **RG:** Y **MK:** unk **PH:** unk **SS:** J-Yorktown Historian **BS:** JLARC 1, 74.

MACHAIN, Claude; b unk; d 1781 **RU:** Seaman, Served on "Magnanime" and died from Yorktown battle **CEM:** French Memorial; GPS 36.81944, -79.39933; Yorktown; York **GS:** U **SP:** No info **VI:** No further data **P:** unk **BLW:** unk **RG:** Y **MK:** unk **PH:** unk **SS:** J-Yorktown Historian **BS:** JLARC 1, 74.

MACKEY, John Sr; b 1767; d 1818 **RU:** Private, Served in 11th Cont Line **CEM:** Lexington; GPS unk; Lexington; Lexington City **GS:** Y **SP:** No info **VI:** No further data **P:** unk **BLW:** unk **RG:** N **MK:** N **PH:** unk **SS:** AS **BS:** 80 vol 3 pg 43.

MACOMB, Alexander; b 27 Jul 1748, County Antrim, Ireland; d 19 Jan 1831 **RU:** Soldier, Probably served fr Detroit in the Navy **CEM:** Arlington National; GPS 38.88377, -77.06535; Jefferson Davis Hwy Rt 110; Arlington **GS:** Y **SP:** 1) Mar (4 May 1773 Detroit) Mary Catherine Navarre (__-17 Nov 1789, NYC) 2) Mar (11 Jul 1791 Trinity Church, NYC) Jane (Marshall) Rucker, widow of John Peter Rucker **VI:** Son of John Macomb and Jane Gordon, emigrated to Albany NY in 1755. Moved with his brother to Detroit where he mar in 1773. Moved to New York City in 1785 where he was a real estate speculator. He suffered ruinous financial setback and moved to his son's home in Georgetown in Washington DC where he died. He and his wife were reinterred fr Old Presbyterian Church in Georgetown to Arlington on 12 May 1892 **P:** unk **BLW:** unk **RG:** Y **MK:** unk **PH:** unk **SS:** J-NSSAR 2000 Reg; NSSAR Ancestor # P-240525 **BS:** JLARC 76; 196.

MACON, William; b 4 Jan 1725; d 25 Nov 1813 **RU:** Patriot, Gave provisions to the cause **CEM:** Fairfield; GPS unk; Sledd Run Sub Div; Hanover **GS:** Y **SP:** Lucy (-----) (9 Jun 1737-1 Dec 1802) **VI:** No further data **P:** N **BLW:** N **RG:** Y **MK:** N **PH:** unk **SS:** G pg 622 **BS:** 31 vol 1 pg 51.

MADDOX, Allison; b c1760, Charles County, MD; d 22 Jan 1843 **RU:** Private, Served in1st MD Line. Drafted fr the Charles Co Militia. Served fr mid-June to 1 Sep 1781 **CEM:** Maddox; GPS unk; Hope Hill Crossing Subdivision, Hope Hill Rd; Prince William **GS:** Y **SP:** Ann Swann (1776-17 Feb 1857) **VI:** Died in Prince William or Fairfax Co **P:** N **BLW:** N **RG:** Y **MK:** Y **PH:** Y **SS:** AK Oct 2015 Cites Archives of MD Vol 18 **BS:** 31.

MADEC, Jean; b unk; d 1781 **RU:** Seaman, Served on "Saint-Esprit" and died from Yorktown battle **CEM:** French Memorial; GPS 36.81944, -79.39933; Yorktown; York **GS:** U **SP:** No info **VI:** No further data **P:** unk **BLW:** unk **RG:** Y **MK:** unk **PH:** unk **SS:** J-Yorktown Historian **BS:** JLARC 1, 74.

MADISON, Ambrose Sr; b 22 Jan 1755, Montpelier Station, Orange Co; d 3 Oct 1793 **RU:** Captain, Was Paymaster 2nd VA Regt 1777-78 and Capt of Regimental Convention Guards in 1779 **CEM:** Montpelier; GPS unk; 11407 Constitution Hwy, Montpelier Station; Orange **GS:** Y **SP:** Mar (11 Nov 1779 Fauquier Co) Mary Willis Lee (27 Jan 1757, Warrenton, Fauquier Co-14 Mar 1798 Montpelier Station, Orange Co) d/o Hancock & Mary (Willis) Lee **VI:** Son of Col James (1723-1801) & Eleanor "Nellie" Rose (Conway) (1731-1829) Madison. Brother to President James Madison Jr. Requested BLW but not recd **P:** N **BLW:** N **RG:** unk **MK:** unk **PH:** unk **SS:** E pg 493 **BS:** 196.

MADISON, James; b 16 Mar 1751, Port Conway, King George Co; d 28 Jun 1836 **RU:** Patriot, Served in 1st Gen Assembly VA 1776, and Exec. Council 1778. Was in Cont Congress 1780-83 **CEM:** Montpelier; GPS unk; 11407 Constitution Hwy, Montpelier Station; Orange **GS:** U **SP:** Dolley Payne Todd Madison **VI:** Secretary of State under Jefferson 1801-09. Fourth president of the US, 1809-1817. Bronze plaque in Wrenn Hall, Williamsburg **P:** unk **BLW:** unk **RG:** Y **MK:** unk **PH:** unk **SS:** J-NSSAR 1993 Reg; NSSAR Ancestor # P-240656 **BS:** JLARC 1, 201 pg 1793.

MADISON, William Strother; b 1758; d 17 Mar 1782 **RU:** Patriot/Private, Was Justice & Sheriff of Botetourt Co & Surveyor of Washington Co. Served in Capt James Gray's Co, 15th VA Regt Jul 1778 **CEM:** Madison; GPS unk; Shawsville; Montgomery **GS:** Y **SP:** Elizabeth Preston (1763-1837) **VI:** Died of smallpox contracted in military service **P:** N **BLW:** N **RG:** unk **MK:** unk **PH:** unk **SS:** CI Muster Roll **BS:** 196.

MADISON, William Taylor; b 5 May 1762 Montpelier, Orange Co; d 20 Jul 1843 **RU:** Lieutenant, Served in State Legion & Regt of Harrison's VA Artillery of VA Line 1781 **CEM:** Montpelier; GPS unk; 11407

RU=Rank/Unit	CEM=Cemetery	GS=Gravestone	SP=Spousal Information
VI=Other Veteran Info	P=Pension	BLW=Bounty/Land Warrant	RG=Registered Grave
MK=SAR/DAR Marker	PH=Photo	SS=Service Source	BS=Burial Source

210

Constitution Hwy, Montpelier Station; Orange **GS:** Y **SP:** 1) Mar (20 Dec 1783 Orange Co) Frances Throckmorton (24 Feb 1765-20 Aug 1832) 2) Mar (1834) Nancy Jarrell **VI:** Son of Col James (1723-1801) & Eleanor "Nellie" Rose (Conway) (1731-1829) Madison. Brother to President James Madison Jr. General in War of 1812. Heirs recd BLW on 29 Aug 1838 of 2666 acres **P:** Y **BLW:** Y **RG:** N **MK**: unk **PH:** unk **SS:** E pg 494 **BS:** 196.

MAGILL, Charles; b 1760; d 2 Apr 1827 **RU:** Major, Served in VA Line. Ent serv Winchester, Frederick Co 1777. Served on Gen Washington Staff as Maj of Calvary **CEM:** Mt Hebron; GPS 39.10916, -78.09497; 305 E Boscawen St; Winchester City **GS:** U **SP:** 1) Mar (29 Apr 1789, Spotsylvania Co) Elizabeth Dangerfield 2) Mar (24 May 1792 Frederick Co) May (Mary) Buckner Thurston, (27 Jul 1772-1850, DC **VI:** Widow appl pen 9 Aug 1838 Fauquier Co. W5336 **P:** Y **BLW:** unk **RG:** Y **MK**: unk **PH:** unk **SS:** J-NSSAR 1993 Reg; CG pg 2165 **BS:** JLARC 1.

MAGILL, James; b c1756; d 24 Aug 1840 **RU:** Private, Served in 12th VA Regt. Ent serv Rockingham Co **CEM:** Old Peaked Mountain; GPS 38.37113, -78.73416; 9843 Town Hall Rd, McGaheysville; Rockingham **GS:** Y **SP:** 1) Betsy Evans 2) Mar (10 Mar 1789 Greene Co, TN) Mary McMeans **VI:** Sol appl pen 4 Sep 1832 Green Co TN age 74 (Probably d and is bur there, not Rockingham Co VA). Widow appl pen 6 May 1844 Walker Co GA age 76 & rejected due to less than six mos service. Pen says he d 24 Aug 1839. Memorialized on common monument.Pen recd R-6827 **P:** Y **BLW:** unk **RG:** unk **MK**: Y **PH:** unk **SS:** K Vol 3 pg 159; N; CG pg 2165 **BS:** 196.

MAGILL, William; b 21 Apr 1748, Augusta Co, VA; d 1797 **RU:** Quartermaster/Patriot, Served in Rockingham Co Militia. Gave material aid to cause **CEM:** Old Peaked Mountain; GPS 38.37113, -78.73416; 9843 Town Hall Rd, McGaheysville; Rockingham **GS:** U **SP:** Mar (1770 Allegheny Co MD) Joan Fowler **VI:** Son of James & (-----) Magill Sr **P:** unk **BLW:** unk **RG:** Y **MK**: unk **PH:** unk **SS:** J-NSSAR 2000 Reg; D Rockingham **BS:** JLARC 76.

MAGNAN, Francois; b unk; d 1781 **RU:** Soldier, Served in Touraine Bn and died fr battle at Yorktown **CEM:** French Memorial; GPS 36.81944, -79.39933; Yorktown; York **GS:** U **SP:** No info **VI:** No further data **P:** unk **BLW:** unk **RG:** Y **MK**: unk **PH:** unk **SS:** J-Yorktown Historian **BS:** JLARC 1, 74.

MAGNAN, Jean; b unk; d 1781 **RU:** Seaman, Served on "Hercule" and died from Yorktown battle **CEM:** French Memorial; GPS 36.81944, -79.39933; Yorktown; York **GS:** U **SP:** No info **VI:** No further data **P:** unk **BLW:** unk **RG:** Y **MK**: unk **PH:** unk **SS:** J-Yorktown Historian **BS:** JLARC 1, 74.

MAGNIEN, Bernard; b c1752, Luneville, France; d 4 Nov 1819 **RU:** Aide de Camp, Was Aide de Camp to Gen Lafayette. Came with Lafayette to serve in Rev **CEM:** Trinity Episcopal; GPS 36.83459, -76.30105; 500 Court St; Portsmouth City **GS:** Y **SP:** Margaret (-----) (__-5 Feb 1819) **VI:** Item 124 in W.B. Butt inventory. From Luneville, France, left to fight in Amer Rev. Was Lt Col in War of 1812. **P:** unk **BLW:** unk **RG:** unk **MK**: Y **PH:** unk **SS:** CD **BS:** JLARC 105127.

MAIDEN, James; b Bet 1750-1755, Augusta Co; d c1797 **RU:** Private, Enl in Rockingham Co 1777. Served in Capt David Laird's and Capt Nathan Lamb's Co 6th & 10th VA Lines **CEM:** Maiden Homestead; GPS unk; Bedor Rd Rt 628, .3 mi fr Rt 33 in Elkton; walk up hill abt .5 mi; Rockingham **GS:** N **SP:** Mar (Aug 1775 or 1776) Theodocia (Docia) Lee (c1753-__). She remar Bazil Hall (__-Aug 1839 Botetourt Co) **VI:** Theodosia was granted L 30 support in Rockingham Co 23 Nov 1779 while he was away in service. Widow appl pen 28 Dec 1843 Rockingham Co age 90. W5098 **P:** Y **BLW:** unk **RG:** unk **MK**: unk **PH:** N **SS:** DAR Ancestor #A072998; K Vol 3 pg 160; BX pg 534; CG pg 2167; DD **BS:** JLARC 4, 64; 51; http://www.heritagecenter.com/cemeteries/cem/cem388.htm.

MAILLET, Marcel; b unk; d 1781 **RU:** Seaman, Served on "Soliaire" and died from Yorktown battle **CEM:** French Memorial; GPS 36.81944, -79.39933; Yorktown; York **GS:** U **SP:** No info **VI:** No further data **P:** unk **BLW:** unk **RG:** Y **MK**: unk **PH:** unk **SS:** J-Yorktown Historian **BS:** JLARC 1, 74.

MAINS, William; b unk; d 1815 **RU:** Private, Served in 3rd & 4th Cont Line **CEM:** Leesburg Presbyterian; GPS 39.11611, -77.56722; 207 W Market St, Leesburg; Loudoun **GS:** Y **SP:** Mary (-----) (__-12 Oct 1827) **VI:** No further data **P:** unk **BLW:** unk **RG:** Y **MK**: N **PH:** unk **SS:** E pg 495 **BS:** 25 pg 190; 196.

RU=Rank/Unit   CEM=Cemetery   GS=Gravestone   SP=Spousal Information
VI=Other Veteran Info   P=Pension   BLW=Bounty/Land Warrant   RG=Registered Grave
MK=SAR/DAR Marker   PH=Photo   SS=Service Source   BS=Burial Source

211

MAIRE, Jacques; b unk; d 1781 **RU**: Seaman, Served on "Northumberland" and died from Yorktown battle **CEM**: French Memorial; GPS 36.81944, -79.39933; Yorktown; York **GS**: U **SP**: No info **VI**: No further data **P**: unk **BLW**: unk **RG**: Y **MK**: unk **PH**: unk **SS**: J-Yorktown Historian **BS**: JLARC 1, 74.

MAISON, Jean; b unk; d 1781 **RU**: Soldier, Served in Foix Bn and died fr battle at Yorktown **CEM**: French Memorial; GPS 36.81944, -79.39933; Yorktown; York **GS**: U **SP**: No info **VI**: No further data **P**: unk **BLW**: unk **RG**: Y **MK**: unk **PH**: unk **SS**: J-Yorktown Historian **BS**: JLARC 1, 74.

MAJOR, Richard Rev; b c1722, Pennsbury, PA; d 3 Dec 1796 **RU**: Patriot, Gave material aid to the cause **CEM**: Hutchison-Major; GPS 38.90569, -77.47508; Pleasant Valley Rd & Lafayette Center Dr, Chantilly; Fairfax **GS**: Y **SP**: Sarah Major (1781-12 Apr 1801) **VI**: SAR Gr marker. Died age 74. He was instrumental in establishing several Baptist congregations in Fairfax and Loudoun counties during his ministry **P**: N **BLW**: N **RG**: Y **MK**: Y **PH**: unk **SS**: G pg 81 **BS**: 61 vol IV, pg CH-20; 196.

MAJOR, William; b 4 Oct 1744; d 19 Mar 1847 **RU**: Private, Served in10th & 14th Cont Lines **CEM**: Major Family; GPS 38.65282, -78.02353; Rt 642, Viewtown Rd nr jct with Ida Belle Ln; Rappahannock **GS**: Y **SP**: Mar (13 Aug 1795) Elizabeth Thatcher Corbin (23 Dec 1779-16 Mar 1869) d/o John (1747-1813) & Frances (Thatcher) (1757-1814) Corbin **VI**: No further data **P**: unk **BLW**: unk **RG**: N **MK**: N **PH**: unk **SS**: E pg 496 **BS**: 163 Major; 196.

MALFROIS, Pierre; b unk; d 1781 **RU**: Seaman, Served on "Languedoc" and died from Yorktown battle **CEM**: French Memorial; GPS 36.81944, -79.39933; Yorktown; York **GS**: U **SP**: No info **VI**: No further data **P**: unk **BLW**: unk **RG**: Y **MK**: unk **PH**: unk **SS**: J-Yorktown Historian **BS**: JLARC 1, 74.

MALLOW, George Sr; b 22 Dec 1727, Griesbach Alasce, France; d Aft 22 Nov 1789 **RU**: Patriot, Gave material aid to cause **CEM**: Mallow Family; GPS unk; McGaheysville; Rockingham **GS**: N **SP**: Mar (21 Apr 1750) France Anna Barbara Muller (26 Sep 1726, France-17 Jan 1797) **VI**: No further data **P**: N **BLW**: N **RG**: Y **MK**: N **PH**: N **SS**: DAR #A073275; O; AL Ct Bk II pg 11, 20, 24 Rockingham Co; DD: cites Levinson Rockingham Co, VA Minute Bk 1778-1786 pg 110, 121 **BS**: 04.

MALONE, Benjamin; b 1756; d 1824 **RU**: Lieutenant, Specific records are at Lib of VA, Auditor's Acct XXII pg 18. Took oath as Lt in Mecklenburg Militia 13 Sep 1779 **CEM**: Canaan Methodist Church; GPS 36.66848, -78.05323; Jct Blackridge Rd & Canaan Church Rd; Mecklenburg **GS**: Y **SP**: No info **VI**: No further data **P**: unk **BLW**: unk **RG**: N **MK**: N **PH**: unk **SS**: E pg 496; CZ pg 295; DB pg 102 **BS**: 54 pg 294.

MANADET, Bernard; b unk; d 1781 **RU**: Soldier, Served in Bourbonnais Bn and died fr battle at Yorktown **CEM**: French Memorial; GPS 36.81944, -79.39933; Yorktown; York **GS**: U **SP**: No info **VI**: No further data **P**: unk **BLW**: unk **RG**: Y **MK**: unk **PH**: unk **SS**: J-Yorktown Historian **BS**: JLARC 1, 74.

MANN, Daniel; b unk; d unk **RU**: Private?, Served in 2nd & 5th Cont Lines **CEM**: Old City; GPS 37.41472, -79.15667; 401 Taylor St; Lynchburg City **GS**: N **SP**: No info **VI**: No further data **P**: unk **BLW**: unk **RG**: N **MK**: N **PH**: N **SS**: E pg 497 **BS**: 62 pg 136.

MANN, Jacob; b unk; d 2 May 1824 **RU**: Private, Served in Capt William McBride's Co at Falls of Ohio in 1782 **CEM**: Back Creek Quaker, aka Gainesboro United Methodist; GPS 39.27861, -78.25694; 166 Siler Ln, Gainesboro; Frederick **GS**: Y **SP**: No info **VI**: No further data **P**: unk **BLW**: unk **RG**: unk **MK**: unk **PH**: unk **SS**: N pg 1266 **BS**: 196.

MANNING, Samuel; b unk; d 1781 **RU**: Private, Served in Capt Chapman's Co, CT Cont line. Died fr the Battle at Yorktown **CEM**: Yorktown Victory Monument Tablet; GPS 38.28350, -78.54150; Yorktown; York **GS**: U **SP**: No info **VI**: BLW 1050-100 **P**: unk **BLW**: Y **RG**: unk **MK**: unk **PH**: unk **SS**: J-Yorktown Historian; DY pg 98, 351 **BS**: JLARC 74.

MANSFIELD, Robert; b 19 Dec 1762, Albemarle Co; d 1 Oct 1833 **RU**: Soldier, Served in VA Line. Ent serv Albemarle Co 1779 **CEM**: Mansfield Family; GPS unk; Nr Barboursville; Orange **GS**: U **SP**: Mar (4 May 1785) Mourning Clark (27 Oct 1763, Albemarle Co-18 Mar 1831) d/o Micajah (27 Feb 1741-1774) & Mildred (Martin) (1741-1827) Clark **VI**: Appl pen 24 Sep 1832 Orange Co age 70. Occupation tailor when appl for pension. S7185 **P**: Y **BLW**: unk **RG**: unk **MK**: unk **PH**: unk **SS**: J- DAR Hatcher; K Vol 3 pg 167; CG pg 2182 **BS**: JLARC 2.

RU=Rank/Unit   CEM=Cemetery   GS=Gravestone   SP=Spousal Information
VI=Other Veteran Info   P=Pension   BLW=Bounty/Land Warrant   RG=Registered Grave
MK=SAR/DAR Marker   PH=Photo   SS=Service Source   BS=Burial Source

212

MANSFIELD, Timothy; b unk; d 11 Oct 1781 **RU:** Private, Served in Col's Co, CT Cont troops and died fr battle at Yorktown **CEM:** Yorktown Victory Monument Tablet; **GPS** 38.28350, -78.54150; Yorktown; York **GS:** U **SP:** No info **VI:** No further data **P:** unk **BLW:** unk **RG:** unk **MK:** unk **PH:** unk **SS:** J-Yorktown Historian; DY pg 213 **BS:** JLARC 74.

MARCHAND, Pierre; b unk; d 1781 **RU:** Seaman, Served on "Hector" and died from Yorktown battle **CEM:** French Memorial; **GPS** 36.81944, -79.39933; Yorktown; York **GS:** U **SP:** no info **VI:** No further data **P:** unk **BLW:** unk **RG:** Y **MK:** unk **PH:** unk **SS:** J-Yorktown Historian **BS:** JLARC 1, 74.

MARCY NARCY, Jean; b unk; d 1781 **RU:** Seaman, Served on "Saint-Esprit" and died from Yorktown battle **CEM:** French Memorial; **GPS** 36.81944, -79.39933; Yorktown; York **GS:** U **SP:** No info **VI:** No further data **P:** unk **BLW:** unk **RG:** Y **MK:** unk **PH:** unk **SS:** J-Yorktown Historian **BS:** JLARC 1, 74.

MARET, Nicolas; b unk; d 1781 **RU:** Soldier, Served in Agenois Bn and died fr battle at Yorktown **CEM:** French Memorial; **GPS** 36.81944, -79.39933; Yorktown; York **GS:** U **SP:** No info **VI:** No further data **P:** unk **BLW:** unk **RG:** Y **MK:** unk **PH:** unk **SS:** J-Yorktown Historian **BS:** JLARC 1, 74.

MARGOT, Pierre; b unk; d 1781 **RU:** Seaman, Served on "Languedoc" and died from Yorktown battle **CEM:** French Memorial; **GPS** 36.81944, -79.39933; Yorktown; York **GS:** U **SP:** No info **VI:** No further data **P:** unk **BLW:** unk **RG:** Y **MK:** unk **PH:** unk **SS:** J-Yorktown Historian **BS:** JLARC 1, 74.

MARIE, Jacques; b unk; d 1781 **RU:** Seaman, Served on "Ville de Paris" and died from Yorktown battle **CEM:** French Memorial; **GPS** 36.81944, -79.39933; Yorktown; York **GS:** U **SP:** No info **VI:** No further data **P:** unk **BLW:** unk **RG:** Y **MK:** unk **PH:** unk **SS:** J-Yorktown Historian **BS:** JLARC 1, 74.

MARIN, Jean de; b unk; d 1781 **RU:** Soldier, Served in Soissonnais Bn and died fr battle at Yorktown **CEM:** French Memorial; **GPS** 36.81944, -79.39933; Yorktown; York **GS:** U **SP:** No info **VI:** No further data **P:** unk **BLW:** unk **RG:** Y **MK:** unk **PH:** unk **SS:** J-Yorktown Historian **BS:** JLARC 1, 74.

MARION, Samuel; b 21 Sep 1756 (pen says Jan 1750) Goochland Co; d 30 Oct 1843 **RU:** Private, Served in VA Line. Ent serv Goochland Co 1776. Served in Capt Morris & Capt Lightfoot's Co **CEM:** Robert Clark, aka Thompson-Whitehead-Wilder; **GPS** unk; Rt 612 7 mi SW of Jonesville; Lee **GS:** Y **SP:** Tabitha Barnet (1762-1843) **VI:** Appl pen 27 May 1834 Lee Co, but also made application in Hawkins Co TN. S4180. Source 4 has pen 1834, and living in Lee Co 1843. Different birth dates on pension and stone **P:** Y **BLW:** unk **RG:** unk **MK:** Y **PH:** Y **SS:** J- DAR Hatcher; B; K Vol 3 pg 169; CG pg 2188 **BS:** JLARC 2; 196.

MARIVAL, Francois; b unk; d 1781 **RU:** Soldier, Served in Agenois Bn and died fr battle at Yorktown **CEM:** French Memorial; **GPS** 36.81944, -79.39933; Yorktown; York **GS:** U **SP:** No info **VI:** No further data **P:** unk **BLW:** unk **RG:** Y **MK:** unk **PH:** unk **SS:** J-Yorktown Historian **BS:** JLARC 1, 74.

MARKS, Abel; b 20 Mar 1760, Montgomery Co, PA; d 20 Mar 1817 **RU:** Soldier, Specific records are at Lib of VA, Auditor's Acct XXV, pg 513 **CEM:** Ketoctin Baptist; **GPS** 39.15746, -77.74870; Ketoctin Church Rd, Purcellville; Loudoun **GS:** Y **SP:** Mary Liddleton (__-1827) **VI:** Son of John & Uriah (Liddleton) Marks **P:** unk **BLW:** unk **RG:** Y **MK:** unk **PH:** unk **SS:** E pg 499; CZ pg 297 **BS:** JLARC 1, 2, 32; 196.

MARKS, George Elisha; b 26 Dec 1744, Loudoun Co; d 18 Oct 1805 **RU:** Corporal, Served in Col Moses Hazen's 2d Canadian Regt **CEM:** Ketoctin Baptist; **GPS** 39.15746, -77.74870; Ketoctin Church Rd, Purcellville; Loudoun **GS:** U **SP:** No info **VI:** Son of John (1716-1788) & (-----) Marks **P:** N **BLW:** N **RG:** unk **MK:** unk **PH:** unk **SS:** CI record book Officers & Men **BS:** 196.

MARKS, Isaiah; b 07 Apr 1754; d 20 Jan 1785 **RU:** Captain, Was 2nd Lt in 11th VA, 11 Nov 1776; 1st Lt 15 Mar 1777; wounded at Brandywine 11 Sep 1777; Regt designated 7th VA 14 Sep 1778; Capt 10 May 1779; transferred to 2nd VA 12 Feb 1781; served to 1 Jan 1783 **CEM:** Ketoctin Baptist; **GPS** 39.15746, -77.74870; Ketoctin Church Rd, Purcellville; Loudoun **GS:** Y **SP:** Never mar/no children **VI:** Brother Thomas appl for pen in 1834 fr Henderson Co, KY. BLW 1655, 300 acres issued 14 Jul 1830 to heirs. R116055 **P:** Y **BLW:** Y **RG:** Y **MK:** Y **PH:** unk **SS:** K Vol 3 pg 170; AK **BS:** 04; JLARC 1, 2, 32.

MARKS, John Jr; b c1716, Germany; d 3 Mar 1788 **RU:** Ensign/Patriot, Took Oath 11 Aug 1777 Loudoun Co Militia. As minister, peached patriotism and espoused Rev War causes **CEM:** Ketoctin

RU=Rank/Unit	CEM=Cemetery	GS=Gravestone	SP=Spousal Information
VI=Other Veteran Info	P=Pension	BLW=Bounty/Land Warrant	RG=Registered Grave
MK=SAR/DAR Marker	PH=Photo	SS=Service Source	BS=Burial Source

213

Baptist; GPS 39.15746, -77.74870; Ketoctin Church Rd, Purcellville; Loudoun **GS:** Y **SP:** Mar (c1740) Uriah Ledyard (__-14 Apr 1788) **VI:** Died in Round Hill, Loudoun Co **P:** unk **BLW:** unk **RG:** Y **MK:** N **PH:** unk **SS:** DAR #A073929; E, pg 500; DD cites Nickols, Legends of Loudoun Valley pg 83, 84 **BS:** 25 pg 192.

MARQUET, Francois; b unk; d 1781 **RU:** Seaman, Served on "Hercule" and died from Yorktown battle **CEM:** French Memorial; GPS 36.81944, -79.39933; Yorktown; York **GS:** U **SP:** No info **VI:** No further data **P:** unk **BLW:** unk **RG:** Y **MK:** unk **PH:** unk **SS:** J-Yorktown Historian **BS:** JLARC 1, 74.

MARQUIS, William; b c1749; d 15 Jan 1815 **RU:** Patriot, Gave provisions to the cause **CEM:** Old Opequon Church; GPS 39.82237, -78.11412; 217 Opequon Church Ln, Kernstown; Frederick **GS:** Y **SP:** Elizabeth Vance (c1745/46 Winchester-c1780) **VI:** No further data **P:** N **BLW:** N **RG:** Y **MK:** N **PH:** unk **SS:** DAR #A074002; AL Ct Bk pg 15, 17 **BS:** 59 pg 209.

MARSH, Ephraim; b unk; d 1781 **RU:** Private, Served in Capt John Abbet's Co, Col John Knickerbacker's Albany, NY Militia Regt and died fr battle at Yorktown **CEM:** Yorktown Victory Monument Tablet; GPS 38.28350, -78.54150; Yorktown; York **GS:** U **SP:** No info **VI:** No further data **P:** unk **BLW:** unk **RG:** unk **MK:** unk **PH:** unk **SS:** J-Yorktown Historian; AX pg 127 **BS:** JLARC 74.

MARSHALL, James Markham; b 12 Mar 1764 Fauquier Co; d 26 Apr 1848 **RU:** Lieutenant, Served in VA Line in artillery co under Maj Nelson, Recd ½ pay indicating disabled in service **CEM:** Marshall Family; GPS unk; Rt 55, Happy Creek Pl, Front Royal; Warren **GS:** U **SP:** Mar (9 Apr 1795) Hester Morris (30 Jul 1774, Philadelphia-13 Apr 1816) **VI:** Appl pen 23 May 1833 Frederick Co. S7173 also VA 1/2 pay (See N.A. Acc #874 #050109 1/2 Pay). Died in Frederick Co **P:** Y **BLW:** unk **RG:** Y **MK:** unk **PH:** unk **SS:** J-NSSAR 1993 Reg, J- DAR Hatcher; CG pg 2197; DD **BS:** JLARC 1 ,2.

MARSHALL, Jesse; b 1765; d 1840 **RU:** Midshipman, Served in VA State Navy **CEM:** Bethel Church; GPS unk; E Washington St; Suffolk City **GS:** N **SP:** No info **VI:** No further data **P:** unk **BLW:** unk **RG:** N **MK:** N **PH:** N **SS:** K pg 174; AR Vol 3 pg 51; BK pg 7; CZ **BS:** 32 e-mail.

MARSHALL, John Curtis; b Sept 24 1755, Westmoreland Co; d Jul 6 1835 **RU:** Captain/Patriot, Ent serv Fauquier Co. Was Lt in Fauquier Independent Co at outbreak of Rev in 1775. Served also in Capt William Pickett's Co. Served w/ father in Culpeper Minute Bn at battle of Great Bridge. Served in winter 1777-78 at Valley Forge w/ George Washington. Comm Lt 3rd Regt 30 Jul 1776. Was Deputy Judge-Advocate 20 Nov 1777. Became Capt 1 Jul 1778 serving in 7th Regt. Retired Feb 12 1781 **CEM:** Shockoe Hill; GPS 37.55190, -77.43170; 4th & Hospital Sts; Richmond City **GS:** U **SP:** Mary Willis Ambler (13 Mar 1776 Yorktown-25 Dec 1831 Richmond) d/o (-----) & Rebecca Burwell (1746-1806) **VI:** Son of Thomas & Mary (Keith) Marshall. 1780, George Wythe's law lectures at William and Mary in Williamsburg. Federalist. House of Rep. Sec of State to John Adams. Awarded BLW 4,000 acres as a capt. Chief Justice of US Supreme Ct in 1801 for 34 yrs, decisions form the basis of Constitutional Law. Sol appl 26 Jan 1833 Washington DC age 77, then living in Richmond. S5731. Died in Philadelphia **P:** Y **BLW:** Y **RG:** Y **MK:** Y **PH:** Y **SS:** K Vol 3 pg 174; CG pg 2198 **BS:** JLARC 1, 4, 77.

MARSHALL, Robert; b unk; d Aft 1783 **RU:** Sergeant, Served in Capt Thomas Craig's Co of Col St Clair's PA Bn 1776 of 4th Cont Line. Was appt Sgt 7 Jan 1776; discharged 18 Jul 1776 **CEM:** Bethel Church aka Old Lyle; GPS unk; Millboro Springs; Bath **GS:** N **SP:** Mar (1792) Jean Vance **VI:** No further data **P:** unk **BLW:** unk **RG:** N **MK:** N **PH:** unk **SS:** A pg 187 **BS:** 80 vol 3 pg 51; 196.

MARSHALL, Thomas; b Apr 2 1730, Westmoreland Co; d Jun 22 1802 **RU:** Colonel/Patriot, Organizer of Culpeper Minuteman. Was Maj at battle of Great Bridge with son John and in 3rd Regt 13 Feb 1776. Was Lt Col Aug 13 1776, Col, 21 Feb 1777. Appt Commander of State Artillery Regt until Feb 1782. Was captured at surrender of Charleston 1780. Gave material aid to the cause **CEM:** Marshall Family; GPS unk; Rt 55, Happy Creek Pl, Front Royal; Warren **GS:** Y **SP:** Mar (1754) Mary Randolph Keith (1737-1809) **VI:** Son of John & Elizabeth (Marham) Marshall. Childhood friend of Geo Washington. Surveyor to Lord Fairfax with help of Washington. Tax collector. High Sheriff. Lt in French & Indian War. Moved to KY after Rev. Died in Old Washington in Mason Co, KY. Memorialized in VA **P:** unk **BLW:** unk **RG:** Y **MK:** N **PH:** unk **SS:** AL Ct Bk pg 15; CE pg 38 **BS:** 113.

MARSHALL, William; b 1753; d 16 May 1796 **RU:** Captain, Commanded a co in York Co Militia Oct 1775 **CEM:** Smyrna; GPS unk; Off Rt 604 Damney's Mill Rd, SE of Corinth Fork; King William **GS:** Y

RU=Rank/Unit	CEM=Cemetery	GS=Gravestone	SP=Spousal Information
VI=Other Veteran Info	P=Pension	BLW=Bounty/Land Warrant	RG=Registered Grave
MK=SAR/DAR Marker	PH=Photo	SS=Service Source	BS=Burial Source

214

SP: No info **VI:** Became a doctor after RW. **P:** unk **BLW:** unk **RG:** unk **MK**: N **PH:** unk **SS:** E pg 502 **BS:** 196.

MARSTELLER, Philip Balthasar or Phillip G; b 4 Jan 1741, Philadelphia Co, PA; d 1803 **RU:** Lieutenant Colonel, Served in PA. Maj, 2nd Battalion, Lancaster Co 1776; Lt Col, 1st Battalion Lancaster Co 1777; Assist Forage Master 1780; Paymaster, Lancaster Co Militia, 1777-1784 **CEM:** Old Christ Church Episcopal; GPS 38.80625, -77.04718; 118 N Washington St; Alexandria City **GS:** Y **SP:** Magdelena Reiss **VI:** Original table stone carried off during Civil War. Member (Lancaster Co) PA Constitutional Convention Jul 1776, Assistant Deputy Quartermaster General, PA Associators in 1777, Lt Col US Army, 1st Batallion (plaque) **P:** unk **BLW:** unk **RG:** Y **MK**: Y **PH:** unk **SS:** BT **BS:** JLARC 1, 25, 86; 20 pg 139; 196.

MARTIN, Alexis; b unk; d 1781 **RU:** Soldier, Served in Foix Bn and died fr battle at Yorktown **CEM:** French Memorial; GPS 36.81944, -79.39933; Yorktown; York **GS:** U **SP:** No info **VI:** No further data **P:** unk **BLW:** unk **RG:** Y **MK**: unk **PH:** unk **SS:** J-Yorktown Historian **BS:** JLARC 1, 74.

MARTIN, Anthony; b 26 Sep 1737, Goochland Co; d 19 Jun 1805 **RU:** Patriot, Gave material aid to the cause **CEM:** Elioch Manor Family; GPS unk; Elioch Manor Dr, end of rd; Powhatan **GS:** Y **SP:** Mar (21 Dec 1758) Sarah Holman (___-aft 1805) **VI:** Son of Peter (1712-1742) & Mary Anne (Rapine) Martin **P:** N **BLW:** N **RG:** N **MK**: N **PH:** unk **SS:** DAR #A074079; D Vol 3 pg 774, 782-4; AL Ct bk pg 5 **BS:** 77, LVA website.

MARTIN, Antoine; b unk; d 1781 **RU:** Seaman, Served on "Marseillais"and died from Yorktown battle **CEM:** French Memorial; GPS 36.81944, -79.39933; Yorktown; York **GS:** U **SP:** No info **VI:** No further data **P:** unk **BLW:** unk **RG:** Y **MK**: unk **PH:** unk **SS:** J-Yorktown Historian **BS:** JLARC 1, 74.

MARTIN, Azariah; b 11 Jan 1742, Amherst Co; d 26 Jul 1824 **RU:** Captain, Commanded Co of militia in Amherst Co 1780 **CEM:** Martin Family; GPS unk; Check property records; Nelson **GS:** U **SP:** Mar (19 Mar 1772) Mary Rodes, (1758, Albemarle Co-1758, Nelson Co) d/o Charles (c1730, Hanover Co-17 Jun 1805, Amherst Co) & Lucy Rhodes **VI:** Son of James (25 Aug 1699-__) & Elizabeth (Crawford) Martin. Rank of Capt confirmed in pen appl by nephew of same name. Pen appl for Clay Co KY 1832 by nephew who served in his Co in Amherst Co. Pen appl by widow Lucy Rodes 28 Feb1840 in KY W554 **P:** Y **BLW:** unk **RG:** Y **MK**: unk **PH:** unk **SS:** J-NSSAR 1993 Reg; K Vol 3 pg 175 **BS:** JLARC 1.

MARTIN, Claude; b unk; d 1781 **RU:** Seaman, Served on "Languedoc" and died from Yorktown battle **CEM:** French Memorial; GPS 36.81944, -79.39933; Yorktown; York **GS:** U **SP:** No info **VI:** No further data **P:** unk **BLW:** unk **RG:** Y **MK**: unk **PH:** unk **SS:** J-Yorktown Historian **BS:** JLARC 1,74.

MARTIN, Henry Andrew; b 1720 Germantown, Fauquier Co; d 1780 **RU:** Patriot, Gave material aid to cause **CEM:** Germantown Glebe; GPS unk; Rt 643 nr Licking Run, Midland; Fauquier **GS:** U **SP:** Mary Ann White (26 Nov 1720 Culpeper Co-1782) **VI:** Son of (-----) & Maria Katherina (Otterbach) (1699-1724) Martin **P:** N **BLW:** N **RG:** unk **MK**: unk **PH:** unk **SS:** AL Certificate Fauquier Co **BS:** 196.

MARTIN, Jean; b unk; d 1781 **RU:** Seaman, Served on "Ville de Paris" and died from Yorktown battle **CEM:** French Memorial; GPS 36.81944, -79.39933; Yorktown; York **GS:** U **SP:** No info **VI:** No further data **P:** unk **BLW:** unk **RG:** Y **MK**: unk **PH:** unk **SS:** J-Yorktown Historian **BS:** JLARC 1,74.

MARTIN, John; b c1735; d 1823 **RU:** Second Lieutenant/Patriot, Gave 180# beef to cause in 1781. Was 2nd Lt Jul 1779 in Capt Weavers' Co, Fauquier Co Militia **CEM:** Martin Family, Germantown; GPS unk; Rt 3 Germantown; Spotsylvania **GS:** N **SP:** 1) Catherine (-----) (___-after 1785 Germantown) 2) Margaret Elliot **VI:** Son of John Joseph & Catherine (-----) Martin. Died in Old Germantown Settlement, Fauquier Co **P:** unk **BLW:** unk **RG:** Y **MK**: N **PH:** N **SS:** D pg 862 **BS:** 10 pg 52; 19 pg 65-66.

MARTIN, Joseph; b c1740; d 1808 **RU:** Brig General/Patriot, Had military duty in the militia as general and public duty as VA agent to the Cherokee Nation in 1777 **CEM:** Martin Family; GPS unk; Leatherwood Downs; Henry **GS:** U **SP:** 1) Susanna Graves (1758-1837) 2) Sarah Lucas (1754-1775) 3) Elizabeth Ward **VI:** Son of Joseph (1700-1761) & Susannah Page (Chiles) (1700-1754) Martin. Martinsville was named in his honor. **P:** unk **BLW:** unk **RG:** unk **MK**: unk **PH:** unk **SS:** E pg 503; CD **BS:** 196.

RU=Rank/Unit	CEM=Cemetery	GS=Gravestone	SP=Spousal Information
VI=Other Veteran Info	P=Pension	BLW=Bounty/Land Warrant	RG=Registered Grave
MK=SAR/DAR Marker	PH=Photo	SS=Service Source	BS=Burial Source

215

MARTIN, Joseph; b 1730, Germantown, Fauquier Co; d 1793 **RU:** Patriot, Gave material aid to cause **CEM:** Germantown Glebe; GPS unk; Rt 643 nr Licking Run, Midland; Fauquier **GS:** U **SP:** Catherine Holtclaw (1734 Germany-1807 Germantown) **VI:** Son of (-----) & Maria Katherina (Otterbach) (1699-1724) Martin **P:** N **BLW:** N **RG:** unk **MK:** unk **PH:** unk **SS:** AL Ct Bk pg 2 Fauquier Co **BS:** 196.

MARTIN, Joseph; b c1755; d 14 Feb 1832 **RU:** Private, Enlisted Alexandria in 6th & 10th VA Cont Line **CEM:** Martin Family; GPS unk; Leatherwood Downs; Henry **GS:** U **SP:** Mar (1 Mar 1782 Loudoun Co) Patsey Baily (1761-aft 1840 Patrick Co) **VI:** Pen both. He appl Henry Co 11 Nov 1811; she appl 26 Feb 1839 Rockingham Co NC **P:** Y **BLW:** unk **RG:** unk **MK:** unk **PH:** unk **SS:** J- DAR Hatcher; E pg 503; AL Ct Bk pg 21, 25 Henry Co; CG pg 2207 **BS:** JLARC 2; AR pg 53.

MARTIN, Louis; b unk; d 1781 **RU:** Soldier, Served in Agenois Bn and died fr battle at Yorktown **CEM:** French Memorial; GPS 36.81944, -79.39933; Yorktown; York **GS:** U **SP:** No info **VI:** No further data **P:** unk **BLW:** unk **RG:** Y **MK:** unk **PH:** unk **SS:** J-Yorktown Historian **BS:** JLARC 1, 74.

MARTIN, Nicolas; b unk; d 1781 **RU:** Seaman, Served on "Destin" and died from Yorktown battle **CEM:** French Memorial; GPS 36.81944, -79.39933; Yorktown; York **GS:** U **SP:** No info **VI:** No further data **P:** unk **BLW:** unk **RG:** Y **MK:** unk **PH:** unk **SS:** J-Yorktown Historian **BS:** JLARC 1, 74.

MARTIN, Orson; b 1735, Goochland Co; d 24 Jul 1786 **RU:** Patriot, Gave material aid to cause **CEM:** Burnt Chimney; GPS unk; Cat Taile Branch; Cumberland **GS:** Y **SP:** Mar (c1763/4) Ann Foushee (07 Mar 1736-25 Aug 1800) **VI:** Son of Valentine Martin & Jane Bridgewater **P:** N **BLW:** N **RG:** N **MK:** N **PH:** unk **SS:** DAR #A074456; AL Ct Bk pg 16, 28 Cumberland Co; AS **BS:** 80 vol 3 pg 53; 196.

MARTIN, Thomas; b 21 Oct 1759, Martins Cree, Northampton Co, PA; d 31 Mar 1856 **RU:** Lieutenant, Served in VA Line at Winchester VA, Jan-Mar 1783 **CEM:** New Providence Presbyterian; GPS 37.95170, -79.30250; 1208 New Providence Rd, Raphine; Rockbridge **GS:** Y **SP:** Letitia Ralston (1771-1861) **VI:** Son of James (1710-1767) & Ann (Miller) (1728-1799) Martin **P:** unk **BLW:** unk **RG:** unk **MK:** unk **PH:** unk **SS:** G pg 676 **BS:** JLARC 63,79; 196.

MARTIN, Thomas; b unk; d 1781 **RU:** Seaman, Served on "Hector" and died from Yorktown battle **CEM:** French Memorial; GPS 36.81944, -79.39933; Yorktown; York **GS:** U **SP:** No info **VI:** No further data **P:** unk **BLW:** unk **RG:** Y **MK:** unk **PH:** unk **SS:** J-Yorktown Historian **BS:** JLARC 1, 74.

MARTIN, Thomas Bryan; b unk; d 4 Sep 1798 **RU:** Patriot, Supplied material goods, including horses, corn, 24, 244 lbs flour, 50 lbs beef, use of wagons, 121 gallons whiskey **CEM:** Greenway Court; GPS unk; Nr Lord Fairfax, White Post; Clarke **GS:** N **SP:** No info **VI:** 1879 letter said he was bur at Greenway Ct Cem. **P:** N **BLW:** N **RG:** N **PH:** N **SS:** AL Cert issued **BS:** 58 pg 10.

MARTIN, Vincent; b unk; d 1781 **RU:** Soldier, Served in Auxonne Bn and died fr battle at Yorktown **CEM:** French Memorial; GPS 36.81944, -79.39933; Yorktown; York **GS:** U **SP:** No info **VI:** No further data **P:** unk **BLW:** unk **RG:** Y **MK:** unk **PH:** unk **SS:** J-Yorktown Historian **BS:** JLARC 1, 74.

MARTIN, William; b unk; d 1804 **RU:** Patriot, Gave material aid to cause **CEM:** Anglican Chapel; GPS unk; Court Street; Lynchburg City **GS:** U **SP:** No info **VI:** No further data **P:** N **BLW:** N **RG:** unk **MK:** unk **PH:** unk **SS:** AL Cert Bedford Co **BS:** JLARC 36.

MASON, George; b 1753; d 5 Dec 1796 **RU:** Captain/Patriot, Commanded a co in Fairfax Co Militia 1775-1776. Gave material aid to cause **CEM:** Gunston Hall; GPS 38.66862, -77.16823; Gunston Rd, Lorton; Fairfax **GS:** Y **SP:** Elizabeth Mary Ann Barnes Hooe (1768-28 May 1814, Lexington) d/o Gerard & Sarah Hooe. She m. 1) George Mason; 2) George Graham of Prince William Co. Memorial Stone **VI:** Son of George & Ann (-----) Mason. Died in his 44th yr in Lexington. Memorial stone **P:** unk **BLW:** unk **RG:** N **MK:** N **PH:** Y **SS:** AL Cert issued; CD **BS:** 61 vol V, pg MN-6; 196.

MASON, George Jr; b 1749; d 24 Mar 1796 **RU:** Captain, Served in Fairfax Co 1774-? commanded by Capt Geo. Washington as ensign. Was Capt in Reg Army 1775-76 **CEM:** Old Christ Church Episcopal; GPS 38.80625, -77.04718; 118 N Washington St; Alexandria City **GS:** Y **SP:** No info **VI:** Resigned Reg Army due to sickness & went to France. Died age 47 **P:** unk **BLW:** unk **RG:** Y **MK:** N **PH:** unk **SS:** E pg 505; H **BS:** 20 pg 139; 196.

RU=Rank/Unit   CEM=Cemetery   GS=Gravestone   SP=Spousal Information
VI=Other Veteran Info P=Pension   BLW=Bounty/Land Warrant RG=Registered Grave
MK=SAR/DAR Marker   PH=Photo   SS=Service Source   BS=Burial Source

216

MASON, George Sr; b 1725; d 7 Oct 1792 **RU:** Patriot, Gave material aid to the cause **CEM:** Gunston Hall; **GPS** 38.66862, -77.16823; Gunston Rd, Lorton; Fairfax **GS:** Y **SP:** 1) Mar (1750) Anna Elbeck; 2) Mar (1780) Sarah Brent **VI:** Son of George & Ann (Thomson) Mason. Justice of Fairfax Co 1754-1759; VA House of Burgesses, 1765 opposed Stamp Act. 1774 Fairfax Resolves, 1775 VA Declaration of Rights. Helped write Constitution **P:** N **BLW:** N **RG:** Y **MK:** N **PH:** Y **SS:** AL Ct Bk pg 15; AJ **BS:** SAR regis; 196.

MASON, Stevens (Stephen) Thomson; b 29 Dec 1760; d 10 May 1803 **RU:** Private, Served in artillery fr Plymouth, MA **CEM:** Raspberry Plain; **GPS** unk; 16500 Agape Ln, Leesburg; Loudoun **GS:** U **SP:** No info **VI:** Served in US Senate fr 1794-1803 **P:** unk **BLW:** Y **RG:** unk **MK:** unk **PH:** unk **SS:** C pg 617; BX pg 546 **BS:** 196.

MASON, Thomas; b unk; d 7 Oct 1781 **RU:** Drummer, Served in Capt Ten Eyck's Co, Col Van Cortlandt's 2d Regt, NY Line. Died fr the battle at Yorktown **CEM:** Yorktown Victory Monument Tablet; **GPS** 38.28350, -78.54150; Yorktown; York **GS:** U **SP:** No info **VI:** No further data **P:** unk **BLW:** unk **RG:** unk **MK:** unk **PH:** unk **SS:** J-Yorktown Historian; AX pg 191 **BS:** JLARC 74.

MASON, Thomson (Thompson); b 17 Aug 1733; d 26 Feb 1785 **RU:** Patriot, Gave material aid to cause **CEM:** Raspberry Plain; **GPS** unk; 16500 Agape Ln, Leesburg; Loudoun **GS:** N **SP:** Mary King Barnes (__-21 Oct 1771) **VI:** Son of George (1690-1735) & Ann (Thomson) (1699-1762) Mason **P:** N **BLW:** N **RG:** unk **MK:** N **PH:** N **SS:** AL Ct Bk pg 50 **BS:** 196.

MASSAL, Jean; b unk; d 1781 **RU:** unk, Served in Touraine Bn and died fr battle at Yorktown **CEM:** French Memorial; **GPS** 36.81944, -79.39933; Yorktown; York **GS:** U **SP:** No info **VI:** No further data **P:** unk **BLW:** unk **RG:** Y **MK:** unk **PH:** unk **SS:** J-Yorktown Historian **BS:** JLARC 1, 74.

MASSEY, Lee; b 22 Sep 1732, probably Stafford Co; d 23 Sep 1814 **RU:** Patriot, Member, Fairfax Co Committee of Safety 1774. Member, committee to care for poor 1775. Provided 7000 lbs of hay to cause **CEM:** Pohick Episcopal; **GPS** 38.42546, -77.11598; 9301 Richmond Hwy, Lorton; Fairfax **GS:** Y **SP:** 1) (-----) 2) (-----) 3) Mar (after 1763) Elizabeth Bronaugh (Brunaugh) **VI:** Rector of Pohick Episcopal Church and thus for George Washington & George Mason. Removed fr burial ground at home "Bradley" on Belmot Bay. Lee rebur under pulpit; Elizabeth in church cem. **P:** N **BLW:** N **RG:** Y **MK:** Y **PH:** Y **SS:** D Fairfax Co **BS:** 04.

MASSIE, Charles; b unk; d 1817 **RU:** Sergeant, Served in 5th Cont Line **CEM:** Johnson Family; **GPS** unk; Rt 658; Goochland **GS:** Y **SP:** No info **VI:** Erected by Jack Jouett Chapt. DAR 1948 **P:** unk **BLW:** unk **RG:** N **MK:** N **PH:** unk **SS:** E pg 506 **BS:** 46 pg 174.

MASSIE, Charles Sr; b 2 Aug 1727, Hanover Co; d 1817 **RU:** Captain/Patriot, Capt 6th VA Regt, 23 Mar 1776. Committee of Safety 1775-76. Gave material aid to cause **CEM:** Spring Valley (Massie Family); **GPS** 37.94277, -78.76863; 3808 Spring Valley Rd Batesville; Albemarle **GS:** Y **SP:** Mar (1755) Mary Davis (__-1817) **VI:** No further data **P:** unk **BLW:** unk **RG:** unk **MK:** unk **PH:** unk **SS:** J- DAR Hatcher; DD cites Paid Supply Tax 1783 Albemarle Co **BS:** JLARC 2; 196.

MASSIE (MASSIE), Thomas; b 11 or 22 Aug 1747, New Kent Co; d 2 Feb 1834 **RU:** Major, Was commissioned Capt 1775 in 6th VA Regt, recruiting soldiers fr New Kent Co. Was Aide to Gen Thomas Nelson. Was present at surrender of Cornwallis, Yorktown 1781. Served in 6th,11th Cont Lines. Appointed Maj 20 Feb 1778. Resigned 25 Jun 1779 **CEM:** Level Green; **GPS** unk; Massies Mill; Nelson **GS:** U **SP:** Mar (11 Apr 1781 Augusta Co) Sarah (Sally) Cocke (c1760-27 Apr 1838) **VI:** Son of William (__-1751) & (-----) Massie. Charter member, Society of the Cincinnati, established by officers of Rev to raise funds for widows & orphans of soldiers. One of first magistrates of Nelson Co when it was formed 1807. BLW of 5333 1/3 acres OH & KY. Sol appl 15 Feb 1833 Nelson Co. Widow appl pen 17 Jan 1837 Nelson Co age 77. W7403 also VA 1/2 Pay. **P:** Y **BLW:** Y **RG:** unk **MK:** Y **PH:** unk **SS:** E pg 506; K Vol 3 pg 187; CG pg 2219 **BS:** JLARC 4, 83.

MATHEWS, Thomas; b 1742, St Christopher's, aka St Kitts, British West Indies; d 20 Feb 1812 **RU:** Captain, Was Capt of Inf 8th Co, 5 Mar 1776-7 Nov 1777; Maj of VA State Artillery Regt in Col Thomas Marshall's Regt 15 Nov 1777; and Lt Col of State Line 8 Nov 1779-15 Apr 1780. Was captured at Charleston **CEM:** St Paul's Episcopal; **GPS** 36.84733, -76.28554; 201 St Paul's Blvd; Norfolk City **GS:** N **SP:** Mar (9 Jul 1773) Mary "Molly" Miller (c1752-8 Jul 1837) **VI:** Son of Samuel Augustus & Mary

RU=Rank/Unit	CEM=Cemetery	GS=Gravestone	SP=Spousal Information
VI=Other Veteran Info	P=Pension	BLW=Bounty/Land Warrant	RG=Registered Grave
MK=SAR/DAR Marker	PH=Photo	SS=Service Source	BS=Burial Source

217

(Gacey) Mathews. Delegate in the General Assembly. Arrived in Norfolk by 1772. Wife permitted pen on applic in 1836. Widow appl 13 Sep 1836 Pasquotank Co NC. W17076 & R16019 also VA 1/2 Pay **P:** Y **BLW:** unk **RG:** N **MK:** N **PH:** N **SS:** J- DAR Hatcher; K Vol 3 pg 189; CB AS; CG pg 2219; CE pg 21, 43, 123, 124, 164; DAR report. **BS:** JLARC 2; DAR report.

MATTHEWS, Richard; b 17 Nov 1761; d 8 Jun 1845 **RU:** Private, Served in Capt William Johnston's Co 11th VA Regt of Foot commanded by Col Morgan, Mar & Apr 1777 **CEM:** Bethel Church; GPS unk; Rt 610; Frederick **GS:** Y **SP:** Mar (c1797) Elizabeth Woolfkill (15 Feb 1777-6 Nov 1820) d/o John (Jun 1752, Germany-1 Jul 1839,Trunbull, OH) & Agnes (Conrad) (1747, PA-__) Woolfkill **VI:** No further data **P:** unk **BLW:** unk **RG:** N **MK:** N **PH:** unk **SS:** AP Service Rec **BS:** 59 pg 212.

MAUBRUCHON, Yves; b unk; d 1781 **RU:** Seaman, Served on "Ville de Paris" and died from Yorktown battle **CEM:** French Memorial; GPS 36.81944, -79.39933; Yorktown; York **GS:** U **SP:** No info **VI:** No further data **P:** unk **BLW:** unk **RG:** Y **MK:** unk **PH:** unk **SS:** J-Yorktown Historian **BS:** JLARC 1, 74.

MAUCHALIN, Yves (or Philibert); b unk; d 1781 **RU:** Soldier, Served in Gatinais Bn and died fr battle at Yorktown **CEM:** French Memorial; GPS 36.81944, -79.39933; Yorktown; York **GS:** U **SP:** No info **VI:** No further data **P:** unk **BLW:** unk **RG:** Y **MK:** unk **PH:** unk **SS:** J-Yorktown Historian **BS:** JLARC 1, 74.

MAUGER, Pierre; b unk; d 1781 **RU:** Seaman, Served on "Auguste" and died from Yorktown battle **CEM:** French Memorial; GPS 36.81944, -79.39933; Yorktown; York **GS:** U **SP:** No info **VI:** No further data **P:** unk **BLW:** unk **RG:** Y **MK:** unk **PH:** unk **SS:** J-Yorktown Historian **BS:** JLARC 1, 74.

MAUPINE, Daniel; b 25 Mar 1700, France; d 20 Sep 1788 **RU:** Patriot, Gave 297# beef for Albemarle Barracks **CEM:** Maupin Family Farm; GPS unk; Morman's River; Albemarle **GS:** Y **SP:** Mar (1775) Margaret Via (c1701-9 Oct 1788) **VI:** No further data **P:** N **BLW:** N **RG:** Y **MK:** N **PH:** unk **SS:** DAR #A075691; AL Ct BK pg 3, 25; Albemarle Co; D vol 3 pg 3 **BS:** SAR Appl.

MAURE, Leon; b unk; d 1781 **RU:** Soldier, Served in Santogne Bn and died fr battle at Yorktown **CEM:** French Memorial; GPS 36.81944, -79.39933; Yorktown; York **GS:** U **SP:** No info **VI:** No further data **P:** unk **BLW:** unk **RG:** Y **MK:** unk **PH:** unk **SS:** J-Yorktown Historian **BS:** JLARC 1, 74.

MAURY, Fontaine; b 3 Feb 1761 Spotsylvania Co; d 1 Jan 1814 **RU:** Private, Aide to Marquis de la Fayette in VA campaign **CEM:** Unknown, probably Fredericksburg; GPS unk; See Fredericksburg newspapers Jan 1814, for obit and burial place; Fredericksburg City **GS:** U **SP:** No info **VI:** Mayor of Fredericksburg Mar 1798 to Mar 1799. **P:** unk **BLW:** unk **RG:** Y **MK:** N **PH:** unk **SS:** AS; SAR regis; NSSAR Ancestor #P-243291 **BS:** SAR regis.

MAURY, Walker; b 20 Jul 1752 Albemarle Co; d 11 Oct 1788 **RU:** Patriot, Gave material aid to cause **CEM:** St Paul's Episcopal; GPS 36.84733, 76.28554; 201 St Paul's Blvd; Norfolk City **GS:** U **SP:** Mary Stith Grimes (25 Aug 1758-23 Sep 1839) d/o Ludwell (1733-1755) 7 Mary (Dawson) (__-1788) Grymes **VI:** Son of James (8 Apr 1717, Ireland,-9 Jun 1769) & (-----) Maury. Was Professor Wm & Mary College. Ordained priest. Died of Yellow Fever. **P:** N **BLW:** N **RG:** unk **MK:** unk **PH:** unk **SS:** AL Ct Bk pg 17 Orange Co **BS:** 196.

MAUSSION, Charles; b unk; d 1781 **RU:** Seaman, Served on "Hector" and died from Yorktown battle **CEM:** French Memorial; GPS 36.81944, -79.39933; Yorktown; York **GS:** U **SP:** No info **VI:** No further data **P:** unk **BLW:** unk **RG:** Y **MK:** unk **PH:** unk **SS:** J-Yorktown Historian **BS:** JLARC 1, 74.

MAXEY, Walter; b 1720, Goochland; d Sep 1791 **RU:** Patriot, Gave material aid to cause **CEM:** Mt Ivy; GPS unk; Scruggs; Franklin **GS:** Y **SP:** Mary Netherland (1720-1798) **VI:** Son of Edward (1660-1740) & (-----) Maxey **P:** N **BLW:** N **RG:** unk **MK:** unk **PH:** unk **SS:** AL Ct Bk pg 8, 10, 11 **BS:** 196.

MAXWELL, David; b 1742; d 28 Jul 1794 **RU:** Private, Served in Illinois in Capt John Kennedy's Co, Col George Rogers Clark's Regt **CEM:** Maxwell Family; GPS unk; Abingdon; Washington **GS:** U **SP:** Elizabeth (-----) **VI:** No further data **P:** unk **BLW:** unk **RG:** Y **MK:** N **PH:** unk **SS:** DAR #A075911; E pg 510 **BS:** DAR report.

MAXWELL, James; b c1729, Northumberland, England; d 4 Oct 1791 **RU:** Captain, Appointed by Navy Board as "Superintendent General of the Shipyard" in Jan. 1777 to supervise construction and fitting of naval vessels. In Jun 1779, was Commissioner of the Navy under the Board of War Jul 1780. **CEM:** St

RU=Rank/Unit   CEM=Cemetery   GS=Gravestone   SP=Spousal Information
VI=Other Veteran Info   P=Pension   BLW=Bounty/Land Warrant   RG=Registered Grave
MK=SAR/DAR Marker   PH=Photo   SS=Service Source   BS=Burial Source

218

Paul's Episcopal; GPS 36.84733, -76.28554; 201 St Paul's Blvd; Norfolk City **GS:** U **SP:** Helen (Calvert) Maxwell Read (1st husband) **VI:** Became Norfolk resident in 1767. Prominent in wife's memoirs. Wore "a cockade in his hat." Granted a special BLW fr VA Governor for naval service to state. William Maxwell appl for pen under his serv for the estate in 1845, which was granted. Recd 1/2 pay, thus probably disabled in service. Heirs also appl for 2nd BLW which was rejected as he already received one. R73 **P:** Y **BLW:** Y **RG:** unk **MK:** unk **PH:** unk **SS:** K Vol 3 pg 195; CB, J- DAR Hatcher; CG pg 2231 **BS:** JLARC 2.

MAXWELL, Thomas; b 1740; d 1781 **RU:** Lieutenant, Served in Capt James Maxwell's Co, Montgomery Co Militia **CEM:** Rural; GPS unk; Maxwell Gap; Montgomery **GS:** U **SP:** No info **VI:** No further data **P:** unk **BLW:** unk **RG:** Y **MK:** unk **PH:** unk **SS:** J-NSSAR 2000 Reg; G pg 237; CZ **BS:** JLARC 76.

MAY, George I; b 1755; d 1815 **RU:** Private, Served in Capt Jonathan Hanby's Co, 3rd Cont Line **CEM:** May Family; GPS unk; May Creek Ln, Criders, Bergton; Rockingham **GS:** Y **SP:** Martha Magdalene (Houghman) **VI:** No further data **P:** unk **BLW:** unk **RG:** Y **MK:** N **PH:** unk **SS:** E pg 510 **BS:** 191 May cem.

MAYER, Jean; b unk; d 1781 **RU:** Seaman, Served on "Ville de Paris" and died from Yorktown battle **CEM:** French Memorial; GPS 36.81944, -79.39933; Yorktown; York **GS:** U **SP:** No info **VI:** No further data **P:** unk **BLW:** unk **RG:** Y **MK:** unk **PH:** unk **SS:** J-Yorktown Historian **BS:** JLARC 1, 74.

MAYO, John; b 21 Oct 1760, Deep Creek, Powhatan Co; d 28 May 1818 **RU:** Patriot, Gave material aid to cause **CEM:** Belleville Estate; GPS unk; See property records for location; Henrico **GS:** U **SP:** Abigail Dellart (1 Mar 1761 Elizabeth Union, NJ-__) **VI:** Son of John (1736 Gloucester Co-__) & Mary (Tabb) (8 Jul 1733-__) Mayo. Rep Henrico Co General Assembly 1785, 1786, and 1791 to 1796. Was Lt Col in War of 1812 **P:** N **BLW:** N **RG:** unk **MK:** unk **PH:** unk **SS:** Al Ct Bk **BS:** 32.

MAYO, John; b 17 Jul 1737, Henrico Co; d 17 Jan 1786 **RU:** Patriot, Gave material to the cause **CEM:** Hollywood; GPS 37.53560, -77.45720; 412 S Cherry St; Richmond City **GS:** Y **SP:** Mary Tabb (8 Jul 1733, Gloucester Co-17 Aug 1792) **VI:** Son of William (1685-1744) & Ann (Perratt) (1700-1773) Mayo. Died in Powhatan Co **P:** N **BLW:** N **RG:** Y **MK:** N **PH:** unk **SS:** E pg 511; D Vol I pg 254 **BS:** 28 pg 198 Appdx.

MAYO, William; b 26 Sep 1757; d 12 Aug 1837 **RU:** Captain, Was Sea Capt 1780-81 **CEM:** St John's Episcopal; GPS 37.53183, -77.41958; 2401 E Broad St; Richmond City **GS:** N **SP:** 1) Elizabeth Poythress 2) Lucy Fitzhugh **VI:** No further data **P:** unk **BLW:** unk **RG:** Y **MK:** Y **PH:** N **SS:** G, pg 288, 291 **BS:** 28 pg 198 Appdx.

MCALEXANDER, James Jr; b 1 May 1756; d 30 Jan 1840 **RU:** Lieutenant, Served as Private in Capt Nicholas Cabell's Co, Albemarle Co Militia Apr 1776. Became Lt before Oct 1781 in Amherst Co. **CEM:** Rockfish Presbyterian; GPS unk; 5016 Rockfish Valley Hwy, Nellysford; Nelson **GS:** Y **SP:** No info **VI:** Son of James Sr (17 Feb 1717-Jan 1798) & (-----) McAlexander. Family monument **P:** unk **BLW:** unk **RG:** unk **MK:** unk **PH:** unk **SS:** E pg 512; DC pg 154 **BS:** 196.

MCALEXANDER, James Sr; b 17 Feb 1717, South Ayrshire, Scotland; d Jan 1798 **RU:** Patriot, Gave material aid to cause **CEM:** Rockfish Presbyterian; GPS unk; 5016 Rockfish Valley Hwy, Nellysford; Nelson **GS:** Y **SP:** No info **VI:** Died in Lovingston, Nelson Co. Family monument **P:** N **BLW:** N **RG:** unk **MK:** unk **PH:** unk **SS:** AL Ct Bk pg 30 Amherst Co **BS:** 196.

MCALEXANDER, John; b 1750, Albemarle Co; d 1834 **RU:** Private, Served in Capt Nicholas Cabell's Co, Albemarle Co Militia Apr 1776 **CEM:** Thompson, Salmons, McAlexander; GPS unk; Rt 719 Woolwine; Patrick **GS:** Y **SP:** Mar (25 Mar 1780) Agnes (Nancy) Burnett (1763-1820) **VI:** Son of James Sr (17 Feb 1717-Jan 1798) & (-----) McAlexander **P:** unk **BLW:** unk **RG:** unk **MK:** unk **PH:** unk **SS:** DC pg 154 **BS:** 196.

MCALLISTER, James; b c1738, Spotsylvania Co; d 1798 **RU:** Private?, Served in Culpeper Militia 1781, and 7th Cont Line **CEM:** McAllister Family; GPS unk; Check property records for burial in or nr Syria; Madison **GS:** N **SP:** Eva (-----) **VI:** No further data **P:** unk **BLW:** unk **RG:** Y **MK:** N **PH:** N **SS:** E pg 512 **BS:** 04.

RU=Rank/Unit	CEM=Cemetery	GS=Gravestone	SP=Spousal Information
VI=Other Veteran Info	P=Pension	BLW=Bounty/Land Warrant	RG=Registered Grave
MK=SAR/DAR Marker	PH=Photo	SS=Service Source	BS=Burial Source

MCCALL, Thomas; b 22 Jul 1757; d 17 Aug 1818 **RU:** Soldier, Enl 29 Jan 1776. Served in Capt Willam Rippey's Co #4 Col Milliam Invenes PA Regt at Mount Independence 23 Nov 1776 **CEM:** Rock Spring; GPS 37.78126, -79.44585; Jct Rt 803 & Liberty Hall Rd, Lodi; Washington **GS:** U **SP:** Agnes Mongomery d/o John & (-----) Montgomery **VI:** Son of Thomas Sr. & (-----) McCall **P:** unk **BLW:** unk **RG:** unk **MK:** unk **PH:** unk **SS:** A pg 209-210; CI Service rec cites PA 7th Regt **BS:** 196.

MCCARTER, James; b unk; d 1781 **RU:** Soldier, Served fr MA, and died fr the Battle at Yorktown **CEM:** Yorktown Victory Monument Tablet; GPS 38.28350, -78.54150; Yorktown; York **GS:** U **SP:** No info **VI:** No further data **P:** unk **BLW:** unk **RG:** unk **MK:** unk **PH:** unk **SS:** J-Yorktown Historian **BS:** JLARC 74.

MCCARTHY (MCCARTY), Daniel; b 24 Aug 1757, Richmond Co; d 13 Mar 1801 **RU:** Lieutenant, Also listed as lieutenant (age 16!) at Brandywine and Germantown battles. Lt, Capt Thomas Triplett's Co, Col William Grayson's Additional Regt. 12 Jan - 1 Dec 1777 **CEM:** Pohick Episcopal; GPS 38.42546, -77.11598; 9301 Richmond Hwy, Lorton; Fairfax **GS:** Y **SP:** Mar (1778 Fairfax Co) Sarah Mason (1760-1823), d/o George, author of Bill of Rights & Ann (Elibeck) Mason **VI:** Son of Col Daniel (1727-1792) & Sinah (Ball) (1728-1798) McCarty of "Mt Air," Fairfax Co. After RW, became Vestryman at Pohick Church in Truro Parish. Bur at "Mt Air" (father's plantation), then moved to "Cedar Grove", then moved to Pohick Church 1991 **P:** unk **BLW:** unk **RG:** Y **MK:** Y **PH:** Y **SS:** E pg 514; AP rec **BS:** JLARC 1, 2,13, 14, 27; 189 pg 91.

MCCARTY, Daniel; b 1727, Popes Creek, Westmoreland Co; d 1792 **RU:** Colonel/Patriot, Gave material aid to cause. Had civil service as Justice of Peace **CEM:** McCarty Family; GPS unk; Longwood, Horners Beach; Westmoreland **GS:** N **SP:** Mar (Jun 1748) Sinah Ball (14 Feb 1727-1798, Fairfax Co) **VI:** Died in Cedar Grove, Fairfax Co **P:** unk **BLW:** unk **RG:** N **MK:** N **PH:** N **SS:** DAR #A074764; AL Ct Bk pg 2, 5 Westmoreland Co; BQ; DD cites Deed abstracts of Fairfax Co **BS:** 189 pg 91.

MCCARTY, Daniel; b 1743; d 1 Mar 1801 **RU:** Patriot, Gave material aid to the cause **CEM:** Old Opequon Church; GPS 39.82237, -78.11412; 217 Opequon Church Ln, Kernstown; Frederick **GS:** Y **SP:** No info **VI:** No further data **P:** N **BLW:** N **RG:** Y **MK:** N **PH:** unk **SS:** AL Ct Bk pg 17 **BS:** 112 pg 6.

MCCAULEY, Daniel; b 1743; d 4 Jul 1829 **RU:** Patriot, Gave material aid to cause **CEM:** Old Opequon Church; GPS 39.82237, -78.11412; 217 Opequon Church Ln, Kernstown; Frederick **GS:** Y **SP:** Elizabeth Marquis (1754 Frederick Co-29 Jul 1829) d/o Thomas & Mary (Colville) McCauley **VI:** No further data **P:** N **BLW:** N **RG:** unk **MK:** N **PH:** unk **SS:** AK **BS:** 04; 112; 196.

MCCHESNEY, James; b 20 Jun 1735, Ireland; d Apr 1805 **RU:** Captain/Patriot, Gave material aid to cause **CEM:** Green Spring Presbyterian; GPS 36.63670, -81.99560; 2007 Green Spring Ch Rd, Abingdon; Washington **GS:** Y **SP:** No info **VI:** No further data **P:** unk **BLW:** unk **RG:** N **MK:** N **PH:** unk **SS:** E pg 515; AL Ct Bk 7 Augusta Co **BS:** 78 pg 275.

McCHESNEY, James; b 1733, Ireland; d 1816 **RU:** Patriot, Gave material aid to cause. Also civil service as road surveyor, 1780 Augusta Co **CEM:** Old Providence; GPS 37.96151, -79.71000; 1005 Spottswood Rd, Spottswood; Augusta **GS:** Y **SP:** Mar (__Ireland) Mary Patterson (__-1781/2) **VI:** Elder of Church in 1776 and Trustee 1793. Newer Govt stone. Name also on SAR cemetery plaque **P:** N **BLW:** N **RG:** N **MK:** Y **PH:** unk **SS:** DAR #A074884; E pg 515; AL Ct Bk pg 7 Augusta Co **BS:** 196.

MCCHESNEY, John; b 1749, PA; d 22 Sep 1822 **RU:** Soldier, Served in PA Line and VA Militia. VA service, Capt William Hendrick's Co **CEM:** Old Providence; GPS 37.96151, -79.71000; 1005 Spottswood Rd, Spottswood; Augusta **GS:** Y **SP:** 1) Rebecca (-----) (1753-1813) **VI:** Recd disability pension in Augusta Co 10 Feb 1810. Newer Govt stone that incorrectly shows he d in 1795. Name also on SAR cemetery plaque **P:** Y **BLW:** unk **RG:** unk **MK:** Y **PH:** unk **SS:** DAR #A074888; B; E pg 515; BT; CG pg 2245; DD **BS:** JLARC 62; 196.

MCCHESNEY, Samuel; b 22 Jun 1753, Ireland; d 4 Apr 1803 **RU:** Captain/Patriot, Commanded a co in Campbell Co Militia. Gave material aid to the cause **CEM:** Green Spring Presbyterian; GPS 36.63670, -81.99560; 2007 Green Spring Ch Rd, Abingdon; Washington **GS:** Y **SP:** Susannah Berry (2 Oct 1757-2 Oct 1822) **VI:** Son of James (1733-1818) & Sarah Mary (Patterson) (1733-__) McChesney **P:** unk **BLW:** unk **RG:** N **MK:** N **PH:** unk **SS:** E pg 515; AL Comm Bk V pg 80 Rockbridge Co **BS:** 78 pg 274; 196.

RU=Rank/Unit	CEM=Cemetery	GS=Gravestone	SP=Spousal Information
VI=Other Veteran Info	P=Pension	BLW=Bounty/Land Warrant	RG=Registered Grave
MK=SAR/DAR Marker	PH=Photo	SS=Service Source	BS=Burial Source

220

MCCLINTIC, William Jr; b 30 Jun 1759, Ireland; d 13 Sep 1786 **RU:** Private, Drafted 28 Feb 1778 Bath Co. Joined army 17 May 1778 under Capt Andrew Wallace 8th VA Regt. VA Line. Ent serv Bath Co in 4th, 8th, 12th Cont Line. Discharged 16 Feb 1779. Volunteered Feb 1781 as rifleman under Capt John Bollar. Wounded at Guilford CH 15 Mar 1781 **CEM:** Warm Springs; GPS 38.05030, -79.78110; Rt 220 Sam Snead Hwy, Warm Springs; Bath **GS:** Y **SP:** Mar (4 Mar 1782) Alice Mann (c1762-__); she mar 2) (14 May 1804) Wm H. Cavendish (__-14 Aug 1818) **VI:** Son of William McClintic (b 1717 Tyrone, Ireland - c1801) & Nancy Shanklin (1723-c1809) Returned to Jackson's River in Bath Co, Mar 1782. The Botetourt Co Ct recommended him for pen but he d before receiving it fr effects of wound received at Battle of Guildford CH. Widow appl pen 21 Dec 1848 Bath Co VA age 86. Pension rejected. R1819 He appl for pension in 1785 or 1786? **P:** N **BLW:** unk **RG:** N **MK:** N **PH:** Y **SS:** E pg 517; K Vol 3 pg 207; CG pg 2248-49 **BS:** 159; 196.

MCCLINTIC (MCCLINTOCK), William Sr; b 1717, Tyrone, Ireland; d 1801 **RU:** Private/Patriot, Served in Battle of Point Pleasant. Gave material aid to cause **CEM:** McClintic Family; GPS unk; 12 mi W of Warm Springs; Bath **GS:** N **SP:** Nancy Shanklin (1723-1809) **VI:** No further data **P:** unk **BLW:** unk **RG:** N **MK:** N **PH:** N **SS:** DAR #A075134; AI, Cert issued; DD cites Poffenbarger Battle of Point Pleasant pg 26 **BS:** 159.

MCCLOUGHRY, John; b unk; d 1781 **RU:** Lieutenant, Served fr NY killed in the battle at Yorktown **CEM:** Yorktown Victory Monument Tablet; GPS 38.28350, -78.54150; Yorktown; York **GS:** U **SP:** No info **VI:** No further data **P:** unk **BLW:** unk **RG:** unk **MK:** unk **PH:** unk **SS:** J-Yorktown Historian **BS:** JLARC 74.

MCCLUER, John; b 1749, Augusta Co; d 4 Jul 1822 **RU:** Private, Served in VA unit in Illinois **CEM:** Falling Springs Presbyterian; GPS 37.68526 -79.44972; 410 Falling Springs Rd, Glasgow; Rockbridge **GS:** Y **SP:** Nancy Agnes Steele (2 Sep 1748-16 Sep 1839) **VI:** Son of John & Nancy (-----) McClurer. SAR marker **P:** unk **BLW:** unk **RG:** Y **MK:** Y **PH:** unk **SS:** J-NSSAR 1993 Reg; CZ pg 282 **BS:** JLARC 1; 196.

MCCLUNG, John; b 1731, Ireland; d 1817 **RU:** Patriot, Gave material aid to cause **CEM:** Timber Ridge Presbyterian; GPS 37.84200, -79.35800; Nr jct Rts 11 & 716, Timber Ridge; Rockbridge **GS:** U **SP:** Mar (1754) Elizabeth Alexander (28 Oct 1735-29 Oct 1802) d/o Archibald (4 Feb 1708-aft 1780) & Margaret (Parks) (__-Aug 1753) Alexander **VI:** No further data **P:** N **BLW:** N **RG:** unk **MK:** unk **PH:** unk **SS:** AL Ct Bk pg 2, 16 Rockbridge Co **BS:** JLARC 63.

MCCLUNG, John Jr; b 1733; d 1832 **RU:** Patriot, Gave material aid to cause **CEM:** McClung Family; GPS unk; nr Millboro; Bath **GS:** U **SP:** Mar (1793 Bath Co) Jane (-----) **VI:** Lived to be 99 **P:** N **BLW:** N **RG:** Y **MK:** unk **PH:** unk **SS:** J-NSSAR 1993 Reg, J- DAR Hatcher; AL Cert Augusta Co **BS:** JLARC 1, 2.

MCCLUNG, William; b c1760, Rockbridge Co; d 1794 **RU:** Ensign, Served in VA Line. Ent serv Rockbridge Co 1780. Received rank of ensign 2 Nov 1779 in Capt James Gilmore's Co **CEM:** Timber Ridge Presbyterian; GPS 37.84200, -79.35800; Nr jct Rts 11 & 716, Timber Ridge; Rockbridge **GS:** Y **SP:** Jean Dun **VI:** Son of James (1700-1779) & Mary (McKy) (1708-1781) McClung. Appl pen 29 Mar 1836, Blount Co, TN. R6628 **P:** Y **BLW:** unk **RG:** unk **MK:** unk **PH:** Y **SS:** K Vol 3 pg 207; AZ pg 228; CG pg 2250 **BS:** JLARC 2,63; 196.

MCCLURE, Alexander; b 1 Aug 1763, Rockbridge Co; d 6 Jul 1842 **RU:** Soldier, Enl Rockbridge Co in VA line **CEM:** Timber Ridge Presbyterian; GPS 37.84200, -79.35800; Nr jct Rts 11 & 716, Timber Ridge; Rockbridge **GS:** U **SP:** No info **VI:** Appl for pen Franklin Co, KY. Died in Franklin Co, KY, memorialized VA. S30575 **P:** Y **BLW:** unk **RG:** unk **MK:** unk **PH:** unk **SS:** K Vol 3 pg 207 **BS:** JLARC 63.

MCCLURE, Andrew; b Jun 1767; d 30 Oct 1847 **RU:** Lieutenant/Patriot, Served in battle of Guilford CH 1781. Gave flour and beef to cause **CEM:** Bethel Presbyterian; GPS 38.04257, -79.17283; 563 Bethel Green Rd, Middlebrook; Augusta **GS:** Y **SP:** Mary Mitchell **VI:** The birth date is probably incorrect. Died age 80 yrs 4 mos **P:** unk **BLW:** unk **RG:** unk **MK:** unk **PH:** unk **SS:** D pg 41 Augusta Co; CZ **BS:** JLARC 62, 63; 196.

MCCLURE, Halbert; b unk; d unk **RU:** Patriot, Gave material aid to cause **CEM:** Timber Ridge Presbyterian; GPS 37.84200, -79.35800; Nr jct Rts 11 & 716, Timber Ridge; Rockbridge **GS:** U **SP:** No

RU=Rank/Unit	CEM=Cemetery	GS=Gravestone	SP=Spousal Information
VI=Other Veteran Info	P=Pension	BLW=Bounty/Land Warrant	RG=Registered Grave
MK=SAR/DAR Marker	PH=Photo	SS=Service Source	BS=Burial Source

221

info **VI**: No further data **P**: N **BLW**: N **RG**: unk **MK**: unk **PH**: unk **SS**: AL Ct Bk II pg 36 Rockingham Co **BS**: JLARC 63.

MCCLURE, John; b 1725; d May 1779 **RU**: Private, Served in militia rolls listed in Virginia's Illinois Dept **CEM**: Fincastle Presbyterian; GPS 37.50017, -79.87558; 108 E Back St, Fincastle; Botetourt **GS**: U **SP**: Mary Allen (1741-1804) d/of Malcom (1712-1792) & Mary Margaret (Cunningham) (1720-1767) Allen **VI**: Son of Halbert Samuel (1684-1754) & Agnes (Steele) (1690-1750) McClure **P**: unk **BLW**: unk **RG**: unk **MK**: unk **PH**: unk **SS**: BY; SAR Ancestor #P-318773 **BS**: 05 cites SAR application; 196.

MCCLURE, John; b 1 Nov 1749; d 4 Jul 1842 **RU**: Private, Served in VA unit in Illinois **CEM**: Stonewall Jackson Memorial; GPS 37.78128, -79.44604; 314 S Main St; Lexington City **GS**: Y **SP**: Mar (1775) Nancy Steele **VI**: Died in Rockbridge Co **P**: unk **BLW**: unk **RG**: unk **MK**: Y **PH**: Y **SS**: J- DAR Hatcher; E pg 517 **BS**: JLARC 2.

MCCLURE, Robert; b unk; d unk **RU**: Patriot, Gave material aid to cause **CEM**: Falling Springs Presbyterian; GPS 37.68526 -79.44972; 410 Falling Springs Rd, Glasgow; Rockbridge **GS**: U **SP**: No info **VI**: No further data **P**: N **BLW**: N **RG**: unk **MK**: unk **PH**: unk **SS**: AL Ct Bk II pg 36 Rockingham Co **BS**: JLARC 63.

MCCLURE, Robert A; b unk; d unk **RU**: Sergeant, Served in Capt Trimble's Co, Augusta Co Militia **CEM**: Timber Ridge Presbyterian; GPS 37.84200, -79.35800; Nr jct Rts 11 & 716, Timber Ridge; Rockbridge **GS**: U **SP**: No info **VI**: Recd BLW **P**: unk **BLW**: Y **RG**: unk **MK**: unk **PH**: unk **SS**: C pg 207; E pg 517 **BS**: JLARC 63.

MCCLURE, Samuel; b 16 May 1748, Augusta Co (Wardell); d unk **RU**: Patriot, Gave material aid to cause **CEM**: Timber Ridge Presbyterian; GPS 37.84200, -79.35800; Nr jct Rts 11 & 716, Timber Ridge; Rockbridge **GS**: U **SP**: No info **VI**: Pensioned Clark Co, IL 1833. S33079 **P**: Y **BLW**: N **RG**: unk **MK**: unk **PH**: unk **SS**: K Vol 3 pg 208; AL Ct Bk pg 2 Rockbridge Co **BS**: JLARC 63.

McCLURG, James; b 1747, Hampton; d 9 Jul 1823 **RU**: Surgeon, Was surgeon Jun 1776 until end of war. Was Superintendent & Inspector of Hospitals in VA **CEM**: St John's Episcopal; GPS 37.53183, -77.41958; 2401 E Broad St; Richmond City **GS**: Y **SP**: Mar (1779) Elizabeth Selden **VI**: Son of Dr. Walter & (-----) McClurg. Recd 6000 acre BLW 21 Oct. 1783. "No pension found for this officer "surgeon", see N.A. Acc #847 #050115 for VA 1/2 pay" (source CG) Was member of Constitutional Convention Philadelphia 1787and Privy Council 1786 & 87. Was Mayor of Richmond 1797, 1800, 1803 **P**: unk **BLW**: Y **RG**: Y **MK**: N **PH**: unk **SS**: E pg 518; L pg 218; AK; CG pg 2251 **BS**: 28 pg 471; 04.

MCCOMB, James; b 8 Aug 1765; d 25 Oct 1846 **RU**: Private, Served in 3rd Cont Line **CEM**: Tinkling Spring Presbyterian; GPS 38.08472, -78.98278; 30 Tinkling Spring Dr, Fishersville; Augusta **GS**: Y **SP**: Susanah Henderson (31 Jul 176_-9 Jun 1848) **VI**: No further data **P**: unk **BLW**: unk **RG**: N **MK**: N **PH**: Y **SS**: E pg 518 **BS**: 142 Tinkling Spr; 208 pg 464; 196.

McCONNEHEY, John; b 15 Apr 1752 Bucks Co, PA; d 1846 **RU**: Private, Entered service in Loudoun Co, 1780 in VA Line **CEM**: McConnehey-Updike; GPS 37.21162, -79.54527; 2730 Chestnut Fork Rd, Chestnut Fork; Bedford **GS**: Y **SP**: Mary Davis **VI**: Moved to Loudoun Co age 10. Moved to Bedford Co 1801 or 1802. Pension appl for 25 Jan 1833 Bedford Co, but suspended for lack of 6 mos service, in Bedford 1836. S16953 **P**: N **BLW**: unk **RG**: N **MK**: N **PH**: unk **SS**: K Vol 3 pg 209 **BS**: 80 vol 3 pg 63.

MCCONNELL, Abram; b 1757; d 7 Aug1830 **RU**: Private, Served in VA Line. **CEM**: Green Spring Presbyterian; GPS 36.63670, -81.99560; 2007 Green Spring Ch Rd, Abingdon; Washington **GS**: U **SP**: Mar (3 Mar 1780 Berkeley Co) Rosanna Fryatt (__-8 May 1846 Washington Co) **VI**: Son of James S. & (------) McConnell. An Abraham McConnell mar Margaret Touchstone in Frederick Co on 15 June 1809 by Alexander Balmain. Lived in Berkeley Co. Appl for pen 25 Feb 1856 Washington Co, R6643. DAR marker **P**: Y **BLW**: unk **RG**: Y **MK**: Y **PH**: unk **SS**: CG pg 2253 **BS**: JLARC 2, 70, 80,101; 78 pg 275.

McCORMICK, Martha (Sanderson); b 1747, Ulster, Ireland; d 1804 **RU**: Patriot, Gave material aid to the cause **CEM**: Old Providence; GPS 37.96151, -79.710; 1005 Spottswood Rd, Spottswood; Augusta **GS**: Y **SP**: Mar (1770) Robert McCormick (1738-12 Oct 1818); s/o Thomas & Elizabeth (Carruth) McCormick **VI**: Daug of George & Catherine (Ross) Sanderson of Scotland. Name also on SAR plaque at cemetery, and Gr has DAR marker **P**: N **BLW**: N **RG**: Y **MK**: Y **PH**: unk **SS**: AS SAR regis **BS**: SAR regis; 196.

RU=Rank/Unit	CEM=Cemetery	GS=Gravestone	SP=Spousal Information
VI=Other Veteran Info	P=Pension	BLW=Bounty/Land Warrant	RG=Registered Grave
MK=SAR/DAR Marker	PH=Photo	SS=Service Source	BS=Burial Source

MCCORMICK, Robert; b 1738, Lancaster Co, PA; d 12 Oct 1818 **RU:** Soldier, Gave material aid to the cause. Served several tours with Associators. Served in Jersey Campaign 1776 in VA Line and Southern Campaign of 1781. Was in Battle of Cowpens **CEM:** Old Providence; GPS 37.96151, -79.710; 1005 Spottswood Rd, Spottswood; Augusta **GS:** Y **SP:** Mar (1770) Martha Sanderson (1747-1804); d/o George & Catherine (Ross) Sanderson **VI:** Son of Thomas & Elizabeth (Carruth) McCormick of Ireland. Elder in Presbyterian Church. Name also on SAR plaque at cemetery **P:** unk **BLW:** unk **RG:** Y **MK:** Y **PH:** unk **SS:** BT; J-NSSAR 1993 Reg; K Vol 3 pg 209 **BS:** JLARC 1; 196.

MCCOUGHRY, John; b unk; d 27 Oct 1781 **RU:** Lieutenant, Served in Capt James Rosekran's 1st Co, Lewis Dubois's 5th NY Line Regt, and died fr battle at Yorktown **CEM:** Yorktown Victory Monument Tablet; GPS 38.28350, -78.54150; Yorktown; York **GS:** U **SP:** No info **VI:** No futher data **P:** unk **BLW:** unk **RG:** unk **MK:** unk **PH:** unk **SS:** J-Yorktown Historian; AX pg 220 **BS:** JLARC App B-5, 74.

MCCOWN, Samuel; b unk; d 1853 **RU:** Private, Served in Capt Smith's Co, Dickerson's VA Regt **CEM:** Stonewall Jackson Memorial; GPS 37.78128, -79.44604; 314 S Main St; Lexington City **GS:** U **SP:** Elizabeth (-----) (18 Jun 1786-8 Jan 1835) **VI:** No further data **P:** unk **BLW:** unk **RG:** unk **MK:** unk **PH:** unk **SS:** B **BS:** JLARC 63; 196.

MCCOY, John; b 1735; d 1796 **RU:** Captain, Commanded a Co in Augusta Co Militia 1777-1779 **CEM:** Doe Hill; GPS 38.25976, -79.26629; Across St fr Doe Hill Methodist Ch Rt 654; Highland **GS:** Y **SP:** No info **VI:** No further data **P:** unk **BLW:** unk **RG:** unk **MK:** Y **PH:** unk **SS:** J- DAR Hatcher; E pg 520 **BS:** JLARC 2.

MCCUE, John; b 1715 Ireland; d Aft 27 Oct 1798 **RU:** Patriot, Civil service as Juror 1775, Amherst Co **CEM:** Tinkling Spring Presbyterian; GPS 38.08472, -78.98278; 30 Tinkling Spring Dr, Fishersville; Augusta **GS:** N **SP:** Mar (8 May 1753) Eleanor Mathews **VI:** No stone **P:** N **BLW:** N **RG:** N **MK:** N **PH:** N **SS:** AS SAR applic; DD cites Sweeny, Amherst Co in the Revolution pg 73 **BS:** SAR Appl; 208 pg 465.

MCCUE, John Rev; b 1752; d 20 Sep 1818 **RU:** Private, Served in Capt Anderson's Co Augusta Co Militia **CEM:** Tinkling Spring Presbyterian; GPS 38.08472, -78.98278; 30 Tinkling Spring Dr, Fishersville; Augusta **GS:** Y **SP:** No info **VI:** Tinkling Springs pastor for 27 yrs **P:** unk **BLW:** unk **RG:** unk **MK:** N **PH:** Y **SS:** E pg 521; CD **BS:** 196.

MCCULLOUGH, Robert; b 2 May 1764; d 29 Aug 1849 **RU:** Private, Fought at Kings Mountain **CEM:** Dunn Family; GPS 36.62560, -81.72640; Abt 1 mi NW of Cherry Tree Gap off Rt 725; Washington **GS:** U **SP:** Sarah Ann Clark (25 Nov 1775-25 Dec 1854) **VI:** Son of Thomas & Isabella (Patrick) McCulloch. **P:** unk **BLW:** unk **RG:** unk **MK:** unk **PH:** unk **SS:** DAR Ancestor #A202096 **BS:** 196.

MCCUNE, John; b 20 Jan 1749; d 25 May 1812 **RU:** First Lieutenant/Patriot, Gave material aid to cause **CEM:** Tinkling Spring Presbyterian; GPS 38.08472, -78.98278; 30 Tinkling Spring Dr, Fishersville; Augusta **GS:** N **SP:** Mar (c1775) Margaret (-----) (__-17 Mar 1812) **VI:** No further data **P:** unk **BLW:** unk **RG:** unk **MK:** N **PH:** N **SS:** AL Cert Augusta Co **BS:** JLARC 62.

MCCUTCHAN, Charles; b 1736; d 29 Jun 1814 **RU:** Soldier, SAR registration did not provide service **CEM:** Glebe Burying Ground; GPS 38.10940, -79.22190; Glebe School Rd Rt 876, Swoopes; Augusta **GS:** Y **SP:** No info **VI:** No further data **P:** unk **BLW:** unk **RG:** unk **MK:** N **PH:** unk **SS:** SAR Ancestor #P-246009; App D 210 pg 394 **BS:** JLARC 8.

MCCUTCHAN, Samuel; b 1744 Ireland; d 2 Mar 1830 **RU:** Captain/Patriot, Commanded a company in Augusta Co Militia. Gave material aid to cause **CEM:** North Mountain; GPS unk; 7 mi S of Staunton on N side Rt 252; Augusta **GS:** Y **SP:** Mar 1) Betsy Blackwood; 2) Rebecca Downey (c1747-10 Jun 1820) d/o Samuel Downey (1722-1773) & Martha McPheeters (__-1801) **VI:** Govt marker **P:** unk **BLW:** unk **RG:** unk **MK:** N **PH:** unk **SS:** DAR #A076139; B; AL Comm Bk II pg 369, 360 Augusta Co **BS:** 196.

MCCUTCHAN, William; b 17 or 27 Nov 1758; d 29 Jun 1848 **RU:** Sergeant, Served in VA Line. Enl Staunton in 1778. Enl Waynesboro in 1780. Served under Capt Samuel McCutcheon (called him "kin" in application) **CEM:** Bethel Presbyterian; GPS 38.04257, -79.17283; 563 Bethel Green Rd, Middlebrook; Augusta **GS:** N **SP:** Mar (20 May 1794 Augusta Co) Jean Finley or Finely (c1770-__), d/o Robert & (-----) Finley/Finely. **VI:** Appl pen 25 Jun 1833 Augusta Co. Widow appl pen 19 Nov 1849 Augusta Co age

RU=Rank/Unit   CEM=Cemetery   GS=Gravestone   SP=Spousal Information
VI=Other Veteran Info   P=Pension   BLW=Bounty/Land Warrant   RG=Registered Grave
MK=SAR/DAR Marker   PH=Photo   SS=Service Source   BS=Burial Source

223

79. W1888 **P:** Y **BLW:** unk **RG:** unk **MK:** unk **PH:** N **SS:** J- DAR Hatcher; SAR Ancestor #P246015; K Vol 3 pg 214; AL Comm Bk II pg 361 Augusta Co; CG pg 2262-63 **BS:** JLARC 2, 4, 62, 63.

MCCUTCHAN (MCCUTCHEN), James; b unk; d unk **RU:** Soldier, Served in Capt James Beatie Co at Kings Mountain **CEM:** Bethel Presbyterian; GPS 38.04257, -79.17283; 563 Bethel Green Rd, Middlebrook; Augusta **GS:** N **SP:** No info **VI:** No further data **P:** unk **BLW:** unk **RG:** unk **MK:** unk **PH:** N **SS:** SAR Ancestor #P-246010; N pg 1241 **BS:** JLARC 62.

MCCUTCHEON, John; b 15 Nov 1758; d 29 Jun 1848 **RU:** Private, Served in Capt John Wilson's Co, Augusta Co Militia **CEM:** North Mountain; GPS unk; 7 mi S of Staunton on N side Rt 252; Augusta **GS:** N **SP:** Jean Finley **VI:** Name is on a copper plate on a monument by DAR chapter listing Rev War soldiers bur in this Glebe **P:** unk **BLW:** unk **RG:** unk **MK:** unk **PH:** N **SS:** G pg 26 **BS:** JLARC 63; 196.

MCDANIEL, George; b 17 May 1722, King William Co; d 22 Nov 1821 **RU:** Major, Served as Sergeant, Cont Line and as Maj in Bedford Co Militia **CEM:** McDaniel Family; GPS unk; Boonesboro Rd; Lynchburg City **GS:** U **SP:** Mar (1748) Margaret Gough (c1728-1821) **VI:** No further data **P:** unk **BLW:** unk **RG:** unk **MK:** unk **PH:** unk **SS:** E pg 522 **BS:** JLARC 36.

MCDANIEL, Thomas; b unk; d 1807 **RU:** Private, Served in Clark's Illinois Regt, 11th Cont Line **CEM:** Back Creek Quaker, aka Gainesboro United Methodist; GPS 39.27861, -78.25694; 166 Siler Ln, Gainesboro; Frederick **GS:** Y **SP:** No info **VI:** No further data **P:** unk **BLW:** unk **RG:** N **MK:** N **PH:** unk **SS:** E pg 522 **BS:** 59 pg 214.

MCDONALD, Bryan; b 8 Jul 1732, New Castle, DE; d Jan 1777 **RU:** Private, Served in Capt John Taylor's Co, Montgomery Co Militia **CEM:** Glebe; GPS 37.45155, -79.96968; Vic jct Rts 779 and 630; Botetourt **GS:** U **SP:** Susanna Ogle (6 May 1728 New Castle, DE-1801) **VI:** Son of Bryan (1732-1777) & Susanna (Ogle) (1728-1801) McDonald **P:** unk **BLW:** unk **RG:** unk **MK:** unk **PH:** unk **SS:** G pg 234-5 **BS:** 196.

MCDONALD, Edward; b 3 Oct 1761; d 19 Apr 1855 **RU:** Private, Served in 7th, 9th, 13th Cont Lines **CEM:** Glebe; GPS 37.45155, -79.96968; Vic jct Rts 779 and 630; Botetourt **GS:** U **SP:** Mary Rowland (11 Mar 1764-11 Apr 1814) d/o of Jame & Margaret (Kyle) Rowland **VI:** Son of Bryan (1732-1777) & Susanna (Ogle) (1728-1801) McDonald **P:** unk **BLW:** unk **RG:** unk **MK:** unk **PH:** unk **SS:** E pg 523 **BS:** 196.

MCDONALD, James; b 18 Jan 1753; d Aug 1777 **RU:** Private, Served in Capt John Montgomery's Co, Montgomery Co Militia **CEM:** Glebe; GPS 37.45155, -79.96968; Vic jct Rts 779 and 630; Botetourt **GS:** N **SP:** No info **VI:** Son of Bryan (1732-1777) & Susanna (Ogle) (1728-1801) McDonald **P:** unk **BLW:** unk **RG:** unk **MK:** unk **PH:** N **SS:** G pg 208 **BS:** 196.

MCDONALD, William; b 24 Sep 1756; d 13 Dec 1833 **RU:** Lieutenant, Served in 1st Lt Dragoons & 7th Cont Line **CEM:** Mt Union; GPS 37.45133, -79.97055; 4614 Catawba Rd, Mt Union; Botetourt **GS:** Y **SP:** Nancy Robinson **VI:** Son of Bryan (1732-1777) & Susanna (Ogle) (1728-1801) McDonald **P:** unk **BLW:** unk **RG:** unk **MK:** N **PH:** unk **SS:** E pg 523 **BS:** JLARC 21, 24; 196.

MCDORMENT (MCDORMAN), David; b 1758, Caroline Co; d 13 Oct 1835 **RU:** Private, Served in 3rd Co, VA line in Capt Field's Co, Col Gaskin's Regt **CEM:** Pine Cliff; GPS 38.28920, -77.64577; Vic jct Rts Jackson Trail Rd and Military Park Rd; Spotsylvania **GS:** Y **SP:** Anne "Nancy" Tiller **VI:** Veterans Admin GS installed 1935. Cemetery is located on private property and reportedly current owner does not allow visitors. Sol recd pension of $80 per annum starting 29 Jan 1829 through Richmond VA Agency. Claim adjudicated through Treasury Dept. No papers at pension bureau. BLW12404 issued 7 Jul 1792 **P:** Y **BLW:** Y **RG:** Y **MK:** N **PH:** unk **SS:** DAR #A201568; K Vol 3 pg 218; AG pg 853; CG pg 2268; Applic for VA GS **BS:** 09 grid 19; 196.

McDOWELL, William; b Bapt 9 Apr 1749, Augusta Co; d 25 Mar 1806 **RU:** Patriot, Was member of Committee of Peace 1777 **CEM:** Trinity Episcopal; GPS 38.14917, -79.07521; 214 Beverley St; Staunton City **GS:** Y **SP:** Mar (1772) Alice (-----) **VI:** No further data **P:** N **BLW:** N **RG:** N **MK:** N **PH:** unk **SS:** DAR #A113373; E pg 524; AL List I pg 2, 6 Augusta Co **BS:** 36 pg 203; 196.

McFADEN (McFADDEN), James; b 1761; d Apr 1799 **RU:** Captain, Served in VA Cont Line **CEM:** Old Presbyterian Meeting House; GPS 38.48528, -77.23532; 323 S Fairfax St; Alexandria City **GS:** N **SP:**

RU=Rank/Unit	CEM=Cemetery	GS=Gravestone	SP=Spousal Information
VI=Other Veteran Info	P=Pension	BLW=Bounty/Land Warrant	RG=Registered Grave
MK=SAR/DAR Marker	PH=Photo	SS=Service Source	BS=Burial Source

224

No info **VI**: Died of consumption age 38, bur 24 Apr 1799. Listed on an SAR plaque in cemetery **P**: unk **BLW**: Y **RG**: Y **MK**: Y **PH**: N **SS**: C pg 357; AK **BS**: 23 pg 105; 196.

McFERRAN, Martin; b unk; d 1788 **RU**: Captain, Co Cmdr in Botetourt Co Militia in 1778 **CEM**: McFerran Family; GPS unk; Rt 220, 6 mi N of Fincastle; Botetourt **GS**: Y **SP**: No info **VI**: No further data **P**: unk **BLW**: unk **RG**: N **MK**: N **PH**: unk **SS**: E pg 526 **BS**: 115 pg 66.

MCGAVOCK, Hugh; b Sep 1761; d 2 Apr 1844 **RU**: Captain, Raised his own Regt 1779. Was Regt Quartermaster 1780 under Col Joseph Crockett, VA Line **CEM**: McGavock Family; GPS unk; NW of jct Rts 610 & 1012, W of Max Meadows; Wythe **GS**: Y **SP**: Nancy Kent (1763-1835) **VI**: Son of James. Appl pen 13 Aug 1834 Wythe Co. S16948 also VA 1/2 pay (See N.A. Acc #874 #050116 1/2 Pay) **P**: Y **BLW**: unk **RG**: unk **MK**: Y **PH**: unk **SS**: K Vol 3 pg 221; CG pg 2275-76 **BS**: JLARC 2, 40,123; 196

MCGAVOCK, James; b 1728, Antrim, Ireland; d 22 Mar 1812 **RU**: Patriot, Was Signer of Fincastle Declaration of Rights. Was Magistrate and Justice for Botetourt and Fincastle Cos **CEM**: McGavock Family; GPS unk; Peppers Ferry Rd, Ft Chiswell, off I-81 12 mi E of Wytheville; Wythe **GS**: Y **SP**: Mar (20 Jan 1760) Mary Cloyd **VI**: No further data **P**: N **BLW**: N **RG**: unk **MK**: Y **PH**: unk **SS**: DAR patriotic index; SAR membership #45571 **BS**: JLARC 2, 40, 101.

MCGOWAN, Samuel; b unk; d unk **RU**: Private, Served in Capt David Grier Co #6, Col Irvine William's Regt at Mount Independence, 28 Nov 1775 **CEM**: Stonewall Jackson Memorial; GPS 37.78128, -79.44604; 314 S Main St; Lexington City **GS**: U **SP**: No info **VI**: No further data **P**: unk **BLW**: unk **RG**: Y **MK**: unk **PH**: unk **SS**: J-NSSAR 2000 Reg; A pg 212 **BS**: JLARC 76.

MCGUFFIN, Thomas Sr; b unk; d 1823 **RU**: Private, Served in Montgomery Co Militia1781 **CEM**: New Providence Presbyterian; GPS 37.95170, -79.30250; 1208 New Providence Rd, Raphine; Rockbridge **GS**: U **SP**: No info **VI**: No further data **P**: unk **BLW**: unk **RG**: unk **MK**: unk **PH**: unk **SS**: G pg 225 **BS**: JLARC 62.

MCILHANEY, James; b 1749; d 16 Sep 1804 **RU**: Captain, Served in Capts Andrew Russell and Lilliam Lae's companies of Fairfax Co in VA Cont Line **CEM**: McIlhaney Family; GPS unk; Nr Hillsboro E side Rt 690 btw Rts 90 & 611; Loudoun **GS**: U **SP**: Mar (25 Dec 1776 Loudoun Co, bond dated 21 Dec 1778) Margaret Williams, a widow (c1760-__). Both of Shelburn Parish when mar **VI**: Wid appl pen 20 Jul 1836 Loudoun Co VA age 76 at pen date R6734. BLW #7770-400 to heirs **P**: Y **BLW**: Y **RG**: unk **MK**: unk **PH**: unk **SS**: K Vol 3 pg 225; BY pg 318; CG pg 2282 **BS**: JLARC 2, 32.

MCINTURF (MCINTURFF), David; b 1729; d 1804 **RU**: Patriot, Gave material aid to cause. **CEM**: Dry Run Church; GPS 38.85929, -78.40075; Rt 678, Fort Valley Rd nr jct with Dry Run Rd, Seven Fountains; Shenandoah **GS**: Y **SP**: No info **VI**: No further data **P**: N **BLW**: N **RG**: N **MK**: N **PH**: unk **SS**: AL **BS**: 04.

MCINTURFF, Frederick; b 1758, Chester Co, PA; d 1 Jul 1816 **RU**: Private, Served in Capt Joseph Bowman's Co **CEM**: Dry Run Church; GPS 38.85929, -78.40075; Rt 678, Fort Valley Rd nr jct with Dry Run Rd, Seven Fountains; Shenandoah **GS**: Y **SP**: Mar (25 Feb 1783) Susannah Carrier (c1768-3 Oct 1816) **VI**: No further data **P**: N **BLW**: N **RG**: N **MK**: unk **PH**: N **SS**: DAR #A077331; DD **BS**: 196.

McIVER, Colin; b unk; d 1788 **RU**: Patriot, Gave material aid to cause **CEM**: Old Christ Church Episcopal; GPS 38.80625, -77.04718; 118 N Washington St; Alexandria City **GS**: N **SP**: No info **VI**: Burial permit issued 9 Jan 1788 **P**: N **BLW**: N **RG**: N **MK**: N **PH**: unk **SS**: AL cert issued **BS**: 20 pg 150.

McKANN, Robert H; b unk; d 1804 **RU**: Private, Served in Capt Joseph Mitchell's Co at Battle of Point Pleasant, Oct 1774 **CEM**: Providence Burial Ground; GPS unk; Waterview; Middlesex **GS**: U **SP**: No info **VI**: No further data **P**: unk **BLW**: unk **RG**: N **MK**: N **PH**: unk **SS**: E pg 350; Z pg 54 **BS**: 88 pg 251.

McKAY, Enos; b unk; d 1804 **RU**: Private, Served in Capt Jacob Springer's Co, VA Cont Line **CEM**: Spring Farm; GPS unk; 2 mi NE of Luray on Turnpike; Page **GS**: N **SP**: No info **VI**: WPA report says d in 1833. **P**: unk **BLW**: unk **RG**: N **MK**: N **PH**: N **SS**: N pg 442 **BS**: 120.

MCKEE, James; b 14 Mar 1752, PA; d 14 Aug 1832 **RU**: Ensign, Served in VA Militia. Lived in Rockbridge Co at enl. Served as sub for brother William McKee **CEM**: McKee, aka Big Springs; GPS unk; Clarence Hardy's farm, off Rt 60 on Rt 63, Kerrs Dist; Rockbridge **GS**: Y **SP**: 1) Jane Telford 2)

RU=Rank/Unit	CEM=Cemetery	GS=Gravestone	SP=Spousal Information
VI=Other Veteran Info	P=Pension	BLW=Bounty/Land Warrant	RG=Registered Grave
MK=SAR/DAR Marker	PH=Photo	SS=Service Source	BS=Burial Source

225

Nancy (Leech) Scott (__-5 Feb 1835) **VI:** Moved with brother William to Rockbridge Co 1774, settling on Kerr's Creek). Pen granted 1835 to children that was due to their mother. S16954 **P:** Y **BLW:** unk **RG:** unk **MK:** Y **PH:** Y **SS:** K Vol 3 pg 226; CG pg 2286 **BS:** JLARC 4,76,126.

MCKEE, Robert; b 18 Aug 1754 Ireland; d Jun 1841 **RU:** First Lieutenant, Took oath as 1st Lt in Rockbridge Co Militia 2 Dec 1778 **CEM:** New Providence Presbyterian; GPS 37.95170, -79.30250; 1208 New Providence Rd, Raphine; Rockbridge **GS:** U **SP:** No info **VI:** No further data **P:** unk **BLW:** unk **RG:** Y **MK:** unk **PH:** unk **SS:** E pg 530 **BS:** JLARC 1, 63; 196.

McKENZIE, Moredock (Mordicai Moredecai Mordock Morodock) Otis; b 1738, Glasgow, Scotland; d 1804 or 1812/1813 **RU:** Private, Was in Battle of Pt. Peasant; 2nd Bn 15th VA Regt and Capt Daniel Smith's Co, Fincastle Co Militia **CEM:** Hare Family; GPS unk; Narrows; Giles **GS:** N **SP:** 1) Jemissa Chapman 2) Mar (1781) Abigail Marrs 3) Mar (1786) Sarah Huet **VI:** No further data **P:** unk **BLW:** unk **RG:** Y **MK:** N **PH:** N **SS:** E pg 531 **BS:** 04.

McKIM, James; b 10 Jul 1754, Brandywine, New Castle Co, DE; d 1804 or 12 Sep 1820 **RU:** Private?, Served in 12th Cont Line in Clark's Illinois Regt **CEM:** McKim Family; GPS unk; Arcola; Loudoun **GS:** Y **SP:** Ruhamah Heath **VI:** Son of Alexander & Jeanette (-----) McKim **P:** unk **BLW:** unk **RG:** Y **MK:** N **PH:** unk **SS:** E pg 200, 532 **BS:** 25 pg 200; 196.

MCKINNEY, James; b unk; d 1804 **RU:** Soldier, Served fr NY, and killed in the battle at Yorktown **CEM:** Yorktown Victory Monument Tablet; GPS 38.28350, -78.54150; Yorktown; York **GS:** U **SP:** No info **VI:** No further data **P:** unk **BLW:** unk **RG:** unk **MK:** unk **PH:** unk **SS:** J-Yorktown Historian **BS:** JLARC 74.

MCKNIGHT, Charles; b unk; d 16 Nov 1791 **RU:** Surgeon, Service in NY. Wounded and entitled to half pay **CEM:** Old Presbyterian Meeting House; GPS 38.48528, -77.23532; 323 S Fairfax St; Alexandria City **GS:** N **SP:** No info **VI:** Listed on an SAR plaque in cemetery. **P:** unk **BLW:** unk **RG:** Y **MK:** Y **PH:** N **SS:** J-NSSAR 1993 Reg; A pg 427, 545; AK **BS:** JLARC 1; 5.

McKNIGHT, William; b c1733; d 25 Jul 1812 **RU:** Private/Patriot, Served in Capt Beatie's Co at Kings Mountain. Gave material aid to cause **CEM:** Presbyterian Church; GPS 38.80015, -77.05791; Wilkes St & Hamilton Ln; Alexandria City **GS:** Y **SP:** 1) Martha Bryan, (c1745-3 Jun 1775); 2) Susannah Evans (1746-10 Nov 1836) **VI:** Death notice in the Alexandria Gazette 27 Jul 1812 **P:** unk **BLW:** unk **RG:** Y **MK:** N **PH:** unk **SS:** N pg 1241; AL Ct Bk pg 88 Loudoun Co **BS:** 23 pg 56; 196.

McLAURINE, James; b 25 Nov 1758,. Cumberland Co; d 1848 **RU:** Private, Lived in Cumberland Co at enl. Ent service 1777, Cumberland Co in 7th VA Regt. Was in Capt Charles Fleming's Co, Col Crockett's 7th VA Regt **CEM:** Petersville; GPS 37.56440, -77.96470; Off Rt 60; Powhatan **GS:** N **SP:** Mar (9 Mar 1789) Catherine Steger (c1769,-aft 1809) **VI:** Appl for pen 26 Jun 1843 Cumberland Co age 84 not received as he had less than 6 mos service. R6780 **P:** N **BLW:** unk **RG:** N **MK:** N **PH:** N **SS:** DAR #A077920; K Vol 3, pg 234; CG Vol 2295 **BS:** SAR corres.

MCLINGAN, James; b unk; d unk **RU:** Soldier, SAR registration did not provide service **CEM:** Arlington National; GPS 38.88377, -77.06535; Jefferson Davis Hwy Rt 110; Arlington **GS:** N **SP:** No info **VI:** No further data **P:** unk **BLW:** unk **RG:** Y **MK:** unk **PH:** N **SS:** J-NSSAR 2000 Reg; NSSAR Ancestor #P-246804 **BS:** JLARC 76.

MCMAHON, Michael; b 1758; d 24 Mar 1786 **RU:** Soldier, Served in 3rd, 5th, 7th, & 11th Cont Lines **CEM:** Old Christ Church Episcopal; GPS 38.80625, -77.04718; 118 N Washington St; Alexandria City **GS:** Y **SP:** No info **VI:** Barber. D age 28. Death notice in the Alexandria Gazette 30 Mar 1786, pg 3 **P:** unk **BLW:** unk **RG:** Y **MK:** unk **PH:** unk **SS:** J-NSSAR 1993 Reg; E pg 535 **BS:** JLARC 1; 20 pg 139.

MCNEIL, Jacob Sr; b Jun 1759; d 1841 **RU:** Indian Spy/Ranger, Served in VA Line. Lived on "Virginia frontier" at enl 1776 as Indian spy and ranger. Served with a Lt John McNeil **CEM:** McNeil Family; GPS unk; Rt 220 N, .1 mi E of MM 25, nr railroad tracks; Franklin **GS:** Y **SP:** Mar (2 Mar 1812 Franklin Co) Peggy Cool (This may be the wife of Jacob Jr.) **VI:** Govt GS says "Guard, Henderson's VA Co" Moved to Franklin Co after RW, where he was pensioned as Jacob, Sr. Sol appl pen 3 Sep 1832 Franklin Co. S5745 **P:** Y **BLW:** unk **RG:** unk **MK:** unk **PH:** Yes **SS:** K Vol 3 pg 238; CG pg 2305 **BS:** JLARC 4, 20.

MCNUTT, Alexander; b 1725, prob Londonderry, Ireland; d 1811 **RU:** Captain, Served in MA & VA Militia **CEM:** Falling Springs Presbyterian; GPS 37.68526 -79.44972; 410 Falling Springs Rd, Glasgow;

RU=Rank/Unit   CEM=Cemetery   GS=Gravestone   SP=Spousal Information
VI=Other Veteran Info   P=Pension   BLW=Bounty/Land Warrant   RG=Registered Grave
MK=SAR/DAR Marker   PH=Photo   SS=Service Source   BS=Burial Source

226

Rockbridge **GS:** Y **SP:** Never mar **VI:** Govt Gr stone **P:** unk **BLW:** unk **RG:** Y **MK:** Y **PH:** Y **SS:** B **BS:** JLARC 1, 63, 79.

MCNUTT, Alexander; b 10 Dec 1754; d 29 Mar 1812 **RU:** Ensign, Was Ens in Capt James Gilmore's Co of VA Militia under command of Gen Morgan in SC, 1780. Also served in Rockbridge Co Militia 1781 **CEM:** Stonewall Jackson Memorial; **GPS** 37.78128, -79.44604; 314 S Main St; Lexington City **GS:** Y **SP:** Rachel Grigsby (c1771 - 7 Jan 1840) **VI:** Son of John (1725-1781) & Katherine (Anderson) (__- 1814) McNutt **P:** unk **BLW:** unk **RG:** unk **MK:** unk **PH:** unk **SS:** CD **BS:** JLARC 2, 63; 196.

MCNUTT, James; b 1740; d 6 Sep 1811 **RU:** Ensign, Served in Capt Mathew Arbuckles Co, at Ft Pleasant 1774 **CEM:** Old Providence; **GPS** 37.96151, -79.71000; 1005 Spottswood Rd, Spottswood; Augusta **GS:** Y **SP:** Margaret McElroy (__-22 Sep 1820) **VI:** Son of Alexander and Jane (-----) McNutt. Name on SAR cemetery plaque **P:** unk **BLW:** unk **RG:** unk **MK:** Y **PH:** unk **SS:** BT **BS:** JLARC 2, 8, 62, 63; 196; 213 pg 461.

MCNUTT, Robert; b unk; d 17 Jan 1781 **RU:** Soldier, Killed at battle of Cowpens, Spartanburg Co, SC **CEM:** Old Providence; **GPS** 37.96151, -79.71000; 1005 Spottswood Rd, Spottswood; Augusta **GS:** Y **SP:** No info **VI:** Died in Cowpens battle in SC. Newer Govt stone. Name also on SAR cemetery plaque **P:** unk **BLW:** unk **RG:** unk **MK:** Y **PH:** unk **SS:** B; BT **BS:** JLARC 2, 63; 196.

MCPHEETERS, William Jr; b 28 Sep 1729, PA; d 28 Oct 1807 **RU:** Soldier/Patriot, Gave material aid to cause **CEM:** Bethel Presbyterian; **GPS** 38.04257, -79.17283; 563 Bethel Green Rd, Middlebrook; Augusta **GS:** U **SP:** Rachel Moore (__-30 Jan 1826) d/o James (1711-1791) & Jane (Walker) (1712-1793) Moore **VI:** Son of William McPheeter (1690-1773) & Rebecca Thompson **P:** unk **BLW:** unk **RG:** unk **MK:** unk **PH:** unk **SS:** AL Comm Bk II pg 361 Augusta Co **BS:** JLARC 62; 196.

MCPHERSON, Hugh; b 2 Mar 1756, Kippochan, County of Argyll and Bute, Scotland; d 20 Feb 1808 **RU:** Soldier, Enl 29 Jul 1782 in Col Moses Hazen's Regt, Cont Troops **CEM:** Trinity Episcopal; **GPS** 36.83459, -76.30105; 500 Court St; Portsmouth City **GS:** Y **SP:** Lilias Blair (1744 Scotland-3 Nov 1822 Norfolk) **VI:** Son of John & Effie (-----) McPherson. Presbyterian minister. Died in Norfolk **P:** unk **BLW:** unk **RG:** unk **MK:** unk **PH:** Y **SS:** CI Service Rec **BS:** 196.

MCREYNOLDS, James; b 1724, Ireland; d 25 Jun 1807 **RU:** Sergeant, Served in Bedford Militia **CEM:** McReynolds Family; **GPS** 37.17360, - 78.5334; Rt 623; Appomattox **GS:** U **SP:** Mar (1749) Mary Bell (27 Feb 1727-10 May 1799) **VI:** No further data **P:** unk **BLW:** unk **RG:** unk **MK:** unk **PH:** unk **SS:** E pg 539 **BS:** JLARC 36.

MCREYNOLDS, John; b 1758; d 1796 **RU:** Captain, Served in Cont Line **CEM:** McReynolds Family; **GPS** unk; Off Rt 623; Campbell **GS:** U **SP:** 1) Mar (6 Dec 1788 (bond)) Jane Campbell d/o James & (-----) Campbell 2) Olivia (-----) **VI:** No further data **P:** unk **BLW:** unk **RG:** unk **MK:** N **PH:** unk **SS:** NSSAR Ancestor # P-247075 **BS:** JLARC 36.

MCREYNOLDS, Joseph; b 1755; d 1776 **RU:** Corporal, Served in 5th Cont line **CEM:** McReynolds Family; **GPS** 37.17360, - 78.5334; Rt 623; Appomattox **GS:** U **SP:** No info **VI:** No further data **P:** unk **BLW:** unk **RG:** unk **MK:** unk **PH:** unk **SS:** E pg 539 **BS:** JLARC 36.

McROBERT, Archibald; b 1736; d 1807 **RU:** Patriot, Gave material aid to cause **CEM:** Hampden-Sydney College Cem; **GPS** unk; Hampden-Sydney; Prince Edward **GS:** Y **SP:** Elizabeth Munford, d/o Robert Munford & Ann Bland **VI:** Charter member of Hampton-Sidney College and Hampton-Sidney Presbyterian Church **P:** N **BLW:** N **RG:** Y **MK:** N **PH:** unk **SS:** AL Ct Bk pg 12, 17 Prince Edward Co; AS **BS:** 80 vol 3 pg 74; 196.

MCROBERTS, Alexander; b unk; d unk **RU:** Private, Served in Col Clark's Illinois Regt **CEM:** Fincastle Presbyterian; **GPS** 37.50017, -79.87558; 108 E Back St, Fincastle; Botetourt **GS:** N **SP:** Mar (3 May 1784 Botetourt Co) Nancy Hillard **VI:** Name is on the SAR plaque at this cemetery **P:** unk **BLW:** unk **RG:** Y **MK:** Y **PH:** N **SS:** E pg 539 **BS:** 196; JLARC 1.

MCROBERTS, John; b 1750; d Aft Aug 1793 **RU:** Soldier/Patriot, Gave material aid to cause **CEM:** Fincastle Presbyterian; **GPS** 37.50017, -79.87558; 108 E Back St, Fincastle; Botetourt **GS:** N **SP:** 1) Mar (12 Apr 1770 Botetourt Co) Sarah McClanahan d/o Francis & (-----) McClanahan 2) Mar (5 Aug

RU=Rank/Unit CEM=Cemetery GS=Gravestone SP=Spousal Information
VI=Other Veteran Info P=Pension BLW=Bounty/Land Warrant RG=Registered Grave
MK=SAR/DAR Marker PH=Photo SS=Service Source BS=Burial Source

227

1793 Botetourt Co) Eunice Crawford **VI:** Name is on the SAR plaque at this cemetery **P:** unk **BLW:** unk **RG:** Y **MK:** Y **PH:** N **SS:** J-NSSAR 1993 Reg; AL Ct Bk pg 15 Augusta Co **BS:** JLARC 1; 196.

MCROBERTS, Samuel; b 1725; d 1784 **RU:** Patriot, Gave material aid to cause **CEM:** Fincastle Presbyterian; GPS 37.50017, -79.87558; 108 E Back St, Fincastle; Botetourt **GS:** N **SP:** No info **VI:** Name is on the SAR plaque at this cemetery **P:** N **BLW:** N **RG:** Y **MK:** Y **PH:** N **SS:** J-NSSAR 1993 Reg; AL Ct Bk pg 1, 11, 16, 19, 21 Botetourt Co **BS:** JLARC 1; 196.

MCSPADDEN, Moses; b 1754, Rockbridge Co; d 24 Aug 1827 **RU:** Soldier, Served in Washington Co Militia **CEM:** Green Spring Presbyterian; GPS 36.63670, -81.99560; 2007 Green Spring Ch Rd, Abingdon; Washington **GS:** Y **SP:** Mar (1776 Rockbridge Co) Sarah Jane Whitesides (1754-1826) **VI:** Son of Thomas (c1720 Ireland-1765) & Dorothy (Edmiston) McSpadden. Farmer & miller near Abingdon VA **P:** unk **BLW:** unk **RG:** unk **MK:** unk **PH:** unk **SS:** CD; CV pg 206,208 **BS:** 196.

MCVEAGH (MCVAY), Jonathan; b 1 Sep 1743, Chester, PA; d 16 Sep 1824 **RU:** Soldier, Served in Capt Evan's Co, Col Thomas Bull's Regt, and 2d Bn Chester Co Militia **CEM:** McVeagh Family Plantation; GPS unk; Not identified by JLARC; Loudoun **GS:** U **SP:** Mar (10 Jan 1770) Elizabeth Bull (20 Aug 1746, PA-14 Dec 1831) **VI:** No further data **P:** unk **BLW:** unk **RG:** Y **MK:** unk **PH:** unk **SS:** J-NSSAR 2000 Reg; DD; AR Vol 3 pg 74 **BS:** JLARC 76.

MCWILLIAMS, William; b 1751; d 17 Apr 1801 **RU:** Lieutenant Colonel, Served in VA Line. Ent serv Fredericksburg. Commanded 7th Co, 3rd VA Regt of Foot Feb 1777-Jan 1777 Spotsylvania Co **CEM:** Masonic Cemetery; GPS 38.30198, -77.46142; 900 Charles St; Fredericksburg City **GS:** U **SP:** Mar (6 Apr 1782) Dorothea B. (-----) (c1765-c Aug 1839). She mar next to George Buckner (___-18 Nov 1828). **VI:** Widow appl pen10 Sep 1838 Caroline Co age 73. R1410 **P:** Y **BLW:** unk **RG:** unk **MK:** unk **PH:** unk **SS:** J- DAR Hatcher; CE pg 39; CG pg 2311 **BS:** JLARC 2.

MEACHUM (MEACHAM), Ichabod; b c1759; d 1827 **RU:** Seaman, Served in 1775, MA Regt 1777 aboard "Trumbull" **CEM:** Meacham Family; GPS unk; Nr Christiansburg; Montgomery **GS:** Y **SP:** No info **VI:** Pen age 59 Montgomery Co 1818. F-S38204 R1702 **P:** Y **BLW:** unk **RG:** Y **MK:** N **PH:** unk **SS:** K Vol 3 pg 242 **BS:** SAR regis.

MEAD, Nicholas; b 16 Feb 1752, Bedford Co; d c1817 **RU:** Sergeant/Patriot, Was recruiting officer Bedford Co Militia. Gave material aid to cause **CEM:** Mead; GPS unk; Near Lowry on Norfolk/Western RR Lines; Bedford **GS:** U **SP:** Mar (18 Jan 1779) Mary Bates (c1753-12 Jan 1850) **VI:** No further data **P:** unk **BLW:** unk **RG:** Y **MK:** N **PH:** unk **SS:** DAR #A076767; J-NSSAR 2000 Reg; AL Ct Bk pg 20 Campbell Co; DD **BS:** JLARC 76.

MEAD, Samuel; b 1761; d unk **RU:** Soldier, Served in Bedford Co Militia **CEM:** Royal Forest; GPS unk; New London; Bedford **GS:** U **SP:** No info **VI:** No further data **P:** unk **BLW:** unk **RG:** unk **MK:** N **PH:** unk **SS:** NSSAR Ancestor # P-247292 **BS:** JLARC 36.

MEAD (MEADE), Everard Sr; b 1 Oct 1748; d Sep 1802 **RU:** Major/Patriot, Served in VA Line. Aide de Camp to Maj Gen Lincoln. Gave material aid to cause **CEM:** Meade Family; GPS unk; Nr Chula; Amelia **GS:** N **SP:** Mary Thornton. Her will dated 1 Sep 1830 **VI:** Son of David & Susannah (Everard) Meade. Sol will 13 Jan 1801 Amelia Co. BLW #2063-300 **P:** unk **BLW:** Y **RG:** Y **MK:** unk **PH:** N **SS:** AL Ct Bk I pg 14 Amelia Co; CG pg 2315 **BS:** JLARC 1, 4, 55; 196.

MEADE, Everard Jr; b unk; d 1834 **RU:** Lieutenant Colonel, Commissioned Capt 8 Mar 1776 in Woodsford's Brigade. Was Lt Col in 2nd VA State Legion 1781-83. Was Aide de Camp to Gen Washington **CEM:** H H Jones Property; GPS unk; Chula; Amelia **GS:** Y **SP:** No info **VI:** Became general after Rev War. Monument erected Sep 1834 by Hedijah Bayliss, fellow Aide de Camp to Gen Lincoln **P:** unk **BLW:** unk **RG:** Y **MK:** unk **PH:** unk **SS:** J-NSSAR 1993 Reg; CD pg 36, 134; NSSAR Ancestor # P-247337 **BS:** JLARC 1.

MEADE, Humberson; b unk; d unk **RU:** Colonel, Service information not listed in SAR Registry **CEM:** Meade Memorial Episcopal; GPS 39.05830, -78.10360; 192 White Post Rd, White Post; Clarke **GS:** U **SP:** No info **VI:** No further data **P:** unk **BLW:** unk **RG:** unk **MK:** N **PH:** unk **SS:** NSSAR Ancestor # P-247343; AR Vol 3 pg 76 **BS:** JLARC 2.

RU=Rank/Unit CEM=Cemetery GS=Gravestone SP=Spousal Information
VI=Other Veteran Info P=Pension BLW=Bounty/Land Warrant RG=Registered Grave
MK=SAR/DAR Marker PH=Photo SS=Service Source BS=Burial Source

228

MEADE, Richard Kidder; b 11 Jul 1746; d 9 Feb 1805 **RU:** Lieutenant Colonel, Served fr 24 Oct 1775 to end of Rev. Capt of 6th Co 2nd VA Regt of Foot 24 Oct 1775. As Lt Col was field officer in 14th VA Regt of Foot, 12 Nov 1776-12 Mar 1777. Capt 2nd VA Regt. Aide-de-Camp to Gen Washington (1777). Assist Gen von Steuben in VA until end of war **CEM:** Meade Memorial Episcopal; GPS 39.05830, -78.10360; 192 White Post Rd, White Post; Clarke **GS:** Y **SP:** No info **VI:** Said to have been originally bur at plantation home "Lucky Hit" which was built after Rev and later moved to White Post **P:** unk **BLW:** unk **RG:** unk **MK:** N **PH:** Y **SS:** CE pg 38, 70 **BS:** JLARC 24; 196.

MEADOWS, James; b 10 Oct 1760, Orange Co; d Oct 1849 **RU:** Private, Ent serv Rockingham Co, May 1781. Served in Capt Garland Burnley's Co, Col Francis Taylor's VA Regt. Also served 3 months in Capt George Huston's Co, Col John Rush's VA Regt. Was in Battles of Burnt Chimneys and Hot Water. Was stationed at Albemarle Barracks. Discharged Apr 1781 **CEM:** James Meadows Sr. Family; GPS unk; 5130 Bear Foot Ln, Elkton; Rockingham **GS:** Y **SP:** Catherine Boswell (Bauswell) (__-1842) **VI:** Son of Francis Sr. (1717-1792) & Mary (-----) Meadows. GS says 1842, but gave 4 affidavits for Am Rev pensions 1843-1846. Birthdates in affidavits varied fr 1756-1762. Earliest affidavit gives birthdate as c1760. Sol appl pen 17 Sep 1832 Rockingham Co. S8895. Widow's pension S6783 or S6683 **P:** Y **BLW:** unk **RG:** no **MK:** N **PH:** Y **SS:** CG pg 2316 **BS:** JLARC 4, 64.

MEADOWS (MEDOWS), Francis; b 1759; d 20 Nov 1836 **RU:** Private, Ent serv Augusta Co, Feb 1777. Served in Capt David Laird's Co, Col Green's 10 VA Regt. Was taken prisoner at Charleston, SC. Also served in 6th Cont Line **CEM:** Peterstown; GPS 37.39470, -80.80140; Off Rt 219 btw Peterstown & Midway, on WV state line; Giles **GS:** Y **SP:** Mar (Fall 1790 or 91 Monroe Co Rockingham Co) Frances Bush (c1771-__) **VI:** Sol appl pen 16 Jun 1816 Monroe Co aged around 64. Died in Monroe Co. Widow appl pen 20 Sep 1841 age 70 in Monroe Co. W5367 **P:** Y **BLW:** unk **RG:** N **MK:** N **PH:** unk **SS:** E pg 541 & AP; CG pg 2316 **BS:** 60 Giles.

MEASE, Robert; b 1746; d 7 Mar 1803 **RU:** Patriot, Signed a legislative petition in Fairfax Co **CEM:** Old Presbyterian Meeting House; GPS 38.48528, -77.23532; 323 S Fairfax St; Alexandria City **GS:** N **SP:** No info **VI:** Died age 57 of decline (Alexandria Gazette, 9 Mar 1803, pg 3) **P:** N **BLW:** N **RG:** N **MK:** N **PH:** N **SS:** BB **BS:** 23 pg 105.

MEASON, Thomas; b 18 Nov 1726, Uniontown PA; d 10 Mar 1813 **RU:** Brigadier General, Served in Cont Army **CEM:** Arlington National; GPS 38.88377, -77.06535; Jefferson Davis Hwy Rt 110; Arlington **GS:** Y **SP:** No info **VI:** PA lawyer. Died in Washington DC. Originally bur in Old Presbyterian Cemetery in Washington DC. Moved to Arlington 12 May 1892. Oldest person bur there **P:** unk **BLW:** unk **RG:** Y **MK:** unk **PH:** unk **SS:** J-NSSAR 1993 Reg; NSSAR Ancestor # P-247455 **BS:** JLARC 1; 196.

MEEK, Samuel; b 1760; d 9 Jul 1812 **RU:** First Lieutenant, Served in Capt James Dysart's Co of Light Horse on tour of NC under command of Col William Campbell May 1781. Govt GS lists service **CEM:** Clark; GPS unk; Cedarville; Washington **GS:** U **SP:** Elizabeth (-----) (1761- 21 May 1831) **VI:** Daughter Mary M. Hopkins of Grainger Co TN appl pen 9 Oct 1856. R7094 **P:** Y **BLW:** unk **RG:** unk **MK:** unk **PH:** unk **SS:** K Vol 3 pg 249; N pg 1262-payroll; CG pg 2320 **BS:** JLARC 4, 34; N pg 184; 196.

MEINER, Francois; b unk; d 1781 **RU:** Soldier, Served in Gatinais Bn and died fr battle at Yorktown **CEM:** French Memorial; GPS 36.81944, -79.39933; Yorktown; York **GS:** U **SP:** No info **VI:** No further data **P:** unk **BLW:** unk **RG:** Y **MK:** unk **PH:** unk **SS:** J-Yorktown Historian **BS:** JLARC 1, 74.

MELVIN, James; b 1764; d 10 May 1826 **RU:** Private, Served 15th Cont Line **CEM:** Nelson Family; GPS unk; New Church; Accomack **GS:** Y **SP:** No info **VI:** Son of Smith & Alaney (-----) Melvin (stone) **P:** unk **BLW:** unk **RG:** N **MK:** N **PH:** unk **SS:** E pg 543 **BS:** 145; 196.

MENAGER, Louis; b unk; d 1781 **RU:** Soldier, Served in Agenois Bn and died fr battle at Yorktown **CEM:** French Memorial; GPS 36.81944, -79.39933; Yorktown; York **GS:** U **SP:** No info **VI:** No further data **P:** unk **BLW:** unk **RG:** Y **MK:** unk **PH:** unk **SS:** J-Yorktown Historian **BS:** JLARC 1, 74.

MENARDIER, Jean; b unk; d 1781 **RU:** Seaman, Served on "Saint-Esprit" and died from Yorktown battle **CEM:** French Memorial; GPS 36.81944, -79.39933; Yorktown; York **GS:** U **SP:** No info **VI:** No further data **P:** unk **BLW:** unk **RG:** Y **MK:** unk **PH:** unk **SS:** J-Yorktown Historian **BS:** JLARC 1, 74.

RU=Rank/Unit	CEM=Cemetery	GS=Gravestone	SP=Spousal Information
VI=Other Veteran Info	P=Pension	BLW=Bounty/Land Warrant	RG=Registered Grave
MK=SAR/DAR Marker	PH=Photo	SS=Service Source	BS=Burial Source

229

MERCER, George; b 1711; d 1777 **RU:** Captain, Appointed Aide de Camp to Col Geo Washington, 17 Sep 1775 at Ft Cumberland. Killed in Battle at Princeton, 3 Jan 1777 **CEM:** St Stephen's Episcopal; GPS unk; 115 N East St, Culpeper; Culpeper **GS:** Y **SP:** No info **VI:** Son of General Hugh Mercer. Some confusion as to who was killed at Battle of Princeton. General Hugh Mercer certainly was killed there. His tombsone says he d age 66, son of Hugh Mercer "who fell at Princeton" **P:** unk **BLW:** unk **RG:** N **MK:** N **PH:** unk **SS:** G pg 357 **BS:** 167 St Stephens; 196.

MERCER, Hugh; b 27 Jan 1726, Roeharty, Scotland; d 12 Jan 1777 **RU:** Brigadier General, Commanded VA 34rd Regt of Foot Dec 1775-6 June 1782. Promoted to Brig Gen Mortally wounded at Princeton **CEM:** City Cemetery; GPS 38.30112, -77.46628; 1000 Washington Ave; Fredericksburg City **GS:** U **SP:** No info **VI:** Died in Princeton NJ. Burial first in Philadelphia. Memorialized on monument on Washington Ave Fredericksburg **P:** unk **BLW:** unk **RG:** unk **MK:** unk **PH:** unk **SS:** CE pg 38 **BS:** 32.

MERCER, James; b 26 Feb 1736, Marlborough, Stafford Co; d 31 Oct 1793 **RU:** Patriot, Was member VA House of Burgesses 1762-75 and 1st Cont Congress 1779 **CEM:** St John's Episcopal; GPS 37.53183, -77.41958; 2401 E Broad St; Richmond City **GS:** Y **SP:** No info **VI:** Judge of VA General Ct 1779-89. Judge of 1st VA Ct of Appeals 1789 until his death. **P:** N **BLW:** N **RG:** Y **MK:** N **PH:** unk **SS:** AQ **BS:** 04 Dec 06; 201 pg 7391.

MERCER, John; b 1736; d 1793 **RU:** Patriot, Gave material aid to cause **CEM:** St John's Episcopal; GPS 37.53183, -77.41958; 2401 E Broad St; Richmond City **GS:** Y **SP:** No info **VI:** No further data **P:** N **BLW:** N **RG:** N **MK:** N **PH:** unk **SS:** N pg 145; AL Ct Bk pg 10 Orange Co **BS:** 32 e-mail 3/06.

MERCIER, Andoche; b unk; d 1781 **RU:** Soldier, Served in Beaujolais Bn and died fr battle at Yorktown **CEM:** French Memorial; GPS 36.81944, -79.39933; Yorktown; York **GS:** U **SP:** No info **VI:** No further data **P:** unk **BLW:** unk **RG:** Y **MK:** unk **PH:** unk **SS:** J-Yorktown Historian **BS:** JLARC 1, 74.

MEREDITH, Elijah; b 1756; d 1796 **RU:** Captain, Served in PA **CEM:** Meredith Family; GPS unk; Check property records; New Kent **GS:** U **SP:** Ann Clopton **VI:** No further data **P:** unk **BLW:** unk **RG:** Y **MK:** unk **PH:** unk **SS:** J-NSSAR 1993 Reg; NSSAR Ancestor #P-247916; CI PA Archives **BS:** JLARC 1.

MEREDITH, James; b 8 Sep 1762; d 20 or 29 Mar 1840 **RU:** Private, Served in VA Line. Ent serv Chesterfield Co **CEM:** Dunham; GPS unk; Rt 630 Cold Harbor; Hanover **GS:** Y **SP:** Mar (27 Dec 1792) Mericha/Merica/Meecha/Megha Hooper (8 Aug 1775 - 5 July 1852) **VI:** Sol appl pen 27 Apr 1833 Hanover Co. Widow appl pen 24 Apr 1843 age 24 Apr 1843 Hanover Co age 68. W3849 **P:** Y **BLW:** unk **RG:** Y **MK:** N **PH:** unk **SS:** E pg 544; K Vol 3 pg 249; CG pg 2327 **BS:** 31 vol 1 pg 35.

MEREDITH, Samuel Garland; b 1732; d 1808 **RU:** Colonel/Patriot, Col of 1st Bn of Minutemen in 1776 of the West Augusta District Bn. Member of Lee's Legion. Gave material aid to cause **CEM:** Winton Plantation; GPS unk; adj Winton Country Club, Clifford; Amherst **GS:** U **SP:** Jane Henry (Jun 1738-12 Aug 1819) d/o John (Aberdeen, Scotland) & Sarah (Winston) (__-1784) Henry **VI:** Brother-in-law of Patrick Henry. BLW #12354 **P:** unk **BLW:** Y **RG:** Y **MK:** unk **PH:** unk **SS:** K Vol 3 pg 250; AL List pg 2 Amherst Co; CE pg 23 **BS:** JLARC 1, 4, 7, 101.

MERIAN, Vincent; b unk; d 1781 **RU:** Seaman, Served on "Sceptre" and died from Yorktown battle **CEM:** French Memorial; GPS 36.81944, -79.39933; Yorktown; York **GS:** U **SP:** No info **VI:** No further data **P:** unk **BLW:** unk **RG:** Y **MK:** unk **PH:** unk **SS:** J-Yorktown Historian **BS:** JLARC 1, 74.

MERIEL, Jean; b unk; d 1781 **RU:** Seaman, Served on "Diademe" and died from Yorktown battle **CEM:** French Memorial; GPS 36.81944, -79.39933; Yorktown; York **GS:** U **SP:** No info **VI:** No further data **P:** unk **BLW:** unk **RG:** Y **MK:** unk **PH:** unk **SS:** J-Yorktown Historian **BS:** JLARC 1, 74.

MERIWETHER, William Douglas; b 2 Nov 1761; d 27 Jan 1845 **RU:** Sergeant, Served in Clark's Illinois Regt 1782 **CEM:** Clover Fields; GPS unk; Rt 22 NE off I-64, W of Charlottesville; Charlottesville City **GS:** N **SP:** Elizabeth Lewis (6 Jun 1769 Henrico Co-27 Mar 1841) d/o Nicholas (1734-1808) & Mary (Walker) (1742-1824) Lewis **VI:** Son of Nicholas Meriwether (1736-1772) & Margaret Douglas (1737-1812) **P:** unk **BLW:** unk **RG:** unk **MK:** unk **PH:** N **SS:** E pg 545 **BS:** JLARC 58; 196.

MERKOT, Georges; b unk; d 1781 **RU:** Soldier, Served in Royal Deaux Ponts Bn and died fr battle at Yorktown **CEM:** French Memorial; GPS 36.81944, -79.39933; Yorktown; York **GS:** U **SP:** No info **VI:** No further data **P:** unk **BLW:** unk **RG:** Y **MK:** unk **PH:** unk **SS:** J-Yorktown Historian **BS:** JLARC 1, 74.

RU=Rank/Unit	CEM=Cemetery	GS=Gravestone	SP=Spousal Information
VI=Other Veteran Info	P=Pension	BLW=Bounty/Land Warrant	RG=Registered Grave
MK=SAR/DAR Marker	PH=Photo	SS=Service Source	BS=Burial Source

MERRITT, Samuel; b c1758; d Aft 1820 **RU:** Soldier, Served in the 2nd VA Regt in1777 **CEM:** Fincastle Presbyterian; GPS 37.50017, -79.87558; 108 E Back St, Fincastle; Botetourt **GS:** N **SP:** Mar (30 Jul 1817 Botetourt Co) Mary Keith (__-Aft 1820) **VI:** Occupation: Laborer. Pensioned 1818 in Botetourt Co, residing there with family 1820. Appl for pen 14 May 1818. S38206. Name is on the SAR plaque at this cemetery **P:** Y **BLW:** unk **RG:** Y **MK:** Y **PH:** N **SS:** K Vol 3 pg 252; CG pg 2337 **BS:** 196; JLARC 1, 4, 60.

MERRYMAN, John; b 1763, MD; d 18 Aug 1849 **RU:** Private?, Served in 1st VA Regt **CEM:** Mt Hebron; GPS 39.10916, -78.09497; 305 E Boscawen St; Winchester City **GS:** Y **SP:** No info **VI:** No further data **P:** unk **BLW:** unk **RG:** N **MK:** N **PH:** unk **SS:** E pg 546 **BS:** 65 Winchester; 196.

MERY, Antoine; b unk; d 1781 **RU:** Soldier, Served in Bourbonnais Bn and died fr battle at Yorktown **CEM:** French Memorial; GPS 36.81944, -79.39933; Yorktown; York **GS:** U **SP:** No info **VI:** No further data **P:** unk **BLW:** unk **RG:** Y **MK:** unk **PH:** unk **SS:** J-Yorktown Historian **BS:** JLARC 1, 74.

MEYERS, John; b unk; d 1828 **RU:** Private, Served in Lee's Legion **CEM:** Mt Zion Church; GPS 36.83461, -81.59338; Old Ebenezer Rd, Marioin; Smyth **GS:** Y **SP:** No info **VI:** No further data **P:** unk **BLW:** unk **RG:** N **MK:** N **PH:** unk **SS:** A pg 115; G pg 650 **BS:** 97 pg 110.

MEYERS, Samuel; b 1748; d 22 Aug 1830 **RU:** Lieutenant, Served in Capt Crogham's Co, Nov 1778 **CEM:** Hebrew; GPS 33.55175, -77.42976; 300 Hospital St; Richmond City **GS:** Y **SP:** No info **VI:** No further data **P:** unk **BLW:** Y **RG:** N **MK:** N **PH:** unk **SS:** C pg 255; E pg 576; AP record; CI Muster Roll reel 119 pg 7 **BS:** 184.

MICHELET, Jean; b unk; d 1781 **RU:** Soldier, Served in Soissonnais Bn and died fr battle at Yorktown **CEM:** French Memorial; GPS 36.81944, -79.39933; Yorktown; York **GS:** U **SP:** No info **VI:** No further data **P:** unk **BLW:** unk **RG:** Y **MK:** unk **PH:** unk **SS:** J-Yorktown Historian **BS:** JLARC 1, 74.

MICKLE, Elijah Watson; b 26 Jul 1740, York Co, PA; d 26 May 1817 **RU:** Soldier, Served in Capt Jame's Elliot's Co in PA **CEM:** Rock Spring; GPS 37.78126, -79.44585; Jct Rt 803 & Liberty Hall Rd, Lodi; Washington **GS:** Y **SP:** Mary Cox (1740-1826) **VI:** No further data **P:** unk **BLW:** unk **RG:** unk **MK:** unk **PH:** Y **SS:** CI PA Archives, CI PA Archives General Index Vol XXI pg 70, 339, 612 **BS:** 196.

MIDDLETON, William; b 1767; d 1832 **RU:** Drummer, Served also as a Coronet in Lee's Legion **CEM:** Old Opequon Church; GPS 39.82237, -78.11412; 217 Opequon Church Ln, Kernstown; Frederick **GS:** Y **SP:** No info **VI:** No further data **P:** unk **BLW:** unk **RG:** unk **MK:** unk **PH:** unk **SS:** J- DAR Hatcher; A pg 288; E pg 548 **BS:** JLARC 2; 196.

MIFFORD, Jacob; b 1764; d 1798 **RU:** Private, Served at age 18 in Frederick Co, MD Regt in Mar 1782 **CEM:** Fincastle Presbyterian; GPS 37.50017, -79.87558; 108 E Back St, Fincastle; Botetourt **GS:** N **SP:** no info **VI:** Name is on the SAR plaque at this cemetery **P:** unk **BLW:** unk **RG:** Y **MK:** Y **PH:** N **SS:** AR Vol 3 pg 83; AP serv Record; J-NSSAR 1993 Reg, J- DAR Hatcher **BS:** JLARC 1, 2; 196.

MILLAN, Thomas; b 01 Mar 1750, Millstone, Somerset Co, NJ; d 27 Apr 1828 **RU:** Ensign, Served in Loudoun Co Militia in Capt William Lane's Co, 1779-1781 **CEM:** Fairfax City; GPS 38.84690, -77.31330; Main St & Page Ave; Fairfax City **GS:** Y **SP:** 1) Mar (c1774) Elizabeth Shedd (1750-1791); 2) Susannah Summers **VI:** Son of William & Elizabeth (Lyle) Millan of Scotland. Older Govt stone marks his grave **P:** N **BLW:** N **RG:** Y **MK:** Y **PH:** Y **SS:** AK; AZ pg 213, CD **BS:** JLARC 1, 2, 14, 27; 04; 196.

MILLAN, William; b 1765; d 28 Jul 1813 **RU:** Patriot, Gave material aid to the cause **CEM:** Millan/Potter Family; GPS unk; 7925 Telegraph Rd; Fairfax **GS:** Y **SP:** No info **VI:** No further data **P:** N **BLW:** N **RG:** N **MK:** N **PH:** unk **SS:** AL Ct Bk pg 26 **BS:** 60 Fairfax Co; 61 vol V pg FB-17.

MILLAN, William; b unk; d 1810 **RU:** Patriot, Gave material aid to cause **CEM:** Fairfax City; GPS 38.84690, -77.31330; Main St & Page Ave; Fairfax City **GS:** N **SP:** No info **VI:** No further data **P:** N **BLW:** N **RG:** Y **MK:** N **PH:** N **SS:** J-NSSAR 2000 Reg; D Loudoun Co **BS:** JLARC 76.

MILLER, Christian; b 1744, near Woodstock, Shenandoah Co; d 26 Apr 1836 **RU:** Sergeant, Served in Shenandoah Co Militia where ent serv **CEM:** Miller Family; GPS unk; Woodstock; Shenandoah **GS:** U **SP:** Mar (1770) Catharine Wisman (__-2 Feb 1839) **VI:** Sol appl pen 10 Sep 1832 Shenandoah Co age

---

RU=Rank/Unit   CEM=Cemetery   GS=Gravestone   SP=Spousal Information
VI=Other Veteran Info   P=Pension   BLW=Bounty/Land Warrant   RG=Registered Grave
MK=SAR/DAR Marker   PH=Photo   SS=Service Source   BS=Burial Source

231

88. Widow appl 28 Jul 1837 Shenandoah Co. W18515 **P:** Y **BLW:** unk **RG:** N **MK:** N **PH:** unk **SS:** E pg 549; CG pg 2349 **BS:** DAR report.

MILLER, Henry; b unk; d 1812 **RU:** Captain, Served in Fraizer's Co, Augusta Co Militia **CEM:** Miller Family; GPS unk; 4998 Scenic Hwy, Bridgewater; Augusta **GS:** Y **SP:** No info **VI:** GS lying flat--needs resetting **P:** unk **BLW:** unk **RG:** unk **MK:** unk **PH:** Y **SS:** E pg 549 **BS:** 196.

MILLER, Henry; b 1726; d 1798 **RU:** Patriot, Gave material aid to cause in Rockbridge Co **CEM:** Miller-Irwin; GPS 37.65116, -79.52014; Dry Well Rd Rt 813, on left at Charles Ln; Lexington City **GS:** Y **SP:** Rebecca Beggs/Boggs (1736-1816) **VI:** Moved fr Lancaster Co to Botetourt (now Rockbridge). Recd BLW 400 acres in Greenlee Grant. Died in Farquier Co. Will proved Oct 1797. New memorial monument **P:** N **BLW:** Y **RG:** unk **MK:** unk **PH:** Y **SS:** AL Ct Bk 4 & 16 **BS:** 196.

MILLER, Henry B Sr; b 14 Jul 1764, Rockingham Co VA; d 18 Sep 1850 **RU:** Private, Ent serv Rockingham Co Aug 1781 Served under Col Nalle and his uncle Capt Michael Coger **CEM:** Elk Run; GPS 38.41042, -78.61033; North St, Elkton; Rockingham **GS:** Y **SP:** 1) Elizabeth (-----) 2) Maria Catharine Price 3) Hanah (-----) (named in will) **VI:** Sol appl pen 21 Aug 1832 Rockingham Co. R7196 **P:** Y **BLW:** unk **RG:** Y **MK:** N **PH:** unk **SS:** AK; E pg 549; CG pg 2354 **BS:** 04.

MILLER, Henry II; b 4 Jan 1759; d 7 Jan 1833 **RU:** Private?, Served in Col Morgan's Rifle Regt **CEM:** Masonic Cemetery; GPS unk; Rt 522, Washington; Rappahannock **GS:** Y **SP:** Mar (14 May 1782, Winchester) Achsah Margaret Warner (1762-23 Feb 1833) **VI:** Son of Henry (1727 Germany-1796 Madison Co) & Susannah (Sibler) (2 Feb 1730, Germany-1796) Miller **P:** unk **BLW:** unk **RG:** Y **MK:** N **PH:** unk **SS:** E pg 549 **BS:** 33.

MILLER, Jacob; b 2 Oct 1748, Washington Co, MD; d 11 Jul 1815 **RU:** Patriot, Gave material aid to the cause **CEM:** Garber Family; GPS unk; Vic Moores Store; Shenandoah **GS:** Y **SP:** Anna Martha Wine (1753 Lancaster Co, PA-1795) d/o Locowich (1724-1792) & Barbara Ann (-----) Miller **VI:** No further data **P:** N **BLW:** N **RG:** N **MK:** N **PH:** unk **SS:** AL ct Bk pg 18 **BS:** 79 pg 24.

MILLER, John; b c1761; d 3 Aug 1841 **RU:** Captain, Probably served in Morgan's Co in Greyson's Regt or in Capt Maybury's Co in May 1778. Served fr July 1775 to Jan 1783. **CEM:** Miller at Mountain Green; GPS unk; Washington; Rappahannock **GS:** Y **SP:** Nancy (-----) (14 Jun 1774 - 22 Sep 1859) **VI:** Grave moved fr Kinloch farm. An original member of Society of Cincinnati **P:** unk **BLW:** unk **RG:** Y **MK:** N **PH:** unk **SS:** E pg 550 **BS:** 33; 163; 210 pg 353.

MILLER, Mathias; b 18 Oct 1743, Berks City, PA; d Dec 1805 **RU:** Private, Served in 3rd PA Regt **CEM:** Rader Lutheran; GPS 38.65073, -78.78055; 17072 Raders Church Rd, Timberville; Rockingham **GS:** Y **SP:** 1) Susanna C. Mueller 2) Catherine Aulenbach 3) (-----) 4) Anna Mariea Moyer Schaeffer **VI:** Moved to VA in 1794-5 **P:** unk **BLW:** unk **RG:** Y **MK:** Y **PH:** Y **SS:** J-NSSAR 1993 Reg; P pg 386; CI Serv Rec Muster Roll **BS:** JLARC 1.

MILLER, Michael; b 1765 York Co PA; d 17 Sep 1817 **RU:** Private, Served in VA unit in Illinois in Capt James Taylor's Co, Col Wayne's PA Bn 1776 **CEM:** Old Weaver Church; GPS 38.44868, -78.90463; Harrisonville; Rockingham **GS:** Y **SP:** Elizabeth Breneman (22 Feb 1773-Mar 1815) D/o Abaham (1744-1815) & Maria (Reiff) (1746-1788) Breneman **VI:** No further data **P:** unk **BLW:** unk **RG:** N **MK:** N **PH:** unk **SS:** E pg 550 **BS:** 191 Shank; 196.

MILLER, Peter; b 1741 PA; d 15 Nov. 1819 **RU:** Patriot, Gave material aid to cause **CEM:** Old Peaked Mountain; GPS 38.37113, -78.73416; 9843 Town Hall Rd, McGaheysville; Rockingham **GS:** Y **SP:** 1) Martha Kropp 2) Rachel Ramsey **VI:** Common monument **P:** N **BLW:** N **RG:** Y **MK:** Y **PH:** unk **SS:** J-NSSAR 2000 Reg; AL Ct Bk II pg 10, 11 Rockingham Co **BS:** JLARC 76.

MILLER, Samuel; b 1738, Lancaster, PA; d 1789 **RU:** Private, Served in Capt Henry Mathias Co, Col Smyser's Regt, PA Militia. **CEM:** Miller Family; GPS unk; Harrisonburg; Harrisonburg City **GS:** Y **SP:** Mar (c1760) Magdalena Wiley (__ York Co, PA-aft 8 Aug 1768) **VI:** No further data **P:** unk **BLW:** unk **RG:** N **MK:** N **PH:** unk **SS:** DAR #A079600; E pg 550; AS SAR applic; CI: PA Archives 6th Series Vol 2 pg 481, 482 **BS:** SAR Appl.

MILLER, Samuel; b 1 Mar 1760, Lancaster Co, PA; d 26 Apr 1846 **RU:** Private, Served in Capt Reuben Harrison's Co, Augusta Co Militia **CEM:** Miller-Irwin; GPS 37.65116, -79.52014; Dry Well Rd Rt 813, on

RU=Rank/Unit	CEM=Cemetery	GS=Gravestone	SP=Spousal Information
VI=Other Veteran Info	P=Pension	BLW=Bounty/Land Warrant	RG=Registered Grave
MK=SAR/DAR Marker	PH=Photo	SS=Service Source	BS=Burial Source

232

left at Charles Ln; Lexington City **GS:** U **SP:** Mar (1 Jan 1787) Margaret Lackey (c1767-1854) d/o Thomas & Agnes (Leech) Lackey **VI:** Son of Henry (1726-1798) & Rebecca (Boggs) (1736-1816) Miller. Died in Rockbridge Co **P:** unk **BLW:** unk **RG:** unk **MK:** unk **PH:** unk **SS:** E pg 550 **BS:** 196.

MILLER, William; b unk; d 1793 **RU:** Captain/Patriot, Served in1st Cont artillery. Gave material aid to cause. **CEM:** Vauter's Episcopal; GPS unk; Rt 368 off Rt 17, Loretto; Essex **GS:** U **SP:** No info **VI:** Grave moved fr family plot **P:** unk **BLW:** unk **RG:** unk **MK:** N **PH:** unk **SS:** D Caroline Co **BS:** JLARC 1, 65.

MILLER, William; b 1 Mar 1757, PA; d 7 Nov 1840 **RU:** Private, Ent serv 1780. Served in Capt Gaines Gilmore Co Rockbridge Co Militia **CEM:** Broad Creek-Miller; GPS unk; Buffalo Dist; Rockbridge **GS:** Y **SP:** Elizabeth Lackey **VI:** Moved to Rockbridge Co c1767. **P:** unk **BLW:** unk **RG:** Y **MK:** N **PH:** unk **SS:** J-NSSAR 1993 Reg; K Vol 3 pg 264 **BS:** JLARC 1.

MILLERT, Michel; b unk; d 1781 **RU:** Soldier, Served in Metz Bn and died fr battle at Yorktown **CEM:** French Memorial; GPS 36.81944, -79.39933; Yorktown; York **GS:** U **SP:** No info **VI:** No further data **P:** unk **BLW:** unk **RG:** Y **MK:** unk **PH:** unk **SS:** J-Yorktown Historian **BS:** JLARC 1, 74.

MILLIOT, Gaspard; b unk; d 1781 **RU:** Soldier, Served in Gatinais Bn and died fr battle at Yorktown **CEM:** French Memorial; GPS 36.81944, -79.39933; Yorktown; York **GS:** U **SP:** No info **VI:** No further data **P:** unk **BLW:** unk **RG:** Y **MK:** unk **PH:** unk **SS:** J-Yorktown Historian **BS:** JLARC 1, 74.

MILLS, John; b c1760, nr Dromore, County Down, Ireland; d 14 Jun 1800 **RU:** Private, Served in Capt Trimble's & Capt Campbell's companies, Augusta Co. Also served in the 12th and 13th Cont Line long enough to receive a pension for service **CEM:** Augusta Stone Presbyterian; GPS 38.23926, -78.97356; 28 Old Stone Church Ln, Ft Defiance; Augusta **GS:** Y **SP:** Frances Hall, d/o John & Elizabeth Hall, d Aug 1843 **VI:** Recd pension in Augusta Co. Memorial stone erected in 1926 says he settled on Middle River abt 1780, gives no date of birth **P:** Y **BLW:** unk **RG:** Y **MK:** unk **PH:** unk **SS:** E pg 551 **BS:** JLARC 1, 2, 8, 23, 62; 196.

MILLS, Robert; b c1760, nr Dromore, County Down, Ireland; d Sep 1785 **RU:** Sergeant, Served in 6th & 11th Cont line. Served as Sgt in Capt Charles Gallahue's Co,12th Cont line, May 1777 **CEM:** Augusta Stone Presbyterian; GPS 38.23926, -78.97356; 28 Old Stone Church Ln, Ft Defiance; Augusta **GS:** Y **SP:** Susannah (------) (___-1799) **VI:** Memorial stone erected in 1926 says he settled on Middle River before 1780. Gives no date of birth **P:** unk **BLW:** unk **RG:** unk **MK:** unk **PH:** unk **SS:** A pg 257; E pg 552 **BS:** JLARC 2, 8; 196.

MILLS, William; b 1760; d 22 Aug 1798 **RU:** Captain, Signed oath as Capt 18 Sep 1777, Spotsylvania Co Miitia. Possibly also served in 6th & 8th Cont Lines **CEM:** Brawner; GPS unk; Rt 1 at Potomac HS; Prince William **GS:** Y **SP:** Peggy Swift **VI:** No further data **P:** unk **BLW:** unk **RG:** Y **MK:** N **PH:** unk **SS:** E pg 552; H **BS:** 15 pg 226.

MILLS, William; b 1760; d unk **RU:** Private, Served in 6th & 8th Cont Line **CEM:** Mill's Family; GPS unk; Standardsville; Greene **GS:** N **SP:** No info **VI:** No further data **P:** unk **BLW:** unk **RG:** N **MK:** N **PH:** N **SS:** E pg 552 **BS:** 192.

MILNER, Thomas; b 1760; d By 1826 **RU:** Private?/Patriot, Served in 4th Cont line. Gave to cause in Isle of Wight Co **CEM:** Eastern State Hospital; GPS 37.25560, -76.71030; S Henry Street; Williamsburg City **GS:** N **SP:** No info **VI:** No further data **P:** unk **BLW:** unk **RG:** N **MK:** N **PH:** N **SS:** E pg 552; AL Ct Bk pg 12 **BS:** 65 Williamsburg.

MIMS, David; b 1 Jan 1701, d Oct 1781 **RU:** Patriot, Gave material aid to cause **CEM:** Mims Family; GPS unk; Manakin; Goochland **GS:** U **SP:** Mar (1721 Goochland Co) Agnes Weldy (1705-1May 1777) **VI:** Son of Thomas & Amelia Anne (Martin) Mims **P:** N **BLW:** N **RG:** unk **MK:** unk **PH:** unk **SS:** AL Ct Bk pg 4 **BS:** 196.

MIMS, David Jr; b 1748, Goochland Co; d 16 Oct 1786 **RU:** Patriot, Gave material aid to cause **CEM:** Mims Family; GPS unk; Licking Hole Creek Farm; Richmond Co **GS:** Y **SP:** Mar (5 Oct 1773) Martha Duiguid (20 Mar 1756-aft 1786) **VI:** No further data **P:** N **BLW:** N **RG:** N **MK:** N **PH:** unk **SS:** DAR #A080131; AL Certificate, Goochland Co; AS **BS:** 80 vol 3 pg 90.

RU=Rank/Unit	CEM=Cemetery	GS=Gravestone	SP=Spousal Information
VI=Other Veteran Info	P=Pension	BLW=Bounty/Land Warrant	RG=Registered Grave
MK=SAR/DAR Marker	PH=Photo	SS=Service Source	BS=Burial Source

233

MINGE, David; b c1746, Charles City Co; d Aft 16 May 1779 **RU:** Captain/Patriot, Was Co Cmdr in May 1779 in Charles City Co Militia. Civil service on County Committee **CEM:** Weyanoke; GPS 37.17300, -77.35600; Rt 619 off Rt 5; Charles City Co **GS:** U **SP:** Mar (1765) Christiana Shields (25 Dec 1745, York Co-aft 1790) **VI:** No further data **P:** unk **BLW:** unk **RG:** N **MK:** N **PH:** unk **SS:** DAR #A080314; E pg 552 **BS:** 127 Minge.

MINIO, Antoine; b unk; d 1781 **RU:** Seaman, Served on "Saint-Esprit" and died from Yorktown battle **CEM:** French Memorial; GPS 36.81944, -79.39933; Yorktown; York **GS:** U **SP:** No info **VI:** No further data **P:** unk **BLW:** unk **RG:** Y **MK:** unk **PH:** unk **SS:** J-Yorktown Historian **BS:** JLARC 1, 74.

MINOR, Garritt; b 11 Mar 1744; d 25 Jun 1799 **RU:** Major, As Capt, commanded a Co of Louisa Co Militia, Oct 1776. Later achieved rank of Major **CEM:** City Cemetery; GPS 38.30112, -77.46628; 1000 Washington Ave; Fredericksburg City **GS:** Y **SP:** Mar (18 May 1769) (both TSs) Mary Overton Terrill (22 May 1760, Louisa Co-30 Oct 1830, Louisa Co) but Sunning Hill Plantation, Louisa Co. **VI:** While bur in different places, he and spouse have nearly identical stones made at the same time, and both give the same marriage date and names of spouse **P:** unk **BLW:** unk **RG:** Y **MK:** unk **PH:** unk **SS:** CE pg 19 **BS:** JLARC 2, 76; 196.

MINOR, John Jr; b 13 May 1761, Topping Forest, Caroline Co; d 8 Jun 1816 **RU:** Soldier/Patriot, Specific service not determined. Gave material aid to cause **CEM:** Masonic Cemetery; GPS 38.30198, -77.46142; 900 Charles St; Fredericksburg City **GS:** Y **SP:** 1) Mary Berkeley of Hanover Co (d mos after wedding) 2) Lucy Landon Carter (29 Apr 1776 - 26 Dec 1855) d/o Landon C. & (-----) Carter of "Cleve", King George Co. **VI:** Member VA House of Delegates; attorney, Presidential Elector for James Monroe. Introduced first bill to emancipate slaves and colonize them elsewhere, which was soundly defeated. Was General in War of 1812. Moved to Masonic Cem fr Hazel Hill in Fredericksburg in 1855. Died in Richmond **P:** unk **BLW:** unk **RG:** Y **MK:** Y **PH:** Y **SS:** D Caroline Co **BS:** JLARC 2, 4, 76, 91.

MINOR, Thomas; b 17 Dec 1751; d 21 Jul 1834 **RU:** Captain/Patriot, Ent serv 1777 in VA Regt. Was commander of Spotsylvania Co 1775. Was also Aide-de-Camp to General Edward Stevens,1781 at the siege of Yorktown. Gave beef to cause Jun 1781. **CEM:** Minor Family; GPS unk; Rt 633, nr Locust Grove homestead; Spotsylvania **GS:** Y **SP:** Mar (1780, probably Caroline Co) Elizabeth Taylor (__-7 Dec 1836) daughter of Col James & (-----) Taylor of Caroline Co **VI:** Recd BLW #5374 & #1679-300 & Pension and VA Half Pay See N.A. Account #874 & #050117 1/2 pay. Filed 15 May 1828 Spottsylvania Co. Widow and surviving children granted pen W5374 **P:** Y **BLW:** Y **RG:** Y **MK:** Y **PH:** unk **SS:** H; K Vol 3 pg 270; CG pg 2374-75; CE pg 15 **BS:** 09 Part 2.

MINOR, Vivion; b 4 Nov 1750; d 29 Sep 1791 **RU:** Captain, Ent serv 1775 Caroline Co. Served in 3rd VA Regt. Was Capt of Caroline Co Militia 1776 **CEM:** Jericho; GPS unk; North Anna River; Caroline **GS:** U **SP:** 1) Mar (11 Feb 1752) Barbara Crosby (11 Feb 1752-21 Sep 1778) d/o David & Mary (-----) Crosby; 2) Mar (31 Mar 1780 at her father's in Caroline Co) Elizabeth Dick (12 Jan 1760-1 Apr 1846) d/o Rev Archibald Dick **VI:** Son of John & Sarah (-----) Minor. Recd pen W-23992, filed 26 Nov 1838 Caroline Co. **P:** Y **BLW:** unk **RG:** unk **MK:** N **PH:** unk **SS:** K Vol 3 pg 270; CG pg 2375; CE pg 15 **BS:** JLARC 4, 15.

MINTER, Anthony; b 1739; d 1808 **RU:** Patriot, Gave material aid to cause **CEM:** Rural; GPS unk; Powhatan; Powhatan **GS:** N **SP:** Mar (19 Dec 1777) Catherine Brownley **VI:** No further data **P:** N **BLW:** N **RG:** Y **MK:** N **PH:** N **SS:** AL Ct Bk pg 24 Powhatan Co; AS SAR regis **BS:** SAR regis.

MION, Pierre; b unk; d 1781 **RU:** Soldier, Served in Touraine Bn and died fr battle at Yorktown **CEM:** French Memorial; GPS 36.81944, -79.39933; Yorktown; York **GS:** U **SP:** No info **VI:** No further data **P:** unk **BLW:** unk **RG:** Y **MK:** unk **PH:** unk **SS:** J-Yorktown Historian **BS:** JLARC 1, 74.

MIOT, Pierre; b unk; d 1781 **RU:** Soldier, Served in Touraine Bn and died fr battle at Yorktown **CEM:** French Memorial; GPS 36.81944, -79.39933; Yorktown; York **GS:** U **SP:** No info **VI:** No further data **P:** unk **BLW:** unk **RG:** Y **MK:** unk **PH:** unk **SS:** J-Yorktown Historian **BS:** JLARC 1, 74.

MITCHELL, James; b 1750, Glasgow, Scotland; d 19 Jun 1787 **RU:** Corporal, Enlisted 25 Jan 1776, served entire war in Cont Line **CEM:** Old Presbyterian Meeting House; GPS 38.48528, -77.23532; 323 S Fairfax St; Alexandria City **GS:** N **SP:** No info **VI:** Recd 400 acres BLW Apr 1785 for 3 yrs service;

RU=Rank/Unit	CEM=Cemetery	GS=Gravestone	SP=Spousal Information
VI=Other Veteran Info	P=Pension	BLW=Bounty/Land Warrant	RG=Registered Grave
MK=SAR/DAR Marker	PH=Photo	SS=Service Source	BS=Burial Source

234

died age 37; death notice in the Alexandria Gazette 21 Jun 1793 **P:** unk **BLW:** Y **RG:** Y **MK**: N **PH:** N **SS:** C pg 474; F pg 48. **BS:** 23 pg 105.

MITCHELL, James; b 1740; d 1806 **RU:** Lieutenant, Served in Lt Tate's Co VA Inf **CEM:** Bethel Presbyterian; GPS 38.04257, -79.17283; 563 Bethel Green Rd, Middlebrook; Augusta **GS:** Y **SP:** Elizabeth Beard **VI:** Govt stone gives yr of death only, thus birth yr is only an estimate. DAR marker placed here. **P:** unk **BLW:** unk **RG:** unk **MK**: Y **PH:** unk **SS:** E pg 554; B; BT **BS:** JLARC 2, 9, 62, 63; 196.

MITCHELL, James; b 1750; d 1795 **RU:** Lieutenant/Patriot, Gave material aid to cause **CEM:** Mitchell Family; GPS unk; Chatham; Pittsylvania **GS:** U **SP:** No info **VI:** According to 76, one mile E of Callands PO **P:** unk **BLW:** unk **RG:** Y **MK:** unk **PH:** unk **SS:** AL Ct Bk pg 3, 14 Pittsylvania Co **BS:** JLARC 2, 76.

MITCHELL, John; b 4 May 1763, Amelia Co; d 6 May 1836 **RU:** Fife Major, Enl Amelia Co 1776 in Capt Roland Ward's Co **CEM:** Wright Family; GPS 36.97658, -80.21693; Pizarro, off Rt 668; Floyd **GS:** U **SP:** Obedience Vaughn (27 Sep 1767 Amelia Co-6 May 1836, Floyd Co) d/o James (1763-1803) & (-----) Vaughan **VI:** Name is on DAR plaque in Cem. Filed for pension Sep 1832 at age 72 **P:** Y **BLW:** unk **RG:** unk **MK:** unk **PH:** unk **SS:** E pg 554; DZ pg 64 **BS:** 196.

MITCHELL, Robert; b 1750; d 29 Apr 1834 **RU:** Ensign, Served in Capt James Kelly's Co, Richmond Co Militia 1776 **CEM:** Bethel Presbyterian; GPS 38.04257, -79.17283; 563 Bethel Green Rd, Middlebrook; Augusta **GS:** Y **SP:** No info **VI:** Age at death on stone is illegible, yr of birth is an estimate **P:** unk **BLW:** unk **RG:** unk **MK:** unk **PH:** unk **SS:** B; E pg 555 **BS:** JLARC 62, 63; 196.

MITCHELL, Robert II; b 1748; d 1827 **RU:** Second Lieutenant, Served in Capt Thomas Belfield's Co, Richmond Co, 3 Nov 1777 **CEM:** Opequon Presbyterian; GPS 39.13938 -78.19494; 217 Opequon Church Ln; Winchester City **GS:** U **SP:** No info **VI:** No further data **P:** unk **BLW:** unk **RG:** unk **MK:** unk **PH:** unk **SS:** J- DAR Hatcher; G pg 314 **BS:** JLARC 2.

MITCHELL, Stephen; b 1754; d 21 Mar 1807 **RU:** Sergeant, Served in Col Charles Lewis, 14th Regt **CEM:** Mitchell Family; GPS unk; Off Rt 764, 1 mi S of Rt 765, Sylvatus; Carroll **GS:** Y **SP:** Mar (13 Mar 1783) Kitturah/Keturah Wade (1768-1834) **VI:** Son of Robert Mitchell (1714-1799) & Mary Enos (1718-1800). Died in Grayson Co. Small Govt marker with rank of Sergeant **P:** unk **BLW:** unk **RG:** unk **MK**: Y **PH:** unk **SS:** AP roll #1082 **BS:** JLARC 2, 11, 43; 196.

MITCHELL, Thomas; b 1732; d 30 Dec 1806 **RU:** Private, Served in Porterfield's Co, 11th VA Inf **CEM:** Bethel Presbyterian; GPS 38.04257, -79.17283; 563 Bethel Green Rd, Middlebrook; Augusta **GS:** Y **SP:** 1) Elizabeth McClanahan Moore; 2) Elizabeth Wales **VI:** Govt stone. No date of birth on stone **P:** unk **BLW:** unk **RG:** unk **MK:** unk **PH:** unk **SS:** B **BS:** JLARC 2,9,62, 63; 196.

MITCHELL, William; b 1750; d Dec 1802 **RU:** Captain, Specific service in Lib of VA Council Journals, 1776-7, pgs 45, 64 **CEM:** Old Presbyterian Meeting House; GPS 38.48528, -77.23532; 323 S Fairfax St; Alexandria City **GS:** N **SP:** No info **VI:** Styled Capt in his burial record. Bur 28 Dec 1802 age 42. Listed on SAR plaque in cemetery **P:** unk **BLW:** unk **RG:** Y **MK**: Y **PH:** N **SS:** J-NSSAR 1993 Reg; AK; CZ pg 313 **BS:** JLARC 1; 23 pg 105; 196.

MITCHELL, William; b 1745 Kilmarnock, East Ayrshire, Scotland; d 10 Feb 1805 **RU:** Captain, Served in Marines as Quartermaster at York. On 12 Jul 1776 supplied Co of Marines with 52 muskets & bayonets **CEM:** St John's Episcopal; GPS 37.53183, -77.41958; 2401 E Broad St; Richmond City **GS:** Y **SP:** Mary Miller **VI:** Burial date on GS **P:** unk **BLW:** unk **RG:** Y **MK**: Y **PH:** unk **SS:** E pg 668; N pg 668 **BS:** 28 pg 481; 196.

MITCHELL, William; b 1793, Augusta Co; d 13 Feb 1834 **RU:** Drummer, Served in Smith's Co, Gist's Cont Troops **CEM:** Bethel Presbyterian; GPS 38.04257, -79.17283; 563 Bethel Green Rd, Middlebrook; Augusta **GS:** Y **SP:** Mar (16 Feb 1826) Sarah Newton (1807 Rockbridge Co-3 Nov 1857) **VI:** Son of James (__Augusta Co-17 Jul 1816) & Susannah (Brownlee) Mitchell. Govt stone, no dates **P:** unk **BLW:** unk **RG:** unk **MK:** unk **PH:** unk **SS:** B **BS:** JLARC 9,62,63; 196.

MOCK, John Harrison; b unk; d 20 Dec 1837 **RU:** Private, served in Capt Thomas Craig's Co, St Clair's PA Regt Jan 1776 **CEM:** Waterford Union of Churches; GPS 39.18557, -77.60802; Fairfax St,

---

RU=Rank/Unit   CEM=Cemetery   GS=Gravestone   SP=Spousal Information
VI=Other Veteran Info   P=Pension   BLW=Bounty/Land Warrant   RG=Registered Grave
MK=SAR/DAR Marker   PH=Photo   SS=Service Source   BS=Burial Source

235

Waterford; Loudoun **GS:** Y **SP:** No info **VI:** No further data **P:** unk **BLW:** unk **RG:** Y **MK:** N **PH:** unk **SS:** A pg 187-8 **BS:** 25 pg 208.

MOFFATT, William Sr; b 1755; d 1839 **RU:** Private, Served in Capt John Blackwell's Co, 3rd VA Regt Jun 1779 **CEM:** Cedar Grove; GPS 36.57204, -80.02599; 301 Fort Lane Rd; Portsmouth City **GS:** U **SP:** No info **VI:** No further data **P:** unk **BLW:** unk **RG:** unk **MK:** unk **PH:** unk **SS:** NSSAR Ancestor #P-250745; AR Vol 3 pg 93 **BS:** JLARC 2, 39.

MOFFETT, George; b 1735; d 26 Aug 1811 **RU:** Colonel/Patriot, Commanded a co in 1776 in the Augusta Co Militia. On16 Jun 1778 took oath as colonel and served to end of war effectively using the militia to protect the citizens of the county fr the Indians. Gave material aid to cause **CEM:** Augusta Stone Presbyterian; GPS 38.23926, -78.97356; 28 Old Stone Church Ln, Ft Defiance; Augusta **GS:** Y **SP:** Sarah McDowell **VI:** Govt stone erected in 1935 styles him Col and indicates Augusta Co Militia **P:** unk **BLW:** unk **RG:** Y **MK:** unk **PH:** unk **SS:** B; E pg 556; AL Cert Augusta Co **BS:** JLARC 1 ,2, 8, 23, 62, 63; 196.

MOFFETT, James; b 30 Aug 1764; d 5 Jul 1826 **RU:** Private, Served in Capt James Ball's Co, Augusta Co Militia **CEM:** Bethel Presbyterian; GPS 38.04257, -79.17283; 563 Bethel Green Rd, Middlebrook; Augusta **GS:** Y **SP:** Mar (29 Dec 1789, Augusta Co) Mary Stewart (19 Dec 1765-15 Sep 1826) d/o of Thomas Steward (1727-1788) and Elizabeth Moore (1725-1805) **VI:** Son of John Moffett (1731-1805) and Jane Ledgerwood (1734-1821. Lived on Christian Creek. Died in Staunton **P:** unk **BLW:** unk **RG:** N **MK:** N **PH:** unk **SS:** E pg 556 **BS:** 142 Bethel; 196.

MOFFETT, Jesse; b 2 Mar 1759; d 6 Dec 1836 or 31 Aug 1852 **RU:** Soldier, Served in VA Line. Served under Capt Harrison 1777 **CEM:** Moffett; GPS unk; Nr Marshall; Fauquier **GS:** Y **SP:** 1) Mar (27 Dec 1782) Hannah (-----) (c1760-__) 2) Mar (27 Dec 1782 Fauquier Co) Elizabeth (-----) **VI:** Sol appl pen 31 Aug 1832 Fauquier Co. Pen says he d 6 Dec 1836. Widow Elizabeth appl pen 30 May 1839 Fauquier Co. W3446 **P:** Y **BLW:** unk **RG:** Y **MK:** unk **PH:** unk **SS:** J-NSSAR 1993 Reg; CG pg 2386; K Vol 3 pg 278 **BS:** JLARC 1.

MOFFETT, John; b 31 Jan 1731; d 10 Oct 1805 **RU:** Private/Patriot, Served in Capt James Trimble's Co. Was Commissioner of the Provision Law for Publick Claims in 1780. Gave material aid to the cause **CEM:** Bethel Presbyterian; GPS 38.04257, -79.17283; 563 Bethel Green Rd, Middlebrook; Augusta **GS:** Y **SP:** 1) Esther Moody d/o James Moody & Rebecca Wilson; 2) Mar (8 May 1760) Jane Ledgerwood (1725-1821) d/o William & Agnes (-----) Ledgerwood **VI:** Son of James Moffett and father of James Moffett, also bur here. Newer marker. Died age 89, "Soldier in Indian Wars" **P:** unk **BLW:** unk **RG:** N **MK:** N **PH:** unk **SS:** AS SAR code dj **BS:** JLARC 62;196.

MOFFETT, William; b 20 Feb 1761; d 20 Jun 1828 **RU:** Private, Served in Capt John Blackwell's Co #4, Col Willaim Heth's 8th VA Regt, Apr 1778. Also served in 3rd and 4th Cont Lines **CEM:** Bethel Presbyterian; GPS 38.04257, -79.17283; 563 Bethel Green Rd, Middlebrook; Augusta **GS:** Y **SP:** 1) Mar (28 Jun 1785 Augusta Co) Elizabeth Gamble, (1761-31 Mar 1790) 2) mar (11 May 1791 Augusta Co) Mary McClanachan (__-1829) **VI:** Son of John (1731-1805) & Jane (Ledgerwood) (1734-1821) Moffett. Recd pen with Mary as his widow **P:** Y **BLW:** unk **RG:** unk **MK:** unk **PH:** unk **SS:** A pg 278; E pg 556; CG pg 2386 **BS:** JLARC 62, 63; 196.

MOFFETT, William Mead; b unk; d 31 Jul 1838 **RU:** Private, Served in Capt Valentine Payton's Co, Mar 1778. Cont Line VA **CEM:** Fairfax Meeting House; GPS 39.18557, -77.60589; Water St & Waterford Rd, Waterford; Loudoun **GS:** Y **SP:** Ellen Mead (-----) (__-13 Jan 1842) **VI:** No further data **P:** unk **BLW:** unk **RG:** Y **MK:** N **PH:** unk **SS:** E pg 556 **BS:** 25 pg 209.

MOINET, Laurent; b unk; d 1781 **RU:** Seaman, Served on "Ville de Paris" and died from Yorktown battle **CEM:** French Memorial; GPS 36.81944, -79.39933; Yorktown; York **GS:** U **SP:** No info **VI:** No further data **P:** unk **BLW:** unk **RG:** Y **MK:** unk **PH:** unk **SS:** J-Yorktown Historian **BS:** JLARC 1, 74.

MOLES, Jeremiah; b 1747, Rockingham Co; d 1825 **RU:** Private, Enlisted 1775, Capt Joseph Crocket, 7th VA Regt, Commanded by Col Dangerfield. Had service at Guinn's Island. Service was fr neighboring Patrick Co **CEM:** Moses Martin; GPS unk; Bassett; Henry **GS:** U **SP:** Mar (18 Jul 1776) Lydia Smith (1750-1819) **VI:** Died in Patrick Co **P:** unk **BLW:** unk **RG:** unk **MK:** unk **PH:** unk **SS:** E pg 506 **BS:** 196.

RU=Rank/Unit	CEM=Cemetery	GS=Gravestone	SP=Spousal Information
VI=Other Veteran Info	P=Pension	BLW=Bounty/Land Warrant	RG=Registered Grave
MK=SAR/DAR Marker	PH=Photo	SS=Service Source	BS=Burial Source

236

MOLIN, Jean; b unk; d 1781 **RU:** Soldier, Served in Beaujolais Bn and died fr battle at Yorktown **CEM:** French Memorial; GPS 36.81944, -79.39933; Yorktown; York **GS:** U **SP:** No info **VI:** No further data **P:** unk **BLW:** unk **RG:** Y **MK:** unk **PH:** unk **SS:** J-Yorktown Historian **BS:** JLARC 1, 74.

MOLLIERE, Antoine; b unk; d 1781 **RU:** Seaman, Served on "Caton" and died from Yorktown battle **CEM:** French Memorial; GPS 36.81944, -79.39933; Yorktown; York **GS:** U **SP:** No info **VI:** No further data **P:** unk **BLW:** unk **RG:** Y **MK:** unk **PH:** unk **SS:** J-Yorktown Historian **BS:** JLARC 1, 74.

MOLTON, Caesar; b unk; d 1781 **RU:** Soldier, Served fr MA, died fr the battle at Yorktown **CEM:** Yorktown Victory Monument Tablet; GPS 38.28350, -78.54150; Yorktown; York **GS:** U **SP:** No info **VI:** No further data **P:** unk **BLW:** unk **RG:** unk **MK:** unk **PH:** unk **SS:** J-Yorktown Historian **BS:** JLARC 74.

MONART, Nicolas; b unk; d 1781 **RU:** Soldier, Served in Touraine Bn and died fr battle at Yorktown **CEM:** French Memorial; GPS 36.81944, -79.39933; Yorktown; York **GS:** U **SP:** No info **VI:** No further data **P:** unk **BLW:** unk **RG:** Y **MK:** unk **PH:** unk **SS:** J-Yorktown Historian **BS:** JLARC 1, 74.

MONCURE, John II; b 22 Jan 1747, Clermont, Stafford Co; d 1784 **RU:** Patriot, Gave 400# beef Nov 1781 **CEM:** Aquia Episcopal; GPS 38.46466, -77.40325; 2938 Jeff Davis Hwy, Aquia; Stafford **GS:** U **SP:** Anne Conway (c1750-__) d/o George & Anne (Heath) Conway **VI:** Son of John I (__ Scotland-10 Mar 1764 VA) & Frances (Brown) Moncure of Charles City, MD. Bur in the Chancel. Originally bur at "Dipple" Cem in Stafford Co. **P:** N **BLW:** N **RG:** unk **MK:** unk **PH:** unk **SS:** D Stafford Co pg 874 **BS:** 196.

MONDRE, Pierre; b unk; d 1781 **RU:** Seaman, Served on "Diademe" and died from Yorktown battle **CEM:** French Memorial; GPS 36.81944, -79.39933; Yorktown; York **GS:** U **SP:** No info **VI:** No further data **P:** unk **BLW:** unk **RG:** Y **MK:** unk **PH:** unk **SS:** J-Yorktown Historian **BS:** JLARC 1, 74.

MONET, Jean; b unk; d 1781 **RU:** Soldier, Served in Soissonnais Bn and died fr battle at Yorktown **CEM:** French Memorial; GPS 36.81944, -79.39933; Yorktown; York **GS:** U **SP:** No info **VI:** No further data **P:** unk **BLW:** unk **RG:** Y **MK:** unk **PH:** unk **SS:** J-Yorktown Historian **BS:** JLARC 1, 74.

MONGER, Henry; b unk; d Aft 1802 **RU:** Patriot, Gave material aid to cause **CEM:** Old Peaked Mountain; GPS 38.37113, -78.73416; 9843 Town Hall Rd, McGaheysville; Rockingham **GS:** Y **SP:** Mar (1802 Rockingham Co) Catherine Fultz d/o George & (-----) Fultz **VI:** No further data **P:** N **BLW:** N **RG:** Y **MK:** Y **PH:** unk **SS:** O pg 120; AL Ct Bk II pg 19 Rockingham Co **BS:** 04.

MONGIN, Jean; b unk; d 1781 **RU:** Soldier, Served in Touraine Bn and died fr battle at Yorktown **CEM:** French Memorial; GPS 36.81944, -79.39933; Yorktown; York **GS:** U **SP:** No info **VI:** No further data **P:** unk **BLW:** unk **RG:** Y **MK:** unk **PH:** unk **SS:** J-Yorktown Historian **BS:** JLARC 1, 74.

MONNIER, Nicolas; b unk; d 1781 **RU:** Seaman, Served on "Auguste" and died from Yorktown battle **CEM:** French Memorial; GPS 36.81944, -79.39933; Yorktown; York **GS:** U **SP:** No info **VI:** No further data **P:** unk **BLW:** unk **RG:** Y **MK:** unk **PH:** unk **SS:** J-Yorktown Historian **BS:** JLARC 1, 74.

MONROE, James; b 28 Apr 1758, Westmoreland Co; d 1831 **RU:** Major/Patriot, Served in 3rd VA Regt. Ent serv 1775. Was wounded at Battle of Harlem Heights. Was in Cont Congress 1783 **CEM:** Hollywood; GPS 37.53560, -77.45720; 412 S Cherry St; Richmond City **GS:** U **SP:** Mar (16 Feb 1786 New York City) Elizabeth Kortright (1768-1830) d/o Laurence & Hannah (Aspinwall) Kortright **VI:** US Senator 1790-94. Minister to France 1794-96 & 1803 and England 1803-07. Was Gov VA 1799-1802, Sec of State under President Madison 1811-17. Sec of War 1814-15. Fifth president of the US 1817-25. President of 2nd Const Conv of VA 1829. Remains moved fr NY to Richmond in 1858. Pen recd by widow's children, Maria H. Governeur & Eliza K. Hay. W26271 **P:** Y **BLW:** unk **RG:** Y **MK:** unk **PH:** unk **SS:** K Vol 3 pg 280 **BS:** JLARC 1, 4, 76; 201 pg 73, 93, 94.

MONROE, William; b c 1760, Westmoreland Co; d 1 Jan 1848 **RU:** Private, Ent serv 1777 and served in a VA Regt **CEM:** North Fork Baptist; GPS 39.06014, -77.68509; 38130 North Folk Rd, North Fork; Loudoun **GS:** Y **SP:** Ann (-----) **VI:** Lived in Westmoreland until age 17. Pen age 72 in 1832 Frederick Co. S5784 **P:** Y **BLW:** unk **RG:** Y **MK:** N **PH:** unk **SS:** K Vol 3 pg 281; CG pg 2388 **BS:** 25 pg 210.

MONTAGUE, Thomas; b c1754, Cumberland Co; d 1839 **RU:** Soldier, Served in VA Line. Lived in Cumberland Co at enl 1775. Source 4 reports death while in RW service of small pox around 1777-78

RU=Rank/Unit	CEM=Cemetery	GS=Gravestone	SP=Spousal Information
VI=Other Veteran Info	P=Pension	BLW=Bounty/Land Warrant	RG=Registered Grave
MK=SAR/DAR Marker	PH=Photo	SS=Service Source	BS=Burial Source

CEM: Olnorary; GPS unk; Old quarry on Old Stage Rd fr CH (see source 4). Behind Cumberland & Cartersville; Cumberland **GS:** U **SP:** Jane Daniel **VI:** Sol appl pen 27 Aug 1832 Cumberland Co age 78. Widow granted pen due arrears in 1841. S5775 **P:** Y **BLW:** unk **RG:** unk **MK:** N **PH:** unk **SS:** K Vol 3 pg 282; CG pg 2389 **BS:** JLARC 2, 4; 04.

MONTCHALEN, Antoine; b unk; d 1781 **RU:** Seaman, Served on "Ville de Paris" and died from Yorktown battle **CEM:** French Memorial; GPS 36.81944, -79.39933; Yorktown; York **GS:** U **SP:** no info **VI:** No further data **P:** unk **BLW:** unk **RG:** Y **MK:** unk **PH:** unk **SS:** J-Yorktown Historian **BS:** JLARC 1, 74.

MONTGOMERY, Francis; b 1761; d 1825 **RU:** Ensign, Served in Capt William Grayson's Co, 1780 **CEM:** Lewis-Montgomery Families (also Manassas Presbyterian Church); GPS 38.46856, -77.30823; 8201 Ashton Ave; Manassas City **GS:** Y **SP:** No info **VI:** No further data **P:** N **BLW:** N **RG:** unk **MK:** unk **PH:** unk **SS:** AZ pg 105 **BS:** 190 by cem name.

MONTGOMERY, Humphrey Jr; b 1750, PA; d 1798 **RU:** Private, Served in Capt Samuel Lapsley's 2nd Co, Col Nathaniel Gist's VA Regt in 1777 **CEM:** Oxford Presbyterian; GPS 37.75302, -79.56023; 18 Churchview Ln, Lexington; Lexington City **GS:** U **SP:** Jean Gay **VI:** Reported as unmarked grave. Bur in area inside iron railing **P:** unk **BLW:** unk **RG:** unk **MK:** unk **PH:** unk **SS:** A pg 285; C pg 257 **BS:** JLARC 126.

MONTGOMERY, John; b unk; d aft 1800 **RU:** Patriot, Gave material aid to cause **CEM:** Montgomery Family; GPS unk; Vic Christianburg; Montgomery **GS:** Y **SP:** No info **VI:** Held title of Colonel **P:** N **BLW:** N **RG:** N **MK:** N **PH:** unk **SS:** AL Comm Bk IV **BS:** 80 vol 3 pg 94.

MONTGOMERY, John; b 1717; d 1802 **RU:** Patriot, Was a member of the Safety Committee for Fincastle Co 1775-1776 **CEM:** Montgomery family; GPS unk; Nr Ft Chiswell in field abt .75 mi behind Ft Chiswell Mansion; Wythe **GS:** U **SP:** No info **VI:** Cem in disrepair, became property of DAR chapter **P:** N **BLW:** N **RG:** unk **MK:** unk **PH:** unk **SS:** G pg 207 **BS:** JLARC 76, 123.

MONTGOMERY, John Rev; b Dec 1752; d 10 Feb 1818 **RU:** Lieutenant / Patriot, Served in VA State Line for 3 yrs. 21 days in Augusta Co. As patriot purchased cattle for army **CEM:** Rocky Spring Presbyterian; GPS 38.11470, -79.24250; 1 mi S of Deerfield; Augusta **GS:** Y **SP:** Agnes Hughart (24 Jan 176_-8 Feb 1824) **VI:** Pastor of Ricky Spring, Lebanon and Windy Grove churches. Trustee and teacher of Liberty Hall Academy. Recd BLW 6000 acres 3 Mar 1784 **P:** unk **BLW:** Y **RG:** N **MK:** N **PH:** unk **SS:** F pg 51; Z pg 93 **BS:** 142 RockySpr; 196.

MONTGOMERY, Joseph; b 1760; d 1842 **RU:** Captain, Served in VA Militia **CEM:** Montgomery Family; GPS unk; Nellysford, near Wintergreen; Nelson **GS:** U **SP:** Jane Woods daughter of Samuel & (-----) Woods, Albemarle Co. **VI:** No further data **P:** unk **BLW:** unk **RG:** Y **MK:** Y **PH:** unk **SS:** J-NSSAR 1993 Reg **BS:** JLARC 1.

MONTGOMERY, Richard; b 1755, York Co, PA; d 8 Feb 1840 **RU:** Soldier, Ent serv York Co PA Line **CEM:** Rocky Spring Presbyterian; GPS 38.11470, -79.24250; 1 mi S of Deerfield; Augusta **GS:** N **SP:** Mar (1787, York Co PA) Elizabeth McCall (__-1855). Became "insane" in widowhood; son appointed her guardian & appl for her **VI:** Moved to Washington Co 1793. Sol appl pen 28 Jan 1833 Washington Co VA age 75. Son Richard Montgomery Jr. appl pen for widow 28 May 1853 Washington Co. BLW appl for 30 Mar 1855 Washington Co. W7485, BLW #26383-160-55 **P:** Y **BLW:** Y **RG:** unk **MK:** N **PH:** N **SS:** JLARC 62, 63, 79; K Vol 3 pg 283; CG pg 2391 **BS:** JLARC 4, 34, 62, 63.

MONTGOMERY, William; b 20 Jan 1732; d 1803 **RU:** Patriot, Gave material aid to cause in Prince William Co **CEM:** Lewis-Montgomery Families (also Manassas Presbyterian Church); GPS 38.46856, -77.30823; 8201 Ashton Ave; Manassas City **GS:** Y **SP:** Mar (8 Nov 1758) Katherina Mars (20 Mar 1742 Aberdeen, Scotland-1800) **VI:** Son of Francis & Elizabeth (-----) Montgomery of London, England **P:** unk **BLW:** unk **RG:** unk **MK:** unk **PH:** unk **SS:** Al Ct Bk pg 10 **BS:** 190 by cem name.

MOODY, John; b 1735; d 1804 **RU:** Private, Served in 3rd, 5th, 7th Cont Line **CEM:** Staunton Baptist; GPS 37.06970, -79.58140; 15267 Smith Mountain Lake Pkwy, Huddleston; Bedford **GS:** N **SP:** Susanna Amoss (1750-1829) **VI:** Son of Edward (1707-1775) & (-----) Moody. SAR plaque **P:** N **BLW:** N **RG:** unk **MK:** Y **PH:** N **SS:** E pg 559 **BS:** 196.

RU=Rank/Unit	CEM=Cemetery	GS=Gravestone	SP=Spousal Information
VI=Other Veteran Info	P=Pension	BLW=Bounty/Land Warrant	RG=Registered Grave
MK=SAR/DAR Marker	PH=Photo	SS=Service Source	BS=Burial Source

238

MOORE, Alexander; b unk; d Jul 1786 **RU:** Captain/Patriot, Served in William Edmiston's Co fr Washington Co at Battle of Point Pleasant, Oct 1774. Gave material aid to cause **CEM:** Moore Family; GPS 37.22110, -81.40170; Adj to RR track E of Tiptop abt halfway to jct Rts 650 & 656; Tazewell **GS:** N **SP:** no info **VI:** Son of Capt James (__-1786) & Martha (Poage) (__-1786) Moore. Killed by Shawnee Indians who attacked family home **P:** N **BLW:** N **RG:** unk **MK:** unk **PH:** N **SS:** Z pg 166; AL Ct Bk pg 1, 5 Rockbridge Co **BS:** 196.

MOORE, Alexander Spotswood; b 1763; d 1799 **RU:** Corporal, Served in 7th & 8th Cont Line **CEM:** Fairfield Plantation; GPS unk; Aylett; King William **GS:** N **SP:** Mar (17 Jul 1787) Elizabeth Aylett (1769-__), said to have mar a Judge Hamilton & moved to Chucky Bend, TN **VI:** Son of Col Bernard & Ann Catherine (Spotswood) Moore. Great uncle of Gen Robert E. Lee. BIL of John Robinson, speaker of House of Burgesses/treasurer of Colony **P:** unk **BLW:** unk **RG:** unk **MK:** unk **PH:** N **SS:** E pg 560 **BS:** 196.

MOORE, Amos Lad; b 13 May 1747, Albemarle Co; d 7 Mar 1836 **RU:** Private?, Served in VA Line. Ent serv Goochland Co **CEM:** Moore Family; GPS unk; Cardwell Rd; Goochland **GS:** Y **SP:** Mar (21 Dec 1775 Albemarle Co) Ann Rogers (c1756-__ of St James Northern Parish) **VI:** Sol appl pen 17 Sep 1832 Goochland Co age 85. Widow appl pen 10 Nov 1841 Goochland Co age 85. W5145 **P:** Y **BLW:** unk **RG:** N **MK:** N **PH:** unk **SS:** E pg 560; K Vol 3 pg 287; CG pg 2397 **BS:** 46 pg 191.

MOORE, Andrew; b 1750; d 10 Aug 1791 **RU:** Captain, Served in VA Militia. Served on Courts Martial in Augusta Co 1776. Served in Rockbridge Co Co at Great Bridge area 1781. Appt Capt 6 May 1778 **CEM:** Old Providence; GPS 37.96151, -79.71000; 1005 Spottswood Rd, Spottswood; Augusta **GS:** Y **SP:** Martha (-----) (176_-1839) **VI:** Name also on SAR plaque at cemetery **P:** unk **BLW:** unk **RG:** unk **MK:** Y **PH:** Y **SS:** E pg 560 **BS:** JLARC 62, 63, 79; 196.

MOORE, Andrew; b Jan 1752 "Cannicello" Rockbridge Co; d 14 Apr 1821 **RU:** Major General, Was a Lt in Capt Samuel McDowell's Co of Rockbridge Co that served at Pt Pleasant 1774. Ent serv Augusta Co (now Rockbridge). Led 9th Va Regt Cont Army under Gen Gates at Battle of Saratoga. Became Maj Gen VA Militia. **CEM:** Stonewall Jackson Memorial; GPS 37.78128, -79.44604; 314 S Main St; Lexington City **GS:** Y **SP:** Mar (31 Mar 1795 Rockbridge Co) Sarah "Sally" Reid (c1777-after 16 Feb 1856), d/o Andrew & (-----) Reid of Rockbridge Co. **VI:** Was member VA House of Delegates 1780-1800; member VA Privy Council 1788; delegate to VA convention which ratified Constitution 1788; served At-Large in US House 1789-1797; US Congressman fr VA 1-4th, 8th Congresses; VA Senate 1800-01; and US Senate 1804-09. Was US Marshall and Trustee Washington & Lee University 1782-1821. Was US Congressman, US Senator. Wid appl pen 4 Sep 1848 Rockbridge Co age 71. W1454, BLW #38539-160-55 **P:** Y **BLW:** Y **RG:** Y **MK:** N **PH:** Y **SS:** K pg 287; Z pg 103; CG pg 2397 **BS:** JLARC 1, 63.

MOORE, Charles; b c1753; d 1790 **RU:** Seaman, Served in VA State Navy **CEM:** St John's Episcopal; GPS 37.53183, -77.41958; 2401 E Broad St; Richmond City **GS:** Y **SP:** No info **VI:** No further data **P:** unk **BLW:** unk **RG:** Y **MK:** N **PH:** unk **SS:** E pg 560; L pg 227 **BS:** 04, Dec 06.

MOORE, James; b 1734, Augusta Co; d 14 Jul 1786 **RU:** Captain, Commanded a co at battles of Cowpens, Guilford CH, Kings Mtn **CEM:** Moore Family; GPS unk; Abb's Valley; Tazewell **GS:** Y **SP:** Martha Poage, massacred by raiding Shawnee Indians **VI:** On obelisk, "Capt James Moore, killed by the Indians 1786." Memorialized on Moore Monument. Abbs Valley in the cemetery **P:** unk **BLW:** unk **RG:** Y **MK:** unk **PH:** Y **SS:** J-NSSAR 2000 Reg; NSSAR Ancestor #P-251537 **BS:** JLARC 76.

MOORE, James; b 1756 or 1757, Chester Co, PA; d 20 May 1813 **RU:** Lieutenant Colonel, Served in PA line 2 Sept 1778 in the rank of Maj. Was in Battles of Brandywine, Germantown, Monmouth, Charleston, Savannah, and Yorktown **CEM:** Northumberland House; GPS 37.5.031, -76. 26194; Cod's Creek, off of Rt 360; Northumberland **GS:** Y **SP:** Mar (18 Oct 1787) Sarah Delaney (c1767-1 Dec 1814) probably PA, d/o Sharp & (-----) Delaney of Philadelphia **VI:** Son of James & Elizabeth (Whitehall) Moore. Was a wine and liquor merchant. DAR marker **P:** unk **BLW:** unk **RG:** unk **MK:** Y **PH:** Y **SS:** AP; AK **BS:** JLARC 2, 93; 200; 04; 47; 196.

MOORE, James; b 20 Sep 1759, Rockbridge Co; d 21 May 1828 **RU:** Private, Capt Cunningham's Co, Augusta Co Militia **CEM:** Stonewall Jackson Memorial; GPS 37.78128, -79.44604; 314 S Main St; Lexington City **GS:** U **SP:** Hannah Barclay (1 Aug 1768-6 Nov 1839) d/o Hugh (1729-1806) & Mary

RU=Rank/Unit   CEM=Cemetery   GS=Gravestone   SP=Spousal Information
VI=Other Veteran Info   P=Pension   BLW=Bounty/Land Warrant   RG=Registered Grave
MK=SAR/DAR Marker   PH=Photo   SS=Service Source   BS=Burial Source

239

(Culbertson) Barclay **VI:** No further data **P:** unk **BLW:** unk **RG:** unk **MK:** unk **PH:** unk **SS:** E pg 561 **BS:** JLARC 63.

MOORE, Jeremiah Rev; b 7 Jun 1746, Stafford Co; d 23 Feb 1815 **RU:** Corporal, Served in Prince William & Fairfax Co Militia. Was Baptist preacher, challenged preeminence of Episcopal Church and preached contrary to British enforcement of religious freedom laws **CEM:** Moore-Hunter Family; GPS 38.88600, -77.27336; 1001 Tapawingo Rd SW, Vienna; Fairfax **GS:** Y **SP:** Lydia French Reno (1745-8 Oct 1835) d/o Francis (1713-1797) & Elizabeth (Bayliss) (__-1764) Reno **VI:** Owned "Moorefield" where this graveyard is located **P:** N **BLW:** unk **RG:** Y **MK:** Y **PH:** Y **SS:** AK; 47, 1933, 1917 **BS:** JLARC 1, 2, 14, 27, 28; 196.

MOORE, John; b 1749; d 1833 **RU:** Patriot, Gave provisions to cause **CEM:** Fincastle Presbyterian; GPS 37.50017, -79.87558; 108 E Back St, Fincastle; Botetourt **GS:** Y **SP:** Mary S. Bright (c1758-Sep 1837) **VI:** Name is on the SAR plaque at this cemetery **P:** N **BLW:** N **RG:** N **MK:** Y **PH:** unk **SS:** Z pg 131 **BS:** 196.

MOORE, John; b 1717, Spotsylvania Co; d 1 Jan 1795 **RU:** Patriot, Gave material aid to cause **CEM:** Beaver Dam Baptist Church; GPS 37.98377, -78.29179; Richmond Rd, Paynes Mill; Fluvanna **GS:** U **SP:** No info **VI:** No further data **P:** N **BLW:** N **RG:** unk **MK:** unk **PH:** unk **SS:** AL Ct Bk pg 3 **BS:** 196.

MOORE, John; b 1754; d Apr 1838 **RU:** Private, Served in Capt Stewart's Co, Augusta Co Militia **CEM:** Fincastle Presbyterian; GPS 37.50017, -79.87558; 108 E Back St, Fincastle; Botetourt **GS:** Y **SP:** Mary S Bright (1765-Sep 1837) **VI:** Died age 84. Name is on VASSAR plaque at cemetery **P:** unk **BLW:** unk **RG:** Y **MK:** Y **PH:** unk **SS:** E pg 561; J-NSSAR 1993 Reg **BS:** 196; 115 pg 16; JLARC 1.

MOORE, Merritt; b Before 1758, York Co; d 1793 **RU:** Patriot, In Apr 1783, gave 4 oxen, a horse, and other items to cause **CEM:** St Luke's Church; GPS 36.93940, -76.58670; 14477 Benns Church Blvd, Smithfield; Isle of Wight **GS:** Y **SP:** Anne Robinson **VI:** Son of Augustine & Mary (Wooley) Moore. Died in York Co **P:** N **BLW:** N **RG:** Y **MK:** N **PH:** unk **SS:** G pg 334 **BS:** 117 pg 6.

MOORE, Reuben; b 10 Jun 1755, Augusta Co or Rockingham Co; d 6 Aug 1803 **RU:** Captain, Served in Rockingham Co Militia under Col Benjamin Harrison. In 1781, was in expedition to North Fork of Potomac against band of Tories. Became Capt 26 Mar 1781 **CEM:** Moore Family; GPS unk; Timberville; Rockingham **GS:** Y **SP:** Mar (1779) Phoebe Harrison (1764-27 Aug 1821) **VI:** No further data **P:** unk **BLW:** unk **RG:** Y **MK:** Y **PH:** unk **SS:** DD cites Levinson Rockingham Co VA Minute Book 1778-1792 Part 1 1778-1786 pg 2, 12, 81, 146, 219 **BS:** JLARC 76.

MOORE, Stephen; b 1751; d 1835 **RU:** Soldier, 1st VA Regt & 9th Cont line **CEM:** Moore Family; GPS 37.97113, -78.63598; 2393 Taylor's Gap Rd, North Garden; Albemarle **GS:** Y **SP:** Elizabeth Royster (1764-1844) **VI:** No further data **P:** unk **BLW:** unk **RG:** unk **MK:** unk **PH:** unk **SS:** E pg 562 **BS:** JLARC 58; 196.

MOORE, William; b 1749, Rockbridge Co; d 1840 or 27 Dec 1842 **RU:** Captain, VA Militia. Lived in Rockbridge Co at enl. Served under Capt Andrew Moore. Served under Gen Lewis at Battle of Point Pleasant. Served under Col John Bowyer. Guarded prisoners fr Battle of Yorktown after Cornwallis surrender **CEM:** Stonewall Jackson Memorial; GPS 37.78128, -79.44604; 314 S Main St; Lexington City **GS:** Y **SP:** Nancy McClung **VI:** Sol appl pen 7 Aug 1832 Rockbridge Co. S5787. Died in Rockbridge Co **P:** Y **BLW:** unk **RG:** Y **MK:** Y **PH:** unk **SS:** J-NSSAR 1993 Reg; CG pg 2409 **BS:** JLARC 1; JLARC 2, 63.

MOORE, William; b unk; d 14 Jul 1786 **RU:** Patriot, Gave material aid to cause **CEM:** Moore Family; GPS 37.22110, -81.40170; Adj to RR track E of Tiptop abt halfway to jct Rts 650 & 656; Tazewell **GS:** U **SP:** No info **VI:** Son of James & Martha (Poage) Moore. Killed by Indians **P:** N **BLW:** N **RG:** N **MK:** unk **PH:** N **SS:** Al Ct Bk pg 2, 25 Montgomery Co **BS:** 196.

MOORE, William; b 1741; d 2 Jan 1827 **RU:** Soldier, Severely wounded and lost leg at Battle of Kings Mountain **CEM:** Rock Spring; GPS 37.78126, -79.44585; Jct Rt 803 & Liberty Hall Rd, Lodi; Washington **GS:** Y **SP:** Elizabeth (-----) (__-11 Oct 18?8 age 76) **VI:** Recd disability pen of $5 per mo. Later increased to $8. DAR Marker. S25312 **P:** Y **BLW:** unk **RG:** N **MK:** Y **PH:** N **SS:** CG pg 2409 **BS:** JLARC 4, 34.

RU=Rank/Unit   CEM=Cemetery   GS=Gravestone   SP=Spousal Information
VI=Other Veteran Info   P=Pension   BLW=Bounty/Land Warrant   RG=Registered Grave
MK=SAR/DAR Marker   PH=Photo   SS=Service Source   BS=Burial Source

240

MOORMAN, Micajah; b 28 Jun 1735 Louisa Co; d 25 Nov 1806 **RU:** Patriot, Performed public service **CEM:** South River Meeting House; **GPS** 37.37246, -79.19194; 5810 Fort Ave; Lynchburg City **GS:** N **SP:** Mar (13 Oct 1754) Susannah Chiles **VI:** Died in Campbell Co **P:** N **BLW:** N **RG:** Y **MK:** N **PH:** unk **SS:** 04 **BY BS:** 04; 137.

MORET, Barthelemy; b unk; d 1781 **RU:** Seaman, Served on "Saint-Esprit" and died from Yorktown battle **CEM:** French Memorial; **GPS** 36.81944, -79.39933; Yorktown; York **GS:** U **SP:** No info **VI:** No further data **P:** unk **BLW:** unk **RG:** Y **MK:** unk **PH:** unk **SS:** J-Yorktown Historian **BS:** JLARC 1, 74.

MORGAN, Daniel; b 1736, County Derry, Ireland or Winter 1736, Hunterdon Co, NJ; d 6 Jul 1802 **RU:** General, Was Capt of VA Riflemen July 1775; prisoner at Quebec 31 Dec 1775; Col 11 CL Nov 12 1776; became Brigadier Gen 13 Oct 1780. Served to close of war **CEM:** Mt Hebron; **GPS** 39.10916, -78.09497; 305 E Boscawen St; Winchester City **GS:** Y **SP:** Abigail Bailey **VI:** Supposedly came to America in early days with father. Served in Craddock's campaign in 1755. Awarded 11,666 acres BLW #1496-850-25 Aug 1789, also BLW Reg #336254-55. Originally buried near Old Stone Presbyterian Church, Winchester **P:** unk **BLW:** Y **RG:** Y **MK:** unk **PH:** Y **SS:** J-NSSAR 1993 Reg E pg 563; CG pg 2415 **BS:** JLARC 1.

MORGAN, Hayes (Haynes); b unk; d 1795 **RU:** Colonel, Served in VA State Line. Commanded 1st State Regt, 5 Jun 1777-1 Jul 1777 **CEM:** Morgan Family; **GPS** unk; Nr White Falls, Banister River; Pittsylvania **GS:** Y **SP:** Mary Thompson (c1750-__), d/o William & (-----) Thompson of Halifax Co. **VI:** Granted BLW 1784. Widow pen in Davis Co, NC, 1837 age 87 **P:** Y **BLW:** Y **RG:** N **MK:** N **PH:** unk **SS:** BY pg 178; G pg 850-1 **BS:** 91 pg 2.

MORGAN, Zackwell; b 1739, Orange Co; d 1 Jan 1795 **RU:** Colonel/Patriot, County Lt Monongalia Co 1777. Also service listed Lib of VA, Auditor's Accts XV, pg 309. Gave material aid to cause **CEM:** Morgantown; **GPS** unk; Morgantown; Fauquier **GS:** U **SP:** Drucilla Springer (9 May 1745, Burlington-1795 Morgantown, Monongalia Co, WV) **VI:** JLARC indicates town of Morgantown is in Fauquier Co, but not found **P:** unk **BLW:** unk **RG:** unk **MK:** unk **PH:** unk **SS:** DAR #A080660; J- DAR Hatcher; D Vol 2 pg 682; E pg 564; CZ pg 318 **BS:** JLARC 2.

MORIN, Jean; b unk; d 1781 **RU:** Seaman, Served on "Diademe" and died from Yorktown battle **CEM:** French Memorial; **GPS** 36.81944, -79.39933; Yorktown; York **GS:** U **SP:** No info **VI:** No further data **P:** unk **BLW:** unk **RG:** Y **MK:** unk **PH:** unk **SS:** J-Yorktown Historian **BS:** JLARC 1, 74.

MORRIS, Nathaniel; b 1744; d 21 Jan 1813 **RU:** Private, Served in 3rd, 4th, 5th, & 9th Cont Lines **CEM:** Morris Family; **GPS** unk; Rt 609 at Vassars; Buckingham **GS:** U **SP:** Nancy Ann Jeffries **VI:** No further data **P:** N **BLW:** N **RG:** unk **MK:** N **PH:** unk **SS:** E pg 565 **BS:** JLARC 2, 33, 59.

MORRIS, William; b 6 Feb 1736; d 25 Apr 1820 **RU:** Private/Patriot, Was in Illinois Regt Co #8, 30 Nov 1778, and discharged Apr 1779. Signed a petition in Hanover Co **CEM:** Morris at Taylor's Creek; **GPS** unk; Bethany Ch Rd; Hanover **GS:** N **SP:** No info **VI:** No further data **P:** unk **BLW:** unk **RG:** Y **MK:** N **PH:** N **SS:** C pg 263; E pg 566 **BS:** 31 vol 2 pg 103.

MORRISOT, Jacques; b unk; d 1781 **RU:** Seaman, Served on "Diademe" and died from Yorktown battle **CEM:** French Memorial; **GPS** 36.81944, -79.39933; Yorktown; York **GS:** U **SP:** No info **VI:** No further data **P:** unk **BLW:** unk **RG:** unk **MK:** unk **PH:** unk **SS:** J Yorktown Historian **BS:** JLARC 2, 33, 59, 74.

MORSON, Arthur; b 1734, Scotland; d 30 May 1798 **RU:** Patriot, Gave material aid to cause **CEM:** Hartwood Presbyterian; **GPS** 38.401883, -77.567450; 50 Hartwood Ch Rd, Fredericksburg; Stafford **GS:** Y **SP:** No info **VI:** Son of Barton Morson and Sarah Stone **P:** N **BLW:** N **RG:** Y **MK:** N **PH:** Y **SS:** D pg 259, 877; AL Ct Bk I pg 27, 28 Stafford Co **BS:** 03 pg 240.

MORTON, George; b c1746, Orange Co; d 1787 **RU:** Patriot, Provided wagon w/ team of horses for Orange Co Militia. Also gave grain to barracks 20 Dec 1780 **CEM:** Soldier's Rest Plantation; **GPS** unk; Rt 620; Orange **GS:** Y **SP:** Jane (-----) (c1756-1802) **VI:** He was a doctor **P:** N **BLW:** N **RG:** Y **MK:** N **PH:** unk **SS:** DAR #A081759; D **BS:** 22 pg 89.

MORTON, James; b 1756; d 21 Jan 1847 **RU:** Captain, Served in VA Line. Was Commander of co in 4th VA Regt **CEM:** High Hill; **GPS** unk; See homeplace property loc; Cumberland **GS:** Y **SP:** No info **VI:** Member Board of Trustees Hampton Sidney Colleges and a civil magistrate. Appl 18 Jul 1828 Prince

RU=Rank/Unit	CEM=Cemetery	GS=Gravestone	SP=Spousal Information
VI=Other Veteran Info	P=Pension	BLW=Bounty/Land Warrant	RG=Registered Grave
MK=SAR/DAR Marker	PH=Photo	SS=Service Source	BS=Burial Source

241

Edward Co. S9035, BLW #1514-200-26 Apr 1798 **P:** Y **BLW:** Y **RG:** N **MK:** N **PH:** unk **SS:** N pg 408; CG pg 2415 **BS:** 157.

MORTON, William; b c1750; d 5 Sep 1835 **RU:** Patriot, Provided wagon and team of three horses for militia fr Aug to 31 Oct 1781 that were not returned **CEM:** Oak Green Farm #1; GPS unk; Rt 663 nr Palmyra Church; Orange **GS:** Y **SP:** No info **VI:** No further data **P:** N **BLW:** N **RG:** N **MK:** N **PH:** unk **SS:** Al App II pg 101 **BS:** 22 pg 77; 196.

MOSBY, Littleberry Jr; b 1757 or 28 Jan 1758; d 1 Oct 1821 **RU:** Captain/Patriot, Served in VA & GA Lines. Was in Cont Line as Lt & Capt and was at Siege of Savannah. Was captured at Charleston or Savannah and later furloughed home to VA. Was in House of Delegates fr Powhatan **CEM:** Mosby Family; GPS unk; Powhatan; Powhatan **GS:** U **SP:** No info **VI:** Son of Benjamin & Mary (Poindexter) Mosby. After Revolution became Col and later General in state militia. BLW #64-300, 4000 acres was awarded **P:** unk **BLW:** Y **RG:** Y **MK:** N **PH:** unk **SS:** E pg 568; K pg 310; CG pg 2436 **BS:** SAR regis.

MOSELEY, Arthur; b 1752, Powhatan Co; d 1803 **RU:** Lieutenant, Drafted 1780 in Capt Robert Hughes Co while crossing Roanoke at Peyton's Ferry. Was in battle at Guilford CH. Promoted to 2nd Lt 29 Jun 1779. Served in Capt John Torbett's Co. Marched to Yorktown 1781 **CEM:** Fincastle Presbyterian; GPS 37.50017, -79.87558; 108 E Back St, Fincastle; Botetourt **GS:** N **SP:** No info **VI:** Pen recd 15 Aug 1832. Name is on the SAR plaque at this cemetery **P:** Y **BLW:** unk **RG:** N **MK:** Y **PH:** N **SS:** AZ pg 78; J-NSSAR 1993 Reg, J- DAR Hatcher **BS:** 196, JLARC 1, 2.

MOSELEY, Arthur; b 9 Nov 1760, Chesterfield Co; d 31 Aug 1829 **RU:** Lieutenant, Served in VA Line. Ent serv Buckingham Co. Was Orderly Sgt in Capt Joh Moseley's Co. Was 2/Lt in VA Militia. Was in Battle of Guilford CH & at Yorktown **CEM:** Moseley Family; GPS unk; "Wheatlands", 10 mi E of Courthouse on Rt 647; Buckingham **GS:** U **SP:** Mar (Dec 1788 Buckingham Co) Sally Perkins (c1722-aft 1855) **VI:** Son of Robert Peter Moseley (1732-1804) & Magdalen Guerrant (1740-1826). Widow appl pen 26 Jan 1848 Buckingham Co & appl there again 20 Mar 1855 for BLW. W7481, BLW #26542-160-55 **P:** Y **BLW:** Y **RG:** unk **MK:** N **PH:** unk **SS:** CG pg 2436 **BS:** JLARC 4, 10, 59, 90; 196.

MOSELEY, Benjamin; b 6 Dec 1755; d 25 Jul 1799 **RU:** First Lieutenant, Served in Cont Artillery **CEM:** Rolfton; GPS unk; Hwy 749; Buckingham **GS:** U **SP:** Mar (25 Dec 1783 Chesterfield Co, bond signed by Peter Branch) Mary Branch (1764-1848) d/o Mr. & Mrs. Ridley Branch **VI:** Sol recd 2666 2/3 acres of BL fr State of VA on VA State BLW $1468. Widow appl pen 11 Feb 1839 Buckingham Co. W5387 Name on memorial stone. BLW #2436-300 **P:** Y **BLW:** Y **RG:** unk **MK:** N **PH:** unk **SS:** CG pg 2436 **BS:** JLARC 4, 10, 59.

MOSELEY, Edward; b 4 May 1718; d 1808 **RU:** Patriot, Clerk of Princess Anne Co Ct, Jul 1775 **CEM:** Moseley Family; GPS unk; Nr Buffalo Creek; Charlotte **GS:** U **SP:** Amey Green **VI:** Son of Arthur (__-1736) & Martha Branch (Cocke) (1688-__) Moseley. Rank of Capt obtained before Rev War **P:** N **BLW:** N **RG:** unk **MK:** unk **PH:** unk **SS:** J- DAR Hatcher; CO pg 46 **BS:** JLARC 2.

MOSELEY, Edward Hack Jr; b 1740; d 1811 or 1814 **RU:** Colonel/Patriot, Commanded Princess Anne Co Militia 1779. Also gave to cause **CEM:** Old Donation Episcopal; GPS 36.86730, -76.12860; 4449 N Witchduck Rd; Virginia Beach City **GS:** U **SP:** 1) Mar (18 Nov 1862) Ann Lovett (1745- by 1774). Charles Gaskin was guardian in 1761 and gave consent for marriage. 2) Mar (May 1774) Martha (Patsey) Westwood (1747-1824) **VI:** Son of Edward Hack (1717-1782) & Amey (Green) Moseley. Served on the House of Burgess. Clerk of Princess Anne Co. Vestryman at Old Donation. Father was loyalist. Plaque placed by broken GS by Princess Anne Co NSDAR Bicentennial Project 1977 **P:** unk **BLW:** unk **RG:** Y **MK:** **PH:** unk **SS:** E pg 568; AL Ct Bk pg 4 Princess Anne Co **BS:** JLARC 1, 78.

MOSELEY, James; b unk; d 1843 **RU:** Sergeant, Served in Bedford Co Militia **CEM:** Old City; GPS 37.41472, -79.15667; 401 Taylor St; Lynchburg City **GS:** Y **SP:** No info **VI:** No further data **P:** unk **BLW:** unk **RG:** N **MK:** N **PH:** unk **SS:** E pg 568 **BS:** 62 pg 60.

MOSELEY, Robert Peter; b 14 Feb 1732, Powhaten Co; d 30 Jan 1804 **RU:** Lieutenant/Patriot, Served in VA Colonial Troops. Gave material aid to cause **CEM:** Moseley Family; GPS unk; Willowlake, Rt 56; Buckingham **GS:** U **SP:** 1) Mary Magdalene Guerrant (31 Aug 1740, Goochland Co-3 Apr 1826) d/o Pierre Sr & Magdalene (Trabue) Guerant 2) Martha Povall, d/o Richard & Tabitha (Hudspeth) Povall **VI:**

RU=Rank/Unit CEM=Cemetery GS=Gravestone SP=Spousal Information
VI=Other Veteran Info P=Pension BLW=Bounty/Land Warrant RG=Registered Grave
MK=SAR/DAR Marker PH=Photo SS=Service Source BS=Burial Source

242

Son of Robert Ligon & Sarah Rachel (Taylor) Moseley **P:** unk **BLW:** unk **RG:** unk **MK:** N **PH:** unk **SS:** AL ct Ck Bk pg 6, 47 **BS:** JLARC 59.

MOSELY, Hildarh (Hillary); b c1760, "prob Princess Anne Co"; d April 1813 **RU:** Patriot, Provided supplies in Norfolk and Princess Anne counties. Filed "Publick Claim" for 260 pounds of beef given to cause.Took oath to the Commonwealth in 1783 as a Common Councilman **CEM:** St Paul's Episcopal; GPS 36.84733, -76.28554; 201 St Paul's Blvd; Norfolk City **GS:** Y **SP:** No info **VI:** "The Order Book and Related Papers of the Common Hall of the Borough of Norfolk Virginia, 1736-1798" lists his public service there **P:** N **BLW:** N **RG:** Y **MK:** Y **PH:** unk **SS:** CB Counciman 1783 **BS:** 178 Jan 11.

MOSHER, William; b unk; d 1781 **RU:** Soldier, Served fr MA, and killed in the battle at Yorktown **CEM:** Yorktown Victory Monument Tablet; GPS 38.28350, -78.54150; Yorktown; York **GS:** U **SP:** No info **VI:** No further data **P:** unk **BLW:** unk **RG:** unk **MK:** unk **PH:** unk **SS:** J-Yorktown Historian **BS:** JLARC 74.

MOSS, John; b c1748 or 1749, York Co; d 11 Dec 1813 **RU:** Captain, Was clothier for VA Cont Line and 1st VA Regt **CEM:** St John's Episcopal; GPS 37.53183, -77.41958; 2401 E Broad St; Richmond City **GS:** U **SP:** Sarah Gibbons **VI:** No further data **P:** unk **BLW:** unk **RG:** unk **MK:** N **PH:** Y **SS:** J-NSSAR 2000 Reg; NSSAR Ancestor #P-253367 **BS:** JLARC 76.

MOSS, Joshua; b 5 Aug 1744, Surry Co; d 5 Feb 1829 **RU:** Sergeant/Patriot, Gave material aid to cause **CEM:** Moss Family; GPS unk; See property records; Sussex **GS:** U **SP:** Mar (15 Jun 1769 Sussex Co) Sarah Pennington (c1752-5 Feb 1829) **VI:** No further data **P:** unk **BLW:** unk **RG:** unk **MK:** unk **PH:** unk **SS:** DAR Ancestor #A081478; J-DAR Hatcher; AL Ct Bk pg 6, 10 Mecklenberg Co **BS:** JLARC 2.

MOSS, Nathaniel; b 1730; d 1807 **RU:** Chaplain/Patriot, Gave material aid to cause **CEM:** Moss Meeting House; GPS unk; N fr Upperville; Fauquier **GS:** U **SP:** No info **VI:** No further data **P:** unk **BLW:** unk **RG:** Y **MK:** unk **PH:** unk **SS:** J-NSSAR 1993 Reg; AL Ct Bk pg 36 Frederick Co **BS:** JLARC 1.

MOTLEY, Joseph; b 1720, Gloucester Co; d Aft 15 Dec 1806 **RU:** Patriot, Gave material aid to cause. Performed civil service as member of Grand Jury, Pittsylvania Co **CEM:** Motley Family; GPS unk; Nr Chatham; Pittsylvania **GS:** Y **SP:** (c1750) Martha Ellington (c1730-1780) **VI:** Son of Joseph (1695-1777) & Elizabeth (Forrest) (1700-__) Motley. Fought with Geo Washington in French & Indian Wars and battle of Braddocks Defeat. Will dated 15 Dec 1806 **P:** N **BLW:** N **RG:** N **MK:** N **PH:** unk **SS:** DAR #A082205; AL Ct Bk pg 14,57; DD **BS:** 80, vol 3, pg 107; 196.

MOUGAL, Nicolas; b unk; d 1781 **RU:** Soldier, Served in Touraine Bn and died fr battle at Yorktown **CEM:** French Memorial; GPS 36.81944, -79.39933; Yorktown; York **GS:** U **SP:** No info **VI:** No further data **P:** unk **BLW:** unk **RG:** Y **MK:** unk **PH:** unk **SS:** J-Yorktown Historian **BS:** JLARC 1, 74.

MOULINS, Antoine; b unk; d 1781 **RU:** Soldier, Served in Touraine Bn and died fr battle at Yorktown **CEM:** French Memorial; GPS 36.81944, -79.39933; Yorktown; York **GS:** U **SP:** No info **VI:** No further data **P:** unk **BLW:** unk **RG:** Y **MK:** unk **PH:** unk **SS:** J-Yorktown Historian **BS:** JLARC 1, 74.

MOUNT, Ezekiel; b 22 Nov 1758, Anwell Twp, NJ; d Aft Aug 1833 **RU:** Soldier, Served in NJ & VA Line. Ent Serv Amwell Twp, NJ **CEM:** Mount Family; GPS unk; Mountville off Rts 733 & 734; Loudoun **GS:** U **SP:** No info **VI:** His family established the town. Appl for pen 13 Aug 1833 Loudoun Co. S11117 **P:** Y **BLW:** unk **RG:** unk **MK:** unk **PH:** unk **SS:** CG pg 2444; NSSAR Ancestor #P-253606 **BS:** JLARC 4.

MOUNTJOY, William; b 17 Apr 1711; d 27 Sep 1777 **RU:** Patriot, Gave material aid to the cause **CEM:** St Paul's Episcopal; GPS 38.33200, -77.12500; 5486 St Paul's Rd off Rt 206; King George **GS:** Y **SP:** No info **VI:** Carried rank of Capt fr Colonial war service. Was originally bur at St Paul's Parrish of Stafford Co **P:** N **BLW:** N **RG:** unk **MK:** unk **PH:** N **SS:** AL Ct Bk 1 pg 5 II pg 2 Cert **BS:** 03 pg 347.

MOUTEL, Liberal; b unk; d 1781 **RU:** Soldier, Served in Foix Bn and died fr battle at Yorktown **CEM:** French Memorial; GPS 36.81944, -79.39933; Yorktown; York **GS:** U **SP:** No info **VI:** No further data **P:** unk **BLW:** unk **RG:** Y **MK:** unk **PH:** unk **SS:** J-Yorktown Historian **BS:** JLARC 1, 74.

MOWRY (MOWREY), Henry; b 19 Jun 1752, Philadelphia, PA; d 1833 **RU:** Private, Served in Capt Joseph Bell's Co & Capt David Bell's Co, Augusta Co Militia **CEM:** Trinity Episcopal; GPS 38.14917, -79.07521; 214 Beverley St; Staunton City **GS:** Y **SP:** Mar (10 Jun 1791) Mary Gibson **VI:** Son of Johann

---

RU=Rank/Unit   CEM=Cemetery   GS=Gravestone   SP=Spousal Information
VI=Other Veteran Info   P=Pension   BLW=Bounty/Land Warrant   RG=Registered Grave
MK=SAR/DAR Marker   PH=Photo   SS=Service Source   BS=Burial Source

243

Peter & Anna Sophia (Germann) Maurer. Gr St shows war service **P:** unk **BLW:** unk **RG:** unk **MK:** unk **PH:** Y **SS:** B; E pg 570 **BS:** JLARC 62; 196.

MOYER, Micheal (William); b 27 Sep 1745 Northampton Co, PA; d 7 Apr 1834 **RU:** Private, Drafted Rockingham Co for 4 mos under Capt Jacob Lincoln, McIntosh Campaign. After Cornwallis's surrender,1781 drafted as Militiaman under Capt Baker. Transferred to Capt Baxter's Co. Sent to Winchester to guard British prisoners **CEM:** Moyer Family; GPS 38.48315,-78.55285; Crab Run Rd, nr Bergton; Rockingham **GS:** Y **SP:** Elizabeth (-----) **VI:** Appl for pen 1 Nov 1833. S18107 **P:** Y **BLW:** unk **RG:** Y **MK:** N **PH:** Y **SS:** K Vol 3 pg 316; CG pg 2447 **BS:** 32 Hutchens 08.

MUIR, James Rev; b 1750, Scotland; d 8 Aug 1820 **RU:** Soldier/Patriot, Signed a Legislative Petition in Alexandria **CEM:** Old Presbyterian Meeting House; GPS 38.48528, -77.23532; 323 S Fairfax St; Alexandria City **GS:** Y **SP:** No info **VI:** Death notice in the Alexandria Gazette 9 Aug 1820 **P:** unk **BLW:** unk **RG:** Y **MK:** unk **PH:** unk **SS:** J-NSSAR 1993 Reg; S- Alexandria **BS:** JLARC 1; 23 pg 106.

MUIR, John; b 1732; d 29 Mar 1791 **RU:** Midshipman, Served in VA State Navy for 3 yrs **CEM:** Old Christ Church Episcopal; GPS 38.80625, -77.04718; 118 N Washington St; Alexandria City **GS:** Y **SP:** No info **VI:** "Here lieth the body of John Muir, late merchant of Alexandria, eldest son of Hugh Muir merchant of Dumfries in Scotland, who departed this life March 20th A.D. 1791 in the 60th yr of his Age". Recd BLW of 2667 acres March 1784 **P:** unk **BLW:** Y **RG:** Y **MK:** N **PH:** unk **SS:** E pg 571 **BS:** 20 pg 139; 196.

MUIR, Robert; b 1748; d 21 Dec 1786 **RU:** Captain, Served in 1779-80, unit not determined **CEM:** Old Christ Church Episcopal; GPS 38.80625, -77.04718; 118 N Washington St; Alexandria City **GS:** Y **SP:** No info **VI:** "Here lieth the body of Robert Muir, son of Hugh Muir, Merchant of Dumfries, Scotland, who departed this life December 21, 1786, aged abt 38 yrs." Vestry minutes indicate grave was moved inside churchyard on 28 Mar 1791. Death notice in the Alexandria Gazette 21 Dec 1786, pg 3 **P:** unk **BLW:** unk **RG:** Y **MK:** N **PH:** unk **SS:** E pg 571 **BS:** 20 pg 140; 196.

MULL, David; b 5 May 1731, Germany; d 27 Dec 1794 **RU:** Patriot, Gave material aid to the cause **CEM:** St James Reformed; GPS 39.27027, -77.62968; Lovettsville Rd, Lovettsville; Loudoun **GS:** Y **SP:** Eva Margaret Boothe (9 Sep 1731-20 Apr 1801) **VI:** No further data **P:** N **BLW:** N **RG:** N **MK:** N **PH:** unk **SS:** AL Ct Bk lt pg 11 **BS:** 25 pg 215; 196.

MULLER, Nicolas; b unk; d 1781 **RU:** Soldier, Served in Royal Deaux Ponts Bn and died fr battle at Yorktown **CEM:** French Memorial; GPS 36.81944, -79.39933; Yorktown; York **GS:** U **SP:** No info **VI:** No further data **P:** unk **BLW:** unk **RG:** unk **MK:** unk **PH:** unk **SS:** J-Yorktown Historian **BS:** JLARC 1, 74.

MULLINS, David; b 11 May 1758, Goochland Co; d 1829 **RU:** Captain, Served in Marks' Co, 14th VA, with Gen Greene. Held rank of Sergeant in 1st, 10th, 14th Cont Lines. Served in Goochland Co Militia. Appt rank of Capt 16 Jun 1783 **CEM:** Single burial; GPS unk; Off Rt 758, 100 yards off Price Rd, nr Horsepasture, Donnybrook Rd, Ridgeway; Henry **GS:** Y **SP:** 1) Mar (30 Aug 1781, Goochland Co.) Susannah Herndon 2) Mary Alexander Burgess **VI:** Son of John & (-----) Mullins. Named one of his sons after Gen Greene. Recd BLW of 100 acres **P:** unk **BLW:** Y **RG:** unk **MK:** unk **PH:** unk **SS:** E pg 571; BY **BS:** JLARC 2, 4, 38.

MULLINS, John; b unk; d 1849 **RU:** Soldier, Served in Over Mountain Men and fought at Kings Mountain **CEM:** John Powers Plantation; GPS unk; Hwy 83, Clintwood; Dickenson **GS:** Y **SP:** Nancy (------) **VI:** Info taken fr roadside plaque. Widow drew pen and BLW **P:** Y **BLW:** Y **RG:** unk **MK:** Y **PH:** Y **SS:** CG pg 2450 **BS:** JLARC 81.

MULLINS, Matthew; b 1720; d 1785 **RU:** Sergeant, As Sgt (perhaps QM Sgt) obtained materials to aid the cause in Culpeper Co **CEM:** Mullins; GPS unk; Nr Fife; Goochland **GS:** U **SP:** Mary Maupin **VI:** No further data **P:** unk **BLW:** unk **RG:** Y **MK:** unk **PH:** unk **SS:** J-NSSAR 2000 Reg; AL Ct Bk 1 pg 25 **BS:** JLARC 76.

MUNFORT (MUNFORD, MONFORT, MONFORD), Robert; b unk; d Aft 1781 **RU:** Colonel/Patriot, Commanded militia at battle of Guilford CH. Was recruiting officer for VA troops. Gave material aid to cause **CEM:** Munfort-Lockett Family; GPS unk; Directions to cem in Source 72. Nr Boydton;

RU=Rank/Unit   CEM=Cemetery   GS=Gravestone   SP=Spousal Information
VI=Other Veteran Info   P=Pension   BLW=Bounty/Land Warrant   RG=Registered Grave
MK=SAR/DAR Marker   PH=Photo   SS=Service Source   BS=Burial Source

244

Mecklenburg **GS:** U **SP:** No info **VI:** No further data **P:** unk **BLW:** unk **RG:** unk **MK:** unk **PH:** unk **SS:** AL Comm Bk IV pg 67, 70 Mecklenburg Co; DB pg 108 **BS:** JLARC 72.

MURPHY, Francis; b c1763, County of Queens, Ireland; d 30 Jun 1837 **RU:** Private, Served in Capt John Bankson's PA Militia Regt, 9 Sep 1777 **CEM:** St Mary's Catholic; GPS 38.79390, -77.04750; 310 S Royal St; Alexandria City **GS:** Y **SP:** No info **VI:** Place of birth fr GS, d in his 75th yr **P:** unk **BLW:** unk **RG:** N **MK:** Y **PH:** Y **SS:** SAR Ancestor #P-334432; AP Muster roll **BS:** 174 pg 111; 196.

MURPHY, Timothy; b 1745; d 1837 **RU:** Private, Served in Capt William Alexander's Co. Col William Irvine's PA Regt Nov 1777, part of VA 9th Regt **CEM:** Murphy Family; GPS 36.59220, -80.93800; Rt 607; Grayson **GS:** U **SP:** No info **VI:** No further data **P:** unk **BLW:** unk **RG:** Y **MK:** unk **PH:** unk **SS:** A pg 215-9 **BS:** 04, Apr 2007.

MURRAY, George; b unk; d Feb 1789 **RU:** Private, Served in VA State Artillery **CEM:** Old Christ Church Episcopal; GPS 38.80625, -77.04718; 118 N Washington St; Alexandria City **GS:** N **SP:** No info **VI:** Burial permit issued 10 Feb 1789, "a poor man" **P:** unk **BLW:** unk **RG:** N **MK:** N **PH:** N **SS:** A pg 355 **BS:** 20 pg 151.

MURRAY, James; b unk; d Jun 1795 **RU:** Private, Served in Capt Reuben Briscoe Co, 3rd Cont Line, commanded by Col Thomas Marshall, Sep 1777-Apr 1778 **CEM:** Old Christ Church Episcopal; GPS 38.80625, -77.04718; 118 N Washington St; Alexandria City **GS:** N **SP:** No info **VI:** Burial permit issued 18 Jun 1795 **P:** unk **BLW:** unk **RG:** N **MK:** N **PH:** N **SS:** A pg 279 **BS:** 20 pg 151.

MURRAY, Reuben; b 1761; d 1845 **RU:** Sergeant, Served 1781 in Capt Turner Morehead's Co at Williamsburg, and on next tour was at Yorktown in Capt James Winn & Capt Linn Sharps Co. Awarded Sgt on this tour. Guarded prisoners on way to Winchester **CEM:** Marshall; GPS 38.86919, -77.83445; Marshall; Fauquier **GS:** Y **SP:** Mar (23 Sep 1795 (bond) Fauquier Co, Thomas Glascock security, Marriage return by John Monroe, minister 24 Sept 1795) Cathrine Chinn Glascock. Called Catherine Glascock on the bond and Catherine Chinn (Glascock) by Gott. **VI:** Claim was rejected for pen 1833. In 1838 he was living in Fauquier Co, where papers were returned. R7524 **P:** N **BLW:** unk **RG:** unk **MK:** unk **PH:** unk **SS:** AZ pg 171-172; CG pg 2461; Fauquier Co Marriages pg 145 **BS:** JLARC 4,16; 196.

MURRAY, Samuel; b unk; d 2 Nov 1808 **RU:** Corporal, Served in Capt Thomas Moultries 5th Co, Col Francis Marion's SC Regt in Nov 1779 **CEM:** Old Stone Methodist; GPS 39.11725, -77.56609; 168 W Cornwall St, Leesburg; Loudoun **GS:** Y **SP:** Mary (-----) (__-13 Dec 1799) **VI:** Justice of Peace in Loudoun Co VA Sep 1809 **P:** unk **BLW:** unk **RG:** Y **MK:** N **PH:** unk **SS:** A pg 290-292 **BS:** 25 pg 216.

MURSON, Arthur; b 1734, Greenook, Scotland; d 30 May 1798 **RU:** Patriot, Gave to cause 10 pairs of shoes, wood, fodder, corn, beef, other items 1775. Was trustee for Falmouth VA **CEM:** Hartwood Presbyterian; GPS 38.40188, -77.56745; 50 Hartwood Ch Rd, Fredericksburg; Stafford **GS:** Y **SP:** No info **VI:** Died in Hartwood, Stafford Co. Pierce found his grave is physically located in Jefferson Co WV. However this is not true as compiler has been to his gr site in Hartwood cem **P:** N **BLW:** N **RG:** unk **MK:** N **PH:** Y **SS:** D Vol II pg 817 Vol 1 pg 754 **BS:** 03 pg 240. 34 pg 211.

MUSE, Battaile; b c1755; d 1805 **RU:** Patriot, Gave material aid to the cause **CEM:** Muse-Lewis "The Moorings"; GPS unk; Lewis Farm nr WV; Clarke **GS:** Y **SP:** No info **VI:** No further data **P:** N **BLW:** N **RG:** N **MK:** N **PH:** unk **SS:** AL Ct Bk pg 18 **BS:** 58 pg 13.

MUSE, Daniel Sr; b 1715, Washington Parish, Westmoreland Co; d 6 Dec 1784 **RU:** Patriot, Gave material aid to cause **CEM:** Muse Family; GPS unk; See property records; Richmond Co **GS:** U **SP:** Mar (1739, Lunenburg Parish, Richmond Co) Hannah Dozier (bef 1720, Westmoreland Co-__) **VI:** Son of Thomas (1665-__) Elizabeth (Sturman) (abt 1680-__) Muse. Died in Lunenburg Parish, Richmond Co **P:** N **BLW:** N **RG:** Y **MK:** unk **PH:** unk **SS:** AL Ct Bk pg 14 Richmond Co **BS:** JLARC 76.

MUSTAIN (MUSTEIN), Avery; b 26 Feb 1756, Pittsylvania Co; d 31 Aug 1833 **RU:** Private, In 1776 served in Capt Thomas Dillard Co. Marched to Gwynns Island against Lord Dunmore. Was in Capt Jesse Heard Co to Holston River against Cherokees. In 1780 was in Capt Isaac Clement's Co in Battle of Camden. In Feb 1781 was in Capt Gabriel Shelton/Capt Thomas Smith Cos. In Aug 1781 was in Capt William Dix/Capt Charles Williams's Cos, in Siege of York. After Cornwallis, surrendered was guard of prisoners on march to Noland's Ferry on Potomac **CEM:** Mustain Barn; GPS 36.56637, -79.18520; Btw

RU=Rank/Unit   CEM=Cemetery   GS=Gravestone   SP=Spousal Information
VI=Other Veteran Info   P=Pension   BLW=Bounty/Land Warrant   RG=Registered Grave
MK=SAR/DAR Marker   PH=Photo   SS=Service Source   BS=Burial Source

245

Gretna & Mt Airy, private property behind barn; Pittsylvania **GS:** Y **SP:** Mar (Mar 1783) Mary Barber **VI:** Sol appl pen 1832. Widow appl pen1839 Pittsylvania Co **P:** Y **BLW:** unk **RG:** N **MK:** N **PH:** unk **SS:** K Vol 3 pg 330-1; AS; AX **BS:** 174.

MUSTOE, Anthony; b unk, Tongue Yard, London, England; d 1807 **RU:** Sergeant, Served in Augusta Co Militia as well as 3rd, 5th, 7th, 12th Cont Lines **CEM:** Mustoe Family; GPS unk; 5 mi S of Healing Springs; Bath **GS:** U **SP:** 1) Mary Wright 2) Mar (13 Mar 1780) Dorothy Silor (6 Feb 1760 Frederick Co MD-25 Jul 1831), d/o Jacob & Dorothy (-----) Silor **VI:** Came to America 1772. Sherriff of Augusta Co. Postmaster in Warm Springs 1796-Oct 1807 **P:** unk **BLW:** unk **RG:** N **MK:** N **PH:** unk **SS:** E pg 576 **BS:** 159 Mustoe.

MYERS, Samuel; b 1748; d 1830 **RU:** Private, Served in VA Line **CEM:** Hebrew; GPS 33.55175, -77.42976; 300 Hospital St; Richmond City **GS:** Y **SP:** No info **VI:** No further data **P:** unk **BLW:** unk **RG:** N **MK:** N **PH:** unk **SS:** E pg 576 **BS:** 168 Hebrew.

MYERS / MYRES, John C; b 1761; d 17 Mar 1802 **RU:** Private, Served in 1st VA Regt of Foot, Mar 1777 **CEM:** Old Christ Church Episcopal; GPS 36.83407, -81.59338; Old Ebenezer Rd Rt 659; Alexandria City **GS:** Y **SP:** Mar (14 Nov 1799) Mrs. Margaret Bowyer, relict of Mr. Henry Bowyer, dec'd **VI:** Died age 41 after a long and painful illness **P:** unk **BLW:** unk **RG:** Y **MK:** N **PH:** unk **SS:** AP RW Roll **BS:** 110 pg 95; 196.

MYTINGER, Daniel; b 14 Dec 1760, Lancaster, PA; d 23 Mar 1836 **RU:** Captain, Specific service not found; Gr St indicates rank **CEM:** German Reformed Church; GPS 39.08150, -78.21840; Mulberry St, Stephen City; Frederick **GS:** Y **SP:** Catherine Elizabeth Campbell (8 Jul 1768-21 Nov 1843) **VI:** Son of George Ludwig & Maria Margaretha (Engelhardt) Meittinger **P:** unk **BLW:** unk **RG:** unk **MK:** unk **PH:** unk **SS:** B **BS:** 112.

NAFUERN, Francois; b unk; d 1781 **RU:** Seaman, Served on "Hextor" and died from Yorktown battle **CEM:** French Memorial; GPS 36.81944, -79.39933; Yorktown; York **GS:** U **SP:** No info **VI:** No further data **P:** unk **BLW:** unk **RG:** Y **MK:** unk **PH:** unk **SS:** J-Yorktown Historian **BS:** JLARC 1, 74.

NALFIN, Remy; b unk; d 1781 **RU:** Soldier, Served in Santogne Bn and died fr battle at Yorktown **CEM:** French Memorial; GPS 36.81944, -79.39933; Yorktown; York **GS:** U **SP:** No info **VI:** No further data **P:** unk **BLW:** unk **RG:** Y **MK:** unk **PH:** unk **SS:** J-Yorktown Historian **BS:** JLARC 1, 74.

NALLE, Martin II; b 1707 Tappahannock, Essex Co; d 15 Sep 1788 **RU:** Captain, Served in 3rd VA Regt **CEM:** Devils Run Farm; GPS unk; Use tax records for location; Culpeper **GS:** U **SP:** Isabelle (-----) (1710-1788) **VI:** Son of Martin (1675 England-1728 Essex Co) & Mary (Aldin) (1681-1734) Nalle **P:** unk **BLW:** unk **RG:** unk **MK:** unk **PH:** unk **SS:** Al Ct Bk I pg 12 **BS:** 196.

NANCE, Reuben; b 8 Jul 1745; d 13 Jan 1812 **RU:** Ensign/Patriot, Served in Henry Co Militia Oct 1777. Gave material aid to cause **CEM:** Nance Plantation Home; GPS unk; Rt 58, 2 mi E of Martinsville; Henry **GS:** U **SP:** 1) Amy Williamson 2) Nancy Brown **VI:** Son of William and Ann (Epps) Nance Jr **P:** unk **BLW:** unk **RG:** unk **MK:** unk **PH:** unk **SS:** E pg 577; AL Ct Bk pg 4 Henry Co **BS:** 196.

NEBLE, Georges; b unk; d 1781 **RU:** Soldier, Served in Royal Deaux Ponts Bn and died fr battle at Yorktown **CEM:** French Memorial; GPS 36.81944, -79.39933; Yorktown; York **GS:** U **SP:** No info **VI:** No further data **P:** unk **BLW:** unk **RG:** Y **MK:** unk **PH:** unk **SS:** J-Yorktown Historian **BS:** JLARC 1, 74.

NEEL, William; b 1761, Lancaster, PA; d 11 Feb 1841 **RU:** Private, Enlisted Augusta Co 1777-8. Served in VA Line **CEM:** Sifford; GPS unk; White Gate; Giles **GS:** U **SP:** Mar (1792 or 93) Rhoda (-----) (__-16 Jan 1846 Giles Co) **VI:** Had lived in Giles Co since 1794. Pen appl for 29 Oct 1832 Giles Co age 71. S15945 **P:** Y **BLW:** unk **RG:** unk **MK:** unk **PH:** unk **SS:** K Vol 4 pg 6; CG Vol 3 pg 2475 **BS:** JLARC 3.

NEFF, Abraham; b c1760; d unk **RU:** Private?, Served in Capt Jacob Holeman's Co, Dunmore Co Militia **CEM:** Neff Family; GPS unk; Vic Stonewall Jackson HS; Shenandoah **GS:** N **SP:** No info **VI:** No further data **P:** unk **BLW:** unk **RG:** N **MK:** N **PH:** N **SS:** C Sec IV pg 608 **BS:** 79 pg 22.

NEFF, Christian; b 1754, Augusta Co; d 21 May 1814 **RU:** Private, Served in Capt Jacob Holeman's Co, Dunmore Co Militia **CEM:** Neff-Kagey; GPS 38.69443, -78.65895; Rt 827, Old Bridge Rd, New Market;

RU=Rank/Unit   CEM=Cemetery   GS=Gravestone   SP=Spousal Information
VI=Other Veteran Info   P=Pension   BLW=Bounty/Land Warrant   RG=Registered Grave
MK=SAR/DAR Marker   PH=Photo   SS=Service Source   BS=Burial Source

246

Shenandoah **GS:** U **SP:** Maria Grabill (1751-24 Jan 1813) **VI:** Son of John Henry (1705-1784) & Ann (-----) (1714-1796) Neff **P:** unk **BLW:** unk **RG:** unk **MK:** unk **PH:** unk **SS:** C pg 607-608 **BS:** 196.

NEFF, Jacob; b 1742, Frederick Co; d 5 Aug 1820 **RU:** Patriot, Paid personal property supply tax, Shenandoah Co, 1782 **CEM:** Neff-Kagey; GPS 38.69443, -78.65895; Rt 827, Old Bridge Rd, New Market; Shenandoah **GS:** Y **SP:** Mar (3 Dec 1765) Barbara Grabill (1742-1804) **VI:** Son of John Henry (1705-1784) & Ann (-----) (1714-1796) Neff. Was a doctor **P:** unk **BLW:** unk **RG:** N **MK:** N **PH:** unk **SS:** DV **BS:** 79 pg 56; 196.

NEFF, Michael; b 15 May 1756, Lancaster Co, PA; d 22 Jan 1825 **RU:** Private, Served in Capt Duck's Co, 1st Co, 3rd Bn, Lancaster Co PA Militia **CEM:** Neff Family; GPS unk; E of Fairview Church on Charles Roberts property, Rural Retreat; Wythe **GS:** U **SP:** Christina Kapp (1746-1830) **VI:** Son of John George & Elizabeth (Stupp) Neff. Death date only on original stone. DAR Plaque **P:** unk **BLW:** unk **RG:** unk **MK:** Y **PH:** unk **SS:** CD **BS:** JLARC 1,2,40,123; 196.

NEHS, Jacob; b 1738, PA; d 1823 **RU:** Private, Served in PA **CEM:** Mt Solomon's Lutheran; GPS 38.44180, -78.44201; Solomon Church Rd & Rt 42, Forestville; Shenandoah **GS:** Y **SP:** Anna Marie Dettamore **VI:** SAR marker **P:** N **BLW:** N **RG:** unk **MK:** Y **PH:** N **SS:** AK - Col James Wood II Nov 2014 **BS:** 04.

NEILL, William; b 20 Oct 1753, Baltimore MD; d 14 May 1824 **RU:** Captain, Commanded a co in William Campbell's Regt **CEM:** Cem Name unk; GPS unk; Rt 58,west ofJonesville; Lee **GS:** Y **SP:** Bathsheba Harrison **VI:** No further data **P:** unk **BLW:** unk **RG:** Y **MK:** N **PH:** unk **SS:** 32 Dec 06 **BS:** 4.

NELSON, Alexander; b 14 Jan 1749; d 2 Jan 1834 **RU:** Private, Enlisted 24 Jan 1776; served in Capt James's Taylor's Co, Col Wayne's PA Battalion until 26 Nov 1776. **CEM:** Augusta Stone Presbyterian; GPS 38.23926, -78.97356; 28 Old Stone Church Ln, Ft Defiance; Augusta **GS:** Y **SP:** Mar (29 Jan 1784) Anne Mathews (17 Jul 1763-9 Jan 1829) d/of Sampson (1737 Ireland-__) & Mary (Lockhart) (__-1781) Mathews **VI:** Died age "nearly 85 yrs" **P:** unk **BLW:** unk **RG:** Y **MK:** unk **PH:** unk **SS:** A pg 200-2; E pg 580; JLARC Report **BS:** JLARC 1, 2, 8, 23, 62; 2 pg 21; 196.

NELSON, Alexander; b 1750; d 12 Sep 1828 **RU:** Private, Enlisted in Army autumn 1780 in Staunton and served in Capt Lapsley's Co, 1st VA Regt **CEM:** Augusta Stone Presbyterian; GPS 38.23926, -78.97356; 28 Old Stone Church Ln, Ft Defiance; Augusta **GS:** Y **SP:** Nancy Mathews (1763-19 Jan 1829) **VI:** Appl pen 23 Aug 1825 Augusta Co. **P:** Y **BLW:** unk **RG:** Y **MK:** unk **PH:** unk **SS:** G pg 60-1; JLARC Report **BS:** JLARC 8, 23.

NELSON, Alexander; b unk; d unk **RU:** Soldier, SAR graves Registry does not provide military or patriotic service **CEM:** New Providence Presbyterian; GPS 37.95130, -79.30250; 1208 New Providence Rd, Raphine; Rockbridge **GS:** U **SP:** No info **VI:** No further data **P:** unk **BLW:** unk **RG:** unk **MK:** unk **PH:** unk **SS:** NSSAR Ancestor #P-255261; SAR application **BS:** JLARC 63, 79.

NELSON, Hugh; b 1750; d 3 Oct 1800 **RU:** Patriot, Gave material aid to cause **CEM:** Grace Episcopal; GPS 37.23560, -76.50750; 115 Church St, Yorktown; York **GS:** U **SP:** Judith Page (7 Mar 1753-19 Mar 1827) d/o John Williamson (1724-1774) & Jane (Byrd) (1729-1774) Page **VI:** Son of William (1711-1772) & Elizabeth (Burwell) (1718-1798) Nelson **P:** N **BLW:** N **RG:** unk **MK:** unk **PH:** unk **SS:** AL Ct Bk II pg 3a **BS:** 196.

NELSON, John; b 1753 or 1756; d 18 Feb 1827 **RU:** Soldier, Served in Cont & VA Lines **CEM:** Bethel Presbyterian; GPS 38.04257, -79.17283; 563 Bethel Green Rd, Middlebrook; Augusta **GS:** N **SP:** Mar (25 Jul 1781, Wm & Mary College chapel) Nancy "Ann" Carter of Williamsburg **VI:** Widow appl pen 13 Nov 1837 Mecklenburg Co age 74. W5414 & VA 1/2 Pay (see N.A. Acc #874 #050124 1/2 Pay). Son of "Secretary Nelson of York" **P:** Y **BLW:** unk **RG:** unk **MK:** unk **PH:** N **SS:** CG Vol 3 pg 2478 **BS:** JLARC 62, 63.

NELSON, Lucy Grymes; b 24 Aug 1743, Brandon, Middlesex Co; d 14 Sep 1830 **RU:** Patriot, Patriotic information not determined, See DAR Senate Document year 1975 for pacifics **CEM:** Fork Episcopal Church; GPS 37.85340, -77.53100; 12566 Old Ridge Rd, Doswell; Hanover **GS:** Y **SP:** Thomas Nelson, Jr (18 Dec 1738 York (later Yorktown-2 Jan 1789 Hanover Co) **VI:** Daug of Philip & Mary (Randolph) Grymes **P:** N **BLW:** N **RG:** N **MK:** N **PH:** unk **SS:** AR Vol 3 pg 117 **BS:** 80 vol 3 pg 117.

RU=Rank/Unit · VI=Other Veteran Info · MK=SAR/DAR Marker · CEM=Cemetery · P=Pension · PH=Photo · GS=Gravestone · BLW=Bounty/Land Warrant · SS=Service Source · SP=Spousal Information · RG=Registered Grave · BS=Burial Source

247

NELSON, Thomas Jr; b 18 Dec 1738, York (later Yorktown); d 2 Jan 1789 **RU:** General/Patriot, At Yorktown seige. Was Signer Declaration of Independence and Wartime Gov of VA. Commander of VA forces during Rev War **CEM:** Grace Episcopal; GPS 37.23560, -76.50750; 115 Church St, Yorktown; York **GS:** Y **SP:** Mar (29 Jul 1762 York Co) Lucy Grymes (24 Aug 1743 Brandon, Middlesex Co-14 Sep 1830 Hanover Co), d/o Philip & Mary (Randolph) Grymes **VI:** Signed Declaration of Independence. Died in Hanover Co **P:** unk **BLW:** unk **RG:** Y **MK:** Y **PH:** unk **SS:** J-NSSAR 1993 Reg, AR Vol3 p118 **BS:** JLARC 1,2; Nelson-Page fam archives.

NELSON, Willaim; b 1754; d 1813 **RU:** Patriot, Gave material aid to cause. Captured by British at Castle Hill, Albemarle Co **CEM:** Grace Episcopal; GPS 37.23560, -76.50750; 115 Church St, Yorktown; York **GS:** U **SP:** 1) Mary Taliaferro (1760 James City Co-1786) d/o Richard (1732-1789) & Rebecca (Cocke) (1725-1818) Taliaferro 2) Abby Byrd d/o Willliam E. & Mary (Willing) Byrd **VI:** Son of William (1711-1772) & Elizabeth (Burwell) (1718-1798) Nelson. Judge of District Ct **P:** N **BLW:** N **RG:** unk **MK:** unk **PH:** unk **SS:** AL Ct Bk Albemarle Co **BS:** 196.

NELSON, William; b unk; d 1854 **RU:** Captain, Served in Fairfax Co Militia 25 Jan 1777 to 21 Jun 1781 **CEM:** Adams-Nelson-Sewell Family; GPS unk; 1443 Layman St, McLean; Fairfax **GS:** Y **SP:** No info **VI:** Died age 76 in 1854 **P:** unk **BLW:** unk **RG:** N **MK:** N **PH:** unk **SS:** A pg 389 **BS:** 61 vol VI, pg MI 90.

NELSON, William; b 11 Apr 1754; d 30 Jun 1831 **RU:** Colonel, Served in 7th VA Regt as Lt in Co. Oct 1776-Oct 1777. Was promoted to Col, 8th VA Regt **CEM:** Nelson Fam at Wingfield; GPS unk; Coatesville; Hanover **GS:** Y **SP:** No info **VI:** No further data **P:** unk **BLW:** unk **RG:** Y **MK:** N **PH:** unk **SS:** E pg 581 **BS:** 31 vol I pg 7.

NELSON, William; b 17 Jun 1746, Yorktown; d 24 Nov 1807 **RU:** Lit Colonel, Served as a Private in a VA Co 1775. Promoted to Maj in 7th Cont Line 29 Feb 1776; to Lt Col 7 Oct 1776; resigned 25 Oct 1777 **CEM:** Forkquarter; GPS unk; Calno Rd Rt 601, Norment Ferry; King William **GS:** U **SP:** Mar (24 Nov 1770) Lucy Chiswell (1752- 4 Apr 1811) d/o Col John & Elizabeth (Randolph) Chiswell. Also bur here **VI:** Son of Thomas (1716-1782) and Lucy (Amistead) Nelson **P:** unk **BLW:** unk **RG:** unk **MK:** unk **PH:** unk **SS:** E pg 581 **BS:** 196.

NELSON, William; b unk; d 1823 **RU:** Major, Served in 7th VA Regt 29 Feb to 7 Oct 1776 **CEM:** Tinkling Spring Presbyterian; GPS 38.08472, -78.98278; 30 Tinkling Spring Dr, Fishersville; Augusta **GS:** N **SP:** No info **VI:** Only stone for William Nelson was b 1785 **P:** unk **BLW:** unk **RG:** N **MK:** N **PH:** N **SS:** G pg 832 **BS:** 142 Tingling Spr.

NELSON, William; b 9 Aug 1763, Yorktown; d 8 Jan 1801 **RU:** Navy Enlisted Man, Served on Brig "Jefferson," Dec 1779, 20 Jan 1780 **CEM:** Grace Episcopal; GPS 37.23560, -76.50750; 115 Church St, Yorktown; York **GS:** N **SP:** Mar (1790) Sally Burwell Page, e/o Gov John & Frances (Burwell) Page **VI:** No further data **P:** unk **BLW:** unk **RG:** unk **MK:** unk **PH:** N **SS:** L pg 230 **BS:** 196.

NESTEL (NESTELL, NESTLE, NISTELL), Peter; b 1750, Albany, NY; d 30 Apr 1817 **RU:** Major, Served in 6th Co, 2nd NY Artillery. Obit records indicate Rev War services at the period of Arnold's defection [as] particularly conspicuous and procured him a prominent place in the favor of Gen Washington, who afterwards gave him many evidences of his esteem and approbation, and to the hour of his death, spoke of him as one of his most faithful co-operators **CEM:** St Paul's Episcopal; GPS 36.84733, -76.28554; 201 St Paul's Blvd; Norfolk City **GS:** N **SP:** 1) Lucy (Nistell) 2) Mary (-----) **VI:** Member of Society of the Cincinnati. Cenotaph marked beside first wife's grave. Educated in Germany **P:** unk **BLW:** unk **RG:** Y **MK:** Y **PH:** N **SS:** CB; G pg 902 **BS:** 32 Jul 2010.

NEUVEU, Edme; b unk; d 1781 **RU:** Soldier, Served in Touraine Bn and died fr battle at Yorktown **CEM:** French Memorial; GPS 36.81944, -79.39933; Yorktown; York **GS:** U **SP:** No info **VI:** No further data **P:** unk **BLW:** unk **RG:** Y **MK:** unk **PH:** unk **SS:** J-Yorktown Historian **BS:** JLARC 1, 74.

NEUVILLE, Jean; b unk; d 1781 **RU:** Seaman, Served on "Magnanime" and died from Yorktown battle **CEM:** French Memorial; GPS 36.81944, -79.39933; Yorktown; York **GS:** U **SP:** No info **VI:** No further data **P:** unk **BLW:** unk **RG:** Y **MK:** unk **PH:** unk **SS:** J-Yorktown Historian **BS:** JLARC 1, 74.

RU=Rank/Unit	CEM=Cemetery	GS=Gravestone	SP=Spousal Information
VI=Other Veteran Info	P=Pension	BLW=Bounty/Land Warrant	RG=Registered Grave
MK=SAR/DAR Marker	PH=Photo	SS=Service Source	BS=Burial Source

248

NEW, Pierre; b unk; d 1781 **RU:** Soldier, Served in Royal Deaux Ponts Bn and died fr battle at Yorktown **CEM:** French Memorial; GPS 36.81944, -79.39933; Yorktown; York **GS:** U **SP:** No info **VI:** No further data **P:** unk **BLW:** unk **RG:** unk **MK:** unk **PH:** unk **SS:** J-Yorktown Historian **BS:** JLARC 1, 74.

NEWELL, James Sr; b 29 Sep 1749, Augusta Co; d 2 Mar 1823 **RU:** Captain/Patriot, Commanded a co in Montgomery Co Militia. Gave material aid to cause **CEM:** Newell-Trigg-Sanders; GPS unk; N side of 619 abt .5 mile W of jct with 636, Austinville; Wythe **GS:** U **SP:** Mar (23 Jan 1771) Sarah Wood (3 Mar 1752-23 mar 1831) d/o William & Martha (Drake) Wood **VI:** Cemetery in grove of trees, enclosed by fence. DAR plaque in cemetery **P:** unk **BLW:** unk **RG:** unk **MK:** unk **PH:** unk **SS:** AL Ct Bk pg 4 Henry Co **BS:** JLARC 2, 40,123;196.

NEWELL, John; b 29 Sep 1743; d 16 Apr 1833 **RU:** Captain, Commanded a company of frontier troops **CEM:** Beeler; GPS unk; Cedar Creek; Frederick **GS:** Y **SP:** 1) Mar (1768) Margaret Ware 2) Sarah Waggoner (1751-1801) 3) Mar (1804) Elizabeth Wright **VI:** No further data **P:** unk **BLW:** unk **RG:** N **MK:** N **PH:** unk **SS:** DAR #A45210; G pg 595 **BS:** 50 pg 75.

NEWLAND, John; b 1743; d 1833 **RU:** Patriot, Gave material aid to cause **CEM:** Newland; GPS unk; 1 mi W on Rt 692 fr jct with Rt 749, on hill on right, Cedar Springs; Wythe **GS:** U **SP:** No info **VI:** Bur on property owned in 1981 by Leroy Sloper **P:** N **BLW:** N **RG:** unk **MK:** unk **PH:** unk **SS:** AL Ct Bk pg 25 Montgomrey Co **BS:** JLARC 123.

NEWMAN, John; b unk; d unk **RU:** Captain, Served in 13th VA Militia Regt **CEM:** David Kagy Farm; GPS unk; Nr New Market; Shenandoah **GS:** U **SP:** No info **VI:** No further data **P:** unk **BLW:** unk **RG:** unk **MK:** unk **PH:** unk **SS:** AR Vol 3 p120; NSSAR Ancestor # P- 255894 **BS:** JLARC 2.

NEWMAN, Walter; b 1742, Augusta Co; d 29 Jul1815 **RU:** Private/Patriot, Gave material aid to cause **CEM:** Arthur Hirsh Family; GPS unk; Nr New Market; Shenandoah **GS:** U **SP:** Mar (c1766) Catherine Lair (5 Nov 1747-1 Feb 1815) d/o Mathias (1714, Palatinate, Germany-25 jun 1787 Rockingham Co) & Catherine Margaretha (Moyer) (__ Germany-1804) Lair **VI:** No further data **P:** unk **BLW:** unk **RG:** Y **MK:** unk **PH:** unk **SS:** J-NSSAR 1993 Reg, J- DAR Hatcher; AL Ct Bk pg 1 Shenandoah Co **BS:** JLARC 1, 2.

NEWTON, Solomon; b unk; d 1781 **RU:** Soldier, Served fr MA, and died fr the Battle at Yorktown **CEM:** Yorktown Victory Monument Tablet; GPS 38.28350, -78.54150; Yorktown; York **GS:** U **SP:** No info **VI:** No further data **P:** unk **BLW:** unk **RG:** unk **MK:** unk **PH:** unk **SS:** J-Yorktown Historian **BS:** JLARC 74.

NEWTON, William; b c1762; d 26 Dec 1814 **RU:** Soldier, Served in Western Bn of State troops **CEM:** Presbyterian Church; GPS 38.80015, -77.05791; Wilkes St & Hamilton Ln; Alexandria City **GS:** Y **SP:** Jane Barr Stuart (c1777-25 Feb 1815) **VI:** Died age 51 (stone.) Death notice in the Alexandria Gazette 29 Dec 1814, pg 3 give death date as 25 Dec. GS reads 26 Dec **P:** unk **BLW:** unk **RG:** Y **MK:** N **PH:** unk **SS:** J-NSSAR 1993 Reg; NSSAR Ancestor # P-256062 **BS:** JLARC 1; 174, pg 60; 23 pg 60.

NICHOLAS, Jacob; b 15 Jul 1724,, Germany (or VA); d 26 Mar 1781 **RU:** Patriot, His estate filed claim for impressed material **CEM:** Old Peaked Mountain; GPS 38.37113, -78.73416; 9843 Town Hall Rd, McGaheysville; Rockingham **GS:** Y **SP:** Barbara Zellers (Sellers) **VI:** Common Monument. Son of John & Margaret (Lorentz) Nicholas **P:** N **BLW:** N **RG:** Y **MK:** Y **PH:** unk **SS:** J-NSSAR 2000 Reg AL pg 38 **BS:** JLARC 76.

NICHOLAS, Jean; b unk; d 1781 **RU:** Seaman, Served on "Ville de Paris" and died from Yorktown battle **CEM:** French Memorial; GPS 36.81944, -79.39933; Yorktown; York **GS:** U **SP:** No info **VI:** No further data **P:** unk **BLW:** unk **RG:** Y **MK:** unk **PH:** unk **SS:** J-Yorktown Historian **BS:** JLARC 1, 74.

NICHOLAS, Lewis; b 1718; d 9 Aug1807 **RU:** Brigadier General, Served in US Army **CEM:** Old Presbyterian Meeting House; GPS 38.48528, -77.23532; 323 S Fairfax St; Alexandria City **GS:** N **SP:** No info **VI:** Died age 90 (Alexandria Gazette, 7 Aug 1807, pg 3). Listed on SAR plaque in cemetery **P:** unk **BLW:** unk **RG:** Y **MK:** Y **PH:** N **SS:** AK **BS:** JLARC 1, 2, 25, 86; 23 pg 106; 196.

NICHOLAS, Lewis; b unk; d Aft 1783 **RU:** Captain & Patriot, Commanded an Independent Co in Albemarle Co according to pension record of Benjamin Harris and James Lewis **CEM:** Fincastle Presbyterian; GPS 37.50017, -79.87558; 108 E Back St, Fincastle; Botetourt **GS:** N **SP:** No info **VI:** Name is on VASSAR plaque at cemetery **P:** unk **BLW:** unk **RG:** N **MK:** Y **PH:** N **SS:** AS Vol 3 pg 121 **BS:** 80 vol 3 pg 117.

RU=Rank/Unit   CEM=Cemetery   GS=Gravestone   SP=Spousal Information
VI=Other Veteran Info   P=Pension   BLW=Bounty/Land Warrant   RG=Registered Grave
MK=SAR/DAR Marker   PH=Photo   SS=Service Source   BS=Burial Source

249

NICHOLAS, Peter; b 5 Apr 1762; d 10 Jul 1852 **RU:** Private, Served in Capt Peachey Gilmer's Co, Augusta Co Militia **CEM:** Old Peaked Mountain; GPS 38.37113, -78.73416; 9843 Town Hall Rd, McGaheysville; Rockingham **GS:** Y **SP:** 1) Mar (1786 Rockingham Co) Euly Boshang d/o Jacob & (-----) Boshang 2) Mar (1782 Rockingham Co) Elizabeth (-----) Sellers, widow of Henry Sellers **VI:** No further data **P:** unk **BLW:** unk **RG:** Y **MK:** Y **PH:** unk **SS:** E pg 584 **BS:** 04.

NICHOLAS, Wilson Cary; b 31 Jan 1761, Williamsburg; d 11 Oct 1820 **RU:** Lieutenant, Commanded a Co in Lt Col George Meade's Legion 1781 **CEM:** Monticello; GPS 38.00829, -78.4552; 931 Thomas Jefferson Pkwy; Charlottesville City **GS:** Y **SP:** Margaret Smith **VI:** No further data **P:** unk **BLW:** unk **RG:** unk **MK:** unk **PH:** unk **SS:** J- DAR Hatcher; DD **BS:** JLARC 2; 196.

NICHOLS, Daniel; b unk; d 1847 **RU:** Private?, Served in 3rd, 4th, 8th, 12th VA Cont Lines **CEM:** Goose Creek; GPS 39.11250, -77.69527; Rt 722, Lincoln; Loudoun **GS:** Y **SP:** No info **VI:** No further data **P:** unk **BLW:** unk **RG:** Y **MK:** N **PH:** unk **SS:** E pg 585 **BS:** 25, pg 221.

NICHOLS, Isaac; b 1720, Chester Co PA; d 9 May 1803 **RU:** Patriot, Paid the Rev War supply and state tax in County of Philadelphia, PA for yrs of 1781, 1782, & 1783. **CEM:** Goose Creek; GPS 39.11250, -77.69527; Rt 722, Lincoln; Loudoun **GS:** U **SP:** Mar (26 Mar 1742, New Castle Co, DE) Margary Cox (1724 PA-1806 Loudoun Co) **VI:** Son of Thomas & Mary (Ludford) Nichols **P:** N **BLW:** N **RG:** unk **MK:** unk **PH:** unk **SS:** Fold 3 PA Archives, series 3 Vol XVI pg 331 **BS:** 196.

NICHOLS, Nathaniel; b unk; d 21 Sep 1846 **RU:** Seaman, Served on the "Hero" Galley 4 Nov 1777 - 13 Feb 1778 **CEM:** Ketoctin Baptist; GPS 39.15746, -77.74870; Ketoctin Church Rd, Purcellville; Loudoun **GS:** Y **SP:** Rachel Chamblin (16 Feb 1800-15 Aug 1887) **VI:** No further data **P:** unk **BLW:** unk **RG:** Y **MK:** N **PH:** unk **SS:** E pg 585; L pg 231 **BS:** 25 pg 223; 196.

NICHOLSON, Jesse or Jessee; b 1759; d 26 Sep 1834 **RU:** Captain, Enl 1776, and served throughout the war. Served fr Brunswick Co, under Lt Binns Jones, 15th VA Regt, Cont line for 3 yrs **CEM:** Cedar Grove; GPS 36.57204, -80.02599; 301 Fort Lane Rd; Portsmouth City **GS:** Y **SP:** Lucy (-----) **VI:** Moved to Portsmouth after Rev War and was Postmaster there. Minister after war. Marker moved 1929 fr Monumental graveyard. Pension recd 16 Jul 1832 Norfolk Co. S5832, BLW #4134-100-22 Mar 1732 through Richmond Land Office. Also BLW #6015, 200 acres for War of 1812 **P:** Y **BLW:** Y **RG:** N **MK:** N **PH:** unk **SS:** N pg 915; AP Serv Rec; CG Vol 3 pg 2499 **BS:** JLARC 3,105; 178 Jan 2011.

NICHOLSON, John; b unk; d Aug 1810 **RU:** Corporal, Served in Capt John Mercer's Co, 3rd VA Regt Cont Line Feb 1778. Had 3 yrs service **CEM:** Nicholson Family; GPS unk; Syria; Madison **GS:** U **SP:** Ann Wiggins **VI:** No further data **P:** unk **BLW:** unk **RG:** unk **MK:** unk **PH:** unk **SS:** A pg 276 **BS:** 196.

NICHOLSON, Robert; b 1725, York Co; d 15 Aug 1798 **RU:** Surgeon, Served in VA Line **CEM:** St John's Episcopal; GPS 37.53183, -77.41958; 2401 E Broad St; Richmond City **GS:** Y **SP:** Mar (21 Apr 1784 James City Co) Elizabeth Digges (c1762-__) **VI:** Died in York Co where he lived for 15 yrs. Prior to that he lived in Williamsburg. Widow pensioned 22 Nov 1838 Gloucester Co age 76 in May 1838. W5422; also VA 1/2 Pay (See N.A. Acc #874 #050127 1/2 Pay) Widow lived in Gloucester Co age 84 when BLW #7774 issued to children 2 Jun 1844 **P:** Y **BLW:** Y **RG:** N **MK:** N **PH:** unk **SS:** E pg 586; K Vol 4 pg 20; CG Vol 3 pg 2499 **BS:** 39 pg 99.

NICOLAS, Pierre; b unk; d 1781 **RU:** Seaman, Served on "Northumberland" and died from Yorktown battle **CEM:** French Memorial; GPS 36.81944, -79.39933; Yorktown; York **GS:** U **SP:** No info **VI:** No further data **P:** unk **BLW:** unk **RG:** Y **MK:** unk **PH:** unk **SS:** J-Yorktown Historian **BS:** JLARC 1, 74.

NICOLE, Jean; b unk; d 1781 **RU:** Soldier, Served in Gatinais Bn and died fr battle at Yorktown **CEM:** French Memorial; GPS 36.81944, -79.39933; Yorktown; York **GS:** U **SP:** No info **VI:** No further data **P:** unk **BLW:** unk **RG:** Y **MK:** unk **PH:** unk **SS:** J-Yorktown Historian **BS:** JLARC 1, 74.

NICOLSON, Thomas; b c1750; d 10 Nov 1808 **RU:** Private, Served in 8th Cont Line **CEM:** St John's Episcopal; GPS 37.53183, -77.41958; 2401 E Broad St; Richmond City **GS:** Y **SP:** No info **VI:** No further data **P:** unk **BLW:** unk **RG:** Y **MK:** N **PH:** Y **SS:** E pg 586 **BS:** 04, Dec 2006.

NIEL, Antoine; b unk; d 1781 **RU:** Seaman, Served on "Duc De Bourgogne" and died from Yorktown battle **CEM:** French Memorial; GPS 36.81944, -79.39933; Yorktown; York **GS:** U **SP:** No info **VI:** No further data **P:** unk **BLW:** unk **RG:** Y **MK:** unk **PH:** unk **SS:** J-Yorktown Historian **BS:** JLARC 1, 74.

RU=Rank/Unit	CEM=Cemetery	GS=Gravestone	SP=Spousal Information
VI=Other Veteran Info	P=Pension	BLW=Bounty/Land Warrant	RG=Registered Grave
MK=SAR/DAR Marker	PH=Photo	SS=Service Source	BS=Burial Source

250

NIXON, George; b 25 Feb 1730, Ireland; d 27 Nov 1800 **RU:** Patriot, Gave material aid to the cause **CEM:** Nixon Family; GPS unk; 19010 Woodburn Rd; Loudoun **GS:** Y **SP:** Mary Combs (1729, Ireland-29 Oct 1804) **VI:** No further data **P:** N **BLW:** N **RG:** N **MK:** N **PH:** unk **SS:** AL Ct Bk pg 31, 58 **BS:** 60 Loudoun; 196.

NIXON, George; b 30 Sep 1751, Loudoun Co; d 17 Nov 1818 **RU:** Private, Served in VA Line **CEM:** Nixon Family; GPS unk; 19010 Woodburn Rd; Loudoun **GS:** Y **SP:** Anna Craven(1778, Loudoun Co-23 Feb 1829) **VI:** Son of George (25 Feb 1730, Ireland-27 Nov 1800) & Mary (Combs) 1729, Ireland-29 Oct 1804) Nixon. Recd BLW **P:** unk **BLW:** Y **RG:** N **MK:** N **PH:** unk **SS:** C pg 258 **BS:** 60 Loudoun; 196.

NIXON, John; b 21 Mar 1755, Ireland; d 27 Aug 1815 **RU:** Private/Patriot, Served in 1st, 10th, 14th Cont Line. Gave material aid to cause **CEM:** Nixon Family; GPS unk; 19010 Woodburn Rd; Loudoun **GS:** Y **SP:** Mar (1778) Rebecca Todd (c1757, MD-__) **VI:** Son of George IV (25 Feb 1730 Ireland-27 Nov 1800) & Mary (Combs) (1729-1804) Nixon **P:** unk **BLW:** unk **RG:** Y **MK:** N **PH:** unk **SS:** DAR #A083895; D Vol 2 pg 599; E pg 587 **BS:** 25 pg 225; 196.

NOEL, Jean; b unk; d 1781 **RU:** Soldier, Served in Bourbonnais Bn and died fr battle at Yorktown **CEM:** French Memorial; GPS 36.81944, -79.39933; Yorktown; York **GS:** U **SP:** No info **VI:** No further data **P:** unk **BLW:** unk **RG:** Y **MK:** unk **PH:** unk **SS:** J-Yorktown Historian **BS:** JLARC 1, 74.

NOLLY, Laurent; b unk; d 1781 **RU:** Soldier, Served in Agenois Bn and died fr battle at Yorktown **CEM:** French Memorial; GPS 36.81944, -79.39933; Yorktown; York **GS:** U **SP:** No info **VI:** No further data **P:** unk **BLW:** unk **RG:** Y **MK:** unk **PH:** unk **SS:** J-Yorktown Historian **BS:** JLARC 1, 74.

NORMAN, Courtney; b 1730; d 1783 **RU:** Soldier, Served in Culpeper Co Militia **CEM:** Fairview; GPS 38.48080,-78.00470; Sperryville Pike Rt 522, Culpeper; Culpeper **GS:** U **SP:** Frances (-----) **VI:** No further data **P:** unk **BLW:** unk **RG:** Y **MK:** unk **PH:** unk **SS:** NSSAR Ancestor #P-256791; SAR applic; DD **BS:** JLARC 76.

NORMAN, George; b Jun 1743, Stafford Co; d Jun 1807 **RU:** Patriot, Gave wagonage to the cause **CEM:** Norman Family # 2; GPS unk; Hope Point Rd; Stafford **GS:** Y **SP:** Elizabeth (-----) (c1749 - cNov 1822) **VI:** No further data **P:** N **BLW:** N **RG:** Y **MK:** N **PH:** Y **SS:** D pg 874, 882 **BS:** 03 pg 296.

NORMAN, Thomas; b 1711-1712 Prob. Stafford Co; d 2 Mar 1785 **RU:** Patriot, Gave for cause beef and 52 lbs bacon **CEM:** Norman Family #1; GPS unk; Quarry Rd; Stafford **GS:** Y **SP:** Elizabeth (-----) (c1714-20 Jun 1771) **VI:** No further data **P:** N **BLW:** N **RG:** Y **MK:** N **PH:** Y **SS:** D pg 881 **BS:** 03 pg 295.

NORTH, Roger; b unk; d 17 Oct 1776 **RU:** Patriot, Gave material aid to the Augusta Co Militia for the Battle of Point Pleasant in 1774 **CEM:** Trinity Episcopal; GPS 38.14917, -79.07521; 214 Beverley St; Staunton City **GS:** Y **SP:** No info **VI:** No further data **P:** N **BLW:** N **RG:** N **MK:** N **PH:** unk **SS:** Z pg 93 **BS:** 142 Trinity; 196.

NORTON, Henry; b unk; d 1 Dec 1781 **RU:** Soldier, Served in 1st NY Regt and died fr Yorktown battle **CEM:** Yorktown Victory Monument Tablet; GPS 38.28350, -78.54150; Yorktown; York **GS:** U **SP:** No info **VI:** No further data **P:** unk **BLW:** unk **RG:** unk **MK:** unk **PH:** unk **SS:** J-Yorktown Historian; AX pg 548 **BS:** JLARC 74.

NORVELL (NORWELL), Henry Holdcraft (Hallcraft); b Jan 1759 VA; d 29 Dec 1846 **RU:** Sergeant, Ent serv 1775 in1st VA Regt, later in 10th Cont Line **CEM:** Old City; GPS 37.41472, -79.15667; 401 Taylor St; Lynchburg City **GS:** Y **SP:** Mary (-----) (Oct 1789-__) **VI:** Pen 1818 Campbell Co. BLW #1796 issued 12 Jun 1783. Died in Campbell Co **P:** Y **BLW:** Y **RG:** Y **MK:** N **PH:** unk **SS:** E pg 589; K Vol 4 pg 28 **BS:** 35 pg 3.

NORWELL (NORVALL), Aquilla; b 1745; d 1795 **RU:** Surgeon, Served for 3 yrs **CEM:** Norvall Family; GPS unk; Nr Dumfries; Prince William **GS:** U **SP:** No info **VI:** No further data **P:** unk **BLW:** unk **RG:** N **MK:** N **PH:** unk **SS:** C pg 481; AS, DAR report **BS:** DAR report.

NUCKOLLS, Charles; b 1745 Louisa Co; d 12 Aug 1820 **RU:** Major, Contact SAR Fincastle Resolution's chapter for service **CEM:** Nuckolls Family; GPS 36.63551, -80.95944; Beyond the end of Wild Turkey Ln, jct US 58 & Rt 94; Grayson **GS:** Y **SP:** Mar (1764) Mary Black (17 Jul 1741 Albemarle

RU=Rank/Unit	CEM=Cemetery	GS=Gravestone	SP=Spousal Information
VI=Other Veteran Info	P=Pension	BLW=Bounty/Land Warrant	RG=Registered Grave
MK=SAR/DAR Marker	PH=Photo	SS=Service Source	BS=Burial Source

251

Co-21 Jun 1824) **VI:** Son of James (c1720, Hanover Co-17 Mar 1810 Louisa Co) & Mary (Henderson) Nuckolls **P:** unk **BLW:** unk **RG:** Y **MK:** N **PH:** unk **SS:** AK Apr 2007 **BS:** 04 Apr 2007; 196.

NUSTER, Claudius; b unk; d unk **RU:** Soldier?, See DAR Senate Report series 10094, vol 5, 1936 for service details **CEM:** Trinity Episcopal; GPS 38.14917, -79.07521; 214 Beverley St; Staunton City **GS:** U **SP:** No info **VI:** No further data **P:** unk **BLW:** unk **RG:** unk **MK:** unk **PH:** unk **SS:** J-DAR Hatcher; NSSAR Ancestor #P -257469 **BS:** JLARC 2.

NUTTER, Zadock (Zadok); b 20 Apr 1759, Somerse,t MD; d 1839 **RU:** Soldier, Served in Capt John Woodgate Co, Col Samuel Patterson's Regt, Delaware. Also in Flying Camp **CEM:** Nutter Property; GPS unk; Pott's Creek; Craig **GS:** U **SP:** Mar (Apr 1794) Catherine Lynn (1765-1846, Botetourt Co) **VI:** No further data **P:** unk **BLW:** unk **RG:** unk **MK:** unk **PH:** unk **SS:** J-DAR Hatcher; DD **BS:** JLARC 2.

O'BANNON, John; b 1735; d Apr 1797 **RU:** Captain, Served in Fauquier Co Militia, possibly promoted to Maj **CEM:** O'Bannon; GPS unk; Warrenton; Fauquier **GS:** Y **SP:** Lydia Duncan (Stampe) (c1742, Prince William Co-aft 1807) **VI:** Son of Joseph (c1720, Orange Co-Sep 1793) & Lydia (-----) (c1773-1797 Fauquier Co) Duncan **P:** unk **BLW:** unk **RG:** Y **MK:** N **PH:** unk **SS:** DAR #A085506; H **BS:** 19 pg 154,151,152, 242.

OBANNON (OBANON), William; b 1730; d 19 Oct 1807 **RU:** Patriot, Gave material aid to cause **CEM:** Obannon-Lawrence; GPS unk; Marshall; Fauquier **GS:** Y **SP:** Mar (1752) Anne Neville (1734 Hampshire Co-__) **VI:** No further data **P:** N **BLW:** N **RG:** unk **MK:** unk **PH:** unk **SS:** DAR #A085510; AL Ct Bk pg 2, 15 Fauquier Co **BS:** 196.

O'BRYANT, Thomas; b 1721, Ireland; d 23 Jan 1793 **RU:** Private, Served in 2nd Cont Line **CEM:** Spears Family; GPS unk; N of Edom Rt 42 7.3 mi; Rockingham **GS:** N **SP:** No info **VI:** No further data **P:** unk **BLW:** unk **RG:** N **MK:** N **PH:** N **SS:** E pg 592 **BS:** 32.

OGLESBY, Daniel; b c1763; d 1859 **RU:** Soldier, Served in militia **CEM:** Old City; GPS 37.41472, -79.15667; 401 Taylor St; Lynchburg City **GS:** U **SP:** No info **VI:** Son of Richard & Susan (-----) Oglesby. Died in Bedford Co **P:** unk **BLW:** unk **RG:** unk **MK:** unk **PH:** unk **SS:** SAR Ancestor #P-262807 **BS:** JLARC 36.

OLIVER, Benjamin; b 2 July 1766; d 9 Sep 1820 **RU:** Private, Served probably in Hanover Co Militia **CEM:** Retreat Farm; GPS unk; Pamunkey River near old church; Hanover **GS:** Y **SP:** No info **VI:** Rank of Capt obtained after war **P:** unk **BLW:** unk **RG:** Y **MK:** N **PH:** unk **SS:** E pg 595 **BS:** 31 vol 1 pg 28.

OLIVER, James; b 1756; d 1827 **RU:** Corporal, Served in VA Line in the Artillery, 6th, 8th, 14th Cont Lines **CEM:** Mt Hebron; GPS 39.18170, -78.15720; 305 E Boscawen St, Winchester; Frederick **GS:** Y **SP:** No info **VI:** Appl pen Frederick Co 11 Jun 1818 #S38269 **P:** Y **BLW:** Y **RG:** unk **MK:** unk **PH:** unk **SS:** C pg 260; E pg 595; CG pg 2536 **BS:** 196.

OLIVER, William; b 10 Apr 1754; d 15 Mar 1842 **RU:** Corporal, Served in 2nd VA State Regt and 3rd Cont Line **CEM:** Old Glade Creek; GPS 37.35989, -79.81828; Grace Hollow Rd, Blue Ridge; Botetourt **GS:** Y **SP:** No info **VI:** No further data **P:** unk **BLW:** unk **RG:** N **MK:** N **PH:** unk **SS:** K Vol 4 pg 40 **BS:** 74 pg 3; 196.

OLLINGER (OLIFER), John Christopher Sr; b 18 Feb 1737, Germany; d 20 Feb 1827 **RU:** Private, Served in Capt James Ewing's Co fr Augusta Co. Served in Bates Co and had service in the 2nd Regt PA Line under Col Seylock and in Col Smith's and Col Lewis's Regt of VA **CEM:** Slemp Memorial; GPS unk; Turkey Cove; Lee **GS:** Y **SP:** Eve Margaret Siler (2 Aug 1754-1 Jun 1854 Lee Co) D/o Jacob Sr & Dorothy (Blubaugh) Siler **VI:** Son of Philip Johann & Juliana (Umberger) Olinger **P:** unk **BLW:** unk **RG:** unk **MK:** Y **PH:** unk **SS:** CA; Z pg 108 **BS:** 196.

OLLIVIER, Paul; b unk; d 1781 **RU:** Seaman, Served on "Duc De Bourgogne" and died from Yorktown battle **CEM:** French Memorial; GPS 36.81944, -79.39933; Yorktown; York **GS:** U **SP:** No info **VI:** No further data **P:** unk **BLW:** unk **RG:** Y **MK:** unk **PH:** unk **SS:** J-Yorktown Historian **BS:** JLARC 1, 74.

OMOHUNDRO, Richard; b 1733; d 1811 **RU:** Ensign/Patriot, Gave material aid to cause **CEM:** Omohundro Family; GPS unk; 400 yds E of Rt 15, 1 mi S of Fork Union, Nr Fork Union 1 mi; Fluvanna

RU=Rank/Unit	CEM=Cemetery	GS=Gravestone	SP=Spousal Information
VI=Other Veteran Info	P=Pension	BLW=Bounty/Land Warrant	RG=Registered Grave
MK=SAR/DAR Marker	PH=Photo	SS=Service Source	BS=Burial Source

252

GS: N **SP:** No info **VI:** No further data **P:** unk **BLW:** unk **RG:** unk **MK:** unk **PH:** N **SS:** AL Ct Bk pg 8, 21 Fluvanna Co **BS:** JLARC 2, 46,100.

ORGAIN, William Derby; b unk; d 20 Dec 1824 **RU:** Patriot, Gave material aid to the cause **CEM:** Orgain Family; GPS 36.86010, -77.94002; Jct Rts 644 & Rt 648, Alberta; Brunswick **GS:** Y **SP:** Elizabeth Neblett, (23 Nov 1746 - 27 May 1815). She is said by legend to haunt this property **VI:** New stone erected 1984 **P:** N **BLW:** N **RG:** unk **MK:** N **PH:** unk **SS:** AL Ct Bk pg 22 Brunswick co **BS:** 196.

ORGAN, unk; b unk; d 1781 **RU:** Soldier, Served fr PA, and died fr the battle at Yorktown **CEM:** Yorktown Victory Monument Tablet; GPS 38.28350, -78.54150; Yorktown; York **GS:** U **SP:** No info **VI:** No further data **P:** unk **BLW:** unk **RG:** unk **MK:** unk **PH:** unk **SS:** J-Yorktown Historian **BS:** JLARC 74.

ORIEUX, Francois; b unk; d 1781 **RU:** Seaman, Served on "Magnanime" and died from Yorktown battle **CEM:** French Memorial; GPS 36.81944, -79.39933; Yorktown; York **GS:** U **SP:** No info **VI:** No further data **P:** unk **BLW:** unk **RG:** Y **MK:** unk **PH:** unk **SS:** J-Yorktown Historian **BS:** JLARC 1, 74.

ORKENSUDE, Erasmus; b unk; d 1781 **RU:** Soldier, Served in Royal Deaux Ponts Bn and died fr battle at Yorktown **CEM:** French Memorial; GPS 36.81944, -79.39933; Yorktown; York **GS:** U **SP:** No info **VI:** No further data **P:** unk **BLW:** unk **RG:** Y **MK:** unk **PH:** unk **SS:** J-Yorktown Historian **BS:** JLARC 1,74.

ORR, John; b c1728, Muirkirk, Scotland; d 20 Jul 1795 **RU:** Patriot, Gave 800# of beef "for public use" in 1780, Loudoun Co **CEM:** St John's Episcopal; GPS 38.84217, -77.42716; 5649 Mt Gilead Rd; Fairfax **GS:** Y **SP:** Susannah Grayson **VI:** "Waterside" was home. Died in Cub Run, Loudoun Co. SAR memorial. GS was moved to St John's Episcopal. He is bur at the Orr family cemetery next to 6709 Jade Post Ln **P:** N **BLW:** N **RG:** N **MK:** Y **PH:** Y **SS:** AL Ct Bk pg 18 **BS:** 61 vol IV pg CN-23.

ORVAULT, Dupe d'; b unk; d 1781 **RU:** Seaman, Served on "Auguste" and died from Yorktown battle **CEM:** French Memorial; GPS 36.81944, -79.39933; Yorktown; York **GS:** U **SP:** No info **VI:** No further data **P:** unk **BLW:** unk **RG:** Y **MK:** unk **PH:** unk **SS:** J-Yorktown Historian **BS:** JLARC 1, 74.

OSBORN (OSBORNE), Enoch; b 1741, Yadkin, Rowan Co, NC; d Sep 1818 **RU:** Captain/Patriot, Commanded a Co in Montgomery Co miltia. Took Oath of Fidelity, Montgomery Co in 1777 **CEM:** Osborn-Cox; GPS unk; Rt 711, Independence; Grayson **GS:** U **SP:** Jane Hash **VI:** No further data **P:** unk **BLW:** unk **RG:** Y **MK:** unk **PH:** unk **SS:** J-NSSAR 1993 Reg, J- DAR Hatcher; B; DD **BS:** JLARC 1, 2;196.

OSBURN, William; b 1750; d 13 Dec 1805 **RU:** Private, Served in PA Regt commanded by Col Lewis Nicola in Apr 1783 **CEM:** Ketoctin Baptist; GPS 39.15746, -77.74870; Ketoctin Church Rd, Purcellville; Loudoun **GS:** Y **SP:** Hannah Gore (1755-1810) **VI:** Son of John (__-1786) and Sarah (Morris) (__-1804) Osburn **P:** unk **BLW:** unk **RG:** unk **MK:** unk **PH:** unk **SS:** A pg 222-224 **BS:** 196.

OSPELL, Mathieu; b unk; d 1781 **RU:** Soldier, Served in Gatinais Bn and died fr battle at Yorktown **CEM:** French Memorial; GPS 36.81944, -79.39933; Yorktown; York **GS:** U **SP:** No info **VI:** No further data **P:** unk **BLW:** unk **RG:** Y **MK:** unk **PH:** unk **SS:** J-Yorktown Historian **BS:** JLARC 1, 74.

OTEY, John Armistead; b 1713 or 1735; d 1817 **RU:** Captain/Patriot, Gave material aid to cause **CEM:** Otey Street; GPS 37.33170, -79.52170; W Franklin St jct with Otey; Bedford **GS:** Y **SP:** Mary F Hopkins (1764-__) d/o John (1791-__) & Jean (Gordon) Hopkins **VI:** No further data **P:** unk **BLW:** unk **RG:** Y **MK:** N **PH:** unk **SS:** J-NSSAR 1993 Reg, J- DAR Hatcher; AL Ct Bk pg 6, 8, 9 Bedford Co **BS:** JLARC 1, 2; 196.

OUDOT, Claude; b unk; d 1781 **RU:** Soldier, Served in Gatinais Bn and died fr battle at Yorktown **CEM:** French Memorial; GPS 36.81944, -79.39933; Yorktown; York **GS:** U **SP:** No info **VI:** No further data **P:** unk **BLW:** unk **RG:** Y **MK:** unk **PH:** unk **SS:** J-Yorktown Historian **BS:** JLARC 1, 74.

OUIN, Jean; b unk; d 1781 **RU:** Seaman, Served on "Saint-Esprit" and died from Yorktown battle **CEM:** French Memorial; GPS 36.81944, -79.39933; Yorktown; York **GS:** U **SP:** No info **VI:** No further data **P:** unk **BLW:** unk **RG:** Y **MK:** unk **PH:** unk **SS:** J-Yorktown Historian **BS:** JLARC 1, 74.

OUVENANT, Rene; b unk; d 1781 **RU:** Seaman, Served on "Hercule" and died from Yorktown battle **CEM:** French Memorial; GPS 36.81944, -79.39933; Yorktown; York **GS:** U **SP:** No info **VI:** No further data **P:** unk **BLW:** unk **RG:** Y **MK:** unk **PH:** unk **SS:** J-Yorktown Historian **BS:** JLARC 1, 74.

RU=Rank/Unit	CEM=Cemetery	GS=Gravestone	SP=Spousal Information
VI=Other Veteran Info	P=Pension	BLW=Bounty/Land Warrant	RG=Registered Grave
MK=SAR/DAR Marker	PH=Photo	SS=Service Source	BS=Burial Source

253

OVERACRE (OVERAKER, OBERAKER, OBERACKER), George; b 15 May 1738 or 15 Apr 1733, Germany; d 15 Oct 1809 **RU:** Private/Patriot, Served in MD and VA. Served in Capt Adam Ott's Co of Select Militia, Washington Co, MD. Provided 870 lbs of beef for Cont Use, Frederick Co, VA **CEM:** Mt Hebron; GPS 39.10916, -78.09497; 305 E Boscawen St; Winchester City **GS:** Y **SP:** Margaret (-----) (9 Jan 1733-16 Jun 1804) **VI:** Died in Frederick Co. Recd BLW **P:** N **BLW:** Y **RG:** Y **MK:** Y **PH:** Y **SS:** AF pg 238; AL CT Bk 17 **BS:** 04; 50 pg 47.

OVERBEY, Peter Z; b 1759; d 13 Jun 1824 **RU:** Patriot, Gave 475# beef to Cont Army **CEM:** Overby & Holt Families; GPS unk; Rt 602 W; Mecklenburg **GS:** Y **SP:** Anne Yancey, d/o Robert & (-----) Yancey **VI:** No further data **P:** N **BLW:** N **RG:** N **MK:** N **PH:** unk **SS:** AL Ct Bk pg 16; DB pg 112 **BS:** 54 pg 223.

OVERBOKER (OFFENBACHER), Frederick; b c1735; d 27 Jun 1831 **RU:** Private, Served in Capt Michael Reader's Co, Dunmore Co Militia **CEM:** Offenbacher; GPS unk; Nr Stanley; Page **GS:** U **SP:** Mar (1796) Elizabeth (-----) (c1745-aft 1796) **VI:** No further data **P:** unk **BLW:** unk **RG:** unk **MK:** unk **PH:** unk **SS:** DAR #A085000; J- DAR Hatcher; C pg 603 **BS:** JLARC 2.

OWEN, James; b 1754, Campbell Co; d 26 Nov 1827 **RU:** Private, Served in 6th and 14th Cont Line **CEM:** Staunton Baptist; GPS 37.06970, -79.58140; 15267 Smith Mountain Lake Pkwy, Huddleston; Bedford **GS:** U **SP:** Mar (23 Oct 1776) Elizabeth Russell (1754 Campbell Co-26 Nov 1827) **VI:** No further data **P:** unk **BLW:** unk **RG:** unk **MK:** unk **PH:** unk **SS:** E pg 599 **BS:** 196.

OWEN, Owen; b 1750, New Castle, Lawrence Co, PA; d 3 Jun 1819 **RU:** Private, Served in Capt Moor's Co, Col Francis' 5th PA Regt **CEM:** Old City; GPS 37.41472, -79.15667; 401 Taylor St; Lynchburg City **GS:** Y **SP:** Jane Hughes (1760, Bedford Co-1835) **VI:** No further data **P:** N **BLW:** N **RG:** N **MK:** unk **PH:** N **SS:** AP payroll **BS:** 196.

OWINGS, Richard; b 13 Nov 1738, Baltimore Co, MD; d 7 Oct 1786 **RU:** Patriot, Performed public service on the Baltimore Circuit Ct in 1775 **CEM:** Old Stone Methodist; GPS 39.11725, -77.56609; 168 W Cornwall St, Leesburg; Loudoun **GS:** U **SP:** Mar (1759, Baltimore) Rachael (-----) (4 Nov 1737, Baltimore-aft Aug 1812, KY) **VI:** Son of Joshua (5 Apr 1704-11 Apr 1785) & Mary (Cockey) (10 Dec 1736-10 Dec 1768) Owings **P:** unk **BLW:** unk **RG:** unk **MK:** unk **PH:** unk **SS:** B plaque in cemetery **BS:** 196.

OZANNE, Pierre; b unk; d 1781 **RU:** Soldier, Served in Gatinais Bn and died fr battle at Yorktown **CEM:** French Memorial; GPS 36.81944, -79.39933; Yorktown; York **GS:** U **SP:** No info **VI:** No further data **P:** unk **BLW:** unk **RG:** Y **MK:** unk **PH:** unk **SS:** J-Yorktown Historian **BS:** JLARC 1, 74.

OZOU, Jean; b unk; d 1781 **RU:** Seaman, Served on "Hercule" and died from Yorktown battle **CEM:** French Memorial; GPS 36.81944, -79.39933; Yorktown; York **GS:** U **SP:** No info **VI:** No further data **P:** unk **BLW:** unk **RG:** Y **MK:** unk **PH:** unk **SS:** J-Yorktown Historian **BS:** JLARC 1, 74.

PABST, Christian; b unk; d 1781 **RU:** Soldier, Served in Royal Deaux Ponts Bn and died fr battle at Yorktown **CEM:** French Memorial; GPS 36.81944, -79.39933; Yorktown; York **GS:** U **SP:** No info **VI:** No further data **P:** unk **BLW:** unk **RG:** Y **MK:** unk **PH:** unk **SS:** J-Yorktown Historian **BS:** JLARC 1, 74.

PACE, John; b 28 May 1751; d 12 Apr 1822 **RU:** Patriot, Took oath of Allegiance 1778 in Henry Co **CEM:** Pace Family; GPS unk; Pace Airport Rd abt .5 mi past airport, Ridgeway; Henry **GS:** U **SP:** Mar (10 Sep 1772) Elizabeth Nunn **VI:** Title of Capt, thus probably served in militia during war period **P:** unk **BLW:** unk **RG:** unk **MK:** unk **PH:** unk **SS:** DAR Ancestor #A085511; DD cites VA Historical Mag Vol 9 pg 142 **BS:** 196.

PACE, William; b 11 Oct 1745, Goochland Co; d Bef 21 Oct 1815 **RU:** Sergeant, Served in VA Militia and as lifeguard for Gen George Washington **CEM:** Jones Family; GPS 36.61690, -82.68580; Rt 635, Yuma, across RR and E of Cowan Branch Baptist Ch; Scott **GS:** Y **SP:** Mary Winiger **VI:** Son of John H (14 Mar 172, Middlesex Co-20 Sep 1790) & Susannah (Houchin) (1723-1809) Pace **P:** unk **BLW:** unk **RG:** Y **MK:** Y **PH:** Y **SS:** H; O; AK **BS:** 04;196.

PACET, Etienne; b unk; d 1781 **RU:** Seaman, Served on "Sceptre" and died from Yorktown battle **CEM:** French Memorial; GPS 36.81944, -79.39933; Yorktown; York **GS:** U **SP:** No info **VI:** No further data **P:** unk **BLW:** unk **RG:** Y **MK:** unk **PH:** unk **SS:** J-Yorktown Historian **BS:** JLARC 1,74.

RU=Rank/Unit
VI=Other Veteran Info
MK=SAR/DAR Marker

CEM=Cemetery
P=Pension
PH=Photo

GS=Gravestone
BLW=Bounty/Land Warrant
SS=Service Source

SP=Spousal Information
RG=Registered Grave
BS=Burial Source

PACKWOOD, Samuel; b 1750; d 15 Aug 1824 **RU:** Private, Served in Capt John Cunningham's Co, Henry Co Militia 1781 **CEM:** Prillaman; GPS 37.01080, -80.06080; Foothills Rd Rt 642 W of Highland United Methodist, Callaway; Franklin **GS:** U **SP:** Mar (c1769) Elizabeth Turner (1747, Amelia Co-2 Aug 1845) d/o Shadrack & Ann (Pollard) Turner of Pittsylvania Co **VI:** Son of Samuel & Penelope (Stout) Packwood **P:** unk **BLW:** unk **RG:** unk **MK:** unk **PH:** unk **SS:** J- DAR Hatcher; G pg 186 **BS:** JLARC 2;196.

PADGETT, Frederick; b 1753 or 1754, Essex Co; d 22 Sep 1846 **RU:** Soldier, Ent Serv Amherst Co in VA Line **CEM:** Millner Estate; GPS unk; See property records; Bedford **GS:** U **SP:** Mar (30 Apr 1787 Amherst Co) Lucia Magan **VI:** Son of Edmund & Mary (-----) Padgett. Pension application 22 Jul 1833 Bedford Co. S8930, possibly pensioned in Bedford in 1828 **P:** Y **BLW:** unk **RG:** unk **MK:** N **PH:** unk **SS:** J- DAR Hatcher; CG Vol 3 pg 2571 **BS:** JLARC 2.

PAGE, Carter; b c1758; d 9 Apr 1825 **RU:** Captain, Served in Capt 3rd Continental Dragoons and Aide-de-Camp to Gen Nelson, and later Lafayette **CEM:** Page Family, "The Fork"; GPS unk; See Source 101; Cumberland **GS:** N **SP:** 1) (-----) 2) mar (14 Dec 1799 Yorktown) Lucy Nelson (c1777-__) d/o General Thomas & (-----) Nelson **VI:** Widow pensioned 11 Jun 1849 Cumberland Co age 72 **P:** Y **BLW:** unk **RG:** unk **MK:** N **PH:** N **SS:** CG Vol 3 pg 2568 **BS:** JLARC 4,101.

PAGE, John; b 17 Apr 1743, "Rosewell" Gloucester Co; d 11 Oct 1808 **RU:** Colonel/Patriot, Was Delegate to VA Const Convention 1776 and Counselor of State by appt by Gov Patrick Henry 5 July 1776. Became Lt Gov VA 76-79. Raised Regt of troops for Gloucestor Co Milita. Was member State House of delegates 1781-83 **CEM:** St John's Episcopal; GPS 37.53183, -77.41958; 2401 E Broad St; Richmond City **GS:** Y **SP:** No info **VI:** Son of (-----) & Alice Grymes (1724-1813). US Rep fr VA 1789-97. Governor of VA 1802-05. Was serving as US Commissioner of Loans for VA at time of death **P:** unk **BLW:** unk **RG:** Y **MK:** N **PH:** unk **SS:** G pg 777 **BS:** 28 pg 493.

PAGE, John; b 1720; d 1780 **RU:** Patriot, Was member Committee of Safety Mathews Co **CEM:** Page home; GPS unk; North portion of Co; Mathews **GS:** U **SP:** Jane Byrd **VI:** No further data **P:** N **BLW:** N **RG:** N **MK:** N **PH:** unk **SS:** AS SAR applic **BS:** SAR Appl.

PAGE, John; b 29 Jun 1760, Hanover Co; d 17 Sep 1838 **RU:** Private, Served in 5th, 7th and 9th Cont Line **CEM:** Old Chapel Episcopal; GPS 39.10670, -78.01470; Jct US 340 & Rt 255, Millwood; Clarke **GS:** U **SP:** Mar (27 May 1784) Maria Horsemanden Byrd (26 Nov 1761, Philadelphia-__) d/o William (6 Sep 1728-1 Jan 1777) & Mary (-----) (10 Sep 1740-Mar 1814) Byrd **VI:** No further data **P:** unk **BLW:** unk **RG:** unk **MK:** unk **PH:** unk **SS:** E pg 601 **BS:** 196.

PAGE, Mann III; b 1749, Gloucester Co; d 1781 **RU:** Colonel/Patriot, Commissioned Col 16 Aug 1781. Elected to Cont Congress 1777 **CEM:** Page Family; GPS unk; Mansfield Hall; Spotsylvania **GS:** Y **SP:** Mary Tayloe (28 Oct 1759-26 Jan 1835) d/o Hon. Joen & (-----) Tayloe of Mt Airy **VI:** Son of Mann (1716-1764) and Ann Corbin (Tayloe) Page (1723-__). Graduate of William & Mary, lawyer. House of Burgesses **P:** unk **BLW:** unk **RG:** N **MK:** N **PH:** unk **SS:** Cont Congress 77; E pg 601 **BS:** 130 Gloucester; 196.

PAGE, Robert; b 4 Feb 1765, Mathews Co; d 8 Dec 1840 **RU:** Captain, Served in Frederick Co Militia **CEM:** Old Chapel Episcopal; GPS 39.10670, -78.01470; Jct US 340 & Rt 255, Millwood; Clarke **GS:** Y **SP:** Mar (1788) Sarah N. Page (16 Feb 1766 Hanover Co-4 Apr 1843) **VI:** Attended College of William & Mary. Served VA House of Delegates and US Congress 1799-1801 **P:** N **BLW:** N **RG:** unk **MK:** unk **PH:** unk **SS:** DAR Ancestor #A985888; E pg 601 **BS:** 196.

PAILLARD, Jean; b unk; d 1781 **RU:** Seaman, Served on "Auguste" and died from Yorktown battle **CEM:** French Memorial; GPS 36.81944, -79.39933; Yorktown; York **GS:** U **SP:** No info **VI:** No further data **P:** unk **BLW:** unk **RG:** Y **MK:** unk **PH:** unk **SS:** J-Yorktown Historian **BS:** JLARC 1, 74.

PAINE, Thomas; b c1739, Spotsylvania Co; d Bef 5 Sep 1815 **RU:** Patriot, Gave material aid to cause **CEM:** Unidentified; GPS unk; Gordonsville; Orange **GS:** Y **SP:** Mar (18 Nov 1773) Elizabeth (-----) **VI:** Son of John (1705-1770) & Frances (Coleman) (1710-1783) Paine. Will probated 5 Sep 1815 **P:** N **BLW:** N **RG:** unk **MK:** unk **PH:** unk **SS:** DAR Newsletter, Sep/Oct 2015 Vol 15 No 5 pg 417 **BS:**196.

RU=Rank/Unit   CEM=Cemetery   GS=Gravestone   SP=Spousal Information
VI=Other Veteran Info P=Pension   BLW=Bounty/Land Warrant   RG=Registered Grave
MK=SAR/DAR Marker   PH=Photo   SS=Service Source   BS=Burial Source

255

PALIS, Paul; b unk; d 1781 **RU:** Seaman, Served in Gatinais Bn and died fr battle at Yorktown **CEM:** French Memorial; GPS 36.81944, -79.39933; Yorktown; York **GS:** U **SP:** No info **VI:** No further data **P:** unk **BLW:** unk **RG:** Y **MK:** unk **PH:** unk **SS:** J-Yorktown Historian **BS:** JLARC 1, 74.

PALMER, Job; b c1759; d 1820 **RU:** Corporal, Served in a RI Regt and was on a prison ship in NY harbor on 18 May 1781 **CEM:** St Paul's Episcopal; GPS 36.84733, -76.28554; 201 St Paul's Blvd; Norfolk City **GS:** Y **SP:** No info **VI:** No further data **P:** unk **BLW:** unk **RG:** N **MK:** N **PH:** unk **SS:** AP RI roll **BS:** 139.

PALUT, Louis; b unk; d 1781 **RU:** Seaman, Served on "Ville de Paris" and died from Yorktown battle **CEM:** French Memorial; GPS 36.81944, -79.39933; Yorktown; York **GS:** U **SP:** No info **VI:** No further data **P:** unk **BLW:** unk **RG:** Y **MK:** unk **PH:** unk **SS:** J-Yorktown Historian **BS:** JLARC 1, 74.

PALY, B; b unk; d 1781 **RU:** Soldier, Served in Gatinais Bn and died fr battle at Yorktown **CEM:** French Memorial; GPS 36.81944, -79.39933; Yorktown; York **GS:** U **SP:** No info **VI:** No further data **P:** unk **BLW:** unk **RG:** Y **MK:** unk **PH:** unk **SS:** J-Yorktown Historian **BS:** JLARC 1, 74.

PANIOLET, Jean; b unk; d 1781 **RU:** Soldier, Served in Bourbonnais Bn and died fr battle at Yorktown **CEM:** French Memorial; GPS 36.81944, -79.39933; Yorktown; York **GS:** U **SP:** No info **VI:** No further data **P:** unk **BLW:** unk **RG:** Y **MK:** unk **PH:** unk **SS:** J-Yorktown Historian **BS:** JLARC 1, 74.

PANKEY, John; b 1736, Goochland Co; d 1810 **RU:** Patriot, Gave material aid to cause **CEM:** Pankey Family; GPS unk; Tower Hill, Appomattox; Appomattox **GS:** U **SP:** Keziah Chambers (c1762-8 Jul 1832) **VI:** Died in Buckingham Co **P:** N **BLW:** N **RG:** unk **MK:** unk **PH:** unk **SS:** AL Ct Bk pg 4, 31 **BS:** 196.

PANNILL, William; b 30 Oct 1738; d 22 Sep 1806 **RU:** Patriot, Donated food to cause **CEM:** Green-Level Family; GPS unk; Rt 663 so of True Blue Corners; Orange **GS:** N **SP:** Ann Morton d/o Jeremiah & Sarah (Mallory) Morton **VI:** Son of William & Sarah (Baily) Pannill of Urbanna, Middlesex Co. Was Sheriff of Orange Co. Burial in family plot known as Green Level **P:** N **BLW:** N **RG:** Y **MK:** N **PH:** N **SS:** D **BS:** 04, Sep 07.

PAON, Jean; b unk; d 1781 **RU:** Seaman, Served on "Saint-Esprit" and died from Yorktown battle **CEM:** French Memorial; GPS 36.81944, -79.39933; Yorktown; York **GS:** U **SP:** No info **VI:** No further data **P:** unk **BLW:** unk **RG:** Y **MK:** unk **PH:** unk **SS:** J-Yorktown Historian **BS:** JLARC 1, 74.

PAPELARD, Jacques; b unk; d 1781 **RU:** Soldier, Served in Agenois Bn and died fr battle at Yorktown **CEM:** French Memorial; GPS 36.81944, -79.39933; Yorktown; York **GS:** U **SP:** No info **VI:** No further data **P:** unk **BLW:** unk **RG:** Y **MK:** unk **PH:** unk **SS:** J-Yorktown Historian **BS:** JLARC 1, 74.

PAPON, Louis; b unk; d 1781 **RU:** Seaman, Served on "Sceptre" and died from Yorktown battle **CEM:** French Memorial; GPS 36.81944, -79.39933; Yorktown; York **GS:** U **SP:** No info **VI:** No further data **P:** unk **BLW:** unk **RG:** Y **MK:** unk **PH:** unk **SS:** J-Yorktown Historian **BS:** JLARC 1, 74.

PARIEL, Leonard; b unk; d 1781 **RU:** Soldier, Served in Touraine Bn and died fr battle at Yorktown **CEM:** French Memorial; GPS 36.81944, -79.39933; Yorktown; York **GS:** U **SP:** No info **VI:** No further data **P:** unk **BLW:** unk **RG:** Y **MK:** unk **PH:** unk **SS:** J-Yorktown Historian **BS:** JLARC 1, 74.

PARIS, Claude; b unk; d 1781 **RU:** Soldier, Served in Auxonne Bn and died fr battle at Yorktown **CEM:** French Memorial; GPS 36.81944, -79.39933; Yorktown; York **GS:** U **SP:** No info **VI:** No further data **P:** unk **BLW:** unk **RG:** Y **MK:** unk **PH:** unk **SS:** J-Yorktown Historian **BS:** JLARC 1, 74.

PARIS, Gabriel; b unk; d 1781 **RU:** Soldier, Served in Santogne Bn and died fr battle at Yorktown **CEM:** French Memorial; GPS 36.81944, -79.39933; Yorktown; York **GS:** U **SP:** No info **VI:** No further data **P:** unk **BLW:** unk **RG:** Y **MK:** unk **PH:** unk **SS:** J-Yorktown Historian **BS:** JLARC 1, 74.

PARIS, Jacques de; b unk; d 1781 **RU:** Soldier, Served in Brie Bn and died fr battle at Yorktown **CEM:** French Memorial; GPS 36.81944, -79.39933; Yorktown; York **GS:** U **SP:** No info **VI:** No further data **P:** unk **BLW:** unk **RG:** Y **MK:** unk **PH:** unk **SS:** J-Yorktown Historian **BS:** JLARC 1, 74.

PARKER, Ebenezer; b 1749, Westford MA; d 29 Dec 1831 **RU:** Private, Served in Capt Jonathan Minot's Co, Col Prescott's MA Regt in Lexington Alarm **CEM:** St John's Episcopal; GPS 37.53183 -

RU=Rank/Unit   CEM=Cemetery   GS=Gravestone   SP=Spousal Information
VI=Other Veteran Info   P=Pension   BLW=Bounty/Land Warrant   RG=Registered Grave
MK=SAR/DAR Marker   PH=Photo   SS=Service Source   BS=Burial Source

256

77.41958; 2401 E Broad St; Richmond City **GS:** U **SP:** Mar (1777) Experience Keep Hildreth (1752-1817) **VI:** No further data **P:** unk **BLW:** unk **RG:** Y **MK:** unk **PH:** unk **SS:** DD **BS:** JLARC 1, 76.

PARKER, Elias; b 3 Jun 1760, Boston, MA; d 8 Dec 1799 **RU:** Lieutenant, Served in Col Joseph Vose's 1st MA Regt **CEM:** Blandford; GPS 37.22433, -77.38604; 319 S Crater St; Petersburg City **GS:** Y **SP:** Mar (29 Sep 1790, Trinity Church, Boston) Mary Brown Parker **VI:** Son of Daniel & Margaret (-----) Parker. Mayor of Petersburg 1796 to 1797. DAR marker. Spouse awarded pen 4 Mar 1843 of $400 a yr **P:** Y **BLW:** unk **RG:** unk **MK:** Y **PH:** unk **SS:** BT **BS:** 196.

PARKER, George; b 28 Oct 1735; d 3 Sep 1784 **RU:** Patriot, Gave material aid to the cause **CEM:** Poplar Cove Wharf; GPS unk; Nr end of Rt 653, Onancock; Accomack **GS:** Y **SP:** Adah Bagwell (12 Sep 1734-26 Aug 1766) **VI:** No further data **P:** N **BLW:** N **RG:** N **MK:** N **PH:** unk **SS:** E pg 603; AL Comm Bk 1 pg 30 **BS:** 37 pg 193.

PARKER, Josiah; b 11 May 1751 Macclesfield, Isle of Wight; d 10 Mar 1810 **RU:** Colonel/Patriot, Served in VA Regt at Trenton. Recd British sword of surrender at Trenton. Fought at Princeton & Brandywine. Was commander of VA Militia south of James 1781. Commanded the unit that defeated Tarleton at Scotts Old Field (1781). Was Nominal Commander at Yorktown. Served in VA House of Delegates (1779-1783). **CEM:** Parker Family; GPS 36.58569, -76.32136; 3.5 mi E of Rescue, Macclesfield; Isle of Wight **GS:** Y **SP:** Mary Pierce Bridger **VI:** Son of Nicolas & Ann (Copeland) Parker. Served as Naval officer in Portsmouth, VA in 1786. Elected to first six US Congresses, serving 1789-1801. Exact location of grave unk. VS12VA **P:** Y **BLW:** unk **RG:** unk **MK:** N **PH:** unk **SS:** AK **BS:** 04.

PARKER, Nicholas; b 31 Oct 1722, Macclesfield, Isle of Wight; d 1789 **RU:** Patriot, Gave material aid to cause **CEM:** Parker Family; GPS 36.58569, -76.32136; 3.5 mi E of Rescue, Macclesfield; Isle of Wight **GS:** N **SP:** Ann Copeland **VI:** Earned rank of Lt Col before Rev War, probably in county militia. Commemorative marker exists **P:** N **BLW:** N **RG:** N **MK:** N **PH:** N **SS:** AK Ct Bk pg 14; AP Roll, SAR Applic **BS:** 04; 153 macclesfield.

PARKER, Thomas; b 1757; d Dec 1819 **RU:** Captain, Served in VA Line fr 1775 to end of war. Was prisoner at Germantown and confined on British ship **CEM:** Poplar Grove; GPS 36.58569, -76.32133; Off Rt 180, Pungoteague, Hack's Neck; Accomack **GS:** Y **SP:** No info **VI:** Recd BLW **P:** unk **BLW:** Y **RG:** N **MK:** N **PH:** unk **SS:** G pg 770; N pg 1028; BY pg 79; CG pg 2596 **BS:** 37 pg 193,194.

PARKER, Thomas; b 1753; d 24 Jan 1820 **RU:** Captain, Served 23 Apr 1778, 5th Cont Line 12 Feb 1781 and 1st Cont Line Jan 1783 **CEM:** St James Episcopal, Old Cemetery; GPS 39.11555, -77.56250; Church St NE, Leesburg; Loudoun **GS:** U **SP:** No info **VI:** Was Brig Gen War of 1812 **P:** unk **BLW:** Y **RG:** unk **MK:** unk **PH:** unk **SS:** E pg 604 **BS:** 196.

PARKER, Timothy; b unk; d 14 Oct 1781 **RU:** Private, Served in Ct Troops Cont line. Died fr the battle at Yorktown **CEM:** Yorktown Victory Monument Tablet; GPS 38.28350, -78.54150; Yorktown; York **GS:** U **SP:** No info **VI:** BLW 259-100 **P:** unk **BLW:** Y **RG:** unk **MK:** unk **PH:** unk **SS:** J-Yorktown Historian; DY 342 **BS:** JLARC 74.

PARKER, William Harwar; b 1759; d 1815 **RU:** Captain, Served in VA Navy on "Tempest." Was wounded **CEM:** McIlhaney Family; GPS unk; Nr Hillsboro E side Rt 690 btw Rts 90 & 611; Loudoun **GS:** U **SP:** No info **VI:** BLW of 2667 acre as Lt for 3 yrs serv was awarded 23 Jun 1783 **P:** unk **BLW:** Y **RG:** unk **MK:** unk **PH:** unk **SS:** E pg 604; G pg 778; L pg 102 **BS:** JLARC 4,32.

PARKINS, Isaac; b Nov 1746, Frederick Co; d 15 Feb 1829 **RU:** Patriot, Gave material aid to the cause in Frederick Co **CEM:** Hollingsworth-Parkins; GPS 39.16600, -78.17490; W Jubal Early Dr; Frederick **GS:** Y **SP:** Mary Steer (1752-1842) **VI:** Died in Winchester, Frederick Co **P:** N **BLW:** N **RG:** unk **MK:** unk **PH:** Y **SS:** AL Ct Bk pg 20, 40 **BS:** 196.

PARKINSON, Joseph Christian; b unk; d 1845 **RU:** Patriot, Gave material aid to cause **CEM:** St John's Episcopal; GPS 37.53183, -77.41958; 2401 E Broad St; Richmond City **GS:** N **SP:** Mar (25 Jan 1842, Richmond) Ann Elizabeth Quarles **VI:** No further data **P:** N **BLW:** N **RG:** N **MK:** N **PH:** N **SS:** D Vol 3 pg 712; AL Ct Bk pg 17 New Kent Co **BS:** 28, pg 351; 196.

RU=Rank/Unit	CEM=Cemetery	GS=Gravestone	SP=Spousal Information
VI=Other Veteran Info	P=Pension	BLW=Bounty/Land Warrant	RG=Registered Grave
MK=SAR/DAR Marker	PH=Photo	SS=Service Source	BS=Burial Source

257

PARKS, John; b 1713; d Jul 1793 **RU:** Patriot, Gave material aid to cause **CEM:** McDowell; GPS 37.86860, -79.31080; Nr jct Rts 11 and 712, Fairfield; Rockbridge **GS:** Y **SP:** No info **VI:** No further data **P:** N **BLW:** N **RG:** unk **MK:** unk **PH:** unk **SS:** Al Ct Bk pg 9 Rockbridge Co **BS:** 196.

PARKS, Joseph; b unk; d 21 Aug 1810 **RU:** Private, Served as Private in Illinois Regt **CEM:** Tinkling Spring Presbyterian; GPS 38.08472, -78.98278; 30 Tinkling Spring Dr, Fishersville; Augusta **GS:** Y **SP:** Rebekah (-----) (1734-Dec 1794) **VI:** Stone nearly illegible and wedged bet tree trunks **P:** unk **BLW:** unk **RG:** unk **MK:** N **PH:** unk **SS:** E pg 605 **BS:** 208 pg 466; 196.

PARMENTER, James; b unk; d 1781 **RU:** Soldier, Served fr MA and died as result of Yorktown battle **CEM:** Yorktown Victory Monument Tablet; GPS 38.28350, -78.54150; Yorktown; York **GS:** U **SP:** No info **VI:** No further data **P:** unk **BLW:** unk **RG:** unk **MK:** unk **PH:** unk **SS:** J-Yorktown Historian **BS:** JLARC 74.

PARRAMORE, William; b 27 Dec 1741; d 4 Jun 1816 **RU:** Colonel, Promoted to Col, Accomack Co Militia on 30 Apr 1782 **CEM:** Belle Vue; GPS unk; Off Rt 646, 7 mi E of Locustville; Accomack **GS:** Y **SP:** Sarah Seymore (c1739-25 Apr 1802 age 63) d/o Digby & Rose Seymore of Northampton Co **VI:** Son of Thomas & Joannah (-----) Parramore **P:** unk **BLW:** unk **RG:** N **MK:** N **PH:** unk **SS:** E pg 605 **BS:** 37 pg 201.

PARRE, Pierre; b unk; d 1781 **RU:** Seaman, Served on "Duc De Bourgogne" and died from Yorktown battle **CEM:** French Memorial; GPS 36.81944, -79.39933; Yorktown; York **GS:** U **SP:** No info **VI:** No further data **P:** unk **BLW:** unk **RG:** Y **MK:** unk **PH:** unk **SS:** J-Yorktown Historian **BS:** JLARC 1, 74.

PASCON (PASCOW, PASCHO), Herbert; b c1741; d 3 Apr or 21 May 1801 **RU:** Lieutenant, Served in VA Navy on Boat "Liberty" 1777 to late 1781 **CEM:** Herbert; GPS 39.01475, -76.35013; Off Armstrong Ln; Hampton City **GS:** N **SP:** Mary (-----) **VI:** Recd BLW of 2666 acres **P:** unk **BLW:** Y **RG:** unk **MK:** unk **PH:** N **SS:** C pg 52; BY **BS:** 202 WPA Hampton City.

PATALIER, Joseph; b unk; d 1781 **RU:** Soldier, Served in Santogne Bn and died fr battle at Yorktown **CEM:** French Memorial; GPS 36.81944, -79.39933; Yorktown; York **GS:** U **SP:** No info **VI:** No further data **P:** unk **BLW:** unk **RG:** Y **MK:** unk **PH:** unk **SS:** J-Yorktown Historian **BS:** JLARC 1, 74.

PATRICK, John; b 1732, PA; d 1809 **RU:** Patriot, Gave material aid to cause **CEM:** Patrick family; GPS unk; Locust Isle, Rt 865 N fr Waynesboro; Waynesboro City **GS:** Y **SP:** Janet McPheeters (1739-Jun 1820) **VI:** Son of Robert & Rachel (-----) Patrick **P:** N **BLW:** N **RG:** unk **MK:** U **PH:** unk **SS:** AL Ct Bk pg 8 Augusta Co **BS:** JLARC 62; 196.

PATRICK, William; b 21 Jan 1763; d 1835 **RU:** Soldier, Ent serv Augusta Co. Served in VA Line **CEM:** Patrick Family; GPS unk; Locust Isle, Rt 865 N fr Waynesboro; Waynesboro City **GS:** U **SP:** No info **VI:** Pension appl 25 Sep 1832 age 69. S5882 **P:** Y **BLW:** unk **RG:** unk **MK:** U **PH:** unk **SS:** K Vol 4 pg 72; CG Vol 3 pg 2616 **BS:** JLARC 4, 8, 62.

PATTERSON, Samuel; b unk; d 26 Mar 1797 **RU:** First Lieutenant, Promoted 1st Lt 01 Sep 1778 **CEM:** Fincastle Presbyterian; GPS 37.50017, -79.87558; 108 E Back St, Fincastle; Botetourt **GS:** Y **SP:** No info **VI:** Name is on the plaque as a 1st Lt **P:** unk **BLW:** unk **RG:** unk **MK:** Y **PH:** unk **SS:** AZ pg 228 **BS:** 196.

PATTERSON, William; b 1752; d 16 Feb 1816 **RU:** Sergeant, Served in Capt John Hay's Co, 9th VA Regt Jun 1777 **CEM:** Trinity United Methodist; GPS 39.13600, -77.00610; 2911 Cameron Mills Rd; Alexandria City **GS:** Y **SP:** Mary (-----) **VI:** No further data **P:** unk **BLW:** unk **RG:** N **MK:** N **PH:** unk **SS:** AP roll **BS:** 23 pg 135.

PATTERSON, William; b 1760, Augusta Co; d 25 Jan 1825 **RU:** Soldier?/Patriot, Gave material aid to cause. He perhaps is the man this name that was a private in the 11th Cont Line or the one who was in General John Clark's Illinois Regt **CEM:** Old Crockett; GPS 37.04161, -80.97662; Rt 600, Crockett's Creek Rd, Wytheville; Wythe **GS:** Y **SP:** Agnes Patton (1765 Botetourt Co-1843 Giles Co) d/o John J. (1689-1757) & Agness (Snodgrass) (1715-___) Patton **VI:** No further data **P:** N **BLW:** N **RG:** unk **MK:** unk **PH:** unk **SS:** AL Ct Bk pg 45 Montgomery Co **BS:** 196.

RU=Rank/Unit	CEM=Cemetery	GS=Gravestone	SP=Spousal Information
VI=Other Veteran Info	P=Pension	BLW=Bounty/Land Warrant	RG=Registered Grave
MK=SAR/DAR Marker	PH=Photo	SS=Service Source	BS=Burial Source

258

PATTESON, David; b 30 Aug 1746, Chesterfield Co; d 2 May 1821 **RU:** First Lieutenant, Served in Chesterfield Militia.Took oath as Lt 30 Oct 1777 **CEM:** Patteson Family; GPS unk; Laurel Meadows; Richmond City **GS:** U **SP:** Eliza Ann Jordan **VI:** Died in Chesterfield Co **P:** unk **BLW:** unk **RG:** Y **MK:** N **PH:** unk **SS:** AC **BS:** 04.

PATTESON, David; b 15 Aug 1758; d 22 Oct 1846 **RU:** Major, Was a Cadet in 1776 **CEM:** Patteson Family; GPS unk; Mt Pleasant; Buckingham **GS:** N **SP:** Judith Dibrel **VI:** Son of Thomas (1735-1790) & (-----) Paterson (Patteson?). No GS but on memorial stone **P:** unk **BLW:** unk **RG:** unk **MK:** N **PH:** N **SS:** E pg 609 **BS:** JLARC 59; 52 pg 443; 196.

PATTESON, Thomas; b 1735; d 1790 **RU:** Captain, Ent serv Buckingham Co. Served in 6th VA Militia **CEM:** Patteson Family; GPS unk; Mt Pleasant; Buckingham **GS:** N **SP:** No info **VI:** Pension appl 24 Jul 1832 Davidson Co, TN. S2011 **P:** Y **BLW:** unk **RG:** unk **MK:** N **PH:** unk **SS:** CG Vol 3 pg 2621; NSSAR Ancestor # P-266801 **BS:** JLARC 59.

PATTON, Henry; b unk; d Aft 1779 **RU:** Captain, Commanded a co in Montgomery Co Militia 7 Sep 1779 **CEM:** Patton Family; GPS unk; nr Dublin; Pulaski **GS:** U **SP:** No info **VI:** No further data **P:** unk **BLW:** unk **RG:** N **MK:** N **PH:** unk **SS:** E pg 609 **BS:** 80 vol 3 pg 155.

PAUL, Nicholas; b 1728 or 1729, PA or Germany; d 1817 **RU:** Second Lieutenant, Was 2nd Lt in 3rd Co, 5th Bn, Northhampton Co, PA Militia 1777. Served in Capt George Noff's 7th Co, 3rd Bn, PA Militia **CEM:** Dayton; GPS 38.42000, -78.94303; Bowman Rd, Dayton; Rockingham **GS:** Y **SP:** 1) Catharine (-----) 2) Barbara Hess. Order unk. **VI:** No further data **P:** unk **BLW:** unk **RG:** Y **MK:** Y **PH:** Y **SS:** J-NSSAR 1993 Reg; S Ancestor #P266934; DAR # A086620 **BS:** JLARC 1.

PAUL, Peter; b 1759 or 1760; d 16 Feb 1844 **RU:** Ensign, Served in Flying Camp of militia in PA. Was Prisoner of War and exchanged 15 Aug 1778 **CEM:** Dayton; GPS 38.42000, -78.94303; Bowman Rd, Dayton; Rockingham **GS:** Y **SP:** Catharine Swope **VI:** No further data **P:** unk **BLW:** unk **RG:** Y **MK:** Y **PH:** Y **SS:** J-NSSAR 1993 Reg; NSSAR Ancestor #P-266937 **BS:** JLARC 1.

PAULARD, Jean; b unk; d 1781 **RU:** Soldier, Served in Gatinais Bn and died fr battle at Yorktown **CEM:** French Memorial; GPS 36.81944, -79.39933; Yorktown; York **GS:** U **SP:** No info **VI:** No further data **P:** unk **BLW:** unk **RG:** unk **MK:** unk **PH:** unk **SS:** J-Yorktown Historian **BS:** JLARC 1, 74.

PAXTON, John; b 1747, Augusta Co; d 8 Aug 1832 **RU:** Captain/Patriot, Commanded co in Rockbridge Co Militia. Served at Point Pleasant in 1777. Gave material aid to cause **CEM:** Glasgow Cemetery; GPS 37.60320, -79.45914; 13th St & Fitzlee, Glasgow; Rockbridge **GS:** Y **SP:** Mar (c1772) Sarah Walker (20 Jun 1750, Augusta Co-24 Nov 1839) **VI:** No further data **P:** unk **BLW:** unk **RG:** unk **MK:** unk **PH:** unk **SS:** DAR #A086701; AL Ct Bk pg 3, 7 Rockbridge Co; AZ pg 42 **BS:** JLARC 79; 196.

PAXTON, John Sr; b 1716, PA; d 13 Feb 1787 **RU:** Patriot, Gave material aid to cause **CEM:** Timber Grove; GPS unk; Buffalo Dist, Timber Ridge; Rockbridge **GS:** N **SP:** Mar (1742 Lancaster, PA) Mary Martha Blair (1726 Ireland-12 Aug 1821) d/o Samuel (1667-1754) & Martha Campbell (Lye) Blair **VI:** No further data **P:** N **BLW:** N **RG:** unk **MK:** unk **PH:** N **SS:** D Vol 3 pg 822, 826 **BS:** 196.

PAXTON, Thomas; b c1719; d 27 Sep 1788 **RU:** Patriot, Gave material aid to cause **CEM:** Paxton Family; GPS 37.71666, -79.40271; Forge Rd, Mechanicsville; Rockbridge **GS:** Y **SP:** 1) Elizabeth McClung (1724-1773) 2) Mary Barclay **VI:** No further data **P:** N **BLW:** N **RG:** unk **MK:** unk **PH:** unk **SS:** DAR Newsletter, Sep/Oct 2015 Vol 15 No 5 pg 417 **BS:** 196.

PAXTON, William; b 7 Apr 1757, Rockbridge Co; d 27 Dec 1838 **RU:** Captain, Commanded a co in Rockbridge Co Militia 5 May 1778 to 1781 **CEM:** Falling Springs Presbyterian; GPS 37.68526 -79.44972; 410 Falling Springs Rd, Glasgow; Rockbridge **GS:** Y **SP:** Mar (Jun 1787) Jane Grigsby, daug of John & (-----) Grigsby **VI:** Pension appl 17 Aug 1832 Rockbridge Co. S5873. Source 2 has him bur on McCormick Farm, Served 3 mos in Whiskey Insurrection in PA in 1794 **P:** Y **BLW:** unk **RG:** Y **MK:** Y **PH:** Y **SS:** CG Vol 3 pg 2625; E pg 610 **BS:** JLARC 1, 2, 63.

PAXTON, William; b unk; d Aft 1781 **RU:** Major/Patriot, Gave material aid to cause **CEM:** Old Graveyard nr Wesley Chapel; GPS unk; Glasgow; Rockbridge **GS:** U **SP:** No info **VI:** No further data **P:** unk **BLW:** unk **RG:** unk **MK:** unk **PH:** unk **SS:** SAR Ancestor #P-267028; AL Ct Bk pg 3 Rockbridge Co **BS:** JLARC 79.

RU=Rank/Unit	CEM=Cemetery	GS=Gravestone	SP=Spousal Information
VI=Other Veteran Info	P=Pension	BLW=Bounty/Land Warrant	RG=Registered Grave
MK=SAR/DAR Marker	PH=Photo	SS=Service Source	BS=Burial Source

259

PAXTON, William Sr; b 1732; d 30 Sep 1795 **RU:** Captain/Patriot, Appointed Capt 5 May 1778 in Rockbridge Co Militia and served to 1781. Gave material aid to the cause **CEM:** Mt Zion Methodist; **GPS** 37.66596, -79.46615; Btw Buffalo & Tinkersville; Rockbridge **GS:** Y **SP:** Elanor (-----) (c1741-13 Aug 1815) **VI:** No further data **P:** unk **BLW:** unk **RG:** N **MK:** N **PH:** unk **SS:** E pg 610; AL Ct Bk pg 3; CZ pg 343 **BS:** JLARC 79; 193; 154 Rockbridge.

PAYNE, Augustine; b 11 Dec 1761; d 16 Mar 1844 **RU:** Private, Ent serv Fauquier Co. Served in John O'Bannon's Co, Fauquier Co Militia, wounded in service **CEM:** Orlean; **GPS** unk; Nr Orlean; Fauquier **GS:** Y **SP:** A man by this name mar (1787 Fauquier Co, bond dated 14 Jan 1789) Catharine "Caty" Young (12 Jul 1769-__) d/o Harmon & (-----) Young **VI:** Pension appl 31 Aug 1832 Fauquier Co. Moved to Parke Co, IN in 1835 and d there in Raccoon Twp. Widow appl pen 19 Dec 1844 Parke Co, IN. W10850 **P:** Y **BLW:** unk **RG:** Y **MK:** N **PH:** unk **SS:** K Vol 4 pg 78; CG Vol 3 pg 2625; Fauquier Co Marriages pg 154 **BS:** JLARC 1.

PAYNE, Daniel; b 1728; d 1796 **RU:** Patriot, In 1777 was named a trustee for Falmouth in Stafford Co. Also was Treasurer **CEM:** Payne Family, aka Cedar Hill; **GPS** 38.13357, -76.97069; Red house, Horners, 2 mi NE of Leedstown; Westmoreland **GS:** U **SP:** Never mar **VI:** One of three to inventory James Hunter's estate in 1785 owner of Hunter Iron Works that provided weapons and equipment during Rev War **P:** N **BLW:** N **RG:** N **MK:** N **PH:** unk **SS:** J pg 211 Pub serv **BS:** 34 pg 211.

PAYNE, Francis; b 1743; d 1816 **RU:** Ensign, Served in Fauquier Co Militia; oath for ensign Feb 1799 **CEM:** Orlean; **GPS** unk; Nr Orlean; Fauquier **GS:** Y **SP:** A man by this name mar (bond 4 Nov 1807, John Nelson security) Patsy Withers **VI:** No further data **P:** unk **BLW:** unk **RG:** Y **MK:** N **PH:** unk **SS:** J-NSSAR 1993 Reg; Fauquier Co Marriages pg 154 **BS:** JLARC 1.

PAYNE, George; b 1743; d 1831 **RU:** Lieutenant Colonel, Appointed Lt Col of Goochland Co Militia, 20 Aug 1781 **CEM:** Grace Episcopal; **GPS** 37.68321, -77.88765; 2955 River Rd West, Goochland CH; Goochland **GS:** Y **SP:** Mar (31 Dec 1765) Betty McCartey-Morton by Rev William Douglas **VI:** No further data **P:** unk **BLW:** unk **RG:** N **MK:** N **PH:** unk **SS:** E pg 610 **BS:** 46 pg 156.

PAYNE, John; b 4 Dec 1713, Goochland Co; d 28 Jul 1784 **RU:** Lieutenant Colonel/Patriot, Was member of House of Burgesses 1752-88. Was Lt Col of Militia and member of Goochland Co Committee of Safety. Gave material aid to cause **CEM:** Payne Family; **GPS** 37.84780, -78.07190; Rt 681 S of Rt 605; Goochland **GS:** U **SP:** 1) Dorothea Spotswood d/o Alexander (1676-1740) Spotswood & Elizabeth Butler (Brayne) Spotwood Thompson (1698-1751) 2) mar (23 Jun 1757) Jane Smith **VI:** Son of George (1680-1744) and Mary (Woodson) (1670-__) Payne. Died in Campbell Co **P:** unk **BLW:** unk **RG:** unk **MK:** unk **PH:** unk **SS:** J- DAR Hatcher; AL Ct Bk pg 1 Goochland Co **BS:** JLARC 2; 196.

PAYNE, John; b 1752 Baynesville, Westmoreland Co; d 21 May 1824 **RU:** Private, Served in 5th & 6th Cont Lines **CEM:** Payne Family, aka Cedar Hill; **GPS** 38.13357, -76.97069; Red house, Horners, 2 mi NE of Leedstown; Westmoreland **GS:** N **SP:** No info **VI:** No further data **P:** unk **BLW:** unk **RG:** N **MK:** N **PH:** N **SS:** E pg 610; AP rec; Application 631 **BS:** 189 pg 110; 196.

PAYNE, John Jr; b unk; d July 1787 or 1788 **RU:** Sailing Master, Served in VA State Navy. Died at Siege of York of smallpox. Master of pilot boat "Hiram" **CEM:** St John's Episcopal; **GPS** unk; 100 W Queen's Way; Hampton City **GS:** U **SP:** No info **VI:** Son of Thomas and (-----) Payne **P:** unk **BLW:** Y **RG:** unk **MK:** unk **PH:** unk **SS:** BY pg 176 **BS:** 32.

PAYNE, Joseph; b 1758; d 5 Apr 1826 **RU:** Ensign, Ent Serv Goochland Co 1776. Served in 8th VA Regt **CEM:** Windy Cove Presbyterian; **GPS** unk; 102 Windy Cove Rd, Millboro; Bath **GS:** N **SP:** Mar (30 Oct or 30 Dec 1779 while prisoner on Long Island) Ann (-----) (c1761-4 Feb 1847) **VI:** Moved to Bath Co in 1807 where appl for pen 12 May 1818 age 59. Widow appl pen 12 Sep 1837 age 76 W18693. DAR plaque on church wall **P:** Y **BLW:** unk **RG:** N **MK:** Y **PH:** N **SS:** E pg 611; K Vol 4 pg 79; CG Vol 3 pg 2626 **BS:** 159 Windy Cove; 196.

PAYNE, Josiah; b 1705; d 1785 **RU:** Patriot, Gave material aid to cause in Goochland Co **CEM:** Robert Payne Plantation; **GPS** unk; Dix Ferry Rd nr Dan River; Danville City **GS:** Y **SP:** No info **VI:** Served in VA House of Delegates 1761-1765 **P:** N **BLW:** N **RG:** N **MK:** N **PH:** unk **SS:** AL Cert Issued **BS:** 81 chart.

RU=Rank/Unit	CEM=Cemetery	GS=Gravestone	SP=Spousal Information
VI=Other Veteran Info	P=Pension	BLW=Bounty/Land Warrant	RG=Registered Grave
MK=SAR/DAR Marker	PH=Photo	SS=Service Source	BS=Burial Source

260

PAYNE, Reuben; b c1756; d 1840 **RU:** Captain, Served in Pittsylvania Co Militia **CEM:** Watkins; GPS unk; Axton; Henry **GS:** U **SP:** Mar (1 Oct 1781 Henry Co) Ann (Nancy) Ray (Rae) **VI:** Operated an Ordinary, Was bur at Payne Cemetery, but was moved to Watkins Cem **P:** unk **BLW:** unk **RG:** unk **MK:** unk **PH:** unk **SS:** G pg 284 **BS:** 196.

PAYNE, Richard; b 18 Jun 1763, Baynesville, Westmoreland Co; d 31 Mar 1843 **RU:** Second Lieutenant, Ent serv Westmoreland 1781. Served in Capt Johnson's Co, Orange Co Militia 24 Mar 1780 **CEM:** Fairview; GPS 38.48080,-78.00470; Sperryville Pike Rt 522, Culpeper; Culpeper **GS:** Y **SP:** Mary Major (1780-1840) **VI:** Appl for pension 15 Aug 1836 Culpeper Co. S8929. Last payment of pension was in 1840. Recd BLW of 777.5 acres. Stone was moved fr near Atlantus where it was found on the WPA Survey **P:** Y **BLW:** Y **RG:** N **MK:** N **PH:** unk **SS:** E pg 611; K Vol 4 pg 80; CG Vol 3 pg 2626 **BS:** 75 Culpeper; 196.

PAYNE, Tarleton; b 21 Feb 1758; d 1812 **RU:** Captain, Served in VA Line. Commanded a co 18 Nov 1777 in 1st VA Regt of Foot, Cont Line **CEM:** Payne Family, Hickory Hill; GPS unk; Rts 609 & 603, Goochland; Goochland **GS:** Y **SP:** Mar (before 28 Jun 1784) Elizabeth Winston **VI:** Son of Joseph & Elizabeth (Fleming) Payne BLW #1737-300 26 Mar 1792. Will probated in 1817 **P:** unk **BLW:** Y **RG:** Y **MK:** N **PH:** unk **SS:** J-NSSAR 1993 Reg; J- DAR Hatcher; N pg 391; CG Vol 3 pg 2626; CE pg 31 **BS:** JLARC 1, 2; 46 pg 164.

PAYNE, William; b 31 Mar 1755, Baynesville, Westmoreland Co; d 19 Sep 1837 **RU:** Captain, Served in VA Line. Ent serv first in 1776 Stafford Co. Moved to Westmoreland in 1780 where he again ent service **CEM:** Payne Farm, Clifton Farm; GPS unk; 5 mi NW of Warrenton; Fauquier **GS:** U **SP:** Marion Andrew Morson (11 Feb 1765, Falmouth-21 Nov 1840) d/o Arthur (1735-1798) & Marion (Andrew) (__-1808) Morson **VI:** After RW, lived in Fredericksburg, then moved to Fauquier Co where pensioned. SAR & DAR markers. Pension application 31 Aug 1832 Stafford Co S8938 **P:** Y **BLW:** unk **RG:** Y **MK:** Y **PH:** unk **SS:** J-NSSAR 1993 Reg; CG Vol 3 pg 2626; K Vol 4 pg 80 **BS:** JLARC 1; 196.

PAYNE, William; b 1762; d 1815 **RU:** Patriot, Gave material aid to cause **CEM:** Payne Family; GPS unk; Chesterbrook; Fairfax **GS:** U **SP:** Elizabeth Adams **VI:** Son of Annias & (-----) Payne **P:** N **BLW:** N **RG:** unk **MK:** unk **PH:** unk **SS:** AL CT Bk, pg 7, 22 Fairfax Co **BS:** 196.

PAYNE, William; b 1758; d Aft 1832 **RU:** Private/Sergeant, Ent serv 1775 Fauquier Co Culpeper Minute Men Bn in Cpt William Pickett's Co. Paid 8 Nov 1775-2 Apr 1776 as Sgt in Capt Hezekiah Turner's Co Fauquier Militia; in 1780 & 81 served as Sgt in Capt John O'Bannon's Co **CEM:** Oak Springs; GPS unk; 770 Fletcher Dr.; Fauquier **GS:** N **SP:** No info **VI:** Pension appl 29 Nov 1832 Fauquier Co S8938.5 **P:** Y **BLW:** unk **RG:** Y **MK:** N **PH:** N **SS:** K Vol 4 pg 80; AV; CG Vol 3 pg 2626; Fauquier Co Marriages pg 156 **BS:** 83 Inv # NF-20.

PAYNE (PAINE), Phillip; b 29 Mar 1760, Goochland Co; d 7 Jul 1840 **RU:** Private/Patriot, Served in Goochland Co Militia. As patriot, was hired to build road to KY during war period **CEM:** Payne Family; GPS unk; "Oak Grove," Rt 659, Altavista; Campbell **GS:** Y **SP:** Elizabeth Dandridge, d/o Nathaniel West & Dorothea (Spotswood) Dandridge (19 Sep 1764 Hanover Co-26 Apr 1833) **VI:** Son of John Payne (1713-1784) & Jane Smith (1736-181). Only the stones are here. Bodies are bur at "Airy Mont" near Gladys **P:** unk **BLW:** unk **RG:** unk **MK:** N **PH:** unk **SS:** N Vol 3 pg 1272 **BS:** JLARC 36; 196.

PEACHY, Thomas G Jr; b 1760; d 1781 **RU:** Patriot, Gave material aid to cause **CEM:** Cedar Grove; GPS 37.26140, -76.70720; Jct Rt 132 and Hunting Cove; Williamsburg City **GS:** Y **SP:** No info **VI:** Son of Thomas (23 Dec 1734-6 Mar 1810) & Elizabeth (Gilliam) (1741-1781) Peachy. Name and family members on monument originally bur behind Randolph home Colonial Williamsburg **P:** N **BLW:** N **RG:** unk **MK:** unk **PH:** unk **SS:** AL Ct Bk I pg 42 Amelia Co **BS:** 196.

PEACHY, Thomas G Sr; b 23 Dec 1734, Richmond Co; d 6 Mar 1810 **RU:** Patriot, Gave material aid to cause also did public service as Clerk of Amelia Co Ct Jul 1776 **CEM:** Cedar Grove; GPS 37.26140, -76.70720; Jct Rt 132 and Hunting Cove; Williamsburg City **GS:** Y **SP:** Elizabeth Gilliam (26 Mar 1741 Farnham Richmond Co-27 May 1781 Farnham, Richmond Co) **VI:** Son of Samuel (1699-1750) & Winnifred Judith (Griffin) (1709-1739) Peachy. Name and family members on monument originally bur behind Randolph home Colonial Williamsburg **P:** N **BLW:** N **RG:** unk **MK:** unk **PH:** unk **SS:** AL Cert Amelia Co; G pg 4 **BS:** 196.

RU=Rank/Unit	CEM=Cemetery	GS=Gravestone	SP=Spousal Information
VI=Other Veteran Info	P=Pension	BLW=Bounty/Land Warrant	RG=Registered Grave
MK=SAR/DAR Marker	PH=Photo	SS=Service Source	BS=Burial Source

261

PEAKE, Humphrey Sr; b 13 Jan 1731; Prince William Co; d 11 Jan 1785 **RU:** Patriot, Gave material aid (125 lbs beef) to the cause **CEM:** Peake Family; GPS 38.73686, -77.08430; Within Martin Luther King Jr Park, 8115 Fordson Rd, path past pool & tennis courts to black metal fencing; Alexandria City **GS:** Y **SP:** Mar (c1755) Mary Stonestreet (1738 Prince George's, MD - 21 Nov 1805, Fairfax Co), d/o Butler & Frances (Tolson) Stonestreet. **VI:** Son of William (bef 1688 Prince William Co - bet 11 Jan-17 Feb, 1761, Bradley, Fairfax) & Sarah (-----) Peake. Died in Fairfax Co **P:** N **BLW:** N **RG:** N **MK:** N **PH:** Y **SS:** AL Ct Bk pg 19 **BS:** 89 vol 5 pg SA 103.

PEAKE, William; b c1762; d 1793 **RU:** Quartermaster Sergeant, Served in 5th Troop, 1st Lt Dragoons. Was wounded in war and taken prisoner 19 Jan 1778 **CEM:** Peake Family; GPS 38.73686, -77.08430; Within Martin Luther King Jr Park, 8115 Fordson Rd, path past pool & tennis cts to black metal fencing, Alexandria City **GS:** Y **SP:** Elizabeth (-----) **VI:** Pension records indicate he d 16 Aug 1816. Appl pen 11 Aug 1788. Recd VA BLW 1796 **P:** Y **BLW:** Y **RG:** N **MK:** N **PH:** Y **SS:** E pg 612; BX pg 623; CU **BS:** 61 Vol. V, pg SA 104; 196.

PEARIS, George; b 1761; d 4 Nov 1810 **RU:** First Lieutenant, Commissioned in Montgomery Co Militia, 3 Mar 1779 **CEM:** Pearis Family; GPS unk; Bluff City; Giles **GS:** Y **SP:** 1) Eleanor Howe 2) Rebecca Clay **VI:** No further data **P:** unk **BLW:** unk **RG:** unk **MK:** Y **PH:** unk **SS:** E pg 613 **BS:** JLARC 2, 26.

PEARSON, Thomas; b 1751; d 1835 **RU:** Lieutenant, Served May 1780, in Cont Line under Col Abraham Buford. Recd arm & head sword wounds at Battle of Waxhaws (SC) against British Lt Col Banastre Talerton **CEM:** Pearson Memorial Park; GPS 36.84000, -79.95030; S off Henry Rd Rt 605; Franklin **GS:** Y **SP:** Mar (3 Aug 1806) Elizabeth Palmer **VI:** Family tradition says was b in Yorkshire, England. Pensioned first in Henrico Co 12 Feb 1813 receiving $60 per annum. Penson continued in Bedford & Franklin Co. Govt grave stone **P:** Y **BLW:** unk **RG:** unk **MK:** unk **PH:** Y **SS:** Rev war service Pen Applic: http://revwarapps.org/va6.pdf; BX pg 624 **BS:** 196.

PECK, Benjamin; b 1761; d 1 Jun 1827 **RU:** Drummer/Patriot, Served in 2nd Regt of Artillery Mar 1780 **CEM:** Fincastle Presbyterian; GPS 37.50017, -79.87558; 108 E Back St, Fincastle; Botetourt **GS:** N **SP:** Mar (1769) Margaret Carper (27 Dec 1751, MD-1820) **VI:** Name is on the SAR plaque at this cemetery **P:** unk **BLW:** unk **RG:** N **MK:** Y **PH:** N **SS:** AP Muster Roll; BT; DL pg 336, 378; AS; DAR report **BS:** DAR report.

PECK, Benjamin; b 1746, Giles Co; d 1824 **RU:** Patriot, Performed public service as Surveyor of Roads and Juror in Botetourt Co **CEM:** Miller; GPS unk; Rt 42, Midway; Craig **GS:** U **SP:** Mar (1769) Margaret Carper (27 Dec 1751, Botetourt Co-after 1824) **VI:** DAR indicates he was b in Sharpsburg, Washington Co, MD **P:** N **BLW:** N **RG:** unk **MK:** unk **PH:** unk **SS:** DAR #A087443; J- DAR Hatcher **BS:** JLARC 2.

PECK, Jacob; b 1723; d 1801 **RU:** Private, Served in Capt Thomas Smith's Co, Augusta Militia **CEM:** Fincastle Presbyterian; GPS 37.50017, -79.87558; 108 E Back St, Fincastle; Botetourt **GS:** Y **SP:** Lydia Borden, b 1723, d 1800. **VI:** Name is on the SAR plaque at this cemetery **P:** unk **BLW:** unk **RG:** Y **MK:** Y **PH:** unk **SS:** E pg 613 **BS:** 04; 196.

PECK, Jacob Sr; b 14 Oct 1739, Frederick Co, MD; d 23 Sep 1827 **RU:** Soldier/Patriot, Served Capt Thomas Smith's Co, Augusta Co Militia. Gave 88 pairs men's shoes & 30 pairs boots 20 Apr 1782 **CEM:** Trinity Episcopal; GPS 38.14917, -79.07521; 214 Beverley St; Staunton City **GS:** Y **SP:** 1) Mar (1778 Orange Co) Mary Coursey 2) mar (9 Mar 1789 Augusta Co) Elizabeth Butt 3) Mar (after 1803 Staunton, Augusta Co) Catherin Fackler Schnebly **VI:** Son of Johann Jacob (1723-1821) & Lydia (Borden) (1728-1800) Peck **P:** unk **BLW:** unk **RG:** unk **MK:** unk **PH:** Y **SS:** E pg 613; CY pg 37 **BS:** JLARC 62, 63; 196.

PECK, John; b 1750; d 1820 **RU:** Ensign/Patriot, Gave material aid to the cause **CEM:** Fincastle Presbyterian; GPS 37.50017, -79.87558; 108 E Back St, Fincastle; Botetourt **GS:** N **SP:** No info **VI:** Name is on the SAR plaque at this cemetery **P:** unk **BLW:** unk **RG:** Y **MK:** Y **PH:** N **SS:** J-NSSAR 1993 Reg, J- DAR Hatcher, AR Vol 3, pg159; AL Ct Bk pg26 **BS:** JLARC 1, 2; 196.

PECK, Joseph; b unk; d 1842 **RU:** Soldier, Service may appear in pension records at Lib VA Vol 2 pg 40 **CEM:** Fincastle Presbyterian; GPS 37.50017, -79.87558; 108 E Back St, Fincastle; Botetourt **GS:** N **SP:** Mar (29 Aug 1792 Botetourt Co) Susanna Franklin **VI:** Recd pension in Augusta Co 1835. Name is on the SAR plaque at this cemetery **P:** Y **BLW:** unk **RG:** Y **MK:** Y **PH:** N **SS:** J-NSSAR 1993 Reg; J-DAR Hatcher AR Vol 3 pg 159; CZ pg 345 **BS:** JLARC 1, 2; 196.

RU=Rank/Unit	CEM=Cemetery	GS=Gravestone	SP=Spousal Information
VI=Other Veteran Info	P=Pension	BLW=Bounty/Land Warrant	RG=Registered Grave
MK=SAR/DAR Marker	PH=Photo	SS=Service Source	BS=Burial Source

262

PEEBLES, Fred; b 1736; d Aft 1780 **RU:** Patriot, Gave material aid to cause **CEM:** Peebles Family; GPS unk; Brink; Greensville **GS:** Y **SP:** No info **VI:** No further data **P:** N **BLW:** N **RG:** unk **MK:** unk **PH:** unk **SS:** AL Ct Bk pg 25 Greenville Co **BS:** 196.

PEIRCE, Joseph; b unk; d Aft 1788 **RU:** Captain/Patriot, Gave material aid to cause **CEM:** Level Green; GPS unk; Kinsale; Westmoreland **GS:** N **SP:** No info **VI:** Was Justice of Peace in Westmoreland Co in 1788 **P:** unk **BLW:** unk **RG:** N **MK:** N **PH:** N **SS:** AL Ct Bk pg 2, 3, 4 Westmoreland Co, AS, DAR report **BS:** DAR report.

PEIRCE, Solomon; b 1742; d 1821 **RU:** Private, Served in Capt Hugh Maxwell's Co,1st MA Battalion commanded by Col John Bailey, 9 Sep 1778. Served total of three years **CEM:** Old Burying Ground; GPS unk; Directions in Senate Doc DAR annual report 1955 vol 4 serial 11912; Arlington **GS:** N **SP:** No info **VI:** No further data **P:** unk **BLW:** unk **RG:** unk **MK:** unk **PH:** N **SS:** J- DAR Hatcher; AP Roll **BS:** JLARC 2.

PEIRCE (PIERCE), David; b 8 Apr 1756 Chester Co, PA; d 28 Oct 1833 **RU:** Private, Served in Capt Joseph Luckie's Co, Flying Camp of Rangers,1776-1782, PA Militia **CEM:** Peirce Family, aka Chaffin; GPS unk; On hill overlooking SR 69 at jct with I-77 in Poplar Camp; Wythe **GS:** U **SP:** Mar (04 Oct 1798) Mary Bell (1778 Montgomery Co-26 Jul 1858) **VI:** No further data **P:** unk **BLW:** unk **RG:** unk **MK:** Y **PH:** unk **SS:** CI, PA Archives 5th series Vol 5 pg 569, 573, 792 **BS:** JLARC 123; 196.

PELHAM, Peter; b 9 Dec 1721, London, Eng; d 28 Apr 1805 **RU:** Patriot, Performed public service as keeper of the jail, Williamsburg, 1775-1780 **CEM:** Bruton Parish Church; GPS 37.27127, -76.70248; 331 W Duke of Gloucester St; Williamsburg City **GS:** U **SP:** Ann Creese (1721-1778) **VI:** Son of Peter (1696-1751) & (-----) Pelham **P:** N **BLW:** N **RG:** unk **MK:** unk **PH:** unk **SS:** Wilkipedia.org **BS:** 196.

PELITIER, Jacques; b unk; d 1781 **RU:** Soldier, Served in Auxonne Bn and died fr battle at Yorktown **CEM:** French Memorial; GPS 36.81944, -79.39933; Yorktown; York **GS:** U **SP:** No info **VI:** No further data **P:** unk **BLW:** unk **RG:** Y **MK:** unk **PH:** unk **SS:** J-Yorktown Historian **BS:** JLARC 1, 74.

PELLETAN, Jean; b unk; d 1781 **RU:** Seaman, Served on "Sceptre" and died from Yorktown battle **CEM:** French Memorial; GPS 36.81944, -79.39933; Yorktown; York **GS:** U **SP:** No info **VI:** No further data **P:** unk **BLW:** unk **RG:** Y **MK:** unk **PH:** unk **SS:** J-Yorktown Historian **BS:** JLARC 1, 74.

PELLETIER, Joseph; b unk; d 1781 **RU:** Seaman, Served on "Citoyen" and died from Yorktown battle **CEM:** French Memorial; GPS 36.81944, -79.39933; Yorktown; York **GS:** U **SP:** No info **VI:** No further data **P:** unk **BLW:** unk **RG:** Y **MK:** unk **PH:** unk **SS:** J-Yorktown Historian **BS:** JLARC 1, 74.

PENCE, George; b 1750; d 1818 **RU:** Captain, Commanded a co Aug 1777 Augusta Co Militia **CEM:** Old Peaked Mountain; GPS 38.37113, -78.73416; 9843 Town Hall Rd, McGaheysville; Rockingham **GS:** U **SP:** Jane Carpenter **VI:** No further data **P:** unk **BLW:** unk **RG:** Y **MK:** Y **PH:** unk **SS:** J-NSSAR 2000 Reg; E pg 615 **BS:** JLARC 76.

PENCE, Henry; b unk; d After 1800 **RU:** Patriot, Gave material aid to cause **CEM:** Old Peaked Mountain; GPS 38.37113, -78.73416; 9843 Town Hall Rd, McGaheysville; Rockingham **GS:** Y **SP:** 1) Mar (1799 Rockingham Co) Cathy Munger d/o Henry Munger 2) Mar (1800 Rockingham Co) Rebecca Dundore d/o Jonathan & (-----) Dundore **VI:** No further data **P:** N **BLW:** N **RG:** Y **MK:** Y **PH:** unk **SS:** O pg 113; AL Ct Bk II pg 13 Rockingham Co **BS:** 04.

PENCE, Jacob; b 20 Dec 1730, Frankfort, Germany; d Feb 1800 **RU:** Private, Served in Capt William Nall's Co, Augusta Co Regt **CEM:** Old Peaked Mountain; GPS 38.37113, -78.73416; 9843 Town Hall Rd, McGaheysville; Rockingham **GS:** U **SP:** Catherine Persinger (1750, Botetourt Co-__) **VI:** Son of Jacob & Catherine (-----) Pence. Died at Cub Run, Rockingham Co **P:** unk **BLW:** unk **RG:** Y **MK:** unk **PH:** unk **SS:** J-NSSAR 2000 Reg **BS:** JLARC 76.

PENCE, Jacob; b c1760; d unk **RU:** Private, Served in Capt Micheal Reader's Co, Shenandoah Co Militia **CEM:** Old Bethel; GPS 38.79113, -78.58904; off Old Bethel Rd (Rt 700), Edinburg; Shenandoah **GS:** Y **SP:** No info **VI:** No further data **P:** unk **BLW:** unk **RG:** N **MK:** N **PH:** unk **SS:** C pg 603 **BS:** 79 pg 92.

RU=Rank/Unit   CEM=Cemetery   GS=Gravestone   SP=Spousal Information
VI=Other Veteran Info   P=Pension   BLW=Bounty/Land Warrant   RG=Registered Grave
MK=SAR/DAR Marker   PH=Photo   SS=Service Source   BS=Burial Source

263

PENCE, James; b unk; d unk **RU:** Corporal, Rank achieved 1777 in Rockingham Co Militia **CEM:** Old Peaked Mountain; GPS 38.37113, -78.73416; 9843 Town Hall Rd, McGaheysville; Rockingham **GS:** U **SP:** No info **VI:** No further data **P:** unk **BLW:** unk **RG:** Y **MK:** unk **PH:** unk **SS:** J-NSSAR 2000 Reg; AZ pg 230 **BS:** JLARC 76.

PENCE, John; b 23 Nov 1755, Augusta Co (now Rockingham); d 10 Jan 1834 **RU:** Soldier, Served in Rockingham Co Militia & VA Regt. Served in Capt William Nall's Co 1778 and in Capt John Rush's Co under Col Sampson Matthews in 1781 **CEM:** Old Peaked Mountain; GPS 38.37113, -78.73416; 9843 Town Hall Rd, McGaheysville; Rockingham **GS:** U **SP:** mar (6 May 1793, same day as marriage bond) Nancy Swisher (Swesher) (c1774-15 Mar 1834) d/o John & (-----) Swisher **VI:** Son of Valentine & Anna Maria Catherine (Oberlin) Pence. Appl for pension Rockingham Co, 20 Aug 1832. Widow appl pen 19 Aug 1839 age 65. W5511, R1906 **P:** Y **BLW:** unk **RG:** unk **MK:** Y **PH:** unk **SS:** K Vol 4 pg 89; CG Vol 3 pg 2650 **BS:** JLARC 4, 64.

PENCE, William; b 1745, Lancaster Co, PA; d 21 May 1820 **RU:** Private, Served in Capt Peachey Gilman's Co, Augusta Co Militia in 1776 **CEM:** Old Peaked Mountain; GPS 38.37113, -78.73416; 9843 Town Hall Rd, McGaheysville; Rockingham **GS:** U **SP:** Elizabeth Price **VI:** Son of Jacob & Catherine (-----) Pence **P:** unk **BLW:** unk **RG:** Y **MK:** Y **PH:** unk **SS:** J-NSSAR 2000 Reg; E pg 615 **BS:** JLARC 76.

PENDLETON, Edmund; b 9 Sep 1721; d 23 Oct 1803 **RU:** Patriot, Was member Comm of Safety for Colony of VA and author of resolutions offered in VA House of Burgesses, 15 May 1776. Was President of Convention 1775 and President VA Ct of Appeals. Was elected to Congress, 1788; President of Convention of VA which met to consider adoption of Federal Constitution; member of Committee that drafted law establishing "Religious Freedom in Virginia" **CEM:** Bruton Parish Church; GPS 37.27127, -76.70248; 331 W Duke of Gloucester St; Williamsburg City **GS:** Y **SP:** 1) Elizabeth Roy (___-17 Nov 1742) 2) Sarah Pollard (4 May 1725-1815) **VI:** Son of Henry & Mary Bishop (Taylor) Pendleton. Was member of House of Representatives for 25 yrs. He and wives were bur first in the Pendleton family cemetery in Caroline Co. Was elected to Congress,1788 and President of Convention of VA which met to consider adoption of Federal Constitution. Was member of Committee that drafted law establishing "Religious Freedom in Virginia" **P:** N **BLW:** N **RG:** Y **MK:** N **PH:** unk **SS:** E pg 615 **BS:** 02 pg 116; 26 pg 143.

PENDLETON, Nathaniel Sr; b 1715 or 1716; d Aug 1794 or 1795 **RU:** Captain/Patriot, Served in 1st VA Regt. Commanded a Co in 3rd VA Regt that was captured at Charleston. Chairman of the Committee of Safety and Correspondence **CEM:** Redwood Plantation; GPS unk; Rt 522 N; Culpeper **GS:** N **SP:** Mar (14 Oct 1744) Elizabeth Clayton (1714-1771) d/o Major Samuel (1685-1735) & Elizabeth (Pendleton) (1684-1761) Clayton. Widow of Joseph Anderson. **VI:** Son of Henry (1683-1721) & Mary Bishop Taylor (1688-1770) Pendleton. Chief magistrate and High Sheriff of Culpeper Co 1765. Author & signer of first protest against the Stamp Act 1765. One of the founders of Fairfax. Issued BLW #1736 on 27 Jul 1795. Records lost in 1800 DC fire. The family cemetery here was in ruins with no stones in 2008 **P:** unk **BLW:** Y **RG:** N **MK:** N **PH:** N **SS:** AL Ct Bk, pg 3, 20; K Vol 4 pg 90; CE pg 41; CF pg 33 **BS:** 80 vol 3 pg 161; 196.

PENDLETON, William; b 1720; d 1780 **RU:** Private, Served in Capt Richard Yancey's Co fr Culpeper Co. Was in Point Pleasant Battle Oct 1774 **CEM:** Old Pendleton; GPS unk; Monroe; Amherst **GS:** U **SP:** Elizabeth Tinsley (1727 New Kent Co-1783) **VI:** Son of John P (1691-1775) & Mary (Tinsley) (1727-1783) Pendleton **P:** N **BLW:** N **RG:** unk **MK:** unk **PH:** unk **SS:** Z pg 87 **BS:** 196.

PENN, Abram or Abraham; b 27 Dec 1743, Drysdale Parrish, Caroline Co; d 26 Jun 1801 **RU:** Colonel, Was Commander of Minute Men Battalion,1776. Served in Henry Co Militia 1780-81. Led Patrick Co troops in Battle at Guilford CH **CEM:** Poplar Grove; GPS unk; W on Rt 626 off Rt 627 Co Line Rd, nr Critz; Patrick **GS:** U **SP:** Ruth Stovall **VI:** DAR Col Abram Penn Chapter is named for him **P:** unk **BLW:** unk **RG:** unk **MK:** unk **PH:** unk **SS:** AZ pg 209; E pg 616 **BS:** JLARC 2, 4, 30.

PENN, Gabriel; b 17 Jul 1741, Drysdale Parrish, Caroline Co; d Jul 1798 **RU:** Lieutenant/Patriot, Served in Amherst Co Militia. Paymaster Buckingham Co Militia, 1775-6. Gave material aid to cause **CEM:** Penn Family; GPS unk; Rt 151, Clifford; Amherst **GS:** U **SP:** Sarah "Betsy" Calloway **VI:** No further data **P:** unk **BLW:** unk **RG:** Y **MK:** N **PH:** unk **SS:** E pg 616, G appendix pg 501; AL Cert 2 Amherst Co **BS:** 04.

RU=Rank/Unit	CEM=Cemetery	GS=Gravestone	SP=Spousal Information
VI=Other Veteran Info	P=Pension	BLW=Bounty/Land Warrant	RG=Registered Grave
MK=SAR/DAR Marker	PH=Photo	SS=Service Source	BS=Burial Source

PENN, George; b 12 Dec 1737, Drysdale Parish, Caroline Co; d 5 Feb 1790 **RU:** Ensign/Patriot, Served in Amherst Co Militia. Gave material aid to cause **CEM:** Penn Family; GPS unk; Rt 151, Clifford; Amherst **GS:** U **SP:** 1) Sara Lea (Lee) 2) Mar (29 May 1783 Amherst Co) Mary Walden, widow **VI:** Family tradition is bur with family at the Gabriel Penn Graveyard **P:** unk **BLW:** unk **RG:** Y **MK:** N **PH:** unk **SS:** G pg 15; AL Cert 1 Amherst Co **BS:** 04.

PENN, John; b 1736; d 1818 **RU:** Cook/Patriot, Served in the USN on the ship "Manley" in 1779. Gave material aid to cause **CEM:** Miller Family; GPS unk; Rt 690; Amherst **GS:** Y **SP:** No info **VI:** No further data **P:** unk **BLW:** unk **RG:** N **MK:** N **PH:** unk **SS:** E pg 616; AL Ct Bk pg 33 Amherst Co **BS:** 01 pg 146.

PENN, William; b 9 Apr 1746, Caroline Co; d 15 Mar 1777 **RU:** Lieutenant/CPT Dragoons, Died fr small pox while serving in Trenton, NJ **CEM:** Penn Family; GPS unk; Rt 151, Clifford; Amherst **GS:** U **SP:** Martha Smith **VI:** Died in Trenton, NJ, and body may not have been carried to cemetery **P:** unk **BLW:** Y **RG:** Y **MK:** N **PH:** unk **SS:** C pg 364 **BS:** 04, May 06.

PENNYWEIGHT (PENNYWITT), Jacob; b 30 Jul 1751; d 27 Jan 1863 **RU:** Captain, Took oath as Capt 31 Aug 1780 Shenandoah Co Militia **CEM:** St Mary Pine Lutheran; GPS 38.74470, -78.68390; 7103 S Middle Rd, Mt Jackson; Shenandoah **GS:** Y **SP:** No info **VI:** No further data **P:** unk **BLW:** unk **RG:** N **MK:** N **PH:** unk **SS:** E pg 616, pg 540 **BS:** 155 Old Pine Church.

PERCHE, Louis; b unk; d 1781 **RU:** Soldier, Served in Soissonnais Bn and died fr battle at Yorktown **CEM:** French Memorial; GPS 36.81944, -79.39933; Yorktown; York **GS:** U **SP:** No info **VI:** No further data **P:** unk **BLW:** unk **RG:** Y **MK:** unk **PH:** unk **SS:** J-Yorktown Historian **BS:** JLARC 1, 74.

PERDUE, Meshack; b 1755 or 1756, Chesterfield Co; d 30 Dec 1837 **RU:** Patriot, Performed patriotic service. Signed Oath of Allegiance Montgomery Co **CEM:** Mark Perdue Farm/Crossroads Burnt Chimney; GPS unk; Rt 672 vic Foxfire Nursery; Franklin **GS:** Y **SP:** Eleanor Dillon **VI:** No further data **P:** N **BLW:** N **RG:** Y **MK:** Y **PH:** unk **SS:** AK Sep 2009; DAR Ancestor # A092290 **BS:** AK Sep 09.

PERKINS, Constantine; b unk; d 1790 **RU:** Major/Patriot, Gave material aid to cause **CEM:** Nicholas Perkins 2d Home; GPS unk; S of Dan River, Danville; Danville City **GS:** U **SP:** No info **VI:** No further data **P:** unk **BLW:** unk **RG:** N **MK:** N **PH:** unk **SS:** 17 81 Militia; AL Ct Bk pg 6, 34, 51, 60 Pittsylvania Co **BS:** 81 chart.

PERKINS, John W; b 31 May 1752; d 17 Mar 1803 **RU:** Lieutenant, Appointed Lt Goochland Co Militia 18 Sep 1777, took oath 16 Feb 1778 **CEM:** Perkins/Hall; GPS unk; Hwy 56; Buckingham **GS:** U **SP:** No info **VI:** No further data **P:** unk **BLW:** unk **RG:** Y **MK:** N **PH:** unk **SS:** E pg 617; H **BS:** 29 pg 453.

PERKINS, Stephen; b unk; d 1821 **RU:** Patriot, Gave material aid to cause in Buckingham Co **CEM:** Perkins family; GPS unk; Vic Rts 600 & 633; Fluvanna **GS:** Y **SP:** No info **VI:** No further data **P:** N **BLW:** N **RG:** N **MK:** N **PH:** unk **SS:** AL Comm Bk I pg 203 **BS:** 66 pg 75.

PERKINSON, Thomas; b 1762 or Oct 1767; d 21 Sep 1816 **RU:** Private, Served 2 mo, 13 days in Bn of MD Militia in Cont Army 29 Nov 1781. **CEM:** Wards Chapel; GPS unk; Crewe; Nottoway **GS:** Y **SP:** No info **VI:** No further data **P:** Y **BLW:** Y **RG:** unk **MK:** unk **PH:** Y **SS:** J- DAR Hatcher; AP Pen & BLW files **BS:** JLARC 2.

PERNOT, Nicolas; b unk; d 1781 **RU:** Soldier, Served in Soissonnais Bn and died fr battle at Yorktown **CEM:** French Memorial; GPS 36.81944, -79.39933; Yorktown; York **GS:** U **SP:** No info **VI:** No further data **P:** unk **BLW:** unk **RG:** Y **MK:** unk **PH:** unk **SS:** J-Yorktown Historian **BS:** JLARC 1, 74.

PEROT, Milan; b unk; d 1781 **RU:** Seaman, Served on "Citoyen" and died from Yorktown battle **CEM:** French Memorial; GPS 36.81944, -79.39933; Yorktown; York **GS:** U **SP:** No info **VI:** No further data **P:** unk **BLW:** unk **RG:** Y **MK:** unk **PH:** unk **SS:** J-Yorktown Historian **BS:** JLARC 1, 74.

PEROTIN, Julien; b unk; d 1781 **RU:** Seaman, Served on "Auguste" and died from Yorktown battle **CEM:** French Memorial; GPS 36.81944, -79.39933; Yorktown; York **GS:** U **SP:** No info **VI:** No further data **P:** unk **BLW:** unk **RG:** Y **MK:** unk **PH:** unk **SS:** J-Yorktown Historian **BS:** JLARC 1, 74.

PEROY, Louis; b unk; d 1781 **RU:** Seaman, Served on "Auguste" and died from Yorktown battle **CEM:** French Memorial; GPS 36.81944, -79.39933; Yorktown; York **GS:** U **SP:** No info **VI:** No further data **P:** unk **BLW:** unk **RG:** Y **MK:** unk **PH:** unk **SS:** J-Yorktown Historian **BS:** JLARC 1, 74.

RU=Rank/Unit	CEM=Cemetery	GS=Gravestone	SP=Spousal Information
VI=Other Veteran Info	P=Pension	BLW=Bounty/Land Warrant	RG=Registered Grave
MK=SAR/DAR Marker	PH=Photo	SS=Service Source	BS=Burial Source

265

PERPETTE, Antoine; b unk; d 1781 **RU:** Seaman, Served on "Palmier" and died from Yorktown battle **CEM:** French Memorial; GPS 36.81944, -79.39933; Yorktown; York **GS:** U **SP:** No info **VI:** No further data **P:** unk **BLW:** unk **RG:** Y **MK:** unk **PH:** unk **SS:** J-Yorktown Historian **BS:** JLARC 1, 74.

PERRIER, Joseph; b unk; d 1781 **RU:** Soldier, Served in Bourbonnais Bn and died fr battle at Yorktown **CEM:** French Memorial; GPS 36.81944, -79.39933; Yorktown; York **GS:** U **SP:** No info **VI:** No further data **P:** unk **BLW:** unk **RG:** Y **MK:** unk **PH:** unk **SS:** J-Yorktown Historian **BS:** JLARC 1, 74.

PERSINGER, Jacob; b 19 Jan 1749, nr Pittsburg, PA; d 3 Jul 1840 **RU:** Corporal, Ent serv Botetourt Co (now Allegheny) 1775. Was in Battle of Point Pleasant 1774. Served in Capt Matthew Arbuckle's Co 1775 to 1 Nov 1776 **CEM:** Persinger Memorial; GPS unk; 3707 Llama Dr; Covington City **GS:** Y **SP:** Mary Kimoerils **VI:** Appl for pension 18 Nov 1833 fr Alleghany Co "where resided since RW". S30019 **P:** Y **BLW:** unk **RG:** Y **MK:** Y **PH:** Y **SS:** K Vol 4 pg 97; CG Vol 3 pg 2667 **BS:** JLARC 1, 4, 51.

PETTETT, John; b unk; d unk **RU:** Private, Served in Fairfax Co Militia **CEM:** Fairfax City; GPS 38.84690, -77.31330; Main St & Page Ave; Fairfax City **GS:** N **SP:** No info **VI:** No further data **P:** unk **BLW:** unk **RG:** N **MK:** N **PH:** N **SS:** E pg 620 **BS:** 61 vol III pg FX-153.

PETTIES (PETTES, PETTUS), Samuel Overton; b 11 Mar 1751, Lunenburg Co; d 12 Feb 1819 **RU:** Lieutenant, Served in Cont Line in an artillery unit **CEM:** Petties Family; GPS unk; Chase City; Mecklenburg **GS:** Y **SP:** Mar (1783) Hannah Minor (Mar 1755-1829) **VI:** Recd BLW **P:** unk **BLW:** Y **RG:** N **MK:** N **PH:** unk **SS:** C pg 135; DB pg 115-6 cites TN USDAR Roster pg 127; AS; CU **BS:** 80 vol 3 pg 167.

PETTITT, William; b 1751; d 11 Nov 1783 **RU:** Private, Served in VA & Cont Lines **CEM:** Bowman's Folly; GPS unk; End of Rt 652, private lane, 2.4 mi NE of Accomac, Joynes Neck; Accomack **GS:** Y **SP:** No info **VI:** Son of William of Northampton Co & Mary (-----) Pettitt **P:** unk **BLW:** unk **RG:** N **MK:** N **PH:** unk **SS:** AP Cont Line VA **BS:** 209; 196.

PETTYPOOL, William; b 1732; d Mar 1813 **RU:** Ensign/Patriot, Served in Capt Richard Jone's Co, Halifax Co Militia. Gave material aid to cause **CEM:** Halifax Town; GPS 36.76403, -78.92668; Check property records; Halifax **GS:** U **SP:** Mar 09 Apr 1772 Sarah Tynes **VI:** No further data **P:** unk **BLW:** unk **RG:** unk **MK:** unk **PH:** unk **SS:** J- DAR Hatcher; AL Ct Bk pg 24 Lunenburg Co **BS:** JLARC 2.

PEYLLARD, Jacques; b unk; d 1781 **RU:** Soldier, Served in Beaujolais Bn and died fr battle at Yorktown **CEM:** French Memorial; GPS 36.81944, -79.39933; Yorktown; York **GS:** U **SP:** No info **VI:** No further data **P:** unk **BLW:** unk **RG:** Y **MK:** unk **PH:** unk **SS:** J-Yorktown Historian **BS:** JLARC 1, 74.

PEYTON, Francis; b 1764; d 26 Aug 1836 **RU:** Lieutenant, Paymaster, Prince William District Bn 1775-76 **CEM:** St Paul's Episcopal; GPS 38.79959, -77.05860; 228 S Pitt St; Alexandria City **GS:** Y **SP:** Sarah West (1776-22 Jun 1849) d/o Hugh & Elizabeth (Minor) West **VI:** Death notice in the Alexandria Gazette 30 Aug 1836, pg 3 **P:** unk **BLW:** unk **RG:** Y **MK:** unk **PH:** unk **SS:** CE pg 22 **BS:** JLARC 1, 2, 25; 196.

PEYTON, Henry; b 1744; d 1814, The Plains **RU:** First Lieutenant/Patriot, Farquier Militia. 1st Lt Oct 1719. Gave material aid to cause **CEM:** Gordonsdale; GPS unk; The Plains; Fauquier **GS:** Y **SP:** A man by this name mar (bond 19 Nov 1796 Fauquier Co) Ann Brent, d/o William Jr. & (-----) Brent **VI:** No further data **P:** unk **BLW:** unk **RG:** Y **MK:** N **PH:** unk **SS:** E pg 621; H; AL Ct Bk pg 3 Fauquier Co; Fauquier Co Marriages pg 158 **BS:** 19 pg 68.

PHARES (PHARIS, FERRIS, FARRIS, FARES), Amariah (Emaria Emeriah Araziah Emerica Amaziah); b 23 May 1778, Middlesex, NJ; d 1 Jan 1824 **RU:** Private, Ent serv 1778 in NJ Mar 1777-1778 in 2nd Regt, Middlesex NJ Militia under Capts Williamson & Gulick. Served in NJ Cont Line 23 May 1778 - 23 Feb 1779. Served in Capt Longstreet's Co, 1st Regt **CEM:** Eastview; GPS unk; Rome; Floyd **GS:** N **SP:** 1) Mar (19 Jun 1780) Sarah Van Zandt 2) Mar (13 Jan 1791 Franklin Co) Elizabeth BeHeler **VI:** At date of enlistment in Cont Line, lived at Cross Road, age 23, height 5'8", light complexion, light eyes, brown hair. Certificate 1542 for depreciation of Cont pay in Middlesex. Pension W5541 Widow appl 26 Dec 1840 Floyd Co VA age 71. Died in Floyd/Montgomery Co **P:** Y **BLW:** unk **RG:** Y **MK:** N **PH:** N **SS:** DAR Ancestor #A204840; SAR Ancestor #P-269370; K Vol 4 pg 103; CG Vol 3 pg 2676, 04 **BS:** 04.

RU=Rank/Unit CEM=Cemetery GS=Gravestone SP=Spousal Information
VI=Other Veteran Info P=Pension BLW=Bounty/Land Warrant RG=Registered Grave
MK=SAR/DAR Marker PH=Photo SS=Service Source BS=Burial Source

266

PHILIPEAU, Gabriel; b unk; d 1781 **RU:** Seaman, Served on "Languedoc" and died from Yorktown battle **CEM:** French Memorial; GPS 36.81944, -79.39933; Yorktown; York **GS:** U **SP:** No info **VI:** No further data **P:** unk **BLW:** unk **RG:** Y **MK:** unk **PH:** unk **SS:** J-Yorktown Historian **BS:** JLARC 1, 74.

PHILIPPE, Pierre; b unk; d 1781 **RU:** Seaman, Served on "Saint-Esprit" and died from Yorktown battle **CEM:** French Memorial; GPS 36.81944, -79.39933; Yorktown; York **GS:** U **SP:** No info **VI:** No further data **P:** unk **BLW:** unk **RG:** Y **MK:** unk **PH:** unk **SS:** J-Yorktown Historian **BS:** JLARC 1, 74.

PHILLIPS, John; b 1749; d 1828 **RU:** Private, Served in Capt John Cropper's Co, Col Dan Morgan's 11th & 15th VA Regt 30 Nov 1788 **CEM:** Old Phillips; GPS unk; Rt 696 NS Troublesome Creek, Evington; Campbell **GS:** U **SP:** 1) Sarah (-----) 2) Margaret (-----) **VI:** No further data **P:** unk **BLW:** unk **RG:** unk **MK:** N **PH:** unk **SS:** A pg 267 **BS:** JLARC 4,36.

PHILLIPS, John; b 1765, Amherst Co; d 22 Nov 1822 **RU:** Private, Served in 6th Cont Line 3 yrs **CEM:** Old Phillips; GPS unk; Rt 696 N side of Troublesome Creek, Evington; Campbell **GS:** N **SP:** Mar (12 Dec 1808, Campbell Co) Margaret Weber (1780-Dec 1833) d/o John & Elizabeth Margaret (-----) Weber **VI:** Recd 100 acres BLW 10 Dec 1785 **P:** unk **BLW:** Y **RG:** unk **MK:** N **PH:** N **SS:** E pg 623; F pg 82; BY **BS:** 196.

PHILLIPS, John M; b c1759; d 1834 **RU:** Patriot, Gave material aid to the cause **CEM:** Shockoe Hill; GPS 37.55190, -77.43170; 4th & Hospital Sts; Richmond City **GS:** Y **SP:** No info **VI:** No further data **P:** N **BLW:** N **RG:** N **MK:** N **PH:** unk **SS:** AL Ct Bk pg 55 **BS:** 57 pg 13.

PHILLIPS, Thomas; b unk; d 1808 **RU:** Patriot, Gave material aid to the cause **CEM:** St John's Episcopal; GPS unk; 100 W Queen's Way; Hampton City **GS:** Y **SP:** No info **VI:** No further data **P:** N **BLW:** N **RG:** N **MK:** N **PH:** unk **SS:** AL Ct Bk 2 pg 3a **BS:** 89 pg 121.

PHILLIPS, Tobias; b 1750; d 12 Feb 1808 **RU:** Soldier, Served in Capt Jonathan Isom's Co, Montgomery Co Militia **CEM:** Tobias Phillips; GPS unk; Rt 619 nr Rt 757; Carroll **GS:** U **SP:** Peggy (-----) (___-12 Feb 1806) **VI:** No further data **P:** unk **BLW:** unk **RG:** unk **MK:** unk **PH:** unk **SS:** G pg 221 **BS:** JLARC 43.

PHILLIPS, William; b 1 Nov 1744; d 30 Dec 1797 **RU:** Lieutenant Colonel/Patriot, Served in Stafford Co Militia. Gave beef & gun to cause **CEM:** Phillips Family; GPS 38.50238, -77.29626; Rt 610, Quantico Marine Base; Stafford **GS:** Y **SP:** Mar (7 Jul 1774) Elizabeth Fowke (___-c1830) **VI:** Sheriff Stafford Co 1792-4, SAR marker **P:** unk **BLW:** unk **RG:** Y **MK:** Y **PH:** Y **SS:** D pg 872; E pg 623 **BS:** 03 pg 300.

PHILLIPS, William; b 12 Nov 1760, Shenandoah Co; d 17 May 1837 **RU:** Soldier, Served in 5th & 8th Cont Line **CEM:** Philllips; GPS unk; Edinburg; Shenandoah **GS:** U **SP:** Christiana Foltz (1768-1837) **VI:** No further data **P:** unk **BLW:** unk **RG:** unk **MK:** unk **PH:** unk **SS:** E pg 623 **BS:** 196.

PHIPPS, William Sr; b 1759; d Aug 1818 **RU:** Private, Served in Capt James Fenley's Co, Montgomery Co Militia **CEM:** Phipps Family; GPS unk; Wytheville; Wythe **GS:** N **SP:** (-----), have children **VI:** Family tradition is bur on his farm. Cemetery is lost **P:** unk **BLW:** unk **RG:** unk **MK:** N **PH:** N **SS:** G pg 232 **BS:** 196.

PHIPPS (PHIPS), Benjamin; b 1761 or 1762, Guilford Co, NC; d 3 May 1838 **RU:** Private, Served in SC & VA Lines **CEM:** Benjamin-Phipps; GPS unk; Saddle Creek Rt 681; Grayson **GS:** U **SP:** Mar (5 July 1782) Jean (-----) **VI:** Appl for pension 24 Sep 1832, Montomery Co, NC (Now Grayson Co) W5539. Widow appl 5 Jul 1844 Grayson Co, VA **P:** Y **BLW:** unk **RG:** Y **MK:** unk **PH:** unk **SS:** J-NSSAR 1993 Reg, J- DAR Hatcher; CG Vol 3 pg 2691 **BS:** JLARC 1, 2.

PHIPPS (PHIPS), John; b 1761; d 1838 **RU:** Private, Served in 10th Cont Line **CEM:** Phipps Family; GPS unk; Saddle Creek; Grayson **GS:** U **SP:** No info **VI:** No further data **P:** unk **BLW:** unk **RG:** Y **MK:** unk **PH:** unk **SS:** J-NSSAR 1993 Reg; E pg 624 **BS:** JLARC 1.

PICHON, Noel; b unk; d 1781 **RU:** Seaman, Served on "Citoyen" and died from Yorktown battle **CEM:** French Memorial; GPS 36.81944, -79.39933; Yorktown; York **GS:** U **SP:** No info **VI:** No further data **P:** unk **BLW:** unk **RG:** Y **MK:** unk **PH:** unk **SS:** J-Yorktown Historian **BS:** JLARC 1, 74.

RU=Rank/Unit	CEM=Cemetery	GS=Gravestone	SP=Spousal Information
VI=Other Veteran Info	P=Pension	BLW=Bounty/Land Warrant	RG=Registered Grave
MK=SAR/DAR Marker	PH=Photo	SS=Service Source	BS=Burial Source

267

PICHON, Pierre; b unk; d 1781 **RU:** Seaman, Served on "Hextor" and died from Yorktown battle **CEM:** French Memorial; GPS 36.81944, -79.39933; Yorktown; York **GS:** U **SP:** No info **VI:** No further data **P:** unk **BLW:** unk **RG:** Y **MK:** unk **PH:** unk **SS:** J-Yorktown Historian **BS:** JLARC 1, 74.

PIELEE, Gilbert; b c1740, Holland; d 22 Feb 1790 **RU:** Patriot, Gave material aid to the cause **CEM:** Tavern Lot; GPS unk; Center of Accomac; Accomack **GS:** Y **SP:** No info **VI:** Native of Holland, d age 40 **P:** N **BLW:** N **RG:** N **MK:** N **PH:** unk **SS:** AL Com Bk I pg 30 **BS:** 37 pg 205.

PIERCE, John; b 1750 or 1760; d 1833 **RU:** Private, Service information not determined **CEM:** Pierce Family; GPS unk; Rt 211, Amissville; Rappahannock **GS:** Y **SP:** Petunia Hune (1769-1808) **VI:** No further data **P:** unk **BLW:** unk **RG:** Y **MK:** N **PH:** unk **SS:** E pg 625 **BS:** 33; 163.

PIERCE (PEIRCE), Joseph; b 1728; d 5 Jun 1798 **RU:** Captain/Patriot, Gave material aid to the cause **CEM:** Old Pierce Homestead; GPS unk; Level Green; Westmoreland **GS:** Y **SP:** Sarah E. Pierce (__-20 Sep 1783) **VI:** Son of William Pierce & (-----) of Westmoreland. Magistrate and Deacon. Liberated a large number of slaves in will. Honorably mentioned in Semples History of Virginia Baptists **P:** unk **BLW:** unk **RG:** N **MK:** N **PH:** unk **SS:** AL Cert Issued **BS:** 107 pg 550, 551.

PIERCY, Henry; b unk; d 17 Jun 1809 **RU:** Captain, Served in 2nd PA Regt until end of war **CEM:** Christ Church Episcopal; GPS 38.80216, -77.05689; Wilkes St & Hamilton Ln; Alexandria City **GS:** N **SP:** Nancy (-----) **VI:** Member of Society of Cinncinatti. Bur with military, Masonic, civil honors (Alexandria Gazette, 20 Jun 1809, pg 3). Entitled to 200 acres bounty land which was issued 1794 to Paul Bentalow. Widow appl pen 1810 and was denied and was advised to take legal action **P:** unk **BLW:** Y **RG:** Y **MK:** N **PH:** N **SS:** E pg 625; BX pg 637 **BS:** 20 pg 110.

PIERROT, Nicholas; b unk; d 1781 **RU:** Seaman, Served on "Diademe" and died from Yorktown battle **CEM:** French Memorial; GPS 36.81944, -79.39933; Yorktown; York **GS:** U **SP:** No info **VI:** No further data **P:** unk **BLW:** unk **RG:** Y **MK:** unk **PH:** unk **SS:** J-Yorktown Historian **BS:** JLARC 1, 74.

PIERSON, Charles; b unk; d 1781 **RU:** Soldier, Served in Gatinais Bn and died fr battle at Yorktown **CEM:** French Memorial; GPS 36.81944, -79.39933; Yorktown; York **GS:** U **SP:** No info **VI:** No further data **P:** unk **BLW:** unk **RG:** Y **MK:** unk **PH:** unk **SS:** J-Yorktown Historian **BS:** JLARC 1, 74.

PIGG, Hezekiah Ford; b 1742, Jones Mill, Pittsylvania Co; d 21 Nov 1785 **RU:** Patriot, Gave material aid to the cause in Pittsylvania Co **CEM:** Pigg Mill Farm; GPS 36.77373, -79.46067; Rt 703, Jones Mill; Pittsylvania **GS:** Y **SP:** 1) Elizabeth Nash 2) Mary Clement 3) Agnes Owen **VI:** Son of Capt John Ghent (1716-1785) & Ann (Clement) Pigg **P:** N **BLW:** N **RG:** N **MK:** N **PH:** unk **SS:** D pg 197; AL CT BK pg 18 **BS:** 82 pg 283; 196.

PIGG, John; b c1720, Amelia Co; d 21 Feb 1785 **RU:** Artillery Captain/Patriot, Provided corn, bacon, flour, brandy for state and continental troops. Was Capt of Militia & VA Artillery **CEM:** Pigg Mill Farm; GPS 36.77373, -79.46067; Rt 703, Jones Mill; Pittsylvania **GS:** Y **SP:** Ann Clement (mar in Amelia) **VI:** Son of Paul and (-----) Pigg **P:** unk **BLW:** unk **RG:** unk **MK:** unk **PH:** unk **SS:** D Pittsylvania Co **BS:** 174, JLARC 20.

PIGGOTT, William; b unk; d 1846 **RU:** Sergeant, Served in VA First Artillery **CEM:** Goose Creek; GPS 39.11250, -77.69527; Rt 722, Lincoln; Loudoun **GS:** Y **SP:** No info **VI:** No further data **P:** unk **BLW:** unk **RG:** Y **MK:** N **PH:** unk **SS:** E pg 625 **BS:** 25 pg 243.

PIGIBIT, Jean; b unk; d 1781 **RU:** Soldier, Served in Soissonnais Bn and died fr battle at Yorktown **CEM:** French Memorial; GPS 36.81944, -79.39933; Yorktown; York **GS:** U **SP:** No info **VI:** No further data **P:** unk **BLW:** unk **RG:** Y **MK:** unk **PH:** unk **SS:** J-Yorktown Historian **BS:** JLARC 1, 74.

PILAU, Jean; b unk; d 1781 **RU:** Soldier, Served in Gatinais Bn and died fr battle at Yorktown **CEM:** French Memorial; GPS 36.81944, -79.39933; Yorktown; York **GS:** U **SP:** no info **VI:** No further data **P:** unk **BLW:** unk **RG:** Y **MK:** unk **PH:** unk **SS:** J-Yorktown Historian **BS:** JLARC 1, 74.

PINCERON, Francois; b unk; d 1781 **RU:** Seaman, Served on "Duc De Bourgogne" and died from Yorktown battle **CEM:** French Memorial; GPS 36.81944, -79.39933; Yorktown; York **GS:** U **SP:** No info **VI:** No further data **P:** unk **BLW:** unk **RG:** Y **MK:** unk **PH:** unk **SS:** J-Yorktown Historian **BS:** JLARC 1, 74.

RU=Rank/Unit	CEM=Cemetery	GS=Gravestone	SP=Spousal Information
VI=Other Veteran Info	P=Pension	BLW=Bounty/Land Warrant	RG=Registered Grave
MK=SAR/DAR Marker	PH=Photo	SS=Service Source	BS=Burial Source

268

PINET, Jean; b unk; d 1781 **RU:** Soldier, Served in Touraine Bn and died fr battle at Yorktown **CEM:** French Memorial; GPS 36.81944, -79.39933; Yorktown; York **GS:** U **SP:** No info **VI:** No further data **P:** unk **BLW:** unk **RG:** Y **MK:** unk **PH:** unk **SS:** J-Yorktown Historian **BS:** JLARC 1, 74.

PINNELL, Thomas; b Nov 1740, Amherst Co; d 12 Nov 1812 **RU:** Private, Served in 2nd Cont Line. Served in Capt Peyton's Co, Col Alexander's Regt and in Col Spotswood's 2d Regt of Foot **CEM:** Amherst; GPS 37.59640, -79.03670; Bus Rt 29, Amherst; Amherst **GS:** U **SP:** Mar (15 Jun 1765) Sarah Clopton (3 Mar 1742, Amherst Co-__) **VI:** No further data **P:** unk **BLW:** unk **RG:** Y **MK:** unk **PH:** unk **SS:** DAR #A089190; J-NSSAR 2000 Reg; E pg 627; DD **BS:** JLARC 76.

PIPER, James; b 11 Feb 1737; d 20 Sep 1825 **RU:** Soldier, Fought at Kings Mountain **CEM:** Sinking Springs; GPS 36.71030, -81.98170; 136 E Main St, Abingdon; Washington **GS:** U **SP:** Margaret Vance (22 Apr 1744-28 Dec 1831) d/o Samuel & Sarah (Colvill) Vance. She mar William Lusk 2nd as widow. **VI:** DAR marker **P:** unk **BLW:** unk **RG:** Y **MK:** Y **PH:** unk **SS:** AR Vol 3 pg 176 **BS:** JLARC 1, 2, 80; 212 pg 76; 196.

PITMAN (PITTMAN), Andrew; b 1760; d 22 Sep 1838 **RU:** Private, Served in Frederick Co Militia. Served also in VA Line **CEM:** German Reformed Church; GPS 39.08150, -78.21840; Mulberry St, Stephen City; Frederick **GS:** Y **SP:** Mar (08 Sep 1829, Frederick Co) Margaret Lefevre (1796-__) her 2d mar to John Minnix **VI:** Former widow appl pen 2 Jan 1860 # W9998; he appl pen 7 Nov 1832, no evidence of receiving **P:** Y **BLW:** unk **RG:** N **MK:** N **PH:** unk **SS:** E pg 628; CG pg 2707-8 **BS:** 112.GerReform.

PITMAN (PITTMAN), Phillip; b unk; d 1820 **RU:** Private, Served in Capt Alexander Machir's Co in the Strasburg District of the Militia **CEM:** Hockmans; GPS unk; vic Lebanon Church; Frederick **GS:** Y **SP:** No info **VI:** No further data **P:** unk **BLW:** unk **RG:** N **MK:** N **PH:** unk **SS:** C pg 606 **BS:** 50 pg 76.

PITOZZEAU, N; b unk; d 1781 **RU:** Seaman, Served on the "Destin" and died from Yorktown battle **CEM:** French Memorial; GPS 36.81944, -79.39933; Yorktown; York **GS:** U **SP:** No info **VI:** No further data **P:** unk **BLW:** unk **RG:** Y **MK:** unk **PH:** unk **SS:** J Yorktown Historian **BS:** JLARC 1, 74.

PITTS, Hezekiah; b 19 Oct 1745; d 1 Oct 1823 **RU:** Captain/Patriot, Served in Northampton Co Militia. Took oath as Capt 14 May 1782. Gave material aid to cause **CEM:** Long Point Farm; GPS unk; Rt 711; Northampton **GS:** Y **SP:** Mar (10 Jun 1773) Mildred Scarburg (26 Feb 1754-29 Jun 1819) **VI:** No further data **P:** unk **BLW:** unk **RG:** N **MK:** N **PH:** unk **SS:** E pg 628; AL Ct Bk pg 4 Northampton Co **BS:** 42 pg 64.

PITTS, Major; b 25 Nov 1755; d 15 Oct 1839 **RU:** Sergeant, Served in VA Line. Ent serv 1775 Northampton Co **CEM:** Wescott Farm; GPS unk; Rt 606 NW of Nassawadox; Northampton **GS:** Y **SP:** No info **VI:** Lived in Northhampton Co. Pen appl for 10 Sep 1832 at age 78. S5931 **P:** Y **BLW:** unk **RG:** N **MK:** N **PH:** unk **SS:** E pg 628; K Vol 4 pg 116; CG Vol 3 2709 **BS:** JLARC 4, 69, 42, pg 64.

PLACET, Claude; b unk; d 1781 **RU:** Seaman, Served on "Hextor" and died from Yorktown battle **CEM:** French Memorial; GPS 36.81944, -79.39933; Yorktown; York **GS:** U **SP:** No info **VI:** No further data **P:** unk **BLW:** unk **RG:** Y **MK:** unk **PH:** unk **SS:** J-Yorktown Historian **BS:** JLARC 1, 74.

PLAGNOLET, Jean; b unk; d 1781 **RU:** Soldier, Served in Soissonnais Bn and died fr battle at Yorktown **CEM:** French Memorial; GPS 36.81944, -79.39933; Yorktown; York **GS:** U **SP:** No info **VI:** No further data **P:** unk **BLW:** unk **RG:** Y **MK:** unk **PH:** unk **SS:** J-Yorktown Historian **BS:** JLARC 1, 74.

PLANTO, Jean; b unk; d 1781 **RU:** Seaman, Served on "Languedoc" and died from Yorktown battle **CEM:** French Memorial; GPS 36.81944, -79.39933; Yorktown; York **GS:** U **SP:** No info **VI:** No further data **P:** unk **BLW:** unk **RG:** Y **MK:** unk **PH:** unk **SS:** J-Yorktown Historian **BS:** JLARC 1, 74.

PLASTER, Michael; b c1724, Germany; d 14 Jun 1803 **RU:** Private?, Took oath of Allegiance **CEM:** Green Hill Primitive Baptist; GPS unk; Patrick Springs; Patrick **GS:** Y **SP:** 1) (-----) 2) Mar (c1770) Tamer Houston (__-1804) **VI:** Died in Franklin Co **P:** unk **BLW:** unk **RG:** N **MK:** N **PH:** unk **SS:** DAR #A089562; B; BE Vol 9 pg 141; VA Mag Hist & Bio Vol 9 pg 141 **BS:** 125 pg 383.

RU=Rank/Unit	CEM=Cemetery	GS=Gravestone	SP=Spousal Information
VI=Other Veteran Info	P=Pension	BLW=Bounty/Land Warrant	RG=Registered Grave
MK=SAR/DAR Marker	PH=Photo	SS=Service Source	BS=Burial Source

269

PLISSON, Jean; b unk; d 1781 **RU:** Seaman, Served on "Sceptre" and died from Yorktown battle **CEM:** French Memorial; GPS 36.81944, -79.39933; Yorktown; York **GS:** U **SP:** No info **VI:** No further data **P:** unk **BLW:** unk **RG:** Y **MK:** unk **PH:** unk **SS:** J-Yorktown Historian **BS:** JLARC 1, 74.

POAGE, Robert; b 1760; d 1836 **RU:** Second Lieutenant, Served in Rockbridge Co Militia 7 Jul 1778 **CEM:** Augusta Stone Presbyterian; GPS 38.23926, -78.97356; 28 Old Stone Church Ln, Ft Defiance; Augusta **GS:** Y **SP:** No info **VI:** Govt stone **P:** unk **BLW:** unk **RG:** Y **MK:** unk **PH:** unk **SS:** AZ pg 228 **BS:** JLARC 1, 2, 8, 23, 62, 63; 196.

POAGE, Thomas; b 1740; d 1803 **RU:** Private/Patriot, Served in Capt Anderson's Co, Augusta Co Militia. Gave material aid to cause **CEM:** Augusta Stone Presbyterian; GPS 38.23926, -78.97356; 28 Old Stone Church Ln, Ft Defiance; Augusta **GS:** Y **SP:** Agnes "Polly" McClanachan (1744-__) **VI:** Govt stone says he was in Capt Anderson's Co. Died in Staunton **P:** unk **BLW:** unk **RG:** Y **MK:** unk **PH:** unk **SS:** B; E pg 629; AL Com Bk II pg 361 Augusta Co **BS:** JLARC 1, 2, 8, 23, 62; 196.

POAGE, William; b 1759; d 23 Sep 1834 **RU:** Private, Served in VA Line. Ent serv 1777 Botetourt Co **CEM:** Poage's Mill; GPS 37.19800, -80.05600; Rt 221, Bent Mountain Rd, village of Poages Mill; Roanoke Co **GS:** U **SP:** Mar (23 Dec 1806 Botetourt Co) Elizabeth Franklin (c1785-10 or 11 Jul 1867) d/o Nathan & (-----) Franklin **VI:** Pension appl for 12 Nov 1832 age 73 Botecourt Co. Widow appl pen 28 Jul 1853 age 68 Roanoke Co. W8502 **P:** Y **BLW:** unk **RG:** unk **MK:** unk **PH:** unk **SS:** J- DAR Hatcher, K Vol 4 pg 117; CG Vol 3 pg 2716 **BS:** JLARC 2.

POAGUE (POAGE), James; b 1747; d 9 Sep 1811 **RU:** Patriot, Gave material aid to cause **CEM:** Old Providence; GPS 37.96151, -79.71000; 1005 Spottswood Rd, Spottswood; Augusta **GS:** N **SP:** No info **VI:** Name is on SAR plaque at cemetery **P:** N **BLW:** N **RG:** unk **MK:** Y **PH:** N **SS:** AL Lists pg 10 Augusta Co; BT **BS:** JLARC 2, 62; 213 pg 460.

POAGUE (POAGE), John; b unk; d 1810 **RU:** Captain, Commanded co in Augusta Co Militia **CEM:** Locust Bottom; GPS unk; Jct Rts 622 & 696; Botetourt **GS:** Y **SP:** No info **VI:** No further data **P:** unk **BLW:** unk **RG:** Y **MK:** N **PH:** unk **SS:** E pg 629 **BS:** 115 pg 12.

POAGUE (POAGE), John Jr; b 1757; d 10 Apr 1827 **RU:** Ensign, Served in Capt Anderson's Co, Augusta Co Militia. Took oath as ensign 18 Sep 1781 **CEM:** Augusta Stone Presbyterian; GPS 38.23926, -78.97356; 28 Old Stone Church Ln, Ft Defiance; Augusta **GS:** U **SP:** 1) Mar (16 Nov 1802 Botetourt Co) Jane Kyle d/o William & (-----) Kyle 2) Mar (20 Jun 1807 Botetourt Co) Catherine Sheets **VI:** Son of John (1726-1789) & (-----) Poague. Govt stone **P:** unk **BLW:** unk **RG:** Y **MK:** unk **PH:** unk **SS:** E pg 629; AZ pg 328 **BS:** JLARC 1, 2, 8, 23, 62, 63; 196.

POHEAGUE, Josias; b unk; d 16 Oct 1781 **RU:** Private, Served in Capt Eldridge Co, CT Cont Line, and died fr battle at Yorktown **CEM:** Yorktown Victory Monument Tablet; GPS 38.28350, -78.54150; Yorktown; York **GS:** U **SP:** No info **VI:** No further data **P:** unk **BLW:** unk **MK:** unk **PH:** unk **SS:** J-Yorktown Historian; DY pg 152 **BS:** JLARC 74.

POIGNARD, Jean or Hector; b unk; d 1781 **RU:** Seaman, Served on "Languedoc" and died from Yorktown battle **CEM:** French Memorial; GPS 36.81944, -79.39933; Yorktown; York **GS:** U **SP:** No info **VI:** No further data **P:** unk **BLW:** unk **RG:** unk **MK:** unk **PH:** unk **SS:** J-Yorktown Historian **BS:** JLARC 1, 74.

POINDEXTER, John Sr; b 1765, Meclenburg Co; d 1817 **RU:** Private, Served in VA Calvary unit in Illinois **CEM:** Poindexter Family; GPS unk; Jct Rts 655 & 834; Franklin **GS:** Y **SP:** Mar (11 Oct 1792 Lunenburg Co) Nancy Neal **VI:** Son of Phillip (c1707-__) & Sarah (Grymes) (20 Aug 1744-__) Poindexter **P:** unk **BLW:** unk **RG:** N **MK:** N **PH:** unk **SS:** E pg 629 **BS:** 82 pg 286; 196.

POINDEXTER, Joseph; b 1736; d 29 Jun 1826 **RU:** Captain, Commanded Co in Bedford Co Militia, oath 28 Sep 1778 **CEM:** Whipping Creek; GPS 37.03430, -79.00180; Rt 633 Epsons Rd nr Long Island; Campbell **GS:** N **SP:** (Order of marriages unk) Elizabeth (-----) & Mar (19 May 1800 Cambell Co (bond)) Frances I. Harrison **VI:** No further data **P:** unk **BLW:** unk **RG:** unk **MK:** N **PH:** N **SS:** E pg 630 **BS:** JLARC 2, 3, 4, 36; 196.

POINDEXTER, Thomas; b 25 May 1760, Elk's Creek, Loudoun Co; d 10 Apr 1843 **RU:** Soldier/Patriot, Ent serv Louisa Co in VA Line. Gave material aid to cause **CEM:** Valetta; GPS unk; Nr Green Springs;

RU=Rank/Unit	CEM=Cemetery	GS=Gravestone	SP=Spousal Information
VI=Other Veteran Info	P=Pension	BLW=Bounty/Land Warrant	RG=Registered Grave
MK=SAR/DAR Marker	PH=Photo	SS=Service Source	BS=Burial Source

270

Louisa **GS:** U **SP:** Mar (18 or 28 Mar 1790) Sarah Ragland (c1769-__) **VI:** Lived in KY after RW for short time, then came back to Loudoun. Appl for pension 15 Jun 1837 W5556. Recd BLW #26961-160-55. Widow appl pen 3 Nov 1846 age 77 W5556 **P:** Y **BLW:** Y **RG:** unk **MK**: unk **PH:** unk **SS:** K Vol 4 pg 129; AL Ct Bk pg 20 Louisa Co; CG Vol 3 pg 2717 **BS:** JLARC 4, 61.

POLLARD, Joseph; b 1758 or 1759; d 6 Sep 1836 **RU:** Private, Ent serv c1779 Goochland Co in a VA regt. Served in 2nd Cont Line in Capt Everard Meades Co in Mar 1777. Brother Robert was discharged fr RW service 1781, went to grandfather's house in Goochland Co, & took supplies to Joseph "who was then serving on retreat of General Lafayette May 1781" **CEM:** Mattaponi Church; GPS unk; Nr Cumnor; King & Queen **GS:** U **SP:** Mar (17 Mar 1791 Hanover Co) Catharine Robinson (__-22 May 1843) **VI:** Pension appl for 10 Dec 1832 age 74 King and Queen Co. Widow appl pen 9 Nov 1840 in King & Queen Co age 71 W5555 **P:** Y **BLW:** unk **RG:** Y **MK**: unk **PH:** unk **SS:** J-NSSAR 1993 Reg; K Vol 4 pg 120; CG Vol 3 pg 2720 **BS:** 196; JLARC 1; E pg 660.

POLLARD, Robert; b 3 Jul 1756, Culpeper Co; d 10 Oct 1847 **RU:** Captain, Served in VA line. Ent serv Culpeper Co 1777 **CEM:** Shockoe Hill; GPS 37.55190, -77.43170; 4th & Hospital Sts; Richmond City **GS:** Y **SP:** Jael Underwood **VI:** Moved Richmond City c1784. Pension appl for 30 Jul 1832 Richmond age 76, S5944 **P:** Y **BLW:** unk **RG:** unk **MK**: N **PH:** Y **SS:** K Vol 4 pg 120; AK; CG Vol 3 pg 2720 **BS:** 04.

POLLARD, William; b c1720; d 1792 **RU:** Patriot, Served as Clerk of Ct, Hanover Co, 1775-1781 **CEM:** Mattaponi Baptist; GPS unk; Vic King & Queen CH; King & Queen **GS:** N **SP:** Mary Anderson **VI:** Son of Joseph (1701-26 Dec 1791) & Priscilla (Holmes) (1701 Caroline Co-26 Jul 1795) Pollard **P:** N **BLW:** N **RG:** unk **MK**: unk **PH:** unk **SS:** DAR Ancestor #A090267; CD **BS:** 196.

POLLET, Denis; b unk; d 1781 **RU:** Seaman, Served on "Duc De Bourgogne" and died from Yorktown battle **CEM:** French Memorial; GPS 36.81944, -79.39933; Yorktown; York **GS:** U **SP:** No info **VI:** No further data **P:** unk **BLW:** unk **RG:** Y **MK**: unk **PH:** unk **SS:** J-Yorktown Historian **BS:** JLARC 1, 74.

POLLOCKFIELD, John Richard Sr; b 4 Jul 1726, Prince George Co, MD; d 1 Jan 1804 **RU:** Private, Served in Lt William Edmiston's Co, Washington Co Militia in Dunmore's War **CEM:** Soloman Litton Hollow; GPS unk; nr Pinnacle Preserve; Russell **GS:** U **SP:** Sarah Ann Wilcoxen (1728-1808) **VI:** Son of Caleb Pollockfield (1678-1763) & Mary Grace Burton (Willett) (1703-1791) Litton. SAR Grave marker. Govt Grave stone lists service **P:** unk **BLW:** unk **RG:** Y **MK**: Y **PH:** unk **SS:** J-NSSAR 2000 Reg; Z pg 152 **BS:** JLARC 76; 196.

POPE, William; b 23 Oct 1762, Louisa Co; d 19 Jul 1852 **RU:** Private, Served in Brig Gen Armand's Command 15 Nov 1783 **CEM:** Dabney at Montpelier; GPS unk; Maiden's Rd, abt 2 mi N of Anderson Hwy, E side of rd, N of Montpelier Plantation; Powhatan **GS:** Y **SP:** Mar (14 Jun 1774 Henrico Co) Ann Woodson (1774-28 Oct 1823) d/o Charles & Nancy (Trotter) Woodson Jr. **VI:** The Commonwelth Attorney of Powhatan Co; also Capt in the War of 1812. Recd 100 acres BLW fr VA, and 100 acres fr US **P:** N **BLW:** Y **RG:** unk **MK**: unk **PH:** unk **SS:** N pg 1253 **BS:** 196.

PORTER, Patrick; b 1 May 1737, Ireland; d 28 Apr 1798 **RU:** Sergeant/Patriot, Served in Capt Joseph Martin's Militia Co; furnished supplies **CEM:** Porter Family; GPS unk; Rt 682 Dungannon; Scott **GS:** Y **SP:** Susannah Walker **VI:** VA historical road sign indicates he had a mill in1774 and built a fort to protect residents fr Indian attacks. DAR plaque **P:** unk **BLW:** unk **RG:** Y **MK**: Y **PH:** Y **SS:** AK Payrolls **BS:** 04, Oct 06; 196.

PORTER, Samuel; b 1764; d 1814 **RU:** Captain, Served in VA unit in Illinois. His Co was with Daniel Boone in KY in the defense of Boonesborough, KY, 1778 **CEM:** Trinity Episcopal; GPS 36.83459, -76.30105; 500 Court St; Portsmouth City **GS:** Y **SP:** No info **VI:** No further data **P:** unk **BLW:** unk **RG:** N **MK**: N **PH:** unk **SS:** B indicates Capt; CZ pg 356; VA Historical Road sign inscription # K18 **BS:** 147 Trinity Ch.

PORTER, Thomas; b 1759, Fauquier Co; d May 1840 **RU:** Sergeant, Served in Col Christian Febiger's 2nd Regt **CEM:** Old Presbyterian Meeting House; GPS 38.48528, -77.23532; 323 S Fairfax St; Alexandria City **GS:** N **SP:** Susannah "Sukey" Nancy (-----) **VI:** Died in Trevilians, Louisa Co. Death notice in Alexandria Gazette 1 May 1800, pg 3. Listed on SAR plaque in cemetery **P:** unk **BLW:** unk **RG:** Y **MK**: Y **PH:** N **SS:** J-NSSAR 1993 Reg; AK; DD **BS:** JLARC 1; 196.

RU=Rank/Unit   CEM=Cemetery   GS=Gravestone   SP=Spousal Information
VI=Other Veteran Info   P=Pension   BLW=Bounty/Land Warrant   RG=Registered Grave
MK=SAR/DAR Marker   PH=Photo   SS=Service Source   BS=Burial Source

271

PORTER, William; b c1749-50, Norfolk Co; d 20 Jun 1807 **RU:** Lieutenant, Ent serv Norfolk Co in Capt Ballard's Co,12th VA Regt until end of war serving over 7 yrs. Was one of oldest Lts **CEM:** Glasgow Street Park; GPS unk; 425 Glasgow St; Portsmouth City **GS:** Y **SP:** Mar (31 Oct 1782 Norfolk Co) Elizabeth Luke d/o Isaac & (-----) Luke **VI:** Son of William & Patience (-----) Porter. Stepfather Joshua Nicholson. Marker moved 1929 fr Monumental graveyard. Ancestor of John Luke Porter; designer of Merrimack; Founding member of Monumental UMC in 1772. Widow appl pen $320/yr 1838 as resident Portsmouth W5159 **P:** Y **BLW:** unk **RG:** Y **MK:** Y **PH:** Y **SS:** K Vol 4 pg 128; Z **BS:** JLARC 2, 4, 39, 105.

PORTERFIELD, Robert; b 22 Feb 1752, Frederick Co; d 13 Feb 1843 **RU:** Captain, Commissioned 2nd Lt in Cont Army 12 Dec 1776 and assigned 11th VA Militia. Promoted 1st Lt 1 Jun 1777. Transferred to 7th VA Regt 14 Sep 1778. Promoted to Capt 16 Aug 1779. Taken as POW at surrender of Charleston SC and kept on prison ship to end of war **CEM:** Thornrose; GPS 38,15120, -79.08460; 1041 W Beverly St; Staunton City **GS:** Y **SP:** 1) Mary Margaret Heth 2) Rebecca Farrar **VI:** Appl pen 16 Jun 1828 Augusta Co. S8965. BLW rec'd 18 Sep 1789, #1738-300. He was re-interred **P:** Y **BLW:** Y **RG:** unk **MK:** N **PH:** Y **SS:** AP Natl Service Records; K Vol 4 pg 129; CG Vol 3 pg 2727 **BS:** JLARC 2, 4, 62, 63.

POTTEN, John; b 1763; d 30 Sep 1835 **RU:** Private, Served in Capt Andrew Fitch's Co, 4th Battalion of CT forces **CEM:** Trinity United Methodist; GPS 39.13600, -77.00610; 2911 Cameron Mills Rd; Alexandria City **GS:** Y **SP:** Sarah (-----) (1775-7 Sep 1829) **VI:** Death notice in Alexandria Gazette 1 Oct 1835, pg 3 **P:** unk **BLW:** unk **RG:** N **MK:** N **PH:** unk **SS:** AP roll **BS:** 23 pg 136.

POTTER, Ebenezer; b Apr 1764; d 7 Oct 1807 **RU:** Private, Served in Illinois Regt & Western Army under Gen George Clark **CEM:** Leesburg Presbyterian; GPS 39.11611, -77.56722; 207 W Market St, Leesburg; Loudoun **GS:** Y **SP:** No info **VI:** No further data **P:** unk **BLW:** unk **RG:** Y **MK:** N **PH:** unk **SS:** G pg 702-3 **BS:** 25 pg 245.

POTTS, Ezekiel; b 8 Jan 1743, Fairfax Co; d 16 Jan 1809 **RU:** Private?/Patriot, Served in Capt Burgess Ball's Co 5th Cont Line. Gave material aid to cause **CEM:** Potts Family; GPS 39.19455, -77.76157; Rts 716 & 714, Hillsboro; Loudoun **GS:** Y **SP:** Mar (29 Nov 1769) Elizabeth Mead (6 Oct 1745-22 Jan 1825 Hillsboro) **VI:** No further data **P:** unk **BLW:** unk **RG:** Y **MK:** N **PH:** unk **SS:** DAR #A091836; E pg 634; AL Ct Bk pg 11 Loudoun Co **BS:** 25 pg 246.

POTTS, John; b 16 Jun 1830 (burial); d 1830 **RU:** Corporal, Served in Capt Portersfield's Co, 30 Nov 1778, Col Morgan's Riflemen, 11th Cont Line. Also served in 2nd VA Brigade and the 7th &15th Cont Lines **CEM:** Shockoe Hill; GPS 37.55190, -77.43170; 4th & Hospital Sts; Richmond City **GS:** Y **SP:** No info **VI:** No further data **P:** unk **BLW:** unk **RG:** N **MK:** N **PH:** unk **SS:** A pg 261; E pg 634 **BS:** 57 pg 8; 196.

POTTS, Jonas; b 22 Aug 1779; d 26 Sep 1828 **RU:** Private, Served on "Romney" in 1775, then joined the Army of the Revolution in Capt Hugh Stephenson's Co **CEM:** Potts Family; GPS 39.19455, -77.76157; Rts 716 & 714, Hillsboro; Loudoun **GS:** Y **SP:** Martha Dowling (28 Dec 1782-15 Mar 1852) **VI:** Son of Ezekiel (1743-1809) & Elizabeth (Mead) (1821-1825) Potts **P:** unk **BLW:** unk **RG:** Y **MK:** N **PH:** unk **SS:** E pg 634 **BS:** 25 pg 247; 196.

POTTS, Nathaniel; b unk; d 1830 **RU:** Patriot, Gave material aid to cause **CEM:** Ketoctin Baptist; GPS 39.15746, -77.74870; Ketoctin Church Rd, Purcellville; Loudoun **GS:** Y **SP:** No info **VI:** No further data **P:** N **BLW:** N **RG:** N **MK:** N **PH:** unk **SS:** D Vol 2 pg 599; AL Ct Bk pg 11 Loudoun Co **BS:** 25 pg 247.

POULAIN, Charles; b unk; d 1781 **RU:** Soldier, Served in Soissonnais Bn and died fr battle at Yorktown **CEM:** French Memorial; GPS 36.81944, -79.39933; Yorktown; York **GS:** U **SP:** No info **VI:** No further data **P:** unk **BLW:** unk **RG:** Y **MK:** unk **PH:** unk **SS:** J-Yorktown Historian **BS:** JLARC 1, 74.

POULAIN, Jean; b unk; d 1781 **RU:** Seaman, Served on "Citoyen" and died from Yorktown battle **CEM:** French Memorial; GPS 36.81944, -79.39933; Yorktown; York **GS:** U **SP:** No info **VI:** No further data **P:** unk **BLW:** unk **RG:** Y **MK:** unk **PH:** unk **SS:** J-Yorktown Historian **BS:** JLARC 1, 74.

POULSON, George B; b unk; d 1801 **RU:** Ensign/Patriot, Was paid for work on Ft Matompkin **CEM:** Ketoctin Baptist; GPS 39.15746, -77.74870; Ketoctin Church Rd, Purcellville; Loudoun **GS:** U **SP:** No info **VI:** No further data **P:** unk **BLW:** unk **RG:** Y **MK:** unk **PH:** unk **SS:** G pg 501 **BS:** JLARC 1, 2, 32.

RU=Rank/Unit   CEM=Cemetery   GS=Gravestone   SP=Spousal Information
VI=Other Veteran Info   P=Pension   BLW=Bounty/Land Warrant   RG=Registered Grave
MK=SAR/DAR Marker   PH=Photo   SS=Service Source   BS=Burial Source

272

POUPON, Francois; b unk; d 1781 **RU:** Soldier, Served in Gatinais Bn and died fr battle at Yorktown **CEM:** French Memorial; GPS 36.81944, -79.39933; Yorktown; York **GS:** U **SP:** No info **VI:** No further data **P:** unk **BLW:** unk **RG:** Y **MK:** unk **PH:** unk **SS:** J-Yorktown Historian **BS:** JLARC 1, 74.

POUVEREAU, Jean; b unk; d 1781 **RU:** Soldier, Served in Santogne Bn and died fr battle at Yorktown **CEM:** French Memorial; GPS 36.81944, -79.39933; Yorktown; York **GS:** U **SP:** No info **VI:** No further data **P:** unk **BLW:** unk **RG:** Y **MK:** unk **PH:** unk **SS:** J-Yorktown Historian **BS:** JLARC 1, 74.

POWELL, John; b 1746; d unk **RU:** Doctor/Captain, Served in Col Meriweathers' Militia 1781, and died fr battle at Yorktown **CEM:** Unidentified; GPS unk; Yorktown; York **GS:** U **SP:** No info **VI:** No further data **P:** unk **BLW:** unk **RG:** Y **MK:** N **PH:** unk **SS:** AS DAR report; AZ pg 143 **BS:** DAR report.

POWELL, Lucas; b 1722; d 1811 **RU:** Patriot, Gave material aid to the cause; also had public service as Juror and member of Committee of Safety **CEM:** Powell Family; GPS unk; Amherst; Amherst **GS:** Y **SP:** Mar (1752) Elizabeth Edwards **VI:** No further data **P:** N **BLW:** N **RG:** Y **MK:** N **PH:** unk **SS:** AL CT BK pg 10; AS; SAR Appl; DD **BS:** SAR Appl.

POWELL, Ptolemy; b c1766 or 1767, King William Co; d 1840 **RU:** Private, Served at age15 fr 1777-1783 **CEM:** Green Level; GPS unk; Rt 652; Spotsylvania **GS:** Y **SP:** Sidney Daniel (1768-1843) Widow of James Leavette **VI:** No further data **P:** unk **BLW:** unk **RG:** Y **MK:** Y **PH:** unk **SS:** 08 Vol 1 pg 417-8 **BS:** 09 Part 2.

POWELL, William; b 1758; d 1829 **RU:** Lieutenant, Served in Co 3, Col Danial Morgan's Regt Jun 1777 **CEM:** Shady Grove Methodist; GPS unk; 11007 W Catharpin, Shady Grove Corner; Spotsylvania **GS:** U **SP:** No info **VI:** Blw 2666 Acres rec'd 08 Mar 1833 **P:** unk **BLW:** Y **RG:** unk **MK:** unk **PH:** unk **SS:** E pg 635 **BS:** 196.

PRADHOUT, Jean; b unk; d 1781 **RU:** Soldier, Served in Touraine Bn and died fr battle at Yorktown **CEM:** French Memorial; GPS 36.81944, -79.39933; Yorktown; York **GS:** U **SP:** No info **VI:** No further data **P:** unk **BLW:** unk **RG:** Y **MK:** unk **PH:** unk **SS:** J-Yorktown Historian **BS:** JLARC 1, 74.

PRATT, Anne Birkett; b 26 Oct 1718; d 8 May 1800 **RU:** Patriot, Provided one day 5 hands to ferry cattle to camp across Rappahannock River and pasturage for 80 cattle for 3 days, plus a beef and two bushels of corn **CEM:** Hungerford-Griffin; GPS unk; 373 Resolutions Rd, Leedstown; Westmoreland **GS:** Y **SP:** Thomas Hungerford (1740-1803) **VI:** Daughter of John (__-1724) & Margaret (Birkett) (__-1749) Pratt **P:** N **BLW:** N **RG:** unk **MK:** unk **PH:** unk **SS:** D pg 2, 9: AL Ct bk pg 1, 4 & Comm Bk V pg 220 **BS:** 196.

PRATT, John Birkett; b 4 Sep 1761; d 15 Jan 1843 **RU:** Corporal, Served in 3rd, 4th, 5th, & 8th Cont Lines for 3 yrs **CEM:** Pratt Family; GPS unk; Rt 686 Camden Rd; Caroline **GS:** U **SP:** Alice Fitzhugh (1789-1845) **VI:** No further data **P:** unk **BLW:** unk **RG:** Y **MK:** N **PH:** unk **SS:** E pg 636; C pg 488 **BS:** 02 pg 117,118; 196.

PRENTIS, Joseph; b 24 Jan 1754, York Co; d 19 Jun 1809 **RU:** Patriot, Was member of VA Convention1775, and Judge of Court of Admiralty during Revolution, and a member of VA House of Delegates 1777-78. Was Speaker of the House 1778, and member of Privy Council under Gov Patrick Henry 1779-81 **CEM:** Green Hill; GPS unk; Nassau St; Williamsburg City **GS:** N **SP:** Mar (16 Dec 1778) Margaret Bowden (27 Nov 1758-27 Aug 1801) **VI:** No further data **P:** N **BLW:** N **RG:** Y **MK:** N **PH:** N **SS:** G pg 546, 47 Vol 6 No 3 pg 190, 199 **BS:** 32.

PRESTON, Francis; b 2 Aug 1765, Botetourt Co; d 26 May 1835 **RU:** Private, Served in Botetourt Co Militia **CEM:** Aspenvale; GPS 36.81420, -81.64000; Rts 641 & 642, Seven Mile Ford; Smyth **GS:** U **SP:** Sarah Buchanan Campbell (1778-1846) d/o Gen William Campbell **VI:** Son of William (1729-1823) & Susanna (Smith) (1740-1823) Preston. Was Brig Gen in War of 1812, VA State Senate 1783, US Congressman 1793-1797. Died in Columbia SC **P:** unk **BLW:** Y **RG:** Y **MK:** unk **PH:** unk **SS:** J-NSSAR 1993 Reg; C pg 617 **BS:** JLARC 1; 97 pg 8; 196.

PRESTON, John; b May 1762; d Mar 1787 **RU:** Captain, Served in Montgomery Co Militia **CEM:** Weaver's; GPS unk; Not identified; Bristol City **GS:** U **SP:** 1) Mary Radford 2) Msr (1811) Elizabeth Ann Carrington of Richmond **VI:** Held rank after war Lt Col and Maj General. Treasurer of VA 1808-1819 **P:** unk **BLW:** unk **RG:** Y **MK:** N **PH:** unk **SS:** J-NSSAR 1993 Reg; AZ pg 131 **BS:** JLARC 1.

RU=Rank/Unit CEM=Cemetery GS=Gravestone SP=Spousal Information
VI=Other Veteran Info P=Pension BLW=Bounty/Land Warrant RG=Registered Grave
MK=SAR/DAR Marker PH=Photo SS=Service Source BS=Burial Source

273

PRESTON, John; b 2 May 1764; d 27 Mar 1827 **RU:** Private, Served in Capt James Bryne's Co in 1781 **CEM:** Greenfield; GPS 37.43750, -79.91420; Off International Pkwy, W of Rt 220, Amsterdam; Botetourt **GS:** U **SP:** No info **VI:** Maj General in War of 1812. Treasurer of VA. Prestonburg, KY named for him **P:** unk **BLW:** unk **RG:** N **MK:** N **PH:** unk **SS:** G pg 241 **BS:** 115 pg 77; 196.

PRESTON, John; b 24 Feb 1750 Buckingham, Bucks Co PA; d 24 Jun 1820 or 1829 **RU:** Private, Served in Capt John Thomas, 2nd Co, 4th Bn, Bucks Co PA **CEM:** South River Meeting House (aka Quaker Memorial Presbyterian); GPS 37.37246, -79.19194; 5810 Fort Ave; Lynchburg City **GS:** Y **SP:** Rebecca Vickers (1753-1834) **VI:** Son of John (1699-1785) & Elizabeth (Tucker) (1728-1752) Preston. Died in Campbell Co. DAR plaque **P:** unk **BLW:** unk **RG:** N **MK:** Y **PH:** N **SS:** CD cites PA service **BS:** JLARC 2, 4, 36; 196.

PRESTON, Robert; b 1750, Ireland; d 16 Dec 1833 **RU:** Private, Served in Capt Thomas Tebb's Co, Col Alexander Spotswood's 2nd VA Regt Jan-Jun 1777. Fought at Point Pleasant and Kings Mountain **CEM:** Walnut Grove; GPS unk; 3012 Lee Hwy Rt 11; Bristol City **GS:** Y **SP:** Margaret Rhea (1757-4 Jun 1822) **VI:** DAR marker **P:** unk **BLW:** unk **RG:** unk **MK:** Y **PH:** unk **SS:** A pg 277 **BS:** JLARC 2, 4, 34, 80; 78 pg 376; 196.

PRESTON, William; b 25 Dec 1729, Lima Vaddy, Ireland; d 1783 **RU:** Colonel/Patriot, Performed civil service as County Lt and a member of Committee of Safety and Justice of Peace **CEM:** Smithfield Plantation; GPS unk; VMI Campus, Blacksburg; Montgomery **GS:** U **SP:** Mar (17 Jul 1761) Susanna Smith (4 Jan 1739-19 Jun 1823) **VI:** No further data **P:** unk **BLW:** unk **RG:** Y **MK:** unk **PH:** unk **SS:** DAR #A092992; J-NSSAR 1993 Reg, J- DAR Hatcher; AL Ct Bk pg 11 Loudoun Co; CZ pg 258 **BS:** JLARC 1, 2.

PRESTON, William; b 1745; d 1781 **RU:** General, Was hero of Kings Mountain. Died near Richmond serving under Gen LaFayette **CEM:** Aspenvale; GPS 36.81420, -81.64000; Rts 641 & 642, Seven Mile Ford; Smyth **GS:** U **SP:** No info **VI:** Remains were brought to Aspenville Cemetery in 1932 **P:** unk **BLW:** unk **RG:** unk **MK:** unk **PH:** unk **SS:** E pg 637 **BS:** JLARC 97; 97 Vol 1 pg 8.

PREVOST, Charles; b unk; d 1781 **RU:** Soldier, Served in Santogne Bn and died fr battle at Yorktown **CEM:** French Memorial; GPS 36.81944, -79.39933; Yorktown; York **GS:** U **SP:** No info **VI:** No further data **P:** unk **BLW:** unk **RG:** Y **MK:** unk **PH:** unk **SS:** J-Yorktown Historian **BS:** JLARC 1, 74.

PRIBBLE (PREBBLE), John; b 1760, MD; d 14 Oct 1850 **RU:** Soldier, Ent Serv 1777 Bedford Co. Militia, VA Line. Served in Capts Charles Watkins, Robert Adams in Cols Calloway and Boones Regts **CEM:** Pribble - Dunn; GPS 37.30800, -79.24700; Castle Craig Quadrant, Evington; Campbell **GS:** U **SP:** Mar (1779, Campbell Co) Elizabeth Mason (1759 Henrico Co-__) **VI:** Lived on Otter River (later Campbell Co). Pensioned Campbell Co age 73 S5951 **P:** Y **BLW:** unk **RG:** unk **MK:** N **PH:** unk **SS:** K Vol 4 pg 143; CG Vol 3 pg 2768; DD **BS:** JLARC 4, 36.

PRICE, Augustine; b 24 Dec 1754; d 8 Feb 1820 **RU:** Teamster/Patriot, Gave material aid to cause **CEM:** Old Peaked Mountain; GPS 38.37113, -78.73416; 9843 Town Hall Rd, McGaheysville; Rockingham **GS:** U **SP:** Margaret Margaret Miller **VI:** Son of Augustice & Anna Elizabeth (Scherp) Preisch. Died in Ohio **P:** unk **BLW:** unk **RG:** Y **MK:** Y **PH:** unk **SS:** J-NSSAR 2000 Reg; AL Ct Bk II pg 25 Rockingham Co; BT plaque **BS:** JLARC 76; 196.

PRICE, Barrett (Barret); b 17 Apr 1749, Henrico Co; d 4 Sep 1794 **RU:** Captain/Patriot, Gave material aid to cause **CEM:** Hollywood; GPS 37.53560, -77.45720; 412 S Cherry St; Richmond City **GS:** U **SP:** Mar (25 Aug 1771) Sarah Graves (1755, Goochland Co-Jul 1852) **VI:** No further data **P:** unk **BLW:** unk **RG:** Y **MK:** unk **PH:** unk **SS:** DAR #A093021; J-NSSAR 1993 Reg; AL Ct Bk pg 9 Henrico Co; DD **BS:** JLARC 1.

PRICE, Joseph; b 1753; d 1828 **RU:** Patriot, Gave material aid to cause **CEM:** Price Family; GPS unk; Nr Cattail Branch & Willis River; Cumberland **GS:** Y **SP:** No info **VI:** No further data **P:** N **BLW:** N **RG:** N **MK:** N **PH:** unk **SS:** AL Ct Bk pg 3, 14, 31 Cumberland Co; AS **BS:** 80 vol 3 pg 190.

PRICE, Joseph; b 1712; d 28 Apr 1783 **RU:** Patriot, Gave material aid to cause **CEM:** Joseph Shores Price Family; GPS unk; Rt 817 or Dillions Mill; Franklin **GS:** U **SP:** Ann Shores (1713-28 Feb 1791) d/o

RU=Rank/Unit	CEM=Cemetery	GS=Gravestone	SP=Spousal Information
VI=Other Veteran Info	P=Pension	BLW=Bounty/Land Warrant	RG=Registered Grave
MK=SAR/DAR Marker	PH=Photo	SS=Service Source	BS=Burial Source

274

Richard (1700-1750) & Susanna (------) Shores **VI:** No further data **P:** N **BLW:** N **RG:** unk **MK:** unk **PH:** unk **SS:** AL Ct Bk pg 5a, 30 Henry Co **BS:** 196.

PRICE, Joseph Shores; b 17 Jul 1734, New Kent Co; d 20 Oct 1801 **RU:** Patriot, Gave material aid to cause **CEM:** Joseph Shores Price Family; GPS unk; Rt 817 or Dillions Mill; Franklin **GS:** U **SP:** Carity Bagby (1735-6 Feb 1803) d/o James M & Marietta (McNail) Bagby **VI:** Son of Joseph (1712-28 Apr 1783) & Ann (Shores) (1713-28 Feb 1791) Price. Died in Buckingham Co **P:** N **BLW:** N **RG:** unk **MK:** unk **PH:** unk **SS:** AL Ct Bk III pg 149 **BS:** 196.

PRICE, Richard; b 1756; d unk **RU:** Sergeant, Served in Capt William Russell's Co, Russell Co Militia **CEM:** Elk Garden; GPS unk; On Red WinePplantation, Elk Garden; Russell **GS:** N **SP:** Priscilla Crabtree (1757, Salt Lick- (__) Elk Garden) **VI:** Became a famous preacher **P:** N **BLW:** N **RG:** unk **MK:** N **PH:** N **SS:** Z pg 154 **BS:** 196.

PRICE, Thomas Sr; b 29 Aug 1754, "Forks of Hanover," Hanover Co; d 21 or 22 Dec 1836 **RU:** Captain, Ent serv Hanover Co 25 Sept 1832. Served in VA Line **CEM:** Fork Episcopal Church; GPS 37.85340, -77.53100; 12566 Old Ridge Rd, Doswell; Hanover **GS:** Y **SP:** Barbara (-----) (__-21 May 1831) **VI:** DAR marker. Pensioned Hanover Co 1832. S5954 **P:** Y **BLW:** Y **RG:** unk **MK:** unk **PH:** N **SS:** J-NSSAR 1993 Reg, J- DAR Hatcher; K Vol 4 pg 146; CG Vol 3 pg 2771 **BS:** JLARC 1, 2; 196; 213 pg 586.

PRICE, William; b c1756; d 27 Jun 1830 **RU:** Major, Served in 1st Va Regt, 1776. Discharged 1783 at Point of Fork **CEM:** Shockoe Hill; GPS 37.55190, -77.43170; 4th & Hospital Sts; Richmond City **GS:** Y **SP:** Sarah Lewis (8 Apr 1772 Goochland Co-26 Jan 1837) d/o Richard & (-----) Lewis of Goochland **VI:** Was register of VA land office for many yrs. Recd BLW of 2666 acres 22 Mar 1783 #1440. Pen fr Richmond City by special Act of Congress, #199. Widow pensioned 1833 by special Act of Congress, no file number **P:** Y **BLW:** Y **RG:** Y **MK:** Y **PH:** unk **SS:** A pg 388 **BS:** 57 pg 8.

PRICE, William; b 22 Jan 1725, Orange Co; d 15 Sep 1807 **RU:** Patriot, Gave material aid to cause **CEM:** Edward Lewis; GPS unk; Nr Heidleback School, Rt 712 Dodson; Patrick **GS:** U **SP:** Mar (1752) Mary Morton (12 Nov 1733, Goochland Co-1815, Prince Edward Co) d/o Joseph (27 Dec 1709 Henrico Co-28 Jun 1782, Charlotte Co) & Mary (Goode) (c1712-1734) Morton **VI:** No further data **P:** N **BLW:** N **RG:** unk **MK:** unk **PH:** unk **SS:** AL Ct Bk pg 28 Pittsylvania Co **BS:** 196.

PRILLAMAN (PRILLMAN), Jacob Sr; b 1721; d Aft Sep 1796 **RU:** Patriot, Gave material aid to cause **CEM:** Prillaman; GPS 37.01080, -80.06080; Foothills Rd Rt 642 W of Highland United Methodist, Callaway; Franklin **GS:** U **SP:** Mar (c1750) Walburga Helm (c1723-22 Mar 1799) **VI:** No further data **P:** N **BLW:** N **RG:** unk **MK:** unk **PH:** unk **SS:** DAR #A093217; AL Ct Bk pg 37 Henry Co **BS:** JLARC 3.

PRINTZ, George; b c Nov1741, Duerhren/Baden, Germany; d 8 May 1834 **RU:** Captain, Was aide to Washington. Also commanded a co in Nelson's Corps of Lt Dragoons **CEM:** Printz or Prince Family; GPS unk; Rt 651 nr Ida; Page **GS:** U **SP:** Mar (1764) Elizabeth Henry, 2) Mary Magdalene Shaffer **VI:** No further data **P:** unk **BLW:** unk **RG:** Y **MK:** unk **PH:** unk **SS:** NSSAR Ancestor #P-273929; DAR #A093238 **BS:** JLARC 1, 2, 94.

PRINTZ (PRINCE), Gottlieb (Cutlip); b 20 Sep 1752 York Co; d 15 Dec 1806 **RU:** Private, Served in Capt Joseph Bowman's Co fr Shenandoah Co, Lt Col William Crawford's Regt, Frederick Co. Was at Point Pleasant 1774. Served at Romney, PA 2 Nov 1775 **CEM:** Printz or Prince Family; GPS unk; Rt 651 nr Ida; Page **GS:** U **SP:** Magdeline Crumm **VI:** No further data **P:** unk **BLW:** unk **RG:** Y **MK:** unk **PH:** unk **SS:** J-NSSAR 1993 Reg, J- DAR Hatcher; N pg 1251; Z pg 51 **BS:** JLARC 1, 2.

PRINTZ (PRINCE), Philip; b 1747; d 1806 **RU:** Private, Served in Michael Reader's Co, Shenandoah Co **CEM:** Printz or Prince Family; GPS unk; Rt 651 nr Ida; Page **GS:** U **SP:** No info **VI:** No further data **P:** unk **BLW:** unk **RG:** Y **MK:** unk **PH:** unk **SS:** SAR Ancestor #P-273932; J-NSSAR 1993 Reg; C pg 603 **BS:** JLARC 1.

PRIOUX, Gilles; b unk; d 1781 **RU:** Seaman, Served on "Ville de Paris" and died from Yorktown battle **CEM:** French Memorial; GPS 36.81944, -79.39933; Yorktown; York **GS:** U **SP:** No info **VI:** No further data **P:** unk **BLW:** unk **RG:** Y **MK:** unk **PH:** unk **SS:** J-Yorktown Historian **BS:** JLARC 1, 74.

RU=Rank/Unit   CEM=Cemetery   GS=Gravestone   SP=Spousal Information
VI=Other Veteran Info   P=Pension   BLW=Bounty/Land Warrant   RG=Registered Grave
MK=SAR/DAR Marker   PH=Photo   SS=Service Source   BS=Burial Source

275

PROU, Joseph; b unk; d 1781 **RU:** Soldier, Served in Bourbonnais Bn and died fr battle at Yorktown **CEM:** French Memorial; GPS 36.81944, -79.39933; Yorktown; York **GS:** U **SP:** No info **VI:** No further data **P:** unk **BLW:** unk **RG:** Y **MK:** unk **PH:** unk **SS:** J-Yorktown Historian **BS:** JLARC 1, 74.

PROUX, Pierre; b unk; d 1781 **RU:** Soldier, Served in Bourbonnais Bn and died fr battle at Yorktown **CEM:** French Memorial; GPS 36.81944, -79.39933; Yorktown; York **GS:** U **SP:** No info **VI:** No further data **P:** unk **BLW:** unk **RG:** Y **MK:** unk **PH:** unk **SS:** J-Yorktown Historian **BS:** JLARC 1, 74.

PROVOL, Charles; b unk; d 1781 **RU:** Soldier, Served in Soissonnais Bn and died fr battle at Yorktown **CEM:** French Memorial; GPS 36.81944, -79.39933; Yorktown; York **GS:** U **SP:** No info **VI:** No further data **P:** unk **BLW:** unk **RG:** Y **MK:** unk **PH:** unk **SS:** J-Yorktown Historian **BS:** JLARC 1, 74.

PRUNTZIGER, Jean; b unk; d 1781 **RU:** Seaman, Served on "Northumberland" and died from Yorktown battle **CEM:** French Memorial; GPS 36.81944, -79.39933; Yorktown; York **GS:** U **SP:** No info **VI:** No further data **P:** unk **BLW:** unk **RG:** Y **MK:** unk **PH:** unk **SS:** J-Yorktown Historian **BS:** JLARC 1, 74.

PRYOR, John; b c1748; d 19 Mar 1823 **RU:** Major, Ent serv 1777 in Cont Artillery. Was Aide-de-Camp to Gen Alexander, 9 Jun 1779. Retired 14 Jan 1783 **CEM:** Shockoe Hill; GPS 37.55190, -77.43170; 4th & Hospital Sts; Richmond City **GS:** Y **SP:** 1) (-----) daughter of Thomas & (-----) Whiting of Gloucester Co, VA 2) mar (22 Feb 1815 Richmond City) Elizabeth Quarles Graves **VI:** BLW issued 10 Aug 1789. W12064, #1750-20-10 for 4555 acres **P:** Y **BLW:** Y **RG:** N **MK:** N **PH:** unk **SS:** E pg 641; K Vol 4 pg 154; CG Vol 3 pg 2782; CD **BS:** 57 pg 1.

PUGH, Job; b 4 Jul 1737, Prince George Co; d 1809 **RU:** Patriot, Gave material aid to cause **CEM:** Back Creek Quaker, aka Gainesboro United Methodist; GPS 39.27861,-78.25694;166 Siler Ln, Gainesboro; Frederick **GS:** Y **SP:** Ruch John (24 Aug 1741 Chester Co, PA-1804 Frederick Co) **VI:** Son of Jessie & Alice (Malin) Pugh/Peugh, both fr Chester Co, PA **P:** N **BLW:** N **RG:** unk **MK:** unk **PH:** unk **SS:** AL Ct Bk pg 18, Shenandoah Co **BS:** 196.

PUGH, Joseph; b c1713; d Aft 7 Jan 1778 **RU:** Patriot, Gave material aid to cause. Also performed public service as High Sheriff, Dunmore Co 1776-1777 **CEM:** Back Creek Quaker, aka Gainesboro United Methodist; GPS 39.27861, -78.25694; 166 Siler Ln, Gainesboro; Frederick **GS:** Y **SP:** Mar (c1750 prob Lancaster Co, PA) Mary Postlethwaite (c1714-aft 28 Dec 1793, Washington Co) **VI:** Bur with other Pughs in cemetery. GS not readable **P:** N **BLW:** N **RG:** unk **MK:** unk **PH:** unk **SS:** DAR #A208784; AL Ct Bk pg 9, 18 Shenandoah Co; DD cites Painter, Shenandoah Co & Its Courthouse pg 12, 13 **BS:** 196.

PUISSANT, Etiene; b unk; d 1781 **RU:** Soldier, Served in Soissonnais Bn and died fr battle at Yorktown **CEM:** French Memorial; GPS 36.81944, -79.39933; Yorktown; York **GS:** U **SP:** No info **VI:** No further data **P:** unk **BLW:** unk **RG:** Y **MK:** unk **PH:** unk **SS:** J-Yorktown Historian **BS:** JLARC 1, 74.

PULLER, John; b 27 Aug 1744; d 5 Mar 1818 **RU:** Patriot, Gave material aid to the cause **CEM:** Puller Family; GPS unk; 1 mi E of Amissville; Culpeper **GS:** Y **SP:** Mar (23 Apr 1772) Ann (-----) (c1749-21 Apr 1829) **VI:** No further data **P:** N **BLW:** N **RG:** N **MK:** N **PH:** unk **SS:** AL Cert **BS:** 167 Puller.

PULLIN, John; b 1763; d 1828 **RU:** Private?, Specific serv may be found at the Lib of VA, Auditors Accts Vol XVIII pg 681 **CEM:** Court Street Baptist Church; GPS unk; 447 Court St; Portsmouth City **GS:** Y **SP:** Margaret Powell (c1775-1849) **VI:** No further data **P:** unk **BLW:** unk **RG:** Y **MK:** N **PH:** unk **SS:** E pg 642; CZ pg 361 **BS:** 27 pg 122.

PURCELL, John; b 1762; d 15 Aug 1838 **RU:** Private?, Ent serv Prince William Co. Served in Lee's Legion and 1st VA Cont Line. Taken prisoner 10 Sep 1778 **CEM:** Upper Ridge; GPS unk; Rt 739; Frederick **GS:** Y **SP:** 1) (-----) 2) mar (1816) Elizabeth Carter (__-1850) **VI:** Awarded BLW 18 Apr 1794 of 100 acres. Widow appl pen 16 Nov 1846 Washington DC **P:** Y **BLW:** Y **RG:** N **MK:** N **PH:** unk **SS:** E pg 642; CG pg 2786 **BS:** 59 pg 264.

PURCELL, Thomas Sr; b Bapt 9 Apr 1720, Hunterdon Co, NJ; d Aft 17 Apr 1779 **RU:** Patriot, Gave material aid to the cause **CEM:** Petts Family; GPS unk; Purcellville; Loudoun **GS:** Y **SP:** Mary Van Hook (1723-__) **VI:** No further data **P:** N **BLW:** N **RG:** N **MK:** N **PH:** unk **SS:** DAR #A092227; AL Ct Bk pg 75 **BS:** SAR Appl.

RU=Rank/Unit	CEM=Cemetery	GS=Gravestone	SP=Spousal Information
VI=Other Veteran Info	P=Pension	BLW=Bounty/Land Warrant	RG=Registered Grave
MK=SAR/DAR Marker	PH=Photo	SS=Service Source	BS=Burial Source

276

PURDIE, George; b by 1758; d Aft 1820 **RU:** Patriot, Gave use of wagon and sundry items for the Nansemond Militia. Also furnished sulfer for public use. On 5 Oct 1780 appt by court to arrange for repair of court house damaged by the enemy **CEM:** St Luke's Church; GPS 36.93940, -76.58670; 14477 Benns Church Blvd, Smithfield; Isle of Wight **GS:** Y **SP:** Mar (1784 Isle of Wight Co) Mary Robinson **VI:** No further data **P:** N **BLW:** N **RG:** N **MK:** N **PH:** unk **SS:** G pg 193 **BS:** 117 pg 6.

QUARLES, John; b 1745, King William Co; d 7 Jan 1798 **RU:** Colonel, Served in Prince William District Bn Mar 1776. May have given to cause **CEM:** Quarles Family; GPS unk; SE fr Bedford; Bedford **GS:** N **SP:** Mar (c1774) Sarah Winston (9 Feb 1747 Hanover Co.-28 Jan 1822) **VI:** No further data **P:** unk **BLW:** unk **RG:** unk **MK:** N **PH:** N **SS:** J- DAR Hatcher; CE pg 22 **BS:** JLARC 2; 196.

QUARLES, John; b unk; d 1844 **RU:** Patriot, Gave material aid to cause **CEM:** St John's Episcopal; GPS 37.53183, -77.41958; 2401 E Broad St; Richmond City **GS:** Y **SP:** No info **VI:** No further data **P:** N **BLW:** N **RG:** N **PH:** unk **SS:** D Vol 2 pg 581; AL Ct Bk pg 11 New Kent Co **BS:** 28 pg 351.

QUARLES, Minor; b 1762; d 1831 **RU:** Patriot, Gave material aid to the cause **CEM:** Carmel Baptist; GPS unk; 24230 Jefferson Davis Pkwy, Ruther Glen; Caroline **GS:** Y **SP:** Sarah Nelson **VI:** Son of William & Merry (Terry) Quarles. Grave reinterred fr homes on the North Anna River. Has newer memorial stone **P:** N **BLW:** N **RG:** Y **MK:** N **PH:** unk **SS:** AL Ct Bk lt II pg 22 **BS:** 14 pg 22; 196.

QUARLES, William; b unk; d 1817 **RU:** Patriot, Gave material aid to cause **CEM:** Carmel Baptist; GPS unk; 24230 Jefferson Davis Pkwy, Ruther Glen; Caroline **GS:** Y **SP:** Merry Terry **VI:** Has newer memorial stone **P:** N **BLW:** N **RG:** Y **MK:** N **PH:** unk **SS:** D pg 857, 862 **BS:** 14 pg 22; 196.

QUENARD, Pierre; b unk; d 1781 **RU:** Soldier, Served in Gatinais Bn and died fr battle at Yorktown **CEM:** French Memorial; GPS 36.81944, -79.39933; Yorktown; York **GS:** U **SP:** No info **VI:** No further data **P:** unk **BLW:** unk **RG:** Y **MK:** unk **PH:** unk **SS:** J-Yorktown Historian **BS:** JLARC 1,74.

QUERJEAN, Herve; b unk; d 1781 **RU:** Seaman, Served on "Hextor" and died from Yorktown battle **CEM:** French Memorial; GPS 36.81944, -79.39933; Yorktown; York **GS:** U **SP:** No info **VI:** No further data **P:** unk **BLW:** unk **RG:** Y **MK:** unk **PH:** unk **SS:** J-Yorktown Historian **BS:** JLARC 1,74.

RADER (RIDER), Adam; b 4 Feb 1761, Germany; d 28 Nov 1817 **RU:** Soldier, Served in 11th Cont Line **CEM:** Rader Family; GPS unk; Past Motts Hill Ln on right, take left on Radar Barn Rd, N of Troutville on Rt 11; Botetourt **GS:** N **SP:** Mar (14 Jan 1789) Mary Hotzenpeller (7 May 1769, Frederick Co-11 Mar 1853) d/o Peter (__-1782) & Anna (-----) Hotzenpeller **VI:** Immigrant Ancestor of Radars in Botetourt Co **P:** unk **BLW:** unk **RG:** unk **MK:** N **PH:** N **SS:** DAR #A093349; E pg 686; BY SAR applic **BS:** JLARC 60, 124.

RADFORD, Richard; b unk; d 19 Nov 1843 **RU:** Patriot, Gave material aid to cause **CEM:** St John's Episcopal; GPS 37.53183, -77.41958; 2401 E Broad St; Richmond City **GS:** N **SP:** No info **VI:** No further data **P:** N **BLW:** N **RG:** N **MK:** N **PH:** N **SS:** D Vol 3 pg 775 **BS:** 28 pg 350.

RAGLAND, John; b 1751; d 2 Jun 1831 **RU:** Private, Served in 10th & 14th Cont Line. Served Capt Winston's Co 14th VA Regt, Cont Line **CEM:** St John's Episcopal; GPS unk; 197 Mountain Rd, Halifax; Halifax **GS:** U **SP:** Mar (1780) Elizabeth Pettus (__Lunenburg Co-1834 Halifax Co) **VI:** No further data **P:** unk **BLW:** unk **RG:** unk **MK:** unk **PH:** unk **SS:** DAR Ancestor #A093390; J- DAR Hatcher; E pg 646; G pg 770 **BS:** JLARC 2.

RAGLAND, John Dudley; b 1761, Hanover Co; d 17 Jun 1832, Goochland Co **RU:** Lieutenant, Ent serv Henrico Co, 1777. Served in 1st VA Regt as Lt **CEM:** Charlie Londeree; GPS unk; DAR and SAR burial sources do not provide location; Buckingham **GS:** U **SP:** Mar (23 Oct 1788, Hanover Co) Margaret S. Thompson (__Goochland Co-18 Nov 1844, Goochland Co) **VI:** Son of John Jr (1721-__) & Ann (Dudley) (4 Jul 1737-__) Ragland, both of Hanover Co. DAR plaque. Pension appl for 15 Sep 1832, Buckingham Co, S5974. Widow also recd pension # W5662 **P:** Y **BLW:** N **RG:** unk **MK:** Y **PH:** unk **SS:** DAR Ancestor #A093392; K Vol 4 pg 172; CG Vol 3 pg 2800 **BS:** JLARC 4, 44, 59.

RAGLAND, Reuben; b c1740, Hanover Co; d Aft 26 Dec 1806 **RU:** Lieutenant/Patriot, Served in Capt James Hill's Co Halifax Co Militia. Gave material aid to cause **CEM:** Ragland Family; GPS unk; Check property records for location. Also see DAR Senate Doc 93, vol 54; Halifax **GS:** U **SP:** Ann (-----) (__Hanover Co-Dec 1806, Halifax Co) **VI:** No further data **P:** unk **BLW:** unk **RG:** unk **MK:** unk **PH:** unk

RU=Rank/Unit   CEM=Cemetery   GS=Gravestone   SP=Spousal Information
VI=Other Veteran Info   P=Pension   BLW=Bounty/Land Warrant   RG=Registered Grave
MK=SAR/DAR Marker   PH=Photo   SS=Service Source   BS=Burial Source

277

SS: DAR Ancestor #A093395; AR Vol 3 pg 199; AL Ct Bk pg 11, 30 Halifax Co; DD cites Halifax Co Order Book 9 pg 261 Jun 1779 **BS:** JLARC 2; 80, vol 3, pg 199.

RAGLAND, William; b 1759; d 1789 **RU:** Private, Served in 6th Cont Line **CEM:** Ragland Family; GPS unk; McDonough; Henry **GS:** N **SP:** No info **VI:** No further data **P:** unk **BLW:** unk **RG:** N **MK:** N **PH:** N **SS:** E pg 647 **BS:** DAR report; 80 vol 3 pg 199.

RAINEY (RAINY), Williamson; b 2 Nov 1760, Mecklenburg Co; d 1847 **RU:** Private, Ent serv Mecklenburg Co 1776-77. Served in VA Line **CEM:** Rainey Family; GPS unk; Rt 627; Mecklenburg **GS:** U **SP:** Mar (23 Nov 1779) Edith Morgan. Francis Rainey, security, note fr Reuben Morgan. **VI:** Pension appl for 23 Oct 1841 Mecklenburg Co R8563 **P:** Y **BLW:** unk **RG:** unk **MK:** unk **PH:** unk **SS:** J- DAR Hatcher; K Vol 4 pg 173; CG Vol 3 pg 2801 **BS:** JLARC 2.

RAMEY, Sanford; b 2 Jan 1759; d 25 Jul 1828 **RU:** Patriot, Gave material aid to cause **CEM:** Catoctin Free Church; GPS 39.16274, -77.64527; Charlestown Pike Rt 9, Paeonian Springs; Loudoun **GS:** Y **SP:** Lydia Wilson (30 Mar 1767-30 Jun 1845) **VI:** No further data **P:** N **BLW:** N **RG:** N **MK:** N **PH:** unk **SS:** D Vol 2 pg 606 **BS:** 25 pg 253; 196.

RAMSAY, Dennis; b 1756; d 1 Sep 1810 **RU:** Colonel, Capt in an Alexandria Regt in Aug 1777. Was capt at battle at Germantown. Later in war may have achieved rank of Col **CEM:** Presbyterian Church; GPS 38.80015, -77.05791; Wilkes St & Hamilton Ln; Alexandria City **GS:** Y **SP:** Jane Allen Taylor (c1768-24 Nov 1848) death notice in Alexandria Gazette 25 Nov 1814, p. 3 **VI:** Son of William (1716-1785) & (-----) Ramsay of Galway Scotland who resided in Alexandria as early as 1744. He possibly made rank of Col after the RW. Death notice in Alexandria Gazette 1 Sep 1840, pg 3 **P:** unk **BLW:** unk **RG:** Y **MK:** unk **PH:** unk **SS:** G pg 263; AK GW Chapter 2015 **BS:** JLARC 86; 23 pg 65; 196.

RAMSAY, Dennis; b c1741, Cumberland Co, NJ; d 25 Nov 1813 **RU:** Officer, Served in NJ Line **CEM:** First Presbyterian Church; GPS 38.79992, -77.05799; 601 Hamilton Ln; Alexandria City **GS:** U **SP:** No info **VI:** No further data **P:** unk **BLW:** unk **RG:** unk **MK:** Y **PH:** unk **SS:** AK GW Chap - 2014 **BS:** 04.

RAMSAY, William; b 1716; d 10 Feb 1785 **RU:** Surgeon/Patriot, Justice of Fairfax Co, Public Service as Surgeon. Was a capt of Independent Co of Fairfax Co in 1774. Gave material aid to cause **CEM:** Old Christ Church Episcopal; GPS 38.80625, -77.04718; 118 N Washington St; Alexandria City **GS:** N **SP:** Ann McCarthy (c1730-2 Apr 1785) **VI:** Son of Dr. William & (-----) Ramsey. Justice of Fairfax Co, overseer of Alex Academy, Postmaster 1772. Resided at SE cnr of King & Fairfax Sts, "oldest house in Alexandria" **P:** unk **BLW:** Y **RG:** Y **MK:** N **PH:** N **SS:** 20, pg 141; E pg 649; H; AL Ct Bk pg 20 Fairfax Co; BY pg 356; CE pg 10 **BS:** 20 pg 141.

RAMSEY, Anthony; b unk; d 18 Sep 1814 **RU:** Soldier, SAR Ancester service not identified **CEM:** Presbyterian Church; GPS 38.80015, -77.05791; Wilkes St & Hamilton Ln; Alexandria City **GS:** N **SP:** Mary (___) **VI:** No further data **P:** unk **BLW:** unk **RG:** Y **MK:** unk **PH:** N **SS:** J-NSSAR 1993 Reg; NSSAR Ancestor # P-275187 **BS:** JLARC 1.

RAMSEY, James Dr; b 1 Apr 1756; d 1815 **RU:** Private, Served in Capt Andrew Wagner's Co, 12th VA Regt **CEM:** Old Lebanon; GPS 38.08090, -79.37545; Off Rt 42, Craigsville; Augusta **GS:** Y **SP:** Mar (178?) Jane Lyle (1758 Rockingham Co-1836) d/o Samuel & Sarah (McClung) Lyle, both of Antrim Co., Ireland **VI:** Newer stone; marker placed 28 Jul 2003 **P:** unk **BLW:** unk **RG:** Y **MK:** Y **PH:** unk **SS:** B; BT; AD **BS:** 04; 196.

RANAUD, Francois; b unk; d 1781 **RU:** Seaman, Served on "Sceptre" and died from Yorktown battle **CEM:** French Memorial; GPS 36.81944, -79.39933; Yorktown; York **GS:** U **SP:** No info **VI:** No further data **P:** unk **BLW:** unk **RG:** unk **MK:** unk **PH:** unk **SS:** J-Yorktown Historian **BS:** JLARC 1, 74.

RANDLE, Henry; b unk; d 16 Oct 1781 **RU:** Private, Served in Capt Elias Van Bunscoten 1st Co, Col Peter Gansevoort's 3rd NY Regt, Died fr battle at Yorktown **CEM:** Yorktown Victory Monument Tablet; GPS 38.28350, -78.54150; Yorktown; York **GS:** U **SP:** No info **VI:** No further data **P:** unk **BLW:** unk **RG:** unk **MK:** unk **PH:** unk **SS:** J-Yorktown Historian; AX pg 198 **BS:** JLARC 74.

RANDOLPH, Beverley; b 1754; d 2 Feb 1797 **RU:** Colonel, Ent serv 1775 Cumberland Co where was col commanding VA unit while also student at William & Mary College. Commanded Cumberland Co Militia until resignation 22 Jan 1781 **CEM:** Westview; GPS unk; Farmville; Prince Edward **GS:** Y **SP:**

RU=Rank/Unit	CEM=Cemetery	GS=Gravestone	SP=Spousal Information
VI=Other Veteran Info	P=Pension	BLW=Bounty/Land Warrant	RG=Registered Grave
MK=SAR/DAR Marker	PH=Photo	SS=Service Source	BS=Burial Source

278

Mar (14 Feb 1775 York Co) Martha "Patty" Cocke, (2 Jun 1753 Henrico Co-21 Sep 1838) d/o James & Ann (Brown) Cocke. **VI:** Son of Peter (1717-1767) and Lucy (Bolling) (1719-__) Randolph. Eighth Governor of Virginia 1788-1791. Died in Green Creek, Cumberland Co. Widow pen 1837 fr Warren Co, while living at Happy Creek Manor. W4774 **P:** Y **BLW:** unk **RG:** N **MK:** N **PH:** unk **SS:** E pg 649; K Vol 4 pg 179-80 **BS:** 130.

RANDOLPH, David Meade; b 1758; d 27 Sep 1830 **RU:** Soldier/Patriot, Service not specified in SAR registry. Gave material aid to cause **CEM:** Bruton Parish Church; GPS 37.27127, -76.70248; 331 W Duke of Gloucester St; Williamsburg City **GS:** U **SP:** Mary Randolph (9 Aug 1762-28 Jan 1828) d/o Thomas Mann & Anne (Cary) (1745-1789) Randolph. **VI:** Son of Richard (1716-1786) and Ann (Cary) Randolph of Curles of Henrico Co. Assigned duties in DC by President Washington after War. Death reported in Whig newspaper 5 Oct 1830. First person bur on grounds that later became Arlington National Cemetery. Not sure which cem contains body **P:** unk **BLW:** unk **RG:** Y **MK:** Y **PH:** unk **SS:** J-NSSAR 1993 Reg; AL Ct Bk pg 40 Chesterfield Co **BS:** JLARC 1; 196.

RANDOLPH, Edmund Jennings; b 10 Aug 1753, Tazewell Hall, Williamsburg; d 13 Sep 1813 **RU:** Colonel/Patriot, Served as Aide-de-Camp to General Washington after Bunker Hill 1775; first VA Attorney General in 1775; Cont Congress 1779. Signed VA Declaration of Rights **CEM:** Old Chapel Episcopal; GPS 39.10677, -78.01470; Jct US 340 & Rt 255, Millwood; Clarke **GS:** Y **SP:** Elizabeth Carter Nicolas (1753-1810) **VI:** Son of John & (-----) Randolph. Was Governor of Virginia 1786, member of Continental Congress 1779. Was Grand Master of Masons in VA 1786. Attended Constitutional Convention 1787, was First Attorney General of US 1789. Served as Secretary of State 1794. Died at Carter Hall at Millwood **P:** unk **BLW:** unk **RG:** Y **MK:** Y **PH:** Y **SS:** E pg 649; DD **BS:** JLARC 1, 24; 196.

RANDOLPH, John; b 29 Jun 1742; d 28 Oct 1775 **RU:** Patriot, Gave material aid to cause **CEM:** Matoax, Randolph Family; GPS unk; Matoaca; Chesterfield **GS:** U **SP:** Mar (9 Mar 1769) Frances Bland (24 Sep 1752-18 Jan 1788) d/o Theodorick & Frances (Bolling) Bland **VI:** No further data **P:** N **BLW:** N **RG:** unk **MK:** unk **PH:** unk **SS:** AL Cert Chesterfield Co **BS:** 196.

RANDOLPH, Peyton; b Sep 1721, Williamsburg; d 22 Oct 1775 **RU:** Patriot, Was President of Conventions 1774, Mar 1775, & Jul 1775 **CEM:** Wren Chapel, College of William & Mary; GPS 37.27070, -76.70910; Sir Christopher Wren Building, W&M campus; Williamsburg City **GS:** Y **SP:** Elizabeth Harrison (__-1783) d/o Benjamin (1694-1745) & Anne (Carter) (1704-1745) Harrison **VI:** Son of Sir John (1693-1737) & Lady Susanna (Beverly) (1692-1754) Randolph. King's Attorney for the Commonwealth in 1745. Member House of Burgesses 1764-1774 & Speaker 1766, President of VA conventions 1774 & 75. President of 1st & 2nd Continental Congresses at time of death. Was Grand Master of Masons 1786 and member Constitutional Convention 1787; Was First US Attorney General 1789 and US Secretary of State 1794. Died in Philadelphia City, PA **P:** N **BLW:** N **RG:** N **MK:** Y **PH:** Y **SS:** N pg 495; AK **BS:** 130.

RANDOLPH, Robert; b 1760, Henrico Co; d 12 Sep 1825 **RU:** Captain, Served in 3rd Lt Dragoons, Cont Line **CEM:** Randolph Family at Eastern View; GPS unk; Nr Casanova; Fauquier **GS:** Y **SP:** Elizabeth Hill Carter **VI:** BLW received for 4000 acres **P:** unk **BLW:** Y **RG:** unk **MK:** unk **PH:** unk **SS:** E pg 649 **BS:** JLARC 16.

RANDOLPH, Thomas Mann; b 1741; d 20 Nov 1793 **RU:** Colonel/Patriot, Served in Goochland Co Militia prior to 20 Sep 1779, when replaced. Gave material aid to cause **CEM:** Tuckahoe Plantation; GPS unk; 12601 River Rd Rt 650, W of Richmond near Manakin; Goochland **GS:** Y **SP:** Anne Cary (1745-6 Mar 1789 Tuckahoe) **VI:** Son of William (1712-1745) and Maria/Mary Judith (Page) (1715-1742) Randolph. Perhaps first person bur on grounds that would later become Arlington National Cem **P:** unk **BLW:** unk **RG:** N **MK:** N **PH:** unk **SS:** E pg 649; AL Cert 1 Albemarle Co **BS:** 46 pg 244; 196.

RANDOLPH, William; b 1737, Elizabeth City Co; d 1795 **RU:** Pilot, Served in 5th & 9th Cont Line **CEM:** Hampton; GPS unk; DAR and SAR burial sources do not provide location; Hampton City **GS:** U **SP:** Mar (c1763) Sarah Minson (c1767-aft 1796) **VI:** No further data **P:** unk **BLW:** unk **RG:** unk **MK:** unk **PH:** unk **SS:** DAR Ancestor #A094332; J-NSSAR 2000 Reg; NSSAR Ancestor #P-275528; AR Vol 3 pg 201; E pg 650 **BS:** JLARC 76.

RU=Rank/Unit	CEM=Cemetery	GS=Gravestone	SP=Spousal Information
VI=Other Veteran Info	P=Pension	BLW=Bounty/Land Warrant	RG=Registered Grave
MK=SAR/DAR Marker	PH=Photo	SS=Service Source	BS=Burial Source

279

RAUSCH (RAUCH), Nicholas; b 1748, Germany; d 31 Oct 1813 **RU:** Private, Served in Capt Esterly's Co, Col Bradford's Regt, Philadelphia PA Militia **CEM:** St Mary Pine Lutheran; **GPS** 38.74470, -78.68390; 7103 S Middle Rd, Mt Jackson; Shenandoah **GS:** U **SP:** Dorothea Reinefeld **VI:** Died in Martinsburg, Berkeley Co WV **P:** unk **BLW:** unk **RG:** Y **MK:** unk **PH:** unk **SS:** J-NSSAR 1993 Reg; NSSAR Ancestor #P-275833; DD **BS:** JLARC 1.

RAUSCH (ROUSH), John Adam; b 1711, Palatinate, Germany; d 19 Oct 1786 **RU:** Patriot, Gave material aid to cause **CEM:** Old St Mary's; **GPS** unk; Mt Jackson; Shenandoah **GS:** U **SP:** No info **VI:** No further data **P:** N **BLW:** N **RG:** Y **MK:** unk **PH:** unk **SS:** DAR Ancestor #A098982; J-NSSAR 1993 Reg; NSSAR Ancestor #P-275831; AL Cert Shenandoah Co **BS:** JLARC 1.

RAUTZ, Francois; b unk; d 1781 **RU:** Seaman, Served on "Duc De Bourgogne" and died from Yorktown battle **CEM:** French Memorial; **GPS** 36.81944, -79.39933; Yorktown; York **GS:** U **SP:** No info **VI:** No further data **P:** unk **BLW:** unk **RG:** Y **MK:** unk **PH:** unk **SS:** J-Yorktown Historian **BS:** JLARC 1, 74.

RAVAN, Jean; b unk; d 1781 **RU:** Seaman, Served on "Sceptre" and died from Yorktown battle **CEM:** French Memorial; **GPS** 36.81944, -79.39933; Yorktown; York **GS:** U **SP:** No info **VI:** No further data **P:** unk **BLW:** unk **RG:** Y **MK:** unk **PH:** unk **SS:** J-Yorktown Historian **BS:** JLARC 1, 74.

RAY, Benjamin; b 1756; d 28 Jan 1841 **RU:** Private, Served in NC Line. Ent serv Surry Co NC 1775. Taken POW and remained so for14 mos **CEM:** Whitt Family; **GPS** unk; Rt 646, W fr Honaker; Russell **GS:** U **SP:** 1) (-----) (c1770-__) 2) mar (31 Jan 1830) Nancy Wilson or Sutherland (a widow) **VI:** Moved fr Surry NC to Russell Co VA 1798. Pension appl for 5 May 1818 Russell Co age 62. BLW issued to widow. Widow appl pen Russell Co 27 Apr 1854 age 72. She appl for BLW 31 Dec 1857. W26355. BLW #79035-160-55 **P:** Y **BLW:** Y **RG:** Y **MK:** unk **PH:** unk **SS:** J-NSSAR 1993 Reg, J- DAR Hatcher; K Vol 4 pg 185; CG Vol 3 pg 2819 **BS:** JLARC 1, 2.

RAYBLET, Philippe; b unk; d 1781 **RU:** Seaman, Served on "Saint-Esprit" and died from Yorktown battle **CEM:** French Memorial; **GPS** 36.81944, -79.39933; Yorktown; York **GS:** U **SP:** No info **VI:** No further data **P:** unk **BLW:** unk **RG:** Y **MK:** unk **PH:** unk **SS:** J-Yorktown Historian **BS:** JLARC 1, 74.

RAYBURN (RAYBORNE, RAYBORN, RAYBURN, RAIBORNE), George; b c1755; d 22 Nov 1828 **RU:** Fifer/Musician, Ent serv Chesterfield Co 1778. Was Fifer in 5th VA Regt and in 3rd and 4th VA Regts. Was captured by British at siege of Charlestown, taken POW and released at end of war **CEM:** Shockoe Hill; **GPS** 37.55190, -77.43170; 4th & Hospital Sts; Richmond City **GS:** Y **SP:** Had wife age 45. (-----) (c1780-__) **VI:** Pen appl for 6 Jun 1818 Richmond, age 62. S38324 **P:** Y **BLW:** unk **RG:** Y **MK:** Y **PH:** unk **SS:** E pg 652; K Vol 4 pg 187; CG Vol 3 pg 2822 **BS:** 57 pg 6.

REA, John; b 1763; d 1826 **RU:** Private, Served in Henry Co Militia in Capt Tarrant's Co **CEM:** Mayo Baptist Church; **GPS** unk; 85 Penn Store Rd, Spencer; Henry **GS:** Y **SP:** No info **VI:** Memorial dedicated by SAR George Waller Chapter 13 Jun 2010 **P:** unk **BLW:** unk **RG:** N **MK:** Y **PH:** unk **SS:** AK correspondence; G pg 187 **BS:** 32 Jun 2010; 196.

REA, William; b 1735; d 1812 **RU:** Private, Served in Capt Page's Co, Col Benjamin Tupper's Regt, 11th Cont Line **CEM:** Cedar Grove; **GPS** 36.57204, -80.02599; 301 Fort Lane Rd; Portsmouth City **GS:** Y **SP:** No info **VI:** No further data **P:** unk **BLW:** unk **RG:** N **MK:** N **PH:** unk **SS:** A pg 129 **BS:** 147.

READ, Edmund (Edmond); b c1756; d 23 Dec 1836 **RU:** Soldier, Ent serv c1772 age 16, Accomack Co, served in VA Regt **CEM:** Chestnut Vale; **GPS** unk; .6 mi N of Rt 605, W of Rt 789, nr Locustville; Accomack **GS:** N **SP:** No info **VI:** Pensioned Accomack Co 1832 age 76. S18564 **P:** unk **BLW:** unk **RG:** unk **MK:** unk **PH:** unk **SS:** K Vol 4 pg 188; CG pg 2826 **BS:** JLARC 4, 5.

READ, John; b unk; d Aft 1781 **RU:** Patriot, Gave material aid to cause **CEM:** Robson Farm; **GPS** unk; Location ot identified in JLARC report; Culpeper **GS:** U **SP:** No info **VI:** No further data **P:** N **BLW:** N **RG:** unk **MK:** unk **PH:** unk **SS:** AL Ct Bk pg 4, 35 Culpeper Co **BS:** JLARC 63.

READ, John; b c 1759; d 14 Dec 1827 or 12 Mar 1831 **RU:** Private/Patriot, Served in Capt William Lowther Co at Nutter's Ft for six mos, 1777. Served again 6 mos in same Co,1780. Volunteered to serve in Capt John D. DeVall at Blockhouse as spy, town of Harrison,1781. Gave material aid to cause **CEM:** Rock Spring; **GPS** 37.78126, -79.44585; Jct Rt 803 & Liberty Hall Rd, Lodi; Washington **GS:** Y **SP:**

RU=Rank/Unit	CEM=Cemetery	GS=Gravestone	SP=Spousal Information
VI=Other Veteran Info	P=Pension	BLW=Bounty/Land Warrant	RG=Registered Grave
MK=SAR/DAR Marker	PH=Photo	SS=Service Source	BS=Burial Source

280

Elizabeth Read (1757-14 Dec 1827) **VI:** Rev War pension **P:** Y **BLW:** unk **RG:** N **MK:** N **PH:** Y **SS:** AL Com Bk IV pg 270; CI - RW Pen **BS:** 78 pg 210; 196.

READ, John K; b c1746, Philadelphia 1758; d 10 Feb 1805 **RU:** Surgeon, Served in 1st Battalion of Minutemen **CEM:** St Paul's Episcopal; GPS 36.84733, -76.28554; 201 St Paul's Blvd; Norfolk City **GS:** Y **SP:** Helen (Calvert) Maxwell Read - 2nd husband **VI:** Moved to Borough of Norfolk c1796. Mayor of Norfolk 1799 **P:** unk **BLW:** unk **RG:** Y **MK:** N **PH:** unk **SS:** CB; G pg 502 **BS:** 87 pg 29.

READ, Samuel; b 31 Mar 1767; d 25 Jan 1831 **RU:** Private, Served in Capt John Robert's Co, Bedford Co Militia **CEM:** Callaway-Steptoe; GPS 37.30560, -79.29470; Rt 460, New London; Bedford **GS:** Y **SP:** Elizabeth (-----) **VI:** Severely weathered stone. Source of service derived fr Campbell Co Historical Society correspondence to JLARC Committee is obviously incorrect. If he was b in 1767, he could not have achieved Capt rank by 1783 at age 16. Perhaps he was in War of 1812 or perhaps birth date incorrect **P:** unk **BLW:** unk **RG:** unk **MK:** N **PH:** unk **SS:** E pg 653 **BS:** JLARC 36; 196.

READ, Thomas; b 21 Nov 1742, Lunenburg Co; d 1817 **RU:** Colonel/Patriot, Was Burgess, member of State Conventions of 1774-76. Committee of Safety for Charlotte Co 1775-76. During RW, served as County Lt. Marched to Petersburg himself. Supplied quotas of that county in men and means to state of VA and Cont Lines. Col of Charlotte Co Millitia 1781 **CEM:** Ingleside, Thomas Read Family; GPS unk; Charlotte CH; Charlotte **GS:** U **SP:** Elizabeth Nash (__-1790), sister of Col Thomas Nash & Mary Nash Read. **VI:** Son of Clement & (-----) Read. Deputy clerk for father in Lunenburg Co, then deputy clerk in Charlotte Co. Clerk in 1770, which office he held until his death in 1817. Member of Constitutional Convention of 1788 **P:** unk **BLW:** unk **RG:** unk **MK:** unk **PH:** unk **SS:** E pg 653 **BS:** 196.

READ, William; b 1720; d 1798 **RU:** Corporal, Served in a VA battalion **CEM:** Read; GPS 37.18220, -79.18510; New London, nr jct Rts 460 & 811; Bedford **GS:** U **SP:** Johanna (-----) **VI:** JLARC site visit could only find stone for his son **P:** unk **BLW:** unk **RG:** Y **MK:** N **PH:** unk **SS:** J-NSSAR 1993 Reg; E pg 653 **BS:** JLARC 1.

REBOUL, Pierre; b unk; d 1781 **RU:** Seaman, Served on "Saint-Esprit" and died from Yorktown battle **CEM:** French Memorial; GPS 36.81944, -79.39933; Yorktown; York **GS:** U **SP:** No info **VI:** No further data **P:** unk **BLW:** unk **RG:** Y **MK:** unk **PH:** unk **SS:** J-Yorktown Historian **BS:** JLARC 1, 74.

REDCROSS, John; b unk; d 1861 **RU:** Private, Served in 2nd VA State Regt **CEM:** Indian Graveyard; GPS unk; Bear Mtn, Rt 643; Amherst **GS:** N **SP:** No info **VI:** Recd BLW #4748 **P:** unk **BLW:** Y **RG:** N **MK:** N **PH:** N **SS:** E pg 655; CZ pg 368 **BS:** 01 pg 70.

REDD, John Franklin; b 25 Oct 1755, Orange Co; d 11 Aug 1850 **RU:** Second Lieutenant, Walked fr Albemarle Co to Henry Co at age 17 to enlist. Served under Gen Joesph Martin. Appted 2nd Lt Apr 1780 in Henry Co. Was at Yorktown 1781 **CEM:** Redd; GPS unk; Fontaine; Henry **GS:** Y **SP:** Mar (24 Aug 1782 Henry Co) Mary Winston Carr Waller (26 Oct 1765 Stafford Co-17 Jul 1828 Henry Co), daughter of Col George (1734-1814) & Ann Winston (Carr) (1735-1839) Waller (1765-1828) **VI:** Son of George (1735-1755) of Orange Co. & Lucy (Franklin) (1737-(-----) Albemarle Co.) Redd. Also served in Indian Wars. Rec'd rank of Maj after RW. Member of court in Henry Co for 40 yrs. Pen Henry Co 1833 **P:** Y **BLW:** unk **RG:** unk **MK:** Y **PH:** unk **SS:** E pg 645; K Vol 4 pg 195 **BS:** JLARC 2, 4, 38,102; 245.

REDIN, John; b 1752, England; d 5 Aug 1832 **RU:** Private?, Served in 6th Cont Line **CEM:** Southern-Shreve; GPS unk; 5300 N 10th St; Arlington **GS:** Y **SP:** Mary (-----) b 1764 England, d 1874 **VI:** No further data **P:** unk **BLW:** unk **RG:** N **MK:** N **PH:** unk **SS:** E pg 655 **BS:** 69 pg 73; 196.

REDMAN, Henry; b unk; d Dec 1790 **RU:** Private, Served in 3rd, 4th, & 8th Cont Lines **CEM:** Old Christ Church Episcopal; GPS 38.80625, -77.04718; 118 N Washington St; Alexandria City **GS:** N **SP:** No info **VI:** Burial permit for "Mr. Redman" issued 15 Dec 1790 to son Thomas Redman **P:** unk **BLW:** unk **RG:** N **MK:** N **PH:** N **SS:** E pg 655 **BS:** 20 pg 152.

REED, William; b c1762, Dunmore (now Shenandoah) Co; d 11 Sep 1839 **RU:** First Sergeant, Ent serv 1778 in Dunmore Co 8th Va Regt. Served in Capt Thomas Bucks Co (Buck's Minute Men), Dunmore Co Militia **CEM:** Stone Chapel Presbyterian; GPS 39.22610, -78.01060; Old Charles Town Rd, Berryville; Clarke **GS:** Y **SP:** Susan (-----) **VI:** Sergeant during French & Indian War and accompanied George

RU=Rank/Unit   CEM=Cemetery   GS=Gravestone   SP=Spousal Information
VI=Other Veteran Info   P=Pension   BLW=Bounty/Land Warrant   RG=Registered Grave
MK=SAR/DAR Marker   PH=Photo   SS=Service Source   BS=Burial Source

281

Rogers Clarke on his Illinois/Indiana campaign **P:** unk **BLW:** unk **RG:** Y **MK:** N **PH:** Y **SS:** E pg 656 **BS:** 50 pg 39.

REEDY, George Peter; b c1749, Goshenhoppen, Montgomery Co, PA; d c1837 **RU:** Sergeant, Served in 7th Co, 6th Bn, Northampton Co PA Militia **CEM:** Reedy; GPS 39.13594, -78.00630; Reedy Groves, Grossy Creek; Grayson **GS:** U **SP:** Mary (Sisk?) (__-after 1840) **VI:** Sol appl BLW Montgomery Co, 25 Jan 1782 (rejected). Purchased 200 acres in Grayson Co **P:** unk **BLW:** N **RG:** unk **MK:** unk **PH:** unk **SS:** PA Archives, Series 5 Vol 8 pg 469, 525 **BS:** 32.

REEVES, George Sr; b 1735, Drewry's Bluff, Chesterfield Co; d 15 Nov 1811 **RU:** Lieutenant, Served in Capt James McDonald's Co, Montgomery Co Militia **CEM:** Reeves Farm; GPS unk; Rt 700, SE of Independence; Grayson **GS:** Y **SP:** Mar (1765) Jane Burton (1745-1811 Independence, VA) **VI:** Son of Thomas (1700-1760) & (-----) Reeves. DAR plaque **P:** unk **BLW:** unk **RG:** Y **MK:** Y **PH:** unk **SS:** DAR Ancestor #A095020; J-NSSAR 1993 Reg, J- DAR Hatcher; E pg 656; CE pg 23; DD; DL pg 766 **BS:** JLARC 1, 2.

REIBAUD, Antoine; b unk; d 1781 **RU:** Seaman, Served on "Victorie" and died from Yorktown battle **CEM:** French Memorial; GPS 36.81944, -79.39933; Yorktown; York **GS:** U **SP:** No info **VI:** No further data **P:** unk **BLW:** unk **RG:** Y **MK:** unk **PH:** unk **SS:** J-Yorktown Historian **BS:** JLARC 1, 74.

REID, Andrew; b 2 Feb 1751 VA; d 1837 **RU:** Patriot, Was Justice of Rockbridge Co Ct and Clerk 7 Apr 1778 **CEM:** Stonewall Jackson Memorial; GPS 37.78128, -79.44604; 314 S Main St; Lexington City **GS:** Y **SP:** Magdalene McDowell (1755-1838) **VI:** Son of Andrew Jr & Sarah (-----) Reid. Died in Rockbridge Co **P:** N **BLW:** N **RG:** unk **MK:** unk **PH:** Y **SS:** G pg 320 **BS:** JLARC 63.

REID, Francis; b 1752; d 1827 **RU:** First Midshipman, Served on "Henry" Galley **CEM:** Reid Family; GPS unk; 9 mi NE of Eagle Rock; Botetourt **GS:** Y **SP:** No info **VI:** Was fr Gloucester Co **P:** unk **BLW:** unk **RG:** N **MK:** N **PH:** unk **SS:** E pg 657; L pg 240 **BS:** 165 Reid.

REID, James; b 1755; d 20 Jul 1821 **RU:** First Lieutenant, Served in 3rd VA Regt Cont Line. Promoted to 1st Lt 01 Mar 1777 **CEM:** Dumfries Public; GPS 38.34110, -77.19964; 17821 Mine Rd, Dumfries; Prince William **GS:** Y **SP:** No info **VI:** SAR monument **P:** unk **BLW:** unk **RG:** Y **MK:** Y **PH:** unk **SS:** AP 3rd VA Regt **BS:** 94 pg 18.

REID, John; b 1762; d 31 Mar 1837 **RU:** Soldier, Ent serv Fairfax Co in 1780. Served in VA Regt **CEM:** Fairfax City; GPS 38.84690, -77.31330; Main St & Page Ave; Fairfax City **GS:** N **SP:** No info **VI:** Pen fr Fairfax Co 1836. Unnamed child granted his pension in arrears S10254 **P:** Y **BLW:** unk **RG:** unk **MK:** N **PH:** N **SS:** K Vol 4 pg 201 **BS:** JLARC 4,14, 27, 28.

REID, Nathan; b 1753; d 1830 **RU:** Captain, Was Capt of 7th Co 28 Jan 1777 in 14th VA Regt of Foot. Later was Capt of 1st Co 1781-2 in Col Thomas Posey's VA Bn. As capt commanded 3rd Co, 1st VA Regt of Foot, Jun-Nov 1779, then 2nd Co 1st VA Regt Jan 1783 **CEM:** Reid Estate "Poplar Grove"; GPS unk; New London; Bedford **GS:** U **SP:** No info **VI:** WPA survey says bur in the old garden, then at Reeves Lemon's home **P:** unk **BLW:** unk **RG:** Y **MK:** N **PH:** unk **SS:** CE pg 32, 33, 71, 92 **BS:** JLARC 1, 2, 36; 75.

REMAIN, Jacques; b unk; d 1781 **RU:** Seaman, Served on "Northumberland" and died from Yorktown battle **CEM:** French Memorial; GPS 36.81944, -79.39933; Yorktown; York **GS:** U **SP:** No info **VI:** No further data **P:** unk **BLW:** unk **RG:** Y **MK:** unk **PH:** unk **SS:** J-Yorktown Historian **BS:** JLARC 1, 74.

REMONT, Charles; b unk; d 1781 **RU:** Soldier, Served in Gatinais Bn and died fr battle at Yorktown **CEM:** French Memorial; GPS 36.81944, -79.39933; Yorktown; York **GS:** U **SP:** No info **VI:** No further data **P:** unk **BLW:** unk **RG:** Y **MK:** unk **PH:** unk **SS:** J-Yorktown Historian **BS:** JLARC 1, 74.

RENARD, Jean; b unk; d 1781 **RU:** Seaman, Served on "Hextor" and died from Yorktown battle **CEM:** French Memorial; GPS 36.81944, -79.39933; Yorktown; York **GS:** U **SP:** No info **VI:** No further data **P:** unk **BLW:** unk **RG:** Y **MK:** unk **PH:** unk **SS:** J-Yorktown Historian **BS:** JLARC 1, 74.

RENOUARD, Jean; b unk; d 1781 **RU:** Seaman, Served on "Hercule" and died from Yorktown battle **CEM:** French Memorial; GPS 36.81944, -79.39933; Yorktown; York **GS:** U **SP:** No info **VI:** No further data **P:** unk **BLW:** unk **RG:** Y **MK:** unk **PH:** unk **SS:** J-Yorktown Historian **BS:** JLARC 1, 74.

RU=Rank/Unit	CEM=Cemetery	GS=Gravestone	SP=Spousal Information
VI=Other Veteran Info	P=Pension	BLW=Bounty/Land Warrant	RG=Registered Grave
MK=SAR/DAR Marker	PH=Photo	SS=Service Source	BS=Burial Source

282

REVEL, Gaspard; b unk; d 1781 **RU:** Seaman, Served on "Caton" and died from Yorktown battle **CEM:** French Memorial; GPS 36.81944, -79.39933; Yorktown; York **GS:** U **SP:** No info **VI:** No further data **P:** unk **BLW:** unk **RG:** Y **MK:** unk **PH:** unk **SS:** J-Yorktown Historian **BS:** JLARC 1, 74.

REYNOLDS, Bernard; b 1763, Caroline Co; d 23 Jan 1833 **RU:** Private, Served in Va Line. Ent serv 1779 Caroline Co **CEM:** Reynolds Family; GPS unk; Hammonville; Russell **GS:** U **SP:** Mar (1 Feb 1787) Lucy (-----) (c1764-__) **VI:** Lived in Henrico Co 1810, then Russell Co 1828. Pension appl for 7 Aug 1832 age 69. She appl pen 26 Dec 1840 age 76 W188904 **P:** Y **BLW:** unk **RG:** unk **MK:** unk **PH:** unk **SS:** J-DAR Hatcher; K Vol 4 pg 205; CG Vol 3 pg 2853 **BS:** JLARC 2.

REYNOLDS, William; b 1757; d 22 Aug 1830 **RU:** Private, Served in Capt Peter Bernard's Co, York Garrison; 2nd VA State Regt Mar & Apr 1778 **CEM:** Old Presbyterian Meeting House; GPS 38.48528, -77.23532; 323 S Fairfax St; Alexandria City **GS:** Y **SP:** No info **VI:** Died age 73 **P:** unk **BLW:** unk **RG:** N **MK:** N **PH:** unk **SS:** AP **BS:** 23 pg 67.

RHODES, Michael; b 1 May 1749; d 11 Oct 1819 **RU:** Private, Served in Michael Reader's Co, VA Cont Line **CEM:** Coffman's Rivermont Farm, Rhodes Family; GPS 38.91623, -78.41480; Fisher Rd Rt 649 to end of state maintenance; Shenandoah **GS:** U **SP:** Anna (Nancy) Stricker **VI:** Son of John (1712-1764) & Eve Catherine (Albright) (1723-1764) Roads **P:** unk **BLW:** Y **RG:** Y **MK:** unk **PH:** unk **SS:** BY pg 306; J-NSSAR 1993 Reg J- DAR Hatcher **BS:** JLARC 1, 2; 196.

RHODES (ROTH), Henry B; b 2 Nov 1747; d 18 Mar 1827 **RU:** Corporal, Served in VA Navy **CEM:** Rhodes (Roth) Family; GPS unk; Vic Broadway Rt 42; Rockingham **GS:** Y **SP:** Elizabeth (-----) **VI:** No further data **P:** unk **BLW:** unk **RG:** Y **MK:** N **PH:** unk **SS:** AK; E pg 660 **BS:** 04; 191 Rhodes.

RIAU, Joseph; b unk; d 1781 **RU:** Seaman, Served on "Saint-Esprit" and died from Yorktown battle **CEM:** French Memorial; GPS 36.81944, -79.39933; Yorktown; York **GS:** U **SP:** No info **VI:** No further data **P:** unk **BLW:** unk **RG:** Y **MK:** unk **PH:** unk **SS:** J-Yorktown Historian **BS:** JLARC 1, 74.

RICE, John Sr; b 1720, Culpeper Co; d 1804 **RU:** Patriot, Gave material aid to the cause **CEM:** Fishback Family; GPS unk; Dayton; Rockingham **GS:** N **SP:** Mar (Shenandoah Valley) Mary Finney (1723-1808), d/o James & Elizabeth (Turner) Finney. **VI:** Son of William (1686-1780) of Hanover Co & Sarah (Nelms or Helms) (1713-1780) of Hampshire Co, WV, Rice **P:** N **BLW:** N **RG:** unk **MK:** unk **PH:** N **SS:** AL CT BK II pg 16 Rockingham Co; CD **BS:** 196.

RICE, Thomas; b 18 Aug 1764; d 3 Dec 1819 **RU:** Private, Served in Capt Robert Powell's Co, 3rd VA Regt under Lt Col Heth. **CEM:** Rice Fam; GPS unk; Rt 743 W of Dayton; Rockingham **GS:** Y **SP:** No info **VI:** No further data **P:** unk **BLW:** unk **RG:** Y **MK:** N **PH:** unk **SS:** AK; A pg 278 **BS:** 04; 191 Rice.

RICHARD, John; b 1762; d 1824 **RU:** Purser, Was in VA Navy on sloop "Scorpian" **CEM:** Shockoe Hill; GPS 37.55190, -77.43170; 4th & Hospital Sts; Richmond City **GS:** Y **SP:** No info **VI:** No further data **P:** unk **BLW:** unk **RG:** N **MK:** N **PH:** unk **SS:** L pg 241 **BS:** 57 pg viii.

RICHARD, Pierre; b unk; d 1781 **RU:** Seaman, Served on "Languedoc" and died from Yorktown battle **CEM:** French Memorial; GPS 36.81944, -79.39933; Yorktown; York **GS:** U **SP:** No info **VI:** No further data **P:** unk **BLW:** unk **RG:** Y **MK:** unk **PH:** unk **SS:** J-Yorktown Historian **BS:** JLARC 1, 74.

RICHARD(S), Henry; b 14 Nov 1753; d 25 Feb 1847 **RU:** Patriot, Gave material aid to the cause **CEM:** Mountain View Methodist; GPS 39.11410, -78.40920; Richards Ln, Mountain Falls; Frederick **GS:** Y **SP:** Catherine Elizabeth Rudolph Keckley (15 Aug 1758, Gadernheim, Germany-21 Apr 1828) d/o Johann (1720-1788) & Margretha (Weimer) (c1732-1788) Rudolph **VI:** Burial site has DAR marker **P:** N **BLW:** N **RG:** N **MK:** Y **PH:** unk **SS:** AL CT Bk pg 12; CD **BS:** 59 pg 271; 196.

RICHARDS, Christian; b 1748; d 18 Aug 1818 **RU:** Private, Served in Capt Jacob Colman's Co, Dunmore Co Militia **CEM:** Red Oak Grove; GPS 36.98184, -80.28639; Off Red Oak Grove Rd Rt 684; Floyd **GS:** U **SP:** Catherine (-----) (1751-1825) **VI:** No further data **P:** unk **BLW:** unk **MK:** unk **PH:** unk **SS:** C pg 608 **BS:** JLARC 29; 196.

RICHARDS, Edward; b 25 Jun 1731, Baltimore Co, MD; d 16 Apr 1812 **RU:** Patriot, Gave material aid to cause **CEM:** Richards Family; GPS unk; 2.5 mi SW of Callaway off Foothills Rd; Franklin **GS:** U **SP:** Elizabeth Stewart (1742-1812) d/o James & (-----) Stuart **VI:** Son of Benjamin (1710-__) & Ann

RU=Rank/Unit   CEM=Cemetery   GS=Gravestone   SP=Spousal Information
VI=Other Veteran Info   P=Pension   BLW=Bounty/Land Warrant   RG=Registered Grave
MK=SAR/DAR Marker   PH=Photo   SS=Service Source   BS=Burial Source

283

(Meryman) (1711-__) Richards **P:** N **BLW:** N **RG:** unk **MK**: unk **PH:** unk **SS:** AL Ct Bk pg 25 Henry Co **BS:** 196.

RICHARDS, George; b unk; d Jul 1789 **RU:** Patriot, Signed Fairfax Co legislative petition during war period **CEM:** Old Christ Church Episcopal; GPS 38.80625, -77.04718; 118 N Washington St; Alexandria City **GS:** N **SP:** No info **VI:** Burial permit issued 4 Jul 1789 **P:** N **BLW:** N **RG:** N **MK:** N **PH:** N **SS:** BB **BS:** 20 pg 152.

RICHARDS, John; b unk; d 1806 **RU:** Patriot, Gave material aid to the cause **CEM:** Williams Family; GPS 38.56808, -77.33511; Williams Wharf; Mathews **GS:** Y **SP:** No info **VI:** No further data **P:** N **BLW:** N **RG:** N **MK:** N **PH:** unk **SS:** AL Ct Bk lt pg 15 **BS:** 48 pg 142.

RICHARDS, John; b 30 Nov 1754; d 22 Jun 1843 **RU:** Soldier, Ent serv 1778 and enlisted in VA Regt **CEM:** Lacy Family; GPS 37.80571, -77.99405; Rt 615; Goochland **GS:** Y **SP:** Mar (before 2 Jul 1781) Ursula Rutherford **VI:** Appl pen 17 Sep 1832, Goochland Co. S15967 **P:** Y **BLW:** unk **RG:** Y **MK:** N **PH:** unk **SS:** E pg 661; CG Vol 3 pg 2871 **BS:** 46 pg 176.

RICHARDS, John; b unk; d 1781 **RU:** Soldier, Served fr MA and died as result of Yorktown battle **CEM:** Yorktown Victory Monument Tablet; GPS 38.28350, -78.54150; Yorktown; York **GS:** U **SP:** No info **VI:** No further data **P:** unk **BLW:** unk **RG:** unk **MK:** unk **PH:** unk **SS:** J-Yorktown Historian **BS:** JLARC 74.

RICHARDSON, George W; b unk; d after 1781 **RU:** Patriot, Gave material aid to the cause **CEM:** Boscobel; GPS unk; Vic Rt 621 Manakin; Goochland **GS:** Y **SP:** Mar (1766) Elizabeth Miller of St James Northern Parish **VI:** No further data **P:** N **BLW:** N **RG:** N **MK:** N **PH:** unk **SS:** AL Ct Bk lt pg 2 **BS:** 46 pg 104.

RICHARDSON, John Sr; b 1 May 1751, Philadelphia Co, PA; d 22 Oct 1837 **RU:** Captain, Served in PA Line. Ent serv 1776 in PA Regt, then moved to Shenandoah Co VA and was made Capt there 28 Feb 1782 **CEM:** Falling Springs Presbyterian; GPS unk; 115 Spring Church Rd, Covington; Covington City **GS:** Y **SP:** Nancy Mossman **VI:** Moved to MD, then Frederick Co VA, then Rockingham Co, then to Botetourt (later Allegheny). Appl pen Alleghany Co 17 Mar 1834. Pension in arrears granted to 3 of 6 children (not named). S18177 **P:** Y **BLW:** unk **RG:** N **MK:** N **PH:** unk **SS:** K Vol 4 pg 216; CG Vol 3 pg 2876 **BS:** 72 vol 2 pg 67.

RICHARDSON, Nightingale; b unk; d 1833 **RU:** Private, Served in PA Line. Served also in Capt Joseph Smith's Co, Col Nathaniel Gist's VA Regt 1777 **CEM:** Goose Creek; GPS 39.11250, -77.69527; Rt 722, Lincoln; Loudoun **GS:** Y **SP:** No info **VI:** BLW #10302-100-11 Jun 1793 **P:** unk **BLW:** Y **RG:** Y **MK:** N **PH:** unk **SS:** E pg 622; CG Vol 3 pg 2878 **BS:** 25 pg 259.

RICHARDSON, Samuel; b 1741; d 1794 **RU:** Captain/Patriot, Commanded a co 18 May 1778, Goochland Co Militia. Signed Oath of Allegiance in Goochland Co 1777 **CEM:** The Oaks; GPS unk; 1.4 mi SE of Tapscott on Rt 603; Goochland **GS:** U **SP:** No info **VI:** No further data **P:** unk **BLW:** unk **RG:** unk **MK:** unk **PH:** unk **SS:** AZ pg 207; DU **BS:** 218.

RICHARDSON, Samuel Marquis; b 1 Feb 1760 ,Frederick Co, MD; d 18 Jan 1831 **RU:** Private, Served in Capt William Rieley Co, Col Hazen's Regt **CEM:** Richardson Family; GPS 38.95750, -78.29610; 1.5 mi fr entrance to GW National Forest, Rt 678 nr Fortsmouth Vol Fire Dept; Warren **GS:** Y **SP:** Mar (3 Jan 1784) Catherine Bainbridge Hal (3 Feb 1760-19 Aug 1837) **VI:** Son of (-----) & Isabell (-----) Calmes (1729-1796). Died in Front Royal **P:** unk **BLW:** unk **RG:** unk **MK:** unk **PH:** unk **SS:** DAR Ancestor #A095733 **BS:** 196.

RICHARDSON, William; b 22 Dec 1750, Stafford Co; d 6 Jul 1821 **RU:** First Lieutenant, Served in Greensville Co Militia Sep 1782 **CEM:** Buck Family; GPS unk; 1 mi W of Buckton Station, Waterlick; Warren **GS:** Y **SP:** 1) Elizabeth Philand 2) Polly Webb (__-1799) **VI:** Son of (-----) and Isabella (Calmes) (__-1796) Richardson **P:** unk **BLW:** unk **RG:** N **MK:** N **PH:** Y **SS:** DAR Ancestor # A097564; AP Serv Rec; DD cites Brown's Sketches of Greensville Co VA 1650-1967 pg 365 **BS:** 113.

RICHARDSON, William Sr; b 1 Sep 1748, Surry Co, NC; d Aug 1835 **RU:** Private, Enl 3 Apr 1777 in Capt Jason Watts' Co. Served 3 yrs. Fought in battle of Kings Mountain 7 Oct 1780 & battle of Point Pleasant 1774 **CEM:** Richardson; GPS 36.93250, 81.53360; Rt 610 Valley Rd; Smyth **GS:** U **SP:** Mar (1764 Washington Co) Rebecca Hays, d/o John & Elizabeth (Bass) Hays (1750-1810) **VI:** Parents unk.

RU=Rank/Unit	CEM=Cemetery	GS=Gravestone	SP=Spousal Information
VI=Other Veteran Info	P=Pension	BLW=Bounty/Land Warrant	RG=Registered Grave
MK=SAR/DAR Marker	PH=Photo	SS=Service Source	BS=Burial Source

284

Warrant of 100 acres of land 10 Feb 1784, "Rich Valley" Smyth Co **P:** unk **BLW:** Y **RG:** unk **MK:** unk **PH:** unk **SS:** F pg 64; N pg 1430; A pg 145 **BS:** 196.

RICKMAN, William Dr; b 1731, England; d 1 Dec 1784 **RU:** Colonel, Served as Col in Cont Line **CEM:** Rickman Family; GPS 37.30529, -77.04826; Kittiewan Plantation, 12104 Weyanoke Rd, Charles City; Charles City Co **GS:** Y **SP:** 1) Mar (1754) Sarah Van Meter 2) Elizabeth Harrison **VI:** Both a newer monument and newer Govt stone mark his grave. His origins in England and the identity of his wife have recently been asserted by the Kittiewan Plantation historian, reflected here. Served as Director of Hospital in VA; Widow Awarded BLW 6,666 acres. Signed Charles City Co petition **P:** unk **BLW:** Y **RG:** unk **MK:** unk **PH:** unk **SS:** E pg663 **BS:** JLARC 110; 196.

RIDDICK, Josiah; b 5 Sep 1748; d 1795 **RU:** Colonel/Patriot, Ent serv during Gen Matthew's invasion. Was captured and sent to New York. Was Commander of Nansemond Co Militia. Gave material aid to cause **CEM:** Riddick Cemetery; GPS 36.68140, -76.55860; Off White Marsh Rd; Suffolk City **GS:** Y **SP:** 1) Elizabeth Godwin, d/o Willis & Mary (Folke) Riddick 2) Anne (-----) (28 Aug 1752-__) **VI:** Son of Mills (1721-1764) & Margaret (Barradall) (__-1764) Riddick. Was granted gratuitiy of 5000 # tobacco 25 Mar 1782 **P:** unk **BLW:** unk **RG:** N **MK:** N **PH:** unk **SS:** E pg 663; AL Ct Bk II pg 9 Nansemond Co; BX pg 674 **BS:** 53 vol I pg 31.

RIDDICK, Mills; b unk; d 1812 **RU:** Lieutenant, Served 3 yrs, units not identified **CEM:** Soldiers Hope; GPS unk; Rt 642, 3.5 mi S of Suffolk; Suffolk City **GS:** Y **SP:** Mary (-----) **VI:** Recd BLW #5921 **P:** unk **BLW:** Y **RG:** N **MK:** N **PH:** unk **SS:** C pg 494 **BS:** 143 Sold Hope.

RIDDLE, Joshua; b unk; d unk **RU:** Soldier, SAR Ancester service not identified **CEM:** Old Presbyterian Meeting House; GPS 38.48528, -77.23532; 323 S Fairfax St; Alexandria City **GS:** N **SP:** No info **VI:** No further data **P:** unk **BLW:** unk **RG:** Y **MK:** unk **PH:** N **SS:** J-NSSAR 1993 Reg; NSSAR Ancestor # P-278993 **BS:** JLARC 1; 5.

RIEBARD, Francois; b unk; d 1781 **RU:** Seaman, Served on "Saint-Esprit" and died from Yorktown battle **CEM:** French Memorial; GPS 36.81944, -79.39933; Yorktown; York **GS:** U **SP:** No info **VI:** No further data **P:** unk **BLW:** unk **RG:** Y **MK:** unk **PH:** unk **SS:** J-Yorktown Historian **BS:** JLARC 1, 74.

RILEY, John; b c1756; d 22 Dec 1825 **RU:** Lieutenant, Received as Lt 25 Nov 1777 In Accomac Co Militia **CEM:** Riley Family; GPS unk; Rt 684, .5 mi W of Rt 658; Accomack **GS:** Y **SP:** Susannah Fletcher, d/o John Fletcher; d 22 Dec 1830 age 75y 10m 26d **VI:** Died age 69 yrs **P:** unk **BLW:** unk **RG:** N **MK:** N **PH:** unk **SS:** E pg 665 **BS:** 38 pg 234.

RINKER, Edward; b unk; d 15 May 1847 **RU:** Sergeant, Served 3 yrs in various units **CEM:** Waterford Union of Churches; GPS 39.18557, -77.60802; Fairfax St, Waterford; Loudoun **GS:** Y **SP:** (-----) Was furnished assistance in Loudoun Co in Apr 1778 **VI:** No further data **P:** unk **BLW:** unk **RG:** Y **MK:** N **PH:** unk **SS:** E pg 666; BX pg 674 **BS:** 25 pg 260.

RINKER, Hans Casper; b 25 Dec 1727, Zurich, Switzerland; d 11 Feb 1804 **RU:** Captain, Commanded a co in Frederick Co Militia 1 Apr 1777 **CEM:** Back Creek Quaker, aka Gainesboro United Methodist; GPS 39.27861, -78.25694; 166 Siler Ln, Gainesboro; Frederick **GS:** Y **SP:** Mar (11 Apr 1757 Germantown, PA) Mary Anna Schultz (28 May 1730, Switzerland-28 Jan 1826) d/o Jacob & Margreth (Huber) Schultz **VI:** No further data **P:** unk **BLW:** unk **RG:** Y **MK:** N **PH:** unk **SS:** E pg 666 **BS:** 59 pg 275; 196.

RINKER, Jacob; b 28 Mar 1749; d 18 Jan 1827 **RU:** Colonel, Appt Col Shenandoah Militia 28 Jun 1781. Took oath 28 Jun 1782, Shenandoah Co Militia **CEM:** Conicville School; GPS 38.8938, -78.69532; Off Rt 703, SW of Conicville nr Swover Creek; Shenandoah **GS:** Y **SP:** Mary Keller (c1753-15 May 1806) **VI:** Marker placed 12 May 2001 **P:** unk **BLW:** unk **RG:** unk **MK:** Y **PH:** unk **SS:** E pg 666 **BS:** JLARC 1, 2, 3.

RINKER, Jacob; b 1723; d 26 Aug 1797 **RU:** Patriot, Gave to the cause **CEM:** Conicville School; GPS 38.8938, -78.69532; Off Rt 703, SW of Conicville nr Swover Creek; Shenandoah **GS:** Y **SP:** Catherine (-----) (c1710-15 Mar 1799) **VI:** GS says he was a "true Republican" **P:** N **BLW:** N **RG:** N **MK:** N **PH:** unk **SS:** AL Ct Bk pg 2, 12 **BS:** 155 Conicville.

RU=Rank/Unit	CEM=Cemetery	GS=Gravestone	SP=Spousal Information
VI=Other Veteran Info	P=Pension	BLW=Bounty/Land Warrant	RG=Registered Grave
MK=SAR/DAR Marker	PH=Photo	SS=Service Source	BS=Burial Source

285

RIORDAN, John; b Feb 1763; d 10 Oct 1803 **RU:** Private, Served in Capt Joseph Anderson's Co, 3rd NJ Regt, Jun 1778 **CEM:** St Mary's Catholic; GPS 38.79390, -77.04750; 310 S Royal St; Alexandria City **GS:** Y **SP:** No info **VI:** Was bur with daughter Mary, age 14. Died age 40 yrs, 6 mos **P:** unk **BLW:** unk **RG:** N **MK:** Y **PH:** Y **SS:** SAR Ancestor #P-33433; AP Roll **BS:** 174 pg 127; 196.

RIOTTE, Pierre; b unk; d 1781 **RU:** Soldier, Served in Gatinais Bn and died fr battle at Yorktown **CEM:** French Memorial; GPS 36.81944, -79.39933; Yorktown; York **GS:** U **SP:** No info **VI:** No further data **P:** unk **BLW:** unk **RG:** Y **MK:** unk **PH:** unk **SS:** J-Yorktown Historian **BS:** JLARC 1, 74.

RIPTON, John; b unk; d 1781 **RU:** Soldier, Served fr PA, killed in the battle at Yorktown **CEM:** Yorktown Victory Monument Tablet; GPS 38.28350, -78.54150; Yorktown; York **GS:** U **SP:** No info **VI:** No further data **P:** unk **BLW:** unk **RG:** unk **MK:** unk **PH:** unk **SS:** J-Yorktown Historian **BS:** JLARC 74.

RITCHEY, David; b unk; d Mar 1807 **RU:** Patriot, Gave material aid to cause **CEM:** Hogshead Family; GPS unk; Off Rt 736 btw Rts 42 & 250, N of Jennings Gap; Augusta **GS:** Y **SP:** No info **VI:** No further data **P:** N **BLW:** N **RG:** N **MK:** N **PH:** unk **SS:** AL Cert **BS:** 142.

RITCHIE, Archibald; b unk, Scotland; d By 20 Apr 1784 **RU:** Patriot, Gave material aid to cause **CEM:** Ritchie Family; GPS unk; Burial vault on lot 18 or 22, Tappahannock; Essex **GS:** U **SP:** Mary Roane (__-1803) **VI:** Was merchant in Tappahannock, by 1766. His vault was opened and coffin contents mutilated by British War of 1812 **P:** N **BLW:** N **RG:** unk **MK:** unk **PH:** unk **SS:** Al Ct bk pg 5 and 6 **BS:** 223 pg 154.

RITCHIE, William; b 1750s; d Fall 1797 **RU:** Private, Served in VA Cont line for 3 yrs **CEM:** Ritchie Family; GPS unk; Burial vault on lot 18 or 22, Tappahannock; Essex **GS:** U **SP:** No info **VI:** Son of Archibald & Mary (Roane) Ritchie (__-1803). this vault was opened and coffin contents mutilated by British War of 1812. BLW issued 20 Jan 1785 100 acres **P:** unk **BLW:** Y **RG:** unk **MK:** unk **PH:** unk **SS:** F pg 65 **BS:** 223 pg 154.

ROANE, John Jr; b 9 Feb 1766, "Uppowac" King William Co; d 15 Nov 1838 **RU:** Private/Patriot, Served in Reg Army appeared on Army Register. Served in VA House of Delegates and was a Delegate to State Constitutional Convention 1788 **CEM:** Uppowac; GPS unk; Rumford; King William **GS:** U **SP:** No info **VI:** Elected Democratic-Republican to Congress 1809-1815. Was Jacksonian Democrat 1827-1831 and Democrat 1835-1837. Son was also Congressman fr VA **P:** unk **BLW:** unk **RG:** unk **MK:** unk **PH:** unk **SS:** C pg 210; E pg 667 **BS:** 196.

ROBERDEAU (ROBERDEAN), Daniel; b 1727, St Christopher; d 5 Jan 1795 **RU:** Brigadier General/Patriot, In Jun 1775 elected Col 2nd Bn of Associators & President of Board of Officers and a Board of Privates, governing Associators. In May 1776 provided provisions for 10,000 men for 3 mos. On 10 Jun 1775 was member PA Council of Safety. Was elected Brig Gen 4 July 1776 Lancaster PA. Advanced $18,000 for Commisioners, never reimbursed. Was member 5 Feb 1777 of Cont Congress **CEM:** Mt Hebron; GPS 39.10916, -78.09497; 305 E Boscawen St; Winchester City **GS:** U **SP:** 1) Mar (3 Oct 1761) Mary Bostwick, d/o Rev Mr. David & Mary (Hinman) Bostwick, (1741_15 Feb 1777 Lancaster PA) 2) Mar (2 Dec 1778 Philadelphia PA) Jane Milligan, prob d/o James & (-----) Milligan (__-3 Sep 1835) **VI:** Son of Isaac & Mary (Cunyngham) Roberdeau **P:** unk **BLW:** unk **RG:** Y **MK:** unk **PH:** unk **SS:** J-NSSAR 1993 Reg, NSSAR Ancestor #P-279849; DAR #A096869 **BS:** JLARC 1, 2.

ROBERTS, Stephen; b 29 Apr 1762; d 15 Jun 1842 **RU:** Sergeant, Enl 2nd SC Regt 1 May 1777. Appt Corporal 6 May 1777 in Grenadier Co. Absent without leave 4 Nov 1777. Promoted to Sergeant 27 June 1778 in Moultrie's Co. Transferred to 1st Vacant Co commanded by Lt Richard Bohun Baker 13 Jul 1778. Reenlisted 1 Nov 1779 under Capt Thomas Moultrie's 6th Co, Col Francis Marion's SC Regt, Nov 1779. Was at siege of Savannah **CEM:** Arnold Grove Episcopal Church; GPS 39.19796, -77.71557; Rt 9, vic jct with Rt 690, Hillsboro; Loudoun **GS:** Y **SP:** Debra Williams (26 Jun 1764-22 Nov 1842) **VI:** No further data **P:** unk **BLW:** unk **RG:** Y **MK:** N **PH:** Y **SS:** E pg 669; Unwanted Patience and Fortitude: Frances Marion's Orderly Book - Patrick O'Kelley **BS:** 25 pg 262; 196.

ROBERTSON, Alexander; b 1753, Augusta Co; d 22 Apr 1801 **RU:** Ensign, Made ensign 16 Dec 1777 in Capt Alexander Robertson's Co in the Augusta Co Militia and then served in Capt Kenny's & Capt Rankin's Cos **CEM:** Augusta Stone Presbyterian; GPS 38.23926, -78.97356; 28 Old Stone Church Ln, Ft Defiance; Augusta **GS:** Y **SP:** Mar (10 Apr 1786) Jean/Jane Cord (c1753-25 Nov 1825) **VI:** Son of

RU=Rank/Unit   CEM=Cemetery   GS=Gravestone   SP=Spousal Information
VI=Other Veteran Info   P=Pension   BLW=Bounty/Land Warrant   RG=Registered Grave
MK=SAR/DAR Marker   PH=Photo   SS=Service Source   BS=Burial Source

286

William (__Ireland-26 Oct 1812, Augusta Co) & Lettice (-----) (__-1809) Robertson. Died age 48 **P:** unk **BLW:** unk **RG:** unk **MK:** unk **PH:** unk **SS:** E pg 670; AZ pg 184 **BS:** JLARC 2 ,8, 23, 62; 196.

ROBERTSON, Alexander; b 1 Mar 1744; d 25 Nov 1816 **RU:** Major/Patriot, Received rank of Maj 21 Oct 1778 in the Augusta Co Militia and served to the end of the war in the 2d Battalion. Was Commissioner of the Provisions Law, Augusta Co 1781 **CEM:** Augusta Stone Presbyterian; GPS 38.23926, -78.97356; 28 Old Stone Church Ln, Ft Defiance; Augusta **GS:** U **SP:** Elizabeth (-----) **VI:** After the war he was promoted to the Lt Col rank **P:** unk **BLW:** unk **RG:** unk **MK:** unk **PH:** unk **SS:** E pg 670; AZ pg 184; AL Cert **BS:** JLARC 2, 8, 23, 62, 63.

ROBERTSON, David; b unk; d 1815 **RU:** Private, Served in Capt John Morton's Co, 4th VA Regt, Jun & Jul 1776 **CEM:** John Conner Family; GPS unk; 200 yds W of jct Rts 616 & 826; Patrick **GS:** Y **SP:** 20 Aug 1796 Patrick Co) Mary Henry d/o John Sr. & (-----) Henry **VI:** No further data **P:** unk **BLW:** unk **RG:** N **MK:** N **PH:** unk **SS:** G pg 679 **BS:** 125 pg 219.

ROBERTSON, Edward; b 1755, Amelia Co; d 1826 **RU:** Private, Served in VA unit paid at Ft Pitt, PA **CEM:** Robertson Family; GPS unk; Dry Fork; Pittsylvania **GS:** Y **SP:** Mar (2 Feb 1782) Mary Ann Jennings **VI:** A Jr and Sr of this same name were in the same unit. Whether he was Jr or Sr not determined **P:** unk **BLW:** unk **RG:** Y **MK:** unk **PH:** unk **SS:** E pg 670; CZ pg 49 **BS:** JLARC 76; 196.

ROBERTSON, James; b 16 Nov 1751, Augusta Co; d unk **RU:** Private, Ent serv 1777 Augusta Co in VA Regt. Served in Capt Rankin's Co, Augusta Co Militia **CEM:** Trinity Episcopal; GPS 38.14917, -79.07521; 214 Beverley St; Staunton City **GS:** N **SP:** Mar (12 Feb 1789 Augusta Co) Mary Russell **VI:** Pensioned Augusta Co 28 Aug 1833 **P:** Y **BLW:** unk **RG:** N **MK:** N **PH:** N **SS:** E pg 670; K Vol 4 pg 239; CG pg 2913 **BS:** 142 trinity.

ROBERTSON, James Sr; b c1744; d 29 Nov 1819 **RU:** Patriot, Gave material aid to cause **CEM:** Robertson Family; GPS unk; Off Rt 641 nr Appomattox CH; Appomattox **GS:** N **SP:** Mar (3 Nov 1763) Rachel Phair (c1749-27 Mar 1822) **VI:** Died in Lynchburg, Campbell Co **P:** N **BLW:** N **RG:** unk **MK:** unk **PH:** N **SS:** DAR Ancestor #A092250; D Vol 1, pg 181-182; AL Ct Bk pg 22 Campbell Co **BS:** JLARC 36.

ROBERTSON, Jeffrey Jr; b 1709; d 16 Dec 1784 **RU:** Patriot, Gave material aid to cause **CEM:** Robertson Farm; GPS 37.367321, -77.607786; Vic jct Robbie Rd & Christina Rd; Chesterfield **GS:** U **SP:** Mar (1734/5) Judith Tanner Mills (c1710-aft 1784 Chesterfield Co) **VI:** No further data **P:** N **BLW:** N **RG:** Y **MK:** N **PH:** unk **SS:** DAR Ancestor #A097253; D Vol 1, pg 248; J-NSSAR 1993 Reg; AL Ct Bk pg 38, 40 Chesterfield Co **BS:** JLARC 1.

ROBERTSON, John; b 1730, PA; d 8 Aug 1828 **RU:** First Lieutenant/Patriot, Served in PA. Appraised beef for the commissioners approving public service claims **CEM:** Shockoe Hill; GPS 37.55190, -77.43170; 4th & Hospital Sts; Richmond City **GS:** Y **SP:** No info **VI:** Was cashier of US Bank in Richmond. **P:** unk **BLW:** unk **RG:** N **MK:** N **PH:** unk **SS:** E pg 670; AL Cert Chesterfield Co **BS:** 57 pg 6; 196.

ROBERTSON, John Jr; b 1763; d 1814 **RU:** First Lieutenant, Was appointed Lt, 6 Aug 1779 Chesterfield Co Militia. Serv in 2nd Cont Line **CEM:** Robertson Family; GPS unk; Off Rt 641 nr Appomattox CH; Appomattox **GS:** Y **SP:** No info **VI:** No further data **P:** unk **BLW:** unk **RG:** N **MK:** N **PH:** unk **SS:** E pg 671 **BS:** 76 Robertson.

ROBERTSON, William; b Dec 1748, Colerain, County Antrim, Ireland; d 12 Nov 1831 **RU:** Captain, Promoted to Capt on 16 Mar 1779, 9th Regt VA Militia. Served as officer fr 1775 until end of war **CEM:** Augusta Stone Presbyterian; GPS 38.23926, -78.97356; 28 Old Stone Church Ln, Ft Defiance; Augusta **GS:** U **SP:** 1) Mar (3 Jun 1788, Augusta Co) Ann Crawford (c1767-10 Dec 1815); 2) Letitice Kerr (12 Jan 1790-18 Dec 1836). Both wives have stones. **VI:** Son of Mathew & Mary (Paxton) Robertson. Recd BLW #1860-200-21 Jan 1790. After the war he served as the county Magistrate. Recd pension of $320 per annum under act of 22 Oct 1828 on Cert #731 while living in Augusta Co **P:** Y **BLW:** Y **RG:** Y **MK:** unk **PH:** unk **SS:** E pg 671; K Vol 4 pg 242; AZ pg 184; CG Vol 3 pg 2915 **BS:** JLARC 1, 8, 23, 62; 196.

ROBERTSON, William; b unk; d 1831 **RU:** Patriot, Gave material aid to cause **CEM:** Stonewall Jackson Memorial; GPS 37.78128, -79.44604; 314 S Main St; Lexington City **GS:** U **SP:** No info **VI:** No further data **P:** N **BLW:** N **RG:** unk **MK:** unk **PH:** unk **SS:** AL Comm Bk II pg 360 Augusta Co **BS:** JLARC 63.

RU=Rank/Unit   CEM=Cemetery   GS=Gravestone   SP=Spousal Information
VI=Other Veteran Info   P=Pension   BLW=Bounty/Land Warrant   RG=Registered Grave
MK=SAR/DAR Marker   PH=Photo   SS=Service Source   BS=Burial Source

287

ROBERTSON, William; b 12 Nov 1748, Charles Co, MD; d 19 Aug 1828 **RU:** Private/Patriot, Served in Capt Belain Posey,Co 3rd MD Militia. Gave material aid to cause **CEM:** Rileyville; GPS 38.76610, -78.38610; At end Cemetery Rd, Luray; Page **GS:** U **SP:** Mar (1779, MD) Mary Timms (1760-1812) **VI:** No further data **P:** unk **BLW:** unk **RG:** unk **MK:** unk **PH:** unk **SS:** DAR Ancestor #A097171; J- DAR Hatcher; AL Ct Bk pg 18 Shenandoah Co; DD cites MD Archives Vol 18 pg 12 **BS:** JLARC 2; 196.

ROBERTSON, William; b 1750; d 1829 **RU:** Second Lieutenant, Served in Capt Ogelby's Co Chesterfield Co Militia **CEM:** Cobbs Family; GPS unk; Bolling Family property, Enon; Chesterfield **GS:** Y **SP:** Elizabeth Bolling **VI:** Son of William & (-----) Robertson Jr. One son Wyndham Robertson became Gov of VA. Another son, Thomas Bolling Robertson became Gov of LA. Family memorial stone-not contemporary. Stones destroyed during Civil War **P:** unk **BLW:** unk **RG:** N **MK:** N **PH:** unk **SS:** G pg 13 **BS:** 56 pg; 196.

ROBICHON, Ferdinand; b unk; d 1781 **RU:** Soldier, Served in Royal Deaux Ponts Bn and died fr battle at Yorktown **CEM:** French Memorial; GPS 36.81944, -79.39933; Yorktown; York **GS:** U **SP:** No info **VI:** No further data **P:** unk **BLW:** unk **RG:** unk **MK:** unk **PH:** unk **SS:** J-Yorktown Historian **BS:** JLARC 1, 74.

ROBINS, Thomas; b 11 Feb 1745; d 8 Nov 1808 **RU:** Private?, Served in 5th Cont Line **CEM:** Robins Family; GPS unk; Robin's Neck; Gloucester **GS:** Y **SP:** Mildred Stubbs **VI:** Son of William & Elizabeth (-----) Robins **P:** unk **BLW:** unk **RG:** N **MK:** N **PH:** unk **SS:** E pg 672 **BS:** 48 pg 53; 213 pg 78.

ROBINSON, Braxton; b c1755; d aft 1795 **RU:** Ensign, Appt Ensign in Greensville Co Militia 23 May 1782 **CEM:** Emporia Tree; GPS unk; Emporia; Emporia City **GS:** Y **SP:** Mar (20 Nov 1789) Frances Walton **VI:** Son of Littleberry & Susanna (-----) Robinson. After war on 27 Jan 1791, promoted to Capt **P:** unk **BLW:** unk **RG:** N **MK:** N **PH:** unk **SS:** G pg 170 **BS:** 80 vol 3 pg 224.

ROBINSON, Isaac; b 8 Oct 1765, Botetourt Co; d 21 Sep 1835 **RU:** Second Lieutenant, Appointed 12 Jul 1781 to 2nd Lt in Botetourt Co Militia **CEM:** North Mountain; GPS unk; 7 mi S of Staunton on N side Rt 252; Augusta **GS:** U **SP:** Mar (6 Sep 1804 Botetourt Co) Eleanor Moffett (20 Mar 1773-3 Sep 1856) d/o John & Jane (Ledgerwood) Moffett **VI:** Cenotaph momument has different dates of 1761-1830 **P:** unk **BLW:** unk **RG:** Y **MK:** N **PH:** unk **SS:** E pg 672 **BS:** 75 No. Mtn; 196.

ROBINSON, James; b 1757, Brunswick Co; d Bef Oct 1801 **RU:** Captain, Commanded a co in Greensville Co Militia **CEM:** Robinson Family; GPS unk; Emporia; Emporia City **GS:** U **SP:** Winnifred Fox **VI:** No further data **P:** unk **BLW:** unk **RG:** unk **MK:** unk **PH:** unk **SS:** J- DAR Hatcher; DD cites Wm & Mary Quarterly Series 1 Vol 27 pg 96 **BS:** JLARC 2.

ROBINSON, John; b 22 Dec 1750; d 1832 **RU:** Lieutenant, Served in VA militia and Cont Line **CEM:** Crossroads Primitive Baptist; GPS 36.60868, -81.01592; Nr Baywood Elem Sch, Rt 624, Baywood; Grayson **GS:** U **SP:** 1) Elizabeth Pyland 2) Polly Webb **VI:** By tradition, Maj Robinson and his wife are bur in unmarked graves in the Robinson-Fields Cemetery. Obtained rank of Maj after RW. Received 2,666 acres BLW **P:** unk **BLW:** Y **RG:** Y **MK:** N **PH:** Y **SS:** E pg 672; AK, Apr 2007 **BS:** 04, Apr 2007; 196.

ROBINSON, John; b 1754 Ireland; d 26 Jun 1826 **RU:** Soldier/Patriot, Gave material aid to cause **CEM:** Washington & Lee Univ Campus; GPS 36.60863, -81.01593; Nr Jefferson St; Lexington City **GS:** U **SP:** No info **VI:** No further data **P:** unk **BLW:** unk **RG:** unk **MK:** unk **PH:** unk **SS:** G pg 770; AL Ct Bk pg 7 **BS:** JLARC 2, 79.

ROBINSON, John; b 1720; d 1795 **RU:** unk, Service information not given in SAR registry **CEM:** Robinson Family; GPS unk; Emporia; Emporia City **GS:** U **SP:** No info **VI:** No further data **P:** unk **BLW:** unk **RG:** unk **MK:** unk **PH:** unk **SS:** NSSAR Ancestor #P-280500; AR Vol 3 pg 225 **BS:** JLARC 2.

ROBINSON, Littlebury; b 1715; d 1792 **RU:** Captain/Patriot, Gave material aid to cause **CEM:** Robinson Family; GPS unk; Emporia; Emporia City **GS:** U **SP:** No info **VI:** No further data **P:** unk **BLW:** unk **RG:** unk **MK:** unk **PH:** unk **SS:** J- DAR Hatcher; AL Ct Bk pg 5 Greenville Co **BS:** JLARC 2.

ROBINSON, Robert; b 1764; d 1808 **RU:** Private, Served in 3rd Artillery Regt, Cont Troops **CEM:** Blandford; GPS 37.22433, -77.38604; 319 S Crater Rd; Petersburg City **GS:** Y **SP:** No info **VI:** No further data **P:** unk **BLW:** unk **RG:** N **MK:** N **PH:** unk **SS:** AP service rec **BS:** 99 pg 33.

RU=Rank/Unit	CEM=Cemetery	GS=Gravestone	SP=Spousal Information
VI=Other Veteran Info	P=Pension	BLW=Bounty/Land Warrant	RG=Registered Grave
MK=SAR/DAR Marker	PH=Photo	SS=Service Source	BS=Burial Source

288

ROBINSON, William; b unk; d Aft 1781 **RU:** Lieutenant Colonel, Commanded Botetourt Co Militia until 12 Apr 1781 **CEM:** Mt Pleasant; **GPS** unk; 6 mi NE of Covington; Covington City **GS:** U **SP:** No info **VI:** No further data **P:** unk **BLW:** unk **RG:** N **MK:** N **PH:** unk **SS:** E pg 673 **BS:** 160 Mt Pleasant.

ROCHE, Jean; b unk; d 1781 **RU:** Soldier, Served in Soissonnais Bn and died fr battle at Yorktown **CEM:** French Memorial; **GPS** 36.81944, -79.39933; Yorktown; York **GS:** U **SP:** No info **VI:** No further data **P:** unk **BLW:** unk **RG:** unk **MK:** unk **PH:** unk **SS:** J-Yorktown Historian **BS:** JLARC 1, 74.

ROCHE, Pierre de; b unk; d 1781 **RU:** Soldier, Served in Soissonnais Bn and died fr battle at Yorktown **CEM:** French Memorial; **GPS** 36.81944, -79.39933; Yorktown; York **GS:** U **SP:** No info **VI:** No further data **P:** unk **BLW:** unk **RG:** unk **MK:** unk **PH:** unk **SS:** J-Yorktown Historian **BS:** JLARC 1, 74.

ROCHEFORT, Jean; b unk; d 1781 **RU:** Seaman, Served on "Auguste" and died from Yorktown battle **CEM:** French Memorial; **GPS** 36.81944, -79.39933; Yorktown; York **GS:** U **SP:** No info **VI:** No further data **P:** unk **BLW:** unk **RG:** unk **MK:** unk **PH:** unk **SS:** J-Yorktown Historian **BS:** JLARC 1, 74.

ROCHELLE, John; b 1746; d unk **RU:** Captain, Was Commissary Officer, VA Troops **CEM:** Rochelle Family, Hermitage Plantation; **GPS** unk; Hwy 671 nr Hansom, Franklin; Franklin City **GS:** Y **SP:** No info **VI:** Son of John & Mary (-----) Rochelle. Govt grave stone, DAR marker **P:** unk **BLW:** unk **RG:** Y **MK:** Y **PH:** unk **SS:** B **BS:** JLARC 76; 196.

ROCHESTER, John Jr; b 1746, Westmoreland Co; d 1794 **RU:** Captain, Served in Westmoreland Co Militia July 1777 **CEM:** Rochester Family; **GPS** unk; Probably old homestead at Lydell's Store, jct Rts 3 & 202; Westmoreland **GS:** U **SP:** 1) Mar (before Jan 1776) Ann Jordan, d/o Robert & (-----) Jordan 2) Anne (-----) McClanahan, widow of William McClanahan **VI:** Son of John (1708-1754) and Hester (Thrift) Rochester **P:** unk **BLW:** unk **RG:** unk **MK:** unk **PH:** unk **SS:** E pg 673; CN pg 85 Westmoreland Co Order Bk **BS:** 80 vol 3 pg 227; 196.

RODES, Charles; b c1730, Hanover Co; d 17 Jun 1805 **RU:** Patriot, Had Civil service as Juror and gave material aid to cause **CEM:** Rodes family; **GPS** unk; See county property records for homeplace; Amherst **GS:** N **SP:** Mar (c1751) Amy Duke (c1733 Hanover Co-13 Nov 1812). SAR applicant indicates also mar Elizabeth Stowe. **VI:** Son of John (6 Nov 1697-aft Feb 1774) & Mary (Crawford) (Mar 1703-__) Rodes. Will dated 19 Mar 1805, Amherst Co **P:** N **BLW:** N **RG:** Y **MK:** N **PH:** N **SS:** DAR Ancestor #A095948; SAR Ancestor #P-280908; D Vol 1 pg 71, 78; AS, SAR applic **BS:** SAR Appl.

RODES (RHODES), John; b 1729; d 1810 **RU:** Fifer/Patriot, Served in Cont Line. Gave material aid to cause **CEM:** Rodes family at Midway Plantation; **GPS** unk; E of Whitehall; Albemarle **GS:** U **SP:** Mar (24 May 1757) Sarah Harris (1735-1803) **VI:** Son of Charles & Amy (Duke) Rodes **P:** unk **BLW:** unk **RG:** Y **MK:** Y **PH:** unk **SS:** J-NSSAR 1993 Reg; AL Ct Bk pg 14 Albemarle Co **BS:** JLARC 1.

RODGERS, Robert; b 29 Jun 1753; d 14 Dec 1827 **RU:** Private, Served in 9th Cont Line **CEM:** Rodgers Plot; **GPS** unk; Rt 180 off Rt 178, .9 mi W of Pungoteague, Hacks Neck; Accomack **GS:** Y **SP:** Mar (31 Oct 1775 (bond) Accomack Co) Tabitha Bundick (22 Jan 1755-28 Nov 1824) d/o Justice Bundick **VI:** Son of Abel & Rosey (-----) Rodgers **P:** unk **BLW:** unk **RG:** N **MK:** N **PH:** unk **SS:** E pg 674 **BS:** 37 pg 218.

ROEBUCK, William; b unk; d 1781 **RU:** Soldier, Served fr VA, killed in the battle at Yorktown **CEM:** Yorktown Victory Monument Tablet; **GPS** 38.28350, -78.54150; Yorktown; York **GS:** U **SP:** No info **VI:** No further data **P:** unk **BLW:** unk **RG:** unk **MK:** unk **PH:** unk **SS:** J-Yorktown Historian **BS:** JLARC 74.

ROGERS, Hamilton; b unk; d 10 Jul 1820 **RU:** Private/Patriot, Served in Capt Henry McCabes Co fr Loudoun Co. Gave material aid to cause **CEM:** North Fork Baptist; **GPS** 39.06014, -77.68509; 38130 North Folk Rd, North Fork; Loudoun **GS:** Y **SP:** No info **VI:** No further data **P:** unk **BLW:** unk **RG:** Y **MK:** N **PH:** unk **SS:** N pg 1267; AL Ct Bk pg 37, 47 Loudoun Co **BS:** 25 pg 263.

ROGERS, James; b unk; d 1804 **RU:** Private?, 9th Cont Line **CEM:** Back Creek Quaker, aka Gainesboro United Methodist; **GPS** 39.27861, -78.25694; 166 Siler Ln, Gainesboro; Frederick **GS:** Y **SP:** no info **VI:** No further data **P:** unk **BLW:** unk **RG:** Y **MK:** N **PH:** unk **SS:** E pg 675 **BS:** 59 pg 283.

ROGERS, John; b 31 Oct 1750, Frederick Co; d 6 Oct 1826 **RU:** Corporal, Serv in Capt John Mercer's Co Feb 1778 of the 3rd VA Regt commanded by Lt Col Heth **CEM:** Back Creek Quaker, aka Gainesboro

RU=Rank/Unit	CEM=Cemetery	GS=Gravestone	SP=Spousal Information
VI=Other Veteran Info	P=Pension	BLW=Bounty/Land Warrant	RG=Registered Grave
MK=SAR/DAR Marker	PH=Photo	SS=Service Source	BS=Burial Source

289

United Methodist; GPS 39.27861, -78.25694; 166 Siler Ln, Gainesboro; Frederick **GS:** Y **SP:** Mar (30 Oct 1787 Frederick Co. by Christian Streit) Mary Olleman **VI:** No further data **P:** unk **BLW:** unk **RG:** Y **MK:** N **PH:** unk **SS:** A pg 276 **BS:** 59 pg 283.

ROGERS, Samual; b unk; d 1781 **RU:** Lieutenant, Served fr MA, and died fr the battle at Yorktown **CEM:** Yorktown Victory Monument Tablet; GPS 38.28350, -78.54150; Yorktown; York **GS:** U **SP:** No info **VI:** No further data **P:** unk **BLW:** unk **RG:** unk **MK:** unk **PH:** unk **SS:** J-Yorktown Historian **BS:** JLARC 74.

ROITOUX, Pierre; b unk; d 1781 **RU:** Soldier, Served in Soissonnais Bn and died fr battle at Yorktown **CEM:** French Memorial; GPS 36.81944, -79.39933; Yorktown; York **GS:** U **SP:** No info **VI:** No further data **P:** unk **BLW:** unk **RG:** Y **MK:** unk **PH:** unk **SS:** J-Yorktown Historian **BS:** JLARC 1, 74.

ROLLER, Conrad; b unk; d Oct 1823 **RU:** Soldier, Ent serv 1781 in VA Line **CEM:** New Jerusalem Lutheran; GPS 39.25736, -77.63891; 12942 Lutheran Church Rd, Lovettsville; Loudoun **GS:** U **SP:** Mar (21 Mar 1779 Loudoun Co by Rev Charles Wildahne, German Lutheran Church) Elizabeth Slats d/o Frederick & (-----) Slates of Pine Run Hundred, Frederick Co. **VI:** Was fr Loudoun Co. Widow appl pen 28 Apr 1840 Loudoun Co age 79. Rec'd BLW. W4325 **P:** Y **BLW:** Y **RG:** unk **MK:** unk **PH:** unk **SS:** C pg 265; K Vol 4 pg 253; CG Vol 3 pg 2941 **BS:** JLARC 4, 32.

ROLSTONE (ROLSTON/RALSTON), David; b 20 Oct 1760, Rockingham Co; d 5 Jun 1849 **RU:** Private, Served in Capts Hopkins and John Rice Cos 1776; Capt Robert Craven's Co under Col Stubblefield 1780; Capt Richard Ragan's Co under Maj Long 1781. Was at the siege of Yorktown. Discharged 20 Oct 1781 **CEM:** Cooks Creek Presbyterian; GPS 38.47472, -78.92997; 4222 Mt Clinton Pike, Harrisonburg; Harrisonburg City **GS:** Y **SP:** Mar (18 Jan 1783. Rockingham Co) Sarah Hinton (__ Shenandoah Co-10 Mar 1804) **VI:** Died in Rockingham Co **P:** unk **BLW:** unk **RG:** Y **MK:** Y **PH:** unk **SS:** E pg 676 **BS:** JLARC 76.

ROSBUCK, William; b unk; d 1781 **RU:** Private, Service unit not identified. Died fr Yorktown battle **CEM:** Yorktown Victory Monument Tablet; GPS 38.28350, -78.54150; Yorktown; York **GS:** Y **SP:** No info **VI:** No further data **P:** unk **BLW:** unk **RG:** N **MK:** N **PH:** unk **SS:** AS; SAR report **BS:** SAR report.

ROSE, Alexander; b Britain; d 28 Nov 1800 **RU:** Major/ Captain, Retired as Maj 14 Sep 1778 **CEM:** St George's Episcopal; GPS unk; 905 Princess Anne; Fredericksburg City **GS:** Y **SP:** 1) Mildred Washington 2) Sarah Fontaine **VI:** Recd 5111 acres BLW #1863-300-3 Mar 1791 **P:** unk **BLW:** Y **RG:** Y **MK:** N **PH:** unk **SS:** E pg 677; CG Vol 3 pg 294 **BS:** 12 pg 113.

ROSE, Henry; b unk; d 4 Feb 1810 **RU:** Soldier, SAR Ancester service not identified **CEM:** Presbyterian Church; GPS 38.80015, -77.05791; Wilkes St & Hamilton Ln; Alexandria City **GS:** N **SP:** No info **VI:** Death notice in Alexandria Gazette 6 Feb 1810, pg 3 **P:** unk **BLW:** unk **RG:** Y **MK:** unk **PH:** N **SS:** J-NSSAR 1993 Reg; NSSAR Ancestor # P-281761 **BS:** JLARC 1.

ROSE, John; b 3 Sep 1761; d 4 Feb 1844 **RU:** Captain, Served in John Clark's III Regt. Was a sea capt in 1780 and was captured by the British **CEM:** Old Stone Methodist; GPS 39.11725, -77.56609; 168 W Cornwall St, Leesburg; Loudoun **GS:** Y **SP:** Anna Beall (3 Feb 1762-22 Jan 1840) d/o George (1729-1807) & (-----) Beale **VI:** Son of Isaac (1729-1805) & Rachel (Grigsby) (1737-1805) Rose. First mayor of Leesburg. Sheriff of Loudoun Co 11 Nov 1822 to 8 Nov 1824 **P:** unk **BLW:** unk **RG:** Y **MK:** N **PH:** unk **SS:** E, pg 677 **BS:** 25, pg 265; 196.

ROSS, Alexander; b 9 Feb 1741; d unk **RU:** Private/Patriot, Service as private in undetermined unit. As a patriot in Frederick Co he furnished the militia paint and iron **CEM:** Augusta Stone Presbyterian; GPS 38.23926, -78.97356; 28 Old Stone Church Ln, Ft Defiance; Augusta **GS:** U **SP:** No info **VI:** No further data **P:** unk **BLW:** unk **RG:** unk **MK:** unk **PH:** unk **SS:** Z pg 77; JLARC report **BS:** JLARC 23; 71; 196.

ROSS, Daniel Sr; b 1740; d 1823 **RU:** Second Lieutenant/Patriot, Appt 2nd Lt Jun 1780, Henry Co Militia. Gave material aid to cause **CEM:** Ross Harbour Methodist; GPS unk; 6260 Elamsville Rd, Stuart; Patrick **GS:** U **SP:** Mar (24 Jul 1798) Nancy Ingram d/o James & (-----) Ingram **VI:** Died in and was probably bur in Missouri. Cemetery has stone memorial to him **P:** unk **BLW:** unk **RG:** unk **MK:** unk **PH:** unk **SS:** AL Comm Bk II pg 153 Henry Co **BS:** JLARC 30,108.

RU=Rank/Unit	CEM=Cemetery	GS=Gravestone	SP=Spousal Information
VI=Other Veteran Info	P=Pension	BLW=Bounty/Land Warrant	RG=Registered Grave
MK=SAR/DAR Marker	PH=Photo	SS=Service Source	BS=Burial Source

290

ROSS, John; b unk; d 25 Feb 1827 **RU:** Private, Served in John Clark's Illinois Regt **CEM:** Ebenezer Baptist; GPS 39.05824, -77.84142; 20421 Airmont Rd, Bluemont; Loudoun **GS:** Y **SP:** Mar (28 Jul 1806 Henry Co) Nancy Woodleif **VI:** No further data **P:** unk **BLW:** unk **RG:** Y **MK:** N **PH:** unk **SS:** E, pg 678 **BS:** 25 pg 266.

ROSS, Peter; b unk; d 1818 **RU:** Private/Patriot, Served in Capt Burnam's Co, 8th VA Regt, for 15 mos, 18 days. Also gave to cause in Fluvanna Co **CEM:** Ross Family; GPS unk; Vic Rts 600 & 633; Fluvanna **GS:** Y **SP:** No info **VI:** No further data **P:** unk **BLW:** unk **RG:** N **MK:** N **PH:** unk **SS:** A, pg 126; AL Comm Bk 1, pg 364 Fluvanna Co **BS:** 66 pg 80.

ROSSIGNOL, Francois; b unk; d 1781 **RU:** Soldier, Served in Bourbonnais Bn and died fr battle at Yorktown **CEM:** French Memorial; GPS 36.81944, -79.39933; Yorktown; York **GS:** U **SP:** No info **VI:** No further data **P:** unk **BLW:** unk **RG:** Y **MK:** unk **PH:** unk **SS:** J Yorktown Historian **BS:** JLARC 1, 74.

ROSSON, Reuben; b 8 Sep 1752; d unk **RU:** Soldier, Ent serv Culpeper 1777. Served in VA Line **CEM:** Farm; GPS unk; Behind Culpeper & Racoon Ford; Culpeper **GS:** U **SP:** No info **VI:** Pensioned Culpeper Co 1832 age 80. Son Edmund gave Power of Attny in Culpeper 1853 to apply for pension in arrears due father S6016 **P:** Y **BLW:** unk **RG:** Y **MK:** unk **PH:** unk **SS:** J-NSSAR 1993 Reg; K Vol 4 pg 264 **BS:** JLARC 1.

ROSZEL (ROSZELL), Stephen G; b unk; d 1792 **RU:** Patriot, Gave material aid to cause **CEM:** Mountain Chapel; GPS unk; Jct Rts 734 & 630; Loudoun **GS:** Y **SP:** No info **VI:** No further data **P:** N **BLW:** N **RG:** N **MK:** N **PH:** unk **SS:** D Vol 2 pg 607; AL Ct Bk pg 47 Loudoun Co **BS:** 25 pg 266.

ROUAY, Charles; b unk; d 1781 **RU:** Soldier, Served in Gatinais Bn and died fr battle at Yorktown **CEM:** French Memorial; GPS 36.81944, -79.39933; Yorktown; York **GS:** U **SP:** No info **VI:** No further data **P:** unk **BLW:** unk **RG:** Y **MK:** unk **PH:** unk **SS:** J-Yorktown Historian **BS:** JLARC 1, 74.

ROUFFE, Gottfried; b unk; d 1781 **RU:** Soldier, Served in Royal Deaux Ponts Bn and died fr battle at Yorktown **CEM:** French Memorial; GPS 36.81944, -79.39933; Yorktown; York **GS:** U **SP:** No info **VI:** No further data **P:** unk **BLW:** unk **RG:** Y **MK:** unk **PH:** unk **SS:** J-Yorktown Historian **BS:** JLARC 1, 74.

ROUSCH (ROUSH), Balser (Balster); b 1745, Shenandoah Co; d 1845 **RU:** Private, Was in battle at Point Pleasant **CEM:** St Mary Pine Lutheran; GPS 38.74470, -78.68390; 7103 S Middle Rd, Mt Jackson; Shenandoah **GS:** U **SP:** No info **VI:** Son of John Adam (__Germany-__) & Susannah (Schlern) Roush. Listed as Palster Rouse in militia **P:** unk **BLW:** unk **RG:** Y **MK:** unk **PH:** unk **SS:** J-NSSAR 1993 Reg; Z pg 162 **BS:** JLARC 1.

ROUSCH (ROUSH), Daniel; b 1754, Shenandoah Co; d Dec 1832 **RU:** Private, Served in 12th Cont Line **CEM:** St Mary Pine Lutheran; GPS 38.74470, -78.68390; 7103 S Middle Rd, Mt Jackson; Shenandoah **GS:** U **SP:** No info **VI:** Son of John Adam (__Germany-__) & Susannah (Schlern) Roush **P:** unk **BLW:** unk **RG:** Y **MK:** unk **PH:** unk **SS:** J-NSSAR 1993 Reg; E pg 679 **BS:** JLARC 1.

ROUSCH (ROUSH), Jacob; b 1746; d 16 Jan 1830 **RU:** Private/Patriot, Was in Battle at Point Pleasant in Capt John Tipton's Co, Shenandoah Co Militia. Gave material aid to cause **CEM:** St Mary Pine Lutheran; GPS 38.74470, -78.68390; 7103 S Middle Rd, Mt Jackson; Shenandoah **GS:** U **SP:** Mar (21 Feb 1776, New Market) Catherine Fox (c1746-__) **VI:** Son of John Adam (__Germany-__) & Susannah (Schlern) Roush **P:** N **BLW:** N **RG:** Y **MK:** unk **PH:** unk **SS:** J-NSSAR 1993 Reg; AL Ct bk pg 1 Shenandoah Co; Z pg 54 **BS:** JLARC 1.

ROUSCH (ROUSH), John; b 1742, PA; d 1816 **RU:** Captain/Patriot, Served in Shenandoah Co Militia 1779-1780. Gave material aid to cause **CEM:** St Mary Pine Lutheran; GPS 38.74470, -78.68390; 7103 S Middle Rd, Mt Jackson; Shenandoah **GS:** U **SP:** No info **VI:** Son of John Adam (__Germany-__) & Susannah (Schlern) Roush **P:** unk **BLW:** unk **RG:** Y **MK:** unk **PH:** unk **SS:** J-NSSAR 1993 Reg; E pg 679; AL Cert 1 Shenandoah Co **BS:** JLARC 1.

ROUSCH (ROUSH), Philip; b 18 Mar 1739, Northampton Co, PA; d 1 Mar 1820 **RU:** Private, Service information not stated in SAR registry **CEM:** St Mary Pine Lutheran; GPS 38.74470, -78.68390; 7103 S Middle Rd, Mt Jackson; Shenandoah **GS:** U **SP:** No info **VI:** Son of John Adam (__Germany-__) & Susannah (Schlern) Roush **P:** unk **BLW:** unk **RG:** Y **MK:** unk **PH:** unk **SS:** J-NSSAR 1993 Reg, J- DAR Hatcher; Z pg 162 **BS:** JLARC 1,2.

RU=Rank/Unit   CEM=Cemetery   GS=Gravestone   SP=Spousal Information
VI=Other Veteran Info   P=Pension   BLW=Bounty/Land Warrant   RG=Registered Grave
MK=SAR/DAR Marker   PH=Photo   SS=Service Source   BS=Burial Source

291

ROUSH, John Adam; b 1711, Germany; d 19 Oct 1786 **RU:** Patriot, Gave material aid to cause **CEM:** St Mary Pine Lutheran; GPS 38.74470, -78.68390; 7103 S Middle Rd, Mt Jackson; Shenandoah **GS:** Y **SP:** Susanne (-----) (1713-1796) **VI:** Emigrant fr Dermstandt, Germany 1736, Early settler of the Shenandoah Valley **P:** N **BLW:** N **RG:** unk **MK:** unk **PH:** unk **SS:** AL Cert **BS:** 155.

ROUSH, Susannah (Schlem); b 1713, Germany; d 1796 **RU:** Patriot, Gave material aid to cause **CEM:** St Mary Pine Lutheran; GPS 38.74470, -78.68390; 7103 S Middle Rd, Mt Jackson; Shenandoah **GS:** Y **SP:** Mar (c1739/40) Johannes Roush (1711 Germany-19 Oct 1786) **VI:** No further data **P:** N **BLW:** N **RG:** Y **MK:** N **PH:** unk **SS:** AS, SAR regis **BS:** SAR regis.

ROUSSE, Antoine; b unk; d 1781 **RU:** Seaman, Served on "Hercule" and died from Yorktown battle **CEM:** French Memorial; GPS 36.81944, -79.39933; Yorktown; York **GS:** U **SP:** No info **VI:** No further data **P:** unk **BLW:** unk **RG:** Y **MK:** unk **PH:** unk **SS:** J-Yorktown Historian **BS:** JLARC 1, 74.

ROUSSEAU, Pierre; b unk; d 1781 **RU:** Seaman, Served on "Diademe" and died from Yorktown battle **CEM:** French Memorial; GPS 36.81944, -79.39933; Yorktown; York **GS:** U **SP:** No info **VI:** No further data **P:** unk **BLW:** unk **RG:** Y **MK:** unk **PH:** unk **SS:** J-Yorktown Historian **BS:** JLARC 1, 74.

ROUSSEL, Jean; b unk; d 1781 **RU:** Soldier, Served in Bourbonnais Bn and died fr battle at Yorktown **CEM:** French Memorial; GPS 36.81944, -79.39933; Yorktown; York **GS:** U **SP:** No info **VI:** No further data **P:** unk **BLW:** unk **RG:** Y **MK:** unk **PH:** unk **SS:** J-Yorktown Historian **BS:** JLARC 1, 74.

ROUSSEL, Vincent; b unk; d 1781 **RU:** Seaman, Served on "Hextor" and died from Yorktown battle **CEM:** French Memorial; GPS 36.81944, -79.39933; Yorktown; York **GS:** U **SP:** No info **VI:** No further data **P:** unk **BLW:** unk **RG:** Y **MK:** unk **PH:** unk **SS:** J-Yorktown Historian **BS:** JLARC 1, 74.

ROUX, Jean; b unk; d 1781 **RU:** Seaman, Served on "Auguste" and died from Yorktown battle **CEM:** French Memorial; GPS 36.81944, -79.39933; Yorktown; York **GS:** U **SP:** No info **VI:** No further data **P:** unk **BLW:** unk **RG:** Y **MK:** unk **PH:** unk **SS:** J-Yorktown Historian **BS:** JLARC 1, 74.

ROUX, Jean; b unk; d 1781 **RU:** Seaman, Served on "Victorie" and died from Yorktown battle **CEM:** French Memorial; GPS 36.81944, -79.39933; Yorktown; York **GS:** U **SP:** No info **VI:** No further data **P:** unk **BLW:** unk **RG:** Y **MK:** unk **PH:** unk **SS:** J-Yorktown Historian **BS:** JLARC 1, 74.

ROWLAND, John; b c1765; d 1834 **RU:** Private, Served in PA Regt commanded by Col Lewis Nicola Apr 1783. Also served in 6th and 13th Cont Lines **CEM:** Shockoe Hill; GPS 37.55190, -77.43170; 4th & Hospital Sts; Richmond City **GS:** Y **SP:** No info **VI:** No further data **P:** unk **BLW:** unk **RG:** N **MK:** N **PH:** unk **SS:** A pg 223 **BS:** 57 pg 13.

ROWLES, William; b c1759; d Aft 1832 **RU:** Private, Served in MD & VA. Entered service 1777, MD State Regt. Served in VA Cont Line Regts 3rd, 5th, & 9th **CEM:** Rowles Family; GPS unk; Markham; Fauquier **GS:** N **SP:** No info **VI:** Pension appl for 28 Nov 1832 Fauquier Co age 73. FS6687RZ094 S6687 **P:** Y **BLW:** unk **RG:** Y **MK:** N **PH:** N **SS:** K Vol 4 pg 268; CG Vol 3 pg 2968 **BS:** 19 og 179.

ROY, Wily; b 12 Jan 1747; d 11 Jan 1816 **RU:** Captain/Patriot, Was Quartermaster Fauquier Co Militia, 1781. Also gave supplies to cause **CEM:** Roy Family; GPS unk; Clover Hill Dr; Stafford **GS:** Y **SP:** Sarah (-----) **VI:** No further data **P:** unk **BLW:** unk **RG:** Y **MK:** N **PH:** unk **SS:** D pg 874 **BS:** 03 pg 341.

ROYALL, John; b c1743; d Aft Aug 1777 **RU:** Second Lieutenant/Patriot, Served in 19th Co of the Amelia Co Militia, May 1764. Gave material aid to cause **CEM:** Royall; GPS unk; Off Promise Land Rd Rt 661, Amelia CH; Amelia **GS:** U **SP:** Mar (May 1764 Amelia Co) Elizabeth Townes **VI:** No further data **P:** unk **BLW:** N **RG:** unk **MK:** unk **PH:** N **SS:** G pg 6; AL Ct Bk I pg 54 Amelia Co **BS:** 196.

ROYALL, Littleberry; b 1742; d 1827 **RU:** Lieutenant, Served in Amelia Co Militia 22 Jun 1780 **CEM:** Royall; GPS unk; Off Promise Land Rd Rt 661, Amelia CH; Amelia **GS:** U **SP:** Mar (25 May 1780 Amelia Co) Elizabeth Jones (__-Sep 1786) **VI:** Son of Littleberry & Mary (Eppes) Royall **P:** unk **BLW:** unk **RG:** unk **MK:** unk **PH:** unk **SS:** G pg 14 **BS:** 196.

ROYER, Jean; b unk; d 1781 **RU:** Seaman, Served on "Reflechi" and died from Yorktown battle **CEM:** French Memorial; GPS 36.81944, -79.39933; Yorktown; York **GS:** U **SP:** No info **VI:** No further data **P:** unk **BLW:** unk **RG:** Y **MK:** unk **PH:** unk **SS:** J-Yorktown Historian **BS:** JLARC 1, 74.

RU=Rank/Unit	CEM=Cemetery	GS=Gravestone	SP=Spousal Information
VI=Other Veteran Info	P=Pension	BLW=Bounty/Land Warrant	RG=Registered Grave
MK=SAR/DAR Marker	PH=Photo	SS=Service Source	BS=Burial Source

292

ROYSTON (ROYSTAN), James; b 1756; d 1800 **RU:** Corporal, Served in MD line **CEM:** City Cemetery; GPS 38.30112, -77.46628; 1000 Washington Ave; Fredericksburg City **GS:** U **SP:** No info **VI:** Drew BLW 5 Sep 1789 **P:** unk **BLW:** Y **RG:** unk **MK:** unk **PH:** unk **SS:** CG pg 2970 **BS:** JLARC 2.

RUBEL (RUBLE), George; b unk; d 20 May 1814 **RU:** Patriot, Gave material aid to the cause **CEM:** Back Creek Quaker, aka Gainesboro United Methodist; GPS 39.27861, -78.25694; 166 Siler Ln, Gainesboro; Frederick **GS:** Y **SP:** Mar (12 Apr 1805 Frederick Co, James Wall, minister) Jane Gobin **VI:** No further data **P:** N **BLW:** N **RG:** Y **MK:** N **PH:** Y **SS:** AL Ct Bk pg 13 **BS:** 59 pg 285.

RUCKER, Ambrose; b 20 Jan 1724, Orange Co; d 14 Dec 1807 **RU:** Captain/Patriot, Served in Va Militia. In 1778, appointed and served as Sheriff of Amherst Co. In 1781-82 was in VA Legislature in House of Delegates representing Amherst Co. Gave material aid to cause **CEM:** Rucker Family; GPS 37.54062, -77.18508; Shepherd Farm Ln off Rt 653 Ambrose Rucker Rd; Amherst **GS:** N **SP:** 1) Mary Clifton Headley 2) Mar (c1760) Mary Tinsley (1738-26 Jul 1818) d/o Edward (1700-1782) & Margaret (Taylor) (1705-1782) Tinsley **VI:** Son of John Rucker (c1700-c1741) & Susannah Phillips. Founded Rucker's Chapel in Amherst Co. (then known as Harris Creek Church, later St Matthew's Chapel) by 1751. In 1791 active in process to establish Warminster Academy in Amherst Co. Findagrave.com entry incorrectly gives his place of birth as Norfolk City **P:** unk **BLW:** unk **RG:** unk **MK:** unk **PH:** N **SS:** E pg 681; D Amherst Co; SAR application 352, 374 **BS:** JLARC 2, 4,115; 196.

RUCKER, Angus; b 1753; d 2 Sep 1836 **RU:** Captain, Served in VA Line. Was living in Culpeper Co at enlistment **CEM:** Rucker, Blakey, Hoffman, Rose; GPS 38.34745, -78.32997; Nr Wolftown; Madison **GS:** U **SP:** No info **VI:** Recd S19068 BLW #1695-300. (Also N.A. Acc #874 #050151 1/2 pay). Pen appl for 26 Feb 1830 Madison Co age 77 **P:** Y **BLW:** Y **RG:** Y **MK:** unk **PH:** unk **SS:** BY pg 87 J-NSSAR 1993 Reg; CG Vol 3 pg 2971 **BS:** JLARC 1.

RUCKER, Anthony Jr; b 1740; d 27 Jan 1821 **RU:** Captain/Patriot, Gave material aid to cause **CEM:** Rucker Family; GPS 37.54062, -77.18508; Shepherd Farm Ln off Rt 653 (Ambrose Rucker Rd); Amherst **GS:** N **SP:** No info **VI:** Son of John Rucker (c1700-c1741) & Susannah Phillips. Original inventory w/ brother of James River Batteau **P:** unk **BLW:** unk **RG:** unk **MK:** unk **PH:** N **SS:** AL Ct Bk pg 6 Amherst Co **BS:** JLARC 115.

RUCKER, Isaac; b Bef 1740; d unk **RU:** Lieutenant Colonel/Patriot, Served in Amherst Co Militia. Lt Col of Co Militia. Ordered to join Gen Lafayette. Gave material aid to cause **CEM:** Rucker Family; GPS 37.54062, -77.18508; Shepherd Farm Ln off Rt 653 (Ambrose Rucker Rd); Amherst **GS:** N **SP:** Mar (28 Jan 1793 Amherst Co as bachelor) Mary Higginbotham, spinster, d/o John & (-----) Higginbotham **VI:** Son of John Rucker (c1700-c1741) & Susannah Phillips. Original inventory w/ brother of James River Batteau **P:** unk **BLW:** unk **RG:** unk **MK:** unk **PH:** N **SS:** JALARC App B pg 4; AL Ct Bk pg 5, 31, 32 Amherst Co **BS:** JLARC 115.

RUCKER, John Sr; b 1720, Orange Co; d Aft 04 Sep 1780 **RU:** Patriot, Civil service as road viewer Amherst Co, 1778 **CEM:** Rucker Family; GPS 37.54062, -77.18508; Shepherd Farm Ln off Rt 653 (Ambrose Rucker Rd); Amherst **GS:** U **SP:** Mar (1747) Eleanor Mildred Warren **VI:** No further data **P:** N **BLW:** N **RG:** unk **MK:** unk **PH:** unk **SS:** DAR ancestor #A099485; SAR ancestor #P-282634; SAR application; DD cites Amherst Co Order Book 1773-1782 pg 325, 336 **BS:** 197.

RUCKMAN, David; b 1747, Summerset, NJ; d 11 Jul 1822 **RU:** Sergeant, Served in Somerset Co, NJ Militia as teamster **CEM:** Ruckman; GPS unk; Little Egypt Rd, US 220 fr Mill Gap to Rt 604, turn left. 2-3 miles grave on right side; Highland **GS:** Y **SP:** Mar (NJ) Susannah Little (1757-1843) **VI:** Son of Samuel (1643-__) & (-----) Ruckman **P:** unk **BLW:** unk **RG:** unk **MK:** unk **PH:** Y **SS:** B; CA; DAR ancestor #A099499, DD **BS:** JLARC 103; 196.

RUFFIN, Edmund Jr; b 2 Jan 1744; d 1807 **RU:** Captain/Patriot, As patriot performed public service as member of House of Delegates **CEM:** Ruffin family, Tar Bay House; GPS unk; 4 mi E of Hopewell; Prince George **GS:** Y **SP:** Mar (c1764) Jane Skipwith (1746-after 1807) **VI:** No further data **P:** unk **BLW:** unk **RG:** N **MK:** N **PH:** unk **SS:** T; G pg 84; AL Cert 1 Dinwiddie Co; AZ pg 47;DAR ancesor #A099662; DD **BS:** 111 Part 3 pg 28.

RU=Rank/Unit	CEM=Cemetery	GS=Gravestone	SP=Spousal Information
VI=Other Veteran Info	P=Pension	BLW=Bounty/Land Warrant	RG=Registered Grave
MK=SAR/DAR Marker	PH=Photo	SS=Service Source	BS=Burial Source

293

RUFFIN, Edmund Sr; b 1713; d 1790 **RU:** Patriot, Gave material aid to cause **CEM:** Ruffin family, Tar Bay House; GPS unk; 4 mi E of Hopewell; Prince George **GS:** Y **SP:** No info **VI:** No further data **P:** N **BLW:** N **RG:** N **MK:** N **PH:** unk **SS:** G pg 83-4; AL Cert I Prince George Co **BS:** 111 Part 3 pg 28.

RUFFNER, Peter Sr; b c1715; d c1781 **RU:** Patriot, Gave material aid to the cause **CEM:** Ruffner Family; GPS unk; Rt 211, Luray; Page **GS:** N **SP:** No info **VI:** No further data **P:** N **BLW:** N **RG:** Y **MK:** N **PH:** N **SS:** AL Ct Bk pg 5,12 **BS:** 79 pg 177,178.

RULLINS, William; b unk; d 1781 **RU:** Soldier, Served fr NY, and died fr the Battle at Yorktown **CEM:** Yorktown Victory Monument Tablet; GPS 38.28350, -78.54150; Yorktown; York **GS:** U **SP:** No info **VI:** No further data **P:** unk **BLW:** unk **RG:** unk **MK:** unk **PH:** unk **SS:** J-Yorktown Historian **BS:** JLARC 74.

RUSH, Charles; b c1730, Germany; d 4 Apr 1806 **RU:** Patriot, Gave material aid to cause **CEM:** Old Peaked Mountain; GPS 38.37113, -78.73416; 9843 Town Hall Rd, McGaheysville; Rockingham **GS:** U **SP:** (Anna) Elizabeth (-----) **VI:** No further data **P:** N **BLW:** N **RG:** Y **MK:** Y **PH:** unk **SS:** J-NSSAR 2000 Reg; AL Ct Bk II pg 26, 27, 35 Rockingham Co **BS:** JLARC 76.

RUSH, John; b 6 Dec 1753, Rockingham (was Augusta Co); d 26 Jun 1835 **RU:** Captain, Served in Capt George Huston's Co and in Col Benjamin Harrison's VA Regt, **CEM:** Old Peaked Mountain; GPS 38.37113, -78.73416; 9843 Town Hall Rd, McGaheysville; Rockingham **GS:** N **SP:** Anna Maria Nicholas **VI:** Son of John Jacob & Anna Barbara (Zeller) Nicholas. App Rockingham Co 23 Nov 1832. R9090. Died in Cub Run, Rockingham Co **P:** Y **BLW:** unk **RG:** N **MK:** N **PH:** N **SS:** E pg 683; CG Vol 3 pg 2981 **BS:** 116 Monument.

RUSSELL, Andrew; b 1716 Ireland; d 20 Nov 1780 **RU:** Patriot, Gave material aid to cause **CEM:** Tinkling Spring Presbyterian; GPS 38.08472, -78.98278; 30 Tinkling Spring Dr, Fisherville; Augusta **GS:** U **SP:** Florence Henderson (1718 Scotland-20 Jul 1764) **VI:** No further data **P:** N **BLW:** N **RG:** unk **MK:** unk **PH:** unk **SS:** AL Commissioners Bk II pg 360 **BS:** 196.

RUSSELL, Joshua; b 1738, Augusta Co; d Bef 15 Oct 1793 **RU:** Private, Served in Capt Johnston's Co, Augusta Co Militia **CEM:** Tinkling Spring Presbyterian; GPS 38.08472, -78.98278; 30 Tinkling Spring Dr, Fisherville; Augusta **GS:** N **SP:** Jane (-----) (1741-__) **VI:** Son of Andrew (1716-1780) & Florence (Henderson) (1718-1764) Russell **P:** N **BLW:** N **RG:** unk **MK:** unk **PH:** N **SS:** E pg 684 **BS:** 196.

RUSSELL, Samuel; b unk; d Bef 23 Feb 1784 **RU:** Sergeant, Served in 9th Cont line for 3 yrs **CEM:** Truro Parish; GPS unk; "On the middle ridge near Ox Road", the present site of Jerusalem Baptist Church off Rt 123; Fairfax **GS:** N **SP:** Sarah (-----) recd aid while he was in service in Loudoun Co in Nov 1780 **VI:** Vestry Minutes Truro Parish 23 Feb 1784 indicate Silvester Gardiner was paid for maintaining him for 13 mos, and for a coffin and burying him **P:** unk **BLW:** unk **RG:** N **MK:** N **PH:** N **SS:** C pg 493; E pg 685; BX pg 697 **BS:** 110 pg 104.

RUSSELL, William; b 1735, Orange Co; d 14 Jan 1793 **RU:** Brigadier General, Capt, Co commander fr Fincastle Co at Battle of Point Pleasant. Commanded substantial forces at Battle of Kings Mountain in 13th & 5th/11th VA Regts. Was Col 13th VA Regt 19 Dec 1776 and 5th VA Regt 14 Sep 1778; taken prisoner Charleston SC 12 May 1780; exchanged Nov 1780; served until 3 Nov 1783. Brevet Brig Gen by act of Cont Congress 3 Nov 1783 **CEM:** Arlington National; GPS 38.88377, -77.06535; Jefferson Davis Hwy Rt 110; Arlington **GS:** Y **SP:** 1) Tabitha Adams (1738-1776) 2) Elizabeth (Henry) Campbell (1749-1825, Chilhowie, Smyth Co) d/o John & Sarah (Winston) Henry. Widow of Gen William Campbell and sister of Patrick Henry **VI:** After War, produced salt in Saltville and served in VA State Senate. Died in Shenandoah Co **P:** unk **BLW:** unk **RG:** Y **MK:** Y **PH:** unk **SS:** AK **BS:** 04; JLARC 1, 2, 114; 196.

RUST, Benjamin; b 1749, Prince William Co; d 21 Jun 1834 **RU:** Private/Patriot, Served in Capt Scott's Co, Fauquier Co Militia. Gave material aid to cause **CEM:** Rust Family; GPS 38.52878, -77.04540; Rt 619, Upperville; Fauquier **GS:** Y **SP:** Hannah (-----) (1757-Jul 1824) **VI:** No further data **P:** unk **BLW:** unk **RG:** N **MK:** N **PH:** unk **SS:** DAR Ancestor #098798; D Fauquier pg 1; AL Cert Fauquier Co **BS:** 19 pg 180.

RUST, Peter; b 1762; d 1828 **RU:** Captain/Patriot, As Sgt, was in the 9th & 10th Cont Lines. Was Signer of Leedstown Resolutions fr Spotsylvania Co **CEM:** Mt Hebron; GPS 39.10916, -78.09497; 305 E Boscawen St; Winchester City **GS:** U **SP:** Mar (9 Jan 1816, Frederick Co) Elizabeth Rust **VI:** Appl for

RU=Rank/Unit   CEM=Cemetery   GS=Gravestone   SP=Spousal Information
VI=Other Veteran Info   P=Pension   BLW=Bounty/Land Warrant   RG=Registered Grave
MK=SAR/DAR Marker   PH=Photo   SS=Service Source   BS=Burial Source

294

pen 10 Dec 1823 Loudoun Co. S25415 **P:** unk **BLW:** unk **RG:** Y **MK**: unk **PH:** unk **SS:** J-NSSAR 2000; Reg; E pg 685; BQ; CG pg 2988 **BS:** JLARC 76.

RUTROUGH, John; b 1756, Chester Co, PA; d 12 Dec 1824 **RU:** Private, Floyd CH Chapter DAR has his specific service **CEM:** Zion Lutheran; GPS 37.13507, -80.41662; Rts 693 & 615, Wades Ln; Floyd **GS:** Y **SP:** Mary Anne Krank (15 May 1755-28 Jan 1839) **VI:** No further data **P:** unk **BLW:** unk **RG:** unk **MK**: unk **PH:** unk **SS:** NSSAR Ancestor # P-283460 **BS:** JLARC 17, 29; 196.

RYMER, George; b 1755, England; d 30 Nov 1845 **RU:** Private, Served in VA Line. Enlisted in Augusta Co **CEM:** Rymer Family; GPS unk; Rt 624. Left through wooden gate to pasture, up over ridge and slightly to right side of mountain. N fr McDowell; Highland **GS:** Y **SP:** 1) (-----) 2) Delilah (-----) **VI:** Came to America 1772. Penson appl 2 Oct 1833 Pendleton Co S9469. Grave pillow type stone, hard to read **P:** Y **BLW:** unk **RG:** unk **MK**: unk **PH:** unk **SS:** CG Vol 3 pg 2993 **BS:** JLARC 103; 196.

SABE, Jean; b unk; d 1781 **RU:** Seaman, Served on "Hercule" and died from Yorktown battle **CEM:** French Memorial; GPS 36.81944, -79.39933; Yorktown; York **GS:** U **SP:** No info **VI:** No further data **P:** unk **BLW:** unk **RG:** Y **MK**: unk **PH:** unk **SS:** J-Yorktown Historian **BS:** JLARC 1, 74.

SAFFROY, Jean; b unk; d 1781 **RU:** Soldier, Served in Bourbonnais Bn and died fr battle at Yorktown **CEM:** French Memorial; GPS 36.81944, -79.39933; Yorktown; York **GS:** U **SP:** No info **VI:** No further data **P:** unk **BLW:** unk **RG:** Y **MK**: unk **PH:** unk **SS:** J-Yorktown Historian **BS:** JLARC 1, 74.

SAGE, James; b 1754, England; d 14 Mar 1820 **RU:** Private, Served in VA Line **CEM:** Sawyers -Elk Creek Community; GPS unk; Hwy 668, Independence; Grayson **GS:** U **SP:** Mar (25 Dec 1780, Montgomery Co) Lovice (Lovise) Ott (Utt) (__-28 Aug 1854 Grayson Co) **VI:** Was baker in London before moving to America. Recd pen #R9140 **P:** Y **BLW:** unk **RG:** Y **MK**: unk **PH:** unk **SS:** J-NSSAR 1993 Reg; J- DAR Hatcher; CG Vol 3 pg 2997 **BS:** JLARC 1, 2.

SALAUN, Francois; b unk; d 1781 **RU:** Seaman, Served on "Citoyen" and died from Yorktown battle **CEM:** French Memorial; GPS 36.81944, -79.39933; Yorktown; York **GS:** U **SP:** No info **VI:** No further data **P:** unk **BLW:** unk **RG:** Y **MK**: unk **PH:** unk **SS:** J-Yorktown Historian **BS:** JLARC 1, 74.

SALE, Bertrand; b unk; d 1781 **RU:** Seaman, Served on "Hercule" and died from Yorktown battle **CEM:** French Memorial; GPS 36.81944, -79.39933; Yorktown; York **GS:** U **SP:** No info **VI:** No further data **P:** unk **BLW:** unk **RG:** Y **MK**: unk **PH:** unk **SS:** J-Yorktown Historian **BS:** JLARC 1, 74.

SALLEMON, Antoine; b unk; d 1781 **RU:** Soldier, Served in Gatinais Bn and died fr battle at Yorktown **CEM:** French Memorial; GPS 36.81944, -79.39933; Yorktown; York **GS:** U **SP:** No info **VI:** No further data **P:** unk **BLW:** unk **RG:** Y **MK**: unk **PH:** unk **SS:** J-Yorktown Historian **BS:** JLARC 1, 74.

SALLES, Jean; b unk; d 1781 **RU:** Soldier, Served in Gatinais Bn and died fr battle at Yorktown **CEM:** French Memorial; GPS 36.81944, -79.39933; Yorktown; York **GS:** U **SP:** No info **VI:** No further data **P:** unk **BLW:** unk **RG:** Y **MK**: unk **PH:** unk **SS:** J-Yorktown Historian **BS:** JLARC 1, 74.

SALMON, Guillaume; b unk; d 1781 **RU:** Seaman, Served on "Solitaire" and died from Yorktown battle **CEM:** French Memorial; GPS 36.81944, -79.39933; Yorktown; York **GS:** U **SP:** No info **VI:** No further data **P:** unk **BLW:** unk **RG:** Y **MK**: unk **PH:** unk **SS:** J-Yorktown Historian **BS:** JLARC 1, 74.

SALMON, John; b 1735; d 24 Jan 1791 **RU:** Captain/Patriot, Commanded a Co in Henry Co Militia in Jun 1780. Had civil service as First Sheriff Henry Co 1776 and Commissioner of Peace of VA, 1777 **CEM:** Salmon Family; GPS unk; See property records; Bedford **GS:** U **SP:** Mar (c1758) Naomi Depriest (c1735, Goochland Co-aft 1791) d/o William & Judith (-----) DePriest **VI:** Son of John (c1700-c1741) (-----) Salmon. Will proves death date **P:** unk **BLW:** unk **RG:** Y **MK**: N **PH:** unk **SS:** DAR Ancestor #A099376; J-NSSAR 1993 Reg; E pg 688 **BS:** JLARC 1.

SALMON, Philibert; b unk; d 1781 **RU:** Soldier, Served in Auxonne Bn and died fr battle at Yorktown **CEM:** French Memorial; GPS 36.81944, -79.39933; Yorktown; York **GS:** U **SP:** No info **VI:** No further data **P:** unk **BLW:** unk **RG:** Y **MK**: unk **PH:** unk **SS:** J-Yorktown Historian **BS:** JLARC 1, 74.

SAMPSON, Seth; b unk; d 1781 **RU:** Soldier, Served fr MA, and killed in the battle at Yorktown **CEM:** Yorktown Victory Monument Tablet; GPS 38.28350, -78.54150; Yorktown; York **GS:** U **SP:** No info **VI:** No further data **P:** unk **BLW:** unk **RG:** unk **MK**: unk **PH:** unk **SS:** J-Yorktown Historian **BS:** JLARC 74.

RU=Rank/Unit	CEM=Cemetery	GS=Gravestone	SP=Spousal Information
VI=Other Veteran Info	P=Pension	BLW=Bounty/Land Warrant	RG=Registered Grave
MK=SAR/DAR Marker	PH=Photo	SS=Service Source	BS=Burial Source

SAMUEL, Vance; b 1749; d 1838 **RU:** Lieutenant, Served in Capt John Lewis Militia Co, Was wounded at the battle of Point Pleasant Oct 1774 **CEM:** Sinking Springs; **GPS** 36.71030, -81.98170; 136 E Main St, Abingdon; Washington **GS:** Y **SP:** No info **VI:** Militia listed him as Samuel Vance instead of Vance Samuel **P:** unk **BLW:** unk **RG:** N **MK:** N **PH:** unk **SS:** AS DAR Report; Z pg 114 **BS:** 80 vol 4 pg 4.

SANDERS, Robert; b 22 Jan 1748; d 20 Oct 1815 **RU:** Patriot, Gave material aid to cause **CEM:** Trigg; **GPS** unk; Wytheville, N side of Rt 619, abt .5 mi W of jct Rts 619 & 636; Wythe **GS:** U **SP:** Catherine Gannaway (1749-1808) **VI:** Son of Thomas (1699-1772 & Anna (Adams) Sanders (__-1769) **P:** N **BLW:** N **RG:** unk **MK:** Y **PH:** Y **SS:** AL Ct Bk pg 33 Montgomery Co **BS:** JLARC 123.

SANDERS (SAUNDERS), Stephen; b 10 May 1747; d 1830 **RU:** Captain/Patriot, Served in Cont Line. Gave material aid to cause **CEM:** Harris; **GPS** unk; SR651, nr SW cnr of jct with SR 690, Cripple Creek; Wythe **GS:** Y **SP:** 1) Miss Adams 2) Isabella Campbell **VI:** Son of Thomas (16 Oct 1699-7 Apr 1772) & Anne (Adams) (__-18 Mar 1769) Sanders. Orig stone not legible, but marker placed 1982 **P:** unk **BLW:** unk **RG:** unk **MK:** Y **PH:** unk **SS:** AL Ct Bk pg 24 Montgomery Co **BS:** JLARC 40,123.

SANFORD, Joseph; b 1744, Westmoreland Co; d 1828 **RU:** Sergeant, Served in Fauntleroy's Co of 5th VA Regt **CEM:** Sanford Family #1; **GPS** unk; Rt 654 to 656, follow 656 S for 3.2 mi; Stafford **GS:** U **SP:** Mar (8 May 1766) Jane Bunbury (12 Nov 1741, King George Co-1818) **VI:** No further data **P:** unk **BLW:** unk **RG:** Y **MK:** unk **PH:** unk **SS:** E pg 690 **BS:** JLARC 1, 48, 73.

SANFORD, Lawrence; b unk; d unk **RU:** Soldier, SAR Ancestor service not identified **CEM:** Old Presbyterian Meeting House; **GPS** 38.48528, -77.23532; 323 S Fairfax St; Alexandria City **GS:** N **SP:** Lavinia Edgerton **VI:** No further data **P:** unk **BLW:** unk **RG:** Y **MK:** unk **PH:** N **SS:** J-NSSAR 1993 Reg; NSSAR Ancestor # P-284436 **BS:** JLARC 1; 5.

SANFORD, Robert; b 12 Mar 1745; d 18 Mar 1792 **RU:** Patriot, Signed a legislative petition in Fairfax Co. Prisoner on ship "Jersey" **CEM:** Old Christ Church Episcopal; **GPS** 38.80625, -77.04718; 118 N Washington St; Alexandria City **GS:** N **SP:** Mar (26 Apr 1768) Jean Sanders (22 Oct 1748-9 Jan 1792) **VI:** Burial permit issued 19 Mar 1792 **P:** N **BLW:** N **RG:** N **MK:** N **PH:** N **SS:** DAR Ancestor #A100086; BB; DD **BS:** 20 pg 152.

SANFORD, Thomas; b unk; d unk **RU:** Second Lieutenant, Served in 2nd VA State Regt 1777-1778 **CEM:** Old Presbyterian Meeting House; **GPS** 38.48528, -77.23532; 323 S Fairfax St; Alexandria City **GS:** N **SP:** no info **VI:** Also could be person this name that was Matross, 1st Artilley **P:** unk **BLW:** unk **RG:** Y **MK:** unk **PH:** N **SS:** J-NSSAR 1993 Reg; E pg 691 **BS:** JLARC 1; 5.

SANSFACON, Jean; b unk; d 1781 **RU:** Soldier, Served in Picardie Bn and died fr battle at Yorktown **CEM:** French Memorial; **GPS** 36.81944, -79.39933; Yorktown; York **GS:** U **SP:** No info **VI:** No further data **P:** unk **BLW:** unk **RG:** Y **MK:** unk **PH:** unk **SS:** J-Yorktown Historian **BS:** JLARC 1, 74.

SANTO, Pierre; b unk; d 1781 **RU:** Seaman, Served on "Auguste" and died from Yorktown battle **CEM:** French Memorial; **GPS** 36.81944, -79.39933; Yorktown; York **GS:** U **SP:** No info **VI:** No further data **P:** unk **BLW:** unk **RG:** Y **MK:** unk **PH:** unk **SS:** J-Yorktown Historian **BS:** JLARC 1, 74.

SARGEANT, Nathaniel; b unk; d 1781 **RU:** Soldier, Served fr MA, and died fr the battle at Yorktown **CEM:** Yorktown Victory Monument Tablet; **GPS** 38.28350, -78.54150; Yorktown; York **GS:** U **SP:** No info **VI:** No further data **P:** unk **BLW:** unk **RG:** unk **MK:** unk **PH:** unk **SS:** J-Yorktown Historian **BS:** JLARC 74.

SATUR, de; b unk; d 1781 **RU:** Soldier, Served in Picardie Bn and died fr battle at Yorktown **CEM:** French Memorial; **GPS** 36.81944, -79.39933; Yorktown; York **GS:** U **SP:** No info **VI:** No further data **P:** unk **BLW:** unk **RG:** Y **MK:** unk **PH:** unk **SS:** J-Yorktown Historian **BS:** JLARC 1, 74.

SAUNDERS, Aaron; b 24 Dec 1757; d 28 Dec 1828 **RU:** Captain/Patriot, Gave material aid to cause **CEM:** Saunders Family; **GPS** unk; Leithtown; Loudoun **GS:** Y **SP:** Susan C (-----) **VI:** Son of James (1719-1778) & Sarah (Gunnell) (1710-1793) Saunders **P:** unk **BLW:** unk **RG:** Y **MK:** N **PH:** unk **SS:** B **BS:** 25 pg 271; 196.

SAUNDERS, David; b Feb 1761, Hanover Co; d 29 Sep 1845 **RU:** Sergeant, Ent Serv Hanover Co 1780. Served as Sergeant of Inf in VA Cont Line **CEM:** Saunders Family; **GPS** 37.31808, -79.43264; Jct

RU=Rank/Unit	CEM=Cemetery	GS=Gravestone	SP=Spousal Information
VI=Other Veteran Info	P=Pension	BLW=Bounty/Land Warrant	RG=Registered Grave
MK=SAR/DAR Marker	PH=Photo	SS=Service Source	BS=Burial Source

296

Rt 460 & Krantz's Corner Rd; Bedford **GS:** Y **SP:** Mar (4 Sep 1788 Bedford Co) Lockey Leftwich (1 Jan 1767 Bedford Co-29 Nov 1853, Bedford) d/o Maj Augustine, Jr & Mary Ann (Turner) Leftwich **VI:** Lived in Charlotte Co during Revolution. Appl pension 21 Aug 1832 Bedford Co. Widow appl pen there 28 Aug 1843 age 70. W3872 **P:** Y **BLW:** unk **RG:** unk **MK:** N **PH:** unk **SS:** J- DAR Hatcher, CG Vol 3 pg 3021; 112 **BS:** JLARC 2; 196.

SAUNDERS, Robert Hyde; b c1757; d Oct 1833 **RU:** Lieutenant, Served in VA State Regt VA Line. Appointed Lt 18 Sep 1777. Resigned Feb 1778 **CEM:** Bruton Parish Church; GPS 37.27127, -76.70248; 331 W Duke of Gloucester St; Williamsburg City **GS:** Y **SP:** No info **VI:** Appl for pen Henrico Co age 74. S6046. Recd BLW of 266 acres **P:** Y **BLW:** Y **RG:** N **MK:** N **PH:** unk **SS:** N pg 461; BG pg 3022; SAR application 71, 119, 140 **BS:** 65, Bruton Par..

SAUNDERS, William; b 1755, King George Co; d 11 May 1819 **RU:** Private, Capt Henry Young's Co, Col Alexander McClannahan's 5th & &7th VA Regts **CEM:** Saunders Family; GPS unk; See property records for location; King George **GS:** U **SP:** 1) Mar (c1790) Sarah Jones (c1770-11 Nov 1827) 2) Nancy Cunningham **VI:** No further data **P:** unk **BLW:** unk **RG:** unk **MK:** unk **PH:** unk **SS:** DAR Ancestor #A100578; BY pg 22; AP rolls #102 & 104; AR Vol 4 pg 8 **BS:** JLARC 2.

SAVAGE, Francis; b c1740; d 20 Sep 1823 **RU:** Lieutenant, Served in Accomack Co Militia. Took oath as Lt 30 Jul 1777 **CEM:** Coal Kiln; GPS unk; 1 mi S jct Rts 607 & 600, R off Rt 600; Accomack **GS:** Y **SP:** Mar (1781, Accomack Co) Leah Custis (1763-31 Aug 1823) **VI:** Died age 73. Styled Capt on his GS **P:** unk **BLW:** unk **RG:** N **MK:** N **PH:** unk **SS:** DAR Ancestor #A100594; E pg 692 **BS:** 37 pg 224.

SAVAGE, Lyttleton; b 1740; d 9 Jan 1805 **RU:** Patriot, Gave material aid to the cause. Took oath as Court Officer on 13 Aug 1776 **CEM:** Cherry Grove; GPS unk; Rt 634; Northampton **GS:** Y **SP:** 1) Mar (14 Jan 1768) Margaret Burton (1747-6 Dec 1772) d/o William & (-----) Burton 2) Mar (11 Dec 1792) Elizabeth Jacob 3) Leah (-----) (1751-5 Jun 1795) **VI:** Styled "Col" on his GS **P:** N **BLW:** N **RG:** N **MK:** N **PH:** unk **SS:** AL Ct bk pg 6,7 **BS:** 42 pg 72.

SAVAGE, Thomas Lytllteton; b 8 Jun 1760; d 20 Jun 1815 **RU:** Private?, Served in 3rd, 5th, 7th Cont Lines **CEM:** Cugley; GPS unk; Rt 634; Northampton **GS:** Y **SP:** 1) Mar (21 May 1789) Mary Burton Savage, d/o Lylleton & (-----) Savage 2) Margaret Teackle (28 Feb 1778-28 Sep 1846) d/o Thomas & (-----) Teackle of Accomack Co. **VI:** A charter member of Phi Beta Kappa in 1779 (Cugley historic landmark plaque) **P:** unk **BLW:** unk **RG:** N **MK:** N **PH:** unk **SS:** E pg 693 **BS:** 42 pg 73; 209.

SAVAGE, William; b 1764; d 15 Nov 1815 **RU:** Private, 4th Cont Line **CEM:** Savage Family; GPS unk; Rt 180, Pungoteaque; Accomack **GS:** Y **SP:** No info **VI:** No further data **P:** unk **BLW:** unk **RG:** N **MK:** N **PH:** unk **SS:** E pg 693; CD **BS:** 145 Savage.

SAVEQUET, Dominique; b unk; d 1781 **RU:** Soldier, Service unit or ship not identified **CEM:** French Memorial; GPS 36.81944, -79.39933; Yorktown; York **GS:** U **SP:** No info **VI:** No further data **P:** unk **BLW:** unk **RG:** Y **MK:** unk **PH:** unk **SS:** J-Yorktown Historian **BS:** JLARC 1, 74.

SAVILLE, Abram (Abraham); b 26 Dec 1763, Chester Co, PA; d 19 Jun 1841 **RU:** Private, Served in Capt Jame Huston's Co, Chester Co PA Militia 1781-1783 **CEM:** Old Anderson farm; GPS unk; W Buffalo Rd; Rockbridge **GS:** N **SP:** Martha Keeble (1765-1841) **VI:** Son of Samuel & Ann (Booth) Saville **P:** unk **BLW:** unk **RG:** Y **MK:** N **PH:** N **SS:** AK; CD **BS:** 04 Oct 06; 196.

SAVOIX, Martiel; b unk; d 1781 **RU:** Soldier, Served in Touraine Bn and died fr battle at Yorktown **CEM:** French Memorial; GPS 36.81944, -79.39933; Yorktown; York **GS:** U **SP:** No info **VI:** No further data **P:** unk **BLW:** unk **RG:** Y **MK:** unk **PH:** unk **SS:** J-Yorktown Historian **BS:** JLARC 1, 74.

SAYERS, Robert; b 1754; d 1826 **RU:** Ensign, Served in Montgomery Co Militia 6 Nov 1781 **CEM:** Crockett Family; GPS 37.01560, -81.05500; Off Rt 600, Crockett's Cove; Wythe **GS:** U **SP:** No info **VI:** Obtained rank of Col after RW. Single stone across fr burying ground **P:** unk **BLW:** unk **RG:** Y **MK:** unk **PH:** unk **SS:** E pg 693 **BS:** JLARC 1, 40, 123; 196.

SAYERS, William; b 1728; d 1781 **RU:** Patriot, Performed public service as a member of the Fincastle Co Committee of Safety 1775-76 **CEM:** Oglesby Sayers; GPS 36.96440, -80.83030; Rt 701, Draper's Valley; Wythe **GS:** U **SP:** No info **VI:** Rank of Ensign dates fr before Rev War period **P:** N **BLW:** N **RG:** Y **MK:** unk **PH:** unk **SS:** J-NSSAR 1993 Reg; G pg 207 **BS:** JLARC 1.

RU=Rank/Unit	CEM=Cemetery	GS=Gravestone	SP=Spousal Information
VI=Other Veteran Info	P=Pension	BLW=Bounty/Land Warrant	RG=Registered Grave
MK=SAR/DAR Marker	PH=Photo	SS=Service Source	BS=Burial Source

297

SAYERS (SAYRES), John Thompson; b 19 Jul 1758; d 20 Mar 1816 **RU:** Lieutenant Colonel, As Maj served in 4th VA Regt of Foot 13 Aug 1776-30 Jan 1777. Promoted to Lt Col in 9th VA Regt serving fr 30 Jan 1777-4 Oct 1777 **CEM:** Oglesby Sayers; GPS 36.96440, -80.83030; Rt 701, Draper's Valley; Wythe **GS:** U **SP:** Susan/Susanna Crockett (26/29 Sep 1764 Wythe Co-14/16 Oct 1828 Wythe Co) **VI:** Report fr 1986 indicated lower sec of cem "overgrown" **P:** unk **BLW:** unk **RG:** Y **MK:** unk **PH:** unk **SS:** DAR Ancestor #A100399; CE pg 18,30,42,58 **BS:** JLARC 1, 40,123; 196.

SCAMMELL, Alexander; b unk; d 1781 **RU:** Colonel, Served fr NH, and died fr the battle at Yorktown **CEM:** Governor's Palace; GPS unk; Williamsburg; Williamsburg City **GS:** U **SP:** No info **VI:** The Governor's Palace was used as a hospital for soldiers wounded in the Yorktown battle. Those that d were bur in a mass grave there **P:** unk **BLW:** unk **RG:** unk **MK:** unk **PH:** unk **SS:** J-Yorktown Historian **BS:** JLARC 74.

SCARA, Michel; b unk; d 1781 **RU:** Seaman, Served on "Marseillais" and died from Yorktown battle **CEM:** French Memorial; GPS 36.81944, -79.39933; Yorktown; York **GS:** U **SP:** No info **VI:** No further data **P:** unk **BLW:** unk **RG:** Y **MK:** unk **PH:** unk **SS:** J-Yorktown Historian **BS:** JLARC 1, 74.

SCARBURGH (SCARBOROUGH), John; b unk; d 1794 **RU:** Lieutenant, Served in 9th Cont Line **CEM:** Scarburgh Farm; GPS unk; Opposite jct Rts 601 & 683, across field to old house "Scarborough"; Northampton **GS:** U **SP:** 1) Mar (26 Jun 1759) Ann Kendall, d/o John & (-----) Kendall 2) Mary (Polly) Jacob, a widow **VI:** Widow Mary appl pen & recd BLW 10 Feb 1823 in OH **P:** Y **BLW:** Y **RG:** Y **MK:** unk **PH:** unk **SS:** J-NSSAR 2000 Reg; E pg 694; CG pg 3033 **BS:** JLARC 76.

SCHOLDER, Francois; b unk; d 1781 **RU:** Soldier, Served in Royal Deaux Ponts Bn and died fr battle at Yorktown **CEM:** French Memorial; GPS 36.81944, -79.39933; Yorktown; York **GS:** U **SP:** No info **VI:** No further data **P:** unk **BLW:** unk **RG:** Y **MK:** unk **PH:** unk **SS:** J-Yorktown Historian **BS:** JLARC 1, 74.

SCHOLFIELD, Thomas; b 1763, Bucks Co PA; d 1810 **RU:** Private, Served in PA units **CEM:** Goose Creek; GPS 39.11250, -77.69527; Rt 722, Lincoln; Loudoun **GS:** N **SP:** Eleanor Flood (1763-1836) **VI:** Recd 400 acres BLW in Northumberland Co, PA **P:** unk **BLW:** Y **RG:** unk **MK:** unk **PH:** N **SS:** CI: PA Archives series 3 Vol XXV pg 320 **BS:** 196.

SCHOLT, Sebastian; b unk; d 1781 **RU:** Soldier, Served in Royal Deaux Ponts Bn and died fr battle at Yorktown **CEM:** French Memorial; GPS 36.81944, -79.39933; Yorktown; York **GS:** U **SP:** No info **VI:** No further data **P:** unk **BLW:** unk **RG:** Y **MK:** unk **PH:** unk **SS:** J-Yorktown Historian **BS:** JLARC 1, 74.

SCHOOLFIELD, John; b 1 Feb 1766, PA; d 8 Dec 1831 **RU:** Midshipman, Served on Frigate "Virginia" 28 Oct 1781 **CEM:** Old City; GPS 37.41472, -79.15667; 401 Taylor St; Lynchburg City **GS:** Y **SP:** No info **VI:** No further data **P:** unk **BLW:** unk **RG:** N **MK:** N **PH:** unk **SS:** M pg 125 **BS:** 172, City Lynch.

SCHULTZ, John; b 3 Dec 1753, PA; d 1840 (will) **RU:** Private, Served in Gen Daniel Morgan's Rifle Co. Was member of Morgan's Dutch mess. Was POW at Siege of Quebec **CEM:** Mt Hebron; GPS 39.10916, -78.09497; 305 E Boscawen St; Winchester City **GS:** Y **SP:** Mar (8 Mar 1791, Frederick Co) Catherine Harr (Return) **VI:** Appl for pen 9 Aug 1832 Winchester in Frederick Co. 56066 **P:** Y **BLW:** unk **RG:** Y **MK:** N **PH:** Y **SS:** J-NSSAR 1993 Reg; CG Vol 3 pg 3039 **BS:** JLARC 1.

SCOTT, Andrew; b 18 Jul 1734; d 4 Mar 1821 **RU:** Private, Served in Capt Lyles Co, Augusta Co **CEM:** McDowell Family; GPS 39.18410, -78.16278; 10 mi N Lexington on Rt 11; Rockbridge **GS:** Y **SP:** No info **VI:** Moved to Rockbridge Co **P:** unk **BLW:** unk **RG:** N **MK:** N **PH:** unk **SS:** E pg 695 **BS:** 154 Rockledge.

SCOTT, George; b 30 Nov 1755; d 13 May 1826 **RU:** Private, Served in Culpeper Co Militia **CEM:** The "Hilton"; GPS unk; vic Rt 15 Madison Mills; Madison **GS:** Y **SP:** Betsey (-----) (27 Oct 1768-26 Jun 1849) **VI:** No further data **P:** unk **BLW:** unk **RG:** N **MK:** N **PH:** unk **SS:** AW Class 103 **BS:** 90 vol 62 pg 211; 213 pg 294.

SCOTT, Gustavus; b 1753, Prince William Co; d 23 Dec 1800 **RU:** Patriot, Performed public service as delegate to MD Convention and as member of MD Council of Safety **CEM:** Fairfax City; GPS 38.84690, -77.31330; Main St & Page Ave; Fairfax City **GS:** Y **SP:** Margaret Hall Caile **VI:** Reinterred Oct 1967 fr family cemetery Strawberry Vale, vic jct VA 123 & I-495. SAR & DAR marker **P:** N **BLW:** N **RG:** Y **MK:** Y **PH:** Y **SS:** AS SAR regis **BS:** SAR regis; 04.

RU=Rank/Unit	CEM=Cemetery	GS=Gravestone	SP=Spousal Information
VI=Other Veteran Info	P=Pension	BLW=Bounty/Land Warrant	RG=Registered Grave
MK=SAR/DAR Marker	PH=Photo	SS=Service Source	BS=Burial Source

SCOTT, James; b 1715, Dipple Parish, Morayshire, Scotland; d Sep 1782 **RU:** Patriot, Gave use of property and 300# beef in Fauquier Co & 3 beeves Prince William Co **CEM:** Aquia Episcopal; GPS 38.46466, -77.40325; 2938 Jeff Davis Hwy, Aquia; Stafford **GS:** Y **SP:** Sarah Brown **VI:** Was a reverend after Rev War. Died in Prince William Co. Originally bur in Scott Family cemetery ("Dipple"). Reinterred to Aquia Cemetery 1942. SAR monument **P:** N **BLW:** N **RG:** Y **MK:** Y **PH:** Y **SS:** D Prince Wm Co **BS:** Fairfax Resolves 2014.

SCOTT, James I; b 12 Aug 1736, Ireland; d 18 Nov 1817 **RU:** Patriot, Gave material aid to cause **CEM:** Scott; GPS unk; Blue Springs; Smyth **GS:** N **SP:** Rachel Holmes (1753-1833) **VI:** Died in Wythe Co **P:** N **BLW:** N **RG:** unk **MK:** unk **PH:** N **SS:** AL Ct Bk pg 6 **BS:** JLARC 114.

SCOTT, John; b 1733, Scotland; d 7 Oct 1799 **RU:** Private, Served in10th VA Regt Jul 1778 **CEM:** Scott Family; GPS unk; Across fr 15000 Conference Center Dr, Washington Technology Park, Chantilly; Fairfax **GS:** Y **SP:** Mary (-----) (c1735-12 Mar 1795 "after a violent illness") **VI:** Died age 66 "after an illness of one hour" **P:** unk **BLW:** unk **RG:** N **MK:** N **PH:** unk **SS:** AP roll **BS:** 61 vol IV pg CH-36.

SCOTT, John; b unk; d 1781 **RU:** Private, Served in 4th NY Regt. Drowned on march to Yorktown **CEM:** Yorktown Victory Monument Tablet; GPS 38.28350, -78.54150; Yorktown; York **GS:** U **SP:** No info **VI:** No further data **P:** unk **BLW:** unk **RG:** unk **MK:** unk **PH:** unk **SS:** J-Yorktown Historian; AX pg 212 **BS:** JLARC 74.

SCOTT, John Baytop; b 26 Sep 1761, Prince Edward Co; d 1813 **RU:** Lieutenant, Served in 1st Light Dragoons, Lee's Legion in 1780. Probably disabled fr wounds **CEM:** Scott Home Site; GPS unk; Off Rt 724, NW fr Scottsburg; Halifax **GS:** Y **SP:** 1) Mar (22 Oct 1782 Halifax Co) Elizabeth Coleman (__-27 Mar 1783 Halifax Co) 2) Mar (29 Sep 1785) Martha "Patsy" Thompson (1769-1817) (2nd cousin to Elizabeth) **VI:** Son of Thomas (21 Mar 1727-__Glouchester Co) & Catherine (Tompkins) (1733-__ VA). Attended Hampden-Sydney College. After Rev, William & Mary College, grad Law degree. Had 2000 acre farm and saw & grist mills on Difficult Creek. Was Lt of Lee's Legion, and Capt in War of 1812,and General of Militia. Was Vice Pres VA Society of the Cincinatti. Headstone was set by Berryman Green Chapter DAR. Recd1/2 pay pension & BLW **P:** Y **BLW:** Y **RG:** unk **MK:** Y **PH:** unk **SS:** J- DAR Hatcher; BG pg 3046 **BS:** JLARC 2; 215.

SCOTT, John E; b unk; d Aft 1805 **RU:** Lieutenant/Patriot, Gave material aid to cause **CEM:** Scott Family; GPS 37.45250, -78.18890; VES Rd; Lynchburg City **GS:** N **SP:** No info **VI:** BLW awarded 18 Nov 1811 **P:** unk **BLW:** Y **RG:** N **MK:** N **PH:** N **SS:** N pg 1361; AL Ct Bk pg 41 Amherst Co **BS:** 131 Scott.

SCOTT, Johnny (Jonny); b 1718, Orange Co; d 1778 **RU:** Captain/Patriot, Served as Commissary in Orange Co Militia. Resigned prior to 23 July 1778. Gave material aid to cause **CEM:** Scott Family; GPS unk; Madison Run; Orange **GS:** U **SP:** Mar (c1750) Mary Hackett (1721-5 Nov 1811) **VI:** No further data **P:** unk **BLW:** unk **RG:** Y **MK:** unk **PH:** unk **SS:** DAR Ancestor #A101609; E pg 696; AL Ct Bk pg 4, 22 Orange Co **BS:** JLARC 76.

SCOTT, Joseph; b 1757; d 15 Oct 1833 **RU:** Private, Served in VA and Cont Lines **CEM:** Scott; GPS unk; Rich Valley; Washington **GS:** U **SP:** Mar (1783) Mary Talbot (__-10 May 1840) **VI:** Son Obediah Scott. Appl for pension 16 May 1853 Washington Co. S9474 **P:** Y **BLW:** unk **RG:** Y **MK:** unk **PH:** unk **SS:** CG Vol 3 pg 3046 **BS:** JLARC 1, 4.

SCOTT, Mathew; b 1751, Ireland; d Feb 1815 **RU:** Sergeant, Served in 4th, 8th, 12th Cont Lines. Perhaps acquired rank as ensign **CEM:** Salem Cemetery; GPS 37.05014, -80.16004; Rt 221, Head of the River Church; Floyd **GS:** U **SP:** Lucretia Ogle (6 Mar 1759-Jun 1836) **VI:** No further data **P:** unk **BLW:** unk **RG:** unk **MK:** unk **PH:** unk **SS:** DAR Ancestor #A101690; E pg 696 **BS:** JLARC 29.

SCOTT, Samuel; b 14 Mar 1754, Caroline Co; d 20 Jun 1822 **RU:** Major, Enl as lieutenant in VA Calvary. In 1777 was Capt in GA Cavalry. Was in battles of Savannah, Guilford CH. Held rank of Major in VA troops. **CEM:** Maj Samuel Scott Family; GPS 37.41330, -79.20304; 2627 Old Forest Rd; Lynchburg City **GS:** Y **SP:** Mar (17 Jun 1794, Spotsylvania Co) Ann Roy (28 Feb 1762-1 Apr 1846) d/o John & Ann (Waller) Roy **VI:** Son of Thomas Scott & Martha Williams. Owned "Locust Thicket" **P:** unk **BLW:** Y **RG:** Y **MK:** Y **PH:** Y **SS:** BY pg 240; AK wid pension **BS:** JLARC 1, 2, 3, 6, 84, 90; 04 Sep 07; 196.

RU=Rank/Unit   CEM=Cemetery   GS=Gravestone   SP=Spousal Information
VI=Other Veteran Info   P=Pension   BLW=Bounty/Land Warrant   RG=Registered Grave
MK=SAR/DAR Marker   PH=Photo   SS=Service Source   BS=Burial Source

299

SCOTT, Samuel; b 7 Dec 1761, Peach Bottom, Lancaster Co, PA; d 1 Aor 1811 **RU:** Private, Served in Capt Cloyd's Co, Montgomery Co Militia 12 Sep 1777 **CEM:** Glade Spring Presbyterian; GPS 36.76720, -81.78720; 33234 Lee Hwy, Glade Spring; Washington **GS:** U **SP:** Mar (1783) Jane Hutton (1765, Morristown, PA-Sep 1844, Cole Co, OH) d/o (-----) & Sarah Dixon (__-17 Aug 1815) **VI:** No further data **P:** N **BLW:** N **RG:** unk **MK:** N **PH:** N **SS:** G pg 215 **BS:** 196.

SCOTT, Stephen; b unk; d 1824 **RU:** Private?, Served in 1st, 10th, & 14th Cont Lines **CEM:** Fairfax Meeting House; GPS 39.18557, -77.60589; Water St & Waterford Rd, Waterford; Loudoun **GS:** Y **SP:** No info **VI:** No further data **P:** unk **BLW:** unk **RG:** Y **MK:** N **PH:** unk **SS:** E pg 696 **BS:** 25 pg 275.

SCOTT, William; b 1766; d 4 Nov 1844 **RU:** Patriot, Gave material aid to the cause **CEM:** Penny Hill; GPS 38.79861, -77.05559; S Payne & Franklin Sts; Alexandria City **GS:** N **SP:** Emma Redman **VI:** Son of Robert Scott & Mary Edwards. Died at Alexandria Hospital **P:** N **BLW:** N **RG:** N **MK:** N **PH:** N **SS:** AL Ct bk pg 17,22 **BS:** 20 pg 45.

SCOTT, William; b c1751, Prince William Co; d 18 Oct 1787 **RU:** Patriot, Gave 545# beef & two horses for five days **CEM:** Aquia Episcopal; GPS 38.46466, -77.40325; 2938 Jeff Davis Hwy, Aquia; Stafford **GS:** Y **SP:** No info **VI:** Died in Fairfax Co. Originally bur 1787 in Scott Family cemetery. Reinterred to Aquia Cemetery 1942 **P:** N **BLW:** N **RG:** Y **MK:** Y **PH:** Y **SS:** D Prince Wm Co; SAR application 886 **BS:** Fairfax Resolves 2014.

SCOTT, William; b unk; d 1798 **RU:** Private/Patriot, Gave material aid to the cause. Wife given allowance for support while he was away in service **CEM:** Dumfries Public; GPS 38.34110, -77.19964; 17821 Mine Rd, Dumfries; Prince William **GS:** N **SP:** No info **VI:** No further data **P:** unk **BLW:** unk **RG:** N **MK:** Y **PH:** N **SS:** D Prince William Co; AL Ct Bk pg 13, 14 **BS:** 96 pg 91.

SCOTT, William E; b 30 Jan 1744, Chesterfield Co; d 1 Jan 1797 **RU:** Lieutenant, Served in Bedford Co Militia **CEM:** Scott Family; GPS unk; Episcopal School Rd 200 yds fr school; Bedford **GS:** N **SP:** Mar (20 May 1784) Elizabeth Wade (c1764-20 May 1814) **VI:** No further data **P:** unk **BLW:** unk **RG:** unk **MK:** unk **PH:** unk **SS:** DAR Ancestor #A101890 **BS:** 131.

SCOTT, William W; b 15 Dec 1756, Caroline Co; d 16 Oct 1817, Campbell Co **RU:** Captain, Ent serv 1776 as 1st Lt under brother Capt Thomas Scott, Prince Edward Co & Charlotte Co. Later served in Col Critten's 3rd Regt of GA Line at battles of Sunbury & Savannah **CEM:** Scott Family; GPS 37.45250, -78.18890; VES Rd; Lynchburg City **GS:** U **SP:** Mar (1 Mar 1781) Ann "Nancy" Jones (13 Mar 1763, Spotsylvania Co-1846, Campbell Co) d/oGabriel (c1740-1777) & Mary Anne (Waller) Jones **VI:** No further data **P:** unk **BLW:** Y **RG:** unk **MK:** unk **PH:** unk **SS:** BY pg 224 **BS:** JLARC 4, 36.

SCRUGGS, Drury; b 1725; d 26 Aug 1782 **RU:** Patriot, Gave material aid to the cause **CEM:** Scruggs Family; GPS unk; Head of Huddy Ck; Cumberland **GS:** Y **SP:** Mar (c1747) Mary (-----) (1720,-24 Jul 1804) **VI:** No further data **P:** N **BLW:** N **RG:** N **MK:** N **PH:** unk **SS:** DAR Ancestor #A100805; AL Com Bk pg 233 **BS:** 80 vol 4 pg 15.

SCRUGGS, Samuel; b 1765; d 20 Mar 1814 **RU:** Private, Served three yrs **CEM:** Old City; GPS 37.41472, -79.15667; 401 Taylor St; Lynchburg City **GS:** Y **SP:** Jane (-----) Had wife in 1828 **VI:** Sol appl pen 1826, Nelson Co age 70. S38357 **P:** Y **BLW:** unk **RG:** N **MK:** N **PH:** unk **SS:** C pg 506; CG pg 3053 **BS:** 162 Methodist.

SCULL, William; b Jun 1739, Philadelphia; d 6 Feb 1813 **RU:** Captain, Was Capt in 11th VA Regt, commanded by Col Richard Hampton, May 1777 **CEM:** Old Presbyterian Meeting House; GPS 38.48528, -77.23532; 323 S Fairfax St; Alexandria City **GS:** N **SP:** Mar (25 Oct 1763, Philadelphia) Jane Lodge **VI:** Died age 75 (Alexandria Gazette, 9 Feb 1813, pg 3) **P:** unk **BLW:** unk **RG:** N **MK:** N **PH:** N **SS:** DAR Ancestor #A205576; AP **BS:** 23 pg 112.

SEABROOK, Nicholas B; b c1733; d 29 Jun 1790 **RU:** Patriot, Gave material aid to cause **CEM:** St John's Episcopal; GPS 37.53183, -77.41958; 2401 E Broad St; Richmond City **GS:** Y **SP:** No info **VI:** No further data **P:** N **BLW:** N **RG:** N **MK:** N **PH:** unk **SS:** D Vol 2 pg 466; AL Cert Henrico Co **BS:** 28 pg 504; 196.

RU=Rank/Unit	CEM=Cemetery	GS=Gravestone	SP=Spousal Information
VI=Other Veteran Info	P=Pension	BLW=Bounty/Land Warrant	RG=Registered Grave
MK=SAR/DAR Marker	PH=Photo	SS=Service Source	BS=Burial Source

300

SEAUCE, Jacques; b unk; d 1781 **RU:** Seaman, Served on "Ville de Paris" and died from Yorktown battle **CEM:** French Memorial; GPS 36.81944, -79.39933; Yorktown; York **GS:** U **SP:** No info **VI:** No further data **P:** unk **BLW:** unk **RG:** Y **MK:** unk **PH:** unk **SS:** J-Yorktown Historian **BS:** JLARC 1,74.

SEAY, Austin Sr; b 1751, Albemarle Co (later Fluvanna); d 1 Feb 1834 **RU:** Sergeant, Ent serv Albemarle Co and served in VA Line **CEM:** Fork Union Military Academy; GPS unk; 4744 James Madison Hwy, Fork Union; Fluvanna **GS:** U **SP:** Mar (1780 or early 1781 in Fluvanna or Goochland Co) Elizabeth Weaver (c1754-c1 Jan 1844) **VI:** Appl pen 24 Jun 1833 age 75, Fluvanna Co. Widow appl pen 4 Oct 1841 age 87. W19341. Source 100 shows dates of 1758-1836 **P:** Y **BLW:** unk **RG:** unk **MK:** Y **PH:** unk **SS:** CG Vol 3 pg 3061 **BS:** JLARC 3,46, 100.

SEBIRE, Martin; b unk; d 1781 **RU:** Seaman, Served on "Ville de Paris" and died from Yorktown battle **CEM:** French Memorial; GPS 36.81944, -79.39933; Yorktown; York **GS:** U **SP:** No info **VI:** No further data **P:** unk **BLW:** unk **RG:** Y **MK:** unk **PH:** unk **SS:** J-Yorktown Historian **BS:** JLARC 1, 74.

SEIGLE, Frederick; b unk; d unk **RU:** Surgeon, Served in Cont Line **CEM:** Mt Hebron; GPS 39.10916, -78.09497; 305 E Boscawen St; Winchester City **GS:** U **SP:** No info **VI:** Recd BLW of 6000 acres, Jul 1797 **P:** unk **BLW:** unk **RG:** Y **MK:** unk **PH:** unk **SS:** J-NSSAR 2000 Reg; NSSAR Ancestor #P-286957 **BS:** JLARC 76.

SELDEN, Wilson Cary; b 1762; d 1835 **RU:** Surgeon, Served in VA State Line as surgeon's mate & full surgeon **CEM:** St James Episcopal, Old Cemetery; GPS 39.11555, -77.56250; Church St NE, Leesburg; Loudoun **GS:** U **SP:** 1) (-----) 2) Mary Mason Page (c1749-17 Sep 1787) **VI:** Pen appl for 13 Jun 1832 in Washington DC age 70. S4815, also VA 1/2 Pay (See N>A. Acc #874 #050159 1/2 pay) Surgeon **P:** Y **BLW:** Y **RG:** unk **MK:** unk **PH:** unk **SS:** BY pg 232; CG Vol 3 pg 3066 **BS:** JLARC 4, 32.

SELIGNET, Jean; b unk; d 1781 **RU:** Soldier, Served in Bourbonnais Bn and died fr battle at Yorktown **CEM:** French Memorial; GPS 36.81944, -79.39933; Yorktown; York **GS:** U **SP:** No info **VI:** No further data **P:** unk **BLW:** unk **RG:** Y **MK:** unk **PH:** unk **SS:** J-Yorktown Historian **BS:** JLARC 1, 74.

SELIQUET, Jean; b unk; d 1781 **RU:** Soldier, Served in Bourbonnais Bn and died fr battle at Yorktown **CEM:** French Memorial; GPS 36.81944, -79.39933; Yorktown; York **GS:** U **SP:** No info **VI:** No further data **P:** unk **BLW:** unk **RG:** unk **MK:** unk **PH:** unk **SS:** J-Yorktown Historian **BS:** JLARC 74.

SELLERS, John Adam; b 1742; d 1821 **RU:** Private/Patriot, Served in 1st Light Dragoons. Gave material aid to cause **CEM:** Old Peaked Mountain; GPS 38.37113, -78.73416; 9843 Town Hall Rd, McGaheysville; Rockingham **GS:** U **SP:** Mar (1792 Rockingham Co) Eve Fifer, prob d/o Adam & (----) Fifer **VI:** Listed on memorial at Peaked Mountain Cemetery as "potentially having been bur there but was not. "Adam Sellers" was b in 1742 and remained in Rockingham Co until early 1817 when he migrated to Clear Creek Twp in Warren Co, Ohio. He d there in April 1821 and was bur in the Salem Reformed Church Cemetery in Warren Co, Ohio. Memorialized on plaque in the cemetery **P:** unk **BLW:** unk **RG:** unk **MK:** Y **PH:** unk **SS:** E pg 700; AL Ct Bk II pg 27, 35 Rockingham Co **BS:** 196.

SEPEDRE, Antoine; b unk; d 1781 **RU:** Soldier, Served in Soissonnais Bn and died fr battle at Yorktown **CEM:** French Memorial; GPS 36.81944, -79.39933; Yorktown; York **GS:** U **SP:** No info **VI:** No further data **P:** unk **BLW:** unk **RG:** Y **MK:** unk **PH:** unk **SS:** J-Yorktown Historian **BS:** JLARC 1, 74.

SERREE, Jacques; b unk; d 1781 **RU:** Soldier, Served in Santogne Bn and died fr battle at Yorktown **CEM:** French Memorial; GPS 36.81944, -79.39933; Yorktown; York **GS:** U **SP:** No info **VI:** No further data **P:** unk **BLW:** unk **RG:** Y **MK:** unk **PH:** unk **SS:** J-Yorktown Historian **BS:** JLARC 1, 74.

SERVE, Antoine; b unk; d 1781 **RU:** Soldier, Served in Gatinais Bn and died fr battle at Yorktown **CEM:** French Memorial; GPS 36.81944, -79.39933; Yorktown; York **GS:** U **SP:** No info **VI:** No further data **P:** unk **BLW:** unk **RG:** Y **MK:** unk **PH:** unk **SS:** J-Yorktown Historian **BS:** JLARC 1, 74.

SEYBERT, Christian; b 1744, Montgomery Co; d 1838 **RU:** Soldier, Served in VA Line. Enl in Montgomery Co, in Capt Issac Taylor's Co, Col John Montgomery's Regt **CEM:** Seybert Family; GPS unk; Gunton Park; Wythe **GS:** U **SP:** Mar (1780) Mary (-----) (1750 Holland-c1830) **VI:** Appl pen 8 Oct 1832 Wythe Co, age 88. S7475. Source 76 has a Christian Scybert bur in Wythe, no city or fam cem. Stones now illegible **P:** Y **BLW:** unk **RG:** unk **MK:** unk **PH:** unk **SS:** DAR Ancestor #A102283; CG Vol 3 pg 3075 **BS:** JLARC 4, 40, 76.

RU=Rank/Unit	CEM=Cemetery	GS=Gravestone	SP=Spousal Information
VI=Other Veteran Info	P=Pension	BLW=Bounty/Land Warrant	RG=Registered Grave
MK=SAR/DAR Marker	PH=Photo	SS=Service Source	BS=Burial Source

301

SEYBERT, Henry; b unk; d 1830 **RU:** Private, Served in Capt Weiser's Co Germ Bn, Cont Troops **CEM:** Seybert Hills Farm; GPS unk; US 200 N fr Monterery to Rt 629, then 1.8 mi; Highland **GS:** U **SP:** No info **VI:** Son of Johan (1717-1758) & Maria Elisabeth (Theiss) (1721-1758) Seybert **P:** unk **BLW:** unk **RG:** unk **MK:** unk **PH:** unk **SS:** NSSAR Ancestor # P-287400; Gov't Gr st gives service **BS:** JLARC 103; 196.

SEYBERT, Nicholas; b 1741, Berks Co, PA; d 1813 **RU:** Captain, Served 7th MD Bn **CEM:** Seybert Chapel; GPS unk; Nr jct Rt 629 Strait Creek and Rt 631, Monterey; Highland **GS:** Y **SP:** No info **VI:** No further data **P:** unk **BLW:** unk **RG:** N **MK:** N **PH:** unk **SS:** E pg 701 **BS:** JLARC 103;181.

SHAKLETT (SHACKLETT), Edward; b 1752; d 23 Apr 1826 **RU:** Sergeant, Served in Cont Line. Entered service Surry Co. Served as Sgt in Col Charles Harrison's Regt of Artillery. Discharged Morristown 10 Jan 1780 **CEM:** Cool Spring Church; GPS unk; .5 mi S of Delaplane; Fauquier **GS:** Y **SP:** Mar (10 May 1782 Farquier Co, bond dated 4 May 1782 Hezekiah Shacklett security) Elizabeth "Betsy" Rector (c1766-24 Oct 1839) **VI:** Widow appl pen 25 Jul 1838 Fauquier Co age 72 W6037 **P:** Y **BLW:** unk **RG:** N **MK:** Y **PH:** Y **SS:** E pg 702; K pg 44; CG Vol 3 pg 3077; Fauquier Co Marriages pg 178 **BS:** 95, Cool Spring; JLARC 2, 4,16.

SHANNON, John; b 1759; d 18 Dec 1832 **RU:** Soldier, Served in VA Line **CEM:** Old Shannon Place; GPS 38.53999, -77.55610; Head of Long Hollow, Rich Valley; Smyth **GS:** U **SP:** Mar (10 Jan 1788 Washington Co) Ann (Nancy) Marshall (c1770-__) **VI:** Widow appl pen 22 Jul 1845 Smyth Co age 75. R9419. Wounded in hip. GSs destroyed **P:** Y **BLW:** unk **RG:** unk **MK:** unk **PH:** unk **SS:** CG Vol 3 pg 3081 **BS:** JLARC 4, 114.

SHANNON, Thomas Reid; b 25 Mar 1753, Albemarle Co; d 12 Nov 1841 **RU:** Captain, Commanded Middle New River Co, Montgomery Co Troops. Also served in Capt Patton's Co, Montgomery Co Militia **CEM:** Shannon-King; GPS 37.21810, -80.74170; Nr Jct Rts 42 & 100, Poplar Hill nr Walker's Creek; Giles **GS:** Y **SP:** Agnes Crowe (17 Jun 1760-16 Oct 1823) **VI:** Son of Samuel (1727 Sadsbury Meeting House, Lancaster Co, PA-1811 Whites Creek, Davidson Co, TN) & Jean (Reid) Shannon.Was a sheriff of Montgomery Co & a state legislator. Name listed on bronze plaque in the cemetery **P:** unk **BLW:** unk **RG:** N **MK:** unk **PH:** unk **SS:** J- DAR Hatcher; G pg 223 **BS:** JLARC 2; 196.

SHARP, John; b 1727; d 18 Oct 1816 **RU:** Soldier, Served in Capt Cunningham's Co, Augusta Co Militia **CEM:** North Mountain; GPS unk; 7 mi S of Staunton on N side Rt 252; Augusta **GS:** Y **SP:** 1) Mar (30 Sep 1797 Augusta Co) Elizabeth Curry; (2) Ann (-----) **VI:** Name inscribed on newer family stone **P:** unk **BLW:** unk **RG:** unk **MK:** N **PH:** unk **SS:** JLARC 62, 63; E pg 703 **BS:** JLARC 62, 63; 196.

SHARP, John Anderson; b 1745; d 1 Dec 1823 **RU:** Ensign, Served in NC Rangers **CEM:** Green Spring Presbyterian; GPS 36.63670, -81.99560; 2007 Green Spring Ch Rd, Abingdon; Washington **GS:** Y **SP:** Elizabeth Laughlin (1748 PA-5 Jan 1825) **VI:** Gov't Gr St shows service **P:** unk **BLW:** unk **RG:** unk **MK:** unk **PH:** unk **SS:** AR Vol 4 pg 22 **BS:** JLARC 2, 70, 80,101; 78 pg 276; 196.

SHARP, Joseph; b 1753; d Oct 1828 **RU:** Soldier, Served in 10th Cont Line **CEM:** Bethel Presbyterian; GPS 38.04257, -79.17283; 563 Bethel Green Rd, Middlebrook; Augusta **GS:** Y **SP:** Mar (30 Sep 1797 Augusta Co) Julianna Scott **VI:** Lower half of stone now missing **P:** unk **BLW:** unk **RG:** unk **MK:** unk **PH:** unk **SS:** E pg 703 **BS:** JLARC 62; 196.

SHARP, Thomas; b 24 Aug 1761; d 24 Jan 1826 **RU:** Lieutenant, Private in Capt Thomas Church's Co, Col Wayne's PA Bn, 1776 and also Hazen's Regt. Was Corporal in 3rd Cont Line. May be person this name promoted to Lt in 1780 **CEM:** Bethel Presbyterian; GPS 38.04257, -79.17283; 563 Bethel Green Rd, Middlebrook; Augusta **GS:** Y **SP:** 1) Jean Wilson 2) Mary Ann Reed (marriages are fr JLARC) **VI:** Recd BLW 8 Nov 1791 **P:** unk **BLW:** Y **RG:** unk **MK:** unk **PH:** unk **SS:** C pg 507; E pg 703; CG pg 3082 **BS:** JLARC 62, 63; 196.

SHAW, James; b unk; d Mar 1793 **RU:** Private, Served as orderly in hospital. Was in consolidated 4th, 8th, 12th VA Regts **CEM:** Old Christ Church Episcopal; GPS 38.80625, -77.04718; 118 N Washington St; Alexandria City **GS:** N **SP:** No info **VI:** Burial permit issued 18 Mar 1793 **P:** unk **BLW:** unk **RG:** N **MK:** N **PH:** N **SS:** AP roll **BS:** 20 pg 152.

SHEETS, Jacob; b unk; d Aft 1781 **RU:** Private/Patriot, Served in Capt Anderson, Augusta Co. Gave material aid to cause **CEM:** Sheets Family; GPS unk; W of Rt 220, Bessemer area; Botetourt **GS:** Y **SP:**

RU=Rank/Unit	CEM=Cemetery	GS=Gravestone	SP=Spousal Information
VI=Other Veteran Info	P=Pension	BLW=Bounty/Land Warrant	RG=Registered Grave
MK=SAR/DAR Marker	PH=Photo	SS=Service Source	BS=Burial Source

302

No info **VI**: No further data **P**: unk **BLW**: unk **RG**: N **MK**: N **PH**: unk **SS**: E pg 705; AL Cert 1 Augusta Co **BS**: 115 pg 82.

SHEETS, Samuel; b unk; d 27 May 1782 **RU**: Patriot, Gave material aid to cause **CEM**: Keezletown; GPS unk; Keezletown; Rockingham **GS**: U **SP**: Elizabeth (-----) (__-1807) **VI**: No further data **P**: N **BLW**: N **RG**: unk **MK**: unk **PH**: unk **SS**: AL Ct Bk pg 28 Albemarle Co **BS**: 96.

SHELBY, Elvan; b 1754; d 1813 **RU**: Patriot, Service information in DAR Senate Document 113, 1973 and 1993 **CEM**: East Hill; GPS 36.59438, -82.17233; E State St on line btw VA and TN; Bristol City **GS**: Y **SP**: No info **VI**: No further data **P**: N **BLW**: N **RG**: N **MK**: N **PH**: unk **SS**: AR Vol 4 pg 26; AS DAR Report **BS**: DAR report.

SHELBY, Evan; b 1754; d 18 Jan 1793 **RU**: General, Was Brig Gen of VA Milita. As Capt commanded an Independent co Sep-Dec 1774. As Maj was in charge of expedition against Indians 1776 and commander of militia unit at Battle of Kings Mountain Oct 1780 **CEM**: East Hill, Sec 1; GPS unk; West of Circles (Source 80 Cem #279A); Washington **GS**: Y **SP**: No info **VI**: Killed by Indians at age 74 after Rev War. First bur where the First Presbyterian Church now stands, and was later removed to this cemetery. Coffin-sized iron mounted over grave **P**: unk **BLW**: unk **RG**: unk **MK**: unk **PH**: unk **SS**: E pg 705; CE pg 24, 141 **BS**: 183; JLARC 80.

SHELBY, Isaac; b 11 Dec 1750, Hagerstown, MD; d 18 Jul 1826 **RU**: Colonel/Patriot, Was in battle at Point Pleasant and was hero at Kings Mountain. Gave material aid to cause **CEM**: East Hill; GPS 36.59438, -82.17233; E State St on line btw VA and TN; Bristol City **GS**: U **SP**: Susanna Hart **VI**: After war became general. Was first governor of Kentucky. Was Secretary of War on Monroe's cabinet. Died in Traveller's Rest, Lincoln Co, KY. Memorialized in the cemetery at the burial site of his father Evan Shelby and Letitia Cox **P**: unk **BLW**: unk **RG**: unk **MK**: N **PH**: unk **SS**: J- DAR Hatcher; Z pg 154; AL Ct Bk pg 1 Montgomery Co; BY **BS**: JLARC 2.

SHELDON, Parker; b 1755; d 1825 **RU**: Soldier, See DAR Senate Document 1930 serial 9337, vol 5 for service **CEM**: Newport; GPS unk; Newport; Giles **GS**: U **SP**: No info **VI**: No further data **P**: unk **BLW**: unk **RG**: Y **MK**: unk **PH**: unk **SS**: J-NSSAR 2000 Reg; NSSAR Ancestor #P-288485; AR Vol 4 pg 27 **BS**: JLARC 76.

SHELOR, Daniel; b 3 Mar 1750, MD; d 13 Dec 1847 **RU**: Captain, Served in MD Cont Line **CEM**: Pine Creek Primitive Baptist; GPS 36.94622, -80.27357; Spangler Mill Rd Rt 682; Floyd **GS**: Y **SP**: Mar (1784) Mary Wickham (1756 Frederick Co, MD-4 Oct 1834) **VI**: Son of Lawrence & (-----) Shelor. Recd pen S6079 **P**: Y **BLW**: unk **RG**: Y **MK**: N **PH**: Y **SS**: NSDAR Patriot Index 2002; Rev War Survivor's Pens Appl File: M804 Roll 2168; JLARC 1, 2, 9 **BS**: JLARC 1, 29; 196.

SHELTON, Eliphaz; b 1741; d 16 Feb 1826 **RU**: Captain/Patriot, Appt Capt Mar 1779 and commanded a co in Henry Co Militia serving until 1781. Gave material aid to cause **CEM**: Eliphaz Shelton-Pilson Family; GPS unk; At foot of Main St, Stuart; Patrick **GS**: U **SP**: Ann (Nancy) (-----) **VI**: Son of Ralph (1709-1789) & Susannah Mary (Daniel) (1713-1787) Shelton. Plaque to him on Patrick CH wall indicates he gave land to build it on **P**: unk **BLW**: unk **RG**: unk **MK**: unk **PH**: unk **SS**: E pg 706; AL Ct Bk pg 22 Henry Co **BS**: JLARC 30; 196.

SHELTON, James; b 1759; d Aft 14 Nov 1840 **RU**: Sergeant, Served in VA Line fr Louisa Co. **CEM**: Woodland; GPS unk; Jackson District; Louisa **GS**: U **SP**: Mar (7 Jun 1798) Elizabeth Thompson (c1774-Jun 1814) **VI**: Was substitute for his brother John. Appl pen Louisa Co 7 May 1836. S10257 **P**: Y **BLW**: unk **RG**: unk **MK**: unk **PH**: unk **SS**: DAR Ancestor #A102788; SAR Ancestor #P-288586; CG pg 3100 **BS**: JLARC 4, 61.

SHELTON, Lemuel; b c1765; d 1848 **RU**: Soldier, Served in VA Line **CEM**: Pine Creek; GPS unk; SAR registration did not give directions; Pittsylvania **GS**: U **SP**: Mar (Aug 1796) Lettis Weeks (__-1815 Pittsylvania Co) **VI**: Son of Gabriel (1740-20 Jun 1803) and Elizabeth (Sheppherd) Shelton. Son Hubbard C. Shelton appl pen 1 Feb 1853 Todd Co KY age 47 R9474 **P**: Y **BLW**: unk **RG**: unk **MK**: unk **PH**: unk **SS**: SAR Ancestor #P-288594; CG Vol 3 pg 3100 **BS**: JLARC 4.

SHELTON, Thomas; b 1738, Old Town, Louisa Co; d 10 Jul 1826 **RU**: Patriot, Gave material aid to cause **CEM**: Roseneath; GPS unk; Jackson District; Louisa **GS**: U **SP**: Mar (12 Mar 1809) Sallie Farrar

RU=Rank/Unit   CEM=Cemetery   GS=Gravestone   SP=Spousal Information
VI=Other Veteran Info   P=Pension   BLW=Bounty/Land Warrant   RG=Registered Grave
MK=SAR/DAR Marker   PH=Photo   SS=Service Source   BS=Burial Source

303

(c1763 Goochland Co-1 Jul 1823) d/o Mathew (29 Oct 1760 Louisa Co-1844) & Martha (Murrell) (c1763-aft 1827) Farrar **VI:** No further data **P:** N **BLW:** N **RG:** unk **MK:** unk **PH:** unk **SS:** DAR Ancestor #A102823; AL Ct Bk pg 21, 24, 30 Lousia Co **BS:** JLARC 61.

SHEPARD, William; b 1740; d 16 Feb 1813 **RU:** Private, Served in Henrico Co Militia **CEM:** Shockoe Hill; GPS 37.55190, -77.43170; 4th & Hospital Sts; Richmond City **GS:** U **SP:** No info **VI:** No further data **P:** unk **BLW:** unk **RG:** unk **MK:** unk **PH:** unk **SS:** E pg 707 **BS:** 196.

SHEPHERD, David; b 1760; d 1823 **RU:** Lieutenant, Served in VA Cont Line **CEM:** Shepherd family; GPS unk; Vic Rts 623 & 659; Fluvanna **GS:** Y **SP:** No info **VI:** Recd BLW 100 acres 31 Jan 1784 **P:** unk **BLW:** Y **RG:** N **MK:** N **PH:** unk **SS:** F pg 68; CZ pg 398 cites Council Journals Lib VA 1777-8 pg 30 **BS:** 66 pg 86.

SHEPHERD, John; b 1738; d 1796 **RU:** Private, Served in Capt John Moore's Co of Militia of Kanawha Co (now WV). Wounded in his hand and thigh **CEM:** Parrish Family; GPS unk; Vic Rts 619 & 660; Fluvanna **GS:** N **SP:** No info **VI:** Appl & recd pen of $40 per annum, 22 Jan 1798 **P:** Y **BLW:** unk **RG:** N **MK:** N **PH:** N **SS:** AN Kanawha Co; CZ pg 398 cites War Files #4 pg 362, 363 Lib VA **BS:** 66 pg 68.

SHIELDS, William; b unk; d unk **RU:** Fife Major, Served in 2nd VA Regt **CEM:** Cub Creek; GPS unk; Off Rt 789 Cub Creek Rd at Beech Grove Community; Nelson **GS:** U **SP:** No info **VI:** No further data **P:** unk **BLW:** unk **RG:** unk **MK:** unk **PH:** unk **SS:** NSSAR Ancestor #P-289160 **BS:** JLARC 83.

SHIPMAN, Benjamin; b Bapt 30 Apr 1749, Morristown, NJ; d 30 Dec 1825 **RU:** Lieutenant, Specific service at Lib of VA, Auditor's Accts, XV, pg 527 **CEM:** Mossy Creek Presbyterian; GPS 38.35331, -79.04914; 372 Kyles Mill Rd, Mt Solon; Augusta **GS:** N **SP:** Mar (c1767) Augusta Mary Osburn (c1747 NJ-28 Sep 1786 Frederick Co) **VI:** No further data **P:** unk **BLW:** unk **MK:** N **PH:** N **SS:** DAR Ancestor #A132451; NSSAR Ancestor #P-289226; DD **BS:** JLARC 62, 63; 196.

SHIPMAN, Jonathan; b 1759; d 19 May 1848 **RU:** Private, Served in Capt John Hopkin's Co, Rockingham Co Militia **CEM:** Mossy Creek Presbyterian; GPS 38.35331, -79.04914; 372 Kyles Mill Rd, Mt Solon; Augusta **GS:** N **SP:** No info **VI:** No further data **P:** unk **BLW:** unk **RG:** unk **MK:** N **PH:** N **SS:** Z pg 100; CZ cites Auditors Acct XXXI pg 356 Lib VA **BS:** JLARC 62, 63; 196.

SHIRKEY, Nicholas; b 1752; d 2 Jul 1830 **RU:** Soldier, Served in VA Line **CEM:** Shirkey-Far; GPS unk; Across James River fr Gala; Botetourt **GS:** U **SP:** Mar (3 Dec 1777) Sarah (-----) (c1761-__) **VI:** Widow appl pen 5 Feb 1844 Botetourt Co age 83. Reappl 2 Sep 1848. W6049 **P:** Y **BLW:** unk **RG:** unk **MK:** N **PH:** unk **SS:** CG Vol 3 pg 3177 **BS:** JLARC 4, 60, 124.

SHIRLEY, Michael; b 1755; d 1842 **RU:** Soldier, Served in 4th & 7th Cont Lines **CEM:** St Peter's Lutheran; GPS 38.22569, -79.16125; 3795 Churchville Ave, Churchville; Augusta **GS:** N **SP:** Submit Bogle **VI:** No further data **P:** unk **BLW:** unk **RG:** unk **MK:** N **PH:** N **SS:** NSSAR Ancestor #P-289308; E pg 709 **BS:** JLARC 62.

SHOMO, Anthony; b 29 Dec 1756, Berks Co, PA; d 14 Apr 1812 **RU:** Ensign, Served in PA 4th Bn 8th Co Berks Co Militia **CEM:** St Mathew's; GPS 36.65131, -78.67121; Breckenridge Ln, New Market; Shenandoah **GS:** Y **SP:** Elizabeth Obold Shomo (__-1842) **VI:** No further data **P:** unk **BLW:** unk **RG:** N **MK:** Y **PH:** unk **SS:** B CD **BS:** 196; 32.

SHORES, Thomas Jr; b 1753; d 15 Oct 1841 **RU:** Private, Enlisted Feb 1776. Capt Matthew Joulett's Co, Col Lewis & Alexander's Regts. Discharged Mar 1778. Also Served in Capt George Rice's Co #9 30 Nov 1778 **CEM:** Shores & Tutwiler Families; GPS 37.74641, -78.38259; Seven Islands; Fluvanna **GS:** N **SP:** Mar (May 1778) Susanna Bugg (Jul 1760 New Kent Co.-5 Aug 1827) d/o William (1711-1796) & Mary (Bacon) (1713-1770) Bugg **VI:** Pensioned Fluvanna Co **P:** Y **BLW:** unk **RG:** unk **MK:** unk **PH:** N **SS:** A pg 264; E pg 710 **BS:** 196.

SHOWALTER, Christain Jr; b 1768; d Aft 1841 **RU:** Private, Listed in 8th Recruiting Class, 9th Bn, Lancaster Co Militia **CEM:** Trissel's Mennonite Ch; GPS unk; Rt 752, Harrisonburg; Harrisonburg City **GS:** N **SP:** Catherine Roadcap **VI:** No further data **P:** unk **BLW:** unk **RG:** Y **MK:** N **PH:** N **SS:** CI PA Archives series V Vol VII **BS:** 04.

RU=Rank/Unit	CEM=Cemetery	GS=Gravestone	SP=Spousal Information
VI=Other Veteran Info	P=Pension	BLW=Bounty/Land Warrant	RG=Registered Grave
MK=SAR/DAR Marker	PH=Photo	SS=Service Source	BS=Burial Source

304

SHREVE, Benjamin Jr; b 7 Oct 1747, Burlington Co, NJ; d 18 Nov 1801 **RU:** Patriot, Signed Legislative Petition City of Alexandria Nov 1778 **CEM:** Quaker Burial Ground; GPS 38.80749, -77.04676; 717 Queen St, Kate Walker Barrett Library; Alexandria City **GS:** U **SP:** 1)Hannah Vail, 2) Susannah Wood **VI:** Son of Benjamin & Sarah (Areson) Shreve. Alexandria merchant. Alexandria Gazette notes burial was in Quaker Cemetery **P:** N **BLW:** N **RG:** unk **MK:** unk **PH:** unk **SS:** BB **BS:** 196.

SHREVE, Samuel; b 25 Jan 1750, Burlington Co, NJ; d 24 Apr 1815 **RU:** Lieutenant Colonel, Capt, 1st Battalion, Gloucester Co; Was Lt Col, in Bn, NJ Militia, Cont Line 5 Feb 1777; resigned 2 Oct 1778 **CEM:** Oakwood; GPS unk; N Roosevelt St; Falls Church City **GS:** Y **SP:** Mira Trout **VI:** Came to Arlington abt 1780 fr New Jersey. Died in Fairfax Co. Sign with info abt him in cemetery nr Fairfax Dr & North Harrison St. Grave moved fr N. Abingdon St **P:** unk **BLW:** unk **RG:** Y **MK:** N **PH:** unk **SS:** AK **BS:** 04; 69 pg 74, 74A; JLARC 2,14, 28.

SHUEY, John Ludwig "Lewis"; b 6 May 1755, Lebanon Co, PA; d 22 Jan 1839 **RU:** Private, Served in the 3rd Co, 2nd Bn, Lancaster Co, PA Militia **CEM:** Glebe Burying Ground; GPS 38.10940, -79.22190; Glebe School Rd Rt 876, Swoopes; Augusta **GS:** Y **SP:** Mar (18 Mar 1780) Anna Maria Loesch (12 Apr 1760-12 Mar 1822) d/o of Johann Balthasar (1734-1804) & Anna Christina (Heyl) (1740-1816) Loesch **VI:** DAR marker **P:** unk **BLW:** unk **RG:** unk **MK:** Y **PH:** unk **SS:** AR Vol 4 pg 32; BT **BS:** JLARC 2, 4, 62; 196.

SHULTZ, John; b c1753; d 03 Nov 1840 **RU:** Private, Served in PA **CEM:** Mt Hebron; GPS 39.10916, -78.09497; 305 E Boscawen St; Winchester City **GS:** Y **SP:** 1) Mar (12 Aug 1788 Frederick Co by Alexander Balmain) Catherine Otto, (c1764-21 Mar 1839) 2) (8 Mar 1791 Frederick Co by Christian Streit) Catherine Haar (Gaar?) **VI:** Was pensioned while residing in Frederick Co **P:** N **BLW:** N **RG:** N **MK:** N **PH:** N **SS:** E pg 694 **BS:** 196,.

SHUMAKER (SCHUMACHER), George; b 26 Oct 1763; d 30 Dec 1834 **RU:** Soldier/Patriot, Served in Capt John Cope's Co of Militia, Frankkoney Twp, Philadelphia, PA **CEM:** Old Presbyterian; GPS 39.27343, -77.69341; Behind Primitive Baptist on S Church St, Lovettsville; Loudoun **GS:** Y **SP:** Mar (7 Jan 1789 Loudoun Co) Magdalena "Mary" Frantz (1773-aft Aug 1839) **VI:** Spouse appl pen 13 Aug 1839, W6004 **P:** Y **BLW:** unk **RG:** Y **MK:** N **PH:** unk **SS:** D Vol 2 pg 599; AP Muster Roll PA Archives series 6 Vol 1; CG pg 3039 **BS:** 25 pg 282.

SHUMATE, Daniel III; b 14 Jun 1751, Fauquier Co; d 1826 **RU:** Second Lieutenant, Served in Fauquier Co Militia. Was Ens Aug 1777, and 2nd Lt 24 Mar 1778. Resigned May 1781 **CEM:** Sunrise Memorial Gardens; GPS unk; Rich Creek; Giles **GS:** Y **SP:** Millicent "Millie" Callison (5 Oct 1758-22 May 1841 Mercer Co, WVA) d/o Isaac & (-----) Callison **VI:** No further data **P:** unk **BLW:** unk **RG:** Y **MK:** N **PH:** unk **SS:** JLARC App B-2 pg 37; E pg 711 **BS:** JLARC 1, 26; 196.

SIDEBOTTOM (SIDEBOTHOM), Joseph; b 1761; d 10 Nov 1848 **RU:** Private, Served in 3rd VA Regt **CEM:** Robinson-Sidebottoms-Hawkins; GPS unk; nr Round Hill; Frederick **GS:** U **SP:** No info **VI:** No further data **P:** unk **BLW:** unk **RG:** unk **MK:** unk **PH:** unk **SS:** E pg 754; CZ pg 400, cites W.F. Boogher's Gleanings of Virginia History Washington DC 1903 pg 177 **BS:** 196.

SIEG, Paul; b 14 Nov 1753; d 22 Sep 1817 **RU:** Soldier, Served in PA Militia **CEM:** St Peter's Lutheran; GPS 38.22569, -79.16125; 3795 Churchville Ave, Churchville; Augusta **GS:** Y **SP:** Susannah Fauber **VI:** Rev War service marker "Private, PA Militia" **P:** unk **BLW:** unk **RG:** unk **MK:** Y **PH:** unk **SS:** B **BS:** JLARC 62; 196.

SIGLER, Michael; b 4 Jan 1754, Berks Co, PA; d 6 Feb 1833 **RU:** Soldier, Served in PA **CEM:** Union Church; GPS 38.44480, -78.38350; Mt Jackson nr jct Main St & Bridge St; Shenandoah **GS:** Y **SP:** Mary Pennywitt (1777-1849) **VI:** No further data **P:** unk **BLW:** unk **RG:** unk **MK:** unk **PH:** Y **SS:** I 519 555; II pg 487; CI PA Archives 6th services Index pg 303 **BS:** 196.

SIMM (SIMMS), James; b 17 Jul 1754; d 2 Dec 1793 **RU:** Private, Served in Capt John Webb's Co of the 5th & 11th Cont Line combined segments Oct 1779 **CEM:** St John's Episcopal; GPS 37.53183, -77.41958; 2401 E Broad St; Richmond City **GS:** Y **SP:** No info **VI:** No further data **P:** unk **BLW:** unk **RG:** N **MK:** N **PH:** unk **SS:** AP **BS:** 28 pg 504; 196.

RU=Rank/Unit   CEM=Cemetery   GS=Gravestone   SP=Spousal Information
VI=Other Veteran Info   P=Pension   BLW=Bounty/Land Warrant   RG=Registered Grave
MK=SAR/DAR Marker   PH=Photo   SS=Service Source   BS=Burial Source

305

SIMMERMAN, Christopher; b 1746; d 1813 **RU:** Soldier, Enl Montgomery Co in Capt Findlay and Capt James Kent Cos **CEM:** St John's Lutheran; **GPS** 36.96500, -81.10110; 405 W Main, Wytheville; Wythe **GS:** Y **SP:** Margaret Reinhardikin (1743-3 Jun 1821) **VI:** Gave 90 acres to establish the town of Evansham, later known as Wytheville in Wythe Co. DAR plaque at home location **P:** N **BLW:** N **RG:** unk **MK:** unk **PH:** unk **SS:** B **BS:** JLARC 3, 40,123; 196.

SIMMERMAN, Earhart (Arehart); b 1762; d 31 Aug 1827 **RU:** Private, Served in Capt James Fenley's Co, Montgomery Co Militia **CEM:** Simmerman, aka Cedar Hill; **GPS** unk; Off I-81 N, open field abt .25 mi east of gravel plant on SR 649; Wythe **GS:** U **SP:** Mary (-----) (c1764-28 Nov 1834) **VI:** No further data **P:** unk **BLW:** unk **RG:** unk **MK:** unk **PH:** unk **SS:** G pg 233 **BS:** JLARC 123.

SIMMERMAN, Stophel (Staphel); b 1759, Montgomery Co; d 4 Feb 1813 **RU:** Private, Served in Capt James Fenley's Co, Montgomery Co Militia **CEM:** Simmerman, aka Cedar Hill; **GPS** unk; Off I-81 N, open field abt .25 mi east of gravel plant on SR 649; Wythe **GS:** Y **SP:** Mar (1774) Anna Margaret Reinhardin (1743 Montgomery Co-3 Jun 1821) **VI:** No further data **P:** unk **BLW:** unk **RG:** N **MK:** N **PH:** unk **SS:** G pg 233 **BS:** 140 Mason B.

SIMMONS, Joshua; b unk; d c1800 **RU:** Private, Served in Chesterfield Co Militia **CEM:** Kirkham Family; **GPS** unk; 1.2 mi N of Disputana; Prince George **GS:** Y **SP:** No info **VI:** No further data **P:** unk **BLW:** unk **RG:** Y **MK:** N **PH:** unk **SS:** E pg 712; CZ pg 401 cites supplement to Chesterfield Co Militia pg 68 **BS:** 111 Part 5 pg 79.

SIMMS, Charles; b 1755, Prince William Co; d 30 Aug 1819 **RU:** Colonel, Served as Maj, 12th Virginia Regt, 12 Nov 1776; Lt Col 6th VA Regt, 29 Sep 1777; transferred to 2nd VA Regt, 14 Sep 1778; resigned 7 Dec 1779 **CEM:** Old Christ Church Episcopal; **GPS** 38.80625, -77.04718; 118 N Washington St; Alexandria City **GS:** Y **SP:** Nancy Ann Douglas **VI:** Inscription on a newer stone: "SACRED to the memory of COL. CHARLES SIMMS, An officer in the Army of Independence and for many yrs an honored Citizen of Alexandria & Mayor of that City in 1811." He d in the yr 1819. He was a member of the Society of the Cincinnati & a friend of General Washington. Original stone is lost. Was also collector at the port of Alexandria **P:** N **BLW:** N **RG:** Y **MK:** Y **PH:** Y **SS:** AK **BS:** JLARC 1, 25, 87; 20 pg 141-2; 196.

SIMMS, Joseph; b 1741; d 1790 **RU:** Private, Enl 29 Aug 1777. Served in Maj Lewis Winder's MD Regt of Foot, Mar 1780 **CEM:** Cloverhill; **GPS** unk; Hastings Dr; Manassas City **GS:** Y **SP:** No info **VI:** SAR marker **P:** unk **BLW:** unk **RG:** Y **MK:** Y **PH:** unk **SS:** AY pg 31 **BS:** 94 appendix pg 3.

SIMMS, Thomas; b 1762; d 5 Apr 1808 **RU:** Sergeant, Served in Grayson's Regt **CEM:** Old Presbyterian Meeting House; **GPS** 38.48528, -77.23532; 323 S Fairfax St; Alexandria City **GS:** N **SP:** Margaret (-----) d 28 Dec 1797 in childbirth **VI:** Died age 46. Listed on SAR plaque in cemetery **P:** unk **BLW:** unk **RG:** Y **MK:** Y **PH:** N **SS:** E pg 713; AK **BS:** 23 pg 107; 196.

SIMPSON, Jeremiah; b 23 Aug 1749; d 25 Feb 1822 **RU:** Sergeant/Patriot, Served three yrs. Signer of Oath of Allegiance. Provided corn to State Troops **CEM:** St Mary's Catholic; **GPS** 38.79390, -77.04750; 310 S Royal St; Alexandria City **GS:** Y **SP:** Rachel (-----) (14 Feb 1752-8 Dec 1806) **VI:** A person this name with similar birth and death dates had patriotic service and d in Pittsylvania Co, thus may be memorialized at this location **P:** unk **BLW:** Y **RG:** unk **MK:** unk **PH:** unk **SS:** DAR Ancestor #A104143; C pg 499 **BS:** 174.

SIMPSON, John; b 1740, Prince William Co; d 18 Feb 1800 **RU:** Private, Served in 4th, 7th, 8th, 10th, 12th, and 15th Cont Lines **CEM:** Simpson Family; **GPS** unk; On original family homeplace, check property records for location; Henry **GS:** U **SP:** Mar (before 1755, Prince William Co) Hannah Roberts (1733-1800) **VI:** No further data **P:** unk **BLW:** unk **RG:** unk **MK:** unk **PH:** unk **SS:** E pg 714 **BS:** 196.

SIMPSON, Thomas; b c1752; d 1824 **RU:** Private, Served in a VA unit in Illinois **CEM:** Grove Baptist Church; **GPS** 36.63750, -79.24924; NW edge of Goldvein; Fauquier **GS:** Y **SP:** A man by this name mar (12 Sep 1799 by Ephraim Abell (Baptist) returned 17 Sep 1799) Hannah Blackwell **VI:** No further data **P:** unk **BLW:** unk **RG:** N **MK:** N **PH:** unk **SS:** E pg 714; CZ pg 402; Fauquier Co Marriages pg 182 **BS:** 95 Grove B. Ch.

RU=Rank/Unit	CEM=Cemetery	GS=Gravestone	SP=Spousal Information
VI=Other Veteran Info	P=Pension	BLW=Bounty/Land Warrant	RG=Registered Grave
MK=SAR/DAR Marker	PH=Photo	SS=Service Source	BS=Burial Source

306

SIMRALL, James Jr; b 3 Feb 1740, PA; d 1 Jul 1798 **RU:** Captain, Commanded a co in Frederick Co Militia **CEM:** Opequon Presbyterian; GPS 39.13938, -78.19494; 217 Opequon Church Ln; Winchester City **GS:** Y **SP:** Mar (18 Mar 1762) Sarah Ferguson (1740-1814 Shelby, KY) **VI:** Died in Kernstown **P:** unk **BLW:** unk **RG:** Y **MK:** Y **PH:** Y **SS:** DAR Ancestor #A104262; J-NSSAR 2000 Reg; E pg 714 **BS:** JLARC 76.

SINCLAIR, John; b 14 Mar 1755, Hampton; d 1819 or 1820 **RU:** Navy Captain/Patriot, Was Privateer. Commanded "Nicholson", a small boat. In 1781 hired as pilot to guide French fleet to Chesapeake **CEM:** Sinclair at "Sherwood"; GPS 37.08370, -78.11672; Selden Post Office; Gloucester **GS:** Y **SP:** 1) Ann Wilson 2) Mary Mackie Ianson **VI:** Died in "Land's End" Gloucester Co. Memorial stone to Capt John Sinclair erected c1937 **P:** unk **BLW:** unk **RG:** Y **MK:** N **PH:** unk **SS:** L pg 247 **BS:** 48 pg 60.

SINCLAIR, Samuel; b 1762; d 27 May 1806 **RU:** Patriot, Gave material aid to cause **CEM:** New Valley Baptist; GPS 39.21918, -77.54746; Bald Hill Rd Rt 673, Lucketts; Loudoun **GS:** Y **SP:** No info **VI:** No further data **P:** N **BLW:** N **RG:** N **MK:** N **PH:** unk **SS:** D Vol 2 pg 612 **BS:** 25 pg 287.

SINGLETON, John; b unk; d unk **RU:** Brigadier General/Patriot, Raised and commanded a body of calvary in 1781. Performed public service as member of Committee of Safety 1775-6 **CEM:** Mt Hebron; GPS 39.10916, -78.09497; 305 E Boscawen St; Winchester City **GS:** U **SP:** No info **VI:** No further data **P:** unk **BLW:** unk **RG:** Y **MK:** unk **PH:** unk **SS:** NSSAR Ancestor #P-290500; CZ pg 402 **BS:** JLARC 76.

SINGLETON, John; b 1758; d Jun 8, 1825 **RU:** Private, Served in Capt John Gregory's Co under Daniel Morgan 1778. Served in other regiments of VA Line until discharge in Philadelphia at end of war **CEM:** St Paul's Episcopal; GPS 36.84733, -76.28554; 201 St Paul's Blvd; Norfolk City **GS:** Y **SP:** Sarah Dyson **VI:** Son of Henry Singleton & Mary Ann Waldron (Reynolds) Singleton **P:** unk **BLW:** unk **RG:** Y **MK:** Y **PH:** unk **SS:** C pg 266-7 **BS:** 178 Jan 11.

SINK, Stephen; b 17 Sep 1758, Chester Co, PA; d 11 Sep 1835 **RU:** Soldier, Enrolled 12 Aug 1780 in 4th Co, 2nd Bn, Chester Co PA Militia **CEM:** Stephen Sink Family; GPS 37.08092, -79.79286; Rt 670 behind house at 956 Three Oaks Rd; Franklin **GS:** U **SP:** Susan Plybon (1752-1843) **VI:** No further data **P:** unk **BLW:** unk **RG:** unk **MK:** unk **PH:** unk **SS:** CD **BS:** JLARC 19; 196.

SIREUIL, Jean de; b unk; d 1781 **RU:** Soldier, Served in Gatinais Bn and died fr battle at Yorktown **CEM:** French Memorial; GPS 36.81944, -79.39933; Yorktown; York **GS:** U **SP:** No info **VI:** No further data **P:** unk **BLW:** unk **RG:** Y **MK:** unk **PH:** unk **SS:** J-Yorktown Historian **BS:** JLARC 1 ,74.

SITLINGTON, Robert; b Nov 1748; d 15 Sep 1833 **RU:** Private, Served in VA Cont Line, Ent serv Augusta Co 1776 as subsitute for Nathan Crawford **CEM:** Sitlington Family; GPS unk; 8.5 mi S of Millboro Springs; Bath **GS:** Y **SP:** No info **VI:** Appl pen 26 Sept 1832 Bath Co. S7517 **P:** Y **BLW:** unk **RG:** N **MK:** Y **PH:** unk **SS:** E pg 715; K Vol 5 pg 80; CG pg 3149 **BS:** 159.

SKINKER, Thomas; b unk; d 1803 **RU:** Patriot, Gave material aid to the cause **CEM:** Grove Baptist Church; GPS 36.63750, -79.24924; NW edge of Goldvein; Fauquier **GS:** Y **SP:** No info **VI:** No further data **P:** N **BLW:** N **RG:** N **MK:** N **PH:** unk **SS:** AL Ct Bk pg 3,13 **BS:** 95 Grove B Ch.

SKINNER, Charles W; b unk; d 1827 **RU:** US Navy, Contact Norfolk Chapter SAR for naval service **CEM:** Cedar Grove; GPS 36.85860, -76.28310; 238 E Princess Anne Rd; Norfolk City **GS:** N **SP:** No info **VI:** No further data **P:** unk **BLW:** unk **RG:** N **MK:** N **PH:** N **SS:** BR 1827 **BS:** 176 1827.

SKINNER, Frederick; b unk; d unk **RU:** Lieutenant, Served in MD Flying Camp in 1776 under Col Charles Griffith's 2nd Bn. By 1758, was in Capt John Brooks Co, MD **CEM:** Fairfax City; GPS 38.84690, -77.31330; Main St & Page Ave; Fairfax City **GS:** N **SP:** Mar (1778 MD) Betty Johns **VI:** No further data **P:** unk **BLW:** unk **RG:** N **MK:** N **PH:** N **SS:** A pg 239 **BS:** 61 vol III pg FX-153.

SKINNER, Henry; b 16 Jan 1760; d Aft Jan 1845 **RU:** Lieutenant, Served in VA Line. Ent serv 1779 in 7th & 8th Cont Lines in 1779. Served in Capt's Reddick and Knott's companies, Col Matthew's Regt **CEM:** Cypress Chapel; GPS 36.61799, -76.59148; 1891 Cypress Chapel Rd; Suffolk City **GS:** Y **SP:** Sarah Augusta Lassiter **VI:** Appl for BLW #2014-100 (BLW claim was indicated as fraudulent). Sol appl for pen 8 Jul 1833 in Nansemond Co age 74. S7521 **P:** Y **BLW:** N **RG:** N **MK:** N **PH:** unk **SS:** DAR Ancestor #A104814; E pg 716; K Vol 5 pg 82; CG Vol 3 pg 3153 **BS:** 144 Henry Skin.

RU=Rank/Unit	CEM=Cemetery	GS=Gravestone	SP=Spousal Information
VI=Other Veteran Info	P=Pension	BLW=Bounty/Land Warrant	RG=Registered Grave
MK=SAR/DAR Marker	PH=Photo	SS=Service Source	BS=Burial Source

307

SKIPWITH, Peyton; b BD unk, Mecklenburg Co; d 11 Oct 1824 **RU:** Lieutenant Colonel, Commanded a Regt in Lawson's Brigade **CEM:** Fincastle Presbyterian; GPS 37.50017, -79.87558; 108 E Back St, Fincastle; Botetourt **GS:** Y **SP:** No info **VI:** Son of Humberston & Lelia (-----) Skipworth of Prestwould, Mecklenburg Co. Name is on the SAR plaque at this cemetery **P:** unk **BLW:** unk **RG:** N **MK:** Y **PH:** unk **SS:** Unit Named in Pension Record **BS:** 196.

SKIPWITH, Peyton Sr; b 11 Dec 1740; d 9 Oct 1805 **RU:** Patriot, Gave material aid to the cause. Performed public service as member of Committee of Safety 8 May 1775, Justice 13 Nov 1775, Sherriff 10 Mar 1777 **CEM:** Prestwould; GPS unk; Clarksville; Mecklenburg **GS:** Y **SP:** Jean (-----) (__-19 May 1826) **VI:** No further data **P:** N **BLW:** N **RG:** N **MK:** N **PH:** unk **SS:** AL Ct Bk pg 2, 18; DB pg 129 **BS:** 54 pg 106; 213 pg 335.

SLACK, Abraham; b 26 Dec 1755 Bucks Co, PA; d 1833 **RU:** Private, Served in Capt Henry Vanhorn's Co, Lt Col Joseph Kirkbride Regt, Buck Co, PA Militia **CEM:** Slack Family, aka Chattin Family; GPS unk; On hillside of Chattin farm, nr Chamblissburg; Bedford **GS:** Y **SP:** Mary Patterson (1743 Bucks Co, PA-1825 Bedford Co) widow of Abraham Huddleston **VI:** No further data **P:** unk **BLW:** unk **RG:** unk **MK:** N **PH:** Y **SS:** J- DAR Hatcher; CI PA Archives 2d series Vol 14 pg 175; DD **BS:** JLARC 2; 196.

SLADE, William; b unk; d Jul 1800 **RU:** Private, Served at Baltimore, May - Sep 1781 **CEM:** Old Christ Church Episcopal; GPS 38.80625, -77.04718; 118 N Washington St; Alexandria City **GS:** N **SP:** No info **VI:** No further data **P:** unk **BLW:** unk **RG:** Y **MK:** N **PH:** N **SS:** AP RW Roll MD **BS:** 20 pg 142.

SLAGLE, George; b c1761, PA; d 21 Apr 1820 **RU:** Drummer, Served in Forman's Troops, York Co, PA **CEM:** Trinity Lutheran; GPS 38.17201, -78.86820; 2564 Rockfish Rd, Crimora; Augusta **GS:** Y **SP:** Catharine Koiner (1766-1855) d/o Michael (1720-1796) & Margaret (Diller) Keinadt (1734-1813) **VI:** No further data **P:** unk **BLW:** unk **RG:** Y **MK:** Y **PH:** unk **SS:** BT **BS:** JLARC 1 ,52, 62; 196.

SLAUGHTER, Augustin(e) Augustus; b c1752-1758; d Bet 23 Nov-27 Dec 1814 **RU:** Surgeon, Served in 7th VA Regt, VA Line, Apr 1776 to Feb. 1777 as supernumerary surgeon **CEM:** St Paul's Episcopal; GPS 36.84733, -76.28554; 201 St Paul's Blvd; Norfolk City **GS:** Y **SP:** No info **VI:** Recd BLW #2168-400 & 2198. Longtime resident of the borough of Norfolk. Was a surgeon **P:** unk **BLW:** Y **RG:** Y **MK:** Y **PH:** unk **SS:** CB, J-NSSAR 1993 Reg; K Vol 5 pg 84; CG Vol 3 pg 3158; SAR application 252, 529 **BS:** JLARC 1.

SLAUGHTER, John Suggart (Suggate); b 2 Nov 1759, Culpeper Co; d 16 Jan 1830 **RU:** Lieutenant Colonel, Enlisted c1776 age 17, and was Lt and Capt Cont Army, Gen Daniel Morgan's Riflemen. Was in battles at Princeton, Trenton, and Saratoga. Was at Valley Forge **CEM:** Slaughter Family "Clover Hill"; GPS unk; Woodville, Hawthorne; Rappahannock **GS:** Y **SP:** Mar (Oct/Nov 1779) Susanna (Susan) Brown **VI:** Mar while stationed in barracks **P:** unk **BLW:** Y **RG:** Y **MK:** N **PH:** unk **SS:** BY pg 57; J-NSSAR 1993 Reg **BS:** JLARC 1.

SLAUGHTER, Philip; b 2 Dec 1758, (pension) or 4 Dec 1748, (TS) Catalpa, Culpeper Co; d 26 Apr or Dec 1849 **RU:** Captain, Served in PA Line. Was Pvt Culpeper Minute Men 1775 and in Col Jameson's Troop of Calvary Spring 1776. Served as Lt in Capt Gabriel Long's Rifle Co 1776 and in 11th Cont Regt 1777. Promoted to Capt 1778 in 7th VA Regt and fought at Brandywine, Germantown, Monmouth, and Stoney Pt. Wintered at Valley Forge **CEM:** Shockoe Hill; GPS 37.55190, -77.43170; 4th & Hospital Sts; Richmond City **GS:** Y **SP:** 1) Margaret French Strother (1759-1835) 2) Elizabeth Towles **VI:** Son of James (1732-1799) & Susannah (Clayton) (1740-1818) Slaughter. Recd BLW #1653-300 8 Jul 1830. Sol had appl BLW Culpeper Co where sol lived during rev. Recd pension 1830 Culpeper Co. W29886. Dau. Ann Mercer Slaughter blind & helpless, pensioned by special act of Congress 8 Feb 1893 **P:** Y **BLW:** Y **RG:** Y **MK:** Y **PH:** unk **SS:** BY pg 283; K Vol 5 pg 85; CG Vol 3 pg 3159 **BS:** JLARC 1, 2, 77.

SLAUGHTER, Robert; b 1748; d 2 Jan 1832 **RU:** Second Lieutenant/Patriot, Served in 3rd Cont Line. Became 2nd Lt 20 Jun 1776, and resigned 18 Dec 1777. Gave material aid to cause **CEM:** Hamilton Family; GPS unk; Rt 636; Spotsylvania **GS:** Y **SP:** Mar (2 Dec 1772) Sarah (-----) (__-17 Nov 1834) **VI:** No further data **P:** unk **BLW:** unk **RG:** Y **MK:** N **PH:** unk **SS:** E pg 718; AL Ct Bk II pg 9 Culpeper Co **BS:** 06 pg 83.

SLOAN, John; b Mar 1758; d 26 Feb 1815 **RU:** Private, Served in 8th Cont Line **CEM:** Trinity United Methodist; GPS 39.13600, -77.00610; 2911 Cameron Mills Rd; Alexandria City **GS:** Y **SP:** Ann Rebecca

RU=Rank/Unit	CEM=Cemetery	GS=Gravestone	SP=Spousal Information
VI=Other Veteran Info	P=Pension	BLW=Bounty/Land Warrant	RG=Registered Grave
MK=SAR/DAR Marker	PH=Photo	SS=Service Source	BS=Burial Source

308

(-----) (3 Sep 1756-26 Feb 1815) **VI:** No further data **P:** unk **BLW:** unk **RG:** Y **MK:** N **PH:** unk **SS:** E pg 718 **BS:** 23 pg 139.

SLUTE, James; b unk; d 1823 **RU:** Ensign, Served in Augusta Co Militia. (Refer to Augusta Co Order books for Militia Co assigned) **CEM:** Old Providence; GPS 37.96151, -79.71000; 1005 Spottswood Rd, Spottswood; Augusta **GS:** N **SP:** No info **VI:** No further data **P:** unk **BLW:** unk **RG:** unk **MK:** unk **PH:** N **SS:** NSSAR Ancestor #P-291228 **BS:** JLARC 63.

SMITH, Abraham; b c1722, Ulster Province, Ireland; d c1783 **RU:** Colonel/Patriot, Was in 1776 Col of Militia. In 1778 was one of the Justices of Rockingham Co and was County Lt, 27 Apr 1778 **CEM:** Smith Family; GPS unk; Rt 727; Rockingham **GS:** Y **SP:** 1) Martha McDowell Reed 2) Charlotte Gamble 3) Sarah Caldwell **VI:** Son of Capt John & (-----) Smith. Capt of Militia Augusta 1756 in French & Indian War. In 1757 prisoner French dominions. In 1758 court marshalled, and acquitted. Died at Egypt Plantation, Rockingham Co **P:** unk **BLW:** unk **RG:** Y **MK:** Y **PH:** Y **SS:** O **BS:** 04.

SMITH, Andrew; b c1756; d 1822 **RU:** Sergeant, Appt Sergeant 9 Feb 1776. Served in Capt John Nelson's Co, PA Regt, commanded by Col John De Haas **CEM:** Shockoe Hill; GPS 37.55190, -77.43170; 4th & Hospital Sts; Richmond City **GS:** Y **SP:** No info **VI:** No pen or BLW **P:** N **BLW:** N **RG:** N **MK:** N **PH:** unk **SS:** A pg 181 **BS:** 57 pg 1.

SMITH, Armistead; b 01 Jan 1737 or 1757, Mathews Co; d 12 Sep 1817 **RU:** Patriot, Gave material aid to cause **CEM:** Ware Episcopal; GPS 37.42275, -76.50789; 7825 John Clayton Mem Hwy; Gloucester **GS:** Y **SP:** Martha Tabb (21 Oct 1757-16 Sep 1821) d/o Edward & Lucy (-----) Tabb **VI:** GS moved fr Toddsbury Plantation on North River in July 1924. He was the 8th Rector of Ware Church 1792-1817. Epitaph recorded 1959 **P:** N **BLW:** N **RG:** Y **MK:** N **PH:** Y **SS:** AL Ct Bk lt pg iii, 2, 17 Gloucester Co; AK **BS:** 48 pg 80; 207.

SMITH, B Egbert; b unk; d 1781 **RU:** Soldier, Served fr NY, killed in the battle at Yorktown **CEM:** Yorktown Victory Monument Tablet; GPS 38.28350, -78.54150; Yorktown; York **GS:** U **SP:** No info **VI:** No further data **P:** unk **BLW:** unk **RG:** unk **MK:** unk **PH:** unk **SS:** J-Yorktown Historian **BS:** JLARC 74.

SMITH, Byrd; b c1762; d 23 Jul 1827 **RU:** Private, Served in Cumberland Co Militia **CEM:** Moses Smith Place; GPS 37.49639, -78.24486; Jct Rt 60 and Stoney Point Rd; Cumberland **GS:** U **SP:** Gillea Arnold (__-bef 1822) **VI:** Son of Robert (1725-1776) & Elizabeth (-----) (__-1804) Smith **P:** unk **BLW:** unk **RG:** N **MK:** N **PH:** unk **SS:** E pg 720; CZ **BS:** 60 Cumberland; 196.

SMITH, Caleb Jr; b 1765; d 14 Jul 1803 **RU:** Private, 2 VA bde, 5th, 7th, 11th, 14th Cont Lines. Also in Col Morgan's Rifleman Regt **CEM:** Old Christ Church Episcopal; GPS 38.80625, -77.04718; 118 N Washington St; Alexandria City **GS:** Y **SP:** No info **VI:** Died age 38 **P:** unk **BLW:** unk **RG:** Y **MK:** N **PH:** unk **SS:** E pg 720 **BS:** 20 pg 142; 196.

SMITH, Edward; b 10 Jun 1752; d 17 Dec 1826 **RU:** Patriot, Gave two guns to Dunmore Co Militia, 1775 **CEM:** Mt Hebron; GPS 39.10916, -78.09497; 305 E Boscawen St; Winchester City **GS:** Y **SP:** Elizabeth (-----) (11 Aug 1761-7 Nov 1832) **VI:** Died in Frederick Co **P:** N **BLW:** N **RG:** Y **MK:** N **PH:** no **SS:** AL CT Bk pg 26, 30; Z pg 80 **BS:** 50 pg 51, 52.

SMITH, Fred; b 1717; d 1794 **RU:** Major, Served in Bedford Co Militia **CEM:** Hat Creek Presbyterian; GPS 37.06570, -78.54240; 6442 Hat Creek Rd, Brookneal; Campbell **GS:** U **SP:** Susanna (-----) **VI:** No further data **P:** unk **BLW:** unk **RG:** unk **MK:** N **PH:** unk **SS:** NSSAR Ancestor #P-291940 **BS:** JLARC 36.

SMITH, George; b 19 Aug 1765; d 30 Aug 1822 or 1828 **RU:** Private, Served in Capt John Hodge's Troop of Light Dragoons 1 Oct 1781 to 14 Feb 1782 **CEM:** Dumfries Public; GPS 38.34110, -77.19964; 17821 Mine Rd, Dumfries; Prince William **GS:** Y **SP:** No info **VI:** SAR Monument (monument is a marker, as well) **P:** N **BLW:** N **RG:** Y **MK:** Y **PH:** Y **SS:** G pg 706 **BS:** 94 pg 18.

SMITH, George W; b unk; d 1833 **RU:** Patriot, Gave material aid to cause **CEM:** Fairfax Meeting House; GPS 39.18557, -77.60589; Water St & Waterford Rd, Waterford; Loudoun **GS:** Y **SP:** No info **VI:** No further data **P:** unk **BLW:** unk **RG:** N **MK:** N **PH:** unk **SS:** D Vol 1 pg 344 **BS:** 25 pg 291.

RU=Rank/Unit	CEM=Cemetery	GS=Gravestone	SP=Spousal Information
VI=Other Veteran Info	P=Pension	BLW=Bounty/Land Warrant	RG=Registered Grave
MK=SAR/DAR Marker	PH=Photo	SS=Service Source	BS=Burial Source

309

SMITH, George William; b 1762, Bathurst, Essex Co; d 26 Dec 1811 **RU:** Private, Served in John Marshall's Co, Fauquier Co Militia **CEM:** Monumental Church; GPS unk; 1224 E Broad St; Richmond City **GS:** U **SP:** 1) Sara Adams 2) Lucy Franklin Read (1733-1845) d/o John Royall & (-----) Read **VI:** Son of Meriwether (1730-1790) & Elizabeth (Daingerfield) Smith. Was VA Governor 1811. Died in theater fire in Richmond **P:** unk **BLW:** unk **RG:** unk **MK:** unk **PH:** unk **SS:** DQ Chapter 1 **BS:** 196.

SMITH, Humphrey (Humphreys); b Sep 1760, Botetourt Co; d Jun 1847 **RU:** Private, Served in 1st Cont Line **CEM:** Smith Chapel; GPS 37.03873, -80.20393; Directions not identified; Floyd **GS:** N **SP:** Mar (5 Jul 1785 Botetourt Co) Eleanor McElhaney (c1740-30 May 1842) d/o Robert (1740-aft Jul 1785) & May (-----) (__-1784) McElhaney **VI:** No further data **P:** unk **BLW:** unk **RG:** unk **MK:** unk **PH:** N **SS:** E pg 721 **BS:** JLARC 29.

SMITH, Isaac; b 4 Nov 1734, Accomack Co; d 23 Mar 1813 **RU:** Paymaster, Served in the Navy **CEM:** Selma; GPS unk; E of Bus Rt 13, .4 mi N of Rt 631 Eastville; Northampton **GS:** Y **SP:** 1) Mar (c1755) Elizabeth Custis Teakle d/o Thomas & Elizabeth (Custis) Teackle 2) Mar (8 May 1790) Elizabeth Goffigon **VI:** Son of Isaac Sr. & Sarah (West) Smith **P:** unk **BLW:** unk **RG:** N **MK:** N **PH:** unk **SS:** E pg 721 **BS:** 42 pg 77.

SMITH, Isaac Watt Sr; b 1760; d 1845 **RU:** Sergeant, Served in 1st, 2d, 3rd and 10th Cont Lines **CEM:** Locust Grove; GPS unk; Locust Grove nr Red Hill Boys Home; Charlotte **GS:** U **SP:** Sarah Hancock (__-1812) **VI:** On pension list of 1835 age 74. Rec'd 200 acres BLW 19 Mar 1784 **P:** Y **BLW:** Y **RG:** unk **MK:** unk **PH:** unk **SS:** E pg 721; F pg 69 **BS:** 226.

SMITH, Jacob; b 1756; d 19 Aug 1836 **RU:** Private, Served in VA Line. Ent serv in Rockingham Co. Served in Capt Burbank's Co,12th Regt. Was taken prisoner 7 Jul 1777 **CEM:** Jollett; GPS unk; Rt 609 N of Jollett; Page **GS:** Y **SP:** Mar (1782 Rockingham Co) Winna (-----) **VI:** Appl pen Rockingham Co 18 Sep 1818 age 59. Widow appl pen 23 Oct 1939 Page Co age 75. W19052 **P:** Y **BLW:** unk **RG:** Y **MK:** N **PH:** unk **SS:** A pg 130-1; CG Vol 3 pg 3192 **BS:** 120 Hartman.

SMITH, James; b c1761; d 11 Jan 1815 **RU:** Patriot, Paid personal property Tax 1782 (considered supply tax for paying Rev War expenses) **CEM:** Smith Family; GPS unk; Mantua Farm Rd; Northumberland **GS:** Y **SP:** No info **VI:** No further data **P:** N **BLW:** N **RG:** unk **MK:** unk **PH:** unk **SS:** EB pg 21 **BS:** 227 pg 124.

SMITH, James; b 1752; d 1833 **RU:** Soldier, Served in Cont Line **CEM:** Blue Spring; GPS 36.65967, -82.41181; Hiltons Area; Scott **GS:** U **SP:** No info **VI:** No further data **P:** unk **BLW:** unk **RG:** unk **MK:** unk **PH:** unk **SS:** E pg 721 **BS:** 196.

SMITH, Jeremiah; b 1711 NJ; d 4 Sep 1787 **RU:** Captain/Patriot, Gave material aid to cause **CEM:** Smith; GPS unk; Gore; Frederick **GS:** U **SP:** Mar (c1752 Frederick Co) (-----) (__-Nov 1769) **VI:** No further data **P:** unk **BLW:** unk **RG:** Y **MK:** unk **PH:** unk **SS:** J-NSSAR 1993 Reg, J- DAR Hatcher; AL Ct Bk pg 36 Frederick Co **BS:** JLARC 1, 2.

SMITH, Jesse; b 1730; d 12 Jun 1821 **RU:** Corporal/Patriot, Served in VA Line. Enl Henry Co 1778 in 3rd VA Regt of VA Light Dragoons. Served in Capt Scott's Co, 3rd Cont Line 1779. Gave material aid to cause **CEM:** Smith family; GPS unk; 1 mi W of Skipwith Rd, 1.5 N of Three Chopt; Henrico **GS:** Y **SP:** 1) Mar (10 Nov 1787, Chesterfield Co) Martha Keys (__-29 Mar 1805 - two days before marrying 2d wife) 2) Mar (31 Mar 1805) Mrs. Lucy Cooke/Cocke (1773-__), wid of Robert Cocke. (Elisha Price signed mar bond with him on 29 Mar 1805 Henrico Co) **VI:** Widow appl pen Jan 1855 Henrico Co age 82. R9789 **P:** Y **BLW:** unk **RG:** N **MK:** N **PH:** unk **SS:** E pg 721; K Vol 5 pg 100; AL Ct Bk pg 9 Henrico Co; CG Vol 3 pg 3196 **BS:** 114; 168 Smith Bur..

SMITH, John; b 07 May 1750, Middlesex Co; d 4 Mar 1836 **RU:** Colonel, Ent serv 1776 Frederick Co as Col of VA Militia. Ent serv Frederick Co in 3rd Div of VA Miltia **CEM:** Mt Hebron; GPS 39.10916, -78.09497; 305 E Boscawen St; Winchester City **GS:** U **SP:** Mar (1782) Animus Anna Bull (1760 PA-15 Sep 1831) **VI:** After RW, obtained rank of Maj General of 3rd Div of Militia in War of 1812. Appl for pen 4 Mar 1833. Lived at "Hackwood". Widower recd pen S6114. Was 15 term member of Congress, VA State Legislature 1779, Senator 1792. Died in Frederick Co **P:** Y **BLW:** unk **RG:** unk **MK:** unk **PH:** unk **SS:** DAR Ancestor #A105975; CG Vol 3 pg 3204-5 **BS:** JLARC 4, 47.

RU=Rank/Unit   CEM=Cemetery   GS=Gravestone   SP=Spousal Information
VI=Other Veteran Info   P=Pension   BLW=Bounty/Land Warrant   RG=Registered Grave
MK=SAR/DAR Marker   PH=Photo   SS=Service Source   BS=Burial Source

310

SMITH, John; b c1745; d 1811 **RU:** Patriot, Gave 3 complete pairs of horse harnesses to cause **CEM:** Smith Family; GPS unk; Rt 688, Orlean; Fauquier **GS:** Y **SP:** No info **VI:** No further data **P:** N **BLW:** N **RG:** N **MK:** N **PH:** unk **SS:** D Fauquier Co pg 18 **BS:** 18 pg 79.

SMITH, John; b c1757; d 1785 **RU:** Patriot, Gave material aid to the cause **CEM:** St Paul's Episcopal; GPS 36.84733, -76.28554; 201 St Paul's Blvd; Norfolk City **GS:** Y **SP:** No info **VI:** No further data **P:** N **BLW:** N **RG:** Y **MK:** N **PH:** unk **SS:** AL Ct Bk I pg 7, 18 **BS:** 87 pg 30.

SMITH, John; b 26 Aug 1753, PA; d 1851 **RU:** Private, Served first in1775 in a PA artillery unit and served one yr fighting Indians. Later served in Capt McCutchen's Co Augusta Co Militia **CEM:** Old Stone Presbyterian; GPS 38.23926, -78.97356; 28 Old Stone Church Ln, Ft Defiance; Augusta **GS:** U **SP:** Mar (13 Sep 1791 Albemarle Co) Martha Wallace (1774-1821) **VI:** He received a pension in 1818 while residing in Ft Defiance. He also resided after the war in Albemarle and Goochland Cos **P:** Y **BLW:** unk **RG:** unk **MK:** U **PH:** unk **SS:** DAR Ancestor #A105935; J- DAR Hatcher; E pg 722; K Vol 5 pg 101 **BS:** JLARC 2.

SMITH, John; b c1761, Frederick Co; d 29 Oct 1812 **RU:** Private, Served in Capt Peter Byron Bruin's Co, 11th VA Regt, commanded by Co Daniel Morgan **CEM:** Stone Chapel Presbyterian; GPS 39.22610, -78.01060; Old Charles Town Rd, Berryville; Clarke **GS:** Y **SP:** Elizabeth (-----) - wife or consort **VI:** No further data **P:** unk **BLW:** unk **RG:** Y **MK:** Y **PH:** Y **SS:** E pg 722 **BS:** 58 pg 95.

SMITH, John; b 1755, England; d Oct 1802 **RU:** Private/Patriot, Served in VA State Militia. Gave material aid to cause **CEM:** Smith Family; GPS unk; Mt Pleasant Farm, now Fentress Naval Auxiliary Airfield; Chesapeake City **GS:** Y **SP:** Mar (__, Norfolk Co) Julia Phillips (__-18 Oct 1802) **VI:** Govt grave stone **P:** unk **BLW:** unk **RG:** unk **MK:** unk **PH:** unk **SS:** DAR Ancestor #A106003; B; D Vol 2, pg 719, 723, 726 **BS:** JLARC 116.

SMITH, John "Dutch"; b Mar 1760, Burke Co, NC; d 1815 **RU:** Private, Served in Capt Mordelia Clarke's Co. Was in Battle of Cowpens, SC. Discharged Mar 1781. Also served 6 mos NC Militia. Served again Apr 1781 & Sep 1781 in NC for total of 12 mos service **CEM:** Spurrier Family; GPS unk; Rt 691, Hiltons; Scott **GS:** Y **SP:** No info **VI:** Recd pen 81931 **P:** Y **BLW:** unk **RG:** Y **MK:** N **PH:** unk **SS:** AK pension rec **BS:** 4-Nov-06.

SMITH, Joseph; b 14 Feb 1761, Berkeley Co; d 20 Jul 1846 **RU:** Private, Served in Col Jehu Eyre Regt, Philadelphia Militia. Was POW **CEM:** Trinity United Methodist; GPS 39.13600, -77.00610; 2911 Cameron Mills Rd; Alexandria City **GS:** Y **SP:** Mary Donahue (Apr 1767-20 Mar 1847) **VI:** Died age 85 yrs 5 mos. Recd pen **P:** Y **BLW:** unk **RG:** N **MK:** N **PH:** unk **SS:** E pg 722; AP Gen Morgan R; CI PA Archive 6th series Vol 1 pg 474-475, 484 Fairfax pension **BS:** 23 pg 140.

SMITH, Joseph; b 1763, MD; d 9 Jul 1842 **RU:** Private, Ent serv Halifax Co. Enl as substitute for Harmon Miller. Ent serv later as substitute for father James Smith. Served in Capt Charles Wall's Co Jan 1781. In Apr 1781 was under Capt Wm Clark. Discharged 28 Jul 1781 by Col Priddy **CEM:** GSA Camp Shawnee; GPS unk; Ringgold; Pittsylvania **GS:** Y **SP:** Mar (5 Jun 1793 Pittsylvania Co) Barsha Humphrey (c1770-__) d/o James & (-----) Humphrey **VI:** Son of James & (-----) Smith. Sol appl pen 17 Sep 1832 Pittsylvania Co. Widow appl pen 26 Aug 1847 Pittsylvania Co age 77. W3725, Recd BLW #13900-160-55. Discharge preserved in pension application **P:** Y **BLW:** Y **RG:** unk **MK:** unk **PH:** unk **SS:** J-NSSAR 2000 Reg; K Vol 5 pg 107; CG Vol 3 pg 3207 **BS:** 174 JLARC 76.

SMITH, Joseph T; b 1722, King George Co; d 6 Jan 1793 **RU:** Lieutenant/Patriot, Appointed as Lt 27 Aug 1781. Gave material aid to cause **CEM:** Mt Eccentric; GPS unk; 2 mi S of The Plains; Fauquier **GS:** N **SP:** Margaret Rowley (__-1793) **VI:** No further data **P:** unk **BLW:** unk **RG:** N **MK:** N **PH:** N **SS:** DAR Ancestor #A106282; AL Ct Bk pg 3, 6 Fauquier Co; AZ pg 201 **BS:** 95 Mt Eccentric.

SMITH, Matthew; b 1745, Edenburg, Scotland; d 1795 **RU:** Private, Served in Lt Col Edward Hand's 1st Regt of Cont Troops, PA **CEM:** White Oak Crossroads; GPS unk; Nr Charlottesville; Charlottesville City **GS:** U **SP:** Mar (1763) Permelia Greene (1746/7-1803) **VI:** No further data **P:** unk **BLW:** unk **RG:** unk **MK:** unk **PH:** unk **SS:** DAR Ancestor #A106441; J- DAR Hatcher; DD **BS:** JLARC 2.

SMITH, Meriwether; b 1730; d 25 Jan 1794 **RU:** Colonel/Patriot, Served as Col of Essex Co Militia. Gave material aid to cause Was member House of Burgesses 1774-75, and delegate to Rev War

RU=Rank/Unit	CEM=Cemetery	GS=Gravestone	SP=Spousal Information
VI=Other Veteran Info	P=Pension	BLW=Bounty/Land Warrant	RG=Registered Grave
MK=SAR/DAR Marker	PH=Photo	SS=Service Source	BS=Burial Source

311

Conventions 1775-76, and member Continental Congress 1778-79 & 1781. **CEM:** Bathhurst Plantation; GPS 37.88976, -76.82628; Nr Dunnsville; Essex **GS:** N **SP:** 1) Mar (c1760) Alice Lee 2) Mar (c1769) Elizabeth Daingerfield **VI:** Born and bur at "Bathurst" nr Dunnsville.Essex Co. Was on Committee of Safety in 1774 and signer of Leedstown Resolves in 1766. Was member House of Delegates 1781-1782, 1785, 1788 **P:** unk **BLW:** N **RG:** N **MK:** N **PH:** N **SS:** AL Ct Bk pg 2 Essex Co; BQ pg 7155 **BS:** JLARC 65;196.

SMITH, Ralph; b 1753; d 28 Feb 1827 **RU:** Patriot, Gave material aid to cause **CEM:** Mt Hermon United Methodist; GPS 37.14500, -79.31170; Rt 712, Lynch Station; Campbell **GS:** Y **SP:** No info **VI:** Founder of Mt Herman Methodist Church 1825 **P:** N **BLW:** N **RG:** N **MK:** unk **PH:** N **SS:** AL Ct Bk pg 3 Pittsylvania Co **BS:** 196.

SMITH, Samuel; b unk; d 1841 **RU:** Lieutenant, Received as Lt 1782, Loudoun Co Militia **CEM:** Goose Creek; GPS 39.11250, -77.69527; Rt 722, Lincoln; Loudoun **GS:** Y **SP:** No info **VI:** No further data **P:** unk **BLW:** unk **RG:** Y **MK:** N **PH:** unk **SS:** E pg 724 **BS:** 25 pg 293.

SMITH, Thomas; b unk; d Aft Jan 1787 **RU:** Captain/Patriot, Appointed Capt Isle of Wight Co Militia, 14 Jul 1782. Gave material aid to cause **CEM:** St Luke's Church; GPS 36.93940, -76.58670; 14477 Benns Church Blvd, Smithfield; Isle of Wight **GS:** Y **SP:** Mar (9 Jan 1787, Isle of Wight Co) Ann Edwards **VI:** No further data **P:** unk **BLW:** unk **RG:** N **MK:** N **PH:** unk **SS:** G pg 194; AL Ct Bk pg 16 Isle of Wight Co **BS:** 117 pg 6.

SMITH, Thomas; b 29 Dec 1719, Powhatan Co; d 25 Sep 1786 **RU:** Patriot, Gave material aid to cause **CEM:** Manakin; GPS 37.56560, -77.71000; Rt 711 vic jct with Rt 635; Powhatan **GS:** U **SP:** Frances Martha Stovall **VI:** Died in Henrico Co **P:** N **BLW:** N **RG:** unk **MK:** unk **PH:** unk **SS:** Al Ct Bk pg 33 Cumberland Co **BS:** 196.

SMITH, Thomas; b 1739; d 20 May 1789 **RU:** Patriot, Was presiding officer over First and Second Committee of Safety 1775, Westmoreland Co **CEM:** Glebe; GPS unk; In garden area of Glebe Parish House, Glebe Creek, Cople Parish; Westmoreland **GS:** U **SP:** Mar (7 Dec 1765) Mary Smith (__-14 Dec 1791) d/o John & Mary (Jacquelin) Smith **VI:** Son of Gregory & Lucy (Cooke) Smith. Rector of Cople Parish 1764 – 1789 **P:** N **BLW:** N **RG:** unk **MK:** unk **PH:** unk **SS:** EC pg 6473 **BS:** 189 pg 57.

SMITH, Thomas; b 1738; d 1789 **RU:** Patriot, Gave material aid to cause **CEM:** Glebe; GPS unk; In garden area of Glebe Parish House, Glebe Creek, Cople Parish; Westmoreland **GS:** N **SP:** Mar (1756 Northumberland Co) Elizabeth Garlington **VI:** No further data **P:** N **BLW:** N **RG:** N **MK:** N **PH:** N **SS:** AL Comm Bk **BS:** 189 pg 56.

SMITH, William; b 5 Feb 1741, Prince William Co; d 22 Feb 1803 **RU:** Ensign, Was in Fauquier Co Militia in 1778 and 1779 **CEM:** Mt Eccentric; GPS unk; 2 mi S of The Plains; Fauquier **GS:** N **SP:** Mar (1773) Elizabeth Doniplan (12 Apr 1744,-15 jan 1809 Fauquier Co) **VI:** No further data **P:** unk **BLW:** unk **RG:** N **MK:** N **PH:** N **SS:** DAR Ancestor #A106143; E pg 725 **BS:** 95 Mt Eccentric.

SMITH, William; b 25 May 1746, prob Gloucester England; d 7 Oct 1802 **RU:** Patriot, Was on Committee for Articles of Confederation 1774. Gave beef to cause and use of stable 1781 **CEM:** St George's Episcopal; GPS unk; 905 Princess Anne; Fredericksburg City **GS:** Y **SP:** Mary (-----) (20 Mar 1750-8 Jul 1822) **VI:** Processioner & vestryman of church. Son Jr was in War of 1812 **P:** N **BLW:** N **RG:** Y **MK:** N **PH:** unk **SS:** D pg 857-8,860 **BS:** 12 pg 114.

SMITH, William; b 1755; d 1835 **RU:** Private, Service information not obtained from pension records **CEM:** Smith Family; GPS unk; 7 mi N of Covington; Alleghany **GS:** N **SP:** No info **VI:** Rec'd pen Alleghany Co **P:** Y **BLW:** unk **RG:** N **MK:** N **PH:** N **SS:** E pg 725 **BS:** 160 Smith.

SMITH, William; b 19 Mar 1743, Farnham Parish, Richmond Co; d 4 Feb 1836 **RU:** Spy-Scout, Entered service 1775 in VA Regt. Began serving as spy at time of Point Pleasant and remained same throughout war **CEM:** Smith Cemetery; GPS 37.86140, -79.98970; Rt 687, Mt Pleasant; Alleghany **GS:** Y **SP:** 1) (-----) 2) Mar (10 Aug 1780) Mary Wright (14 Jun 1759, Botetourt Co-6 Oct 1858) **VI:** Son of David Smith and Mary Bryant. Sol appl pen 17 Nov 1832. Widow appl pen Jun 1842 Alleghany Co. W6094, 16897. Vet Admin monument, reads "Continental Line." Mary Wright's name inscribed on this stone as well **P:** Y **BLW:** unk **RG:** Y **MK:** N **PH:** Y **SS:** K pg 119; K Vol 5 pg 119; CG Vol 3 pg 3235; B **BS:** 196.

RU=Rank/Unit   CEM=Cemetery   GS=Gravestone   SP=Spousal Information
VI=Other Veteran Info P=Pension   BLW=Bounty/Land Warrant RG=Registered Grave
MK=SAR/DAR Marker   PH=Photo   SS=Service Source   BS=Burial Source

312

SMITH, William Henry; b unk; d 1808 **RU:** Soldier, Contact George Washington SAR Chapter for service for men listed on their cemetery plaque **CEM:** Old Presbyterian Meeting House; GPS 38.48528, -77.23532; 323 S Fairfax St; Alexandria City **GS:** Y **SP:** No info **VI:** Listed on SAR plaque in cemetery **P:** unk **BLW:** unk **RG:** Y **MK:** Y **PH:** unk **SS:** J-NSSAR 1993 Reg; AK **BS:** JLARC 1; 23 pg 108; 196.

SMITH (SMYTH), Adam B; b 1720; d 1785 **RU:** Chaplain, Served in Botetourt Co Militia 1777 **CEM:** Fincastle Presbyterian; GPS 37.50017, -79.87558; 108 E Back St, Fincastle; Botetourt **GS:** N **SP:** No info **VI:** Name is on the SAR plaque in cemetery **P:** unk **BLW:** unk **RG:** Y **MK:** Y **PH:** N **SS:** E pg 749; AR Vol 4 pg 41 **BS:** JLARC 2, 76.

SNAPP, George; b Feb 1752, Bucks Co, PA; d unk **RU:** Private, Enlisted Frederick Co **CEM:** Mt Hebron; GPS 39.10916, -78.09497; 305 E Boscawen St; Winchester City **GS:** Y **SP:** Mar (07 Dec 1804, Frederick Co) Anna Meyers (Return) **VI:** Appl for pen 23 Oct 1833 & 1837 **P:** Y **BLW:** unk **RG:** Y **MK:** unk **PH:** unk **SS:** J-NSSAR 2000 Reg; NSSAR Ancestor #P-293546 **BS:** JLARC 76.

SNAPP, Lawrence Sr; b 1723, Mulhausen, Departement du Bas Rhin, Alsace, France; d May 1782 **RU:** Captain, Served in Dunmore (Shenandoah) Co Militia in Capt Alexander Machir's Co, Strasburg District. Later commanded a co there **CEM:** St Paul's Lutheran; GPS 38.99140, -78.36250; 156 W Washington, Strasburg; Shenandoah **GS:** U **SP:** Mar (1746 Frederick Co) Margaret Stephens (1724/25 Rhineland, Germany-Jun 1801 Shenandoah Co), d/o Hans Peter & Maria Christina (-----) Stephens **VI:** Member of Frederick Co Militia on 24 July 1758 in French and Indian War. Vestryman of Beckford Parish in St Paul's Lutheran Church in Strasburg, Shenandoah Co. Probably bur there or on family farm, long since disappeared **P:** unk **BLW:** unk **RG:** unk **MK:** unk **PH:** unk **SS:** C pg 606 **BS:** 196.

SNEAD, Robert; b 23 May 1762 "within 9 mi of Hanover Court House"; d 19 Jan 1841 **RU:** Private, Ent serv 1778 as substitute for brother John, later brother Richer, later brother-in-law Elijah Pridee. Was at Battle of Yorktown Oct 1781 **CEM:** Snead Family; GPS unk; Rt 624 nr Hylas, nr main road; Hanover **GS:** U **SP:** Mar (1 Mar 1792) Sophia (-----) (28 Jun 1777-12 Mar 1844) **VI:** DAR marker placed at grave 1978. Pensioned 1832 Hanover Co, when living nr Ground Squirrel. Widow appl pen 1843 fr Hanover, Co age 65. Pension rejected - no reason given. R9891 **P:** N **BLW:** unk **RG:** Y **MK:** Y **PH:** unk **SS:** K Vol 5 pg 124 **BS:** JLARC 1, 2, 71.

SNIDOW, Christian; b 15 Mar 1760; d Oct 1836 **RU:** Lieutenant, Ent serv Montgomery Co 1776. Served in Giles Co Militia **CEM:** Horseshoe; GPS unk; Pembroke; Giles **GS:** Y **SP:** Mar (24 Aug 1784 Montgomery, Kanawha Co, WVA) Mary Burk (22 Jan 1762-3 May 1825) d/o Thomas (1741-1808) & Clara (Frazer) (1742-1811) Burke **VI:** Son of John Jacob & Mary Elizabeth (Helm) Snidow. Sol appl pen 26 May 1834 Giles Co. S17112. Represented Giles Co in VA House of Delegates. Gov't Gr st; DAR plaque. A Lt Col in War of 1812 **P:** Y **BLW:** unk **RG:** Y **MK:** Y **PH:** unk **SS:** K Vol 5 pg 127; CG Vol 3 pg 3241 **BS:** JLARC 1,2,26; 196.

SNIDOW, Jacob; b 15 Nov 1763, Lancaster Co, PA; d 1847 **RU:** Soldier, Ent serv Montgomery (later Giles) Co. Enlisted 1780, 81, 82 "to fight Indians". Also served in VA Line **CEM:** Snidow Farm, "Sugar Maple"; GPS unk; Rt 460 on Lilly Hill, Pembroke; Giles **GS:** U **SP:** Clara Burk **VI:** Sol appl pen 23 Nov 1835. R9903. Pension denied, prob because not part of regularly constituted military unit **P:** N **BLW:** unk **RG:** unk **MK:** unk **PH:** unk **SS:** K Vol 5 pg 127; CG Vol 3 pg 3241 **BS:** JLARC 2,4,26.

SNIDOW, Philip; b 1756, Lancaster Co, PA; d 28 Oct 1792 **RU:** Private, Served in Capt John Lucas's Co, Montgomery Co Militia **CEM:** Snidow Farm, "Sugar Maple"; GPS unk; Rt 460 on Lilly Hill, Pembroke; Giles **GS:** U **SP:** Mar (14 Feb 1782 Henry Co) Barbara (Prillarman) Martin (1764-1848) **VI:** Son of John Jacob & Mary Elizabeth (Helm) Snidow. DAR plaque **P:** unk **BLW:** unk **RG:** unk **MK:** Y **PH:** Y **SS:** J- DAR Hatcher; B; G pg 234 **BS:** JLARC 2; 196.

SNODGRASS, David; b 1725, Washington Co; d 18 Oct 1814 **RU:** Patriot, Gave beef to cause 1776 **CEM:** Glade Spring Presbyterian; GPS 36.76720, -81.78720; 33234 Lee Hwy, Glade Spring; Washington **GS:** U **SP:** Margaret Glenn (1740-1816) **VI:** Son of William (1697-1766) & Catherine (Patterson) (1705-1783) Snodgrass **P:** N **BLW:** N **RG:** unk **MK:** unk **PH:** unk **SS:** DD cites Draper Papers, VA MSS, 5225, reel 121 **BS:** 196.

SNODGRASS, James; b 31 Oct 1762; d 3 Jul 1828 **RU:** Lieutenant, Was at King's Mountain under Campbell **CEM:** Rock Spring; GPS 37.78126, -79.44585; Jct Rt 803 & Liberty Hall Rd, Lodi; Washington

RU=Rank/Unit   CEM=Cemetery   GS=Gravestone   SP=Spousal Information
VI=Other Veteran Info   P=Pension   BLW=Bounty/Land Warrant   RG=Registered Grave
MK=SAR/DAR Marker   PH=Photo   SS=Service Source   BS=Burial Source

313

GS: U **SP:** Ann Long (23 May 1766-14 Oct 1845) **VI:** Son of David (1725-1814) & Margaret Ann (Glenn) (1740-1816) Snodgrass **P:** Y **BLW:** unk **RG:** unk **MK:** unk **PH:** unk **SS:** CI Rev War pen VA **BS:** 196.

SNODGRASS, John Jr; b 1746 or 1747, Jones Springs, Berkeley Co, WV; d 1796 **RU:** Patriot, Gave material aid to cause **CEM:** Glade Spring Presbyterian; GPS 36.76720, -81.78720; 33234 Lee Hwy, Glade Spring; Washington **GS:** U **SP:** Mary Miller (1747-1838) **VI:** Son of John (1726-1788) & Elizabeth (-----) (1726-1787) Snodgrass. Wrote will 8 Jun 1795 **P:** N **BLW:** N **RG:** unk **MK:** unk **PH:** unk **SS:** AL Cert Berkeley Co WV **BS:** 196.

SNODGRASS, William; b 10 May 1760 Frederick Co (later Berkeley Co); d 18 Sep 1849 **RU:** Soldier, Lived in Washington Co at enl 1775 & 1776. Served in VA Line **CEM:** Snodgrass; GPS unk; Bristol (or Blountsville, TN); Bristol City **GS:** U **SP:** No info **VI:** Sol appl pen 22 Aug 1832, Sullivan Co, TN **P:** Y **BLW:** unk **RG:** unk **MK:** unk **PH:** unk **SS:** J- DAR Hatcher; K Vol 5 pg 127; CG Vol 3 pg 3242 **BS:** JLARC 2; 196.

SNOW, Edward; b unk; d 1781 **RU:** Soldier, Served fr MA, and killed in the battle at Yorktown **CEM:** Yorktown Victory Monument Tablet; GPS 38.28350, -78.54150; Yorktown; York **GS:** U **SP:** No info **VI:** No further data **P:** unk **BLW:** unk **RG:** unk **MK:** unk **PH:** unk **SS:** J-Yorktown Historian **BS:** JLARC 74.

SNOW, Richard; b Jun 1753; d Aft 28 Sep 1833 **RU:** Private, Served in Albemarle Co Militia commencing spring 1777 for 20 mos on several re-enlistments. Was at seige of Yorktown Oct 1781 in Capt John Harris's Co, VA Cont Line **CEM:** Snow Johnson Family; GPS unk; S base Buck Mountain, approx .5 mi behind house; Albemarle **GS:** N **SP:** Lorana Davis (c1765-__) **VI:** No GS, thus no specific burial proof. Son or eldest grandson of John Snow. Pen recd 1832 #514540 **P:** unk **BLW:** unk **RG:** unk **MK:** unk **PH:** N **SS:** DAR Ancestor #A201695; G pg 755; AP pen rec; CG pg 3244 **BS:** 32 Sheap Mar 2015.

SOLNE, Andre; b unk; d 1781 **RU:** Soldier, Served in Gatinais Bn and died fr battle at Yorktown **CEM:** French Memorial; GPS 36.81944, -79.39933; Yorktown; York **GS:** U **SP:** No info **VI:** No further data **P:** unk **BLW:** unk **RG:** Y **MK:** unk **PH:** unk **SS:** J-Yorktown Historian **BS:** JLARC 1,74.

SOMERVILLE, James; b 25 Feb 1742, Glascow, Scotland; d 4 Apr 1798 **RU:** Patriot, Gave use of warehouse Dec 1779-Apr 1781. Alderman in Fredericksburg 1782 **CEM:** Masonic Cemetery; GPS 38.30198, -77.46142; 900 Charles St; Fredericksburg City **GS:** Y **SP:** No info **VI:** Died in Port Royal **P:** N **BLW:** N **RG:** Y **MK:** N **PH:** unk **SS:** D pg 867 **BS:** 11 pg 107-9.

SOMMERS, Simon; b 23 Nov 1747; d 2 Dec 1836 **RU:** Adjutant, Served in VA Line. Appt 1776 Adjutant 6th VA Regt, served to end of campaign in 1781 **CEM:** Sommers Family; GPS 38.52828, -77.10295; 115 E Fairfax St, Falls Church; Fairfax **GS:** Y **SP:** Elizabeth (-----) (1762-1831) **VI:** Appl pen 28 Dec 1828 Alexandria Co (then DC but now in VA) W9705, Recd 4000 acres bounty land. BLW #1480-200. Died in Alexandria Co **P:** Y **BLW:** Y **RG:** N **MK:** Y **PH:** Y **SS:** K Vol 4 pg 129; CG Vol 3 pg 3248 **BS:** 80 vol 4 pg 58.

SORBETZ, Barthelemy; b unk; d 1781 **RU:** Soldier, Served in Gatinais Bn and died fr battle at Yorktown **CEM:** French Memorial; GPS 36.81944, -79.39933; Yorktown; York **GS:** U **SP:** No info **VI:** No further data **P:** unk **BLW:** unk **RG:** Y **MK:** unk **PH:** unk **SS:** J-Yorktown Historian **BS:** JLARC 1, 74.

SORIN, Pierre; b unk; d 1781 **RU:** Seaman, Served on "Victorie" and died from Yorktown battle **CEM:** French Memorial; GPS 36.81944, -79.39933; Yorktown; York **GS:** U **SP:** No info **VI:** No further data **P:** unk **BLW:** unk **RG:** Y **MK:** unk **PH:** unk **SS:** J-Yorktown Historian **BS:** JLARC 1, 74.

SOULIGNAC, Mathieu; b unk; d 1781 **RU:** Soldier, Served in Beaujolais Bn and died fr battle at Yorktown **CEM:** French Memorial; GPS 36.81944, -79.39933; Yorktown; York **GS:** U **SP:** No info **VI:** No further data **P:** unk **BLW:** unk **RG:** Y **MK:** unk **PH:** unk **SS:** J-Yorktown Historian **BS:** JLARC 1, 74.

SOURSON, Jean; b unk; d 1781 **RU:** Soldier, Served in Soissonnais Bn and died fr battle at Yorktown **CEM:** French Memorial; GPS 36.81944, -79.39933; Yorktown; York **GS:** U **SP:** No info **VI:** No further data **P:** unk **BLW:** unk **RG:** Y **MK:** unk **PH:** unk **SS:** J-Yorktown Historian **BS:** JLARC 1, 74.

RU=Rank/Unit   CEM=Cemetery   GS=Gravestone   SP=Spousal Information
VI=Other Veteran Info   P=Pension   BLW=Bounty/Land Warrant   RG=Registered Grave
MK=SAR/DAR Marker   PH=Photo   SS=Service Source   BS=Burial Source

314

SOUTHER, Micheal; b c1754, Culpeper Co; d 1813 **RU:** Patriot, Furnished supplies to the Cont Army & performed public service **CEM:** John Robertson Property; GPS unk; Ruth; Madison **GS:** N **SP:** Mary Fisher **VI:** No further data **P:** N **BLW:** N **RG:** Y **MK:** N **PH:** N **SS:** D Vol I pg 26, 33 **BS:** 04.

SOWDER, Jacob; b 1734, PA; d 1819 **RU:** Private, Served in 4th, 8th, & 12th Cont lines **CEM:** Mt Pleasant Church; GPS 37.13289, -80.30640; 1024 Mt Pleasant Rd, Shawsville; Montgomery **GS:** N **SP:** Elizabeth (-----) Sowder (1738-1785) **VI:** No further data **P:** N **BLW:** N **RG:** N **MK:** unk **PH:** N **SS:** E pg 729 **BS:** JLARC 29; 196.

SOWERS, George; b c1742; d 29 Aug 1822 **RU:** Patriot, Provided material aid to cause **CEM:** Mt Hebron; GPS 39.10916, -78.09497; 305 E Boscawen St; Winchester City **GS:** Y **SP:** No info **VI:** Bur in the Centenary Reformed UCC portion of the Mt Hebron Cemetery **P:** N **BLW:** N **RG:** N **MK:** N **PH:** N **SS:** AL Ct Bk pg 18 **BS:** 196.

SOWERS, George; b 1750, York Co, PA; d 18 Mar 1834 **RU:** Private, Served in Capt Andrew Forman, York Co, PA Militia **CEM:** Zion Lutheran; GPS 37.13507, -80.41662; Rts 693 & 615, Wades Ln; Floyd **GS:** Y **SP:** Elizabeth Spangler (1764 MD-Nov 1857 Floyd Co) **VI:** Govt grave stone **P:** unk **BLW:** unk **RG:** unk **MK:** unk **PH:** Y **SS:** B Rev War Marker **BS:** JLARC 17, 29; 196.

SPANGLER, Daniel; b c1753; d 1823 **RU:** Patriot, Gave material aid to the cause **CEM:** Pine Creek Primitive Baptist; GPS 36.94622, -80.27357; Spangler Mill Rd Rt 682; Floyd **GS:** Y **SP:** Mary Nofsinger **VI:** Son of Daniel (1716-1787) & Mary (Noffsinger) (1720-1820) Spangler. Died in Franklin Co **P:** N **BLW:** N **RG:** Y **MK:** N **PH:** unk **SS:** AL Ct Bk **BS:** 64 pg 120; 196.

SPANGLER, Daniel; b 1716; d 3 Nov 1787 **RU:** Patriot, Gave material aid to cause **CEM:** Pigg River Primitive Baptist; GPS 36.96913, -80.07368; Rt 750 nr Callaway; Franklin **GS:** U **SP:** No info **VI:** No further data **P:** N **BLW:** N **RG:** Y **MK:** N **PH:** unk **SS:** AK; AL Ct Bk pg 30 Henry Co **BS:** 04, Oct 06.

SPANGLER, Jacob; b 3 Apr 1756; d 14 Jan 1827 **RU:** Private, Served in Capt Thomas Ingles Co, Montgomery Co Militia, Apr 1781 **CEM:** Sharon Lutheran; GPS 37.05800, -81.20590; Rt 42 W of Ceres; Bland **GS:** Y **SP:** Margaret Groseclose (1760 Lancaster Co, PA-11 Aug 1838 Wythe Co), d/o Peter Sr (1730-1803) & Mary Magdalena (Ott) (1732-1805) Gloseclose **VI:** No further data **P:** unk **BLW:** unk **RG:** Y **MK:** N **PH:** unk **SS:** E pg 729 **BS:** 60 Bland Co; 196.

SPANGLER, Peter Jr; b 1742, Berks Co, PA; d 1833 **RU:** Private, Served in Capt Thomas Ingles Co, 7 Apr 1781, Montgomery Co Militia **CEM:** Zion Lutheran; GPS 36.84110, -81.22310; 1417 Zion Church Rd, Crockett; Wythe **GS:** U **SP:** Mar (22 Sep 1773 Shenandoah Co) Elizabeth (Pheiffer, Piper, or Pfeiferin) Huddle **VI:** Generally believed to have d in Wythe Co, though one source says he d in Ohio **P:** unk **BLW:** unk **RG:** unk **MK:** unk **PH:** unk **SS:** G pg 227 **BS:** 196.

SPANGLER (SPENGER), Daniel; b c1747, PA; d 14 Feb 1823 **RU:** Patriot, Performed public service Henry Co **CEM:** Pine Creek Primitive Baptist; GPS 36.94622, -80.27357; Spangler Mill Rd Rt 682; Floyd **GS:** Y **SP:** Sarah Bolt (1753, 8 May 1823 age 80+) **VI:** Son of Daniel Spangler (1716-1787) and Mary Noftsinger (1720-1839) **P:** N **BLW:** N **RG:** unk **MK:** N **PH:** unk **SS:** AL Ct Bk **BS:** 196.

SPEAR (SPEARS), James; b 30 Jul 1759; d 29 Oct 1836 **RU:** Soldier, Served in 2nd Bn under Col Moses McClean **CEM:** Rock Spring; GPS 37.78126, -79.44585; Jct Rt 803 & Liberty Hall Rd, Lodi; Washington **GS:** U **SP:** No info **VI:** Pensioned Washington Co, as Vet Admin Ltr 13 April 1835 lists him as recd pension certificate **P:** Y **BLW:** unk **RG:** unk **MK:** unk **PH:** unk **SS:** CI **BS:** 196.

SPEARS, John; b 12 Feb 1759; d 4 Oct 1842 **RU:** Soldier, Served in VA Line. Ent serv Chesterfield Co 1778 **CEM:** Bethel Baptist; GPS 37.50986, -77.71166; 1100 Huguenot Springs Rd, Midlothian; Chesterfield **GS:** U **SP:** Mar (12 Apr 1804, Chesterfield Co) Susannah (Sussanah) Womack (c1779-__) **VI:** Sol appl pen 26 Jan 1833 Chesterfield Co. Widow appl pen there 30 Apr 1853 age 74 & BLW 17 Apr 1855 there. W2363, BLW #26915-160-55. DAR marker **P:** Y **BLW:** Y **RG:** unk **MK:** Y **PH:** unk **SS:** K Vol 5 pg 134; CG Vol 3 pg 3261 **BS:** JLARC 2, 4,12, 35; 196.

SPEED, Joseph; b 27 May 1750, Mecklenburg Co; d 23 Apr 1806 **RU:** Patriot, Was in May 1776 in VA Convention **CEM:** Speed Family; GPS unk; Check property records for family land; Mecklenburg **GS:** Y **SP:** Mar (3 Dec 1782 in NC) Ann Bignall **VI:** Son of John & Mary (Taylor-Mintry) Speed **P:** N **BLW:** N **RG:** N **MK:** N **PH:** unk **SS:** AR Vol 4 pg 62; AT Vol 1 pg 153 **BS:** DAR Rpt.

RU=Rank/Unit	CEM=Cemetery	GS=Gravestone	SP=Spousal Information
VI=Other Veteran Info	P=Pension	BLW=Bounty/Land Warrant	RG=Registered Grave
MK=SAR/DAR Marker	PH=Photo	SS=Service Source	BS=Burial Source

315

SPENCE, John; b 11 Jul 1766 1766, Scotland; d 18 May 1829 **RU:** Private, Served in Capt Samuel Booker's Co Nov 1778. Served in 5th, 11th, and 15th Cont Lines **CEM:** Tebbsdale Plantation; GPS unk; Rt 633 off US 1 Dumfries; Prince William **GS:** Y **SP:** Mary Fushee Tebbs **VI:** Was a physician. SAR marker **P:** unk **BLW:** unk **RG:** Y **MK:** Y **PH:** unk **SS:** E pg 730 **BS:** 94 pg 471; 196.

SPENGLER, Philip; b 17 Mar 1761, York, York Co PA; d 1823 **RU:** Private, Served in PA Line **CEM:** Mt Zion United Methodist; GPS unk; 399 W Queens St, Strasburg; Shenandoah **GS:** Y **SP:** Regina Stover, d/o Peter & (-----) Stover **VI:** Son of Phillip Sr. and Anna Margaret Salome (Dinkel) Spengler. Was Lt Col, 6th VA Milita Regt War of 1812 **P:** unk **BLW:** unk **RG:** unk **MK:** unk **PH:** Y **SS:** B **BS:** 196.

SPERRY, Jacob; b 1751; d 3 Apr 1808 **RU:** Captain, Served in VA Line. Ent serv 1775 in Winchester. Was prisoner of war in Quebec **CEM:** Mt Hebron; GPS 39.10916, -78.09497; 305 E Boscawen St; Winchester City **GS:** U **SP:** Mar (23 Aug 1790, Winchester) Elizabeth Lauck (c1766 or c1779-__) **VI:** Widow appl pen 3 Nov 1838, Winchester, age 59. Widow appl for BLW in 1855 age 89. W3470, BLW #26042-160-55 **P:** Y **BLW:** Y **RG:** unk **MK:** unk **PH:** unk **SS:** K Vol 5 pg 141; CG Vol 3 pg 3271 **BS:** JLARC 4, 47.

SPERRY, John; b 10 Nov 1757, Frederick Co; d 14 Nov 1842 **RU:** Soldier, Ent serv 1775 Frederick Co for 2 yrs in 8th VA Regt serving part of time for Capt Charles M Thurston **CEM:** Mt Hebron; GPS 39.10916, -78.09497; 305 E Boscawen St; Winchester City **GS:** Y **SP:** Mar (29 Sep 1779) Sarah Maria Orrbetter (__-3 Mar 1836 Winchester), d/o Valentine & Catherine (Foltz or Stoltz) Urlettig **VI:** Originally bur in Presbyterian Cemetery next to German Reformed Church Cem in Mt Hebron. Remains removed to Presbyterian reburial site along with 71 others in 1912. Sol never appl for pen however heirs appl pen. R9992 **P:** Y **BLW:** unk **RG:** unk **MK:** Y **PH:** unk **SS:** NARA M804; K Vol 5 pg 141; CG Vol 3 pg 3271-2 **BS:** JLARC 1, 2, 4, 47.

SPILMAN, James; b c1725, Germantown, Fauquier Co; d 20 Sep 1790 **RU:** Patriot, Gave material aid to cause **CEM:** Campbell, also Roy Neff Farm; GPS 38.46970, -77.99190; N of Jeffersonville, Rt 45 on left; Fauquier **GS:** U **SP:** 1) Martha (-----) (__, Jeffersonton, Culpeper Co-7 Sep 1771) 2) Alice Huffman **VI:** No further data **P:** N **BLW:** N **RG:** unk **MK:** unk **PH:** unk **SS:** AL Cert Culpeper Co; DAR Newsletter Sep/Oct 2015, Vol 15 #5 pg 418 **BS:** 196.

SPITLER, Jacob; b 1766; d 1840 **RU:** Private, Served in Capt Michael Reader's Co, Shenandoah Co Militia **CEM:** Union Presbyterian; GPS 39.10916, -78.09497; Churchville; Augusta **GS:** N **SP:** Mar (21 Sep 1800, Augusta Co) Elizabeth Crist **VI:** No further data **P:** unk **BLW:** unk **RG:** N **MK:** N **PH:** N **SS:** C pg 603 **BS:** 142.

SPOONER, Charles; b 1741; d 15 Oct 1800 **RU:** Captain, Contact George Washington SAR Chapter for service for men listed on their cemetery plaque **CEM:** Old Presbyterian Meeting House; GPS 38.48528, -77.23532; 323 S Fairfax St; Alexandria City **GS:** N **SP:** No info **VI:** Called "Capt Spooner" in burial record, without first name. Bur 27 Apr 1798 age 40. Died of dropsey. Listed on SAR plaque in cemetery **P:** unk **BLW:** unk **RG:** Y **MK:** Y **PH:** N **SS:** SAR Ancestor #P-295200; J-NSSAR 1993 Reg; AK **BS:** JLARC 1; 23 pg 108; 196.

SPRAGINS (SPRAGANS), Thomas; b Bef 1755; d 17 Dec 1793 **RU:** Patriot, Gave material aid to cause **CEM:** Clarkton; GPS unk; Rt 632, Clarkton; Halifax **GS:** N **SP:** Maacah Abney (__-21 Sep 1794) d/o Danney & (-----) Abney **VI:** Son of William (__-1755) & Martha (Abney) (1705-__) Spragins **P:** N **BLW:** N **RG:** unk **MK:** unk **PH:** N **SS:** AL Ct Bk pg 40 **BS:** 196.

SPRAKER (SPRECHER), John Christopher; b 11 Jun 1738, Linn, Fayette Co, PA; d 11 May 1830 **RU:** unk, Probably served in Montgomery Co Militia, specific service at the Kegley Room, Wytheville Community College **CEM:** Zion Lutheran; GPS 36.84110, -81.22310; 1417 Zion Church Rd, Crockett; Wythe **GS:** Y **SP:** Catherina Reichart (11 Jun 1738 Linn, Fayette Co, PA-11 May 1830) **VI:** Son of Johan Christopher & Maria Ernestine (Beck) Sprecher. Died in Cripple Creek, Wythe Co **P:** unk **BLW:** unk **RG:** unk **MK:** unk **PH:** unk **SS:** JLARC 123 **BS:** JLARC 123; 196.

SPROUL, William; b c1731 Ireland; d 1806 **RU:** Patriot, Gave material aid to cause **CEM:** Airy Knoll; GPS unk; E of Rt 252 abt .4 mi N of Rt 620, S of Newport; Augusta **GS:** Y **SP:** 1) Mar (1757 Augusta Co) Jane (-----) 2) Mar (1773 Augusta Co) Susannah (-----) **VI:** Was in Colonial War **P:** N **BLW:** N **RG:** unk **MK:** unk **PH:** unk **SS:** AL Cert Augusta Co **BS:** 32 e-mail 28 Sep 2011.

RU=Rank/Unit	CEM=Cemetery	GS=Gravestone	SP=Spousal Information
VI=Other Veteran Info	P=Pension	BLW=Bounty/Land Warrant	RG=Registered Grave
MK=SAR/DAR Marker	PH=Photo	SS=Service Source	BS=Burial Source

316

ST CLARE, Robert; b 1755; d 1817 **RU:** Private, Served in VA Militia at Ft Pitt, PA 1775 **CEM:** St Clare Family; GPS unk; Appomattox; Appomattox **GS:** U **SP:** No info **VI:** No further data **P:** unk **BLW:** unk **RG:** unk **MK:** unk **PH:** unk **SS:** NSSAR Ancestor #P-295647; E pg 734 **BS:** JLARC 2.

STAFFORD, Ralph Sr; b 1757; d 1794 **RU:** Private?, Served in Cont Line **CEM:** Staffville; GPS unk; Hillsville; Giles **GS:** Y **SP:** No info **VI:** No further data **P:** unk **BLW:** unk **RG:** Y **MK:** N **PH:** unk **SS:** E pg 754 **BS:** 55 pg 165.

STALLARD, Samuel; b c1745, Essex Co; d Aft 28 Oct 1815 **RU:** Patriot, Gave material aid to cause **CEM:** Stallard-Moore; GPS 36.81155, -82.46172; Nr jct Rts 780 & 671 nr Nickelsville, Dungannon; Scott **GS:** Y **SP:** Jael Ellen Duncan (1751, Culpeper-1851) d/o Raleigh & (-----) Duncan **VI:** Son of Walter (1720-1807) & Elizabeth (Williams) (1720-1748) Stallard **P:** N **BLW:** N **RG:** unk **MK:** unk **PH:** unk **SS:** DAR Newsletter Sep/Oct 2015 Vol 15 #5 pg 418 **BS:** 196.

STANARD, Larkin; b May 1760, Spotsylvania Co; d Aft 1833 **RU:** Captain/Patriot, Served in VA Line 1776 in 6th VA Regt. Ent serv Spotsylvania Co. Was Cadet in Col Mordecei, Buckner's Regt. Was member House of Delegates **CEM:** Stanard (Stanfield) Family; GPS unk; Rt 646; Spotsylvania **GS:** N **SP:** Elizabeth Parrot Chew, d/o Robert & (-----) Chew **VI:** Appl pen 6 Aug 1833, Spotsylvania Co. S7807 **P:** Y **BLW:** unk **RG:** Y **MK:** N **PH:** N **SS:** H; K Vol 5 pg 149; CG Vol 3 pg 3290 **BS:** 09 part 2.

STANFIELD, Thomas; b 1747; d 1796 **RU:** Lieutenant/Patriot, Gave material aid to cause **CEM:** Stanfield Family, Boyd Farm; GPS unk; Rt 658, 2 mi S of Turbeville; Halifax **GS:** U **SP:** No info **VI:** Gr St indicates was Lt **P:** unk **BLW:** unk **RG:** Y **MK:** unk **PH:** unk **SS:** J-NSSAR 1993 Reg, J- DAR Hatcher; AL Ct Bk pg 13 Halifax Co **BS:** JLARC 1,2; 215.

STAPLES, Samuel; b 23 Mar 1762, Buckingham Co; d 23 Mar 1825 **RU:** Major, Served in 6th Cont Line. Also served as private in Capt Nicolas Cabell's Co, Albemarle Co Militia, Apr 1776. Was at seige at Yorktown and for gallantry there was promoted to Maj Oct 1781 **CEM:** Stuart Town; GPS unk; Chestnut St, Stuart; Patrick **GS:** Y **SP:** Lucinda Penn (1771-1850) **VI:** Son of John & Keziah (Norman) Staples. GS moved fr home cemetery **P:** unk **BLW:** unk **RG:** N **MK:** N **PH:** unk **SS:** E, pg 735; CD; DC pg 154 **BS:** JLARC 30; 60 Patrick; 196.

STARK, William; b 1757; d 1 Aug 1844 **RU:** Second Lieutenant, Enl serv in Dinwiddie Co 1776. Served in 6th VA Regt, VA Line. Was severely wounded at Battle of Brandywine and resigned fr Army 1778 **CEM:** Cedar Grove; GPS 36.85860, -76.28310; 238 E Princess Anne Rd; Norfolk City **GS:** N **SP:** (-----) Mar during RW. **VI:** Sol appl pen 23 Jul 1832 Norfolk age 75. S7592 **P:** Y **BLW:** unk **RG:** N **MK:** N **PH:** N **SS:** K Vol pg 151; BR 1827; CG Vol 3 pg 3300 **BS:** 176.

STARK (STARKE), William; b 14 Dec 1754; d 29 Dec 1838 **RU:** Sergeant, VA Line. Ent serv Stafford Co 1781 **CEM:** Stark-Payne; GPS unk; On Quantico Marine Base opposite Ruby fire station; Stafford **GS:** U **SP:** Mar (16 Feb 1786) Mary Kendall (1770-__) d/o John & (-----) Kendall **VI:** Widow appl pen 18 Aug 1852 age 92 & appl for BLW 3 Dec 1855. Pen #R10059 **P:** Y **BLW:** Y **RG:** unk **MK:** unk **PH:** unk **SS:** K Vol 5 pg 152; CG pg 3300 **BS:** JLARC 48, 63; 3 pg 365.

STAUTZER, Jacob; b unk; d 1781 **RU:** Soldier, Served in Royal Deaux Ponts Bn and died fr battle at Yorktown **CEM:** French Memorial; GPS 36.81944, -79.39933; Yorktown; York **GS:** U **SP:** No info **VI:** No further data **P:** unk **BLW:** unk **RG:** unk **MK:** unk **PH:** unk **SS:** J-Yorktown Historian **BS:** JLARC 1, 74.

STEELE, Alexander; b c1735, Brunswick Co; d 25 Jun 1808 **RU:** First Lieutenant, Private in Capt John Peyton's Co 3rd VA Regt, commanded by Col George Weedon, Oct 1776 to 1 Jan 1777 **CEM:** Second Concord Presbyterian; GPS 37.34209, -78.96585; Phoebe Pond Rd Rt 609 E of Concord; Appomattox **GS:** Y **SP:** Mar (15 May 1758 (probably) Bedford Co) Elizabeth Carson Helm **VI:** No further data **P:** unk **BLW:** unk **RG:** unk **MK:** unk **PH:** unk **SS:** AP **BS:** JLARC 36; 196.

STEELE, Andrew; b 1743; d 13 Feb 1800 **RU:** Soldier, Served in Bedford Militia **CEM:** Old Providence; GPS 37.96151, -79.71000; 1005 Spottswood Rd, Spottswood; Augusta **GS:** Y **SP:** Mary Ramsey **VI:** Newer Govt stone. Name also on SAR cemetery plaque **P:** unk **BLW:** unk **RG:** unk **MK:** Y **PH:** unk **SS:** B; BT **BS:** JLARC 62; 196.

STEELE, David; b 1756; d 1840 **RU:** Private/Rifleman, Served in VA Cont Line and Lee's Regt VA Vol. Severely wounded by numerous saber cuts at Guilford CH and taken as prisoner **CEM:** Old Providence;

RU=Rank/Unit	CEM=Cemetery	GS=Gravestone	SP=Spousal Information
VI=Other Veteran Info	P=Pension	BLW=Bounty/Land Warrant	RG=Registered Grave
MK=SAR/DAR Marker	PH=Photo	SS=Service Source	BS=Burial Source

317

GPS 37.96151, -79.71000; 1005 Spottswood Rd, Spottswood; Augusta **GS**: Y **SP**: No info **VI**: Invalid pen 4 Sep 1790. Increased under act of 16 Apr 1816. S7605. Has Govt stone with no dates. Name in on SAR plaque at cemetery **P**: Y **BLW**: unk **RG**: unk **MK**: unk **PH**: unk **SS**: B; K pg 155; CG Vol 3 pg 3310 **BS**: JLARC 2, 8, 9, 62, 63.

STEELE, James Wendle; b 1752; d 10 Jan 1823 **RU**: Lieutenant, Served in Capt Tate's Co, Augusta Co **CEM**: Old Providence; GPS 37.96151, -79.71000; 1005 Spottswood Rd, Spottswood; Augusta **GS**: Y **SP**: Mar (17 May 1781) Margaret "Maggie" Parks (1765-1848), d/o John & (-----) Parks **VI**: One of 12 Augusta Co Justices. Newer Govt stone. Name also on SAR cemetery plaque **P**: unk **BLW**: unk **RG**: unk **MK**: Y **PH**: Y **SS**: B; BT; K pg 213 **BS**: JLARC 2 ,8, 62; 196.

STEELE, John; b unk; d 1814 **RU**: Lieutenant, Served in Augusta Co Militia and 8th & 9th VA Regt **CEM**: Tinkling Spring Presbyterian; GPS 38.08472, -78.98278; 30 Tinkling Spring Dr, Fishersville; Augusta **GS**: N **SP**: No info **VI**: Person same name and death yr has Gov't Grave stone in the Old Providence cemetery in Augusta Co, thus perhaps only memorialized there or in this cemetery, Perhaps was promoted to Capt before Oct 1783. Rec'd 2667 acres BLW 20 May 1783 for 3 yrs service and on 12 Feb 1808, 387 acres for an additional 7 mos service **P**: unk **BLW**: Y **RG**: unk **MK**: unk **PH**: N **SS**: NSSAR Ancestor #P-296718; C pg 113; N pg 44 **BS**: JLARC 62, 63.

STEELE, John; b unk; d 1804 **RU**: Soldier/Patriot, Gave use of horse for 29 days **CEM**: Tinkling Spring Presbyterian; GPS 38.08472, -78.98278; 30 Tinkling Spring Dr, Fishersville; Augusta **GS**: N **SP**: No info **VI**: No further data **P**: unk **BLW**: unk **RG**: unk **MK**: N **PH**: N **SS**: D pg 66 Augusta Co **BS**: JLARC 62; 196.

STEELE, John Jr; b unk; d 1814 **RU**: Private, Served in Capt Tate's Co, Augusta Co Militia **CEM**: Old Providence; GPS 37.96151, -79.71000; 1005 Spottswood Rd, Spottswood; Augusta **GS**: Y **SP**: No info **VI**: Newer Govt stone. Name also on SAR cemetery plaque. Person same name and death yr bur in Tinkling Springs cemetery but believed not to be him **P**: unk **BLW**: unk **RG**: unk **MK**: Y **PH**: unk **SS**: B; BT **BS**: 196.

STEELE, John Sr; b 1755; d 1804 **RU**: Private, Served in Capt Tate's Co, Augusta Militia **CEM**: Old Providence; GPS 37.96151, -79.71000; 1005 Spottswood Rd, Spottswood; Augusta **GS**: Y **SP**: No info **VI**: Newer Govt stone. Name also on SAR cemetery plaque **P**: unk **BLW**: unk **RG**: unk **MK**: Y **PH**: unk **SS**: B; BT; E pg 737 **BS**: 44;196.

STEELE, Nathaniel; b 1722; d 30 May 1796 **RU**: Soldier/ Patriot, Gave material aid to cause **CEM**: Old Providence; GPS 37.96151, -79.71000; 1005 Spottswood Rd, Spottswood; Augusta **GS**: Y **SP**: 1) Lydia Pratt 2) Rosannah (-----) (__-1808) **VI**: Son of David & Janet (-----) Steele. Stone nearly destroyed. Name on SAR plaque at cemetery **P**: unk **BLW**: unk **RG**: unk **MK**: Y **PH**: unk **SS**: SAR Ancestor #P-296737; BT **BS**: JLARC 8;196.

STEELE, Robert; b 1730 or 1733; d 10 Apr 1800 **RU**: Private, Served in Capt Campbell's Co, Augusta Co Militia **CEM**: Old Providence; GPS 37.96151, -79.71000; 1005 Spottswood Rd, Spottswood; Augusta **GS**: U **SP**: Elizabeth Wendel **VI**: No further data **P**: unk **BLW**: unk **RG**: unk **MK**: unk **PH**: unk **SS**: E pg 738 **BS**: 196.

STEELE, Robert; b 1750; d 11 Jun 1821 **RU**: Soldier, Served in Capt John Adam's Co, Montgomery Co Militia **CEM**: Steele Family; GPS unk; nr Bland; Wythe **GS**: U **SP**: 1) Mary Keeling 2) Rebecca Oury **VI**: No further data **P**: unk **BLW**: unk **RG**: Y **MK**: unk **PH**: unk **SS**: J-NSSAR 2000 Reg; DD cites VA Mag Hist & Blog Vol 47 2nd series pg 160 **BS**: JLARC 76.

STEELE, Samuel Jr; b 1747; d 8 Jun 1837 **RU**: Captain, Commanded a company of Rockbridge Militia, 5 May 1778. Resigned commission on 5 May 1779 **CEM**: Old Providence; GPS 37.96151, -79.71000; 1005 Spottswood Rd, Spottswood; Augusta **GS**: Y **SP**: Margret Campbell **VI**: Son of Samuel Steele, Sr & Margaret Fulton **P**: unk **BLW**: unk **RG**: unk **MK**: Y **PH**: unk **SS**: BT **BS**: JLARC 2, 8, 62, 63; 196.

STEELE, Samuel Jr; b unk; d 1823 **RU**: Private, Served in a VA Regt and Capt Smith's Co, Augusta Co Militia **CEM**: Old Providence; GPS 37.96151, -79.71000; 1005 Spottswood Rd, Spottswood; Augusta **GS**: Y **SP**: No info **VI**: Govt grave stone **P**: N **BLW**: N **RG**: N **MK**: N **PH**: N **SS**: E pg 738 **BS**: 196.

RU=Rank/Unit CEM=Cemetery GS=Gravestone SP=Spousal Information
VI=Other Veteran Info P=Pension BLW=Bounty/Land Warrant RG=Registered Grave
MK=SAR/DAR Marker PH=Photo SS=Service Source BS=Burial Source

318

STEELE, Samuel Sr; b 1707; d 16 Feb 1790 **RU:** Patriot, Gave material aid to cause **CEM:** Old Providence; **GPS** 37.96151, -79.71000; 1005 Spottswood Rd, Spottswood; Augusta **GS:** Y **SP:** 1) Sarah Campbell (1720-1748) 2) Margraret Fulton 3) Martha Fulton, sister of Margaret **VI:** No further data **P:** N **BLW:** N **RG:** unk **MK:** Y **PH:** unk **SS:** AL Ct Bk pg 7 Augusta Co **BS:** JLARC 8 ,9, 62, 63; 196.

STEELE, Thomas; b 1750; d 1834 **RU:** Private, 3rd Regt, 3rd Cont Line **CEM:** Old Methodist Church; GPS 39.08620, -78.21670; 5291 Main St, Stephens City; Frederick **GS:** Y **SP:** Possible marriage (24 Feb 1816 Frederick Co by George M. Frye) Sarah Carver **VI:** No further data **P:** unk **BLW:** unk **RG:** N **MK:** N **PH:** unk **SS:** E pg 738; AP roll 3rd Regt **BS:** 112; 196.

STEELE, Thomas; b 3 Jun 1747; d 4 Jul 1799 **RU:** Soldier, Ent serv Rockbridge Co on 2 Nov 1779 **CEM:** Old Providence; GPS 37.96151, -79.71000; 1005 Spottswood Rd, Spottswood; Augusta **GS:** Y **SP:** Jane Moore (1750-2 Jan 1826) **VI:** Son of David & Janet (-----) Steele. Name is on SAR plaque at cemetery **P:** unk **BLW:** unk **RG:** unk **MK:** Y **PH:** unk **SS:** BT **BS:** JLARC 62, 63; 196.

STEELE, William; b unk; d 1818 **RU:** Private, Served in Capt Tate's Co, Augusta Co Militia **CEM:** Old Providence; GPS 37.96151, -79.71000; 1005 Spottswood Rd, Spottswood; Augusta **GS:** Y **SP:** No info **VI:** Newer Govt stone. Name is on SAR cemetery plaque **P:** unk **BLW:** unk **RG:** unk **MK:** Y **PH:** unk **SS:** B; E pg 738; BT **BS:** JLARC 63; 196.

STEERS, Isaac; b 1757; d 1824 **RU:** Patriot, Gave material aid to cause **CEM:** Fairfax Meeting House; GPS 39.18557, -77.60589; Water St & Waterford Rd, Waterford; Loudoun **GS:** Y **SP:** No info **VI:** No further data **P:** N **BLW:** N **RG:** N **MK:** N **PH:** unk **SS:** D Vol 2 pg 602; AL Ct Bk pg 2, 21 Loudoun Co **BS:** 25 pg 298.

STEFFEY, John; b 21 Dec 1745, Lancaster Co, PA; d 6 Jun 1836 **RU:** Private, Ent serv Lancaster Co PA in PA Line. Served in Capt Farnstsler's Co PA Militia **CEM:** St Paul's Lutheran; GPS 36.91173, -81.23484; 330 St Pauls Church Rd, Rural Retreat; Wythe **GS:** U **SP:** 1) (-----) 2) Mar (10 Jan 1813 Wythe Co VA while in service War of 1812) Rosanna (Rosena) Philippy (c1780-__) **VI:** Also had War of 1812 service. Sol appl pen 26 May 1834 Wythe Co. Widow appl pen 24 Jan 1854 Wythe Co VA age 74. W7205, Recd BLW #26543-160-55 **P:** Y **BLW:** Y **RG:** unk **MK:** unk **PH:** unk **SS:** K Vol 5 pg 157; CG Vol 3 pg 3314 **BS:** JLARC 4, 40,123.

STEIN, Jean; b unk; d 1781 **RU:** Soldier, Served in Royal Deaux Ponts Bn and died fr battle at Yorktown **CEM:** French Memorial; GPS 36.81944, -79.39933; Yorktown; York **GS:** U **SP:** No info **VI:** No further data **P:** unk **BLW:** unk **RG:** Y **MK:** unk **PH:** unk **SS:** J-Yorktown Historian **BS:** JLARC 1, 74.

STEPHAN, Guillaume; b unk; d 1781 **RU:** Seaman, Served on "Auguste" and died from Yorktown battle **CEM:** French Memorial; GPS 36.81944, -79.39933; Yorktown; York **GS:** U **SP:** No info **VI:** No further data **P:** unk **BLW:** unk **RG:** Y **MK:** unk **PH:** unk **SS:** J-Yorktown Historian **BS:** JLARC 1, 74.

STEPHENS, Lawrence; b 1755, Frederick Co; d 1847 **RU:** Corporal, Served in VA Line 1st VA Regt. Lived in Fincastle Co (later Montgomery) at enl 1775 in Frederick Co **CEM:** Stephens aka Hurst; GPS unk; SR 100 S to SR 607 E to Jett farm, Wytheville, nr Carroll Co line; Wythe **GS:** U **SP:** Joanna (-----) **VI:** Sol appl pen10 Dec 1832 Wythe Co. S7639 **P:** Y **BLW:** unk **RG:** unk **MK:** unk **PH:** unk **SS:** K Vol 5 pg 159; CG Vol 3 pg 3315 **BS:** JLARC 2, 4, 40, 43,123.

STEPHENSON, John; b 1710; d 23 Nov 1778 **RU:** Patriot, Paid for recruiting doctor in Western Augusta Co, Mar 1776 and gave 120# flour 26 Aug 1782 **CEM:** Cross Keys; GPS unk; Cross Keys; Rockingham **GS:** U **SP:** 1) Sarah Waite d/o James & Catherine (Rothgab) Waite. 2) Esther (Waite) Taylor, widow of John Taylor & d/o James & Catherine (Rothgab) Waite (Sarah's sister) **VI:** Signed the Orange Co Importation books in 1740 with wife Mary & daughter Sarah **P:** N **BLW:** N **RG:** unk **MK:** unk **PH:** unk **SS:** E pg 739; CY pg 100 **BS:** 196.

STEPTOE, James Jr; b 16 Jul 1750, Westmoreland Co; d 9 Feb 1826 **RU:** Patriot, Had civil service as Clerk of Bedford Co **CEM:** Callaway-Steptoe; GPS 37.30560, -79.29470; Rt 460, New London; Bedford **GS:** Y **SP:** No info **VI:** Clerk of Bedford Co Ct 54 yrs. Died in Campbell Co **P:** N **BLW:** N **RG:** unk **MK:** unk **PH:** unk **SS:** DAR #A108749; DD **BS:** 196.

RU=Rank/Unit	CEM=Cemetery	GS=Gravestone	SP=Spousal Information
VI=Other Veteran Info	P=Pension	BLW=Bounty/Land Warrant	RG=Registered Grave
MK=SAR/DAR Marker	PH=Photo	SS=Service Source	BS=Burial Source

319

STERRETT, William; b c1757; d Apr 1818 **RU**: Private, Served in Capt Bell's Co, Augusta Co Militia **CEM**: Hebron Presbyterian; **GPS** 38.14140, -79.15500; 423 Hebron Rd; Staunton City **GS**: Y **SP**: No info **VI**: No further data **P**: unk **BLW**: unk **RG**: N **MK**: N **PH**: unk **SS**: E pg 740 **BS**: 36 pg 67; 196.

STEVENS, Edward; b 1745, Culpeper Co; d 17 Aug 1820 **RU**: Colonel/Patriot, Was Lt Col in Culpeper District Bn 1775. Served in battles at Great Bridge, Brandywine, Camden, Guilford CH, and siege of Yorktown. As public servant signed Culpeper Co petitions **CEM**: Masonic Cemetery; **GPS** 38.48530, -77.99470; 950 N Main, Culpeper; Culpeper **GS**: U **SP**: Gilly Coleman, d/o Robert Esq & (-----) Coleman **VI**: Name is on VA Historical Road sign; SAR marker **P**: unk **BLW**: Y **RG**: Y **MK**: Y **PH**: Y **SS**: J-NSSAR 1993 Reg; AL Ct Bk I pg 1, 52 Culpeper Co; CE pg 16; CZ pg 417 **BS**: JLARC 1; 196.

STEVENS, John; b 1746; d Sep 1831 **RU**: Private, Served in Capt Daniel Trigg's Co, Montgomery Co Militia **CEM**: Northern Methodist; **GPS** 38.35777, -78.94344; Rt 867 Old Bridgewater Rd, Mt Crawford; Rockingham **GS**: N **SP**: No info **VI**: No further data **P**: N **BLW**: N **RG**: N **MK**: unk **PH**: N **SS**: G pg 221 **BS**: 196.

STEVENSON, James; b 1740; d Jun 1809 **RU**: Patriot, Paid the personal property tax which included Rev War supply tax, Culpeper Co, 1783 **CEM**: Masonic Cemetery; **GPS** 38.30198, -77.46142; 900 Charles St; Fredericksburg City **GS**: U **SP**: Mar (1759) Francis Littlepage **VI**: Listed as a Reverend on Culpeper Co tax lists. Died in Culpeper Co **P**: unk **BLW**: unk **RG**: unk **MK**: unk **PH**: unk **SS**: DAR Ancestor #A109240; NSSAR Ancestor #P-297556; DV Culpeper Co 1783 **BS**: JLARC 2.

STEVENSON (STEPHENSON), William Jr; b unk; d 1805 **RU**: Lieutenant/Patriot, Had Recruiting duty 13 Feb 1777. Later served in Col Charles Harrison's Regt of Artillery in York Co, serving until 1783. Gave material aid to cause **CEM**: Stephenson Family; **GPS** unk; Clayton Rd; Southampton **GS**: N **SP**: No info **VI**: Recd BLW 2666 acres **P**: unk **BLW**: Y **RG**: N **MK**: N **PH**: N **SS**: N pg 454; AL Ct Bk pg 12 Southampton Co; CZ pg 419 **BS**: 53 vol I pg 37.

STEWART, Charles; b c1730, Norfolk; d Feb 1801 **RU**: Second Lieutenant, Served 28 Jun 1777 in 15th VA Regt which later became the 11th Regt, serving 3 yrs. Stone says served in "11 Va. Mil. Inf" **CEM**: Stewart Family; **GPS** unk; Beechwood Plantation on Dismal Swamp Trail; Chesapeake City **GS**: N **SP**: Martha Foreman **VI**: Recd BLW 2666 acres **P**: unk **BLW**: Y **RG**: N **MK**: N **PH**: N **SS**: DAR Ancestor #A109390; N pg 1211 **BS**: DAR Rpt, JLARC 88; 63 pg 101.

STEWART, John; b 1746; d Sep 1800 **RU**: Captain, Served as Marine officer US Navy and appointed Capt 24 Aug 1776 **CEM**: Old Presbyterian Meeting House; **GPS** 38.48528, -77.23532; 323 S Fairfax St; Alexandria City **GS**: N **SP**: No info **VI**: Bur 12 Sep 1800, age 54. Listed on SAR plaque in cemetery **P**: unk **BLW**: unk **RG**: Y **MK**: Y **PH**: N **SS**: J-NSSAR 1993 Reg; AK; CI General Navy Register **BS**: JLARC 1; 23 pg 108; 196.

STEWART, William; b c1749; d 14 Nov 1824 **RU**: Private, Served in Capt Pierce's Co, Montgomery Co, 6 Apr 1781 **CEM**: Glade Spring Presbyterian; **GPS** 36.76720, -81.78720; 33234 Lee Hwy, Glade Spring; Washington **GS**: Y **SP**: Susan (-----) (9 Sep 1760-1821) **VI**: No further data **P**: N **BLW**: N **RG**: N **MK**: N **PH**: unk **SS**: E pg 472; G pg 241 **BS**: 78, pg 188.

STICKLEY, Benjamin; b c1750; d c1796 **RU**: Lieutenant/Patriot, Was Lt 31 May 1782, Shenandoah Co Militia. Gave material aid to cause **CEM**: Stickley Family; **GPS** unk; Strasburg; Shenandoah **GS**: U **SP**: Mar (1772) Ann Stover (__, Strasburg-aft 1796) **VI**: No further data **P**: unk **BLW**: unk **RG**: Y **MK**: U **PH**: unk **SS**: DAR Ancestor #A109762; D Vol 3 pg 841; E pg 742 **BS**: 04.

STIFF, James; b 1757, Cumberland Co; d 19 May 1837 **RU**: Private, Ent Serv Bedford Co 1775 in 5th VA Regt **CEM**: Stiff Family; **GPS** unk; Union Church Rd 1 mi past Union Methodist, Thaxton; Bedford **GS**: Y **SP**: Mar (1 Sep 1779) Mary "Molly" Lewis (bc1760-24 May 1841) **VI**: Appl pen 12 Feb 1833, Russell Parish, Bedford Co, age 76. Widow appl pen 20 Jun 1839 Bedford Co age 79. W4344 Stone reads "Jas. Stiff, Fowler's Co. 5 VA Regt. Rev War" **P**: Y **BLW**: unk **RG**: unk **MK**: N **PH**: unk **SS**: B; K Vol 5 pg 169-70; CG Vol 3 pg 3341 **BS**: JLARC 2; 196.

STIGLEMAN (STICKLEMAN, STIGGLEMAN, STRICKLEMAN, STEICHELMAN), Philip (Phillip); b c1758, Germany; d Bef 1841 **RU**: Private, Served in Capt Alexander Martin & Col Peter Grub's cos of Lancaster Co, PA Militia. Destined for "Camp in ye Jerseys" 13 Aug 1776 **CEM**: Goodykoontz; **GPS**

RU=Rank/Unit	CEM=Cemetery	GS=Gravestone	SP=Spousal Information
VI=Other Veteran Info	P=Pension	BLW=Bounty/Land Warrant	RG=Registered Grave
MK=SAR/DAR Marker	PH=Photo	SS=Service Source	BS=Burial Source

320

unk; Rt 729; Floyd **GS:** N **SP:** Margaret Weaver d/o Peter & (-----) Weaver **VI:** Died in Floyd/Montgomery Co. Widow moved to Wayne Co IN & bur there **P:** unk **BLW:** unk **RG:** unk **MK:** N **PH:** N **SS:** NSSAR Ancestor #P-298023 **BS:** JLARC 29.

STITH, Buckner; b 1722, Rockspring, Brunswick Co; d Jul 1791 **RU:** Captain, Appointed Capt in Brunswick Co Militia Jan 1782 **CEM:** Mt Vernon Unitarian; **GPS** unk; 1909 Winhill Ln; Alexandria City **GS:** N **SP:** Susanna Munford **VI:** No further data **P:** unk **BLW:** unk **RG:** N **MK:** N **PH:** N **SS:** NSSAR Ancestor #P-298268; DAR #A110256; G pg 80 **BS:** 61 FX 298.

STITH, Griffin; b 24 Aug 1753, Northampton Co; d 18 Jun 1794 **RU:** Patriot, Was Clerk of Northampton Co 13 Mar 1777. Was paid for moving prisoners fr Eastern Shore **CEM:** Kings Creek; **GPS** unk; Cape Charles; Northampton **GS:** U **SP:** Ann Stratton (Sep 1757-1779) **VI:** Son of Griffin (1720-1784) & Mary (Blaikley) (1726-1784) Stith **P:** N **BLW:** N **RG:** unk **MK:** unk **PH:** unk **SS:** N pg 538; G pg 563 **BS:** 196.

STOBO, Jacob; b c1760; d 30 Jan 1794 **RU:** Captain, Taken prisoner when US Sloop "Washington" was captured 29 May 1781 in NY. Was sent to Old Mill Prison in England **CEM:** Trinity Episcopal; **GPS** 36.83459, -76.30105; 500 Court St; Portsmouth City **GS:** Y **SP:** Mar (12 Oct 1783 Baltimore MD) Sarah Hughes **VI:** Resided in Philadelphia PA before coming to VA. Died in Gosport, Portsmouth **P:** unk **BLW:** unk **RG:** N **MK:** N **PH:** unk **SS:** B gives rank; CI Revolution Navy & Privateer Records **BS:** 92 stone 15; 196.

STOHER, Balthazar; b unk; d 1781 **RU:** Soldier, Served in Royal Deaux Ponts Bn and died fr battle at Yorktown **CEM:** French Memorial; **GPS** 36.81944, -79.39933; Yorktown; York **GS:** U **SP:** No info **VI:** No further data **P:** unk **BLW:** unk **RG:** Y **MK:** unk **PH:** unk **SS:** J-Yorktown Historian **BS:** JLARC 1, 74.

STOKES, Christopher C; b 18 May 1749; d 1820 **RU:** Corporal, Served in Capt Samuel Eddeni's Co at Valley Forge, 3 Jun 1778 **CEM:** Cedar Grove; **GPS** 36.57204, -80.02599; 301 Fort Lane Rd; Portsmouth City **GS:** Y **SP:** No info **VI:** Son of Thomas & Ann (-----) Stokes. A man with this name also served in State Navy **P:** unk **BLW:** unk **RG:** Y **MK:** N **PH:** unk **SS:** A pg 342; C pg 371; N pg 172 **BS:** 27 pg 109.

STONE, Hawkin/Hawkins/Hawken; b 1735 Charles Co MD; d 10 Mar 1810 **RU:** Patriot, Provided 5 beeves one time and 3 another time to cause **CEM:** Aquia Episcopal; **GPS** 38.46466, -77.40325; 2938 Jeff Davis Hwy, Aquia; Stafford **GS:** Y **SP:** 1) (-----) 2) Jemima Smith 3) Elizabeth (Burroughs) **VI:** Originally bur in Scott Family cem at Dipple. Reinterred to Aquia Cemetery in 1942.Son of Barton Stone and Sarah (___) **P:** N **BLW:** N **RG:** Y **MK:** Y **PH:** Y **SS:** D Vol 3 pg 876 **BS:** 03 pg 129.

STONE, Jeremiah; b 1742; d 1827 **RU:** Private, Served in Capt Love's Co, Montgomery Co Militia **CEM:** Stone Family; **GPS** unk; Elk Creek; Grayson **GS:** U **SP:** Susannah (-----) (1744-18 Sep 1809) **VI:** Son of Barton & Sarah (-----) Stone **P:** unk **BLW:** unk **RG:** Y **MK:** unk **PH:** unk **SS:** D Fr Wm Co; G pg 233; AK Fairfax Resolves 2014 **BS:** JLARC 1, 3; 94; 196.

STONE, John; b 25 Nov 1754, Richmond Co; d 10 Jul 1824 **RU:** Private/Patriot, Served in Cont Line. Received money for services as soldier in infantry, Nov 1782 **CEM:** Hubbard-Stone; **GPS** unk; Rt 650 Hermosa; Pittsylvania **GS:** Y **SP:** Dollie Hoskins (10 Nov 1761-4 Apr 1862) **VI:** Son of Joshua & Dolly (Hoskins) Stone **P:** unk **BLW:** unk **RG:** Y **MK:** U **PH:** unk **SS:** J-NSSAR 2000 Reg; NSSAR Ancestor #P-298626; DAR Ancestor #A110087 **BS:** JLARC 76.

STONE, Joshua; b 1744; d 20 Oct 1821 **RU:** Captain, Was 2nd Lt 23 Oct 1777 in Capt Joseph Farris Co and 1st Lt 20 Jun 1780 Capt John Buckley Co. Later Capt of militia himself **CEM:** Stone Family; GPS unk; Nr Mulberry Church; Pittsylvania **GS:** Y **SP:** Mary Hoskins **VI:** Son of Josiah & Wilmoth (Bryant) Stone **P:** unk **BLW:** unk **RG:** N **MK:** N **PH:** unk **SS:** G pg 269 **BS:** 174 AS, AW.

STONE, William; b c1765; d 23 May 1827 **RU:** Private, Ent serv 1777 in1st VA Regt & 8th, 10th, 14th Cont Lines **CEM:** City Cemetery; **GPS** 38.30112, -77.46628; 1000 Washington Ave; Fredericksburg City **GS:** Y **SP:** Mar (1781) Mary McGuire (c1751 or c1761-___) **VI:** Sol appl pen 8 May 1818 Stafford Co age 59. Pen rec 1829 or 1830, Stafford Co. Widow appl pen 7 Dec 1838 Harrison Co KY age 77. However in 1839 she gave age as abt 88. W8752 **P:** Y **BLW:** unk **RG:** Y **MK:** N **PH:** unk **SS:** A pg 195; E pg 744; CG Vol 3 pg 3358 **BS:** 06 pg 29.

STONE, William B; b 8 Sep 1757; d 15 Oct 1793 **RU:** unk, Served in 1st VA State Regt and 8th, 10th 14th Cont Lines **CEM:** Edrington Family; **GPS** 38.44378, -77.38064; End of Rt 692, Quarry Rd, across fr

RU=Rank/Unit	CEM=Cemetery	GS=Gravestone	SP=Spousal Information
VI=Other Veteran Info	P=Pension	BLW=Bounty/Land Warrant	RG=Registered Grave
MK=SAR/DAR Marker	PH=Photo	SS=Service Source	BS=Burial Source

34 Edrington Court; Stafford **GS:** Y **SP:** No info **VI:** Son of Barton & Sarah (-----) Stone. Recd pen in Stafford Co **P:** Y **BLW:** unk **RG:** N **MK:** N **PH:** Y **SS:** E pg 744 **BS:** 03 pg 196.

STONEBRIDGE, John; b unk; d 1805 **RU:** Patriot, Gave material aid to the cause **CEM:** Back Creek Quaker, aka Gainesboro United Methodist; GPS 39.27861, -78.25694; 166 Siler Ln, Gainesboro; Frederick **GS:** Y **SP:** No info **VI:** No further data **P:** N **BLW:** N **RG:** Y **MK:** N **PH:** unk **SS:** AL Ct Bk pg 40 **BS:** 59 pg 319.

STORKE, William; b c1753; d 27 Aug 1822 **RU:** Patriot, Gave beef to cause, King George Co, 1781 **CEM:** Masonic Cemetery; GPS 38.30198, -77.46142; 900 Charles St; Fredericksburg City **GS:** Y **SP:** 1) Anna Rosetta Bryson 2) Elizabeth Washington **VI:** Vestryman St George Church. Son of John & Frances (-----) Storke **P:** N **BLW:** N **RG:** Y **MK:** N **PH:** unk **SS:** D pg 568 **BS:** 11 pg 114-5.

STOUDERT, Claude; b unk; d 1781 **RU:** Soldier, Served in Gatinais Bn and died fr battle at Yorktown **CEM:** French Memorial; GPS 36.81944, -79.39933; Yorktown; York **GS:** U **SP:** No info **VI:** No further data **P:** unk **BLW:** unk **RG:** unk **MK:** unk **PH:** unk **SS:** J-Yorktown Historian **BS:** JLARC 1, 74.

STOUTSENBERGER (STOUSEBERGER), John; b 1762; d 3 Mar 1837 **RU:** Drum major, Ent serv 1778. Was Drum Major PA Artillery Regt **CEM:** New Jerusalem Lutheran; GPS 39.25736, -77.63891; 12942 Lutheran Church Rd, Lovettsville; Loudoun **GS:** U **SP:** Maria Margaretha Kitchinden (c1762-c1847) **VI:** Widow pen 1838 Loudoun Co. 3 children appl pen,1854. W6207 **P:** Y **BLW:** unk **RG:** unk **MK:** unk **PH:** unk **SS:** K Vol 5 pg 179 **BS:** JLARC 4, 32.

STOVER, Peter; b 1715; d 1799 **RU:** Patriot, Gave material aid to cause **CEM:** Riverview; GPS 38.98420, -78.36140; Grounds of Riverview HS, Strasburg; Shenandoah **GS:** U **SP:** No info **VI:** No further data **P:** N **BLW:** N **RG:** unk **MK:** unk **PH:** unk **SS:** Al Ct Bk pg 2-4, 8-10, 12, 13, 20 **BS:** 196.

STOVER, Peter; b 1763; d 1814 **RU:** Private, Served in Capt Alexander Machir's Co, Strasburg District, Shenandoah Co. **CEM:** Mt Zion United Methodist; GPS unk; 399 W Queens St, Strasburg; Shenandoah **GS:** Y **SP:** No info **VI:** No further data **P:** unk **BLW:** unk **RG:** N **MK:** N **PH:** unk **SS:** C pg 607 **BS:** 65 Strasburg.

STRANGE, John Alloway; b 15 Jan 1727, Goochland Co; d 1 Sep 1811 **RU:** Patriot, Gave material aid to cause **CEM:** Oak Hill; GPS 37.70690, -78.25360; Rt 655; Fluvanna **GS:** N **SP:** Mar (22 Sep 1756, New Kent Co) Ann Mildred Mitchell (3 Jan 1727-29 Apr 1782) **VI:** No further data **P:** N **BLW:** N **RG:** unk **MK:** unk **PH:** N **SS:** DAR Ancestor #A202286; AL Ct bk pg 5, Fluvanna Co **BS:** 196.

STRATTON, Henry; b 1735, Dale Parish, Chesterfield Co; d 1799 **RU:** Lieutenant/Patriot, Took oath as Lt 14 Sep 1766, Bedford Co Militia. Gave material aid to cause **CEM:** Stratton Family; GPS unk; Jct Rts 122 & 736; Bedford **GS:** N **SP:** Sarah Hampton **VI:** No further data **P:** unk **BLW:** unk **RG:** Y **MK:** N **PH:** N **SS:** AL Ct Bk pg 7, 19 Bedford Co; AK Bedford Mus. **BS:** 04 Sep 07.

STRATTON, John Handley; b 1745, Chesterfield Co; d 6 Apr 1805 **RU:** Trooper/Patriot, Served in First Lt Dragoons, 25th VA Regt Cont Line. Gave material aid to cause **CEM:** Stratton Family; GPS unk; New Canton; Buckingham **GS:** U **SP:** Susan Ann Douglass **VI:** No further data **P:** unk **BLW:** unk **RG:** N **MK:** N **PH:** unk **SS:** AL Ct Bk pg 18 Amherst Co; AS SAR Report; NSSAR Ancestor #P-299349; DAR #A111137 **BS:** unk.

STREIT (STRAIGHT), Christian; b 07 Jun 1749, NJ; d 15 Mar 1812 **RU:** Chaplain, Served in 8th Cont Line, 1 Aug 1776 - Jul 1777 **CEM:** Mt Hebron; GPS 39.10916, -78.09497; 305 E Boscawen St; Winchester City **GS:** Y **SP:** Mar (15 Oct 1789, Frederick Co) Susannah Barr, (Return) **VI:** No further data **P:** unk **BLW:** unk **RG:** unk **MK:** N **PH:** Y **SS:** J-NSSAR 1993 Reg. E, pg 745-746 NARA M246 **BS:** 50 pg 50; JLARC 1.

STRICKLER, Benjamin; b 21 Jan 1726, W. Hempfield Twp, Lancaster Co, PA; d 11 Apr 1791 **RU:** Patriot, Gave material aid to cause **CEM:** Beaver-Brubaker (Mauck's Mill); GPS 39.18343, -78.16278; Rt 615, vic Luray; Page **GS:** N **SP:** Mary Baidler **VI:** Tradition states that Benjamin Strickler is bur at Strickler Cemetery on Massanutten Tract, where Isaac Strickler is bur. More likely bur with wife & children and memorialized there **P:** N **BLW:** N **RG:** Y **MK:** N **PH:** unk **SS:** C pg 603 **BS:** 79 pg 174-6.

RU=Rank/Unit   CEM=Cemetery   GS=Gravestone   SP=Spousal Information
VI=Other Veteran Info   P=Pension   BLW=Bounty/Land Warrant   RG=Registered Grave
MK=SAR/DAR Marker   PH=Photo   SS=Service Source   BS=Burial Source

STRICKLER, Isaac; b 15 Aug 1749, Egypt Bend, Page Co; d 1 May 1817 **RU:** Private, Served in Michael Reader's Co, Shenandoah Co Militia **CEM:** Strickler Monument; GPS unk; SW side of Rts 615 & Rt 211, Ft Egypt; Page **GS:** N **SP:** 1) Mar (24 Dec 1779 Linville, Rockingham Co) Susanna Brubaker (15 Jul 1759 Lancaster Co PA-8 Aug 1805 Massanutten Heights, Shenandoah Co) d/o Abraham & Barbara (Long) Brubaker 2) Mar (11 Jul 1807, Luray, Shenandoah Co) Catherine Mauck Beaver (widow of Christian Beaver) (29 Jan 1764 Shenandoah Co-29 May 1829) d/o Daniel & Barbara (Harnsbarger) Mauck **VI:** Son of Isaac & Magdalena (Neff) Strickler. Died in Egypt Bend, Page Co **P:** unk **BLW:** unk **RG:** Y **MK:** N **PH:** N **SS:** C pg 603 **BS:** 79 pg 174-6.

STRICKLER, Jacob; b 9 Dec 1728, W. Hempfield Co, Lancaster Co, PA; d 29 Jan 1784 **RU:** Patriot, Gave material aid to cause **CEM:** Strickler Monument; GPS unk; SW side of St Rt 615, Rt 211, Ft Egypt; Page **GS:** N **SP:** 1) Nancy Kauffman 2) Magdalena Moomaw **VI:** Died in Fortt Egypt, Page Co **P:** N **BLW:** N **RG:** Y **MK:** N **PH:** N **SS:** H **BS:** 79 pg 235, 236.

STRICKLER, Joseph; b 1 Sep 1731, W. Hempfield Twp, Lancaster Co PA; d 30 Aug 1795 **RU:** Patriot, Gave material aid to cause **CEM:** Strickler Monument; GPS unk; SW side of St Rt 615, Rt 211, Ft Egypt; Page **GS:** N **SP:** 1) Mar (1 Feb 1755 Shenandoah Co) Elizabeth Stoeckli (Stickley) d/o Johannes & Barbara (Morgan) Stoeckli (25 Jan 1733 PA-21 Jan 1773 Egypt Bend, Dunmore Co) 2) Mar (21 Jun 1774 Shenandoah Co) Barbara Harnish d/o Christian & Barbara (Hiestand) Hamish Jr (c1753-aft Aug 1807) **VI:** Son of Abraham & Anna Maria (Ruffner) Strickler. Died in Egypt Plantation, Page Co **P:** N **BLW:** N **RG:** Y **MK:** N **PH:** N **SS:** C, pg 603 **BS:** 79, pg 197.

STROBIA, John; b 1742; d 10 Mar 1809 **RU:** Patriot, Was Legislative Petitioner for Rev War supplies furnished western counties **CEM:** St John's Episcopal; GPS 37.53183, -77.41958; 2401 E Broad St; Richmond City **GS:** U **SP:** Mary P-----) (1762-1795) **VI:** No further data **P:** N **BLW:** N **RG:** unk **MK:** unk **PH:** unk **SS:** S VA Legislative Petitions **BS:** 196.

STRODE, John; b 1734 PA, Chester Co; d c1820 **RU:** Patriot, Ran an ironworks during war and gave much material to the cause **CEM:** Fairview; GPS 38.48080,-78.00470; Sperryville Pike Rt 522, Culpeper; Culpeper **GS:** Y **SP:** Anne (-----) **VI:** Originally buried at "Fleetwood" in Culpeper Co. He may have d in North Carolina **P:** N **BLW:** N **RG:** Y **MK:** N **PH:** Y **SS:** 34 pg 114-5 **BS:** 34 pg 114, 115.

STROTHER, French; b 1733; d 3 Jun 1800 **RU:** Colonel/Patriot, Served in VA militia as he received pension. Member of VA Constitution Conventions 1776 and 1788. As patriot gave to the cause in Culpeper Co **CEM:** St George's Episcopal; GPS unk; 905 Princess Anne; Fredericksburg City **GS:** Y **SP:** Lucy Coleman daughter of Gilly C & (-----) Coleman. Also Ann (-----) **VI:** Son of James (__-1761 Culpeper Co.) & Margaret (French) Strother. Represented Culpeper Co in General Assembly for 25 yrs. Served as County Justice and County Lt. **P:** Y **BLW:** unk **RG:** Y **MK:** N **PH:** unk **SS:** H **BS:** 12 pg 114.

STROTHER, John; b 1758; d 1790 **RU:** Captain, Commanded a co 24 Oct 1776 in Culpeper Co Militia **CEM:** Strother-Jones; GPS unk; Stephens City; Frederick **GS:** Y **SP:** Hellen Piper (1768-after 1840) **VI:** No further data **P:** unk **BLW:** unk **RG:** N **MK:** N **PH:** unk **SS:** E pg 747 **BS:** 59 pg 322.

STROTHER, John Dabney Sr; b 31 Dec 1721; d Apr 1795 **RU:** Captain/Patriot, Member of Committee of Safety for Culpeper 1775. Gave material aid to cause Culpeper Co **CEM:** Wadefield, Strother Family; GPS unk; Nr Washington; Rappahannock **GS:** U **SP:** Mar (1741) Mary Wade **VI:** Son of Francis & Suzanne (Dabney) Strother. Father was Lt in Colonial militia. Was Capt in French and Indian War. One of 16 Culpeper justices who signed the 1765 Stamp Act Protest. Was Justice and Sheriff of Co **P:** unk **BLW:** unk **RG:** unk **MK:** unk **PH:** unk **SS:** J- DAR Hatcher; D pg 238; AL Ct Bk I pg 5 Culpeper Co **BS:** JLARC 2; 196.

STROUD, Thomas A; b 1765; d 1838 **RU:** Private, Served in Capt Felix Warley's Co, 3rd Carolina Regt of Cont Line Jul 1779 **CEM:** Blandford; GPS 37.22433, -77.38604; 319 S Crater Rd; Petersburg City **GS:** Y **SP:** Susanna (Susan) Bacon Bishop (15 Aug 1770 Woodstock, Windham Co, CT-19 Jul 1847, Petersburg) **VI:** No further data **P:** unk **BLW:** unk **RG:** N **MK:** N **PH:** unk **SS:** AP roll SC Cont Line **BS:** 128 pg 1; 196.

STUART, Archibald; b 19 Mar 1757; d 11 Jul 1832 **RU:** Private, Served in Augusta & Rockbridge Co Militias, Was at the Battle of Guilford CH in NC, Mar 1781 **CEM:** Trinity Episcopal; GPS 38.14917, -79.07521; 214 Beverley St; Staunton City **GS:** Y **SP:** Eleanor Briscoe (1768-1858) **VI:** Son of Alexander

RU=Rank/Unit	CEM=Cemetery	GS=Gravestone	SP=Spousal Information
VI=Other Veteran Info	P=Pension	BLW=Bounty/Land Warrant	RG=Registered Grave
MK=SAR/DAR Marker	PH=Photo	SS=Service Source	BS=Burial Source

323

(1734-1822) & (-----) Stuart. Attended College of William and Mary fr 1777-1780. A lawyer and judge. Read law under Thomas Jefferson. Member of VA federal convention of 1788. Favored ratification of US Constitution **P:** unk **BLW:** unk **RG:** unk **MK:** unk **PH:** Y **SS:** B **BS:** JLARC 62, 63; 196.

STUART, Benjamin; b 1736, PA; d 12 Dec 1808 **RU:** Private/Patriot, Served as private in First Light Dragoons. Gave material aid to cause **CEM:** Tinkling Spring Presbyterian; GPS 38.08472, -78.98278; 30 Tinkling Spring Dr, Fishersville; Augusta **GS:** N **SP:** Eleanor Tate **VI:** Son of Archibald Stuart (1696-1761) & Janet Brown **P:** unk **BLW:** unk **RG:** unk **MK:** N **PH:** N **SS:** E pg 747; AL Comm Bk II pg 360 Augusta Co **BS:** JLARC 62, 63; 196; 208 pg 467.

STUART, John; b 1756, Glasgow Scotland; d 1 Feb 1814 **RU:** Private, Served in Capt Robert Powell's Co, 3rd VA Regt of Foot, commanded by Col William Heath Feb 1779. Also served in 15th VA Regt **CEM:** Blandford; GPS 37.22433, -77.38604; 319 S Crater Rd; Petersburg City **GS:** Y **SP:** No info **VI:** Merchant in Petersburg **P:** unk **BLW:** unk **RG:** N **MK:** N **PH:** unk **SS:** E pg 747; AP Payroll and service rec **BS:** 188 # 1358; 196.

STUART, John Ainsworth; b unk, Belfast Ireland; d unk **RU:** Soldier, SAR registry did not provide service **CEM:** Old Presbyterian Meeting House; GPS 38.48528, -77.23532; 323 S Fairfax St; Alexandria City **GS:** N **SP:** No info **VI:** No further data **P:** unk **BLW:** unk **RG:** Y **MK:** unk **PH:** N **SS:** J-NSSAR 1993 Reg; NSSAR Ancestor # P-299893 **BS:** JLARC 1; 5.

STUART, Robert; b 1759; d 28 Oct 1827 **RU:** Sergeant, Served in 8th Cont Line **CEM:** Stuart Family; GPS unk; Rt 727, Blackwells property; Rockbridge **GS:** Y **SP:** No info **VI:** Son of Alexander Sr (27 Aug 1734 Chester PA-1822) & (-----) Stuart **P:** unk **BLW:** unk **RG:** unk **MK:** unk **PH:** unk **SS:** E pg 747 **BS:** 196.

STUART, William David; b 13 Dec 1723 Stafford Co; d 1799 **RU:** Patriot, Performed public service as member of Committee of Safety **CEM:** Stuart-Grymes Family; GPS 38.33601, -77.13407; Rt 218 on Cedar Grove Farm; King George **GS:** Y **SP:** Mar (26 Nov 1750) Sarah Foote (29 Jun 1732 Cedar Grove, Stafford Co-aft 1799 St Paul's Parish) **VI:** Son of William (1723-1799) & Sarah (Foote) (1732-__) Stuart. Was a reverend **P:** N **BLW:** N **RG:** unk **MK:** unk **PH:** unk **SS:** DAR Ancestor #A109740; AL Ct Bk pg 4 King George Co **BS:** 196.

STUBERT, Adam; b unk; d 1781 **RU:** Soldier, Served in Royal Deaux Ponts Bn and died fr battle at Yorktown **CEM:** French Memorial; GPS 36.81944, -79.39933; Yorktown; York **GS:** U **SP:** No info **VI:** No further data **P:** unk **BLW:** unk **RG:** Y **MK:** unk **PH:** unk **SS:** J-Yorktown Historian **BS:** JLARC 1, 74.

SUMMERS, Francis; b 3 Mar 1732; d 10 Sep 1800 **RU:** Soldier/Patriot, Overseer of the Poor for Fairfax Co 1776. VA, donated 750 lbs of beef **CEM:** Summers Family; GPS 38.49150, -770828; Lincolnia, nr Deming Avenue and Rt 613; Fairfax **GS:** Y **SP:** Jane Watkins Charlton (1736-22 Aug 1814) **VI:** Son of John & (-----) Summers. DAR marker by Thomas Lee Chapter **P:** unk **BLW:** unk **RG:** Y **MK:** Y **PH:** unk **SS:** NSDAR #A032424; AK; BT **BS:** JLARC 1, 3,14, 25, 27, 28; 04; 47 pg 55.2.

SUMMERS, Horsey; b 1762, Somerset Co, MD; d 25 Feb 1852 **RU:** Soldier, MD Line. Lived in Somerset Co, MD at enl. Was age 15 at time **CEM:** Parksley; GPS unk; .5 mi N of Rt 176, W of Rt 678, NE fr Parksley; Accomack **GS:** N **SP:** Mar (Accomac Co) (-----) **VI:** Appl pen 12 Sep 1851, Accomac Co, age 89. Children granted pen in arrears. S7664 **P:** Y **BLW:** unk **RG:** unk **MK:** unk **PH:** N **SS:** K Vol 5 pg 192; CG Vol 3 pg 3389 **BS:** JLARC 4 , 5.

SUMMERS, John; b 14 Nov 1687, Middlesex Co; d 4 Dec 1790 **RU:** Patriot, Gave material aid to the cause **CEM:** Summers Family; GPS 38.49150, -770828; Demming Ave & Lincolnia Rd; Alexandria City **GS:** N **SP:** No info **VI:** Son of John & Elizabeth (-----) Summers. Died at 103 yrs old in "Summers Grove" nr Annanndale, Alexandria, Fairfax Co **P:** N **BLW:** N **RG:** N **MK:** N **PH:** N **SS:** AL Ct Bk lt, pg 2, 6 **BS:** 20 pg 194.

SUMMERS, John; b 13 Dec 1746; d 28 Jan 1806 **RU:** Soldier/Patriot, Served in Capt McCuthen's Co, Augusta Co Militia. Gave material aid to cause **CEM:** St John's Reformed UCC; GPS 38.05081, -79.17761; 1515 Arbor Hill Rd, Middlebrook; Augusta **GS:** Y **SP:** Mar (1770) Elizabeth Reidenauer (Ridenour) (28 Jan 1752-28 Dec 1812) **VI:** Eroded stone. Son of Johan George & Maria Margaretha (----

RU=Rank/Unit   CEM=Cemetery   GS=Gravestone   SP=Spousal Information
VI=Other Veteran Info   P=Pension   BLW=Bounty/Land Warrant   RG=Registered Grave
MK=SAR/DAR Marker   PH=Photo   SS=Service Source   BS=Burial Source

324

-) Summers **P:** unk **BLW:** unk **RG:** unk **MK:** unk **PH:** Y **SS:** DAR Ancestor #A110926; D Vol 1 pg 98; E pg 750; CD **BS:** JLARC 62; 196.

SUMMERS, William J; b unk; d 3 Jun 1805 **RU:** Bombardier, Appointed bombardier Dec 1776, in Capt John Canter's Co of Artillery at Valley Forge **CEM:** Sharon; GPS unk; Middleburg; Loudoun **GS:** Y **SP:** No info **VI:** No further data **P:** unk **BLW:** unk **RG:** Y **MK:** N **PH:** unk **SS:** E pg 750 **BS:** 25 pg 302.

SUMMERS (SOMMERS), Simon; b 23 Nov 1747, Fairfax Co; d 2 Dec 1836 **RU:** Major or Adjutant/Patriot, Served as the Adjutant, 6th VA Regt fr 21 Mar 1776 to end of campaign in 1781. Also donated "waggon and team 13 days hawling public stores." - Fairfax Co. Ct claim Feb 1782 **CEM:** Falls Church Episcopal; GPS 38.88077, -77.17166; 115 E Fairfax St; Falls Church City **GS:** Y **SP:** Elizabeth Ferguson **VI:** Died in Fairfax Co VA. Find a Grave says he d in 1806. Govt Grave Stone. Rec pen S905 and BLW 1480-200 **P:** Y **BLW:** Y **RG:** Y **MK:** Y **PH:** unk **SS:** AK M805 Roll 758; BY; AL Ct Bk; A pg 507; CD **BS:** 04; JLARC 1, 2,14, 27, 28, 45.

SWAN, Caleb; b 2 Jul 1758, Fryeburg, York Co, MA (now Oxford Co, ME); d 29 Nov 1809 **RU:** Ensign, Served as Corporal and Sergeant 9th MA Regt, 1 Feb 1777; appointed Ensign 26 Nov 1779; transferred to 8th MA 1 Jan 1781; transferred to 3rd MA 12 Jun 1783; retained in Jackson's Cont Regt Nov 1783 **CEM:** Arlington National; GPS 38.88377, -77.06535; Jefferson Davis Hwy Rt 110; Arlington **GS:** Y **SP:** No info **VI:** Died in DC. Bur at Old Presbyterian Cem in DC. Reinterred 12 May 1892. Fryeburg was located in York Co. MA prior to 1804 (formation of Oxford Co.). Area of MA became ME in 1820 **P:** unk **BLW:** unk **RG:** Y **MK:** N **PH:** unk **SS:** J-NSSAR 1993 Reg, J- DAR Hatcher **BS:** JLARC 1, 2; 196.

SWIFT, Thomas; b 1765; d 28 May 1804 **RU:** Marine, Served in shipyard at Portsmouth **CEM:** Trinity Episcopal; GPS 36.83459, -76.30105; 500 Court St; Portsmouth City **GS:** U **SP:** No info **VI:** GS indicates rank of capt probably obtained after war period **P:** unk **BLW:** unk **RG:** unk **MK:** unk **PH:** unk **SS:** See burial source 57 **BS:** 57.

SYDNOR, Joseph; b 17 Oct 1740, Lancaster Co; d 1787 **RU:** Patriot, Gave material aid to cause **CEM:** Sydnor - Young Family; GPS unk; Petersburg National Battlefield; Dinwiddie **GS:** N **SP:** Ann Chowning (1751-__) **VI:** Son of Anthony Sydnor (1711-1779) and Elizabeth Taylor (1722-1785) **P:** N **BLW:** N **RG:** unk **MK:** Y **PH:** N **SS:** Comm Bk V pg 239 Dinwiddie Co **BS:** 192; 196.

SYDNOR, William; b c1734; d Jun 1794 **RU:** Patriot, Signer of Leedstown Resolutions 1766. Served on Lancaster Co Committee of Safety during war period **CEM:** St Mary's Whitechapel Episcopal; GPS 37.44782, -76.33181; 5940 White Chapel Rd, Lively; Lancaster **GS:** N **SP:** Mar (12 Oct 1763 (bond) Richmond Co) Ellen Fauntleroy (__-14 Dec 1807 Fairfax Co) d/o Capt Moore & Ann (Heale) Fauntleroy **VI:** Son of William & Cathrine (-----) Sydnor **P:** N **BLW:** N **RG:** N **MK:** N **PH:** N **SS:** BQ pg 7157 **BS:** Serv Source BQ pg 7158.

SYME (SIMS, SYMES), John II; b 25 Dec 1729; d 25 Nov 1805 **RU:** Colonel/Patriot, Gave material aid to cause **CEM:** Syme; GPS unk; Rts 6763 & 703 nr Rockville, Rocky Mills; Hanover **GS:** N **SP:** 1) Mildred Thornton Meriwether (1739-1760) 2) Sarah Hoops (1747-1810) **VI:** Son of John (1690-1732) & Sarah (Winston) (1710-1784) Syme **P:** unk **BLW:** unk **RG:** unk **MK:** unk **PH:** N **SS:** AL Ct Bk I pg 22-26, 38 Hanover Co **BS:** JLARC 71.

TABB, Edward; b 03 Feb 1719; d 21 Dec 1782 **RU:** Patriot, Gave material aid to cause In Gloucester Co **CEM:** Ware Episcopal; GPS 37.42275, -76.50789; 7825 John Clayton Mem Hwy; Gloucester **GS:** Y **SP:** Lucy Todd (20 Nov 1721-18 Feb 1791) d/o Christopher (1690-1743) & (-----) Todd **VI:** Son of John & Martha (-----) Tabb. Stone moved fr Toddsbury on North River in August 1924. Epitaph recorded 1959 **P:** N **BLW:** N **RG:** Y **MK:** N **PH:** Y **SS:** AL Ct Bk pg iii,15 **BS:** 48 pg 81; 196; 207.

TABB, Philip (Phillip); b 6 Nov 1750; d 25 Feb 1822 **RU:** Captain/patriot, Served in Capt Gloucester Co Militia, 25 Jul 1775 to 1776. Appointed Lt 13 Sep 1775. Also gave material aid to cause **CEM:** Ware Episcopal; GPS 37.42275, -76.50789; 7825 John Clayton Mem Hwy; Gloucester **GS:** Y **SP:** Mary Mason Wythe (7 Sep 1751-22 Sep 1814) d/o Nathaniel & Elizabeth (-----) Wythe. **VI:** Son of Edward and Lucy (-----) Tabb. Died in "Toddsbury" Gloucester Co. Stone moved fr Toddsbury on North River in August 1924. Epitaph recorded 1959 **P:** N **BLW:** N **RG:** Y **MK:** N **PH:** Y **SS:** E pg 755; AK; AL Ct Bk pg iii, 12 **BS:** 48 pg 83; 207.

RU=Rank/Unit   CEM=Cemetery   GS=Gravestone   SP=Spousal Information
VI=Other Veteran Info   P=Pension   BLW=Bounty/Land Warrant   RG=Registered Grave
MK=SAR/DAR Marker   PH=Photo   SS=Service Source   BS=Burial Source

325

TABB, Thomas; b 1755, Seaford, Gloucester Co; d 1818/1819 **RU:** Ensign/Patriot, Served in Gloucester Co Militia 1775. Performed recruiting services in Amelia & Lunenburg Co in 1776. Delegate fr Lunenburg Co to VA Legislature 1775 **CEM:** Toddsbury Plantation; GPS unk; Elmington; Mathews **GS:** U **SP:** Elizabeth H.Teakle, d 04 Dec 1824, **VI:** Death date determined by Mathews Co tax record **P:** unk **BLW:** unk **RG:** unk **MK:** unk **PH:** unk **SS:** E pg 755 **BS:** 196.

TAFT, Nathan; b unk; d 1781 **RU:** Soldier, Served fr MA and died fr Yorktown battle **CEM:** Yorktown Victory Monument Tablet; GPS 38.28350, -78.54150; Yorktown; York **GS:** U **SP:** No info **VI:** No further data **P:** unk **BLW:** unk **RG:** unk **MK:** unk **PH:** unk **SS:** J-Yorktown Historian **BS:** JLARC 74.

TALBOTT, Samuel; b 1726; d 30 Dec 1777 **RU:** Captain, Served in 2nd PA Regt; died at Valley Forge Dec 1777 **CEM:** Falls Church Episcopal; GPS 38.88077, -77.17166; 115 E Fairfax St; Falls Church City **GS:** U **SP:** Mary Magdalene Demoville (__-2 Jul 1791) d/o Samuel & Rose (Neale) Demoville **VI:** Son of Benjamin & Hannah Elizabeth (Neale) Talbott. He d fr exposure and his family awarded half pay. Was member Society Cincinnati **P:** Y **BLW:** unk **RG:** unk **MK:** unk **PH:** unk **SS:** A pg 434, 488 **BS:** 196.

TALIAFERRO, Lawrence; b 9 Dec 1734; d 8 Apr 1798 **RU:** Colonel, Appointed Lt Col 28 May 1778. Col Commandant of the Minute Men raised in Orange, Culpeper, Fauquier Co **CEM:** Rose Hill; GPS unk; Rapidan; Orange **GS:** Y **SP:** 1) Mar (1758) Mary Jackson 2) mar (3 Feb 1774) Sarah Dade **VI:** Son of Francis & Elizabeth (Hay) Taliaferro, of "Epson". Gov't and SAR markers **P:** unk **BLW:** unk **RG:** Y **MK:** Y **PH:** unk **SS:** SAR Ancestor #P-301602; J-NSSAR 2000 Reg **BS:** JLARC 76; 196.

TALIAFERRO, Walker; b unk; d Bef 13 Mar 1826 **RU:** Colonel/Patriot, Served in Caroline Co Militia. Col rank given 14 Aug 1777. Member House of Burgesses **CEM:** Taliaferro Family; GPS unk; Rt 654; Caroline **GS:** N **SP:** Sallie Turner d/o Thomas Turner, Jr. & Sallie (-----) **VI:** Member of Masonic Lodge **P:** unk **BLW:** unk **RG:** Y **MK:** N **PH:** unk **SS:** E pg 756; H **BS:** 02 pg 143.

TALLEY (TALLY), Nathaniel (Nathan); b unk; d c1823 **RU:** Sergeant, Served in Taylor's VA Regt **CEM:** Cowlands Site; GPS unk; Rt 613; Spotsylvania **GS:** U **SP:** Mollie (-----) **VI:** No further data **P:** unk **BLW:** unk **RG:** Y **MK:** N **PH:** unk **SS:** E pg 757; SAR application 454 **BS:** 09 grid 32.

TANKARD, John Dr; b 1752; d 24 Apr 1836 **RU:** Colonel, Enl serv nr Williamsburg as surgeon in 1778 for the Flying Hospital and was deputy director for VA hospitals at time he enlisted. Surgeon for the VA State troops, stationed at Williamsburg. Also was with LaFayette when he retreated to mountains in Orange Co **CEM:** Tankard's Rest; GPS unk; Exmore; Northampton **GS:** U **SP:** 1) Zillah (-----) 2) Mar (12 Feb 1778) Sarah (-----) Andrews, widow of Southy Andrews **VI:** Was Surgeon. Pen 1834 Northampton Co. S48512. DAR Grave marker says he was in the 8th VMR, LaFayette's Division **P:** Y **BLW:** Y **RG:** unk **MK:** unk **PH:** unk **SS:** K Vol 5 pg 207; CG Vol 3 pg 3418; BT **BS:** JLARC 2, 4, 69; 42 pg 82; 209.

TANNER, Abraham; b Feb 1759, Culpeper Co; d 1844 **RU:** Private, Ent serv Culpeper Co (later Madison Co) 1779-80. Served in Culpeper Militia 1781 **CEM:** Tanner Family; GPS unk; Hebron Valley; Madison **GS:** N **SP:** Elizabeth (-----) **VI:** Son of Christopher Sr. (__-1792) & Elizabeth Aylor Tanner. Appl pen 23 Aug 1832 Madison Co. S6190 **P:** Y **BLW:** unk **RG:** Y **MK:** N **PH:** N **SS:** E pg 757; K Vol 5 pg 208; CG Vol 3 pg 3418 **BS:** 04.

TANNER, Christopher; b c1751; d 1781 **RU:** Sergeant, Was listed in Culpeper recruiting classes. Died in service 1781 **CEM:** Williamsburg Land Conservancy; GPS unk; 5000 New Point Rd; Williamsburg City **GS:** N **SP:** Mary Cook (14 Dec 1753-__) d/o George & Mary Sarah (Reiner) Cook. **VI:** Son of Christopher Sr. (__-1792) & Elizabeth Aylor Tanner. Memorialized at Yorktown Victory Monument Tablet **P:** unk **BLW:** unk **RG:** N **MK:** N **PH:** N **SS:** AU Will Chap; J-Yorktown Historian **BS:** JLARC 74.

TAPP (TOPP), Vincent; b 1757; d Mar 1824 **RU:** Sergeant-Major, Served in VA Line. Ent serv Wheeling, OH 1776 **CEM:** Trinity Episcopal; GPS 38.14917, -79.07521; 214 Beverley St; Staunton City **GS:** U **SP:** Mar (Charlottesville, VA) Susanna Gamble (__-Apr 1835) **VI:** Prob son of Vincent Tapp (__-1757 Frederick Co, MD). His grandfather was William Tatico (__-1719) of Northumberland Co, last King of Wicomico Indians. Disability pen fr 16 Jul 1811 for severe wound to arm at Battle of Brandywine. Granted regular pension fr Augusta Co in 1820, age 63, as resident of Staunton. Reapplied 19 Jan 1820, Staunton VA age 63. S41231. Moved to Albemarle Co after RW. After Rev taught school nr Charlottesville. Clerk of the Ct of Hustings at Staunton **P:** Y **BLW:** unk **RG:** Y **MK:** unk **PH:** unk **SS:** K Vol 5 pg 210; CG Vol 3 pg 3420 **BS:** JLARC 1, 4, 62, 63.

RU=Rank/Unit	CEM=Cemetery	GS=Gravestone	SP=Spousal Information
VI=Other Veteran Info	P=Pension	BLW=Bounty/Land Warrant	RG=Registered Grave
MK=SAR/DAR Marker	PH=Photo	SS=Service Source	BS=Burial Source

TATE, John; b 1725, Hanover Co; d 1794 **RU:** Private, Served in Capt Tate's Co, Augusta Militia **CEM:** Tinkling Spring Presbyterian; GPS 38.08472, -78.98278; 30 Tinkling Spring Dr, Fishersville; Augusta **GS:** N **SP:** No info **VI:** No further data **P:** unk **BLW:** unk **RG:** unk **MK:** N **PH:** N **SS:** E pg 758; J- DAR Hatcher **BS:** 196; JLARC 2.

TATE, John; b 6 Aug 1761 (1731 per GS), Augusta Co; d end of Aug 1836 **RU:** Soldier, Served in VA Line. Lived in Augusta Co at enl in 1777. Served under James Tate (relative). Moved with father to Botetourt Co where enl again 1781 **CEM:** Bethel Presbyterian; GPS 38.04257, -79.17283; 563 Bethel Green Rd, Middlebrook; Augusta **GS:** U **SP:** No info **VI:** Appl pen 7 Sep 1832, Botetourt Co. S6191 This is not the same John Tate bur at Bethel with Govt stone, dates 1739-1802, with RW service **P:** Y **BLW:** unk **RG:** unk **MK:** unk **PH:** unk **SS:** E pg 758; K Vol 5 pg 212; CG Vol 3 pg 3423 **BS:** JLARC 62,63.

TATE, John; b 25 Feb 1749 (baptized); d 13 Dec 1802 **RU:** Soldier, Served in brother James Tate's Co, Augusta Co Militia & in Capt May's Co Botetourt Co. Was in Battle at Kings Mountain in Yorktown **CEM:** Old Providence; GPS 37.96151, -79.710; 1005 Spottswood Rd, Spottswood; Augusta **GS:** Y **SP:** Mar (1774) Jane Steele (__-1834) **VI:** Son of John & Mary (Doak) Tate. Trustee of Saunton Academy 1792, VA Legislator 1798.Newer Govt stone. Name also on SAR cemetery plaque **P:** unk **BLW:** unk **RG:** Y **MK:** Y **PH:** unk **SS:** B; BT **BS:** JLARC 1, 2, 8, 62, 63; 196.

TATE, John; b 1743, Augusta Co; d 15 Dec 1828 **RU:** Soldier, Served in Oct 1780 Washington Co, Militia. In 1776 built Tate's Fort. Was in Battle of Kings Mountain, SC **CEM:** Tate-Burdine; GPS unk; Lebanon; Russell **GS:** Y **SP:** Mar (c1766 VA) Mary Bracken (1742-1817), d/o John & Martha (Green) Bracken. **VI:** Son of Robert & Mary (-----) Tate. Moved to Moccasin Valley in Russell Co, Nov 1772. In 1789 was Capt in 72nd Regt of VA Militia. In 1795, was Maj in 2nd Bn 72nd Regt VA Militia. In 1801-3 was Sheriff & Collector of Revenue for Russell Co. In 1802 was Lt Col Commandant 72 Regt, 3rd Div VA Militia by appt of Gov (later President) James Monroe. In 1826-8 again became Sheriff & Collector **P:** N **BLW:** N **RG:** unk **MK:** unk **PH:** Y **SS:** CD **BS:** 196.

TATE, Robert; b Mar 1753; d 8 or 20 Jul 1832 **RU:** Private, Served in Co commanded by his brother, James Tate and in William Tate's Co, Augusta Co Militia **CEM:** Bethel Presbyterian; GPS 38.04257, -79.17283; 563 Bethel Green Rd, Middlebrook; Augusta **GS:** Y **SP:** Margaret Alexander McClug (5 Oct 1755 Greenville, Augusta Co-23 Sep 1839) d/o John & Elizabeth (Alexander) McClung **VI:** Birth & death data fr 11 Aug 1936 WPA survey of cemetery by Scioto M. Herndon, available at Library of VA **P:** unk **BLW:** unk **RG:** unk **MK:** unk **PH:** Y **SS:** G pg 772 **BS:** JLARC 62, 63; 196.

TATE, Thomas; b 1740; d Aft 1781 **RU:** Private/Patriot, Gave material aid to cause **CEM:** Tinkling Spring Presbyterian; GPS 38.08472, -78.98278; 30 Tinkling Spring Dr, Fishersville; Augusta **GS:** N **SP:** Elizabeth Caldwell **VI:** No further data **P:** unk **BLW:** unk **RG:** unk **MK:** N **PH:** N **SS:** SAR Ancestor #P-301961; AL Cert Augusta Co **BS:** JLARC 2, 63.

TATE, William; b 20 Nov 1753, Augusta Co; d 11 Feb 1830 **RU:** Captain, Took oath as Capt in Augusta Co Miltia 21 Aug 1781. Served to end of war **CEM:** Tate Family, nr Buchanan House; GPS unk; Broadford; Smyth **GS:** N **SP:** Dorcas Mitchell **VI:** No further data **P:** unk **BLW:** unk **RG:** unk **MK:** unk **PH:** N **SS:** DAR Ancestor #A112194; E pg 758 **BS:** JLARC 11, 14.

TATE, William; b 1747; d 15 Sep 1803 **RU:** Lieutenant Colonel, Served in Washington Co Militia 1776 **CEM:** Glenwood; GPS unk; Clarksville; Washington **GS:** U **SP:** Elizabeth (-----) (1755-1840) **VI:** No further data **P:** unk **BLW:** unk **RG:** unk **MK:** unk **PH:** unk **SS:** E pg 758 **BS:** 196.

TAVINER (TAVENNER), Ritchard (Richard); b unk; d 1844 **RU:** Private, Served in Capt Samuel Noland's Co, Loudoun Co Militia **CEM:** Goose Creek; GPS 39.11250, -77.69527; Rt 722, Lincoln; Loudoun **GS:** Y **SP:** No info **VI:** No further data **P:** unk **BLW:** unk **RG:** Y **MK:** N **PH:** unk **SS:** N pg 1254 **BS:** 25 pg 306.

TAYLOE, John; b 28 May 1721, Richmond Co; d 12 Apr 1779 **RU:** Patriot, Had public serv as member of First Council of State under Gov Patrick Henry. Resigned 9 Oct 1776. Gave tools to the cause Nov 1778 **CEM:** Tayloe Family; GPS 37.58200, -76.4729; Mt Airy, Rt 360, Warsaw; Richmond Co **GS:** U **SP:** Mar (11 Jul 1747) Rebecca Plater (8 Aug 1731-22 Jan 1787) **VI:** No further data **P:** N **BLW:** N **RG:** unk **MK:** unk **PH:** unk **SS:** DAR Ancestor #A112260; G pg 518; DD cites VA Hist Mag Vol 1 pg 64 **BS:** 196.

RU=Rank/Unit   CEM=Cemetery   GS=Gravestone   SP=Spousal Information
VI=Other Veteran Info   P=Pension   BLW=Bounty/Land Warrant   RG=Registered Grave
MK=SAR/DAR Marker   PH=Photo   SS=Service Source   BS=Burial Source

327

TAYLOR, Alexander; b 1737; d 1801 **RU:** Patriot, Gave material aid to cause, Prince George Co **CEM:** Blandford; **GPS** 37.22433, -77.38604; 319 S Crater Rd; Petersburg City **GS:** Y **SP:** No info **VI:** No further data **P:** N **BLW:** N **RG:** N **MK:** N **PH:** unk **SS:** AL Comm Bk IV 364 Prince George Co **BS:** 99 pg 30.

TAYLOR, Charles; b 3 Jan 1755, Orange Co; d 27 Jan 1821 **RU:** Surgeon, Was Surgeon of the Regt of Convention, Cont Line.and the Surgeon of Albemarle Barracks **CEM:** Christ Church; **GPS** 37.61019, -76.54606; 420 Christ Church Rd, Weems; Lancaster **GS:** Y **SP:** Mar (11 May 1777) Sarah Conway **VI:** Son of George & Rachel (Gibson) Taylor. Recd BLW. Family Physician of President Madison **P:** unk **BLW:** Y **RG:** unk **MK:** Y **PH:** Y **SS:** E pg 759; AK **BS:** JLARC 2; 200; 04.

TAYLOR, Edmund; b 16 Aug 1741; d 28 Jan 1822 **RU:** Patriot, Gave material aid to cause **CEM:** Taylor Family; **GPS** 37.40850, -76.25405; VAQ 738 Old Ridge Rd; Hanover **GS:** Y **SP:** Mar (16 May 1771) Ann Day (18 Mar 1753 Hanover Co-12 Jul 1835) **VI:** No further data **P:** N **BLW:** N **RG:** Y **MK:** unk **PH:** Y **SS:** DAR Ancestor #A112406; J-NSSAR 2000 Reg; AL Ct Bk I pg 30 Hanover Co **BS:** JLARC 76.

TAYLOR, Erasmus; b 5 Sep 1715, Rapidan, Culpeper Co; d 18 Dec 1794 **RU:** Patriot, Gave material aid to cause **CEM:** Greenfields Family; **GPS** 38.25335, -78.10039; Rt 2021, back of cem on Madex Dr; Orange **GS:** Y **SP:** Jane Moore (22 Dec 1728-19 Sep 1812) d/o John & Rebecca (Catlett) Moore **VI:** Son of James (1675-1729) & Martha (Thompson) (1679-1762) Taylor **P:** N **BLW:** N **RG:** N **MK:** N **PH:** unk **SS:** Al Comm Bk IV, pg 188 Orange Co **BS:** 22 pg 64; 196.

TAYLOR, George; b 1745 Wales; d 12 Apr 1824 **RU:** First Lieutenant, Served in Capt Dillard's Co Henry Co Militia. Perhaps the George Taylor, who served as 1st Lt, Henry Co Militia **CEM:** Taylor; **GPS** unk; George Taylor Hwy; Henry **GS:** Y **SP:** Mar (1767) Elizabeth Anyon of Wales (__-aft 1823) **VI:** Died in Mayo, Henry Co **P:** unk **BLW:** unk **RG:** unk **MK:** Y **PH:** unk **SS:** DAR Ancestor #A112488; Z pg 210, 230; AZ pg 210 **BS:** JLARC 102.

TAYLOR, George; b 11 Feb 1711, King & Queen Co; d 4 Nov 1792 **RU:** Patriot, Gave material aid to the cause in Orange Co. Served as Clerk of Ct 1776 **CEM:** Greenfield; **GPS** unk; Rapidan; Culpeper **GS:** N **SP:** Mar (28 Feb 1738) Rachel Gibson (4 May 1717-16 Feb 1761) **VI:** Son of James & Martha (Thompson) Taylor. Was not a Col in the Revolution but held the rank of Sgt. Was Col in the French & Indian War and was with Washington at Braddock's defeat. Died in Orange Co **P:** unk **BLW:** unk **RG:** unk **MK:** N **PH:** N **SS:** DAR Ancestor #A112475; AL recd Cert Orange Co; DD cites Joyner First Settlers of Orange Co VA pg 242 **BS:** 196.

TAYLOR, James; b 2 Mar 1739, Ireland; d 23 Feb 1801 **RU:** Corporal, Served in Capt Joseph Smith's Co, Col Nathaniel Gist's Regt **CEM:** Taylor Family; **GPS** unk; Short Hill Mountain; Rockbridge **GS:** U **SP:** Mar (20 Jun 1775) Anna Paul (30 Aug 1753, Botetourt Co-15 Dec 1828) **VI:** No further data **P:** unk **BLW:** unk **RG:** unk **MK:** unk **PH:** unk **SS:** DAR #A112628; E pg 760; AP roll 72 **BS:** 196.

TAYLOR, James; b cAug 1737; d 13 Nov 1814 **RU:** Patriot, Was Mayor of Norfolk during War (1778, 1780, 1782). Submitted claims for losses incurred during burning of Norfolk **CEM:** St Paul's Episcopal; **GPS** 36.84733, -76.28554; 201 St Paul's Blvd; Norfolk City **GS:** Y **SP:** No info **VI:** "The Order Book and Related Papers of the Common Hall of the Borough of Norfolk, Virginia 1736-1798" shows public service. Mayor of Norfolk after war in 1790 **P:** N **BLW:** N **RG:** Y **MK:** Y **PH:** unk **SS:** CB; AL Ct Bk pg 2 **BS:** 87 pg 30.

TAYLOR, James; b 27 Dec 1732, Caroline Co; d 12 Mar 1814 **RU:** Patriot/Colonel, Commander Caroline Co Militia. Gave material aid to cause **CEM:** Taylor-Quarles Family; **GPS** 38.25629, -78.05394; End of Bloomsbury Rd; Caroline **GS:** U **SP:** Mar (Jun 1758) Ann Berry Hubbard (26 Mar 1738-27 May 1789) **VI:** Son of James (1703-1784) & Alice (Thornton) (1708-1739) Taylor **P:** unk **BLW:** unk **RG:** unk **MK:** unk **PH:** unk **SS:** E pg 760: AL List II pg 1 Caroline Co **BS:** 196.

TAYLOR, Jesse; b unk; d 24 Dec 1787 **RU:** Patriot, Signed legislative petition Alexandria **CEM:** Old Christ Church Episcopal; **GPS** 38.80625, -77.04718; 118 N Washington St; Alexandria City **GS:** U **SP:** No info **VI:** No further data **P:** N **BLW:** N **RG:** unk **MK:** unk **PH:** unk **SS:** BB **BS:** 110 pg 91.

TAYLOR, Jesse; b 1741; d Oct 1800 **RU:** Patriot, Gave material aid to cause **CEM:** Old Presbyterian Meeting House; **GPS** 38.48528, -77.23532; 323 S Fairfax St; Alexandria City **GS:** N **SP:** No info **VI:**

RU=Rank/Unit	CEM=Cemetery	GS=Gravestone	SP=Spousal Information
VI=Other Veteran Info	P=Pension	BLW=Bounty/Land Warrant	RG=Registered Grave
MK=SAR/DAR Marker	PH=Photo	SS=Service Source	BS=Burial Source

328

Died of biious fever, bur 15 Oct 1800, age 49. Listed on SAR plaque in cemetery **P:** N **BLW:** N **RG:** Y **MK:** Y **PH:** N **SS:** J-NSSAR 1993 Reg; AL Ct Bk pg 7, 14 Fairfax Co; AK **BS:** JLARC 1; 23 pg 108; 196.

TAYLOR, John; b 19 Dec 1753; d 21 Aug 1824 **RU:** Lieutenant Colonel & Paymaster, Paymaster, Caroline Co Bn 1775-6. Commander, Caroline & Militia 1780 **CEM:** Hazelwood; GPS 38.18667, -77.22639; Hazelwood Ln at Rt 674, Port Royal; Caroline **GS:** Y **SP:** Mar (4 Dec 1783) Lucy Penn (17 Oct 1766 Mt Airy, Caroline Co- Aug 1831 Hazelwood, Port Royal) d/o John (2 Sep 1741 Caroline Co-14 Sep 1788, NC) & Susannah (Lyme) (c1745 Caroline Co-1 Mar 1784, NC) Penn **VI:** US Senator fr VA 1792-94. In Jun 1803, appointed to fill vacancy caused by death of Stevens T. Mason & served until Dec 1803. Served again fr 1822 until death 1824 **P:** unk **BLW:** unk **RG:** Y **MK:** N **PH:** unk **SS:** E pg 761 **BS:** 60.

TAYLOR, Nimrod; b 1756, Fauquier Co; d 16 Jul 1834 **RU:** Private, Ent serv 1780 Fauquier Co in Col Edmonds' Regt of Militia. Served in Capt Balls Co for 23 days **CEM:** Carter Family; GPS unk; Rt 649, Rye Cove; Scott **GS:** Y **SP:** Mar (1777) Mary Lutz (__-7 Sep 1840 Scott Co) **VI:** Appl for pension 12 Dec 1832 Scott Co. R10422 **P:** Y **BLW:** unk **RG:** unk **MK:** Y **PH:** Y **SS:** H pg 3436; K Vol 5 pg 223; N pg 1347-8 **BS:** JLARC 2, 22.

TAYLOR, Peter; b c1752; d 30 May 1823 **RU:** Soldier, Enl Accomack Co, and served in 3rd, 4th, 8th, and 12th Cont Lines **CEM:** Lincoln Memorial; GPS 36.80830, -76.32810; Jct Kirby St and Deep Creek Blvd; Portsmouth City **GS:** N **SP:** Mar (Jul 1783 Accomack Co) Elizabeth Kelly (1766-1 Sep 1855) **VI:** Obit indicates soldier in the Revolution. He appl for pen 25 Oct 1818 in Norfolk. Spouse appl pen 21 Aug 1843 at Portsmouth **P:** Y **BLW:** Y **RG:** unk **MK:** unk **PH:** unk **SS:** C pg 273; E pg 761; CG pg 3436 **BS:** 196.

TAYLOR, Robert; b 8 May 1749; d 10 Oct 1826 **RU:** Patriot, Publicly toasted "the Congress, General Washington, success to the American Arms, etc" Was Mayor of Norfolk during War (1778, 1780, 1782). Submitted claims for losses incurred during burning of Norfolk. Gave material aid to the cause **CEM:** St Paul's Episcopal; GPS 36.84733, -76.28554; 201 St Paul's Blvd; Norfolk City **GS:** Y **SP:** "Sally Curle Barraud" likely "Sarah Crull Taylor" fr St Paul's Churchyard **VI:** Was Mayor of Norfolk 1784, 1789, 1793 **P:** N **BLW:** N **RG:** Y **MK:** Y **PH:** unk **SS:** CB; AL Ct Bk pg 12 **BS:** 87 pg 30.

TAYLOR, Robert; b 29 Apr 1763, Orange Co; d 3 Jul 1845 **RU:** Sergeant, Served at Yorktown in Alcock's Regt Oct 1781 **CEM:** Taylor Family, Meadow Farm; GPS 38.22898, -78.07895; 16823 Monrovia Rd; Orange **GS:** Y **SP:** Mar (7 Jul 1784) Frances Pendleton (1767-1831) **VI:** Son of Erasmus (1715-1794) & (-----) Taylor. Served in VA State Senate 1804-1812. Served US Legislature 1825-1827 **P:** unk **BLW:** unk **RG:** N **MK:** N **PH:** unk **SS:** C pg 576 **BS:** 22 pg 91; 196.

TAYLOR, Sarah Crull (Croel (Curle Barraud) Huitt); b c1755; d Jan. 15, 1787, Norfolk **RU:** Patriot, Submitted claim for losses suffered during the burning of Norfolk **CEM:** St Paul's Episcopal; GPS 36.84733, -76.28554; 201 St Paul's Blvd; Norfolk City **GS:** Y **SP:** Probably mar to Mayor Robert Taylor **VI:** No further data **P:** N **BLW:** N **RG:** Y **MK:** Y **PH:** unk **SS:** CB Friend Amer Cause **BS:** 178 Jan 11.

TAYLOR, Stacy; b 28 Feb 1757, Bucks Co, PA; d 1836 **RU:** Private, Served in Capt Jacob Bennet's Light Dragoons fr Bucks Co, PA **CEM:** Goose Creek; GPS 39.11250, -77.69527; Rt 722, Lincoln; Loudoun **GS:** Y **SP:** Ruth Beans (1775-1846) **VI:** Son of Timothy & Letitia (Kirkbride) Taylor **P:** unk **BLW:** unk **RG:** N **MK:** N **PH:** unk **SS:** CI PA Archives pg 208 **BS:** 196.

TAYLOR, Thomas; b c1751; d 31 Dec 1802 **RU:** Private, Served in Capt Samuel Noland's Co, Loudoun Co Militia **CEM:** Level Green Farm; GPS unk; 6275 Old Centerville Rd, Chantilly; Fairfax **GS:** Y **SP:** No info **VI:** No further data **P:** unk **BLW:** unk **RG:** N **MK:** N **PH:** unk **SS:** N pg 1254 **BS:** 61 Vol IV pg CN-22.

TAYLOR, Timothy II; b 11 Jan 1761, Newtown, Bucks Co, PA; d 8 Jun 1838 **RU:** Private, Served in 12th VA Regt, Cont Line **CEM:** Goose Creek; GPS 39.11250, -77.69527; Rt 722, Lincoln; Loudoun **GS:** Y **SP:** Mar (Feb 1780 Bucks Co, PA) Achrah (-----) (5 Feb 1759-16 May 1826) **VI:** Commissioned Lt Col 25 May 1810 in War of 1812 and commanded 56th VA Regt **P:** unk **BLW:** unk **RG:** N **MK:** N **PH:** unk **SS:** E pg 762; Serv Record Card **BS:** 196.

RU=Rank/Unit	CEM=Cemetery	GS=Gravestone	SP=Spousal Information
VI=Other Veteran Info	P=Pension	BLW=Bounty/Land Warrant	RG=Registered Grave
MK=SAR/DAR Marker	PH=Photo	SS=Service Source	BS=Burial Source

329

TAYLOR, William; b c1738; d 11 Sep 1820 **RU:** Patriot, Was a county clerk during war period. Gave material aid to the cause **CEM:** Taylor Family; GPS unk; 18 mi S of Kenbridge; Lunenburg **GS:** Y **SP:** Martha Waller (28 Nov 1747 James City Co-11 Mar 1828) **VI:** Son of M. Daniel (1704-1742) & Alice (Littlepage) (1708-1787) Taylor **P:** N **BLW:** N **RG:** N **MK:** N **PH:** unk **SS:** Al Ct Bk pg 14, 17; BN WPA report **BS:** 196; 172 The Taylor.

TAYMAN (LAYMAN, LAYMON), George; b 1760, Frederick, Frederick Co, MD; d 15 Jul 1854 **RU:** Private/Patriot, Military service not determined. As patriot gave material aid to cause under name Laymon **CEM:** Temontown; GPS unk; Laymantown; Botetourt **GS:** U **SP:** Mar (1785 MD) Barbara Baumgardner (Sep 1763-Mar 1852) **VI:** Son of George Hans & Salome (-----) Lehman **P:** unk **BLW:** unk **RG:** unk **MK:** N **PH:** unk **SS:** DAR Ancestor #A067530; SAR Ancestor #P-302658; AL cert Botetourt Co under name Lymon; AR DAR Application; AR pg 102; BY **BS:** JLARC 2.

TEACKLE, Arthur; b 28 Feb 1755; d 31 Jan 1791 **RU:** First Lieutenant, Served in 9th Cont Line for 7 yrs. Was 1st Lt 26 Jul 1776. **CEM:** Teackle House; GPS unk; Rt 1709 & Brooklyn St, Wachapreague; Accomack **GS:** Y **SP:** Elizabeth Read (27 Feb 1760-10 May 1815) **VI:** Recd BLW of 3111 acres for 7 yrs service **P:** unk **BLW:** Y **RG:** N **MK:** N **PH:** unk **SS:** C pg 118; E pg 762 **BS:** 37 pg 252.

TEACKLE (TEAKLE), Levin; b 1717; d 28 Sep 1794 **RU:** Patriot, Gave material aid to the cause **CEM:** Teackle House; GPS unk; Rt 1709 & Brooklyn St, Wachapreague; Accomack **GS:** Y **SP:** Joyce (-----) (Feb 1735-Dec 1760) **VI:** Son of John & (-----) Teackle. Died age 70 **P:** N **BLW:** N **RG:** N **MK:** N **PH:** unk **SS:** AL Com Bk 1 pg 32 **BS:** 37 pg 252.

TEBBS, Willoughby; b 1759, prob Dumfries, Prince William Co; d 22 Oct 1803 **RU:** Lieutenant, Served 1 Mar 1777-21 Sep 1778, Grayson's Cont Regt. Was Regt QM Jul 1778 and 2nd Lt 8 Jun 1777. Resigned 21 Sep 1778 **CEM:** Tebbsdale Plantation; GPS unk; Rt 633 off US 1 Dumfries; Prince William **GS:** Y **SP:** Mar (16 Oct 1771, however, pen info says 1787 Dumfries) Betsey Carr (c1780-18 Mar 1858) d/o of William & (-----) Carr. (Wm Carr signed mar bond with sol on 30 Aug 1786 in Prince William Co). **VI:** Practiced law in Dumfries VA. Later after War, Col of Prince William Co. Militia. Son of Foushee & Mary (Baxter) Tebbs. W6284. Widow pen 1840 Loudoun Co age 60. BLW #4946 issued to brother John Tebbs then to heirs **P:** Y **BLW:** Y **RG:** Y **MK:** Y **PH:** Y **SS:** K Vol 5 pg 231; CG Vol 3 pg 3423; SAR Patriot Index CD **BS:** JLARC 4, 31.

TEBBS, Willoughby William; b c1750; d 1832 **RU:** Captain, Gave material aid to the cause **CEM:** Tebbsdale Plantation; GPS unk; Rt 633 off US 1 Dumfries; Prince William **GS:** Y **SP:** No info **VI:** No further data **P:** unk **BLW:** unk **RG:** N **MK:** N **PH:** unk **SS:** AL,Ct Bk pg 14 as Capt **BS:** 94 pg 471.

TEETER, John; b 1753 Rhine Valley, Germany; d 6 Aug 1818 **RU:** Patriot, Served as juryman and constable Washington Co 1777-1783 **CEM:** Teeter Family; GPS 36.66470, -82.12080; Vic Clear Creek Dam; Washington **GS:** Y **SP:** Mar (20 May 1769) Eve Turner/Tournai (1753-aft 6 May 1818) **VI:** No further data **P:** N **BLW:** N **RG:** Y **MK:** N **PH:** unk **SS:** I; AR Vol 4 pg 102; DD **BS:** 78 pg 382.

TEPHANY, Remy; b unk; d 1781 **RU:** Seaman, Served on "Pluton" and died from Yorktown battle **CEM:** French Memorial; GPS 36.81944, -79.39933; Yorktown; York **GS:** U **SP:** No info **VI:** No further data **P:** unk **BLW:** unk **RG:** Y **MK:** unk **PH:** unk **SS:** J-Yorktown Historian **BS:** JLARC 1, 74.

TERRELL, David Jr; b 10 Jun 1829; d 14 Feb 1805 **RU:** Patriot, Gave material aid to cause **CEM:** South River Meeting House; GPS 37.37246, -79.19194; 5810 Fort Ave; Lynchburg City **GS:** Y **SP:** Jane Johnson (30 May 1762-2 Jun 1850) **VI:** No further data **P:** N **BLW:** N **RG:** N **MK:** unk **PH:** N **SS:** AL Cert Caroline Co **BS:** 196; 221.

TERRELL, Samuel; b By 1766; d unk **RU:** Patriot, Provided material support to the cause fr Louisa Co **CEM:** Golansville Meeting House; GPS unk; Golansville on US1; Caroline **GS:** N **SP:** Mar (7 May 1800) Elizabeth Harris **VI:** Son of Pleasant & (-----) Terrell **P:** N **BLW:** N **RG:** N **MK:** N **PH:** unk **SS:** Al Ct Bk pg 42 Louisa Co **BS:** 14 pg 44.

TERRY, Nathaniel Sr; b 1724; d 21 Apr 1780 **RU:** Patriot, Was member of the House of Burgesses **CEM:** Terry Family; GPS unk; 1154 N Terry Rd, Halifax; Halifax **GS:** Y **SP:** 1) Lucy Hatcher 2) Mar (1746) Sarah Royale (3 feb 1715-16 Jun 1778) **VI:** DAR marker & VA Historical Rd sign **P:** N **BLW:** N

RU=Rank/Unit	CEM=Cemetery	GS=Gravestone	SP=Spousal Information
VI=Other Veteran Info	P=Pension	BLW=Bounty/Land Warrant	RG=Registered Grave
MK=SAR/DAR Marker	PH=Photo	SS=Service Source	BS=Burial Source

330

RG: Y **MK:** Y **PH:** Y **SS:** DAR Ancestor #A113709; J-NSSAR 1993 Reg; AR Vol 4 pg 105; DD cites VA Mag Hist & Bio Vol 37 No 1 pg 27 **BS:** JLARC 1, 2.

TERRY, Royal; b 1754; d 1825 **RU:** Private, Service information not listed in SAR registry **CEM:** Terry Family; GPS unk; 1154 N Terry Rd, Halifax; Halifax **GS:** U **SP:** No info **VI:** No further data **P:** unk **BLW:** unk **RG:** Y **MK:** unk **PH:** unk **SS:** J-NSSAR 2000 Reg; NSSAR Ancestor #P-303163 **BS:** JLARC 76.

TERRY, William; b 1752, Cumberland Co; d 1814 **RU:** Captain, Commanded a company in Bedford Co Militia. Took oath as capt 28 May 1781 **CEM:** Terry Family; GPS unk; Oakwood; Bedford **GS:** N **SP:** Susan Turner (1755 Bedford Co-1814) **VI:** No further data **P:** unk **BLW:** unk **RG:** unk **MK:** N **PH:** N **SS:** J- DAR Hatcher; E pg 765 **BS:** JLARC 2; 80 vol 4.

TERRY, William E; b unk; d 1845 **RU:** Patriot, Gave material aid to cause **CEM:** St John's Episcopal; GPS 37.53183, -77.41958; 2401 E Broad St; Richmond City **GS:** N **SP:** No info **VI:** No further data **P:** N **BLW:** N **RG:** N **MK:** N **PH:** N **SS:** D Vol 2, pg 572 **BS:** 28 pg 351.

TERVILLE, Andre; b unk; d 1781 **RU:** Soldier, Served in Bourbonnais Bn and died fr battle at Yorktown **CEM:** French Memorial; GPS 36.81944, -79.39933; Yorktown; York **GS:** U **SP:** No info **VI:** No further data **P:** unk **BLW:** unk **RG:** unk **MK:** unk **PH:** unk **SS:** J-Yorktown Historian **BS:** JLARC 74.

TESTELIN, Louis; b unk; d 1781 **RU:** Soldier, Served in Bourbonnais Bn and died fr battle at Yorktown **CEM:** French Memorial; GPS 36.81944, -79.39933; Yorktown; York **GS:** U **SP:** No info **VI:** No further data **P:** unk **BLW:** unk **RG:** Y **MK:** unk **PH:** unk **SS:** J-Yorktown Historian **BS:** JLARC 1,74.

TETER (TETOR), Paul; b c1730, PA; d 27 Nov 1784 **RU:** Corporal/Patriot, Gave material aid to cause **CEM:** Old Peaked Mountain; GPS 38.37113, -78.73416; 9843 Town Hall Rd, McGaheysville; Rockingham **GS:** N **SP:** Mar (c1760) Rebecca Hinkle (5 Oct 1736-aft 29 Mar 1797 S Clair, IL) d/o Justus (10 Feb 1706 Germany; 24 Aug 1778 German Valley, VA) & Mary Margareta (Eshman) Hinkle **VI:** No further data **P:** unk **BLW:** unk **RG:** N **MK:** N **PH:** N **SS:** AL Ct Bk I pg 7,14 Rockingham Co; AZ pg 184 **BS:** 116 Monument.

TEYO, Rene; b unk; d 1781 **RU:** Seaman, Served on "Palmier" and died from Yorktown battle **CEM:** French Memorial; GPS 36.81944, -79.39933; Yorktown; York **GS:** U **SP:** No info **VI:** No further data **P:** unk **BLW:** unk **RG:** Y **MK:** unk **PH:** unk **SS:** J-Yorktown Historian **BS:** JLARC 1, 74.

THATCHER, Stephen; b 2 Dec 1765; d 2 May 1845 **RU:** Private, Served in Capt Samuel Noland's Co, Loudoun Co Militia **CEM:** Ebenezer Baptist; GPS 39.05824, -77.84142; 20421 Airmont Rd, Bluemont; Loudoun **GS:** Y **SP:** Alcy Chew (5 Nov 1744-5 Apr 1829) d/o James & (-----) Chew **VI:** Son of Richard & (-----) Thatcher. Died in Bloomfield or Bluemont, Loudoun Co **P:** unk **BLW:** unk **RG:** Y **MK:** N **PH:** unk **SS:** N pg 1254 **BS:** 25 pg 310; 196.

THEVENIN, Louis; b unk; d 1781 **RU:** Soldier, Served in Agenois Bn and died fr battle at Yorktown **CEM:** French Memorial; GPS 36.81944, -79.39933; Yorktown; York **GS:** U **SP:** No info **VI:** No further data **P:** unk **BLW:** unk **RG:** Y **MK:** unk **PH:** unk **SS:** J-Yorktown Historian **BS:** JLARC 1, 74.

THOMAS, Francis; b 23 Mar 1743; d 27 Jun 1835 **RU:** Private, Served in Bn of VA forces commanded by Col James Hendricks May 1777 **CEM:** Fincastle Presbyterian; GPS 37.50017, -79.87558; 108 E Back St, Fincastle; Botetourt **GS:** Y **SP:** Grace Metcalfe (14 Mar 1741-6 Sep 1829) **VI:** Name is on SAR plaque in cemetery **P:** unk **BLW:** unk **RG:** Y **MK:** Y **PH:** unk **SS:** J-NSSAR 1993 Reg, J- DAR Hatcher, AR Vol 4 pg 108; AP Serv Record **BS:** JLARC 1, 2; 196.

THOMAS, Giles; b 30 Nov 1763, Harford Co, MD; d 21 Mar 1842 **RU:** Private, Served in MD Cont Line. Served under General Nathaniel Greene in battles at Guilford, Camden, and Ninety Six **CEM:** Westview; GPS 37.23390, -80.40830; Blacksburg; Montgomery **GS:** Y **SP:** Mar (4 Jun 1786, Blacksburg) Nancy Anne Wheeler (10 May 1762-12 Jun 1845) d/o Benjamin & Mary (Neale) Wheeler **VI:** Son of David & Hannah (Greene) Thomas. Gov't Gr Stone. Appl for pen Aug 1832. Recd BLW # 1747 **P:** Y **BLW:** Y **RG:** unk **MK:** unk **PH:** unk **SS:** SAR Ancestor #P-303628; SAR applic **BS:** 196.

THOMAS, Harrison; b 1760; d 1809 **RU:** Sergeant, Served in the 10th Regt. Perhaps also served as Capt **CEM:** Old Thomas Farm; GPS unk; N of Rt 617, NW of Weirwood; Northampton **GS:** Y **SP:** 1) (----

RU=Rank/Unit   CEM=Cemetery   GS=Gravestone   SP=Spousal Information
VI=Other Veteran Info   P=Pension   BLW=Bounty/Land Warrant   RG=Registered Grave
MK=SAR/DAR Marker   PH=Photo   SS=Service Source   BS=Burial Source

331

-) 2) Elizabeth Downing **VI:** No further data **P:** unk **BLW:** unk **RG:** unk **MK**: N **PH:** unk **SS:** NSSAR Ancestor #P-303630 **BS:** JLARC 2, 69; 42 pg 83.

THOMAS, John; b 8 Apr 1757, Buckingham Co; d 13 Sep 1849 **RU:** Captain, Ent serv 1779 as Ensign in VA Line. Lived Albemarle Co 1778 at enl. Served in the Regt of Guards at the Albemarle Barracks under Col Francis Taylor **CEM:** Martin Marietta's Land; GPS unk; Nr Red Hill; Albemarle **GS:** U **SP:** No info **VI:** Sol appl pen 6 May 1833 Albemarle Co. Rejected due to less than six mos service. R10502. Recd BLW that indicates he d c1849 Buckingham Co **P:** N **BLW:** Y **RG:** unk **MK:** unk **PH:** unk **SS:** DAR Ancestor #A113057; SAR Ancestor #P-303742; K Vol 5 pg 245; BY pg 373; J- DAR Hatcher; CG Vol 3 pg 3565 **BS:** JLARC 2.

THOMAS, John; b 1764; d 1850 **RU:** Ensign, Served in Albemarle Co Militia **CEM:** Thomas Family; GPS unk; Nr Red Hill; Albemarle **GS:** U **SP:** No info **VI:** No further data **P:** unk **BLW:** unk **RG:** unk **MK**: unk **PH:** unk **SS:** E pg 767 **BS:** JLARC 2.

THOMAS, John; b 16 Oct 1733, Southampton Co; d 9 Jul 1821 **RU:** Private, Served in Capt Faunteroy's Co 5th & 9th VA Regts 1778 **CEM:** St Clair Bottom Primitive Baptist; GPS 36.76098, -81.64556; Jct Rts 600 & 660, Chilhowie; Smyth **GS:** Y **SP:** Mary Robinette (1740 Southampton Co-9 Jul 1821) **VI:** No further data **P:** unk **BLW:** unk **RG:** unk **MK:** unk **PH:** unk **SS:** AP payroll **BS:** 196.

THOMAS, John Sr; b 1760, Montgomery Co, PA; d 1829 **RU:** Private, Served in Capt B Raug's Co, PA Milita **CEM:** Ebenezer Baptist; GPS 39.05824, -77.84142; 20421 Airmont Rd, Bluemont; Loudoun **GS:** U **SP:** Mar (c1790) Leah Jones **VI:** Son of Japhet & Mary (Drake) Thomas. Arr in Loudoun Co 1794 **P:** unk **BLW:** unk **RG:** unk **MK:** unk **PH:** unk **SS:** AP **BS:** 196.

THOMAS, Richard; b 29 Aug 1764; d 25 Feb 1840 **RU:** Private, Served in 11th Cont Line **CEM:** Thomas Family; GPS unk; nr Timberville; Rockingham **GS:** Y **SP:** Elizabeth (-----) (1769-1840) **VI:** No further data **P:** unk **BLW:** unk **RG:** Y **MK:** N **PH:** unk **SS:** AK; E pg 767 **BS:** 04; 191 ThomasFam.

THOMAS, William; b 1752; d 1834 **RU:** Patriot, Gave material aid to cause **CEM:** Thomas-Lowry Farm; GPS unk; E fr Bedford; Bedford **GS:** U **SP:** Elizabeth (-----) (__-26 Sep 1836) **VI:** No further data **P:** N **BLW:** N **RG:** unk **MK:** N **PH:** unk **SS:** DAR Ancestor #A133859; J- DAR Hatcher; AL Ct Bk pg 8, 27 Bedford Co **BS:** JLARC 2.

THOMPSON, Alexander; b 1732; d 5 May 1824 **RU:** Lieutenant Colonel, In charge of Augusta Co Militia 1776 & 1777 **CEM:** Tinkling Spring Presbyterian; GPS 38.08472, -78.98278; 30 Tinkling Spring Dr, Fishersville; Augusta **GS:** N **SP:** No info **VI:** No further data **P:** unk **BLW:** unk **RG:** N **MK:** N **PH:** N **SS:** E pg 768; CZ pg 434 **BS:** 142 Tinkling Spr; 208 pg 467.

THOMPSON, Amos Rev; b 7 Aug 1731 New Haven CT; d 8 Sep 1804 **RU:** Chaplain, Appointed Chaplain 23 Jul 1776 in Bn commanded by Col Hugh Stevenson **CEM:** Leesburg Presbyterian; GPS 39.11611, -77.56722; 207 W Market St, Leesburg; Loudoun **GS:** Y **SP:** Jane Evans of MD **VI:** Son of Amos Thompson (1702-1795) & Sarah Alling (1702-1787). Baptized in New Haven, CT on 31 Oct 1731. Died shortly after Leesburg Presbyterian was organized **P:** unk **BLW:** unk **RG:** Y **MK:** unk **PH:** unk **SS:** Journal Congress 9/7/1776 pg 585 **BS:** JLARC 1, 2, 32; 196.

THOMPSON, Andrew; b 1750, Ireland; d 1840 **RU:** Ensign/Patriot, Served in Capt Thomas Ingles Co, Montgomery Co Mlitia 7 Apr 1781. Also served in Battle of Pt Pleasant Oct 1774. Had public service as Justice of Peace, Montgomery Co **CEM:** Bird; GPS unk; Rt 42 2.5 mi E of Bland village; Bland **GS:** U **SP:** Ann (-----) (1755-1840) **VI:** DAR marker **P:** unk **BLW:** unk **RG:** unk **MK:** Y **PH:** unk **SS:** SAR Ancestor #P-303981; DAR Ancestor #A113833; J- DAR Hatcher; G pg 227 **BS:** JLARC 2; 196.

THOMPSON, Archibald; b 10 Jun 1764; d 4 Aug 1846 **RU:** Private, Served in Capt Daniel Trigg's Co, Montgomery Co Militia 7 Apr 1781 **CEM:** Thompson Family; GPS unk; Thompson Valley; Tazewell **GS:** U **SP:** Mar (29 Mar 1796) Rebecca Perry (Jul 1778-12 Nov 1836) **VI:** No further data **P:** unk **BLW:** unk **RG:** Y **MK:** unk **PH:** unk **SS:** SAR Ancestor #P-303992; DAR Ancestor #A113848; J-NSSAR 2000 Reg; G pg 227 **BS:** JLARC 76; 196.

THOMPSON, Daniel; b 1755; d c1835 **RU:** Private, Served in 1st VA State Regt for 3 yrs. Served under Capt Thomas Ewell, Col George Gibson Regt 1775-1778 **CEM:** Thompson Family; GPS 38.87201, -77.26178; Vic jct Rt 29 & Nutley St; Fairfax **GS:** N **SP:** Mar (1782) Sarah Blundon (1759, Fairfax Co-

RU=Rank/Unit   CEM=Cemetery   GS=Gravestone   SP=Spousal Information
VI=Other Veteran Info   P=Pension   BLW=Bounty/Land Warrant   RG=Registered Grave
MK=SAR/DAR Marker   PH=Photo   SS=Service Source   BS=Burial Source

332

1785) **VI:** Son of Samuel Pierce (__-1705) & Nanie (Ballinger) Thompson. Recd 100 acres BLW **P:** unk **BLW:** Y **RG:** N **MK:** N **PH:** N **SS:** DAR Ancestor #A113923; C pg 377; E pg 768; F pg 73 **BS:** 60 Fairfax Cem.

THOMPSON, Hugh; b unk; d 25 Dec 1823 **RU:** Sergeant, Served in Capt Jeremiah Talbott's Co, 30 Nov 1777. Served also in a VA unit in the IL Department **CEM:** Potts Family; GPS unk; Rts 716 & 714, Hillsboro; Loudoun **GS:** Y **SP:** No info **VI:** No further data **P:** unk **BLW:** unk **RG:** Y **MK:** N **PH:** unk **SS:** A pg 217; CZ pg 436 **BS:** 25 pg 313.

THOMPSON, James; b 1732; d 1824 **RU:** Colonel, Service information not listed in SAR registry **CEM:** Tinkling Spring Presbyterian; GPS 38.08472, -78.98278; 30 Tinkling Spring Dr, Fishersville; Augusta **GS:** N **SP:** No info **VI:** No further data **P:** unk **BLW:** unk **RG:** unk **MK:** N **PH:** N **SS:** NSSAR Ancestor #P-304136 **BS:** JLARC 62,63.

THOMPSON, James; b c1750; d 1831 **RU:** Private/Patriot, Gave material aid to cause **CEM:** Thompson-Ford Family; GPS unk; Green Branch Farm; Fauquier **GS:** N **SP:** No info **VI:** No further data **P:** unk **BLW:** unk **RG:** N **MK:** N **PH:** N **SS:** E pg 768; AL Ct Bk pg 26 Fauquier Co **BS:** 83 e-mail 07.

THOMPSON, James Paxton; b 1 Sep 1736, Spotsylvania Co; d 1814 **RU:** Captain, Service information not determined. See DAR Senate Doc for year 1950 ser 11507, vol 6 for unit **CEM:** Thompson Family; GPS unk; Not identified; Tazewell **GS:** U **SP:** 1) Rebecca Gray 2) Elizabeth Shantafer **VI:** No further data **P:** unk **BLW:** unk **RG:** Y **MK:** unk **PH:** unk **SS:** DAR Ancestor #A115416; SAR Ancestor #P-304169; J-NSSAR 2000 Reg **BS:** JLARC 76.

THOMPSON, John; b 27 Feb 1764, Augusta Co; d 16 Jul 1850 **RU:** Captain, Served in VA Line. Ent serv 1780 Montgomery Co **CEM:** Thompson Family; GPS unk; Thompson Valley; Tazewell **GS:** U **SP:** Mar (1789) Louisa Bowen (c1767-1812) d/o Rees (1737, MD-7 Oct 1780 Kings Mountain, NC) & Louisa (Smith) (c1741, Augusta Co-16 Feb 1830) Bowen **VI:** Appl pen 31 Mar 1834 Tazewell Co, age 70. Pension rejected R10540 **P:** N **BLW:** unk **RG:** unk **MK:** unk **PH:** unk **SS:** J- DAR Hatcher; K Vol 5 pg 253-4; CG Vol 3 pg 3478 **BS:** JLARC 2.

THOMPSON, Robert; b unk; d 1847 **RU:** Captain, Commanded a company 1776-1780 in Augusta Co Militia. Resigned 21 Mar 1780 **CEM:** Tinkling Spring Presbyterian; GPS 38.08472, -78.98278; 30 Tinkling Spring Dr, Fishersville; Augusta **GS:** N **SP:** No info **VI:** No further data **P:** unk **BLW:** unk **RG:** unk **MK:** N **PH:** N **SS:** E pg 769 **BS:** JLARC 62, 63.

THOMPSON, Samuel; b 1705; d unk **RU:** Patriot, Signed Legislative petition **CEM:** Thompson Family; GPS 38.87201, -77.26178; Vic jct Rt 29 & Nutley St; Fairfax **GS:** Y **SP:** No info **VI:** No further data **P:** N **BLW:** N **RG:** N **MK:** N **PH:** unk **SS:** BB Legislative Pet **BS:** 60 Fairfax Co.

THOMPSON, Smith; b 1748; d 1840 **RU:** Soldier, Served in VA Line in 16th VA Regt. Lived in Augusta Co at enl 1777. **CEM:** Trinity Episcopal; GPS 38.14917, -79.07521; 214 Beverley St; Staunton City **GS:** U **SP:** Nancy McCullock **VI:** Occupation weaver. Sol appl pen 26 Jul 1819 Augusta Co. S38438. Widow made inquiry 11 Dec 1840 fr Staunton VA **P:** unk **BLW:** unk **RG:** unk **MK:** unk **PH:** unk **SS:** K Vol 5 pg 255 **BS:** JLARC 2, 62.

THOMPSON, William; b unk; d 11 Sep 1831 **RU:** Corporal, Served in John Clark's Illinois Regt 1782 **CEM:** Potts Family; GPS unk; Rts 716 & 714, Hillsboro; Loudoun **GS:** Y **SP:** No info **VI:** No further data **P:** unk **BLW:** unk **RG:** Y **MK:** N **PH:** unk **SS:** E pg 770 **BS:** 25 pg 313.

THOMPSON, William; b 1722, Ireland; d 9 Jul 1798 **RU:** Lieutenant/Patriot, Signed Oath of Allegiance Montgomery Co **CEM:** Thompson Family; GPS unk; Thompson Valley; Tazewell **GS:** U **SP:** 1) Margaret (-----) 2) Lydia Ward (c1743-12 Oct 1830) **VI:** No further data **P:** unk **BLW:** unk **RG:** Y **MK:** unk **PH:** unk **SS:** SAR Ancestor #P-304457; DAR Ancestor #A114675; J-NSSAR 2000 Reg **BS:** JLARC 76.

THOMPSON, William; b 1734; d 23 Nov 1800 **RU:** Private/Patriot, Served in Capt Given's Co, Augusta Co Militia. Gave material aid to cause **CEM:** Falling Springs Presbyterian; GPS 37.68494, -79.45105; 410 Falling Springs Rd, Glasgow; Rockbridge **GS:** Y **SP:** Margaret (-----) (1743-5 Oct 1815) **VI:** No further data **P:** N **BLW:** N **RG:** unk **MK:** unk **PH:** unk **SS:** E pg 770 **BS:** 204.

RU=Rank/Unit	CEM=Cemetery	GS=Gravestone	SP=Spousal Information
VI=Other Veteran Info	P=Pension	BLW=Bounty/Land Warrant	RG=Registered Grave
MK=SAR/DAR Marker	PH=Photo	SS=Service Source	BS=Burial Source

THOMPSON, William; b 12 Sep 1742, Augusta Co; d 26 Jun 1815 **RU:** Soldier/Patriot, Gave material aid to cause **CEM:** Bethel Presbyterian; GPS 38.04257, -79.17283; 563 Bethel Green Rd, Middlebrook; Augusta **GS:** N **SP:** Mar (16 Jun 1771) Rachel Allen (19 Oct 1740, Augusta Co-__) d/of James (__-18 Oct 1791) & Mary (-----) Allen **VI:** No further data **P:** unk **BLW:** unk **RG:** unk **MK:** unk **PH:** N **SS:** SAR Ancestor #P-304454; J- DAR Hatcher; AL Cert 2 Augusta Co **BS:** JLARC 2.

THOMPSON (THOMASSON), John; b 1753; d 1840 **RU:** Drummer/Patriot, Served in Capt Johnson's Co, Louisa Co Milita. Gave material aid to cause **CEM:** Little River Baptist; GPS unk; Bumpass; Louisa **GS:** Y **SP:** Grizel Ellis **VI:** Govt grave stone **P:** unk **BLW:** unk **RG:** unk **MK:** unk **PH:** unk **SS:** SAR Ancestor #P-304215; NSSAR Ancestor #P-304453; J- DAR Hatcher; AL Ct Bk pg 21 Louisa Co; CD serv on Gr St **BS:** JLARC 2; JLARC 1, 2, 4, 61; 196.

THOMSON, Daniel; b unk; d 1781 **RU:** Soldier, Served fr MA and died fr Yorktown battle **CEM:** Yorktown Victory Monument Tablet; GPS 38.28350, -78.54150; Yorktown; York **GS:** U **SP:** No info **VI:** No further data **P:** unk **BLW:** unk **RG:** unk **MK:** unk **PH:** unk **SS:** J-Yorktown Historian **BS:** JLARC 74.

THOMSON, James; b Jan 1739, Glasgow, Scotland; d Feb 1812 **RU:** Chaplain/Patriot, Served in a VA unit in Illinois. Gave material aid to cause and performed public service as member of Committee of Safety 1775-6 **CEM:** Globe Farm; GPS unk; Nr The Plains; Fauquier **GS:** U **SP:** Mar (1769) Mary Ann Farrow **VI:** No further data **P:** unk **BLW:** unk **RG:** unk **MK:** unk **PH:** unk **SS:** DAR Ancestor #A114174; J- DAR Hatcher; D Vol 1 pg 357; E pg 770; AR pg 112; CZ pg 436 **BS:** JLARC 2.

THORNHILL, Jesse; b 13 Oct 1763, Buckingham Co; d 5 Jun 1837 **RU:** Soldier, Ent Serv Buckingham Co. Served in VA Line **CEM:** Thornhill Family; GPS unk; Off Rt 656, Rustburg; Campbell **GS:** N **SP:** Elizabeth Stevens (7 May 1766-12 Jun 1845) **VI:** Sol appl pen 14 Aug 1832, Campbell Co. S14679 **P:** Y **BLW:** unk **RG:** unk **MK:** N **PH:** N **SS:** CG Vol 3 pg 3487 **BS:** JLARC 4, 21 ,36; 196.

THORNTON, Anthony; b 15 Nov 1727, Ormesby, Caroline Co; d 1782 **RU:** Lieutenant Colonel/Patriot, Was County Lt in 1781, according to a letter fr him to Governor Thomas Nelson in 1781. Had public service as Chairman of Committee of Safety. Gave material aid to cause,1775 **CEM:** Thornton Family; GPS unk; Ormsby; Caroline **GS:** Y **SP:** Mar (31 Dec 1746) Sarah Taliaferro (17 May 1728-c1760) **VI:** No further data **P:** unk **BLW:** unk **RG:** N **MK:** N **PH:** unk **SS:** DAR Ancestor #A200971; D Vol 1 pg 193; G pg 105; CZ pg 436 cites Calendar of VA State papers pg 439 **BS:** 80 vol 4 pg 113.

THORNTON, George; b 18 Nov 1752, Guinea's Bridge, Caroline Co; d 30 Aug 1853 **RU:** Lieutenant, Served in VA Line. Ent serv 1775 Caroline Co in brother Capt Anthony Thornton's Co. Ent serv again 1781 as 1st Lt in that Co **CEM:** Thornton; GPS unk; Haney property, E side of Rt 619, btw South River Bridge & Dundee Graveyard; Greene **GS:** U **SP:** Mar (9 Jan 1774) Margaret (-----) (20 Jun 1758-29 Jan 1823) **VI:** Sol appl pen 14 Jun 1845, Greene Co. S7709 **P:** Y **BLW:** unk **RG:** unk **MK:** unk **PH:** unk **SS:** K Vol 5 pg 258; CG Vol 3 pg 3487 **BS:** JLARC 113.

THOROUGHGOOD, Adam; b 1750; d c1785 **RU:** Colonel, Served under Gen Washington during Battle of Yorktown 1781. Was one of 56 wounded **CEM:** Old Donation Episcopal; GPS 36.86730, -76.12860; 4449 N Witchduck Rd; Virginia Beach City **GS:** U **SP:** No info **VI:** No further data **P:** unk **BLW:** unk **RG:** unk **MK:** unk **PH:** unk **SS:** Amy Waters Yarsinske, Virginia Beach: "A History of Virginia's Golden Shore" pg 78 **BS:** Church Historian.

THRIFT, Jeremiah; b 24 Dec 1719, North Farnham Parish, Richmond Co; d 10 Feb 1806 **RU:** Patriot, Gave material aid to the cause **CEM:** Old Ball Burying Ground; GPS unk; 3427 Washington Blvd, behind American Legion Bldg; Arlington **GS:** U **SP:** Ann Trammel **VI:** Son of Nathaniel & Elizabeth (Parsons) Thrift. Name is on monument **P:** N **BLW:** N **RG:** unk **MK:** unk **PH:** unk **SS:** AL Ct Bk TBA **BS:** 196.

THROCKMORTON, William; b 1755; d 1812 **RU:** Private, Served in 6th Troop, 1st Regt Lt Dragoons **CEM:** Ware Episcopal; GPS 37.42275, -76.50789; 7825 John Clayton Mem Hwy; Gloucester **GS:** U **SP:** Mary Dixon (1762-__) **VI:** Son of John & Rebecca (Richardson) Throckmorton **P:** unk **BLW:** unk **RG:** unk **MK:** unk **PH:** unk **SS:** J- DAR Hatcher; C pg 511 **BS:** JLARC 2; 196.

THURMAN, Richard Sr; b 18 Dec 1743, Lynchburg; d 14 Aug 1830 **RU:** Captain, Served in VA Regt under LaFayette. Was capt in Cont Line in Col Holcombe's Regt **CEM:** Old City; GPS 37.41472, -79.15667; 401 Taylor St; Lynchburg City **GS:** Y **SP:** Mar (1762) Ann Brown (5 Apr 1745-7 Jun 1790) **VI:**

RU=Rank/Unit	CEM=Cemetery	GS=Gravestone	SP=Spousal Information
VI=Other Veteran Info	P=Pension	BLW=Bounty/Land Warrant	RG=Registered Grave
MK=SAR/DAR Marker	PH=Photo	SS=Service Source	BS=Burial Source

334

No further data **P:** unk **BLW:** unk **RG:** Y **MK:** N **PH:** unk **SS:** DAR Ancestor #115121; C pg 525; DD cites newspaper article Richmond Enquirer 29 Oct 1824 **BS:** 35 pg 4.

THURMAN, Robert; b 1753; d 19 Oct 1817 **RU:** Patriot, Signed Legislative Petition 14 Oct 1779 to move county court house. As patriot paid personal Property Tax (Rev War Supply tax) 1783, Prince William Co **CEM:** Thurman Family; GPS unk; Glen-Gery Brick Co, 9905 Godwin Dr; Manassas City **GS:** Y **SP:** No info **VI:** No further data **P:** N **BLW:** N **RG:** unk **MK:** unk **PH:** unk **SS:** DV **BS:** 190 cem name.

TILDEN, John Bell; b 9 Dec 1762, Philadelphia, PA; d 21 Jul 1838 **RU:** Lieutenant, Served as an officer in the PA Line and was at Yorktown. Was a Lt of the 2nd PA Regt at the close of war **CEM:** Stephens City United Methodist; GPS 39.08620, -78.21670; 5291 Main St, Stephens City; Frederick **GS:** Y **SP:** Jane (-----) (18 Dec 1766-26 May 1827) **VI:** Son of __ and Anna (-----) Bell. Sol appl pen 22 Jul 1828, Frederick Co. S42497. Recd BLW #2200-300-10 Oct 1796. Also recd PA State BLW **P:** Y **BLW:** Y **RG:** Y **MK:** N **PH:** unk **SS:** A, pg 434, CG Vol 3 pg 3499 **BS:** 59 pg 329.

TILFORD, David; b Bef 1765; d after 1783 **RU:** Soldier, Rank & serv unk, but Co Hist Soc indicates soldier bur in county cem **CEM:** Tilford Cub Creek; GPS unk; Cub Creek Rd Rt 789, Tyro; Nelson **GS:** U **SP:** No info **VI:** No further data **P:** unk **BLW:** unk **RG:** unk **MK:** unk **PH:** unk **SS:** G pg 538 **BS:** JLARC 83 Nelson Co Hist Soc.

TILFORD, James; b Aft 1739, Ireland; d 4 Jun 1787 **RU:** Patriot, Gave rifle to the cause 7 Nov 1775 **CEM:** Tilford Cub Creek; GPS unk; Cub Creek Rd Rt 789, Tyro; Nelson **GS:** U **SP:** Elizabeth (-----) **VI:** No further data **P:** N **BLW:** N **RG:** unk **MK:** unk **PH:** unk **SS:** DAR Ancestor #A115441; G pg 538; DD cites VA Mag of Hist & Biog Vol 26, #1 pg 58, 66, 68 **BS:** JLARC 83 Nelson Co Hist Soc.

TILQUAZ, Nicolas; b unk; d 1781 **RU:** Soldier, Served in Soissonnais Bn and died fr battle at Yorktown **CEM:** French Memorial; GPS 36.81944, -79.39933; Yorktown; York **GS:** U **SP:** No info **VI:** No further data **P:** unk **BLW:** unk **RG:** Y **MK:** unk **PH:** unk **SS:** J-Yorktown Historian **BS:** JLARC 1, 74.

TINCELIN, Jean; b unk; d 1781 **RU:** Soldier, Served in Gatinais Bn and died fr battle at Yorktown **CEM:** French Memorial; GPS 36.81944, -79.39933; Yorktown; York **GS:** U **SP:** No info **VI:** No further data **P:** unk **BLW:** unk **RG:** Y **MK:** unk **PH:** unk **SS:** J-Yorktown Historian **BS:** JLARC 1, 74.

TINIER, Joseph; b unk; d 1781 **RU:** Soldier, Served in Gatinais Bn and died fr battle at Yorktown **CEM:** French Memorial; GPS 36.81944, -79.39933; Yorktown; York **GS:** U **SP:** No info **VI:** No further data **P:** unk **BLW:** unk **RG:** Y **MK:** unk **PH:** unk **SS:** J-Yorktown Historian **BS:** JLARC 1, 74.

TINSLEY, Parker; b unk; d aft 1813 **RU:** unk, Service not listed in SAR registry **CEM:** Spring Grove; GPS 39.10916, -78.09970; Rockville; Hanover **GS:** U **SP:** No info **VI:** JLARC site visit reveals govt grave stone indicates service after Rev War. (See Report, App D pg 12) He had 1812 service **P:** unk **BLW:** unk **RG:** unk **MK:** unk **PH:** unk **SS:** SAR Ancestor #P-305452; JLARC 71 **BS:** JLARC 71.

TINSLEY, Thomas; b 4 Sep 1755; d 17 Dec 1822 **RU:** Captain/Patriot, Was Capt 1782/83 Hanover Co Militia. Gave material aid to cause **CEM:** Spring Grove; GPS 39.10916, -78.09970; Rockville; Hanover **GS:** Y **SP:** Susanna Thomson (5 Dec 1765-29 Jul 1844) d/o John & Ann (Garland) Thompson **VI:** No further data **P:** unk **BLW:** unk **RG:** unk **MK:** unk **PH:** unk **SS:** SAR Ancestor #P-305455; AL Ct Bk II pg 13 Hanover Co **BS:** JLARC 71; 196.

TINSLEY, William; b 1762; d 15 Jul 1836 **RU:** Fifer, Enlisted Cumberland Co. Served in VA Bn, Taylor's Regt **CEM:** Spring Grove; GPS 39.10916, -78.09970; Rockville; Hanover **GS:** Y **SP:** Deliah (-----) (__- after 1837) **VI:** After RW, became capt of Co A, 2nd Bn, Hanover Grenadiers in 74th VA Line, 1789. Appl pen 26 Jun 1818. S41255 **P:** Y **BLW:** Y **RG:** unk **MK:** unk **PH:** unk **SS:** E pg 774; CG pg 3506; CZ pg 438 **BS:** 196.

TISSIER, Jacques; b unk; d 1781 **RU:** Seaman, Served on "Citoyen" and died from Yorktown battle **CEM:** French Memorial; GPS 36.81944, -79.39933; Yorktown; York **GS:** U **SP:** No info **VI:** No further data **P:** unk **BLW:** unk **RG:** Y **MK:** unk **PH:** unk **SS:** J-Yorktown Historian **BS:** JLARC 1, 74.

TISSIER, Jacques; b unk; d 1781 **RU:** Soldier, Served in Beaujolais Bn and died fr battle at Yorktown **CEM:** French Memorial; GPS 36.81944, -79.39933; Yorktown; York **GS:** U **SP:** No info **VI:** No further data **P:** unk **BLW:** unk **RG:** Y **MK:** unk **PH:** unk **SS:** J-Yorktown Historian **BS:** JLARC 1, 74.

RU=Rank/Unit	CEM=Cemetery	GS=Gravestone	SP=Spousal Information
VI=Other Veteran Info	P=Pension	BLW=Bounty/Land Warrant	RG=Registered Grave
MK=SAR/DAR Marker	PH=Photo	SS=Service Source	BS=Burial Source

TOBLER (DOBLER), Jacob Sr; b 14 May 1764; d 7 Feb 1820 **RU:** Private, Served in James Cox Co, Montgomery Co Militia **CEM:** Kimberling; GPS 36.91750, -81.30440; Rt 617, Rural Retreat; Wythe **GS:** U **SP:** Maria Magdalene Roush **VI:** Son of Jacob & Anna (Hough) Tobler. Name on stone spelled Dobler **P:** unk **BLW:** unk **RG:** unk **MK:** unk **PH:** unk **SS:** DAR Ancestor #A116115; BW pg 9 **BS:** JLARC 123; 196.

TODD, Charles; b unk; d 1817 **RU:** Captain/Patriot, Commanded a Co Caroline Co Militia May 1782. Gave material aid to cause **CEM:** Hickory Grove; GPS unk; Hickory Grove Plantation; Caroline **GS:** N **SP:** Mary (-----) (__-1821) **VI:** Son of Dr George (1711-1790) & (----) Todd **P:** unk **BLW:** unk **RG:** unk **MK:** N **PH:** N **SS:** E pg 1775; AL Ct Bk II pg 9, 30 Caroline Co; CD **BS:** 196.

TODD, George Dr; b 1711; d 10 Mar 1790 **RU:** Patriot/Physician, Gave material aid to cause. Treated soldiers during Rev **CEM:** Hickory Grove; GPS unk; Hickory Grove Plantation; Caroline **GS:** N **SP:** No info **VI:** Deputy Sheriff in Co 1737-1747. Physician **P:** unk **BLW:** unk **RG:** unk **MK:** N **PH:** N **SS:** AL Ct Bk I pg. 268,269; CD **BS:** 196.

TODD, Mallory; b 1 Jan 1742 Battery Park; d 4 Nov 1817 **RU:** Patriot, Gave material aid to cause **CEM:** Wrenn's Cemetery; GPS unk; Rt 10, 5 mi N of Smithfield; Isle of Wight **GS:** Y **SP:** Ann (-----) (8 Feb 1761-6 Sep 1832) **VI:** Cured first Smithfield ham **P:** N **BLW:** N **RG:** Y **MK:** N **PH:** N **SS:** AL Ct Bk pg 20; AK **BS:** 153 Wrenn's Ch.

TOLON, Francois; b unk; d 1781 **RU:** Seaman, Served on "Languedoc" and died from Yorktown battle **CEM:** French Memorial; GPS 36.81944, -79.39933; Yorktown; York **GS:** U **SP:** No info **VI:** No further data **P:** unk **BLW:** unk **RG:** Y **MK:** unk **PH:** unk **SS:** J-Yorktown Historian **BS:** JLARC 1, 74.

TOMPKINS, Christopher; b 27 Oct 1740, Chilesburg, Caroline Co; d 5 Apr 1823 **RU:** Colonel, Served in Cont Army, and participant in siege of Yorktown. Commanded a Co King William Co Militia 1775-1776 **CEM:** Fleet Street, Plantation Grounds; GPS 37.78166, -77.25359; Rt 604 S of Webb Creek, Etna Mills, on Rt 4 1 mi fr Jct Rt 30; King William **GS:** U **SP:** Mar (25 Nov 1774) Ann Temple Fleet (23 Nov 1752, King & Queen Co-21 Oct 1822) d/o William (1726-1773) & Ann (Temple) (1726-1754) Fleet **VI:** Son of Christopher (1705-1779) & Joyce (Reade) (1701-1771) Tompkins. Died in Etna Mills, Enfield, King William Co **P:** N **BLW:** N **RG:** N **MK:** unk **PH:** N **SS:** E pg 776-7; CZ **BS:** 196.

TOMPKINS, Christopher; b 17 Oct 1705, Gloucester Co; d 16 Mar 1779 **RU:** Patriot, Gave material aid to cause **CEM:** Maple Swamp; GPS unk; Chilesburg; Caroline **GS:** U **SP:** Joyce Reade (6 Mar 1701, Gloucester Co-8 Aug 1771) d/o Thomas (1649-1716) & Lucy (Gwynne) (1651-1731) Reade **VI:** Son of Christopher (1662-__) & Lucy (Gwynne) (1670-1750) Tompkins **P:** N **BLW:** N **RG:** unk **MK:** unk **PH:** unk **SS:** Ak Ct Bk Pgs 8, 29 **BS:** 196.

TOMPKINS, Harry; b 1777; d 17 Apr 1829 **RU:** Patriot, Was Clerk of Henrico Co and Committee of Safety 1775-6 **CEM:** Shockoe Hill; GPS 37.55190, -77.43170; 4th & Hospital Sts; Richmond City **GS:** N **SP:** Fanny Taylorson **VI:** Son of William Overton & Mary (Michie) Tompkins. Member #1219 Clan of Tomkyns, vol 1, bur 18 Apr 1829 age 52 **P:** N **BLW:** N **RG:** unk **MK:** unk **PH:** unk **SS:** E pg 777; CZ pg 440 **BS:** 196.

TONEY, Archibald; b unk; d 24 Mar 1811 **RU:** Private?, Served in 1st, 10th, 14th Cont Lines fr Goochland Co **CEM:** St John's Episcopal; GPS 37.53183, -77.41958; 2401 E Broad St; Richmond City **GS:** Y **SP:** No info **VI:** No further data **P:** unk **BLW:** unk **RG:** N **MK:** N **PH:** unk **SS:** E pg 777 **BS:** 28 pg 512.

TONEY, John; b 1758; d 1832 **RU:** Private, Served in 7th Cont Line 7 Apr 1781 **CEM:** Toney Family; GPS unk; Glen Lyn; Giles **GS:** U **SP:** Mary Toney (c1765-unk, Giles Co) **VI:** He or the John Toney fr Powhatan Co drew a BLW **P:** unk **BLW:** Y **RG:** unk **MK:** unk **PH:** unk **SS:** SAR Ancestor #P-306019; J-DAR Hatcher; A pg 258; C pg 221; E pg 777; AZ pg 179 **BS:** JLARC 2.

TOTTEN, John; b unk; d 1823 **RU:** Private, Served in Capt Thomas Ingles Co, Montgomery Co Militia 7 Apr 1781 **CEM:** Totten Family; GPS unk; Vic jct Rts 610 & 687; Smyth **GS:** Y **SP:** No info **VI:** No further data **P:** unk **BLW:** unk **RG:** N **MK:** N **PH:** unk **SS:** G pg 227 **BS:** 97 pg 183.

RU=Rank/Unit	CEM=Cemetery	GS=Gravestone	SP=Spousal Information
VI=Other Veteran Info	P=Pension	BLW=Bounty/Land Warrant	RG=Registered Grave
MK=SAR/DAR Marker	PH=Photo	SS=Service Source	BS=Burial Source

336

TOUGARE, Francis; b unk; d 1781 **RU:** Seaman, Served on "Diademe" and died from Yorktown battle **CEM:** French Memorial; GPS 36.81944, -79.39933; Yorktown; York **GS:** U **SP:** No info **VI:** No further data **P:** unk **BLW:** unk **RG:** Y **MK:** unk **PH:** unk **SS:** J-Yorktown Historian **BS:** JLARC 1, 74.

TOURNIS, Jacques; b unk; d 1781 **RU:** Soldier, Served in Angoumois Bn and died fr battle at Yorktown **CEM:** French Memorial; GPS 36.81944, -79.39933; Yorktown; York **GS:** U **SP:** No info **VI:** No further data **P:** unk **BLW:** unk **RG:** Y **MK:** unk **PH:** unk **SS:** J-Yorktown Historian **BS:** JLARC 1, 74.

TOUSSET, Jean; b unk; d 1781 **RU:** Soldier, Served in Gatinais Bn and died fr battle at Yorktown **CEM:** French Memorial; GPS 36.81944, -79.39933; Yorktown; York **GS:** U **SP:** No info **VI:** No further data **P:** unk **BLW:** unk **RG:** Y **MK:** unk **PH:** unk **SS:** J-Yorktown Historian **BS:** JLARC 1, 74.

TOUTIN, Eustache; b unk; d 1781 **RU:** Seaman, Served on "Saint-Esprit" and died from Yorktown battle **CEM:** French Memorial; GPS 36.81944, -79.39933; Yorktown; York **GS:** U **SP:** No info **VI:** No further data **P:** unk **BLW:** unk **RG:** Y **MK:** unk **PH:** unk **SS:** J-Yorktown Historian **BS:** JLARC 1, 74.

TOWLER, Joseph; b 1743; d 1843 **RU:** Private, Served in Cont line, commanded by Col Fowler **CEM:** Towler Family; GPS unk; Nr Anthony's Ford; Pittsylvania **GS:** U **SP:** Francis Dixon **VI:** No further data **P:** unk **BLW:** unk **RG:** Y **MK:** unk **PH:** unk **SS:** J-NSSAR 2000 Reg; E pg 778 **BS:** JLARC 76.

TOWLES, Oliver; b c1741; d 18 Nov 1821 **RU:** Colonel, Served in VA Line. Was Capt of Spotsylvania Co Miltia 1775, Maj of 6th Regt of Foot 15 Aug 1777. Was in Battle of Germantown 4 Oct 1777. Taken prisoner Germantown Dec 1777 to fall 1780, promoted to Col 5th VA Regt 12 Feb 1781. Present at surrender Yorktown **CEM:** Towles Family; GPS unk; See DAR Senate Report 1954, serial 11831, vol 4 for loc; Lynchburg City **GS:** Y **SP:** Mar (bef 1770) Mary Chew d/o Larkin & Mary (Beverly) Chew **VI:** Son of Oliver Towles (c1710-1770) & Mary (-----) Gilleson, a widow, of Caroline and Spotsylvania Cos. Attorney. Recd BLW #2213-450-7 Dec 1791, records lost in DC fire 1814. Moved to Lynchburg **P:** unk **BLW:** Y **RG:** N **MK:** N **PH:** unk **SS:** K Vol 5 pg 276; CG Vol 3 pg 3522; CE pg 15, 48, 49 **BS:** DAR Rpt.

TOWN, Asce; b unk; d 1781 **RU:** Soldier, Served fr MA, and died fr the Battle at Yorktown **CEM:** Yorktown Victory Monument Tablet; GPS 38.28350, -78.54150; Yorktown; York **GS:** U **SP:** No info **VI:** No further data **P:** unk **BLW:** unk **RG:** unk **MK:** unk **PH:** unk **SS:** J-Yorktown Historian **BS:** JLARC 74.

TOWNES, John; b 1761; d 1845 **RU:** Ensign, Served in Amelia Co Militia. Appt Ensign 25 May 1780 in Capt William Johnston's Co, Col Morgan's VA Regt 1777. In 1778 taken prisoner Charleston **CEM:** Townes; GPS unk; Rt 38 at Level Mount Estates, Amelia CH; Amelia **GS:** U **SP:** Mar (1780) Elizabeth Leigh (1760 Farmville-1795) d/o John (1737-1785) & Elizabeth (Greenhill) (1740-1820) Leigh **VI:** Recd BLW 2,666 acres **P:** unk **BLW:** Y **RG:** unk **MK:** unk **PH:** unk **SS:** G pg 13 **BS:** 196.

TOWNSEND, Henry; b 1765; d 5 Jul 1831 **RU:** Private, Served in 2nd VA Regt **CEM:** Royal Oak; GPS unk; Behind Marion Baptist Church; Washington **GS:** Y **SP:** Mar (1785) Catherine (-----) (__-7 Jun 1835) **VI:** Sol appl 4 Mar 1830, Washington Co. R10658. Died in Marion **P:** Y **BLW:** unk **RG:** Y **MK:** N **PH:** unk **SS:** K pg 277; CG Vol 3 pg 3525 **BS:** 97 vol 1 pg 140.

TRAIL, Thomas; b c1746, Frederick Co, MD; d Aft 1835 **RU:** Private, Ent serv in Amherst Co in Capt John Loving's Co, then to Capt Baret's Co, Gen Nelson's Command. Was at the surrender of Cornwallis in Oct 1781 **CEM:** Wright Family; GPS 36.97658, -80.21693; Pizarro off Rt 668; Floyd **GS:** U **SP:** No info **VI:** Memorialized by DAR plaque in cem. Age 86 on 17 Sep 1832 on pension listing, # S7748 **P:** Y **BLW:** unk **RG:** unk **MK:** Y **PH:** unk **SS:** E pg 780 **BS:** 196 for John Mitchell.

TREASURE, Richard; b unk; d 1781 **RU:** Soldier, Served fr DE, killed in the battle at Yorktown **CEM:** Yorktown Victory Monument Tablet; GPS 38.28350, -78.54150; Yorktown; York **GS:** U **SP:** No info **VI:** No further data **P:** unk **BLW:** unk **RG:** unk **MK:** unk **PH:** unk **SS:** J-Yorktown Historian **BS:** JLARC 74.

TREMPER, Laurence (Lawrence); b 1753; d 15 Jan 1841 **RU:** Lieutenant, Served in NY Line. Ent serv Rhineback NY where resided. Was Lt in NY Militia. Moved to VA nr end of war where ent serv again **CEM:** Trinity Episcopal; GPS 38.14917, -79.07521; 214 Beverley St; Staunton City **GS:** U **SP:** Unmarried **VI:** Lived at Rhinebeck in Dutchess Co, NY during Rev War. Moved soon after the war to Staunton, Augusta Co where he was postmaster for many yrs. S7754 **P:** Y **BLW:** unk **RG:** unk **MK:** unk **PH:** unk **SS:** K Vol 5 pg 281; CG Vol 3 pg 3536 **BS:** JLARC 2, 4 62.

RU=Rank/Unit	CEM=Cemetery	GS=Gravestone	SP=Spousal Information
VI=Other Veteran Info	P=Pension	BLW=Bounty/Land Warrant	RG=Registered Grave
MK=SAR/DAR Marker	PH=Photo	SS=Service Source	BS=Burial Source

TRENT, Thomas; b unk; d 28 Jun 1820 **RU:** Sergeant, Served in 15th VA Regt for three yrs **CEM:** Old Trent Mill Farm; GPS unk; Rt 631; Appomattox **GS:** U **SP:** Elizabeth (-----) **VI:** Awarded gratuity of L250 in addition to pay on 2 Nov 1779 for loss of both arms in battle at Monmouth **P:** Y **BLW:** Y **RG:** unk **MK:** unk **PH:** unk **SS:** SAR Ancestor #P-306962; C pg 510; BX pg 812; CZ pg 442 **BS:** JLARC 33.

TRIBBLE, Andrew; b 1740; d 1822 **RU:** Chaplain/Patriot, Gave material aid to cause **CEM:** Tribble Family, Shirley Durbin Farm; GPS unk; 2 mi S jct Rts 25 & 75; Madison **GS:** U **SP:** Sarah Ann **VI:** No further data **P:** unk **BLW:** unk **RG:** unk **MK:** unk **PH:** unk **SS:** AL Ct Bk pg 15 Albemarle Co **BS:** JLARC 99.

TRIGG, Daniel; b 14 Aug 1749, Bedford Co; d 3 Apr 1819 **RU:** Captain/Patriot, Was Capt in Montgomery Co Militia. Gave material aid to cause **CEM:** Trigg Family; GPS unk; Abingdon; Washington **GS:** Y **SP:** Helen Hancock Dillinger **VI:** After war in 1788 was Col of Militia in Montgomery Co. Became practicing physician in Johnson City TN **P:** unk **BLW:** unk **RG:** Y **MK:** N **PH:** unk **SS:** N pg 1245; AL Ct Bk pg 46 Montgomery Co **BS:** SAR regis.

TRIGG, John (Johns); b 1748, New London, Caroline Co; d 28 Jun 1804 **RU:** Captain, Recommended rank of capt 24 Feb 1778 Bedford Co Militia **CEM:** Trigg Family (aka Old Liberty Plantation); GPS unk; Nr Liberty; Bedford **GS:** U **SP:** Dinah (Dianna) Ayers (1757-1809) **VI:** Was a VA State Representative **P:** unk **BLW:** unk **RG:** unk **MK:** N **PH:** unk **SS:** J- DAR Hatcher; E pg 781; AZ pg 189 **BS:** JLARC 2; 196.

TRIMBLE, James; b Bef 1730, Armagh, Ireland; d 9 Apr 1776 **RU:** Captain/Patriot, Commanded co Augusta Co Militia. Gave material aid to cause **CEM:** Old Monmouth Presbyterian; GPS 37.80810, -79.47280; Jct Rts 60 & 669; Lexington City **GS:** U **SP:** Mar (c1745) Sarah Kersey (c 1727-aft 7 Dec 1787) **VI:** No further data **P:** unk **BLW:** unk **RG:** unk **MK:** unk **PH:** unk **SS:** AL Ct Bk pg 7 Bedford Co; CZ pg 443 cites Lib VA Auditors Accts, Vol XV pg 103 **BS:** JLARC 63.

TRIMBLE, John; b 1742; d 22 Apr 1824 **RU:** Private, Served in Capt James Bell's Co **CEM:** Glebe Burying Ground; GPS 38.10940, -79.22190; Glebe School Rd Rt 876, Swoopes; Augusta **GS:** Y **SP:** 1) (probably) Mary (-----) (__-18 Feb 1770) 2) (probably) Clarissa Sidney Claypoole **VI:** Died aged abt 82 yrs **P:** unk **BLW:** unk **RG:** unk **MK:** unk **PH:** unk **SS:** SAR Ancestor #P-307072; E pg 781 **BS:** JLARC 8; 210 pg 395; 196.

TRIMBLE, Sarah (nee Kersey); b c 1727; d Aft 7 Dec 1787 **RU:** Patriot, Gave material aid to cause **CEM:** Old Monmouth Presbyterian; GPS 37.80810, -79.47280; Jct Rts 60 & 669; Lexington City **GS:** U **SP:** Mar (c1745) James Trimble (bef 1730-1776) **VI:** No further data **P:** N **BLW:** N **RG:** unk **MK:** unk **PH:** unk **SS:** DAR Ancestor #A203233; D Vol 3 pg 824 **BS:** 196.

TRIPLETT, Simon; b 1740, King George Co; d 14 May 1810 **RU:** Colonel/Patriot, Served as Capt in Prince William District Bn fr Loudoun Co, Mar 1776. Later became Colonel and performed public service as member Committee of Safety 1775-6. Gave material aid to cause **CEM:** Rock Quarry on Goose Creek; GPS unk; Mt Pleasant; Loudoun **GS:** U **SP:** Mar (aft 20 Apr 1764) Martha Lane (__ Truro Parish-aft 1810) **VI:** No further data **P:** unk **BLW:** unk **RG:** Y **MK:** unk **PH:** unk **SS:** DAR Ancestor #A116621; J-NSSAR 1993 Reg; AL Ct Bk pg 51 Loudoun Co; CE pg 22 **BS:** JLARC 1.

TRIPLETT, William; b 1730; d 1803 **RU:** Lieutenant/Patriot, Served as Ens, 1 Nov 1777, Lt 10 May 1778, Paymaster 10 Jan 1779, in Grayson's Additional Regt. Transferred to Capt Thomas Bell's Co, Gist's Regt 22 Apr 1779. Was Lt & Adjutant, Capt John Steed's Co, 2nd VA Brigade (Col Christian Febiger) Dec 1779-Mar 1780. Retired 1 Jan 1781. Provided 550# beef 26 Apr 1781 **CEM:** Triplett Family; GPS 38.74246, 77.14318; On grounds of Humphrey's Engineer Center at John J. Kingman Rd nr the gate to the Army Geospatial Center at Fort Belvoir; Fairfax **GS:** Y **SP:** Mar (c1762) Sarah Massey **VI:** Both SAR & DAR markers on gravesite **P:** unk **BLW:** unk **RG:** Y **MK:** Y **PH:** Y **SS:** 47 Vol 21 pg 115 **BS:** JLARC 1,13,14, 27, 28.

TROTTER, John; b unk; d Aft 1781 **RU:** Patriot, Gave material aid to cause **CEM:** Trinity Episcopal; GPS 38.14917, -79.07521; 214 Beverley St; Staunton City **GS:** U **SP:** No info **VI:** No further data **P:** N **BLW:** N **RG:** unk **MK:** unk **PH:** unk **SS:** J- DAR Hatcher; AL Ct Bk pg 6 Augusta Co **BS:** JLARC 2.

TROUT (TROUTT), (George) Michael; b 1740 Augusta Co; d 1822 **RU:** Ensign, Served in Capt Laird's Co, Augusta Co Militia **CEM:** Trout or Kline family; GPS unk; 5180 Trissels Rd, Broadway; Rockingham

RU=Rank/Unit · CEM=Cemetery · GS=Gravestone · SP=Spousal Information
VI=Other Veteran Info · P=Pension · BLW=Bounty/Land Warrant · RG=Registered Grave
MK=SAR/DAR Marker · PH=Photo · SS=Service Source · BS=Burial Source

338

GS: Y **SP:** Elizabeth Bear (Baer) **VI:** 1999 SAR marker shows two George Michael Trouts, one b in VA, one b in PA Both b 1750 mar to Eliz. Baer **P:** unk **BLW:** unk **RG:** Y **MK:** N **PH:** Y **SS:** E pg 783, AK Jan 209 **BS:** 04, Jan 2009.

TROUTWINE (TROUTVINE), George Jacob; b c1739, Prussia; d 8 Oct 1783 **RU:** Surgeon's Mate, Served in 11th Cont Line 13 Nov 1776. Resigned 22 Nov 1777 **CEM:** Mt Hebron; GPS 39.10916, -78.09497; 305 E Boscawen St; Winchester City **GS:** U **SP:** Lucy Martin **VI:** No further data **P:** unk **BLW:** unk **RG:** Y **MK:** unk **PH:** unk **SS:** DAR Ancestor #A132357; J-NSSAR 2000 Reg; NSSAR Ancestor #P-307226 **BS:** JLARC 76.

TROWBRIDGE, Samuel; b c1746, Morristown, Morris Co, NJ; d 8 Nov 1822 **RU:** Patriot, Gave material aid to the cause **CEM:** Little Mountain United Methodist; GPS 39.27280, -78.18910; 259 Little Mountain Church Rd, Cedar Grove; Frederick **GS:** Y **SP:** 1) Mar (1768 Winchester) Jane Ruble 2) Mar (1786) Christianna Dumire **VI:** No further data **P:** N **BLW:** N **RG:** Y **MK:** N **PH:** unk **SS:** AL Ct Bk pg 18 **BS:** 59 pg 331.

TUCKER, Daniel; b 1755; d 1800 **RU:** Private, Served in 4th Cont line **CEM:** Tucker; GPS 37.71440, -79.08610; Rt 621, Indian Creek; Amherst **GS:** N **SP:** Mar (15 Sep 1792 Amherst Co as bachelor) Judith Coleman, widow **VI:** Son of Drury (1719-1801) & Susanna Douglass (1722-1765) Tucker. Likely at Tucker Cemetery historic graveyard adjacent to old Tucker homeplace in Amherst VA **P:** unk **BLW:** unk **RG:** unk **MK:** unk **PH:** N **SS:** E pg 783 **BS:** 196.

TUCKER, St George; b 10 Jul 1752, Southampton Parish, Bermuda; d 20 Nov 1827 **RU:** Lieutenant Colonel, Was Secretary & Aide de Camp to Gen Nelson 1779. Served in VA Militia 1780-81. Wounded in Gilford CH battle 15 Mar 1781 **CEM:** Cabell Family; GPS unk; Edgewood, 3008 Warminster Dr, Wingina; Nelson **GS:** Y **SP:** No info **VI:** Son of Bermuda & (-----) Tucker. Professor of Law, College Wm & Mary 1790-1804. Justice of VA Court of Appeals 1803-1811. Judge US District Court 1813-1825. Died in Warminster, Albemarle Co **P:** unk **BLW:** unk **RG:** N **MK:** Y **PH:** N **SS:** E pg 784 **BS:** 32 email Oct. 2013.

TULLOSS (TULLOS), Rodham Jr; b unk; d Dec 1815 **RU:** Ensign, Served in Fauquier Co Militia, recorded as ensign 24 Mar 1778 **CEM:** Tulloss Family; GPS unk; Somerville; Fauquier **GS:** N **SP:** Mar (bond 21 Aug 1764, Peter Grant security) Ann Finnie **VI:** No further data **P:** unk **BLW:** unk **RG:** Y **MK:** N **PH:** N **SS:** 19 pg 243; Fauquier Co Marriages pg 202 **BS:** 19 pg 243.

TUMELIN, Nicolas; b unk; d 1781 **RU:** Soldier, Served in Bourbonnais Bn and died fr battle at Yorktown **CEM:** French Memorial; GPS 36.81944, -79.39933; Yorktown; York **GS:** U **SP:** No info **VI:** No further data **P:** unk **BLW:** unk **RG:** Y **MK:** unk **PH:** unk **SS:** J-Yorktown Historian **BS:** JLARC 1,74.

TURBERVILLE, George Lee; b 7 Sep 1760, Hague, Westmoreland Co; d 26 Mar 1798 **RU:** Major, Served 6 yrs, 11 mos in Cont Line. Was Capt in VA Line **CEM:** Hickory Hill, aka Epping; GPS unk; Hague; Westmoreland **GS:** U **SP:** Elizabeth "Betty" Tayloe Corbin (1764-1798) d/o Gawin & Johanna (Tucker) Corbin **VI:** Son of John (1737-1799) & Martha (Corbin) (1738-1792) Turberville. Member VA House of Delegates 1785-87 and Sheriff of Richmond Co 1798. Held rank as Col at end of life. BLW of 4611 acres awarded to daughters.BLW 2153 & 2508 issued 15 Jul 1789 **P:** unk **BLW:** Y **RG:** unk **MK:** unk **PH:** unk **SS:** G pg 904; DAR Ancestor # A116986; K Vol 5 pg 296 **BS:** 196.

TURBERVILLE, John; b 14 Sep 1737, Hickory Hill, Hague, Westmoreland Co; d 10 Jul 1799 **RU:** Second Lieutenant/Patriot, Was member Committee of Safety fr Westmoreland Co along with brother George Richard Turberville, 31 Jan 1775. Was 2/Lt in Capt John Rice's Co, Westmoreland Co Militia Aug 1777 **CEM:** Hickory Hill, aka Epping; GPS unk; Hague; Westmoreland **GS:** U **SP:** 1) Martha Corbin (1738-1792), d/o Hon. Col John & Lettice (Lee) Corbin 2) Anne Ballentine **VI:** Son of Maj George & Martha (Lee) Turberville. Listed as Major, A stipulation of burial was that he be next to first wife Martha Corbin, with whom he had 10 children. Court action was needed to divide property even though he had will **P:** unk **BLW:** unk **RG:** unk **MK:** unk **PH:** unk **SS:** CN pg 85 **BS:** 196.

TURNER, Hezekiah; b 23 Jul 1739, Charles Co, MD; d c1817 **RU:** Captain/Patriot, Was Paymaster, 3rd VA Regt, Sep 1777-May 1778. Performed public service as Justice of the Commission of Peace, Fauquier Co **CEM:** Turner Family; GPS unk; Delaplane; Fauquier **GS:** N **SP:** Mar (29 Apr 1764)

RU=Rank/Unit	CEM=Cemetery	GS=Gravestone	SP=Spousal Information
VI=Other Veteran Info	P=Pension	BLW=Bounty/Land Warrant	RG=Registered Grave
MK=SAR/DAR Marker	PH=Photo	SS=Service Source	BS=Burial Source

339

Henrietta Chunn (1736 Charles Co, MD-aft 1817 Culpeper Co) **VI:** No further data **P:** unk **BLW:** unk **RG:** Y **MK:** N **PH:** N **SS:** DAR Ancestor #A117060; A pg 276; C pg 139; CG pg 3558 **BS:** 19 pg 343.

TURNER, James; b 7 May 1759; d 8 Jan 1828 **RU:** Patriot, Gave material aid to cause **CEM:** Longwood; GPS 37.34170, -79.51190; Nr jct Oakwood & Longwood Ave Rt 122; Bedford City **GS:** Y **SP:** Sarah Frances "Sally" Leftwich (20 Jan 1762-27 Nov 1834) d/o William (1737-1820) & Elizabeth "Betsey" (Haynes) (1737-1820) Leftwich **VI:** Son of Richard (1730-1769) & Ann Nancy (Johns) (1732-1822) Turner **P:** N **BLW:** N **RG:** unk **MK:** unk **PH:** unk **SS:** AL Ct Bk pg 10,17 Bedford Co **BS:** 196.

TURNER, John; b c1751; d 1781 **RU:** Patriot, Gave material aid to the cause **CEM:** Moore House; GPS unk; Rt 238, Yorktown; York **GS:** Y **SP:** No info **VI:** No further data **P:** N **BLW:** N **RG:** N **MK:** N **PH:** unk **SS:** AL Ct Bk pg 10 **BS:** 65 Yorktown.

TURNER, John L; b 13 Jul 1755, Mathews Co; d 16 Jul 1820, Mathews Co **RU:** Private, Served in Capt George Armstrong's 3rd MD Regt. Enlisted Middlebrook MD 14 Jan 1778, and trained at Camp Charlotte. Served 3 yrs Cont Army **CEM:** Turner Family; GPS unk; Rt 14, W end Horn Branch; Mathews **GS:** Y **SP:** Elizabeth (-----) (__-14 Oct 1817) **VI:** Pen recd 1818 Mathews Co. S41273 **P:** Y **BLW:** unk **RG:** Y **MK:** N **PH:** Y **SS:** K Vol 5 pg 298 **BS:** 43 pg 190.

TURNER, Mattocks; b unk; d 1781 **RU:** Soldier, Served fr DE, and killed in the battle at Yorktown **CEM:** Yorktown Victory Monument Tablet; GPS 38.28350, -78.54150; Yorktown; York **GS:** U **SP:** No info **VI:** No further data **P:** unk **BLW:** unk **RG:** unk **MK:** unk **PH:** unk **SS:** J-Yorktown Historian **BS:** JLARC 74.

TURNER, Nathaniel; b c1739; d 27 Apr 1795 **RU:** Patriot, Gave material aid to cause **CEM:** Turner Family; GPS unk; Eastern View; Hanover **GS:** Y **SP:** No info **VI:** He is listed in the War files # 4, Lib VA so may have had service **P:** unk **BLW:** unk **RG:** Y **MK:** N **PH:** unk **SS:** E pg 786; AL Ct Bk II pg 15 Hanover Co; CZ pg 446 **BS:** 31 vol 1 pg 30.

TUTWILER, Leonard; b 10 Jan 1739 Switzerland; d 25 Jan 1804 **RU:** Private, Served in Dunmore Co's Independent Co, and Capt George Baxter's Co, Col Harrison's Regt, Rockingham, Co and was in battle of Cowpens **CEM:** Friedens United Church of Christ; GPS 38.34848, -78.87653; 3960 Friedens Church Rd; Rockingham **GS:** Y **SP:** Catherine (-----) **VI:** No further data **P:** unk **BLW:** unk **RG:** unk **MK:** unk **PH:** unk **SS:** DAR Ancestor #A117496; G pg 144 **BS:** 196.

TYLER, John; b 28 Feb 1747, York Co; d 6 Jan 1813 **RU:** Captain, Commanded co in Charles Co Militia Co Sep 1775 **CEM:** Greenway; GPS 37.20190, -77.05200; Rt 5, Charles City CH; Charles City Co **GS:** Y **SP:** Mary Armistead (1761-1777) **VI:** Son of John Tyler (1714-1773) & Anne Contesse. Was an attorney; member VA House of Delegates 1778-86; was Speaker fr 1781-85; Judge VA Admiralty Ct 1776 & 1786-88; Judge of State Supreme Ct 1788; Vice President of state conv called to ratify US Constitution; 1788-1808 Chief Judge of VA General Ct; VA Governor 1808-11. In 1812 appointed by President Madison as VA US District Ct Judge. Tyler Co WV named for him. Father of US President John Tyler **P:** unk **BLW:** unk **RG:** N **MK:** N **PH:** unk **SS:** E pg 787 **BS:** JLARC 110; SAR Appl; 196.

TYLER, John; b 15 Jun 1761, Prince William, Co; d 19 Aug 1830 **RU:** First Lieutenant, Served in Capt Scott Co as private and as 1st Lt in 3rd VA Regt **CEM:** Davies; GPS unk; Nr Elon; Amherst **GS:** Y **SP:** Mar (bond dated 2 Feb 1780, Amherst Co) Elizabeth "Betsey" Dillard (__-5 Feb 1849) d/o William & (----) Dillard **VI:** Vet Admin GS, does not give date of birth, inscribed "Served at Charlottesville, The Surrender at Yorktown, and Winchester." Widow appl pen 21 Apr 1845. W6328 **P:** Y **BLW:** unk **RG:** unk **MK:** unk **PH:** unk **SS:** AP; CG pg 3568 **BS:** 196.

TYLER, John; b c1749; d 1809 **RU:** Major, Served as 1st Lt 3rd VA Regt, Major serv not determined. Gave material aid to cause **CEM:** Sharon; GPS unk; Middleburg; Loudoun **GS:** Y **SP:** Mar (2 Feb 1789 Amherst Co as bachelor) Elizabeth Dillard, spinster d/o William & (-----) Dillard. Buried lot 53 **VI:** Son of Charles & (-----) Tyler. **P:** unk **BLW:** unk **RG:** N **MK:** N **PH:** unk **SS:** AL Cert Issued; AP **BS:** 65 pg 87.

UMBERGER (UMBARGER), Henry; b 1752, Lebanon TWP, Lancaster Co, PA; d bef 23 Mar 1837 **RU:** Lieutenant Colonel, Served in Capt John Harkerader's Co, Lancaster Co, PA Militia. Also took Oath of Allegiance **CEM:** Rose Hill; GPS unk; Kegley farm 840 Rose Hill Rd, Wytheville; Wythe **GS:** U **SP:** 1) Ann Margaret Baurin 2) Catherine Neff **VI:** No further data **P:** unk **BLW:** unk **RG:** unk **MK:** unk **PH:** unk

RU=Rank/Unit   CEM=Cemetery   GS=Gravestone   SP=Spousal Information
VI=Other Veteran Info   P=Pension   BLW=Bounty/Land Warrant   RG=Registered Grave
MK=SAR/DAR Marker   PH=Photo   SS=Service Source   BS=Burial Source

340

SS: AP PA Archives 2d Ser, Vol 13 pg 403-4 Muster roll; AR Vol 4 pg 135 DAR applic; BY-SAR applic **BS:** JLARC 2, 40.

UPSHUR, Arthur IV; b 1726, Warwick, Accomack Co; d 15 Jan 1784 **RU:** Lieutenant/Patriot, Public service as member of Committee of Safety **CEM:** Warwick House; GPS unk; Rt 605 1 mi S of Quinby, Upshur Bay; Accomack **GS:** Y **SP:** Mar (c1755) Leah Custis (1728-24 Apr 1792) **VI:** No further data **P:** unk **BLW:** unk **RG:** N **MK:** N **PH:** unk **SS:** DAR #A118083; AL Comm Bk I pg 13 Accomack Co; BG pg 200 **BS:** 145 Quimby.

UPSHUR, Caleb; b 1744; d 17 Oct 1778 **RU:** Patriot, Specific service not identified **CEM:** Warwick House; GPS unk; Rt 605 1 mi S of Quinby, Upshur Bay; Accomack **GS:** Y **SP:** No info **VI:** No further data **P:** N **BLW:** N **RG:** N **MK:** N **PH:** unk **SS:** BH Upshur pg 4 **BS:** 145 Quimby.

UPSHUR, John; b 1741, Northampton Co; d 5 Sep 1799 **RU:** Patriot, Justice of Peace and Justice of Ct of Oyer & Terminor 1778 and Commissioner of Grain Tax 1781 **CEM:** Quimby; GPS unk; Painter; Accomack **GS:** U **SP:** 1) Ann Emmerson (1745-1775) 2) Mar (17 Mar 1781) Margaret Downing (1753-1789) **VI:** Son of Abel (1702-1753) & Rachael (Revell) (1702-1749) Upshur **P:** N **BLW:** N **RG:** unk **MK:** unk **PH:** unk **SS:** DAR Ancestor #A118099; DD cites Northampton Co Minute Book 1777-1778 pg 44 and Calendar VA State Papers Vol 2 pg 454 **BS:** 196.

UPSHUR, Thomas; b 2 Jul 1739; d 19 Dec 1792 **RU:** Captain, Commanded Inf Co in VA State Troops **CEM:** Brownsville Family; GPS unk; .25 mi N on Rt 600 fr Exmore; Northampton **GS:** U **SP:** Mar (29 Jan 1761) Anne Stockley **VI:** No further data **P:** unk **BLW:** Y **RG:** unk **MK:** unk **PH:** unk **SS:** C pg 537 **BS:** 42 pg 87.

URVOY, Jean; b unk; d 1781 **RU:** Seaman, Served on "Soliaire" and died from Yorktown battle **CEM:** French Memorial; GPS 36.81944, -79.39933; Yorktown; York **GS:** U **SP:** No info **VI:** No further data **P:** unk **BLW:** unk **RG:** Y **MK:** unk **PH:** unk **SS:** J-Yorktown Historian **BS:** JLARC 1, 74.

VACHERE, Andre; b unk; d 1781 **RU:** Soldier, Served in Gatinais Bn and died fr battle at Yorktown **CEM:** French Memorial; GPS 36.81944, -79.39933; Yorktown; York **GS:** U **SP:** No info **VI:** No further data **P:** unk **BLW:** unk **RG:** unk **MK:** unk **PH:** unk **SS:** J-Yorktown Historian **BS:** JLARC 74.

VADEN, Burwell; b 2 Sep 1733, Henrico Co; d c1824 **RU:** Private/Patriot, Signed the Oath of Allegiance. In 1777 served in Capt Reuben Payne's Co. Also served on Grand Jury of Inquest in 1781 **CEM:** Chatham; GPS 36.81900, -79.39900; Ennis Dr, Chatham; Pittsylvania **GS:** Y **SP:** Mar (1758) Sarah (-----) (1742-6 Feb 1824) **VI:** No further data **P:** unk **BLW:** unk **RG:** Y **MK:** N **PH:** Y **SS:** DAR Ancestor #A116714; Y Bk 4 pg 387; AW **BS:** 174; 04.

VAISSE, Jean; b unk; d 1781 **RU:** Seaman, Served on "Magnanime" and died from Yorktown battle **CEM:** French Memorial; GPS 36.81944, -79.39933; Yorktown; York **GS:** U **SP:** No info **VI:** No further data **P:** unk **BLW:** unk **RG:** unk **MK:** unk **PH:** unk **SS:** J-Yorktown Historian **BS:** JLARC 74.

VALENTINE, Batchelder; b 1750; d 1807 **RU:** Patriot, Gave material aid to cause **CEM:** Hollywood; GPS 37.53560, -77.45720; 412 S Cherry St; Richmond City **GS:** Y **SP:** Ann Satterwhite (1752-1829) d/o Mann (of York Co) & Ann (Palmer) Satterwhite **VI:** Listed on obelisk with other family members **P:** N **BLW:** N **RG:** unk **MK:** unk **PH:** unk **SS:** AL Ct Bk pg 20 King William Co **BS:** 196.

VALENTINE, Edward; b 1763; d 1832 **RU:** Captain, Served in artillery unit in Cont Line. Was wounded **CEM:** Trinity Episcopal; GPS 38.14917, -79.07521; 214 Beverley St; Staunton City **GS:** U **SP:** no info **VI:** Restitution for back pay to his estate 29 Nov 1850 of $3952.50 was made. R18626. Recd 1/2 pay NARA Acct #874 and #050179 **P:** Y **BLW:** unk **RG:** unk **MK:** unk **PH:** unk **SS:** SAR Ancestor #P-309065; C pg 585, 3578 **BS:** JLARC 8, 51, 62, 63.

VALEOT, Jean; b unk; d 1781 **RU:** Seaman, Served on "Languedoc" and died from Yorktown battle **CEM:** French Memorial; GPS 36.81944, -79.39933; Yorktown; York **GS:** U **SP:** No info **VI:** No further data **P:** unk **BLW:** unk **RG:** unk **MK:** unk **PH:** unk **SS:** J-Yorktown Historian **BS:** JLARC 74.

VALLANCE, William; b unk; d 1781 **RU:** Soldier, Served fr NY, killed in the battle at Yorktown **CEM:** Yorktown Victory Monument Tablet; GPS 38.28350, -78.54150; Yorktown; York **GS:** U **SP:** No info **VI:** No further data **P:** unk **BLW:** unk **RG:** unk **MK:** unk **PH:** unk **SS:** J-Yorktown Historian **BS:** JLARC 74.

RU=Rank/Unit	CEM=Cemetery	GS=Gravestone	SP=Spousal Information
VI=Other Veteran Info	P=Pension	BLW=Bounty/Land Warrant	RG=Registered Grave
MK=SAR/DAR Marker	PH=Photo	SS=Service Source	BS=Burial Source

341

VALLE, Jean; b unk; d 1781 **RU:** Seaman, Served on "Hercule" and died from Yorktown battle **CEM:** French Memorial; GPS 36.81944, -79.39933; Yorktown; York **GS:** U **SP:** No info **VI:** No further data **P:** unk **BLW:** unk **RG:** unk **MK:** unk **PH:** unk **SS:** J-Yorktown Historian **BS:** JLARC 74.

VALLEE, Pierre; b unk; d 1781 **RU:** Seaman, Served on "Ville de Paris" and died from Yorktown battle **CEM:** French Memorial; GPS 36.81944, -79.39933; Yorktown; York **GS:** U **SP:** No info **VI:** No further data **P:** unk **BLW:** unk **RG:** unk **MK:** unk **PH:** unk **SS:** J-Yorktown Historian **BS:** JLARC 74.

VALLEE, Vincent; b unk; d 1781 **RU:** Seaman, Served on "Citoyen" and died from Yorktown battle **CEM:** French Memorial; GPS 36.81944, -79.39933; Yorktown; York **GS:** U **SP:** No info **VI:** No further data **P:** unk **BLW:** unk **RG:** unk **MK:** unk **PH:** unk **SS:** J-Yorktown Historian **BS:** JLARC 74.

VAN LEAR (VANLEAR), Jacob; b unk; d 1822 **RU:** Private, Served in Capt Long's Co, Augusta Co Militia **CEM:** Tinkling Spring Presbyterian; GPS 38.08472, -78.98278; 30 Tinkling Spring Dr, Fishersville; Augusta **GS:** N **SP:** Jane (-----) **VI:** No further data **P:** unk **BLW:** unk **RG:** unk **MK:** N **PH:** N **SS:** E pg 791 **BS:** JLARC 62.

VAN VOST, Christian; b unk; d 1781 **RU:** Private, Served in 1st Regt NY Line. Killed in the battle at Yorktown **CEM:** Yorktown Victory Monument Tablet; GPS 38.28350, -78.54150; Yorktown; York **GS:** U **SP:** No info **VI:** No further data **P:** unk **BLW:** unk **RG:** unk **MK:** unk **PH:** unk **SS:** J-Yorktown Historian; AX pg 348 **BS:** JLARC 74.

VANCE, James D; b 1752, Orange Co; d 21 Dec 1816 **RU:** Private, Served in 4th, 8th, 12th Cont Lines **CEM:** Opequon Presbyterian; GPS 39.13938, -78.19494; 217 Opequon Church Ln; Winchester City **GS:** Y **SP:** No info **VI:** Died in Frederick Co **P:** unk **BLW:** unk **RG:** Y **MK:** N **PH:** unk **SS:** E pg 790 **BS:** 59 pg 333; 196.

VANCE, John; b 12 Feb 1736; d 28 Aug 1823 **RU:** Lieutenant, Served in Capt James Dysart's Co of Light Horse on tour of NC under command of Col William Campbell. Was listed on payroll of 21 May 1781 **CEM:** Vance Family; GPS unk; Rt 695; Washington **GS:** Y **SP:** Jane (-----) (12 Feb 1741-2 Feb 1824) **VI:** No further data **P:** N **BLW:** N **RG:** N **MK:** unk **PH:** N **SS:** N pg 1262-payroll; CI Muster Roll **BS:** 212 pg 108.

VANCE, Robert; b 1728; d 18 Aug 1818 **RU:** Patriot, Was Commissioner in 1780-81, Berkeley Co **CEM:** Montour; GPS unk; Not identified by SAR source; Winchester City **GS:** U **SP:** Jean White (1747 Culpeper-__) **VI:** Son of Samuel & Sarah (Covllie) Vance **P:** N **BLW:** N **RG:** unk **MK:** unk **PH:** unk **SS:** DAR Ancestor #A117359; SAR Ancestor #P-310142; J- DAR Hatcher; AL Ct Bk I pg 9 **BS:** JLARC 2.

VANCE, Samuel; b 1734, Ireland; d 1807 **RU:** Captain/Patriot, Served in 8th Cont Line. Gave material aid to cause **CEM:** Opequon Presbyterian; GPS 39.13938, -78.19494; 217 Opequon Church Ln; Winchester City **GS:** U **SP:** Sarah Byrd **VI:** No further data **P:** unk **BLW:** unk **RG:** Y **MK:** Y **PH:** unk **SS:** J-NSSAR 2000 Reg; AL Cert 1 Frederick Co **BS:** JLARC 76.

VANCE, Samuel; b 1749; d 8 Dec 1838 **RU:** Soldier, Was in battles at Point Pleasant & Kings Mountain **CEM:** Sinking Springs; GPS 36.71030, -81.98170; 136 E Main St, Abingdon; Washington **GS:** U **SP:** Margaret Laughlin **VI:** No further data **P:** unk **BLW:** unk **RG:** unk **MK:** Y **PH:** unk **SS:** NSSAR Ancestor # P-310151 **BS:** JLARC 2, 80.

VANCE, William; b 1741; d Oct 1792 **RU:** Captain, Served in 8th VA Regt Frederick Co Militia. Took oath as ensign 4 Aug 1779 **CEM:** Old Opequon Church; GPS 39.82237, -78.11412; 217 Opequon Church Ln, Kernstown; Frederick **GS:** Y **SP:** 1) Nancy Gilkeson 2) Mary Colville 3) Ann Glass **VI:** No inscription on GS. No record of pension **P:** unk **BLW:** unk **RG:** Y **MK:** Y **PH:** Y **SS:** J-NSSAR 2000 Reg; E pg 790 **BS:** JLARC 76.

VANDEVANTER (VANDEVINDER, VAN DEVENTER, VANDEVENTER), Isaac; b 8 Feb 1747, Hunterdon Co, NJ; d 12 Jul 1803 **RU:** Second Lieutenant/Patriot, Served in Loudoun Co Militia, and took oath as 2nd Lt, 15 Sep 1778. Also gave 335# beef to cause **CEM:** Fairfax Meeting House; GPS 39.18557, -77.60589; Water St & Waterford Rd, Waterford; Loudoun **GS:** Y **SP:** Elizabeth McGeath **VI:** No further data **P:** unk **BLW:** unk **RG:** Y **MK:** N **PH:** unk **SS:** D pg 2; E pg 191; AZ pg 212; AL Ct BK pg 3 Loudoun Co **BS:** 25 pg 323.

RU=Rank/Unit	CEM=Cemetery	GS=Gravestone	SP=Spousal Information
VI=Other Veteran Info	P=Pension	BLW=Bounty/Land Warrant	RG=Registered Grave
MK=SAR/DAR Marker	PH=Photo	SS=Service Source	BS=Burial Source

342

VANMETER, Henry Jr; b 12 May 1754, Frederick Co; d 17 May 1830 **RU:** Private/Patriot, Served in militia. Gave to cause in Berkeley Co **CEM:** Miller Family; GPS unk; Mountain View Farm, vic Front Royal; Warren **GS:** Y **SP:** Elizabeth Miller (19 Nov 1755-24 Jan 1808) **VI:** No further data **P:** unk **BLW:** unk **RG:** Y **MK:** N **PH:** unk **SS:** E pg 791; AL Ct Bk pg 6 **BS:** 01 pg 36.

VANPELT, Peter; b unk; d 4 Apr 1831 **RU:** Private, Ent serv Amherst Co. In fall of 1777, served 3 mos in Capt Robert Cravens Co at Tygart's Valley VA. Enlisted April 1778, and served18 mos in Capts David Stephenson's and John Steed's Cos, Col Neville's VA Regt. Was at Battle of Monmouth **CEM:** Frank Harman Place; GPS unk; Rt 42 N, Harrisonburg; Harrisonburg City **GS:** N **SP:** Mar (13 Mar 1778) Agnes (Agness) (c1761-25 Aug 1840) **VI:** Died in Rockingham Co. Widow appl pen 17 Apr 1837 Buckingham Co, age 76. W18198 **P:** Y **BLW:** unk **RG:** Y **MK:** N **PH:** N **SS:** E pg 791; AK; CG Vol 3 pg 3599 **BS:** 04; 191 Fr Harman.

VANPELT, Tunis; b unk; d 1840 **RU:** Patriot, Gave material aid to cause **CEM:** Frank Harman Place; GPS unk; Rt 42 N, Harrisonburg; Harrisonburg City **GS:** Y **SP:** No info **VI:** No further data **P:** N **BLW:** N **RG:** Y **MK:** unk **PH:** unk **SS:** AL Cert Berkeley Co **BS:** 219.

VANSICKLER, Ferdinand (Fernandus); b 11 May 1738, NJ; d 1818 **RU:** Private, Probably served in Loudoun Co Militia **CEM:** North Fork Baptist; GPS 39.06014, -77.68509; 38130 North Folk Rd, North Fork; Loudoun **GS:** U **SP:** Mar (10 Jun 1757) Eleanor WinKoop, d/o Philip & Margaret (Conover) Wynkoop **VI:** No further data **P:** unk **BLW:** unk **RG:** unk **MK:** unk **PH:** unk **SS:** BY cites DAR Mag **BS:** JLARC 32.

VAQUIER, Francois; b unk; d 1781 **RU:** Seaman, Served on "Diademe" and died from Yorktown battle **CEM:** French Memorial; GPS 36.81944, -79.39933; Yorktown; York **GS:** U **SP:** No info **VI:** No further data **P:** unk **BLW:** unk **RG:** unk **MK:** unk **PH:** unk **SS:** J-Yorktown Historian **BS:** JLARC 74.

VARNER, Joseph; b 1758; d 1848 **RU:** Soldier, Served in Cont & VA Lines. Ent serv Charlotte Co **CEM:** Varner Family; GPS unk; Nr jct of Rts 696 & 626, btw Critz & Salem Church, Locust Grove; Patrick **GS:** N **SP:** Mar (7 Oct 1790) Polly (Molly) Kinney (c1772-_) **VI:** Also served in the War of 1812. Listed as a pensioner in 1840. Sol appl pen Apr 1820 Halifax Co age 56. Widow appl pen 4 Mar 1850 Patrick Co age 78 and BLW 11 Apr 1855 age 85 Patrick Co. W1762, BLW #12641-100 & BLW #139-60-55. Unmarked grave **P:** Y **BLW:** Y **RG:** unk **MK:** unk **PH:** N **SS:** CG Vol 3 pg 3608 **BS:** JLARC 4, 30.

VARNER (WERNER), Phillip; b 1746, Alsace, Germany; d 1830 **RU:** Patriot, Gave material aid to the cause **CEM:** James Varner Family; GPS unk; SE of Luray; Page **GS:** Y **SP:** Barbara Hottel **VI:** No further data **P:** N **BLW:** N **RG:** Y **MK:** N **PH:** unk **SS:** AL Ct Bk pg 6, 120 **BS:** 120 Hartman.

VARRENNES, Jean; b unk; d 1781 **RU:** Soldier, Served in Beaujolais Bn and died fr battle at Yorktown **CEM:** French Memorial; GPS 36.81944, -79.39933; Yorktown; York **GS:** U **SP:** No info **VI:** No further data **P:** unk **BLW:** unk **RG:** unk **MK:** unk **PH:** unk **SS:** J-Yorktown Historian **BS:** JLARC 74.

VAUGHAN, James; b c1738-1741; d 1803 **RU:** Sergeant, Rank obtained 1778. Serv in 3rd & 4th Cont Line **CEM:** Vaughan Family; GPS unk; Not identified; Amelia **GS:** Y **SP:** 1) Mar (c1771) Ann Hill (__-1782) d/o James & (-----) Hill, 2) Mar (bef 14 Mar 1783) Lucy Jeter d/o Thomas & (-----) Jeter **VI:** Son of Robert (c1705, Prince George Co-1779) & Martha (-----) Vaughan **P:** unk **BLW:** Y **RG:** N **MK:** N **PH:** unk **SS:** DAR Ancestor #A118308; E pg 793 **BS:** 80 vol 4 pg 144.

VAUGHAN (VAUGHN), William Jr; b 18 Nov 1760, Hanover Co; d 22 Mar 1841 **RU:** Sergeant, Ent serv Bedford Co 1780. Served in Webber's VA Co, 4th Cont Line and wounded at seige of 96 **CEM:** Vaughan Family; GPS 36.44200, -81.41660; Fries, Spring Valley Community; Grayson **GS:** Y **SP:** Mar (8 May 1794) Elizabeth "Betsey" Fielder (17 Feb 1777-__) d/o John & (-----) Fielder **VI:** Son of William & Mary (-----) Vaughan. Sol appl pen 24 Sep 1832 Grayson Co. Widow appl pen 27 Jan 1851, and for BLW 19 Apr 1855 both in Grayson Co. W2708 in 1851. BLW 29019-160 (55) **P:** Y **BLW:** Y **RG:** unk **MK:** Y **PH:** unk **SS:** J- DAR Hatcher; E pg 173, 793; CG Vol 3 pg 3611 **BS:** 199, JLARC 2.

VAUGHN, James; b c1756; d 14 Dec 1830 **RU:** Sergeant, Promoted in 1778 and served in 3rd & 4th Cont Lines **CEM:** Shockoe Hill; GPS 37.55190, -77.43170; 4th & Hospital Sts; Richmond City **GS:** Y **SP:** No info **VI:** No further data **P:** unk **BLW:** unk **RG:** Y **MK:** N **PH:** unk **SS:** E pg 793 **BS:** 57 pg 9.

RU=Rank/Unit	CEM=Cemetery	GS=Gravestone	SP=Spousal Information
VI=Other Veteran Info	P=Pension	BLW=Bounty/Land Warrant	RG=Registered Grave
MK=SAR/DAR Marker	PH=Photo	SS=Service Source	BS=Burial Source

343

VAUGHN, William; b unk; d unk **RU:** Sergeant, Served in Spencer's Regt, Cont Troops **CEM:** Fairmont Baptist; **GPS** unk; 3948 Findlay Gap Dr, Shipley; Nelson **GS:** Y **SP:** No info **VI:** No further data **P:** unk **BLW:** unk **RG:** N **MK:** N **PH:** unk **SS:** AP roll **BS:** 182.

VAWTER, Benjamin; b unk; d 1830 **RU:** Private, Served in 2nd VA State Regt **CEM:** Old City; **GPS** 37.41472, -79.15667; 401 Taylor St; Lynchburg City **GS:** N **SP:** No info **VI:** No further data **P:** unk **BLW:** unk **RG:** Y **MK:** N **PH:** N **SS:** E pg 793 **BS:** 62 pg 173.

VAWTER, John; b unk; d 1834 **RU:** Private?, Served 3 yrs in VA Cont Line **CEM:** Old City; **GPS** 37.41472, -79.15667; 401 Taylor St; Lynchburg City **GS:** Y **SP:** No info **VI:** Heir, Beverly Vawter recd BLW of 100 acres for his service **P:** unk **BLW:** Y **RG:** Y **MK:** N **PH:** unk **SS:** C pg 213; E pg 793; F pg 77 **BS:** 62 pg 173.

VBEL, Geroges; b unk; d 1781 **RU:** Soldier, Served in Royal Deux Ponts Bn and died fr battle at Yorktown **CEM:** French Memorial; **GPS** 36.81944, -79.39933; Yorktown; York **GS:** U **SP:** No info **VI:** No further data **P:** unk **BLW:** unk **RG:** unk **MK:** unk **PH:** unk **SS:** J-Yorktown Historian **BS:** JLARC 74.

VEALE, Thomas; b 1725, Norfolk Co; d 16 Dec 1793 **RU:** Patriot, Gave material aid to cause in Norfolk **CEM:** Trinity Episcopal; **GPS** 36.83459, -76.30105; 500 Court St; Portsmouth City **GS:** Y **SP:** Mar (15 Nov 1763. Norfolk) Bethiah Edwards **VI:** Capt in Colonial War. Was Burgess fr Norfolk Co 1762-1765. One of the Trustees of Portsmouth **P:** N **BLW:** N **RG:** unk **MK:** unk **PH:** unk **SS:** D pg 255 **BS:** 57.

VEINTEFFER, JH; b unk; d 1781 **RU:** Seaman, Served on "Auguste" and died from Yorktown battle **CEM:** French Memorial; **GPS** 36.81944, -79.39933; Yorktown; York **GS:** U **SP:** No info **VI:** No further data **P:** unk **BLW:** unk **RG:** unk **MK:** unk **PH:** unk **SS:** J-Yorktown Historian **BS:** JLARC 74.

VENABLE, Abraham Bedford Jr; b 20 Nov 1758; d 28 Dec 1811 **RU:** Patriot, Gave material aid to cause **CEM:** Monumental Church; **GPS** unk; 1224 E Broad St; Richmond City **GS:** Y **SP:** No info **VI:** Son of Nathaniel (1733-1804) & Elizabeth Michaux (Woodson) (1740-1791) Venable. Was US Congressman & US Senator and elected to represent VA's 6th & 7th Districts & at-Large in US House of Representatives, 1791-99. Was US Senator fr VA fr 1803-4. Died in theater fire in Richmond 26 Dec 1811 **P:** N **BLW:** N **RG:** unk **MK:** unk **PH:** unk **SS:** AL Ct Bk pg 30 Prince Edward Co **BS:** 196.

VENABLE, Nathaniel; b 1 Nov 1733, Lousia Co; d 26 Dec 1804 **RU:** Patriot, Gave material aid to cause **CEM:** Venable-Slate Hill Plantation; **GPS** unk; Worsham; Prince Edward **GS:** Y **SP:** Elizabeth Michaux Woodson (6 Jun 1740-29 Sep 1791) d/o Richard & Anne Madeline (Michaux) Woodson. **VI:** Son of Abraham (II) & Martha (Davis) Venable. Was member of House of Burgesses; VA House of Delegates 1766, 1769, 1776; and a State Senator fr P.E. Co fr 1780-85. One of founders of Hampden-Sydney College **P:** N **BLW:** N **RG:** unk **MK:** unk **PH:** unk **SS:** AL Ct Bk pg 29, 37 Prince Edward Co **BS:** 196.

VERDAVOIR, Oger; b unk; d 1781 **RU:** Soldier, Served in Agenois Bn and died fr battle at Yorktown **CEM:** French Memorial; **GPS** 36.81944, -79.39933; Yorktown; York **GS:** U **SP:** No info **VI:** No further data **P:** unk **BLW:** unk **RG:** unk **MK:** unk **PH:** unk **SS:** J-Yorktown Historian **BS:** JLARC 74.

VERDIER, Jacques; b unk; d 1781 **RU:** Seaman, Served on "Marseillais" and died from Yorktown battle **CEM:** French Memorial; **GPS** 36.81944, -79.39933; Yorktown; York **GS:** U **SP:** No info **VI:** No further data **P:** unk **BLW:** unk **RG:** unk **MK:** unk **PH:** unk **SS:** J-Yorktown Historian **BS:** JLARC 74.

VERRIER, Joseph; b unk; d 1781 **RU:** Soldier, Served in Bourbonnais Bn and died fr battle at Yorktown **CEM:** French Memorial; **GPS** 36.81944, -79.39933; Yorktown; York **GS:** U **SP:** No info **VI:** No further data **P:** unk **BLW:** unk **RG:** unk **MK:** unk **PH:** unk **SS:** J-Yorktown Historian **BS:** JLARC 74.

VERSIN, Pierre; b unk; d 1781 **RU:** Seaman, Served on "Hextor" and died from Yorktown battle **CEM:** French Memorial; **GPS** 36.81944, -79.39933; Yorktown; York **GS:** U **SP:** No info **VI:** No further data **P:** unk **BLW:** unk **RG:** unk **MK:** unk **PH:** unk **SS:** J-Yorktown Historian **BS:** JLARC 74.

VEXLIN, Emmanuel; b unk; d 1781 **RU:** Seaman, Served on "Soliaire" and died from Yorktown battle **CEM:** French Memorial; **GPS** 36.81944, -79.39933; Yorktown; York **GS:** U **SP:** No info **VI:** No further data **P:** unk **BLW:** unk **RG:** unk **MK:** unk **PH:** unk **SS:** J-Yorktown Historian **BS:** JLARC 74.

RU=Rank/Unit   CEM=Cemetery   GS=Gravestone   SP=Spousal Information
VI=Other Veteran Info   P=Pension   BLW=Bounty/Land Warrant   RG=Registered Grave
MK=SAR/DAR Marker   PH=Photo   SS=Service Source   BS=Burial Source

344

VEXTAIN, Emmanuel; b unk; d 1781 **RU:** Soldier, Served in Gatinais Bn and died fr battle at Yorktown **CEM:** French Memorial; GPS 36.81944, -79.39933; Yorktown; York **GS:** U **SP:** No info **VI:** No further data **P:** unk **BLW:** unk **RG:** unk **MK:** unk **PH:** unk **SS:** J-Yorktown Historian **BS:** JLARC 74.

VIA, William; b 1761; d 27 Jun 1836 **RU:** Private, Served in VA Line Bn **CEM:** Via Family; GPS unk; Brown's Cove; Albemarle **GS:** U **SP:** Mar (7 Dec 1781) Mary Craig **VI:** Appl pen 7 Dec 1828 and recd same in Albemarle Co age 67. Widow appl pen 5 Aug 1829 **P:** Y **BLW:** unk **RG:** unk **MK:** unk **PH:** unk **SS:** J- DAR Hatcher; E pg 794; CG pg 3616 **BS:** JLARC 2.

VIAL, Pierre; b unk; d 1781 **RU:** Soldier, Served in Soissonnais Bn and died fr battle at Yorktown **CEM:** French Memorial; GPS 36.81944, -79.39933; Yorktown; York **GS:** U **SP:** No info **VI:** No further data **P:** unk **BLW:** unk **RG:** unk **MK:** unk **PH:** unk **SS:** J-Yorktown Historian **BS:** JLARC 74.

VIGOUREUX, Francois; b unk; d 1781 **RU:** Soldier, Served in Gatinais Bn and died fr battle at Yorktown **CEM:** French Memorial; GPS 36.81944, -79.39933; Yorktown; York **GS:** U **SP:** No info **VI:** No further data **P:** unk **BLW:** unk **RG:** unk **MK:** unk **PH:** unk **SS:** J-Yorktown Historian **BS:** JLARC 74.

VILATON, Jean; b unk; d 1781 **RU:** Soldier, Served in Santogne Bn and died fr battle at Yorktown **CEM:** French Memorial; GPS 36.81944, -79.39933; Yorktown; York **GS:** U **SP:** No info **VI:** No further data **P:** unk **BLW:** unk **RG:** unk **MK:** unk **PH:** unk **SS:** J-Yorktown Historian **BS:** JLARC 74.

VILLARET, Joseph; b unk; d 1781 **RU:** Soldier, Served in Bourbonnais Bn and died fr battle at Yorktown **CEM:** French Memorial; GPS 36.81944, -79.39933; Yorktown; York **GS:** U **SP:** No info **VI:** No further data **P:** unk **BLW:** unk **RG:** unk **MK:** unk **PH:** unk **SS:** J-Yorktown Historian **BS:** JLARC 74.

VILLEDIEU, Jean; b unk; d 1781 **RU:** Seaman, Served on Caton and died from Yorktown battle **CEM:** French Memorial; GPS 36.81944, -79.39933; Yorktown; York **GS:** U **SP:** no info **VI:** No further data **P:** unk **BLW:** unk **RG:** unk **MK:** unk **PH:** unk **SS:** J-Yorktown Historian **BS:** JLARC 74.

VILLEON, de la; b unk; d 1781 **RU:** Seaman, Served on "Diademe" and died from Yorktown battle **CEM:** French Memorial; GPS 36.81944, -79.39933; Yorktown; York **GS:** U **SP:** No info **VI:** No further data **P:** unk **BLW:** unk **RG:** unk **MK:** unk **PH:** unk **SS:** J-Yorktown Historian **BS:** JLARC 74.

VINCE, Joseph; b unk; d 1781 **RU:** Seaman, Served on "Ville de Paris" and died from Yorktown battle **CEM:** French Memorial; GPS 36.81944, -79.39933; Yorktown; York **GS:** U **SP:** No info **VI:** No further data **P:** unk **BLW:** unk **RG:** unk **MK:** unk **PH:** unk **SS:** J-Yorktown Historian **BS:** JLARC 74.

VINCENT, Nicolas; b unk; d 1781 **RU:** Seaman, Served on "Solitaire" and died from Yorktown battle **CEM:** French Memorial; GPS 36.81944, -79.39933; Yorktown; York **GS:** U **SP:** No info **VI:** No further data **P:** unk **BLW:** unk **RG:** unk **MK:** unk **PH:** unk **SS:** J-Yorktown Historian **BS:** JLARC 74.

VINEYARD, George; b 21 Jun 1759; d 1852 **RU:** Private, Served in VA Line. Ent serv Rockbridge Co **CEM:** Vineyard; GPS unk; Gate City; Scott **GS:** U **SP:** No info **VI:** Sol appl 13 Feb 1844 Scott Co age 84. S7794 **P:** Y **BLW:** unk **RG:** unk **MK:** unk **PH:** unk **SS:** CG Vol 3 pg 3619 **BS:** JLARC 4.

VINYARD, Christain; b unk, Palatinate, Germany; d 27 Feb 1798 **RU:** Patriot, Performed patriotic service to VA Militia. Furnished supplies 11 Apr 1782 **CEM:** Vinyard Family; GPS unk; Lauderale Ave; Roanoke Co **GS:** Y **SP:** Mar (1772) Chritiania Tabler **VI:** No further data **P:** N **BLW:** N **RG:** Y **MK:** N **PH:** unk **SS:** D Roanoke area **BS:** 04.

VINYARD, Christian; b unk; d 1837 **RU:** Patriot, Gave material aid to the cause **CEM:** Vinyard Family; GPS unk; Vinton; Roanoke Co **GS:** U **SP:** No info **VI:** No further data **P:** N **BLW:** N **RG:** Y **MK:** N **PH:** unk **SS:** AL Ct Bk pg 25 **BS:** DAR report.

VITRE, Jean; b unk; d 1781 **RU:** Soldier, Served in Gatinais Bn and died fr battle at Yorktown **CEM:** French Memorial; GPS 36.81944, -79.39933; Yorktown; York **GS:** U **SP:** No info **VI:** No further data **P:** unk **BLW:** unk **RG:** unk **MK:** unk **PH:** unk **SS:** J-Yorktown Historian **BS:** JLARC 74.

VITRIER, Andre; b unk; d 1781 **RU:** Soldier, Served in Gatinais Bn and died fr battle at Yorktown **CEM:** French Memorial; GPS 36.81944, -79.39933; Yorktown; York **GS:** U **SP:** No info **VI:** No further data **P:** unk **BLW:** unk **RG:** unk **MK:** unk **PH:** unk **SS:** J-Yorktown Historian **BS:** JLARC 74.

RU=Rank/Unit   CEM=Cemetery   GS=Gravestone   SP=Spousal Information
VI=Other Veteran Info   P=Pension   BLW=Bounty/Land Warrant   RG=Registered Grave
MK=SAR/DAR Marker   PH=Photo   SS=Service Source   BS=Burial Source

345

VIVANSON, Bernard; b unk; d 1781 **RU:** Soldier, Served in Touraine Bn and died fr battle at Yorktown **CEM:** French Memorial; GPS 36.81944, -79.39933; Yorktown; York **GS:** U **SP:** No info **VI:** No further data **P:** unk **BLW:** unk **RG:** unk **MK:** unk **PH:** unk **SS:** J-Yorktown Historian **BS:** JLARC 74.

VIZET, Joseph; b unk; d 1781 **RU:** Seaman, Served on "Diademe" and died from Yorktown battle **CEM:** French Memorial; GPS 36.81944, -79.39933; Yorktown; York **GS:** U **SP:** No info **VI:** No further data **P:** unk **BLW:** unk **RG:** unk **MK:** unk **PH:** unk **SS:** J-Yorktown Historian **BS:** JLARC 74.

VON EFFINGER, John; b unk; d unk **RU:** Corporal, Served in Voneffinge's unitr **CEM:** Woodstock; GPS unk; Woodstock; Shenandoah **GS:** U **SP:** no info **VI:** No further data **P:** unk **BLW:** unk **RG:** unk **MK:** unk **PH:** unk **SS:** J-NSSAR 2000 Reg; AR Vol 4 pg 147 **BS:** JLARC 76.

VORRIOT, Pierre; b unk; d 1781 **RU:** Seaman, Served on "Hextor" and died from Yorktown battle **CEM:** French Memorial; GPS 36.81944, -79.39933; Yorktown; York **GS:** U **SP:** No info **VI:** No further data **P:** unk **BLW:** unk **RG:** unk **MK:** unk **PH:** unk **SS:** J-Yorktown Historian **BS:** JLARC 74.

VOWELL, John G; b unk; d 1806 **RU:** Soldier, Served in 6th Cont Line **CEM:** Old Presbyterian Meeting House; GPS 38.48528, -77.23532; 323 S Fairfax St; Alexandria City **GS:** N **SP:** No info **VI:** No further data **P:** unk **BLW:** unk **RG:** Y **MK:** unk **PH:** N **SS:** J-NSSAR 2000 Reg; NSSAR Ancestor #P-311198; E pg 796 **BS:** JLARC 1; 5.

WADDELL, D James; b 2 Jul 1752, Lancaster Co; d 21 Feb 1813 **RU:** Soldier/Patriot, Served in Capt Thomas Massie's Co of Foot, 6th Cont line, commanded by Col James Hendrick. Also gave 330# of beef, (5 quarters) 20 Apr 1782 **CEM:** Trinity Episcopal; GPS 38.14917, -79.07521; 214 Beverley St; Staunton City **GS:** Y **SP:** Mary Gordon (__-1813) **VI:** No further data **P:** unk **BLW:** unk **RG:** unk **MK:** unk **PH:** Y **SS:** CI Muster Roll Fold 3 CY pg 33 **BS:** 196.

WADE, Isaac Sr; b c1758; d 9 Aug 1823 **RU:** Private, Ent ser 1777 in Bedford Co Militia and was in 14th VA Regt. Served at battles of Brandywine and Germantown. Ent serv again 1781 Bedford Co. Wounded at Yorktown **CEM:** Woodford/Wade; GPS unk; 11477 Falling Creek Rd; Bedford **GS:** N **SP:** Mar (11 Feb 1779 Bedford Co) Polly Gibbs, widow of Thomas Stevens. Source CG says marriage date is 11 Feb 1779. **VI:** Son of Isaac listed in records as War of 1812 veteran also bur here. Widow appl pen 1 May 1839 Bedford Co, age 78. W6389 **P:** Y **BLW:** unk **RG:** Y **MK:** N **PH:** N **SS:** AK, Bedford Mus; E pg 797; K Vol 6 pg 27; CG Vol 3 pg 3628 **BS:** 04, Sep 07.

WADE, Stephen; b unk; d 12 Oct 1781 **RU:** Private, Served in Ct Cont line and died fr battle at Yorktown **CEM:** Yorktown Victory Monument Tablet; GPS 38.28350, -78.54150; Yorktown; York **GS:** U **SP:** No info **VI:** No further data **P:** unk **BLW:** unk **RG:** unk **MK:** unk **PH:** unk **SS:** J-Yorktown Historian; DY pg 340 **BS:** JLARC 74.

WAFORD, George; b 1737; d Jan 1810 **RU:** Soldier, Served in Capt Thomas Hill's Co, Col McClanahan's 7th Regt, 7th Cont line, Nov 1776-Jan 1777. Also was in Lt Thomas Buckmerson's Co at Morristown **CEM:** Trinity Episcopal; GPS 38.14917, -79.07521; 214 Beverley St; Staunton City **GS:** Y **SP:** No info **VI:** No further data **P:** unk **BLW:** unk **RG:** unk **MK:** unk **PH:** Y **SS:** E pg 7, 98; CI **BS:** 196.

WAGENER (WEGENER), Peter; b 1730 or 10 Oct 1744, Prince William Co; d 1797/98 **RU:** Colonel/Patriot, Appointed 4 July 1777 to Col, Fairfax Co Militia. He imported cannon fr Annapolis, MD to Alexandria. Was clerk of the county **CEM:** Pohick Episcopal; GPS 38.42546, -77.11598; 9301 Richmond Hwy, Lorton; Fairfax **GS:** Y **SP:** Mar (14 Apr 1774 Fairfax Co) Sarah McCarty **VI:** Succeeded father as clerk, Fairfax Co fr 1744 through war. Was Associate, Fairfax Co, VA 1770; Still listed as County Lt 22 Jul 1783. Memorial marker Pohick Church Cem, Alexandria **P:** unk **BLW:** unk **RG:** unk **MK:** Y **PH:** Y **SS:** NSSAR Ancestor #P-311506 **BS:** JLARC 2, 4,14, 27, 28, 45.

WAITE, William; b 1 Jan 1700 England; d 11 Oct 1782 **RU:** Patriot, Gave material aid to cause **CEM:** Waite Family; GPS 38.42539, -77.11615; Bristerburg; Fauquier **GS:** Y **SP:** No info **VI:** No further data **P:** N **BLW:** N **RG:** Y **MK:** N **PH:** unk **SS:** D Vol 1 pg 360 Vol 2 pg 251 **BS:** 19 pg 205.

WAITT, William; b unk; d 16 Apr 1800 **RU:** Patriot, Gave the use of a stable for the cause **CEM:** Masonic Cemetery; GPS 38.30198, -77.46142; 900 Charles St; Fredericksburg City **GS:** Y **SP:** Catherine (-----) (c1736-27 May 1792) **VI:** No further data **P:** N **BLW:** N **RG:** Y **MK:** N **PH:** unk **SS:** D pg 861 **BS:** 08 vol 3 pg 299.

RU=Rank/Unit	CEM=Cemetery	GS=Gravestone	SP=Spousal Information
VI=Other Veteran Info	P=Pension	BLW=Bounty/Land Warrant	RG=Registered Grave
MK=SAR/DAR Marker	PH=Photo	SS=Service Source	BS=Burial Source

346

WALES, Andrew; b 1737; d Nov 1799 **RU:** Patriot, Gave material aid to cause **CEM:** Old Presbyterian Meeting House; GPS 38.48528, -77.23532; 323 S Fairfax St; Alexandria City **GS:** N **SP:** Margaret (-----), b c1737, bur 3 Mar 1798 **VI:** Died age 57, bur 23 Nov 1799 **P:** N **BLW:** N **RG:** Y **MK:** N **PH:** N **SS:** AL pg 232 Ct Bk lt pg 5 **BS:** 23 pg 110.

WALKE, Anthony II; b 3 Jan 1725; d 2 Oct 1779 **RU:** Patriot, Performed public service and gave to cause **CEM:** Greenwich; GPS unk; Euclid Station; Virginia Beach City **GS:** U **SP:** 1) Jane Bolling Randolph (1729-1756) 2) Mary Mosely **VI:** Son of Col Anthony I & (-----) Walke. Member of VA House of Burgesses. United with Patrick Henry, Mason, Madison, Marshall, Jefferson, & other patriots resisting British oppression **P:** N **BLW:** N **RG:** unk **MK:** unk **PH:** unk **SS:** AL Cert Princess Anne Co **BS:** 220.

WALKE, Thomas IV; b 1760, Richmond; d 1797 **RU:** Captain, Commissioned Capt 1780 Princess Anne Co Militia **CEM:** Old Donation Episcopal; GPS 36.86730, -76.12860; 4449 N Witchduck Rd; Virginia Beach City **GS:** U **SP:** Elizabeth (-----) (1797-1815) no children **VI:** Son of Thomas III & (-----) Walke. One of 2 representatives to the VA Convention. Helped VA ratify US Constitution by narrow margin. Was Vestryman & Warden of Lynnhaven Parish. Helped design & build Eastern Shore Chapel **P:** Y **BLW:** unk **RG:** unk **MK:** unk **PH:** unk **SS:** Fold 3 Rev war pen files **BS:** Church Historian.

WALKER, Alexander; b 19 May 1716, Londonderry, Newry, Down, N Ireland; d 1784 **RU:** Patriot, Provided equipment & supplies **CEM:** Walker Creek; GPS unk; Walker Creek; Rockbridge **GS:** Y **SP:** Mar (8 Jan 1747 Augusta Co) Jane Hammer **VI:** Son of John and Catherine (Rutherford) Walker **P:** N **BLW:** N **RG:** Y **MK:** N **PH:** unk **SS:** E pg 799; AL Ct Bk Rockbridge Co pg 3, 5 **BS:** SAR Appl.

WALKER, Alexander; b 1718, Scotland; d 1820 **RU:** Soldier, Served in Capt Samuel Mc'Dowell's Co, Augusta Co Militia. Also served in VA unit at Point Pleasant Oct 1774, and wounded in battle there **CEM:** Augusta Stone Presbyterian; GPS 38.23926, -78.97356; 28 Old Stone Church Ln, Ft Defiance; Augusta **GS:** Y **SP:** Mar (Sep 1777 Augusta Co) Jane Stuart (__-13 Dec 1843(d/o Alexander & (-----) Stuart **VI:** Private in the French & Indian war, Capt James Allen's Co 1756-1758 (Gov't GS). Ran Little Run Plantation. Death date given in SAR and DAR Ancestor files are incorrect as pension records give date of 1820 a more accurate source. Widow Jane recd pen #R11040 **P:** Y **BLW:** unk **RG:** unk **MK:** unk **PH:** unk **SS:** Z pg 199; CG pg 3642 **BS:** JLARC 1, 8, 23, 62; 196.

WALKER, Francis; b 22 Jun 1764, Castle Hill, Albemarle Co; d Mar 1806 **RU:** Soldier, Probably served in county militia **CEM:** Castle Hill; GPS 38.05683, -78.31828; 1625 Country Club Dr, can be seen 150 yds E of Wood Ln, Farmington; Albemarle **GS:** Y **SP:** Jane Byrd Nelson (May 1775-Jun 1808) **VI:** No further data **P:** unk **BLW:** unk **RG:** unk **MK:** unk **PH:** unk **SS:** NSSAR Ancestor #P-312087 **BS:** JLARC 58; 196.

WALKER, George; b 1753, Germany; d 29 Dec 1839 **RU:** Fifer, Served as Fifer in Capt Thomas B. Bowen's Co 9, Oct 1777. Fought with Bedford Co, PA Militia **CEM:** Leffel; GPS 37.48080, -80.13970; Off Cumberland Gap Rd, Meadow Creek; Craig **GS:** U **SP:** Mar (1780, Hagerstown, MD) Margaret Heefner (c1763-1830) **VI:** Known as Col George Walker. Emigrated to the Colonies fr Germany 1765-70. Moved fr PA to MD where he met and mar Margaret Heefner. Around 1798 moved to Botetourt Co, Walker homestead on Craigs Creek, and to Valley of Sinking Creek, Botetourt Co, at New Castle, VA. This portion of Botetourt Co is now Craig Co. Received BLW **P:** unk **BLW:** Y **RG:** unk **MK:** N **PH:** unk **SS:** AP payroll; CU Vol 5 pg 96-103; CV Vol 23 pg 236 **BS:** 196.

WALKER, George Reynolds; b 3 Apr 1760, Princess Anne Co; d 4 Mar 1822 **RU:** Lieutenant, Served in VA Line. Was Ensign in VA Troops 1777. and commissioned Lt 1778 in VA Co **CEM:** Walker Farm; GPS 37.25327, -79.49419; 1972 Montevido Rd, Rt 667; Bedford **GS:** U **SP:** 1) Mar (7 Aug 1782, Princess Anne Co) Judith Haynes (1765-20 Jul 1787) d/o Maj Erasmus & (-----) Haynes; 2) Mar (26 Jan 1788, Blunt Point, Warwick Co) Lucy West (c1770-Apr 1849 Johnson Co, KY) d/o Col John & (-----) West of Blunt Point, Warwick Co **VI:** Son of Thomas (__-28 Jan 1788) & Sarah (Reynolds) (__-1792) Walker. Buried on his farm in Bedford Co. Widow appl pen 13 Jul 1844 Johnson Co KY age 75. She had moved to Floyd Co, KY to live with son but was living in Johnson Co, KY when applying. R11046 **P:** Y **BLW:** unk **RG:** unk **MK:** N **PH:** unk **SS:** K Vol 6 pg 38; CG Vol 3 pg 3644 **BS:** JLARC 4.

WALKER, Henry; b 1760; d Jun 1803 **RU:** Major, Served in 6th & 10th Cont Lines. Was at Valley Forge 1777-79 **CEM:** Walker Family; GPS unk; Covington; Covington City **GS:** N **SP:** Martha Woods (22 Dec

RU=Rank/Unit CEM=Cemetery GS=Gravestone SP=Spousal Information
VI=Other Veteran Info P=Pension BLW=Bounty/Land Warrant RG=Registered Grave
MK=SAR/DAR Marker PH=Photo SS=Service Source BS=Burial Source

347

1761 Albemarle Co-13 Dec 1834 Fincastle, Botetourt Co) d/o Andrew (1722-1781) & Martha (Poage) (1728-1818) Woods. **VI:** Son of William (1725-1810) & Mary Levenia (Bartley) (1732-1808) Walker **P:** unk **BLW:** unk **RG:** unk **MK:** unk **PH:** N **SS:** E pg 800 **BS:** 196.

WALKER, James; b 5 Apr 1726, King & Queen Co; d 18 Dec 1801 **RU:** Patriot, Was member of Committee of Safety, Orange Co, VA 1775 **CEM:** Walker United Methodist; **GPS** 38.29328, -78.16756; Nr Bent Tree; Madison **GS:** Y **SP:** Sarah Jane Ware (1740-1819) **VI:** Member VA House of Burgesses 1761-1771. Died in Orange Co **P:** N **BLW:** N **RG:** Y **MK:** N **PH:** unk **SS:** J-NSSAR 2000 Reg **BS:** JLARC 76.

WALKER, John; b 13 Feb 1744, Cobham, Albemarle Co; d 2 Dec 1809 **RU:** Colonel/Patriot, Aide to Gen George Washington, 1777. Gave 107 cords of wood furnished for officers of Convention troops **CEM:** Belvoir; **GPS** unk; 5172 Stony Point Pass, Cismont; Albemarle **GS:** Y **SP:** Mar (c1764) Elizabeth Moore (21 Oct 1746, King William Co-10 Sep 1809, Belvoir, Cismont, Albemarle Co.) d/o Col Bernard & Ann Catherine (Spotswood) Moore of King William Co **VI:** Graduated College of William & Mary in 1764. Was delegate to Continental Congress 1780. Was attorney, and planter. Was appointed to fill a vacant US Senate seat, Mar 1790, serving there until Nov 1790. Died in Madison Run, Orange Co **P:** unk **BLW:** unk **RG:** unk **MK:** Y **PH:** unk **SS:** NSSAR Ancestor #P-312151; DAR # A119424 **BS:** JLARC 1, 2; 196.

WALKER, John Sr; b 1714 Scotland; d 1797 **RU:** Patriot, Gave material aid to cause **CEM:** Walkerland; **GPS** 37.94613, -79.38794; Vic jct Rts 602 & 724, behind Maxwelton Cabins; Rockbridge **GS:** Y **SP:** Mary Culton (1717-__) **VI:** Known as Gunstalker **P:** N **BLW:** N **RG:** unk **MK:** unk **PH:** unk **SS:** AL Ct Bk pg 2 **BS:** 196.

WALKER, Joseph; b c1748, Lancaster Co, PA; d Aft 1815 **RU:** Patriot, Paid supply tax Rockbridge Co, 1783 **CEM:** Falling Springs Presbyterian; **GPS** 37.68494, -79.45105; 410 Falling Springs Rd, Glasgow; Rockbridge **GS:** Y **SP:** Mar (1772 PA) Jane Moore (c1749 Chester Co, PA-aft 18 Feb 1818) **VI:** No further data **P:** N **BLW:** N **RG:** unk **MK:** unk **PH:** unk **SS:** DAR Ancestor #A119491; DD **BS:** BY.

WALKER, Martha; b 2 May 1760; d 1829 **RU:** Patriot, Provided housing and food for Jack Jouett and assistants enroute to warn Thomas Jefferson of the coming of the British **CEM:** Castle Hill; **GPS** 38.05683,-78.31828; 1625 Country Club Dr, can be seen 150 yds E of Wood Ln, Farmington; Albemarle **GS:** Y **SP:** Mar (1780) George Divers (1747-2 May 1830) **VI:** Daug of Thomas (1715-1794) & Mildred (Thornton) (1721-1778) Walker **P:** N **BLW:** N **RG:** unk **MK:** unk **PH:** unk **SS:** BT- DAR is marking her grave as patriot 2016 **BS:** 196.

WALKER, Thomas; b 15 Jan 1715, Walkerton, King and Queen Co; d 9 Nov 1794 **RU:** Patriot, Gave material aid to cause **CEM:** Castle Hill; **GPS** 38.05683, -78.31828; 1625 Country Club Dr, can be seen 150 yds E of Wood Ln, Farmington; Albemarle **GS:** Y **SP:** 1) Mar (1741) Midred (Thornton) Meriweather (1721-1778), widow of Nicholas Meriweather & cousin to George Washington; 2) mar (c1781) Elizabeth Mary Gregory **VI:** Son of Col Thomas (1650-1734) & Susannah (Peachy) (1688-1736) Walker. Named Cumberland Gap. Built 1st KY log cabin, 1750. Was a Surgeon. Served VA House of Burgesses three times. Was Commissary to VA troops French & Indian War. Was guardian to young Thomas Jefferson. Signed peace treaties w/ Indians VA & Ohio. Was delegate fr Albemarle Co to VA House of Delegates along w/ Jefferson. Died in Cismont, Albemarle Co **P:** N **BLW:** N **RG:** Y **MK:** N **PH:** unk **SS:** AL Ct Bk pg 4, 5, 12, 38 **BS:** 67 vol 2 pg 282; 196.

WALKER, William; b 26 Feb 1757, Cumberland Co; d 1840 **RU:** Captain, Ent serv 1778 Cumberland Co, serving in 4th VA Regt. Was at Battle of Trenton, Iron Hill, Brandywine, White Horse, Germantown, Yorktown **CEM:** Walker Family; **GPS** unk; Farmville; Cumberland **GS:** U **SP:** No info **VI:** Capt in Cumberland Militia after the war. Lived within one mi of Airygreen when he appl for pen,14 Jul 1832 "where he had always lived." Pen last paid in 1839. **P:** Y **BLW:** unk **RG:** Y **MK:** N **PH:** unk **SS:** J-NSSAR 1993 Reg; K Vol 6 pg 44; CG Vol 3 pg 3651 **BS:** JLARC 1.

WALKER, William; b 19 Dec 1725, Lancaster Co, PA; d 17 Aug 1810 **RU:** Patriot, Gave material aid to cause **CEM:** Caldwell family; **GPS** unk; End of Rt 611 across Craig Creek fr Camp Easter Seals; Botetourt **GS:** Y **SP:** Mary Levenia Bartley (19 Jan 1732-1810) **VI:** No further data **P:** N **BLW:** N **RG:** N **MK:** unk **PH:** N **SS:** AK Ct Bk pg 8, 24 **BS:** 196.

RU=Rank/Unit	CEM=Cemetery	GS=Gravestone	SP=Spousal Information
VI=Other Veteran Info	P=Pension	BLW=Bounty/Land Warrant	RG=Registered Grave
MK=SAR/DAR Marker	PH=Photo	SS=Service Source	BS=Burial Source

348

WALKER, William; b unk; d 1848 **RU:** Patriot, Gave material aid to the cause **CEM:** St John's Episcopal; **GPS** 37.53183, -77.41958; 2401 E Broad St; Richmond City **GS:** U **SP:** No info **VI:** No further data **P:** N **BLW:** N **RG:** N **MK:** N **PH:** unk **SS:** AL, Ct Bk pg 7,8 **BS:** 28 pg 351.

WALKER, William; b 1758; d 17 Apr 1837 **RU:** Private, Served in Capt Holcomb's Co, 4th VA Regt, Nov 1777 **CEM:** Walkerland, Maxwelton Farm; **GPS** 37.94613, -79.38794; Vic jct Rts 602 & 724, behind Maxwelton Cabins; Rockbridge **GS:** U **SP:** No info **VI:** No further data **P:** unk **BLW:** unk **RG:** unk **MK:** unk **PH:** unk **SS:** AP Payroll **BS:** 196.

WALKER, William; b 1757, Dinwiddie Co; d 10 Oct 1850 **RU:** Soldier, Served in Bedford Co Militia **CEM:** Walker Family; **GPS** 37.28481, -79.51186; Rt 723, Boxwood Hill, Five Forks; Bedford **GS:** Y **SP:** Elizabeth Rice (1784-__) d/o Benjamin (1735-1827) & (-----) Rice **VI:** Styled Capt on his GS, died age 92 yrs **P:** unk **BLW:** unk **RG:** unk **MK:** N **PH:** unk **SS:** J- DAR Hatcher; E pg 801 **BS:** JLARC 2; 196.

WALL, John C; b 1758; d Aft 1815 or c1840 **RU:** Private, Volunteered 1776. Enlisted 1 Apr 1777 and served in co of Regulars commanded by Capt John Washington, in 4th VA Regt commanded by Col Thomas Elliott. Enlisted again in 1780, fought in Battle of Guilford CH in March 1781, marched fr there to Ramsey's Mills in Deep River, then to Yorktown. After surrender guarded prisoners to Winchester. **CEM:** Mt Hebron; **GPS** 39.10916, -78.09497; 305 E Boscawen St; Winchester City **GS:** Y **SP:** Mary (-----) (c1806-16 Jun 1849) **VI:** Appl for pension,but was rejected Also served in War of 1812 **P:** unk **BLW:** unk **RG:** Y **MK:** N **PH:** Y **SS:** B Volunteer 1776; E pg 801 **BS:** 50 pg 47.

WALL, Peter; b 1754, Dinwiddie Co; d 19 Jul 1848 **RU:** Private, Served in VA Line. Ent Serv Dinwiddie Co 1781 in VA Regt **CEM:** Wall Family; **GPS** 39.18335, -78.16268; Vic Danville; Danville City **GS:** U **SP:** Mar (Dec 1825) Elizabeth Daly (or Dailey) **VI:** Moved to Brunswick Co, then Mecklenburg Co, then to Rockingham Co, NC, then to Pittsylvania Co. Died in Pittsylvania Co. Widow appl pen 18 Aug 1855 age 80. W25857. Recd BLW 35678-160-55 **P:** Y **BLW:** Y **RG:** N **MK:** N **PH:** unk **SS:** K Vol 4 pg 46; CG Vol 3 pg 3652; AS **BS:** VASSAR Roster 2007.

WALLACE, Gustavus Brown; b 9 Nov 1751, Ellerslie Pt, King George Co; d 17 Aug 1802 **RU:** Lieutenant Colonel, Served as Capt of 5th Co, 3rd VA Regt of Foot 20 Feb 1776-Jan 1777 in King George Co. Served in 2nd VA Regt of Foot, 12 Feb 1781-1 Jan 1783. Was captured at Charleston SC May 1780 **CEM:** Masonic Cemetery; **GPS** 38.30198, -77.46142; 900 Charles St; Fredericksburg City **GS:** U **SP:** No info **VI:** BLW #24122-450-13, Dec 1791 awarded to Francis Greaves **P:** unk **BLW:** Y **RG:** Y **MK:** unk **PH:** unk **SS:** DAR Ancestor #A119888; K Vol 6 pg 46; CE pg 39; CG Vol 3 pg 3653 **BS:** JLARC 1, 2, 48, 91.

WALLACE, John; b 19 Jan 1761; d 4 May 1829 **RU:** Private, Served in Capts William Payne's and Charles Ewell's Companies, Col George Gibson's 1st VA Regt **CEM:** Liberty Hall; **GPS** unk; Rt 652 abt 1.4 mi fr jct Rt 653, and .5 mi N, nr Wallace farm rd; Stafford **GS:** U **SP:** Mar (1792) Elizabeth Hooe (c1766-3 Sep 1850) d/of Howson (c1725-5 Sep 1796) & Mary (Dade) Hooe **VI:** No further data **P:** unk **BLW:** unk **RG:** unk **MK:** unk **PH:** unk **SS:** DAR Ancestor #A119926; E pg 802; AP-roll #918 **BS:** JLARC 48.

WALLACE, John D; b 1754, Scotland; d 29 Jan 1829 **RU:** Private, Served in 1st or 9th Cont line. Served in Capt James Dysart's Co of Light Horse on tour of NC under command of Col William Campbell, 21 May 1781 **CEM:** Wallace; **GPS** 38.15972, -77.79558; 8630 Peppertree Rd, Wilderness Corner; Spotsylvania **GS:** Y **SP:** Anne Hammond **VI:** Died in Chancellorsville, Spotsylvania Co **P:** N **BLW:** unk **RG:** Y **MK:** N **PH:** Y **SS:** E pg 802 **BS:** 09 part 2, 196.

WALLACE, Robert; b 1744, Botetourt Co; d Feb 1812 **RU:** Private, Was in Battle at Point Pleasant 1774 in Capt John Murray's Co of Rockbridge Co **CEM:** Old Lebanon; **GPS** 38.08090 -79.37545; Off Rt 42, Craigsville; Augusta **GS:** Y **SP:** Esther Boyd (1750-1824) d/o Robert & Eleanor (Porterfield) Boyd **VI:** Son of Samuel & Elizabeth Jane (Archer) Wallace **P:** unk **BLW:** unk **RG:** Y **MK:** N **PH:** Y **SS:** Z pg103 **BS:** 04; 196.

WALLACE, William; b unk; d 1831 **RU:** Soldier, Was Lt in Capt Samuel McDowell's Co of Rockbridge Co. Served in 1st VA State Regt. Then served in 3rd, 4th, 10th, & 14th Cont Lines **CEM:** Stonewall Jackson Memorial; **GPS** 37.78128, -79.44604; 314 S Main St; Lexington City **GS:** U **SP:** No info **VI:** No further data **P:** unk **BLW:** unk **RG:** unk **MK:** unk **PH:** unk **SS:** E pg 802 **BS:** JLARC 63.

RU=Rank/Unit	CEM=Cemetery	GS=Gravestone	SP=Spousal Information
VI=Other Veteran Info	P=Pension	BLW=Bounty/Land Warrant	RG=Registered Grave
MK=SAR/DAR Marker	PH=Photo	SS=Service Source	BS=Burial Source

349

WALLER, George; b 1732; d 18 Nov 1814 **RU:** Major/Patriot, Served as Adjutant to Col Abram Penn. Gave material aid to cause **CEM:** Oakwood; GPS 39.68690, -78.88000; 199 Cemetery St; Martinsville City **GS:** Y **SP:** Ann Winston Carr, dates on cenotagph say b. 1735, d 1839 **VI:** SAR/DAR markers on stone **P:** unk **BLW:** unk **RG:** Y **MK:** Y **PH:** unk **SS:** AL Ct bk pg 7a, 9, 38 Henry Co **BS:** JLARC 1, 2, 4, 38; 196.

WALLER, Thomas Carr; b unk; d 1787 **RU:** Patriot, Gave material aid to cause **CEM:** Meadowbrook Memorial Gardens; GPS 36.82940, -76.46640; 4569 Shoulders Hill Rd; Suffolk City **GS:** U **SP:** Sarah (-----) d/o John & Ann (Harris) (-----) **VI:** Son of John & Agnes (Carr) Waller **P:** N **BLW:** N **RG:** unk **MK:** unk **PH:** unk **SS:** AL Ct Bk pg 5, 6, 24 Spotsylvania Co **BS:** 196.

WALLER, William Edmund; b 1747, Newport, Spotsylvania Co; d 11 Aug 1830 **RU:** Private, Served in Lt Walker Scott's Co & Capt Thomas Minor's Co, Col Gregory Smith's 2nd VA State Regt. Also served in 1st VA State Regt & Cont Line for 3 yrs **CEM:** Prospect Hill; GPS unk; Waller Rd, nr Forest Green, Partlow; Spotsylvania **GS:** U **SP:** Mildred Smith (1755-1804) d/o Stephen & Phoebe (Hawkins) Smith **VI:** Son of Edmund (1718-1771) & Mary (Pendleton) (1720-1808) Waller. Baptist Minister. Moved to KY & later returned where to Louisa Co. Recd 447,200 acres BLW **P:** unk **BLW:** Y **RG:** unk **MK:** unk **PH:** unk **SS:** DAR Ancestor #A120071; N pg 1433, 1056, 1057 **BS:** 196.

WALLER, William Jr; b 1766; d 1815 **RU:** Private, Served in 1st VA Regt. Was at Charlestown 26 May 1783. Discharged 11 July 1783 **CEM:** Olde Concord Road; GPS unk; Rt 721; Stafford **GS:** Y **SP:** No info **VI:** Was a Baptist clergyman fighting for religious freedom **P:** unk **BLW:** unk **RG:** N **MK:** N **PH:** unk **SS:** N pg 1057; Archives Lib of VA **BS:** 03 pg 183; 196.

WALLER, William Sr; b 26 Nov 1740, Stafford Co; d 4 Aug 1817 **RU:** Corporal/Patriot, Served in 11th and 15th Cont Lines and Capt George Rice's Co # 9, VA Battalion. Gave 425 pounds of beef to cause **CEM:** Waller Family; GPS 38.43891, -77.38353; Rt 721; Stafford **GS:** Y **SP:** 1) Elizabeth Allen 2) Margaret (-----) 3) Ursula Withers **VI:** Cemetery originally listed as Concord **P:** unk **BLW:** unk **RG:** Y **MK:** N **PH:** Y **SS:** A pg 264; D pg 855,884; E pg 803 **BS:** 196; 30 pg 55:2.

WALLIS, Colley; b unk; d 1781 **RU:** Soldier, Served fr MA, killed in the battle at Yorktown **CEM:** Yorktown Victory Monument Tablet; GPS 38.28350, -78.54150; Yorktown; York **GS:** U **SP:** No info **VI:** No further data **P:** unk **BLW:** unk **RG:** unk **MK:** unk **PH:** unk **SS:** J-Yorktown Historian **BS:** JLARC 74.

WALTERS, Michael; b c1750, Germany; d Aug 1798 **RU:** Private, Served in Doack's VA Militia **CEM:** Browning's Mill; GPS unk; Old Stage Rd; Wythe **GS:** Y **SP:** Mar (as 2nd husband) Catherine Creger/Krieger (9 Jun 1754-8 Feb 1841) **VI:** Gov't Gr St shows service **P:** unk **BLW:** unk **RG:** unk **MK:** unk **PH:** unk **SS:** NSSAR Ancestor #P-312919; DAR #A120169 **BS:** JLARC 40,123; 196.

WALTON, Jesse; b 10 Nov 1739, Hanover Co; d 30 April 1821 or 1822 **RU:** Lieutenant, Was on War Dept supernumary list as Lt, 16 Sep 1777. Also provided material aid to cause **CEM:** Walton Family; GPS unk; probably "Whitmel"; Pittsylvania **GS:** Y **SP:** Mar (c1764/1765) Ann Pleasant **VI:** Son of William & (-----) Walton **P:** unk **BLW:** unk **RG:** Y **MK:** N **PH:** unk **SS:** E pg 804 **BS:** SAR application

WALTON, Joel; b 20 Sep 1759, Hanover Co; d 13 Apr 1840 **RU:** Soldier, Lived Louisa Co at enl, 1780 in 2nd VA Regt. Served in Battle of Camden SC in VA Line **CEM:** Spring Valley; GPS unk; Cuckoo District; Louisa **GS:** U **SP:** Sarah Sims (__-10 Mar 1840) **VI:** Son of John (1 Apr 1738-23 Sep 1793) & Mary (Baker) (5 Dec 1739-1812) Walton. Moved to Louisa Co as child. Appl pen 11 Feb 1833. S3627 **P:** Y **BLW:** unk **RG:** unk **MK:** unk **PH:** unk **SS:** K Vol 6 pg 54; CG Vol 3 pg 3664 **BS:** JLARC 4, 61.

WALTON, John B; b 1758; d 27 Mar 1836 **RU:** Private/Patriot, Gave material aid to cause **CEM:** Walton Family; GPS unk; Nr Ft Lewis; Salem City **GS:** Y **SP:** Mary L (-----) (1758-21 Aug 1824) **VI:** No further data **P:** unk **BLW:** unk **RG:** unk **MK:** unk **PH:** unk **SS:** J- DAR Hatcher; D Bedford Co **BS:** JLARC 2; 123 pg 68; 196.

WALTON, William; b 1751; d 1836 **RU:** Lieutenant, Specific service in DAR 1973 in Senate Document serial #93, -Doc 113 **CEM:** Walton Family; GPS unk; Nr Ft Lewis; Salem City **GS:** U **SP:** No info **VI:** No further data **P:** unk **BLW:** unk **RG:** unk **MK:** unk **PH:** unk **SS:** AR Vol 4 pg 157 **BS:** JLARC 2.

WALTON, William Sr; b 25 Oct 1749; GA; d 29 Jan 1845 **RU:** Second Lieutenant/Patriot, Served in Capt John Lewis Co, Botetourt Co. As patriot was Commissioner of Peace **CEM:** Walton Family; GPS

RU=Rank/Unit CEM=Cemetery GS=Gravestone SP=Spousal Information
VI=Other Veteran Info P=Pension BLW=Bounty/Land Warrant RG=Registered Grave
MK=SAR/DAR Marker PH=Photo SS=Service Source BS=Burial Source

350

unk; Nr Ft Lewis; Salem City **GS:** Y **SP:** Mary Lefwich (1758-1824) **VI:** No further data **P:** unk **BLW:** unk **RG:** unk **MK:** unk **PH:** Y **SS:** J- DAR Hatcher; DL part 1 pg 295, 297, 34 **BS:** JLARC 2; 123 pg 68.

WAMPLER, Hans George Michael; b 19 Nov 1724, Hinsingen, Alsace, France; d Dec 1789 **RU:** Soldier, Served in PA Militia **CEM:** St John's Lutheran; GPS 36.96500, -81.10110; 405 W Main, Wytheville; Wythe **GS:** U **SP:** Mar (1746) Anna Elizabeth Steffey (__-1807) **VI:** Son of Hans Peter Sr. (1701-1749) & Veronica (Lung) (1703-1743) Wampler. Lived in Lebanon Twp, Lancaster Co, PA and moved by 1771 to Fincastle Co, of which Montgomery Co was formed. Was on William Crockett's list of tithables in 1771. He served in Lord Dunsmore's War in 1774. He was an Elder in his Church in 1782 **P:** unk **BLW:** unk **RG:** unk **MK:** unk **PH:** unk **SS:** NSSAR Ancestor #P-313064; DAR #A120379 **BS:** JLARC 123; 196.

WANGER, Henry; b 1753 PA; d 9 Aug 1819 **RU:** Private, Served in Capt Alexander Milvain's Co, 5th Battalion, Lancaster Co PA Militia **CEM:** Early; GPS 38.39536, -78.90465; 3588 Early Rd, Pleasant Valley; Rockingham **GS:** U **SP:** No info **VI:** No further data **P:** unk **BLW:** unk **RG:** unk **MK:** unk **PH:** unk **SS:** PA Archives Series 5, Vol VII, pg 520 **BS:** 196.

WAPLES, Samuel; b 1755; d 11 Aug 1834 **RU:** Lieutenant, Served in VA Line. Lived Accomack Co at enl. Ent serv 1776 as Lt 9th VA Regt and was in battles of Brandywine & Germantown where taken prisoner but escaped. Was also Lt in 1777 **CEM:** Onancock; GPS unk; Rts 718 & 638, Onancock; Accomack **GS:** Y **SP:** Mar (20 Aug 1822 Accomack) Sabra P. Townsend (3 May 1791-24 Dec 1856) d/o Henry & Sally (-----) Townsend [TS] **VI:** Styled "Capt" on his GS which reads "of the Revolution." Sol appl pen 17 Jun 1828 Accomack Co age 70. Widow appl pen 25 Apr 1853 Accomack Co, age 62 & appl BLW 7 Apr 1855. W6427. BLW #1733-200 & BLW #14529-160-55 **P:** Y **BLW:** Y **RG:** Y **MK:** unk **PH:** unk **SS:** K Vol 6 pg 57; CG Vol 3 pg 3666; BT **BS:** JLARC 1, 4, 5; 209.

WARD, Henry; b 5 Apr 1751, Bedford Co; d 12 Apr 1823 **RU:** Major/Commissary/Patriot, QM in Bedford Co Militia. As patriot was Co Sheriff **CEM:** Adams-Ward; GPS 37.13210, -79.24073; Mansion Bridge Rd Rt 640, Altavista; Campbell **GS:** Y **SP:** Mar (1781) Martha Barber/Barbour (__-1851) **VI:** No further data **P:** unk **BLW:** unk **RG:** unk **MK:** N **PH:** unk **SS:** DD **BS:** JLARC 36; 196.

WARD, John; b 1716; d Bef 23 Jan 1807 **RU:** Major, Served in Bedford Co Militia **CEM:** Adams-Ward; GPS 37.13210, -79.24073; Mansion Bridge Rd Rt 640, Altavista; Campbell **GS:** Y **SP:** 1) Ann Harrelson Chiles, (__-1765); 2) Sarah (Clark) Lynch (1716-20 Jan 1792) d/o Christopher Clark and widow of Charles Lynch **VI:** No further data **P:** unk **BLW:** unk **RG:** unk **MK:** N **PH:** unk **SS:** NSSAR Ancestor #P-313227 **BS:** JLARC 36; 196.

WARD, William; b 30 May 1753; d 21 Dec 1817 **RU:** Captain, Served in Montgomery Co Militia 6 Nov 1781 **CEM:** Black Lick Rural Retreat; GPS 36.94435, -81.24377; 2390 Black Lick Rd; Wythe **GS:** Y **SP:** Mar (1775) Jean Watson (2 Mar 1758-12 Apr 1836) **VI:** Grave stone not found in 1997 **P:** unk **BLW:** unk **RG:** unk **MK:** unk **PH:** unk **SS:** DAR Ancestor #A120748; SAR Ancestor #P-313363; E pg 805; DL Vol 1 pg 754 **BS:** JLARC 1123.

WARD, William; b 1725, Ireland; d 1795 **RU:** Lieutenant Colonel/ Patriot, In charge of Montgomery Co Militia, 15 Feb 1782. Was Commissioner of Land Tax 15 Feb 1782 **CEM:** Ward's Cove; GPS unk; Thompson Valley; Tazewell **GS:** Y **SP:** No info **VI:** Sergeant in Co of Rangers 1756 and 1757 **P:** unk **BLW:** unk **RG:** Y **MK:** N **PH:** unk **SS:** C pg 274; E pg 805; AR Vol 4 pg 158 **BS:** SAR application

WARDLOW (WARDLAW), William; b Jun 1745, Augusta Co; d 7 Feb 1819 **RU:** Patriot, Gave material aid to cause. Was also a justice during war period **CEM:** New Providence Presbyterian; GPS 37.95130, -79.30250; 1208 New Providence Rd, Raphine; Rockbridge **GS:** U **SP:** Mary Coalter (__-15 May 1808) **VI:** No further data **P:** N **BLW:** N **RG:** unk **MK:** unk **PH:** unk **SS:** DAR Ancestor #A206516; AL Ct Bk pg 5 Rockbridge Co **BS:** JLARC 79.

WARE, John; b 12 Dec 1736, Gloucester Co; d 17 Jun 1816 **RU:** Captain/Patriot, Commanded a co in Albemarle Co Militia, Sep 1775. Gave material aid to cause **CEM:** Ben Glade; GPS unk; Rock Castle; Goochland **GS:** Y **SP:** 1) Mar (27 May 1756 Caroline Co "on the Byrd in this County") Ann Harrison 2) mar (6 Apr 1762 Maniken Town, Henrico Co) Mary Watson **VI:** No further data **P:** unk **BLW:** unk **RG:** unk **MK:** N **PH:** unk **SS:** J- DAR Hatcher; CE pg 14; AL Ct Bk pg 3, 41 Goochland Co **BS:** JLARC 2; 196.

RU=Rank/Unit   CEM=Cemetery   GS=Gravestone   SP=Spousal Information
VI=Other Veteran Info P=Pension   BLW=Bounty/Land Warrant RG=Registered Grave
MK=SAR/DAR Marker PH=Photo   SS=Service Source   BS=Burial Source

351

WARREN, Jesse; b 1751 Surry Co; d June 1832 **RU:** Patriot, Gave material aid to cause **CEM:** Lawn's Creek Parish Church; GPS unk; Hog Island (no public access); Surry **GS:** Y **SP:** Martha Phillips (1788-15 Dec 1863) **VI:** No further data **P:** N **BLW:** N **RG:** Y **MK:** N **PH:** Y **SS:** Al Ct Bk pg 4 **BS:** 196; 133.

WARWICK, Jacob; b 1743, Augusta Co; d 11 Jan 1826 **RU:** Captain, Commanded a company Augusta Co Milita after 1779. Rank of Capt 20 Mar 1777 **CEM:** Fort Dinwiddie; GPS 38.09228, -79.83140; NE of jct of Dinwiddie Trail & River Rd, Warm Springs; Bath **GS:** Y **SP:** Mar (1765) Mary Vance (1743-11 Jan 1823) **VI:** Styled "Maj" on GS **P:** unk **BLW:** unk **RG:** Y **MK:** N **PH:** unk **SS:** DAR Ancestor #A121754; E pg 807; AZ pg 185 **BS:** SAR regis.

WASHINGTON, Bushrod; b 5 Jun 1762; d 26 Nov 1829 **RU:** Private, Enl in Cont Army nr end of Rev War. Present at surrender of Cornwallis at Yorktown **CEM:** Mt Vernon; GPS 38.42280, -77.05090; Mt Vernon Estate; Fairfax **GS:** U **SP:** Anna Blackburn (8 Dec 1768 Woodbridge, Prince William Co-28 Nov 1829 Darby, Delaware Co, PA) **VI:** Son of John Augustine (1736-1787) & Hanna (Bushrod) (1738-1801) Washington. Elected to VA House of Delegates. Served as delegate to VA Convention with ratified the Constitution in 1788. President John Adams nominated him to Supreme Ct for 30 yrs, until his death at age 67 in Philadelphia, PA. Memorialized in cemetery at Mt Vernon **P:** unk **BLW:** unk **RG:** unk **MK:** unk **PH:** unk **SS:** CD **BS:** 196.

WASHINGTON, Edward; b c1712, Westmoreland Co; d Bef 18 Sep 1792 **RU:** Patriot, Gave equipment and/or supplies **CEM:** Huntington; GPS unk; 3 mi fr Pohick Church; Fairfax **GS:** Y **SP:** Mary (Stone) Barry/Barre (c1718-__) d/o Edward & (-----) Barre of France **VI:** Son of Edward (c1693 Prince George Co, MD-__) & (-----) Washington. Collected taxes as sub sheriff in Prince William Co, 1730. Will probated 18 Sep 1792 in Truro Parish **P:** N **BLW:** N **RG:** Y **MK:** N **PH:** unk **SS:** SAR Ancestor #P-314186; AL Ct Bk pg 21 BY **BS:** 8 vol 4 pg 163.

WASHINGTON, George; b 22 Feb 1732, Pope's Creek Plantation, Westmoreland Co; d 14 Dec 1799 **RU:** General, Commander in Chief of VA forces 1755; VA House of Burgesses 1758-74; 1st, 2nd Cont Congress. Commander in chief of all forces raised or to be raised 1775 **CEM:** Mt Vernon; GPS 38.42280, -77.0509; Mt Vernon Estate; Fairfax **GS:** U **SP:** Mar (8 Jan 1755) Martha (Dandridge) Custis (2 Jun 1731-22 May 1802) d/o John (1700-1756) & Frances (Jones) (1710-1785) Dandridge and widow of Daniel Parke Custis (1711-1757). **VI:** Son of Augustine (1694-1743) & Mary (Ball) (c1708-1789) Washington. Family moved to "Ferry Farm" in Stafford Co when he was a young boy. Had service in French & Indian War. Inaugurated as President 30 Apr 1789 & 1792 **P:** unk **BLW:** unk **RG:** Y **MK:** unk **PH:** unk **SS:** NSSAR Ancestor #P-314188; DAR #A121962 **BS:** JLARC 1,13, 23; 201 pg 7391-7392.

WASHINGTON, George Augustine; b 1758; d 15 Jun 1793 **RU:** Aide-de-camp, Aide-de-camp to General Lafayette **CEM:** Mt Vernon; GPS 38.42280, -77.0509; Mt Vernon Estate; Fairfax **GS:** U **SP:** Mar (15 Oct 1785. Mount Vernon) Frances Bassett (19 Dec 1767-1796) **VI:** Son of Charles (21 May 1738, Westmoreland Co-1800) & Mildred (Thornton) (__Spotsylvania Co-__) Washington. Bur in Washington family vault **P:** unk **BLW:** unk **RG:** unk **MK:** unk **PH:** unk **SS:** NSSAR Ancestor # P-314189 **BS:** JLARC 14; 196.

WASHINGTON, John A; b unk, Leedstown; d 26 Jun 1787 **RU:** Colonel/Patriot, Gave beef to the army **CEM:** Bushfield; GPS unk; Nomini River; Westmoreland **GS:** U **SP:** Nancy Constant **VI:** Will dated 3 Jul 1785 provided other information **P:** unk **BLW:** unk **RG:** unk **MK:** unk **PH:** unk **SS:** J- DAR Hatcher; AL Certificate Westmoreland Co **BS:** JLARC 2.

WASHINGTON, John Augustine; b 13 Jan 1736, Stafford Co; d 10 Jan 1797 **RU:** Colonel/Patriot, Served in VA Militia, and was member VA Conventions 1775-6. Gave material aid to cause **CEM:** Pohick Episcopal; GPS 38.42546, -77.11598; 9301 Richmond Hwy, Lorton, Mt Holly; Fairfax **GS:** U **SP:** Mar (14 Apr 1756 Westmoreland Co) Hannah Bushrod (1738-1801) d/o John & Hannah (Corbin) Bushrod. **VI:** Son of Augustine (1694-1743) & Mary (Ball) (c1708-1789) Washington. Will dated 31 Jul 1787. Died in Mount Holly, Westmoreland Co **P:** unk **BLW:** unk **RG:** unk **MK:** unk **PH:** unk **SS:** AL Ct Bk pg 1, 4 Westmoreland Co **BS:** JLARC 14, 28; 196.

WASHINGTON, John H; b unk; d 1830 **RU:** Patriot, Gave material aid to the cause **CEM:** Washingon Family; GPS unk; Potomac View; King George **GS:** Y **SP:** No info **VI:** No further data **P:** N **BLW:** N **RG:** Y **MK:** N **PH:** unk **SS:** AL Ct Bk pg 2 **BS:** 17 pg 63.

RU=Rank/Unit	CEM=Cemetery	GS=Gravestone	SP=Spousal Information
VI=Other Veteran Info	P=Pension	BLW=Bounty/Land Warrant	RG=Registered Grave
MK=SAR/DAR Marker	PH=Photo	SS=Service Source	BS=Burial Source

352

WASHINGTON, Martha (Dandridge); b 21 Jul 1732, New Kent Co; d 22 May 1802 **RU:** Patriot, Wife of George Washington. Spearheaded relief efforts for soldiers, giving them soup, medicine, and clothes while in the field with her husband **CEM:** Mt Vernon; GPS 38.42280, -77.0509; Mt Vernon Estate; Fairfax **GS:** Y **SP:** 1) Mar (15 May 1750, New Kent Co) Daniel Parke Custis (1700-1756); 2) Mar (6 Jan 1759, New Kent Co) George Washington (11 Feb 1732 Pope's Creek, Westmoreland Co-14 Dec 1799, Mt Vernon) son of Augustine (1694-1743) & Mary (Ball) (c1708-1789) Washington **VI:** Daughter of John Dandridge (1700-1756) and Frances Jones **P:** N **BLW:** N **RG:** Y **MK:** unk **PH:** unk **SS:** AS SAR regist **BS:** 196.

WASHINGTON, Mary (Ball); b c1708; d 25 Aug 1789 **RU:** Patriot, As patriot knitted socks for Militia and furnished supplies **CEM:** Kenmore Plantation; GPS unk; 1500 Washington Ave; Fredericksburg City **GS:** Y **SP:** Mar 6 Mar 1731 (bible) to Augustine Washington b 12 Nov 1694, d 12 Apr 1743, Ferry Farm, King George (now Stafford) Co **VI:** D/o Joseph Ball (24 May 1649-1711, Lancaster Co) & Mary (----) Johnson Ball Hews (__-1721 Cherry Point, Northumberland Co). Mother of Gen George Washington. Her exact burial location is not known, but monument erected at "Mediation Rock" where she is said to have gone to contemplate. The monument was begun in the 1830s, the project abandoned, the land sold and offered for auction in 1889, which was halted by court order and public outrage, and the monument finally completed **P:** N **BLW:** Y **RG:** Y **MK:** N **PH:** unk **SS:** D Vol 3 pg 869 **BS:** 196; Historical site.

WASHINGTON, William Augustine; b 25 Nov 1757; d 2 Oct 1810 **RU:** Lieutenant Colonel, Served in VA Line. Was Capt of 6th Co 3rd VA Regt of Foot, 26 Feb 1776-Sep 1778, fr Westmoreland Co. Later was Lt Col in VA 3rd Regt of Light Dragoons 20 Nov 1778-9 Nov 1782. This unit served in Carolinas in 1779. He later commanded the combined 1st & 3rd Regts at Charleston **CEM:** Mt Vernon; GPS 38.42280, -77.0509; Mt Vernon Estate; Fairfax **GS:** U **SP:** 1) Mar (25 Sep 1777) Jane "Jenny" Washington (1764-1795), cousin 2) Mar (10 Jul 1792) Mary Lee (1775-1791) 3) Mar (11 May 1799) Sarah "Sally" Tayloe (1765-1834) **VI:** Son of Augustine II (1720-1762) & Anne (Aylett) (1724-1774) Washington & nephew of George Washington. Bur in vault at Mt Vernon 4 Oct 1810 & removed to new vault 1824. Recd BLW #2421-450-7 Mar 1798 **P:** unk **BLW:** Y **RG:** unk **MK:** unk **PH:** unk **SS:** CE pg 39, 104, 105, 181; CG Vol 3 pg 3690 **BS:** JLARC 14.

WASSON, James; b unk; d 1781 **RU:** Private, Served in Lt Inf fr CT Cont Line. Killed in the battle at Yorktown **CEM:** Yorktown Victory Monument Tablet; GPS 38.28350, -78.54150; Yorktown; York **GS:** U **SP:** (-----) Ames **VI:** Widow recd BLW #152-60-55 **P:** unk **BLW:** Y **RG:** unk **MK:** unk **PH:** unk **SS:** J-Yorktown Historian; DY pg 121, 156, 351 **BS:** JLARC 74.

WATKINS, John; b 1732; d 10 Mar 1785 **RU:** Patriot, Gave equipment and/or supplies **CEM:** Littlepage; GPS unk; Nr Pamunkey R, Cumberland; New Kent **GS:** Y **SP:** Betty Clairbourne, d/o Philip Whitehead & (-----) Claiborne Esq. of King William Co. **VI:** No further data **P:** N **BLW:** N **RG:** Y **MK:** N **PH:** unk **SS:** AL Ct Bk pg 17,18,20 **BS:** 104 pg 359.

WATKINS, Samuel; b 21 Jan 1748, MD; d 1830 **RU:** Private, Served in Capts John Gerault's & Edward Worthington's companies, VA Illinois Regt **CEM:** Petersville; GPS 37.56440, -77.96470; Off Rt 60; Powhatan **GS:** U **SP:** Mary McClure **VI:** No further data **P:** unk **BLW:** unk **RG:** unk **MK:** unk **PH:** unk **SS:** SAR Ancestor #P-314527 cites Geo Rogers Clark papers, 1781-1783 VA Series; E pg 810 **BS:** 80 vol 4, pg 165.

WATKINS, Samuel; b 26 Apr 1750, Cumberland Co; d Jan 1795 **RU:** Second Lieutenant/Patriot, Served in Amelia Co Militia. Recd rank 23 Nov 1780. Gave material aid to cause **CEM:** Petersville; GPS 37.56440, -77.96470; Off Rt 60; Powhatan **GS:** U **SP:** Mar (26 Jul 1773) Elizabeth Goode (1 Jan 1760-Jan 1792) **VI:** No further data **P:** unk **BLW:** unk **RG:** unk **MK:** unk **PH:** unk **SS:** DAR Ancestor #A122393; J- DAR Hatcher; E pg 810; AL Ct Bk I pg 17 Amelia Co **BS:** JLARC 2.

WATKINS, Thomas J; b unk; d 19 Nov 1821 **RU:** Patriot, Gave material aid to cause **CEM:** Ben Lomond; GPS unk; Off Rt 600 on Rt 627; Goochland **GS:** Y **SP:** Ruth Hail (__-16 Nov 1821) **VI:** No further data **P:** N **BLW:** N **RG:** Y **MK:** N **PH:** unk **SS:** AL Ct Bk II, pg 23 **BS:** 46 pg 100.

WATKINS, William J; b unk; d 1838 **RU:** Patriot, Gave material aid to cause **CEM:** Ben Lomond; GPS unk; Off Rt 600 on Rt 627; Goochland **GS:** Y **SP:** No info **VI:** No further data **P:** N **BLW:** N **RG:** Y **MK:** N **PH:** unk **SS:** AL Cert Issued **BS:** 46 pg 100.

RU=Rank/Unit   CEM=Cemetery   GS=Gravestone   SP=Spousal Information
VI=Other Veteran Info   P=Pension   BLW=Bounty/Land Warrant   RG=Registered Grave
MK=SAR/DAR Marker   PH=Photo   SS=Service Source   BS=Burial Source

353

WATLINGTON (WADLINGTON), John; b 1756; d 6 Feb 1812 **RU:** Captain, Served in VA Line. Ent serve Halifax Co 1777, Served as Lt of Artillery and later as Capt of Artillery. Served in Battles of Camden and Guilford CH as well as Gate's defeat **CEM:** Watlington Family; GPS unk; Halifax town; Halifax **GS:** Y **SP:** 1) Elizabeth Allen 2) Mar (6 Sep 1792, Caswell Co NC) Elizabeth "Betsey" Donohu d/o Thomas & Keisiah (-----) Donohu **VI:** Son of Col Armistead & (-----) Watlington, Esf 1777 Halifax Co, where resided. Widow recd pen W4097, also VA 1/2 pay (see N.A. Acc #874 #050186 1/2 pay) **P:** Y **BLW:** Y **RG:** Y **MK:** N **PH:** unk **SS:** K Vol 6 pg 73; AK Vol 4, pg 73-4; CG Vol 3 pg 3700 **BS:** DAR Rpt.

WATSON, Benjamin; b 1767; d 10 Mar 1838 **RU:** Private, Served in 3rd Cont Line **CEM:** Colonna Family aka Wakefield Farm; GPS unk; 1 mi east of Pennyville, Hacks Neck; Accomack **GS:** Y **SP:** Susan (-----) (1775-11 Apr 1837). TS "wife of Benjamin Watson" **VI:** No further data **P:** unk **BLW:** unk **RG:** N **MK:** N **PH:** unk **SS:** E pg 810 **BS:** 145 Colonna; 196.

WATSON, John; b 1737, England; d 1824 **RU:** Private, Served in Mathews Co Militia and VA Line **CEM:** Trinity Episcopal; GPS 37.41069, -76.33578; Off Rt 614 nr jct Khyber Pass Trail; Mathews **GS:** U **SP:** Mar (Feb 1776) Hannah Tabor (1749-__) **VI:** Pen recd by spouse, #W18258, at $40 per annum **P:** Y **BLW:** unk **RG:** unk **MK:** unk **PH:** unk **SS:** CG pg 3702 **BS:** 196.

WATSON, Joseph; b c1758; d 8 Apr 1828 **RU:** Corporal/Patriot, Served in Capt Harris Co 19-21 Sep 1781 at Williamsburg. Also gave material aid to cause **CEM:** Shockoe Hill; GPS 37.55190, -77.43170; 4th & Hospital Sts; Richmond City **GS:** Y **SP:** No info **VI:** No further data **P:** unk **BLW:** unk **RG:** Y **MK:** N **PH:** unk **SS:** AL Ct Bk I pg 3; N pg 1246-7 **BS:** 57 pg 6.

WATSON, Robert; b unk; d unk **RU:** Corporal, Served in 5th & 11th VA Cont Lines **CEM:** Watson Family; GPS unk; Vic Rts 678 & 625; Fluvanna **GS:** Y **SP:** Belle (-----) **VI:** No further data **P:** unk **BLW:** unk **RG:** Y **MK:** N **PH:** unk **SS:** E pg 811 **BS:** 66 pg 96.

WATSON, William; b 1755; d 25 Aug 1844 **RU:** Private/Patriot, Served in VA Line. Ent serv Powhatan Co in Capts Robert Hughes & Richard Crump's Cos, Powhatan Co Militia. Also gave material aid to cause **CEM:** Watson-Perrow; GPS unk; Gunter Mountain; Buckingham **GS:** Y **SP:** 1) Christiana Clelland 2) Fannie Wilkerson (1759-1840) **VI:** Sol appl 13 Aug 1832 Buckingham Co age 77. R11211. Newer Govt stone **P:** Y **BLW:** unk **RG:** unk **MK:** N **PH:** unk **SS:** DAR Ancestor #A003855; SAR Ancestor #P-314744; D Vol 3 pg 784, 785; E pg 811; CG Vol 3 pg 3704 **BS:** JLARC 4, 59; 196.

WATSON, William J; b unk; d 27 Oct 1838 **RU:** Soldier, Ent serv Powhatan Co 1777. Later ent serv in "Virginia Regt" and served at Battle of Guilford CH. Gave material aid to cause **CEM:** Ben Lomond; GPS unk; Off Rt 600 on Rt 627; Goochland **GS:** U **SP:** Mar (17 Dec 1767) Martha Pleasants, surety Richard Pleasants **VI:** Pen rejected because service less than six mos **P:** N **BLW:** unk **RG:** unk **MK:** unk **PH:** unk **SS:** AL **BS:** 46 pg 100.

WATTERS, William; b 16 Oc 1751; d 29 Mar 1827 **RU:** Private, Served in 2nd & 12th Cont Lines, VA **CEM:** Watters-Adams Family; GPS unk; 6444 Linway Terr, McLean; Fairfax **GS:** Y **SP:** Sarah Adams **VI:** Stone erected by Virginia Conference of the Methodist Episcopal Church. Epitaph- "He was a pioneer, leading the way for the vast army of American Methodist Itinerates having the Everlasting Gospel to preach" **P:** unk **BLW:** unk **RG:** Y **MK:** Y **PH:** unk **SS:** E pg 811; AR **BS:** 61 vol I pg ML-43.

WATTERSON, Henry; b 1744, Augusta Co; d 1791 **RU:** Captain/Patriot, Commanded a co in Botetourt Co Militia. Gave material aid to cause **CEM:** Watterson Family; GPS unk; Christiansburg; Montgomery **GS:** Y **SP:** Mar (1764) Agnes Reaburn (__-4 Feb 1817) **VI:** SAR applic indicates rank of Capt **P:** unk **BLW:** unk **RG:** Y **MK:** N **PH:** unk **SS:** DAR Ancestor #A122674; AS SAR applic; DF pg 123, 126, 130, 134 **BS:** 80 vol 4 pg 166.

WATTS, John; b 1752, Dinwiddie Co; d 8 Jun 1830 **RU:** Captain, Ent serv Bedford Co. Served as Capt 1st VA Regt of Dragoons. Wounded at Eutaw Springs, nr Savannah, GA **CEM:** Gravelly Hill; GPS unk; Town of Gravelly Hill; Bedford **GS:** U **SP:** No info **VI:** After war served rank of Lt Col US Army Light Dragoons 8 Jan 1799. Pen in Bedford Co.Recd BLW #243 of 4,944 acres issued 27 Aug 1795. Records lost in DC fire of 1800 **P:** Y **BLW:** Y **RG:** Y **MK:** N **PH:** unk **SS:** SAR Ancestor #P-314802; J-NSSAR 1993 Reg; K Vol 6 pg 80; CG pg 3706 **BS:** JLARC 1.

RU=Rank/Unit	CEM=Cemetery	GS=Gravestone	SP=Spousal Information
VI=Other Veteran Info	P=Pension	BLW=Bounty/Land Warrant	RG=Registered Grave
MK=SAR/DAR Marker	PH=Photo	SS=Service Source	BS=Burial Source

354

WAX, Henry Sr; b 1744, Baden-Wurtenburg, Germany; d 1796 **RU:** Sergeant, Sgt in Capt Daniel DeTurcks' Co of Berks Co PA 1776-1778 and promoted to Capt after the War period on 5 Jan 1784 **CEM:** Fincastle Presbyterian; GPS 37.50017, -79.87558; 108 E Back St, Fincastle; Botetourt **GS:** Y **SP:** 1) Mar (11 May 1767 Alace, Berks Co, PA) Margaret Geshwind (1750 Berks Co, PA-10 Feb 1791) 2) Mar (1 May 1791) Catherine Kerns Keyser **VI:** Son of Johann Philippus Wachs. Moved to VA in 1786 **P:** unk **BLW:** unk **RG:** Y **MK:** Y **PH:** unk **SS:** J-NSSAR 1993 Reg; J- DAR Hatcher; AR Vol 4 pg 166 **BS:** JLARC 1, 2; 196.

WAYLAND, John; b 1725; d 1804 **RU:** Patriot, Gave material aid to cause **CEM:** Hebron Lutheran; GPS 38.40676, -78.24808; 899 Blankenbaker Rd, Madison; Madison **GS:** N **SP:** Cayherine Broyles (1730-1830) d/o Hans Jacob (1705-1763) & Maria Caterhine (Fleishman) (1705-1710) Broyles **VI:** A member of the church when he died with burial there likely but not proved **P:** N **BLW:** N **RG:** unk **MK:** unk **PH:** N **SS:** ALCt Bk 1 pg 33, 35 **BS:** 196.

WEATHERFORD, John William; b 4 May 1747, Charlotte Co; d 23 Jan 1833 **RU:** Chaplain or Soldier, Served in VA Line. Ent serv 1779 Henry Co in VA Regt to fight Indians. Moved to Pittsylvania Co & enl there again **CEM:** Shockoe Baptist; GPS 36.80960, -79.26590; Rt 640, Chatham; Pittsylvania **GS:** U **SP:** Martha Patsy Sublette (1752, Charlotte Co-Nov 1829) d/o William (__-1751) & Susannah (Allen) (__-1803) Sublett **VI:** Appl pen 20 Feb 1845 Bartholomew Co at age 97 on 5 May 1844. R11231. Baptist preacher for 70 yrs. Early advocate for religious liberty. Jailed five mos in 1773 for preaching. Release secured by Patrick Henry. Memorialized at burial site in VA **P:** Y **BLW:** unk **RG:** unk **MK:** Y **PH:** Y **SS:** K Vol 6 pg 84-5; CG Vol 3 pg 3710 **BS:** JLARC 96,99; 196.

WEAVER, John Peter; b 1745; d 1815 **RU:** Private, Served in Capt Tate's Co of Miliitia, Augusta Co **CEM:** St John's Reformed UCC; GPS 38.05081, -79.17761; 1515 Arbor Hill Rd, Middlebrook; Augusta **GS:** Y **SP:** Elizabeth (-----) (1746-1814) **VI:** No further data **P:** unk **BLW:** unk **RG:** unk **MK:** N **PH:** unk **SS:** DAR Ancestor #A123365; E pg 813 **BS:** JLARC 9, 62; 196.

WEAVER, Peter; b c1736, Orange Co; d 1817 **RU:** Private/Patriot, Served in Culpeper Co Militia 1781. Gave material aid to cause **CEM:** Hebron Valley; GPS unk; Hebron Valley; Madison **GS:** N **SP:** Mary Barbara Huffman **VI:** Son of German immigrant John & (-----) Weaver of Culpeper Co (later Madison Co). **P:** unk **BLW:** unk **RG:** Y **MK:** N **PH:** N **SS:** D; AS SAR appl; AM pg 30 **BS:** 04, Feb 1994.

WEAVER, Tilman Jr; b c1745, Germantown, Prince William Co (later Fauquier Co); d 1809 **RU:** Captain, Served in Fauquier Co Militia, obtained Capt rank 24 Mar 1778 **CEM:** Germantown Glebe; GPS unk; Rt 643 nr Licking Run, Midland; Fauquier **GS:** Y **SP:** Elizabeth (-----) (__-bef 1809, Germantown) **VI:** Son of Tilman Sr. (1703-1760) & Ann Elizabeth (Cuntze) (1708 Germany-__) Weaver **P:** unk **BLW:** unk **RG:** unk **MK:** U **PH:** unk **SS:** E pg 813 **BS:** 19 pg 66.

WEBB, Henry "Hal"; b c1750, Franklin Co; d c1845 **RU:** Private, Served in VA Militia under Capt Jonathan Isom **CEM:** Thompson-Bolt; GPS 36.81040, -80.55030; Off Bannon Rd Rt 625, Willis; Carroll **GS:** Y **SP:** Susannah Cocke **VI:** Son of Jacob Webb & Mary Austin. Died in Grayson Co **P:** unk **BLW:** unk **RG:** Y **MK:** N **PH:** Y **SS:** DAR Ancestor #A123781; SAR Ancestor #P-315165; G pg 221; DD cites VA Mag of Hist & Biog Vol 46 #4 pg 345-6 **BS:** 196; 04; 196.

WEBB, John; b 1750, Frederick Co, MD; d 1803 **RU:** Private, Served in MD Line. Ent serv Frederick Co, MD 1776. Was in Battle at Trenton, NJ in Capt Neely's Co and in his father-in-law, Capt William Duvall's Co **CEM:** Hebron United Methodist; GPS unk; Rt 606 jct Bobcat Ln; Craig **GS:** U **SP:** Mar (15 or 16 Jun 1775 Frederick Co MA) Susannah Duvall (1757-__) **VI:** Died in Botetourt Co. Widow appl pen 1 Apr 1848 Belmont Co OH & BLW 15 Mar 1855 Belmont Co. W4384. BLW #530-160-55 **P:** Y **BLW:** Y **RG:** unk **MK:** unk **PH:** unk **SS:** NSSAR Ancestor # P-315198; CG Vol 3 pg 3717 **BS:** JLARC 4, 60.

WEBB, Tapley (Tarpley); b 1763, Richmond City; d 2 Mar 1836 **RU:** Seaman, Served in VA State Navy **CEM:** Cedar Grove; GPS 36.57204, -80.02599; 301 Fort Lane Rd; Portsmouth City **GS:** U **SP:** Mar (16 Dec 1809 Portsmouth) Elizabeth W. Poiner (1787-1836) **VI:** Vet's daughter Mrs. Ann P. Young appl pen 4 Sep 1856 Norfolk Co. She was issued BLW 9776 13 Oct 1856. S36113 **P:** Y **BLW:** Y **RG:** unk **MK:** unk **PH:** unk **SS:** K Vol 6 pg 90; BY pg 240; CG Vol 3 pg 3719 **BS:** JLARC 4; 196.

RU=Rank/Unit   CEM=Cemetery   GS=Gravestone   SP=Spousal Information
VI=Other Veteran Info   P=Pension   BLW=Bounty/Land Warrant   RG=Registered Grave
MK=SAR/DAR Marker   PH=Photo   SS=Service Source   BS=Burial Source

355

WEBB, Thomas T; b 1745; d 1796 **RU:** Corporal, Capt Thomas Posey's Co, 7th VA Regt **CEM:** Old Christ Church Episcopal; GPS 38.80625, -77.04718; 118 N Washington St; Alexandria City **GS:** N **SP:** No info **VI:** No further data **P:** unk **BLW:** unk **RG:** N **MK:** N **PH:** N **SS:** A -7th VA Regt **BS:** 110 pg 96.

WEBB, William; b unk; d 26 Apr 1805 **RU:** Captain/Patriot, Mil serv not identified. Gave material aid to cause **CEM:** St John's Episcopal; GPS 37.53183, -77.41958; 2401 E Broad St; Richmond City **GS:** Y **SP:** No info **VI:** No further data **P:** unk **BLW:** unk **RG:** unk **MK:** unk **PH:** unk **SS:** AL Ct Bk lt pg 13 **BS:** 28.

WEBB, William; b unk; d 1796 **RU:** Patriot, Gave material aid to the cause **CEM:** St John's Episcopal; GPS 37.53183, -77.41958; 2401 E Broad St; Richmond City **GS:** Y **SP:** N o info **VI:** No further data **P:** N **BLW:** N **RG:** Y **MK:** N **PH:** unk **SS:** AL Ct Bk lt pg 13 **BS:** 28 pg 517.

WEBB, William Warren; b 1699, Isle of Wight Co; d Aft 28 Aug 1783 **RU:** Patriot, Gave material aid to cause **CEM:** Blue Run Baptist; GPS unk; Rt 20 N of jct with Rt 655, Barboursville; Orange **GS:** N **SP:** Mar (c1727) Mary Jane Elizabeth Crittenden (1702, Spotsylvania Co-__) **VI:** Son of John & Martha (Riggens) Webb **P:** N **BLW:** N **RG:** unk **MK:** unk **PH:** N **SS:** DAR Ancestor #A201743; AL Ct Bk pg 27, 29 Orange **BS:** Church records

WEBBER, William; b 15 Aug 1747, Goochland Co; d 28 Feb 1808 **RU:** Soldier/Patriot, Served in VA infantry during RW. Gave material aid to cause **CEM:** Webber Family; GPS unk; W Rt 6 fr Richmond 9.2 mi, right Rt 621 3.5 mi; Goochland **GS:** U **SP:** Mar (23 Jan 1773) Mary Woolfolk (21 Oct 1752, Spotsylvania Co-c1833) d/o John (6 Nov 1727, Spotsylvania Co-18 Jan 1816) & Elizabeth (Wigglesworth) (17 Mar 1732-10 Aug 1791) Woolfolk **VI:** Baptist minister. Recd BLW **P:** unk **BLW:** Y **RG:** unk **MK:** unk **PH:** unk **SS:** DAR Ancestor #A134528; C pg 274; AL Ct Bk pg 16 Goochland Co; DD **BS:** JLARC 99.

WEBSTER, George; b unk; d 1796 **RU:** Soldier, Served fr MA, and died fr the Battle at Yorktown **CEM:** Yorktown Victory Monument Tablet; GPS 38.28350, -78.54150; Yorktown; York **GS:** U **SP:** No info **VI:** No further data **P:** unk **BLW:** unk **RG:** unk **MK:** unk **PH:** unk **SS:** J-Yorktown Historian **BS:** JLARC 74.

WEDDLE (WADDELL, WODLE, WEDEL), Benjamin; b 1751, Lancaster Co, PA; d 1807 **RU:** Private, Served in Capt James Byrn's Co, Montgomery Co. Also served in Capt John Lucas Co, Col William Preston's Regt **CEM:** Weddle Family; GPS unk; Bent Mountain; Roanoke Co **GS:** N **SP:** Mar (__ Lancaster Co, PA) Annie Mary Eiler (1751-1834) **VI:** Died in Montgomery Co on return trip fr Richmond with wagonload of supplies. Monument in Weddle Family Cem. Indicates he is bur on Bent Mountain in Roanoke Co in unk location **P:** unk **BLW:** unk **RG:** Y **MK:** N **PH:** N **SS:** DAR Ancestor #A119631; SAR Ancestor #P-315551; Montgomery Cthse; G pg 241; DD cites VA Mag of Hist & Biog Vol 47 pg 154 **BS:** 04; 196.

WEEDON, George; b 1734 or 1735; d 1793 or 1796 **RU:** Brig General, Was in charge of Stafford Co & Fredericksburg Militia, Cont Line 3 yrs. Commanded VA 3rd Regt of Foot 13 Aug 1776 to 21 Feb 1777. Was Brigade Commander as well Oct 1776 at Trenton **CEM:** Masonic Cemetery; GPS 38.30198, -77.46142; 900 Charles St; Fredericksburg City **GS:** Y **SP:** Mar (Fredericksburg) Catherine Gordon (__-1797) **VI:** Owned and operated tavern in Fredericksburg until 1776 and again after war. Mayor of Fredericksburg after war. Recd 10,000 acres BLW #2418-850-3 May 1791. Records lost in 1800 DC fire **P:** unk **BLW:** Y **RG:** Y **MK:** Y **PH:** Y **SS:** F pg 77; K Vol 6 pg 91; CE pg 38, 39; CG Vol 3 pg 3727 **BS:** 13 pg 18.

WEIR, Hugh; b 1746; d 16 Jul 1822 **RU:** Captain, Commanded a co in Rockbridge Co Militia 7 Aug 1781 **CEM:** McKee, aka Big Springs; GPS unk; Clarence Hardy's farm, off Rt 60 on Rt 63, Kerrs Dist; Rockbridge **GS:** U **SP:** Mary McKee (1746-2 Aug 1822) **VI:** No further data **P:** N **BLW:** N **RG:** unk **MK:** unk **PH:** unk **SS:** E pg 815 **BS:** 204.

WEISER, Henry; b 15 Apr 1755, Pulaski Co; d 12 Jan 1844 **RU:** Private, Served in Capts Berry, Bell, Long & Knox's Cos, Col Bowman's Regt, 8th Cont Line under General Morgan **CEM:** Bell Farm; GPS unk; Dublin; Pulaski **GS:** U **SP:** Mar (1778) Barbara Ann Ripseed (14 Feb 1758-10 May 1837) **VI:** Recd Pen #S7854 **P:** Y **BLW:** unk **RG:** unk **MK:** unk **PH:** unk **SS:** DAR Ancestor #A121737; E pg 815; DD cites pension rec as serv source **BS:** JLARC 2.

RU=Rank/Unit   CEM=Cemetery   GS=Gravestone   SP=Spousal Information
VI=Other Veteran Info   P=Pension   BLW=Bounty/Land Warrant   RG=Registered Grave
MK=SAR/DAR Marker   PH=Photo   SS=Service Source   BS=Burial Source

356

WEISS, Matthias; b 12 Mar 1752, Bethlehem Twp, Northampton Co, PA; d 5 May 1831 **RU:** Private, Served in Capt Jacob Weidman's Co, Lt Col Robert Knox Regt, Philadelphia Militia **CEM:** Weiss Family; GPS unk; Rt 637 or 736, Independence; Grayson **GS:** U **SP:** Rachel Bonham Ball **VI:** No further data **P:** unk **BLW:** unk **RG:** Y **MK:** unk **PH:** unk **SS:** J-NSSAR 1993 Reg, J- DAR Hatcher; AP Muster Roll PA Archives 6th series Vol 1 pg 401-2 **BS:** JLARC 1, 2.

WELBURN (WELBOURNE), William Sr; b 11 Oct 1762; d 11 Oct 1839 **RU:** Captain, Served in VA Line. Ent serv Accomack Co 1777-8. Capt Thomas Marshall's Co. Later was Capain in Accomack Co Militia **CEM:** Welburn or Welbourne Family; GPS unk; Rts 709 & 679, Horntown; Accomack **GS:** Y **SP:** Mar (5 Feb 1784 Accomac Co (bond) Coleburn Lang, security) Sabra Corbin (__-bef 11 Oct 1839) **VI:** Appl pen 1 Aug 1832 Accomack Co age 70. S7856 **P:** Y **BLW:** unk **RG:** unk **MK:** unk **PH:** N **SS:** K Vol 6 pg 93; CG Vol 3 pg 3731 **BS:** JLARC 4, 6.

WELCH, Sylvester Sr; b 15 Mar 1764; d 19 Apr 1834 **RU:** Soldier, Served in Cont Line. Ent Serv Northumberland Co 1777. Served in 1st VA Regt **CEM:** Marshall; GPS 38.86919, -77.83445; Marshall; Fauquier **GS:** Y **SP:** A man by this name mar (bond 25 Nov 1793, Joseph Jackson security) Sarah Jackson **VI:** Sol appl pen 1 Dec 1832 in Fauquier Co age 77. S6342 **P:** Y **BLW:** unk **RG:** Y **MK:** Y **PH:** Y **SS:** K Vol 6 pg 95; CG Vol 3 pg 3735; Fauquier Co Marriages pg 210 **BS:** JLARC 1,16; 196.

WELCH, Thomas; b 1 Feb 1753, Orange Co; d 10 Jul 1821 **RU:** Private, Served in Col Daniel Morgan's 11th & 15th VA Regts. 7th Cont Line **CEM:** Falling Springs Presbyterian; GPS 37.68494, -79.45105; 410 Falling Spring Rd, Glasgow; Rockbridge **GS:** Y **SP:** Sarah Grigsby, d/o John & (-----) Grigsby **VI:** Son of Thomas & (-----) Welch Sr **P:** unk **BLW:** unk **RG:** Y **MK:** Y **PH:** unk **SS:** J-NSSAR 1993 Reg; E pg 803 **BS:** JLARC 1; 196.

WELLFORD, Robert; b 12 Apr 1753, Ware, Hertfordshire, England; d 24 Apr 1823 **RU:** Patriot, Was British surgeon, treated American soldiers due to poor treatment by British captors, gave horse & beef to cause. Resigned fr British Army **CEM:** Willis Hill, Fredericksburg National Military Park; GPS unk; Marye Heights; Fredericksburg City **GS:** Y **SP:** Catherine Randolph Yates (24 Mar 1760-11 Feb 1831) **VI:** Son of William (1726-1790) & Jane (Brasenar) (1724-1783) Welford. Came to colonies with First Royal Grenadiers. Friend of Col Spotswood during RW and later accompanied Gen Washington, who gave letters of introduction to friends in Fredericksburg. During Whiskey Rebellion (1794), became Surgeon General of Army raised to surpress uprising **P:** N **BLW:** N **RG:** Y **MK:** N **PH:** Y **SS:** D pg 873,861 **BS:** 06 pg 95, 96; 196.

WELLS, Zachariah; b 1739; d Oct 1813 **RU:** Private, Served in VA Line. Ent serv Loudoun Co 1776. Was in Battles of Brandywine & Germantown. Ent serv again 1778 in VA Cavalry unit on KY frontier **CEM:** Wells Family; GPS 36.84640, -82.81720; Rt 739 abt 1 mi S of jct with 605; Wise **GS:** U **SP:** Rebecca (-----) (__-before 1813) **VI:** Son of Zachariah (__-1781) & (-----) Wells though DNA evidence shows his parents may be George & Susannah (Ward) Wells. Wells & Ward families together in MD. Appl pen 29 Mar 1825 Sullivan Co TN age 80 S39119. Died in Sullivan Co, TN or Wilkes Co, NC. BLW recd 1784 **P:** Y **BLW:** Y **RG:** unk **MK:** unk **PH:** unk **SS:** J- DAR Hatcher; K Vol 6 pg 100; CG Vol 3 pg 3745 **BS:** JLARC 2; 196.

WENDREWECK, Armand; b unk; d 1796 **RU:** Soldier, Served in Gatinais Bn and died fr battle at Yorktown **CEM:** French Memorial; GPS 36.81944, -79.39933; Yorktown; York **GS:** U **SP:** No info **VI:** No further data **P:** unk **BLW:** unk **RG:** Y **MK:** unk **PH:** unk **SS:** J-Yorktown Historian **BS:** JLARC 1,74.

WENGER, Henry; b 15 Aug 1753, Lancaster Co, PA; d 9 Aug 1819 **RU:** Private, Served in10th PA Regt **CEM:** Early; GPS 38.39536, -78.90465; 3588 Early Rd, Pleasant Valley; Rockingham **GS:** Y **SP:** Anna Huber (1758 Lancaster Co, PA-20 Jun 1824) **VI:** No further data **P:** unk **BLW:** unk **RG:** unk **MK:** unk **PH:** unk **SS:** AP Serv Record NARA M881 Roll 0832 **BS:** 196.

WESCOTT, John; b c1741, Cumberland Co, NJ; d 25 Nov 1813 **RU:** Captain/ Patriot, Served as Cumberland Co NJ Board of Freeholders, 1775; and on a Deerfield Twp Committee on Observation & Correspondence, 17 Sep 1775, Served in rank of Lt in 1st Western Co of Artillery, NJ State Troops, 1 May 1776, and as Capt Oct. 1776 and 1777 **CEM:** Old Presbyterian Meeting House; GPS 38.48528, -77.23532; 323 S Fairfax St; Alexandria City **GS:** Y **SP:** Annie (-----) of Cumberland Co., NJ **VI:** No further data **P:** unk **BLW:** unk **RG:** unk **MK:** Y **PH:** unk **SS:** AS; BT **BS:** JLARC 86; 23 pg 84.

RU=Rank/Unit	CEM=Cemetery	GS=Gravestone	SP=Spousal Information
VI=Other Veteran Info	P=Pension	BLW=Bounty/Land Warrant	RG=Registered Grave
MK=SAR/DAR Marker	PH=Photo	SS=Service Source	BS=Burial Source

357

WEST, Abel; b 30 May 1734; d 30 May 1816 **RU:** Lieutenant, Oath as Lt Accomack Militia 30 Sep 1777 **CEM:** Old West Place, aka Cedar View; GPS unk; N of Craddockville off Rt 616; Accomack **GS:** Y **SP:** Nanney (-----) (23 Oct 173_-20 Dec 1805) **VI:** No further data **P:** unk **BLW:** unk **RG:** Y **MK:** N **PH:** unk **SS:** E pg 817 **BS:** 37 pg 274.

WEST, Anthony Jr; b 24 Aug 1760; d 2 Feb 1795 **RU:** Patriot, Provided equipment and/or supplies **CEM:** West Family; GPS unk; Deep Creek; Accomack **GS:** Y **SP:** No info **VI:** Son of Anthony & Eleanor (-----) West Sr **P:** N **BLW:** N **RG:** Y **MK:** N **PH:** unk **SS:** AL cert issued **BS:** 106 pg 538; 47 Vol 3 pg. 259.

WEST, John; b 7 Nov 1753; d 17 Dec 1835 **RU:** Soldier, Ent serv 1776 in Philadelphia PA **CEM:** Goose Creek; GPS 39.11250, -77.69527; Rt 722, Lincoln; Loudoun **GS:** U **SP:** Mar (24 Oct 1791) Hannah (-----) **VI:** Pensioned Loudoun Co 1833 W6453 **P:** Y **BLW:** unk **RG:** unk **MK:** unk **PH:** unk **SS:** K Vol 6 pg 102 **BS:** JLARC 4, 32.

WEST, Joseph; b 1 Jan 1719, Chadds Ford, Delaware Co, PA; d 12 Sep 1802 **RU:** Patriot, Gave material aid to cause **CEM:** West Plantation; GPS unk; Straightstone; Pittsylvania **GS:** U **SP:** 1) Elizabeth Hazard 2) Mar (6 Mar 1740 Chester Co PA) Jane Owen (1720-1791), d/o John & Hannah (Maris) Owen **VI:** Son of John (1690-1776) & Sarah (Pearson) West **P:** N **BLW:** N **RG:** unk **MK:** unk **PH:** unk **SS:** J- DAR Hatcher; NSSAR Ancestor # P-316746 **BS:** JLARC 2.

WEST, Thomas Wade; b 1745; d 28 Jul 1799 **RU:** Patriot, Performed public service **CEM:** Old Christ Church Episcopal; GPS 38.80625, -77.04718; 118 N Washington St; Alexandria City **GS:** N **SP:** No info **VI:** Manager of the Virginia & South Carolina Companies of Comedians, killed when he fell fr the upper story to the stage in his new Alexandria theater, age 54 (Alexandria Gazette, 29 Jul 1799 pg 3) **P:** N **BLW:** N **RG:** N **MK:** N **PH:** N **SS:** BB Legislative Pet. **BS:** 20 pg 143.

WEST, William; b 1762; d 1815 **RU:** Patriot, Gave material aid to cause **CEM:** Good Hope United Methodist; GPS unk; 1633 Benefit Rd; Chesapeake City **GS:** Y **SP:** No info **VI:** No further data **P:** N **BLW:** N **RG:** unk **MK:** unk **PH:** unk **SS:** Al Ct Bk pg 6 Princess Anne Co **BS:** 20 pg 153.

WEST, William; b unk; d 1790 **RU:** Patriot, Gave material aid to the cause **CEM:** Dumfries Public; GPS 38.34110, -77.19964; 17821 Mine Rd, Dumfries; Prince William **GS:** N **SP:** No info **VI:** Name on SAR monument **P:** N **BLW:** N **RG:** Y **MK:** Y **PH:** N **SS:** AL Ct Bk I pg 18 **BS:** 96 pg 74.

WESTON, Lewis; b unk; d Jul 1795 **RU:** Patriot, Signed a Legislative Petition in Alexandria **CEM:** Old Christ Church Episcopal; GPS 38.80625, -77.04718; 118 N Washington St; Alexandria City **GS:** N **SP:** no info **VI:** Burial permit issued 13 Jul 1792 **P:** N **BLW:** N **RG:** N **MK:** N **PH:** N **SS:** BB; S-Alexandria **BS:** 20 pg 153.

WETHERBEE, James; b unk; d 1781 **RU:** Soldier, Served fr MA, and died fr the Battle at Yorktown **CEM:** Yorktown Victory Monument Tablet; GPS 38.28350, -78.54150; Yorktown; York **GS:** U **SP:** No info **VI:** No further data **P:** unk **BLW:** unk **RG:** unk **MK:** unk **PH:** unk **SS:** J-Yorktown Historian **BS:** JLARC 74.

WHALEY, Zedekaih (Zadock); b unk; d 30 Nov 1782 **RU:** Commodore, US Navy, MD, was killed in Naval "Battle of the Barges" **CEM:** Scott Hall; GPS unk; Daugherty Rd, Onancock; Accomack **GS:** Y **SP:** no info **VI:** Son of William & Mary (Radcliffe) Whaley **P:** Y **BLW:** unk **RG:** Y **MK:** Y **PH:** unk **SS:** B DAR marker **BS:** 37 pg 276.

WHARTON, John Esq; b 25 Nov 1762; d 25 Feb 1811 **RU:** Private, Capt Wallace's Co, 3rd VA Regt, commanded by Col Geo Weeden, 8 Oct -7 Dec 1776 **CEM:** Wharton Family; GPS unk; Assawoman Creek; Accomack **GS:** Y **SP:** Mar (10 Jun 1784) Elizabeth Williams (24 May 1746-13 Nov 1831) d/o William & Margaret (-----) Williams **VI:** Died in Philadelphia and body moved to cem here **P:** unk **BLW:** unk **RG:** N **MK:** N **PH:** unk **SS:** AP roll **BS:** 145 Wharton; 196.

WHARTON, Samuel; b 27 Jul 1761; d 10 Dec 1841 **RU:** Soldier, Ent serv Spotsylvania Co 1777. Severely wounded by cannonball at siege of Yorktown **CEM:** Whartons; GPS unk; Christopher Run; Louisa **GS:** U **SP:** Mar (8 Mar 1786 Spotsylvania Co) Letitia "Letty" Hutcherson d/o William & Sarah (-----) Hutcherson **VI:** Widow appl pen 16 Jun 1842 Louisa Co. age abt 74, and for increase in 1849 Louisa

RU=Rank/Unit   CEM=Cemetery   GS=Gravestone   SP=Spousal Information
VI=Other Veteran Info   P=Pension   BLW=Bounty/Land Warrant   RG=Registered Grave
MK=SAR/DAR Marker   PH=Photo   SS=Service Source   BS=Burial Source

358

Co. She appl for BLW 1855. W6488. BLW #38832-160-55 **P:** Y **BLW:** Y **RG:** unk **MK:** unk **PH:** unk **SS:** K Vol 6 pg 106; CG Vol 3 pg 3764 **BS:** JLARC 4, 61.

WHEELER, Drummond; b 1727, Truro, Fairfax Co; d 1804 **RU:** Patriot, Paid personal Property Tax (Rev War Supply Tax) 1782 and 1783, Fairfax Co **CEM:** Wheeler-Greenville Family; GPS 38.47755, -77.32458; 7300 Old Compton Rd; Prince William **GS:** Y **SP:** Mar (5 Jun 1750 Fairfax Co) Jean Wesley (c1725-May 1799) **VI:** Son of Richard & Rebecca (Frizzell) Wheeler **P:** unk **BLW:** unk **RG:** unk **MK:** unk **PH:** unk **SS:** DV **BS:** 190 by cem name.

WHEELER, John Sr; b c1746; d 3 May 1819 **RU:** Private, Served in Capt John Brent, Col Lawson Regt, Cont Line **CEM:** Wheeler-Pugh-Jennings; GPS unk; Off Rt 663 nr Bear Creek, down little dirt rd; Charlotte **GS:** U **SP:** Mar (aft 1765) Mary Trisdale (c1745-1804) **VI:** No further data **P:** unk **BLW:** unk **RG:** unk **MK:** unk **PH:** unk **SS:** DAR Ancestor #A064914; JLARC Rpt App B-2 pg 27; C pg 278; CU 1806 **BS:** JLARC 118.

WHEELER, William; b unk; d Aug 1796 **RU:** Surgeon, Served as surgeon in Col Ebenezer's Regt of NY Artillery. Commissioned 4 Sep 1777, resigned 8 Jan 1779 **CEM:** Old Christ Church Episcopal; GPS 38.80625, -77.04718; 118 N Washington St; Alexandria City **GS:** N **SP:** No info **VI:** Burial permit issued 15 Aug 1796 **P:** unk **BLW:** unk **RG:** N **MK:** N **PH:** N **SS:** A pg 155 **BS:** 20 pg 153.

WHIDDON, John; b 19 Sep 1730; d 14 May 1796 **RU:** Patriot, Gave material aid to cause **CEM:** Old Massenburgh; GPS unk; South Norfolk; Norfolk City **GS:** Y **SP:** Mary (-----) (c1740-13 Jan 1818) **VI:** No further data **P:** N **BLW:** N **RG:** Y **MK:** N **PH:** unk **SS:** AL Ct Bk pg 10 **BS:** 63 pg 110.

WHITACRE, John III; b 1737, Makefield, Bucks Co, PA; d 1785 **RU:** Private, Served in 8th & 9th Cont Lines **CEM:** Goose Creek; GPS 39.11250, -77.69527; Rt 722, Lincoln; Loudoun **GS:** U **SP:** Mar (c1758 NJ) Keziah Taylor (1738-__) **VI:** Son of John II (1704-1768) & Naomi (Hulme) (1713-1789) Taylor. Moved with parents to VA 1761 **P:** unk **BLW:** unk **RG:** unk **MK:** unk **PH:** unk **SS:** C pg 275; E pg 820 **BS:** 196.

WHITACRE (WHITAKER), George; b 1745 Bucks Co, PA; d 12 Sep 1785 **RU:** Patriot, Gave material aid to cause **CEM:** Goose Creek; GPS 39.11250, -77.69527; Rt 722, Lincoln; Loudoun **GS:** N **SP:** Mar (c1765) Ruth (-----) (1749-__) **VI:** No further data **P:** N **BLW:** N **RG:** unk **MK:** unk **PH:** N **SS:** DAR Ancestor #A124215; AL Ct Bk pg 5 **BS:** 196.

WHITAKER, James; b 1753, Buckingham Co; d 4 May 1842 **RU:** Private, Ent serv Buckingham Co and served in VA Line in Capts Winston's, Miller's and Moseley's Cos, Col Charles Fleming's Regt. Served at Siege of Yorktown **CEM:** Whitaker Family Farm; GPS unk; Not identified; Campbell **GS:** U **SP:** Mar (10 Mar 1791 Buckingham Co by Rev William Flowers) Susannah Beckham **VI:** Sol appl pen 14 Aug 1832 Campbell Co age 69. Widow appl pen 2 Jun 1843 Campbell Co age 74. W3482 **P:** Y **BLW:** unk **RG:** Y **MK:** N **PH:** unk **SS:** DAR Ancestor #A124219; J-NSSAR 2000 Reg; K Vol 6 pg 112; CG Vol 3 pg 3780 **BS:** JLARC 76.

WHITAKER, John; b unk; d Oct 14 1781 **RU:** Private, Served in Capt Aaron Ogden's Co, Lt Col Francis Barber's Battalion, NJ Cont Line. Died fr service at Yorktown **CEM:** Yorktown Victory Monument Tablet; GPS 38.28350, -78.54150; Yorktown; York **GS:** U **SP:** No info **VI:** No further data **P:** unk **BLW:** unk **RG:** unk **MK:** unk **PH:** unk **SS:** J-Yorktown Historian; DX pg 24 **BS:** JLARC 74.

WHITE, Alexander; b 1738; d 9 Oct 1804 **RU:** Patriot, Gave material aid to cause. Member of House of Delegates 1782-83 **CEM:** Woodville Estate; GPS unk; Winchester; Frederick **GS:** U **SP:** No info **VI:** Son of Robert (1689-1755) & Margaret (Hoge) (1700-1752) White. Delegate to state convention that considered adoption of US Constitution. President Washington appointed White to commission that laid out Washington DC and oversaw construction of first public buildings. Member of VA House of Delegates again 1799-1801 **P:** N **BLW:** N **RG:** unk **MK:** unk **PH:** unk **SS:** AL Ct Bk pg 8, 17 Frederick Co **BS:** 196.

WHITE, Ambrose; b 1754, Caroline Co; d 2 Jun 1823 **RU:** First Lieutenant, Served in Caroline Co Militia **CEM:** Greenlawn; GPS 38.07030, -77.33830; Lakewood Rd, Bowling Green; Caroline **GS:** Y **SP:** Mar (Jan 1776) Ann Jones (1754 Caroline Co-22 Jun 1827) **VI:** New monument with DAR insignia was

RU=Rank/Unit   CEM=Cemetery   GS=Gravestone   SP=Spousal Information
VI=Other Veteran Info   P=Pension   BLW=Bounty/Land Warrant   RG=Registered Grave
MK=SAR/DAR Marker   PH=Photo   SS=Service Source   BS=Burial Source

359

placed in 1971,that gives rank as Lieutenant of Militia **P:** unk **BLW:** unk **RG:** unk **MK**: Y **PH:** unk **SS:** DAR Ancestor #A124572; J-NSSAR 2000 Reg; NSSAR Ancestor #P-317974 **BS:** JLARC 76; 196.

WHITE, Benjamin; b 14 May 1760, Loudoun Co; d 1837 **RU:** Private, Served in Clark's Illinois Regt & possibly 13th & 15th Cont Lines **CEM:** Goose Creek; GPS 39.11250, -77.69527; Rt 722, Lincoln; Loudoun **GS:** Y **SP:** Mary (-----) **VI:** Son of Richard & Rebekah (Canthron) White **P:** unk **BLW:** unk **RG:** N **MK**: N **PH:** N **SS:** E pg 821 **BS:** 196.

WHITE, Isaac; b unk; d 1781 **RU:** Soldier, Served fr PA, and died fr the Battle at Yorktown **CEM:** Yorktown Victory Monument Tablet; GPS 38.28350, -78.54150; Yorktown; York **GS:** U **SP:** No info **VI:** No further data **P:** unk **BLW:** unk **RG:** unk **MK**: unk **PH:** unk **SS:** J-Yorktown Historian **BS:** JLARC 74.

WHITE, Jacob; b 1765; d 2 Jun 1832 **RU:** Captain, Ent serv 1778 in VA Line. Ent serv again 1781 in "VA Co" and served in Battle of Guilford CH **CEM:** White Family; GPS 37.28400, -79.24130; Nr Charlemont, jct 638 & 637; Bedford **GS:** Y **SP:** Mar (1775) Mary Allen (__-14 Dec 1840). Widow mar 2nd to John Lafoy/Lafo/Lafoe in 1804 or 1805 **VI:** Served in Siege of '96 (District, SC). Widow granted pen 1849 W8076 **P:** Y **BLW:** unk **RG:** unk **MK**: unk **PH:** Yes **SS:** J- DAR Hatcher; K Vol 6 pg 115; CG Vol 3 pg 3789 **BS:** JLARC 2.

WHITE, John; b Mar 1756, Kingston Parish, Gloucester Co; d 12 Jun 1834 **RU:** 2nd LT, Enl serv 1776 VA Line. Was in Gloucester Co Militia. Served a six month tour at Gwynn's Island when Lord Dunmore invaded; was involved in ousting Dunmore fr VA in 1776. In 1781 served under Capt Hungerford & Col Mercer. Was in Cont Army at Battle of Sewell's Old Field, nr Tyndall's Point (now Gloucester Point). Left service after Siege of Yorktown in Oct 1781, however commissioned 2nd Lt May 1782 in Capt Edmund Jones Co **CEM:** White Family (Whitehaven); GPS unk; 160 Pine View Dr; Mathews **GS:** U **SP:** Mar (26 Mar 1791 Norfolk by Minister James McBride, Church of England) Elizabeth Davenport (27 Nov 1771 Norfolk-1843) d/o Capt William (20 Sep 1746-5 July 1787) and Mary (Hunley) (1752-1843) Davenport. **VI:** Son of William and Elizabeth (Bartlett) White. Sol appl pen 13 Aug 1832 Mathews Co. Widow appl there 13 Aug 1838 age 66. W6476 **P:** Y **BLW:** unk **RG:** unk **MK**: unk **PH:** unk **SS:** E pg 822; K Vol 6 pg 118; J- DAR Hatcher; CG Vol 3 pg 3792; CQ pg 187 **BS:** JLARC 2.

WHITE, Joseph; b 1755, Amelia Co; d 26 Mar 1844 **RU:** Private, Served in Capt Thomas Buford's Co at Battle of Point Pleasant, Oct 1774; also later in Capts John Trigg's Co, Bedford Co Militia **CEM:** White Family; GPS unk; Stewartsville; Bedford **GS:** U **SP:** Mar (14 Mar 1826, Bedford Co) Penalope Angel (1771-aft 1866) **VI:** He appl pen 11 Sep 1822 and d in Otterville, Bedford Co. She appl pen 18 Jun 1853 #W11809; Widow appl BLW 3 Apr 1855 # 26168-160-55 **P:** Y **BLW:** Y **RG:** unk **MK**: unk **PH:** unk **SS:** DAR Ancestor A125221; CG pg 3793; DD; Z pg 125 **BS:** 196.

WHITE, Josiah (Josias); b 1 Feb 1760; d 7 Sep 1820 **RU:** Patriot, VA, gave material to cause **CEM:** Ketoctin Baptist; GPS 39.15746, -77.74870; Ketoctin Church Rd, Purcellville; Loudoun **GS:** Y **SP:** No info **VI:** No further data **P:** N **BLW:** N **RG:** Y **MK**: N **PH:** unk **SS:** D, Vol 2, pg 612 **BS:** 25, pg 338.

WHITE, Michael; b 1750; d 2 Apr 1832 **RU:** Sergeant/Patriot, 6th & 10th VA Regts; served at Valley Forge, PA. Paid supply tax 1783 **CEM:** St John's Lutheran; GPS 39.15310, -78.36520; 3623 Buck Mountain Rd, Hayfield; Frederick **GS:** Y **SP:** Mar (9 Sep 1783) Elizabeth Fry (1765-1817) **VI:** Son of Michael & Catherine (-----) White. DAR plaque on grave site **P:** unk **BLW:** unk **RG:** unk **MK**: Y **PH:** unk **SS:** DAR Ancestor #A208022; E pg 822; DD **BS:** 196.

WHITE, Robert; b c1734; d 5 Aug 1815 **RU:** Lieutenant, Served in 2nd, 5th, 6th, 9th, 11th, 15th Cont Lines **CEM:** White Family; GPS unk; Rt 615; Frederick **GS:** Y **SP:** Mar (9 Sep 1783 Frederick Co by John Montgomery) Elizabeth Fry **VI:** Drew pension Frederick Co **P:** Y **BLW:** unk **RG:** Y **MK**: N **PH:** unk **SS:** E pg 822-3 **BS:** 59 pg 350.

WHITE, Robert; b c1759; d 2 Nov 1831 **RU:** Lieutenant Colonel, Served in VA Line. Ent serv 20 Jan 1775 for one yr under Hugh Stephenson. Promoted to Lt in Capt Joseph Mitchell's Co, 12th VA Regt 1776. Severely wounded Jun 1777,which disqualified him fr further service. Promoted to Lt Col 4 Aug 1779, Frederick Co Militia **CEM:** Mt Hebron; GPS 39.10916, -78.09497; 305 E Boscawen St; Winchester City **GS:** Y **SP:** unk **VI:** Recd BLW #1678-300. Was judge after war. Pensioned 1828 Frederick Co #S7893. Died in Frederick Co abt age 72. Originally bur in Presbyterian cem next to German Reformed

RU=Rank/Unit   CEM=Cemetery   GS=Gravestone   SP=Spousal Information
VI=Other Veteran Info   P=Pension   BLW=Bounty/Land Warrant   RG=Registered Grave
MK=SAR/DAR Marker   PH=Photo   SS=Service Source   BS=Burial Source

360

Cem in Mt Hebron. Moved to present location 1912 with 71 other people. S. 7,893 **P:** Y **BLW:** Y **RG:** Y **MK:** N **PH:** Y **SS:** A pg 551; E pg 822; K Vol 6 pg 120-1; CG Vol 3 pg 3795 **BS:** JLARC 1, 4, 47.

WHITE, Thomas; b 20 May 1760; d 21 Mar or 23 Apr 1825 **RU:** Captain, Ent serv Fauquier Co 1776 in 1st VA Regt at age 17 Was at Seige of Yorktown, **CEM:** Spring Grove; GPS 39.10916, -78.09970; Rockville; Hanover **GS:** N **SP:** 1) Elizabeth Cross 2) mar Feb 1783 Elizabeth Blackwell (c1763-1842) **VI:** Member of House of Delegates and magistrate for many yrs. Later held rank of Brigadier-General. Justice of Peace. Obit in Richmond Enquirer 23 Apr 1825 pg 3 says "died at his seat, Spring Grove, Hanover Co, on 21st..." Died at "Spring Grove" Hanover Co. Widow pensioned 1840 age 77 but rejected due to insufficient proof of service. R11409 **P:** N **BLW:** unk **RG:** Y **MK:** N **PH:** N **SS:** G pg 774; K Vol 6 pg 122 **BS:** 31 vol 1 pg 21.

WHITE, William; b 1 Jun 1762, Caroline Co; d Oct 1781 **RU:** Captain, Served in VA Line. Ent serv 1775 as Sgt, later promoted to Lt, 1st VA Regt. A person this name died fr battle at Yorktown believed to be him **CEM:** Yorktown Victory Monument Tablet; GPS 38.28350, -78.54150; Yorktown; York **GS:** U **SP:** Agnes Cardwell **VI:** Widow age 71 appl pen 19 Jan 1838 Hanover Co & appl BLW 24 Mar 1855. W4099. BLW #3190-160-55 to widow, BLW #2213-200 to heirs **P:** Y **BLW:** Y **RG:** unk **MK:** unk **PH:** unk **SS:** J-Yorktown Historian; K Vol 6 pg 124; CG Vol 3 pg 3801 **BS:** JLARC 74.

WHITING, James; b unk; d 1781 **RU:** Soldier, Served fr MA, and died fr the Battle at Yorktown **CEM:** Yorktown Victory Monument Tablet; GPS 38.28350, -78.54150; Yorktown; York **GS:** U **SP:** No info **VI:** No further data **P:** unk **BLW:** unk **RG:** unk **MK:** unk **PH:** unk **SS:** J-Yorktown Historian **BS:** JLARC 74.

WHITNEY, Silas; b unk; d 1781 **RU:** Soldier, Served fr MA, and died fr the Battle at Yorktown **CEM:** Yorktown Victory Monument Tablet; GPS 38.28350, -78.54150; Yorktown; York **GS:** U **SP:** No info **VI:** No further data **P:** unk **BLW:** unk **RG:** unk **MK:** unk **PH:** unk **SS:** J-Yorktown Historian **BS:** JLARC 74.

WHITTEN, Thomas Sr; b 10 Sep 1719, Prince George Co, MD; d 1794 **RU:** Patriot, Signed Oath of Allegiance 30 Sep 1777. Also was Commissioner for Supply Distribution, Montgomery Co **CEM:** Maplewood; GPS 37.12803, -81.52104; nr Jct Rts 19, 460, & 16 Tazewell Ave; Tazewell **GS:** U **SP:** Mar (1742 MD) Elizabeth Cecil (15 Mar 1720-__) **VI:** No further data **P:** N **BLW:** N **RG:** unk **MK:** unk **PH:** unk **SS:** DAR Ancestor #A125475; D Vol 2 pg 609; G pg 209 **BS:** 196.

WHITWORTH, Thomas; b 26 Jun 1726, King William Co; d 4 Jul 1801 **RU:** Patriot, Gave material aid to cause **CEM:** Whitworth; GPS unk; Paineville; Amelia **GS:** N **SP:** Elizabeth Southerland (1726-1819) **VI:** Died in Lunenburg Co **P:** N **BLW:** N **RG:** unk **MK:** unk **PH:** N **SS:** AL Ct Bk 1 pg 10 in Amelia Co **BS:** 196.

WIATT, John; b 1740, Gloucester Co; d Mar 1827 **RU:** Colonel/Patriot, Was in Battle of Guilford CH. Gave material aid to cause **CEM:** Wiatt-Norvell; GPS unk; City Farm Quadrant; Campbell **GS:** U **SP:** Mar (c1794 Buckingham Co) Wilhelmina Jordan (1750, Buckingham Co-1836 Lynchburg) d/o Samuel & Judith (Scott) Jordan **VI:** Find a Grave.com indicates he is bur in the Radchiffe cem in Lynchburg & source DD indicates he was b 1750 in Spotsylvania Co and d in Lynchburg **P:** unk **BLW:** unk **RG:** unk **MK:** N **PH:** unk **SS:** AL Cert Amherst Co **BS:** JLARC 36.

WIATT, Thomas; b unk; d 1828 **RU:** Captain, Commanded a Co King & Queen Co Militia **CEM:** Avoca; GPS unk; Altavista; Campbell **GS:** U **SP:** Mary (18 May 1793 Campbell Co (bond)) Sarah/Sally Miller d/o John & (-----) Miller **VI:** No further data **P:** unk **BLW:** unk **RG:** unk **MK:** N **PH:** unk **SS:** NSSAR Ancestor #P-319429 **BS:** JLARC 36.

WICKLIFF(E) (WYCLIFFE), Arrington (Aaron); b c1752; d unk **RU:** Private, Served in 2nd VA Regt 3 yrs under Capt Davis & Lt Tyler in 8th Regt at Baltimore. Was in Battles of Brandywine, Germantown, Monmouth. Believed to have served under Gen Daniel Morgan in 1776 with brothers **CEM:** Wickliff Family; GPS 38.46243, -77.24409; Behind 13220 Yates Ford Rd, Clifton; Fairfax **GS:** Y **SP:** Catherine Davis **VI:** DAR gr marker in Cem and Gov't Gr Stone **P:** unk **BLW:** unk **RG:** Y **MK:** Y **PH:** unk **SS:** AK **BS:** JLARC 1, 2, 13, 14, 27.

WICKLIFF(E) (WYCLIFFE), Moses; b unk; d 13 Feb 1796 **RU:** Private, Served in 2nd VA Regt 3 yrs under Capt Davis & Lt Tyler in 8th Regt at Baltimore. Was in Battles of Brandywine, Germantown, Monmouth. Believed to have served under Gen Daniel Morgan in 1776 with brothers **CEM:** Wickliff

RU=Rank/Unit CEM=Cemetery GS=Gravestone SP=Spousal Information
VI=Other Veteran Info P=Pension BLW=Bounty/Land Warrant RG=Registered Grave
MK=SAR/DAR Marker PH=Photo SS=Service Source BS=Burial Source

361

Family; GPS 38.46243, -77.24409; Behind 13220 Yates Ford Rd, Clifton; Fairfax **GS:** Y **SP:** No info **VI:** DAR gr marker in cem and Gov't gr stone **P:** unk **BLW:** unk **RG:** Y **MK:** Y **PH:** Y **SS:** AK **BS:** JLARC 1,2,13, 14, 27.

WIDENER, Michael; b 1 Jun 1758, Rockingham Co; d 12 Apr 1843 **RU:** Private, Served in VA Line **CEM:** Pleasant View; GPS 36.68670, -81.74970; Vic jct Rts 801 & 605, Glade Spring; Washington **GS:** U **SP:** Mar (13 Jan 1823-1825, Washington Co) Elizabeth Callahan **VI:** Son of John & Elizabeth (Worrell) Widner. Soldier appl pen 26 Nov 1832, widow appl pen 28 Jun 1853 W8303. Widow appl BLW in 1855 # 26617-160-55 **P:** Y **BLW:** Y **RG:** unk **MK:** unk **PH:** unk **SS:** CG pg 3821 **BS:** 196.

WIDENER, Samuel; b unk; d 1833 **RU:** Sergeant, Served in Capt Thomas Church Co, Col Wayne's PA Battalion 1776 **CEM:** Widener's Valley; GPS unk; Cem #239 in Source 80; Washington **GS:** U **SP:** No info **VI:** DAR marker placed by Ft Chiswell Chapt at foot of crude native stone **P:** unk **BLW:** unk **RG:** unk **MK:** Y **PH:** unk **SS:** NSSAR Ancestor #P-319509; A pg 196 **BS:** JLARC 80.

WIGGINTON, John; b c1758, Prince William Co; d 19 Aug 1843 **RU:** Private, Served in Cont Line in Capt George Hardy's Co, Lee's Partison Legion. Ent serv again Prince William Co 1780 **CEM:** Wigginton Family; GPS unk; Off Rt 7, Huddleston; Bedford **GS:** Y **SP:** Mar (6 Sep 1787 Bedford Co) Margaret McGeorge (c1764 Hanover Co-17 Oct 1851) **VI:** Sol appl pen 14 Jun 1828 Bedford Co. Widow appl pen 29 Nov 1843 Bedford Co. Patriot Pensioned 14 Jul 1828. Widow recd pension of $100 per yr. W6547. He perhaps is the person this name that drew BLW # 12673-100-14, 14 Jul 1792 **P:** Y **BLW:** unk **RG:** Y **MK:** N **PH:** unk **SS:** DAR Ancestor #A126013; SAR Ancestor #P-319589; J-NSSAR 2000 Reg; K Vol 6 pg 135; CG Vol 3 pg 3823, 3825 **BS:** JLARC 4, 36, 76.

WIGGINTON, John Sr; b 1741; d 27 Apr 1825 **RU:** Patriot, Gave material aid to cause. Served as Tax Assessor 1783 **CEM:** Wigginton; GPS unk; Rt 29, Lakota; Culpeper **GS:** Y **SP:** Elizabeth Botts (__-15 Jul 1824) **VI:** No further data **P:** N **BLW:** N **RG:** Y **MK:** N **PH:** unk **SS:** D Vol 1 pg 267; E pg 826 **BS:** 29, pg 28; 33.

WILCOX, John; b unk; d 1781 **RU:** Soldier, Served fr NY, and killed in the battle at Yorktown **CEM:** Yorktown Victory Monument Tablet; GPS 38.28350, -78.54150; Yorktown; York **GS:** U **SP:** No info **VI:** No further data **P:** unk **BLW:** unk **RG:** unk **MK:** unk **PH:** unk **SS:** J-Yorktown Historian **BS:** JLARC 74.

WILHOITE (WILHOIT), Daniel; b c1744, Orange Co; d Bef 1796 **RU:** Private?, Listed in Culpeper Classes 1781, VA Militia **CEM:** Wilhoite Family; GPS unk; Hebron Valley; Madison **GS:** N **SP:** Mary Blankenbeckler (c1747-__) d/o Michael & Elizabeth Barbara (Gaar) Blankenbaker **VI:** Son of John & Margaret (Weaver) Wilhoit **P:** unk **BLW:** unk **RG:** Y **MK:** N **PH:** N **SS:** See BS 04 **BS:** 04.

WILHOITE (WILHOIT), John; b c1745, Orange Co; d 1820 **RU:** Private, Listed in Culpeper Classes 1781, VA Militia **CEM:** Wilhoite Family; GPS unk; Hebron Valley; Madison **GS:** N **SP:** Mary Fishback (__-1838 Madison Co) d/o Harman & Kathrina (-----) Fishback **VI:** Son of John & Margaret (Weaver) Wilhoit **P:** unk **BLW:** unk **RG:** Y **MK:** N **PH:** N **SS:** See BS 29 pg 41 **BS:** 04.

WILKINS, Willis; b 1 Feb 1757; d 4 Apr 1815 **RU:** Patriot, Gave material aid to cause **CEM:** Deer Crossing; GPS unk; Adjacent to 2017 Coral Ivy Ln; Chesapeake City **GS:** Y **SP:** No info **VI:** Was Capt of the Sliver Greys fr Deep Creek during War of 1812 **P:** N **BLW:** N **RG:** N **MK:** N **PH:** unk **SS:** H Public Servant **BS:** 75 Portsmouth; 196.

WILKINSON, John; b 8 Feb 1757, Sussex Co; d 23 Jan 1823 **RU:** Private, Served in 4th Co, 3rd VA Regt, Baylor's Dragoons **CEM:** Salem Methodist; GPS unk; 19312 Templeton Rd; Prince George **GS:** Y **SP:** Martha "Patsey" Rives (1767 Sussex Co-1829) **VI:** Gov't Gr Stone **P:** N **BLW:** unk **RG:** unk **MK:** N **PH:** unk **SS:** NSSAR Ancestor #P-320287 **BS:** JLARC 116; 196.

WILKINSON, Thomas; b unk; d Jun 1790 **RU:** Private, Served in 15th VA Regt **CEM:** Old Christ Church Episcopal; GPS 38.80625, -77.04718; 118 N Washington St; Alexandria City **GS:** N **SP:** Sarah (-----); **VI:** Burial permit issued 4 Jun 1790. Widow pensioned file # not determined **P:** Y **BLW:** unk **RG:** Y **MK:** N **PH:** N **SS:** G pg 722 **BS:** 20 pg 154.

WILKINSON, William; b 1745; d 1823 **RU:** Private, Served in VA Line, 6th VA Regt. Ent serv Greensville Co. Served in Illinois **CEM:** Wilkinson Family; GPS unk; Rt 610, Gold Hill; Buckingham **GS:**

RU=Rank/Unit   CEM=Cemetery   GS=Gravestone   SP=Spousal Information
VI=Other Veteran Info   P=Pension   BLW=Bounty/Land Warrant   RG=Registered Grave
MK=SAR/DAR Marker   PH=Photo   SS=Service Source   BS=Burial Source

362

Y **SP:** No info **VI:** Plaque on remnants of old stone **P:** unk **BLW:** unk **RG:** unk **MK:** Y **PH:** unk **SS:** B; E pg 829; CG Vol 3 pg 3841; BY **BS:** JLARC 59;196.

WILKISON, William Sr; b Jun 1766; d 11 Mar 1857 **RU:** Private?, Served in a VA unit in Illinois **CEM:** North Fork Baptist; GPS 39.06014, -77.68509; 38130 North Folk Rd, North Fork; Loudoun **GS:** Y **SP:** No info **VI:** No further data **P:** unk **BLW:** unk **RG:** Y **MK:** N **PH:** unk **SS:** E pg 829 **BS:** 25, pg 341.

WILKS, Samuel; b 24 Oct 1761, Loudoun Co; d 1 Jul 1837 **RU:** Soldier, Ent Serv Bedford Co 1780-1781 in VA Line **CEM:** Wilks Family; GPS unk; Nr Leftwich Church; Bedford City **GS:** U **SP:** 1) Elizabeth (-----) 2) Mar (11 Oct 1826 Bedford Co by Rev William Leftwich) Margaret Witt (c1785 or c1789-before 1 Nov 1858) **VI:** Sol appl pen 28 Mar 1833 Bedford Co. Widow appl pen 21 Jan 1854 age 65 (in 1857 said she was 72.) R11553 **P:** Y **BLW:** unk **RG:** unk **MK:** N **PH:** unk **SS:** SAR Ancestor #P-320297; K Vol 6 pg 139; CG Vol 3 pg 3841 **BS:** JLARC 4, 36.

WILLIAMS, James; b 1758, "Cedar Farm" Culpeper Co; d 22 Mar 1822 **RU:** Captain, Was 2nd Lt 10th VA Regt Dec 1776; 1st Lt 18 Mar 1777; and Capt 2 Jan 1778, Regt 6th VA. Appointed Capt 19 Sep 1778 & served to close of war. Served also in 8th and 10th VA Regt **CEM:** Williams Family, "Soldier's Rest Farm"; GPS unk; Rt 620; Orange **GS:** Y **SP:** 1) Eleanor Green 2) Elizabeth Bruce (4 Feb 1777 "Soldier's Rest" Orange Co-1823 Orange Co) d/o Charles & Frances (Stubblefield) Bruce. She mar (3 Jun 1795) James Williams as his second wife. She is bur at Soldiers Rest Plantation Grounds, Orange Co. **VI:** Son of William & Lucy (Clayton) Williams. Was an original member of the Society of the Cincinatti. Served as a Maj General of Miltia in War of 1812. Recd BLW 2 Oct 1807 of 5054 acres. Died at "Soldier's Rest" Orange Co **P:** unk **BLW:** Y **RG:** Y **MK:** unk **PH:** unk **SS:** E pg 83; CG Vol 3 pg 3857 **BS:** JLARC 1, 98.

WILLIAMS, James; b unk; d 21 Jul 1818 **RU:** Major/Patriot, Was staff officer in brigade. Gave material aid to cause **CEM:** Blandford; GPS 37.22433, -77.38604; 319 S Crater Rd; Petersburg City **GS:** Y **SP:** No info **VI:** Member VA Society of Cincinati **P:** Y **BLW:** unk **RG:** unk **MK:** N **PH:** Y **SS:** E pg 831; G ps 407, 676, 714, 879; AL Comm Bk IV pg 256 Prince George Co **BS:** 196.

WILLIAMS, James; b unk; d 1781 **RU:** Sergeant, Served fr MA, and died fr the Battle at Yorktown **CEM:** Yorktown Victory Monument Tablet; GPS 38.28350, -78.54150; Yorktown; York **GS:** U **SP:** No info **VI:** No further data **P:** unk **BLW:** unk **RG:** unk **MK:** unk **PH:** unk **SS:** J-Yorktown Historian **BS:** JLARC 74.

WILLIAMS, James Mastin; b 23 Sept 1763, Pittsylvania Co (then Hallifax); d 12 Jan 1838 **RU:** Private, Ent serv PA 1781 for brother John Williams. Served at Battle of Guilford CH, Feb 1781. Discharged Rockingham Co, NC. Reinlisted for brother in Capt William Dix's Co, under Col Nathaniel Cocke, Gen Stephens Brigade. Discharged Mar 1781 at Ramsey's Mill, Deep River. Guarded British prisoners under Capt Morton **CEM:** Williams Family; GPS unk; SR 698 Cliff Hetzel Farm, Pickway; Pittsylvania **GS:** Y **SP:** Mar (2 Dec 1784) Wilmouth or Wilmoth, d/o (-----) & Catharine Walker (Oct 1768-__) She was living in PA in 1845 & 1849. **VI:** Sol appl pen 6 Sep 1832, Pittsylvania Co. Widow appl pen 14 Oct 1840 Pittsylvania Co. W6505 **P:** Y **BLW:** unk **RG:** Y **MK:** unk **PH:** unk **SS:** J-NSSAR 2000 Reg; K Vol 6 pg 146; CG Vol 3 pg 3857 **BS:** 174; JLARC 76.

WILLIAMS, John; b 1747 Studley, Hanover Co; d 30 Apr 1795 **RU:** Patriot, Gave material aid to cause **CEM:** Williams-Knight Family; GPS unk; Vic jct Rt 623 & Eubanks Rd; Lunenberg **GS:** U **SP:** Mar (4 Jan 1768 Charlotte Co) Frances Hughes **VI:** Son of Joseph (1720-1792) & Henrietta (Jouett) Williams (1727-1778). One of earliest Baptist ministers of Lunenberg, Charlotte and Mecklenberg. He and father founded Meherrin Baptist Church when no other Baptist church existed in these counties. Died at Ft Mitchell, Lunenberg Co **P:** N **BLW:** N **RG:** unk **MK:** unk **PH:** unk **SS:** AK Ct Bk pg 25 Lunenburg Co **BS:** 196.

WILLIAMS, Joseph; b 1748; d Aft 29 Jun 1829 **RU:** Patriot, Gave beef to cause **CEM:** Morgan Family; GPS 36.76690, -81.43750; 1.5 mi fr Teas on private rd beyond Rt 601; Smyth **GS:** Y **SP:** Catherine E (-----) (1751-1823) **VI:** No further data **P:** N **BLW:** N **RG:** Y **MK:** N **PH:** unk **SS:** AS SAR regis; D Vol 2 pg 599 **BS:** SAR reg; 196.

WILLIAMS, Richard; b 1730, Bucks Co, PA; d Aft 9 May 1797 **RU:** Patriot, Gave material aid to cause **CEM:** Morgan; GPS unk; Rye Valley; Smyth **GS:** U **SP:** Mar (3rd 12 Dec 1772, Northampton Co) Margaret Nottingham (c1752-1 Oct 1810, Mathews Co) **VI:** Appears widow moved body fr Gloucester

RU=Rank/Unit	CEM=Cemetery	GS=Gravestone	SP=Spousal Information
VI=Other Veteran Info	P=Pension	BLW=Bounty/Land Warrant	RG=Registered Grave
MK=SAR/DAR Marker	PH=Photo	SS=Service Source	BS=Burial Source

363

Co to her cemetery in Mathews Co or he is memorialized there **P:** N **BLW:** N **RG:** unk **MK**: unk **PH:** unk **SS:** DAR Ancestor #A13400; NSSAR Ancestor #P-321027 **BS:** JLARC 114.

WILLIAMS, Samuel; b unk; d 19 May 1789 **RU:** Patriot, Gave material aid in Gloucester Co **CEM:** Williams Family; GPS 38.56808, -77.33511; Williams Wharf; Mathews **GS:** Y **SP:** No info **VI:** Died in Kingston Parish, Gloucester Co **P:** N **BLW:** N **RG:** N **MK:** N **PH:** unk **SS:** AL Ct Bk pg iii,9 **BS:** 48 pg 141.

WILLIAMS, Sarah; b c1741; d 13 Jul 1812 **RU:** Patriot, Gave a beef and contributed material support to the cause **CEM:** Dumfries Public; GPS 38.34110, -77.19964; 17821 Mine Rd, Dumfries; Prince William **GS:** Y **SP:** No info **VI:** SAR monument **P:** N **BLW:** N **RG:** Y **MK:** Y **PH:** Y **SS:** D Vol 3 pg 808 **BS:** 04.

WILLIAMS, Thomas; b 1745; d Bef Oct 1784 **RU:** Major, Gave material aid to cause. Served as Grand Juror and Overseer of Roads **CEM:** Williams Family; GPS 38.56808, -77.33511; See 1938 DAR Senate doc 10448, vol 2; Nottoway **GS:** U **SP:** Alice (-----) **VI:** No further data **P:** unk **BLW:** unk **RG:** unk **MK**: unk **PH:** unk **SS:** J- DAR Hatcher; DN pg 409, 411 **BS:** JLARC 2.

WILLIAMS, Thomas S; b 4 May 1762, Kingston Parish, Gloucester Co; d 19 Aug 1823 **RU:** Private, Served in Gloucester Co Militia under Capt John Billups **CEM:** Williams Family; GPS 38.56808, -77.33511; Williams Wharf; Mathews **GS:** Y **SP:** 1) Mar (15 Jun 1793) Susannah Billups (__-1804) 2) mar (18 Oct 1804) Mary Lilly Billups (21 Jan 1785 Kingston Parish, Gloucester Co-23 Jun 1857 Mathews Co) d/o Joseph & Joice (Respess) Billups **VI:** Son of Samuel & Sarah (Haggoman) Williams. **P:** unk **BLW:** unk **RG:** N **MK:** N **PH:** unk **SS:** E pg 833 **BS:** 134 pg 8; 196.

WILLIAMS, William M; b unk; d 1801 **RU:** Private, Served in Gloucester Co Militia under Capt John Billups **CEM:** Williams Family; GPS 38.56808, -77.33511; Williams Wharf; Mathews **GS:** Y **SP:** No info **VI:** No further data **P:** unk **BLW:** unk **RG:** Y **MK:** N **PH:** unk **SS:** N pg 1264 **BS:** 48 pg 140.

WILLIS, Lewis; b 11 Nov 1734; d 15 Jan 1813 **RU:** Colonel, Lt Col in Caroline District Bn Feb-Sep 1776. Was commander of 10th VA Regt **CEM:** Willis Hill, Fredericksburg National Military Park; GPS unk; Marye Heights; Fredericksburg City **GS:** N **SP:** 1) Mary Champe 2) Elizabeth Carter **VI:** Died in Spotsylvania Co. Listed on grave stone of Col Byrd C Willis, thus probably his son **P:** unk **BLW:** unk **RG:** Y **MK:** N **PH:** N **SS:** H; CE pg 15 **BS:** 08 vol 3 pg 416.

WILLOUGHBY, William; b 1758; d 14 Jun 1800 **RU:** Ensign/Patriot, Signer of Leedstown Resolutions in 1766. Served in Capt James Dysart's Co of Light Horse, Col William Campbells Regt May 1781 **CEM:** St Paul's Episcopal; GPS 36.84733, -76.28554; 201 St Paul's Blvd; Norfolk City **GS:** Y **SP:** Margaret (-----) (1766-11 Jan 1827) **VI:** No further data **P:** unk **BLW:** unk **RG:** Y **MK:** N **PH:** unk **SS:** N pg 1252 **BS:** 87 pg 31; 196.

WILLSON, John Sr; b c1749; d 12 Jul 1826 **RU:** Corporal, Served in 9th Cont Line **CEM:** Second Concord Presbyterian; GPS 37.34209, -78.96585; Phoebe Pond Rd Rt 609 E of Concord; Appomattox **GS:** Y **SP:** Elizabeth (-----) (c1748-22 Nov 1814) **VI:** Died age 77 **P:** unk **BLW:** unk **RG:** unk **MK**: unk **PH:** unk **SS:** E pg 835 **BS:** 196; 199.

WILLSON, Matthew; b Augusta Co; d 1825 **RU:** Patriot, Gave material aid to cause **CEM:** Bethel Presbyterian; GPS 38.04257, -79.17283; 563 Bethel Green Rd, Middlebrook; Augusta **GS:** U **SP:** No info **VI:** Son of James & Rebecca (-----) Willson **P:** N **BLW:** N **RG:** unk **MK:** unk **PH:** unk **SS:** AL Comm Bk II pg 360 Augusta Co **BS:** 196.

WILLSON, Moses; b 1754; d 4 Mar 1826 **RU:** Private?/Patriot, Capt Charles Campbell's Co, Augusta Co Militia. Patriot service as Constable, Augusta Co 1 Jul 1778 **CEM:** New Providence Presbyterian; GPS 37.95170, -79.30250; 1208 New Providence Rd, Raphine; Rockbridge **GS:** Y **SP:** Elizabeth (-----) (__-1837) **VI:** Son of James (1717-1801) & Rebeccal (-----) (1728-1820) Willson **P:** unk **BLW:** unk **RG:** unk **MK:** unk **PH:** unk **SS:** E pg 836 **BS:** 196.

WILLSON, William; b 6 Nov 1745; d 13 Dec 1832 **RU:** Major, Ent serv Augusta Co 1774 & served at Battle of Point Pleasant. Ent serv again Augusta Co 1776 & served in seige of Jamestown **CEM:** Willson Family; GPS 38.07283, -79.12096; Rt 697 White Oak Gap Rd, W of Rt 11, Mint Spring; Augusta **GS:** U **SP:** Margaret Kerr Shields **VI:** Was pensioned 1832 Augusta Co where he had always lived. S6393 **P:** Y **BLW:** unk **RG:** unk **MK:** N **PH:** unk **SS:** K Vol 6 pg 164 **BS:** JLARC 62; 196.

RU=Rank/Unit	CEM=Cemetery	GS=Gravestone	SP=Spousal Information
VI=Other Veteran Info	P=Pension	BLW=Bounty/Land Warrant	RG=Registered Grave
MK=SAR/DAR Marker	PH=Photo	SS=Service Source	BS=Burial Source

WILLSON (WILSON), John; b 1753, PA; d 19 Jun 1826 **RU:** Major, Was 2nd Lt Rockbridge Co Militia, 4 Aug 1778 and was Maj Augusta Co Militia in 2nd Bn 20 Mar 1781 **CEM:** New Providence Presbyterian; GPS 37.95170, -79.30250; 1208 New Providence Rd, Raphine; Rockbridge **GS:** Y **SP:** Rachel Downey **VI:** Delegate to VA Legislature 1797. Sheriff 1811; Justice 1795-1801 **P:** unk **BLW:** unk **RG:** unk **MK:** Y **PH:** unk **SS:** NSSAR Ancestor #P-321925 **BS:** 196.

WILMER, William Holland; b 9 Mar 1734 Chester Towne, MD; d 24 Jul 1827 **RU:** Private, Served in MD Militia **CEM:** Bruton Parish Church; GPS 37.27127, -76.70248; 331 W Duke of Gloucester St; Williamsburg City **GS:** Y **SP:** Marion Hannah Cox (1796-15 Sep 1821 Alexandria) **VI:** Was President of William & Mary College; Rector of Bruton Parish Church **P:** unk **BLW:** unk **RG:** N **MK:** N **PH:** unk **SS:** BJ pg 106 **BS:** 170 Bruton; 196.

WILSON, Abraham Sr; b King & Queen Co; d Apr 1793 **RU:** Private, Served in Spotsylvania Co Militia **CEM:** Clark-Jayne; GPS unk; Jonesville; Lee **GS:** U **SP:** Mar (c1768 Botetourt Co) Catherine Livingston (1760-1815) **VI:** Died in Smyth Co **P:** unk **BLW:** unk **RG:** unk **MK:** unk **PH:** unk **SS:** E pg 836 **BS:** 196.

WILSON, Daniel; b 1735; d 1807 **RU:** Ensign, In Jan 1781 served in Capt Charles Wall's Co at Cabin Point and then at Portsmouth under General Mullenberg **CEM:** Old Monmouth Presbyterian; GPS 37.80810, -79.47280; Jct Rts 60 & 669; Lexington City **GS:** Y **SP:** No info **VI:** No further data **P:** unk **BLW:** unk **RG:** N **MK:** N **PH:** unk **SS:** AZ pg 161-2 **BS:** 154 Rockbridge.

WILSON, David; b c1740; d 4 Feb 1820 **RU:** Sergeant, Capt William Henshaw's Co, Col Wm Craford's Regt fr Frederick Co in Oct 1774 at Ft Charlotte **CEM:** Long-Stephens; GPS unk; Stephens City; Frederick **GS:** Y **SP:** Mar (11 March 1783 Frederick Co by Rev John Montgomery) Mary Henning (4 Aug 1766-14 Apr 1843) **VI:** Oldest graveyard in Stevens City. Cemetery also known as Long-Stephens **P:** unk **BLW:** unk **RG:** Y **MK:** N **PH:** unk **SS:** Z pg 53 **BS:** 122; 59, pg 355.

WILSON, Elibabb (Eli); b c1755, Augusta Co; d 11 Nov 1845 **RU:** Soldier, Ent serv Pendleton Co 1776 & 1781 at Bull Pasture **CEM:** Unidentified; GPS 37.96151, -79.71000; Nr Doe Hill; Highland **GS:** U **SP:** No info **VI:** Pen 1832 Pendleton Co age 77. Bur in Highland Co which was formed in 1842 fr Pendleton & Bath Cos **P:** Y **BLW:** unk **RG:** Y **MK:** unk **PH:** unk **SS:** K Vol 6 pg 167 **BS:** JLARC 76.

WILSON, Hugh; b 1740; d 1809 **RU:** Lieutenant, Was commissioned Lt 1 Apr 1783. Served in Capt Samuel McDowell's Co of Rockbridge Co and also in Frederick Co Militia, **CEM:** Old Monmouth Presbyterian; GPS 37.80810, -79.47280; Jct Rts 60 & 669; Lexington City **GS:** Y **SP:** No info **VI:** No further data **P:** unk **BLW:** unk **RG:** N **MK:** N **PH:** unk **SS:** E pg 836 **BS:** 154 Rockbridge.

WILSON, James; b 22 Dec 1739; d 6 Aug 1824 **RU:** Patriot, Gave material aid to the cause **CEM:** Sharon Lutheran; GPS 37.05800, -81.20590; Rt 42 W of Ceres; Bland **GS:** Y **SP:** Elizabeth Poage (1739-12 May 1824) **VI:** No further data **P:** N **BLW:** N **RG:** Y **MK:** N **PH:** unk **SS:** AL Ct Bk pg 10 **BS:** 60, Bland Co; 196.

WILSON, James; b unk; d 1799 **RU:** Patriot, Gave material aid to the cause **CEM:** St Paul's Episcopal; GPS 36.84733, -76.28554; 201 St Paul's Blvd; Norfolk City **GS:** Y **SP:** No info **VI:** No further data **P:** N **BLW:** N **RG:** Y **MK:** N **PH:** unk **SS:** AL Ct Bk pg 3, 28 **BS:** 87 pg 31.

WILSON, James; b 1760; d 1818 **RU:** Sergeant, Served Oct 1779 in 6th VA Regt **CEM:** St John's Episcopal; GPS 37.53183, -77.41958; 2401 E Broad St; Richmond City **GS:** Y **SP:** No info **VI:** No further data **P:** unk **BLW:** unk **RG:** N **MK:** N **PH:** unk **SS:** AP **BS:** 28 pg 516.

WILSON, James; b 1767; d 9 Jul 1805 **RU:** Soldier, SAR registry did not provide service **CEM:** Old Presbyterian Meeting House; GPS 38.48528, -77.23532; 323 S Fairfax St; Alexandria City **GS:** N **SP:** Eliza John Taylor, d/o Jesse & (-----) Taylor **VI:** Died of fever age 38 (Alexandria Gazette, 10 Jul 1805, pg 2). Merchant of Alexandria. Listed on SAR plaque in cemetery **P:** unk **BLW:** unk **RG:** Y **MK:** Y **PH:** N **SS:** J-NSSAR 1993 Reg; AK **BS:** JLARC 1; 23 pg 110; 196.

WILSON, James R; b unk; d 17 Aug 1819 **RU:** US Navy, Specific service in the Navy not determined **CEM:** Arlington National; GPS 38.88377, -77.06535; Jefferson Davis Hwy Rt 110; Arlington **GS:** N **SP:** No info **VI:** Findagrave indicates he was in the US Navy but lists no birth year or gravestone, thus could be War of 1812 veteran not Rev War veteran **P:** unk **BLW:** unk **RG:** Y **MK:** unk **PH:** N **SS:** J-NSSAR 2000 Reg; NSSAR Ancestor # P-321856 **BS:** JLARC 76; 196.

RU=Rank/Unit	CEM=Cemetery	GS=Gravestone	SP=Spousal Information
VI=Other Veteran Info	P=Pension	BLW=Bounty/Land Warrant	RG=Registered Grave
MK=SAR/DAR Marker	PH=Photo	SS=Service Source	BS=Burial Source

WILSON, John; b 1740, Pittsylvania Co; d 21 May 1820 **RU:** Colonel/Patriot, Served in Pittsylvania Co Militia 1777-78. Gave material aid to cause **CEM:** Dan's Hill; **GPS** unk; Danville at Wilson's ferry; Danville City **GS:** Y **SP:** Mar (2 Apr 1767) Mary Lumpkin (1749 King & Queen Co-4 Jan 1827) **VI:** Son of Peter of the Ferry Farm. Was County Lt (in charge of all military affairs for the county) fr 1779 until end of Rev War. In 1783 was member of Constitutional Convention. Died in Pittsylvania Co **P:** unk **BLW:** unk **RG:** Y **MK:** N **PH:** unk **SS:** E pg 836; AL Ct Bk pg 18, 60 Pittsylvania Co **BS:** 81 Chart.

WILSON, John; b Dec 1732, , Chester Co, PA; d 21 Jan 1820 **RU:** Major, Took oath as Maj 20 Mar 1781 Augusta Co Militia **CEM:** Stony Run; GPS 38.22920, -79.7003; US Rt 220, N of jct with 607; Highland **GS:** Y **SP:** 1) Isabella Seawright, 2) Mar (1785) Sally Alexander **VI:** Son of William & Barbara (McKane) Wilson of Dublin, Ireland. Gov't Gr St **P:** unk **BLW:** unk **RG:** unk **MK:** unk **PH:** unk **SS:** E pg 837; AZ pg 185 **BS:** 196.

WILSON, John; b 1748; d 1826 **RU:** Soldier, Served in Cont Line **CEM:** Old Concord Presbyterian; GPS unk; Rt 648, Concord; Campbell **GS:** N **SP:** Mar (18 Mar 1793 Pittsylvania Co) Sarah Lynch **VI:** No further data **P:** unk **BLW:** unk **RG:** unk **MK:** N **PH:** N **SS:** NSSAR Ancestor # P-321917 **BS:** JLARC 36.

WILSON, John Sr; b 1753, Staunton; d 23 Sep 1799 **RU:** Colonel/Patriot, Took oath as Maj in Militia 20 Mar 1781. Gave material aid to cause **CEM:** Glebe Burying Ground; GPS 38.10940, -79.22190; Glebe School Rd Rt 876, Swoopes; Augusta **GS:** U **SP:** Mar (25 Oct 1775) Druscilla Swearington (1755-1826 KY) **VI:** Son of George (1728 Scotland-Feb 1777 NJ) & Elizabeth Crawford (McCreavy) (__Scotland-__) Wilson **P:** unk **BLW:** unk **RG:** Y **MK:** N **PH:** unk **SS:** E pg 837; AL Cert 3 Augusta Co **BS:** 80 vol 4 pg 203; AR.

WILSON, Nathaniel; b 1764; d 5 Apr 1803 **RU:** Patriot, Mended uniforms for Capt John Edmonds Co at Norfolk **CEM:** Wilson Family; GPS unk; 701 Saunders Rd, City Prison Farms, St Brides Plantation; Chesapeake City **GS:** U **SP:** Margaret Bartee (1 Dec 1768-6 Jan 1816) d/o Thomas & Ann (Keeling) Bartee **VI:** Son of Malichi & Lidia (-----) Wilson **P:** N **BLW:** N **RG:** Y **MK:** N **PH:** N **SS:** G pg 521 **BS:** 63 pg 97; 196.

WILSON, Richard; b Dec 1762, Caroline Co; d 1836 **RU:** Orderly Sergeant, Ent serv Caroline Co 1779. Served in VA Line as Orderly Sgt **CEM:** Wilson Family, R.L. Bowling Property; GPS unk; Rt 659; Amherst **GS:** U **SP:** No info **VI:** Moved to Amherst Co in 1796. Appl pen 23 Aug 1832 Amherst Co. S6416 **P:** Y **BLW:** unk **RG:** unk **MK:** unk **PH:** unk **SS:** K Vol 6 pg 173; CG Vol 3 pg 3894 **BS:** JLARC 4, 7.

WILSON, Robert; b unk; d unk **RU:** Colonel/Patriot, Gave material aid to cause **CEM:** Wilson; GPS unk; Dans Hill; Danville City **GS:** U **SP:** 1) Ruth Hairston 2) Catherine Ann Pannill **VI:** Son of John (1740-1820) & Mary (Lumpkin) Wilson. Died in Pittsylvania Co **P:** unk **BLW:** unk **RG:** unk **MK:** unk **PH:** unk **SS:** AL Ct Bk pg 11 Henry Co **BS:** 196.

WILSON, Samuel; b 16 Apr 1750; d 6 Apr 1826 **RU:** Captain, Commanded a company in Augusta Co Militia,and served at Battle of Point Pleasant Oct 1774 **CEM:** Old Providence; GPS 37.96151, -79.71000; 1005 Spottswood Rd, Spottswood; Augusta **GS:** Y **SP:** Mary Wilson (1759-23 Jul 1819). Shared stone with husband **VI:** Name on SAR plaque at cemetery **P:** unk **BLW:** unk **RG:** unk **MK:** Y **PH:** unk **SS:** Z pg 101; BT **BS:** JLARC 2, 8 ,62, 63, 79; 196.

WILSON, Samuel; b 1735, Northern Ireland; d Nov 1807 **RU:** Soldier, Served in Capt Adam Clemson's Co, Bedford Co Militia **CEM:** Old Monmouth Presbyterian; GPS 37.80810, -79.47280; Jct Rts 60 & 669; Rockbridge **GS:** U **SP:** Mar (1788) Mary Mackey (1737-1820) **VI:** Will veriies death year and place **P:** unk **BLW:** unk **RG:** unk **MK:** unk **PH:** unk **SS:** E pg 837 **BS:** 196.

WILSON, Thomas; b unk; d 1830 **RU:** Corporal, Served in Col Daniel Morgan's Regt **CEM:** Goose Creek; GPS 39.11250, -77.69527; Rt 722, Lincoln; Loudoun **GS:** Y **SP:** No info **VI:** No further data **P:** N **BLW:** N **RG:** unk **MK:** unk **PH:** unk **SS:** E pg 837 **BS:** 196.

WILSON, Thomas; b 1727; d 1800 **RU:** Patriot, Gave material aid to the cause **CEM:** Old Monmouth Presbyterian; GPS 37.80810, -79.47280; Jct Rts 60 & 669; Lexington City **GS:** Y **SP:** No info **VI:** No further data **P:** N **BLW:** N **RG:** N **MK:** N **PH:** unk **SS:** AL Ct Bk pg 2, 4 **BS:** 154 Old Mon'th.

RU=Rank/Unit	CEM=Cemetery	GS=Gravestone	SP=Spousal Information
VI=Other Veteran Info	P=Pension	BLW=Bounty/Land Warrant	RG=Registered Grave
MK=SAR/DAR Marker	PH=Photo	SS=Service Source	BS=Burial Source

366

WILSON, Wallis; b c1755; d Jul 1846 **RU:** Private, Served in VA Line. Ent serv Halifax Co in VA Regt 1781. Served at Siege of Yorktown. Served in Capts Standfield, Wall, Powell, Gains, and Faulkner's Cos, Col Peter Rodger's Regt **CEM:** Wallis Wilson Family; GPS unk; By Rt 737, 4 mi fr Mecklenburg line; Halifax **GS:** Y **SP:** 1) Mar (c1785) Rebecca Wall (__-1812) 2) Mar (12 Jun 1812) Sarah Wade (1775-__) **VI:** Appl pen 19 Dec 1832 age 76 or 77. S6418 **P:** Y **BLW:** unk **RG:** Y **MK:** N **PH:** Y **SS:** SAR Ancestor #P-322129; K Vol 4 pg 175; CG Vol 3 pg 3897 **BS:** SAR regis; 196.

WILSON, William; b 1 Aug 1751; d 1 Dec 1835 **RU:** Captain, Commanded a company Augusta Co Militia 15 Apr 1783 **CEM:** Augusta Stone Presbyterian; GPS 38.23926, -78.97356; 28 Old Stone Church Ln, Ft Defiance; Augusta **GS:** U **SP:** 1) Isabella Larrabee 2) Mar (14 Jun 1786) Elizabeth Poage (c1768-1 Dec 1835) d/o Thomas (1740-24 Dec 1803) & Agnes (McClanahan) (__-19 Sep 1792) Poage **VI:** Obtained the rank of major after the war period. Second pastor of Presbyterian Stone Church fr 1780-1810. Appl pen 25 Sep 1832 Augusta Co. S6393. On plaque to pastors on Augusta Stone Church. Discrepency on birth date and yr **P:** Y **BLW:** unk **RG:** unk **MK:** unk **PH:** unk **SS:** SAR Ancestor #P-322165; E pg 837; CG Vol 3 pg 3883 **BS:** JLARC 8;196.

WILSON, William; b c1765 or 1760, or 6 Dec 1761, Norfolk Co; d 19 Jul 1838 **RU:** Captain, Served in 11th Regt VA Line. Was taken prisoner 7 Jul 1777 **CEM:** Cedar Grove; GPS 36.57204, -80.02599; 301 Fort Lane Rd; Portsmouth City **GS:** Y **SP:** Nancy Wormington (1765-26 Jan 1840) **VI:** Son of John & (-----) Wilson. Sol appl pen 19 May 1834 in Portsmouth, Norfolk Co. R11686. Govt grave stone. **P:** Y **BLW:** unk **RG:** Y **MK:** N **PH:** Y **SS:** C Sec 2 pg 214; CG Vol 3 pg 3899 **BS:** 27 pg 29; 196.

WILSON, William; b 1760; d 1824 **RU:** Private, Served in Capt Hugh Caperton's Co, New River Valley Men, Indian Wars (this would be in Rev War timeframe considering his age). Also probably the man of this name who served in Capt John Lewis's Co of Rangers **CEM:** Peterstown; GPS 37.39470, -80.80140; Off Rt 219 btw Peterstown & Midway, on WV state line; Giles **GS:** Y **SP:** Mar (23 Mar 1793) Mary Doak **VI:** Govt grave stone. **P:** N **BLW:** N **RG:** unk **MK:** unk **PH:** Y **SS:** Z pg 129 **BS:** 195.

WILSON, Willis; b 1748; d 1798 **RU:** Colonel, Had VA sea serv. Was Capt of the galley "Caswell." Served also in 5th Regt of Artillery **CEM:** Trinity Episcopal; GPS 36.83459, -76.30105; 500 Court St; Portsmouth City **GS:** U **SP:** No info **VI:** Pen granted 1845 to his son William of Norfolk. R109. Also VA 1/2 pay (see N.A. Acct #837 Va State Navy-YS File VA 1/2 Pay) Stone 57 in W.B. Butt inventory **P:** Y **BLW:** unk **RG:** unk **MK:** unk **PH:** unk **SS:** K Vol 6 pg 176; CG Vol 3 pg 3899 **BS:** JLARC 127.

WILSON, Willis; b 1757; d 1822 **RU:** Lieutenant, Served in Cumberland Co Militia **CEM:** Bonbrook House; GPS unk; 7.5 mi N of Cumberland; Cumberland **GS:** Y **SP:** No info **VI:** No further data **P:** unk **BLW:** unk **RG:** N **MK:** N **PH:** unk **SS:** E pg 838 **BS:** 157 Bonbrook.

WILSON (WILLSON), John; b 1753; d 19 Jun 1826 **RU:** Second Lieutenant, Served in Rockbridge Co Militia, 4 Aug 1778 **CEM:** New Providence Presbyterian; GPS 37.95130, -79.30250; 1208 New Providence Rd, Raphine; Rockbridge **GS:** U **SP:** Rachel Downey **VI:** Delegate to VA Legislature 1797 **P:** unk **BLW:** unk **RG:** Y **MK:** unk **PH:** unk **SS:** SAR Ancestor #P-321925; E pg 835 **BS:** JLARC 1, 63.

WINGFIELD, Charles; b 3 Dec 1728, Hanover Co; d 5 Dec 1803 **RU:** Patriot, Was signer of Albemarle Co Declaration of Independence 1779. Also gave material aid to cause **CEM:** Wingfield Family; GPS unk; 531 Woodlands Rd; Charlottesville City **GS:** U **SP:** Mar (27 Feb 1750, Hanover Co) Rachel Joyner (1728-__) **VI:** Son of John (c1695 New Kent Co-1700) & Martha (Hudson) (1704-1779) Wingfield **P:** N **BLW:** N **RG:** unk **MK:** unk **PH:** unk **SS:** DAR Ancestor #A128457; AL Cert Albemarle Co; CD **BS:** 196.

WINGFIELD, John; b 13 Feb 1742; d 7 Feb 1814 **RU:** Private/Patriot, Served in 10th Cont Line and Capt John Winston's Co, 14th Cont Line. Signed Albemarle Co Declaration of Independence **CEM:** Wingfield Family; GPS unk; Shepard Property, Slaughter Pen Creek; Charlottesville City **GS:** U **SP:** Mar (7 Mar 1764) Robina Langford (1747 Albemarle Co-1817) **VI:** No further data **P:** unk **BLW:** unk **RG:** unk **MK:** unk **PH:** unk **SS:** DAR Ancestor #A128478; SAR Ancestor #P-322508; E pg 839 **BS:** JLARC 58.

WINGFIELD, John M; b 6 May 1765; d 26 July 1849 **RU:** Private, Enl in Goochland Co **CEM:** Shepherd Family; GPS unk; Batesville; Albemarle **GS:** U **SP:** No info **VI:** Sol appl pen 22 May1845, Hanover Co # R11715 **P:** Y **BLW:** unk **RG:** unk **MK:** unk **PH:** unk **SS:** NSSAR Ancestor #P-322509 **BS:** JLARC 58; 196.

RU=Rank/Unit   CEM=Cemetery   GS=Gravestone   SP=Spousal Information
VI=Other Veteran Info   P=Pension   BLW=Bounty/Land Warrant   RG=Registered Grave
MK=SAR/DAR Marker   PH=Photo   SS=Service Source   BS=Burial Source

367

WINGFIELD, Thomas Jr; b 1750; d 1825 **RU:** Captain, Commanded a co in Hanover Co Militia **CEM:** Marl Ridge; GPS unk; Rt 54, Ashland; Hanover **GS:** Y **SP:** Rhoda Davis (1760-1830) **VI:** Son of John & Mary (Hudson) Winfield. One large stone with many names inscribed **P:** unk **BLW:** unk **RG:** Y **MK:** N **PH:** unk **SS:** E pg 839 **BS:** 31 vol 1 pg 91.

WINGFIELD, Thomas Sr; b 1740, Walnut Shade, Hanover Co; d 1830 **RU:** Patriot, Gave material aid to cause and signed a legislative petition **CEM:** Walnut Shade; GPS unk; Walnut Shade Ln off Rt 54; Hanover **GS:** U **SP:** Ann Davis (1754-1831) **VI:** Son of John (c1695) New Kent Co & Martha Hudson (1704-1779) Wingfield. Rev War service may pertain to individual with same name b 1750 in the county **P:** unk **BLW:** unk **RG:** unk **MK:** unk **PH:** unk **SS:** E pg 839; AL Cert 2 Hanover Co **BS:** 196.

WINGFIELD, Willam; b 28 Jul 1758; d 8 Mar 1836 **RU:** Patriot, Was signer of Albemarle Co Declaration of Independence 1779 **CEM:** Wingfield Family; GPS 36.84838, -79.78482; Off Bonfield Dr Rt 890; Franklin **GS:** U **SP:** Mary Wingfield, his first cousin **VI:** Son of Charles (1728-1803) & Rachel (Joyner) Wingfield **P:** N **BLW:** N **RG:** unk **MK:** unk **PH:** unk **SS:** CD **BS:** 196.

WINN, James; b 15 Apr 1757; d 14 Jun 1815 **RU:** Sergeant, Served in 6th Cont Line **CEM:** Oakwood; GPS 36.38690, -79.88000; 199 Cemetery St; Martinsville City **GS:** Y **SP:** No info **VI:** GS shows military service **P:** N **BLW:** N **RG:** unk **MK:** unk **PH:** unk **SS:** E pg 838 **BS:** 196.

WINN, Jesse Durrett; b 13 Apr 1752; d 22 Nov 1823 **RU:** Soldier, Served in 74th VA Light Inf **CEM:** Spring Grove; GPS 39.10916, -78.09970; Rockville; Hanover **GS:** Y **SP:** Deborah Harris **VI:** No further info **P:** unk **BLW:** unk **RG:** unk **MK:** unk **PH:** unk **SS:** NSSAR Ancestor #P-322554 **BS:** JLARC 71; 196.

WINN, Minor Jr; b 1730; d 25 Oct 1813 **RU:** First Lieutenant, Served in Fauquier Co Militia as 1st Lt Oct 1779 and took oath on Mar 1780 **CEM:** Winn Family; GPS unk; Probably at Rock Hill Rt 626 nr Halfway; Fauquier **GS:** N **SP:** Mar (bond 7 Oct 1766, James Withers, security) Elizabeth "Betty" Withers (c1748-c1803) d/o Thomas (15 Feb 1723 Stafford Co-12 Nov 1794) & Elizabeth (Williams) (__-27 Mar 1783) Withers **VI:** Son of Minor, Sr (1704 Westmoreland Co-1788) & Margaret (Connor) Winn. Cemetery has vanished **P:** unk **BLW:** unk **RG:** Y **MK:** N **PH:** N **SS:** Fauquier Co Marriages pg 216 **BS:** 19 pg 243.

WINN, Richard; b 1753; d 1816 **RU:** Sergeant, Served in 5th & 9th Cont Line **CEM:** White-Yancey-Jones Family; GPS unk; Rt 49 S fr Chase City, left on 697 at Reese's old store, 2.5 mi on right at old homeplace; Mecklenburg **GS:** U **SP:** Priscilla McKinney **VI:** No further data **P:** unk **BLW:** unk **RG:** unk **MK:** unk **PH:** unk **SS:** SAR Ancestor #P-322585; E pg 829; AZ pg 180 **BS:** JLARC 72.

WINN, Thomas; b 27 Dec 1753, Hanover Co; d 16 Nov 1824 **RU:** First Lieutenant, Served in Fluvanna Co Militia 8 Apr 1782. (DAR plaque at GS shows service fr 1776 to 1783) **CEM:** Winnsville; GPS unk; Rts 612 and 671, Fork Union; Fluvanna **GS:** Y **SP:** Elizabeth Dabney Anderson (17 Dec 1753-30 Nov 1819) **VI:** No further data **P:** unk **BLW:** unk **RG:** unk **MK:** Y **PH:** unk **SS:** DAR Ancestor #A128769; E pg 829 **BS:** JLARC 1, 3, 18, 46; 196.

WINNIFORD, David; b 1750; d 26 Apr 1794 **RU:** Sergeant, Served in VA Line. Ent serv Powhatan Co "in VA unit" (no yr), then entered serv Cumberland Co as Sergeant 1779. Served at Battle of Brandywine where wounded **CEM:** Winniford Family; GPS 37.71653, -78.16861; Fork of Willis Baptist Church, jct Rts 660 & 713; Cumberland **GS:** U **SP:** Mar (16 Nov 1780 Cumberland Co) Judith (-----) (c1763-__). She was living in Adair Co KY with her daughter in 1852. **VI:** Widow moved to KY in 1800 where pen 14 Aug 1840, Adair Co, KY age 77, living 12 mi fr Columbia. W9021 **P:** Y **BLW:** unk **RG:** Y **MK:** N **PH:** unk **SS:** J-NSSAR 1993 Reg; K Vol 6 pg 182-3; CG Vol 3 pg 3908 **BS:** JLARC 1.

WINSTON, Geddes; b 1724, Hanover Co; d 6 Jun 1784 **RU:** Private/Patriot, Mil serv not determined. Was Sheriff, Hanover Co 1782 **CEM:** St John's Episcopal; GPS 37.53183, -77.41958; 2401 E Broad St; Richmond City **GS:** Y **SP:** Mary Jordan (c1742-9 Dec 1811 Richmond) **VI:** Recd pen Hanover Co **P:** Y **BLW:** unk **RG:** Y **MK:** N **PH:** unk **SS:** DAR Ancestor #A128885; E pg 840; AL Ct Bk I pg 50 Hanover Co **BS:** 39, pg 100.

WINSTON, William Overton; b 1747; d 1815 **RU:** Captain, Commanded a co in Hanover Co Militia, May 1779 **CEM:** Blenheim-Winston; GPS unk; Rt 646, Hanover; Hanover **GS:** Y **SP:** Mar (1 Dec 1770) Joanna Robinson (1755-1794) **VI:** Son of John (1724-1772) & Alice (Bickerton) (1730-1773) Winston **P:** unk **BLW:** unk **RG:** Y **MK:** N **PH:** unk **SS:** E pg 840 **BS:** 31 vol 1 pg 55; 196.

RU=Rank/Unit	CEM=Cemetery	GS=Gravestone	SP=Spousal Information
VI=Other Veteran Info	P=Pension	BLW=Bounty/Land Warrant	RG=Registered Grave
MK=SAR/DAR Marker	PH=Photo	SS=Service Source	BS=Burial Source

368

WIRE, William; b c1753; d 27 Feb 1840 **RU:** Private, Served in Capt J Lewis in 7th Co, VA Regt fr Frederick Co, VA **CEM:** St James Reformed; GPS 39.27027, -77.62968; Lovettsville Rd, Lovettsville; Loudoun **GS:** Y **SP:** No info **VI:** No further data **P:** unk **BLW:** unk **RG:** Y **MK:** N **PH:** unk **SS:** G pg 373 **BS:** 25 pg 344; 196.

WISE, John; b c1765; d 30 Mar 1812 **RU:** Corporal, Served in 9th Cont Line **CEM:** Wise Family; GPS unk; Chesconessex; Accomack **GS:** Y **SP:** Mar (18 Apr 1799) Sarah Corbin Cropper (21 Mar 1777 Bowman's Folly, Accomack Co-21 Jan 1813) d/o John Jr (23 Dec 1755-15 Jan 1821) & Margaret Douglas (Pettitt) (12 Apr 1755-3 Jun 1784) Cropper **VI:** Son of John & Margaret (Douglas) Wise. GS inscription indicates he had rank of Maj and was Speaker of House and Clerk of County Ct (Major rank perhaps obtained after war period) **P:** unk **BLW:** unk **RG:** Y **MK:** N **PH:** unk **SS:** E pg 840 **BS:** 37 pg 284.

WITCHER, William Jr; b 1739; d 1820 **RU:** Major, Raised a co of militia in 1775. Promoted 16 Nov 1779 to Maj in Pittsylvania Co Militia. Resigned 19 Sep 1780 **CEM:** Witcher Family; GPS unk; nr Sandy Level Post Office; Pittsylvania **GS:** Y **SP:** Mar (1 Apr 1782 Pittsylvania Co) Molly or Polly Dalton **VI:** Was vestryman of Camden District Parish 1763 **P:** unk **BLW:** unk **RG:** Y **MK:** N **PH:** unk **SS:** N pg 1228;AS; AW **BS:** 174.

WITCHER, William Sr; b 1724; d 8 Jun 1808 **RU:** Major/Patriot, Served in VA Militia. Provided equipment and/or supplies **CEM:** Witcher family; GPS 36.57047, -79.35798; Penhook; Franklin **GS:** Y **SP:** Ann Majors **VI:** Was Justice, Franklin Co **P:** unk **BLW:** unk **RG:** Y **MK:** N **PH:** unk **SS:** AL Ct Bk pg I, 56 **BS:** SAR Application

WITHAM, William; b unk; d 1781 **RU:** Private, Served in Col Peter Gansevort's 3rd NY Regt. Died fr the battle at Yorktown **CEM:** Yorktown Victory Monument Tablet; GPS 38.28350, -78.54150; Yorktown; York **GS:** U **SP:** No info **VI:** No further data **P:** unk **BLW:** unk **RG:** unk **MK:** unk **PH:** unk **SS:** J-Yorktown Historian; AX pg 46 **BS:** JLARC 74.

WITHERS, Lewis; b 1758; d 4 May 1821 **RU:** Private, Served in Winn's Co, Fauquier Co Militia 1781 and wounded at Battle of Cowpens **CEM:** Withers-Nelson family; GPS unk; 9337 James Madison Hwy; Fauquier **GS:** Y **SP:** Katherine Potts **VI:** No further data **P:** unk **BLW:** unk **RG:** Y **MK:** N **PH:** Y **SS:** AV **BS:** 83 Inv # 58.

WITHERS, William; b 6 Apr 1726; d 5 Jan 1804 **RU:** Sergeant, Served in Grayson's Regt, Cont Line **CEM:** Withers-Nelson family; GPS unk; 9337 James Madison Hwy; Fauquier **GS:** Y **SP:** Mar (15 Dec 1756 or 1777 Fauquier Co) Elizabeth Hord Barbey or Barbee (22 Sep 1732-17 Oct 1871) d/o Andrew & Jane Lacey (Dulaney) Barbee **VI:** Son of Capt James & Elizabeth (Keene) Withers, Sr **P:** unk **BLW:** unk **RG:** Y **MK:** Y **PH:** Y **SS:** E pg 841; AV; Fauquier Co Marriages pg 217 **BS:** 83 Inv # 58.

WITTEN, James; b 7 Jan 1759, MD; d 15 Mar 1830 **RU:** Private, Served in Capt James Maxwell's Co, Montgomery Co Militia **CEM:** Witten Family; GPS unk; Plum Creek nr his cabin; Tazewell **GS:** U **SP:** Mar (1783) Rebecca Cecil (1765 MD-1840) **VI:** No further data **P:** unk **BLW:** unk **RG:** unk **MK:** unk **PH:** unk **SS:** DAR Ancestor #A125451; SAR Ancestor #P-323120; J- DAR Hatcher; E pg 237; BW pg 27, 56 **BS:** JLARC 2.

WITTEN, Thomas Jr; b 23 Jan 1753, Prince George Co, MD; d 6 Oct 1841 **RU:** Ensign, Served in VA Line. Ent serv Tazewell Co 1776 as Ens and served in Capt James Maxwell's Co Montgomery Co. Fought in Battle of King's Mountain under Lt Rees Bowen and Tazwell Comar, 29 Mar 1774, Fincastle Co **CEM:** W. A. Leece Family; GPS unk; Off Rt 91 south of Rt 460, Fort Witten, Paintlick; Tazewell **GS:** U **SP:** Mar (29 Mar 1774 Augusta, Fincastle Co) Eleanor "Nellie" Cecil (1755-1836) **VI:** Son of Thomas (1719-1794) & Elizabeth Bean (Cecil) Witten. Rec pen for protecting frontier settlements fr Indians. He and David Ward were first representatives fr Tazewell Co elected to VA legislature 1801, 02, 03. Appl pen 15 Oct 1832 Tazewell Co. S6407. Source 89 has death in 1844 for Thomas Witten Jr **P:** Y **BLW:** unk **RG:** unk **MK:** unk **PH:** unk **SS:** E pg 825; G pg 237; K Vol 6 pg 190; CG Vol 3 pg 3920 **BS:** JLARC 4, 89; 196.

WLOVASSE, Jean; b unk; d 1781 **RU:** Seaman, Served on "Ville de Paris" and died from Yorktown battle **CEM:** French Memorial; GPS 36.81944, -79.39933; Yorktown; York **GS:** U **SP:** No info **VI:** No further data **P:** unk **BLW:** unk **RG:** Y **MK:** unk **PH:** unk **SS:** J-Yorktown Historian **BS:** JLARC 1, 74.

RU=Rank/Unit	CEM=Cemetery	GS=Gravestone	SP=Spousal Information
VI=Other Veteran Info	P=Pension	BLW=Bounty/Land Warrant	RG=Registered Grave
MK=SAR/DAR Marker	PH=Photo	SS=Service Source	BS=Burial Source

369

WONEYCUTT, Edward; b unk; d 1 Jun 1811 **RU:** Captain, Was 1st Lt & Capt 1777-78 on "Greyhound" and "Hornet" **CEM:** Cedar Grove; GPS 36.57204, -80.02599; 301 Fort Lane Rd; Portsmouth City **GS:** U **SP:** No info **VI:** Pen granted to heirs 1849. Also recd 1/2 pay for being disabled or wounded. R110 **P:** Y **BLW:** unk **RG:** unk **MK:** unk **PH:** unk **SS:** K Vol 6 pg 191; CG Vol 3 pg 3924 **BS:** JLARC 4, 39.

WOOD, Benjamin; b 15 Mar 1761; d 29 Apr 1829 **RU:** Soldier, Served in 1st VA Regt **CEM:** Wood-Conn; GPS unk; Rileyville, 9 mi Luray; Page **GS:** Y **SP:** 1) Mar (25 Jan 1792) Sarah Fallis (1766-1822) 2) Mar (18 Jun 1823) Elizabeth Pasquette Abbott (1789-1871) **VI:** Son of Nehemiah (1731-1816) and Abigale (Grigsby) Wood **P:** unk **BLW:** unk **RG:** Y **MK:** Y **PH:** Y **SS:** E pg 842 **BS:** JLARC 76.

WOOD, James; b 28 Jan 1741, Winchester City; d 16 Jun or 16 Jul 1813 **RU:** Brig General, Commander 12th VA Regt as Col, 12 Nov 1776. Served until 1 Jan 1783, afterwards commanded 1st VA Regt to end of war **CEM:** St John's Episcopal; GPS 37.53183, -77.41958; 2401 E Broad St; Richmond City **GS:** Y **SP:** Jean Moncure **VI:** Governor of Virginia 1796-1799. BLW awarded 14 Feb 1792 for 7,777 acres. No GS, however plaque inside church indicates burial **P:** unk **BLW:** Y **RG:** Y **MK:** Y **PH:** unk **SS:** E pg 843; N pg 293; CE pg 33 **BS:** 32 e-mail 06.

WOOD, Jeremiah; b unk; d unk **RU:** unk, SAR registry did not provide service. See DAR US Senate Doc serial 10000, vol 2, 1935 for service **CEM:** Harkin (Heathering) Hill; GPS unk; Peaks of Otter; Bedford **GS:** U **SP:** Mar (28 Dec 1796 Bedford Co) Mary Dooley d/o John & (-----) Dooley **VI:** No further data **P:** unk **BLW:** unk **RG:** unk **MK:** N **PH:** unk **SS:** AR, vol 4, pg 210; NSSAR Ancestor #P-323556 **BS:** JLARC 2.

WOOD, John; b 1763, Anne Arundel CO, MD; d 28 Jul 1843 **RU:** Private, Private, in Mackell's Co, MD Regt **CEM:** Wood Family; GPS 38.20279, -78.53238; Off Markwood Rd Rt 664, Earlysville; Albemarle **GS:** Y **SP:** Mar (22 Apr 1783 Calvert Co, MD) Elizabeth "Betsey" Sunderland (c1764-1855) **VI:** GS reads "Mackell's Co, MD Regiment. DAR Marker. Spouse pen #W6573 & BLW # 9525-160-55 **P:** Y **BLW:** Y **RG:** Y **MK:** Y **PH:** unk **SS:** DAR Ancestor #A128002; J-NSSAR 1993 Reg; BT **BS:** JLARC 1; 196.

WOOD, Jonathan Sr; b 1744, Fairfax Co; d 13 Nov 1804 **RU:** Private, Served in Capt Rowland's Co, Botetourt Co Militia. Was in Capt James Thompson's Co fr Scott Co in 1774 during battle of Point Pleasant. Also was in battle at King's Mountain **CEM:** Wood; GPS 36.71720, -82.36940; Rt 613; Scott **GS:** U **SP:** Nancy Davidson Wood (1746-17 Apr 1827 Scott Co) **VI:** No further data **P:** unk **BLW:** unk **RG:** unk **MK:** unk **PH:** unk **SS:** DAR Ancestor #A128050; SAR Ancestor #P-323618; E pg 843 **BS:** 196.

WOOD, Nehemiah; b 1731, Prince William Co; d 3 Oct 1816 **RU:** Private/Patriot, Served in 8th Cont Line. Gave material aid to cause **CEM:** Fairview; GPS unk; Rileyville, 7 mi fr Luray; Page **GS:** Y **SP:** Mar (c1755) Abigale Grigsby (c1735-28 Jul 1800) **VI:** No further data **P:** N **BLW:** unk **RG:** Y **MK:** Y **PH:** unk **SS:** DAR Ancestor #A128108; D Vol 3 pg 841; E pg 843 **BS:** JLARC 76.

WOOD, Robert; b 27 Jul 1747, Winchester; d 1801 **RU:** Patriot, Furnished equipment and/or supplies. Was Commissioner of Peace, Frederick Co **CEM:** Wood Family; GPS unk; Glen Burnie nr Winchester; Frederick **GS:** Y **SP:** 1) Mar (2 Apr 1774) Comfort Welsh (1751-c1840) 2) Abigail Rudd **VI:** No further data **P:** N **BLW:** N **RG:** Y **MK:** N **PH:** unk **SS:** DAR Ancestor #A128143; SAR Ancestor #P-323714; AL Ct Bk pg 18, 48 **BS:** 80 vol 4 pg 212.

WOOD, Thomas; b unk; d 1817 **RU:** Patriot, Gave material aid to cause **CEM:** Wood family; GPS unk; Vic jct Rts 659 & 610; Fluvanna **GS:** Y **SP:** Mary Hope (__-1823) **VI:** No further data **P:** N **BLW:** N **RG:** Y **MK:** N **PH:** unk **SS:** AL Ct Bk pg 1,45 **BS:** 66 pg 102.

WOOD, Thomas; b 1753, Lunenburg Co; d 26 Jan 1824 **RU:** Private, Served in VA Line. Ent Serv Lunenburg Co 1780 where then living. Served in Battles of Camden, Guilford CH, and Siege of Yorktown **CEM:** Old Wood Family; GPS 36.50000, -79.46520; Rodgers Chapel Rd btw Rts 605 & 608, Clover; Halifax **GS:** U **SP:** Mar (1774 or 1775 Lunenburg Co by Rev Craig, Episcopal) Mary Moore (c1759-__) **VI:** Widow appl pen 30 Jan 1839 Halifax Co age 80. W6568, Govt Gr Stone **P:** Y **BLW:** unk **RG:** Y **MK:** unk **PH:** unk **SS:** DAR Ancestor #A128234; SAR Ancestor #P-323784; J-NSSAR 1993 Reg; K Vol 6 pg 198; CG Vol 3 pg 3957 **BS:** JLARC 1 App D pg 12.

RU=Rank/Unit   CEM=Cemetery   GS=Gravestone   SP=Spousal Information
VI=Other Veteran Info   P=Pension   BLW=Bounty/Land Warrant   RG=Registered Grave
MK=SAR/DAR Marker   PH=Photo   SS=Service Source   BS=Burial Source

370

WOOD, William Sr; b unk; d 1811 **RU:** Second Lieutenant, Served in Capt Anderson's Militia Co 1778 **CEM:** Wood; GPS unk; Rt 620 nr Rt 616, Rodophil; Amelia **GS:** N **SP:** Ann Wood **VI:** Son of William Wood Jr. Lived at Ingleside in Amelia Co. **P:** unk **BLW:** unk **RG:** unk **MK:** unk **PH:** N **SS:** AZ pg 180 **BS:** 196.

WOODARD, William; b 1710, Dublin, County Dublin, Ireland; d 1818 **RU:** Patriot, Gave material aid to cause in Princess Anne Co before moving to Rappahannock Co **CEM:** Woodard; GPS unk; James Woodard Farm, off Co Rd 600 in field N of "Caboose Pond"; Rappahannock **GS:** U **SP:** Olive Butt **VI:** Ran away fr home & came to VA as indentured servant on plantation in East VA for seven yrs. Then moved to Piedmont area. Died in Sperryville, Rappahannock Co **P:** N **BLW:** N **RG:** unk **MK:** unk **PH:** unk **SS:** JLARC 116; AL Comm Bk IV Princess Anne Co **BS:** JLARC 116.

WOODDELL, Thomas; b c1730; d 1785 **RU:** Patriot, Gave material aid to cause **CEM:** Mossy Creek Presbyterian; GPS 38.35331, -79.04914; 372 Kyles Mill Rd, Mt Solon; Augusta **GS:** Y **SP:** Mar (c1752) PA Alise (-----) (__-1818 Bath Co) **VI:** No further data **P:** N **BLW:** N **RG:** Y **MK:** N **PH:** unk **SS:** SAR Ancestor #P-323972; AS SAR regist **BS:** 80 vol 4 pg 213; 196.

WOODFIN, Samuel; b 21 Sep 1752; d 13 Jan 1832 **RU:** Patriot, Gave material aid to cause **CEM:** Muddy Creek Baptist; GPS unk; 3470 Rt 629, Powhatan; Powhatan **GS:** N **SP:** Obedience Gaithright (7 Nov 1753-15 Dec 1827) **VI:** No further data **P:** N **BLW:** N **RG:** unk **MK:** unk **PH:** N **SS:** AL Ct Bk pg 24 Powhatan Co **BS:** 196.

WOODFORD, William; b 1734; d 30 Nov 1780 **RU:** Brig General, Promoted to Brig Gen 21 Feb 1777, 1st VA Brigade comprised 2nd, 3rd, 6th, 11th, 15th Regts in 1779. After White Plains rearrangements, Regts were 2nd, 3rd, 4th, 5th, 7th, 8th, 9th. Taken prisoner at Charleston. Died as prisoner in NY in Nov 1780 **CEM:** White Hall; GPS unk; 2.4 mi N of Woodford; Caroline **GS:** N **SP:** No info **VI:** Died in Charleston SC. Contrary to statement that Gen Woodford was bur in Trinity Churchyard, NYC, is the tradition that he is bur in graveyard in "White Hall" **P:** unk **BLW:** unk **RG:** Y **MK:** N **PH:** N **SS:** G pg 401, 792; CE pg 34 **BS:** 98 Caroline.

WOODHOUSE, William; b 1750; d 1783 **RU:** Captain/Patriot, Gave material aid to cause. Commanded a co in Princess Anne Co, Militia 1777 **CEM:** Old Donation Episcopal; GPS 36.86984, -76.13316; 4449 N Witchduck Rd; Virginia Beach City **GS:** U **SP:** Mar (c1774) Susan Pallett (__-1820) **VI:** No further data **P:** unk **BLW:** unk **RG:** unk **MK:** unk **PH:** unk **SS:** DAR Ancestor #A128492; J- DAR Hatcher; E pg 844; AL Comm Bk IV pg 228 Princess Anne Co; DD cites VA Mag Hist & Biog Vol 15, Oct 1907, pg 188 **BS:** JLARC 2.

WOODRUFF, David Jr; b c1762; d 14 Nov 1814 **RU:** Captain, Served in Amherst Co Militia **CEM:** Monument Hill; GPS 37.55115, -79.09496; Nr jct Rt 663 on Stable Ln, Sweet Briar College; Amherst **GS:** Y **SP:** Judith McDaniel (c1786-3 Jun 1844) **VI:** Son of David Sr & Clary (Powell) Woodruff **P:** unk **BLW:** unk **RG:** Y **MK:** N **PH:** unk **SS:** E pg 844; AL cert issued **BS:** 01 pg 167.

WOODS, Andrew Sr; b 1722; d 10 Apr 1781 **RU:** Private/Patriot, Served in Capt Daniel Smith's Co, Fincastle Co Militia in Lord Dunmore's war at Point Pleasant. Also was in Capt James Robertson's Co. Was Sheriff of Botetourt Co. Gave material aid to cause **CEM:** Buchanan; GPS unk; Buchanan; Botetourt **GS:** U **SP:** Mar (31 Jan 1747 Staunton) Martha Poage (1728 Augusta Co-15 Apr 1818) **VI:** High Sheriff **P:** unk **BLW:** unk **RG:** Y **MK:** unk **PH:** unk **SS:** DAR Ancestor #A128819; AL Ct Bk pg 4,10,28 Botetourt Co; DF pg 456 **BS:** JLARC 76.

WOODS, Samuel; b 17 May 1727, Ireland; d 10 Jan 1781 **RU:** Sergeant, Enl 25 Jan 1776 in Co 2, Col Wm Irvine's PA Regt. Served in Canada Campaign. Captured 10 Jun 1776 at Three Rivers on St Lawrence River **CEM:** Woods Family; GPS unk; Rockfish Presbyterian Church S of Afton; Nelson **GS:** Y **SP:** Mar (1760) Mary (-----) (1742-20 Apr 1779) **VI:** Died in Albemarle Co **P:** unk **BLW:** unk **RG:** Y **MK:** N **PH:** unk **SS:** A pg 202 **BS:** 01 pg 191.

WOODS, William; b 31 Dec 1744; d 4 May 1837 **RU:** Ensign, Appt ensign in Albemarle Co Militia 8 Mar 1781 **CEM:** Woods Family; GPS unk; .5 mi S of Mechum River; Fluvanna **GS:** Y **SP:** No info **VI:** No further data **P:** unk **BLW:** unk **RG:** N **MK:** N **PH:** unk **SS:** E pg 845 **BS:** 164 Woods.

RU=Rank/Unit	CEM=Cemetery	GS=Gravestone	SP=Spousal Information
VI=Other Veteran Info	P=Pension	BLW=Bounty/Land Warrant	RG=Registered Grave
MK=SAR/DAR Marker	PH=Photo	SS=Service Source	BS=Burial Source

371

WOODS, William; b 2 Nov 1715, Dunshaughlin, County Meath, Ireland; d 12 Apr 1783 **RU:** Lieutenant Colonel, Probably served in Albemarle Co Militia **CEM:** St Paul's; **GPS** 38.05830, -78.59580; 851 Owensville Rd, Ivy; Albemarle **GS:** U **SP:** Mar (1 Oct 1735 Augusta Co VA) Susannah Wallace d/o Peter & Elizabeth (Woods) Wallace **VI:** Son of Michael Marion (1684-1762) & Mary Catherine (Campbell) (1690-1742) Woods. Was a Minister. Plaque in cem lists his descendants **P:** unk **BLW:** unk **RG:** unk **MK:** unk **PH:** unk **SS:** CD **BS:** 196.

WOODSON, Jacob; b 11 May 1748; d 5 Dec 1838 **RU:** Captain, Commanded a co Prince Edward Co Militia in 1780 **CEM:** Woodson Family; **GPS** unk; Farmville; Prince Edward **GS:** U **SP:** Elizabeth Morton (28 Nov 1754-12 Feb 1845) d/o Capt John Morton **VI:** Was a justice & magistrate. Signed the Statute for Religious Freedom written by Thomas Jefferson. **P:** unk **BLW:** unk **RG:** unk **MK:** unk **PH:** unk **SS:** E pg 845 **BS:** 196.

WOODSON, John; b 28 Feb 1763, Goochland Co; d Aft 23 Oct 1832 **RU:** Ensign, Served in Capts Miller, Curd, Pleasants, & Duke companies **CEM:** Deanery Family; **GPS** unk; Cartersville on James River; Cumberland **GS:** Y **SP:** Mar (30 Mar 1786 Hanover Co) Mary Lightfoot Anderson (c1760, Louisa Co-__ Hanover Co) **VI:** Appl pen 23 Oct 1832 #S6434 **P:** Y **BLW:** unk **RG:** N **MK:** N **PH:** unk **SS:** DAR Ancestor #A205266; E pg 845; CG pg 3950 **BS:** 157 Deanery.

WOODSON, Tarleton; b 22 Mar 1758, Goochland Co; d 1795 **RU:** Sergeant, Served under Col Patrick Henry & Capt Charles Scott **CEM:** Woodson; **GPS** unk; Directions not identified; Albemarle **GS:** N **SP:** Annis Shepard (__-aft 1830) **VI:** Son of John & Elizabeth (Bailey) Woodson, both of Goochland Co **P:** unk **BLW:** Y **RG:** unk **MK:** unk **PH:** N **SS:** DAR Ancestor #A129220, SAR Ancestor #P- 324342; J- DAR Hatcher; BY pg 344 **BS:** JLARC 2.

WOODWARD, James; b unk; d Mar 1788 **RU:** Captain, Served in 1st VA Regt **CEM:** Old Christ Church Episcopal; **GPS** 38.80625, -77.04718; 118 N Washington St; Alexandria City **GS:** N **SP:** No info **VI:** Burial permit for Capt James Woodward issued 19 Mar 1788 to Capt Joseph Greenway **P:** unk **BLW:** Y **RG:** Y **MK:** N **PH:** N **SS:** E pg 846 **BS:** 20 pg 154.

WOODWARD, William; b 1746, Rappahannock Co; d during or after war **RU:** Private, Served in 6th VA Regt **CEM:** Smith Family; **GPS** 36.69923, -76.11877; Mt Pleasant Farm, now Fentress Naval Auxiliary Airfield; Chesapeake City **GS:** Y **SP:** No info **VI:** Govt GS shows service **P:** unk **BLW:** unk **RG:** unk **MK:** unk **PH:** unk **SS:** E pg 844 **BS:** 196.

WOODY, Martin; b 31 Mar 1758, Goochland Co; d 6 Dec 1846 **RU:** Soldier, Enlisted 1777-78 Amherst Co where he then lived, then enlisted 1781 Bedford Co Militia **CEM:** Woody Family; **GPS** unk; Plantation Rd, Rocky Mount; Franklin **GS:** U **SP:** Mar (27 Oct 1785 Henry Co by Rev Robert Jones) Susanna Roberson (1765 Franklin Co-15 Jul 1852 Franklin Co) **VI:** Son of Henry & (-----) Woody. Soldier appl pen 6 May 1833 in Franklin Co age 75. Widow appl pen 3 May 1847 age 76. W3912 **P:** Y **BLW:** unk **RG:** unk **MK:** unk **PH:** unk **SS:** K Vol 6 pg 206; CG Vol III **BS:** JLARC 4,19; 196.

WOOLFOLK, John George; b 1750; d 1819 **RU:** Second Lieutenant, Took oath 13 Jan 1779 in Caroline Co Militia **CEM:** Woolfolk Family; **GPS** unk; Rt 721 Sparta Rd, DeJarnette; Caroline **GS:** U **SP:** Elizabeth Powers Boadnax **VI:** No further data **P:** unk **BLW:** unk **RG:** Y **MK:** N **PH:** unk **SS:** E pg 847 **BS:** JLARC 76.

WOOLSLEY, Thomas; b 1719, Weschester Co, NY; d 26 Feb 1794 **RU:** Private, Served in 1st Light Dragoons of VA **CEM:** Riverbend; **GPS** unk; Vic jct Rts 650 & 660; Smyth **GS:** Y **SP:** 1) Mar (1739 Bedford NY) Elizabeth Waters 2) Mar (1782 Radford VA) Sarah Pierce (__-1794) d/o John & Sarah (-----) Pierce **VI:** Son of Richard & Sarah (Fowler) Woolsey. Was pioneer and Baptist Minister. Recd 100 acres BLW **P:** unk **BLW:** Y **RG:** Y **MK:** N **PH:** unk **SS:** E pg 847 **BS:** 97 vol 1 pg 120; 196.

WORMELEY, Ralph V; b c1744; d 19 Jan 1806 **RU:** Patriot, Furnished equipment and supplies to cause **CEM:** Tayloe Family; **GPS** 37.58200, -76.47290; Mt Airy, Rt 360, Warsaw; Richmond Co **GS:** Y **SP:** Eleanor Tayloe (16 Oct 1756-25 Feb 1815) d/o John II & Rececca Plater (Addison) Tayloe **VI:** Son of Ralph IV & Jane (Boles) Wormeley. Served several times as a member of the House of Delegates and in the Virginia Convention of 1788. Died in Middlesex Co. He and his wife have a gravetone in the Christ Church Cemetery in Saluda, Middlesex Co, thus perhaps only memorialized at Mt Airy **P:** N **BLW:** N **RG:** Y **MK:** N **PH:** unk **SS:** AL Ct Bk pg 6 **BS:** 84 pg 98; 196.

RU=Rank/Unit	CEM=Cemetery	GS=Gravestone	SP=Spousal Information
VI=Other Veteran Info	P=Pension	BLW=Bounty/Land Warrant	RG=Registered Grave
MK=SAR/DAR Marker	PH=Photo	SS=Service Source	BS=Burial Source

372

WORRELL, James; b 1752, Chester Co, PA; d 31 Jan 1802 **RU:** Private, Served in 6th Battalion of PA Militia **CEM:** Worrell Family; GPS 36.78290, -80.66173; Off Pils Trail Rt 673, .6 mi S of Rt 221, Eona; Carroll **GS:** Y **SP:** 1) Barbary Pennicic 2) Elizabeth Crandell **VI:** Son of Peter Worrell & Mary Trego. DAR plaque on small stone **P:** unk **BLW:** unk **RG:** unk **MK:** Y **PH:** unk **SS:** NSDAR **BS:** JLARC 2, 4, 43; 68; 196.

WORSHAM, Essex; b 1758, Amelia Co; d Aft 1832 **RU:** Private, Ent serv Amelia Co 1778 as substitute for brother Henry Worsham. Ent serv again in 1781 as substitute for brother Cannon Worsham **CEM:** Worsham Family; GPS unk; Check county property rec for loc; Pittsylvania **GS:** Y **SP:** Mar (28 Dec 1786) Elizabeth Dunnavant, d/o Hodges & (-----) Dunnavant **VI:** Lived in Amelia for 10 yrs after RW, then moved to Prince Edward where he lived 15 yrs, then Pittsylvania Co. Appl pen 17 Nov 1832 in Pittsylvania Co. S6447 **P:** Y **BLW:** unk **RG:** N **MK:** N **PH:** unk **SS:** K Vol 6 pg 211; CG Vol 3 pg 3962-3 **BS:** DAR Rpt.

WORSHAM, George; b c1757; d Oct 1822 **RU:** Patriot, Gave material aid to cause **CEM:** Shockoe Hill; GPS 37.55190, -77.43170; 4th & Hospital Sts; Richmond City **GS:** Y **SP:** No info **VI:** No further data **P:** N **BLW:** N **RG:** Y **MK:** N **PH:** unk **SS:** AL Ct Bk pg 44 **BS:** 57 pg 1.

WORSHAM, William; b 16 Jun 1752, Chesterfield Co; d 27 Aug 1836 **RU:** Captain/Patriot, As QM Sgt, served under Joseph Scott, 1st Cont Dragoons Jan 1777. Was taken prisoner 15 mos later. Was Capt of Prince Edward Co Militia. Gave material aid to cause **CEM:** Worsham Family Square; GPS 37.32163, -78.44328; Vic Rts 665 & 15 Farmville Rd, Worsham; Prince Edward **GS:** N **SP:** Margaret Jones (1758-1827) **VI:** Pen recd by son Richard.Also recd BLW 2666 acres **P:** Y **BLW:** Y **RG:** unk **MK:** unk **PH:** N **SS:** E pg 848; AL Ct Bk pg 52 Chesterfield Co; CG pg 3963 **BS:** 196.

WORTHINGTON, William; b unk; d 29 May 1825 **RU:** Matross, Served in Co #6, John Dandridge Co at Valley Forge in Jun 1778 **CEM:** Ketoctin Baptist; GPS 39.15746, -77.74870; Ketoctin Church Rd, Purcellville; Loudoun **GS:** Y **SP:** No info **VI:** The GS inscription can be read as dying in the 14th yr of his age however it is believed to be in error and should read 74th yr of his age **P:** unk **BLW:** unk **RG:** Y **MK:** N **PH:** unk **SS:** A pg 248 **BS:** 25 pg 347.

WRAY, David; b 1751, Brunswick Co; d 3 Sep 1833 **RU:** Private, Ent serv Apr or May 1778 then again in 1780. Was in expedition against Indians in western part of VA called New River in Capt John Donlison's Co. In 1780 volunteered in Henry Co under Capt Wm Witcher and sent to NC, then SC. Then guarded prisoners fr Battle of Cowpens. Also was in Battle of Guilford CH **CEM:** Wray Family; GPS unk; Check Co property rec for loc; Pittsylvania **GS:** Y **SP:** Mar (11 Feb 1797 Botetourt Co) Elizabeth Carvin **VI:** Appl for pen 17 Sep 1832 age 81 Henry Co (now Pittsylvania Co). S7973 **P:** Y **BLW:** unk **RG:** N **MK:** N **PH:** unk **SS:** E pg 848; K Vol 6 pg 212; CG Vol 3 **BS:** DAR Rpt.

WREN, James; b c1728, Fairfax Co; d Bef 21 Nov 1815 **RU:** Captain/Patriot, Served in Fairfax Co Militia. Gave material aid to cause **CEM:** Wren Family; GPS unk; Hillsman Dr and Mahala Ln; Falls Church City **GS:** U **SP:** 1) Mar (27 Mar 1753) Catherine Brent (13 Jan 1729, Stafford Co-c1770 Fairfax Co 2) Sarah Jones **VI:** No further data **P:** unk **BLW:** unk **RG:** unk **MK:** unk **PH:** unk **SS:** DAR Ancestor #A130667; D Vol 2 pg 346; AL Ct Bk pg 27 Fairfax Co; DD cites pen of Samuel Barker Davis as source **BS:** JLARC 14.

WRIGHT, John; b 8 Aug 1767; d Bef 23 Jun 1851 **RU:** Private, Served in Col Daniel Gaines Regt, Amherst Co Militia **CEM:** Moore; GPS unk; Fort Edmiston; Washington **GS:** U **SP:** Mar (1792, Washington Co) Mary Kincannon (10 Sep 1774, Washington Co-aft 1840) d/of Francis (21 Mar 1750 York Co, PA-___ Hardin Co, TN) & Martha (Snodgrass) (___-26 Aug 1817, Maury Co, TN) Kincannon **VI:** No further data **P:** unk **BLW:** unk **RG:** unk **MK:** unk **PH:** unk **SS:** DN pg 409, 411 **BS:** JLARC 2.

WRIGHT, Joseph; b 1752; d 8 Oct 1826 **RU:** Private, Served in Capt Trimble's Augusta Co Militia **CEM:** Hebron Presbyterian; GPS 38.14140, -79.15500; 423 Hebron Rd; Staunton City **GS:** Y **SP:** Ruth Evans **VI:** Died age 74 (stone) **P:** unk **BLW:** unk **RG:** unk **MK:** unk **PH:** unk **SS:** E pg 850 **BS:** JLARC 62, 63; 196.

WRIGHT, Robert Mosley Sr; b 1766; d 20 Jan 1838 **RU:** Soldier, Ent serv Caroline Co **CEM:** Elmwood; GPS unk; Rt 651, 5.3 mi S of DeJarnette; Caroline **GS:** N **SP:** Margaret Hawkins Boutwell, d/o William

RU=Rank/Unit	CEM=Cemetery	GS=Gravestone	SP=Spousal Information
VI=Other Veteran Info	P=Pension	BLW=Bounty/Land Warrant	RG=Registered Grave
MK=SAR/DAR Marker	PH=Photo	SS=Service Source	BS=Burial Source

373

Boutwell (1773-29 Oct 1855) **VI:** Son of Robert & Mary Catherine (Bell) Wright. Appl for pen Caroline Co 8 Oct 1832 age 69 **P:** Y **BLW:** unk **RG:** unk **MK:** N **PH:** N **SS:** CG Vol 3 pg 3975 **BS:** 196.

WRIGHT, Stephen; b 24 Dec 1763, Craney Island, Norfolk Co; d Aft 1852 **RU:** Colonel, Ent Sea Service at Craney Island where he lived as Ens, VA Militia. Served on small navy cruiser with his guardian, Capt W Westcott. Captured by British and held on prison ship until 1783. Obtained rank of Colonel **CEM:** Cedar Grove; GPS 36.85860, -76.28310; 238 E Princess Anne Rd; Norfolk City **GS:** Y **SP:** Mar (12 Jun 1795, Norfolk Co) Abigail O'Conner **VI:** Son of Steven & Anne (Phripp) Wright. Was in Legislature fr county for abt 50 yrs. Was County Justice. Appl for pen 4 Aug 1849 Norfolk where he then lived and was known as "Col" and was presiding Magistrate "for many yrs." Pen applic rejected due to insufficient proof. R11907. He was living in 1852 **P:** N **BLW:** unk **RG:** Y **MK:** N **PH:** unk **SS:** K Vol 6 pg 222; BR; CG Vol 3; see Burial source 136 **BS:** 136 2009 newsltr.

WRIGHT, William; b 18 Nov 1740, York Co; d 29 Aug 1806 **RU:** Sergeant/Patriot, Served in Fauquier Co Militia. Gave material aid to cause **CEM:** Dermonte Burying Ground; GPS unk; Liberty; Fauquier **GS:** U **SP:** Mar (25 Dec 1768 New York Co, VA) Elizabeth Lloyd (7 Nov 1750 York Co-25 Jul 1830 Fauquier Co) d/o William & Sarah (Chowning) Lloyd **VI:** Son of John & Ann (-----) Wright **P:** unk **BLW:** unk **RG:** unk **MK:** unk **PH:** unk **SS:** J- DAR Hatcher, E pg 850; AL Ct Bk pg 26 Fairfax Co **BS:** JLARC 2; 196.

WYATT, John; b c1740, Stafford Co; d 1808 **RU:** Soldier, Served 3 yrs in VA Cont Lines 3rd, 4th, 8th, 12th, & 2nd VA State Regt **CEM:** Wyatt; GPS unk; Rt 601, 3.6 mi S of South Boston; Halifax **GS:** U **SP:** Mar (25 Jan 1790 Halifax Co) Leah Younger d/o William & Patience (-----) Younger **VI:** Son of William Edward & Lettice (-----) Wyatt. John's will in Hallifax Co, drawn 24 Feb 1801, proved 22 Feb 1808. VA Recd BLW of 100 acres, 30 May 1783 **P:** unk **BLW:** Y **RG:** unk **MK:** unk **PH:** unk **SS:** E pg 851; F pg 78 **BS:** 196.

WYCKLIFFE (WICKLIFF), Aaron; b unk; d unk **RU:** Private, Served in 11th VA Regt **CEM:** Wickliff Family; GPS 38.46243, -77.24409; Behind 13220 Yates Ford Rd, Clifton; Fairfax **GS:** Y **SP:** No info **VI:** DAR Marker **P:** unk **BLW:** unk **RG:** N **MK:** Y **PH:** unk **SS:** AS DAR Report **BS:** DAR report.

WYCKLIFFE (WICKLIFF), Moses; b unk; d unk **RU:** Private, Served in 11th VA Regt **CEM:** Wickliff Family; GPS 38.46243, -77.24409; Behind 13220 Yates Ford Rd, Clifton; Fairfax **GS:** Y **SP:** No info **VI:** DAR Marker **P:** unk **BLW:** unk **RG:** N **MK:** Y **PH:** unk **SS:** AS DAR Report **BS:** DAR report.

WYLIE, Samuel; b unk; d 1781 **RU:** Private, Killed in Battle of Green Springs nr Williamsburg **CEM:** Williamsburg Land Conservancy; GPS unk; 5000 New Point Rd; Williamsburg City **GS:** N **SP:** No info **VI:** Name is on the monument erected in Williamsburg **P:** unk **BLW:** unk **RG:** N **MK:** N **PH:** N **SS:** AU Will Chap **BS:** 32.

WYNNE, Edmund; b 26 Mar 1744; d 6 May 1763 **RU:** Patriot, Gave material aid to cause **CEM:** Essex Lodge, aka Washington's Lodge; GPS unk; See property records for loc; York **GS:** N **SP:** Mary Llewellyn (19 Jan 1750-21 Mar 1809) **VI:** Son of John & Lucy (Hill) Wynne **P:** N **BLW:** N **RG:** unk **MK:** unk **PH:** N **SS:** AL Ct Bk II pg 1, 7 Warwick Co **BS:** 32 Frederick W Bolt, Historian York Co Dec 2004.

WYNNE, Thomas; b c1742; d Jan 1794 **RU:** Patriot, Gave material aid to cause **CEM:** Essex Lodge, aka Washington's Lodge; GPS unk; See property records; York **GS:** N **SP:** Frances Harwood (c1732-aft 1792) **VI:** Son of John & Lucy (Hill) Wynne **P:** N **BLW:** N **RG:** unk **MK:** unk **PH:** N **SS:** AL Ct Bk II pg 1, 7 Warwick Co **BS:** 32 Frederick W Bolt, Historian York Co Dec 2004.

WYNNE, Thomas H; b c1720; d bet 1826-1860 **RU:** Patriot, Provided equipment & supplies **CEM:** St John's Episcopal; GPS 37.53183, -77.41958; 2401 E Broad St; Richmond City **GS:** Y **SP:** No info **VI:** No further data **P:** N **BLW:** N **RG:** Y **MK:** N **PH:** unk **SS:** AL Ct Bk 1 pg 1, 7 **BS:** 28 pg 349.

WYNNE (WYNN), William Jr; b 25 Feb 1762, Pittsylvania Co; d 1835 **RU:** Private, Served in Capt Thomas Mastin's Co of Militia stationed at Wynn's Garrison fort fr 1779 to end of war in 1783 **CEM:** Wynn-Peery; GPS 37.12620, -81.4988; Campbell Ln, Tazewell; Tazewell **GS:** Y **SP:** No info **VI:** Son of William Sr. & Cynthia (Harmon) Wynn (1735 Montgomery Co-__). Appl pen 4 Apr 1834 R11920 **P:** Y **BLW:** unk **RG:** unk **MK:** unk **PH:** unk **SS:** CG pg 3983 **BS:** 196.

WYNNE (WYNN), William Sr; b 10 Aug 1729; d 8 Jul 1808 **RU:** Patriot, Gave material aid to cause **CEM:** Wynn-Peery; GPS 37.12620, -81.4988; Campbell Ln, Tazewell; Tazewell **GS:** Y **SP:** 1) Cynthia

RU=Rank/Unit   CEM=Cemetery   GS=Gravestone   SP=Spousal Information
VI=Other Veteran Info P=Pension   BLW=Bounty/Land Warrant RG=Registered Grave
MK=SAR/DAR Marker   PH=Photo   SS=Service Source   BS=Burial Source

374

Harmon (1735 NC-17 Jul 1776) 2) Mar (1 Jan 1782, Montgomery Co) Phyllis Marrs (20 Sep 1763-12 Jan 1855) **VI:** Son of William (1699-26 Nov 1778, Pittsylvania Co) & Francis (Reade) Wynne **P:** unk **BLW:** unk **RG:** N **MK:** N **PH:** unk **SS:** AL Ct Bk pg 43, 44, 45 Montgomery Co; AS SAR applic **BS:** 80 vol 4 pg 221; 196.

WYSONG, Feidt (Fyette); b 1754 or 1759, York PA; d 1837 **RU:** Soldier, Drafted and served under Capt Josiah Swearington in Col Morrison's Regt for abt 5 mos. Marched to Ft McIntosh to the Muskingum and was discharged there. In Jul 1781, drafted and marched under Capt Looney to Bottom's Bridge below Richmond then to Yorktown and was at the seige. **CEM:** Fincastle Presbyterian; GPS 37.50017, -79.87558; 108 E Back St, Fincastle; Botetourt **GS:** N **SP:** Mar (27 May 1814 Botetourt Co) Susanna Coffman d/o Henry & (-----) Coffman **VI:** Name is on SAR plaque at this cemetery. Pensioned 3 Sep 1832 **P:** N **BLW:** N **RG:** Y **MK:** Y **PH:** N **SS:** AZ pg 127 **BS:** JLARC 1; 196.

WYSOR (WEYSOR, WEIZER), Henry; b 1756; d 12 Jan 1844 **RU:** Sergeant, Served in Frederick Co, Feb 1776 in Capt Berry's Co, Col Muhlenburg's 8th VA Cont Line. Was at Charleston at Ft Moultrie attack. Later with Gen Morgan, at Saratoga at surrender of Burgoyne, and at Valley Forge. In 1781 rejoined and was at siege at Yorktown. Had 5 tours serving 28 mos **CEM:** Wysor; GPS unk; Dublin; Pulaski **GS:** U **SP:** Mar (31 May 1811 Montgomery Co) Cynthia Charlton (3 Nov 1787-14 Jan 1866) **VI:** He moved to Montgomery Co after the war and was a Lt in War of 1812. Appl for pension 3 Sep 1832 age 78. His1833 address was at Christiansburg. S7854 **P:** Y **BLW:** unk **RG:** unk **MK:** unk **PH:** unk **SS:** E pg 851; K Vol 6 pg 228; AZ pg 164; CG Vol III **BS:** 196.

WYTHE, George; b 1726; d 8 Jun 1806 **RU:** Patriot, Was Signer of Declaration of Independence. Provided supplies to Maj Nelson's Troops of Horse & Gen Steven's Brigade **CEM:** St John's Episcopal; GPS 37.53183, -77.41958; 2401 E Broad St; Richmond City **GS:** U **SP:** Elizabeth Eggleston Taliaferro (1739 Willamsburg-Aug 1787, James City Co) d/o Richard & (-----) Taliaferro **VI:** No further data **P:** N **BLW:** N **RG:** Y **MK:** N **PH:** Y **SS:** E pg 851 **BS:** 28 pg 349.

YAGER, John Sr; b 15 Sep 1732, Madison Co; d 17 Aug 1826 **RU:** Patriot, Gave material aid to cause **CEM:** Hebron Lutheran; GPS 38.40676, -78.24808; 899 Blankenbaker Rd, Madison; Madison **GS:** U **SP:** Mar (c1757 Madison Co) Mary Margaret Wilhoit, d/o John Christian & Walburga (Weaver) Wilhoit (1737-1800) **VI:** Son of Adam Sr (1708-1794) & Susanna (Kobler) Yager (1710-__). Known as "Blind" John Yeager in old age **P:** unk **BLW:** unk **RG:** unk **MK:** unk **PH:** unk **SS:** AL Ct Bk 1 pg 43 Culpeper Co **BS:** 196.

YANCEY, Charles; b 10 May 1741; d 9 Jan 1814 **RU:** Captain, Commanded a Co in the Louisa Co Militia 1781-1782 **CEM:** Yancey/Crawford Family; GPS unk; Yanceyville; Louisa **GS:** N **SP:** Mary Crawford (8 Aug 1742-1841) **VI:** Son of Robert (__-1746) & Temperance (Dumas) Yancey **P:** N **BLW:** N **RG:** unk **MK:** N **PH:** N **SS:** CZ pg 486 **BS:** 196.

YANCEY, Charles Sr; b 1732; d 15 Apr 1805 **RU:** Patriot, Gave material aid to the cause **CEM:** Yancey Family; GPS 38.51709, -77.95532; Off Rt 685 Aubern Rd, 3.5 mi WNW of Brandy Station; Culpeper **GS:** Y **SP:** Mar (1740) Caroline Powers **VI:** No further data **P:** N **BLW:** N **RG:** N **MK:** N **PH:** unk **SS:** DAR Ancestor #A108720; AL Ct Bk I pg 16 **BS:** 167 Yancey; 196.

YANCEY, Lewis Davis; b 1689; d 1784 **RU:** Patriot, Provided beef and cattle to the army **CEM:** Yancey Family; GPS 38.51709, -77.95532; Off Rt 685 Auburn Rd, 3.5 mi WNW of Brandy Station; Culpeper **GS:** Y **SP:** Mar (c1710) Mildred Winifred Cavenaugh (1710-1780) **VI:** No further data **P:** N **BLW:** N **RG:** Y **MK:** N **PH:** unk **SS:** AK **BS:** 29 pg 28; 196.

YANCEY, Mary; b 8 Aug 1742; d 1841 **RU:** Patriot, Gave material aid to cause **CEM:** Yancey/Crawford Family; GPS unk; Yanceyville; Lousia **GS:** U **SP:** Charles Yancey (10 May 1741-9 Jan 1814 **VI:** No further data **P:** N **BLW:** N **RG:** unk **MK:** unk **PH:** unk **SS:** AL Ct Bk pg 16, 24 Lousia Co **BS:** 196.

YANCEY, Robert; b 1 Jan 1742, Hanover Co; d 20 Jul 1818 **RU:** Patriot, Performed public service by viewing, making report on alterations on Gillis Rd as ordered by Mecklenburg Co Ct on 13 May 1776 **CEM:** Yancey Family; GPS unk; Hwy 736 S fr 602 abt 2.5 mi, Averett; Mecklenburg **GS:** Y **SP:** Mar (aft 5 Mar 1765) Philadelphia Jones (c1754- aft 1818) d/o John (c1715, Mecklenburg Co-1791) & (-----) Jones **VI:** Cem in wooded area with periwinkle **P:** N **BLW:** N **RG:** unk **MK:** unk **PH:** unk **SS:** Mecklenburg Co Order Book #4 (1773-79) pg 337; DAR Patriot Index Vol 3 pg 3047 **BS:** 196.

RU=Rank/Unit	CEM=Cemetery	GS=Gravestone	SP=Spousal Information
VI=Other Veteran Info	P=Pension	BLW=Bounty/Land Warrant	RG=Registered Grave
MK=SAR/DAR Marker	PH=Photo	SS=Service Source	BS=Burial Source

375

YANCEY, William Layton (Leighton); b 1754, Lousia or Rockingham Co; d 4 Apr 1813 **RU:** Lieutenant, Served in 1st Regt of Light Dragoons under Col Theodrick Bland. Taken prisoner at Charleston 12 May 1780 and was prisoner on parole to end of war. Perhaps became a Capt before war ended **CEM:** Hilltop-Yancey Farm; GPS unk; Elkton; Rockingham **GS:** Y **SP:** Fanny Lynn Lewis (17 May 1763-30 Aug 1845) d/o Thomas (1718-1790) & Jane (Strother) (1732-1820) Lewis **VI:** Recd pen W7380. Awarded 4000 acres BLW #4894, 22 May 1799 & 1333 acres and # 2921 for 2667 acres. **P:** Y **BLW:** Y **RG:** unk **MK:** Y **PH:** unk **SS:** NSSAR Ancestor # P-325756 **BS:** JLARC 2, 4, 64, 76; 196.

YATES, Charles; b 20 Apr 1727, Whitehaven, England; d 11 Jan 1809 **RU:** Patriot, Was member Committee of Correspondence for Fredericksburg Jun 1774 **CEM:** Masonic Cemetery; GPS 38.30198, -77.46142; 900 Charles St; Fredericksburg City **GS:** Y **SP:** No info **VI:** Son of Rev Francis & Anne (Offeur) Yates **P:** N **BLW:** N **RG:** Y **MK:** N **PH:** Y **SS:** D pg 870 **BS:** 11 pg 124-7; 196.

YATES, Enoch; b 1761; d 27 Jan 1852 **RU:** Soldier, Served in Augusta Co Militia. **CEM:** Bell; GPS 38.26140, -78.95560; Rt 11, Mt Sidney; Augusta **GS:** Y **SP:** Mar (20 Jan 1803) Sally Wilson **VI:** Listed in "Burials in Augusta Co Cemeteries" pub by the county historical society 1979 and 1985 **P:** unk **BLW:** unk **RG:** unk **MK:** N **PH:** unk **SS:** NSSAR Ancestor #P-325818 **BS:** JLARC 8; 196.

YATES, John III; b 1715, New Kent Co; d 25 Oct 1777 **RU:** Patriot, Gave material aid to cause **CEM:** Richardson-Yates Family; GPS unk; Ringhold; Pittsylvania **GS:** U **SP:** Elizabeth Kilgore (1720 Orange Co. NC-3 Sep 1793 Pittsylvania Co.) **VI:** No further data **P:** N **BLW:** N **RG:** unk **MK:** unk **PH:** unk **SS:** AL Ct Bk pg 16 New Kent Co **BS:** 196.

YATES, William; b 1744; d 2 Dec 1789 **RU:** Lieutenant Colonel, Served on Washington's staff. Also in VA Cont Line **CEM:** Abingdon Episcopal; GPS 37.33355, -76.51364; 4645 George Washington Mem Hwy Rt 17; Gloucester **GS:** U **SP:** 1) Mar (22 Jun 1777) Ann Isham Poythress (__-24 Jun 1764) 2) Mar (21 Sep 1785) Elizabeth Booth **VI:** Son of Bartholomew (24 Aug 1676-__) & Elizabeth (Randolph) Yates. Graduated William & Mary College 1764 and later was Justice, Amelia Co **P:** unk **BLW:** Y **RG:** unk **MK:** unk **PH:** unk **SS:** N pg 415CZ pg 486 **BS:** 196.

YEARY, Benedict; b 1732; d 1802 **RU:** Patriot, Supplied horse for 14 days **CEM:** Benedict Yeary; GPS unk; Nr Rocky Station Fort; Lee **GS:** N **SP:** Mary (-----) (__-1799) **VI:** No further data **P:** N **BLW:** N **RG:** unk **MK:** unk **PH:** N **SS:** CD **BS:** 196.

YEARY, Henry Jr; b 1765, Fairfax Co VA; d 11 Jul 1840 **RU:** Private, Served in Gen William Campbell's Regt fr Abingdon as waterboy to Battle of Kings Mountain, 7 Oct 1780 **CEM:** Yeary Family; GPS unk; W fr Ewing; Lee **GS:** Y **SP:** Martha Ball **VI:** Son of Henry David (1730, Fairfax Co-1799, Boones Path, Lee Co) & (-----) Yeary **P:** unk **BLW:** unk **RG:** Y **MK:** Y **PH:** Y **SS:** J-NSSAR 1993 Reg NSSAR Ancestor #P-325874; J- DAR Hatcher **BS:** JLARC 1, 2.

YEARY, Henry Sr; b c1725 or 1730; d 1799 **RU:** Private/Patriot, USDAR records indicate service, details unk. Allowed 15# for a horse lost in service **CEM:** Ball Family; GPS unk; Rt 684 vic Ewing; Lee **GS:** Y **SP:** Mar (1760 Washington Co) Elizabeth Croxall (Croxtall) (1729 MD-1805) **VI:** No further data **P:** unk **BLW:** unk **RG:** Y **MK:** N **PH:** unk **SS:** DAR Ancestor #A133186; AK Nov 06 **BS:** 04, Nov 06.

YEATMAN, Thomas Muse; b 1762; d 14 Sep 1812 **RU:** Lieutenant/patriot, Served in Westmoreland Co Militia. Appt Lt 1777 and commanded Co. Also gave a beef to cause in Westmoreland Co **CEM:** Ware Episcopal; GPS 37.42275, -76.50789; 7825 John Clayton Mem Hwy; Gloucester **GS:** Y **SP:** Mary Tompkins (1765-Oct 1796) d/o John & (-----) Tomkins **VI:** Stone moved fr Yeatman plantation to Ware Episcopal Church cemetery **P:** N **BLW:** N **RG:** N **MK:** N **PH:** unk **SS:** E pg 853 **BS:** 48 pg 143; 196; 207.

YOUEL, William; b 1734, Sterling, Scotland; d 1 Sep 1834 **RU:** Soldier, Served in Capt James Gilmore's Co at Battle of Cowpens in Gilmore Rifles **CEM:** Youel Family, Meadow Lawn Farm; GPS unk; Rt 601, Goshen; Rockbridge **GS:** U **SP:** Mar (8 Aug 1774) Elizabeth Nelson (1736 Scotland-aft 9 Jan 1834) **VI:** No further data **P:** unk **BLW:** unk **RG:** Y **MK:** Y **PH:** unk **SS:** DAR Ancestor #A129687; J-NSSAR 1993 Reg; NSSAR Ancestor #P-326076; J- DAR Hatcher; N pg 1249 **BS:** JLARC 1,2.

YOUNG, Ezekiel; b Bef1736, England; d Jun 1800 **RU:** Private, Served in James MaCorkle Co, Montgomery Co, 5 Dec 1777 **CEM:** Young Family; GPS unk; Nr jct Rts 711 & 680; Grayson **GS:** U **SP:**

RU=Rank/Unit	CEM=Cemetery	GS=Gravestone	SP=Spousal Information
VI=Other Veteran Info	P=Pension	BLW=Bounty/Land Warrant	RG=Registered Grave
MK=SAR/DAR Marker	PH=Photo	SS=Service Source	BS=Burial Source

376

Ruth Whitehead **VI:** No further data **P:** unk **BLW:** unk **RG:** Y **MK:** N **PH:** unk **SS:** A pg 212; H Apr 07 **BS:** 4-Apr-07.

YOUNG, Henry; b 1741 Essex Co VA; d 15 Nov 1817 **RU:** Quartermaster General, Entered Conl Army as Lt in 1776, promoted to Capt 28 Dec 1776. Was appt Quartermaster of VA 1781 by Gov Digges. Served in 5th Regt, Cont Line **CEM:** Young Family; GPS unk; Walkerton; King & Queen **GS:** Y **SP:** No info **VI:** Son of Henry & Rachel (Smith) Young. Member of King and Queen Co court. Records lost in DC fire of 1800. Recd BLW #32466 on 3 Jun 1695 of 6666 acres. R18332 **P:** Y **BLW:** Y **RG:** unk **MK:** unk **PH:** unk **SS:** K Vol 6 pg 236; N pg 412 **BS:** 196.

YOUNG, James; b unk; d 1790 **RU:** Second Lieutenant, Served in Lt Young's Co of troops. Appt in Augusta Co militia rank of 2nd Lt, 20 Oct 1778 in Capt Patterson's Co. Served also in Capt John Young's Co **CEM:** Augusta Stone Presbyterian; GPS 38.23926, -78.97356; 28 Old Stone Church Ln, Ft Defiance; Augusta **GS:** Y **SP:** No info **VI:** Govt stone **P:** unk **BLW:** unk **RG:** Y **MK:** Y **PH:** Y **SS:** E pg 854 **BS:** JLARC 1, 2, 8, 23, 62; 196.

YOUNG, John; b 25 Mar 1737; d 25 Dec 1824 **RU:** Captain?, Service not listed in SAR registry **CEM:** Glebe Burying Ground; GPS 38.10940, -79.22190; Glebe School Rd Rt 876, Swoopes; Augusta **GS:** Y **SP:** 1) Mar (13 Sep 1763) Mary Elizabeth White (1746-2 Apr 1779) d/o Isaac White 2) Mar (23 Jan 1781) Mary Sitlington (15 Sep 1759-25 Jul 1838) **VI:** Son of Hugh Young (1699-1756) & Agnes Sitlington. VA DAR plaque styles him Capt **P:** unk **BLW:** unk **RG:** unk **MK:** Y **PH:** unk **SS:** NSSAR Ancestor # P-326247 **BS:** JLARC 8, 62, 63; 196.

YOUNG, John; b 1760; d unk **RU:** Private, Served in Capt Simpson's Co, Augusta Co Militia **CEM:** Trinity Episcopal; GPS 38.14917, -79.07521; 214 Beverley St; Staunton City **GS:** U **SP:** No info **VI:** No further data **P:** unk **BLW:** unk **RG:** unk **MK:** unk **PH:** unk **SS:** E pg 854 **BS:** JLARC 2, 8.

YOUNG, John; b 1760, Paris, Fauquier Co; d aft 1822 **RU:** Soldier, SAR registry did not provide service **CEM:** Old Presbyterian Meeting House; GPS 38.48528, -77.23532; 323 S Fairfax St; Alexandria City **GS:** N **SP:** Euphemia Humphrey (1770, Loudoun Co-16 Apr 1822) d/o Thomas (2 Jun 1742 PA-6 Jun 1823) & Mary (Marks) (12 Jul 1742,-5 Sep 1811) Humphrey **VI:** No further data **P:** unk **BLW:** unk **RG:** Y **MK:** unk **PH:** N **SS:** J-NSSAR 1993 Reg ; NSSAR Ancestor #P-326234 **BS:** JLARC 1; 5.

YOUNG, Thomas; b 6 Apr 1766; d 16 Apr 1840 **RU:** Soldier, Service not listed in SAR registry **CEM:** Glebe Burying Ground; GPS 38.10940, -79.22190; Glebe School Rd Rt 876, Swoopes; Augusta **GS:** Y **SP:** Mary (-----) (27 May 1759-10 Mar 1831) (Gr st says wife of Thomas Young) **VI:** DAR plaque **P:** unk **BLW:** unk **RG:** unk **MK:** Y **PH:** unk **SS:** NSSAR Ancestor #P-326403 **BS:** JLARC 62, 63; 210 pg 394; 196.

YOUNG, William; b 2 May 1740; d c1810 **RU:** Patriot, Gave material aid to cause **CEM:** Young Family; GPS unk; Ruther Glen; Caroline **GS:** U **SP:** Jane Mickelborough (15 Jan 1752 Middlesex Co-9 Nov 1835) d/o Henry (10 Feb 1705 Middslesex Co-1783) & Susanna (Daniel) Mickleborough **VI:** Died in Middlesex Co **P:** N **BLW:** N **RG:** unk **MK:** unk **PH:** unk **SS:** AL Ct Bk II pg 33 **BS:** 196.

YOUNG, William; b unk; d unk **RU:** Private/Patriot, Served in Capt Trimble's Co, Augusta Co Militia, Gave material aid to cause **CEM:** Glebe Burying Ground; GPS 38.10940, -79.22190; Glebe School Rd Rt 876, Swoopes; Augusta **GS:** N **SP:** No info **VI:** Name is on DAR plaque **P:** unk **BLW:** unk **RG:** Y **MK:** N **PH:** N **SS:** E pg 855; AL Comm Bk II pg 30 Augusta Co **BS:** 36 pg 28, 32.

YOUNT, Jacob; b c1755, PA; d 7 Oct 1821 **RU:** Soldier, Served in York Co PA in 1778. Served in Capt Adam Serfoos' Co 1781 **CEM:** Yount Family; GPS unk; Rts 253 & 278, 2.8 mi E; Rockingham **GS:** N **SP:** Catherine Dagen **VI:** No further data **P:** unk **BLW:** unk **RG:** Y **MK:** N **PH:** N **SS:** AK **BS:** 4.

YOWELL (YOWEL), William; b 1 May 1763, Culpeper Co; d 6 Mar 1845 **RU:** Private, Ent serv 1779 Culpeper Co. Served at battle of Petersburg & Siege of Yorktown **CEM:** Yowell Family; GPS 38.19420, -78.49120; Syria; Madison **GS:** N **SP:** Mar (Jul 1782, nr Slate Mills, Culpeper Co) Nellie (Nelly) Crane (15 Apr 1763-__) **VI:** He was pen Madison Co 1832. Widow appl pen 19 Jun 1847 Madison Co, Recd BLW 16 Mar 1855. W5551. BLW 26208-160-55 **P:** Y **BLW:** Y **RG:** Y **MK:** N **PH:** N **SS:** K Vol 6 pg 242; AK; CG Vol 3 pg 4055 **BS:** 4.

RU=Rank/Unit	CEM=Cemetery	GS=Gravestone	SP=Spousal Information
VI=Other Veteran Info	P=Pension	BLW=Bounty/Land Warrant	RG=Registered Grave
MK=SAR/DAR Marker	PH=Photo	SS=Service Source	BS=Burial Source

377

YVES, Andre; b unk; d 1781 **RU:** Seaman, Served on "Ville de Paris" and died from Yorktown battle **CEM:** French Memorial; GPS 36.81944, -79.39933; Yorktown; York **GS:** U **SP:** No info **VI:** No further data **P:** unk **BLW:** unk **RG:** Y **MK:** unk **PH:** unk **SS:** J-Yorktown Historian **BS:** JLARC 1, 74.

ZANE, Isaac II; b 24 Apr 1743, Philadelphia PA; d 10 Aug 1795 **RU:** Brigadier General/Patriot, Was in 1773 in House of Burgesses. During War his Marlboro Iron Works produced four and six pound ordnance, shot, kettles, salt pans, camp stoves, and cannons. In 1794 was Brig Gen of Frederick Co VA Militia. Gave material aid to cause **CEM:** Mt Pleasant Meeting House; GPS 39.12080, -78.30440; Rt 622, Mt Pleasant; Frederick **GS:** U **SP:** With mistress Elizabeth McFarland (c1762-10 Oct 1831) had a child **VI:** Son of Isaac & Sarah (Elfreth) Zane **P:** unk **BLW:** unk **RG:** unk **MK:** unk **PH:** unk **SS:** AL Ct Bk pg 5 & 10 Shenandoah Co **BS:** 196.

ZEA, Martin; b c1756 or 1760, Lancaster Co, PA; d 3 Nov 1838 **RU:** Soldier, Served in VA Line **CEM:** St Pauls Lutheran; GPS 38.99140, -78.36250; 156 W Washington, Strasburg; Shenandoah **GS:** Y **SP:** Mar (30 Jan 1787) Ann Stockshlager (3 Feb 1766-10 Jul 1842 Strasburg, Shenandoah Co) **VI:** Moved to Shenandoah Co with parents before RW. Appl for pen Shenandoah Co 7 Oct 1833. Wife's pen rejected because she was not a widow at date of the act **P:** Y **BLW:** unk **RG:** unk **MK:** unk **PH:** Y **SS:** E pg 544; CG Vol 3 pg 4005 **BS:** 196.

ZELL, John; b unk; d 1781 **RU:** unk, Was killed in the Battle at Yorktown **CEM:** Yorktown Victory Monument Tablet; GPS 38.28350, -78.54150; Yorktown; York **GS:** U **SP:** No info **VI:** No further data **P:** unk **BLW:** unk **RG:** unk **MK:** unk **PH:** unk **SS:** J-Yorktown Historian **BS:** JLARC 74.

ZIMMERMAN, Christopher; b 1719, Spotsylvania Co; d 1781 **RU:** Patriot, Gave material aid to cause **CEM:** Hebron Lutheran; GPS 38.40676, -78.24808; 899 Blankenbaker Rd, Madison; Madison **GS:** U **SP:** No info **VI:** Son of Johann (1692-1748) & Anna (Albrecht) (1687-1757) Zimmerman. Died in Culpeper Co **P:** N **BLW:** N **RG:** unk **MK:** unk **PH:** unk **SS:** AL Ct Bk I pg 24, 27 **BS:** 196.

ZIMMERMAN, Henry; b 1755; d 16 Nov 1806 **RU:** Ensign, Served in PA **CEM:** Old Christ Church Episcopal; GPS 38.80625, -77.04718; 118 N Washington St; Alexandria City **GS:** N **SP:** Mar (1803) Elizabeth Fairhurst (__ Loudoun Co-1850) d/o Jeremiah & Ann (Slaughter) Fairhurst **VI:** GS indicates he d 16 Nov 1806, age 51 **P:** unk **BLW:** unk **RG:** Y **MK:** N **PH:** N **SS:** A pg 543; A pg 144 **BS:** 20 pg 144.

ZIMMERMAN, John; b 1737, Orange Co; d 1819 **RU:** Patriot, Gave material aid to cause **CEM:** Hebron Lutheran; GPS 38.40676, -78.24808; 899 Blankenbaker Rd, Madison; Madison **GS:** U **SP:** No info **VI:** Son of Johann (1692-1748) & Anna (Albrecht) (1687-1757) Zimmerman **P:** N **BLW:** N **RG:** unk **MK:** unk **PH:** unk **SS:** AL Ct Bk I pg 24,27 **BS:** 196.

ZIRKLE, George Adam; b Sep 1738, Telford, Montgomery Co, MD; d 8 Sep 1800 **RU:** Private, Served in MD **CEM:** Zirkle Family; GPS 38.65900, -78.69580; River Rd, New Market; Shenandoah **GS:** Y **SP:** Elizabeth Rettenour/Reidenauer (1752-1829) **VI:** Son of Johan Ludwig (1705-1747) & Maria Eva (Bear) (1709-1771) Zirkle. SAR marker **P:** N **BLW:** N **RG:** unk **MK:** Y **PH:** N **SS:** AK - Col James Wood II Nov 2014 **BS:** 04; 196.

RU=Rank/Unit	CEM=Cemetery	GS=Gravestone	SP=Spousal Information
VI=Other Veteran Info	P=Pension	BLW=Bounty/Land Warrant	RG=Registered Grave
MK=SAR/DAR Marker	PH=Photo	SS=Service Source	BS=Burial Source

378

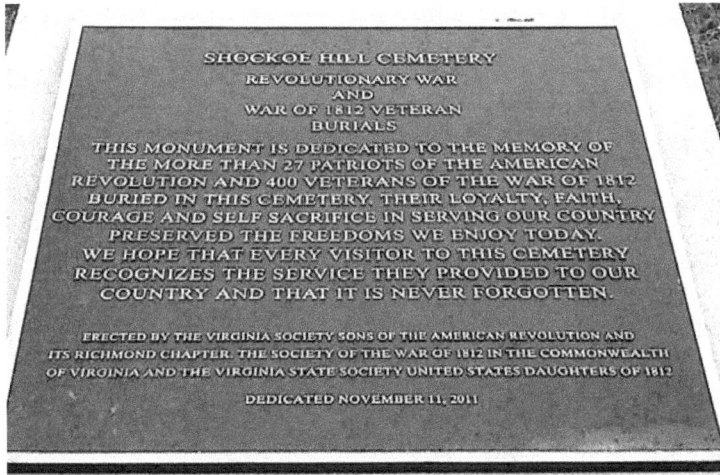

Plaque on monument dedicated to Revolutionary War and War of 1812 burials at Shockoe Hil Cemetery (City of Richmond)

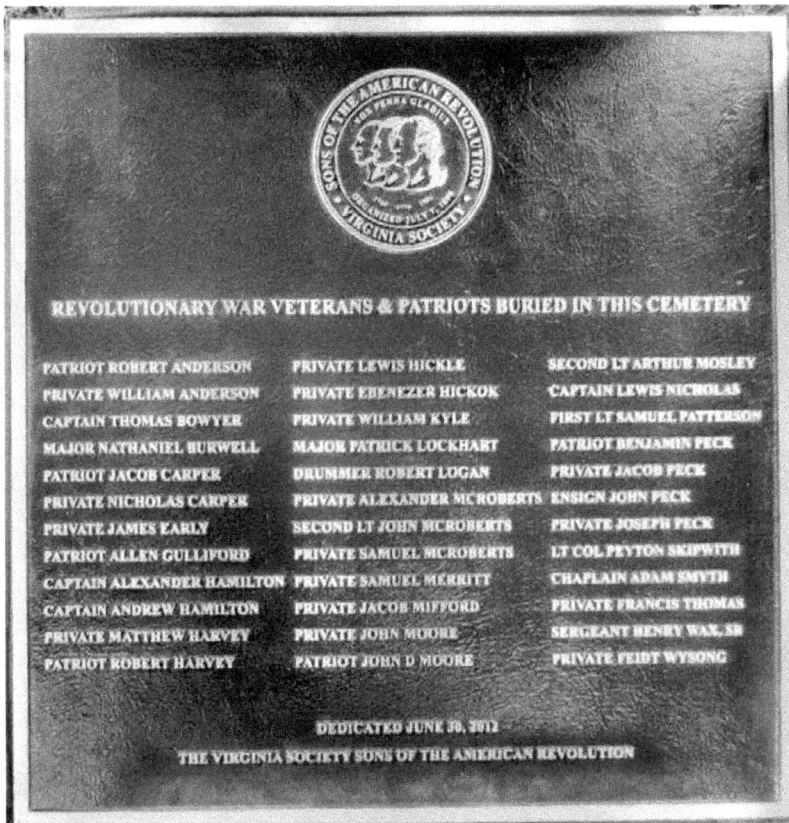

Plaque listing Revolutionary War Veterans and Patriots at Fincastle Presbyterian Church (Fincastle, Botetourt County)

REVOLUTIONARY WAR PATRIOTS AND WAR OF 1812 VETERANS BURIED IN THIS CEMETERY

REVOLUTIONARY WAR

PRIVATE SAMUEL CARSON
PRIVATE ROBERT COOPER
CAPTAIN PATRICK HALL
CAPTAIN WILLIAM HALL
PRIVATE JAMES MCCHESNEY
PRIVATE JOHN MCCHESNEY
PATRIOT MARTHA MCCORMICK
PRIVATE ROBERT MCCORMICK

ENSIGN JAMES MCNUTT
PRIVATE ROBERT MCNUTT
CAPTAIN ANDREW MOORE
PRIVATE JAMES POAGE
PRIVATE ANDREW STEELE
PRIVATE DAVID STEELE
ENSIGN JAMES W. STEELE
PRIVATE JOHN STEELE, JR.

PRIVATE JOHN STEELE, SR.
PRIVATE NATHANIEL STEELE
CAPTAIN SAMUEL STEELE
PRIVATE SAMUEL STEELE, JR.
PRIVATE THOMAS STEELE
PRIVATE WILLIAM STEELE
PRIVATE JOHN TATE
CAPTAIN SAMUEL WILSON

WAR OF 1812

SERGEANT DAVID CARSON
PRIVATE ELIJAH CARSON
PRIVATE JOHN CARSON
LIEUTENANT SAMUEL CARSON, SR.
PRIVATE JOHN COOPER
PRIVATE RICHARD GIBBS

PRIVATE ROBERT HALL
PRIVATE WILLIAM HALL
PRIVATE THOMAS JACKSON
PRIVATE WILLIAM LUSK
SERGEANT WILLIAM MCCHESNEY
CORPORAL WILLIAM MCCORMICK
PRIVATE ROBERT MCNUTT

PRIVATE WILLIAM MOORE
PRIVATE WILLIAM MOORE
PRIVATE JAMES E. POAGUE
PRIVATE JOHN POAGUE
PRIVATE WILLIAM STEELE
PRIVATE JOHN M. WILSON

FUNDED BY THE NATIONAL SOCIETY SONS OF THE AMERICAN REVOLUTION (SAR) GEORGE WASHINGTON ENDOWMENT FUND, VIRGINIA SOCIETY SAR KNIGHT-PATTY TRUST FUND AND THE SOCIETY OF THE WAR OF 1812 IN THE COMMONWEALTH OF VIRGINIA.
DEDICATED MAY 15, 2010

Plaque listing Revolutionary War Patriots and War of 1812 Veterans at the
Old Providence Reformed Presbyterian Church (Spotswood, Augusta County)

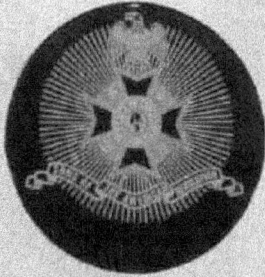

BURIALS OF REVOLUTIONARY WAR PATRIOTS IN THIS
HISTORICAL CEMETERY

SERGEANT DANIEL ANDERSON
PRIVATE DAVID ANDERSON
LT COLONEL JOHN BANISTER
CAPTAIN ROBERT BOLLING
SERGEANT JOHN CAMERON
PRIVATE ROBERT DONALDSON
MATROSS EDWARD HAMMON
CAPTAIN WILLIAM HARRISON
PRIVATE JESSE HEATH
CAPTAIN JOHN JEFFERS
PRIVATE ANDREW JOHNSON
GENERAL JOSEPH JONES
PRIVATE EDWARD LEE
PRIVATE ROBERT ROBINSON
PRIVATE THOMAS STROUD
PRIVATE JOHN STUART
PATRIOT ALEXANDER TAYLOR
MAJOR JAMES WILLIAMS
CAPTAIN ERASMUS GILL
DEDICATED BY THE VIRGINIA SOCIETY SONS
OF THE AMERICAN REVOLUTION

This VASSAR monument located at the Blandford Cemetery in Petersburg names the
Revolutionary War Patriots buried there. It was dedicated on April 16, 2016.

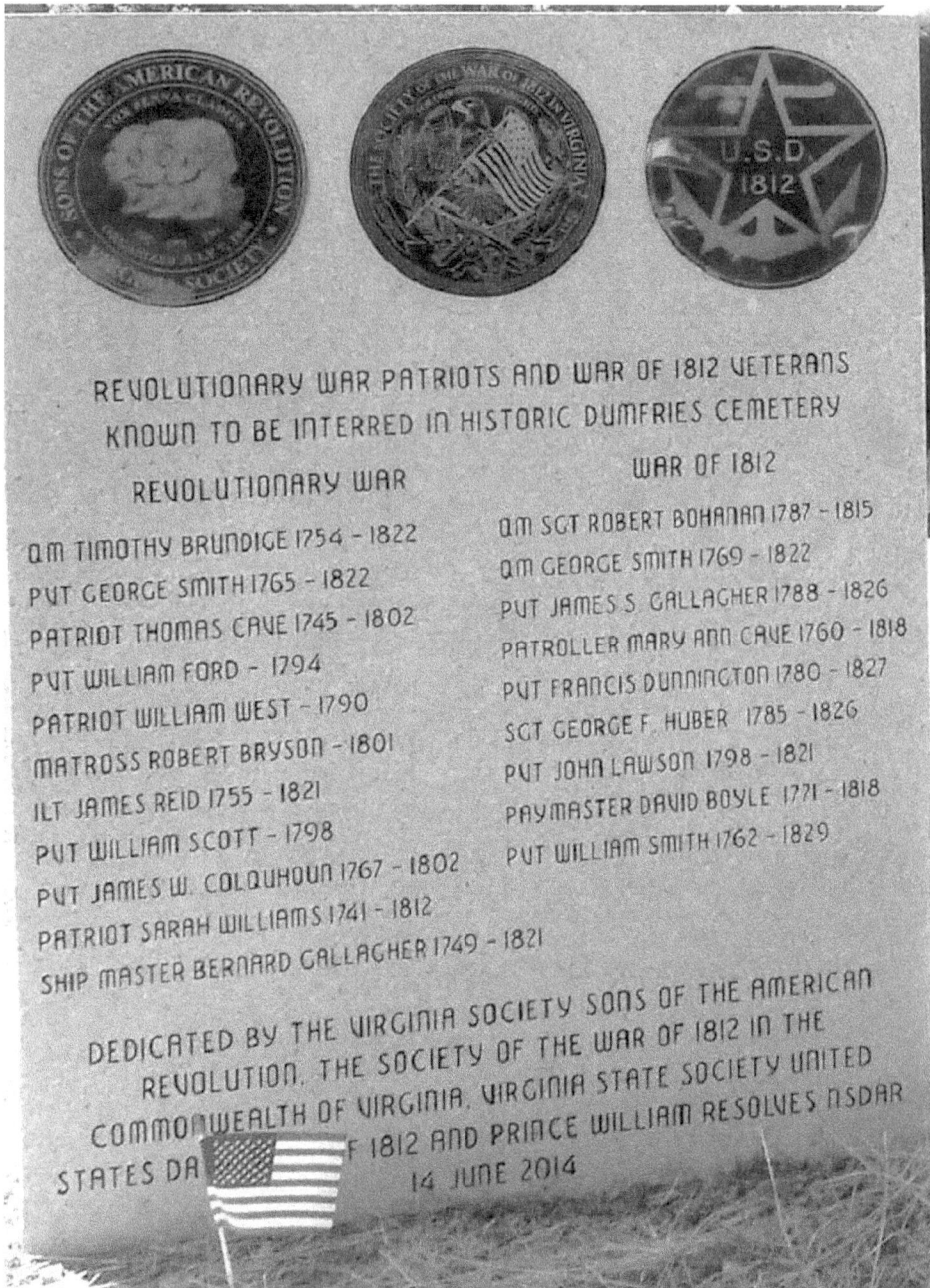

REVOLUTIONARY WAR PATRIOTS AND WAR OF 1812 VETERANS
KNOWN TO BE INTERRED IN HISTORIC DUMFRIES CEMETERY

REVOLUTIONARY WAR

QM TIMOTHY BRUNDIGE 1754 - 1822
PVT GEORGE SMITH 1765 - 1822
PATRIOT THOMAS CAVE 1745 - 1802
PVT WILLIAM FORD - 1794
PATRIOT WILLIAM WEST - 1790
MATROSS ROBERT BRYSON - 1801
1LT JAMES REID 1755 - 1821
PVT WILLIAM SCOTT - 1798
PVT JAMES W. COLQUHOUN 1767 - 1802
PATRIOT SARAH WILLIAMS 1741 - 1812
SHIP MASTER BERNARD GALLAGHER 1749 - 1821

WAR OF 1812

QM SGT ROBERT BOHANAN 1787 - 1815
QM GEORGE SMITH 1769 - 1822
PVT JAMES S. GALLAGHER 1788 - 1826
PATROLLER MARY ANN CAVE 1760 - 1818
PVT FRANCIS DUNNINGTON 1780 - 1827
SGT GEORGE F. HUBER 1785 - 1826
PVT JOHN LAWSON 1798 - 1821
PAYMASTER DAVID BOYLE 1771 - 1818
PVT WILLIAM SMITH 1762 - 1829

DEDICATED BY THE VIRGINIA SOCIETY SONS OF THE AMERICAN
REVOLUTION, THE SOCIETY OF THE WAR OF 1812 IN THE
COMMONWEALTH OF VIRGINIA, VIRGINIA STATE SOCIETY UNITED
STATES DA   F 1812 AND PRINCE WILLIAM RESOLVES NSDAR
14 JUNE 2014

This monument in the Dumfries City Cemetery (Prince William County)
shows Revolutionary War Patriots and War of 1812 Veterans buried there.
It was dedicated in June 2014.

This plaque listing Revolutionary Patriots and War of 1812 Veterans is mounted
on a pole at the entrance of the Masonic Cemetery in Fredericksburg.
It was dedicated on May 16, 2015

REVOLUTIONARY WAR PATRIOTS MEMORIALIZED IN THIS HISTORIC CEMETERY

PRIVATE JAMES ALLEN

CAPTAIN ANDREW ANDERSON

CAPTAIN DAVID BELL

CAPTAIN JOSEPH BELL, JR

PRIVATE JOSEPH BELL, SR

PRIVATE JOSEPH BELL

PRIVATE WILLIAM BELL

PATRIOT ARTHUR CONNALY, SR

PRIVATE JAMES CRAIG, JR

PRIVATE JAMES CRAIG, SR

PRIVATE JOHN CRAIG

PRIVATE WILLIAM CRAIG

PRIVATE GEORGE CRAWFORD, JR

MAJOR JOHN CRAWFORD

PATRIOT PATRICK CRAWFORD

CAPTAIN ROBERT CURRY

CAPTAIN JOHN GAMBLE

PRIVATE JOHN GIBBONS

CAPTAIN JOHN GIVENS

PRIVATE ROBERT HARNSBERGER

PRIVATE WILLIAM HOOK

PRIVATE WILLIAM HOOKE, SR

PRIVATE ROBERT HOOK(HOOKE), SR

PRIVATE ROBERT KENNY

PRIVATE JAMES KERR

PRIVATE JOHN KERR, JR

PRIVATE JOHN KERR, SR

PRIVATE JOSEPH KERR

CAPTAIN ROBERT KENNEY

PRIVATE JOHN MILLS

SERGEANT ROBERT MILLS

COLONEL GEORGE MOFFETT

PRIVATE ALEXANDER NELSON

PRIVATE ALEXANDER NELSON

ENSIGN JOHN POAGE, JR

2D LIEUTENANT ROBERT POAGE

PRIVATE THOMAS POAGE

ENSIGN ALEXANDER ROBERTSON

LT COL ALEXANDER ROBERTSON, SR

LIEUTENANT WILLIAM ROBERTSON

PRIVATE ALEXANDER ROSS

PRIVATE JOHN SMITH

PATRIOT ALEXANDER WALKER

MAJOR WILLIAM WILSON

LIEUTENANT JAMES YOUNG

DEDICATED JULY 25, 2015

BY THE VIRGINIA SOCIETY
SONS OF THE AMERICAN
REVOLUTION

This pole-mounted plaque in the Old Stone Presbyterian Church Cemetery
(Fort Defiance, Augusta County) was dedicated by VASSAR on 25 Jul 2015.

REVOLUTIONARY WAR PATRIOTS

KNOWN TO BE INTERRED OR MEMORIALIZED
IN THIS HISTORIC BURIAL GROUND

MAYOR GEORGE ABYVON
PATRIOT MARIAM ABYVON
PATRIOT HARRISON ALLMAND
PATRIOT SAMUEL BACON
CAPTAIN JOHN CALVERT
COUNCILMAN THOMAS CALVERT
LIEUTENANT GEORGE CHAMBERLAIN
SURGEON'S MATE CARY H. HANSFORD
CAPTAIN MILES KING, SR.
PATRIOT JOHN LAWRENCE
PATRIOT JOHN LEE
LIEUTENANT COLONEL THOMAS MATHEWS
CAPTAIN JAMES MAXWELL
PATRIOT HILLARY MOSELY
CAPTAIN LIEUTENANT PETER NESTELL
SURGEON JOHN K. READ
PRIVATE JOHN SINGLETON
SURGEON AUGUSTIN SLAUGHTER
MAYOR JAMES TAYLOR
ALDERMAN ROBERT TAYLOR
PATRIOT SARAH C. TAYLOR
UNNAMED MINUTEMAN
UNNAMED MINUTEMAN
UNNAMED SOLDIER

NORFOLK CHAPTER AND VIRGINIA SOCIETY
SONS OF THE AMERICAN REVOLUTION

DEDICATED DECEMBER 3, 2011

This VASSAR plaque identifying burials of Revolutionary War Patriots
is mounted on the wall of Historic St. Paul's Episcopal Church in Norfolk.
It was dedicated Dec 3 2011.

REVOLUTIONARY WAR PATRIOTS AND WAR OF 1812 VETERANS BURIED
IN THIS HISTORIC CEMETERY
REVOLUTIONARY WAR
PATRIOT ANNE BIRKETT PRATT HUNGERFORD
CAPTAIN JOHN PRATT HUNGERFORD
CAPTAIN THOMAS HUNGERFORD
PRIVATE WILLIAM KENDALL

WAR OF 1812
BRIGADIER GENERAL JOHN PRATT HUNGERFORD
MAJOR HENRY HUNGERFORD
AIDE DE CAMP JOHN WASHINGTON HUNGERFORD

Dedicated by the James Monroe Chapter,
Virginia Society Sons of the American Revolution
and the Society War of 1812 in the Commonwealth of Virginia

This plaque lists Revolutionary War Patriots and War of 1812 Veterans
buried in the Hungerford Pratt Cemetery (Westmoreland County)

This monument in the Mount Hebron Cemetery in Winchester lists the Revolutionary War Patriots buried there. It was dedicated on Aug 24, 2013.

APPENDIX A – VETERAN LIST BY COUNTY / INDEPENDENT CITY

About Virginia Counties and Independent Cities:

In 1634, the Virginia Colony was divided into eight "shires" later renamed counties. Today the Commonwealth of Virginia has 95 Counties and 38 Independent Cities. Unlike in most states, Virginia's cities are not part of counties. Incorporated cities are independent jurisdictions with their own political and administrative systems and are equal to counties as governmental subdivisions of the state. They have their own court systems, and with a few exceptions, their own record repositories.

Confusion can occur because some cities and counties are named the same, yet may or may not be geographically contiguous. Also, a county's seat (courthouse) is sometimes located within the boundaries of a city. For example, Fairfax County surrounds the City of Fairfax City and its county seat is located there. However, Richmond County and the City of Richmond are in different parts of the state, as are Franklin County and the City of Franklin. Also, the names of James City County and Charles City can be misleading. Two of the originial shires, they have always been counties and never incorporated cities.

Research sources for county/city information in this section include *The Hornbook of Virginia History* published by the Library of Virginia and *Encyclopedia Virginia* published online by the Virginia Foundation for the Humanities.

ACCOMACK COUNTY. Original 1634 shire of Accawmack or Accomac County comprised Virginia's Eastern Shore. Name changed to Northampton County in 1643. Split into the present Accomack and Northampton Counties in 1663. County seat is Accomac (23301).

ANDREWS, Robert	JOYNES, Levin S	TEACKLE, Arthur
ANDREWS, William	KENNAHORN, William Jr	TEACKLE (TEAKLE), Levin
BAGWELL, Isaiah	KENNAHORN, William Sr	UPSHUR, Arthur IV
BENSON, James Sr	KER, Edward	UPSHUR, Caleb
BRADFORD, Thomas A	KER, John Shepard	UPSHUR, John
BURTON, Thomas	LAWS, John	WAPLES, Samuel
CAMPBELL, Archibald	MELVIN, James	WATSON, Benjamin
COLONNA, Benjamin	PARKER, George	WELBURN (WELBOURNE),
CORBIN, George	PARKER, Thomas	William Sr
CROPPER, John	PARRAMORE, William	WEST, Abel
CROPPER, Sebastian	PETTITT, William	WEST, Anthony Jr
CUSTIS, Henry	PIELEE, Gilbert	WHALEY, Zedekaih (Zadock)
CUSTIS, Thomas	READ, Edmund (Edmond)	WHARTON, John Esq
ELLIOTT, William	RILEY, John	WISE, John
FLOYD, Matthew	RODGERS, Robert	
FOREMAN, Robert	SAVAGE, Francis	
GALI (GALLIN, GALING),	SAVAGE, William	
Samuel	SUMMERS, Horsey	

ALBEMARLE COUNTY. Formed in 1744 from Goochland County. County seat is Charlottesville (22902). **See also CHARLOTTESVILLE CITY.**

ANDERSON, Edmund	HARDING, Isaac	THOMAS, John
BOWEN, Micajah	HARRIS, Benjamin	VIA, William
BROCKMAN, William Sr	HARRIS, William	WALKER, Francis
BROWN, Bernis	HUDSON, Christopher	WALKER, John
BROWN, Brightberry	HUDSON, John	WALKER, Martha
CHILDRESS, Benjamin	LEWIS, Charles	WALKER, Thomas
DIVERS, George	MASSIE, Charles Sr	WINGFIELD, John M
EARLY, James	MAUPINE, Daniel	WOOD, John
EPPERSON, David	MOORE, Stephen	WOODS, William
GARLAND, Nathaniel	RODES (RHODES), John	WOODSON, Tarleton
GENTRY, James	SNOW, Richard	
HAMNER, Nicholas	THOMAS, John	

ALEXANDRIA CITY (22314). Incorporated as a town in 1779 in portion of Fairfax County which became part of District of Columbia, then Alexandria County, then Arlington County. Achieved Independent City status from Arlington County in 1852. Court records begin in 1780. **See also ARLINGTON COUNTY and FAIRFAX COUNTY.**

ALLISON, Robert
ANDERSON, James
ARELL, David
ARELL, H (Henry)
ARELL, Samuel
AYRES, William
BAILLIE, Robert
BARTLEMAN, William
BENNETT, Charles
BIRD, William
BLACK, Benjamin
BLACK, David
BLUNT, Washer
BOYAR (BOYARS), John
BOYER, Henry
BRAWNER, William Henry
BROOKS, John Turpin
BURNES (BURNS), John
BUTCHER, John
CALLENDER, John
CAMPBELL, James
CARLYLE, John
CHAPIN, Benjamin
CHEW, Rodger
CONNELL, William
CONNER, James
COOK, Jacob
COOPER, Samuel
CRAIG, Samuel
CRAIK, James Dr
CRAWFORD, Thomas
CREIGHTON, Robert Dr
CROUCHER, Thomas
DEAN, Joseph
DELAGNEL, Julius Adolphus
DICK, Elisha Cullen Dr
DOUGLASS, Daniel
DUNLOP, John
DUNN, William
EVANS, John
FAW, Abraham
FENDALL, Philip Richard
FITZGERALD, John
FLEMING, Andrew
GILLIES (GILLES), James Dr
GILPIN, George
GRAHAM, David
GRIMES, John
HAGAN, Francis Ignatius
HAGERTY, Patrick
HANNAH, Alexander

HARPER, Edward
HARPER, John
HARPER, Joseph
HARPER, William
HARTSHORNE, William
HAYLEY, James
HERBERT, William
HESS, Jacob
HILTON, Samuel
HOOF, Lawrence
HUNTER, Alexander
HUNTER, George
HUNTER, John
HUNTER, William
HUNTER, William Jr
HURDLE, Lawrence
IRWIN, James
JANNEY, Abel
JOHNSON, Dennis
JORDAN, John
KEITH, Alexander
KENNEDY, James Dr
KIDD, James
KINCAID, John
LACROIX, Pierre
LADD, William
LAWRASON, James
LEWIS, Edward
LONGDEN, John
MARSTELLER, Philip
    Balthasar or Phillip G
MASON, George Jr
MCFADEN (McFADDEN),
    James
MCIVER, Colin
MCKNIGHT, Charles
MCKNIGHT, William
MCMAHON, Michael
MEASE, Robert
MITCHELL, James
MITCHELL, William
MUIR, James Rev
MUIR, John
MUIR, Robert
MURPHY, Francis
MURRAY, George
MURRAY, James
MYERS (MYRES), John C
NEWTON, William
NICHOLAS, Lewis
PATTERSON, William

PEAKE, Humphrey Sr
PEAKE, William
PEYTON, Francis
PIERCY, Henry
PORTER, Thomas
POTTEN, John
RAMSAY, Dennis
RAMSAY, Dennis
RAMSAY, William
RAMSEY, Anthony
REDMAN, Henry
REYNOLDS, William
RICHARDS, George
RIDDLE, Joshua
RIORDAN, John
ROSE, Henry
SANFORD, Lawrence
SANFORD, Robert
SANFORD, Thomas
SCOTT, William
SCULL, William
SHAW, James
SHREVE, Benjamin Jr
SIMMS, Charles
SIMMS, Thomas
SIMPSON, Jeremiah
SLADE, William
SLOAN, John
SMITH, Caleb Jr
SMITH, Joseph
SMITH, William Henry
SPOONER, Charles
STEWART, John
STITH, Buckner
STUART, John Ainsworth
SUMMERS, John
TAYLOR, Jesse
TAYLOR, Jesse
VOWELL, John G
WALES, Andrew
WEBB, Thomas T
WESCOTT, John
WEST, Thomas Wade
WESTON, Lewis
WHEELER, William
WILKINSON, Thomas
WILSON, James
WOODWARD, James
YOUNG, John
ZIMMERMAN, Henry

ALEXANDRIA COUNTY. Renamed in 1920. **See ARLINGTON COUNTY.**

ALLEGHANY COUNTY. Formed in 1822 from Bath County and Botetourt County. Includes the former independent city of Clifton Forge (1906) which reverted in 2001 to a town within the County. County seat is Covington (24426). **See also COVINGTON CITY.**

HAYNES, Benjamin	HUMPHREY, William	SMITH, William
HAYNES, Joseph	KING, John	SMITH, William

AMELIA COUNTY. Formed in 1735 from Brunswick County and Prince George County. County seat is Amelia (23002).

ARCHER, John	GILES, William Branch	ROYALL, John
AVARY, Wiliam	GREEN, John	ROYALL, Littleberry
BOOKER, George	GREEN, Thomas	TOWNES, John
BOOKER, Richardson	GREEN, William	VAUGHAN, James
(Richerson)	JACKSON, Francis	WHITWORTH, Thomas
CHAPPELL, John Sr	JONES, Peter	WOOD, William Sr
EGGLESTON, Joseph	MEAD(E), Everard Sr	
GILES, William	MEADE, Everard Jr	

AMHERST COUNTY. Formed in 1761 from Albemarle County. County seat is Amherst (24521).

BURTON, Samuel	LOVING, William	RODES, Charles
CABELL, William Jr	MEREDITH, Samuel Garland	RUCKER, Ambrose
CRAWFORD, Ann (Anderson)	PENDLETON, William	RUCKER, Anthony Jr
DILLARD, James B	PENN, Gabriel	RUCKER, Isaac
ELLIS, Josiah B	PENN, George	RUCKER, John Sr
FRANKLIN, James	PENN, John	TUCKER, Daniel
HENRY, William	PENN, William	TYLER, John
HIGGINBOTHAM, James	PINNELL, Thomas	WILSON, Richard
JOHNS, William	POWELL, Lucas	WOODRUFF, David Jr
LAINE, William	REDCROSS, John	

APPOMATTOX COUNTY. Formed in 1845 from parts of Buckingham, Campbell, Charlotte, and Prince Edward Counties. A fired destroyed all county records in 1892. County seat is Appomattox (24552).

AKERS, William	KELSO, Robert	ROBERTSON, John Jr
CARSON, James	MCREYNOLDS, James	ST CLARE, Robert
FLOOD, Henry	MCREYNOLDS, Joseph	STEELE, Alexander
HARRIS, John C	PANKEY, John	TRENT, Thomas
HOLLAND, Richard	ROBERTSON, James Sr	WILLSON, John Sr

ARLINGTON COUNTY. Formed from a portion of Fairfax County, including the town of Alexandria, that was ceded by Virginia to the federal government in 1789. Became part of the District of Columbia in 1801 and named **ALEXANDRIA COUNTY** by Congress. Returned to Viriginia jurisdiction in 1847. Name changed to Arlington County in 1920. County seat is Arlington (22210). **See also ALEXANDRIA CITY.**

ADAMS, William	FOLLIN, Catherine (Sandford)	MEASON, Thomas
AULD, Hugh Sr	FOLLIN, John	PEIRCE, Solomon
BALL, John	GREEN, John	REDIN, John
BALL, Moses	HOUSE, James	RUSSELL, William
BURROWS, William Ward	JONES, Edward	SWAN, Caleb
CARLETON, Joseph	L'ENFANT, Pierre Charles	THRIFT, Jeremiah
CARLIN, William	LINGAN, James McCubbin	WILSON, James R
CASSIN, John	MACOMB, Alexander	
DAVIS, John A	MCLINGAN, James	

AUGUSTA COUNTY. Created in 1738 from Orange County. County government formed in 1745. County seat is Staunton (24401). **See also STAUNTON CITY and WAYNESBORO CITY.**

ALEXANDER, Archibald
ALEXANDER, Gabriel
ALLEN, James
ANDERSON, Alexander
ANDERSON, Andrew
ANDERSON, George
ANDERSON, George
ANDERSON, John
ANDERSON, William
ARMSTRONG, William
BALSLEY (BALSEY),
  Christian
BARGER, Jacob
BASKIN, Charles
BELL, David
BELL, David
BELL, James
BELL, Joesph
BELL, John
BELL, Joseph Jr
BELL, Joseph Sr
BELL, Samuel
BELL, William
BERRY, John
BLACK, John
BLAIR, William
BRATTON, Robert
BREEDEN, George
BUCHANAN, Andrew
BUMGARDNER, Christian
BUMGARDNER, Jacob
CARSON, Samuel
CHRISTIAN (CHRISTAIN),
  John
COCHRAN, James
COCHRAN, William
CONNALY, Arthur Sr
COOPER, Robert
CRAIG, Alexander
CRAIG, James Jr
CRAIG, James Sr
CRAIG, John
CRAIG, John
CRAIG, Samuel
CRAIG, William
CRAWFORD, George Jr
CRAWFORD, John
CRAWFORD, John
CRAWFORD, Patrick
CURRY, Robert
DAVIS, Walter
DAVIS, William D
DOAK, Robert
DOAK, Samuel
DOAK (DOACK), David

ERVIN, William
EWING, James
EWING, James
EWING, James
EWING, William
FALL, George
FINLEY, John
FISHBURNE, Dietrick
  (Detrich)
FRAZIER, James
FULTON, James
FULWEIDER, Johannes
GAMBLE, John
GIBBONS, John
GILKESON, Hugh
GILKESON, William
GIVENS, John
GLENN, George
GOLLADAY, David
GRAHAM, Andrew
GUTHRIE, John
HALL, Patrick
HALL, William
HALL, William Sr
HAMILTON, Alexander
HAMILTON, David
HAMILTON, James
HAMILTON, James
HAMILTON, John
HAMILTON, William
HANGER, Frederick Jr
HANGER, Peter
HANNA, Joseph
HANNA, Robert
HARNSBERGER, Robert
HOGSHEAD, David Jr
HOGSHEAD, Michael
HOOK, William
HOOK(E), Robert Sr
HOOK(E), William Sr
HOUSTON, Samuel
HUFFER (HUFFORD,
  HUFFERT), Jacob
HUGHART, Thomas
HUMPHREYS (HUMPHRIES),
  David
HUNTER, Samuel
IRVINE (ERWIN, IRWIN),
  Edward
JOHNSTON, William Z
KELLER, Frederick Sr
KELLER, George
KELLER, George
KENNEY (KENNY, KINNEY),
  Robert

KENNEY (KENNY, KINNEY),
  Robert
KERR, James
KERR, John Jr
KERR, John Sr
KERR, Joseph
KERR, William
KILPATRICK, Ann
KOINER, George Adam
KOINER, George Michael
KOINER, Kasper
LANDES, John
LEWIS, John
LINK, Matthias
LOCKRIDGE, Andrew
LOGAN, John
LONG, Joseph Sr
MCCHESNEY, James
MCCHESNEY, John
MCCLURE, Andrew
MCCOMB, James
MCCORMICK, Martha
  (Sanderson)
MCCORMICK, Robert
MCCUE, John
MCCUE, John Rev
MCCUNE, John
MCCUTCHAN, Charles
MCCUTCHAN, Samuel
MCCUTCHAN, William
MCCUTCHAN, James
MCCUTCHEON, John
MCNUTT, James
MCNUTT, Robert
MCPHEETERS, William Jr
MILLER, Henry
MILLS, John
MILLS, Robert
MITCHELL, James
MITCHELL, Robert
MITCHELL, Thomas
MITCHELL, William
MOFFETT, George
MOFFETT, James
MOFFETT, John
MOFFETT, William
MONTGOMERY, John Rev
MONTGOMERY, Richard
MOORE, Andrew
NELSON, Alexander
NELSON, Alexander
NELSON, John
NELSON, William
PARKS, Joseph
POAGE, Robert

(AUGUSTA, continued)

POAGE, Thomas
POAGUE (POAGE), James
POAGUE (POAGE), John Jr
RAMSEY, James Dr
RITCHEY, David
ROBERTSON, Alexander
ROBERTSON, Alexander
ROBERTSON, William
ROBINSON, Isaac
ROSS, Alexander
RUSSELL, Andrew
RUSSELL, Joshua
SHARP, John
SHARP, Joseph
SHARP, Thomas
SHIPMAN, Benjamin
SHIPMAN, Jonathan
SHIRLEY, Michael
SHUEY, John Ludwig "Lewis"
SIEG, Paul
SLAGLE, George
SLUTE, James
SMITH, John
SPITLER, Jacob

SPROUL, William
STEELE, Andrew
STEELE, David
STEELE, James Wendle
STEELE, John
STEELE, John
STEELE, John Jr
STEELE, John Sr
STEELE, Nathaniel
STEELE, Robert
STEELE, Samuel Jr
STEELE, Samuel Jr
STEELE, Samuel Sr
STEELE, Thomas
STEELE, William
STUART, Benjamin
SUMMERS, John
TATE, John
TATE, John
TATE, John
TATE, Robert
TATE, Thomas
THOMPSON, Alexander
THOMPSON, James

THOMPSON, Robert
THOMPSON, William
TRIMBLE, John
VAN LEAR (VANLEAR),
   Jacob
WALKER, Alexander
WALLACE, Robert
WEAVER, John Peter
WILLSON, Matthew
WILLSON, William
WILSON, John Sr
WILSON, Samuel
WILSON, William
WOODDELL, Thomas
YATES, Enoch
YOUNG, James
YOUNG, John
YOUNG, Thomas
YOUNG, William

BATH COUNTY. Formed in 1791 from Augusta County, Bedford County and Greenbriar County (WV). County Seat is Warm Springs (24484).

ARBUCKLE, Mathew
BOLAR, John
BRADLEY, William
BRATTON, James
CAMERON, Charles
CRAWFORD, Nathan
DICKINSON, John
GIVEN, William

GLASSBURN, David
KEYSER (KEYSOR), William
LAVERTY, Ralph
MARSHALL, Robert
MCCLINTIC, William Jr
MCCLINTIC (MCCLINTOCK),
   William Sr
MCCLUNG, John Jr

MUSTOE, Anthony
PAYNE, Joseph
SITLINGTON, Robert
WARWICK, Jacob

BEDFORD [CITY] (24523). Achieved Independent City status in 1968, then in 2013 reverted to a town within Bedford County in 2013. **See also BEDFORD COUNTY.**

FUQUA, Joseph
GRAHAM, Michael

TURNER, James
WILKS, Samuel

BEDFORD COUNTY. Formed in 1754 from Lunenburg County. Part of Albemarle County was added in 1755. County seat is town of Bedford (24523).

ANDERSON, Nelson
ANDREWS, Thomas
ARTHUR, Thomas Sr
BARTON, Elisha
BLANKENSHIP, Abraham Sr
BROWN, Henry
BUFORD, Henry
BURNETT, Williamson
CALLAWAY (CALLOWAY),
   James
CALLAWAY (CALLOWAY),
   William

CALLAWAY (CALLOWAY),
   William Jr
CAMPBELL, Thomas
CHAPMAN, Nathan
COBBS, John L
COFER, George
COX, Valentine
CREWS, Joseph
DAWSON, Martin
DICKERSON, Joseph
EWING, Robert Sr
FRANTZ, Christian

FUQUA, Ralph Jr
GOGGIN, Stephen Jr
GROOM, Jonathan
HARDY, Joseph Austin
HARDY, Joshua
HURT, Moses
JETER, Henry
LEE, William
LEFTWICH, Augustine Jr
LEFTWICH, Joel
LEFTWICH, Thomas
LEFTWICH, Uriah

(BEDFORD, continued)

LEFTWICH, William
LOGWOOD, Thomas
LOYD, Henry
McCONNEHEY, John
MEAD, Nicholas
MEAD, Samuel
MOODY, John
OTEY, John Armistead
OWEN, James
PADGETT, Frederick
QUARLES, John
READ, Samuel

READ, William
REID, Nathan
SALMON, John
SAUNDERS, David
SCOTT, William E
SLACK, Abraham
STEPTOE, James Jr
STIFF, James
STRATTON, Henry
TERRY, William
THOMAS, William
TRIGG, John (Johns)

WADE, Isaac Sr
WALKER, George Reynolds
WALKER, William
WATTS, John
WHITE, Jacob
WHITE, Joseph
WIGGINTON, John
WOOD, Jeremiah

BLAND COUNTY. Formed in 1861 from Giles County, Tazewell County, and Wythe County. County seat is Bland (24315).

GROSECLOSE, Peter Jr
GROSECLOSE, Peter Sr

HARMAN, Henry Sr
SPANGLER, Jacob

THOMPSON, Andrew
WILSON, James

BOTETOURT COUNTY. Formed 1770 from Augusta County. County seat is Fincastle (24090).

ABENDSCHON
  (OBENSHAIN), Samuel
ALLEN, Hugh
ALLEN, James
ALLEN, John
ALLEN, Malcolm
ALLEN, Robert
ANDERSON, Robert
ANDERSON, William
BAKER, Henry Sr
BELL, James
BOWYER, Henry
BOYER (BOWYER), Thomas
BRECKENRIDGE, James
BRICKEY, Peter
BROUGH, Daniel
BRUGH, Daniel Sr
BRUGH, Hermanus
CAHOON, Charles
CARLOCK, Hanchrist
CARPER, Jacob
CARPER, Nicholas
CARTER, Nicholas
CROSS, William
EARLY, James Matten
GISH, Jacob
GUILIFORD, Allen

HAMILTON, Alexander
HAMILTON, Andrew
HARVEY, Matthew
HARVEY, Robert
HICKLE, Lewis
HICKOK, Ebenezer
HUME(S), William
JORDAN, John
KAYSER (KEYSER), John J
KESSLER, John
KYLE, William
LAYMAN, George
LEE, Zachariah Jr
LEMON, Jacob
LOCKHART, Patrick
LOGAN, Robert
MCCLURE, John
MCDONALD, Bryan
MCDONALD, Edward
MCDONALD, James
MCDONALD, William
MCFERRAN, Martin
MCROBERTS, Alexander
MCROBERTS, John
MCROBERTS, Samuel
MERRITT, Samuel
MIFFORD, Jacob

MOORE, John
MOORE, John
MOSELEY, Arthur
NICHOLAS, Lewis
OLIVER, William
PATTERSON, Samuel
PECK, Benjamin
PECK, Jacob
PECK, John
PECK, Joseph
POAGUE (POAGE), John
PRESTON, John
RADER (RIDER), Adam
REID, Francis
SHEETS, Jacob
SHIRKEY, Nicholas
SKIPWITH, Peyton
SMITH (SMYTH), Adam B
TAYMAN (LAYMAN,
  LAYMON), George
THOMAS, Francis
WALKER, William
WAX, Henry Sr
WOODS, Andrew Sr
WYSONG, Feidt (Fyette)

BRISTOL CITY (24201). Achieved Independent City status in 1890. City boundaries include part of Tennessee. **See also WASHINGTON COUNTY.**

PRESTON, John
PRESTON, Robert

SHELBY, Elvan
SHELBY, Isaac

SNODGRASS, William

BRUNSWICK COUNTY. Formed in 1720 from Prince George County. County government formed in 1732. County seat is Lawrenceville (23868).

ABERNATHY, John D Jr	BISHOP, Mathew	LEWIS, Benjamin
ABERNATHY, John Sr	CLAIBORNE, Thomas	ORGAIN, William Derby
BISHOP, John	LANIER, Benjamin Bird	

BUCHANAN COUNTY. Formed in 1858 from Russell County and Tazewell County. County seat is Grundy (24614).

No known veteran burials.

BUCKINGHAM COUNTY. Formed in 1761 from Albemarle County. County seat is Buckingham (23921).

AGEE, Jacob	EVANS, William	MOSELEY, Arthur
AGEE, James	FLOOD, Noah	MOSELEY, Benjamin
BOATWRIGHT, Reuben	FORBES, Alexander	MOSELEY, Robert Peter
BRANCH, Olive	GLOVER, Anthony	PATTESON, David
BROWN, Benjamin	GLOVER, Samuel Jr	PATTESON, Thomas
CABELL, John	HARRISON (later STARKS),	PERKINS, John W
CHAMBERS, John	William	RAGLAND, John Dudley
COLEMAN, Julius	HOOPER, George	STRATTON, John Handley
COLEMAN, Robert	JONES, Michael	WATSON, William
ELDRIDGE, Rolfe	MORRIS, Nathaniel	WILKINSON, William

BUENA VISTA CITY. Achieved Independent City status in 1892. **See also ROCKBRIDGE County.**

No known veteran burials.

CAMPBELL COUNTY. Formed in 1782 from Bedford County. County seat is Rustburg (25688). **See also LYNCHBURG CITY.**

ADAMS, Robert "Old Robin"	DRISKILL, Daniel	LEWIS, William J
ALEXANDER, Robert	EARLY, Jeremiah	LYNCH, Anselm
ANTHONY, John	EVANS, Daniel	LYNCH, Charles Sr
BLANKENSHIP, Hudson	EVANS, Reese	MCREYNOLDS, John
BROWN, Henry	FIELDS, Andrew	PAYNE (PAINE), Phillip
BROWN, John	FRANKLIN, Thomas	PHILLIPS, John
CALLAWAY (CALLOWAY),	HADEN, Anthony	PHILLIPS, John
John	HADEN, Benjamin	POINDEXTER, Joseph
CARDWELL, Robert	HADEN, John Sr	PRIBBLE (PREBBLE), John
CARWILE(S), Jacob Sr	HANKS, Abraham	SMITH, Fred
CLARK, John	HANKS, Abraham	SMITH, Ralph
CLEMENT, Adam Sr	HEATH (HAYTH), Thomas	THORNHILL, Jesse
COBBS, Charles	HOWARD, James	WARD, Henry
COBBS, Jesse	HUNTER, John Jr	WARD, John
COBBS, John Sr	HUNTER, Robert	WHITAKER, James
COBBS, Robert	IRVINE, John Jr	WIATT, John
CREASY, William	IRVINE, John Sr	WIATT, Thomas
DEARING (DEERING), James	JONES, Thomas	WILSON, John
DIUGUID, George	LEE, John	
DIXON, James	LEFTWICH, Augustine Sr	

CAROLINE COUNTY. Formed in 1728 from Essex County, King and Queen County, and King William County. County seat is Bowling Green (22427). Many older records are housed at the Central Rappahannock Heritage Center in Fredericksburg.

BAYLOR, George	DICK, Archibald	TAYLOR, James
BAYLOR, John	GEORGE, Reuben	TAYLOR, John
BAYLOR, Walker	GILCHRIST, Robert	TERRELL, Samuel
BAYNHAM, Richard	HILL, Humphrey	THORNTON, Anthony
BOULWARE, Mark	HOOMES, John	TODD, Charles
BOUTWELL, John T	HOOMES, John	TODD, George Dr
BOUTWELL, William	LOMAX, Thomas	TOMPKINS, Christopher
BRIDGES, Richard	MINOR, Vivion	WHITE, Ambrose
BUCKNER, George	PRATT, John Birkett	WOODFORD, William
BURKE, Thomas	QUARLES, Minor	WOOLFOLK, John George
CHEWNING, Samuel	QUARLES, William	WRIGHT, Robert Mosley Sr
DEJARNETTE, Joseph Jr	TALIAFERRO, Walker	YOUNG, William

CARROLL COUNTY. Formed in 1842 from Grayson County. County seat is Hillsville (24343).

BLAIR, Thomas	DALTON, William	HUFFMAN, Barnard
BOBBITT, John	EDWARDS, Elias	KENNY, William
BOBBITT, Robert	EDWARDS, Isaac	MITCHELL, Stephen
BOBBITT, William Sr	FARMER, James	PHILLIPS, Tobias
BOWMAN, Robert	FROST, John	WEBB, Henry "Hal"
COLLIER, Aaron	GARDNER, James	WORRELL, James
COX, Enoch Sr	HANKS, Joshua	
COX, Solomon	HILL, James	

CHARLES CITY COUNTY. An original 1634 shire. County seat is Charles City (23030).

BISHOP, Billy	CRUTCHFIELD, John	MINGE, David
CARTER, Charles	CRUTCHFIELD, Lewis	RICKMAN, William Dr
CARTER, Edward	HARRISON, Benjamin	TYLER, John
CHRISTIAN, James	HARRISON, Benjamin	
CHRISTIAN, Joseph	LIGHTFOOT, William	

CHARLOTTE COUNTY. Formed in 1765 from Lunenburg County. County seat is Charlotte Court House (23923).

BEDFORD, Thomas Sr	CALDWELL, John F	READ, Thomas
BOULDIN, Thomas Sr	CARRINGTON, Paul	SMITH, Isaac Watt Sr
BOULDIN, Wood	GAINES, Richard	WHEELER, John Sr
BOULDIN (BOUDLIN),	HENRY, Patrick	
Thomas	MOSELEY, Edward	

CHARLOTTESVILLE CITY. Achieved Independent City status in 1888. **See also ALBEMARLE COUNTY.**

BROWN, Bazael (Bazel)	LEWIS, Jesse Pitman	MERIWETHER, William
BRYAN, John Patterson	LEWIS, Mary	Douglas
CARR, Dabney Jr	LEWIS, Nicholas	NICHOLAS, Wilson Cary
CARR, John	LEWIS, Taliaferro	SMITH, Matthew
GILMER, George Dr	LEWIS, Thomas Walker	WINGFIELD, Charles
JEFFERSON, Thomas	LEWIS, William	WINGFIELD, John

CHESAPEAKE CITY (23320). Formed in 1963 by the consolidation of Norfolk County (created in 1691) and South Norfolk City (created in 1921), which both then became extinct.

BUTT, Epaphroditus	SMITH, John	WILKINS, Willis
HALSTEAD (HOLSTEAD), Matt	STEWART, Charles	WILSON, Nathaniel
	WEST, William	WOODWARD, William

CHESTERFIELD COUNTY. Formed in 1749 from Henrico County. County seat is Chesterfield Court House (23823).

BAILEY, Benjamin	FLEMING, William	RANDOLPH, John
BOLLING, Thomas	FRANKLIN, John Sr	ROBERTSON, Jeffrey Jr
BROOKS, Elias	GATES, William	ROBERTSON, William
CLARKE, William	GOODE, Francis	SPEARS, John
CLAY, Eleazer	GOODE, John	
DUNCAN, Charles	HUNDLEY, Josiah	
FERGUSSON (FARGUSSON FURGUS(S)ON), Moses	KABLER, Frederick	
	LOCKETT, Edmund Sr	

CLARKE COUNTY. Formed in 1836 from Frederick County. Part of Warren County added in 1860. County seat is Berryville (22611).

ANDERSON, Joseph Edward Sr	FROST, William	MEADE, Richard Kidder
	HAY, William	MUSE, Battaile
BERRY, Benjamin	HOLKER, John	PAGE, John
BLAKEMORE, George	HUNSICKER, Peter	PAGE, Robert
BLAKEMORE, Thomas Sr	IRELAND, James	RANDOLPH, Edmund Jennings
BURWELL, Nathaniel	JACKSON, Thomas	
BUTLER, Lawrence (Lance)	LARUE, Isaac	REED, William
BYRD, Thomas Taylor	MARTIN, Thomas Bryan	SMITH, John
CHANDLER, Carter	MEADE, Humberson	

COLONIAL HEIGHTS CITY (23834). Achieved Independent City status in 1948. **See also CHESTERFIELD COUNTY.**

No known veteran burials.

COVINGTON CITY (24426). Achieved Independent City status in 1952. **See also ALLEGHANY COUNTY.**

BROWN, James	PERSINGER, Jacob	ROBINSON, William
DAMERON, John	RICHARDSON, John Sr	WALKER, Henry

CRAIG COUNTY. Formed in 1851 from Botetourt County, Giles County, Roanoke County, and part of Monroe County (WV). County seat is New Castle (24127).

ALLEN, Moses	PECK, Benjamin	WEBB, John
NUTTER, Zadock (Zadok)	WALKER, George	

CULPEPER COUNTY. Formed in 1749 from Orange County. County seat is Culpeper (22701).

BROWN, Daniel	FORD, John Thomas	JAMESON, John
CLAYTON, Phillip	GAINES, Thomas	JONES, Gabriel Jr
COLVIN, Daniel	GARNETT, James Rev	JONES, Thomas
COVINGTON, Francis L	GARNETT, Reuben	LEWIS, Betty (Washington)
DAWSON, Benjamin	HALL, Thomas Sr	MERCER, George
DILLARD, George	HANSB(O)ROUGH, William	NALLE, Martin II
DILLARD, John	HUDSON, James	NORMAN, Courtney
DUNCAN, Charles	HUME, Francis	PAYNE, Richard
FISHBACK, John Frederick	INSKEEP, James	PENDLETON, Nathaniel Sr
FISHBACK, Martin	JAMESON, David	PULLER, John

(CULPEPER, continued)

READ, John	STRODE, John	YANCEY, Charles Sr
ROSSON, Reuben	TAYLOR, George	YANCEY, Lewis Davis
STEVENS, Edward	WIGGINTON, John Sr	

CUMBERLAND COUNTY. Formed in 1749 from Goochland County. County seat is Cumberland (23040).

ANDERSON, James	HOLMAN, John	SMITH, Byrd
ANDERSON, Thomas	MARTIN, Orson	WALKER, William
BOATWRIGHT, Daniel	MONTAGUE, Thomas	WILSON, Willis
BOOKER, E Nash	MORTON, James	WINNIFORD, David
BOOKER, Edward	PAGE, Carter	WOODSON, John
CARRINGTON, George Jr	PRICE, Joseph	
HARRISON, Carter Henry	SCRUGGS, Drury	

DANVILLE CITY. Achieved Independent City status in 1890. **See also PITTSYLVANIA COUNTY.**

CLAY, Matthew	PERKINS, Constantine	WILSON, John
PAYNE, Josiah	WALL, Peter	WILSON, Robert

DICKENSON COUNTY. Formed in 1880 from Buchanan County, Russell County, and Wise County. County seat is Clintwood (24228).

MULLINS, John

DINWIDDIE COUNTY. Formed in 1752 from Prince George County. County seat is Dinwiddie (23841).

COUSINS, Henry	GRIGG, Abner	SYDNOR, Joseph
CUTLER, William	GRIGG, William Sr	
GOODWYN, Joseph	JARRETT (JARRATT),	
GOODWYN, Peterson	Devereux	
GREENWAY, James	KING, Elisha	

DUNMORE COUNTY. Renamed in 1778. **See SHENANDOAH COUNTY.**

ELIZABETH CITY COUNTY (extinct). See HAMPTON CITY. An original 1634 shire, consolidated in 1952 with Hampton.

EMPORIA CITY. Achieved Independent City status in 1967. **See also GREENSVILLE COUNTY.**

ROBINSON, Braxton	ROBINSON, John
ROBINSON, James	ROBINSON, Littlebury

ESSEX COUNTY. Formed in 1692 from [Old] Rappahannock County which formed from Lancaster County. County seat is Tappahannock (22560).

BOOKER, Lewis	GARNETT, Muscoe	RITCHIE, Archibald
CAMPBELL, Hugh	GARRETT, William	RITCHIE, William
DISHMAN, Sarah	MILLER, William	SMITH, Meriwether

FAIRFAX CITY (22030). Achieved Independent City status in 1961. **See also FAIRFAX COUNTY.**

BOWIE, William S Sr	MILLAN, Thomas	REID, John
CHAPMAN, Thomas	MILLAN, William	SCOTT, Gustavus
ELLIS, Richard	PETTETT, John	SKINNER, Frederick

FAIRFAX COUNTY. Formed in 1742 from Prince William County. County seat is Fairfax (22030). **See also FAIRFAX CITY.**

ADDISON, John
ALEXANDER, Charles Sr
BARKER, Nathaniel
BROADWATER, Charles
BROADWATER, Charles Lewis
BROWN, William
CHAPMAN, George
CHICHESTER, Richard "Hard"
COCKBURN, Martin
COFFER, Thomas W
CONNER (CONNOR), Patrick
DULANEY, John
FITZHUGH, William
GARY (GERY), James
GUNNELL, Henry M
GUNNELL, William
HALEY, James
HALLEY, Henry Simpson
HALLEY, James Jr
HOLLIDAY, Israel Ellsworth
HUNT, James
HUNTER, Elizabeth (Chapman)
HUNTER, George Dr
HUNTER, John Chapman

HUNTER, Nathaniel Chapman
HURST, John
HUTCHESON, Benjamin
JOHNSTON, William
LANE, William
LEE, Richard Bland
LEE, William "Billy"
LINDSAY, Thomas
LINDSAY, William
LINDSAY, William
MAJOR, Richard Rev
MASON, George
MASON, George Sr
MASSEY, Lee
MCCARTY (MCCARTHY) Daniel
MILLAN, William
MOORE, Jeremiah Rev
NELSON, William
ORR, John
PAYNE, William
RUSSELL, Samuel
SCOTT, John
SOMMERS, Simon
SUMMERS, Francis
TAYLOR, Thomas

THOMPSON, Daniel
THOMPSON, Samuel
TRIPLETT, William
WAGENER (WEGENER), Peter
WASHINGTON, Bushrod
WASHINGTON, Edward
WASHINGTON, George
WASHINGTON, George Augustine
WASHINGTON, John Augustine
WASHINGTON, Martha (Dandridge)
WASHINGTON, William Augustine
WATTERS, William
WICKLIFF(E) (WYCLIFFE), Arrington (Aaron)
WICKLIFF(E) (WYCLIFFE), Moses
WYCKLIFFE (WICKLIFF), Aaron
WYCKLIFFE (WICKLIFF), Moses

FALLS CHURCH CITY (22046). Achieved Independent City status in 1948. **See also FAIRFAX COUNTY.**

BOWIE, James
SHREVE, Samuel

SUMMERS (SOMMERS), Simon

TALBOTT, Samuel

FAUQUIER COUNTY. Formed in 1759 from Prince William County. County seat is Warrenton (22186).

ASBURY (ASHBURY), Joseph
ASH, Francis
ASH, George
ASHBY, John
BALL, John
BLACKWELL, Joseph Jr
BLACKWELL, Joseph Sr
BRONOUGH, Thomas
BURKE, William
CHILTON, John
CHUNN, John Thomas
COMBS, Robert
COURTN(E)Y, William
DARNALL, Jeremiah
DIGGES, Edward
EASTHAM, George
EDMONDS, Elias Jr
EDMONDS, John
EDMONDS, William

ESKRIDGE, Margaret (Mrs Kenner)
FOSTER, James
GEORGE, Benjamin
GLASCOCK, Hezekiah
GLASCOCK, John
GLASSCOCK (GLASCOCK), George
GLASSCOCK (GLASCOCK), Thomas
HATHAWAY, John
HAWKINS, John
HICKS, Kimble
HITT, Peter
HORNER, Gustavus Brown
JAMES, John
JENNINGS, Lewis
KEITH, Thomas Randolph
KEMPER (KAMPER), Charles Sr

KENNER, Howson Francis
LEE, Charles
LEWIS, William
LINN, William Sr
LOVE, Charles
LOVE, Samuel
MARTIN, Henry Andrew
MARTIN, Joseph
MOFFETT, Jesse
MORGAN, Zackwell
MOSS, Nathaniel
MURRAY, Reuben
O'BANNON, John
OBANNON (OBANON), William
PAYNE, Augustine
PAYNE, Francis
PAYNE, William
PAYNE, William

(FAUQUIER, continued)

PEYTON, Henry
RANDOLPH, Robert
ROWLES, William
RUST, Benjamin
SHAKLETT (SHACKLETT), Edward
SIMPSON, Thomas
SKINKER, Thomas

SMITH, John
SMITH, Joseph T
SMITH, William
SPILMAN, James
THOMPSON, James
THOMSON, James
TULLOS(S), Rodham Jr
TURNER, Hezekiah

WAITE, William
WEAVER, Tilman Jr
WELCH, Sylvester Sr
WINN, Minor Jr
WITHERS, Lewis
WITHERS, William
WRIGHT, William

FINCASTLE COUNTY (extinct). Formed in 1772 from Botetourt County. Became extinct in 1776 when divided to form Montgomery County, Washington County, and Kentucky County (now the state of Kentucky). **See MONTGOMERY COUNTY and WASHINGTON COUNTY.**

FLOYD COUNTY. Formed in 1831 from Montgomery County. County seat is Floyd (24091).

BANKS, John
BISHOP, Henry
BOOTH, George
CONNOR, Daniel
DICKERSON, Elijah
DICKERSON, Moses
DUNCAN, John
EDWARDS, Benjamin
GOODSON, Thomas H II
GOODSON, Thomas Washington I
HEARD, John
HOWARD, Peter Rev
HOWARD, Robert

HOWARD, William Lawrence
HOWELL, Daniel Sr
HUNGATE, William
JONES, Robert
KENNON, Richard
KING, John
MITCHELL, John
PHARES (PHARIS, FERRIS, FARRIS, FARES), Amariah (Emaria(h), Araziah, Emerica, Amaziah)
RICHARDS, Christian
RUTROUGH, John
SCOTT, Mathew

SHELOR, Daniel
SMITH, Humphrey (Humphreys)
SOWERS, George
SPANGLER, Daniel
SPANGLER (SPENGER), Daniel
STIGLEMAN (STICKLEMAN, STIGGLEMAN, STRICKLEMAN, STEICHELMAN), Philip (Phillip)
TRAIL, Thomas

FLUVANNA COUNTY. Formed in 1777 from Albemarle County. County seat is Palmyra (22963).

ADAMS, James Sr
ASHLIN, John
BOWLES, Knight
BURGESS, John
BYBEE, Pleasant
CARY, Wilson Miles
DUNCAN, George
EASTON, William

JONES, George
MOORE, John
OMOHUNDRO, Richard
PERKINS, Stephen
ROSS, Peter
SEAY, Austin Sr
SHEPHERD, David
SHEPHERD, John

SHORES, Thomas Jr
STRANGE, John Alloway
WATSON, Robert
WINN, Thomas
WOOD, Thomas
WOODS, William

FRANKLIN CITY (23851). Achieved Independent City status in 1961. **See also SOUTHAMPTON COUNTY.**

ROCHELLE, John

FRANKLIN COUNTY. Formed in 1786 from Bedford County and Henry County. County seat is Rocky Mount (24151).

ABSHIRE, Abraham
ANGLE (ANGELL), Peter
BERNARD, Walter
BOOTH, John
BRIZENDINE, William Sr
CANNADAY, James
COOK, Benjamin
COOPER, William Sterling

CRAGHEAD, John
DILLON, Jesse
ENGLISH, William
GREER, Moses Sr
GRIFFITH, Benjamin
HATCHER, Elijah Sr
HILL, Robert
HILL, Thomas

HILL, Violet (Linus)
HOLLAND, Thomas
HOOK, John
HOUGH (HUFF), John
HUFF, John
JONES, Robert Jr
JONES, Thomas
KING, Stephen

(FRANKLIN, continued)

LESUEUR, Martel
LUMSDEN, John
MAXEY, Walter
MCNEIL, Jacob Sr
PACKWOOD, Samuel
PEARSON, Thomas

PERDUE, Meshack
POINDEXTER, John Sr
PRICE, Joseph
PRICE, Joseph Shores
PRILLAMAN (PRILLMAN),
   Jacob Sr

RICHARDS, Edward
SINK, Stephen
SPANGLER, Daniel
WINGFIELD, Willam
WITCHER, William Sr
WOODY, Martin

FREDERICK COUNTY. Formed in 1738 from Orange County. County seat is Winchester (22601).
   See also WINCHESTER CITY.

ADAMS, William
BAKER, Joseph
BROWNLEY, John Jr
BRYARLY (BRYERLY),
   Thomas
BUCHER, Philip Peter
BUCK, Thomas
CARTNELL (CARTMELL,
   CARTMILL), Nathaniel
CATHER, Jasper
COOLE, John M
COOPER, John Jr
CRUMLEY, William
DANNER (TANNER), Jacob
DARLINGTON, Gabriel
DAVIS, David
DEHAVEN, Isaac
DEHAVEN, Peter
DELONG, John Nicholas
FISHER, John
FRIEZ (FREIS, FREISE,
   FREIZE), Martin
HAMILTON, James
HELM, Meridith Jr
HITE, Isaac
HITE, Isaac

HOGE, Edward
HOGE, James
HOGE, William
HOGE (HOGG), James Sr
HOTT, George
JACKSON, George
JACKSON, Josiah
JONES, Strother
KEARFOOT (KERFOOT),
   William
KERFOOT (KEARFOOT),
   William
KLINE, Jacob
KRIM (GRIM, CRIM), John
LARRICK, Casper
LIGHT, Peter
MANN, Jacob
MARQUIS, William
MATTHEWS, Richard
MCCARTY, Daniel
MCCAULEY, Daniel
MCDANIEL, Thomas
MIDDLETON, William
MYTINGER, Daniel
NEWELL, John
OLIVER, James

PARKINS, Isaac
PIT(T)MAN, Andrew
PIT(T)MAN, Phillip
PUGH, Job
PUGH, Joseph
PURCELL, John
RICHARD(S), Henry
RINKER, Hans Casper
ROGERS, James
ROGERS, John
RUBEL (RUBLE), George
SIDEBOTTOM
   (SIDEBOTHOM), Joseph
SMITH, Jeremiah
STEELE, Thomas
STONEBRIDGE, John
STROTHER, John
TILDEN, John Bell
TROWBRIDGE, Samuel
VANCE, William
WHITE, Alexander
WHITE, Michael
WHITE, Robert
WILSON, David
WOOD, Robert
ZANE, Isaac II

FREDERICKSBURG CITY (22401). Achieved Independent City status in 1879. **See also**
   SPOTSYLVANIA COUNTY.

BARTON, Seth
BROOKE, Robert
BRUCE, Charles
CALLENDER, Eleazer
CARTER, Charles
CHEW, John Jr
CHEW, Robert Beverly
DAY, Benjamin
DRUMMOND, William
DUNCANSON, James
FOX, Samuel
GRINNAN, Daniel Sr
HENDERSON, David
HOLLADAY, Lewis
JENKINS, William

JONES, Joseph
JONES, William (John) Paul
JULIAN, John
LEGG, John
LEWIS, Fielding
LEWIS, George Washington
LITTLEPAGE, Lewis
MAURY, Fontaine
MCWILLIAMS, William
MERCER, Hugh
MINOR, Garritt
MINOR, John Jr
ROSE, Alexander
ROYSTON (ROYSTAN),
   James

SMITH, William
SOMERVILLE, James
STEVENSON, James
STONE, William
STORKE, William
STROTHER, French
WAITT, William
WALLACE, Gustavus Brown
WASHINGTON, Mary (Ball)
WEEDON, George
WELLFORD, Robert
WILLIS, Lewis
YATES, Charles

GALAX CITY (24333). Achieved Independent City status in 1954. **See also CARROLL COUNTY and GRAYSON COUNTY**

No known veteran burials.

GILES COUNTY. Formed in 1806 from Montgomery County, Tazewell County, and Monroe County (WV). County seat is Pearisburg (24134).

ALBERT, Jacob Allen	HULL, Henry	PEARIS, George
BURK (BURKE), Thomas	HUTCHESON, William	SHANNON, Thomas Reid
CHAPMAN, Isaac	JOHNSTON, David	SHELDON, Parker
CHAPMAN, John	KIRK, John II	SHUMATE, Daniel III
CLAY, Mitchell	LUCAS, Parker	SNIDOW, Christian
CLAY, William M Sr	LYBROOK, John	SNIDOW, Jacob
FARLEY, Thomas Jr	MCKENZIE, Moredock	SNIDOW, Philip
FRENCH, Matthew	(Mordicai, Moredecai,	STAFFORD, Ralph Sr
HALE, Edward	Mordock, Morodock) Otis	TONEY, John
HARE, Joseph	ME(A)DOWS, Francis	WILSON, William
HAYS, John	NEEL, William	

GLOUCESTER COUNTY. Formed in 1651 from York County. County seat is Gloucester (23061).

ANDERSON, Matthew	DIGGES, Dudley Power	SMITH, Armistead
(Mathew)	HUDSON, Vincent	TABB, Edward
BOOTH, George W	JONES, William	TABB, Philip (Phillip)
CAFFEE, William	LEWIS, Warner II	THROCKMORTON, William
CLARK, James	ROBINS, Thomas	YATES, William
CURTIS, William	SINCLAIR, John	YEATMAN, Thomas Muse

GOOCHLAND COUNTY. Formed in 1728 from Henrico County. County seat is Goochland (22063).

GAY, William	MASSIE, Charles	RICHARDSON, George W
GEORGE, William	MIMS, David	RICHARDSON, Samuel
HOLMAN, William Jr	MOORE, Amos Lad	WARE, John
HOLMAN, William Sr	MULLINS, Matthew	WATKINS, Thomas J
ISBELL, Joseph	PAYNE, George	WATKINS, William J
ISBELL, William	PAYNE, John	WATSON, William J
LACY, Mathew	PAYNE, Tarleton	WEBBER, William
LEAKE, Josiah	RANDOLPH, Thomas Mann	
LEAKE (LEAK), Elisha	RICHARDS, John	

GRAYSON COUNTY. Formed in 1793 from Wythe County. County seat is Independence (24348).

ANDERSON, Jacob	HASH, John Sr	REEDY, George Peter
BREWER, Lewis	HASH, William	REEVES, George Sr
BROWN, John	JACKSON, William Sullivan	ROBINSON, John
BYRD, William	LUNDY, John	SAGE, James
CAMPBELL, John	MURPHY, Timothy	STONE, Jeremiah
COMER, John	NUCKOLLS, Charles	VAUGHAN (VAUGHN),
CORNET(T), James Jr	OSBORN (OSBORNE), Enoch	William Jr
COX, David	PHIPPS (PHIPS), Benjamin	WEISS, Matthias
HALE, Lewis	PHIPPS (PHIPS), John	YOUNG, Ezekiel

GREENE COUNTY. Formed in 1838 from Orange County. Count seat is Stanardsville (22973).

BEADLES, John	DAVIS, Isaac	MILLS, William
BURTON, May Jr	ESTES, William	THORNTON, George

GREENSVILLE COUNTY. Formed in 1781 from Brunswick County. County seat is Emporia (23847). **See also EMPORIA CITY**.

GRIGG, Burwell	IVEY, John	PEEBLES, Fred

HALIFAX COUNTY. Formed in 1752 from Lunenburg County. Includes the former independent city of South Boston (1960) which reverted in 1995 to a town within the County. County seat is Halifax (24558).

ADAMS, Nipper (Napier)	EASLEY, Robert	PETTYPOOL, William
BARKSDALE, Beverly	ESTES, George	RAGLAND, John
BARKSDALE, Peter	FAULKNER, Jacob	RAGLAND, Reuben
BETTS, Spencer	FERRELL (FERRILL),	SCOTT, John Baytop
BROOKS, John	William H	SPRAGINS (SPRAGANS),
CARRINGTON, George	FIT(T)ZPATRICK, John	Thomas
CARRINGTON, Paul	GREEN(E), Berryman	STANFIELD, Thomas
CLARK, John	JONES, William	TERRY, Nathaniel Sr
CLARK, Thomas	KEATTS, William Sr	TERRY, Royal
COLE, William	KENT, Luke	WATLINGTON
COLES, Walter	KENT, Robert	(WADLINGTON), John
DAVENPORT, Bedford	LIGHTFOOT, Mildred Howell	WILSON, Wallis
DAVENPORT, Catrin	LOGAN, William	WOOD, Thomas
(Catherine)	LOVELACE, Thomas	WYATT, John

HAMPTON CITY (23669). Achieved Independent City status in 1908 when separated from Elizabeth City County, but remained the county seat and shared many services with the county. In 1952, Hampton City and Elizabeth City County reunited and consolidated, along with town of Phoebus, into an enlarged independent Hampton City.

BOOKER, George	JENNINGS, William	PAYNE, John Jr
BOOKER, John	JENNINGS, William	PHILLIPS, Thomas
BROWN, Benjamin	JONES, John	RANDOLPH, William
HERBERT, Pascow (Pasco)	PASCON (PASCOW,	
JENNINGS, Charles	PASCHO), Herbert	

HANOVER COUNTY. Formed in 1721 from New Kent County. County seat is Hanover (23069).

ANDERSON, Robert	FONTAINE, William	NELSON, William
BELL, George	FULCHER, William	OLIVER, Benjamin
BERKELEY, Nelson	GOODALL, Parke	PRICE, Thomas Sr
BLACKWELL, David	GREEN, Fortunatus	SNEAD, Robert
BOWLES, Thomas	GRUBBS, Hensley (Henry)	SYME(S) (SIMS), John II
BOWLES, Thomas Philip	GRUBBS (VAN KRUPPS),	TAYLOR, Edmund
BOWLES (BOLLS), William	William	TINSLEY, Parker
BRADFORD, John	HARRIS, Jordan	TINSLEY, Thomas
BROCK, John P	HARRIS, William E	TINSLEY, William
BROWN, Isaac	HOWARD, James	TURNER, Nathaniel
BUMPASS, Samuel	JONES, John	WHITE, Thomas
CHRYSTIE, Thomas	MACON, William	WINGFIELD, Thomas Jr
DABNEY, Charles	MEREDITH, James	WINGFIELD, Thomas Sr
DAVENPORT, David	MORRIS, William	WINN, Jesse Durrett
DIGGES (DIGGS), Dudley Jr	NELSON, Lucy Grymes	WINSTON, William Overton

HARRISONBURG CITY (22801). Achieved Independent City status in 1916. **See also ROCKINGHAM COUNTY.**

CHRISMAN, George	ROLSTONE (ROLSTON,	VANPELT, Peter
HARRISON, Thomas	RALSTON), David	VANPELT, Tunis
MILLER, Samuel	SHOWALTER, Christain Jr	

HENRICO COUNTY. An original 1634 shire. County seat was Varina until 1752, then Richmond until 1974, and now Henrico (23228).

ANDREWS, Benjamin	CRADDOCK, Robert	LAFAYETTE, James
ANDREWS, Bullard	FRAYSER (FRAZIER), Jesse	MAYO, John
BRACKETT, John I	GEORGE, Byrd	SMITH, Jesse

HENRY COUNTY. Formed in 1776 from Pittsylvania County. County seat is Martinsville (24112). **See also MARTINSVILLE CITY.**

ANGLIN, Philip II or Jr	FULFERSON, Frederick	NANCE, Reuben
BARKSDALE, Thomas Henry	GRAVELY, Joseph	PACE, John
BOULDIN, Thomas Jr	HAIRSTON, George	PAYNE, Reuben
COX, Charles	HOLLANDSWORTH, Thomas	RAGLAND, William
COX, Charles II	KING, George	REA, John
DESHAZO, William	KING, John Sr	REDD, John Franklin
DILLARD, John	MARTIN, Joseph	SIMPSON, John
DYER, George	MARTIN, Joseph	TAYLOR, George
EDWARDS, Ambrose	MOLES, Jeremiah	
FRANKLIN, Lewis	MULLINS, David	

HIGHLAND COUNTY. Formed in 1847 from Bath County and Pendleton County (WV). County seat is Monterey (24465).

ARBOGAST, Michael	HEMPENSTALL, Abraham	RUCKMAN, David
ARMSTRONG, John	HEYDE (HIDY), Johann	RYMER, George
ARMSTRONG, John	Henrich (John)	SEYBERT, Henry
CARLISLE (CARLILE,	HULL, George	SEYBERT, Nicholas
CARLYLE), James	HULL, Peter	WILSON, Elibabb (Eli)
GILMOR(E) (GILMER),	JONES, Henry	WILSON, John
Samuel	KINHEAD (KINKEAD),	
GUM, Isaac	Thomas	
GWIN(N), David	MCCOY, John	

HOPEWELL CITY (23860). Originally known as City Point. Achieved Independent City status in 1916. **See also PRINCE GEORGE COUNTY.**

No known veteran burials.

ISLE OF WIGHT COUNTY. An original 1634 shire as Warrosquyoake County. Renamed in 1637. County seat is Isle of Wight (23397).

BARLOW, Jesse	MOORE, Merritt	PURDIE, George
BENN, George	PARKER, Josiah	SMITH, Thomas
HUBARD, William	PARKER, Nicholas	TODD, Mallory

JAMES CITY COUNTY. An original 1634 shire. County seat is Williamsburg (23185). **See also WILLIAMSBURG CITY.**

JONES, Daniel

KING AND QUEEN COUNTY. Formed in 1691 from New Kent County. County seat is King and Queen Court House (23085).

COLLINS, Thomas	FLEET, William	POLLARD, Joseph
DEW, Thomas	HOSKINS, Robert	POLLARD, William
FAUNTLEROY, Samuel Griffin	LYNE, William	YOUNG, Henry

KING GEORGE COUNTY. Formed in 1721 from Richmond County. Count seat is King George (22485).

ARNOLD, William	DISHMAN, Samuel	JONES, William
ASHTON, Henry Alexander	GRYMES, Benjamin Jr	MOUNTJOY, William
BRAXTON, Carter	HARVEY, Mungo	SAUNDERS, William
DAVIS, Jesse	HIPKINS, John	STUART, William David
DAVIS (DAVIES), Jesse	HOOE, Gerard (Garrard)	WASHINGTON, John H

KING WILLIAM COUNTY. Formed in 1702 from King and Queen County. County seat is King William (23086).

AYLETT, William	FOX, John	ROANE, John Jr
BROWNE, William Burrnett	HILL, James	TOMPKINS, Christopher
BURWELL, Nathaniel	LANGBORNE, William	
CLAIBORNE, William	MARSHALL, William	
DANDRIDGE, William	MOORE, Alexander	
EDWARDS, Ambrose	Spotswood	
EUBANK(S), Richard	NELSON, William	

LANCASTER COUNTY. Formed in 1651 from Northumberland County and York County. The portion from York County (south of the Rappahannock River) became Middlesex County in 1669. County seat is Lancaster (22503).

BALL, James	DOWNMAN, Rawleigh	SYDNOR, William
BALL, James	GORDON, James (Colonel)	TAYLOR, Charles
CHOWNING, William	KELLEY, James	

LEE COUNTY. Formed in 1793 from Russell County. County seat is Jonesville (24263).

BAKER, Andrew II	ELY, William	NEILL, William
BALES, Jonathan	EWING, William	OLLINGER (OLIFER), John
BALL, George	FRITTS, John	Christopher Sr
BALL, John	GIBSON, George	WILSON, Abraham Sr
CAMPBELL, James	GILBERT, Samuel	YEARY, Benedict
CARMACK, William	HOBBS, Vincent	YEARY, Henry Jr
DUFF, Robert	MARION, Samuel	YEARY, Henry Sr

LEXINGTON CITY (24450). Achieved Independent City status in 1966. **See also ROCKBRIDGE COUNTY.**

ALEXANDER, Andrew	HOSTETTER, Ulrich	MONTGOMERY, Humphrey Jr
ALEXANDER, John	IRVINE, William	MOORE, Andrew
ALEXANDER, William	JOHNSTON (JOHNSON),	MOORE, James
ANDERSON, Thomas	Zachariah	MOORE, William
BERRYHILL, John	LEACH, John	REID, Andrew
BOWYER, Henry	LEE, Henry III	ROBERTSON, William
BOWYER, John	LOGAN, James	ROBINSON, John
BRADLEY, William	LOGAN, James	TRIMBLE, James
CAMPBELL, Alexander	MACKEY, John Sr	TRIMBLE, Sarah (Kersey)
FIX, Phillip	MCCLURE, John	WALLACE, William
FLINT, John	MCCOWN, Samuel	WILSON, Daniel
GRAHAM, William	MCGOWAN, Samuel	WILSON, Hugh
HALL, James	MCNUTT, Alexander	WILSON, Thomas
HARRIS, James	MILLER, Henry	
HILL, John Berry	MILLER, Samuel	

LOUDOUN COUNTY. Formed in 1747 from Fairfax County. County seat is Leesburg (22075).

ALDRIDGE, John
ANDERSON, Andrew
ANSLEY, William
AXLINE, John
BALL, Burgess
BEANS, William
BENEDUM, Peter
BERRY, David
BINNS, Charles
BROWN, Isaacher
BROWN, John
CAMPBELL, Aeneas
CARR, John
CARR, John
CARR, Thomas Sr
CARTER, Edward
CARTER, James
CARTER, Richard
CHEW, John
CHEW, John Sr
CLAPHAM, Josias
COCHRAN, Samuel R
COPELAND, James (Jas)
CURTIS, James
DAVIS, James
DELANY, John
DONOHOE, John V
DOUGLAS(S), Hugh
DRAKE, Thomas
DUNN, John
ELGIN, Francis Jr
ELGIN, Gustavus
ELGIN, Walter
ELLZEY, William
EWER (EWERS), John
FAULEY (FAWLEY), John
FURR, Enoch
GARDNER, John
GIBSON, Joseph
GIDEON, Peter
GORE, Joshua Sr
GRADY, James Sr
GREEN, John
GREEN, Samuel
GREGG, John
GREGG, John C
HANDLEY, John
HATCHER, James Sr
HEATON, James
HELM, Meridith Sr

HEREFORD, John E
HIXON, Timothy
HOGE, William
HOUGH, Benjamin
HOUGH (HUFF), William
HUGHES, Isaac
HUGHES, Thomas A
HUMPHREY, Jesse
HUMPHREY(S), Abner
HUMPHREY(S), Thomas
JAMES, Thomas
LANE, Joseph
LEE, Ludwell
LOVE, James
MAINS, William
MARKS, Abel
MARKS, George Elisha
MARKS, Isaiah
MARKS, John Jr
MASON, Stevens (Stephen)
  Thomson
MASON, Thomson
  (Thompson)
MCILHANEY, James
MCKIM, James
MCVEAGH (MCVAY),
  Jonathan
MOCK, John Harrison
MOFFETT, William Mead
MONROE, William
MOUNT, Ezekiel
MULL, David
MURRAY, Samuel
NICHOLS, Daniel
NICHOLS, Isaac
NICHOLS, Nathaniel
NIXON, George
NIXON, George
NIXON, John
OSBURN, William
OWINGS, Richard
PARKER, Thomas
PARKER, William Harwar
PIGGOTT, William
POTTER, Ebenezer
POTTS, Ezekiel
POTTS, Jonas
POTTS, Nathaniel
POULSON, George B
PURCELL, Thomas Sr

RAMEY, Sanford
RICHARDSON, Nightingale
RINKER, Edward
ROBERTS, Stephen
ROGERS, Hamilton
ROLLER, Conrad
ROSE, John
ROSS, John
ROSZEL(L), Stephen G
SAUNDERS, Aaron
SCHOLFIELD, Thomas
SCOTT, Stephen
SELDEN, Wilson Cary
SHUMAKER (SCHUMACHER),
  George
SINCLAIR, Samuel
SMITH, George W
SMITH, Samuel
STEERS, Isaac
STOUTSENBERGER
  (STOUSEBERGER), John
SUMMERS, William J
TAVINER (TAVENNER),
  Ritchard (Richard)
TAYLOR, Stacy
TAYLOR, Timothy II
THATCHER, Stephen
THOMAS, John Sr
THOMPSON, Amos Rev
THOMPSON, Hugh
THOMPSON, William
TRIPLETT, Simon
TYLER, John
VANDEVANTER
  (VANDEVINDER,
  VANDEVENTER), Isaac
VANSICKLER, Ferdinand
  (Fernandus)
WEST, John
WHITACRE, John III
WHITACRE (WHITAKER),
  George
WHITE, Benjamin
WHITE, Josiah (Josias)
WILKISON, William Sr
WILSON, Thomas
WIRE, William
WORTHINGTON, William

LOUISA COUNTY. Formed in 1742 from Hanover County. County seat is Louisa (23093).

ANDERSON, David Jr	GOODWYN (GOODWIN),	POINDEXTER, Thomas
BAGBY, John	Robert	SHELTON, James
BARRAT (BARRET), John	GUNNELL, John II	SHELTON, Thomas
BOXLEY, Joseph I Sr	GUNNELL (GUNNILL),	THOMPSON (THOMASSON),
BULLOCK, David	John Sr	John
CAMPBELL, Francis Lee	HANCOCK, Austin	WALTON, Joel
DABNEY, Samuel	JACKSON, Thomas	WHARTON, Samuel
DAVIS, Abraham	JACKSON, William	YANCEY, Charles
DICKINSON, James	JERDONE, Francis	YANCEY, Mary
GIBSON, William	JOHNSON, Thomas Jr	WILLIAMS, John Rev

LUNENBURG COUNTY. Formed in 1746 from Brunswick County. County seat is Lunenburg (23952).

BOSWELL, John Iverson	DEGRAFENREIDT, Tscharner	WILLIAMS, John Rev
CLARK, John Shadrock	HITE, Julius	
(Shadrick)	TAYLOR, William	

LYNCHBURG CITY (24505). Achieved Independent City status in 1852. **See also CAMPBELL COUNTY.**

BAILEY, John	JONES, Thomas C Sr	SCHOOLFIELD, John
BALLARD, William Jr	LYNCH, John	SCOTT, John E
BURKE, Richard H	MANN, Daniel	SCOTT, Samuel
CHILTON (CHELTON),	MARTIN, William	SCOTT, William W
Richard Sr	MCDANIEL, George	SCRUGGS, Samuel
DANIEL, William Sr	MOORMAN, Micajah	TERRELL, David Jr
DAVIS, William	MOSELEY, James	THURMAN, Richard Sr
DOUGLASS, Achilles	NORVELL (NORWELL),	TOWLES, Oliver
DUFFEL, Edward	Henry Holdcraft (Hallcraft)	VAWTER, Benjamin
DUFFEL, James C	OGLESBY, Daniel	VAWTER, John
GEORGE, Reuben	OWEN, Owen	
GRAY, Francis	PRESTON, John	

MADISON COUNTY. Formed in 1793 from Culpeper County. County seat is Madison (22727).

AYLOR, Jacob	GAAR, Andrew	SOUTHER, Micheal
BEALE, Reuben	GAAR, Johann (John) Adam	TANNER, Abraham
BLANKENBAKER, Michael	GAAR, John (Johannes)	TRIBBLE, Andrew
CAMPBELL, Cammuel	GAINES, James	WALKER, James
Elias Sr	GRAVES, John	WAYLAND, John
CAMPBELL, Elias	HARRISON, John Sr	WEAVER, Peter
CAMPBELL, John	HOUSE, Matthias	WILHOITE (WILHOIT), Daniel
CARPENTER, Samuel	LILLARD, James	WILHOITE (WILHOIT), John
CROW, James	MCALLISTER, James	YAGER, John Sr
FORD, John	NICHOLSON, John	YOWELL (YOWEL), William
FRAY, Ephraim	RUCKER, Angus	ZIMMERMAN, Christopher
FRY, Henry	SCOTT, George	ZIMMERMAN, John

MANASSAS CITY (22110). Achieved Independent City status in 1975. **See also PRINCE WILLIAM COUNTY.**

ALEXANDER, William	HENRY, Isaac	MONTGOMERY, William
BALL, Spencer	HOOE, Bernard	SIMMS, Joseph
CARTER, Landon Jr	HOOE, Robert Howson	THURMAN, Robert
DOGAN, Henry	MONTGOMERY, Francis	

MANASSAS PARK CITY (20111). Achieved Independent City status in 1975. **See also PRINCE WILLIAM COUNTY.**

No known veteran burials.

MARTINSVILLE CITY (24112). Achieved Independent City status in 1928. **See also HENRY COUNTY.**

JONES, Benjamin Dr   WALLER, George   WINN, James

MATHEWS COUNTY. Formed in 1791 from Gloucester County. County seat is Mathews (23109).

BILLUPS, Joseph	JAMES, Thomas	WHITE, John
BILLUPS, Joseph Jr	PAGE, John	WILLIAMS, Samuel
DIXON, John	RICHARDS, John	WILLIAMS, Thomas S
FORREST, George	TABB, Thomas	WILLIAMS, William M
FOSTER, Isaac	TURNER, John L	
FOSTER, Peter G	WATSON, John	

MECKLENBURG COUNTY. Formed in 1765 from Lunenburg County. County seat is Boydton (23917).

ANDREWS, Benjamin	DAVIS (DAVIES), William	PETTIES (PETTES, PETTUS), Samuel Overton
ANDREWS, Varney Sr	GOODE, Samuel	RAINEY (RAINY), Williamson
ANDREWS, William A	GREGORY, Roger	SKIPWITH, Peyton Sr
BASKERVILLE, William	KEEN, Abraham (Abram)	SPEED, Joseph
BENNETT, Jordan	LEWIS, John T	WINN, Richard
BOYD, Alexander	MALONE, Benjamin	YANCEY, Robert
BOYD, Francis	MUNFORT (MUNFORD, MONFORT, MONFORD), Robert	
BOYD, Robert		
BRAME, Richens	OVERBEY, Peter Z	
BURWELL, Lewis		

MIDDLESEX COUNTY. Formed in 1669 from the portion of Lancaster County south of the Rappahannock River that had formed from York County in 1651. County seat is Saluda (23149).

BERKELEY, Edmund	DAME, George	LEE, Arthur
CORBIN, Gawin Tayloe	GRYMES, Philip Ludwell	MCKANN, Robert H
CORBIN, Richard	HEALY, James	
COSBY, Overton	JACKSON, John	

MONTGOMERY COUNTY. Formed in 1776 from Fincastle County, which became extinct at that time. County seat is Christianburg (24073).

ALTIZER (ALTHAUSEN), Emery (Emera)	GILES, Thomas	LUCAS(S), John
BARGER, Philip	HALL, Asa Sr	MADISON, William Strother
BLACK, John	HALL, Jesse	MAXWELL, Thomas
BOOTHE, George	HANCOCK, George	MEACHUM (MEACHAM), Ichabod
BRATTON, James	HARLESS, David Anthony	MONTGOMERY, John
CRAIG, James	HARLESS (HORLESS), Philip	PRESTON, William
CROCKETT, Hugh	HENDERSON, John	SOWDER, Jacob
DAVIES, Joseph Sr	HOWARD, William	THOMAS, Giles
GARDNER, John	KINSER (KENSOR), Michael	WATTERSON, Henry
	LESTER, John	

NANSEMOND COUNTY (extinct). See SUFFOLK CITY. Formed in 1637 as Upper Norfolk County from New Norfolk County, which formed from Elizabeth City County (an original 1634 shire). Renamed Nansemond County in 1646. Suffolk was the county seat from 1750 to 1972. County became the City of Nansemond in 1972, then merged with the City of Suffolk in 1974. A good deal of Nansemond County historical records are housed at the David R. Rubenstein Rare Books and Manuscript Library at Duke University, Durham, NC.

NELSON COUNTY. Formed in 1808 from Amherst County. County seat is Lovingston (22949).

BALLARD, Proctor	FORTUNE, Thomas	MASSIE (MASSIE), Thomas
CABELL, Nicholas	HARRIS, William	MCALEXANDER, James Jr
CABELL, Samuel Jordan	HILL, Nathaniel	MCALEXANDER, James Sr
CABELL, William Sr	HILL, William	MONTGOMERY, Joseph
CLARKE, Christopher	JACOBS, George	SHIELDS, William
CLARKSON, James	JACOBS, John	TILFORD, David
COFFEY (COFFEE), Edmund	JONES, Charles	TILFORD, James
COLEMAN, Hawes	JONES, Thomas	TUCKER, St George
ESTES, Elisha	LOVINGS (LOVING), John Jr	VAUGHN, William
FORTUNE, Benjamin	MARTIN, Azariah	WOODS, Samuel

NEW KENT COUNTY. Formed in 1654 from York County. County seat is New Kent (23124).

CLOPTON, John	DENNETT, John	WATKINS, John
CLOPTON, William	MEREDITH, Elijah	

NEWPORT NEWS CITY (23607). Achieved Independent City status in 1896 from Warwick County. Enlarged in 1958 when it reconsolidated with Warwick City which was the former Warwick County.

CARY, John	CARY, Richard Jr	DIGGS, Edward
CARY, Richard	CARY, Thomas Jr	

NORFOLK CITY (23510). Created as the Borough of Norfolk by royal charter in 1736 in Norfolk County. Achieved Independent City status in 1845.

ABYVON, George	GRIMES, James S	READ, John K
ABYVON (ABYNON), Marrim	HANSFORD, Cary H	SINGLETON, John
(Miriam, Manim, Meriam,	HARVEY, John	SKINNER, Charles W
Marsam)	HENLEY, James	SLAUGHTER, Augustin(e)
ALLMAND, Harrison	HOWELL, John F	(Augustus)
BACON, Samuel	KING, Miles Sr	SMITH, John
BURT, John M	LAWRENCE, John	STARK, William
CALVERT, John Salvage	LEE, John	TAYLOR, James
CALVERT, Thomas	MATHEWS, Thomas	TAYLOR, Robert
CHAMBERLAIN(E), George	MAURY, Walker	TAYLOR, Sarah Crull (Croel,
CONSTABLE, Thomas	MAXWELL, James	Curle) Barraud Huitt
DOUGHERTY (DOUGHTY),	MOSELY, Hildarh (Hillary)	WHIDDON, John
Edward	NESTEL (NESTELL, NESTLE,	WILLOUGHBY, William
DOUGLAS, William	NISTELL), Peter	WILSON, James
FERGUSON, Daniel	PALMER, Job	WRIGHT, Stephen

NORFOLK COUNTY (extinct). See CHESAPEAKE CITY. Formed in 1691 from Lower Norfolk County, which formed from New Norfolk County, which formed from Elizabeth City County (an original 1634 shire). County seat was Portsmouth. Over time, the county was reduced as several cities split off. In 1963, the remaining county consolidated with South Norfolk city as the new City of Chesapeake.

NORTHAMPTON COUNTY. Original 1634 shire of Accawmack or Accomac County comprised Virginia's Eastern Shore. Name changed to Northampton County in 1643. Split into the present Accomack and Northampton Counties in 1663. County seat is Eastville (23347).

BAIN, William	PITTS, Hezekiah	STITH, Griffin
BELL, George	PITTS, Major	TANKARD, John Dr
BELL, William	SAVAGE, Lyttleton	THOMAS, Harrison
DARBY, John	SAVAGE, Thomas Lytllteton	UPSHUR, Thomas
DARBY, Nathaniel	SCARBURGH	
HOLLAND, Nathaniel	(SCARBOROUGH), John	
KENDALL, George	SMITH, Isaac	

NORTHUMBERLAND COUNTY. Formed in 1649 from the Chickacoan (Indian) District, the early 17th-century name for the region between the Potomac and Rappahannock Rivers. "Mother County" of the Northern Neck. County seat is Heathsville (22473).

BALL, David	HAYNIE, Bridgar II	SMITH, James
BLACKWELL, William	JONES, Walter Dr	
COX, Peter	MOORE, James	

NORTON CITY (24273). Achieved Independent City status in 1954. **See also WISE COUNTY.**

No known veteran burials.

NOTTOWAY COUNTY. Formed in 1789 from Amelia County. County seat is Nottoway (23955).

ALLEN, Charles	EPES (EPPES), Francis	PERKINSON, Thomas
DUPUY, James	HENDERSON, James	WILLIAMS, Thomas

ORANGE COUNTY. Formed in 1735 from Spotsylvania County. County seat is Orange (22960).

BROCKMAN, Samuel Jr	HOLLOWAY, George	PAINE, Thomas
BRUCE, Charles	JONES, Churchill	PANNILL, William
CAMPBELL, William	JONES, William	SCOTT, Johnny (Jonny)
COOPER, James	LINDSAY, Reuben	TALIAFERRO, Lawrence
COWHERD, Francis Kirtley	MADISON, Ambrose Sr	TAYLOR, Erasmus
CRITTENDEN, William	MADISON, James	TAYLOR, Robert
DADE, Francis L	MADISON, William Taylor	WEBB, William Warren
DAVIS, Thomas	MANSFIELD, Robert	WILLIAMS, James
GORDON, Nathaniel	MORTON, George	
HEAD, Benjamin Sr	MORTON, William	

PAGE COUNTY. Formed in 1831 from Rockingham County and Shenandoah County. County seat is Luray (22835).

ALESHIRE, John Conrad	OVERBOKER	STRICKLER, Benjamin
COURTNEY, William	(OFFENBACHER),	STRICKLER, Isaac
GROVE, Marcus	Frederick	STRICKLER, Jacob
GROVE (GROFF), Christian	PRINTZ, George	STRICKLER, Joseph
Sr (Christley)	PRINTZ (PRINCE), Gottlieb	VARNER (WERNER), Phillip
KEYSER, Andrew Sr	(Cutlip)	WOOD, Benjamin
KEYSER, Charles Jr	PRINTZ (PRINCE), Philip	WOOD, Nehemiah
KIBLER, Henry	ROBERTSON, William	
LONG, Philip	RUFFNER, Peter Sr	
MCKAY, Enos	SMITH, Jacob	

PATRICK COUNTY. Formed in 1791 from Henry County. County seat is Stuart (24171).

ADAMS, Jacob	HUGHES, Archelaus	PRICE, William
BRYANT, William	LETCHER, William	ROBERTSON, David
CORN, Jesse Sr	LEWIS, Edward	ROSS, Daniel Sr
CRITZ, Hamon Jr (Herman)	MCALEXANDER, John	SHELTON, Eliphaz
HANBY, Jonathan	PENN, Abram or Abraham	STAPLES, Samuel
HANCOCK, John	PLASTER, Michael	VARNER, Joseph

PETERSBURG CITY (23803). Achieved Independent City status in 1850. Formed from parts of Chesterfield County, Dinwiddie County, and Prince George County. Records begin in 1784.

ANDERSON, Daniel	BASS, William	DONALDSON, Robert
ANDERSON, David	BOLLING, Robert	GILL, Erasmus
BANISTER (BANNISTER),	BURK, John Daly	HAMMON, Edward
John Monroe	CAMERON, John	HARRISON, William

(PETERSBURG, continued)

HEATH, Jesse
JEFFERS (JEFFRIES), John
JOHNSON, Andrew
JONES, Joseph

LEE, Edward
PARKER, Elias
ROBINSON, Robert
STROUD, Thomas A

STUART, John
TAYLOR, Alexander
WILLIAMS, James

PITTSYLVANIA COUNTY. Formed in 1767 from Halifax County. County seat is Chatham (24531).
See also CITY OF DANVILLE.

AARON, Abraham Sr
ADAMS, Robert Jr
ADKINS, William
BERGER, Jacob
BOAZ, Thomas
BRUCE, John
BUCKLEY, James Jr
BUCKLEY, James Sr
BUCKLEY, John
BULLINGTON, Robert
CALLAND(S), Samuel
CALLAWAY (CALLOWAY),
    Charles
CARTER, Thomas
CHENEY (CHANEY),
    Abram (Abraham)
CIRCLE (CIRKLE), Peter
CLARK, William
CLEMENT(S), Benjamin
CLOPTON, Robert
COLEMAN, Daniel
COLEMAN, Isaac

COLEMAN, Stephen
COLES, Isaac Sr
DAVIS, Benjamin
DAVIS, Joseph
DAVIS, William
DICKENSON, Griffith
DOVE, William
EAST, Thomas
FITZ (FITTS), Robert Walker
FITZGERALD, Edmund
    (Edmond)
GARDNER, Nathanial
HAMPTON, Thomas
HARRIS, Samuel
HOPKINS, James
HOSKINS, Thomas Coleman
HUNT, David
HUTCHINGS, Moses
HUTCHINS (HUTCHINGS),
    Christopher
JONES, Thomas Sr
KEESEE (KEEZEE), Jeremiah

MITCHELL, James
MORGAN, Hayes (Haynes)
MOTLEY, Joseph
MUSTAIN (MUSTEIN), Avery
PIGG, Hezekiah Ford
PIGG, John
ROBERTSON, Edward
SHELTON, Lemuel
SMITH, Joseph
STONE, John
STONE, Joshua
TOWLER, Joseph
VADEN, Burwell
WALTON, Jesse
WEATHERFORD, John
    William
WEST, Joseph
WILLIAMS, James Mastin
WITCHER, William Jr
WORSHAM, Essex
WRAY, David
YATES, John III

POQUOSON CITY. Achieved Independent City status in 1975. **See also YORK COUNTY.**

No known veteran burials.

PORTSMOUTH CITY (23704). Established as a town in 1752 in Norfolk County. Achieved Independent City status in 1858, but remained the county seat until 1963.

ASHLEY, Warren
BALLARD, Edward
BARRON, James
BENSON, Robert
BILISOLY, Antonio S
BLOW, Richard
BRAIDFOOT, John
BROWN, Henry
DAVIS, Samuel
DICKINSON, Thomas Bowers
DICKSON, Henry
FOWLER, Samuel

GRICE, Joseph
GRIMES, Thomas
HILL, Thomas M or H
JARVIS, John Sr
KEARNES, John
KEY, John
LUKE, Issac Sr
MAGNIEN, Bernard
MCPHERSON, Hugh
MOFFATT, William Sr
NICHOLSON, Jesse(e)
PORTER, Samuel

PORTER, William
PULLIN, John
REA, William
STOBO, Jacob
STOKES, Christopher C
SWIFT, Thomas
TAYLOR, Peter
VEALE, Thomas
WEBB, Tapley (Tarpley)
WILSON, William
WILSON, Willis
WONEYCUTT, Edward

POWHATAN COUNTY. Formed in 1777 from Cumberland County. County seat is Powhatan (23139).

HARRIS, Francis E
HOBSON (HOPSON), Joseph
    Calip/Caleb
MARTIN, Anthony

MCLAURINE, James
MINTER, Anthony
MOSBY, Littleberry Jr
POPE, William

SMITH, Thomas
WATKINS, Samuel
WATKINS, Samuel
WOODFIN, Samuel

PRINCE EDWARD COUNTY. Formed in 1754 from Amelia County. County seat is Farmville (23901).

ALLEN, Charles	LEIGH, John	VENABLE, Nathaniel
ALLEN, James Jr	McROBERT, Archibald	WOODSON, Jacob
LANCASTER, John	RANDOLPH, Beverley	WORSHAM, William

PRINCE GEORGE COUNTY. Formed in 1703 from Charles City County. County seat is Prince George (23875).

ALDRIDGE, James	HARRISON, Nathaniel	RUFFIN, Edmund Jr
BLAND, Richard Jr	HARRISON, Robert	RUFFIN, Edmund Sr
EPPES, Francis	HARRISON, William H	SIMMONS, Joshua
GLOVER, Joseph	HEATH, Henry	WILKINSON, John
HARRISON, Benjamin	LEE, Nathaniel	

PRINCE WILLIAM COUNTY. Formed in 1731 from King George County and Stafford County. County seat is Manassas (22110). **See also MANASSAS CITY.**

ALEXANDER, William	FITZHUGH, Thomas	MADDOX, Allison
ASHMORE, William	FLOURANCE, George Jr	MILLS, William
ATKINSON, George	FLOURANCE (FLORENCE,	NORWELL (NORVALL),
BEAVER(S), John Sr	FLORANCE), William	Aquilla
BLACKBURN, Thomas	FORD, William	REID, James
BRUNDIGE, Timothy	GALLAGHER, Bernard	SCOTT, William
BRYSON, Robert	GRAYSON, Spencer	SMITH, George
CAVE, Thomas	GRAYSON, William	SPENCE, John
CLARKE, Christopher	GRAYSON, William	TEBBS, Willoughby
COLQUHOUN, James W	HENDERSON, Alexander	TEBBS, Willoughby William
DAVIS, Hugh	HOWISON, Stephen	WEST, William
EWELL, Jesse	LEE, Henry II	WHEELER, Drummond
FAIRFAX, William	LUCKETT, John B	WILLIAMS, Sarah

PRINCESS ANNE COUNTY (extinct). See VIRGINIA BEACH CITY. Formed in 1691 from Lower Norfolk County, which formed from New Norfolk County, which formed from Elizabeth City County (an original 1634 shire). Consolidated in 1963 with the City of Virginia Beach.

PULASKI COUNTY. Formed in 1839 from Montgomery County and Wythe County. County seat is Pulaski (24301).

BELL, Robert	HOGE, James	PATTON, Henry
BROOK, Edmund (Edmond)	HOGG (HOGE), James Jr	WEISER, Henry
CADDELL, Samuel	HONAKER, Henry S Sr	WYSOR (WEYSOR,
CECIL, John	HONAKER (HONEGGER),	WEIZER), Henry
CECIL, Samuel Witten Sr	Hans Jacob	
CLOYD, Joseph	HOWE, Daniel	

RADFORD CITY. Achieved Independent City status in 1892. **See also MONTGOMERY COUNTY.**

No known veteran burials.

RAPPAHANNOCK COUNTY. Formed in 1833 from Culpeper County. County seat is Washington (22747).

AMIS(S), Joseph	CORDER, John	MILLER, Henry II
AMIS(S), Levi	DEARING, John	MILLER, John
ANDERSON, Elijah	GRIFFIN, Henry	PIERCE, John
BROWNING, John	HITT, Nimrod(s)	SLAUGHTER, John Suggart
COLVIN, Mason	HOTTENSTEIN, Jacob	(Suggate)
CORBIN, John	LILLARD, Benjamin	STROTHER, John Dabney Sr
CORBIN, William	MAJOR, William	WOODARD, William

[OLD] RAPPAHANNOCK COUNTY (extinct). Formed in 1656 from Lancaster County. Became extinct in 1692 when it was divided to form Essex County and Richmond County.

RICHMOND CITY (23219). Founded in 1742, became capital in 1780. Incorporated as a town in 1782 in Henrico County, but called a city. Achieved Independent City status in 1842. Includes the former independent city of Manchester (1874) which was consolidated in 1910.

ABBOTT, Joseph
ALLEGREE, William
AMBLER, John Esq
AMES, Isaac
ANDREE, John G
BAILEY, Ansel Anselm
Ansolem Anselem
BAKER, Hilary (Hillary) Jr
BALL, David
BARKER, William
BARTON, Richard
BEALE, John
BELL, Nathaniel Nathan
BELL, Robert
BLAIR, John
BLANKENSHIP, James W
BROWN, Richard
BROWN, William
BURTON, John P
BUTLER, James F
CALL, Daniel
CARRINGTON, Edward
CARRINGTON, George
CARTER, William
CARTER, William
CHAMBERLAYNE, William
CLAIBORNE, William
COLQUITT, John
COPLAND, Charles
COURTNEY, John
CURRIE, James
DAVIS, Augustine
DRAKE, James Sr
DUNCAN, Andrew
DUVAL, Plilip Jr
EGE, Jacob
EGE, Samuel
ELLIOTT (ELLIOT), Thomas
EPPES, Peter
FOSTER, Joseph

FOUSHEE, William
FRANCISCO, Peter
GAMBLE, Robert
GEDDES, Winston
GIBBON, James
GRAHAM, William
GRAY, James
GREENHOW, Robert
GRIFFIN, Thomas
HAGAN, Michael
HARRIS, David
HARVIE, John
HERON, James
HOLLOWAY, Daniel
HOPKINS, Walter
JONES, Charles G
LANE, Anna Maria
LANE, John
LAWRENCE, John
LAWSON, Robert
LESTER, John
LOVELL, Joseph
MARSHALL, John Curtis
MAYO, John
MAYO, William
McCLURG, James
MERCER, James
MERCER, John
MEYERS, Samuel
MITCHELL, William
MONROE, James
MOORE, Charles
MOSS, John
MYERS, Samuel
NICHOLSON, Robert
NICOLSON, Thomas
PAGE, John
PARKER, Ebenezer
PARKINSON, Joseph
    Christian

PATTESON, David
PHILLIPS, John M
POLLARD, Robert
POTTS, John
PRICE, Barrett (Barret)
PRICE, William
PRYOR, John
QUARLES, John
RADFORD, Richard
RAYBURN(E) (RAYBORN(E),
    RAIBORNE), George
RICHARD, John
ROBERTSON, John
ROWLAND, John
SEABROOK, Nicholas B
SHEPARD, William
SIMM(S), James
SLAUGHTER, Philip
SMITH, Andrew
SMITH, George William
STROBIA, John
TERRY, William E
TOMPKINS, Harry
TONEY, Archibald
VALENTINE, Batchelder
VAUGHN, James
VENABLE, Abraham
    Bedford Jr
WALKER, William
WATSON, Joseph
WEBB, William
WEBB, William
WILSON, James
WINSTON, Geddes
WOOD, James
WORSHAM, George
WYNNE, Thomas H
WYTHE, George

RICHMOND COUNTY. Formed in 1692 from [Old] Rappahannock County which formed from Lancaster County. County seat is Warsaw (22572).

BEALE, Robert
BEALE, William Jr
BELFIELD, John
BELFIELD, Sydnor
BELFIELD, Thomas Wright

BROCKENBROUGH, John
BROCKENBROUGH, William
CARTER, Landon
FAUNTLEROY, Moore
FLOOD, Nicholas Dr

LEE, Francis Lightfoot
MIMS, David Jr
MUSE, Daniel Sr
TAYLOE, John
WORMELEY, Ralph V

ROANOKE CITY (24101). Achieved Independent City status in 1884. **See also ROANOKE COUNTY**.

COLLINS, Benjamin	FLEMING, William	HARSHBARGER, Christian Sr

ROANOKE COUNTY. Formed in 1838 from Botetourt County. County seat is Salem (24153).

DEVERLE (DEYERLE), Peter	LEWIS, Andrew Jr	WEDDLE (WADDELL,
ESOM (ESCOM), Hannah	POAGE, William	WODLE, WEDEL),
HANNAN, Esom	VINYARD, Christain	Benjamin
LEWIS, Andrew	VINYARD, Christian	

ROCKBRIDGE COUNTY. Formed in 1778 from Augusta County and Botetourt County. County seat is Lexington (24450). **See also LEXINGTON CITY.**

ALBRIGHT, Frederick	HOUSTON, James	PAXTON, John
ALEXANDER, Archibald	HOUSTON, John Sr	PAXTON, John Sr
BARCLAY, Hugh	HOUSTON, Samuel	PAXTON, Thomas
BENNINGTON, Job	HOUSTON, Samuel	PAXTON, William
BERRY, Charles	HUGHES, John W	PAXTON, William
CAMPBELL, Charles	JONES, Nicholas	PAXTON, William Sr
CAMPBELL, Charles	KINCAID, John	SAVILLE, Abram (Abraham)
CLOYD, David	KIRKPATRICK, Robert	SCOTT, Andrew
COINER, Conrad	LAIRD, James	STUART, Robert
COX, Philip	LEECH, John Sr	TAYLOR, James
CRAWFORD, Alexander	MARTIN, Thomas	THOMPSON, William
CROSS, William	MCCLUER, John	WALKER, Alexander
DEDERICK, Jacob	MCCLUNG, John	WALKER, John Sr
DRYDEN, James Jr	MCCLUNG, William	WALKER, Joseph
FLEET, William	MCCLURE, Alexander	WALKER, William
FOREHAND, John Sr	MCCLURE, Halbert	WARDLOW (WARDLAW),
FRAZIER, John	MCCLURE, Robert	William
GILMORE, James	MCCLURE, Robert A	WEIR, Hugh
GLASGOW, Arthur	MCCLURE, Samuel	WELCH, Thomas
GRIGSBY, John	MCGUFFIN, Thomas Sr	WILLSON, Moses
HAMILTON, William T	MCKEE, James	WILLSON (WILSON), John
HARRIS, Robert	MCKEE, Robert	WILSON, Samuel
HENRY, James Jr	MCNUTT, Alexander	WILSON (WILLSON), John
HICKMAN, Jacob	MILLER, William	YOUEL, William
HIGHT, George	NELSON, Alexander	
HOUSTON, George	PARKS, John	

ROCKINGHAM COUNTY. Formed in 1778 from Augusta County. County seat is Harrisonburg (22801). **See also HARRISONBURG CITY.**

ANDES, Andrew	BOWMAN, Peter	FLOOK (FLUCK), Henry (John
ARMENTROUT, George	BRENEMAN, Abraham	Henry)
ARMENTROUT, Henry	BRIGHT, John	GIBBONS, Isaac
ARMENTROUT, John Henry	BROCK, John Sr	GORDON, Thomas
ARMENTROUT, Peter	BRYAN, Thomas	GREEN, Joseph
ARMENTROUT	CONRAD, Henry	HAINES, Casper
(ERMENTRAUDT), Philip	CONRAD, John Peter	HAINES, George
BAKER, John Sr	CONRAD (CONROD), John	HAINES, John
BAKER, Michael	Stephen Jr	HAINES, Jonas
BEAR (BAER), Jacob Sr	CONRAD (CONROD,	HAINES, Joseph
BEARD, James	COONROD), Jacob	HAINES (HAINS), Peter M
BERRY, Benjamin	CRAWFORD, William	HAINES (HAYNES), Frederick
BERRY, John	CRIM (KRIM, GRIM), Johann	HAMMER, Henry
BERRY (BEERY), Abraham	Peter	HARMON, Henry
BIBLE, Adam Jr	CUSTER (CUSTARD),	HARMON, Jacob Jr
BOWMAN, John	Richard Sr	HARNSBERGER, Adam

(ROCKINGHAM, continued)

HARRISON, Benjamin
HARRISON, John Peyton
HARRISON, Reuben
HARRISON, Reuben
HEADRICK, Charles
HERRING, Bethual (Bethuel Bethuard)
HERRING, Leonard
HERRING, William
HINKLE, Isaac
HINKLE, Yost
HOLSINGER, Micheal
HOPKIN(S), Archibald
HOPKIN(S), John
HUFFMAN (HOOFMAN), Valentine (Valentin)
KAYLOR, Micheal
KING, John
KISLING (KISSLING), Jacob
KISSLING, Ditrick
KISSLING, John
KLEIN, George Jr
KRING, John
KYGER, Christian
KYLE, David Sr

LAYMAN, John
LEE, Zephaniah
LEHMAN, Ludwick
LEWIS, Thomas
LINCOLN, Jacob
LONG, Mary
MAGILL, James
MAGILL, William
MAIDEN, James
MALLOW, George Sr
MAY, George I
MEADOWS, James
MILLER, Henry B Sr
MILLER, Mathias
MILLER, Michael
MILLER, Peter
MONGER, Henry
MOORE, Reuben
MOYER, Micheal (William)
NICHOLAS, Jacob
NICHOLAS, Peter
O'BRYANT, Thomas
PAUL, Nicholas
PAUL, Peter
PENCE, George

PENCE, Henry
PENCE, Jacob
PENCE, James
PENCE, John
PENCE, William
PRICE, Augustine
RHODES (ROTH), Henry B
RICE, John Sr
RICE, Thomas
RUSH, Charles
RUSH, John
SELLERS, John Adam
SHEETS, Samuel
SMITH, Abraham
STEPHENSON, John
STEVENS, John
TETER (TETOR), Paul
THOMAS, Richard
TROUT(T), (George) Michael
TUTWILER, Leonard
WANGER, Henry
WENGER, Henry
YANCEY, William Layton (Leighton)
YOUNT, Jacob

RUSSELL COUNTY. Formed in 1786 from Washington County. County seat is Lebanon (24266).

BICKLEY, Charles
BICKLEY, John
BICKLEY, Sebastian
BROWNING, Francis
DAVIS, James
DICKINSON (DICKSON), Henry

DORTON, William Jr
KELLY, Edward
LITTON, Martha (Duncan)
LITTON (LINTON), Burton Caleb Sr
LITTON (LINTON), Solomon Caleb Sr

LITTON (LITION), Thomas W
POLLOCKFIELD, John Richard Sr
PRICE, Richard
RAY, Benjamin
REYNOLDS, Bernard
TATE, John

SALEM CITY (24153). Achieved Independent City status in 1968. **See also ROANOKE COUNTY.**

BRYAN, William Jr
GARST, Frederick

JOHNSTON, John
WALTON, John B

WALTON, William
WALTON, William Sr

SCOTT COUNTY. Formed in 1814 from Lee County, Russell County, and Washington County. County seat is Gate City (24251).

BROWN, William
CARTER, Joseph
CARTER, Thomas
COCKE, David
ENGLAND, John
FREEMAN, William
GATES, Elijah

GODSEY, Austin
HENSLEY, Samuel
LANE, Corbin
LAWSON, William II
LAWSON, William Sr
LIVINGSTON, Peter
PACE, William

PORTER, Patrick
SMITH, James
SMITH, John "Dutch"
STALLARD, Samuel
TAYLOR, Nimrod
VINEYARD, George
WOOD, Jonathan Sr

SHENANDOAH COUNTY. Originally named Dunmore County when formed in 1772 from Frederick County. Renamed in 1778. County seat is Woodstock (22664).

BLY, John
BUCK, Charles Jr
DELLINGER, Christian Jr
EFFINGER, John Ignatius
FRYE, Benjamin
FUNK, Jacob
FUNKHOUSER, Abraham
FUNKHOUSER, Jacob Jr
FUNKHOUSER, Jacob Sr
FUNKHOUSER, John III
GOLLADAY (GOLLIDAY),
   Jacob
GOLLADAY (GOLLODAY),
   Joseph
GRANDSTAFF (GRINSTAFF),
   George
GRAY (GREY), Daniel
HARRISON, Benjamin
HENKEL, Paul Rev
HOTTEL, Johann
HOTTEL, John Jacob
HOTTEL, Joseph
HOUCK, George Michael
HUDSON, Thomas
JEFF, Henry

KELLER, George
KELLER, George Jr
KIPPS (KEPPS, KIPS), Jacob
KULLERS (CULLERS), Jacob
KULLERS (KULLER,
   CULLERS), John
LAYMAN, Benjamin
MCINTURF (MCINTURFF),
   David
MCINTURFF, Frederick
MILLER, Christian
MILLER, Jacob
NEFF, Abraham
NEFF, Christian
NEFF, Jacob
NEHS, Jacob
NEWMAN, John
NEWMAN, Walter
PENCE, Jacob
PENNYWEIGHT
   (PENNYWITT), Jacob
PHILLIPS, William
RAUSCH (RAUCH), Nicholas
RAUSCH (ROUSH), John
   Adam

RHODES, Michael
RINKER, Jacob
RINKER, Jacob
ROUSCH (ROUSH), Balser
   (Balster)
ROUSCH (ROUSH), Daniel
ROUSCH (ROUSH), Jacob
ROUSCH (ROUSH), John
ROUSCH (ROUSH), Philip
ROUSH, John Adam
ROUSH, Susannah (Schlem)
SHOMO, Anthony
SIGLER, Michael
SNAPP, Lawrence Sr
SPENGLER, Philip
STICKLEY, Benjamin
STOVER, Peter
STOVER, Peter
VON EFFINGER, John
ZEA, Martin
ZIRKLE, George Adam

SMYTH COUNTY. Formed in 1832 from Washington County and Wythe County. County seat is Marion (24354).

BISHOP, John
BLANKENBECKLER
   (BLANKENBAKER),
   Zachariah Jr
BOWEN, Arthur
BRODY, John
BUCHANAN, Alexander
BUCHANAN, John
CAMPBELL, John
CAMPBELL, William
COLE, Hugh
COLE, Joseph Jr
CRABTREE, Jacob

CROWE, Edward
DUNGAN (DUNCAN), Elisha
GREEVER (GREWER),
   Phillip Sr
HARMON, Mathias
HENINGER (HENEGAR)
   (HENNINGAR), Jacob
IRONS, John
JAYNE, Henry
KILLINGER, George
LAMM (LAMIE), John
LAMME, James
MEYERS, John

PRESTON, Francis
PRESTON, William
RICHARDSON, William Sr
SCOTT, James I
SHANNON, John
TATE, William
THOMAS, John
TOTTEN, John
WILLIAMS, Joseph
WILLIAMS, Richard
WOOLSLEY, Thomas

SOUTHAMPTON COUNTY. Formed in 1749 from Isle of Wight County. County seat is Courtland (23837).

BOYKIN, Simon
BOYKIN, Simon
CARY, George

DENSON, Jordan
FERGUSON, Robert
FORT, Lewis

STEVENSON (STEPHENSON),
   William Jr

SPOTSYLVANIA COUNTY. Formed in 1721 from Essex County, King and Queen County, and King William County. County seat is Spotsylvania (22552).

ALSOP, Benjamin	HOLLADAY, Joseph	POWELL, Ptolemy
BALLARD, James	HOLLADAY, Lewis	POWELL, William
BROOKE, Francis Taliaferro	LIPSCOMB, John	SLAUGHTER, Robert
CHANCELLOR, John	LIPSCOMB, Thomas	STANARD, Larkin
COLSON, Thomas	MARTIN, John	TALLEY (TALLY), Nathaniel
ESTES, Richard	MCDORMENT	(Nathan)
HERNDON, Edward Jr	(MCDORMAN), David	WALLACE, John D
HERNDON, Edward Sr	MINOR, Thomas	WALLER, William Edmund
HERNDON, William	PAGE, Mann III	

STAFFORD COUNTY. Formed in 1664 from Westmoreland County. County seat is Stafford (22554).

BENSON, William (Willis) Lee	HARRISON, Thomas	PHILLIPS, William
BOLES, William	HEDGES, John	ROY, Wily
BOWEN, John Pratt	HORE, Elias	SANFORD, Joseph
BRENT, Richard	HUNTER, James	SCOTT, James
BRIGGS, David	KING, Robert	SCOTT, William
CURTIS, John	LEE, Thomas Ludwell	STARK (STARKE), William
DANIEL, Frances (Moncure)	MONCURE, John II	STONE, Hawkin(s) (Hawken)
DANIEL, Travers D Sr	MORSON, Arthur	STONE, William B
DEBAPTIST (deBAPTIST,	MURSON, Arthur	WALLACE, John
D. BAPTIST), John	NORMAN, George	WALLER, William Jr
GASKINS, John	NORMAN, Thomas	WALLER, William Sr

STAUNTON CITY. Achieved Independent City status in 1871. **See also AUGUSTA COUNTY.**

ARGENBRIGHT	HOOVER, Michael	ROBERTSON, James
(ARGENTINE), Augustus	HUFF, Francis Jr	STERRETT, William
(Augustine)	HUGHART, Thomas	STUART, Archibald
BELL, Samuel	HUGHES, James	TAPP (TOPP), Vincent
BLACKBURN, Samuel	KING, William Sr	THOMPSON, Smith
BUSTER, Claudius	LEWIS, Thomas	TREMPER, Laurence
CLARK, James	LOHR, Johan Peter	(Lawrence)
CLARKE, James	LONG, John	TROTTER, John
CRAWFORD, John	MCDOWELL, William	VALENTINE, Edward
GARDINER, Francis	MOWRY (MOWREY), Henry	WADDELL, D James
HANGER, Peter	NORTH, Roger	WAFORD, George
HARMAN, Michael	NUSTER, Claudius	WRIGHT, Joseph
HAYS, John	PECK, Jacob Sr	YOUNG, John
HEISKELL (HISKILL), Peter	PORTERFIELD, Robert	

SUFFOLK CITY (23434). Founded in 1742 as a town in Nansemond County and became county seat in 1750. Achieved Independent City status in 1910, but remained the county seat until 1972 when Nansemond County changed to a city. In 1974, the cities of Suffolk and Nansemond consolidated as an enlarged City of Suffolk.

COWLING, Josiah	RIDDICK, Josiah	SKINNER, Henry
MARSHALL, Jesse	RIDDICK, Mills	WALLER, Thomas Carr

SURRY COUNTY. Formed circa 1652 from James City County. County seat is Surry (23883).

BOOTH, Beverly	COCKE, John Hartwell
BROWNE, William	WARREN, Jesse

SUSSEX COUNTY. Formed in 1754 from Surry County. County seat is Sussex (22884).

CLAIBORNE, Augustine	JONES, Holmes	MOSS, Joshua

TAZEWELL COUNTY. Formed in 1800 from Russell County and Wythe County. County seat is Tazewell (24651).

BAILEY, Richard	HARMAN (HARMON), Daniel	WARD, William
BOWEN, Rees	MOORE, Alexander	WHITTEN, Thomas Sr
BROOKS, William	MOORE, James	WITTEN, James
BROWN, Low (Lowe)	MOORE, William	WITTEN, Thomas Jr
GILLESPIE (GILLASPY),	THOMPSON, Archibald	WYNN(E), William Jr
Thomas II	THOMPSON, James Paxton	WYNN(E), William Sr
HARMAN, Daniel Conrad	THOMPSON, John	
HARMAN, Mathias (Matthias)	THOMPSON, William	

VIRGINIA BEACH CITY (23456). Oceanside resort incorporated as a town in 1906 in Princess Anne County. Achieved Independent City status in 1952. Enlarged in 1963 by reconsolidation with Princess Anne County, which became extinct at that time.

ACKISS, John	KEELING, Jacob	WALKE, Thomas IV
ACKISS, John	MOSELEY, Edward Hack Jr	WOODHOUSE, William
BOUSH, William Sr	THOROUGHGOOD, Adam	
JAMES, Edward	WALKE, Anthony II	

WARREN COUNTY. Formed in 1836 from Frederick County and Shenandoah County. County seat is Front Royal (22630).

ALLEN, Thomas	MARSHALL, James Markham	RICHARDSON, William
CLOUD, Daniel	MARSHALL, Thomas	VANMETER, Henry Jr
HONAKER, John	RICHARDSON, Samuel	
JACOBS, William H	Marquis	

WARWICK COUNTY AND WARWICK CITY (extinct). See NEWPORT NEWS CITY. An original 1634 shire as Warwick River County; renamed in 1643. County became an independent city in 1952, then consolidated with Newport News City in 1958.

WASHINGTON COUNTY. Formed in 1776 from Fincastle County which became extinct at that time. County seat is Abingdon (24210).

BAKER, Isaac	DOUGLASS, John	LAUGHLIN, Alexander
BARKER, Edward	DUFF, Samuel	LEONARD, Frederick
BEATIE, David	DUNKIN, John Jr	MAXWELL, David
BEATTY (BEATTIE), William	DUNKIN, John Thomas	MCCALL, Thomas
BERRY, John	EVINS, William	MCCHESNEY, James
BRADLEY, John	FARRIS, Gideon	MCCHESNEY, Samuel
BUCHANAN, John	FLEENOR, Michael	MCCONNELL, Abram
CAMPBELL, James	FULKERSON, James	MCCULLOUGH, Robert
CAMPBELL, John	(Jacobus)	MCSPADDEN, Moses
CARMACK, John	GAMBLE, George	MEEK, Samuel
CARSON, Charles	HAYTER, Israel	MICKLE, Elijah Watson
CLAPP, Earl B	HOBBS, Ezekiel	MOORE, William
CLARK, James	HOPE, Adam	PIPER, James
CLARK, Peter	HOPE, James	READ, John
CONN, William Young	JOHNSTON (JOHNSON),	SAMUEL, Vance
CRAIG, Robert	Peter	SCOTT, Joseph
CUMMINGS, Charles Rev	KELLY, John	SCOTT, Samuel
DAVIES, James II	KING, William	SHARP, John Anderson

(WASHINGTON, continued)

SHELBY, Evan	STEWART, William	VANCE, John
SNODGRASS, David	TATE, William	VANCE, Samuel
SNODGRASS, James	TEETER, John	WIDENER, Michael
SNODGRASS, John Jr	TOWNSEND, Henry	WIDENER, Samuel
SPEAR(S), James	TRIGG, Daniel	WRIGHT, John

WAYNESBORO CITY. Achieved Independent City status in 1948. See also AUGUSTA COUNTY.

ALLEN, Robert	PATRICK, John
CULLEN (CULLINS), John	PATRICK, William

WESTMORELAND COUNTY. Formed in 1653 from Northumberland County. County seat is Montross (22520).

BANKHEAD, James	LEE, Richard Henry	ROCHESTER, John Jr
CARTER, Robert III	MCCARTY, Daniel	SMITH, Thomas
HUNGERFORD, John Pratt	PAYNE, Daniel	SMITH, Thomas
HUNGERFORD, Thomas	PAYNE, John	TURBERVILLE, George Lee
KENDALL, William	PEIRCE, Joseph	TURBERVILLE, John
LEE, George Fairfax	PIERCE (PEIRCE), Joseph	WASHINGTON, John A
LEE, Philip Ludwell	PRATT, Anne Birket	

WILLIAMSBURG CITY (23185). Founded as Middle Plantation in James City County and York County in 1633. Established as Williamsburg when the capital move there in 1699. Capital of Virginia from 1699 to 1780. Granted a royal charter in 1722 as a borough, but called a city. Achieved Independent City status in 1884. See also JAMES CITY COUNTY.

AMBLER, Jacquelin	HARRIS, John	PELHAM, Peter
ANDERSON, James	HENDERSON, James	PENDLETON, Edmund
ASLIN, Samuel	HENLEY, Leonard	PRENTIS, Joseph
BLAIR, John Jr	JONES, Richard	RANDOLPH, David Meade
BURWELL, Thomas H N	JONES, William	RANDOLPH, Peyton
CABEL, Joseph	LAWSON, William	SAUNDERS, Robert Hyde
EALEY, John	LETCHER, William	SCAMMELL, Alexander
GALT, John Minson	MILNER, Thomas	TANNER, Christopher
GREENHOW, John	PEACHY, Thomas G Jr	WILMER, William Holland
GRIFFIN, Cyrus	PEACHY, Thomas G Sr	WYLIE, Samuel

WINCHESTER CITY (22601). Achieved Independent City Status in 1874. Also see FREDERICK COUNTY.

ALLEN, John	GRIM, Charles	LUCAS, Basil
ALLEN, Robert	GRIM, John	MAGILL, Charles
ALLEN, Robert	HAMILTON, James	MERRYMAN, John
BAKER, Henry	HELPHENSTINE	MITCHELL, Robert II
BAKER, William Henry	(HELVESTON,	MORGAN, Daniel
BALDWIN, Cornelius Dr	HELPHENSTIEN), Peter	OVERACRE (OVERAKER,
BALL, William	HOFF, Lewis	OBERAKER,
BEATTY, Henry	HOLLENBACH	OBERACKER), George
CHIPLEY, William	(HOLLENBECK), Daniel	ROBERDEAU
COPENHAVER	HOLMES, Hugh	(ROBERDEAN), Daniel
(COPENHAVEN), Michal	HOOVER, John	RUST, Peter
(Michael)	HOOVER, John Henry	SCHULTZ, John
EWING, Samuel	HUFF, John	SEIGLE, Frederick
FAIRFAX, Thomas	KREMER (KRAMER), Conrad	SHULTZ, John
FRY, Christopher	KURTZ, Adam	SIMRALL, James Jr
GILKESON, John	LAUCK, Simon	SINGLETON, John
GILKESON, Samuel	LAUCK (LAUK), Peter	SMITH, Edward

(WINCHESTER, continued)

SMITH, John
SNAPP, George
SOWERS, George
SPERRY, Jacob
SPERRY, John

STREIT (STRAIGHT),
  Christian
TROUTWINE (TROUTVINE),
  George Jacob
VANCE, James D

VANCE, Robert
VANCE, Samuel
WALL, John C
WHITE, Robert

WISE COUNTY. Formed in 1856 from Lee County, Russell County, and Scott County. County seat is Wise (24293).

BOWLING, James

WELLS, Zachariah

WYTHE COUNTY. Formed in 1790 from Montgomery County. Count seat is Wytheville (24382).

BEAN, Mordecai
BROWN, Christopher Sr
CASSELL, Michael
COOK, Henry
CREGER, George
CROCKETT, John
CROCKETT, Joseph
DARTER (TARTER), Nicholas
DOAK, David D
DOAK, David Sr
DOAK, Joseph
DOAK, William
DOBLER, Jacob
ETTER, Daniel
GLEAVES, Michael
GLEAVES, William Benjamin
GRAHAM, Robert
HARKRADER (HARKRIDER),
  John
HILLENBERG
  (HILLENBURG), Daniel
HOPPESS, John

HOUNSHELL, John
KEESLING, Conrad
KING, John
KING, Robert
KING, William
KISLING, George
KISSLING (KISLING,
  KESLING), Hugh Conrad
MCGAVOCK, Hugh
MCGAVOCK, James
MONTGOMERY, John
NEFF, Michael
NEWELL, James Sr
NEWLAND, John
PATTERSON, William
PEIRCE (PIERCE), David
PHIPPS, William Sr
SANDERS, Robert
SANDERS (SAUNDERS),
  Stephen
SAYERS, Robert
SAYERS, William

SAYERS (SAYRES), John
  Thompson
SEYBERT, Christian
SIMMERMAN, Christopher
SIMMERMAN, Earhart
  (Arehart)
SIMMERMAN, Stophel
  (Staphel)
SPANGLER, Peter Jr
SPRAKER (SPRECHER),
  John Christopher
STEELE, Robert
STEFFEY, John
STEPHENS, Lawrence
TOBLER (DOBLER), Jacob Sr
UMBERGER (UMBARGER),
  Henry
WALTERS, Michael
WAMPLER, Hans George
  Michael
WARD, William

YORK COUNTY. An original 1634 shire as Charles River County; renamed in 1643. County seat is Yorktown (23490).

ADAM, Paul
ADAMS, Jesse
AGNES, Jean
AIMONT, Jean
ALAIN, Georges
ALARDIOT, Antoine
ALLARD, Andre
ALLEN, Joseph
AMIRAUD, Philippe
ANDRE, Jean
ANDREW, Seth
ANDUTEAU, Jacques
ANGEVAISE, Nicolas
ANGIBAUD, Joseph
ANIBEL, William
ANIEER, William
ARISMENDY, Jean
ARTEAU, Andre

ASSELIN, Claude
ATHEAN, Claude
AUBIN, Jean
AUDIGER, Henri
AUDIOT, Jean
AUGE, Jean
AUGER, Etienne
AUGER, Pierre
AUVRAY, Louis
BAGGAGE, Jean
BAGOUS, Michel
BAORTON, Robert
BARBARAN, Francois
BARBATON, Joseph
BARCY, (-----)
BARDOU, Michel
BARNUM, Zeanas
BARON, Bernard

BARRETT, John
BARTHELEMY, Louis
BATTEZ, Pierre
BATTLES, James
BEAUJEARD, Francois
BEAUMARTIN, Jean
BEDEL, Etienne
BEDEL, Jacques
BEDEL, Jean
BEDESQUE, Vincent
BEGA, Nicolas
BEGAIN, Francois
BEHER, Pierre
BELANGER, Vincent
BELLEDENT, Pierre
BENNETT, William
BENTON, Calab
BERGER, Jacques

(YORK, continued)

BERNAN, Julien
BERTHELOT, Francois
BERTIN, Jean
BESARD, Jean
BESCOND, Jean
BESSARD, Claude
BEVEL, Abel
BEZE, Antoine
BIDEAU, Ange
BIDOT, Jean
BILLEBOUX, Oliver
BIS, Georges
BLANCHET, Louis
BLANDELET, Jean
BLEUTAU, Henri
BLEVEL, Guillaume
BLEVENET, Paul
BLONDEL, Pierre
BLONDELLE, Nicolas
BOCQ, Jean
BODEVER, Bernard
BOHEU, Chretian
BOISSARD, Michel
BOISSEAU, Pierre
BONET, Guillaume
BONGAR, Francois
BONNET, Jean
BOUCAULT, Mathieu
BOUILLOT, Benoist
BOULAIRE, Julien
BOULANGER, Nicolas
BOUQUET, Marcel
BOURDER, Jean
BOURDIN, Nicolas
BOURGAIN, Jean
BOURHIS, Francois
BOURHIS, Gregoire
BOURIGEOT, Francois
BRASSON, Jean
BRIAN, Louis
BROSTMAN, Jean
BROWN, Jonas
BRULON, Francois
BRUN, Jean
BRUNET, Jean
BUIS, Louis
BULLE, Jean
BURCK, Justus
BURNLEY, Joel Terrell
BURT, John
CABANNES, Jean
CABARE, Francois
CABON, Yves
CAILLET, Jean
CAIN, Abel
CALAGHAN, John

CALLINAN, Guillaume
CAMBERNON, Antoine
CAMPBELL, William
CANNELLE, Jean
CANTON, Antoine
CANYS, Pierre
CARBONEL, Louis
CARPIER, Gilles
CARRE, Rene
CATEL, Jean
CAVALIER, Francois
CHABRIER, Fleury
CHAMOIS, Claude
CHANPEAU, Francois
CHARET, Gilbert
CHARLES, Jean
CHASE, Jonathan
CHATILLON, Jacques
CHATTE, Pierre
CHAUNIET, Guillaume
CHAUVIN, Julien
CHAVAILLARD, Thomas
CHEMITTE, Jean
CHERET, Andre
CHEROT, Jean
CHEVALIER, Joseph
CHEVALIER, Paul
CHRISTOL, Jacques
CHUMARD, Thomas
CLEACH, Jean
CLOARET, Jean
COCQ, Antoine
COFFEY, Jean
COLAR, Andre
COLERAN, Jean
COLUE, Andre
COMBOT, Bernard
COMBRUN, Jean
CONDE, Pierre
CORLAIX, Jean
CORNISH, Daniel
COSTAIL, Sidet
COSTE, Vidal
COUILLARD, Jacques
COURBET, Antoine
COURTOIS, Etienne
COUTEL, Guillaume
CRAFFORD, Carter
CRAFFORD, Charles
CREANCE, Guillaume
CREPEL, Pierre
CRESPOT, Francois
CURDINET, Francois
CURDON, Louis
CURTIS, John Parke
DAGGETT, Ebenezer

DAGONARD, Claude
DANIEL, Marie
DANIK, Pierre
DARAY, Bertrand
DAUCAN, Guillaume
DAULIN, Jean
DAUSSENT, Pierre
DAUVERGNE, Jacques
DAVID, Francois
DAVID, Yves
DAVIS, Thomas
DE BERTHELOT, Augustin
DEBASE, Pierre
DECOUNE, Louis
DEGRES, Michel
DELAHAYE, Pierre
DELAPORT, Ubal
DELTRIEUX, Pierre
DEMARET, Nicolas
DEMBRE, Pierre
DEREUT, Pierre
DERINIER, Louis
DESCHAMPS, Joseph
DESHAY, Francois
DESMONT, Antoine
DESRIEU, Louis Sr
DETERMINE, Nicolas
DEVAISE, Joseph
DEVILLIERS, Gabriel
DEZE, Andre
DIALE, Jean
DIAMOND, Moses
DIDIERRE, Nicolas
DILTZER, Jean
DIQUE-DOUNIER, Francois
DIRONDELLES, Francois
DIVET, Henri
DOMINO, Jean
DOWNER, Ezra
DREUILHET, Dominique
DUBEAU, Pierre
DUBOURG, Nicolas
DUCROS, Lue
DUFOUR, Charles
DUFUT, Michel
DUGUE, Joseph
DULAC, Jean
DUMONT, Denis
DUPLAT, Michel
DUPREX, Joseph
DUPUIS, Jean
DURAND, Pierre
EDMON, Maurice
EGGERS, Elijah
EGRE, Paul
ELIE, Claude

(YORK, continued)

ELLIS, Jacob
ENAUD, Antoine
ENSORIEL, Espirit
EVERLET, Gaspard
FABRE, Paul
FAISSANS, Maurice
FELIX, (-----)
FERET, Dominique
FERRAND, Antoine
FERREY, Claude
FINCOMB, Amos
FISSY, Antoine
FLAGLY (FLAGLEY), John
FLORI, Pierre
FOLE, Nicolas
FONTENAY, Guillaume
FOURNIER, Charles
FOWLES, James
FRIMIER, John
FROLEAUX, Julien
FROMENT, Pierre
FUGENOT, Noel
GABIANT, Benoit
GAGUEBEY, Bernard
GALBURE, Jean
GALOTET, Jean
GALTIER, Jean
GAREL, Julien
GARIQUE, Jacques
GAUDARD, Jean
GAUSSE, Philippe
GAUTIER, Jean
GAVAUDANT, Michel
GELLY, Jacques
GENIES, Joseph
GENTIL, Joseph
GEOFFROY, Jean
GERAUD, Guillaume
GERRY, Philippe
GERTHIER, Francois
GILLES, Pierre
GILLET, Guillaume
GINBERT, Julien
GIRARD, Joseph
GIRAUD, Joseph
GLANET, Louis
GODARD, Jean
GODEAU, Nicolas
GOODRICH, David
GORRELIER, Pierre
GOSSAN, Jean
GOULD, William
GOUYA, Antoine
GOUZER, Albin
GRANBON, Claude
GRANDY, James

GRENON, Andre
GREROUA, Jean
GRIGNON, Thomas
GROSNIER, Jacques
GROSSETETE, Antoine
GROULT, Jean
GUBIAUD, Benoist
GUEGUEN, Joachim
GUELIN, Nicolas
GUENARD, Pierre
GUIBOISEAU, Francois
GUILLAUME, Joseph
GUILLERAUX, Joseph
GUILLON, Francois
GUILLOT, Mathieu
GUINELS, Francois
GULLAMEBOURG, Antoine
GUY, Rene
HAGUENEAU, Jerome
HAMMOND, Stephen
HAMON, Guenole
HAMON, Yves
HARDING, Aesop
HAUTVILLE, Joseph
HAWKINS, Issac
HAYWARD, James
HELEH, Jean
HENNONE, Jean
HENRY, Didier
HERMAIN, Jean
HERRINGTON, William
HERVE, Guillaume
HERVE, Jean
HERVE, Michel
HIELDEN, (------)
HIGGINS, Thomas
HIGIE, Richard
HILL, Amos
HILTZENBERGER, Francois
HIX, James
HOAGON, Cyprien
HOFFMAN, Andre
HONORE, Jean
HOUBA, Remy
HOUCHOIS, Charles
HOUPILLARD, Jacques
HUBERT, Jean
HUGUETT, Louis
HULL, Johiel
HURSIN, Francois
JACOBS, John
JACOBY, Nicolas
JAGOUS, Francois
JAMAIS, Sebastian
JAUBERT, Jean
JAUBERT, Joseph

JAUNEAU, Julien
JEAN, Jean
JEAN, Pierre
JERIFAFIN, Jean
JOBART, Joseph
JOLIVET, Francois
JOLY (JOLLEY), (-----)
JONES, Jacob
JOSEPH, Jean
JOSSARD, Jean
JOSSE, Jean
JOSSE, Oliver
JOUE, Jean
JOULIN, Jean
JULIEN, Claude
JUND, Francois
JUPIN, Laurent
JUVET, Barthelemy
KELL, Michel
KIMBALL, Benjamin
KYNION, William
LABBE, Jean
LACOSTE, Jean
LACROIX, Guillaume
LACROIX, Jean
LAFOSSE, Antoine
LAFOSSE, Charles
LAFRANCE, Nicolas
LAGADENE, Jean
LAGNEL, Louis
LAINE, Philippe
LALOGE, Pierre de
LAMBERT, Blaise
LAMESSE, Etienne
LAMY, Pierre
LANGLOIS, Jacques
LANNOY, Jean de
LAROCHE, Etienne
LAROSE, Jean
LATAUPE, Gilbert
LAURENCEAU, Jean
LAURENS, Jean
LAURENT, Daniel
LAURENT, Jacques
LEBAIL, Guillaume
LEBARS, Louis
LEBERRE, Yves
LEBIHAN, Isaac
LEBOURG, Jacques
LEBREHEL, Pierre
LEBRUN, Edme
LECAMUS, Francois
LECLAIR, Francois
LECOEUR, Jean
LECOMTE, Pierre
LECOURTOIS, Philippe

(YORK, continued)

LECUNFF, Joseph	MARCY (NARCY), Jean	MOSHER, William
LEDUC, Jean	MARET, Nicolas	MOUGAL, Nicolas
LEDUC, Jean	MARGOT, Pierre	MOULINS, Antoine
LEE, David	MARIE, Jacques	MOUTEL, Liberal
LEE, John	MARIN, Jean de	MULLER, Nicolas
LEFERME, Pierre	MARIVAL, Francois	NAFUERN, Francois
LEFEVRE, Jean	MARQUET, Francois	NALFIN, Remy
LEFEVRE, Joseph	MARSH, Ephraim	NEBLE, Georges
LEFLOCH, Francois	MARTIN, Alexis	NELSON, Hugh
LEGOFF, Jean	MARTIN, Antoine	NELSON, Thomas Jr
LEGROSS, Pierre	MARTIN, Claude	NELSON, Willaim
LEGUEN, Louis	MARTIN, Jean	NELSON, William
LEGUERN, Guillaume	MARTIN, Louis	NEUVEU, Edme
LEGUILLOUX, Rene	MARTIN, Nicolas	NEUVILLE, Jean
LEHUP, Pierre	MARTIN, Thomas	NEW, Pierre
LEJORE, Jean	MARTIN, Vincent	NEWTON, Solomon
LELAYER, Yves	MASON, Thomas	NICHOLAS, Jean
LEMAY, Jacques	MASSAL, Jean	NICOLAS, Pierre
LEMAY, Julien	MAUBRUCHON, Yves	NICOLE, Jean
LEMINGNON, Jean	MAUCHALIN, Yves	NIEL, Antoine
LEMOING, Jean	(or Philibert)	NOEL, Jean
LENOIR, Rene	MAUGER, Pierre	NOLLY, Laurent
LEPAGE, Pierre	MAURE, Leon	NORTON, Henry
LEPARC, Jean	MAUSSION, Charles	OLLIVIER, Paul
LEPELLE, Julien	MAYER, Jean	ORGAN, unk
LERICHE, Jacques	MCCARTER, James	ORIEUX, Francois
LEROUX, Etienne	MCCLOUGHRY, John	ORKENSUDE, Erasmus
LEROUX, Jean	MCCOUGHRY, John	ORVAULT, Dupe d'
LERSNE, Augustin	MCKINNEY, James	OSPELL, Mathieu
LESAGNE, Pierre	MEINER, Francois	OUDOT, Claude
LESOURD, Sebastien	MENAGER, Louis	OUIN, Jean
LETOUX, Clement	MENARDIER, Jean	OUVENANT, Rene
LEVENT, Jean	MERCIER, Andoche	OZANNE, Pierre
LEWIS, Benjamin	MERIAN, Vincent	OZOU, Jean
LIEBERT, Jean	MERIEL, Jean	PABST, Christian
LIGNOT, Pierre	MERKOT, Georges	PACET, Etienne
LINSEY, Stephen	MERY, Antoine	PAILLARD, Jean
LIVERNOIS, Jacques	MICHELET, Jean	PALIS, Paul
LORIVAT, Jean	MILLERT, Michel	PALUT, Louis
LORMIER, Augustin	MILLIOT, Gaspard	PALY, B
LORRAIN, Georges	MINIO, Antoine	PANIOLET, Jean
LOUIS, Jean	MION, Pierre	PAON, Jean
LYONNOIS, Jean	MIOT, Pierre	PAPELARD, Jacques
LYONNOIS, Pierre	MOINET, Laurent	PAPON, Louis
MACHAIN, Claude	MOLIN, Jean	PARIEL, Leonard
MADEC, Jean	MOLLIERE, Antoine	PARIS, Claude
MAGNAN, Francois	MOLTON, Caesar	PARIS, Gabriel
MAGNAN, Jean	MONART, Nicolas	PARIS, Jacques de
MAILLET, Marcel	MONDRE, Pierre	PARKER, Timothy
MAIRE, Jacques	MONET, Jean	PARMENTER, James
MAISON, Jean	MONGIN, Jean	PARRE, Pierre
MALFROIS, Pierre	MONNIER, Nicolas	PATALIER, Joseph
MANADET, Bernard	MONTCHALEN, Antoine	PAULARD, Jean
MANNING, Samuel	MORET, Barthelemy	PELITIER, Jacques
MANSFIELD, Timothy	MORIN, Jean	PELLETAN, Jean
MARCHAND, Pierre	MORRISOT, Jacques	PELLETIER, Joseph

(YORK, continued)

PERCHE, Louis
PERNOT, Nicolas
PEROT, Milan
PEROTIN, Julien
PEROY, Louis
PERPETTE, Antoine
PERRIER, Joseph
PEYLLARD, Jacques
PHILIPEAU, Gabriel
PHILIPPE, Pierre
PICHON, Noel
PICHON, Pierre
PIERROT, Nicholas
PIERSON, Charles
PIGIBIT, Jean
PILAU, Jean
PINCERON, Francois
PINET, Jean
PITOZZEAU, N
PLACET, Claude
PLAGNOLET, Jean
PLANTO, Jean
PLISSON, Jean
POHEAGUE, Josias
POIGNARD, Jean or Hector
POLLET, Denis
POULAIN, Charles
POULAIN, Jean
POUPON, Francois
POUVEREAU, Jean
POWELL, John
PRADHOUT, Jean
PREVOST, Charles
PRIOUX, Gilles
PROU, Joseph
PROUX, Pierre
PROVOL, Charles
PRUNTZIGER, Jean
PUISSANT, Etiene
QUENARD, Pierre
QUERJEAN, Herve
RANAUD, Francois
RANDLE, Henry
RAUTZ, Francois
RAVAN, Jean
RAYBLET, Philippe
REBOUL, Pierre
REIBAUD, Antoine
REMAIN, Jacques
REMONT, Charles
RENARD, Jean
RENOUARD, Jean
REVEL, Gaspard
RIAU, Joseph
RICHARD, Pierre
RICHARDS, John

RIEBARD, Francois
RIOTTE, Pierre
RIPTON, John
ROBICHON, Ferdinand
ROCHE, Jean
ROCHE, Pierre de
ROCHEFORT, Jean
ROEBUCK, William
ROGERS, Samual
ROITOUX, Pierre
ROSBUCK, William
ROSSIGNOL, Francois
ROUAY, Charles
ROUFFE, Gottfried
ROUSSE, Antoine
ROUSSEAU, Pierre
ROUSSEL, Jean
ROUSSEL, Vincent
ROUX, Jean
ROUX, Jean
ROYER, Jean
RULLINS, William
SABE, Jean
SAFFROY, Jean
SALAUN, Francois
SALE, Bertrand
SALLEMON, Antoine
SALLES, Jean
SALMON, Guillaume
SALMON, Philibert
SAMPSON, Seth
SANSFACON, Jean
SANTO, Pierre
SARGEANT, Nathaniel
SATUR, de
SAVEQUET, Dominique
SAVOIX, Martiel
SCARA, Michel
SCHOLDER, Francois
SCHOLT, Sebastian
SCOTT, John
SEAUCE, Jacques
SEBIRE, Martin
SELIGNET, Jean
SELIQUET, Jean
SEPEDRE, Antoine
SERREE, Jacques
SERVE, Antoine
SIREUIL, Jean de
SMITH, B Egbert
SNOW, Edward
SOLNE, Andre
SORBETZ, Barthelemy
SORIN, Pierre
SOULIGNAC, Mathieu
SOURSON, Jean

STAUTZER, Jacob
STEIN, Jean
STEPHAN, Guillaume
STOHER, Balthazar
STOUDERT, Claude
STUBERT, Adam
TAFT, Nathan
TEPHANY, Remy
TERVILLE, Andre
TESTELIN, Louis
TEYO, Rene
THEVENIN, Louis
THOMSON, Daniel
TILQUAZ, Nicolas
TINCELIN, Jean
TINIER, Joseph
TISSIER, Jacques
TISSIER, Jacques
TOLON, Francois
TOUGARE, Francis
TOURNIS, Jacques
TOUSSET, Jean
TOUTIN, Eustache
TOWN, Asce
TREASURE, Richard
TUMELIN, Nicolas
TURNER, John
TURNER, Mattocks
URVOY, Jean
VACHERE, Andre
VAISSE, Jean
VALEOT, Jean
VALLANCE, William
VALLE, Jean
VALLEE, Pierre
VALLEE, Vincent
VAN VOST, Christian
VAQUIER, Francois
VARRENNES, Jean
VBEL, Geroges
VEINTEFFER, JH
VERDAVOIR, Oger
VERDIER, Jacques
VERRIER, Joseph
VERSIN, Pierre
VEXLIN, Emmanuel
VEXTAIN, Emmanuel
VIAL, Pierre
VIGOUREUX, Francois
VILATON, Jean
VILLARET, Joseph
VILLEDIEU, Jean
VILLEON, de la
VINCE, Joseph
VINCENT, Nicolas
VITRE, Jean

(YORK, continued)

VITRIER, Andre
VIVANSON, Bernard
VIZET, Joseph
VORRIOT, Pierre
WADE, Stephen
WALLIS, Colley
WASSON, James
WEBSTER, George

WENDREWECK, Armand
WETHERBEE, James
WHITAKER, John
WHITE, Isaac
WHITE, William
WHITING, James
WHITNEY, Silas
WILCOX, John

WILLIAMS, James
WITHAM, William
WLOVASSE, Jean
WYNNE, Edmund
WYNNE, Thomas
YVES, Andre
ZELL, John

APPENDIX B – CEMETERY LIST BY COUNTY / INDEPENDENT CITY

Cemetery Name	GPS Coordinates	Location/Directions

ACCOMACK COUNTY

Cemetery Name	GPS Coordinates	Location/Directions
Belle Vue	unk	Off Rt 646, 7 mi E of Locustville
Benson Family	unk	Nr Jct Cattail Rd Rt 690 & Whites Crossing Rd Rt 690
Bowman's Folly	unk	End of Rt 652, private lane, 2.4 mi NE of Accomac, Joynes Neck
Bradford-Burton	unk	Rt 182 and Rt 605, N fr Quinby
Burton Private	unk	Wachapreague
Chestnut Vale	unk	.6 mi N of Rt 605, W of Rt 789, nr Locustville
Coal Kiln	unk	1 mi S jct Rts 607 & 600, R off Rt 600
Colonna Family, aka Wakefield Farm	unk	1 mi east of Pennyville, Hacks Neck
Deep Creek Plantation	unk	Onancock
Foreman Plot	unk	NW of jct Rts 709 & 708, nr Miona
Joynes-Bayne	unk	W end of Meadville Dr, Onancock
Kennahorn Family	unk	N side of Rt 638, .4 mi E of 637, W fr Cashville
Laws Family	unk	Rt 13 nr Nelsonia
Melrose & Ker Family	unk	Abt 2 mi SW Pungoteaque
Morrison Hill	unk	.8 mi S of Rt 622, W of Rt 600, Frogstool
Mt Custis	unk	Off Rt 622 2.5 mi of Rt 13, Bayley's Neck
Mt Holly	37.70485, -75.74185	Hill St, Onancock
Nelson Family	unk	New Church
Old West Place, aka Cedar View	unk	N of Craddockville off Rt 616
Onancock	unk	Rts 718 & 638, Onancock
Parksley	unk	.5 mi N of Rt 176, W of Rt 678, NE fr Parksley
Poplar Cove Wharf	unk	Nr end of Rt 653, Onancock
Poplar Grove	36.58569, -76.32133	Off Rt 180, Pungoteague, Hack's Neck
Quimby	unk	Painter
Riley Family	unk	Rt 684, .5 mi W of Rt 658
Rodgers Plot	unk	Rt 180 off Rt 178, .9 mi W of Pungoteague, Hacks Neck
Savage Family	unk	Rt 180, Pungoteaque
Scott Hall	unk	Daugherty Rd, Onancock
Scott Hall, aka Edward Snead	37.71115; -75.75250	Nr River btw Mt Prospect Ave and South St, Onancock
Tavern Lot	unk	Center of Accomac
Teackle House	unk	Rt 1709 & Brooklyn St, Wachapreague
Thomas Parker Family	unk	Rt 180 nr Pungoteague
Warwick House	unk	Rt 605 1 mi S of Quinby, Upshur Bay
Waterfield Farm	unk	1.4 mi N of Rt 614, W of Rt 617, SE fr Pennyville
Welburn or Welbourne Family	unk	Rts 709 & Rt 679, Horntown
West Family	unk	Deep Creek
Wharton Family	unk	Assawoman Creek
Wise Family	unk	Chesconessex

ALBERMARLE COUNTY (See also Charlottesville City)

Belvoir	unk	5172 Stony Point Pass, Cismont
Berry Hill	unk	1.5 mi N of Sweet Briar College
Blue Ridge Farm	unk	Rt 261, 2.1 mi off Rt 250 W, Greenwood
Bowen Farm	unk	Red Hill
Brightberry Brown Family	38.20972, -78.67243	5525 Brown's Gap Turnpike, Brown's Cove
Brockman-Mitchell	unk	Petty's Creek Annex, Stony Point
Brown Family #2	unk	Rt 810, Brown's Cove
Castle Hill	38.05683, -78.31828	1625 Country Club Dr, can be seen 150 yds E of Wood Ln, Farmington
Garland Family	unk	Check property records
Hamner Family	unk	Carter's Bridge, Keene
Harris Family	37.81867, -78.66393	Irish Rd, Esmont
Locust Hill	unk	Off Rt 676 N of Rt 250, Ivy
Martin Marietta's Land	unk	Nr Red Hill
Maupin Family Farm	unk	Morman's River
Moore Family	37.97113, -78.63598	2393 Taylor's Gap Rd, North Garden
Mt Air	unk	Hardware River, Keene, NW of Scottsville
Mt Zion Methodist	37.80220, -78.59140	Rt 170 off Portress Rd Rt 627, Esmont
Old Hardin (Shirley) Property	unk	Nr Greenwood
Rockgate	38.06170, -78.70170	981 Crozet Ave, Crozet
Rodes Family, Midway Plantation	unk	E of Whitehall
Shepherd Family	unk	Batesville
Snow Johnson Family	unk	S base Buck Mtn, abt .5 mi behind house
Spring Valley, Massie Family	37.94277, -78.76863	3808 Spring Valley Rd, Batesville
St Paul's Church	38.05830, -78.59580	851 Owensville Rd, Ivy
Thomas Family	unk	Nr Red Hill
Via Family	unk	Brown's Cove
Wakefield Cemetery	unk	Wakefield Farm Rd, Earlysville
Wood Family	38.20279, -78.53238	Off Markwood Rd Rt 664, Earlysville
Woodson	unk	Not identified

ALEXANDRIA CITY (See also Arlington County)

Christ Church Episcopal	38.80216, -77.05689	Wilkes St & Hamilton Ln
Fendall Family	unk	614 N Washington St
First Presbyterian	38.79992, -77.05799	601 Hamilton Ln
Mt Vernon Unitarian	unk	1909 Winhill Ln
Old Christ Church Episcopal	36.83407, -81.59338	Old Ebenezer Rd Rt 659
Old Christ Church Episcopal	38.80625, -77.04718	118 N Washington St
Old Presbyterian Meeting House	38.48528, -77.23532	323 S Fairfax St
Peake Family	38.73686, -77.08430	M L King Jr Park, 8115 Fordson Rd, past pool & tennis cts to black metal fence
Penny Hill	38.79861, -77.05559	S Payne & Franklin Sts
Presbyterian Church	38.80015, -77.05791	Wilkes St & Hamilton Ln
Quaker Burial Ground	38.80749, -77.04676	717 Queen St, Kate Walker Barrett Library
St Marys Catholic Church	38.79390, -77.04750	310 S Royal St
St Paul's Episcopal	38.79959, -77.05860	228 S Pitt St
Summers Family	38.49150, -77.08280	Demming Ave & Lincolnia Rd
Trinity United Methodist	39.13600, -77.00610	2911 Cameron Mills Rd

ALLEGHANY COUNTY (See also Covington City)

Humphries Lone Grave	unk	11 mi SW of Covington
Mountain View	37.81360, -79.81390	Clifton Forge
Smith Cemetery	37.86140, -79.98970	Rt 687, Mt Pleasant
Smith Family	unk	7 mi N of Covington
Stull Family	unk	10 mi S of Lowmoor

AMELIA COUNTY

Archer, Red Lodge	unk	Red Lodge Rd
Avary Family	unk	Avary Church Rd
Booker	unk	Rt 612
Booker Family	unk	Grub Hill Church Rd, check property records for location of plantation
Chappell	unk	Fowlkes Bridge Rd, Paineville
Green Family	unk	Rt 622
Grub Hill	37.39940, -77.97030	Grub Hill Church Rd Rt 609
H H Jones Property	unk	Chula
Jackson Family	unk	6101 Buckskin Rd, Rt 640, Jetersville
Jeter-Cadwell	unk	Giles Rd Rt 636
Locust Grove	unk	Rt 66 abt 5 mi S of Victoria
Meade Family	unk	Nr Chula
Royall	unk	Off Promise Land Rd Rt 661, Amelia CH
Townes	unk	Rt 38 at Level Mount Estates, Amelia CH
Vaughan Family	unk	Not identified
Whitworth	unk	Paineville
Wigwam Estate	unk	Amelia CH
Wood	unk	Rt 620 nr Rt 616, Rodophil

AMHERST COUNTY

Amherst	37.59640, -79.03670	Bus Rt 29, Amherst
Burton Family	unk	1 mi SW jct Genitoe and Brick Church Ln, property of Roger Epperson in a .5 acre lot
David Crawford Plantation	unk	Check property records for plantation location
Davies	unk	Nr Elon
Franklin	unk	Amherst
Higginbotham Family	37.69140, -79.14280	Rt 617 N of jct with 761, Amherst
Indian Graveyard	unk	Bear Mtn, Rt 643
Laine Family	unk	Amherst
Mansion House	unk	Buffalo Island
Miller Family	unk	Rt 690
Monument Hill	37.55115, -79.09496	Stable Ln nr jct Rt 663, Sweet Briar College
Old Keys Church	unk	Jct Rts 647 & 722
Old Pendleton	unk	Monroe
Penn Family	unk	Rt 151, Clifford
Powell Family	unk	Amherst
Rodes family	unk	Check property records
Rucker Family	37.54062, -77.18508	Shepherd Farm Ln off Rt 653 Ambrose Rucker Rd
Shelton-Ellis-Watts	unk	Winesap Rd
Tucker	37.71440, -79.08610	Rt 621, Indian Creek
Wilson Family, R.L. Bowling Property	unk	Rt 659
Winton Plantation	unk	adj Winton Country Club, Clifford

APPOMATTOX COUNTY

First Concord Presbyterian	unk	Hwy 460 E fr Lynchburg City.
Flood Family	unk	Vera
Kelso Family	unk	1 mi N of Pamplin on Rt 600
Liberty Baptist	37.35181, -78.82862	1709 Church St, Appomatox
McReynolds Family	37.17360, - 78.5334	Rt 623
Old Trent Mill Farm	unk	Rt 631

(APPOMATTOX COUNTY, CONTINUED)

Old Walker Home	unk	5 mi N of Pamplin on Rt 600, then .4 mi W on Rt 627, then .4 mi NW on Rt 628
Pankey Family	unk	Tower Hill, Appomattox
Robertson Family	unk	Off Rt 641 nr Appomattox CH
Second Concord Presbyterian	37.34209, -78.96585	Phoebe Pond Rd Rt 609 E of Concord
St Clare Family	unk	Appomattox

ARLINGTON COUNTY (See also Alexandria City)

Arlington National	38.88377, -77.06535	Jefferson Davis Hwy Rt 110
Ball-Carlin Family	unk	300 S Kensington St
Old Ball Burying Ground	unk	3427 Washington Blvd, behind American Legion Bldg
Old Burying Ground	unk	See Senate Doc DAR annual report 1955 vol 4 serial 11912
Southern-Shreve	unk	5300 N 10th St

AUGUSTA COUNTY (See also Staunton City and Waynesboro City)

Airy Knoll	unk	E of Rt 252 abt .4 mi N of 620, just to S of Newport
Augusta Stone Presbyterian	38.23925, -78.97356	28 Old Stone Church Ln, Ft Defiance
Bell	38.26140, -78.95560	Rt 11, Mt Sidney
Bethel Presbyterian	38.04256, -79.17283	563 Bethel Green Rd, Middlebrook
Bratton Family	unk	Nr Goshen
Buchanan Family	unk	Nr Rockbridge Co line, possibly on Ben Jacobs' land, btw Rts 602 & 681
Emmanuel	unk	Mt Solon
Fishburne	unk	End of Rt 847, behind Verona Methodist Church, Verona
Glebe Burying Ground	38.10940, -79.22190	Glebe School Rd Rt 876, Swoopes
Hanger Family	unk	Rt 670, near Greenville
Hanna Family	unk	Nr Grottoes
Hogshead Family	unk	Off Rt 736 btw Rts 42 & 250, N of Jennings Gap
John Sterrett Family	unk	1 mi W of Craigsville
Jones-Van Lear	unk	Rt 613, .3 mi S jct with Rt 742, farm of Alfred Ryder
Keller Family	unk	Dr Knopp's Farm, Churchville
Landes Family	38.30110, -78.97170	W fr Burketown 2 mi, near Weyers Cave
Leland Brown Farm	unk	Nr Weyers Cave
Lewis Family	unk	Nr Staunton
Miller Family	unk	4998 Scenic Hwy, Bridgewater
Mossy Creek Presbyterian	38.35331 -79.04914	372 Kyles Mill Rd, Mt Solon
North Mountain	unk	7 mi S of Staunton on N side Rt 252
Old Lebanon	38.08090 -79.37545	Off Rt 42, Craigsville
Old Link	unk	.5 mi W of Ft Defiance
Old Providence	37.96151, -79.710	1005 Spottswood Rd, Spottswood
Old Stone Presbyterian	38.23926, -78.97356	28 Old Stone Church Ln, Ft Defiance
Rocky Spring Presbyterian	38.11470, -79.24250	1 mi S of Deerfield
Samuel Bell Family	38.22770, -78.89085	Nr NW jct Craigshop Rd & Rt 608 toward Middle River
Schutterle Community	38.22030, -79.10470	Off Rt 728 SE of Rt 732, Franks Mill
Shenandoah Methodist	38.98160, -78.95773	1919 Howardsville Turnpike, Sherando
St James Methodist	unk	3777 Churchville Ave, Churchville
St John's Reformed UCC	38.05081, -79.17761	1515 Arbor Hill Rd, Middlebrook
St Peter's Lutheran	38.22569, -79.16125	3795 Churchville Ave, Churchville
Tinkling Spring Presbyterian	38.08472, -78.98278	30 Tinkling Spring Dr, Fishersville

(AUGUSTA COUNTY, CONTINUED)

Trinity Lutheran	38.17201, -78.86820	2564 Rockfish Rd, Crimora
Union Presbyterian	39.10916, -78.09497	Churchville
West Augusta Cemetery	38.26670, -79.33330	Rt 716 W Augusta Rd, 8 mi N of Staunton
Willson Family	38.07283, -79.12096	Rt 697 White Oak Gap Rd, W of Rt 11, Mint Spring

BATH COUNTY

Augusta	unk	See DAR Senate Doc year 1959
Bethel Church aka Old Lyle	unk	Millboro Springs
Bratton	37.99750, -79.56170	Rts 39 & 42 Mountain Valley Rd 4 mi E of Millboro Springs
Fort Dinwiddie	38.09228, -79.83140	NE of jct of Dinwiddie Trail & River Rd, Warm Springs
George Revercomb Property	unk	McClintic by Jackson River
Cleek	38.19310, -79.73220	Rt 220 Sam Snead Hwy, Warm Springs
Keyser Family	37.96885, -79.83694	Nr Jct Rts 612 & 618, Warm Springs
Laverty Farm	unk	Cow pasture
Mallow Tract	unk	Nr Hot Springs
McClintic Family	unk	12 mi W of Warm Springs
McClung Family	unk	Nr Millboro
Mustoe Family	unk	5 mi S of Healing Springs
Sitlington Family	unk	8.5 mi S of Millboro Springs
Warm Springs	38.05030, -79.78110	Rt 220 Sam Snead Hwy, Warm Springs
Windy Cove Presbyterian	unk	102 Windy Cove Rd, Millboro

BEDFORD COUNTY AND BEDFORD CITY

Anderson Family	37.38970, -79.39045	2370 Cifax Rd, Goode
Andrews Family	unk	Evington
Blankenship Family	unk	Nr Montvale
Brown Family	unk	Off New London Rd Rt 709, Forest
Callaway-Steptoe	37.30560, -79.29470	Rt 460, New London
Campbell Family	unk	Nr Irving
Chapman Family	unk	Goodview
Cox Family	unk	Forest across fr Lake Vista
Crews Family	unk	Nr Big Island
Dickerson Family	unk	Nr Moneta
Ewing-Patterson	unk	Penick's Mill
Frantz Family	unk	Check property records
Fuqua Family	37.33344, -79.48352	Orange Street
Gravelly Hill	unk	Town of Gravelly Hill
Groom Family	unk	Nr Shady Grove Church
Hardy Family	37.23460, -79.30230	State Rts 122 & 640, Forbes Mill
Harkin (Heathering) Hill	unk	Peaks of Otter
Hurt Family	unk	Nr Mobley's Creek
Jeter Family	unk	Btw Centerville & Otterville
Lee Family	unk	New London
Leftwich Family	unk	Mt Airy, nr Leesville
Locust Level	37.23180, -79.43420	Rt 460, nr Montvale
Logwood Family	unk	Locust Hill
Longwood	37.34170, -79.51190	Nr jct Oakwood & Longwood Ave Rt 122
McConnehey-Updike	37.21162, -79.54527	2730 Chestnut Fork Rd, Chestnut Fork
McManaway Family	unk	Chamblissburg
Mead	unk	Near Lowry on Norfolk/Western RR Lines
Millner Estate	unk	Check property records
Otey Street	37.33170, -79.52170	W Franklin St jct with Otey

(BEDFORD COUNTY AND BEDFORD CITY, CONTINUED)

Quaker Baptist	37.20619, -79.51623	4665 Chestnut Fork Rd, Chestnut Fork
Quarles Family	unk	SE fr Bedford
Read	37.18220, -79.18510	New London, nr jct Rts 460 & 811
Reid Estate, "Poplar Grove"	unk	New London
Royal Forest	unk	New London
Rural	unk	Check property records
Salmon Family	unk	Check property records
Saunders Family	37.31808, -79.43264	Jct Rt 460 & Krantz's Corner Rd
Scott Family	unk	Episcopal School Rd 200 yds fr school
Slack Family, aka Chattin Family	unk	On hillside of Chattin farm, nr Chamblissburg
St Stephen's Episcopal	37.37811, -79.30831	1694 Perrowville Rd, Forest
St Steven's Episcopal	unk	Jct Rts 663 and 221
Staunton Baptist	37.06970 -79.58140	15267 Smith Mountain Lake Pkwy, Huddleston
Stiff Family	unk	Union Church Rd 1 mi past Union Methodist, Thaxton
Stratton Family	unk	Jct Rts 122 & 736
Terry Family	unk	Oakwood
Thomas-Lowry Farm	unk	E fr Bedford
Trigg Family, aka Old Liberty Plantation	unk	Nr Liberty
Valentine Cox	unk	Forest
Walker Family	37.28481, -79.51186	Rt 723, Boxwood Hill, Five Forks
Walker Farm	37.25327, -79.49419	1972 Montevido Rd, Rt 667
White Family	37.28400, -79.24130	Nr Charlemont, jct 638 & 637
White Family	unk	Stewartsville
Wigginton Family	unk	Rt 7, Huddleston
Wilks Family	unk	Nr Leftwich Church
Woodford-Wade	unk	11477 Falling Creek Rd

BLAND COUNTY

Bird	unk	Rt 42 2.5 mi E of Bland village
Holly Brook	unk	Rt 606 off Hwy 42 adj Holly Brook Community Center
Sharon Lutheran	37.05800, -81.20590	Rt 42 W of Ceres

BOTETOURT COUNTY

Abendschon Family	unk	Nr Mill Creek Baptist
Allen Family	unk	5.5 mi S of Buchanan
Allen-Carper	unk	Rt 43 nr Eagle Rock
Allen-Lauderdale	unk	Fincastle
Baker-Ferry Family	unk	East of Rt 779, Daleville
Breckenridge Family	unk	Grove Hill Farm, Rt 606 1 mi NW of Fincastle
Brickey Family	unk	Check property records
Brickey-Lee	unk	Rt 779, McAfees Knob
Buchanan	unk	Buchanan
Cahoon Family	unk	Glade Creek nr Bedford Co line
Caldwell family	unk	End of Rt 611 across Craig Creek fr Camp Easter Seals
Carlock Family	unk	Lick Run
Cross Family Farm	unk	Nr Roanoke
Daleville	37.39869, -79.91069	Roanoke Rd Rt 220 nr Kroger store, Daleville
Fincastle Presbyterian	37.50017, -79.87558	108 E Back St, Fincastle

(BOTETOURT COUNTY, CONTINUED)

Glebe	37.45155, -79.96968	Vic jct Rts 779 and 630
Greenfield	37.43750, -79.91420	Off International Pkwy, W of Rt 220, Amsterdam
Kessler Family	unk	Nr Brick Union Ch
Laymantown	37.36278, -79.84909	Laymontown Rd, Laymantown
Lemon Family	37.77126, -79.78160	Nr jct Rts 220 & 698 Lick Run Rd, Lick Run
Locust Bottom	unk	Jct Rts 622 & 696
Locust Bottom Church	37.74170, -79.8150	Eagle Rock
McFerran Family	unk	Rt 220, 6 mi N of Fincastle
Mt Union	37.45133, -79.97055	4614 Catawba Rd, Mt Union
Old Dutch	unk	W side of Rt 11 at Mill Creek, 9 mi S of Buchanan
Old Glade Creek	37.35989, -79.81828	Grace Hollow Rd, Blue Ridge
Rader Family	unk	Past Motts Hill Ln on right, take left on Radar Barn Rd, N of Troutville on Rt 11
Reid Family	unk	9 mi NE of Eagle Rock
Sheets Family	unk	W of Rt 220, Bessemer area
Shirkey-Far	unk	Across James River fr Gala
Simmons-Brugh	unk	Nr Mill Creek Baptist Church
Temontown	unk	Laymantown

BRISTOL CITY (See also Washington County)

East Hill	36.59438, -82.17233	E State St on line btw VA and TN
Snodgrass	unk	Bristol (or Blountsville, TN)
Walnut Grove	unk	3012 Lee Hwy Rt 11
Weaver's	unk	Not identified

BRUNSWICK COUNTY

Abernathy Family	36.50420, -77.88047	400 yds W of Preswood Rd, Rt 646, 1.2 mi N of Linerty Rd, Rt 634
Bishop Family	36.62640, -77.95580	Rt 644, Brunswick
Claiborne Family	unk	Nr jct Rts 713 & 715, Lawrenceville
Flournoy	unk	Rt 58
Lanier Family	unk	Nr Smoky Ordinary & Poarch Store
Lewis Family	38.80276, -77.96242	Woodstock Plantation, Meredithville
Orgain Family	36.86010, -77.94002	Jct Rts 644 & Rt 648, Alberta

BUCKINGHAM COUNTY

Agee Family	unk	Nr Dillwyn
Anthony Glover Cem	unk	Dirt lane 1 mi S of Alcoma
Boatwright Family	unk	Nr Mt Zion Church, 6277 Cartersville Rd, New Canton
Branch	37.58250, -78.49000	Rt 631, Manteo
Chambers Family	unk	Rt 659, 2.75 mi W of Ransons
Charlie Londeree	unk	Not identified by DAR and SAR sources
Coleman Family	unk	Nr Salem Methodist Church
Coleman Family	unk	Bent Creek
Eldridge Family	unk	Fork of North & Slate Rivers
Flood Family, "Toga"	unk	Rt 24
Grace Church	unk	Manteo
Greenfield	unk	On Rocky Creek nr Penlan
Greenhill	unk	James River State Park
Hooper Family	unk	Hooper's Mount, Arcanum
Jones	unk	Rt 24, S of Togson, abt 2.5 mi then 1.5 mi on private road

(BUCKINGHAM COUNTY, CONTINUED)

Loch Lomond	unk	Check property records
Merionette	unk	Nr Willis Mountain
Morris Family	unk	Rt 609 at Vassars
Moseley Family	unk	Willowlake, Rt 56
Moseley Family	unk	"Wheatlands", Rt 647 10 mi E of CH
Patteson Family	unk	Mt Pleasant
Perkins-Hall	unk	Hwy 56
Physics Springs	unk	Buckingham
Rolfton	unk	Hwy 749
Samuel Glover	unk	Rt 742
Stratton Family	unk	New Canton
Watson-Perrow	unk	Gunter Mountain
Wilkinson Family	unk	Rt 610, Gold Hill

CAMPBELL COUNTY (See also Lynchburg City)

Adams-Ward	37.13210, -79.24073	Mansion Bridge Rd Rt 640, Altavista
Alexander-Adams	unk	Rt 652, Gladys
Avoca	unk	Altavista
Blankenship-Oldham	unk	Winfall
Blenheim	37.13150, -78.5700	Rt 648, Gladys
Brown Family	unk	Off Rt 705
Brown Family-Thompson Valley	unk	New London
Carwile	37.08470, -78.58020	Rt 708 Seamster Rd, go to end, abt 1 mi walk, Noruna
Clark Family	37.29563, -79.21086	Cnr Lawyer's Rd and Missionary Manor
Cobbs Family	unk	Plain Dealing, Naruna
Cobbs Hall	unk	Nr Rt 643, Brookneal
Concord Presbyterian #2	unk	.5 mi S of Hunter's Tavern
Concord Presbyterian #3	unk	4909 Reedy Spring Rd, Sprout Springs
Creasy Family	unk	Nr jct Rts 615 and 648
Deering Family	unk	At Otterburne, Old Deering Place on Otter River, Altavista nr Evington
Diuguid	unk	On Barry Jones Farm near Rt 460, on Co Rd 757 btwn Concord & Lynchburg City
Dixon Family	37.18420, -79.59310	Off Rt 658, Concord quadrant, nr Rustburg
Driskill	unk	SE of Rt 40, Dog Creek
Falling River Baptist	37.07531, -78.91543	2874 Wickliffe Ave, Brookneal
Franklin Family	37.07200, -79.05100	SW Rt 646 3.2 mi N of Rt 615, Gladys quadrant
Goose Creek	unk	Lynch Station
Haden family	unk	Phillips Farm, Evington
Harper Family	unk	Nr Hat Creek Church, Brookneal
Hat Creek Presbyterian	37.06570, -78.54240	6442 Hat Creek Rd, Brookneal
Howard Family	unk	Nr Campbell Co CH, Rustburg
Jones Family	unk	Gladys Twp
Lee Family	unk	Leesville
Lynch Family	37.12946, -79.26853	Avoca Museum, 1514 Main St, Altavista
McReynolds Family	unk	Off Rt 623
Mt Athos	unk	Rt 460, Kelly
Mt Zion United Methodist	unk	5662 Red House Rd, Rustburg
Mt Hermon United Methodist	37.14500, -79.31170	Rt 712, Lynch Station
Oakdale	37.17076, -79.04768	Mollies Creek Rd, Gladys
Old Concord Presbyterian	unk	Rt 648, Concord
Old Phillips	unk	Rt 696 N side of Troublesome Creek, Evington
Otter Oaks	unk	Nr Evington

(CAMPBELL COUNTY, CONTINUED)

Payne Family	unk	"Oak Grove," Rt 659, Altavista
Pribble - Dunn	37.30800, -79.24700	Castle Craig Quadrant, Evington
Thornhill Family	unk	Off Rt 656, Rustburg
Walnut Hill	unk	Anthony home on Otter River, Evington
Whipping Creek	37.03430, -79.00180	Rt 633 Epsons Rd nr Long Island
Whitaker Family Farm	unk	Not identified
Wiatt-Norvell	unk	City Farm Quadrant
Wyndholm, aka Early Family	unk	Flat Creek nr Evington

CAROLINE COUNTY

Baylor Family	unk	Newmarket, Rt 2, 6 mi S of Bowling Green
Baynham Family	unk	Rt 653, Ruther Glen
Boutwell-Smith Family	unk	Rt 17, 3.1 mi S of Port Royal
Buckner-Washington-Burke	unk	Off Rt 2, W on Rt 626 Woodford Rd for 4 mi to gate of "Braynefield"
Burke Family	unk	1 mile N of Burke's Bridge, on Burke's Bridge Rd Rt 654, Bowling Green
Carmel Baptist	unk	24230 Jefferson Davis Pkwy, Ruther Glen
Cool Spring Farm	unk	10065 Rozell Rd, Woodford
DeJarnette Family	unk	Rt 2, 5.5 mi fr Bowling Green
Dick-Smith Family	unk	Bullock's Rd
Elmwood	unk	Rt 651, 5.3 mi S of DeJarnette
Fairford	unk	Nr Penola
Golansville Meeting House	unk	Golansville on US1
Greenlawn	38.07030, -77.33830	Lakewood Rd, Bowling Green
Hazelwood	38.18667, -77.22639	Hazelwood Ln at Rt 674, Port Royal
Hickory Grove	unk	Hickory Grove Plantation
Hill Family	37.93764, -77.55152	5498 MtAiry Dr, Mt Airy, Ruther Glen
Jericho	unk	North Anna River
Lomax-White	unk	Rt 758, Port Tobago
Maple Swamp	unk	Chilesburg
Old Mansion	unk	S end of Main St, Bowling Green
Pratt Family	unk	Rt 686 Camden Rd
Samuel Chewning Estate	unk	See tax map for location
Taliaferro Family	unk	Rt 654
Taylor-Quarles Family	38.25629, -78.05394	End of Bloomsbury Rd
Thornton Family	unk	Ormsby
Townsfield Farm	unk	Port Royal
White Hall	unk	2.4 mi N of Woodford
Woolfolk Family	unk	Rt 721 Sparta Rd, DeJarnette
Young Family	unk	Ruther Glen

CARROLL COUNTY

Blair	unk	Cliffview
Bobbitt Family	36.47841, -80.40554	Rt 682 E of Rt 52, Hillsville
Bowman-Fariss Family	36.66541, -80.66541	Blue Ridge Pkwy MM 194, Volunteer Rd W side btw Alpine Court Rd & Boundary Rd
Collier Family	36.78160, -80.59830	Jct Rts 628 & 624, Dugspur
Gardner Family	36.76610, -80.72080	End of Lynhaven Rd, Hillsville
Glenwood Methodist	36.62769, -80.88667	.1 mile E of jct Rt 608 Coal Creek Rd and Rt 609 Peaks Mountain Rd
John Frost	36.71845, -80.89540	Roseberry Ln nr Hillsville
Kenny Family	unk	Vic jct Rts 802 & 709
Mitchell Family	unk	Off Rt 764, 1 mi S of Rt 765, Sylvatus
North End	36.77234, -80.73866	101 Beaver Dam Rd, Hillsville
Old Quaker	36.64067, -80.88620	Off Old Quaker Rd Rt 727, Pipers Gap

(CARROLL COUNTY, CONTINUED)

Thompson-Bolt	36.81040, -80.55030	Off Bannon Rd Rt 625, Willis
Tobias Phillips	unk	Rt 619 nr Rt 757
William Dalton	36.79595, -80.64369	Off Rt 221, Dugspur
Worrell Family	36.78290, -80.66173	Off Pils Trail Rt 673, .6 mi S of Rt 221, Eona

CHARLES CITY COUNTY

Belle Air Plantation	37.20490, -77.34000	Rt 5, New Hope
Berkeley Plantation	37.31450, -77.17840	Rt 5, Harrison Landing Rd
Greenway	37.20190, -77.05200	Rt 5, Charles City CH
Lightfoot Family	unk	Teddington, Sandy Point
Rickman Family	37.30529, -77.04826	Kittiewan Plantation, 12104 Weyanoke Rd
Shirley Plantation	unk	Rt 5 SE of Richmond
Soldier's Rest	unk	Blanks Crossroads
Weyanoke	37.17300, -77.35600	Rt 619 off Rt 5

CHARLOTTE COUNTY

Cub Creek	37.03220, -78.75830	Rt 616 Cub Creek Church Rd, Brookneal
Golden Hills Estate	unk	Drakes Branch
Henry Family	unk	Red Hill Plantation, 1250 Red Hill Rd, Brookneal
Ingleside, Thomas Read Family	unk	Charlotte CH
Locust Grove	unk	Drakes Branch
Locust Grove	unk	Locust Grove nr Red Hill Boys Home
Moseley Family	unk	Nr Buffalo Creek
Mulberry Hill	36.88629, -78.70353	Staunton River Battlefield State Park, 1035 Fort Hill Trail, Randolph
Wheeler-Pugh-Jennings	unk	Off Rt 663 nr Bear Creek, down dirt rd

CHARLOTTESVILLE CITY (See also Albermarle County)

Brown Family #1	unk	Mt Fair nr Charlottesville
Bryan Family	unk	Farmington Country Club, 10th tee
Carr Family	unk	Stoney Pt Rd Rt 20 nr Charlottsville
Clover Fields	unk	Rt 22 NE off I-64, W of Charlottesville
Gilner Family	38.04851, -78.44964	Pen Park off Rio Rd
Lewis Family, University Heights	38.02390, -78.31000	Jct 250 W and Colonnade Dr, nr Old Ivy Rd
Lewis-Clarkson	38.04407, -78.51706	Collonade Dr
Monticello	38.00829, -78.45520	931 Thomas Jefferson Pkwy
Riverview	38.02610, -78.45810	1701 Chesapeake St
White Oak Crossroads	unk	Nr Charlottesville
Wingfield Family	unk	531 Woodlands Rd
Wingfield Family	unk	Shepard Property, Slaughter Pen Creek

CHESAPEAKE CITY

Butt Family	unk	Old Brooks Farm, St Julian Creek
Deer Crossing	unk	Adj to 2017 Coral Ivy Ln
Good Hope United Methodist	unk	1633 Benefit Rd
Halstead Family	unk	Pond Lake
Smith Family	36.69923, -76.11877	Mount Pleasant Farm, now Fentress Naval Auxiliary Airfield
Stewart Family	unk	Beechwood Plantation, Dismal Swamp Trail
Wilson Family	unk	701 Saunders Rd, City Prison Farms, St Brides Plantation

CHESTERFIELD COUNTY

Bailey Family	37.37075, -77.77635	Matoaca
Bethel Baptist	37.50986, -77.71166	1100 Huguenot Springs Rd, Midlothian
Brooks Family	unk	North of Walmsley Blvd. Btw Angus and Shackleford roads
Clarke Family	37.24354, -77.44655	Ravensbourne Dr, Ettrick
Clay Family	unk	At his homeplace, check property records
Cobbs Family	unk	Bolling Family property, Enon
Duncan Family	unk	Roslyn Ave, 2 mi E of Town Hall, Chester
Farguson Family	unk	12951 Blue Stack Ct.
Fleming Family	unk	Midlothian
Franklin Family	unk	Twp 50
Gates Family	unk	Rt 614, .4 mi west on private road next to "Fairfield" Farm
Kabler Family	unk	Check property records for homeplace
Lockett Family	unk	Brandermill, cnr of Long Gate & Huntgate
Matoax, Randolph Family	unk	Matoaca
Robertson Farm	37.367321, -77.607786	Vic jct Robbie Rd & Christina Rd
Skinquarter Baptist	37.40916, -77.792655	6900 Moseley Rd, Moseley

CLARKE COUNTY

Anderson Family	39.85160, -77.52350	"Springfield Farm," Rt 608 nr Morgan Spring Run, Webbtown
Berryville Baptist	39.94700, -77.53700	114 Academy St, Berryville
Blakemore Family	39.10216, -77.59246	Byrd Farm vic Rt 7, Moreland
Blakemore Family	39.17245, -77.99008	Blakemore Ln, off Rt 7, Berryville
Butler Family	39.53680, -78.63850	Family farm in SE part of Co, named as Dearmont Farm by one source
Chandler Family	39.1121, -78.03	Helvestine Farm, Rt 7 vic Rt 633
Frost	unk	Vic Hopewell
Grace Episcopal	39.15220, -77.98060	110 N Church St, Berryville
Green Hill	39.15810, -77.97690	Berryville
Greenway Court	unk	Nr Lord Fairfax, White Post
Meade Memorial Episcopal	39.05830, -78.10360	192 White Post Rd, White Post
Muse-Lewis, "The Moorings"	unk	Lewis Farm nr WV
Old Buck Marsh Meeting House	39.94730, -77.58370	nr Barryville Meeting House
Old Chapel Episcopal	39.10670, -78.01470	Jct US 340 & Rt 255, Millwood
Stone Chapel Presbyterian	39.22610, -78.01060	Old Charles Town Rd, Berryville

COVINGTON CITY (See also Alleghany County)

Dameron Family	unk	20 mi W of Covington
Falling Springs Presbyterian	unk	115 Spring Church Rd
Mt Pleasant	unk	6 mi NE of Covington
Persinger Memorial	unk	3707 Llama Dr
Samuel Brown Family	unk	9 mi W of Covington
Walker Family	unk	Covington

CRAIG COUNTY

Allen Family	unk	Off Craig Creek, nr Oriskany
Hebron United Methodist	unk	Rt 606 jct Bobcat Ln
Leffel	37.48080, -80.13970	Off Cumberland Gap Rd, Meadow Creek
Miller	unk	Rt 42, Midway
Nutter Property	unk	Pott's Creek

CULPEPER COUNTY

Brown	unk	Rt 636 1 mi NW of Reva, 2 mi NW to gate
Catalpa Plantation	unk	His homeplace on mountain nr town, check property records
Coons Family	unk	vic Rixeyville Rt 640
Covington Family	unk	Reported nr Washington CH but that would place it in Rappahannock Co, not Culpeper. Not in findagrave. Check JLARC report
Crooked Run Baptist	unk	7351 James Madison Hwy, Rapidan
Dawson Family	unk	Culpeper
Devils Run Farm	unk	Check tax records for location
Duncan	38.59068, -77.96277	Nr Oakshade
Fairview	38.48080,-78.00470	Sperryville Pike Rt 522, Culpeper
Farm	unk	Behind Culpeper & Racoon Ford
Fleetwood	unk	Fleetwood Ln off Rt 621, Jeffersonton
Ford Family	unk	Merrimac
Garnett Family	unk	Rt 648, 10 mi off Rt 15
Greenfield	unk	Rapidan
Hall Family	unk	Rt 658 vic Winston
Hudson Family	unk	Rt 721
Hume	unk	Nr Remington on James Madison St
Jones Family	unk	Crooked Run
Masonic Cemetery	38.48530, -77.99470	950 N Main, Culpeper
Puller Family	unk	1 mi E of Amissville
Redwood Plantation	unk	Rt 522 N
Robson Farm	unk	Not identified, not in findagrave
Slaughter-Jones Family	38.45500, -77.84131	Stone's Mill Rd Rt 676, LaGrange
St Mark's, aka Little Fork Church	unk	See DAR Senate Doc 1956, serial 11999 vol 8
St Stephen's Episcopal	unk	115 N East St, Culpeper
Stevensburg Baptist	unk	Stevensburg
Western View	unk	17434 Boldaker Ln
Wigginton	unk	Rt 29, Lakota
Yancey Family	38.51709, -77.95532	Off Rt 685 Aubern Rd, 3.5 mi WNW of Brandy Station

CUMBERLAND COUNTY

Bonbrook House	unk	7.5 mi N of Cumberland
Booker Family	unk	Rt 641 outside Cumberland CH
Boston Hill Plantation	unk	Cartersville
Burnt Chimney	unk	Cat Taile Branch
Clifton	37.40752, -78.07579	Off Rt 690 N of Hamilton
Cotton Town	unk	Holman Square
Deanery Family	unk	Cartersville on James River
High Hill	unk	Check property records for homeplace
James Anderson Family	unk	Reeds
Moses Smith Place	37.49639, -78.24486	Jct Rt 60 and Stoney Point Rd
Olnorary	unk	Old quarry on Old Stage Rd fr CH. Behind Cumberland & Cartersville
Page Family, "The Fork"	unk	Check Source 101
Price Family	unk	Nr Cattail Branch & Willis River
Scruggs Family	unk	Head of Huddy Ck
Walker Family	unk	Farmville
Winniford Family	37.71653, -78.16861	Fork of Willis Baptist Ch, jct Rts 660 & 713

DANVILLE CITY (See also Pittsylvania County)

Clay Family	unk	Danville
Dan's Hill	unk	Danville at Wilson's ferry
Nicholas Perkins, 2nd Home	unk	S of Dan River, Danville
Robert Payne Plantation	unk	Dix Ferry Rd nr Dan River
Wall Family	39.18335, -78.16268	Vic Danville
Wilson	unk	Dans Hill

DICKENSON COUNTY

John Powers Plantation	unk	Hwy 83, Clintwood

DINWIDDIE COUNTY

Fleetwood Plantation	unk	6630 Brills Rd, McKenney
Goshen Family	unk	8 mi S of Petersburg and W of Old Stage Rd on the "Goshen" site
Mt Pleasant	unk	Rt 609
Old Saponey Church	36.97110, -77.63610	E of Rt 709 on Rt 692
Sweden Plantation	37.15854, -77.54751	Nr jct Claiborne & White Oak rds, Sutherland
Sydnor-Young Family	unk	Petersburg National Battlefield
The Grove	unk	Rt 662, 12 mi S of Dinwiddie

EMPORIA CITY (See also Greensville County)

Emporia Tree	unk	Emporia
Robinson Family	unk	Emporia

ESSEX COUNTY

Bathhurst Plantation	37.88976, -76.82628	Nr Dunnsville
Campbell Family	unk	Lot 44, Tappahannock
Dishman Family	unk	Pine Hill Hunt Club
Garnett Family	unk	Elmwood, Loretto
Pitts Farm	unk	Nr Slaydo
Ritchie Family	unk	Burial vault on lot 18 or 22, Tappahannock
St Paul's Episcopal	37.82921, -76.96836	7924 Richmond-Tappahannock Hwy, Millers Tavern
Vauter's Episcopal	unk	Rt 368 off Rt 17, Loretto

FAIRFAX COUNTY, FAIRFAX CITY, AND FALLS CHURCH CITY

Adams-Nelson-Sewell Family	unk	1443 Layman St, McLean
Addison Family	unk	Homeplace Oxen Hill on the Potomac River opposite Mt Vernon
Belle Vale	unk	Belle Vale Manor, Doeg's Run
Broadwater Family	38.88940, -77.2610	Cnr of Tapawingo Rd and Frederick St SW, Vienna
Cockburn Family	unk	"Springfield," Gunston Rd Rt 242, W of Gunston Hall, Mason Neck
Dranesville United Methodist	39.00240, -77.35082	11720 Sugarland Rd, Dranesville
Dulaney Family	unk	See DAR Senate Doc 1956, serial 11999 vol 8
Fairfax City	38.84690, -77.31330	Main St & Page Ave, Fairfax
Falls Church Episcopal	38.88077, -77.17166	115 E Fairfax St, Falls Church
Flint Hill	38.88190, -77.29390	Chain Bridge Rd, Oakton
Frying Pan Meeting House	38.56240, -77.24480	2615 Centreville Rd, Herndon
Gary Family	unk	Centreville
Gunnell Family	unk	600 Innsbrook Ave, Great Falls

(FAIRFAX COUNTY, FAIRFAX CITY, AND FALLS CHURCH CITY, CONTINUED)

Gunston Hall	38.66862, -77.16823	Gunston Rd, Lorton
Haley/Halley Family	unk	4422 San Carlos Rd, Fairfax
Huntington	unk	3 mi fr Pohick Church
Hutchinson-Whaley	unk	Next to 4319 General Kearney Ct, Chantilly
Hutchison-Major	38.90569, -77.47508	Pleasant Valley Rd & Lafayette Center Dr, Chantilly
Lane Family	38.90658, -77.38822	12700 Franklin Farm Rd, Centreville
Laurel Hill	38.70961, -77.23464	Former Lorton Reformatory grounds, Lorton
Level Green Farm	unk	6275 Old Centerville Rd, Chantilly
Lindsay Family	38.70958, -77.23767	Off Lorton Rd nr Laurel Golf Club, Lorton
Millan-Potter Family	unk	7925 Telegraph Rd
Moore-Hunter Family	38.88600, -77.27336	1001 Tapawingo Rd SW, Vienna
Mt Air	38.73340, -77.17533	Newington Rd, Newington
Mt Vernon	38.42280, -77.0509	Mt Vernon Estate
Oakwood	unk	N Roosevelt St, Falls Church
Payne Family	unk	Chesterbrook
Pleasant Green Farm, Popes Head Run	unk	Nr Occoquan
Pohick Episcopal	38.42546, -77.11598	9301 Richmond Hwy, Lorton
Scott Family	unk	Across fr 15000 Conference Center Dr, Washington Technology Park, Chantilly
Sommers Family	38.52828, -77.10295	115 E Fairfax St, Falls Church
St John's Episcopal	38.84217, -77.42716	5649 Mt Gilead Rd
Sully Plantation	unk	Sully Rd Rt 28, adj Dulles National Airport, Chantilly
Summers	38.82121, -77.14098	Jct Rt 613 & Beaugard St, Lincolnia
Summers Family	38.49150, -770828	Lincolnia, nr Deming Avenue and Rt 613
The Mount	unk	2312 Col Lindsey Ct, Falls Church
Thompson Family	38.87201, -77.26178	Vic jct Rt 29 & Nutley St
Triplett Family	38.74246, 77.14318	On grounds of Humphrey's Engineer Center at John J. Kingman Rd nr the gate to the Army Geospatial Center at Fort Belvoir
Truro Parish	unk	"On the middle ridge near Ox Road", the present site of Jerusalem Baptist Church off Rt 123
Walnut Tree Farm	unk	Btw Vienna & Oakton
Watters-Adams Family	unk	6444 Linway Terr, McLean
Wickliff Family	38.46243, -77.24409	Behind 13220 Yates Ford Rd, Clifton
Wren Family	unk	Hillsman Dr and Mahala Ln, Falls Church

FAUQUIER COUNTY

Ash-Blackmore	unk	Delaplane
Ashby Family, Belmont	unk	Greenland Farm, nr Rt 724, Delaplane
Ball-Shumate	38.66382, -77.79851	On a knoll W & slightly S of Rts 15, 29, & 17 where it crosses Licking Run Stream
Blackwell Family	unk	The Meadows, E of Rt 628 at the first farm past Bethel United Methodist Church
Bronough Family	unk	Blue Ridge
Burke-Shaw	unk	Rt 688
Campbell, also Roy Neff Farm	38.46970, -77.99190	N of Jeffersonville on Rt 45 on left
Chunn Family	unk	Behind Mt Independence on Rt 17, N of Delaplane
Clascock, "Glenmore"	unk	Rectortown
Clermont	unk	Warrenton
Combs Family	unk	Hopewell
Cool Spring Church	unk	.5 mi S of Delaplane

(FAUQIUER COUNTY, CONTINUED)

Courtney Family	unk	Hartwood Airfield
Dermonte Burying Ground	unk	Liberty
Diggs Family	unk	Cliff Mill
Eastman Family	unk	Jct Rts 17 & 660
Edmonds Family	unk	Warrenton
George Family	unk	Catlett
Germantown Glebe	unk	Rt 643 nr Licking Run, Midland
Glasscock Family Farm	unk	Nr Marshall
Globe Farm	unk	Nr The Plains
Gordonsdale	unk	The Plains
Grove Baptist Church	36.63750, -79.24924	NW edge of Goldvein
Hawkins Family	38.77367, -77.62359	Buckland Farm, 6342 Pleasant Colony Ln, Warrenton
Hitt Family	unk	Rt 645
James Family	unk	Midland
Jennings-Foster Family	unk	11446 FreemansFord
Kemper Family	unk	Rt 802 Nr Warrenton
Kenner	unk	Rt 616, Somerville
Kenner Family	unk	2452 Kenner Ln
Lewis Family	unk	Little Georgetown
Linn Family Farm	unk	Morgantown
Love Family	38.43950, -77.40266	Buckland Farm, 6342 Pleasant Colony Ln, Warrenton
Marshall	38.86919, -77.83445	Marshall
Moffett	unk	Nr Marshall
Morgantown	unk	Morgantown
Moss Meeting House	unk	N fr Upperville
Mt Eccentric	unk	2 mi S of The Plains
Oak Springs	unk	770 Fletcher Dr
O'Bannon	unk	Warrenton
Obannon-Lawrence	unk	Marshall
Orlean	unk	Nr Orlean
Paris Community	unk	Paris
Payne Farm, Clifton Farm	unk	5 mi NW of Warrentown
Randolph Family, Eastern View	unk	Nr Casanova
Rockburn	unk	Rockburn Farm, 224 Crenshaw Rd, Rectortown
Rockburn (Rachburn)	unk	Nr Warrenton
Rockspring	unk	Check property records
Rowles Family	unk	Markham
Rust Family	38.52878, -77.04540	Rt 619, Upperville
Sherman-Hicks Family, aka Liberty Farm	unk	Paris
Smith Family	unk	Rt 688, Orlean
The Hatherage	unk	Warrenton
Thompson-Ford Family	unk	Green Branch Farm
Tulloss Family	unk	Somerville
Turner Family	unk	Delaplane
Waite Family	38.42539, -77.11615	Bristerburg
Warrenton	unk	Chestnut St, Warrenton
Whitewood	unk	2 mi N of The Plains
Winn Family	unk	Probably at Rock Hill Rt 626 nr Halfway
Withers-Nelson family	unk	9337 James Madison Hwy

FLOYD COUNTY

Eastview	unk	Rome
Goodson Family	unk	Pine Creek, near Turtle Rock
Goodykoontz	unk	Rt 729
Hungate Family	unk	Rt 615 nr Little River
King	unk	Nr MM 141 on Blue Ridge Pkwy
Pine Creek Primitive Baptist	36.94622, -80.27357	Spangler Mill Rd Rt 682
Red Oak Grove	36.98184, -80.28639	Off Red Oak Grove Rd Rt 684
Salem Cemetery	37.05014, -80.16004	Rt 221, Head of the River Church
Smith Chapel	37.03873, -80.20393	Not identified
Sumpter	unk	Rt 619, Floyd
Wade-Cox	unk	Check property records
Wimmer King	unk	Copper Hill
Wright Family	36.97658, -80.21693	Pizarro off Rt 668
Zion Lutheran Church	37.13507, -80.41662	Rts 693 & 615, Wades Ln

FLUVANNA COUNTY

Adams	unk	Bybee
Ashlin Family	unk	End Rt 606
Beaver Dam Baptist	37.98377, -78.29179	Richmond Rd, Paynes Mill
Bybee Family	unk	Nr Rt 633, Troy Neighborhood
Cary Family	unk	Carysbrook
Duncan Family	unk	Nr Hardware River
Eastin Family	unk	Rt 601
Fork Union Military Academy	unk	4744 James Madison Hwy, Fork Union
Lyles Church	37.84793, -78.20337	Palmyra
Oak Hill	37.70690, -78.25360	Rt 655
Old Jones Place	unk	Rt 600 nr Troy
Omohundro Family	unk	400 yds E of Rt 15, 1 mi S of Fork Union
Parrish Family	unk	Vic Rts 619 & 660
Perkins family	unk	Vic Rts 600 & 633
Ross Family	unk	Vic Rts 600 & 633
Shepherd family	unk	Vic Rts 623 & 659
Shores & Tutwiler Families	37.74641, -78.38259	Seven Islands
Unmarked Grave	unk	Overlooking Hardware River N of Rt 6.
Watson Family	unk	Vic Rts 678 & 625
Winnsville	unk	Rts 612 and 671, Fork Union
Wood family	unk	Vic jct Rts 659 & 610
Woods Family	unk	.5 mi S of Mechum River

FRANKLIN CITY (See also Southampton County)

Rochelle Family, Hermitage Plantation	unk	Hwy 671, nr Hansom

FRANKLIN COUNTY

Abshire	unk	Boones Mill
Angle Family	37.06940, -79.86310	Rt 699
Booth Family	unk	Rt 666 nr Smith Mountain Lake
Cook Family	unk	Rt 630 nr Rt 890, nr Sago
Cooper Family	unk	Snow Creek
Dillon Family	unk	Rt 900
Elsie Jones	unk	Nr Endicott Assembly of God Ch, Rt 793
English Family	unk	Kemps Mill
Graghead Family	unk	Rt 1361 nr Radford
Greer Family	unk	.5 mi W of Rts 812 & 919
Hatcher Family	unk	Scruggs

(FRANKLIN COUNTY, CONTINUED)

Holland Family	unk	Rt 616 nr HancockCem
Hook Family	unk	Rt 122 nr US Cellular
John Fisher Farm	37.03640, -79.72470	Rt 669
Joseph Shores Price Family	unk	Rt 817 or Dillions Mill
Mark Perdue Farm, Crossroads Burnt Chimney	unk	Rt 672 vic Foxfire Nursery
McNeil Family	unk	Rt 220 N, .1 mi E of MM 25, nr RR tracks
Mt Ivy	unk	Scruggs
Overfelt	37.07377, -79.94785	Grassy Hill Rd, Helm
Pearson Memorial Park	36.84000, -79.95030	S off Henry Rd Rt 605
Pigg River Primitive Baptist	36.96913, -80.07368	Rt 750 nr Callaway
Poindexter Family	unk	Jct Rts 655 & 834
Prillaman	37.01080, -80.06080	Foothills Rd Rt 642 W of Highland United Methodist, Callaway
Prillman-Turner	unk	Btw Ferrun & Philpott Res
Private	unk	Nr Glade Hill
Ramsey-Stanley	unk	Rt 764 nr Rt 606
Richards Family	unk	2.5 mi SW of Callaway off Foothills Rd
Stephen Sink Family	37.08092, -79.79286	Rt 670 behind house at 956 Three Oaks Rd
Tanyard-Barnard-Hill	unk	Rocky Mount
Ward Feazell	unk	Ferrum
Wingfield Family	36.84838, -79.78482	Off Bonfield Dr Rt 890
Witcher Family	36.57047, -79.35798	Penhook
Woody Family	unk	Plantation Rd, Rocky Mount

FREDERICK COUNTY (See also Winchester City)

Back Creek Quaker, aka Gainesboro United Methodist	39.27861, -78.25694	166 Siler Ln, Gainesboro
Baker Tomb	unk	Albin
Beeler	unk	Cedar Creek
Bethel Church	unk	Rt 610
Bucher	unk	Mountain Falls
Burnt Factory United Methodist	38,18490, -78.07550	1943 Jordan Springs Rd Rt 664, Burnt Factory
Buckton Graveyard	unk	Not identified
Castleman's Farm	unk	Berryville
Cooper Family	unk	W side of Back Mtn Rd, 1 mi N of Mountain Falls
George Hott	unk	Rt 654 fr Nain 7 mi to Pleasant Valley Church, on right on top of hill
German Reformed Church	39.08150, -78.21840	Mulberry St, Stephens City
Hite Family	unk	Middletown
Hockmans	unk	Vic Lebanon Church
Hollingsworth-Parkins	39.16600, -78.17490	W Jubal Early Dr
Jones Family	unk	Vanchese
Little Mountain United Methodist	39.27280, -78.18910	259 Little Mountain Ch Rd, Cedar Grove
Long-Stephens	unk	Stephens City
Milburn Chapel	39.22360, -78.11360	Milburn Rd Rt 622, Stephenson
Mountain View Methodist	39.11410, -78.40920	Richards Ln, Mountain Falls
Mt Carmel	39.03170, -78.28720	3rd & Commerce St, Middletown
Mt Hebron	39.18170, -78.15720	305 E Boscawen St, Winchester
Mt Olive	39.22610, -78.72000	327 Mt Olive Rd, Hayfield
Mt Pleasant Meeting House	39.12080, -78.30440	Rt 622, Mt Pleasant
Old Hite Farm	unk	Long-Meadows, Middletown
Old Methodist Church	39.08620, -78.21670	5291 Main St, StephenS City
Old Opequon Church	39.82237, -78.11412	217 Opequon Church Ln, Kernstown

(FREDERICK COUNTY, CONTINUED)

Old Stone Church	39.30110, -78.16750	Nr 461 Green Spring Rd, Green Spring
Pughtown	unk	Gainesboro
Robinson-Sidebottoms-Hawkins	unk	Nr Round Hill
Smith	unk	Gore
St John's Lutheran	39.15310, -78.36520	3623 Buck Mountain Rd, Hayfield
Stephens City United Methodist	39.08620, -78.21670	5291 Main St, Stephens City
Strother-Jones	unk	Stephens City
Trinity Evangelical Lutheran	39.08280, -78.21679	Mulberry St Stephens City
Upper Ridge	unk	Rt 739
Walnut Grove Plantation	unk	White Post
White Family	unk	Rt 615
White Post, aka Wheeler Family	39.71170, -78.5419	Nr White Post, nr Clarke-Frederick co line, Dearfield Farm
Wood Family	unk	Glen Burnie nr Winchester
Woodville Estate	unk	Winchester

FREDERICKSBURG CITY (See also Spotsylvania County)

City Cemetery	38.30112, -77.46628	1000 Washington Ave
Holladay Family	unk	Bellefont House
Kenmore Plantation	unk	1500 Washington Ave
Masonic Cemetery	38.30198, -77.46142	900 Charles St
St George's Episcopal	unk	905 Princess Anne
Fredericksburg Natl Military Park	unk	Willis Hill, Marye Heights

GILES COUNTY

Birchlawn Burial Park	39.32610, -80.71080	Wenonah Ave Rt 460, Pearisburg
Boyd, Wolf Creek	unk	Wolf Creek Rd nr Narrows
Cloverhollow	37.33470, -80.47580	Rt 715 Deerfield Ln before first sharp turn
Doe Mountain Farm	unk	Nr Pembroke
French (possibly same as Boyd)	unk	Wolf Creek nr Curve
Hale Farm	unk	Wolf Creek nr Narrows
Hare Family	unk	Narrows
Horseshoe	unk	Pembroke
Indian Bottom Farm	unk	Walkers Creek District Twp
Kirk Burial Grounds	unk	Chapman-Straley Farm Rt 730, nr Eggleston Springs
Lybrook Family	37.33385, -80.61087	End Rt 65, Pembroke
Mt Prospect	unk	Rt 634, Old Strother Farm, Ripplemeade
Newport	unk	Newport
Old Hoges Chapel	unk	Mount Lake Rd
Pearis Family	unk	Bluff City
Peterstown	37.39470, -80.80140	Off Rt 219 btw Peterstown & Midway, on WV state line
Phlegar Farm	unk	Rt 626, Ripplemead
Private Grave	unk	Nr Celanese, Pearisburg
Shannon-King	37.21810, -80.74170	Nr Jct Rts 42 & 100, Poplar Hill nr Walker's Creek
Sifford	unk	White Gate
Snidow Farm, "Sugar Maple"	unk	Rt 460 on Lilly Hill, Pembroke
Staffville	unk	Hillsville
Sugar Run, Farmer Family	unk	Staffordsville
Sunrise Memorial Gardens	unk	Rich Creek
Toney Family	unk	Glen Lyn

GLOUCESTER COUNTY

Abingdon Episcopal	37.33355, -76.51364	4645 George Washington Mem Hwy Rt 17
Bellamy Methodist Church	37.40149, -76.58883	4870 Chestut Fork Rd
First United Baptist Church	37.37133, -76.53449	6188 George Washington Mem Hwy Rt 17
Highgate	unk	Cash Post Office
Marlfield Plantation	37.44928, -76.62239	Rt 610 at 3780 Pebble Ln, Marlfield
Robins Family	unk	Robin's Neck
Sinclair, "Sherwood"	37.08370, -78.11672	Selden Post Office
Toddbury	unk	On North River
Union Baptist	37.27882, -76.44331	9524 Guinea Rd, Achilles
Ware Episcopal	37.42275, -76.50789	7825 John Clayton Mem Hwy
Warner Hall	37.20403, -76.28539	4750 Warner Hall Rd

GOOCHLAND COUNTY

Ben Glade	unk	Rock Castle
Ben Lomond	unk	Rt 627 off Rt 600
Boscobel	unk	Vic Rt 621 Manakin
Fairfield	unk	5.5 mi W of Goochland Rt 6 to Rt 614 .4 mi
Friendship Rest	unk	Rt 623
Grace Episcopal	37.68321, -77.88765	2955 River Rd West, Goochland CH
Holman Family	unk	Rt 645
Isbell Family	unk	Rt 619
Johnson Family	unk	Rt 658
Lacy Family	37.80571, -77.99405	Rt 615
Mims Family	unk	Manakin
Moore Family	unk	Cardwell Rd
Mullins	unk	Nr Fife
Payne Family	37.84780, -78.07190	Rt 681 S of Rt 605
Payne Family, Hickory Hill	unk	Rts 609 & 603, Goochland
Rocky Spring Leake	unk	Jct Rts 6 & 600
The Oaks	unk	1.4 mi SE of Tapscott on Rt 603
Tuckahoe Plantation	unk	12601 River Rd Rt 650, W of Richmond near Manakin
Webber Family	unk	W Rt 6 fr Richmond 9.2 mi, right on Rt 621 3.5 mi
Woodlawn	unk	Jct Rts 250 & 612

GRAYSON COUNTY

Anderson-Hash	36.66593, -81.33110	Flatridge & Old Bridle Creek Rd
Benjamin-Phipps	unk	Saddle Creek Rt 681
Brown-Osborne	unk	1168 White Pine Rd
Comer	unk	Rt 662, Elk Creek
Cornett Family	36.72401, -81.23889	Rt 662
Cox Family Farm	unk	Rt 629 W of Baywood
Crossroads Primitive Baptist	36.60868, -81.01592	Nr Baywood Elem Sch, Rt 624, Baywood
Hale Family	unk	Nr Elk Creek
Jackson Family	unk	Rt 658, along Bear Creek
Murphy Family	36.59220, -80.93800	Rt 607
Nuckolls Family	36.63551, -80.95944	Beyond the end of Wild Turkey Ln, jct US 58 & Rt 94
Osborn-Cox	unk	Rt 711, Independence
Phipps Family	unk	Saddle Creek
Reedy	39.13594, -78.00630	Reedy Groves, Grossy Creek
Reeves Farm	unk	Rt 700, SE of Independence
Rudy	unk	Rt 660 near Elk Creek, Independence
Samuel Byrd Family	unk	Old Colonial Rd
Sauger	unk	Elk Creek

(GRAYSON COUNTY, CONTINUED)

Sawyers-Elk Creek Community	unk	Hwy 668, Independence
Silas Ward Family	unk	Bridle Creek
Stone Family	unk	Elk Creek
Vaughan Family	36.44200, -81.41660	Fries, Spring Valley Community
Weiss Family	unk	Rt 637 or 736, Independence
Young Family	unk	Nr jct Rts 711 & 680

GREENE COUNTY

Beadles Family	unk	Btw Green Acres Rd & N side of Green Acres Lake, Greene Hills
Burton Graveyard	38.16240, -78.20570	NE cnr of Rt 29 N and Rt 609 E
Locust Grove	unk	From Rt 623 take 641 .4 mi to Locust Grove farm rd, .35 mi
Mill's Family	unk	Standardsville
Thornton	unk	Haney property, E side of Rt 619, btw South River Bridge & Dundee Graveyard
Unidentified	unk	South/left side Rt 648 after crossing Buffalo River fr Rt 604

GREENSVILLE COUNTY (See also Emporia City)

Grigg Family	unk	Jarratt
Ivey Family	unk	Rt 611 5.5 mi W of Emporia
Peebles Family	unk	Brink

HALIFAX COUNTY

Adams Family	unk	Check property records
Barksdale Family	unk	End of Rt 689 at Depot, Cedar View, South Boston
Betts Family, Snow Hill	36.35465, -78.57311	2091 Snow Hill Rd, Cluster Springs
Brooks Private	unk	Rt 681 West of Halifax, Cluster Springs
Carrington Family	unk	Bruce Estate "Berry Hill" W of South Boston, off Rt 659, on the "River Rd" E of the house
Clark Family	unk	Bannister Lodge
Clark Plantation	unk	Strawberry Br
Clarkton	unk	Rt 632, Clarkton
Cole Family	unk	Off Rt 672, NW of Asbury Church nr Halifax
Coles-Carrington	unk	Mildendo Plantation
Cross Road Baptist	36.62690, -79.04780	1098 Flint Rock Rd, South Boston
Davenport Family	unk	Nr jct Rts 360 & 344, Scottsburg
Faulkner Family	unk	Nr Cherry Hill, 1 mi W of Hyco, nr Omega
Ferrell Family	unk	Cherry Hill, W of Halifax
Fitzpatrick Family	unk	Nathalie
Halifax Town	36.76403, -78.92668	Check property records
Keatts Family	unk	Nr Mulberry Baptist Church, nr Pittsylvania
Kent Family	unk	Poplar Creek
Logan Family	unk	Off Rt 672, NE jct with Rt 666, .4 mi on private Rd
Lovelace Family	unk	Off Rt 676, W of Asbury Church
Oak Hill	unk	South Boston
Oak Ridge	36.71912, -78.90321	Main St & Hamilton St, South Boston
Old Wood Family	36.50000, -79.46520	Rodgers Chapel Rd btw Rts 605 & 608, Clover
Ragland Family	unk	Check property records and DAR Senate doc 93, vol 54
Scott Home Site	unk	Off Rt 724, NW fr Scottsburg

(HALIFAX COUNTY, CONTINUED)

St John's Episcopal	unk	197 Mountain Rd, Halifax
Stanfield Family, Boyd Farm	unk	Rt 658, 2 mi S of Turbeville
Terry Family	unk	1154 N Terry Rd, Halifax
Wallis Wilson Family	unk	By Rt 737, 4 mi fr Mecklenburg line
Watlington family	unk	Halifax town
Wyatt	unk	Rt 601, 3.6 mi S of South Boston

HAMPTON CITY

Herbert	39.01475, -76.35013	Off Armstrong Ln
Sherwood Cemetery	37.07384, -76.34973	Langley Air Force Base
St John's Episcopal	unk	100 W Queen's Way

HANOVER COUNTY

Airwell	unk	Rt 738
Aldingham	unk	Check property records
Beaver Dam	unk	Rt 738
Blackwell Family	unk	Spring Grove
Blenheim-Winston	unk	Rt 646, Hanover
Bowles Family	unk	Waterloo, Chickahominy Point
Brock Spring	unk	Old Telegraph Rd
Brown Family	unk	New Castle
Cherrydale	unk	Rt 667
Dunham	unk	Rt 630 Cold Harbor
Fairfield	unk	Sledd Run Sub Div
Fork Episcopal	37.85340, -77.53100	12566 Old Ridge Rd, Doswell
Goldmine farm	unk	Rt 271, Rockville
Goodall's Tavern Property	unk	.75 mi W of jct Rts 623 & 33
Green	unk	Greenlands Farm, abt 4 mi N Ashland
Grubbs Family, aka Spring Grove	37.43510, 77.36520	Spring Grove #2 Farm, nr Calvary Christian jct Rts 623 & 624
Jones Family	unk	Rt 742 Nicholas St
Longrow	unk	Rt 658
Marl Ridge	unk	Rt 54, Ashland
Morris at Taylor's Creek	unk	Bethany Ch Rd
Nelson Fam at Wingfield	unk	Coatesville
Pleasant Valley	unk	Mechanicsville
Retreat Farm	unk	Pamunkey River near old church
Snead Family	unk	Rt 624 nr Hylas, nr main road
Spring Grove	39.10916, -78.09970	Rockville
St Paul's Episcopal	37.76570, -77.37120	8050 St Paul's Rd, Hanover
Still House Spring	unk	Rt 669
Studley	37.40100, -77.17270	Studley Farm Rd, under tree in front yard of Mr. J.A. Francieni, Jr residence (as of 1978)
Syme	unk	Rts 6763 & 703 nr Rockville, Rocky Mills
Taylor Family	37.40850, -76.25405	VAQ 738 Old Ridge Rd
Turner Family	unk	Eastern View
Union Baptist	37.94660, -77.65160	16230 Union Church Rd, Beaverdam
Walnut Shade	unk	Walnut Shade Ln off Rt 54

HARRISONBURG CITY (See also Rockingham County)

Cooks Creek Presbyterian	38.47472, -78.92997	4222 Mt Clinton Pike
Frank Harman Place	unk	Rt 42 N
Miller Family	unk	Harrisonburg
Trissel's Mennonite	unk	Rt 752
Woodbine	38.44803, -78.86244	Jct Rt 33 & Reservoir St

HENRICO COUNTY

Afro-American, aka East End	37.53640, -77.38640	Bulheller Rd
Andrews Family	unk	Thomas Andrews Plantation, Appomattox River
Belleville Estate	unk	Check property records
Craddock Family	unk	Off Darbytown Rd 5.6 mi SE of Richmond
George Family	unk	Rt 60, Briel's Farm Rd 9.7 mi E of Richmond
Glendale/Frayser Farm Family	unk	Rt 5, 11 mi SE of Richmond
Rural	unk	Check property records for plantation
Smith family	unk	1 mi W of Skipwith Rd, 1.5 mi N of Three Chopt Rd

HENRY COUNTY (See also Martinsville City)

Anglin Plantation	unk	Nr Patrick Co line
Barksdale Family	unk	Camden Parish
Blackberry Creek Private	unk	Bassett
Cox Family	unk	Cox, nr Turkey Pen Branch & Smith River
DeShazo	unk	Leatherwood
Dyer Family	36.45261, -79.48125	Foxpipe Rd, Leatherwood
Font Hill	unk	Leatherwood Creek, Irisburg
Franklin Family	36.71597,-79.94299	Off US 57 btw Shadyview Rd Rt 1404 & US 220 Bypass, behind "Old Franklin Home Place," nr community of Fieldale
Grassy Creek	36.64716, -79.91943	Nr Horsepasture, Rt 829, Drakes Branch
Hairston Family	unk	SR 208, Beaver Creek, N of Martinsville
King	unk	Leatherwood
Leatherwood Plantation	36.44534, -79.4558	Nr Martinsville
Martin Family	unk	Leatherwood Downs
Mayo Baptist Church	unk	85 Penn Store Rd, Spencer
Moses Martin	unk	Bassett
Nance Plantation Home	unk	Rt 58 2 mi E of Martinsville
Pace Family	unk	Pace Airport Rd abt .5 mi past airport, Ridgeway
Ragland Family	unk	McDonough
Redd	unk	Fontaine
Simpson Family	unk	Family homeplace, check property records
Single burial	unk	Off Rt 758, 100 yards off Price Rd, nr Horsepasture, Donnybrook Rd, Ridgeway
Taylor	unk	George Taylor Hwy
Watkins	unk	Axton

HIGHLAND COUNTY

Arbogast Family	unk	Wimer Mountain Rd, Blue Grass
Armstrong Family	unk	N of McDowell
Armstrong Family	unk	Stonewall District
Clover Creek Church	unk	Clover Creek Rt 678 S of McDowell, 7.7 mi, right side
Doe Hill	38.25976, -79.26629	Rt 654, across from Doe Hill Methodist
Gilmore Family	unk	In woods in back of Briscoe's Grocery Store Rt 84, Mill Gap
Gum Family, aka Walker Wilfong Family	unk	Hightown
Heyde	unk	Rt 644, Blue Grass
Hull Family	unk	Rt 640 to Rt 637, .9 mi to Elmer Ruckman farm
Jones Family	unk	Farm of Clay Botkins, left fr US 250 on Rt 614 traveling fr McDowell

(HIGHLAND COUNTY, CONTINUED)

Ruckman	unk	Little Egypt Rd, US 220 fr Mill Gap to Rt 604, turn left, 2 to 3 miles grave on right
Rymer Family	unk	Rt 624 N fr McDowell. Left through wooden gate to pasture, up over ridge and slightly to right side of mountain.
Seybert Chapel	unk	Nr jct Rt 629 Strait Creek & Rt 631, Monterey
Seybert Hills Farm	unk	US 200 N fr Monterery to Rt 629, 1.8 mi
Shinaberry	unk	3 mi N Hightown, Crabbottom
Stony Run	38.22920, -79.7003	US Rt 220, N of jct with 607
Unidentified	37.96151, -79.71000	Nr Doe Hill

ISLE OF WIGHT COUNTY

Benns United Methodist	36.56170, -76.35100	1457 Benns Church Blvd, Smithfield
Parker Family	36.58569, -76.32136	3.5 mi E of Rescue, Macclesfield
St Luke's Church	36.93940, -76.58670	14477 Benns Church Blvd, Smithfield
Wrenn's Cemetery	unk	Rt 10, 5 mi N of Smithfield

JAMES CITY COUNTY

Jones-Nunn Family	37.21246, -76.47290	Farmville Ln, Norge

KING AND QUEEN COUNTY

Bird-Boyd-Todd Family	unk	Popular Grove Plantation, Stevensville
Collins Family	unk	Check property records
Dewsville plantation	unk	Newtown
Fauntleroy Family, Farmers Mount Plantation	unk	Whitehall
Goshen	unk	Check property records and Senate Doc 1952, serial 11670 vol 3
Lyne Family	unk	Check property records
Mattaponi Baptist	unk	Vic King & Queen CH
Mattaponi Church	unk	Nr Cumnor
Young Family	unk	Walkerton

KING GEORGE COUNTY

Braxton Estate	unk	Chericoke
Davis Family	unk	Edgehill
Dishman Family, Pine Hill	unk	Off Rt 621, Shiloh
Eagle's Nest	unk	Rt 218 E to Rt 242 N to Rt 682
Emmanuel Episcopal	unk	US 301, Port Conway
Mt Mariah Plantation	unk	Rt 619, 10 mi NE of King George
Saunders Family	unk	Check property records
St Paul's Episcopal	38.33200, -77.12500	5486 St Paul's Rd off Rt 206
Stuart-Grymes Family	38.33601, -77.13407	Rt 218 on Cedar Grove Farm
Unidentified, Private	unk	Edgehill
Washingon Family	unk	Potomac View
Willow Hill	unk	Jct Kennedy Dr and Van Buren Dr, Presidential Lake subdiv

KING WILLIAM COUNTY

Claiborne Family	unk	Sweet Hall, Rocky Mount
Edwards Family	unk	Cherry Grove
Elsing Green Plantation	37.61608, -77.04073	Off Mt Olive Cohoke Rd Rt 632
Fairfield Plantation	unk	Aylett

(KING WILLIAM COUNTY, CONTINUED)

Fleet Street, Plantation Grounds	37.78166, -77.25359	Rt 604 S of Webb Creek, Etna Mills, on Rt 4 1 mi fr Jct Rt 30
Forkquarter	unk	Calno Rd Rt 601, Norment Ferry
Huntington, aka Old Fox	unk	On Mattaponi River
Langborne Family	unk	At Langborne on bank of Pamunkey River
Retreat	unk	Aylett
Smyrna	unk	Off Rt 604 Damney's Mill Rd, SE of Corinth Fork
Springfield	unk	Abt 2 mi S of King William CH, on right side of Rt 621, leading fr Skyron to Palls
Uppowac	unk	Rumford
Vermont Plantation	unk	W River Rd Rt 600, .5 mi E of Dorrel Rd Rt 628, River Hill

LANCASTER COUNTY

Chowning Ferry Farm	unk	Chownings Ferry Rd
Christ Church	37.61019, -76.54606	420 Christ Church Rd, Weems
Morrattico House	unk	Morattico
Old St John's Cemetery	37.68920, -76.38530	Off Rt 1066 Harris Rd abt .5 mi S of DMV Dr
St Mary's Whitechapel Episcopal	37.44782, -76.33181	5940 White Chapel Rd, Lively

LEE COUNTY

Ball Family	unk	Rt 684 vic Ewing
Benedict Yeary	unk	Nr Rocky Station Fort
Brooks	unk	Ewing on Kesterson Rd Rt 690, 3 mi fr town
Campbell-Hobbs	unk	Rt 682, vic Ewing
Clark-Jayne	unk	Jonesville
Clifton Neff Farm	unk	Ewing
Duff family	unk	3.2 mi E on Rt 612, fr jct Rts 58E and 421 E, Stickleyville
Ewing-McClure, aka Friendship Church	unk	Jonesville
Fritts Family	unk	Maybe adj to federal prison, check property records
Gibson Family	unk	Gibson Station
Hobbs family, aka Debusk Family	unk	Dryden
Jonathan Bales Family	unk	Rt 682 vic Ewing
Robert Clark, aka Thompson-Whitehead-Wilder	unk	Rt 612 7 mi SW of Jonesville
Russell Family	unk	Rt 58, Rose Hill
Slemp Memorial	unk	Turkey Cove
Tritt-Gilbert	unk	Rt 642, Woodway
Yeary Family	unk	W fr Ewing
Unidentified	unk	Rt 58, W of Jonesville

LEXINGTON CITY (See also Rockbridge County)

Hostetter Family	unk	Lexington
Lexington	unk	Lexington
Miller-Irwin	37.65116, -79.52014	Dry Well Rd Rt 813, on left at Charles Ln
New Monmouth Presbyterian	37.83960, -79.48586	2343 West Midland Rd
Old Monmouth Presbyterian	37.80810, -79.47280	Jct Rts 60 & 669
Oxford Presbyterian	37.75302, -79.56023	18 Churchview Ln, Lexington
Stonewall Jackson Memorial	37.78128, -79.44604	314 S Main St
Washington & Lee Univ Campus	36.60863, -81.01593	Nr Jefferson St

LOUDOUN COUNTY

Arnold Grove Episcopal Church	39.19796, -77.71557	Rt 9, vic jct with Rt 690, Hillsboro
Ball Burial Ground	39.14404, -77.54690	Off Rt 15 nr N Spring Behavioral Healthcare
Benedum Family	unk	Leesburg
Campbell-Belt Estate	unk	Rock Hill, Leesburg
Carter Family	unk	Nr Middleburg
Catoctin Free Church	39.16274, -77.64527	Charlestown Pike Rt 9, Paeonian Springs
Ebenezer Baptist	39.05824, -77.84142	20421 Airmont Rd, Bluemont
Elgin Family	unk	Kingdom Farm, Evergreen Mill Rd, Sycolin, S of Leesburg
Ellzey Family	unk	Rt 621, Middleton
Fairfax Meeting House	39.18557, -77.60589	Water St & Waterford Rd, Waterford
Fox Family	unk	Waterford S on Hwy 62, Paeonian Springs
Goose Creek	39.11250, -77.69527	Rt 722, Lincoln
Hixon Family	unk	Check property records
Ketoctin Baptist	39.15746, -77.74870	Ketoctin Church Rd, Purcellville
Lane Family	unk	Leithtown
Leesburg Presbyterian	39.11611, -77.56722	207 W Market St, Leesburg
McIlhaney Family	unk	Nr Hillsboro E side Rt 690 btw Rts 90 & 611
McKim Family	unk	Arcola
McVeagh Family Plantation	unk	Not identified by JLARC
Mount Family	unk	Mountville off Rts 733 & 734
Mountain Chapel	unk	Jct Rts 734 & 630
New Jerusalem Lutheran	39.25736, -77.63891	12942 Lutheran Church Rd, Lovettsville
New Valley Baptist	39.21918, -77.54746	Bald Hill Rd Rt 673, Lucketts
Nixon Family	unk	19010 Woodburn Rd
North Fork Baptist	39.06014, -77.68509	38130 North Folk Rd, North Fork
Old Presbyterian	39.27343, -77.69341	Behind Primitive Baptist, S Church St, Lovettsville
Old Stone Methodist	39.11725, -77.56609	168 W Cornwall St, Leesburg
Petts Family	unk	Purcellville
Potts Family	39.19455, -77.76157	Rts 716 & 714, Hillsboro
Raspberry Plain	unk	16500 Agape Ln, Leesburg
Richard Carter Property	unk	Nr Leesburg
Rock Quarry, Goose Creek	unk	Mt Pleasant
Rokeby	unk	Nr Leesburg
Saunders Family	unk	Leithtown
Sharon	unk	Middleburg
South Fork Meeting House	39.02640, -77.80220	Rt 630, Unison
St James Episcopal, Old Cemetery Lot	39.11555, -77.56250	Church St NE, Leesburg
St James Reformed	39.27027, -77.62968	Lovettsville Rd, Lovettsville
Union Cemetery	39.12046, -77.56239	323 N King St, Leesburg
Unison	unk	Unison
Upperville Methodist	unk	11134 Delaplane Grade Rd, Upperville
Waterford Union of Churches	39.18557, -77.60802	Fairfax St, Waterford

LOUISA COUNTY

Anderson	unk	Nr South Anna River, Rt 642
Belle Isle	unk	Nr Frederick Hall
Bullock Family	unk	Rt 758, Walnut Hill
Clover Hill	unk	S Anna River, Rt 647
Dabney Family	unk	4.3 mi NE of Orchid
Gibson Farm	unk	Louisa
Goodwyn house cem	unk	Rt 16, 3.4 mi fr Louisa
Gunnell Family	unk	Buckner
Hermitage	unk	Cedar Hill Rd, Pendleton

(LOUISA COUNTY, CONTINUED)

Jackson Family	unk	Catalpa Hall, Rt 522
Jerdone Castle	unk	4.4 mi NW of Buckner
Little River Baptist	unk	Bumpass
Mt Air/Pleasant View	unk	Overton Fork, Rt 723 Bohannon Rd nr Lake Anna
Roseneath	unk	Jackson District
Roundabout Castle	unk	3998 Yanceyville Rd
Spring Valley	unk	Cuckoo District
Tolersville Tavern Burial Ground	38.01321, -77.90345	Rt 677 nr Mineral Baptist, Mineral
Valetta	unk	Nr Green Springs
Whartons	unk	Christopher Run
Woodland	unk	Jackson District
Yancey-Crawford Family	unk	Yanceyville
Williams-Knight Family	unk	Vic jct Rt 623 & Eubanks Rd

LUNENBURG COUNTY

Boswell Family	unk	Off Rt 634, SE of Rebobeth
DeGrafenreidt Family	unk	Check property records
Hite Family	unk	Forksville
Taylor Family	unk	18 mi S of Kenbridge

LYNCHBURG CITY (See also Campbell County)

Anglican Chapel	unk	Court Street
Chilton-Moorman	unk	Off Rt 221
Maj Samuel Scott Family	37.41330, -79.20304	2627 Old Forest Rd
McDaniel Family	unk	Boonesboro Rd
Old City	37.41472, -79.15667	401 Taylor St
Presbyterian Church	37.40206, -79.13848	2020 Grace St
Scott Family	37.45250, -78.18890	VES Rd
South River Meeting House, aka Quaker Memorial Presbyterian	37.37246, -79.19194	5810 Fort Ave
Towles Family	unk	See DAR Senate Report 1954, serial 11831, vol 4

MADISON COUNTY

Aylor Family	unk	.75 mi N of Novum Post Office
Carpenter Family	unk	on first patent land complied 1940, VA346
Ford Family	unk	Nr Leon
Fry Family	unk	Meander Plantation
Gaar Mountain	38.43374, -78.29048	Mulatto Run nr Beamer Hd Rd
Gaines Family	unk	Check tax map for location
Graves Family	unk	Check property records
Harrison Family	38.43373, -78.29048	Shelby
Hebron Lutheran	38.40676, -78.24808	899 Blankenbaker Rd, Madison
Hebron Valley	unk	Hebron Valley
House Hollow Farm	unk	Slate Mills
Jillard-Weakley	unk	Rt 600 Syria
John Robertson Property	unk	Ruth
Lillard Family	unk	Nethers
Lillard Family	unk	Syria
Lorenz Gaar Family	unk	Mulatto Run nr Beamer Hd Rd
McAllister Family	unk	Check property records near Syria
Mt Pisgah Church	38.39265, -78.30396	Rt 652 nr intersection of Ruth Rd
Nicholson Family	unk	Syria
Repton Family	unk	Vic Pratts Post Office

(MADISON COUNTY, CONTINUED)

Rucker, Blakey, Hoffman, Rose	38.34745, -78.32997	Nr Wolftown
Tanner Family	unk	Hebron Valley
The "Hilton"	unk	vic Rt 15 Madison Mills
Tribble Family, Shirley Durbin Farm	unk	2 mi S jct Rts 25 & 75
Walker United Methodist	38.29328, -78.16756	Nr Bent Tree
Wilhoite Family	unk	Hebron Valley
Yowell Family	38.19420, -78.49120	Syria

MANASSAS CITY (See also Prince William County)

Ball Family	38.80945, -77.50895	Manassas Battlefield, off Vandor Ln across fr Strayer University
Bethel Luthern	unk	8712 Plantation Ln
Cloverhill	unk	Hastings Dr
Hooe Family	38.80555, -77.53451	Chinn Ridge, Manassas National Battlefield Park
Lewis-Montgomery Families, Manassas Presbyterian	38.46856, -77.30823	8201 Ashton Ave
Mayfield Plantation	38.75290, -77.35571	Mayfield Park
Pittsylvania (Carter)	38.49711, -77.31305	Manassas National Battlefield Park
Stonewall Memory Gardens	38.81530, -77.55170	12004 Lee Hwy
Thurman Family	unk	Glen-Gery Brick Co, 9905 Godwin Dr

MARTINSVILLE CITY (See also Henry County)

Oakwood	36.38690, -79.88000	199 Cemetery St

MATHEWS COUNTY

Foster	unk	Check property records
James Family	37.35835, -76.33166	End of Bar Neck Rd, Susan
Old Billups	unk	Rt 643, Moon
Page Home	unk	North portion of Co
Richard Foster	unk	Rt 650, Hicks Wharf Rd, Rose Hill Plantation
St James Church	unk	Mathews CH
Toddsbury Plantation	unk	Elmington
Trinity Episcopal	37.41069, -76.33578	Off Rt 614 nr jct Khyber Pass Trail
Turner Family	unk	Rt 14, W end Horn Branch
White Family (Whitehaven)	unk	160 Pine View Dr
Williams Family	38.56808, -77.33511	Williams Wharf

MECKLENBURG COUNTY

Andrews Family	36.78894, -78.13494	Whittles Mill Rd, South Hill
Bennett Family	unk	Check property records
Boyd Family	unk	Behind Health Dept Bldg, Boyton
Boyd Family	unk	Hwy 895, end of Rt 875
Boydton Presbyterian	36.40101, -78.23127	Boydton
Burwell Family	unk	Stoneland
Canaan Methodist	36.66848, -78.05323	Jct Blackridge Rd & Canaan Church Rd
Gregory Family	unk	Jct Rts 655 & 657
Invernay Family Center	unk	Rt 138 at Invernay Post Office
Keen Family	unk	Rt 92
Lewis Family	unk	Rt 727
Munfort-Lockett Family	unk	Nr Boydton, see Source 72
Overby-Holt Family	unk	Rt 602 W
Petties Family	unk	Chase City

(MECKLENBURG COUNTY, CONTINUED)

Prestwould	unk	Clarksville
Rainey Family	unk	Rt 627
Speed Family	unk	Check property records
St James Episcopal	36.66626, -78.38683	Boydton
White-Yancey-Jones Family	unk	Rt 49 S fr Chase City, left on 697 at Reese's old store, 2.5 mi on right at old homeplace
Whittle-Davis Family	unk	Left of old Whittle House off Hwy 636
William A. Andrews 1400 acres	36.78894, -78.13494	South Hill
Yancey Family	unk	Hwy 736 S fr 602 abt 2.5 mi, Averett
Young-Brame Family	unk	5 mi E of Boydton, 1 mi S of Antlers

MIDDLESEX COUNTY

Christ Church	37.60968, -76.54643	Rt 33 2 mi E of Saluda
Clark's Neck	unk	Check property records
Landsdowne House	unk	Virginia St, Urbanna
Providence Burial Ground	unk	Waterview

MONTGOMERY COUNTY

Barger Family	unk	Blacksburg
Barnett Family	36.80751, -80.15219	Alleghany Spring Rd, Sisson Farm
Blacksburg	unk	Nr Blacksburg
Boothe Family	unk	Little River, Christiansburg
Broce-Kenser	37.23061, -80.45373	Boxwood Dr, Blacksburg
Craig	unk	Christiansburg
Craig Family	37.13390, -80.39220	East Park Ln
Fortheringay	37.19101, -80.23193	Nr Graham St, Shawsville
Harless Family	37.21331, -80.54910	Vic jct Rt 744 & Long Shop Rd, Blacksburg
Henderson	unk	Catawba Rd Rt 785 Blacksburg
Howard-Palmer	37.05575, -80.50448	4165 Piney Woods Rd, behind House, Childress
Lester	37.11698, -80.25156	S fr Riner
Lucas Family or Old Cooper	unk	S or E fr Riner
Mack Creek Village	unk	W fr Snowvilleon Lead Mine Rd abt 5 mi to Little River Dam Rd, then N .7 mi, on left just past Burleigh Ln
Madison	unk	Shawsville
Meacham Family	unk	Nr Christiansburg
Montgomery Family	unk	Vic Christianburg
Mt Pleasant Church	37.13289, -80.30640	1024 Mt Pleasant Rd, Shawsville
Oakley-Altizer	unk	Chestnut Ridge, Riner
Rural	unk	Maxwell Gap
Rural	unk	Reed Creek
Smithfield Plantation	unk	VMI Campus, Blacksburg
Sunset	37.12390, -80.40420	South Franklin near 1-81, Christiansburg
Watterson Family	unk	Christiansburg
Westview	37.23390, -80.40830	Blacksburg
White	37.15829, -80.25423	Rt 637, S of Shawsville

NELSON COUNTY

Cabell Family	unk	Edgewood, 3008 Warminster Dr, Wingina
Cabell Family	unk	Norwood
Clarkson-Meeks, aka Clarkson #2	unk	5 mi N of Massies Mill cross Tye River Bridge
Coffey Family	unk	Cub Creek Rd Rt 789, Tyro

(NELSON COUNTY, CONTINUED)

Cub Creek	unk	Off Cub Creek Rd Rt 789 at Beech Grove Community
Estes Family	unk	Check property records and DAR 1959 Senate Doc serial 12260 vol 5
Fairmont Baptist	unk	3948 Findlay Gap Dr, Shipley
Fortune	unk	Lovingston
Hill Family	unk	Cub Creek Rd Rt 789, Tyro
Jones-Clarkson	37.79438, -78.98530	Persimmon Hill Rd, Roseland
Level Green	unk	Massies Mill
Lovings Gap	unk	Lovington
Martin Family	unk	Check property records
Montgomery Family	unk	Nellysford, near Wintergreen
Old Bardstown City	unk	Bardstown
Rockfish Presbyterian	unk	5016 Rockfish Valley Hwy, Nellysford
Soldier's Joy	unk	Wingina
Tilford Cub Creek	unk	Cub Creek Rd Rt 789, Tyro
Tompkins Family	unk	Shipman at Burk Homestead
Warminster	37.68360, -78.69420	Warminster, Norwood
Wintergreen	unk	Rt 151 beyond Nellysford
Woods Family	unk	Rockfish Presbyterian S of Afton

NEW KENT COUNTY

Littlepage	unk	Nr Pamunkey R, Cumberland
Meredith Family	unk	Check property records
St Peter's Episcopal	unk	8400 St Peters Ln, Quinton

NEWPORT NEWS CITY (formerly Warwick County)

Denbigh United Presbyterian	unk	302 Denbigh Blvd
Peartree Hall	unk	Nr Warwick Hall CH and Tabbs Ln
Windmill Point	unk	N of jct Warwick River and Lucas Creek and S of Rt 173

NORFOLK CITY

Cedar Grove	36.85860, -76.28310	238 E Princess Anne Rd
Dick Warren Farm	unk	Lake Drummond
Harvey Family	unk	Not identified
Old Massenburgh	unk	South Norfolk
Sanderson Home	unk	Near NC line
St Paul's Episcopal	36.84733, 76.28554	201 St Paul's Blvd

NORTHAMPTON COUNTY

Brownsville Family	unk	.25 mi N on Rt 600 fr Exmore
Cherry Grove	unk	Rt 634
Cugley	unk	Rt 634
Darby's Wharf Farm	unk	Nr Shields Bridge, Belle Haven
Fatherly Farm	unk	Wierwood
Kendall Grove	unk	Rt 674
Kings Creek	unk	Cape Charles
Long Point Farm	unk	Rt 711
Maria Robins House	unk	1 mi N of center of Eastville
Old Thomas Farm	unk	N of Rt 617, NW of Weirwood
Poplar Hill	unk	Rt 631, Cherrystone
Red Bank Church	unk	Jct Rts 600 & 617
Scarburgh Farm	unk	Opposite jct Rts 601 & 683,across field to old house "Scarborough"

(NORTHAMPTON COUNTY, CONTINUED)

Selma	unk	E of Bus Rt 13, .4 mi N of Rt 631 Eastville
Tankard's Rest	unk	Exmore
Wescott Farm	unk	Rt 606 NW of Nassawadox

NORTHUMBERLAND COUNTY

Ball Family	37.45912, -76.19536	Cress Field, Bay View on Balls Neck
Cox Homestead	unk	Cherry Point
Hayfield	unk	Nr Callao
Haynie Family	unk	Heathsville
Northumberland House	37.50310, -76. 26194	Cod's Creek, off of Rt 360
Roseland	37.51131, -76.16576	Reedville
Smith Family	unk	Mantua Farm Rd

NOTTOWAY COUNTY

Blendon	37.14110, -78.08030	Rt F656 & Rt 460 Nottoway Court House Rd
Dupuy	unk	Jennings Ordinary, NW 647 for 1 mi to Carrington home
Lakeview	37.07091, -78.01143	8th St, Blackstone
The Old Place	unk	5 mi NW of Blackstone
Wards Chapel	unk	Crewe
Williams Family	38.56808, -77.33511	See 1938 DAR Senate doc 10448, vol 2

ORANGE COUNTY

Blue Run Baptist	unk	Rt 20 N of jct with Rt 655, Barboursville
Brockman Family	unk	Greenway, Monrovia
Campbell Family	unk	Campbellton near Barboursville
Cowherd Family, "Oak Hill"	unk	Gordonsville
Dade Family	unk	Rose Hill
Ellwood Burial Ground	unk	Wilderness Battlefield
Greenfields Family	38.25335, -78.10039	Rt 2021, back of cem on Madex Dr
Green-Level Family	unk	Rt 663 S of True Blue Corners
Holloway Family	unk	Orange
Lidsay Family, Springfield Farm	unk	W fr Gordonsville
Mansfield Family	unk	Nr Barboursville
Maplewood	38.14640, -78.20060	Rt 33 W Gordonsville
Montpelier	unk	11407 Constitution Hwy, Montpelier Station
Mount Valley	unk	Vic jct Rts 663 & 522
New Hope	unk	Orange
Oak Green Farm #1	unk	Rt 663 nr Palmyra Church
Rose Hill	unk	Rapidan
Schuler Place	unk	Rt 705
Scott Family	unk	Madison Run
Soldier's Rest Plantation	unk	Rt 620
Taylor Family, Meadow Farm	38.22898, -78.07895	16823 Monrovia Rd
Unidentified	unk	Gordonsville
Westover United Methodist	38.28130, -78.38607	2801 Fredericksburg Rd
Williams Family, "Soldier's Rest Farm"	unk	Rt 620

PAGE COUNTY

Aleshire Family	unk	E of Rt 616, 8 mi S of Luray, in back of canning factory
Beaver-Brubaker, Mauck's Mill	39.18343, -78.16278	Rt 615, vic Luray
Courtney Family	unk	Nr N Bank Hamshill Creek
Fairview	unk	Rileyville, 7 mi fr Luray

(PAGE COUNTY, CONTINUED)

Grove Family	unk	Meadow Mills off Rt 340, S fr Luray
Grove Family	unk	Slade Farm Rt 615 near Luray, Bixler's Ferry
James Varner Family	unk	SE of Luray
Jollett	unk	Rt 609 N of Jollett
Keyser Family	unk	Rt 684 NW fr Luray 8 mi
Long Family Price Farm	unk	Rt 616, Alma
Offenbacher	unk	Nr Stanley
Printz or Prince Family	unk	Rt 651 nr Ida
Rileyville	38.76610, -78.38610	At end of Cemetery Rd, Luray
Robert T Kemp Farm	unk	Luray
Ruffner Family	unk	Rt 211, Luray
Spring Farm	unk	2 mi NE of Luray on Turnpike
Strickler Monument	unk	SW side of Rts 615 & 211, Ft Egypt
Wood-Conn	unk	Rileyville, 9 mi from Luray

PATRICK COUNTY

Adams-Graves-Pilson Families	unk	.5 mi south of Rt 717, N side of Goblintown Creek nr Fairystone Park
Bryant Family	unk	Charity, behind Heidelbach School
Creasey's Chapel	unk	Stuart
Critz Baptist Church	unk	3294 Dogwood Rd, Critz
Delionback Home	36.34040, -80.33240	End of Rt 749 on Ararat River
Edward Lewis	unk	Nr Heidleback School, Rt 712 Dodson
Eliphaz Shelton-Pilson Family	unk	Main St, Stuart
Green Hill Primitive Baptist	unk	Patrick Springs
Hughesville	unk	Hwy 631 nr Stuart
John Conner Family	unk	200 yds W of jct Rts 616 & 826
Lewis Family	unk	712 Heidleback School Rd, Dodson
Liberty Primitive Baptist	36.69494, -80.16269	Patrick Springs
Patrick Henry Allied Memorial	unk	Fairy Stone State Park
Poplar Grove	unk	W on Rt 626 off Rt 627 Co Line Rd, nr Critz
Ross Harbour Methodist	unk	6260 Elamsville Rd, Stuart
Stuart Town	unk	Chestnut St, Stuart
Thompson-Salmons-McAlexander	unk	Rt 719 Woolwine
Varner Family	unk	Nr jct Rts 696 & 626, btw Critz & Salem Church, Locust Grove

PETERSBURG CITY

Bass Family	unk	Bass St, Appomattox River at Exeter Mills
Blandford	37.22433, -77.38604	319 S Crater Rd

PITTSYLVANIA COUNTY (See also Danville City)

Alta Vista Plantation	unk	Altavista
Berger Burial Ground	36.92909, -79.25041	Rt 685, or plot on Rt 927 E of Chalk Level, E fr Gretna 6 mi
Bergers	36.95748, -79.48408	Nr Siloan Church nr Rt 605
Boaze Family	36.71055, -79.55003	1148 Couny Rd 945, Dry Fork
Brightwood	unk	Marilla Ln, Chatham
Buckley Family	36.95506, -79.14145	Rt 40, Mt Airy
Bullington Family	unk	Nr Sandy River
Callands Family	36.85587, -79.62549	NE of Callands
Chatham	36.81900, -79.39900	Ennis Dr, Chatham
Cheney Family	unk	Nr Keeling

(PITTSYLVANIA COUNTY, CONTINUED)

Clark Family	36.84823, -79.32198	Pineville nr Chatham
Clement Hill	unk	Rt 29 N, btw Chatham & Hurt
Clopton Family	unk	Slatesville Rd, N of jct US Rt 360
Coleman Family	unk	Nr Riceville
Coleman Family	unk	Off Yeats Store Rd, Java
Coles	36.54722, -79.16470	8 mi NE of Chatham. Off Rt 690 (Source 76) or Rt 685 at Chalk Level, Java (Source 101)
Davis Family	unk	Cherrystone Plantation
Dews Family	unk	13 mi SE of Gretna Rt 677
Easley Family	unk	Callands
Fitts	36.58428, -79.69962	Rt 621 off Rt 610, Aiken Summit
Fitzgerald Family	36.80353, -79.24233	1 mi E of Shockoe on Rt 832
George Family	unk	Gretna
Glenrock	36.80060, -79.44548	E of Rt 824, .5 mi S of Greenbuck Branch
GSA Camp Shawnee	unk	Ringgold
Hampton Family	unk	Cascade
Harris Family	unk	SR 816 or on Rt 703,10 mi fr Chatham nr Chatham HS
Hopkins	unk	Behind Thomas Muse house near Franklin Co Line, Sago
Hubbard-Stone	unk	Rt 650 Hermosa
Hunt	37.00709, -79.22413	Rt 640 Mount Airy nr Renan
Hutchings, Jack Crane Farm	36.74674, -79.42226	Rt 718 Dry Fork
Jones Family	36.84300, -79.26227	Nr Mtn Top, 7 mi E of Chatham
Keesee Family	36.87683, -79.52109	Nr Green Pond
Locust Bottom	37.74148, -79.81456	Jct Rts 633 & 696
Mill Meeting House	unk	Nr Chatham
Mitchell Family	unk	Chatham
Morgan Family	unk	Nr White Falls, Banister River
Motley Family	unk	Nr Chatham
Mustain Barn	36.56637, -79.18520	Btw Gretna & Mt Airy, private property behind barn
Pigg Mill Farm	36.77373, -79.46067	Rt 703, Jones Mill
Pine Creek	unk	Not identified in SAR registration
Richardson-Yates Family	unk	Ringhold
Robertson Family	unk	Dry Fork
Rock Wall	unk	Dry Fork
Shockoe Baptist	36.80960, -79.26590	Rt 640, Chatham
Stone Family	unk	Nr Mulberry Church
Towler Family	unk	Nr Anthony's Ford
Walton Family	unk	probably "Whitmel"
Ward	37.05492, -79.43637	Hurt
West Plantation	unk	Straightstone
William Atkins Family	unk	Rt 649 nr Cooper's Store, Callands
Williams Family	unk	SR 698 Cliff Hetzel Farm, Pickway
Witcher Family	unk	Nr Sandy Level Post Office
Worsham Family	unk	Check property records
Wray Family	unk	Check property records

PORTSMOUTH CITY

Cedar Grove	36.57204, -80.02599	301 Fort Lane Rd
Cedar Grove	36.83860, -76.30810	Salter St
Court Street Baptist	unk	447 Court St
Glasgow Street Park	unk	425 Glasgow St
Lincoln Memorial	36.80830, -76.32810	Jct Kirby St and Deep Creek Blvd
Trinity Episcopal	36.83459, -76.30105	500 Court St

POWHATAN COUNTY

Dabney, Montpelier	unk	Maiden's Rd, abt 2 mi N of Anderson Hwy, E side of rd, N of Montpelier Plantation
Elioch Manor Family	unk	Elioch Manor Dr, end of rd
Manakin	37.56560, -77.71000	Rt 711 vic jct Rt 635
Mosby Family	unk	Powhatan
Muddy Creek Baptist	unk	3470 Rt 629, Powhatan
Old Hobson	unk	Blenheim, nr Balleville
Patrick Harris Homesite	unk	Dirt Rd off Rt 614 abt 3 mi
Petersville	37.56440, -77.96470	Off Rt 60
Rural	unk	Powhatan

PRINCE EDWARD COUNTY

Allen Family	unk	Vic Farmville
Allen-Watkins Family	unk	Farmville
Clover Forest	unk	3 mi W of Farmville nr Sandy Fork Bridge
Hampden-Sydney College	unk	Hampden-Sydney campus
Leigh Family	unk	Base of Leigh Mountain, Farmville
Venable-Slate Hill Plantation	unk	Worsham
Westview	unk	Farmville
Woodson Family	unk	Farmville
Worsham Family Square	37.32163, -78.44328	Vic Rts 665 & 15 Farmville Rd, Worsham

PRINCE GEORGE COUNTY

Aldridge Family	unk	Off Rt 607, 2 mi E of Rt 654
Bicars	unk	75 yds behind house on private road off Rt 641, Huntington
Bland Family	unk	2 mi E of Hopewell on Rt 10, 1.2 mi N on Rt 36, then 10 ft E
Brandon Plantation	37.15271, -76.59362	Burrowsville
Eppes Family	unk	Off Rt 616, 3.9 mi SE of jct with Rt 37
Harrison Family	unk	5.5 mi NE Burrowsville
Harrison-Pinkards	unk	4.5 mi E Prince George, then N
Heath Family	unk	See Senate Doc 1938 serial 10448 vol 2
Kirkham Family	unk	1.2 mi N of Disputana
Nathaniel Lee Home	unk	NE of Carson
Ruffin Family, Tar Bay House	unk	4 mi E of Hopewell
Salem Methodist Church	unk	19312 Templeton Rd
Tooker Family, Brandon Home	unk	5 mi NE of Burrowsville

PRINCE WILLIAM COUNTY (See also Manassas City)

Bacon Race	38.69145, -77.46439	Davis Ford Rd & Bacon Race Rd
Beaver Family	38.66118, -77.47324	13380 Bristol Rd, Nokesville
Blackburn-Atkinson	38.36878, -77.16685	Rippon Lodge off Rt 638, Woodbridge
Brawner	unk	Rt 1 at Potomac HS
Camp Glen Kirk	38.77367, -77.62360	Gainesville, Rt 29 N, Linter Hall Rd
Carver	38.52735, -77.56054	Rt 610 vic jct with Rt 612
Clarke Family	unk	Nr Woodbridge PO, Woodbridge
Davis Family	unk	Wolf Run Shoals Rd
Dumfries Public	38.34110, -77.19964	17821 Mine Rd, Dumfries
Effingham Plantation	38.38393, -77.31290	1 mi E of Adan, 14325 Trotter's Ridge Place, Nokesville
Ewell-Weems	unk	Rt 640
Fitzhugh Plantation	unk	Check property records
Flourance Family	38.71577, -77.46386	Lake Jackson

(PRINCE WILLIAM COUNTY, CONTINUED)

Grayson	38.64775, -77.27648	West Longview Dr, Woodbridge
Henderson	unk	Mountclair
Howison Family	38.63313, -77.38399	Minniville Rd
Lane Family	unk	Cement Rd
Leesylvania Plantation	38.35240, -77.15200	On a ridge overlooking Occoquan Bay, Woodbridge
Luckett	unk	Nr Quantico Marine Base
Maddox	unk	Hope Hill Crossing Subdiv, Hope Hill Rd
Norvall Family	unk	Nr Dumfries
Tebbsdale Plantation	unk	Rt 633 off US 1 Dumfries
Wheeler-Greenville Family	38.47755, -77.32458	7300 Old Compton Rd

PULASKI COUNTY

Bell Family, Dunkards Bottom	37.05702, -80.62087	Claytor Lake State Park, Dublin
Bell Farm	unk	Dublin
Caddall	unk	Thornspring Farm
Cecil Family	unk	Nr Radford and Dublin
Cecil Family Farm #2	unk	Neck's Creek, Belspring
Cloyd	37.16166, -80.70583	Rt 100 Cleyburne Blvd N of Dublin
Honaker	unk	Draper
Patton Family	unk	nr Dublin
Sunnyside	unk	Btw Radford and Dublin at Old Joseph Howe place, Back Creek
Unidentified	unk	Snowville
Wysor	unk	Dublin

RAPPAHANNOCK COUNTY

Browning Family	unk	Nr Salem Baptist Ch
Corder-Pierce Family	unk	Amissville
Dearing Family	unk	Caledonia Farm, 47 Dearing Rd, Flint Hill
Elijah Anderson	38.45380, -77.5833	27 Shurgen Ln, Amissvile
Hot Mountain	unk	Nethers
Lutheran	unk	Washington
Major-Corbin	38.65282, -78.02353	Rt 642 Viewtown Rd nr jct with Ida Belle Ln, Amissville
Masonic Cemetery	unk	Rt 522, Washington
Miller	unk	Rt 248, Harris Hollow, Washington
Miller, Mountain Green	unk	Washington
Pierce Family	unk	Rt 211, Amissville
Slate Mills	unk	Vic Woodville
Slaughter Family, "Clover Hill"	unk	Woodville, Hawthorne
Tapp-Griffin Families	unk	Vic Amissville
Unidentified	unk	Amissville
Wadefield-Strother Family	unk	Nr Washington
Woodard	unk	James Woodard Farm, off Co Rd 600 in field N of "Caboose Pond"

RICHMOND CITY

Hebrew	33.55175, -77.42976	300 Hospital St
Hollywood	37.53560, -77.45720	412 S Cherry St
Monumental Church	unk	1224 E Broad St
Patteson Family	unk	Laurel Meadows
Shockoe Hill	37.55190, -77.43170	4th & Hospital Sts
St John's Episcopal	37.53183 -77.41958	2401 E Broad St
Unidentified	37.32337, -77.26132	Nr State Capitol

RICHMOND COUNTY

Beale Family	unk	Chestnut Hill, E of Ethel
Belfield Family	unk	2804 County Bridge Rd, Warsaw
Doctor's Hall	unk	Nr jct Rappahannock River & Creek
Farnham Episcopal	unk	231 N Farnham Church Rd, Farnham
Lower Lunenburg Parish	37.96066, -76.76920	Off N side Rt 360, Warsaw
Mims Family	unk	Licking Hole Creek Farm
Muse Family	unk	Check property records
North Farnham Episcopal	unk	Farnham
Tayloe Family	37.58200, -76.4729	Mt Airy, Rt 360, Warsaw

ROANOKE CITY (See also Roanoke County)

Belmont	unk	Frank Rd, Roanoke
Old German	unk	Roanoke
Old Lick, aka First Baptist	37.28250, -79.93690	Hart Ave btw 2nd & 4th St

ROANOKE COUNTY (See also Roanoke City and Salem City)

Deyerle Family	unk	W part of Co
Esom Family	unk	Nr Cave Spring
Greenwood Family	unk	Cave Springs
King	unk	Bent Mtn, S fr Roanoke
Old German	unk	Roanoke
Old Lick, aka First Baptist	37.28250, -79.93690	Hart Ave btw 2nd & 4th St, Roanoke
Poage's Mill	37.19800, -80.05600	Rt 221, Bent Mtn Rd, Poages Mill village
Vinyard Family	unk	Lauderale Ave
Vinyard Family	unk	Vinton
Weddle Family	unk	Bent Mtn

ROCKBRIDGE COUNTY (See also Lexington County)

Alone Community, aka Bethany Lutheran	unk	Rts 602 & 525, Kerrs Dist part 6
Bennington-Gaylor	unk	Waterloo Rd
Broad Creek-Miller	unk	Buffalo Dist
Dryden Family	unk	See DAR Senate Doc 1958 serial 12259, vol 4
Falling Springs Presbyterian	37.68494, -79.45105	410 Falling Springs Rd, Glasgow
Glasgow Cemetery	37.60320, -79.45914	13th St & Fitzlee, Glasgow
Hattan Family	unk	Rt 629, behind house on Frances Hostetters property, Kerrs Dist
High Bridge Presbyterian	37.62420, -79.58610	67 High Bridge Rd, Natural Bridge
McDowell	37.86860, -79.31080	Nr jct Rts 11 & 712, Fairfield
McDowell Family	39.18410, -78.16278	10 mi N Lexington on Rt 11
McKee, aka Big Springs	unk	Clarence Hardy's farm, off Rt 60, on Rt 631, Kerrs Distr
Mt Zion Methodist	37.66596, -79.46615	Btw Buffalo & Tinkersville
Muse, aka Irvine Family, Timber Grove, or Timber Ridge Presbyterian	unk	9 mi N of Lexington off Rt 11, SW of jct Rts 11 & 716, 73 Sam Huston Way, Buffalo Dist
Neriah Baptist	37.78778, -79.36482	Jct Rts 631 & 706, South River
New Providence Presbyterian	37.95130, -79.30250	1208 New Providence Rd, Raphine
Old Anderson farm	unk	W Buffalo Rd
Old Monmouth Presbyterian	37.80810, -79.47280	Jct Rts 60 & 669
Old Stone Presbyterian	unk	73 Sam Huston Way
Oxford Presbyterian	37.75302, -79.56023	18 Churchview Ln, Lexington
Paxton Family	37.71666, -79.40271	Forge Rd, Mechanicsville
Stuart Family	unk	Rt 727, Blackwells property
Taylor Family	unk	Short Hill Mountain

(ROCKBRIDGE COUNTY, CONTINUED)

Timber Grove	unk	Buffalo Dist, Timber Ridge
Timber Ridge Presbyterian	37.84200, -79.35800	Nr jct Rts 11 & 716, Timber Ridge
Unidentified, Old Graveyard	unk	Nr Wesley Chapel, Glasgow
Unidentified, Private Graveyard	unk	Nr St Stephens Church, Goshen
Walker Creek	unk	Walker Creek
Walkerland, Maxwelton Farm	37.94613, -79.38794	Vic jct Rts 602 & 724, behind Maxwelton Cabins
Youel Family, Meadow Lawn Farm	unk	Rt 601, Goshen

ROCKINGHAM COUNTY

Bear Family	unk	Bear Lithia Spr
Bethel Cemetery	38.47592, -78.75641	3061 Armentrout Path, Keezletown
Bible Family	unk	Dull Hunt Rd at Fulks Run
Bowman Family	unk	War Branch, Peaked Mountain Rt 726 abt 1 mi fr jct with Rt 613 on private rd
Brenneman Mennonite	38.62620, -78.87588	Brenneman Church Rd
Brock Family	36.71055, -79.55003	2401 Indian Trail Rd, Keezletown 22832
Crawford Family #2	unk	Rt 726 .6 mi fr jct with Rt 613 on Sam Brown property, Peaked Mountain
Cross Keys	unk	Cross Keys
Custer Family	unk	Dry River S of Rt 259, Fulks Run
Dayton	38.42000, -78.94303	Bowman Rd, Dayton
Early	38.39536, -78.90465	3588 Early Rd, Pleasant Valley
East Point	unk	Rt 602 left fr Rt 33 E, Elkton
Elk Run	38.41042, -78.61033	North St, Elkton
Fishback Family	unk	Dayton
Friedens United Church of Christ	38.34848, -78.87653	3960 Friedens Church Rd
Greenwood	38.38470, -78.97610	Vic Green St & North Grove St, Bridgewater
Harley Good Farm	unk	Brock's Gap, SW side of SR 259
Harrison Family, Smith's Creek	38.4200, -78.94303	Nr Lacey Springs
Hilltop-Yancey Farm	unk	Elkton
Holsinger Family	38.61139, -78.76164	2805 Holsinger Rd, Broadway
James Meadows Sr. Family	unk	5130 Bear Foot Ln, Elkton
Keezletown	unk	Keezletown
Kline Family	38.58118, -78.82895	Rt 1415 nr Broadway
Kring Salvage	unk	Off John Deere Dr, behind Harman Machinery, Broadway
Lacey Springs	38.54475, -78.77072	Lacey Springs
Lewis Family	unk	Rts 708 & 340
Lincoln Family	36.68726, -82.56917	7884 Harpine Rd Rt 42, Linville, 3 mi S of Broadway on SR 42, N of Edom exit
Lindale Mennonite	unk	Jesse Bennett Way, Linville
Maiden Homestead	unk	Bedor Rd Rt 628, .3 mi fr Rt 33 in Elkton, walk up hill abt .5 mi
Mallow Family	unk	McGaheysville
Massanutten Cross Keys	38.35817, -78.84124	Rt 679 at Cross Keys, vic jct Rts 276 & 679
May Family	unk	May Creek Ln, Criders, Bergton
Moore Family	unk	Timberville
Moyer Family	38.48315,-78.55285	Crab Run Rd, nr Bergton
Mt Olivet Church of Brethren	unk	2977 Pineville Rd, McGayesville
Northern Methodist	38.35777, -78.94344	Rt 867 Old Bridgewater Rd, Mt Crawford
Old Peaked Mountain	38.37113, -78.73416	9843 Town Hall Rd, McGaheysville
Old Weaver Church	38.44868, -78.90463	Harrisonville
Rader Lutheran	38.65073, -78.78055	17072 Raders Church Rd, Timberville
Rhodes (Roth) Family	unk	Vic Broadway Rt 42

(ROCKINGHAM COUNTY, CONTINUED)

Rice Fam	unk	Rt 743 W of Dayton
Salem Presbyterian	unk	Cooks Creek
Smith Family	unk	Rt 727
Spears Family	unk	N of Edom Rt 42 7.3 mi
Thomas Family	unk	Nr Timberville
Trout or Kline family	unk	5180 Trissels Rd, Broadway
Union Church	unk	Rt 679 Battlefield Rd
Woodbine	unk	Cnr of E Market St and Ott St, Harrisonburg
Yount Family	unk	Rts 253 & 278, 2.8 mi E

RUSSELL COUNTY

Bickley Family	36.88530, -82.27780	Rt 615 across fr Rt 640, Castlewood
Dickinson Family	unk	Nr Old Courthouse
Dorton	unk	Rt 71 near Dickensonville
Elk Garden	unk	Red Wine Plantation, Elk Garden
Kelly	36.95690, -82.09360	Off Rt 621 on Sandy Ridge, nr home of Rev & Mrs Gonan Kelly
Reynolds Family	unk	Hammonville
Soloman Litton Hollow	unk	nr Pinnacle Preserve
Tate-Burdine	unk	Lebanon
Thomas Family	unk	Poor Farm Rd, Lebanon
Unidentified	unk	Morefield
Whitt Family	unk	Rt 646, W fr Honaker

SALEM CITY (See also Roanoke County)

Garst Family	unk	Kesler Mill Rd up hill near RR tracks
Walton Family	unk	Nr Ft Lewis
West Hill	37.29313, -80.06753	Boon St

SCOTT COUNTY

Blue Spring	36.65967, -82.41181	Hiltons Area
Brown Family	unk	Eagle hills
Carter Family	unk	Rt 649, Rye Cove
Cocke Family	unk	Ft Blackmore
England	36.60323, -82.94029	Looneys Gap #14
Freeman Family	unk	Rt778, Weber City
Godsey Family	unk	Rt 613, Nickelsville
Hensley	36.64426, -82.71960	Sleepy Hollow Ln
Jones Family	36.61690, -82.68580	Rt 635, Yuma, across RR and E of Cowan Branch Baptist Ch
Lawson Confederate Memorial	36.68728, -82.50114	Rt 71, Snowflake
Livingston Family	36.67987, -82.35273	Rt 689, Mendota
Pendleton	36.67145, -82.66248	Rt 664, Manville
Porter Family	unk	Rt 682 Dungannon
Spurrier Family	unk	Rt 691, Hiltons
Stallard-Moore	36.81155, -82.46172	Nr jct Rts 780 & 671 nr Nickelsville, Dungannon
Vineyard	unk	Gate City
Wood	36.71720, -82.36940	Rt 613

SHENANDOAH COUNTY

Arthur Hirsh Family	unk	Nr New Market
Boehm	unk	Nr Clary
Buckton Family	unk	1 mi W of Buckton Station
Clover Hill	unk	Saumsville

(SHENANDOAH COUNTY, CONTINUED)

Coffman's Rivermont Farm, Rhodes Family	38.91623, -78.41480	Fisher Rd Rt 649 to end of state maintenance
Conicville School	38.8938, -78.69532	Off Rt 703, SW of Conicville nr Swover Crk
David Kagy Farm	unk	Nr New Market
Dellinger Family	38.5037, -78.4054	Madison Dist, Conicville
Dry Run Church	38.85929, -78.40075	Rt 678, Ft Valley Rd nr jct with Dry Run Rd, Seven Fountains
Frye Family	unk	Wheatfield
Funk Family	unk	behind Travel Trailer Park, vic Strasburg
Funkhouser Family	38.801981, -78.78390	Resort Dr Rt 835, Basye
Funkhouser Family	unk	Mt Jackson
Funkhouser Family	unk	Vic Fishers Hill
Funkhouser Family	unk	Waxwing Ln on Shipe farm
Garber Family	unk	Vic Moores Store
Grandstaff Family	unk	Narrow Pass Creek
Keller	38.56480, -78.46220	Tom's Brook, nr Mt Olive
Keller Family	38.49457, -78.25335	Burner Ln off Fort Valley Rd
Keller Family	38.96580, -78.46220	Sand Ridge Rd, Mt Olive
Miller Family	unk	Woodstock
Mt Solomon's Lutheran	38.44180, -78.44201	Solomon Church Rd & Rt 42, Forestville
Mt Zion United Methodist	unk	399 W Queens St, Strasburg
Neff Family	unk	Vic Stonewall Jackson HS
Neff-Kagey	38.69443, -78.65895	Rt 827, Old Bridge Rd, New Market
Old Bethel	38.79113, -78.58904	Off Old Bethel Rd Rt 700, Edinburg
Old St Mary's	unk	Mt Jackson
Philllips	unk	Edinburg
Rinker	unk	Conicville
Riverview	38.98420, -78.36140	Grounds of Riverview HS, Strasburg
St Martin's Lutheran	38.64480, -78.67124	2235 River Rd, New Market
St Mary Pine Lutheran	38.74470, -78.68390	7103 S Middle Rd, Mt Jackson
St Mathew's	36.65131, -78.67121	Breckenridge Ln, New Market
St Paul's Lutheran	38.99140, -78.36250	156 W Washington, Strasburg
St Paul's Reformed Church	38.87780, -78.50663	Cnr S Church Sr & E South St, Woodstock
Stickley Family	unk	Strasburg
Union Church	38.44480, -78.38350	Mt Jackson nr jct Main St & Bridge St
Woodstock	unk	Woodstock
Zirkle Family	38.65900, -78.69580	River Rd, New Market

SMYTH COUNTY

Allison	36.91140, -81.75170	W of plaster mine, Locust Cove Rd private property with closed gate, E of Saltville
Aspenvale	36.81420, -81.64000	Rts 641 & 642, Seven Mile Ford
Bowen Family	36.81420, -81.64000	Aspenvale
Brody Family	unk	Saltville
Buchanan Family	36.95610, -81.54470	New Cove, E of Saltville
Greever	36.79250, -81.69860	Rt 1019 off Rt 11, Chilhowie
Harmon Family	36.95470, -81.40080	Rt 610 Old Valley Rd, S of Hamon Creek nr Bland Co line
Lamie Family	unk	2 mi E of Saltville
Locust Grove	unk	W fr Chatham Hill
Morgan	unk	Rye Valley
Morgan Family	36.76690, -81.43750	1.5 mi fr Teas on private rd beyond Rt 601
Mt Zion Church	36.83461, -81.59338	Old Ebenezer Rd, Marioin
Old Grewer (Greever) Burial Ground	36.79250, -81.69860	W end of Skyview Dr, Chilhowie
Old Shannon Place	38.53999, -77.55610	Head of Long Hollow, Rich Valley

(SMYTH COUNTY, CONTINUED)

Rich Valley Presbyterian	36.90248, -81.62490	3811 Valley Rd, Saltville
Richardson	36.93250, 81.53360	Rt 610 Valley Rd
Riverbend	unk	Vic jct Rts 650 & 660
Royal Oak	36.84315, -81.49660	Behind Marion Baptist Church, Marion
Scott	unk	Blue Springs
St Clair Bottom Primitive Baptist	36.76098, -81.64556	Jct Rts 600 & 660, Chilhowie
Tate Family	unk	Nr Buchanan House, Broadford
Totten Family	unk	Vic jct Rts 610 & 687

SOUTHAMPTON COUNTY (See also Franklin City)

Boykin Family	unk	Rt 460, across river fr Zuni
Ferguson Family	unk	31356 Rochelle Swamp Rd, Vic Newsoms
George Cary Family	unk	4.5 mi W of Courtland
Jerico	unk	Courtland
Mason Family	unk	Rt 612 Fortsville Rd, 4 mi NW of Adam Grove
Stephenson Family	unk	Clayton Rd

SPOTSYLVANIA COUNTY

Alsop	unk	Lake View Estates subdivision in small grove, Snow Hill
Ballard Family	unk	Nr Catherine Furnace, see property records
Bellefonte	unk	Leiston
Belvoir House	unk	Jct Rts 608 E & 635
Brooke Family	unk	Rt 2, 6 mi N Fredericksburg, E side of St Julian house
Cowlands Site	unk	Rt 613
Elmwood	unk	Rt 614
Fairview	unk	Rt 3
Gordon Herndon	38.15467, -77.65341	Rt 656 S off Rt 208, Post Oak
Green Level	unk	Rt 652
Greenfield	unk	Fawn Lake Pwy
Hamilton Family	unk	Rt 636
Laurel Hill, Nywood Farm	unk	Rt 210 3.3 mi E of CH
Martin Family, Germantown	unk	Rt 3 Germantown
Meadow Hill Estate	unk	Off Rt 613, 1.8 mi N of Luck's Store
Minor Family	unk	Rt 633, nr Locust Grove homeplace
Page Family	unk	Mansfield Hall
Pine Cliff	38.28920, -77.64577	Vic jct Jackson Trail Rd and Military Park Rd
Prospect Hill	unk	Waller Rd nr Forest Green, Partlow
Shady Grove Methodist	unk	11007 W Catharpin, Shady Grove Cnr
Stanard (Stanfield) Family	unk	Rt 646
Vauxhall Site	unk	Rt 607
Wallace	38.15972, -77.79558	8630 Peppertree Rd, Wilderness Cnr

STAFFORD COUNTY

Aquia Episcopal	38.46466, -77.40325	2938 Jeff Davis Hwy, Aquia
Belleview Plantation	unk	Rt 604
Cedar Run	38.36299, -77.33694	Quantico Marine Base
Crows Nest	unk	Crows Nest area
Edrington Family	38.44378, -77.38064	End of Rt 692, Quarry Rd, aross fr 34 Edrington Court
Fairview	unk	Chopawamic Creek
Hartwood Presbyterian	38.40188, -77.56745	50 Hartwood Ch Rd, jct rts 705 & 612

(STAFFORD COUNTY, CONTINUED)

Hedges Family	unk	Quantico Marine Base
Jett Family #2	unk	End of Broad Oak Ln, see property records
King Family	unk	Rt 658 Brent Point Rd
Liberty Hall	unk	Rt 652 abt 1.4 mi fr jct Rt 653 and .5 mi N nr Wallace farm rd
Norman Family #1	unk	Quarry Rd
Norman Family #2	unk	Hope Point Rd
Olde Concord Road	unk	Rt 721
Phillips Family	38.50238, -77.29626	Rt 610, Quantico Marine Base
Pratt Family, aka Glebe	38.29934, -77.34450	1374 White Oak
Richland, aka Brent Family	unk	Rt 637, Aquia
Roy Family	unk	Clover Hill Dr
Sanford Family	unk	#1 Rocky Pen area
Sanford family #1	unk	Rt 654 to 656, follow 656 S for 3.2 mi
Stark-Payne	unk	Quantico Marine Base opp Ruby fire station
Stony Hill	unk	Stony Hill Rd nr Curtis Lake
Union Church	38.32268, -77.46615	Carter St, Falmouth
Waller Family	38.43891, -77.38353	Rt 721

STAUNTON CITY (See also Augusta County)

Hebron Presbyterian	38.14140, -79.15500	423 Hebron Rd
Stone House Plantation	unk	Hill behind Hays Creek, nr Staunton
Thornrose	38,15120, -79.08460	1041 W Beverly St
Trinity Episcopal	38.14917, -79.07521	214 Beverley St
Western State Hospital	38.14299, -79.06571	Village Dr

SUFFOLK CITY (formerly Nansemond County)

Bethel Church	unk	E Washington St
Cedar Hill	36.73640, -76.58000	105 Mahan St
Cypress Chapel	36.61799, -76.59148	1891 Cypress Chapel Rd
Meadowbrook Mem Gardens	36.82940, -76.46640	4569 Shoulders Hill Rd
Riddick Cemetery	36.68140, -76.55860	Off White Marsh Rd
Soldiers Hope	unk	Rt 642, 3.5 mi S of Suffolk

SURRY COUNTY

Cocke Family	unk	Mount Pleasant
Four Mile Tree	unk	Off Swan's Point Rd
Lawn's Creek Parish Church	unk	Hog Island, no public access
Rogers Family	unk	Off Rt 40

SUSSEX COUNTY

Claiborne Family	unk	Check property records
Jones Family	unk	See DAR Senate 1937 serial 10173 vol 1
Moss Family	unk	Check property records

TAZEWELL COUNTY

Bowen Family	unk	Cove Creek
Brooks	unk	Rt 604, .2 mi fr grocery behind silo, Thompson Valley
Dry Fork, Sayer's Farm, or Harman	unk	Rt 637, Dry Fork, State Marker nearby
Henry Harmon	unk	Fourway
Hezekiah Harman	unk	In front of HS off Rtst 460 & 19, Tazewell
Leatherwood Farm	unk	Rt 460, Bluefield

(TAZEWELL COUNTY, CONTINUED)

Maplewood	37.12803, -81.52104	Nr Jct Rts 19, 460, & 16 Tazewell Ave
Moore	37.22110, -81.40170	Adj to RR track E of Tiptop abt halfway to jct Rts 650 & 656
Moore Family	unk	Abb's Valley
Sayer's Farm	unk	Mouth of Thompson Valley, foot of Clinch Mountain, Dry Fork
Thompson Family	unk	Not identified
Thompson Family	unk	Thompson Valley
W. A. Leece Family	unk	Off Rt 91 S of Rt 460, Fort Witten, Paintlick
Ward's Cove	unk	Thompson Valley
Witten Family	unk	Plum Creek nr his cabin
Wynn-Peery	37.12620, -81.4988	Campbell Ln, Tazewell

VIRGINIA BEACH CITY (formerly Princess Anne County)

Greenwich	unk	Euclid Station
Old Baptist Meeting House	36.61001, -76.03494	Vic 664 Princess Anne Rd, Creeds
Old Donation Episcopal	36.86730, -76.12860	4449 N Witchduck Rd
Keeling Family	unk	Back of Laurel Manor
Lynhaven House	unk	Shore Dr
Red Mill Farm	unk	Hedgelawn Rd
Kempsville Skirmish Monument	unk	Pleasant Hall

WARREN COUNTY

Buck Family	unk	1 mi W of Buckton Station, Waterlick
Cloud Family	unk	1.5 mi West Front Royal
Marshall Family	unk	Rt 55, Happy Creek Pl, Front Royal
Millar Family	unk	W Main St, Front Royal
Miller Family	unk	Mountain View Farm, vic Front Royal
Richardson Family	38.95750,-78.29610	1.5 mi fr entrance to GW National Forest, Rt 678 nr Fortsmouth Vol Fire Dept
Trenary Farm	unk	Bayard Post Office

WASHINGTON COUNTY (See also Bristol City)

Baker Family, aka Spring Creek	unk	N Jct with 647 Bristol-Abingdon Rd
Buchanan Family	36.84163, -81.75199	Rt 696, S of Saltville
Burson Family, orig Fulkerson	36.66440, -82.17500	Nr Jct of Rt 633 & Spur Strap Rd, Burson's Corner
Carmack	unk	Nr Bristol
Clark	unk	Cedarville
Davies Farm	unk	Check property records nr Abingdon
Dunn Family	36.62560, -81.72640	Abt 1 mi NW of Cherry Tree Gap off Rt 725
East Hill, Sec 1	unk	West of Circles, see Source 80 Cem #279A
Ebbing Spring	unk	N side of middle fork of Holstein River, vic Glade Spring
Fleenor	unk	North Fork, Holston
Glade Spring Presbyterian	36.76720, -81.78720	33234 Lee Hwy, Glade Spring
Glenwood	unk	Clarksville
Green Spring Presbyterian	36.63670, -81.99560	2007 Green Spring Ch Rd, Abingdon
Hayter-Litton	36.84443, -81.92628	Nr the Litton Home, 7261 Hayter's Gap Rd
Hobbs	unk	North Fork, Holston River
Jackson Lewis	unk	Taylors Valley
John Douglass	unk	100 yds N of John B Douglass Wayside Rt 19, 9 mi N of Abingdon
Johnston	unk	1 mi on ext of Valley St, Abingdon
Malone Family	unk	Three Springs

(WASHINGTON COUNTY, CONTINUED)

Maxwell Family	unk	Abingdon
Moore	unk	Fort Edmiston
Pleasant View	36.68670, -81.74970	Vic jct Rts 801 & 605, Glade Spring
Rock Spring	37.78126, -79.44585	Jct Rt 803 & Liberty Hall Rd, Lodi
Royal Oak	unk	Behind Marion Baptist Church
Scott	unk	Rich Valley
Sinking Springs	36.71030, -81.98170	136 E Main St, Abingdon
Teeter family	36.66470, -82.12080	Vic Clear Creek Dam
Trigg Family	unk	Abingdon
Vance Family	unk	Rt 695
Walnut Grove	unk	Lee Hwy, Bristol
Widener's Valley	unk	See Source 80, Cem #239

WAYNESBORO CITY (See also Augusta County)

Allen Marker	unk	E Waynesboro at Winchester Heights, lot 4, Elkin Ave
Bethleham Lutheran	38.05454, -78.95222	1148 Ladd Rd
Patrick Family	unk	Locust Isle, Rt 865 N fr Waynesboro

WESTMORELAND COUNTY

Burnt House Field	unk	Hague
Bushfield	unk	Nomini River
Dishman Family	unk	Forest Glen
Glebe	unk	In garden area of Glebe Parish House, Glebe Creek, Cople Parish
Hickory Hill, aka Epping	unk	Hague
Hungerford-Griffin	unk	373 Resolutions Rd, Leedstown
Lee Family	unk	Stratford Hall
Level Green	unk	Kinsale
McCarty Family	unk	Longwood, Horners Beach
Nomini Hall Graveyard	unk	Hague
Old Pierce Homestead	unk	Level Green
Payne Family, aka Cedar Hill	38.13357, -76.97069	Redhouse Horners, 2 mi NE of Leedstown
Rochester Family	unk	Probably old homestead at Lydell's Store, jct Rts 3 & 202
Unidentified	unk	Rt 675, nr Lee Creek, Hague

WILLIAMSBURG CITY

Bruton Parish Church	37.27127, -76.70248	331 W Duke of Gloucester St
Cedar Grove	37.26140, -76.70720	Jct Rt 132 and Hunting Cove
Eastern State Hospital	37.25560 -76.71030	S Henry Street
Governor's Palace	unk	Colonial Williamsburg Historic Area
Green Hill	unk	Nassau St
Jamestown Church	unk	3827 Ironbound Rd, Williamsburg
Williamsburg Land Conservancy	unk	5000 New Point Rd
Wren Chapel, William & Mary	37.27070, -76.70910	College of William & Mary, nr jct Jamestown Rd and Richmond Rd

WINCHESTER CITY (See also Frederick County)

Christ Episcopal, Courtyard	unk	114 W Boscawen St
Ewing Family	unk	Off Stickley Dr to Hayvenhurst Ct
Montour	unk	Not identified by SAR source
Mt Hebron	39.10916, -78.09497	305 E Boscawen St
Opequon Presbyterian	39.13938 -78.19494	217 Opequon Church Ln

WISE COUNTY

Benjamin Bolling	37.07721, -82.70543	Sulpher Springs Dr., Flat Gap
Wells Family	36.84640, -82.81720	Rt 739 abt 1 mi S of jct with Rt 605

WYTHE COUNTY

Black Lick Rural Retreat	36.94435, -81.24377	2390 Black Lick Rd
Browning's Mill	unk	Old Stage Rd
Crockett	unk	SR 649, turn left to cross RR tracks, to Suthers home
Crockett Family	37.01560, -81.05500	Off Rt 600, Crockett's Cove
Dobler Family	unk	nr Kimbersville
Gleaves Farm	unk	Dunkley farm, Cripple Creek
Harris	unk	SR 651, near the SW cnr of jct with SR 690, Cripple Creek
Hillenberg	unk	Maybe SW of Crockett
Horseshoe Bend, Graham Family	36.94917, -80.90010	N side of Reed Creek on Formato Dr near jct with E Lee Hwy
Keesling	unk	Grahams Forge
Keesling	unk	Rural Retreat
Kimberling	36.91750, -81.30440	Rt 617, Rural Retreat
King	unk	W side Rt 625, S of jct with Rt 667, Crockett
McGavock Family	unk	NW of jct of Rts 610 & 1012, W of Max Meadows
McGavock Family	unk	Peppers Ferry Rd, Ft Chiswell, off I-81, 12 mi E of Wytheville
Montgomery family	unk	Nr Ft Chiswell, in field abt .75 mi behind Ft Chiswell Mansion
Neff Family	unk	E of Fairview Church on Charles Roberts property, Rural Retreat
Newell-Trigg-Sanders	unk	N side of Rt 619 abt .5 mi W of jct with Rt 636, Austinville
Newland	unk	1 mi W on 692 fr jct with SR 749, on hill on right, Cedar Springs
Oglesby Sayers	36.96440, -80.83030	Rt 701, Draper's Valley
Old Crockett	37.04161, -80.97662	Rt 600, Crockett's Creek Rd, Wytheville
Old Keesling	unk	unk
Peirce Family, aka Chaffin	unk	On hill overlooking SR 69 at jct with I-77 in Poplar Camp
Phipps Family	unk	Wytheville
Rose Hill	unk	Kegley farm 840 Rose Hill Rd, Wytheville
Seybert Family	unk	Gunton Park
Simmerman, aka Cedar Hill	unk	Off I-81 N, open field abt .25 mi E of gravel plant on SR 649
St John's Lutheran	36.96500, -81.10110	405 W Main, Wytheville
St Paul's Lutheran	36.91173, -81.23484	330 St Pauls Church Rd, Rural Retreat
Steele Family	unk	nr Bland
Stephens, aka Hurst	unk	SR 100 S to SR 607 E to Jett farm, Wytheville, nr Carroll Co line
Trigg	unk	Wytheville, N side of Rt 619, abt .5 mi W of jct Rts 619 & 636
West End	36.94140, -81.11670	Off Rt 11, Wytheville
Zion Lutheran	36.84110, -81.22310	1417 Zion Church Rd, Crockett

YORK COUNTY

Carter Crafford	unk	Fort Eustis SW of golf course maint shop
Essex Lodge, aka Washington's Lodge	unk	Check property records
French Memorial	36.81944, -79.39933	Yorktown
Grace Episcopal	37.23560, -76.50750	115 Church St, Yorktown
Moore House	unk	Rt 238, Yorktown
Old Kiskiak	unk	Nr Yorktown
Yorktown Victory Monument	38.28350, -78.54150	Yorktown

APPENDIX C - CODE TO & BIBLIOGRAPHY OF SERVICE SOURCES

(Note: volume, issue, type, pages, etc. for many of these sources are listed in the main patriot text)

A   Saffell, W.T.R. *Records of the Revolutionary War.* 1894. Reprint, Bowie, MD: Clearfield Co., Inc., 1996.

B   Gravestone Inscriptions.

C   Brumbaugh, Gaius Marcus. *Revolutionary War Records, Volume I, Virginia.* 1936. Reprint, Baltimore: Genealogical Publishing Company, 1967.

D   Abercrombie, Janice L. & Richard Slatten. *Virginia Revolutionary Publick Claims.* Athens, GA: Iberian Publishing Company, 1992. This source includes authors *Index to Virginia Revolutionary War Publick Claims.*

E   Gwathmey, J.H. *Historical Register of Virginians in the Revolution 1775-1783.* Richmond, VA: The Dietz Press, 1938.

F   Wilson, Samuel M., *Catologue of Revolutionary Soldiers and Sailors of the Commonwealth of Virginia to Whom Land Bounty Warrants Were Granted by Virginia for Military Services in the War for Independence.* 1953. Reprint, Baltimore: Southern Book Company, 2002.

G   *Virginia Military Records.* Baltimore: Clearfield Publishing, 2002. Arranged by county. Compiled articles originally published in *The Virginia Magazine of History and Biography*, the *William and Mary College Quarterly*, and *Tyler's Quarterly*.

H   SAR Patriot Index, Edition III, 2000.

I   SAR Revolutionary War Graves Register, NASSAR, edition 2000

J   Eby Jerri Lyn. *Laying the Hoe: A Century of Iron Manufacturing, Stafford County, Virginia, With Genealogical Notes on Over 300 Families.* Westminster, MD: Willowbend Books, 2003.

K   Wardell, Patrick G. *Virginia/West Virginia Genealogical Data from Revolutionary War Pension and Bounty Land Warrant Records.* 6 volumes. Bowie, MD: Heritage Books, Inc., 1988-1998.

L   Stewart, Robert Armistead. *The History of Virginia's Navy in the Revolution.* Richmond: Mitchell & Hoskiss Printers, 1933.

M   United States War Department. *The Pension Rolls of 1835.* 4 volumes. 1835. Reprint, Baltimore: Genealogical Publishing Co., Inc., 2002.

N   Burgess, Louis A. *Virginia Soldiers of 1776.* 3 volumes. 1927. Reprint, Baltimore: Clearfield Company, 1994.

O   Rockingham County, Virginia. Minute Book 1, 1778-1786. County Records, microfilm reel 25. Richmond: Library of Virginia.

P   Wayland, John W. *Virginia Valley Records, Genealogical and Historical Materials of Rockingham County, Virginia.* Baltimore: Genealogical Publishing Company, 1965.

Q   Thwaite, Reuben Gold and Louis Phelps Kellogg. *Documentary History Lord Dunmore's War 1774.* 1905. Reprint, Harrisonburg, VA: Wisconsin Historical Society, 1974.

R   Virginia. Fairfax County Court Booklet 1782.

S   NASSAR Graves Registry Patriot & Graves Index http://patriot.sar.org/fmi/iwp/cgi?-db=Grave%20Registry&-loadframes (this site reflects latest up-dates and should be used rather than source BY. Also it provides the NASSAR assigned patriot number.)

T   Funkhouser, Jacob. *A Historical Sketch of the Funkhouser Family.* Harrisonburg, VA: Rockingham Register Press, 1902.

U   Wayland, John Walter. *Men of Mark and Representative Citizens of Harrisonburg and Rockingham County, Virginia; Portraits and Biographies of Men and Women*. Staunton, VA: McClure Co., 1943.

V   Halifax County Commissioner's Book.

W   Handbook Stratford Hall Plantation & Lees of Virginia, pub 2004.

X   Grigsby, Hugh Blair. "Thomas Lewis." *The History of the Virginia Federal Convention of 1788*. Vol. II. 1890. Abridged, New York: DeCapo Press, 1969.

Y   Pittsylvania County Court Book

Z   Skidmore, Warren with Donna Kaminsky. *Lord Dunmore's Little War of 1774*. Bowie, MD: Heritage Books, Inc., 2002.

AA   Montgomery County Revolutionary War Records. *Southern Campaign American Revolution Pension Statements & Rosters* pertains to Montgomery County, VA http://www.rootsweb.ancestry.com/~vamontgo/southerncampaignamericanrevolutionpensionstatements.

AB   Wayland, John Walter. *A History of Rockingham County, Virginia*. Dayton, VA: Ruebush-Elkins Co., 1912.

AC   Cabell, James Branch. *The Majors and Their Marriages*. Richmond, VA: Hill Printing Co., 1915.

AD   Waddell, Joseph Addison. *Annals of Augusta County, Virginia, From1726 to 1871*. 2d Ed, Staunton, Va : Caldwell, 1902,c1901

AE   *Virginia Genealogy Society Quarterly*, volume 2 (Richmond, VA: Virginia Genealogical Society, 1964.

AF   Clements, S. Eugene and F. Edward Wright. *The Maryland Militia in the Revolutionary War*. Silver Spring, MD: Family Line Publications, 1987.

AG   Family Tree Maker CD #145, *Military Records: Revolutionary War Pension Lists*

AH   Bockstruck, Lloyd D. *Virginia's Colonial Soldiers*. Baltimore: Genealogical Publishing Co., Inc., 1988.

AI   Scott, W. W. *A History of Orange County, Virginia*. Richmond, VA: Everett Waddey Company, 1907.

AJ   Office of the Secretary of State. *Massachusetts Soldiers and Sailors of the Revolutionary War: A Compilation from the Archives*. Boston: Wright & Potter Printing Company, State Printers, 1896-1898.

AK   VASSAR Graves Registration Submissions

AL   *Revolutionary War Public Service Claims*. "On-line Catalog: Images and Indexes." Library of Virginia. Searchable by name only, giving County and citation to the County Court Booklet and State Auditor's Commissioners Book. Original images are on microfilm. http://www.lva.virginia.gov/ : 2015.

AM   McIlwaine, Henry Read, *Executive Journals of the Council of Colonial Virginia*, Vol II, VA State Library, 1864-1934, pub 1925.

AN   *Virginia Revolutionary War State Pensions*. "Images and Indexes." Library of Virginia. Not to be confused with federal pensions at the National Archives. Original images are on microfilm. http://www.lva.virginia.gov/ : 2015.

AO   Lineage Books, NSDAR, Vol I & II, Ancestors Index.

AP   National Archives Records Administration, Washington, D.C. Revolutionary War Compiled Military Service Record and/or Pension File. File numbers given in the text.

AQ   *Biographical Directory of the United States Congress 1774 to Present.* Washington, DC: U.S. Government Printing Office. On line http://bioguide.congress.gov : 2015.

AR   Hatcher, Patricia Law. *Abstract of Graves of Revolutionary Patriots.* 4 volumes. Dallas, TX: Pioneer Heritage Press, 1987. Also available at ancestry.com (subscription service).

AS   Rev War Graves Committee, NSSAR *Master Roster of Patriots of Rev War,* Jan 2007.

AT   *Virginia Genealogies and Biographies 1500's-1900's.* Genealogy.com. Novato, UT: Brøderbund Software, 2000. This 2-CD bundle is a compilation of 22 Genealogical Publishing Company volumes. Applies to: see text for patriot.

AU   Williamsburg Chapter VASSAR, "Study of Burials from Green Springs Battle", Ltr Feb 2007.

AV   CMM SAR Chapter *CMM Battalion Roster,* prepared 2005, revised 2007.

AW   Hurt, Frances Hallum. *An Intimate History of the American Revolution in Pittsylvania County, Virginia.* Danville, VA: Womack Press, 1976.

AX   *New York in the Revolution and the War of 1812.* CD-ROM. Family Tree Maker. Novato, UT: Brøderbund Software, 2000.

AY   Brumbaugh, Gaius Marcus. *Genealogical Records: Maryland Settlers & Soldiers 1700s-1800s.* CD-ROM. Novato, CA: Genealogy.com, 2000. Muster rolls and other records of service.

AZ   McAllister, Joseph Thompson. *Virginia Militia in the Revolutionary War.* Hot Springs, VA: McAllister Publishing Company, 1913.

BA   Virginia Historical Inventory. WPA Survey Reports of Burials in Prince George County, Library of Virginia, Richmond.

BB   Fairfax Resolves Chapter, VASSAR *Legislative Petitions Alexandria & Fairfax County, VA* 2009.

BC   Lewis Preston et al. *Annals of Southwest Virginia, 1769-1800.* Vol. I. 1929. Reprint, Baltimore: Genealogical Publishing Co., Inc., 1996.

BD   Berg, Fred Anderson. *Encyclopedia of Continental Army Units—Battalions, Regiments and Independent Corps.* Harrisburg, PA: Stackpole Books, 1992.

BE   Stewart, Robert Armistead, *Virginia Navy in the Revolution,* Virginia Magazine of History and Biography. Richmond: Virginia Historical Society. Also at Ancestry.com. *Virginia Navy in the Revolution* [database on-line]. Provo, UT, USA: Ancestry.com Operations Inc., 1998.

BF   *Maryland and Delaware Revolutionary Patriots 1775-1783, Military Records.* CD-ROM. Genealogy.com. Novato, UT: Brøderbund Software, 2001.

BG   Boddie, John Bennett. *Historical Southern Families,* volume X. (For page numbers see text for patriot).

BH   *Southern Genealogies 1600-1800. (*For volume and page numbers see text for patriot).

BI   Dixon, Joan M. *National Intelligencer Newspaper Abstracts 1814-1817.* Westminster, MD: Heritage Books, 2006.

BJ   Newman, Harry Wright. *Maryland Revolutionary Records.* 1938. Reprint, Baltimore: Genealogical Publishing Co., Inc, 2002.

BK   Virginia Historical Inventory. WPA Survey Reports of Burials in Russell County, Library of Virginia, Richmond.

BL   Stryker, William S. *Official Register of the Officers and Men of New Jersey in the Revolutionary War.* New Jersey Historical Records Project, Adjutant-Generals Office. Trenton, NJ: W. T. Nicholson & Co., 1872.

BM   Virginia Historical Inventory. WPA Survey Reports of Burials in Bath County, Library of Virginia, Richmond.

BN   Virginia Historical Inventory. WPA Survey Reports of Burials in Lunenburg County, Library of Virginia, Richmond.

BO   Virginia Historical Inventory. WPA Survey Reports of Burials in Rappahannock County, Library of Virginia, Richmond.

BP   Henley, B. J. *Obituaries from VA Newspapers,* on Microfilm Lib of VA. (For name of reel; Reel #, etc. see text for patriot).

BQ   Charles R. Sydnor, Jr. "Northern Neck of Virginia Historical Society, February 27, 2009, Annual Commemoration of the Leedstown Resolutions." Text of Mr. Sydnor's address reprinted in the *Northern Neck of Virginia Historical Magazine* LIX (December 2009), 7153-7163. (Contains biographical information on some of the signers).

BR   *American Beacon & Norfolk Daily Advertizer (Obituaries.or Death Notices?)* Microfilm# Reel # see text for patriot.

BS   Bushman, Katherine Gentry. *Augusta County, Virginia Court of Claims, 1782-1785.* Staunton, VA: Virginia Daughters of the American Revolution, Col. Thomas Hughart Chapter, 1970.

BT   Daughters of the American Revolution grave markers.

BU   Hanks, Chris W. "Patriots' Graves in Pittsylvania County." *Pittsylvania County History.com.* http://pittsylvaniacountyhistory.com/patriots/: 1 March 2015. Email: cwhanks@gmail.com.

BV   Chiarito, Marian Dodson, "Oaths of Allegiance - 1777 Pittsylvania County, VA." *Magazine of Virginia Genealogy* 23 (February, 1985). Retyped and digitized by Cynthia Hubbard Headen at rootsweb.ancestry.com under the same title at http://www.rootsweb.ancestry.com/~vapittsy/Oaths.html : 2015.

BW   Kegley, Mary B. *Militia of Montgomery County, Virginia, 1777-1790.* 1970. Reprint, Dublin, VA: private printing, 1997.

BX   Bockstruck, Lloyd Dewitt. *Revolutionary War Pensions Awarded By State Governments 1775-1884, The General and Federal Governments Prior to 1814, and by Private Acts of Congress Prior to 1905.* Baltimore: Genealogical Publishing Co, Inc., 2011.

BY   "Patriot Grave Search." *National Society of the Sons of the American Revolution.* https://memberinfo.sar.org/patriotsearch/search.aspx : 2015.

BZ   DAR Records 56th-77th Annual Reports DAR. Senate documents (United States Congress, Senate). Government Printing Office: Washington, DC.

CA   National Society of the Sons of the American Revolution. Louisville, KY. Approved membership applications.

CB   Hogandobler, Matt. "Service for Veterans & Patriots Buried at St Paul's Church, Norfolk, VA, Dec 2011." Unpublished copy for compiler.

CC   Prince William County, Virginia. Order Book 1778-1784. Prince William County Records, microfilm reel 88. Richmond: Library of Virginia.

CD   Find A Grave. www.findagrave.com. Memorials giving biographical information that include documented service in the Revolutionary War.

CE   Sanchez-Saavedra, E. M. *A Guide to Virginia Military Organizations in the American Revolution, 1774-1787*. Richmond: Virginia State Library, 1978.

CF   Arlington National Cemetery Interment Cards. "U.S., Burial Registers, Military Posts and National Cemeteries Internment Cards, and National Cemeteries, 1862-1960." *Ancestry.com*. http://search.ancestry.com/search/db.aspx?dbid=3135 : 2015. Under an agreement reached in 2002 between the Veterans Administration and Ancestry.com, all burial records for national cemeteries were merged into a single database. Users must enter the name of the deceased veteran and the name of the cemetery to narrow the search to a specific person and cemetery.

CG   White, Virgil D. *Genealogical Abstracts of Revolutionary War Pension Files*. 3 vols. Waynesboro, TN: National Historical Publishing Co., 1990-1992.

CH   Hay, Gertrude May (Sloan). *Roster of Soldiers from North Carolina in the American Revolution, with an appendix containing a collection of miscellaneous records*. Durham, NC: private printing, 1932.

CI   "Revolutionary War." *Fold3.com*. Online index and images. Fold3.com by ancestry.com. There are 21 sources, (For particular source with volumes, pages, etc., see text for patriot).

CJ   Adam, Robert. "Naval Office on the Potomac." *William & Mary Quarterly* 2, 2nd Series (October 1922): 292-295.

CK   Cartmell, T.K. *Shenandoah Valley Pioneers & Their Descendants: A History of Frederick County, Virginia from Its Formation in 1738 to 1908*. Berryville, VA: Chesapeake Book Co., 1963.

CL   Hamilton, Clay and Marti Hiatt. *Claims Presented to the Court of Augusta: 21 March 1782 to March 1785*. Richmond: Virginia Genealogical Society, 2005.

CM   Chalkley, Lyman. *Chronicles of the Scottish-Irish Settlement in Virginia 1745-1800; Extracted from the Original Court Records of Augusta County*. 3 vols. 1912. Reprint, Baltimore: Genealogical Publishing Co, Inc., 1965. (For vol # and page # see text for patriot).

CN: Crozier, William Armstrong. *Virginia County Records: Westmoreland County*. New Series, Vol. I. 1913. Reprint, Baltimore: Genealogical Publishing Co., Inc., 2008.

CO   James, Edward Wilson. *The Lower Norfolk County, Virginia Antiquary,* pub. 1895. Richmond: Whittet & Shepperson, 1895-1906. (For volume # and name of article see text for patriot).

CP   *Dunmore's War (Virginia Payrolls/Public Service Claims, 1775)*. "Online Catalog: Images & Indexes." The Library of Virginia. http://lva1.hosted.exlibrisgroup.com/F/YY5IQP14B3S4JQNSF2DBRNC5QYRNVVV2NQ XR4MLUVCH YQ8GM9E-22624?func=file&file_name=find-b-clas36&local_base=CLAS36: 2015. Part of Record Group 1. Online database and images contains the names of Virginia citizens or soldiers from the counties of Augusta, Bedford, Botetourt, Culpeper, Dunmore (now Shenandoah), Fincastle and Kentucky who were compensated in 1775 for supplies or service during Dunmore's Expedition against the Delaware, Mingo and Shawnee tribes in 1774. Entries in the volume typically include names, county of residence, name of commander, length of service or item being compensated for, and the amount of compensation.

CQ   Hadfield, Kathleen Halverson, ed. *Historical Notes on Amelia County, Virginia*. Amelia, VA: Amelia County Historical Committee, 1982.

CR   Egle, William Henry. *Some Pennsylvania Women During the War of the Revolution,* Harrisburg, PA: Harrisburn Publishing Co., 1898.

CS   SAR grave marker or cemetery plaque.

CT   Egle, William Henry, ed. *Provincial Papers: Supply, and State Tax Lists of the City and County of Philadelphia for the Years 1781, 1782 and 1783.* Pennsylvania Archives, Third Series, volume XVI. Philadelphia: Secretary of the Commonwealth by W. S. Ray, state printer, 1898.

CU   *Revolutionary War Bounty Warrants.* "On-Line Catalog: Images & Indexes." The Library of Virginia: http://lva1.hosted.exlibrisgroup.com/F/H4BCGKCX18A5AF7IDJLE2FM4KP24SN2CYCV1 IG7JJS3N2KY6VF-26256?func=file&file_name=find-b-clas39&local_base=CLAS39: 2015

CV   Palmer, William Pitt, ed. *Calendar of Virginia State Papers & Other Manuscripts.* Volumes 1 & 2 (1652-1781). 1875-1878. Reprint, New York: Kraus Reprint Corp., 1968.

CW   Liles, Frankie. "Washington County Militia at Kings Mountain." *Magazine of Virginia Genealogy* 52 (Feb 2014), 78-82.

CX   Harman, John Newton. *Annals of Tazewell County, Virginia, 1800-1922.* Richmond: W. C. Hill Printing, 1923. [Original was one volume. Followed up with another author with two volumes, and a later version by Nellie Schreiner-Yantis] (See text for patriot).

CY   Saunders, William L, ed. *The Colonial Records of North Carolina, 1662-1776.* 10 Vols. Raleigh, NC: Trustees of the Public Libraries, pub by State of NC, 1886-1890.

CZ   Eckenrode, James Hamilton, archivist. Virginia State Library, Archives Division. *List of Revolutionary Soldiers of Virginia: Special Report of the Department of Archives and History for 1911.* Richmond: D. Bottom, Superintendent of Public Printing, 1912.

DA   Thomas, William H. B. *Patriots of the Upcountry: Orange County, Virginia in the Revolution.* Orange, VA: Orange County Bicentennial Commission, 1976.

DB   Elliott, Katherine B. *Revolutionary Records, Mecklenburg County, Virginia.* South Hill, VA: private printing by Prestwood Chapter, US Daughters of the American Revolution, 1964.

DC   Little, Barbara Vines. "Amherst County Minute Men, 1776." *Magazine of Virginia Genealogy,* 52 (May 2014), 153-154.

DD   Daughters of the American Revolution. "Ancestor Search." On line database. Index to approved applications. http://services.dar.org/public/dar_research/search/?Tab_ID=1 : 2015.

DE   Rockingham County Minute Books. (See text for patriot for specific record and page numbers).

DF   Stoner, Robert Douthat. *A Seed Bed of the Republic: A Study of the Pioneers in the Upper (Southern) Valley of Virginia.* Roanoke, VA: Roanoke County Historical Society, 1962.

DG   Hill, Judith Parks America. *A history of Henry County, Virginia: With Biographical Sketches of its Most Prominent Citizens and Genealogical Histories of Half a Hundred of its Oldest Families.* 1925. Reprint, Baltimore: Regional Publishing Co., 1962.

DH   Draper, Lyman C. *Kings Mountain and Its Heroes: History of the Battle of Kings Mountain, October 7th 1780 and the Events that Led to It.* Cincinnati: Peter G. Thompson Publishers, 1881.

DI   PA Historical Museum Commission http://phmc.info/historicpreservation.

DJ   *Culpeper County Classes, 1781.* "On-Line Catalog: Images & Indexes." The Library of Virginia. http://www.lva.virginia.gov/ : 2015. Index only, made from a typed transcript from a Photostat copy of the original, which contains errors. Original manuscript is on Revolutionary War Public Service Claims, microfilm reel 7. For an accurate and complete transcript, see: John V. Blankenbaker, *The Culpeper Classes in Culpeper County for January 1781 for Recruiting this State's Quota of Troops to serve in the Continental Army.* Chad's Ford, PA: private printing, 1999 for a complete transcript.

DK   Brumbaugh, Gaius Marcus. *Maryland Settlers & Soldiers 1700s-1800s.* Family Archives CD. *Baltimore:* Genealogical Publishing Co, Inc., 2000.

DL   Summers, Lewis Preston et al. *Annals of Southwest Virginia, 1769-1800.* Vol. II. Johnson City, TN: Overmountain Press, 1929. Has undergone several reprints. (See text for patriot for specifics).

DM   Pedigo, Virginia G. and Lewis Gravely Pedigo, *History of Patrick and Henry Counties, Virginia.* 1933. Reprint, Baltimore: Clearfield Co., 2002.

DN   Evans, James. *Historical and Geographical Encyclopedia, Illustrated.* Chicago: H. H. Hardesty, 1883.   Includes Amherst County, VA families and history.

DO   Ancestry.com. *Partial list of early settlers, Revolutionary soldiers and the graves of Augusta County soldiers located to date* [database on-line]. Provo, UT: Ancestry.com Operations Inc., 2005. Original data: King, Fannie Bayly, *Partial List of Early Settlers, Revolutionary Soldiers and the Graves of Augusta County Soldiers located to date.* Staunton, Va.: private printing, 1935. Ancestry.com. http://search.ancestry.com/search/db.aspx?dbid=10553 : 2015.

DP   Minnis, M. Lee. *The First Regiment of Foot 1775-1783.* [Continental Line, Virginia.] Westminster, MD: Willow Bend Books, 1998.

DQ   Bell, John W. *Memoirs of Governor William Smith, of Virginia. His Political, Military, and Personal History.* New York: The Moss Engraving Co., 1891.

DR   Rager, Susan Godman. "Leedstown Resolves: 1766." *Northern Neck of Virginia Law Page.* Online transcript. http://www.ragerlaw.com/leedstownresolutionspage.htm : Accessed September 2015.

DS   Rev. Horace Edwin Hayden. *Virginia Genealogies.* 1885. Reprint, Baltimore: Southern Book Co., 1959.

DT   Will of Rawleigh Downman, signed 10 March 1781, proved 19 April 1791. Will Book 20, p. 188a-189, Circuit Clerk's Office, Lancaster County Court House, Lancaster, VA.

DU   Reid, R. J., *Oaths of Allegiance, Goochland Co, VA,* Papers,1777-1870, Accession 22032, Personal Papers Collection, The Library of VA.

DV   Binns Genealogy, *1782 and 1783 Personal Property and land Tax Lists Fairfax County, VA,,* These taxes used to support cost of Rev War proving patriotic service; http://www.binnsgenealogy.com/MembersOnlyArea/pdfs/Fairfax/1782Personal/06.pdf

DW   See source AD.

DX   Styker, William Scudder, *New Jersey Continental Line in the Virginia Campaign of 1781,* Jan 20, 2012.

DY   Family Archives CD, *New York in the Revolution as a Colony & State,* vol I the Militia.

DZ   Worrell, Anne Lowry, *Over Mountain Men Their Early Court Records in Southwest Virginia,* Genealogy Publishing Co, Inc., Baltimore, 1976.

EA   Lela C. Adams, Compiler, "1778-1780 Tax Lists of Henry County, Virginia," (Bassett, VA: privately published, 1973).

EB   The Bulletin of the Northumberland County Historical Society, vol 9, 1972, *Northumberland County Tax List, 1782.*

EC: Lohrenz, Otto, *Reverend Thomas Smith of Revolutionary Virginia: A case Study in Social Rank,* Northern Neck of Virginia Historical Magazine, 2004, pgs 6458-6475.

ED: Bryant, William C., Jr, *Packett Family Graveyard-Sabine Hall,* Northern Neck of Virginia Historical Magazine, 2006, pgs 6734-675.

EE: Hopkins, William Lindsay, *Virginia Revolutionary War Land Grant Claims 1783-1850 (Rejected),* Privately printed Richmond, VA 1988.

EF   Jones, Mary Stephens, Complier, Editor, *"18^(th) Century Perspective: Culpeper County,* Culpeper County Historical Society, 1976.

EG   Lillard, Dewey, *Culpeper Classes for 1781: An In Depth Study,* Sep 2001, unpublished, lists classes pertaining to Madison County inhabitants.

EH   Transcribed by Clay Hamilton and Marty Hiatt, *Book of Claims Presented to the Court of Augusta County 1782-1785,* Virginia Genealogical Society, 2005.

APPENDIX D - CODE TO & BIBLIOGRAPHY OF BURIAL SOURCES

JLARC, "Special Report: Preservation of Revolutionary War Veteran Gravesites." Virginia. Joint Legislative and Audit Review Commission of the Virginia General Assembly. House Document 42. Also available as a downloadable pdf file at *JLARC.* http://jlarc.virginia.gov/reports/Rpt264.pdf : January 2001. This report used 127 sources, which are numbered in Appendix B of the report. For example, a burial in this book reading JLARC 4, 154 means that sources #4 and #154 were used for that individual.

01   Moxley, J. M. *Gravestone Inscriptions in Amherst County, VA. 1985. Gravestone Inscriptions in Amherst County, Virginia.* Amherst, VA: Amherst County Museum and Historical Society, 1999.

      This has since been supplemented with: "Gravestone Inscriptions in Amherst County— Gravestones 2." *Amherst County Museum and Historical Society.* Online database. http://www.amherstcountymuseum.org/gravestones.html : 2015. With GPS coordinates. Users will need the original book to use this web site. From the website: "The digital edition contains cemeteries not found in the 1999 edition, corrections to the 1999 edition, and in some instances a cemetery has been re-surveyed. The digital edition will be revised periodically as corrections are noted and new cemeteries and burials are recorded. For this reason, instead of citing by page numbers (which may change as revisions occur), references are to the cemetery number."

02   Collins, Herbert Ridgeway. *Cemeteries of Caroline County, Volume 2, Private Cemeteries.* Westminster, MD: Family Line Publishers, 1995. (Now published by Colonial Roots, Lewes, DE)

03   Musselman, Homer D. *Stafford County, Virginia Veterans and Cemeteries.* Fredericksburg, VA: Bookcrafters, 1994. Source also includes data from an unpublished addendum by the author in May 2002.

04   SAR Rev War Graves Register Completed Forms, VASSAR.

05   SAR Rev War Graves Register. NASSAR, 2000 Edition.

06   Klein, Margaret C. *Tombstone Inscriptions of Spotsylvania County, Virginia.* Palm Coast, FL: private printing, 1983.

07   Bowers, D. "Pillars of the Past." Fredericksburg (VA) *Free Lance Star*, Nov. 4, 2000, p. 2-3.

08   Virginia Historical Inventory. WPA Cemetery Survey Reports, Spotsylvania County. Library of Virginia, Richmond. See Service Code 75.

09   Durrett, Virginia Wright and Sonya V. Harvison. *Handbook of Historic Sites in Spotsylvania County, Virginia.* Spotsylvania, VA: Spotsylvania Historical Association, 1987.

10   Holtzclaw, B. C. and W. B. Hackley. *Germantown Revisited.* Germanna Record, No. 2, 1962 . Reprint: Locust Grove, VA: Memorial Foundation of the Germanna Colonies, 1980.

11   Jett, Dora Chinn. *Minor Sketches of Major Folk and Where They Sleep: The Old Masonic Burying Ground, Fredericksburg, Virginia.* Richmond: Old Dominion Press, 1928.

12   Quenzel, Carol H. *The History and Background of St, George's Episcopal Church, Fredericksburg, Virginia.* Richmond: for the Vestry, 1951.

13   Hodges, Robert Allen. *The Masonic Cemetery of Fredericksburg, Virginia.* Fredericksburg, VA: private printing, 1991—original entry here said published 1951.

14   Collins, Herbert Ridgeway. *Cemeteries of Caroline County, Virginia.* Vol. 1, Public Cemeteries. Westminster, MD: Family Line Publications, 1994. Currently published by Colonial Roots, Lewes, Delaware.

15   Turner, Ronald R. *Prince William County, Virginia Burial index 1800-2001.* Manassas, VA: private printing, 2001.

16   Conners, E.R., III. *One Hundred Old Cemeteries of Prince William County, Virginia.* Manassas, VA: private printing, 1981.

17   Klein, Margaret C. *Tombstone Inscriptions of King George County, Virginia.* Baltimore: Genealogical Publishing Co., Inc., 1979.

18   Baird, Nancy Chappalear, Carol Jordan and Joseph Scherer. *Fauquier County, Virginia Tombstone Inscriptions.* Vol. I. Bowie, MD: Heritage Books, 2000.

19   Baird, Nancy Chappalear, Carol Jordan and Joseph Scherer. *Fauquier County, Virginia Tombstone Inscriptions.* Vol. II. Bowie, MD: Heritage Books, 2000.

20   Pippenger, Wesley E. *Tombstone Inscriptions of Alexandria, Virginia.* Vol. III. Westminster, MD: Family Line Publications, 1992.

21   Rudd, Alice B. *Shockoe Cemetery, Richmond, Virginia: Register of Internments, April 10 1822 –December 31, 1950.* 2 volumes. Washington, DC: private printing, 1960.

22   Klein, Margaret C. *Tombstone Inscriptions of Orange County, Virginia.* 1979. Reprint, Baltimore: Clearfield Publishing Co., Inc., 2001.

23   Pippenger, Wesley E. *Tombstone Inscriptions of Alexandria, Virginia.* Vol, I. Westminster, MD: Family Line Publications, 2000.

24   Pearson, Virginia Drewry McGeorge. "Family and Cemetery Records." *Northern Neck of Virginia Historical Magazine,* XX (1970), xxxx. Used for Wellford Family Cemetery at Sabine Hall" in Warsaw, Richmond County.

25   Thomas Balch Library. *Loudoun County, Virginia Cemeteries: A Preliminary Index.* Lovettsville, VA: Willow Bend Books, 1996.

26   Goodwin, William Arthur Rutherford. *Bruton Parish Church Restored & Its Historic Environment.* Petersburg, VA: The Franklin Press, 1907. *Historical Sketch of Bruton Church, Williamsburg, VA,* pub 1903.

27   Matthews, Bettie Jo. *Cedar Grove Cemetery, Portsmouth, Virginia Plot Book 1 and Book 2.* Bowie, M: Heritage Books, 1992.

28   Moore, J. Staunton and L. W. Burton. The *Annals and History of Henrico Parish, Diocese of Virginia, and St. John's Church P.E. Church.* 1904. Reprint, Baltimore: Genealogical Publishing Co., Inc., 1997.

29   Jones, Mary Stevens. *An 18th Century Perspective: Culpeper County.* Culpeper, VA: Culpeper Historical Society, 1976.

30   Eby, Jerrilyn. *They Called Stafford Home: The Development of Stafford County, Virginia from 1600 until 1865.* Bowie, MD: Heritage Books, Inc., 1997.

31   Yates, Helen Kay and W. E. Winfrey. *Family Graveyards in Hanover County, Virginia.* 2 volumes. Hanover, VA: Hanover County Historical Society, 1995, 2000.

32   Letters and e-mail correspondence from submitters. Compiler's files.

33   Cemetery Files. Rappahannock County Historical Society, 328 Gay St., Washington, VA.

34   Eby, Jerrilyn. *Laying the Hoe: A Century of Iron Manufacturing, Stafford County, Virginia, With Genealogical Notes on Over 300 Families.* Westminster, MD: Willowbend Books, 2003.

35   Delaney, T. *Veteran Burials in Old City Cemetery, Lynchburg, VA,* revised list of 2005.

36   *Burials in Augusta County, Virginia Cemeteries*. Staunton, VA: Augusta County Historical Society, 1985. Original entry was: Hamrick, R. M. Jr., *Burials in Augusta County, VA Cemeteries, Part I.*

37   Mihalyka, Jean Merritt and Faye Downing Wilson. *Graven Stones of Lower Accomack County, Virginia*. Pub 1986.

38   Cary, Mary Frances with Moody K. Miles III and Barry W. Miles. *Tombstone Inscriptions of Upper Accomack County, Virginia*. Bowie, MD: Heritage Books, 1995.

39   Wright, F. Edward. *Quaker Records of Henrico Monthly Meeting, And Other Church Records of Henrico, New Kent and Charles City Counties, Virginia*. Lewes, MD: Colonial Roots, 2002.

40   Hill, Margaret Lester and Clyde H. Ratcliffe. *In Remembrance: Gravestone Inscriptions and Burials of Lancaster County, Virginia*. White Stone, VA: private printing, 2002.

41   Miles, Barry W. with James H. Mero and Joseph A. Atkins. *Cemeteries City of Hampton, VA, Formally Elizabeth County*. Bowie, MD: Heritage Books, 1999.

42   Mihalyka, Jean Merrit. *Gravestone Inscriptions in Northampton County, Virginia*. Richmond: Virginia State Library, 1984.

43   Sheridan, Christine L. and Elsie W. Ernst. *Tombstones of Mathews County, Virginia, 1711-1986*. Mathew, VA: Mathews County Historical Society, 1988.

44   Augusta County Historical Society. *Burials in Augusta County, Virginia Cemeteries*. Staunton, VA: The Society, 1985.Original entry was: Hamrick, R.M. Jr., *Burials in Augusta County, VA Cemeteries, Part II.*

45   Miles, Barry W. & Gertrude Stead. *Cemeteries of the City of Newport News, Formerly Warwick County, Virginia*. Bowie, MD: Heritage Books, 1999.

46   Hamner, Ann K. *Grave Sites and Cemeteries in Goochland County, Virginia*. Goochland, VA: private printing, 1990.

47   *William & Mary Quarterly*. See text for patriot for volume, pages, etc.

48   Branch, Joseph Bryan. Association for the Preservation of Virginia Antiquities. *Epitaphs of Gloucester and Mathews Counties, Virginia, Through 1865*. Richmond: Virginia State Library, 1959.

49   Murphy, W.A., Mrs. & Fanny Bayly King. *Glebe Burying Ground, 1749*. [Augusta County.] Staunton, VA: Col. Thomas Hughart Chapter, Virginia Daughters of the American Revolution, 1934.

50   Winchester-Frederick Co Historical Society. *2200 Gravestone Inscriptions from Winchester and Frederick County, Virginia,* also *Gravestone Inscriptions from 61 Graveyards in Frederick Co.* Both were published by Winchester-Frederick County Historical Society in 1960.

51   Not used.

52   Hull, Janice J. R. *Buckingham Burials, A Survey Cemeteries in Buckingham County, Virginia*. Vol. I. Alexandria, VA: Hearthside Press, 1997.

53   "Southampton County Historical Society Cemetery Project." *Southampton County Historical Society—Rootsweb*. http://www.rootsweb.ancestry.com/~vaschs/cemetery.htm : 2015.

54   Moore, Munsey Adams. *Cemetery and Tombstone Records of Mecklenburg County, Virginia*. 2 vols. Chase City, VA: Munsey Moore pub., 1982-1987.

55   Research Committee, Giles County Historical Society. *Giles County, Virginia, History—Families*. No place: Giles County Historical Society, 1982.

56   Lipowicz, Rachel Baker. *Gone But Not Forgotten, Gravestone Inscriptions and Burials of Chesterfield County, Virginia.* Chesterfield, VA: Chesterfield County Historical Society Cemetery Committee, 1998.

57   Not used.

58   Royston, Donald R and Mary L. Royston. *Cemeteries of Clarke County, Virginia.* Athens, GA: New Papyrus Publishing, 2005.

59   Delaney-Painter, Nancy and Susan L. McCabe. *Index to Burials in Frederick County, Virginia.* Westminster, MD: Willow Bend Books, 2004.

60   "Virginia Cemetery Records." On-line database, searchable by county / independent city. *Interment.net.* http://interment.net/us/va/index.htm : 2015.

61   Fairfax Genealogical Society. *Fairfax County, Virginia Gravestones.* 6 volumes. Merrifield, VA: The Society, 1994-1998.

62   Baber, Lucy H. M. *Behind the Old Brick Wall: A Cemetery Story.* Lynchburg Committee of the Colonial Dames of America in the Commonwealth of Virginia, 1968. Whittet & Shepperson printers, Richmond.

63   *Tombstone Inscriptions of Norfolk, County, Virginia.* Norfolk, VA: Norfolk County Historical Society of Chesapeake, Virginia and National Society of the Daughters of the American Revolution (Norfolk, VA), 1979.

64   *Cemeteries King George County.* Vol. 1, Church Cemeteries. King George, VA: King George County Historical Society, 2000.

65   Rootsweb, VA Tombstone Photo Project Index

66   *Family Cemeteries in Fluvanna County, Virginia.* Palmyra, VA: Fluvanna County Historical Society and US Daughters of the American Revolution, Point of Fork Chapter (Fort Union), by Seven Islands Publishing, 1996.

67   Early, Mrs. John E. and Mrs. Gordon F. Harris. *Records of Cemeteries in Albemarle County, Virginia, including Charlottesville.* 12 volumes. Charlottesville, VA: US Daughters of the American Revolution, Jack Jouett Chapter (Charlottesville), 1971-72.

68   Burow, Suzanne. Carroll County Historical Society. *Cemetery Records of Carroll County, Virginia.* Baltimore: Gateway Press, 1990.

69   Arlington Genealogy Club. *Graveyards of Arlington County, Virginia.* Arlington, VA: National Genealogical Society, 1985.

70   US Daughters of the American Revolution, Frances Bland Chapter (Petersburg). *Dinwiddie County, Virginia Graveyard Records.* Petersburg, VA: The Society, 1945.

71   Rudolph, Mrs. C. F. *Record Tombstone Inscriptions in the Old Fort Defiance Cemetery, Fort Defiance, Augusta County, Virginia.* No place: private printing, 1952.

72   Alleghany Highlands Genealogical Society. *Survey of Various Cemeteries of Alleghany County. Virginia.* 3 volumes. Covington, VA: The Society, 1995-97.

73   McNeely, Mike. "The Brugh Cemetery, Botetourt County, Virginia." Text file. *The Tombstone Transcription Project, Virginia, Botetourt County. USGenWeb Archives.* http://files.usgwarchives.net/va/botetourt/cemeteries/brugh.txt : 2015

74   Ayers, Charles Linard and Ruth G. Hale. "Old Glade Creek Cemetery Additions— Botetourt County." Text file. *The Tombstone Transcription Project, Virginia, Botetourt County. USGenWeb Archives.* http://files.usgwarchives.net/va/botetourt/cemeteries/oldglade02.txt : 2015.

75   Virginia Historical Inventory. WPA Cemetery Survey Reports. Library of Virginia, Richmond. Available at Library of Virginia>online Catalog> Indexes and Images>Virginia

Historical Inventory, search word "cemeteries." Alphabetical listing by county.
http://www.lva.virginia.gov/

76   Early, Ruth Hairston. *Campbell Chronicles & Family Sketches, 1782-1926*. 1927, Reprint.
      Baltimore: Regional Publishing Company, 1978.

77   Nowery, Catherine Lynn. *Tombstone Inscriptions of Powhatan County, Virginia*. 2
      volumes. Rock Hill, SC: privately printed, 1996-97.

78   McConnell, Catherine S. *High on A Windy Hill*. Bristol, TN: The King Printing Company,
      1968. Washington County Historical Society. High on A Windy Hill: Cemeteries of
      Washington County, Vol. II, 2002? Or the 1968 book plus addendum which is: Niemann,
      John P. and Rubinette Miller Neimann. *High on A Windy Hill: Index and Addendum,
      Washington County, Virginia Cemeteries*. Abingdon, VA: Washington County Historical
      Society, 1989. Original entry read: *High on a Windy Hill (Cem Washington, Co, VA)*, pub
      1968, additions 1999 [not 1989].

79   Borden, Duane Lyle. *Tombstone Inscriptions of Shenandoah & Page Counties, Virginia*.
      Ozark, MO: Yates Publishing Co., 1984.

80   Hatcher, Patricia Law. *Abstract of Graves Revolutionary Patriots*. 4 volumes.
      Westminster, MD: Willow Bend Books, 2001. Citations in the book refer to volume and
      page number. These volumes are consolidations of annual reports made by the DAR to
      the U.S. Senate from 1900 to 1974.

81   Ricketts, R. D. "Danny". *Dan River Plantations, Danville & Pittsylvania Co, VA*. He also
      has a blog site called Ricketts.com

82   Franklin County Heritage Society. *Cemeteries of Franklin County, Va*. Henry, VA: B & C
      Publishing Co., 1998.

83   Payne, L. C. & L. W. *Fauquier family Cemeteries of Rev War,* Mar 2007.

84   The National Society of the Colonial Dames of America in the State of Virginia. *The
      Parish Register of Christ Church, Middlesex County, Va. from 1653 to 1812*. 1897.
      Reprint with revised index, Easley, SC: Southern Historical Press, 1988.

85   The National Society of the Colonial Dames of America in the State of Virginia. *Parish
      Register of St Peter's Parish, New Kent County, Virginia 1680-1787*. Richmond: Wm.
      Ellis Jones, Book and Job Printer, 1904.

86   Clarke, Peyton Neale. *Old King William Homes & Families: An Account of Some of the
      Old Homesteads and Families of King William County, From Its Earliest Settlement.*1897.
      Reprint, Baltimore: Regional Publishing Company, 1964.

87   "St. Paul's Church." *The Key* (December 1984). Norfolk Genealogical Society.

88   Gray, Louise E., Richard H. Genders et al. Middlesex County Board of Supervisors.
      Historic Buildings in Middlesex County, Virginia 1650-1875. Charlotte, NC: Delmar
      Printing Co., 1978.

89   The Hugh S. Watson, Jr. Genealogical Society of Tidewater, Virginia. *Gravestone
      Inscriptions From the Cemetery of St Johns Episcopal Church, Hampton, Virginia.
      Hampton, VA: Thomas Nelson Community College, 1975.*

90   *Tombstone Inscriptions from the Family Cemetery at 'Hilton,' Madison County, Virginia*.
      Virginia Magazine of History and Biography 62 (April 1954), 211-212.

91   Pittsylvania Historical Society. "Gravestones in Pittsylvania County." *The Quill Pen*. This
      is a quarterly journal started in 1982, now called the *Pittsylvania Packet*. Name changed
      in August 1991.

92   Butt, Marshall W. and Dean Burgess, D. *Surviving Gravestones at Trinity Church,
      Portsmouth, Virginia*. Portsmouth, VA: private printing, 2000.

93 "Cemetery Records." Photos and transcripts of inscriptions of tombstones, often annotated with additional biographical data. Listed in alphabetical order by cemetery name. *Carol's House.* http://carolshouse.com/cemeteryrecords/ : 2015.

94 Virginia Historical Inventory. WPA Cemetery Survey Reports, Prince William County. Library of Virginia, Richmond. See Service Code 75.

95 Virginia Historical Inventory. WPA Cemetery Survey Reports, Fauquier County. Library of Virginia, Richmond. See Service Code 75.

96 *Records of Dettingen Parish, Prince William County, Virginia 1745-1802.* Dumfries, VA: Historic Dumfries, 1976.

97 Sturgill, Mack Howard and Kenneth Lee. *Smyth County Virginia Cemeteries.* 4 vols. No place: private printing, 1993-1994.

98 Virginia Historical Inventory. WPA Cemetery Survey Reports, Caroline County. Library of Virginia, Richmond. See Service Code 75.

99 *Virginia Vital Records, Compiled from Virginia Magazine of History & Biography, William & Mary Quarterly and Tyler's Quarterly.* Baltimore: Clearfield Publishing, 2007. From:C. G. Chamberlayne. "Old Blandford Tombstones," *William and Mary Quarterly* 5, 1st Series (April 1897), 230-240.

100 *Virginia Vital Records.* From: Lyon G. Tyler. "Inscriptions on Old Tombs in Gloucester Co.,Virginia," *William and Mary Quarterly* 3, 1st Series (July 1894), 28-43.

101 *Virginia Vital Records.* Taken from: Rev. S. O. Southall. "Tombstones. New Castle, Hanover County." Tyler's Quarterly 3 (1921), 69.

102 *Virginia Vital Records.* From: George H. S. King. "Tombstone Inscriptions From the Family Cemetery at 'Jerdone Castle,' Louisa County, Virginia." *Virginia Magazine of History and Biography* 62 (Apr 1954), 208-209.

103 *Virginia Vital Records.* From: Lenora Higginbotham Sweeney. "Epitaphs Copied from the Family Cemetery at Soldier's Joy, Nelson County, Virginia." *Virginia Magazine of History and Biography* 64 (Apr 1956), 208-209.

104 *Virginia Vital Records.* From: Lyon G. Tyler. *"Old Tombstones in New Kent County."* William and Mary Quarterly 5, 1st Series (1896), 77-81.

105 *Virginia Vital Records.* From: "Early Tombstones in Northumberland, County." *William and Mary Quarterly* 8, 1st Series (Jul 1899), 42-47.

106 *Virginia Vital Records.* From: "Old Tombstones in Northampton & Accomac Counties, Va." *William and Mary Quarterly* 3, 1st Series (Apr 1895), 256-262.

107 *Virginia Vital Records.* From: G. W. Beale. "Inscriptions on Old Tombstones in Westmorelandand Northumberland Counties." *William and Mary Quarterly* 9 (Jul 1990), 25-31.

108 *Virginia Vital Records.* From: G.W. Beale. "Early Tombs in Westmoreland, Richmond and Northumberland Counties." *William and Mary Quarterly* 11, 1st Series (Oct 1902), 123-130; (Jan 1903), 191-195.

109 *Virginia Vital Records,* Appendix A. From: "Inscriptions From Tombstones in King & Queen, Westmoreland, Hanover and Albemarle Counties." *William and Mary Quarterly* 9, 1st Series (Jan 1901), 25-31.

110 Wright, F. Edward, and Wesley E. Pippenger. *Early Church Records of Alexandria City and Fairfax County, Virginia.* Westminster, MD: Family Line Publications, 1996.

111 Virginia Historical Inventory. WPA Cemetery Survey Reports, Prince George County. Library of Virginia, Richmond. See Service Code 75.

112   Virginia Historical Inventory. WPA Cemetery Survey Reports, Frederick County. Library of Virginia, Richmond. See Service Code 75.

113   Virginia Historical Inventory. WPA Cemetery Survey Reports, Warren County. Library of Virginia, Richmond. See Service Code 75.

114   Virginia Historical Inventory. WPA Cemetery Survey Reports, Henrico County. Library of Virginia, Richmond. See Service Code 75.

115   Botetourt County American Bi-Centennial Commission. *Botetourt County History Before 1900 Through County Cemetery Records.* Fincastle, VA: Publications Committee, 1978.

116   Revolutionary War Monument, Peaked Mountain Cemetery, McGaheysville, Rockingham County, Virginia. Bronze plaque commemorating patriots known to be buried here. Erected by the Massanutton Chapter NSDAR on 12 Oct 1981. Original stones are not extant.

117   "Old St. Luke's Church Cemetery" Benn's Church Blvd, Gravestone Study Task Force, Isle of Wight County Historical Society, 2006.

118   Fitzgerald, Magdalene V. *Cole's Burial Ground, Pittsylvania County,* VA (Publisher not determined).

119   Chart of Revolutionary War Soldiers Buried in Mt Hebron Cemetery, Winchester, VA http://www.historicalmarkerproject.com/markers/HMHU6_revolutionary-war-soldiers-in-mt-hebron-cemetery_Winchester-VA.html

120   Virginia Historical Inventory. WPA Cemetery Survey Reports, Page County. Library of Virginia, Richmond. See Service Code 75.

121   Levy, Andrew. *The Great Emancipator: The Forgotten Story of Robert Carter III, The Founding Father Who Freed his Slaves.* New York: Random House, 2005.

122   Roanoke Valley Historical Society. *Roanoke County Graveyards Through 1920.* Roanoke, VA: The Society, 1986.

123   Worrell, Anne Lowry, comp. *Over The Mountain Men: Their Early Court Records in Southwest Virginia.* Baltimore: Genealogical Publishing Co., Inc., 1976.

124   Matheny, Emma R. & Helen K. Yates. *Kingston Parish Register, Gloucester and Matthews Counties, 1749-1827.* Richmond: the authors, 1963.

125   Pilson, O. E. *Tombstone Inscriptions of the Cemeteries in Patrick County, Virginia.* Baltimore:Gateway Press, 1984.

126   Pippenger, Wesley E. *Tombstone Inscriptions of Alexandria, Virginia.* Vol. 2. Westminster, MD: Family Line Publications, 1992.

127   Charles City County Revolutionary War Roster http://www.charlescity.org/rwr/rwr-search.php?button=go&page=1

128   Morrison, Carol A. *Miscellaneous Headstone Inscriptions, Old Blandford Cemetery, Petersburg, Virginia.* Online document: http://vagenweb.petersburghistory.com/old/cemetery/blandfd2.htm. Email: camorrison@ibm.net. June, 2015.

129   Harris, Malcomb H. *Old New Kent County, Virginia: Some Account of the Planters and Plantations in King William County, Virginia.* Vol. I. West Point, VA: private printing, 1977.

130   Virginia county websites, *Burials of Virginia Politicians* http://politicalgraveyard.com/geo/VA

131   "Bedford County Cemetery Listings." On-line database. *USGENWEB Tombstone Transcription Project.* http://www.usgwtombstones.org/virginia/bedford.html - June 2015.

132   Fairfax Resolves Chapter, VASSAR *Virginia Legislative Petitions for Alexandria and Fairfax County.*

133   "Surry County, VA, Cemeteries." *Rootsweb.ancestry.com.* Online database. http://www.rootsweb.ancestry.com/~vaschsm/cemetery.html - June 2105. Compiled by Surry County Historical Society, Surry, VA.

134   Princess Anne Chapter USDAR. *Old Tombstone Records Mathews County, VA,* 1970.

135   Wilson, Thurman Robert & Ruth Boyd Wilson. *Tazewell County Cemeteries.* 3 Vols. No place: private printing, 1992-1994.

136   Friends of Norfolk Historic cemeteries, *Cedar Grove Cemetery Rev War Veterans* 2009 newsletter. For name of newsletter, publication data (issue/volume, number, page number, etc. place published See text for patriot).

137   Letter Jun 2001, Historian Poquoson Presbyterian church.

138   Not used.

139   Virginia Historical Inventory. WPA Cemetery Survey Reports, City of Norfolk. Library of Virginia, Richmond. See Service Code 75.

140   Virginia Historical Inventory. WPA Cemetery Survey Reports, Wythe County. Library of Virginia, Richmond. See Service Code 75.

141   Virginia Historical Inventory. WPA Cemetery Survey Reports, Greenville County. Library of Virginia, Richmond. See Service Code 75.

142   Virginia Historical Inventory. WPA Cemetery Survey Reports, Augusta County. Library of Virginia, Richmond. See Service Code 75.

143   Virginia Historical Inventory. WPA Cemetery Survey Reports, Suffolk County. Library of Virginia, Richmond. See Service Code 75.

144   Virginia Historical Inventory. WPA Cemetery Survey Reports, Southampton County. Library of Virginia, Richmond. See Service Code 75.

145   Virginia Historical Inventory. WPA Cemetery Survey Reports, Accomack County. Library of Virginia, Richmond. See Service Code 75.

146   Dixon, Joan M. *National Intelligencer Newspaper Abstracts 1814-1817.* Bowie, MD: Heritage Books, 2006.

147   Virginia Historical Inventory. WPA Cemetery Survey Reports, City of Portsmouth. Library of Virginia, Richmond. See Service Code 75.

148   Virginia Historical Inventory. WPA Cemetery Survey Reports, Prince Edward County. Library of Virginia, Richmond. See Service Code 75.

149   Virginia Historical Inventory. WPA Cemetery Survey Reports, Louisa County. Library of Virginia, Richmond. See Service Code 75.

150   Virginia Historical Inventory. WPA Cemetery Survey Reports, Floyd County. Library of Virginia, Richmond. See Service Code 75.

151   Virginia Historical Inventory. WPA Cemetery Survey Reports, Nottoway County. Library of Virginia, Richmond. See Service Code 75.

152   Virginia Historical Inventory. WPA Cemetery Survey Reports, Orange County. Library of Virginia, Richmond. See Service Code 75.

153   Virginia Historical Inventory. WPA Cemetery Survey Reports, Isle of Wight County. Library of Virginia, Richmond. See Service Code 75.

154   Virginia Historical Inventory. WPA Cemetery Survey Reports, Rockbridge County. Library of Virginia, Richmond. See Service Code 75.

155   Virginia Historical Inventory. WPA Cemetery Survey Reports, Shenandoah County. Library of Virginia, Richmond. See Service Code 75.

156   Virginia Historical Inventory. WPA Cemetery Survey Reports, Pittsylvania County. Library of Virginia, Richmond. See Service Code 75.

157   Virginia Historical Inventory. WPA Cemetery Survey Reports, Cumberland County. Library of Virginia, Richmond. See Service Code 75.

158   Virginia Historical Inventory. WPA Cemetery Survey Reports, Russell County. Library of Virginia, Richmond. See Service Code 75.

159   Virginia Historical Inventory. WPA Cemetery Survey Reports, Bath County. Library of Virginia, Richmond. See Service Code 75.

160   Virginia Historical Inventory. WPA Cemetery Survey Reports, Alleghany County. Library of Virginia, Richmond. See Service Code 75.

161   Virginia Historical Inventory. WPA Cemetery Survey Reports, Amherst County. Library of Virginia, Richmond. See Service Code 75.

162   Virginia Historical Inventory. WPA Cemetery Survey Reports, City of Lynchburg. Library of Virginia, Richmond. See Service Code 75.

163   Virginia Historical Inventory. WPA Cemetery Survey Reports, Rappahannock County. Library of Virginia, Richmond. See Service Code 75.

164   Virginia Historical Inventory. WPA Cemetery Survey Reports, Fluvanna County. Library of Virginia, Richmond. See Service Code 75.

165   Virginia Historical Inventory. WPA Cemetery Survey Reports, Botetourt County. Library of Virginia, Richmond. See Service Code 75.

166   Virginia Historical Inventory. WPA Cemetery Survey Reports, Dinwiddie County. Library of Virginia, Richmond. See Service Code 75.

167   Virginia Historical Inventory. WPA Cemetery Survey Reports, Culpeper County. Library of Virginia, Richmond. See Service Code 75.

168   Virginia Historical Inventory. WPA Cemetery Survey Reports, City of Richmond. Library of Virginia, Richmond. See Service Code 75.

169   Virginia Historical Inventory. WPA Cemetery Survey Reports, Madison County. Library of Virginia, Richmond. See Service Code 75.

170   Virginia Historical Inventory. WPA Cemetery Survey Reports, City of Williamsburg. Library of Virginia, Richmond. See Service Code 75.

171   Virginia Historical Inventory. WPA Cemetery Survey Reports, Amelia County. Library of Virginia, Richmond. See Service Code 75.

172   Virginia Historical Inventory. WPA Cemetery Survey Reports, Lunenburg County. Library of Virginia, Richmond. See Service Code 75.

173   Virginia Historical Inventory. WPA Cemetery Survey Reports, Buckingham County. Library of Virginia, Richmond. See Service Code 75.

174   Pippenger, Wesley E. *Tombstones of Alexandria Virginia*. Vol V. Bowie, MD: Heritage Books,   2005. Used for St. Mary's Catholic Church.

175   Burial Register St Mary's Catholic Church, Alexandria, VA. http://www.alexandriagazette.com/news/2015/dec/09/column-founding-father-st-marys-catholic-church-an/

176   "Cedar Grove Cemetery." Norfolk Bureau of Cemeteries' [sic] Interment Database. From Cedar Grove Cemetery web page, City of Norfolk web site http://www.norfolk.gov/Facilities/Facility/Details/46 : "The Norfolk Bureau of Cemeteries' interment database is now available online via WebCemeteries.com. [Not searchable by cemetery.] The Bureau's database does not include obituaries or monument photographs. USGenWeb Archives, a cooperative network of volunteers that provides genealogical information on the internet, provides many of these in its interment catalog of Cedar Grove Cemetery." http://www.usgwarchives.net/va/norfolkcity/cemeteries/elmwoodcedargrove/elmcg08-a-bap.html -: June 2015.

177.   Obituaries in American Commercial Beacon & Portsmouth Advertiser http://ldsgenealogy.com/cgi-bin/News-VA.cgi?43036_American_Beacon_and_Norfolk_and_Portsmouth_Daily_Advertiser. (Norfolk, Va.) 1827-1851.

178   VASSAR Burial Committee for St Paul's Church Graveyard (Compiler a member).

179.   Virginia Historical Inventory. WPA Cemetery Survey Reports, Shockoe Hill Cemetery, City of Richmond. Library of Virginia, Richmond. See Service Code 75.

180.   Burial Cards Hollywood Cemetery, City of Richmond. Burial cards on microfilm. Business Records from 1847-2012 (includes interments). On Misc. Reels 626-628, 1015-1024, 1025-1027, 1130-1131, 1829, 4656, 4657, 5403, 6146. (23 reels total). http://lva1.hosted.exlibrisgroup.com/F/AYNNF89VD3EVPVLLD3SLN92BBV1V7TYG877 CFVSYBG5CMSDJ1L-38154?func=full-set-set&set_number=003537&set_entry=000042&format=999

181   Virginia Historical Inventory. WPA Cemetery Survey Reports, Highland County. Library of Virginia, Richmond. See Service Code 75.

182   Virginia Historical Inventory. WPA Cemetery Survey Reports, Nelson County. Library of Virginia, Richmond. See Service Code 75.

183   Virginia Historical Inventory. WPA Cemetery Survey Reports, Bristol Cemetery, Washington County. Library of Virginia, Richmond. See Service Code 75.

184   Virginia Historical Inventory. WPA Cemetery Survey Reports, Hebrew Cemetery, City of Richmond. Library of Virginia, Richmond. See Service Code 75.

185   Virginia Historical Inventory. WPA Cemetery Survey Reports, Roanoke County. Library of Virginia, Richmond. See Service Code 75.

186   Virginia Historical Inventory. WPA Cemetery Survey Reports, Rockingham County. Library of Virginia, Richmond. See Service Code 75.

187   Virginia Historical Inventory. WPA Cemetery Survey Reports, Powhatan County. Library of Virginia, Richmond. See Service Code 75.

188   Virginia Historical Inventory. WPA Cemetery Survey Reports, Blandford County. Library of Virginia, Richmond. See Service Code 75.

189   Mallory, Dalton W. *Westmoreland County, Virginia Cemeteries, Vol. 1*. Athens, GA: New Papyrus Publishing, 2009.

190   Prince William County cemetery website. *http://www.historicprincewilliam.org/cemeteries.html*

191   Rockingham County Historical Society 2011 rootsweb.ancestry.com

192   Norfolk/Portsmouth Obituaries Journal *https://www.genealogybank.com/explore/newspapers/historical-obituaries/usa/virginia/norfolk*

193   *Death Notices from Richmond, Virginia Newspapers 1821-1840.* Special Publication No. 9. Richmond: Virginia Genealogical Society, 1987.

194   Chris Hanks. *Pittsylvania County History.* http://www.PittsylvaniaCountyHistory.com

195   Wikipedia, the free encyclopedia. *https://en.wikipedia.org/wiki/Home_page*

196   Find A Grave. http://findagrave.com/index.html

197   NSSAR Patriot Grave Search https://memberinfo.sar.org/patriotsearch/search.aspx

198   Not used.

199   http://usgwtombstone.org/virginia/virginia.html VA tombstone Transcription Project (WPA Reports).

200   William & Mary Quarterly. See text for patriot for specifics.

201   Virginia Historical Inventory. WPA Cemetery Survey Reports, Appomattox County. Library of Virginia, Richmond. See Code 75.

202   Virginia Historical Inventory. WPA Cemetery Survey Reports, Hampton [City]. Library of Virginia, Richmond. See Code 75.

203   Arlington National Cemetery Interment Cards. "U.S., Burial Registers, Military Posts and National Cemeteries Internment Cards, and National Cemeteries, 1862-1960." *Ancestry.com.* http://search.ancestry.com/search/db.aspx?dbid=3135 : 2015. Under an agreement reached in 2002 between the Veterans Administration and Ancestry.com, all burial records for national cemeteries were merged into a single database. Users must enter the name of the deceased veteran and the name of the cemetery to narrow the search to a specific person and cemetery.

204   Not used.

205   Mt Hebron Cemetery, Winchester, VA website Internment Records http://mthebroncemetery.org

206   Charles Randolph Hughes, *Gravestone Records from Old Chapel Cemetery, Located at Berryville, Clarke Co., Virginia,* Berryville, VA printed by Blue Ridge Press, 1906.

207   *Gravestones in the Cemetery, Ware Episcopal Church* [Gloucester County]. Alphabetical listing by name, with plot numbers. http://warechurch.org - June 2015.

208   Wilson, Howard McKnight. *The Tinkling Spring, Headwater of Freedom: The Study of a Church and Her People 1732-1952.* Fisherville, VA: private printing, 1954.

209   Stith, Wayne. "Cemetery Documentation Project—Gravestones of the Eastern Shore of Virginia." *Easternshore.com.* Accomack County. *http://easternshorestuff.com/cemeteryproject/acccems.htm*

210   Chalkley, Lyman. *Chronicles of the Scotch-Irish Settlement in Virginia.* Vol. II. 1912. Reprint, Baltimore: Genealogical Publishing Co., Inc., 1965.

211   Frain, Elizabeth R. *Union Cemetery, Leesburg, Loudoun County, Virginia: Plats A & B 1784-1995.* Lovettsville, VA: 1995

212   Green, Laurie Boush & Virginia Bonney West. *Old Churches, Their Cemeteries and Family Graveyards of Princes Anne County, Virginia.* Virginia Beach: the authors, 1985.

213   Mary R. Miller. *Place Names of the Northern Neck.* Richmond: Virginia State Library, 1983.

214   Downman Family Bible. Photostat of original. Mary Ball Washington Museum & Library, Lancaster, VA.

215   Dew, Allen, *Halifax County, VA Cemeteries.* Website
        http://cemeterycensus.com/va/halif/index.htm

216   Culpeper Co, VA Genealogy Family Search; Tombstone Transcription Project
        https://familysearch.org/learn/wiki/en/Culpeper_County,_Virginia_Genealogy#Cemeteries

217   Chamberlayne, C. G., *Burials in Old Blandford Church Graveyard,* 1896, transcribed by
        K. Torp *http//genealogytrails.com/vir/Dinwiddie/cem_oldblandfordchurch.html;* (Reprinted
        William & Mary Quarterly, 2 volumes, Vol 5, No 4, (Apr 1897) and Vol 6, No1 (Jul 1897)

218   Tombstone Transcription Project, Goochland Co, VA
        http://usgwtombstones.org/virginia/goochland.html

219   *http://www.heritagecenter.com/cemeteries/*

220   *www.genealogy.com/forum/surnames/topics*

221   U.S Genealogical Web Archives for Virginia. *http://www.usgwarchives.net/va/*

APPENDIX E – GENERAL BIBLIOGRAPHY OF OTHER SOURCES

Note: Books by the same author are denoted with "-----" after the first entry.

Adams, Lela C. *Marriages of Patrick County, Virginia 1791-1850*. Bassett, VA: Private printing, 1972.

Ashby, Bernice M. *Shenandoah County Virginia Marriage Bonds 1772-1850*. Berryville, VA: Virginia Book Company, 1967. Marriages are arranged in chronological order.

Baber, Lucy Harrison Miller and Hazel Letts Williamson. *Marriages of Campbell County, Virginia 1782-1810*. Lynchburg, VA: Private printing, 1971.

Biographical Directory of the American Congress 1774-Present. Alexandria, VA: Congressional Quarterly Staff. Biographies of the members of the Continental Congress from September 5, 1774 to October 21, 1788 and the United States Congress from March 4, 1789 to the present. Available on line at: <http://bioguide.congress.gov/biosearch/biosearch.asp> Active as of June 2012.

Chalkley, Lyman. *Chronicles of the Scotch-Irish Settlement in Virginia, Extracted from the Original Court Records of Augusta County 1745-1800*. 3 Vols. 1912, Reprint. Baltimore: Genealogical Publishing Company, Inc., 1965.

Chamberlayne, Churchill Gibson. *The Vestry Book and Register of Bristol Parish, Virginia 1720-1789*. 1898, Reprint. Greensville, SC: Southern Historical Press, Inc., 1994.

Chapman, Blanche Adams. *Marriages of Isle of Wight County, Virginia, 1628-1800*. 1933, Reprint with Revised Index by Anita Comois. Baltimore: Genealogical Publishing Co., Inc., 1976.

Chiarito, Marian Dodson and James Headley Prendergast. *Marriages of Halifax County Virginia 1801-1831*. Nathalie, VA: The Clarkton Press, 1985.

Davis, Eliza Timberlake. *Frederick County, Virginia, Marriages 1771-1825*. Baltimore: Genealogical Publishing Co., Inc., 1975.

Dennis, Earl S. and Jane E. Smith. *Marriage Bonds of Bedford County, Virginia 1755-1800*. 1933, Reprint with Index to Wills from 1754 to 1830 by Rowland D. Buford. Baltimore: Genealogical Publishing Co., Inc., 1981. Marriages are arranged alphabetically by first letter of last name and thereafter in no discernable order.

Dodd, Virginia Anderson. *Henry County Marriage Bonds 1778-1849*. Richmond, VA: Private printing, 1953.

Elliott, Katherine B. *Marriage Records 1749-1840 Cumberland County Virginia*. South Hill, VA: Private printing, 1969.

First Marriage Record of Augusta County, VA. 1785-1813. Verona, VA: McClure Press for the Col. Thomas Hughart Chapter, D.A.R., 1970. Marriages are arranged chronologically, with an every name index.

Fisher, Theresa A. *Marriage Records of the City of Fredericksburg, and of Orange, Spotsylvania Counties, Virginia 1722-1850*. Bowie, MD: Heritage Books, Inc., 1990.

------. *Marriages of Caroline County, Virginia, 1777-1853*. Bowie, MD: Heritage Books, Inc., 1998.

Fothergill, Augusta B. *Marriage Records of Brunswick County, Virginia 1730-1852*. 1953, Revised. Baltimore: Genealogical Publishing Co., Inc., 1976

Hill, Margaret Lester. *Ball Families of Virginia's Northern Neck: An Outline*. Private printing, 1990.

Hopkins, William Lindsay. *Caroline County Court Records and Marriages, 1787-1810*. Richmond, VA: Private printing, 1987.

Hodge, Robert A. *The Church Register of Rev. Silas M. Bruce for 1832-1881*. Locust Grove, VA: Germania Community College, 1975, Transcript of marriages. Index omits many names.

Jewell, Mrs. Walter Towner. *Loudoun County, Virginia Marriage Bonds 1762-1850*. Berryville, VA: Chesapeake Book Company, 1962.

Kiblinger, William H. and Janice L. Abercrombie. *Marriages of Louisa County, Virginia 1815-1861*. Orange, VA: Central Virginia Newspapers, Inc., 1969. Entries in this book are arranged in chronological order by only. Indexed.

Kilby, Craig M. "The Kelley Brothers and the American Colonization Society: From Northumberland to Liberia." *The Bulletin of the Northumberland County Historical Society*, 45 (2008), 34-53.

Kilby, Craig M. and Jane Langloh. "Lancaster County Estates 1835-1865." Lancaster, VA: Mary Ball Washington Museum & Library. On line at: http://mbwm.org/estates.asp Active as of June 2012.

King, George Harrison Sanford. *Marriages of Richmond County, Virginia 1668-1853*. Fredericksburg, VA: Private Printing, 1964.

Knorr, Catherine L. *Marriages of Brunswick County Virginia 1750-1810*. Pine Bluff, AR: The Perdue Company, 1953.

-----. *Marriages of Charlotte County Virginia 1764-1815*. Pine Bluff, AR: The Perdue Company, 1951.

-----. *Marriages of Halifax County Virginia 1753-1800*. Pine Bluff, AR: The Perdue Company, 1957.

-----. *Marriages of Chesterfield County, Virginia 1771-1815*, Pine Bluff, AR: The Perdue Company, 1958.

-----. *Marriages of Fredericksburg Virginia 1782-1850*. Pine Bluff, AR: Private printing, 1954.

-----. *Marriages of Halifax County Virginia 1753-1800*. Pine Bluff, AR: The Perdue Company, 1957.

-----. *Marriages of Orange County Virginia 1747-1810*. Pine Bluff, AR: The Perdue Company, 1959.

-----. *Marriages of Pittsylvania County Virginia 1767-1805*. Pine Bluff, AR: The Perdue Company, 1956.

-----. *Marriages of Powhatan County Virginia 1777-1830*. Pine Bluff, AR: The Perdue Company, 1957.

-----. *Marriages of Prince Edward County Virginia 1754-1810*. Pine Bluff, AR: The Perdue Company, 1950.

-----. *Marriages of Southampton County Virginia 1750-1810*. Pine Bluff, AR: The Perdue Company, 1955.

-----. *Marriages of Surry County Virginia 1768-1825*. Pine Bluff, AR: The Perdue Company, 1960.

Lee, Elizabeth Nuckolls, *King George County Virginia Marriages, Vol. I, Marriages Book 1, 1786-1850 (including ministers' returns)*. Athens, GA: Iberian Publishing Company, 1995. Arranged alphabetically by first letter of groom's surname, then chronologically. Indexed.

------. *King George County Virginia, Vol. II, Implied Marriages*. Athens, GA: Iberian Publishing Company, 1995.

Lewis, James F. "Westmoreland County, Virginia, Marriages." *The Virginia Genealogist*, Vol. 10, No. 1, 24-56 (January-March, 1966). This article supplements *Westmoreland County Marriages* published by Stratton Nottingham in 1928

Lindsay, Joyce H. *Marriages of Henrico County Virginia 1680-1808*. Richmond, VA: Private printing, 1960.

Marriage Notices from Richmond, Virginia Newspapers 1821-1840. Special Publication No. 10. Richmond, VA: Virginia Genealogical Society, 1988.

Marriages and Deaths from Lynchburg, Virginia Newspapers 1794-1836. Baltimore: Genealogical Publishing Co., Inc., for the Randall Holt Chapter, National Society Daughters of the American Colonists, 1993.

Marriages and Deaths from Richmond, Virginia Newspapers 1780-1820. Special Publication No. 8. Richmond, VA: Virginia Genealogical Society, 1983. Deaths comprise pages 1-175. Marriages comprise pages 176-266. Index to brides comprises pages 267-285. There is no comprehensive index.

Marriage Records 1811-1853, Mecklenburg County Virginia. South Hill, VA: Preswould Chapter of Daughters of the American Revolution, 1962.

Marriages of Middlesex County, Virginia 1740-1852, Special Publication No. 3. Richmond, VA: Virginia Genealogical Society, 1965. The information for this book comes from the Marriage Register compiled from original bonds by the WPA in the 1930s, which is known to contain errors.

Matheny, Emma R. and Helen K. Yates. *Marriages of Lunenburg County Virginia 1746-1853*. Richmond, VA: Private printing, 1967.

McCarty, William M. and Kathleen Much. *McCartys of the Northern Neck, 350 Years of a Virginia Family*. 2005. Revised. Baltimore: Otter Bay Books, 2010.

McGinnis, Carol. *Virginia Genealogy, Sources & Resources*. Baltimore: Genealogical Publishing Co., Inc., 1993.

McIlwaine, H. R. *Index to Obituary Notices in the Richmond Enquirer from May 9, 1804 through 1828 and the Richmond Whig from January, 1824, through 1838*. 1921, Reprint. Baltimore: Genealogical Publishing Co., Inc., 1974. Originally published in the Bulletin of the Virginia State Library Vol. XIV, No. 4, October 1921.

Mihalyka, Jean M. *MARRIAGES Northampton County, Virginia 1660-1854*. 1991, Revised. Bowie, MD: Heritage books, Inc., 2000. This book –itself revised--is a major revision of the work of Stratton Nottingham in 1929.

Morten, Oren F. *A History of Rockbridge County Virginia*. Staunton, VA: The McClure Co., Inc., 1920.

Nance, Joanne Lovelace. *Charlotte County, Virginia 1816-1850, Marriage Bonds and Ministers' Returns (with additions to marriages 1764-1815)*. Charlottesville, VA: The N. W. Lapin Press, 1987.

Nottingham, Stratton. *The Marriage License Bonds of Lancaster County, Virginia from 1701 to 1848*. 1927, Reprint. Baltimore: Clearfield Publishing Company, Inc., 2002.

-----. *The Marriage License Bonds of Mecklenburg County, Virginia from 1765-1810*. Onancock, VA: Private printing,1926.

-----. *The Marriage License Bonds of Northampton County, Virginia from 1706 to 1854*. 1929, Reprint. Baltimore: Genealogical Publishing Company, Inc., 1974. This work was considerably enhanced and revised by Jean M. Mihalyka, see above. Mihalyka' s book is considered the superior source.

-----. *The Marriage License Bonds of Northumberland County, Virginia, from 1783 to 1850*. 1929, Reprint. Baltimore: Genealogical Publishing Co., Inc., 1976.

-----. *The Marriage License Bonds of Westmoreland County 1786-1850*. Onancock, VA: Private printing, 1929. This work was supplemented by James F. Lewis in 1966 (see above.)

Pippenger, Wesley E. *Death Notices from Richmond, Virginia Newspapers 1841-1853*. Richmond: Virginia Genealogical Society, 2002.

-----. *Index to Virginia Estates 1800-1865*. Ten vols. Richmond, VA: Virginia Genealogical Society, 2001-2010.

Pollock, Michael E. *Marriage Bonds of Henrico County, Virginia 1782-1853*. Baltimore: Genealogical Publishing Co., Inc., 1984.

Reddy, Anne Waller and Andrew Lewis Riffe. *Virginia Marriage Bonds Richmond City,* Vol 1. Staunton, VA: The McClure Co., Inc., 1939. Covers years 1797-1853. Entries are in chronological order. Indexed.

Second Marriage Record of Augusta County, VA. 1813-1850. Verona, VA: McClure Press for the Col. Thomas Hughart Chapter, D.A.R., 1972. The entries in the book are in chronological order only.

Strickler, Harry M. *Old Tenth Legion Marriages. Marriages in Rockingham County, Virginia From 1778 to 1816, Taken from the marriage bonds*. Dayton, VA: Joseph K. Ruebush Co., 1928.

Sweeny, Lenora Higginbotham. *Marriage Records of Amherst County, Virginia 1815-1821 And Subscription for Building St. Mark's Church Amherst County, Virginia*. Lynchburg, VA: J. P. Bell Company, Inc., 1961.

Sweeny, William Montgomery. *Marriage Bonds and Other Marriage Records of Amherst County, Virginia 1763-1800*. 1937, Reprint. Baltimore: Genealogical Publishing Company, Inc., 1973.

Turman, Nora Miller. *Marriage Records of Accomack County, Virginia 1776-1854, Recorded in Bonds, Licenses and Ministers' Returns*. Bowie, MD: Heritage Books, Inc., 1994.

Tyler, Lyon G., ed. *Encyclopedia of Virginia Biography*. 4 vols. NY: Lewis Historical Publishing Co., 1915.

Virginia: A Guide to the Old Dominion. Federal Writers' Project. 1941. Reprint. Richmond: Library of Virginia, 1991. Also on line in hypertext format and searchable as *The WPA Guide to the Old Dominion*, University of Virginia, American Studies Program (1999) at: <http://xroads.virginia.edu/~hyper/VAGuide/frame.html> Active as of June 2012.

"Virginia, Marriages, 1785-1946." Salt Lake City, UT: Genealogical Society of Utah. Index based on data collected by the Genealogical Society of Utah. Sources in this collection are varied and noted in the batch number of each entry. It is searchable online at: <https://familysearch.org/search/collection/show#uri=http://familysearch.org/searchapi/se arch/collection/1708698> Active as of June 21012.

Vogt, John and T. William Kethley, Jr. *Albemarle County Marriages 1780-1853*. 3 vols. Athens, GA: Iberian Publishing Co., 1991.

-----. *Virginia Historic Marriage Register: Clarke County Marriages, 1836-1850*. Athens, GA: Iberian Press, 1983. Clarke County was formed in 1836 from Frederick County.

-----. *Culpeper County Marriages, 1780-1853*. Athens, GA: Iberian Publishing Company, 1986.

-----. *Virginia Historic Marriage Register: Fluvanna County Marriages 1781-1849*. Athens, GA: Iberian Press, 1984.

-----. *Virginia Historic Marriage Register: Frederick County Marriages 1738-1850*. 1984, Revised. Athens, GA: Iberian Press, 1987.

-----. *Virginia Historic Marriage Register: Greene County Marriages 1838-1850*. Athens, GA: Iberian Press, 1984.

-----. *Virginia Historic Marriage Register: Madison County Marriages 1792-1850*. Athens, GA: Iberian Press, 1983.

-----. *Virginia Historic Marriage Register: Nelson County Marriages, 1808-1850*. Athens, GA: Iberian Publishing Company, 1985.

-----. *Virginia Historic Marriage Register: Orange County Marriages, 1747-1850*. Athens, GA: Iberian Press, 1984.

-----. *Virginia Historic Marriage Register: Rappahannock County Marriages, 1833-1850*. Athens, GA: Iberian Press, 1984.

-----. *Virginia Historic Marriage Register: Roanoke County Marriages, 1838-1850*. Athens, GA, Iberian Press, 1984.

-----. *Virginia Historic Marriage Register: Smyth County Marriages, 1832-1850*. Athens, GA, Iberian Press, 1984. Smyth County was formed in 1832 from Washington and Wythe Counties.

-----. *Virginia Historical Marriage Register: Warren County Marriages, 1836-1850*. Athens, GA: Iberian Press, 1983. Warren County was formed from Shenandoah County in 1836. Negative research.

-----. *Virginia Historical Marriage Register: York County Virginia Marriages, volume 1, Bond & Ministers' Returns 1769-1853*. Athens, GA: Iberian Publishing Company, 1994.

Wertz, Mary Alice. *Marriages of Loudoun County, Virginia 1757-1853*. Baltimore: Genealogical Publishing Co., Inc., 1985.

Wingo, Elizabeth B. *Marriages of Norfolk County, Va. (Now City of Chesapeake), 1788, 1793-1817*. Norfolk, VA: Private printing, 1963.

-----. *Marriages of Princess Anne County Virginia 1749-1821*. Norfolk, VA: Private printing, 1961. Princess Anne County became extinct in 1963 and became part of Virginia Beach.

Williams, Kathleen Booth. *Marriages of Amelia County, Virginia 1735-1815*. Private printing, 1961.

-----. *Marriages of Goochland County Virginia 1733-1815*. Private printing, 1960.

-----. *Marriages of Louisa County Virginia 1766-1815*. Alexandria, VA: Private printing, 1959.

-----. *Marriages of Orange County Virginia 1747-1810*. Private printing, 1959.

-----. *Marriages of Pittsylvania County Virginia 1767-1805*. Private printing, 1956.

-----. *Marriages of Pittsylvania County Virginia 1806-1830*. Private printing, 1965.

Wingfield, Marshall. *A History of Caroline County Virginia*. Baltimore: Regional Publishing Co., 1969.

Worrell, Anne Lowry. *A Brief of Wills and Marriages in Montgomery and Fincastle Counties, Virginia 1773-1831*. 1932, Reprint. Berryville, VA: Virginia Book Company, no date

-----. *Early Marriages, Wills, and Some Revolutionary War Records, Botetourt County, Virginia.* Baltimore: Genealogical Publishing Co., Inc., 1975. Marriages generally go no later than 1812.

Yates, William A. "Wythe County, Virginia Marriages, 1790-1800." The Ridge Runners, Vol. 4, No. 1, 58-61 (May 1975).

APPENDIX G – ADDENDA AND ERRATA

Additions:

ALLEMONG, Jacob; b 1754, Northampton, PA, d 8 Mar 1808 **RU:** Patriot, Gave material aid to cause, Frederick Co **CEM:** Heironmous family, GPS unk; Whitacre Farm, Whitacre; Frederick **GS:** Y **SP:** Elizabeth Rinker (6 Nov 1761-1848) **VI:** No further data **P:** N **BLW:** N **RG:** N **MK:** N **PH:** no **SS:** D; AL Comm Bk II, pg 168 Frederick Co **BS:** 221 Frederick Cemeteries.

ARMENTROUT, Frederick: b 16 Oct 1759, PA, d 22 Dec 1838; **RU:** Patriot, Gave material aid to cause, Rockingham Co **CEM:** Armentrout family, GPS unk; Potts Creek; Alleghany **GS:** Y **SP:** No info **VI:** No further data **P:** N **BLW:** N **RG:** N **MK:** N **PH:** no **SS:** D vol 1 **BS:** 196.

BIRCHETT, Drury; b 23 Jul 1762, d 10 Dec 1836 **RU:** Patriot, Gave material aid to cause **CEM:** Birchett Family, GPS unk; Rt 603, 1.6 mi East fr jct with Rt 460; Prince George **GS:** Y **SP:** Catherine (__) **VI:** Was Capt in War of 1812 **P:** N **BLW:** N **RG:** N **MK:** N **PH:** no **SS:** AL Comm Bk IV, pg 361, Prince George Co **BS:** 111.

BRUCE, James; b 20 Mar 1763 Charlotte Co, d 12 May 1837 **RU:** Patriot Gave material aid to cause **CEM:** Bruce Family West of South Boston, Rt 659 at Berry Hill Plantation; Halifax **GS:** Y **SP:** 1) Sarah Coles (1770-1806), 2) Mar Apr 1819, Elvira Cabell (10 Sep 1783-2 Oct 1853) **VI:** Son of Charles Bruce. Died in Philadelphia, buried there, body brought back to Berry Hill 100 years later and reinterred. He owned country stores, flour mills, a fertilizer-plaster factory, a blackmith shop, lumber mills, a cotton factory, and two taverns. **P:** N **BLW:** N **RG:** unk **MK:** unk **PH:** unk **SS:** Al Ct Bk pg 13, 47 **BS:** 196.

CARR, Peter; b 20 Oct 1740, died 1812 **RU:** Private/Patriot Served in Capt Henry McCabe's Co, Col Dabney's Regt, 1st Militia Brigade, Provided beef and a gun to the cause **CEM:** Union; GPS 39.12046,-77.56237; 323 North King St, Leesburg; Loudoun; **GS:** Y **SP:** Rachel Callwell (--12 Mar 1798) **VI:** Son of John Carr (1694-1794). Listed on monument with other family names **P:** N **BLW:** N **RG:** unk **MK:** unk **PH:** unk **SS:** DAR Ancestor #A019628, D vol 2, pg 610, 616; N pg 1267 **BS:** 196.

CRAWFORD, John; b 1741, Augusta Co, d 13 Jan 1832 **RU:** Captain. Served in Lt Col Richard Campbell's 2d VA Regt. Was captured at Charleston, exchanged Jul 1781 and served to Jun 1783 **CEM:** Hebron; GPS 38.14140, -79.15500; 423 Hebron Rd; Staunton City **GS:** Y **SP:** 1) Margaret "Peggy" Crawford daug of Patrick Crawford and Sally Wilson, 2) Sarah Newman (1767-1850) **VI:** Son of Alexander Crawford and Mary McPheeters **P:** unk **BLW:** unk **RG:** N **MK:** unk **PH:** unk **SS:** DP pg 208 **BS:** 196.

CROW, Thomas, Sr; b unk, d 1811 **RU:** Private, Enlisted in C. Minnis's Co, Col Fleming's 1st VA Regt, Feb 1778. Served to Jan 1779 **CEM:** Scott; GPS 36.88110, -81.38720; Across I-81 from rest stop Phipps Rd, Atkins :Smyth **GS:** N **SP:** No info **VI:** Son of Robert Crow and Mary (__) **P:** unk **BLW:** unk **RG:** N **MK:** N **PH:** N **SS:** DP pg 209 **BS:** 196.

DOAK, David, b 9 Dec 1740, d 1787 **RU:** Patriot, Gave use of horse for 22 days and hauled supplies for 6 days **CEM:** North Mountain; GPS unk; One mi N of Mt Tabor on Rt 620; Augusta **GS:** U **SP:** 1) Jennet Alexander, 2) Janet Davis **VI:** Son of Samuel Doak and Jane Mitchell. His name is on monument in cem with others at site of North Mountain Meeting House **P:** N **BLW:** N **RG:** unk **MK:** unk **PH:** unk **SS:** DY pg 125 **BS:** 142; 196.

FLOHR, George Daniel; b 30 Aug 1762, d 30 Apr 1826 **RU:** Soldier Served in the French Royal Deux-Ponts Regiment supporting American cause **CEM:** St Johns Lutheran Church; GPS 36.96500,-81.10110; 405 W Main, Wytheville; Wythe **GS:** Y **SP:** Elizabeth (__) (19 Jun 1777-25 Jul 1858) **VI:** Served as Pastor of church from 1799 to death in 1826. His log cabin home about a mile away was dismantled and re-erected in cemetery. **P:** N **BLW:** N **RG:** N **MK:** N **PH:** N **SS:** Letter 26 Apr 2011, Wythe B Sharitz, President of the Church Cemetery Board. Correspondence from Historian Dr Robert Selig **BS:** 196.

HOGSETT, James; b unk, d 18 Dec 1807 **RU:** Patriot, Gave beef and a wagon for two days for militia use **CEM:** Hogshead Family. GPS unk; Nr jct Rts 736/250 outside Parnassus, Jennings Gap; Augusta **GS:** U **SP:** No info **VI:** No further data **P:** N **BLW:** N **RG:** unk **MK:** unk **PH:** unk **SS:** DY pg 29 **BS:** 142.

LEDGERWOOD, James; b 1738, Ireland, d 14 Sep 1805, Botetourt Co **RU:** Private Served in 14th Cont Line in IL **CEM:** North Mountain; GPS unk; One mi N of Mt Tabor on Rt 620; Botetourt **GS:** U **SP:** No info **VI:** Son of William Ledgerwood (1700-1792) and Agness Mitchell **P:** N **BLW:** N **RG:** N **MK:** N **PH:** no **SS:** E pg 464 **BS:** 196

LEDGERWOOD, William; b 1700, Ireland, d 4 Dec 1792, **RU:** Private Served in IL **CEM:** North Mountain; GPS unk; One mi N of Mt Tabor on Rt 620 **GS:** U **SP:** Agness Mitchell **VI:** Arrived with family in Augusta Co 1740. Served also in Colonial War **P:** N **BLW:** N **RG:** N **MK:** N **PH:** no **SS:** E pg 464 **BS:** 196

NORTHEN, Peter; b 23 Aug 1750, Farnham, d 8 Sep 1811 **RU:** Ensign Took oath as ensign 1 Oct 1781, Capt Brockenbrough's Co, Richmond Co Militia **CEM:** Fernwood, aka Capt Peter Northen Burial Grd; GPS 37.94117, -76.74268; 13548 Historyland Hwy, Rt 3, Cobham Park; Richmond Co **GS:** Y **SP:** Jane Alderson **VI:** Son of William Northen and Abigail Minty. Made rank of Capt after war period. Govt gr st **P:** N **BLW:** N **RG:** N **MK:** N **PH:** no **SS:** D vol III, pg 816; E pg 589 **BS:** 196

Deletions:

KAYLOR, Michael; Determined to be too young to have served

www.ingramcontent.com/pod-product-compliance
Lightning Source LLC
Chambersburg PA
CBHW082349270326
41935CB00013B/1559